Lecture Notes in Computer Science 9953

Commenced Publication in 1973
Founding and Former Series Editors:
Gerhard Goos, Juris Hartmanis, and Jan van Leeuwen

More information about this series at http://www.springer.com/series/7407

Tiziana Margaria · Bernhard Steffen (Eds.)

Leveraging Applications of Formal Methods, Verification and Validation

Discussion, Dissemination, Applications

7th International Symposium, ISoLA 2016
Imperial, Corfu, Greece, October 10–14, 2016
Proceedings, Part II

 Springer

Editors
Tiziana Margaria
Lero
Limerick
Ireland

Bernhard Steffen
TU Dortmund
Dortmund
Germany

ISSN 0302-9743   ISSN 1611-3349   (electronic)
Lecture Notes in Computer Science
ISBN 978-3-319-47168-6   ISBN 978-3-319-47169-3   (eBook)
DOI 10.1007/978-3-319-47169-3

Library of Congress Control Number: 2016953300

LNCS Sublibrary: SL1 – Theoretical Computer Science and General Issues

Printed on acid-free paper

This Springer imprint is published by Springer Nature
The registered company is Springer International Publishing AG
The registered company address is: Gewerbestrasse 11, 6330 Cham, Switzerland

Preface

Welcome to ISoLA 2016, the 7th International Symposium on Leveraging Applications of Formal Methods, Verification and Validation, that was held in Corfu, Greece during October 10–14, 2016, endorsed by EASST, the European Association of Software Science and Technology.

This year's event followed the tradition of its forerunners held 2004 and 2006 in Cyprus, 2008 in Chalkidiki, 2010 and 2012 in Crete, and 2014 in Corfu, and the series of ISoLA Workshops in Greenbelt (USA) in 2005, Poitiers (France) in 2007, Potsdam (Germany) in 2009, in Vienna (Austria) in 2011, and 2013 in Palo Alto (USA).

As in the previous editions, ISoLA 2016 provided a forum for developers, users, and researchers to discuss issues related to the *adoption and use of rigorous tools and methods* for the specification, analysis, verification, certification, construction, test, and maintenance of systems from the point of view of their different application domains. Thus, since 2004 the ISoLA series of events serves the purpose of bridging the gap between designers and developers of rigorous tools, on one hand, and users in engineering and in other disciplines on the other hand. It fosters and exploits synergetic relationships among scientists, engineers, software developers, decision makers, and other critical thinkers in companies and organizations. By providing a specific, dialogue-oriented venue for the discussion of common problems, requirements, algorithms, methodologies, and practices, ISoLA aims in particular at supporting researchers in their quest to improve the usefulness, reliability, flexibility, and efficiency of tools for building systems and users in their search for adequate solutions to their problems.

The program of the symposium consisted of a collection of *special tracks* devoted to the following hot and emerging topics:

- Correctness-by-Construction and Post-Hoc Verification: Friends or Foes?
  (Organizers: Maurice ter Beek, Reiner Haehnle, Ina Schaefer)
- Static and Runtime Verification: Competitors or Friends?
  (Organizers: Dilian Gurov, Klaus Havelund, Marieke Huisman, Rosemary Monahan)
- Testing the Internet of Things
  (Organizers: Michael Felderer, Ina Schieferdecker)
- Rigorous Engineering of Collective Adaptive Systems
  (Organizers: Stefan Jähnichen, Martin Wirsing)
- RVE: Runtime Verification and Enforcement, the (Industrial) Application Perspective
  (Organizers: Ezio Bartocci, Ylies Falcone)
- ModSyn-PP: Modular Synthesis of Programs and Processes
  (Organizers: Boris Düdder, George Heineman, Jakob Rehof)
- Variability Modelling for Scalable Software Evolution
  (Organizers: Ferruccio Damiani, Christoph Seidl, Ingrid Chieh Yu)
- Statistical Model Checking
  (Organizers: Kim Larsen, Axel Legay)

- Detecting and Understanding Software Doping
  (Organizers: Christel Baier, Holger Hermanns)
- Formal Methods and Safety Certification: Challenges in the Railways Domain
  (Organizers: Alessandro Fantechi, Stefania Gnesi)
- Semantic Heterogeneity in the Formal Development of Complex Systems
  (Organizers: Idir Ait Sadoune, Paul Gibson, Marc Pantel)
- Privacy and Security Issues in Information Systems
  (Organizers: Axel Legay, Fabrizio Biondi)
- Evaluation and Reproducibility of Program Analysis and Verification
  (Organizers: Markus Schordan, Dirk Beyer, Jonas Lundberg)
- Towards a Unified View of Modeling and Programming
  (Organizers: Manfred Broy, Klaus Havelund, Rahul Kumar, Bernhard Steffen)
- Learning Systems: Machine-Learning in Software Products and Learning-Based
  Analysis of Software Systems
  (Organizers: Falk Howar, Andreas Rausch, Karl Meinke)

The following embedded events were also hosted:

- RERS: Challenge on Rigorous Examination of Reactive Systems (Falk Howar,
  Markus Schordan, Bernhard Steffen, Jaco van de Pol)
- Doctoral Symposium and Poster Session (Anna-Lena Lamprecht)
- Tutorial: Automata Learning in Practice (Falk Howar, Karl Meinke)
- Industrial Day (Axel Hessenkämper)

Co-located with the ISoLA Symposium was:

- STRESS 2016 – 4th International School on Tool-Based Rigorous Engineering of
  Software Systems (J. Hatcliff, T. Margaria, Robby, B. Steffen)

In addition to the contributions of the main conference, the proceedings also comprise contributions of the four embedded events and tutorial papers for STRESS. We thank the track organizers, the members of the Program Committee and their reviewers for their effort in selecting the papers to be presented, the local organization chair, Petros Stratis, and the EasyConferences team for their continuous precious support during the week as well as during the entire two-year period preceding the events, and Springer for being, as usual, a very reliable partner for the publication of the proceedings. Finally, we are grateful to Kyriakos Georgiades for his continuous support for the website and the program, and to Markus Frohme, Johannes Neubauer, and Julia Rehder for their help with the online conference service (OCS).

Special thanks are due to the following organizations for their endorsement: EASST (European Association of Software Science and Technology) and Lero – The Irish Software Research Centre, and our own institutions – the TU Dortmund and the University of Limerick.

October 2016

Tiziana Margaria
Bernhard Steffen

Organization

Symposium Chair

Tiziana Margaria   Lero, Ireland

Program Chair

Bernhard Steffen   TU Dortmund, Germany

Program Committee

Yamine Ait Ameur	IRIT-ENSEEIHT, France
Idir Ait-Sadoune	SUPELEC, France
Christel Baier	TU Dresden, Germany
Ezio Bartocci	TU Wien, Austria
Dirk Beyer	LMU Munich, Germany
Fabrizio Biondi	Inria, France
Manfred Broy	TUM, Germany
Ferruccio Damiani	University of Turin, Italy
Boris Duedder	TU Dortmund, Germany
Ylies Falcone	University of Grenoble, France
Alessandro Fantechi	Università di Firenze, Italy
Michael Felderer	University of Innsbruck, Austria
Paul Gibson	Telecom Sud Paris, France
Stefania Gnesi	CNR, Italy
Kim Guldstrand Larsen	Aalborg University, Denmark
Dilian Gurov	KTH Royal Institute of Technology, Sweden
Klaus Havelund	Jet Propulsion Laboratory, USA
George Heineman	WPI, USA
Holger Hermanns	Saarland University, Germany
Axel Hessenkämper	Hottinger Baldwin Messtechnik GmbH, Germany
Falk Howar	Clausthal University of Technology, Germany
Marieke Huisman	University of Twente, The Netherlands
Reiner Hähnle	TU Darmstadt, Germany
Stefan Jaehnichen	TU Berlin, Germany
Jens Knoop	TU Wien, Austria
Anna-Lena Lamprecht	University of Limerick, Ireland
Axel Legay	Inria, France
Martin Leucker	University of Lübeck, Germany
Jonas Lundberg	Linneaus University, Sweden
Tiziana Margaria	Lero, Ireland

Karl Meinke	KTH Royal Institute of Technology, Sweden
Rosemary Monahan	NUI Maynooth, Ireland
Marc Pantel	Université de Toulouse, France
Jakób Rehof	TU Dortmund, Germany
Ina Schaefer	TU Braunschweig, Germany
Ina Schieferdecker	Fraunhofer FOKUS/TU Berlin, Germany
Markus Schordan	Lawrence Livermore National Laboratory, USA
Christoph Seidl	TU Braunschweig, Germany
Bernhard Steffen	TU Dortmund, Germany
Maurice ter Beek	ISTI-CNR, Italy
Martin Wirsing	LMU, Germany
Ingrid Chieh Yu	University of Oslo, Norway

Additional Reviewers

Vahdat Abdelzad	University of Ottawa, Canada
Michał Antkiewicz	University of Waterloo, Canada
Davide Basile	ISTI-CNR Pisa, Italy
Bernhard Beckert	Karlsruhe Institute of Technology, Germany
Lenz Belzner	LMU, Germany
Saddek Bensalem	Verimag, France
Gérard Berry	Collège de France, France
Marius Bozga	Verimag, France
Tomas Bures	Charles University Prag, Czech Republic
Laura Carnevali	STLAB, Italy
Sofia Cassel	Uppsala University, Sweden
Vincenzo Ciancia	ISTI-CNR, Italy
Loek Cleophas	TU Eindhoven, The Netherlands
Francesco Luca De Angelis	University Geneva, Switzerland
Rocco De Nicola	IMT Lucca, Italy
Julien Delange	CMU-SEI, USA
Giovanna Di Marzo Serugendo	CUI, Switzerland
Maged Elaasar	Modelware Solutions, USA
Hilding Elmqvist	Mogram AB, Sweden
Uli Fahrenberg	Inria, France
Alessio Ferrari	CNR, Italy
John Fitzgerald	Newcastle University, UK
Thomas Given-Wilson	Inria, France
Sorren Hanvey	University of Limerick, Ireland
Anne E. Haxthausen	Technical University of Denmark, Denmark
Robert Heinrichs	TU Berlin, Germany
Rolf Hennicker	LMU, Germany
Phillip James	Swansea University, UK
Einar Broch Johnsen	University of Oslo, Norway
Gabor Karsai	Vanderbilt University, USA

Contents – Part II

Formal Methods and Safety Certification: Challenges in the Railways Domain

RVE: Runtime Verification and Enforcement, the (Industrial) Application Perspective

Variability Modeling for Scalable Software Evolution

Detecting and Understanding Software Doping

Learning Systems: Machine-Learning in Software Products and Learning-Based Analysis of Software Systems

Testing the Internet of Things

Doctoral Symposium

Industrial Track

RERS Challenge

STRESS

Contents – Part I

Evaluation and Reproducibility of Program Analysis and Verification

ModSyn-PP: Modular Synthesis of Programs and Processes

Semantic Heterogeneity in the Formal Development of Complex Systems

Correctness-by-Construction and Post-hoc Verification: Friends or Foes?

Privacy and Security Issues in Information Systems

Towards a Unified View of Modeling and Programming

Towards a Unified View of Modeling and Programming (Track Summary)

Manfred Broy[1], Klaus Havelund[2(✉)], Rahul Kumar[3], and Bernhard Steffen[4]

[1] Technische Universität München, Munich, Germany
[2] Jet Propulsion Laboratory, California Institute of Technology, Pasadena, USA
klaus.havelund@jpl.nasa.gov
[3] Microsoft Research, Redmond, USA
[4] TU Dortmund University, Dortmund, Germany

1 Motivation and Goals

Since the 1960s we have seen a tremendous amount of scientific and methodological work in the fields of specification, design, and programming languages. In spite of the very high value of this work, however, this effort has found its limitation by the fact that we do not have a sufficient integration of these languages, as well as tools that support the development engineer in applying the corresponding methods and techniques. A tighter integration between specification and verification logics, graphical modeling notations, and programming languages is needed.

In a (possibly over) simplified view, as an attempt to impose some structure on this work, we can distinguish between three lines of work: formal methods, model-based engineering, and programming languages. Formal methods include, usually textual, formalisms such as VDM, CIP, Z, B, Event-B, ASM, TLA+, Alloy, and RAISE, but also more or less automated theorem proving systems such as Coq, Isabelle, and PVS. Such formalisms are usually based on mathematical concepts, such as functions, relations, set theory, etc. A specification typically consists of a signature, i.e. a collection of names and their types, and axioms over the signature, constraining the values that the names can denote. A specification as such denotes a set of models, each providing a binding of values to the names, satisfying the axioms. Such formal methods usually come equipped with proof systems, such that one can prove properties of the specifications, for example consistency of axioms, or that certain theorems are consequences of the axioms. A common characteristic of these formalisms is their representation as text, defined by context-free grammars, and their formalization in terms of semantics and/or logical proof systems. In parallel one has seen several model checkers appearing, such as SPIN, SMV, FDR, and UPPAAL. These usually prioritize efficient verification algorithms over expressive and convenient specification languages. Exceptions are more recent model checkers for programming languages, including for example Java PathFinder (JPF).

K. Havelund–The research performed by this author was carried out at Jet Propulsion Laboratory, California Institute of Technology, under a contract with the National Aeronautics and Space Administration.

© Springer International Publishing AG 2016
T. Margaria and B. Steffen (Eds.): ISoLA 2016, Part II, LNCS 9953, pp. 3–10, 2016.
DOI: 10.1007/978-3-319-47169-3_1

Starting later in the 1980s, the model-based engineering community developed graphical formalisms, most prominently represented by UML and later SysML. These formalisms offer graphical notation for defining data structures as "nodes and edge" diagrams, and behavioral diagrams such as state machines and message sequence diagrams. These formalisms specifically address the ease of adoption amongst engineers. It is clear that these techniques have become more popular in industry than formal methods, in part likely due to the graphical nature of these languages. However, these formalisms are complex (the standard defining UML is much larger than the definition of any formal method or programming language), are incomplete (the UML standard for example has no expression-language, although OCL is a recommended add-on), and they lack commonly agreed up semantics. This is not too surprising as UML has been designed on the basis of an intuitive understanding of the semantics of its individual parts and concepts, and not under the perspective of a potential formal semantics ideally covering the entire UML. This leaves users some freedom of interpretation, in particular concerning the conceptual interplay of individual model types and often leads to misunderstandings, but it has still been sufficient in practice in order to support tool-based system development, even by providing, e.g., partial code generation. On the other hand, it is also responsible for the only very partial successes of the decades of attempts to provide formal semantics to UML. One may, therefore, argue that (the abstract syntax and intuitive semantics of) UML, as it stands, is not adequately designed to support a foundation in terms of a formal semantics. It would therefore be interesting to reconsider the design of UML with the dedicated goal to provide a formal semantics and thereby reach a next level of maturity.

Finally, programming languages have evolved over time, starting with numerical machine code, then assembly languages, and transitioning to higher-level languages with FORTRAN in the late 1950s. Numerous programming languages have been developed since then. The C programming language has since its creation in the early 1970s conquered the embedded software world in an impressive manner. Later efforts, however, have attempted to create even higher-level languages. These include language such as Java and Python, in which collections such as sets, lists and maps are built-in, either as constructs or as systems libraries. Especially the academic community has experimented with functional programming languages, such as ML, OCaml, and Haskell, and more recently the integration of object-oriented programming and functional programming, as in for example Scala.

Each of the formalisms mentioned above have advantageous features not owned by other formalisms. However, what is perhaps more important is that these formalisms have many language constructs in common, and to such an extent that one can ask the controversial question: *Should we strive towards a unified view of modeling and programming?* It is the goal of the meeting to discuss the relationship between modeling and programming, with the possible objective of achieving an agreement of what a unification of these concepts would mean at an abstract level, and what it would bring as benefits on the practical level.

What are the trends in the three domains: formal specification and verification, model-based engineering, and programming, which can be considered to support a unification of these domains. We want to discuss whether the time is ripe for another attempt to bring things closer together.

2 Contributions

The paper contributions in this track are introduced below. The papers are ordered according to the sessions of the track: (1) opinions, (2) more concrete, (3) meta-level considerations, (4) domain-specific approaches, (5) tools and frameworks view, and (6) panel. Within each track the papers are ordered to provide a natural flow of presentations.

2.1 Opinions

Selic [16] (*Programming* $\subset$ *Modeling* $\subset$ *Engineering*) takes the position that models and modeling have a much broader set of purposes than just programming. It points out that there is a direct conflict between modeling and programming, as modeling is based on abstracting away irrelevant details whereas programming requires full implementation oriented details. In the end, the paper investigates the question of the complex relationship between modeling and programming. Finally it comes up with the question of whether modelers can become programmers, and it concludes that it has to deal with the question whether high level modeling languages can be used as implementation languages.

Seidewitz [15] (*On a Unified View of Modeling and Programming – Position Paper*) considers a unified view of modeling and programming. Seidewitz takes the position that some software models specify behavior precisely enough that they can be executed, and that all programs can be considered models, at least of the execution they specify. He concludes that modeling and programming are actually not so different after all, and there might be conversions. He claims that the language design legacy of UML is largely grounded on the old view of sharply separating models and programs, complicating their future convergence, and that it is perhaps time to move forward in the direction of new generations of unified modeling and programming languages.

Haxthausen and Peleska [5] (*On the Feasibility of a Unified Modelling and Programming Paradigm*) argue that we should not expect there to be a single "best" unified modeling, programming and verification paradigm in the future. They, on the contrary, argue that a multi-formalism approach is more realistic and useful. Amongst the reasons mentioned is that multiple stake holders will not be able to agree on a formalism. The multi-formalism approach requires to translate verification artifacts between different representations. It is illustrated by means of a case study from the railway domain, how this can be achieved, using concepts from the theory of institutions, formalized in category theory.

2.2   More Concrete

Elaasar and Badreddin [3] (*Modeling Meets Programming: A Comparative Study in Model Driven Engineering Action Languages*) compare two approaches, Alf and Umple, where modeling meets programming. They start from the remark that modeling and programming have often been considered two different domains. They point out, that this is true when modeling is primarily meant for human communication, but is not the case when modeling is meant for execution. In their paper they discuss two approaches that specifically address execution. In particular they consider the language Alf, that has evolved from the modeling community to make models executable, and Umple, that has evolved from the academic community to introduce abstractions of modeling into programming languages. The paper discusses critical differences, and ideas for future evolution of model oriented programming languages.

Lattmann, Kecskés, Meijer, Karsai, Völgyesi, and Lédeczi [8] (*Abstractions for Modeling Complex Systems*) present three abstraction methods for improving the scalability of the modeling process and the system models themselves. The abstractions, crosscuts, model libraries, and mixins, are part of the WebGME framework, and the paper describes how these abstractions are incorporated into this framework.

Leavens, Naumann, Rajan, and Aotani [9] (*Specifying and Verifying Advanced Control Features*) discuss the problem of verifying programs that are written with design patterns such as higher-order functions, advice, and context dependence. Such concepts allow for greater modularity and programming convenience, but tend to be harder to verify. They propose the use of Greybox specifications and techniques for verification of such programs.

2.3   Meta-Level Considerations

Rouquette [13] (*Simplifying OMG MOF-based Metamodeling*) discusses the complexity of UML, the meta-model MOF used to define it, and the XML Metadata Interchange (XMI) standard used for serializing UML models. He alternatively suggests to define the abstract syntax of a modeling language as a normalized relational schema, and to consider a particular model as tabular instance of that schema. He finally suggests leveraging recent advances in functional programming languages, such as Scala, in order to modernize the traditional practice of model-based programming with the Object Constraint Language (OCL) and the Query/View/Transformation (QVT) standards.

Prinz, Møller-Pedersen, and Joachim Fischer [12] (*Modelling and Testing of Real Systems*) elaborate on OMG-style modeling conventions, in particular by introducing the distinction between description and prescription in order to deal with partially realized systems. Whereas the former is intended for capturing already existing parts of a foreseen system, the latter specifies to be realized parts. This distinction is also used in their testing approach which reminds of hardware in the loop or back-to-back testing, where real and simulated parts are simultaneously used. The power of this approach depends on the executability level of the underlying (modeling) languages, which ranges from mere presentation to dual executability as required for fully exploiting the presented testing approach. In this sense, the corresponding 5-level hierarchy can be regarded as a specific top-level view for merging the modeling and programming landscapes.

Kugler [6] (*Unifying Modelling and Programming: A Systems Biology Perspective*) suggests to explore the topic of unifying modeling and programming in the context of computational systems biology, which is a field in its early stages, and therefore potentially more receptive to new ideas. Here, for example cells can be effectively described as biological programs. Software and system development share several of the main challenges that computational systems biology is facing: making models amendable to formal and scalable reasoning, using visual languages, combining different programming languages, rapid prototyping, and program synthesis.

2.4 Domain-Specific Approaches

Berry [1] (*Formally Unifying Modeling and Design for Embedded Systems - a Personal View*) shows the direct and formal connection between model-based design and programming in the synchronous languages framework, which is tailored for the embedded system domain. In this setting higher-level models can comfortably be designed, verified, and subsequently transformed to high quality system code. That this actually works as described has been witnessed in the past, and it is the foundation for the Kieler framework, where the design of hardware circuits is targeted. On the one hand, Berry's work impressively demonstrates the synergies between modeling and programming. On the other hand, the author explicitly admits that the success of his overall framework is domain-specific, and cannot easily be generalized.

Rybicki, Smyth, Motika, Schulz-Rosengarten, and Hanxleden [14] (*Interactive Model-Based Compilation Continued Incremental Hardware Synthesis for SCCharts*) present an extension of the Kieler development framework, which further strengthens its meta-modeling based approach for stepwise translating high level descriptions to hardware. Remarkable is its user-orientation: not only can the effect of the (M2M) transformations steps be controlled via sophisticated graphical visualization, but also subsequent simulation runs can be followed at each of the intermediate levels. Thus Kieler can be regarded as a framework where models are "morphed" to programs and even hardware by automatic transformation. At the practical side this illustrates the maturity of Eclipse's meta-modeling facilities, which, in the meantime, can effectively be used to integrate domain-specific languages into a development framework.

Larsen, Fitzgerald, Woodcock, Nilsson, Gamble, and Foster [7] (*Towards Semantically Integrated Models and Tools for Cyber-Physical Systems Design*) argue that the modeling of specifically embedded cyber-physical systems best can be done using multiple formalisms. A case study of a small unmanned aerial vehicle is used to demonstrate the need for multiple formalisms, namely a formalism for defining control, in this case VDM-RT, and a formalism for continuous behavior defined by differential equations, in this case 20-sim. The integration is founded in the semantic framework of Unifying Theories of Programming (UTP). Combined systems are suggested simulated via a co-simulation framework.

2.5 Tools and Frameworks View

Lethbridge, Abdelzad, Orabi, Orabi, and Adesina [10] (*Merging Modeling and Programming using Umple*) present Umple, a programming and modeling language that has been created by introducing modeling constructs in programming and vice-versa. Umple aims at maintaining model-code and text-diagram duality. Several examples and uses of Umple are provided with a broad discussion.

Elmqvist, Henningsson, and Otter [4] (*Systems Modeling and Programming in a Unified Environment based on Julia*) present a new methodology for modeling cyber physical systems using a Modelica-like extension of the powerful Julia programming language – a language extension they call Modia. A good discussion is provided by the authors regarding the needs of a Model Based Systems Engineering approach, along with a strong description of the features and implementation of the Modia language. Examples and illustrations are also provided in great detail.

Naujokat, Neubauer, Margaria, and Steffen [11] (*Meta-Level Reuse for Mastering Domain Specialization*) reflect on the distinction between modeling and programming in terms of WHAT and HOW, and emphasize the importance of perspectives: what is a model (a WHAT) for the one, may well be a program (a HOW) for the other. In fact, attempts to pinpoint technical criteria like executability or abstraction for clearly separating modeling from programming seem not to survive modern technical developments. Rather, the underlying conceptual cores continuously converge. What remains is the distinction of WHAT and HOW, separating true purpose from its realization, i.e. providing the possibility of formulating the primary intent without being forced to over-specify. The paper argues that no unified general-purpose language can adequately support this distinction in general, and propose a meta-level framework for mastering the wealth of required domain-specific languages.

2.6 Panel

The panel section started with a presentation by Broy, Havelund, and Kumar [2] (*Towards a Unified View of Modeling and Programming*), who present an argument for unifying modeling and programming in one formalism. They highlight relevant developments in the fields of formal methods, model-based engineering, and programming languages. They subsequently illustrate how modeling can be perceived as programing via examples in the Scala programming language. The paper concludes with a summary of issues considered important to reflect on in any attempt to unify modeling and programming. They specifically highlight the need to combine textual and visual languages, the need for allowing definition of domain-specific languages, and the need for analysis support.

References

1. Berry, G.: Formally unifying modeling and design for embedded systems - a personal view. In: Margaria, T., Steffen, B. (eds.) 7th International Symposium On Leveraging Applications of Formal Methods, Verification and Validation, ISoLA 2016, Corfu, Greece, 10–14 October, LNCS. Springer (2016). These proceedings
2. Broy, M., Havelund, K., Kumar, R.: Towards a unified view of modeling and programming. In: Margaria, T., Steffen, B. (eds.) 7th International Symposium On Leveraging Applications of Formal Methods, Verification and Validation, ISoLA 2016, Corfu, Greece, 10–14 October, LNCS. Springer (2016). These proceedings
3. Elaasar, M., Badreddin, O.: Modeling meets programming: a comparative study in model driven engineering action languages. In: Margaria, T., Steffen, B. (eds.) 7th International Symposium On Leveraging Applications of Formal Methods, Verification and Validation, ISoLA 2016, Corfu, Greece, 10–14 October, LNCS. Springer (2016). These proceedings
4. Elmqvist, H., Henningsson, T., Otter, M.: Systems modeling and programming in a unified environment based on Julia. In: Margaria, T., Steffen, B. (eds.) 7th International Symposium On Leveraging Applications of Formal Methods, Verification and Validation, ISoLA 2016, Corfu, Greece, 10–14 October, LNCS. Springer (2016). These proceedings
5. Haxthausen, A.E., Peleska, J.: On the feasibility of a unified modelling and programming paradigm. In: Margaria, T., Steffen, B. (eds.) 7th International Symposium On Leveraging Applications of Formal Methods, Verification and Validation, ISoLA 2016, Corfu, Greece, 10–14 October, LNCS. Springer (2016). These proceedings
6. Kugler, H.: Unifying modelling, programming: a systems biology perspective. In: Margaria, T., Steffen, B. (eds.) 7th International Symposium On Leveraging Applications of Formal Methods, Verification and Validation, ISoLA 2016, Corfu, Greece, 10–14 October, LNCS. Springer (2016). These proceedings
7. Larsen, P.G., Fitzgerald, J., Woodcock, J., Nilsson, R., Gamble, C., Foster, S.: Towards semantically integrated models and tools for cyber-physical systems design. In: Margaria, T., Steffen, B. (eds.) 7th International Symposium On Leveraging Applications of Formal Methods, Verification and Validation, ISoLA 2016, Corfu, Greece, 10–14 October, LNCS. Springer (2016). These proceedings
8. Lattmann, Z., Kecskés, T., Meijer, P., Karsai, G., Völgyesi, P., Lédeczi, Á.: Abstractions for modeling complex systems. In: Margaria, T., Steffen, B. (eds.) 7th International Symposium On Leveraging Applications of Formal Methods, Verification and Validation, ISoLA 2016, Corfu, Greece, 10–14 October, LNCS. Springer (2016). These proceedings
9. Leavens, G.T., Naumann, D., Rajan, H., Aotani T.: Specifying and verifying advanced control features. In: Margaria, T., Steffen, B. (eds.) 7th International Symposium On Leveraging Applications of Formal Methods, Verification and Validation, ISoLA 2016, Corfu, Greece, 10–14 October, LNCS. Springer (2016). These proceedings
10. Lethbridge, T.C., Abdelzad, V., Orabi, M.H., Orabi, A.H., Adesina, O.: Merging modeling and programming using Umple. In: Margaria, T., Steffen, B. (eds.) 7th International Symposium On Leveraging Applications of Formal Methods, Verification and Validation, ISoLA 2016, Corfu, Greece, 10–14 October, LNCS. Springer (2016). These proceedings

11. Naujokat, S., Neubauer, J., Margaria, T., Steffen, B.: Meta-level reuse for mastering domain specialization. In: Margaria, T., Steffen, B. (eds.) 7th International Symposium On Leveraging Applications of Formal Methods, Verification and Validation, ISoLA 2016, Corfu, Greece, 10–14 October, LNCS. Springer (2016). These proceedings

12. Prinz, A., Møller-Pedersen, B., Fischer, J.: Modelling and testing of real systems. In: Margaria, T., Steffen, B. (eds.) 7th International Symposium On Leveraging Applications of Formal Methods, Verification and Validation, ISoLA 2016, Corfu, Greece, 10–14 October, LNCS. Springer (2016). These proceedings

13. Rouquette, N.F.: Simplifying OMG MOF-based metamodeling. In: Margaria, T., Steffen, B. (eds.) 7th International Symposium On Leveraging Applications of Formal Methods, Verification and Validation, ISoLA 2016, Corfu, Greece, 10–14 October, LNCS. Springer (2016). These proceedings

14. Rybicki, F., Smyth, S., Motika, C., Schulz-Rosengarten, A., von Hanxleden, R.: Interactive model-based compilation continued - incremental hardware synthesis for SCCharts. In: Margaria, T., Steffen, B. (eds.) 7th International Symposium On Leveraging Applications of Formal Methods, Verification and Validation, ISoLA 2016, Corfu, Greece, 10–14 October, LNCS. Springer (2016). These proceedings

15. Seidewitz, E.: On a unified view of modeling and programming - position paper. In: Margaria, T., Steffen, B. (eds.) 7th International Symposium On Leveraging Applications of Formal Methods, Verification and Validation, ISoLA 2016, Corfu, Greece, 10–14 October, LNCS. Springer (2016). These proceedings

16. Selic, B.: Programming $\subset$ modeling $\subset$ engineering. In: Margaria, T., Steffen, B. (eds.) 7th International Symposium On Leveraging Applications of Formal Methods, Verification and Validation, ISoLA 2016, Corfu, Greece, 10–14 October, LNCS. Springer (2016). These proceedings

Programming ⊂ Modeling ⊂ Engineering

Bran Selić[✉]

Malina Software Corp., Nepean, ON, Canada
selic@acm.org

Abstract. The proven ability of some modeling languages to be used as both design and implementation languages has raised hopes of a seamless blending between design and implementation, a capability that only seems possible in the domain of software engineering. In turn, this has led to methodological questions on how best to take advantage of models and modeling technologies in the development of complex software systems. To provide some insight into this question, we start with a review of the role and types of models that are found in traditional engineering disciplines and compare that to current practices in model-based software engineering in industrial practice. The conclusion reached is that, despite some very unique characteristics of software, there does not seem to be any compelling reason to treat the handling of models in software engineering in a radically different way than what is done in engineering in general.

Keywords: Model-based engineering · Software engineering methodology · Modeling languages

1 Introduction

"The design *is* the implementation," we would proclaim triumphantly to our colleagues, most of whom, being experienced practitioners of software development, remained skeptical. This took place during the early days of our experience with a new computer language, which we had devised for our own domain-specific purposes. In today's terminology this language would qualify as a *domain-specific modeling language*. It was intended specifically for writing of complex real-time applications in the telecommunications space (e.g., implementing communications protocols) [12]. The language had all the features of a truly modern high-level language: it was object oriented and component based. The *high-level structure* (architecture) of a system was specified by hierarchical networks of interconnected parts captured as reusable classes, while the *high-level behavior* of these classes was specified using a simplified custom variant of Harel's statecharts [4]. It departed from traditional programming language conventions of the time (1980's and 1990's) in that it relied fundamentally on a visual syntax for rendering its high-level concepts. Since these were based on graph-like formalisms, a graphical syntax was a natural choice. This allowed us to bypass the tedious and error-prone manual translation of such specifications into equivalent linear programming language text, while at the same time enabling a more direct visualization of design intent. The language was executable and expressive enough to support creation of complete production-quality implementations.

© Springer International Publishing AG 2016
T. Margaria and B. Steffen (Eds.): ISoLA 2016, Part II, LNCS 9953, pp. 11–26, 2016.
DOI: 10.1007/978-3-319-47169-3_2

At the time, most telecom software development proceeded according to the conventional waterfall approach: once the requirements were defined and frozen, a high-level design was first produced and documented. This documentation was then used as a basis for further refinement, wherein the individual elements of the high-level design were detailed out and, when that was complete, the results were captured in a set of detailed design documents. At that point a design "freeze" would be declared and the implementation phase would commence, typically using a third-generation programming language such as C. One of the most vexing issues was that, due in great part to the semantic gap between the implementation language and the language of the design, it was easy for the implementation to diverge from the design. This corruption of design intent typically occurred gradually and silently, since it is often very difficult to detect these types of flaws by human inspection of program code.

The motivation that led to the introduction of our new domain-specific language was to avoid these shortcomings and to accelerate development. By using this *modeling* language, we envisaged that one simply had to start by specifying the high-level design and, through a process of continual incremental refinement, eventually conclude with a complete final implementation. Because all such refinement occurred in the context of the original high-level design while using the same specification language, the likelihood of undetected design corruption was significantly lowered. Moreover, since a highly intuitive diagrammatic form was used to specify the high-level (architectural) elements, we thought that the design, when supplemented with appropriate descriptive text, could be discerned directly from the implementation. And, as a final step, the corresponding implementation would be generated automatically by a computer-based code generator, which translated the final design specification (i.e., model) into an executable program.

However, as users accumulated experience with the language, this compellingly simple and highly appealing vision of software development proved to be naïve and incomplete. In this essay, we examine the reasons why this was the case and some steps that need to be taken to make such an approach practical.

2   On Models and Their Use in Engineering Practice

Models have been an integral and critical element of general engineering practice since time immemorial. And, although *software* engineering is undoubtedly unique in many ways, it is, nonetheless, a form of engineering[1]. Consequently, before we focus on the use of models in software development, it is helpful to review the role of models in traditional engineering disciplines and what benefits (and pitfalls) this brings.

Reaching deep into the history of engineering, we encounter the instructive case noted by Marcus Vitruvius Polio. He was an "architect" in Ancient Rome at the time of Emperor Augustus (circa the first century BC). Vitruvius' legacy lives on through his

---

[1] The American Heritage Dictionary® of the English Language (5th edition) defines engineering as "the application of scientific and mathematical principles to practical ends such as the design, manufacture, and operation of efficient and economical structures, machines, processes, and systems." (http://www.thefreedictionary.com/engineering).

book, *De Architectura*, which is probably the oldest surviving engineering text. In Book X of this opus, he discusses a case of the use of models in engineering practice and concludes:

"For not all things are practicable on identical principles, but there are some things which, when enlarged in imitation of small models, are effective, others cannot have models but are constructed independently of them, while there are some which appear feasible in models, but when they have begun to increase in size are impracticable..."[2]

The specific case behind these conclusions was the failure of what originally seemed to be a very clever siege defense mechanism: a rotating crane mounted on a city's wall that would grab an enemy's siege device as it was approaching the wall and then bring it "within the wall(s)" to be dealt with. This was based on a convincing demonstration of the effectiveness of such a device using a small scale model. Unfortunately for the defenders, in this particular case the enemy responded by constructing a siege engine of such exceptional proportions that it was simply not feasible to construct a crane of appropriate size that could deal with it.

What we can glean from Vitruvius' here is that: (a) models were used as "proof of concept" devices to stakeholders even in Antiquity (and probably earlier), (b) models sometimes served as "blueprints" to guide construction of the actual artifacts, and (c) that we have to be careful with predictions made using models.

2.1 What Is a Model?

It is helpful to define what we mean here by the term *model* in the engineering sense:

Definition: An <u>engineering model</u> *is a selective representation of some system intended to capture accurately and concisely all of its essential properties of interest for a given set of concerns.*

A key component in this definition is the view that a model should be constructed *for a particular purpose* (i.e., for a "set of concerns"). A useful model reduces the amount of information that needs to be absorbed by removing or hiding from view those properties and elements of the modeled system that are deemed inessential *for the purposes of that model*. We discuss below the different purposes that engineering models serve, but, invariably, these include some type of analysis or examination of the model, based on which predictions can be made. Engineers want to ask questions of their models (Will it do what it is supposed to do? Will it be strong enough? How much will it cost?). By reducing the amount of information to be considered, answering such questions can be made easier, whether the analysis is performed by humans or computers.

When considering engineering models, we must not underestimate the human side of modeling, because the model itself as well as the results of model analyses typically have to be viewed and understood by humans. For example, stakeholders of a systems

---

[2] Taken from clause 5, Chap. 16, Book X, in [7].

must be able to unambiguously specify their concerns and requirements. Since it is often the case that they may not have the requisite technical background to understand technical specifications, human-centric ones are needed. Even in situations where models and analysis results are being examined by engineering experts, there is still a crucial need to facilitate understanding. This and other critical concerns pertaining to engineering models are discussed in the following section.

2.2   The Essential Properties of Useful Engineering Models

We postulate here that the following are essential properties that a *useful* engineering model must possess:

1. An engineering model must have *clearly defined purpose*. This is because the purpose of a model determines which elements of the modeled system are to be included in the model and which ones are to be excluded. A model that is intended to serve too many different kinds of analyses will result in an excess of information, hindering practical analyses. This naturally leads to the conclusion that we will likely multiple models for any given system.

2. Engineering models must be *abstract*. As discussed previously, a good model should contain only information about the modeled system and its immediate environment that is relevant to the purposes of the model.

3. Engineering models must be *accurate*. Obviously, the information contained in the model must be sufficiently faithful in its representation of the modeled elements such that the results of the analyses performed on the model can be trustworthy.

4. Engineering models must be *analyzable*. That is, the model must be constructed in such a manner that it is conducive to the desired analyses to be performed on it. These analyses are typically used to predict the properties of interest of the modeled system.

5. Engineering models must be *understandable* to their human stakeholders, because practically all design involves human judgement. Hence, models must be presented in a form that matches the worldview and intuition of its target audience. Models that are cryptic and difficult to decipher may obscure crucial flaws and misunderstandings. For models specified using computer-based modeling languages, this usually implies using a domain-specific syntax. After all, the concrete syntax of a language is the most immediate interface between human readers and underlying computer representations. Reducing the gap between these two reduces what Fred Brooks refers to as "accidental" (i.e., needless) complexity [1].

6. Last but certainly not least, an engineering model must be *cost effective* to construct. Clearly, it must be substantially cheaper and more efficient to construct a model than it is to construct the modeled system.

2.3   How Engineering Models Are Used

They following summarizes the various purposes behind engineering models:

1. Models are needed to assist in the *understanding* of both complex problems and corresponding systems. Determining what a system is doing (or, what it is supposed to do) and how it does it, is a major hurdle even when dealing with moderately complex systems. By reducing the amount of information presented, a model reduces the degree of complexity that needs to be comprehended.

2. Engineering models are also used to make *predictions* about the system under consideration. These predictions can be generated in many different ways; by using mathematical models, logical inference, search-based methods, or even informal reasoning and intuition. Predictions derived from models are used in two distinct cases: (a) to determine whether or not a proposed design choice will lead to a desirable solution, or, (b) to validate that a proposed model corresponds to reality (i.e., the prediction matches a known data point of the modeled system).

3. In addition, engineering models are often used to *communicate* knowledge and intent between human stakeholders. The design of complex systems typically involves different categories of stakeholders with different and sometimes conflicting sets of concerns, who ultimately have to reach consensus. For example, an architect may present a small scale model of a proposed design for a building, which can then serve as a basis for discussion of possible changes and alternatives. Once again, this means that it is critical that the model can be in a form that is understood by stakeholders.

4. Models can also serve as "blueprints" used to guide *implementation*. In this case, the model captures the design intent, which is to be realized by the implementers. In most engineering disciplines, design and implementation are distinct: they typically require different sets of expertise, different tools, and different processes. Consequently, transferring and conserving design intent during implementation can be a difficult and error-prone process. To minimize the likelihood of corruption of design intent, implementation-oriented models need to be sufficiently detailed and precise to be properly interpreted by the implementers.

2.4   The Two Categories of Engineering Models

There is an important difference between models used for implementation (item 4 above) and models used for the other purposes listed. Namely, whereas the first three purposes require *abstract* models that are designed to *minimize* the amount of irrelevant information, models used as blueprints should be sufficiently *complete and detailed* to ensure correct realization of the specified design intent. In this sense, these two types of models are in opposition to each other, although they serve complementary functions. We refer to the models used for understanding, prediction, and communication as *descriptive* models, since their ultimate purpose is to facilitate human comprehension. In contrast, models that are used for implementation are referred to here as *prescriptive* models. This is a very useful and important distinction, since it can serve as a guide when constructing models, helping us, among other things, to avoid mixing of multiple contradictory purposes within a single model.

To illustrate the contrast between the two kinds of models, consider the case of a modern submarine as representative of the type of complex engineering system being built nowadays. Figures 1 and 2 show two different models of this system. The model in Fig. 1 is a descriptive model. Its primary purpose is to explain the basic principles of submarine operation. To that end, the model includes only the information essential to that purpose. (Note, however, that, despite the need to reduce the amount information presented, the model uses silhouettes of the submarine cross-section and of the waterline to help us understand the model more easily – this is the human aspect of modeling mentioned earlier.)

In contrast, the model in Fig. 2 is rich with detail, since it is intended to be used in the construction of the actual system. Clearly, models of this type tend to be much more difficult to understand and, hence, are not well suited to analytical reasoning or formal treatment.

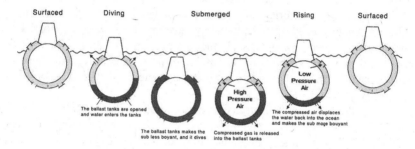

Fig. 1. A descriptive model of a submarine

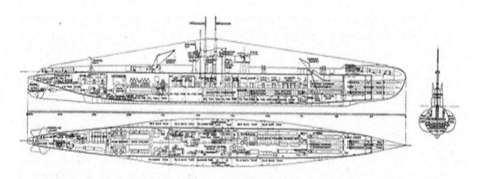

Fig. 2. A prescriptive model of a submarine

3   On Complex Engineering Systems and Their Models

It is interesting to contrast the highly intricate model shown in Fig. 2 with the far simpler one in Fig. 1. Why does a system that is conceptually so simple result in such a complex implementation? Where does all that additional complexity come from and is it really necessary? To answer these questions, we must examine what distinguishes a professional real-world engineering system from, say, a prototype or one built by non-experts.

3.1   On the Complexity of Engineering Systems and Its Sources

Modern engineering systems are becoming increasingly sophisticated and, conse-quently, more complex. For our discussion, it is helpful to single out the notion of the *primary functionality* of a system. This is the behavior of a system that is typically captured through use cases, and represents its *raison d'etre*. In case of submarine, for example, this is simply the ability to dive under water and re-surface as required.

Needless to say, if a system must support numerous different use cases, the primary functionality of an engineering system can be a source of great complexity. However, in practice it is rarely the only one. The other main source of complexity stems from the fact that industrial-grade engineering systems are generally required to be *dependable* and *practical*. By "dependable" we simply mean that a system is able to perform its primary functionality correctly when required. On the other hand, a system is deemed "practical" if operating it does not involve unwarranted or unreasonable effort (a form of accidental complexity) or excessive cost. For instance, a submarine whose internal cabin temperature exceeds 50°C would not be considered practical, no matter how well it performs its primary functionality.

Ensuring that a complex engineering system is both dependable and practical is usually achieved through additional ancillary mechanisms that supplement and support its primary functionality (e.g., air conditioning in submarines, power steering in automobiles, safety brakes in elevators). They exist solely to support the primary functionality and do not have a meaningful purpose outside the context of their system. In this essay, we shall refer to the set of such mechanisms as the *infrastructure* of a system.

Experienced professional engineers are fully aware of the importance and impact of a well-designed infrastructure. This is especially true given that, in many complex engineering systems, it is the case that *the complexity of the infrastructure exceeds by far the complexity of a system's primary functionality* (e.g., consider the models in Figs. 1 and 2)[3].

---

[3] Sadly, this is something that is still not well understood by many software engineers, where it is common practice to focus exclusively on use cases before any other considerations. The result is often a cumbersome and ineffective infrastructure.

3.2 Infrastructure in Complex Software Systems

But, is it meaningful to talk about the infrastructure in software systems? Surely, this is all handled by the underlying hardware, leaving software designers to worry only about implementing the primary functionality. This view has even led some software practitioners to conclude that software development is a discipline that transcends engineering[4]. Thus, one of the pioneers of computer science, Edsger Dijkstra, put it: "I see no meaningful difference between programming methodology and mathematical methodology"[5]. By this, he meant that software should be developed by a process that consists of designing computational algorithms and then proving their correctness using formal mathematical arguments.

While this approach may hold for certain limited categories of software applications, it definitely does not stand up in case of software that interacts directly with the physical world, such as the embedded software found in various *cyber-physical systems* [6]. Because these systems are typically required to interact continually with their environment, physical phenomena can have a major impact on their design, resulting in a significant amount of infrastructure to ensure dependability (e.g., fault-tolerance mechanisms, security mechanisms, performance-enhancing mechanisms (e.g., memory caches, pre-fetching mechanism)) and practicality (e.g., user interfaces).

However, there is typically much more to the infrastructure of software applications than just the mechanisms for coping with physical phenomena. Underlying most of today's software is at least an operating system and, possibly, one or more application frameworks. These provide much of the needed infrastructure in support of dependability and practicality. They are typically very sophisticated software programs whose complexity often exceeds that of most applications that run on top of them. Although from an application point of view an operating system hides behind its application programming interface (API) – an abstraction interface – its dependability and practicality characteristics must be accounted for in application design. For example, when considering the response time of a software application, the performance overheads of the underlying operating system can play a significant part.

Even more relevant is the fact that not all infrastructure functionality can be relegated to the operating system or application framework. As explained in the "end-to-end" argument by Saltzer et al., given that an operating system is designed to be generic (i.e., application independent), it cannot take on infrastructure functions that are specific to a particular application [11]. For example, the handling of a particular component failure may require non-standard application-specific recovery procedures. Therefore, such functions must be included directly in the application code.

In summary, we conclude that software systems also need an infrastructure, and that this can contribute in a major way to the overall system complexity.

---

[4] "Because [programs] are put together in the context of a set of information requirements, *they observe no natural limits* other than those imposed by those requirements. Unlike the world of engineering, *there are no immutable laws to violate*", Wei-Lung Wang in a letter to the editor published in the Communications of the ACM (vol. 45, 5), 2002.

[5] In EWD1209 (http://www.cs.utexas.edu/~EWD/).

3.3   Modeling Software Infrastructure

Because the infrastructure plays an ancillary role in an engineering system and does not directly contribute to the primary functionality of a system (although it can influence it), it is often omitted from or merely implied in many descriptive models. For example, when specifying the functionality of some software application, we rarely go into the complex details of how the operating system performs its job.

Consider, for example, the simple model of a software application depicted in Fig. 3, which shows two components, **PeerA** and **PeerB,** exchanging a simple high-level message ("hello"). However, what actually happens in this system involves a number of infrastructure (operating system) elements that are not visible in the application model. A typical "complete" scenario of such a situation might proceed as shown in Fig. 4. Here, we can see that the roles of components **PeerA** and **PeerB** are actually realized by two operating system threads, which use a set of ancillary operating system entities to transfer the high-level message from one end to the other using a reliable positive acknowledgement communications protocol.

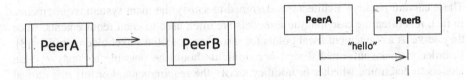

Fig. 3. A descriptive model of a software application

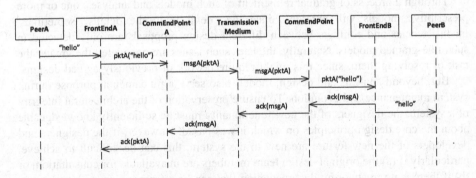

Fig. 4. A prescriptive model of the system shown in Fig. 3

The standard approach for dealing with this type of situation is to model the software system as being structured in a set of hierarchically arranged layers and then representing what happens within each layer separately, as shown in Fig. 5. Thus, the model in Fig. 3 only shows the content of the application layer, while completely hiding the presence and operation of the underlying operating system layer.

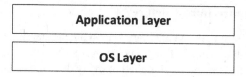

Fig. 5. A layered (descriptive) model of a software system

However, the use of layering is merely a modeling pattern used in descriptive models [13]. It does not in any way reduce the overall complexity of the underlying system, but merely helps us in understanding the system. (In fact, although commonly used in practice, software layers are a purely conceptual construct (i.e., an abstraction) that is not supported as a first-class concept in any standard programming language.)

3.4   Prescriptive and Descriptive Models in Industrial Practice

In the process of design, designers invariably start with high-level descriptive models. These capture putative architectures designed to satisfy the main system requirements. In fact, it is often the case that these models are often used to elicit requirements, since they serve as a convenient focal points for resolving potential stakeholder conflicts [8]. In order to make informed design decisions, it should be possible to analyze these models to determine whether or not they satisfy the requirements. For this it is critical that such models are analyzable for the properties of interest. Note that there are typically many different descriptive models serving different purposes, which have to be reconciled eventually – often a non-trivial task[6].

Through a process of gradual refinement of such models and analyses, one or more prescriptive models will emerge. Since the "devil is in the details" sometimes, inconsistencies and conflicts between different design proposals are only detected in such fine-grained models. Naturally, the later such issues are uncovered the greater the task of resolving them, since this might require rework of previously agreed designs.

But, beyond analysis and design, models also serve a fundamental purpose during system maintenance and evolution. To ensure preservation of the architectural integrity of a system, the designers of the new functionality must be sufficiently knowledgeable about the core design principles on which it was based. However, if the designers and developers of the new feature are new to the system, this can be difficult to achieve, particularly if (a) the original design team members are unavailable for consultation, or (b) if there is no trustworthy documentation that can be referenced. In such situations, descriptive models are crucial as teaching aids.

---

[6] The difficulty with this approach is that the independently derived solutions to the sub-problems may not be independent of each other. This leads to subsequent integration problems. As Michael Jackson noted: "Having divided to conquer, we must reunite if we wish to rule" [5].

4   On Model-Based Software Engineering

There can be no doubt that software is unique among engineering disciplines in a number of regards. The most obvious is the fact that software involves minimal production costs. When implementing software there is no heavy material to be lifted, carried, or bent into shape; no chemicals to be obtained, combined, or processed in some complex manner; no expensive scaffolding to put up. This is, of course, an important benefit, but it can also have disadvantages. Chief among these is that, unhampered by physical production constraints, it is easy to generate complexity in software merely by writing code.

A proven method of reducing complexity, is to use of higher-level computer languages, which are closer to human reasoning and to domain-specific concepts. This was the original motivation behind so-called third-generation programming languages. However, these have not proven effective for descriptive purposes resulting in the emergence of modern *modeling languages*.

4.1   Modeling Languages vs. Programming Languages

There is some debate whether there is a fundamental difference between modeling and programming. After all, a program is a human-readable textual *representation* of the binary data that is actually stored and executed in a computer. Thus, it can be argued that by programming, we are abstracting away the details (i.e., modeling) of the underlying computing instruction set and data representations. Given that, it can be argued that programs *are* models. So, is this conceptually any different from the case where a model written in some computer-based modeling language is used to generate code?

The simple answer to that question is "no"; i.e., programming *is* indeed a kind of modeling. However, that question may be too narrowly focused, since it fails to account for the full range of purposes of models. The fact is that programming languages are intended primarily and almost exclusively for prescriptive purposes, which means that they tend to be more technology facing than human facing. As a result, their constructs and their syntax are designed to be sufficiently precise and detailed to ensure an unambiguous specification of the desired implementation. Note that practically all common programming languages use a strictly textual syntax, which is generally much easier to process by a computer than a graphical syntax. This despite the proven fact that some aspects of a system may be much more naturally expressed using graphical forms.

For example, compare the two representations of a component-based network structure shown in Fig. 6. The diagram on the left uses a typical graphical notation, such as found in a modeling language like UML. The right-hand side shows an equivalent textual specification of the same network as might be expressed in some programming language. Most human readers would agree that the mixed graphical-textual representation of on the left is more intuitive and, therefore, easier to understand.

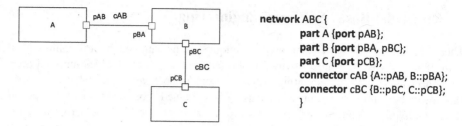

Fig. 6. A component diagram (left) and its textual representation (right)

Thus, one key distinction between modeling languages and programming languages is that the former have a concrete syntax that is much more oriented to human needs. Furthermore, because the definitions of modeling languages often separate their abstract syntax from their concrete syntax, it is even possible to use multiple different concrete syntaxes for a given modeling language, based on the purpose of a model. This is particularly useful, since it allows us to view a given model using different concrete representations, depending on concerns.

There is another important distinction that can differentiate the two categories of languages: the degree of enforcement of formal syntactical rules. In case of programming languages, there is little flexibility: a compiler will not proceed with code generation until every last syntactical flaw has been removed. That is, before a program can be useful, it must be both complete and syntactically correct.

Most descriptive models, on the other hand, tend to be incomplete and may even be left inconsistent. For example, we may be using a modeling language just to "sketch out" a vague idea in the form of a model, so that it can be discussed by stakeholders. In such situations, we would definitely prefer not to be burdened in placing unnecessary effort in ensuring full conformance to the various syntactical rules, since we are not interested in using such a model for prescription. Ideally, exploration of the design space should be made as lightweight and as efficient as possible, especially in the early phases of development – something that is difficult to achieve if a programming language is used for this purpose because of the need to make even early prototypes complete and correct at all levels of detail. Hence, we are left with less time for exploring different design alternatives.

One alternative, of course, is to use completely informal specifications in natural language text, pseudocode, or informal diagrams to capture a design idea during design space exploration. This, unfortunately, relies exclusively on all-too-fallible human reasoning and is less reliable. Clearly, the optimum seems to lie somewhere in the middle; that is, something that allows us to take advantage of the power of computers to help with correctness, yet does not tie us down too much with a bureaucratic-like formality, at least not until necessary.

There are two ways of achieving this option. One possibility is simply to define fewer syntactic rules in the language, such that it is possible to define models that are incomplete, yet can still be partially checked for syntactic consistency. An example of such a language is standard UML, which has numerous formal syntactic rules expressed as OCL constraints that can be validated, but still leaves the possibility of incomplete models [9]. Some UML tools provide a refinement of this approach, by allowing modelers to define which of the OCL rules are to be enforced and which ones not. The other strategy is similar: it consists of defining a complete set of formal syntactic rules that a fully valid model must obey, but to group these rules into different levels of strictness. Modelers can then select the degree of strictness that they would like to enforce at a given point. During early phases of development, the level would be set low and increased gradually over time as the design solidifies.

4.2 From Models to Code: A Seamless Thread?

As discussed in the introduction, my colleagues and I had anticipated a "seamless" process, whereby both design and programming (i.e., implementation) would be done using a single high-level domain specific language. In fact, there are a number of successful examples of pragmatic feasibility of this approach in industrial practice (e.g., [2, 16]).

This does indeed represent a unification of modeling and implementation. But, this only applies to *prescriptive models*, which, as we argued, are only one type of model needed in the engineering process.

A key lesson that emerged from our experiences with using an implementation-oriented modeling language is that the resulting prescriptive models are *not* suitable for descriptive purposes. Not only do they contain too much detail, but they are also expressed in a language that is not suitable for the wide variety of different descriptive purposes. Different stakeholders are focused on different concerns and, hence, prefer languages that more directly capture and reflect those concerns. In our experience, implementation models, with their abundance of detail required to specify the infrastructure and primary system functionality, have proven almost as complex and difficult to understand as traditional program code. This means that, while the modeling language can simplify an implementer's task, it does not do much for other stakeholders.

However, if we introduce multiple models specified in a variety of languages, there is the obvious danger of inconsistencies between such models and the implementation. This renders descriptive models as untrustworthy, which greatly diminishes their value. A putative but not fully proven solution to this problem is described next.

4.3 Resolving the Multiple Models Dilemma

Multiple mutually inconsistent sources of information for a given system present a dilemma to the reader: which source is to be trusted, if any? Duplicated information quickly becomes unsynchronized despite the most meticulous procedural strictures designed to prevent that. The only pragmatic solution to this problem is to have *exactly one reference source of information* for an element of the system. This does not mean that such information only appears in one place, which would clearly be too restrictive. Instead, it means that all representations of that information except for the reference itself, whatever their context and concrete form, are formally (i.e., automatically) derived from the reference source. One approach to achieve this is that the basic source of all information about a system is contained in the final implementation (prescriptive) model itself. If full automated model-to-code generation is used, then the equivalent computer program is a fully derived artifact. Any changes to the model will be accurately reflected in the code. This approach could also be applied in the reverse direction to produce the necessary descriptive models from either the code or the implementation model.

Clearly, this requires sophisticated automatable model-to-model transformations. Particularly challenging are abstraction transformations, that is, transformations that generate abstract representations of detailed models into less detailed ones suitable for descriptive purposes. This means not only that they perform abstraction, but also that they translate from one modeling language to another.

To perform the necessary abstraction transformation for this case requires a precise definition of the various element-to-element mappings. For example, the elements **PeerA**, **FrontEndA**, and **CommEndPointA** in Fig. 4, are all "merged" into element **PeerA** in Fig. 3. To reduce overhead and effort, these types of mappings can often be based on standard abstraction patterns such as those described in [12].

To assist in performing such transformations, one approach that has proven successful in practice is the use of *concern-specific annotations* attached to the implementation model. These are used as "hints" to the transformation engine when constructing the domain-specific model. In case of the UML modeling language a facility that is suitable for this purpose is the *profile mechanism* [9, 10]. A UML profile can be used to provide a domain-specific interpretation of selected elements of a model. Furthermore, this can be supplemented with domain-specific data needed for analysis. For example, when analyzing the timing properties of a proposed software design, it is possible to identify time-consuming elements of a system as well as the amount of time that they consume, by marking them with appropriate annotations defined in the industry-standard MARTE profile of UML [9, 14]. This information can be used by a model-to-model transform program to produce a corresponding timing model of the system expressed in a language suited to that purpose. And, because UML profiles can be dynamically applied to a model (and also "un-applied" subsequently) without affecting the underlying model in any way, it is possible to provide many different domain-specific interpretations for a single implementation model.

Although there are numerous practical *ad hoc* solutions to model transformations, it is still primarily a research topic. Fortunately, there is some excellent work on the theoretical foundations of model transformations that should eventually wind its way into practice and industrial-strength tools (e.g., [3, 15]).

However, one major drawback of this approach is that it is practical only once the implementation model is in place. That is, it cannot be used in the forward direction. For example, numerous high-level concern-specific models might be used during the design process, expressed using domain-specific modeling languages. If accepted, such models must be refined and converted to the modeling language of the implementation and inserted into the overall implementation model. The problem of ensuring that such a transformation is semantics (i.e., design intent) preserving has no general solution.

However, once the conversion has taken place, it may be possible to capture it formally, so that it can be used subsequently to automatically derive the required descriptive view.

5 Conclusions

The ability of modeling languages to be used in the development of complex software systems has been answered in the affirmative in industrial practice numerous times (e.g., [2, 16]). This has raised the prospects of a potentially "seamless" progress from models to code, characterized by a continuous process of refinement starting with high-level models and terminating with model-based implementations. This is an appealing innovation since it avoids some of the most critical error-prone discontinuities that have plagued engineering from time immemorial, since they often lead to failure to accurately reflect design intent in the final implementation.

In this essay, we examined the role of models and modeling in the development of software systems by first analyzing how these are treated in more traditional forms of engineering. Along the way, we also reviewed the role and kinds of models used in software engineering practice. Based on this and despite all the idiosyncrasies and unique features of software relative to more traditional engineering technologies, we are driven to a conclusion that there does not seem to be any compelling reason why software engineering should approach models and modeling any differently in this regard. The only substantive distinction that uniquely characterizes software seems to be that production costs are practically negligible. However, since production occurs once the design is completed, this does not seem to affect what needs to be modeled or how it is done.

Acknowledgement. The author would like to express his gratitude to Prof. Manfred Broy and Dr. Gerard Berry on their very helpful and constructive reviews of the original version of this text. All remaining flaws are solely the responsibility of the author.

References

1. Brooks, F.: The Mythical Man-Month. Addison-Wesley, Reading (1995)
2. Corcoran, D.: The good, the bad, and the ugly: experiences with model-driven development in large scale projects at Ericsson. In: Proceedings of the 6th European Conference on Modelling Foundations and Applications (ECMFA 2010) (2010)
3. Czarnecki, K., Helsen, S.: Feature-based survey of model transformation approaches. IBM Syst. J. **45**(3), 621–645 (2006)
4. Harel, D.: Statecharts: a visual formalism for complex systems. Sci. Comput. Program. **8**(3), 231–274 (1987)
5. Jackson, M.: CASE tools and development methods. In: Spurr, K., Layzell, P. (eds.) CASE on Trial, Chap. 8. John Wiley & Sons (1990)
6. Lee, E.A., Seshia, S.A.: Introduction to Embedded Systems, A Cyber-Physical Systems Approach, 2nd edn. (2015). http://LeeSeshia.org. ISBN 978-1-312-42740-2

7. Morgan, M.H. (translator): Vitruvius: The Ten Books on Architecture. Dover Publications, Inc., New York (1914). (An on-line version of this volume can be found in the Project Gutenburg repository at http://www.gutenberg.org/files/20239/20239-h/29239-h.htm)
8. Nuseibeh, B.: Weaving together requirements and architectures. IEEE Comput. **34**(3), 115–117 (2001)
9. Object Management Group (OMG): UML Profile for MARTE™: Modeling and Analysis of Real-time Embedded Systems™, Version 1.1, OMG document no.: formal/2011-06-02 (2011). (http://www.omg.org/spec/MARTE/1.1/PDF)
10. Object Management Group (OMG): OMG Unified Modeling Language™ (OMG UML), Version 2.5, OMG document no.: formal/2015-03-01 (2015). (http://www.omg.org/spec/UML/2.5/PDF)
11. Saltzer, J., et al.: End-to-end arguments in system design. In: Proceedings of the Second International Conference on Distributed Computing Systems, pp. 509–512. IEEE Computer Society (1981)
12. Selic, B., Gullekson, G., Ward, P.: Real-time Object-Oriented Modeling. John Wiley & Sons, Hoboken (1994)
13. Selic, B.: A short catalogue of abstraction patterns for model-based software engineering. Int. J. Inf. **5**(1–2), 313–334 (2011)
14. Selic, B., Gerard, S.: Modeling and Analysis of Real-Time and Embedded Systems with UML and MARTE: Developing Cyber-physical Systems. The MK/OMG Press (2013)
15. Syriani, E., Vangheluwe, H., LaShomb, B.: T-Core: a framework for custom-built model transformation engines. J. Softw. Syst. Model. **14**(3), 1215–1243 (2015)
16. Weigert, T., Weil, F.: Practical experience in using model-driven engineering to develop trustworthy systems. In: Proceedings of IEEE International Conference on Sensor Networks, Ubiquitous, and Trustworthy Computing (SUTC 2006), pp. 208–217. IEEE Computer Society (2006)

On a Unified View of Modeling and Programming Position Paper

Ed Seidewitz[✉]

nMeta LLC, 14000 Gulliver's Trail, Bowie, MD 20720, USA
ed-s@modeldriven.com,
ed@nmeta.us

Abstract. In the software community, modeling and programming are generally considered to be different things. However, some software models specify behavior precisely enough that they can be executed in their own right. And all programs can be considered models, at least of the executions that they specify. So perhaps modeling and programming are not actually so different after all. Indeed, there is a modeling/programming convergence going on right now in the Unified Modeling Language (UML) community, with a recent series of specifications on precise execution semantics for a growing subset of UML. But the language design legacy of UML is largely grounded in the old view that sharply separates models and programs, complicating the new convergence. It is perhaps now time to move forward to a new generation of unified modeling/programming languages.

Keywords: Programming languages · Modeling languages · UML · fUML · Alf · Action language · Modeling tools

I think it is safe to say that most software developers consider models to be something quite different from programs. However, let's consider what a "model" really is.

A model is always *about* something, which I term the *system under study* (SUS). For our purposes here, we can consider a model to consist of a set of statements about the SUS expressed in some *modeling language*. These statements make assertions about certain properties of the SUS, but say nothing about other properties that are not mentioned.

A model thus *abstracts* from the SUS it models by the selection of statements it makes. The model is useful to the extent that the properties not considered by the model are simply not important for the purpose of the model or can be chosen or determined independently of the model. (For further discussion of this view of modeling for software, and it's relation to how modeling is done in other fields, see [6].)

A modeling language can be textual, graphical or a combination of the two. Depending on the expressivity of the language, it may be possible to make statements about an SUS that range from very precise to quite loose. A precise model simply makes more detailed assertions that place tighter, less ambiguous constraints on the SUS.

T. Margaria and B. Steffen (Eds.): ISoLA 2016, Part II, LNCS 9953, pp. 27–31, 2016.
DOI: 10.1007/978-3-319-47169-3_3

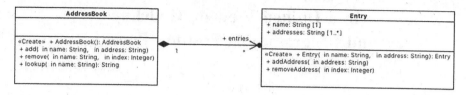

Fig. 1. UML class model of an AddressBook

Consider the simple class model shown in Fig. 1, in which the Unified Modeling Language (UML) [2] is used as the modeling language. What does this model mean? That depends on how you *interpret* it.

One interpretation is that this is a problem domain model of address books. Under this interpretation, the model states that an address book can have zero or more entries; that each entry must include one name and at least one address; that addresses can be added to, removed from and looked up in an address book; and so forth.

But now suppose that I add behavioral models for the operations specified in the classes in Fig. 1. For example, Fig. 2 shows a UML activity model for the behavior of the AddressBook lookup operation. What is this a model of? Effectively, it is a model of the *computation* to be carried out in order to perform the lookup operation.

Indeed, this activity is within the so-called *Foundational UML* (fUML) subset of UML, for which there are precisely-defined, standard execution semantics [5]. If behavioral models are provided for all the operations shown in Fig. 1, then the result is a completely *executable* UML model, with standard semantics.

Now, the diagram in Fig. 2 may seem to be a somewhat awkward way to specify behavior at this level of detail. However, there is also a standard *Action Language for Foundational UML* (Alf) [1], which provides a fully textual notation for writing such activity models. For instance, the activity drawn in Fig. 2 can be written as follows in Alf:

```
namespace AddressBook;
activity lookup(in name: String): String[0..*] {
   return this.entries->
           select e (e.name == name).addresses;
}
```

This now looks a lot like code. However, the *meaning* of this textual notation is, in fact, defined by mapping it to executable UML models. The Alf text given above essentially maps to the UML activity model shown in Fig. 2, and execution of the Alf text has exactly the semantics of executing the corresponding UML activity. Thus, Alf is not a separate programming language, but, rather, a textual notation for writing UML models.

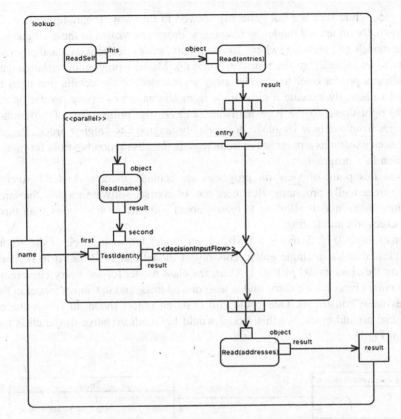

Fig. 2. UML activity model for the AddressBook lookup operation

Further, Alf also includes textual notation for structural UML modeling elements. For example, the AddressBook class can be notated in Alf as follows:

```
class AddressBook {

public entries: compose Entry[0..*];

@Create public AddressBook();
public add(in name: String, in address: String);
public remove(in name: String, in index: Integer);
public lookup(in name: String): String[0..*];

}
```

So, it is clear that a modeling language does not have to be graphical, and that models can be executable. So how is this different than programming?

In fact, while they are not generally viewed in this way, programming languages are essentially *all* textual modeling languages. Programs written in these languages are precise models of *execution* (where, for simplicity, I consider both data and algorithmic aspects to be included in the term "execution"). Modern programming languages, in fact, allow a programmer to abstract away a great deal of the details that need to be handled to actually execute a program – from language processing, to the operating system, right down to the bare hardware. Indeed, the progression of programming languages from machine language, to assembly language to "higher order" languages can be seen exactly as a progression in increasing the abstraction possible for modeling execution in a program.

From this point of view *all* programs are actually models. And all *executable* models are actually programs. But there are, of course, software models that are *not* programs. Such models allow us to reason about software in ways other than through direct execution and testing.

For example, Fig. 3 shows a UML object model for an instance of the Address-Book class that has a single entry. This object model can be *deduced* to be correct, based on the class model in Fig. 1. Thus, the class model for the Entry class requires that an entry object have a name and at least one address, and the object model in Fig. 3 satisfies these constraints. One could still draw an object model in which the entry object had no addresses, but this model would be *invalid* relative to the class model given in Fig. 1.

Fig. 3. UML object model for an AddressBook

Thus, UML object models can be given precise semantics that are not necessarily execution semantics. There can also be requirements models, architecture models and business models with precise semantics that may or may not be execution semantics. But a major advantage of considering execution in the context of a wider modeling language is that it allows deductive or inductive reasoning on models to be combined with execution and testing, within a single, consistent semantic framework. On the other hand, the semantics of most programming languages are *entirely* execution semantics, other than, perhaps, "static semantic" checks that may be provided by the language compiler (such as type checking).

To maximize the effectiveness of a combined modeling/programming language, one would like a language that takes the best experience with the design of both traditional modeling and programming languages. I would suggest that the following characteristics are particularly important for such a language.

- It should be designed to express both problem and solution domain models, not just as an abstraction of hardware computing paradigms.

- It should have a formal semantics that allows reasoning about models, but also provide a (consistent) execution semantics for models (or segments of models) in which execution behavior is fully specified.
- It should provide a textual notation for representing and reasoning on all types of models, but should also provide graphical notations where those are most appropriate, allowing multiple views of the same model.

With the adoption of the fUML and Alf specifications, as well as a growing set of additional "precise semantics" specifications built on that foundation [3, 4], such a convergence of programming and modeling language design is actually already taking place for UML. However, UML was not originally designed with executability in mind and it has become a very complicated language (especially since version 2.0). Further, even in the latest base UML standard [2], the specifications of semantics is informal and largely imprecise. This makes it considerably more difficult to create separate precise semantics specification for UML, while maintaining general compatibility with the language as it has existed for many years. And it limits how far the community can practically go in achieving the goals I listed above.

It is, perhaps, time we moved on to something better – both for modeling and for programming.

References

1. Object Management Group. Action Language for Foundational UML (Alf): Concrete Syntax for a UML Action Language, Version 1.0.1, October 2013. http://www.omg.org/spec/ALF/1.0.1/
2. Object Management Group. OMG Unified Modeling Language™ (OMG UML), Version 2.5 (2015). http://www.omg.org/spec/UML/2.5/
3. Object Management Group. Precise Semantics of UML Composite Structures (PSCS), Version 1.0 (2015). http://www.omg.org/spec/PSCS/1.0/
4. Object Management Group. Precise Semantics of UML State Machines, Request for Proposals (2015). http://doc.omg.org/ad/2015-3-2
5. Object Management Group. Semantics of a Foundational Subset for Executable UML Models (fUML), v1.2.1, January 2016. http://www.omg.org/spec/FUML/1.2.1/
6. Seidewitz, E.: What models mean. IEEE Softw. **20**, 26–32 (2003)

On the Feasibility of a Unified Modelling and Programming Paradigm

Anne E. Haxthausen[1]([✉]) and Jan Peleska[2]

[1] DTU Compute, Technical University of Denmark, Kongens Lyngby, Denmark
aeha@dtu.dk
[2] Department of Mathematics and Computer Science, University of Bremen,
Bremen, Germany
jp@cs.uni-bremen.de

Abstract. In this article, the feasibility of a unified modelling and programming paradigm is discussed from the perspective of large scale system development and verification in collaborative development environments. We motivate the necessity to utilise multiple formalisms for development and verification, in particular for complex cyber-physical systems or systems of systems. Though modelling, programming, and verification will certainly become more closely integrated in the future, we do not expect a single formalism to become universally applicable and accepted by the development and verification communities. The multi-formalism approach requires to translate verification artefacts (assertions, test cases, etc.) between different representations, in order to allow for the verification of emergent properties based on local verification results established with different methods and modelling techniques. It is illustrated by means of a case study from the railway domain, how this can be achieved, using concepts from the theory of institutions. This also enables the utilisation of verification tools in different formalisms, despite the fact that these tools are usually developed for one specific formal method.

1 Introduction

State of Practise. "Programs are models" - this is a well known slogan of model-driven development, and it is well-founded, since several modelling formalisms allow for automated code generation, where the code is just regarded as a less abstract (textual) model. Refinement relations between abstract and more concrete models can be specified with mathematical rigour, so that the code can be traced back to the original model without any ambiguities. This suggests a unified approach to constructing models and software code during the development life cycle, and it also indicates that a comprehensive approach to developing new modelling formalisms as well as new programming languages should be adopted.

Both ideas, however, cannot be considered as state of practise today. Despite all efforts to provide a seamless modelling and programming environment, tool support for high-level modelling is still very heterogeneous and controversially discussed, with issues such as

© Springer International Publishing AG 2016
T. Margaria and B. Steffen (Eds.): ISoLA 2016, Part II, LNCS 9953, pp. 32–49, 2016.
DOI: 10.1007/978-3-319-47169-3_4

- SCADE or Simulink/Stateflow or UML?
- Domain-specific languages or wide-spectrum languages?
- Semi-formal of fully formal modelling semantics?

In contrast to this, we experience a growing consensus about the effectiveness of programming languages (C++, Java, Haskell) and the usability of integrated development environments (IDEs), such as Eclipse, Microsoft Developer, or X-code, all of them offering effective support for software development, debugging, and various aspects of testing. Last, but not least, powerful re-usable libraries have been built for supporting efficient software programming, while the higher-level formalisms only provide very basic packages that can be re-used when creating models[1].

Summarising, we agree with the authors of [7] that it will take another 10 years until graphical high-level modelling tools will have reached a level of perfection that is comparable to current state-of-the art IDEs. According to our understanding, the reluctant acceptance of high-level modelling techniques is less caused by a reluctance to adopt formal concepts, but simply by the fact that the user experience is more satisfactory and the feeling of productiveness is higher when working on the level of software code than when working with more abstract formalisms.

Advocating the Multi-formalism Approach. This position paper is less about the closer integration of modelling, programming, and verification, because this is not the only problem to be solved: from our perspective, an even more severe problem consists in the fact that as of today, there is no preferred modelling formalism the majority of the development and verification communities might be willing to agree upon. On the contrary, development and verification projects for large and complex systems involving heterogeneous components, such as cyber-physical systems or systems of systems [12] suggest that a multi-formalism approach – supported by collaborative distributed development environments – may become the preferred solution in the future. This enables development and verification teams to use optimised methods and tools for developing and verifying specific system components. While this obviously helps to avoid endless discussions about which modelling language to choose in a project, the multi-formalism approach also comes with a down-side: verification results locally obtained for system components by means of different formalisms need to be translated into other representations when emergent system properties have to be derived from local component-specific assertions.

The main message of this paper is that the advantages of the multi-formalism approach outweigh this translation effort, because systematic methods for transferring theories and verification results between formalisms exist and can be efficiently applied. They even help to re-use tools built for one formalism in

---

[1] It is interesting to note that the Z specification language already provided extensive libraries, as can be seen in its early reference books like [16]. This, however, has not become a standard requirement for designing new formalisms.

the context of another. We expect further that the necessity to translate verification artefacts between different formalisms will advance the integration of modelling and programming, because these translations can only be defined and applied on the more abstract level of modelling.

Our thesis is supported further by the growing interest in model-driven systems engineering [13]: currently, manufacturers in the aircraft, railways, and automotive domains express considerable interest in a model-based approach to developing large-scale complex systems or even systems of systems. This interest is motivated by the desire to analyse executable models for early detection of conceptual errors and to exchange semantically precise models instead of or in addition to informal textual documents with suppliers. This general acceptance of the importance of formalised modelling is expected to accelerate the elaboration of integrated modelling and programming approaches. Moreover, at least for the avionic domain and for the domain of railway control systems, model-based systems engineering is always discussed in multi-formalism context, where tool-supported methods like Simulink/Stateflow, SCADE, SysML, and B are applied to different modelling, code generation, and verification tasks in large-scale development projects.

Overview. In Sect. 2, the necessity for a multi-formalism approach to large-scale system developments is justified. We analyse the possibilities to apply multiple high-level formalisms when developing and verifying complex systems in a collaborative development environment. In Sect. 3, a case study is presented that will be used to illustrate the verification of emergent properties in the next Sect. 4 using the linking approach which allows to translate assertions elaborated in one formalism to equivalent assertions of another. In Sect. 5, the linking approach is applied again: it is described how verification tools can interact to support different formalisms with a maximal degree of re-use. As an example, we consider test strategies for finite state machines with guaranteed fault coverage and show how the resulting test strategies can be translated to other formalisms while preserving the fault coverage properties. In Sect. 6 the conclusions are presented.

2   A Multi-formalism Approach to Large-Scale System Developments

For large-scale system developments, as needed for complex distributed cyber-physical systems (CPS) or systems of systems, several modelling formalisms, and associated development and verification methods with corresponding tool support are needed. We see the following main reasons for this assessment.

- Sub-components should be modelled, developed, and verified with formalisms that are optimised for their specific requirements. For CPS, these components may be very heterogeneous, from smart sensors to discrete or hybrid (mixed discrete and time-continuous observables) control components, supported by database servers and mathematical constraint solvers.

- Different development and verification teams will work on large scale developments, each group preferring to use their "favourite" methods and associated tool box.

In a development campaign for an aircraft, for example, hybrid control tasks might be modelled with Simulink/Stateflow, local synchronous discrete control with SCADE, and integration aspects (such as asynchronous data exchange between flight deck and cabin) with SysML. This example shows that the multi-formalism approach is not so much a vision but more like an established fact today. What is missing is a systematic approach allowing for mathematically sound integration of development artefacts and for sound interpretation of local verification results in the global system context:

- For the verification of *emergent properties* – these are properties that can only be derived from the collaborative behaviour of all interacting system components – it is necessary to take local verification results into account which have been developed using different formalisms to express the assertions guaranteed by the sub-components.

Apart from this essential prerequisite for developing safe systems using the multi-formalism approach, there is another, more efficiency-oriented challenge to be solved:

- Complex automation algorithms available in a tool supporting a specific formalism need to be made available for other formalisms as well.

Three Approaches Supporting Multi-formalism Development and Verification. We see at least three possible major approaches for semantic integration of development and verification artefacts based on different formalisms:

1. The *linking approach* uses mechanisms to translate models and assertions between different formalisms. It can be based, for example, on the theory of institutions [4–6] with its foundations in mathematical category theory, or on the Unifying Theories of Programming (UTP) [8] which relies on lattice theory and the equivalence between programming languages and logic.
2. The *megamodel approach* maps the meta models (i.e. semantic models) of different formalisms into the same meta-meta model, usually denoted as a megamodel in the software engineering communities [1]. Megamodels contain the semantic representations of models elaborated in different formalisms; moreover, they contain transformations relating elements of the different models. This allows for verifying emergent properties on the megamodel representations of all sub-component assertions.
3. The *wide-spectrum approach* combines multiple "sub-formalisms" in one and provides a common "heavy weight" semantic meta model.

The three approaches are illustrated in Fig. 1.

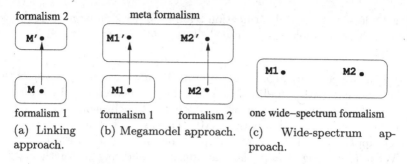

Fig. 1. Three approaches for semantic integration.

From today's perspective, we consider the linking approach as the most promising one, because it has been elaborated in the most thorough way and exercised – sometimes only heuristically – in practise. The megamodel approach is still a fairly new research topic, and many investigations are only concerned with static model semantics, while the linking approach fully supports the translation of facts about behavioural semantics. Finally, the wide-spectrum approach (UML/SysML are prominent examples from this class) never seems to cover all modelling features that people may need in a specific development and verification undertaking. Moreover, the integration of sub-formalisms automatically results in complex semantic models. This can be seen in the UML and SysML standards published by the Object Management Group, where only the static semantics is fully formalised, while the behavioural semantics of language elements is only specified in natural language style.

The linking approach is illustrated by means of an example in the paragraphs below. We use linking techniques based on the theory of institutions. This should not suggest, however, that we consider this as the preferred linking method; the UTP-based method seems to be equally well-suited, as can be seen from case studies like [2].

3   Case Study – On-board Train Controller for Speed and Brakes

Consider an on-board control system for high-speed trains. This typically comprises several controllers communicating over some local bus system. In Fig. 2, a vital part of the on-board control system is shown, consisting of the *ceiling speed monitor (CSM)* and the *brake controller (BC)*. The former compares the train's current speed v against the maximal speed v_m currently admissible according to the commands received from the radio block centre. If the speed is too high, the CSM first sends warning messages to the train engine driver (N = Normal, O = Overspeed, W = Warning), and then – if the train is speeding even more – transits to intervention mode (I), where a braking command $b := ON$ is transmitted on the bus. The conditions to release the brakes after an intervention by the CSM depend on the train's location; this is reflected by a Boolean parameter *nva* ("national value allowing early release of brakes") sent by the radio block centre. Its meaning is discussed below when presenting the behavioural CSM model. We assume that the CSM interface is realised according to the shared variable paradigm: the inputs are polled regularly, and the output variables are written to at the end of each processing cycle.

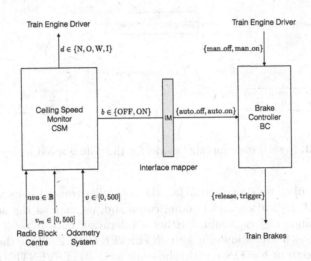

Fig. 2. Interfaces of the on-board train control system.

For illustrating certain aspects of theory linking, we assume that the BC has an event-based interface: it receives commands to trigger or release the brakes from both the CSM and the train engine driver as events auto_on, auto_off (automated trigger and release of the brakes) and man_on, man_off (manual trigger and release events), respectively. To map the state-based CSM output b to input events of the BC, an interface mapper (IM) observes changes of b and creates the corresponding auto_on, auto_off events for the BC. The IM could be implemented, for example, as a lower software layer of the BC which reads state data from the communication bus (realised, for example, as a reflective memory), and creates events for the BC software accordingly.

The CSM behaviour is specified by means of a SysML state machine communicating via shared variables, as shown in Fig. 3. Initially, the controller is in state **NORMAL**, and the outputs to train engine driver and BC are N and OFF, respectively. As soon as the actual speed exceeds the maximal speed allowed $(v > v_m)$, the controller changes into state **OVERSPEED** and changes the indication to the train engine driver to O. If the actual speed exceeds $v_m + dW(v_m)$ (dW is a continuous non-negative function depending on v_m), the indication changes to W. Speeding further until the threshold $v_m + dI1(v_m)$ is violated leads to a transition into the first intervention state: the indication changes to I, and the output b to the BC is set to ON.

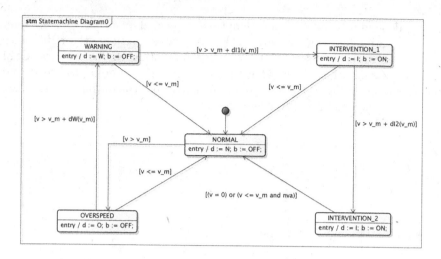

Fig. 3. SysML state machine model for the ceiling speed monitor.

In the control states described so far, the controller transits back to NORMAL and resets both indication and braking command, as soon as the actual speed is in normal range $v \leq v_m$ again. Further acceleration until $v > v_m + dI2(v_m)$, however, enforces a transition into state INTERVENTION_2. There the indication $d = I$ and the output $b = ON$ remain the same as in INTERVENTION_1, but the transition back to normal is only allowed when the train has come to a standstill, or if the country-dependent value nva has been set to **true** and $v \leq v_m$ holds again.

The brake controller BC is modelled as a deterministic finite state machine (DFSM) in Mealy Machine style, as shown in Fig. 4. In initial state RELEASED, the brakes are released, and repeated auto_off, man_off events do not change this. On reception of the man_on event from the train engine driver, the brakes are triggered. In the corresponding DFSM state TRIGGERED, the brakes may only be released again by the train engine driver: auto_off commands from the CSM are ignored. If however, the CSM also sends a braking command via event auto_on, the DFSM transits into state TRIGGERED_AUTO, and now only the auto_off command can release the brakes again. If the BC is in state RELEASED and gets the command to trigger the brakes from the CSM, it directly transits to TRIG-GERED_AUTO. Again, only the CSM command can initiate the release of the brakes in this situation, and commands from the train engine driver are ignored.

4   Emergent Property Verification

In the case study introduced above, consider the safety-related verification obligation

> *Whenever the CSM indicates intervention (I) on output d, the emergency brakes are triggered in the next system state at the latest.*

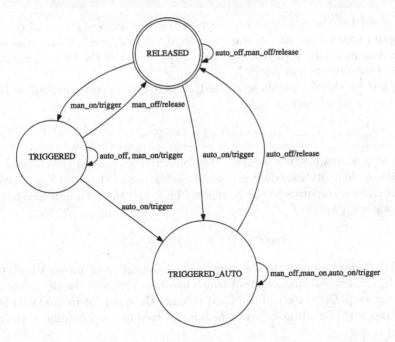

Fig. 4. Finite state machine model of the brake controller.

This is an emerging property, because its validity cannot be decided by analysis of the CSM or the BC alone: the CSM knows about d, but it has no control over the trigger event to the brakes. On the contrary, the BC knows when the trigger event has been fired, but doesn't know about d-indications.

Furthermore, we observe that the CSM and the BC have been modelled with different formalisms, since the latter has DFSM semantics, while the former is represented as a SysML state machine with a shared variable interface. The behavioural semantics of SysML state machines can be represented conveniently by Kripke Structures (see [10] for a detailed description of the CSM semantics) whose states are variable valuation functions and whose atomic propositions have CSM variables and control state names as free variables. We choose the semantic variant where outputs changed while passing through transient states are not observable. Assume, for example, that the CSM is in state NORMAL and receives a new actual speed value $v > v_m + dI2(v_m)$. Then it passes through states OVER-SPEED, WARNING, and INTERVENTION_1 until it ends up in INTERVENTION_2 where it becomes stable. Only then the associated outputs $d = I, b = ON$ become visible. Moreover, input changes only become visible while the CSM resides in a stable state.

We decide to use Kripke Structures to represent the semantics of the complete system S and specify assertions by means of LTL formulas over variable symbols of S. The variables of S are the interface variables of the CSM plus auxiliary Boolean variables a_{on} (if true, the last input event on the IM-BC interface was auto_on, if false, the last input on this interface was auto_off), m_{on} (if true, the last input event to the BC on the train engine driver interface was man_on, if false, it was man_off), r (if true, the last output event of the BC was release, if false, the last output was trigger).

With these variable symbols at hand, the safety property specified textually above can be formalised as

$$\varphi_S \equiv \mathbf{G}\big(\neg(d = I) \vee \mathbf{X}\neg r\big) \tag{1}$$

Let us now assume that local verification activities have already shown that the CSM implementation conforms to the SysML model shown in Fig. 3, the BC implementation conforms to the model in Fig. 4, and that the interface mapper implementation fulfils

$$\varphi_{IM} \equiv \mathbf{G}\big((b = ON) \Leftrightarrow \mathbf{X}a_{on}\big) \tag{2}$$

Formula (2) specifies that the IM reacts on a change of CSM output b from OFF to ON by creating an auto_on event which becomes visible to the BC in the next processing step. Conversely, if the CSM changes the b output from ON to OFF, the IM generates an auto_off event which is reflected by $\neg a_{on}$ holding in the next processing step.

Using k-induction [14], we can prove by model checking that the CSM model satisfies the invariant

$$\varphi_{CSM} \equiv \mathbf{G}\big(\neg(d = I) \vee (b = ON)\big) \tag{3}$$

when interpreted in the semantics where intermediate transient processing steps are not observable.

It remains to establish a suitable LTL assertion for the BC. This is not straightforward, since the DFSM semantics is represented by the state machine's *language* $L(BC)$, consisting of all finite traces of input/output events that can be performed by the BC. In contrast to this, LTL formulas are interpreted over infinite sequences π of sets of valid atomic propositions. We observe, however, that the violation of every *LTL safety property* can already be decided on a finite prefix of π. Conversely, every finite execution prefix not violating a safety formula can be extended to an infinite execution π which is a model for the safety formula [15]. Since all LTL formulas which are of interest in our context are safety formulas, this suggests that the DFSM language $L(BC)$ can be interpreted to fulfil a safety property, if this property is not violated by any I/O trace of the language.

This concept will now be realised formally by mapping DFSMs with the signature of the BC to associated Kripke structures with atomic propositions a_{on}, m_{on}, r. The construction follows the recipes of the theory of institutions [4–6]. An institution defines some essential aspects of a logic system: signatures, sentences (over a given signature), models (over a given signature), and the satisfaction relation between models and sentences of the same signature. Mappings between two institutions can be defined, by defining maps translating signatures, sentences and models between the two institutions, respectively. The linking approach performed in this section, uses this idea to first define a model map μ translating DFSM models having the signature Σ_{BC}[2] of the BC DFSM to Kripke models over a corresponding Kripke signature Σ_K[3]. We can then use this model translation map to translate the DFSM model of the BC to a corresponding Kripke model for which we can formulate a suitable LTL assertion. To ensure that the behaviour of the translated model is consistent with the original model, we also define a sentence translation map σ from Kripke sentences (LTL assertions) over Σ_K to DFSM sentences over Σ_{BC} and prove a satisfaction condition that expresses that model satisfaction of sentences is "invariant under change of formalism". The translation of models and sentences is illustrated in Fig. 5.

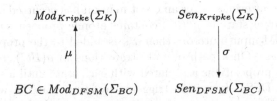

Fig. 5. Model and sentence translation. $Mod_{Kripke}(\Sigma_K)$ is the set of all Kripke models over Σ_K, $Mod_{DFSM}(\Sigma_{BC})$ is the set of all DFSM models over Σ_{BC}, $Sen_{Kripke}(\Sigma_K)$ is the set of all Kripke sentences over Σ_{BC}, and $Sen_{DFSM}(\Sigma_{BC})$ is the set of all DFSM sentences over Σ_{BC}.

Model Map. As a first step, the *model map* μ mapping DFSMs over signature Σ_{BC} to Kripke Structures over signature Σ_K is created. Let $M = (Q, q_0, \Sigma_I, \Sigma_O, h)$ be a DFSM with finite state space Q, initial state $q_0 \in Q$, input alphabet $\Sigma_I = \{auto\_on, auto\_off, man\_on, man\_off\}$, output alphabet $\Sigma_O = \{release, trigger\}$, and transition relation $h \subseteq Q \times \Sigma_I \times \Sigma_O \times Q$. Then $\mu(M)$ is defined as the Kripke Structure $\mu(M) = (S, s_0, R, L, AP)$ with

1. Atomic proposition set $AP = \{a_{on}, m_{on}, r\}$
2. State space $S \subseteq Q \times 2^{AP}$
3. Initial state $s_0 = (q_0, \{r\})$
4. Labelling function $L : S \to 2^{AP};\quad (q, A) \mapsto A$
5. Transition relation $R \subseteq S \times S$ specified by

---

[2] The signature of a DFSM model consists of its input alphabet and output alphabet. For the BC model, we have $\Sigma_{BC} = (\Sigma_I, \Sigma_O) = (\{auto\_on, auto\_off, man\_on, man\_off\}, \{release, trigger\})$.

[3] A Kripke signature consists of those input variables, local variables and output variables that can be used in a model over that signature. For the corresponding Kripke signature Σ_K it is the variables a_{on}, m_{on}, and r.

$$R = \{((q, A), (q', A')) \in S \times S \mid (q, \text{man\_on}, \text{release}, q') \in h \land A' = A \cup \{m_{\text{on}}, r\}\}$$
$$\cup \; \{((q, A), (q', A')) \in S \times S \mid (q, \text{man\_on}, \text{trigger}, q') \in h \land A' = (A \setminus \{r\}) \cup \{m_{\text{on}}\}\}$$
$$\cup \; \{((q, A), (q', A')) \in S \times S \mid (q, \text{man\_off}, \text{release}, q') \in h \land A' = (A \setminus \{m_{\text{on}}\}) \cup \{r\}\}$$
$$\cup \; \{((q, A), (q', A')) \in S \times S \mid (q, \text{man\_off}, \text{trigger}, q') \in h \land A' = (A \setminus \{m_{\text{on}}, r\})\}$$
$$\cup \; \{((q, A), (q', A')) \in S \times S \mid (q, \text{auto\_on}, \text{release}, q') \in h \land A' = A \cup \{a_{\text{on}}, r\}\}$$
$$\cup \; \{((q, A), (q', A')) \in S \times S \mid (q, \text{auto\_on}, \text{trigger}, q') \in h \land A' = (A \setminus \{r\}) \cup \{a_{\text{on}}\}\}$$
$$\cup \; \{((q, A), (q', A')) \in S \times S \mid (q, \text{auto\_off}, \text{release}, q') \in h \land A' = (A \setminus \{a_{\text{on}}\}) \cup \{r\}\}$$
$$\cup \; \{((q, A), (q', A')) \in S \times S \mid (q, \text{auto\_off}, \text{trigger}, q') \in h \land A' = (A \setminus \{a_{\text{on}}, r\})\}$$

The Kripke Structure created via μ from the BC DFSM is shown in Fig. 6. The initial state is (RELEASED, $\{r\}$). Its reachable states are the pairs (q, A) of BC states and subsets $A \subseteq AP$, such that the latter are always consistent with the latest input events: after an event man_on has occurred on DFSM level, the associated target state in $\mu(BC)$ contains atomic proposition m_{on}. If this is followed by DFSM input auto_on, then a_{on} is added to the propositions of the $\mu(BC)$ target state. On a path of state transitions in $\mu(BC)$, m_{on} remains in the set of atomic propositions associated with each state until a state transition corresponds to a DFSM transition triggered by input man_off, whereupon m_{on} is removed from the propositions of the target state reached by $\mu(BC)$.

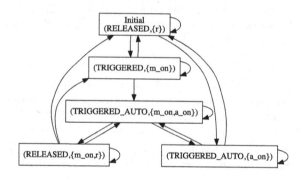

Fig. 6. Kripke Structure $\mu(BC)$.

Sentence Translation Map. In the second step of the linking approach, a *sentence translation map* σ is created. This is a map allowing us to translate assertions defined for Kripke Structures into assertions about DFSMs. For the purpose of this small example we can restrict the sentences of interest to LTL invariants $G\psi$, where ψ is a proposition in negation normal form, built from the atomic propositions of $AP = \{a_{\text{on}}, m_{\text{on}}, r\}$.

On the DFSM level, sentences are predicates over I/O-traces ι, implicitly quantified over all $\iota \in L(M)$, where $L(M)$ is the set of all I/O-traces of the model M under consideration. Again, we restrict these predicates to invariants that are written in LTL style; more precisely:

1. Sentences over a signature (Σ_I, Σ_O) are of the form $\mathbf{G}\alpha$, where α is a predicate in negation normal form using atomic propositions from the set

$$APM = \{x = c \mid c \in \Sigma_I\} \cup \{y = e \mid e \in \Sigma_O\}$$

2. The satisfaction relation between models M and sentences $\mathbf{G}\alpha$ consists of invariant assertions over $L(M)$ for DFSMs models M written in the form $M \models \mathbf{G}\alpha$ which is interpreted as

$$M \models \mathbf{G}\alpha \equiv \forall \iota \in L(M) : \mathbf{G}\alpha(\iota)$$

where $\mathbf{G}\alpha(\iota)$ is interpreted as

$$\mathbf{G}\alpha(\iota) \equiv \forall i = 1, \ldots, n : \alpha[x_i/x, y_i/y]$$

for $\iota = (x_1, y_1).(x_2, y_2)\ldots(x_n, y_n)$. In this definition, $\alpha[x_i/x, y_i/y]$ denotes the proposition α with every occurrence of x replaced by the actual input event x_i, and every y replaced by the actual output y_i.

Take, for example, the assertion

$$BC \models \mathbf{G}(\neg(x = \text{man\_off}) \vee (y = \text{release}))$$

This assertion is not fulfilled, because the BC can perform the I/O-trace

$$(x_1, y_1).(x_2, y_2).(x_3, y_3) \cdots = (\text{man\_on}, \text{trigger}).(\text{auto\_on}, \text{trigger}).(\text{man\_off}, \text{trigger})\ldots$$

Evaluating $\alpha[x_3/x, y_3/y]$ results in

$$\alpha[x_3/x, y_3/y] \equiv \neg(\text{man\_off} = \text{man\_off}) \vee (\text{trigger} = \text{release}) \equiv \texttt{false}$$

Let W_K denote the invariant LTL formulas $\mathbf{G}\psi$ over Kripke Structures, and W_M the invariant formulas $\mathbf{G}\alpha$ over I/O-sequences of DFSMs. Then the sentence translation map can be defined as follows.

$$\sigma : W_K \longrightarrow W_M; \qquad \mathbf{G}\psi \mapsto \mathbf{G}(\sigma'(\psi))$$
$$\sigma' : \text{Propositions}(AP) \longrightarrow \text{Propositions}(AP_M)$$
$$m_{\text{on}} \mapsto (x = \text{man\_on})$$
$$\neg m_{\text{on}} \mapsto (x = \text{man\_off})$$
$$a_{\text{on}} \mapsto (x = \text{auto\_on})$$
$$\neg a_{\text{on}} \mapsto (x = \text{auto\_off})$$
$$r \mapsto (y = \text{release})$$
$$\neg r \mapsto (y = \text{trigger})$$
$$\psi \wedge \psi' \mapsto \sigma'(\psi) \wedge \sigma'(\psi')$$
$$\psi \vee \psi' \mapsto \sigma'(\psi) \vee \sigma'(\psi')$$

Satisfaction Condition. Having constructed model map and sentence translation map, the so-called *satisfaction condition* has to be proven. The satisfaction condition states in our case that

$$\mu(M) \models \mathbf{G}\psi \text{ if and only if } M \models \sigma(\mathbf{G}\psi)$$

It is straightforward to see that this follows directly from the way μ and σ have been constructed. The satisfaction condition is illustrated in Fig. 7.

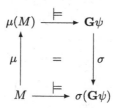

Fig. 7. Satisfaction condition for model and sentence translation.

Other Conditions. It also to be proven that the model map μ is properly defined in the sense that it preserves the "natural" morphisms between models. For DFSMs, these morphisms are arrows indicating I/O-equivalence: $M_1 \longrightarrow M_2$ if and only if $L(M_1) = L(M_2)$, and therefore also an arrow $M_2 \longrightarrow M_1$ exists. On the level of Kripke Structures, the corresponding morphisms are bisimulations between Kripke Structures defined over the same atomic propositions. It is easy to see that μ maps I/O-equivalent DFSMs to bisimilar Kripke Structures, so this condition is fulfilled. The condition is illustrated in Fig. 8.

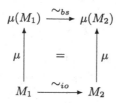

Fig. 8. The model map μ translates I/O-equivalent DFSMs to bisimilar Kripke Structures. $\sim_{io}$ denotes the io-equivalence relation and $\sim_{bs}$ denotes the bisimulation relation.

Proof of Emergent Property. Having established the satisfaction condition, we are now in the position to represent properties of the BC by means of LTL invariants over atomic propositions from AP, and every invariant that can be shown for $\mu(BC)$ is ensured by the BC itself, just in the slightly differing syntactic representation of W_M-formulas.

Analysing the transition graph of $\mu(BC)$ in Fig. 6, it can be immediately deduced that the invariant

$$\varphi_{BC} \equiv \mathbf{G}\left(\neg a_{on} \vee \neg r\right) \tag{4}$$

is fulfilled. Collecting now the assertions established in (2), (3), and (4), it is easy to see that together they imply the desired safety property specified in (1).   □

The example above illustrated the application of the theory of institutions in a linking approach to verify emergent properties in a large scale system development, where different formalisms are used for modelling different system components. In the next section, another application of this approach will be described: the cooperation of tools, each of them fulfilling verification tasks for specific formalisms.

5   Collaborative Development and Verification Environments – Next Generation

Large scale system developments require *collaborative development environments (CDEs)*, where geographically distributed development teams can work locally on their specific components and cooperate on integration tasks. We expect that the CDE paradigm will become even more popular in the future, because it will also enable collaboration of tools, with the objective to support the multi-formalism approach. This might be particularly beneficial for verification tools.

Complete DFSM Test Strategies. To illustrate this point, let us consider a model-based test automation tool available for DFSMs, that applies so-called *complete test strategies*: this means that a test suite generated from a reference model M

1. accepts every implementation M' fulfilling the given conformance relation $M' \leq M$ (soundness), and
2. rejects every implementation M' violating $M' \leq M$ by letting at least one test case fail (exhaustiveness).

For black-box testing, completeness is always defined in relation to a fault domain. For DFSMs with I/O-equivalence as conformance relation, for example, complete test strategies usually depend on the fault domain $\mathcal{D}(\Sigma_I, \Sigma_O, m)$ containing all DFSMs over signature (Σ_I, Σ_O), whose minimised equivalent DFSM contains at most m states. For this fault domain, several practically implementable test strategies exist [3,11,17].

Complete Test Strategies for the CSM. Suppose that the model-based DFSM testing tool was available and could be applied for testing the brake controller BC. The superior test strength of complete test suites suggests to investigate whether such a strategy might also be available for the ceiling speed monitor CSM. This requires some consideration, since the CSM has inputs v, v_m which are of floating point type. Therefore it is infeasible to enumerate all possible

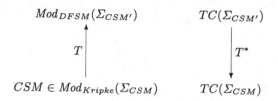

Fig. 9. Model translation T and test case translation T^*. Σ_{CSM} is the signature of the CSM model (including the input variables nva, v, and v_m, and the output variables b and d) and $\Sigma_{CSM'}$ is the corresponding DFSM signature. $Mod_{Kripke}(\Sigma_{CSM})$ is the set of all Kripke models over the signature Σ_{CSM}, $Mod_{DFSM}(\Sigma_{CSM'})$ is the set of all DFSM models over $\Sigma_{CSM'}$, $TC_{Kripke}(\Sigma_{CSM})$ is the set of all Kripke test cases over Σ_{CSM}, and $TC_{DFSM}(\Sigma_{CSM'})$ is the set of all DFSM test cases over $\Sigma_{CSM'}$.

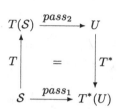

Fig. 10. Satisfaction condition for model and test case translation.

input combinations during a test suite, so we cannot simply represent the CSM as another DFSM. It is possible, however, to construct input equivalence classes for the SysML state machine, because only the CSM inputs cannot be enumerated, but the internal states and its outputs are finite. The construction of these classes has been elaborated in [10], and it has been shown that this enables an abstraction of the SysML state machine to a DFSM with a signature $\Sigma_{CSM'}$ having input equivalence classes as inputs and with an output alphabet corresponding to the finite value assignments to the CSM outputs d and b. In the light of the linking approach, this result can be re-phrased as follows and as illustrated in Fig. 9.

1. Every deterministic Kripke Structure S with infinite input domains but finite internal state values and finite outputs can be mapped by the model translation map T to a minimised DFSM. This DFSM take input equivalence classes of S as inputs and operates on the same outputs as S.
2. The model translation map T respects I/O-equivalence as conformance relation: if Kripke Structure S' conforms to the reference model S, then the DFSM $T(S')$ conforms to the reference DFSM $T(S)$, as illustrated in Fig. 11.
3. Sentences in this scenario are test cases and the sentence translation map is the *test case map* T^* which translates DFSM test cases into test cases running against implementations with Kripke Structure semantics.
4. Satisfaction relations are now of the form "FSM M passes a test case" or "Implementation S passes a test case".

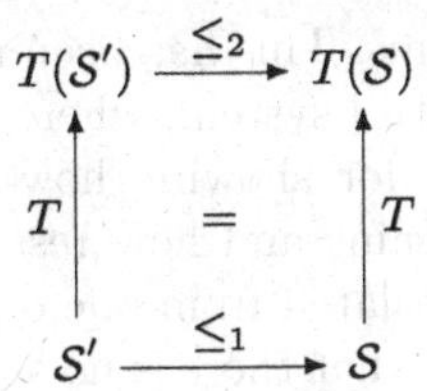

$$T(\mathcal{S}') \xrightarrow{\leq_2} T(\mathcal{S})$$

$$T \Big\uparrow \quad = \quad \Big\uparrow T$$

$$\mathcal{S}' \xrightarrow{\leq_1} \mathcal{S}$$

Fig. 11. Model translation preserves conformance relation.

5. The diagram in Fig. 10 commutes; this implies that (T, T^*) fulfil the satisfaction condition: the DFSM abstraction $T(\mathcal{S})$ of implementation $\mathcal{S}$ passes a DFSM test case U, if and only if the implementation $\mathcal{S}$ also passes the translated test case $T^*(U)$ on Kripke Structures.
6. The satisfaction condition now implies that complete test strategies derived from reference DFSM $T(\mathcal{S})$ are translated via T^* to likewise complete test strategies for implementations with Kripke Structure semantics. This shows that not only assertions about specific models, but also whole *theories* can be transferred from one institution to the other.

As a result of these theoretical considerations (they have been elaborated in more detail in [9]), we can construct a tool for testing implementations against SysML state machine models similar to the CSM model as follows.

1. Input reference model $\mathcal{S}$.
2. Calculate DFSM abstraction $T(\mathcal{S})$.
3. Send DFSM $T(\mathcal{S})$ to the DFSM testing tool to calculate the associated complete DFSM test suite $\mathbf{TS}(T(\mathcal{S}))$.
4. Receive $\mathbf{TS}(T(\mathcal{S}))$ from the DFSM testing tool and translate it to a complete test suite $T^*(\mathbf{TS}(T(\mathcal{S})))$ that can be executed against implementation $\mathcal{S}'$.

In [2], a similar approach to re-using tools in different formalisms is described; this is based on the Unifying Theories of Programming UTP. The role of the morphisms and co-morphisms between institutions is taken on by Galois connections between lattices in UTP.

6 Conclusions

In this contribution, the aspect of using multiple formalisms in large-scale system developments with collaborative development environments has been discussed. For the domain of cyber-physical systems, we consider the multi-formalism approach as essential for such undertakings, because special methods and associated modelling techniques are needed to optimise the development and verification of system components possessing a considerable structural and behavioural variety – from smart sensors via mechatronics controllers to database servers. We have argued that the multi-formalism approach requires some theoretical support for verifying emergent system properties and re-using verification tools in the context of different formalisms. This has been illustrated by means of a case study for an on-board train control system, where the theory of institutions has been applied as one possibility for showing how assertions can be translated between different semantic domains and how test suites with guaranteed fault detection properties can be translated from one domain into another.

These considerations suggest that there is no single "best" unified modelling, programming and verification paradigm to be expected in the future. Instead, system development and verification according to the multi-formalism approach will become more and more natural. The examples show that this trend will automatically foster the integration between modelling and programming: the transfer of verification artefacts between different formalisms requires a level of abstraction which is significantly higher than that of typical programming languages.

Nevertheless, considerable work is still necessary to achieve a degree of usability and integration for modelling and verification techniques that is already available today for "conventional" programming in integrated development environments. In particular, it cannot be expected that the institution morphisms and co-morphisms together with their satisfaction conditions will be elaborated manually from scratch for every new large scale system development. Instead, a library of existing inter-formalism transformations is needed, and the (usually routine) proofs of satisfaction conditions need to be mechanised.

Acknowledgements. The first author's research has been funded by the Robust-RailS project granted by Innovation Fund Denmark. The second author's contribution has been elaborated within project *ITTCPS – Implementable Testing Theory for Cyber-physical Systems* (http://www.cs.uni-bremen.de/agbs/-projects/ittcps/index.html) which has been granted by the University of Bremen in the context of the German Universities Excellence Initiative (http://en.wikipedia.org/wiki/German_Universities_Excellence_Initiative).
Some diagrams in this paper were created using Paul Taylors diagrams package.

References

1. Bézivin, J., Jouault, F., Valduriez, P.: On the need for megamodels. In: OOP-SLA/GPCE: Best Practices for Model-Driven Software Development Workshop (2004)
2. Cavalcanti, A., Huang, W., Peleska, J., Woodcock, J.: CSP and kripke structures. In: Leucker, M., Rueda, C., Valencia, F.D. (eds.) ICTAC 2015. LNCS, vol. 9399, pp. 505–523. Springer, Heidelberg (2015). doi:10.1007/978-3-319-25150-9_29
3. Chow, T.S.: Testing software design modeled by finite-state machines. IEEE Trans. Softw. Eng. **SE-4**(3), 178–186 (1978)
4. Diaconescu, R.: Institution-independent Model Theory. Birkhäuser Verlag AG, Basel, Boston, Berlin (2008)
5. Goguen, J.A., Burstall, R.M.: Institutions: abstract model theory for specification and programming. J. Association Comput. Mach. **39**, 95–146 (1992). Predecessor. LNCS **164**, 221–256 (1984)
6. Goguen, J., Roşu, G.: Institution morphisms. Formal Aspects Comput. **13**(3), 274–307 (2014)

7. Grönniger, H., Krahn, H., Rumpe, B., Schindler, M., Völkel, S.: Textbased modeling. CoRR, abs/1409.6623 (2014)
8. Hoare, C.A.R., Jifeng, H.: Unifying Theories of Programming. Prentice-Hall, Englewood Cliffs (1998)
9. Huang, W., Peleska, J.: Complete model-based equivalence class testing for nondeterministic systems. Formal Aspects of Computing. (Under review)
10. Huang, W., Peleska, J.: Complete model-based equivalence class testing. STTT 18(3), 265–283 (2016)
11. Luo, G., Bochmann, G.V., Petrenko, A.: Test selection based on communicating nondeterministic finite-state machines using a generalized Wp-method. IEEE Trans. Softw. Eng. 20(2), 149–162 (1994)
12. Nielsen, C.B., Larsen, P.G., Fitzgerald, J., Woodcock, J., Peleska, J.: Systems of systems engineering: basic concepts, model-based techniques, and research directions. ACM Comput. Surv. 48(2), 18:1–18:41 (2015)
13. Schmidt, D.C.: Model-driven engineering. IEEE Comput. 39(2), 25–31 (2006)
14. Sheeran, M., Singh, S., Stålmarck, G.: Checking safety properties using induction and a SAT-solver. In: Hunt, W.A., Johnson, S.D. (eds.) FMCAD 2000. LNCS, vol. 1954, pp. 127–144. Springer, Heidelberg (2000). doi:10.1007/3-540-40922-X_8
15. Sistla, A.P.: Safety, liveness and fairness in temporal logic. Formal Aspects Comput. 6(5), 495–511 (1994)
16. Spivey, J.M.: The Z Notation: A Reference Manual. Prentice-Hall Inc., Upper Saddle River (1989)
17. Vasilevskii, M.P.: Failure diagnosis of automata. Kibernetika (Transl.) 4, 98–108 (1973)

Modeling Meets Programming:
A Comparative Study in Model Driven
Engineering Action Languages

Maged Elaasar[1(✉)] and Omar Badreddin[2]

[1] Modelware Solutions, La Canada Flintridge
CA 91011, USA
`melaasar@gmail.com`
[2] Electrical Engineering and Computer Science Department,
University of Texas at El Paso, El Paso, USA
`obbadreddin@utep.edu`

Abstract. Modeling and programming have often been considered two different activities. While this may be true when modeling is primarily meant for human communication and early design explorations, it is not the case when modeling is meant for execution. Some approaches have been specifically developed to address this latter case with variable successes. In this paper, we discuss two such approaches, namely ALF and Umple. ALF has evolved from the modeling community to provide a textual syntax for an executable subset of UML called Foundation UML (fUML). Umple has evolved from the academic community to introduce the abstractions of modeling into programing languages. We compare both approaches, highlight their critical differences, and discuss their contribution to the evolution of model oriented programming languages.

Keywords: Modeling · Programming · UML · ALF · Umple · Model Driven Engineering · Action language

1 Introduction

A model is a simplified representation of a more complex system. It is frequently used to abstract and analyze a system by focusing on one or more aspects. Models are used to understand, communicate, simulate, calibrate, evaluate, test, validate and explore alternatives for system development. Modelers use a wide variety of models to explore different aspects of the system such as requirements, structure, behavior, event, time, security, flow, process, activity, performance, quality, usability, etc. These models can be expressed in many forms including textual and visual representations.

Model Driven Engineering (MDE) [1] is a well-accepted engineering approach, where models are used to understand and comprehend parts of a complex system under development. Modeling languages raise the level of abstraction for the specification of a system to help manage system complexity and evolution. Modeling languages are typically defined in terms of their abstract syntax (metamodel), concrete syntax (or notation) and semantics (or rules). While some modeling languages are executable, like

© Springer International Publishing AG 2016
T. Margaria and B. Steffen (Eds.): ISoLA 2016, Part II, LNCS 9953, pp. 50–67, 2016.
DOI: 10.1007/978-3-319-47169-3_5

the foundational subset of UML (fUML) [2], others are not. This, according to some, is one criterion that distinguishes modeling languages from programming languages.

Programming, on the other hand, is the activity of developing executable software. Programs are written in a programming language, which is a set of rules for expressing computations in a human-readable form that can be translated unambiguously to a machine-readable form. A programming language is defined in terms of its, typically textual syntax, defined with some grammar formalism like BNF [3], and its semantics defined by translation to some mathematical formalism.

There is often confusion in distinguishing between modeling and programming languages [4]. For example, there is a misconception that textual languages are always programming languages and that graphical languages are always modeling languages. This distinction becomes more challenging when domain-specific languages (DSLs) are considered [5]. DSLs can be either visual, textual, or both; and may or may not be executable. It quickly becomes evident that a single criterion is not sufficient for distinguishing modeling and programming. However, there have been some criteria suggested in the literature [22] that could potentially be used to give a more accurate classification including: (a) whether the language has a textual or visual notation, (b) how the language syntax and semantics are defined, (c) the extent to which the language is executable, (d) the language's level of abstraction, (e) the underlying fundamental concepts of the language, (f) how the language is used in each phase of development, and (g) whether the language supports multiple viewpoints. Such criteria will result in a number of categories of languages.

One category embeds code into modeling languages. An example of this approach is the *Rational Rose RealTime* [6], whereby one can specify snippets of code in some programming language (like C) as body of UML operations, derivation of UML properties or specification of UML actions. The resulting model is translated into code in that programming language, with the code snippets being integrated in the generated code. A key drawback of this approach is that the code snippets are at a different semantic level than the model elements, making the specification and debugging difficult. Moreover, synchronizing changes between the model and the code become challenging. Finally, the platform independence of the models is compromised (a workaround is to use different UML profiles to add code in different languages).

Another category embeds modeling concepts into programming languages. A notable example here is the Umple language [7]. Umple allows embedding modeling concepts from UML (e.g., class and state machine concepts) into native code of a programming language (e.g., Java, C++). The mix is translated into code before being executed. This approach allows developers to incrementally adopt modeling practices without giving up on code. It also blurs the line between modeling and programming, since an Umple module can be all-code, all-model or anything in between. A key drawback, like the previous category, is that platform independence is lost.

A third category gives modeling languages the appearance of a programming language. An example here is the ALF language [2], which is an OMG standard. ALF is a textual syntax for the foundational subset of UML (fUML), which has well-defined execution semantics. ALF's textual syntax is parsed into instances of its abstract syntax, which maps to the abstract syntax of fUML. ALF allows the textual expression of the structure (e.g., class diagram) as well as the behavior (e.g., state machines) of fUML models. ALF programs can be executed by fUML engines, which come with UML modeling tools, such as *Papyrus* [8] and *MagicDraw* [9].

Approaches in the first category have been well explored for a long time, and have not had detrimental success in bridging the gap between the communities of modeling and programming. Therefore, we focus on approaches in the relatively newer second and third categories, most notably: Umple and ALF. The goal of both Umple and ALF is to provide an executable modeling language, with which an engineer can design and specify system behavior. Both approaches allow for visual and textual modeling and development. Umple has been developed in Academia following an evidence-based approach [16], where it has been driven by the need to improve comprehension of code [4]. ALF has been developed by the OMG, as a result of merging two proposals from IBM and BridgePoint [17], where it has been driven by the need to have a model-based action language.

Both programming and modeling have their unique strengths and weaknesses. Programming typically results in an executable artifact that can be tested, while models can sometimes be ambiguous and incomplete. Hence, there is potentially significant value in merging the two approaches and harness their strengths. In this paper, we focus on such approaches that provide formalisms that reduce or eliminate the distinction between modeling and programming. These formalisms can be either textual, visual, or both. Our contribution is to compare these two previously mentioned approaches, highlight their critical differences and discuss ideas for their evolution.

The rest of this paper is organized as follows: in Sect. 2, we give an overview of related works; we define a running example in Sect. 3; in Sect. 4, we describe the ALF language approach; we also describe the Umple language approach in Sect. 5; in Sect. 6, we compare the two approaches and highlight their critical differences; finally, we conclude and outline future work in Sect. 7.

2 Related Works

Adoption of MDE approaches in practice remains very limited [10]. Outside of a few niche domains (such as safety critical and embedded systems), MDE has not witnessed broad adoption. Open Source development for example has remained entirely code-centric [11]. In education, MDE pedagogies' results have been mixed, and students' perception of the role of UML in software development has been declining [27].

Challenges with adoption of MDE can be attributed to many factors, including: (1) synchronization of modeling and coding artifacts. Forward and reverse engineering technologies face many open challenges [12]. As a result, engineers find it increasingly difficult and time consuming to maintain the synchronization between model and code artifacts. (2) Challenges related to versioning and merging of large modeling artifacts. By contrast, versioning and merging of code artifacts has become widely adopted [13, 14]. (3) Challenges in applying MDE practices in agile and small size projects, and

(4) perceived failure of educating future engineers and convincing them of the value of MDE methodologies [15, 27]. To mitigate some of those challenges, a number of approaches have been proposed that merge both coding and modeling into the same development environment.

textUML provides an API and a library for creating UML diagrams using Java syntax [18]. Systems developed using *textUML* run over JVM, and the tool provides debugging facilities. *BridgePoint* is an executable modeling tool based on Shlaer-Mellor methodology [19]. It provides a visual editor only for UML constructs, and supports a proprietary syntax for action definitions. Both *textUML* and *BridgePoint* provide an executable platform mixing code and modeling concepts.

tUML is another approach whereby both models and code are defined in the same artifact [20]. *tUML*, like ALF, defines a subset of UML for which it provides a textual syntax. The main goal of *tUML* is to facilitate the fixing of sketchy models, by providing a familiar textual syntax.

PlantUML is yet another textual modeling and coding environment [21]. The distinctive feature of *PlantUML* is that it is very permissive and verbose. Actions in *PlantUML* can be defined using unstructured text. As a result, *PlantUML* does not strictly follow the UML metamodel.

3 Running Example

The running example is an Ecommerce ordering system that is loosely based on the Online Bookstore Domain case study given in Appendix B of [24]. The example, shown in (Fig. 1) with a UML class diagram, describes a set of classes involved in an

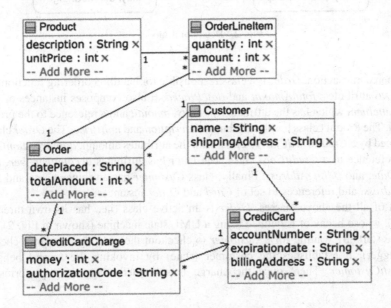

Fig. 1. Structural and behavioral models

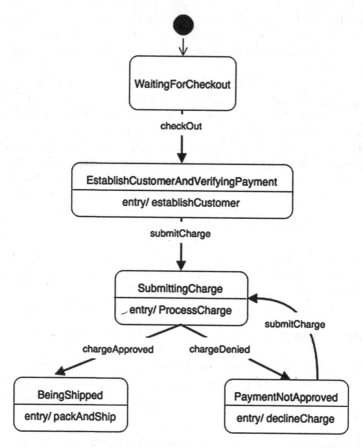

Fig. 2. Behavioral model

Ecommerce transaction. *Order* is a class responsible for handling ordering functionality. It has two attributes: *totalAmount* and *datePlaced*. It also composes instances of class *OrderLineItem*, which has the attributes *quantity*, *amount* and a reference to the product ordered. The Product class has the attributes *description* and *unitPrice*. The *Order* class is referenced by a *CreditCardCharge* class, with the attributes amount, *authorizationCode*, and a reference to a *CreditCard* class. The latter has attributes *accountNumber*, *expirationDate*, and *billingAddress*. Finally, class *Customer* has attributes name and *shippingAddress*, and references to set of *Card* and *Order* instances.

Out of all the above classes, *Order* is an active class (i.e., has its own thread of control), whose behavior is defined using a UML state machine (shown in Fig. 2). The machine starts by waiting for a *Customer* to checkout the order (state). Once checked out (trigger), it establishes the customer (state) by invoking the (entry) behavior *EstablishCustomer*. Then, once the charge is submitted (trigger), it performs the submitting charge (state) by invoking the (entry) behavior *ProcessCharge*. At that point, if the charge is approved (trigger), it prepares for shipping (state) by invoking the (entry) behavior *PackAndShip*. On the other hand, if the charge is declined (trigger), it indicates that the payment has not been approved (state) and invokes the (entry) behavior *DeclineCharge*. This may prompt the customer to re-enter the payment information and resubmit the charge (trigger), which goes back to being processed (state).

Each one of those behaviors invoked by each state can itself be a behavior specified using a UML state machines, a UML activity, or an expression in some action language. For example, the *EstablishCustomer* behavior is specified as a UML Activity diagram (Fig. 3). The activity creates an instance of class *Order*, populates its collection of *OrderLineItem* instances, and sets its *datePlaced* to current date and its *totalAmount* to the sum of the amounts for each line item in the order. The reader may notice that this visual activity modeling may not be the most convenient way of specifying this activity. This is further discussed in subsequent sections.

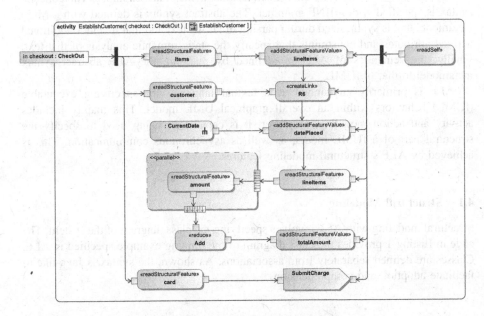

Fig. 3. Activity modeling for *EstablishCustomer*

4   ALF: UML Action Language

ALF [2] is a standard action language, defined as a textual surface syntax for foundational UML (fUML) [23]. fUML is an executable subset of standard UML that can be used to define, in an operational style, the structural and behavioral semantics of systems. fUML is a computationally complete language. It has a Kernel module that provides basic object-oriented capabilities, a Common Behavior module that provides general behavior and synchronous communication capabilities and an Activities module that provides activity-modeling capabilities. Other modules being standardized include one for Composite Structure modeling [26] capabilities and one for State Machine modeling capabilities [25].

The motivation for ALF as a textual syntax for fUML is clear: the graphical notation of fUML (e.g., the activity diagram in Fig. 3) is not convenient for detailed programming. The textual syntax on the other hand is more suitable for the specification of detailed computations and algorithms. However, what distinguishes ALF from other action languages (e.g., regular programming languages) is that it is at the same semantic level as the rest of the model. This is achieved by mapping the ALF textual syntax directly to the abstract syntax (metamodel) of fUML. Alf also provides standard libraries for primitive types (e.g., string, boolean, integer, real, etc.) and primitive behaviors (boolean, string, arithmetic, and collection functions). It also provides basic asynchronous communication support based on the concept of channels.

ALF is defined by its concrete syntax, abstract syntax and semantics. The concrete syntax is specified with a BNF grammar. The abstract syntax is defined with a MOF metamodel that is synthesized during parsing of an Alf text and that includes additional derived attributes and constraints that specify the static semantic analysis of that text. Finally, the semantics of ALF are defined by mapping the ALF abstract syntax metamodel to that of fUML.

ALF is primarily envisioned as a textual language for specifying executable (fUML) behaviors within an overall graphical UML model. This mainly includes activity and action modeling. However, it is capable of being used to specify the structural part of a fUML model, as well as asynchronous communication. This is achieved by ALF's structural modeling features.

4.1   Structural Modeling

Structural modeling with ALF involves specifying the class diagram of the system. The code in Listing 1 provides the class diagram of the running example specified in ALF. Classes are defined separately from associations. As shown, the syntax is Java-like to facilitate adoption and comprehension.

```
active class Order {
   public datePlaced: Date;
   public totalAmount: Money; }

class OrderLineItem {
   public quantity: Integer;
   public amount: Money; }

class Product {
   public description: String;
   public unitPrice: Money; }

class CreditCardCharge {
   public amount: Money;
   public authorizationCode: String[0..1] }

class CreditCard {
   public accountNumber: String;
   public expirationDate: Date;
   public billingAddress: Address; }

class Customer {
   public name: PersonalName;
   public shippingAddress: Address[0..1] }

assoc R1 {
   public product: Product;
   public orderlineItem: OrderLineItem[*]; }

assoc R2 {
   public lineItems: compose OrderLineItem[*];
   public order: Order; }

assoc R3 {
   public order: Order;
   public charge: CreditCardCharege[*]; }

assoc R4 {
   public card: CreditCard;
   public charge: CreditCardCharege[*]; }

assoc R5 {
   public card: Card [*];
   public customer: Customer;}

assoc R6 {
   public customer: Customer;
   public order: Order[*]; }
```

Listing 1. Structural modeling in ALF

4.2 Behavioral Modeling

ALF provides textual syntax for the specification of behavior models that are supported by fUML. Up to version 1.2.1, the fUML specification supports activity models but not state machines (or interactions). However, ongoing work at the OMG on the specification of the precise semantics of state machine will change that in an upcoming revision of fUML and consequently ALF. Meanwhile, ALF can be used for specifying standalone activity models and in specific areas of state machines, most notably to specify guard conditions for transitions, and *entry*, *exit* and *do* behaviors of states, in the form of activities.

In the running example, the behavior of the Order class is specified with a state machine, so it cannot itself be specified in ALF. However, some of its entry actions, e.g., *EstablishCustomer*, (Fig. 3) are activities, hence can be expressed more concisely in ALF code. The code in Listing 2 creates an instance of the class *Order* and populates it based on the input parameter *checkOut*. This shoes that a textual syntax is more concise and comprehensible than the corresponding visual notation.

```
activity EstablishCustomer(checkOut: CheckOut) {
    this.lineItems = checkOut.items;
    R6.addLink(checkout.customer, this);
    this.datePlace = CurrentDate();
    this.totalAmount = this.lineItems.amount->reduce Add;
    this.SubmitCharge(checkOut.card); }
```

Listing 2. Behavioral modeling in ALF

5 Umple: UML Programming

Umple is a model oriented programming language. It integrates modeling and programming by introducing model-level concepts and embedding them textually as part of modern Object Oriented programming languages [7]. The result is a language that blurs the distinction between code and modeling abstractions. The key premise of this approach is to enable software engineers that are mostly accustomed to textual coding environments to take advantage of modeling abstractions and MDE methodologies.

To demonstrate the approach, we represent the running example presented in Sect. 3 encoded in the Umple language.

5.1 Structural Modeling

Listing 3 shows the structural part (class diagram) of the running example.

```
class Product {
  1 -- * OrderLineItem;
  description;
  int unitPrice; }

class OrderLineItem {
  * -- 1 Order;
  int quantity;
  int amount; }

class Order {
  1 -- * CreditCardCharge;
  datePlaced;
  int totalAmount;  }

class CreditCardCharge {
  * -> 1 creditCard;
  int money;
  authorizationCode; }

class Customer {
  name;
  shippingAddress; }

class CreditCard {
  * -- 1 Customer;
  accountNumber;
  expirationdate;
  billingAddress; }
```

Listing 3. Structural modeling in Umple

Like ALF, Umple also adopts a Java-like syntax to promote adoption and comprehension. Associations are defined within either of the participating classes as shown in Listing 3. Alternatively, associations can be grouped under 'association' header (as shown in Listing 4). Associations can be named, and associations role names are optional on both ends.

```
association {
  1 Product -- * OrderLineItem;
  * OrderLineItem -- 1 Order;
  1 Order -- * CreditCardCharge;
  * CreditCardCharge -> 1 creditCard;
  * CreditCard -- 1 Customer;
}
```

Listing 4. Grouping of associations in Umple

Umple supports primitive types (such as int, string, date, etc.). Umple defaults attributes to string type if a type is not provided.

5.2 Behavioral Modeling

In Umple, active classes, those that own their thread of execution, can have a state machine associated with them. In our running example, the class *Order* is an Active class. Hence, its state machine can be defined as in Listing 5.

```
class Order {
  1 -- * CreditCardCharge;
  datePlaced;
  int totalAmount;

  OrderStatus {
    WaitingForCheckOut {
      checkout -> EstablishCustomerAndVerifyingPayment;
    }
    EstablishCustomerAndVerifyingPayment {
      entry/ {establishCustomer();}
      submitCharge -> SubmittingCharge;
    }
    SubmittingCharge {
      entry/{ProcessCharge();}
      chargeApproved -> BeingShipped;
      chargeDenied -> PaymentNotApproved;
    }
    BeingShipped {
      entry/{PackAndShip();}
    }
    PaymentNotApproved {
      entry/{declineCharge();}
      submitCharge -> SubmittingCharge; } }

  // methods to implement state machine actions
    private void establishCustomer () {
      this.lineItems = checkOut.items;
      order.addOrderLineItem(aOrderLineItem);
      this.datePlace = CurrentDate();
      this.totalAmount = this.lineItems.amount += Add;
      this.SubmitCharge(checkOut.card); }

    private void ProcessCharge() {
  // method action code here } }
```

Listing 5: Behavioral Modeling in Umple

5.3   Execution Semantics for Umple

Umple has been developed to be an executable language, just like ALF. However, since it is not a standard, we like to shed some lights on its execution semantics. Recall that an Umple module can mix modeling concepts with some programming language. Umple currently has integration with Java, C++, C#, Ruby, and PhP. For purposes of this paper, we use Java as an example language. When an Umple module is compiled, the compiler first translates the modeling parts of the module to corresponding code in the same programming language. Umple supports both an Eclipse-based and a web-based development platform. The code provided in this paper can be inserted into the web-based platform for a quick demonstration of the approach.

In Umple, model and code parts can be mixed in the same module or in separate modules. In this paper, we present the structural code and behavioral code separately, but they can also be combined in the same module. As shown in Listing 5, the state machine defines the behavior of the order instances, as represented by the *OrderStatus* state variable. In this class, you can see an association between *Order* class and *CreditCard* class, in addition to the state machine.

The state machine defines the states, transitions and actions. Umple also support an arbitrary number of nesting levels and concurrent regions.

By default, the first state specified in a module is considered the start state. Transitions' trigger events are specified as methods that return a Boolean value; true if the event was processed and false otherwise. Transitions' entry, exit and do actions require definition using an action language. Since we are using Java as an action language, such actions are defined in Java. Listing 5 shows two methods; *establishCustomer* and *ProcessCharge*. The method *establishCustomer* is implemented in Java (syntactically it looks very similar to ALF).

Action methods can interplay with the structural and behavioral modeling constructs by calling the interface generated by Umple. For example, to manipulate an association membership, the action method can call the *add* or *remove* interface made available by the language. In our example, the method *addOrderLineItem* is generated from Umple's structural model and is implemented in the generated code in Java as follows.

```
public boolean addOrderLineItem(OrderLineItem aOrderLineItem) {
    boolean wasAdded = false;
    if (orderLineItems.contains(aOrderLineItem)) { return false; }
    Order existingOrder = aOrderLineItem.getOrder();
    boolean isNewOrder = existingOrder != null
    && !this.equals(existingOrder);
    if (isNewOrder) {
      aOrderLineItem.setOrder(this); }
    else {
      orderLineItems.add(aOrderLineItem); }
    wasAdded = true;
    return wasAdded; }
```

Listing 6: Implementation of *addOrderItem*

Umple language supports both bi-directional, Uni-directional and composition associations. Associations can be declared in either of the two participating classes, or alternatively can be grouped under one class named *Associations*. Umple allows all combinations of association multiplicities.

6 Comparison and Discussion

In this section, we compare both ALF and Umple with respect to their motivation, approach to integration with modeling languages, language artifacts, abstract syntax, textual syntax, graphical syntax and semantics. Table 1 summarizes those differences.

Table 1. Comparison between ALF and Umple

	ALF	Umple
Textual representation	YES	YES
Textual manipulation	YES	YES
Visual representation	YES (fUML notation)	YES (UML notation)
Visual manipulation	YES, partially through the fUML visual notation	YES. Changes are automatically synchronized since both visual and textual representations are semantically equivalent.
Standalone	YES, but can also be used to specify parts of a UML model specified visually	YES
Executable	YES	YES
Action language syntax	New textual Syntax	New textual syntax embedded in OO language, such as Java, C, C++, Ruby.
Syntax origin	Industrial proposals from IBM and BridgePoint, refined and managed by OMG	Evidence based, where syntax evolves based on empirical user studies
Activity support	YES	YES through embedding programming language
State machine support	Under development	YES
Meta-model conformance	fUML	Umple meta-model that closely resembles a subset of UML meta model
Code injection	YES but injected code is passed along unparsed	YES but injected code is natively part of the module
Platform	ALF execution engine	The same compiler/interpreter of the embedding Language with a front – end translation of modeling code to the language

6.1   Motivation

Both ALF and Umple are motivated by the need to bridge the gap between programming and modeling. In the case of ALF, a need was identified for a language to specify actions in UML models while staying within the boundary of the UML abstract syntax. Historically, UML tools used to support specifying those actions using programming languages. However, this has proved hard and inconvenient due to the differences in syntax between UML and those languages.

Umple, on the other hand, came in response to the less than satisfactory adoption of modeling among the software development community. The traditional forward engineering (i.e., code generation from model) approaches were not enough to convince developers to model first. For example, a recent study on the adoption of modeling practices by the open-source community revealed that only 0.3 % of commits were XML based [11], suggesting that model based commits are negligible. Even when applied, the produced models tend to be low in abstraction (as detailed as code).

6.2   Approach to Integration with Modeling Languages

ALF provides a textual grammar (specified in BNF) for the executable subset of UML (fUML), which covers mainly activity diagrams. However, instead of modeling those activities using the graphical notation, it proved much more convenient to specify them using the ALF textual syntax. An ALF program is a fUML model that can be executed according to the execution semantics of fUML. The idea is that developing ALF programs may appeal to software developers who are used to programming using textual languages (like Java or C++). However, unlike those languages, which have small specifications, fUML is still considered a large and complex specification.

On the other hand, Umple provides another strategy to help software developers gradually adopt modeling practices. It allows them to slowly replace parts of their code with more concise modeling abstractions that can be translated to equivalent code before execution. For example, bi-directional associations in UML can be considered higher in abstraction than two properties in the associated classes that are opposite to each other (have opposite cross references). By doing so, developers can control when and how fast they adopt modeling approaches. A valid Umple module can be made up of all code, all modeling concepts or anywhere in between.

6.3   Language Artifacts

ALF can be used either as a standalone programming language, specifying the structure and behavior of a system textually, or can be used to specify some behaviors textually in an otherwise visually specified structural fUML model. However, we suspect that the latter use case is still the predominant one.

Umple, on the other hand allows the specification of programs as standalone textual artifacts. The artifacts can include only model abstractions, only code abstractions, or a mix of both. As programmers get more comfortable with modeling abstractions, and understand the corresponding generated code, they may switch (refactor) their code to add more model-based abstractions. It is interesting to mention that the Umple code-base itself is writing in Umple, i.e., in a mix of model and code fashion.

6.4 Abstract Syntax

Although ALF's grammar is defined in BNF, the specification provides a full mapping from that grammar to the abstract syntax of fUML. This means that the AST implied by the BNF grammar is fully mapped to the abstract syntax of fUML, specified as a MOF metamodel. This mapping made it possible, for example, to develop an ALF support for the Papyrus tool using Xtext [28], a technology that allows developing textual syntaxes that map to Ecore (Eclipse implementation of Essesntial MOF). fUML supports structural modeling in addition to some behavioral modeling (e.g., using activity diagrams). There is undergoing work at OMG to add more coverage of the UML behavioral models. ALF also supports code injection (injecting code of other languages, like Java or C).

On the other hand, Umple's abstract syntax is a mix of the BNF grammar of the programming language and one that is defined for the modeling concepts. The latter corresponds to an Umple-specific metamodel that resemble the UML metamodel. In other words, the modeling parts of an Umple program are parsed into an AST that conforms to a BNF grammar which maps to the Umple metamodel. Before compilation, that AST is traversed and converted to code in the same embedding programming language. Umple currently supports structural modeling in addition to behavioral modeling using state machines (activity modeling is achieved by embedding a programming language). Umple supports code injection only for the target language.

To support a close interplay between the code and the model, Umple generates a number of 'methods' from the modeling elements that can be called by the coding elements. For example, the state machine model in Umple will generate methods to support querying the current state, or first state, or the number of states in a particular state machine. Similarly, in the class diagram, the associations will generate methods to return the member instances on either end of the association, and methods to add and remove members. These methods can then be called by the code to implement a specific behavior.

6.5 Textual Syntax

ALF's textual syntax for action definitions uses Java-like conventions. The rationale is to be familiar to OO languages. However, it is not parsed with a Java parse; it has its own parser (for its grammar); and hence stay platform independent.

Umple uses the target language syntax for the non-modeling parts. The rationale is to improve adoption and comprehension (this has also educational benefits where students are likely to already know Java for example). Furthermore, Umple syntax has been driven by comprehensive empirical studies (grounded theory, subject interviews, controlled experimentations, surveys, etc.).

6.6   Graphical Syntax

ALF is just a textual concrete syntax for the fUML abstract syntax, which has a visual concrete syntax (notation) as well. This means that ALF programs can be visualized using the fUML graphical notation, and an fUML model specified visually can also be edited through the ALF textual notation.

Umple code can be manipulated visually or textually. Textual editors include both the modeling abstractions as well as the programming language code. The visual editors show only the modeling abstractions. Since the code can be of any arbitrary object oriented language, this code does not have corresponding visual elements. Edits on the textual or visual side are automatically synchronized, so that both remain in synch.

6.7   Execution Semantics

ALF uses it's a separate execution engine that interprets its programs based on the fUML execution semantics. Despite the fact that fUML's, and more generally UML's, abstract syntax implementation might be different between modeling tools (which is what is happening in practice), the problem may not transcend to ALF, if those tools supported the same BNF grammar, at least as far as parsing is concerned. There is always a risk of differences in execution semantics interpretation.

Umple, on the other hand, relies mostly on the native compiler/interpreter of the embedding programming language; after all modeling code has been translated into that language. This gives it consistency in execution semantics. This is also helped by the fact that only one team is managing the implementation of Umple. Of course, exposing Umple to different implementations may make it suffer similar problems to fUML and ALF.

7   Conclusion

Action languages are motivated by the need to bridge the gaps between programming and modeling. These languages have the potential to raise the abstraction level, and enable software developers to effectively adopt design level abstractions introduced by modeling languages, such as UML.

This paper discussed two such action languages, ALF and Umple. ALF has emerged from the modeling community and is managed by the OMG. Umple has emerged from academia in an effort to bring modeling closer to the mainstream programming community. Both languages have a concrete textual syntax, but they differ in key points.

ALF is designed to function either independently, or within the context of a UML structural model. Umple is designed to function as a complete executable language where structural modeling is part of the language. Moreover, Umple supports two concrete syntaxes, textual and visual, although they are not standard On the other hand, ALF also supports textual and graphical notations, albeit both are standardized.

ALF adopts a Java-like syntax, where in the case of Umple, the action language syntax is identical to the embedding OO language. The motivation in both cases is to facilitate adoption, and ease the learning curve for new comers.

Action languages have not yet been widely adopted. We are only aware of a handful of courses that offer action language training. In the future, we plan to develop such courses. We also plan to use both languages to develop a large case study where we specify a system's structure and behavior and report on the findings. We also plan to carry an empirical study where we ask software developers to program certain problems in both languages (after some initial training) and report on our findings.

References

1. France, R., Rumpe, B.: Model-driven development of complex software: a research roadmap. In: 2007 Future of Software Engineering. IEEE Computer Society (2007)
2. Seidewitz, E.: UML with meaning: executable modeling in foundational UML and the Alf action language. ACM SIGAda Ada Lett. **34**(3), 61–68 (2014)
3. Zaytsev, V.: BNF was here: what have we done about the unnecessary diversity of notation for syntactic definitions. In: Proceedings of the 27th Annual ACM Symposium on Applied Computing. ACM (2012)
4. Badreddin, O., Forward, A., Lethbridge, T.C.: Model oriented programming: an empirical study of comprehension. In: Proceedings of the 2012 Conference of the Center for Advanced Studies on Collaborative Research. IBM Corp. (2012)
5. Karsai, G., Krahn, H., Pinkernell, C., Rumpe, B., Schindler, M., Völkel, S.: Design guidelines for domain specific languages (2014). arXiv preprint: arXiv:1409.2378
6. Bichler, L., Radermacher, A., Schuerr, A.: Evaluating UML extensions for modeling real-time systems. In: Proceedings of the Seventh International Workshop on Object-Oriented Real-Time Dependable Systems (WORDS 2002). IEEE (2002)
7. Badreddin, O., Lethbridge, T.C.: Model oriented programming: bridging the code-model divide. In: Proceedings of the 5th International Workshop on Modeling in Software Engineering. IEEE Press (2013)
8. Lanusse, A., Tanguy, Y., Espinoza, H., Mraidha, C., Gerard, S., Tessier, P., Terrier, F.: Papyrus UML: an open source toolset for MDA. In: Proceedings of the Fifth European Conference on Model-Driven Architecture Foundations and Applications (ECMDA-FA 2009), pp. 1–4 (2009)
9. Neuendorf, D.: Review of MagicDraw UML® 11.5 professional edition. J. Object Technol. **5**(7), 115–118 (2006)
10. Tilley, S., Murphy, S., Huang, S.: 5th international workshop on graphical documentation: determining the barriers to adoption of UML diagrams. In: Proceedings of the 23rd Annual International Conference on Design of Communication: Documenting & Designing For Pervasive Information. ACM (2005)
11. Badreddin, O., Lethbridge, T.C., Elassar, M.: Modeling practices in open source software. In: Petrinja, E., Succi, G., El Ioini, N., Sillitti, A. (eds.) OSS 2013. IFIP AICT, vol. 404, pp. 127–139. Springer, Heidelberg (2013)
12. CanforaHarman, G., Di Penta, M.: New frontiers of reverse engineering. In: 2007 Future of Software Engineering. IEEE Computer Society (2007)

13. Oliveira, H., Murta, L., Werner, C. Odyssey-VCS: a flexible version control system for UML model elements. In: Proceedings of the 12th International Workshop on Software Configuration Management. ACM (2005)

14. Badreddin, O., Lethbridge, T.C., Forward, A.: A novel approach to versioning and merging model and code uniformly. In: 2014 2nd International Conference on Model-Driven Engineering and Software Development (MODELSWARD). IEEE (2014)

15. Laforcade, P., Choquet, C.: Next step for educational modeling languages: the model driven engineering and reengineering approach. *null*. IEEE (2006)

16. Badreddin, O., Lethbridge, T.C.: Combining experiments and grounded theory to evaluate a research prototype: Lessons from the umple model-oriented programming technology. In: Proceedings of the First International Workshop on User Evaluation for Software Engineering Researchers. IEEE Press (2012)

17. Badreddin, O., Lethbridge, T.C., Forward, A.: Investigation and evaluation of UML action languages. In: 2014 2nd International Conference on Model-Driven Engineering and Software Development (MODELSWARD). IEEE (2014)

18. Chaves, R.: TextUML (2009). http://abstratt.github.io/textuml/readme.html

19. Fayad, M.E., Hawn, L.J., Roberts, M.A., Klatt, J.R.: Using the Shlaer-Mellor object-oriented analysis method. IEEE Softw. **10**(2), 43–52 (1993)

20. Jouault, F., Delatour, J.: Towards fixing sketchy UML models by leveraging textual notations: application to real-time embedded systems. In: OCL@ MoDELS (2014)

21. PlantUML modeling tool. http://plantuml.com/

22. Sun, Y., Demirezen, Z., Mernik, M., Gray, J., Bryant, B.: Is my DSL a modeling or programming language? In: Proceedings of 2nd International Workshop on Domain-Specific Program Development, Nashville, US, p. 4 (2008)

23. Lazăr, C.-L., Lazăr, I., Pârv, B., Motogna, S., Czibula, I.-G.: Tool support for fUML models. Int. J. Comput. Commun. Control **5**(5), 775–782 (2010)

24. Mellor, S., Balcer, M.: Executable UML: A Foundation for Model-Driven Architecture, 1st edn. Addison-Wesley, Reading (2002)

25. OMG, Precise Semantics of UML State Machine RFP, ad/15-03-02

26. OMG, Precise Semantics of UML Composite Structures v1.0, formal/2015-10-02

27. Badreddin, O.B., Sturm, A., Hamou-Lhadj, A., Lethbridge, T., Dixon, W., Simmons, R.: The effects of education on students' perception of modeling in software engineering. In: First International Workshop on Human Factors in Modeling (HuFaMo 2015). CEUR-WS, pp. 39–46 (2015)

28. Eysholdt, M., Behrens, H.: Xtext: implement your language faster than the quick and dirty way. In: Proceedings of the ACM International Conference Companion on Object Oriented Programming Systems Languages and Applications Companion. ACM (2010)

Abstractions for Modeling Complex Systems

Zsolt Lattmann, Tamás Kecskés, Patrik Meijer, Gábor Karsai,
Péter Völgyesi, and Ákos Lédeczi[✉]

Institute for Software Integrated Systems, Vanderbilt University,
Nashville, TN 37212, USA
{zsolt.lattmann,tamas.kecskes,patrik.meijer,gabor.karsai,
peter.volgyesi,akos.ledeczi}@vanderbilt.edu
http://www.isis.vanderbilt.edu

Abstract. The ever increasing popularity of model-based system- and software engineering has resulted in more and more systems—and more and more complex systems—being modeled. Hence, the problem of managing the complexity of the models themselves has gained importance. This paper introduces three abstractions that are specifically targeted at improving the scalability of the modeling process and the system models themselves.

Keywords: Model · Metamodel · DSML · Inheritance

1   Introduction

Model Driven Engineering (MDE) and a related technique called Model Integrated Computing (MIC) are begin applied in more and more domains. MIC advocates the use of domain specific modeling languages (DSML) relying on a tool infrastructure configured automatically by metamodels [22]. The MIC open source toolsuite centered on the Generic Modeling Environment (GME) [11] has been applied successfully in a broad range of domains by Vanderbilt [8,10,12,14,15] and others [1,2,4,6,19,23]. Design space exploration of embedded systems [16] and the seamless integration of multiple complex simulators [7] are some of the most compelling examples of the power of MIC.

The recent trend in computing is to move away from desktop tools to cloud- and web-based architectures for better scalability, maintainability and seamless platform support. The latest generation MIC toolsuite called WebGME follows this trend. It is a web-based software infrastructure to support the collaborative modeling, analysis, and synthesis of complex, large-scale information systems. The number one design goal of WebGME was to better support the modeling of complex systems. This includes features targeted specifically for an enhanced modeling process including collaborative editing similar to Google Docs and a git-like database backend supporting model version control. WebGME also introduced a number of novel abstractions to support the scalability of the models of complex systems which themselves are necessarily complex. The focus of this paper is exactly these abstractions: crosscuts, model libraries, and *mixins*.

© Springer International Publishing AG 2016
T. Margaria and B. Steffen (Eds.): ISoLA 2016, Part II, LNCS 9953, pp. 68–79, 2016.
DOI: 10.1007/978-3-319-47169-3_6

Cross-cutting concepts are always difficult to model and visualize. WebGME introduces the concept of a crosscut that is a collection of objects that the modeler wishes to view together independent of where they are located in the hierarchical model structure. As a simple example, consider a system with software and hardware models. A crosscut is a straightforward way to capture the assignment of software components to hardware units even though they reside in disjoint model hierarchies.

A unique feature of GME has been its support for prototypical inheritance. Each model at any point in the composition hierarchy is a prototype that can be derived to create an instance model. Derivation creates a copy of the model (and all of its parts recursively, i.e., a deep copy), but it establishes a dependency relationship between the corresponding objects. Any changes in the prototype automatically propagate to the instance. WebGME extended this concept to merge metamodels with models. Meta-information, that is language specification, can be captured anywhere in the model composition and inheritance hierarchies. It is exactly the mechanism of inheritance that enforces the language rules by propagating it down the inheritance hierarchy. Consequently, metamodels and models are tightly integrated and any changes in the former are immediately propagated to the latter.

However, the combination of the model composition hierarchy and prototypical inheritance introduces quite interesting inter-dependencies among models. For this reason, GME only allowed multiple-inheritance for metamodels. Since WebGME merged metamodels and models and since multiple inheritance for metamodels proved to be a highly valuable feature, WebGME introduces mixins that provide the useful attributes of multiple inheritance for metamodels, but avoid its pitfalls.

The rest of the paper is organized as follows. Section 2 describes the main ideas behind WebGME and its architecture. Section 3 describes the crosscut abstraction. Section 4 covers model libraries. Section 5 is dedicated to the mixin concept. Finally, a brief overview of related work and conclusions are presented.

2   Overview

The metamodel specifies the domain-specific modeling language. The metamodeling language consists of a set of elementary modeling concepts. These are the basic conceptual building blocks of any given approach and corresponding tools. It is the meta-metamodel that defines these fundamental concepts. These may include composition, inheritance, a variety of associations, attributes, and other concepts. Which of these concepts to include, how to compose them, what editing operations are to operate on them and which are the most important design decisions that affect all aspects of the infrastructure and the domain modelers who will use it.

Hierarchical decomposition is the most widely used technique to handle complexity. This is the fundamental organization principle in WebGME, too. Copying, moving, or deleting a model will copy, move, or delete its constituent parts.

To help manage the complexity of any one model, aspects are also supported. An aspect is a view of a model where only a certain subset of its children are visible. For example, the model of a car can have separate aspects for the mechanical, electric and hydraulic components.

Prototypical inheritance is a unique feature that lets the modeler reuse and refine models. Just as there is a single composition tree, there is a single inheritance tree with a single object at its root. Rules specified by the metamodel, as well as actual model parts, propagate down this tree. Deleting a model will delete all of its descendants in the inheritance hierarchy too.

This approach is markedly different from inheritance in OO programming languages or in other modeling languages such as UML. First of all, it combines composition and inheritance. Note that Smalltalk and JavaScript have prototypical inheritance also, but that does not create new instances down the composition hierarchy. Second, inheritance is a live relationship between models that is continuously maintained during the modeling process. That is, any changes to a model propagate down the inheritance tree immediately.

The novel idea in WebGME is to blur the line where metamodeling ends and domain modeling begins by utilizing inheritance to capture the meta-model/model relationship. Every model in a WebGME project is contained in a single inheritance hierarchy rooted at a model called *FCO*, for First Class Object. Metamodel information can be provided anywhere in this hierarchy. An instance of any model inherits all of the rules and constraints from its base (recursively all the way up to *FCO*) and it can further refine it by adding additional metamodeling information. This is a form of multi-level metamodeling with a theoretically infinite number of levels. As a result of this approach, (1) metamodel changes propagate automatically to every model; (2) metamodels can be refined anywhere in the inheritance and composition hierarchies; (3) partially built domain models can become first class language elements to serve as building blocks; and (4) different (meta)model versions can peacefully coexist in the same project.

Note that while the concept of inheritance and prototypical inheritance has been developed in the context of OO languages, their use in the context of domain-specific modeling is different. The purpose of the domain-specific modeling is to create domain models (that roughly correspond to the object instances at run-time) that are based on metamodels (that roughly correspond to the classes created at design-time) - but these are created and edited in the same tool environment and coexist in the same database. Statically typed, compiled OO languages often draw a distinction between classes and instances and instances cannot be edited in the same editors as the one used for editing the class definitions, although some dynamic OO languages (like Python) have some capabilities that allow such operations.

Other important concepts in the meta-metamodel are pointers which are one to one associations and sets which are one to many associations. A pair of pointers can be visualized as a connection. For example, the default WebGME editor takes any object with two pointers with the reserved names of src and dst, displays the object as a connection and supports the customary editing operations.

Otherwise, connections are ordinary models; they can contain children, have other pointers and can be derived, etc. Therefore, the connection concept as such is not part of the meta-metamodel. However, pointers may cut across the hierarchy and hence, are not easily visualizable in an intuitive manner. The next section will describe the crosscut abstraction that were designed to overcome this problem.

Finally, textual attributes can be attached to models as well. Just as a simple illustration of the power of inheritance, there is a textual attribute called name added to the root object of the inheritance tree. The result is that every single modeling object has a name attribute. So, the actual WebGME application code does not need to have a specific concept for a model name.

3   Crosscuts

Cross-cutting concepts are always difficult to model. The typical way to capture relationships between models in different branches and/or levels of the composition hierarchy is through pointers and sets. However, the visual depiction of such associations is not intuitive at all since most tools display models according to composition, that is, they usually show the children of one model in one window (grandchildren may show up as ports). The target of a pointer can be indicated by its name and navigation to it can be supported, for example, by a double click operation, but an intuitive visual depiction of such relationships is sorely missing. For example, a connection between far away objects is supported by the meta-metamodel, yet there is no way to actually show it. To address this problem, WebGME introduces the concept of *crosscuts*.

A crosscut is a collection of objects that the modeler wishes to view together. The selection can be manual, that is, the user can drag objects into a crosscut view. Alternatively, a script can be provided that executes a one-time query to collect models from anywhere in the composition hierarchy. Existing associations between objects in a crosscut are depicted by various lines between the objects. For example, inheritance is shown similar to UML class diagrams, while pointers are visualized with lines and arrows. In addition to visualization, the main utility of crosscuts is that they serve as association editors. The target of pointers and set membership can be edited here. Deleting a model from a crosscut does not delete the object from the project, it simply removes it from the given crosscut.

Each crosscut has a context model, the designated container for new model elements created in the crosscut. (Note that it is atypical to create new models since a crosscut is meant to be a collection of already existing models. However, a connection is a model with two pointers, so allowing new connections in crosscuts was the motivation behind this design decision.) The default context is the root of the composition hierarchy called the *ROOT*. As *ROOT* can contain anything, crosscuts can be freely constructed. However, if the modeler chooses a context different from *ROOT*, the composition rules of the metamodel apply (even though crosscut containment is not composition). This is actually a great way to control and manage crosscuts. On the flip side, if one wants a crosscut with no constraints, but wants to avoid creating too many crosscuts in *ROOT*, one can simply create a model and specify that it can contain First Class Objects (*FCO*) which is the root of the inheritance hierarchy. Any instance of such a model can now serve as the context for unconstrained crosscuts.

One special use for crosscuts in WebGME is for metamodeling. Recall that meta information can be specified anywhere in the composition hierarchy. Therefore, there is no single model to show to edit the metamodel of the DSML. In WebGME, a crosscut is created for the metamodel where the user drags in all models that need to contain DSML specification. It is there and only there, where meta information can be specified. Of course, the metamodel is a special crosscut, because a new association created there does not actually create a new instance of a pointer, for example, but instead specifies that the given kind of pointer of a model can point to the selected model (and its instances).

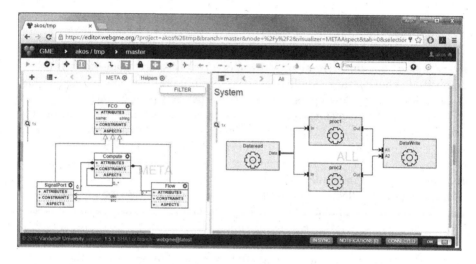

Fig. 1. Hierarchical Signal Flow Graph

Consider Fig. 1 that depicts the metamodel of a simple hierarchical signal flow graph (SF) on the left and an example SF domain model on the right. The metamodel shows that Compute nodes, SignalPorts and Flows are all derived from *FCO*. Note that unlike in any other tool we are aware of, this inheritance relationship was not drawn explicitly by the user. Instead, when these models were created in the first place, they were instantiated from a model, in this case, *FCO*. The metamodel displays these already existing inheritance relationships but they can be edited as well. On the other hand, the associations in Fig. 1 were created in the meta crosscut. For example, the *src* and *dst* pointer specifications were drawn by the user specifying that a Flow represents a relationship between two SignalPorts. The default WebGME editor, in turn, will show these as connections (explained above) as expected in an signal flow graph.

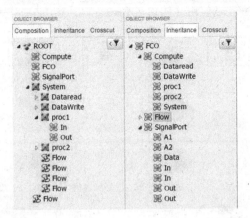

Fig. 2. Composition and Inheritance Trees

The composition and inheritances trees of this simple example are shown in Fig. 2. The composition hierarchy on the left shows that Root has four children, Compute, SignalPort, Flow and System. The metamodel in the previous figure only showed the first three. That is exactly because a metamodel is a crosscut and we only needed to specify meta information for these models. The System model is an instance of the Compute model (the inside of which is shown on he right side of Fig. 1 above). The inheritance hierarchy on the right side of Fig. 2 shows this as well as the four other instances of the Compute model that are in turn contained by System.

Finally, we present a domain model example to illustrate the utility of crosscuts. The introduction outlined the use case of modeling a component based software system and a simple parallel hardware architecture that uses multiple compute nodes. If we want to explicitly model the assignment of software component to hardware nodes, we need a placeholder for expressing that relation. Since the hardware and software models should have their own model composition hierarchy, a crosscut is a straightforward way to specify the assignment. Figure 3 shows the crosscut created for this purpose. Note the assignment connections that connect software components to a hardware nodes. A crosscut is an only place where they can be visualized since the source and destination models as well as the connections themselves have different parents in the composition hierarchy. Creating a modeling concept specifically for this purpose is feasible, but it would unnecessarily complicate the metamodel.

4   Libraries

The concept of software libraries have been used widely for decades because of its utility in code reuse and evolution. There is a similar need for reusing models and modeling languages. Since the concepts of the metamodel and model are merged in WebGME, that is, the modeling language specification is embedded in the

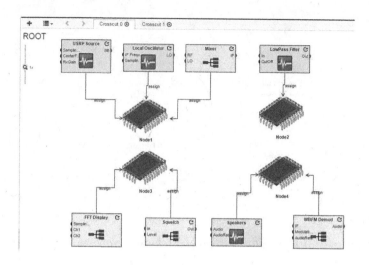

Fig. 3. Software to Hardware Assignment Example

actual domain models, it is even more important to support model libraries for reuse and language evolution. Hence, WebGME supports model libraries in a seamless and intuitive manner.

Creating a library is as easy as identifying a subset of a project and exporting it. A library is defined along the composition hierarchy. This means that any meta- or domain model can be designated as a library and its complete containment sub-tree will be included automatically. The library, in turn, can be imported into another project. Pointers and sets that refer to models in the library from outside of it are not affected at all. Instances of models contained in a library that reside outside of the library cause no problems either. However, what happens when a prototype of a model in the library is not part of the library? Or if a pointer or set refer from inside to the outside of the library? The design decision was made to allow this situation, but importing such a library would only work where the container project also has the exact same models so that these outward pointing relations can be restored. In other words, this works for very closely related projects. The recommended and most typical use of model libraries are for cases when this does not happen. For example, exporting a metamodel does not run into this problem because metamodels are inherently self contained. The other most typical use is collecting a set of basic domain models as a component library where the only external dependencies are to the metamodels. In those cases, the metamodels are typically contained in a library and domain models in another and they are updated at the same time. Note that the ROOT and the FCO are present in all WebGME projects, so external references to those are fine.

Library updates are not generating notifications automatically but users of the library can request updates when the source of the library is updated. These updates are automatically propagated through the whole project, so the new features are available instantly for the existing instance models while the outdated features will be removed automatically. Any custom extensions of the library will remain intact as long as their prototypes are still present in the library.

This style of model libraries provide a good basis for domain composition. It can be seen, that as long as a metamodel library depends only on the *FCO*, any other metamodel library becomes compatible with it allowing quick and easy integration. Any associations between such metamodels in the target project are transparently supported without losing the ability to evolve with the original metamodels. Section 5 will present an example of how such metamodel composition works.

5   Mixins: Multiple Inheritance for Metamodels

To enhance the overall re-usability of modeling concepts, WebGME implements a *mixin* feature as an extension to prototypical inheritance. Mixins augment the desirable features of single inheritance, but they only apply to metamodels. Mixins allow metamodels to share specifications, be derived from multiple sources, or extend each other's behavior. Mixins provide a tradeoff to successfully address the problems inherent to multiple inheritance [18] when it comes to prototypical inheritance between object models while keeping the end result as simple as possible.

We can extend the specifications of a metamodel by assigning multiple mixin nodes to it. The resulting node will not only inherit its definitions from its prototype, but from its mixins as well. However, as opposed to prototypical inheritance, the metamodel will not inherit any actual children of the mixins.

The mixin definition is an ordered array of nodes, so if a given meta rule could be derived from multiple sources, the first occurrence will always be used. Also, the specification inherited from the prototype has priority over the specifications obtained from the mixins. Hence, prototypical inheritance is not affected by mixins. It also takes care of the problem of repeated inheritance as any data can only be inherited from a single base, so even if the mixin nodes define colliding properties, the source of every rule remains clear. Furthermore, as metamodels are never pre-compiled in WebGME, the tool is able to give immediate feedback if a rule collision happens as a result of a change in the mixin definitions or the mixins themselves.

Mixins support combining existing domains to model complex systems in a seamless manner. Take the example language of a hierarchical signal flow graph shown in Fig. 1. If we want to combine this language with a hierarchical state machine language—shown in Fig. 4—where the behavior of a *State* can be modeled by a signal flow graph, we just need to import the two languages as libraries into a new project and define the mixin relation among the elements of the two domains as shown in Fig. 5.

As we can see in Fig. 5, the mixin relation is visualized similarly to the inheritance relation, but with a dashed line to make a distinction. These relations

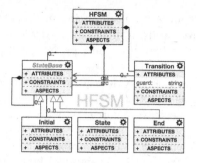

Fig. 4. Hierarchical Finite State Machine

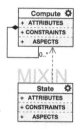

Fig. 5. Combining two languages

can be freely added or removed at any point with the following two exceptions. No node can be in a mixin relation of itself or any of its ancestors in the pro- totypical inheritance tree, as that kind of relation will not add anything to the already existing rule-set. On the other hand, cycles among the mixin relations are allowed, even though they are not necessarily meaningful, because even with these loops, the order of definitions remains unambiguous and consistent.

Figure 6 shows a simple domain model for the combined state machine-signal flow graph DSML. There is a state machine model on the left side, while on the right, the inside of the state *Processing* is shown that contains the example signal flow from Fig. 1. So mixins enabled the composition of the two domains by performing a few simple steps.

6   Related Work

AToMPM [21], a web-based metamodeling and transformation tool, is the most closely related to our work. While many of the design decisions that guided the development of the tool are similar to ours, the fusion of metamodeling and prototypical inheritance, mixins, and crosscuts are unique to WebGME.

To the best of our knowledge, very little work is being done on abstractions to handle model complexity beyond the traditional hierarchical decomposition. Collaborative editing also helps in building large complex models and there is rel- evant work in the technical literature on this aspect. Various collaborative tools

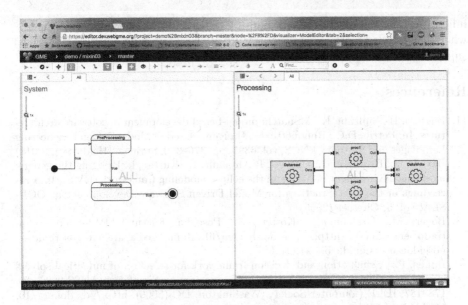

Fig. 6. SF with SM together

are used in specific domains such as mechanical engineering [13], automotive industry [9], and UML [3]. SLIM [24] is a prototype of a collaborative environment executed in a web browser. The Connected Data Objects (CDO) [20] is a model repository and a run-time persistence framework for EMF. It supports locking, offline scenarios, various persistence backends, such as Hibernate, and pluggable fail-over adapters to multiple repositories. CAMEL [5] is also an eclipse plugin that supports collaborative interaction via modeling, drawing, chatting, posterboards, whiteboards, and it is capable of replaying online meetings. Its focus is on collaborative communications rather than versioning and collaborative use of domain-specific languages.

7   Conclusions

The paper presented three abstractions specifically designed to support the management of complexity of large system models. When the modeling language itself has hundreds of concepts and domain models reach tens of thousands of objects [17], traditional methods such as hierarchical decomposition are no longer sufficient to ensure a manageable modeling process. The purpose of crosscuts is to provide an intuitive way to capture and visualize relations between models in different parts of the composition hierarchy. Model libraries are extremely helpful in managing metamodels, i.e., modeling languages, and support reusable repositories of component models. Combined with prototypical inheritance, they enable modeling language and model evolution in a seamless fashion. The mixin feature presents a trade off between full-scale multiple inheritance and single inheritance. Essentially it enables multiple inheritance for metamodels which is where it is needed most. This novel feature allows combining existing DSMLs to support the modeling of truly complex systems.

References

1. Bagheri, H., Sullivan, K.: Monarch: model-based development of software architectures. In: Petriu, D.C., Rouquette, N., Haugen, Ø. (eds.) Model Driven Engineering Languages and Systems. LNCS, vol. 6395, pp. 376–390. Springer, Heidelberg (2010)
2. Bézivin, J., Brunette, C., Chevrel, R., Jouault, F., Kurtev, I.: Bridging the generic modeling environment (GME) and the eclipse modeling framework (EMF). In: Proceedings of the Best Practices for Model Driven Software Development at OOPSLA, vol. 5, Citeseer (2005)
3. Boger, M., Graham, E., Köster, M.: Poseidon for uml. Pode ser encontrado em (2000). http://gentleware.com/fileadmin/media/archives/userguides/poseidon_users_guide/book1.html
4. Bunus, P.: A simulation and decision framework for selection of numerical solvers in. In: Proceedings of the 39th Annual Symposium on Simulation ANSS 2006, pp. 178–187. IEEE Computer Society, Washington, DC (2006). http://dx.doi.org/10.1109/ANSS.2006.9
5. Cataldo, M., Shelton, C., Choi, Y., Huang, Y.Y., Ramesh, V., Saini, D., Wang, L.Y.: Camel: a tool for collaborative distributed software design. In: Fourth IEEE International Conference on Global Software Engineering, ICGSE 2009, pp. 83–92. IEEE (2009)
6. Czarnecki, K., Bednasch, T., Unger, P., Eisenecker, U.: Generative programming for embedded software: an industrial experience report. In: Batory, D., Consel, C., Taha, W. (eds.) GPCE 2002. LNCS, vol. 2487, pp. 156–172. Springer, Heidelberg (2002). doi:10.1007/3-540-45821-2_10
7. Hemingway, G., Neema, H., Nine, H., Sztipanovits, J., Karsai, G.: Rapid synthesis of high-level architecture-based heterogeneous simulation: a model-based integration approach. Simulation 88(2), 217–232 (2012)
8. Karsai, G., Sztipanovits, J., Ledeczi, A., Bapty, T.: Model-integrated development of embedded software. Proc. IEEE 91(1), 145–164 (2003)
9. Kong, S., Noh, S., Han, Y.G., Kim, G., Lee, K.: Internet-based collaboration system: press-die design process for automobile manufacturer. Int. J. Adv. Manufact. Technol. 20(9), 701–708 (2002)
10. Lattmann, Z., Nagel, A., Scott, J., Smyth, K., Porter, J., Neema, S., Bapty, T., Sztipanovits, J., Ceisel, J., Mavris, D., et al.: Towards automated evaluation of vehicle dynamics in system-level designs. In: ASME 2012 Computers and Information in Engineering Conference, pp. 1131–1141. ASME (2012)
11. Lédeczi, Á., Bakay, A., Maroti, M., Volgyesi, P., Nordstrom, G., Sprinkle, J., Karsai, G.: Composing domain-specific design environments. Computer 34(11), 44–51 (2001)
12. Levendovszky, T., Balasubramanian, D., Coglio, A., Dubey, A., Otte, W., Karsai, G., Gokhale, A., Nyako, S., Kumar, P., Emfinger, W.: Drems: a model-driven distributed secure information architecture platform for managed embedded systems. IEEE Softw. 31, 1 (2014)
13. Li, M., Wang, C.C., Gao, S.: Real-time collaborative design with heterogeneous CAD systems based on neutral modeling commands. J. Comput. Inf. Sci. Eng. 7(2), 113–125 (2007)

14. Long, E., Misra, A., Sztipanovits, J.: Increasing productivity at Saturn. Computer **31**(8), 35–43 (1998)
15. Mathe, J.L., Ledeczi, A., Nadas, A., Sztipanovits, J., Martin, J.B., Weavind, L.M., Miller, A., Miller, P., Maron, D.J.: A model-integrated, guideline-driven, clinical decision-support system. IEEE Softw. **26**(4), 54–61 (2009)
16. Mohanty, S., Prasanna, V., Neema, S., Davis, J.: Rapid design space exploration of heterogeneous embedded systems using symbolic search and multi-granular simulation. ACM SIGPLAN Not. **37**(7), 18–27 (2002)
17. Neema, H., Lattmann, Z., Meijer, P., Klingler, J., Neema, S., Bapty, T., Sztipanovits, J., Karsai, G.: Design space exploration and manipulation for cyber physical systems. In: IFIP First International Workshop on Design Space Exploration of Cyber-Physical Systems (IDEAL 2014), Springer, Heidelberg (2014)
18. Singh, G.B.: Single versus multiple inheritance in object oriented programming. ACM SIGPLAN OOPS Messenger **6**(1), 30–39 (1995)
19. Stankovic, J., Zhu, R., Poornalingam, R., Lu, C., Yu, Z., Humphrey, M., Ellis, B.: Vest: an aspect-based composition tool for real-time systems. In: Proceedings of the 9th IEEE Real-Time and Embedded Technology and Applications Symposium, 2003, pp. 58–69, May 2003
20. Stepper, E.: Connected data objects (cdo), November 2012. http://www.eclipse.org/cdo/documentation/index.php
21. Syriani, E., Vangheluwe, H., Mannadiar, R., Hansen, C., Van Mierlo, S., Ergin, H.: Atompm: a web-based modeling environment. MODELS (2003)
22. Sztipanovits, J., Karsai, G.: Model-integrated computing. Computer **30**(4), 110–111 (1997)
23. Thramboulidis, K., Perdikis, D., Kantas, S.: Model driven development of distributed control applications. Int. J. Adv. Manufact. Technol. **33**(3), 233–242 (2007)
24. Thum, C., Schwind, M., Schader, M.: Slima lightweight environment for synchronous collaborative modeling. In: Schürr, A., Selic, B. (eds.) Model Driven Engineering Languages and Systems. LNCS, vol. 5795, pp. 137–151. Springer, Heidelberg (2009)

Specifying and Verifying Advanced Control Features

Gary T. Leavens[1(✉)], David Naumann[2], Hridesh Rajan[3], and Tomoyuki Aotani[4]

[1] Department of Computer Science, University of Central Florida, Orlando, FL 32816, USA
leavens@cs.ucf.edu
[2] Department of Computer Science, Stevens Institute of Technology, Hoboken, NJ 07030, USA
naumann@cs.stevens.edu
[3] Department of Computer Science, Iowa State University, Ames, IA 50011, USA
hridesh@iastate.edu
[4] Department of Mathematical and Computing Sciences, Tokyo Institute of Technology, Tokyo 152-8552, Japan
aotani@is.titech.ac.jp
http://www.cs.ucf.edu/~leavens,
https://www.cs.stevens.edu/~naumann/,
http://web.cs.iastate.edu/~hridesh/,
https://taotani.wordpress.com/

Abstract. Advances in programming often revolve around key design patterns, which programming languages embody as new control features. These control features, such as higher-order functions, advice, and context dependence, use indirection to decrease coupling and enhance modularity. However, this indirection makes them difficult to verify, because it hides actions (and their effects) behind an abstraction barrier. Such abstraction barriers can be overcome in a modular way using greybox specification techniques, provided the programming language supports interfaces as a place to record specifications. These techniques have previously allowed specification and modular verification of higher-order functional and object-oriented programs, as well as aspect-oriented and context-oriented programs.

Keywords: Greybox specification · Modular verification · JML language

1 Introduction

With advances in computing, come ever-increasing complexity for software and ever-increasing demands for new ways to manage that complexity. Furthermore, with computers becoming more tightly integrated into daily life (through smartphones and sensors), the consequences of incorrect software loom ever larger.

© Springer International Publishing AG 2016
T. Margaria and B. Steffen (Eds.): ISoLA 2016, Part II, LNCS 9953, pp. 80–96, 2016.
DOI: 10.1007/978-3-319-47169-3_7

One response to these looming consequences is formal methods: using mathematics to specify and verify the correctness of programs. In particular, the refinement calculus [5,26] provides a very attractive way to integrate programming and specification into a single unified language.

However, formal methods have a difficult time keeping up with trends in programming, which have proposed advanced control features to help modularize complex, modern software. These advanced control features include higher-order functions and higher-order methods, aspect-oriented advice, and context-oriented programming. In particular, higher-order features are a way that language designers can give programmers the power to design their own control abstractions.

Greybox specification techniques [11], based on work in the refinement calculus, support modular specification and verification of programs that use advanced control features [33]. In this paper we survey the application of greybox techniques to higher-order, aspect-oriented, and context-oriented programming, demonstrating how a carefully designed combination of specification language and programming language features enables modular verification.

Classical Hoare-style specification and verification techniques [18] work well for simple first-order imperative languages. Specification languages adapted these techniques to imperative languages with procedural abstractions, writing contracts for procedures in the form of pre- and postconditions plus frame axioms [1,16,19,35]. The design by contract methodology [23,24] is a well-known popularization of these ideas.

However, more advanced styles of programming, including higher-order programming, some object-oriented (OO) design patterns, and aspect-oriented and context-oriented features make it difficult to apply classical Hoare-style specification and verification techniques. In particular, as Shaner et al. [33] noted, a key difficulty is specifying that calls to certain functions or methods are *mandatory*; i.e., that these calls must take place in certain states. The problem is that Hoare logic only specifies required state transformations; it does not specify the kind of control flow details that would allow clients to make strong conclusions about mandatory calls.

1.1 The Client-Reasoning Problem

The client-reasoning problem is for clients to statically draw strong conclusions about uses of advanced control features. To illustrate this problem in the context of higher-order programming, consider the forEach method from the class ArrOps (shown in Fig. 1). The forEach method calls the run method of the procedure parameter p with the array and each index as arguments; these calls are made in increasing order of the indexes. The interface AProc is given in Fig. 2 on the next page. The specification of the method forEach will be discussed further below.

In order to understand the client-reasoning problem for such examples, consider the client of ArrOps shown in Fig. 3. This client uses the type APMax (see Fig. 4 on the next page), which implements the AProc interface. The run

```
public class ArrOps<T> {
    /*@ extract @*/
    public void forEach(T[] a, AProc<T> p) {
        //@ maintaining 0 <= i && i <= a.length;
        //@ decreasing a.length - i;
        for (int i = 0; i < a.length; i++) {
            p.run(a, i);
        }
    }
}
```

Fig. 1. The type ArrOps, in Java with JML Annotations. JML annotations are written as special comments that start with an at-sign (@).

```
public interface AProc<T> {
    /*@ public normal_behavior
      @    requires 0 <= i && i < a.length;
      @    assignable a[i], objectState;   @*/
    void run(T[] a, int i);
}
```

Fig. 2. The interface type AProc, which specifies the precondition and frame of the run method. In JML such method specifications appear before the method header. In multi-line JML annotations, the at-signs (@) at the beginning of lines are ignored.

```
Integer[] mya = new Integer[2];
mya[0] = 5; mya[1] = 4;
ArrOps<Integer> ao = new ArrOps<Integer>();
APMax pm = new APMax();
ao.forEach(mya, pm);
//@ assert pm.getMax() == 5;
System.out.println("max is " + pm.getMax());
```

Fig. 3. A client of ArrOps that uses forEach.

function of APMax sets the field maxSeen to the maximum of the array element at the given index and the current value of maxSeen. Thus, as shown in the assertion in Fig. 3, after calling forEach, the value of maxSeen should be 5 (and thus the program will print "max is 5").

However, standard Hoare logic does not make it easy to statically prove the assertion in Fig. 3, due to the abstraction barrier that is the specification of AProc's run method. This method has a very weak specification, which only says that the index is required to be a legal index into the array argument and that it may assign to the array at the given index, and to locations in the data group objectState, which represents the state owned by the AProc object. (The data group objectState is built-in to the type Object.) This specification is very weak, so as to permit arbitrary subtypes of AProc with vastly different behaviors for run.

```
public class APMax implements AProc<Integer> {
    protected /*@ spec_public @*/ Integer maxSeen = Integer.MIN_VALUE;
                                //@ in objectState;

    /*@ also
      @    requires 0 <= i && i < a.length;
      @    assignable maxSeen;
      @    ensures maxSeen == Math.max(\old(maxSeen),a[i]); @*/
    public void run(Integer[] a, int i) {
        if (a[i] > maxSeen) {
            maxSeen = a[i];
        }
    }
    //@ ensures \result == maxSeen;
    public /*@ pure @*/ Integer getMax() { return maxSeen; }
}
```

Fig. 4. The type APMax, which implements the interface AProc<Integer>.

In order to statically verify the assertion in Fig. 3, one must use the specification of APMax's run method, not the specification of run in AProc. However, standard logics do not support such reasoning [33]. The problem is that the modular Hoare logic rule for method calls uses the specification of the called method and does not take into account the indirection due to dynamic dispatch in this example. Thus one can only prove a weak specification for forEach, one that is insufficient to prove the assertion in Fig. 3.

This incompleteness in standard specification and verification techniques is important in many real examples. Not only does it affect higher-order programming, but it also occurs in several common OO design patterns, such as the Observer, Template Method, and Chain of Responsibility patterns [33]. Furthermore it also affects other innovative styles of programming, such as aspect-oriented and context-oriented programming.

2 Related Work

The formal methods literature offers some ways around this static verification problem for the case of higher-order procedures in simple imperative and in OO languages.

2.1 Higher-Order Logic Techniques

One solution is to use higher-order logic to write specifications that are parameterized by the specifications of argument methods [12,13,27]. In our example, this would mean writing the specification of forEach using the pre- and postcondition specifications of its AProc argument. The postcondition of forEach would then be expressed using those argument specifications, as shown in Fig. 5 on the next page. However, such specifications are often more complex than the code

```
/*@ requires (\forall int i; 0 <= i && i < a.length; p.run.pre(a,i)
  @               && ((p.run.post(a,i) && (i+1) < a.length)
  @                   ==> p.run.pre(a,i+1)));
  @ assignable p.objectState, a[*];
  @ ensures (\forall int i; 0 <= i && i < a.length; p.run.post(a,i));
  @*/
public void forEach(T[] a, AProc<T> p) {
```

Fig. 5. Specification of `ArrOps`'s `forEach` method in the style of Ernst et al. [13]. The notations `.pre` and `.post` refer to the pre- and postconditions of an (actual argument) method, which are treated as a function of the method's arguments. The JML notation for quantifiers is used, with a range condition between the semicolons.

they specify [33], especially if the argument methods can update state, because a precise general specification of the higher-order method needs to describe sequencing of the state updates. Furthermore, technically such specifications do not specify that mandatory calls must be made, only that the required state transformations happen. Finally, we are not aware of work using higher-order specifications that deals with frame conditions, with the exception of the frame conditions that are implicit in higher order separation logics [3,22].

Findler and Felleisen [14] also use a higher-order logic, but for dynamic contract checking instead of static verification. Their specification technique does not allow for the specification of mandatory calls. By contrast Barnett and Schulte [10] use specifications similar to model programs (in AsmL) to specify mandatory calls, but their contracts are enforced dynamically.

2.2   Trace-Based Techniques

Another solution is to augment specifications with traces. Soundarajan and Fridella [34] use two specifications for such higher-order methods: a functional specification and an extended specification that specifies traces of what methods must be called; this "e-specification" can be used to reason about the effects of those mandatory calls. For example, the e-specification of `ArrOps`'s `forEach` method in their style would look like Fig. 6. In this figure, the trace τ has n elements, where n is the length of the array parameter a. The `run` method would have to be declared as a "hook method," which explains the notation `.hm` used in the specification. Soundarajan and Fridella's enrichment rule (R2) allows proving assertions like the assertion in Fig. 3. One problem with this solution is that it makes specifications of higher-order methods, such as `forEach`

$$epre.\texttt{ArrOps.forEach(a, p)} \equiv [(\texttt{a} \neq \texttt{null} \wedge \texttt{p} \neq \texttt{null}) \wedge \tau = \epsilon]$$
$$epost.\texttt{ArrOps.forEach(a,p)} \equiv [(|\tau| = \texttt{a.length}) \wedge (\forall i : 0 \leq i \wedge i \leq \texttt{a.length} :$$
$$(\tau[i+1].hm = \texttt{p.run(a,i)}))]$$

Fig. 6. An e-specification of `ArrOps`'s `forEach` method in the style of Soundarajan and Fridella [34].

somewhat complex and unintiutive. Another problem with this solution is that correctness proofs involve intricate reasoning about traces [33].

2.3 Greybox Techniques

Greybox specifications are a way around the difficulties of these other techniques.

Büchi and Weck's original paper on greybox specifications [11] developed the insight that abstract programs from the refinement calculus [5, 26], possibly containing specification statements, are a good way to specify higher-order programs. Büchi and Weck originally gave a semantics based on traces and a proof system that relied on proofs of refinement (and thus higher-order logic).

Shaner et al. [33] adapted the greybox technique to JML by adding two features: *model program* specifications (which are JML's embodiment of greybox specifications) and refining statements (which are the way that specification statements from the refinement calculus are implemented in JML). Their work simplified Büchi and Weck's idea by restricting what programs could be considered to correctly implement a greybox specification. The main restriction is that all statements other than specification statements, including method calls, that appear in a model program must appear in a correct implementation. This restriction makes it easy for model programs to specify mandatory calls; such calls are simply written into the model program and thus must appear in a correct implementation. In cases where the model program does not contain specification statements, the model program will thus be identical to the correct code.

Like greybox specifications, JML model programs may contain specification statements, which can be used to abstract from program details. The matching of model program statements that is involved in proving correctness of an implementation (and enforcing mandatory calls) is aided by requiring that each specification statement in the model program must be replaced by a corresponding **refining** statement in a correct implementation. A refining statement has the general form **refining** *spec* { *S* }, where *spec* is a pre- and postcondition specification, and *S* is a statement; such a statement corresponds in the matching process to the specification statement *spec*, which makes matching of model program specifications and implementations trivial. In addition, JML requires that the body of each refining statement must correctly implement its specification. Clients can reason about calls to a method with a model program specification by substituting the model program for the call, using the copy rule [25]; doing so allows the verifier to reach strong conclusions by combining properties known in the call's context with the model program [33].

For the ArrOps example, the forEach method contains no refining statements, and thus its model program specification is the same as its code. In general model program specifications can be extracted from JML annotated code automatically, which is indicated by using the **extract** keyword [33]. The extracted specification is shown in Fig. 7 on the next page. Comparing this with Fig. 1, one can see that the model program contains the same code as the method. Thus the calls to p are mandatory and their exact order is also specified.

```
/*@ public model_program {
  @    maintaining 0 <= i && i < a.length;
  @    decreasing a.length - i;
  @    for (int i = 0; i < a.length; i++) {
  @        p.run(a, i);
  @    }
  @ } @*/
public void forEach(T[] a, AProc<T> p);
```

Fig. 7. The model program specification extracted for the forEach method of the type ArrOps.

3   Applicability of Greybox Techniques

Recall that the client-reasoning problem is caused by the weak specification used for AProc's run method. The problem is that the usual and modular rule for verification of method calls uses the specification of the called method from the module that the caller directly refers to, in this case AProc. However, the verification of the assertion in Fig. 3 requires use of the specification of the actual parameter, APMax (see Fig. 4).

Advanced styles of programming often aim to separate programs into parts that can be combined in flexible ways. Functional programming, for example, allows the definition of higher-order functions, such as map and foldr, which can apply functions to elements of a list in some standard pattern. The higher-order function, such as map, does not need any prior knowledge of the function parameter, which is passed to it as an argument. The parameter function is thus called indirectly by the higher-order function.

In object-oriented (OO) programs "higher-order methods" [33] are used in several design patterns, such as the Template Method pattern, the Chain of Responsibility pattern [15,33], and the Composite pattern [15,32]. In these patterns, the code corresponding to a higher-order method makes "mandatory calls" [33] to some parameter's method(s). Again, the result is that the higher-order method needs only limited prior knowledge of the object passed to it and its methods. As in the case of functional programming, this allows for great flexibility in combining program parts.

Similarly, in aspect-oriented (AO) programs, advice may be invoked in a very indirect manner, by the occurrence of an event [20]. Similar kinds of indirection occur in implicit invocation [28,31] and in context-oriented programs [17].

In all these kinds of programs, indirection tends to make specification and verification incomplete. The difficulty is that the parameter specification is weak (like the specification in AProc), in order to allow maximum flexibility, but such weak specifications are not sufficient to draw strong conclusions (like the assertion in Fig. 3). In order to draw such strong conclusions, the specification needs to make the calls to the parameter mandatory, so that the reasoning technique can count on the actual parameter being called. Shaner et al. combined model program specifications, which specify mandatory calls, with a copy rule, which makes it possible for knowledge of the dynamic type of the actual arguments to be used in reasoning about calls [33].

Our experience with using greybox specification techniques is that they solve this problem, not only for functional and OO languages, but also for new kinds of programming techniques, such as aspect-oriented, implicit invocation, and context-oriented programming. In the rest of this paper we review such greybox specification and verification techniques in the context of OO programming, and then in aspect-oriented and context-oriented programming. These advanced control features lend support to our thesis that greybox specification and verification techniques are useful for the specification and modular verification of advanced control features. Indeed, we conjecture that adaptations of such greybox techniques will be useful for as yet unknown control features that will be developed in the future. We also point out the programming language features that help apply this technique.

4   Greybox Techniques in OO Programming

This section reviews the application of greybox specification techniques [11] to the verification of Object-Oriented (OO) programs, based on the work of Shaner et al. [33].

For verification of method implementations against model program specifications, Shaner et al. use a two-step process. First the implementation is matched against the model program; for the implementation to be correct, each statement that is not a specification statement must appear literally in the implementation, and specification statements must each match a corresponding **refining** statement (i.e., one which contains that specification). Second, the bodies of **refining** statements are verified to correctly implement their specifications.

For verification of calls to methods with model program specifications, a copy rule [25] is used; that is, the model program is copied to the call site, with an appropriate substitution of actuals for formal parameters.[1] For example to reason about the client code in Fig. 3, one copies the body of the model program specification (see Fig. 7 on the previous page) to the call site, substituting the actuals for the formals, and obtains the code shown in Fig. 8. In that code, lines 5–9 are the model program specification of forEach, with the actuals mya and pm substituted for the formals a and p, respectively. As can be seen in Fig. 8, the call on line 8 now uses pm's run method, so the specification for the run method in its type, APMax (see Fig. 4), can be used to reason about its effects. In this case one would need to add an additional loop invariant, such as

```
//@ maintaining (\forall int j; 0 <= j && j <= i; a[j] <= pm.getMax());
```

to finish the proof of the assertion in line 10.

---

[1] This copying can be used repeatedly if the model program contains recursive calls. In general the substitution of actuals for formals may need to rename locals to avoid capture.

```
1       Integer[] mya = new Integer[2];
2       mya[0] = 5; mya[1] = 4;
3       ArrOps<Integer> ao = new ArrOps<Integer>();
4       APMax pm = new APMax();
5       //@ maintaining 0 <= i && i < mya.length;
6       //@ decreasing mya.length - i;
7       for (int i = 0; i < mya.length; i++) {
8           pm.run(mya, i);
9       }
10      //@ assert pm.getMax() == 5;
11      System.out.println("max is " + pm.getMax());
```

Fig. 8. Code from Fig. 3 with the model program specification substituted for the call to forEach.

There are a few other important points to be taken from the Shaner et al. paper [33]. As has already been noted, by using refining statements and JML's **extract** keyword, one can simultaneously specify and implement a higher-order method, without the redundancy that would appear if one writes a model-program specification explicitly that contains specification statements. Second the Shaner et al. paper formalizes the logic for reasoning about OO programs with model program specifications; it also contains a soundness proof for the logic. Finally, the technique can be used with only first-order reasoning and does not require "explicit reasoning in the style of refinement calculi" [33, Sect. 5.1]. Refinement style reasoning could be a viable alternative in some cases, because the benefit of not requiring refinement calculus style reasoning comes at a cost: correct implementations of a model program specification cannot use different control structures than those in the model program specification, since matching on such non-specification statements is literal. Nevertheless, the technique is quite practical and the Shaner et al. paper shows examples of specification and verification for three design patterns: Observer, Template Method, and Chain of Responsibility.

Finally, it is important to point out how modular verification interacts with the language features of Java. Because Java method calls name the method called and because the static type of the receiver is known, a client can find the model program specification by looking up the (JML) specification for the method being called in the class of the receiver. When a model program specification is found, the client can use the copy rule as described above.

5   Greybox Techniques in Aspect-Oriented Programming

Aspect-oriented programming aims to modularize concerns (or policies) in programs [20]. One way to modularize such concerns is to use the Observer pattern, calling registered handlers whenever an interesting event occurs. The Observer pattern is directly supported by AspectJ's control features: pointcuts and advice [21]. *Pointcuts* specify events in the execution of a program, such as method calls, method body executions, and variable access. *Advice* is code that can be declared to be run before, after, or instead of the code that would normally run for an event. These features make verification difficult [7], because events are pervasive in a program's execution (many events can occur in the execution of even a small section of code) and also announced implicitly (there is no indication in the code of their presence [31]).

Implicit invocation languages, such as Ptolemy [28,29], announce events explicitly,[2] and thus make clear in the code where events may happen. Ptolemy also features event interface declarations, which allows both static type checking of handlers (the analogue of advice in Ptolemy) and provides a place where specifications for event handlers can be written.

For our purposes, the most interesting thing about Ptolemy is the specification and verification technique for it called "translucid contracts" [7–9]. In the remainder of this section we review that work on translucid contracts and relate it to greybox specifications. Translucid contracts combine Hoare-style pre- and postcondition specifications with model programs. The model programs specify the "control effects" of handlers: in particular they specify when a handler invokes the next handler in the chain of handlers for an event. Even without formal reasoning about correctness, knowing whether a handler must invoke the next handler is useful for reasoning about what happens when multiple handlers are registered to handle an event, as it answers questions such as "will all the registered handlers run?"

To give a concrete example, we reproduce the first example from Shaner et al.'s paper [33] in PtolemyJ,[3] a variant of Ptolemy. Consider the event declaration given in Fig. 9. This event has a single parameter, a `Counter` named `ctr`. Its translucid contract consists of a precondition (following **requires**), a model program, which is the block following **assumes**, and a postcondition (following **ensures**). The model program has a specification statement, **preserves** `ctr.getCount() >= 0;`, which is shorthand for

```
requires ctr.getCount() >= 0;
ensures ctr.getCount() >= 0;
```

This specification statement is followed by `next.invoke()`, which is a mandatory call to the next handler (if there is one) or the original announced code (otherwise).

Events in Ptolemy occur when an **announce** statement is executed. An example appears in Fig. 10 on the next page, which is a class that implements a simple counter. The **announce** statement in the method bump runs all handlers registered for the `Bumped` event; it passes the context (**this**) to the handlers.

The class `LastVal` (Fig. 11 on the next page) has a handler, `handleBump`, that can handle `Bumped` events, due to the **when** declaration at the end of the class. As required by the translucid contract's model program specification,

---

[2] Which handlers are invoked is implicit in implicit invocation languages, but where they are invoked from is evident in the source code. See Sanchez and Leavens's paper [31] for a general discussion of the reasoning tradeoffs involved.

[3] See http://web.cs.iastate.edu/~ptolemy/ for details about PtolemyJ.

```
public void event Bumped {
  Counter ctr;

  requires ctr.getCount() >= 0
  assumes {
    preserves ctr.getCount() >= 0;
    next.invoke();
  }
  ensures ctr.getCount() >= 0
}
```

Fig. 9. PtolemyJ declaration of an event Bumped with a translucid contract.

```
public class Counter {
  private /*@ spec_public @*/ int count = 0;

  //@ requires count < Integer.MAX_VALUE;
  //@ assignable count, handlers[*].objectState;
  //@ ensures count == \old(count+1);
  public void bump() {
    announce Bumped(this) {
      this.count = this.count+1;
    }
  }
  //@ ensures \result == count;
  public /*@ pure @*/ int getCount() { return count; }
}
```

Fig. 10. PtolemyJ code for a class Counter with JML style annotations.

```
public class LastVal {
  private /*@ spec_public @*/ int val = 0; //@ in objectState;

  //@ ensures \result == this.val;
  public /*@ pure @*/ int getVal() { return this.val; }

  public void handleBump(Bumped next) {
    refining preserves next.ctr.getCount() >= 0;
    { val = next.ctr.getCount(); }
    next.invoke();
  }
  when Bumped do handleBump;
}
```

Fig. 11. PtolemyJ code for the class LastVal containing a handler.

it consists of a **refining** statement that corresponds to the specification statement in the model program and an invocation of the next handler. Thus the handler matches the model program specification, which is required for correctness.

```
Counter c = new Counter();
LastVal lv = new LastVal();
register(lv);
c.bump();
//@ assert lv.val == 1;
```

Fig. 12. A PtolemyJ client with an assertion to be verified.

Reasoning about client code also uses a copy rule for **announce** statements and for invocations of next.**invoke**(); the model program specification is substituted for the announcement (with actuals replacing formals). As with the Shaner et al. paper, the advantage of this style of client reasoning is that it permits strong conclusions to be drawn if one knows what the handlers are. For example, in this example, one could verify the last assertion in Fig. 12.

Bagherzadeh and his coauthors have also applied this technique to AspectJ (and OO languages with built-in support for events, such as C#) in a *FOAL* paper [6]. This application relies on some programming conventions that make modular reasoning possible; for example making the types of events that a handler can handle statically visible. One way to make these types visible is to pass an object of the event type to the handler, so that the event type appears in the handler's type signature. In conclusion, from a programming language design viewpoint, it is important to have some feature, such as event types, to support modular verification, by statically linking types of events to handlers.

6   Greybox Techniques in Context-Oriented Programming

Context-oriented programming (COP) [17] is an approach to modularizing context-dependent behavior. A *context* is some property of the program's state or environment that may vary over time, such as whether a user has purchased a software license, whether the computer (or smartphone) running the program is plugged in to a power outlet, or the time of day. One way to have the program's behavior vary based on contexts is to use delegation, as in the Strategy pattern [15], and update the object to which the program delegates behavior as the context varies, but languages such as JCop [4] automate this by providing several control features. Programmers can write *partial methods*, which can dynamically override the behavior of methods, and *layers*, which group partial methods, and which can be dynamically activated.

Programs written in a COP language make modular reasoning difficult because the COP mechanisms hide whether partial methods are overriding the behavior of other methods. Since contexts can change dynamically, the text of the program will not indicate which layers are active.

Aotani et al., in a forthcoming *FTfJP* paper [2], which we review here, address these reasoning problems by adopting the approach we are highlighting in this paper. Layer interfaces are introduced, and these can contain model program specifications of partial methods (similar to translucid contracts), in

```
public class Seat allows SalePricing {
    protected /*@ spec_public @*/ Money price;

    /*@ assignable price; ensures price.equals(p); @*/
    public Seat(Money p) { price = p; }

    /*@ ensures \result.equals(price); @*/
    Money /*@ pure @*/ getPrice(){ return price; }
}
```

Fig. 13. The Seat class.

```
1  public layerinterface SalePricing {
2    /*@ public model_program {
3    @    double percent;
4    @    /*@ assignable percent;
5    @    @ ensures 0.0 < percent && percent <= 1.0; @*/
6    @    return Money.discount(proceed(), percent);
7    @ } @*/
8    Money /*@ pure @*/ Seat.getPrice();
9  }
```

Fig. 14. The SalePricing layer interface, which has a model program specification with a specification statement on lines 4–5.

```
1  public layer HalfOff implements SalePricing {
2    Money /*@ pure @*/ Seat.getPrice() {
3      double percent;
4      /*@ refining assignable percent;
5      @            ensures 0.0 < percent && percent <= 1.0; @*/
6      { percent = 0.5; }
7      return Money.discount(proceed(), percent);
8    }
9  }
```

Fig. 15. The HalfOff layer, which implements the override of Seat's getPrice method. Note the refining statement, in lines 4–5, which corresponds to the specification statement in the SalePricing interface.

order to allow modular reasoning. A partial method implements a model program specification if its code matches the model program specification (as above). Thus model programs specify control effects, and a copy rule can be used to reason about calls to methods that have such specifications. A class must use an **allows** declaration to say which layer interfaces can override methods in the class. When combined with knowledge of what layers may be active, such model program specifications permit verification of strong properties of client code.

As an example, consider an airline reservation system, with a class Seat, shown in Fig. 13. This class allows the layer interface SalePricing.

The layer interface SalePricing, shown in Fig. 14 declares a partial method that overrides Seat's getPrice method, with a model program specification. The model program specification contains a specification statement on lines 4–5. This layer interface satisfies an important technical condition on layer interfaces, which is that whenever a layer interface declares a partial method that overrides a method in a class, then that class must declare that it allows that layer interface. For example, since SalePricing overrides a method of class Seat, then Seat must allow SalePricing. This guarantees that methods can only be overridden by allowed layer interfaces.

Conversely, layers must declare which layer interfaces they implement, and layers cannot declare partial methods that are not declared in all layer interfaces that they implement. This guarantees that layers do not add extraneous partial methods. For example, the layer HalfOff, shown in Fig. 15 implements the partial method for Seat.getPrice, as specified in the layer interface SalePricing. Note that the **refining** statement on lines 4–6 implements the specification statement in the model program in Fig. 14 (lines 4–5).

7   Conclusions

Greybox techniques are an effective way to reason about programs written with advanced control features. Our prior work, some of which is reviewed in this paper, shows how model program specifications are effective in reaching strong conclusions about programs that use higher-order procedures, higher-order OO design patterns, aspect-oriented and implicit invocation features, context-oriented programming, and also web-services [30].

The basic recipe for our approach is as follows:

1. Provide interfaces that represent the common behavior and are a place to write specifications. In OO design patterns these are normal Java methods, in Ptolemy these are event types, in COP these are layer interfaces.
2. Use greybox specifications to specify these higher-order interfaces.
3. Verify an implementation of a greybox specification by a two step process: (a) code matching of the implementation against the greybox specification, and (b) checking that refining statements are correctly implemented [33]. Code matching permits reasoning about control effects. Checking of refining statements allows verification of implementations using first-order logic tools like SMT solvers.
4. Make greybox specifications visible to clients statically. In Ptolemy this is done by linking handlers to event types, where the translucid contracts are written [7], and in context-oriented programming this is done by linking layers to layer interfaces where model program specifications are recorded [2].
5. Use a copy rule for verification of calls to methods with greybox specifications. This permits drawing strong conclusions [33] about client code by combining the context of the call with the model program.

For language designers, points 1 and 4 are the most important; they also allow informal reasoning to be modular. The other points are more important for formal methods.

Based on our experience with different kinds of advanced control features, we hypothesize that this same recipe will work for as yet unknown advanced control features.

Acknowledgments. Thanks to Luke Meyers and Klaus Havelund for comments on an earlier draft. Special thanks to Steve Shaner, who co-developed the theory behind this paper with Leavens and Naumann [33]. Thanks to Mehdi Bagherzadeh and Jose Sanchez, who helped us apply greybox specification techniques to Ptolemy and AspectJ. The work of Leavens was supported in part by US NSF grants CNS1228695 and CCF1518897. The work of Naumann was supported in part by NSF CNS 1228930. The work of Rajan was supported in part by NSF grants CCF-15-18897, CNS-15-13263, CCF-14-23370, CCF-11-17937, and CCF-08-46059. The work of Aotani was supported by the Core Research for Evolutional Science and Technology (CREST) Program, "Software development for post petascale supercomputing — Modularity for supercomputing" by the Japan Science and Technology Agency.

References

1. Ambler, A.L., Good, D.I., Browne, J.C., Burger, W.F., Choen, R.M., Hoch, C.G., Wells, R.E.: Gypsy: a language for specification and implementation of verifiable programs. In: Proceedings of the ACM Conference on Language Design for Reliable Software (1977)
2. Aotani, T., Leavens, G.T.: Towards modular reasoning for context-oriented programs. In: Formal Techniques for Java-like Programs, July 2016 (to appear)
3. Appel, A.W.: Program Logics - for Certified Compilers. Cambridge University Press, Cambridge (2014)
4. Appeltauer, M., Hirschfeld, R., Linckeb, J.: Declarative layer composition with the JCop programming language. J. Object Technol. **12**(2), 4:1–4:37 (2013)
5. Back, R.-J., von Wright, J.: Refinement Calculus: A Systematic Introduction. Graduate Texts in Computer Science. Springer, New York (1998)
6. Bagherzadeh, M., Leavens, G.T., Dyer, R.: Applying translucid contracts for modular reasoning about aspect andobject oriented events. In: 10th International Workshop on Foundations of Aspect-Oriented Languages (2011a)
7. Bagherzadeh, M., Rajan, H., Leavens, G.T., Mooney, S.: Translucid contracts: expressive specification and modularverification for aspect-oriented interfaces. In: 10th International Conference on Aspect-Oriented Software Development (2011b)
8. Bagherzadeh, M., Rajan, H., Darvish, A.: On exceptions, events and observer chains. In: 12th International Conference on Aspect-Oriented Software Development (2013)
9. Bagherzadeh, M., Dyer, R., Fernando, R.D., Sanchez, J., Rajan, H.: Modular reasoning in the presence of event subtyping. In: 14th International Conference on Modularity (2015)
10. Barnett, M., Schulte, W.: Runtime verification of.NET contracts. J. Syst. Softw. **65**(3), 199–208 (2003)

11. Büchi, M., Weck, W.: The greybox approach: when blackbox specifications hide too much. Technical Report 297, Turku Center for Computer Science (1999)
12. Damm, W., Josko, B.: A sound and relatively complete Hoare-logic for a language with higher type procedures. Acta Informatica 20(1), 59–101 (1983)
13. Ernst, G.W., Navlakha, J.K., Ogden, W.F.: Verification of programs with procedure-type parameters. Acta Informatica 18(2), 149–169 (1982)
14. Findler, R.B., Felleisen, M.: Contracts for higher-order functions. In: ACM International Conference on Functional Programming (2002)
15. Gamma, E., Helm, R., Johnson, R., Vlissides, J.: Design Patterns: Elements of Reusable Object-Oriented Software. Addison-Wesley, Reading (1995)
16. Guttag, J.V., Horning, J.J.: A tutorial on Larch and LCL, a Larch/C interface language. In: Prehn, S., Toetenel, H. (eds.) VDM 1991. LNCS, vol. 552, pp. 1–78. Springer, Heidelberg (1991). doi:10.1007/BFb0019995
17. Hirschfeld, R., Costanza, P., Nierstrasz, O.: Context-oriented programming. J. Object Technol. 7(3), 125–151 (2008)
18. Hoare, C.A.R.: An axiomatic basis for computer programming. Commun. ACM 12(10), 576–580 (1969)
19. Jones, C.B.: Systematic Software Development Using VDM. Prentice-Hall, Englewood Cliffs (1986)
20. Kiczales, G., Lamping, J., Mendhekar, A., Maeda, C., Lopes, C., Loingtier, J.-M., Irwin, J.: Aspect-oriented programming. In: Akşit, M., Matsuoka, S. (eds.) ECOOP 1997. LNCS, vol. 1241, pp. 220–242. Springer, Heidelberg (1997). doi:10.1007/BFb0053381
21. Kiczales, G., Hilsdale, E., Hugunin, J., Kersten, M., Palm, J., Griswold, W.G.: An overview of AspectJ. In: Knudsen, J.L. (ed.) ECOOP 2001. LNCS, vol. 2072, pp. 327–354. Springer, Heidelberg (2001). doi:10.1007/3-540-45337-7_18
22. Krishnaswami, N.R., Aldrich, J., Birkedal, L., Svendsen, K., Buisse, A.: Design patterns in separation logic. In: International Workshop on Types in Languages Design and Implementation (2009)
23. Meyer, B.: Applying 'design by contract'. Computer 25(10), 40–51 (1992)
24. Meyer, B.: Object-Oriented Software Construction, 2nd edn. Prentice Hall, Upper Saddle River (1997)
25. Morgan, C.: Procedures, parameters, abstraction: separate concerns. Sci. Comput. Program. 11(1), 17–27 (1988)
26. Morgan, C.: Programming from Specifications, 2nd edn. Prentice Hall, Hertfordshire (1994)
27. Naumann, D.A.: Predicate transformers and higher order programs. Theor. Comput. Sci. 150, 111–159 (1995)
28. Rajan, H., Leavens, G.T.: Quantified, typed events for improved separation of concerns. Technical Report 07-14c, Iowa State University, Department of Computer Science, October 2007. ftp://ftp.cs.iastate.edu/pub/techreports/TR07-14/TR.pdf
29. Rajan, H., Leavens, G.T.: Ptolemy: a language with quantified, typed events. In: Vitek, J. (ed.) ECOOP 2008. LNCS, vol. 5142, pp. 155–179. Springer, Heidelberg (2008). doi:10.1007/978-3-540-70592-5_8
30. Rajan, H., Tao, J., Shaner, S., Leavens, G.T.: Tisa: a language design and modular verification technique for temporal policies in web services. In: Castagna, G. (ed.) ESOP 2009. LNCS, vol. 5502, pp. 333–347. Springer, Heidelberg (2009). doi:10.1007/978-3-642-00590-9_24
31. Sánchez, J., Leavens, G.T.: Reasoning tradeoffs in languages with enhanced modularity features. In: 15th International Conference on Modularity (2016)

32. Shaner, S., Rajan, H., Leavens, G.T.: Model programs for preserving composite invariants. In: 7th International Workshop on Specification and Verification of Component-Based Systems, Technical report CS-TR-08-07, University of Central Florida (2008)

33. Shaner, S.M., Leavens, G.T., Naumann, D.A.: Modular verification of higher-order methods with mandatory calls specified by model programs. In: International Conference on Object-Oriented Programming, Systems, Languages and Applications (2007)

34. Soundarajan, N., Fridella, S.: Incremental reasoning for object oriented systems. In: Owe, O., Krogdahl, S., Lyche, T. (eds.) From Object-Orientation to Formal Methods. LNCS, vol. 2635, pp. 302–333. Springer, Heidelberg (2004). doi:10.1007/978-3-540-39993-3_15

35. Wing, J.M.: Writing Larch interface language specifications. ACM Trans. Prog. Lang. Syst. 9(1), 1–24 (1987)

Simplifying OMG MOF-Based Metamodeling

Nicolas F. Rouquette[✉]

Jet Propulsion Laboratory, California Institute of Technology,
Pasadena, CA, USA
`nicolas.f.rouqette@jp.nasa.gov`

Abstract. This paper advocates for a unification of modeling & programming from the perspective of normalized, implementation-neutral database schemas: representing programs and models in terms of irreducible and independent tables. This idea departs from the mainstream of modeling & programming, which typically revolves around Application Program Interface (API) ecosystems for operational needs and external serialization for interchange needs. Instead, this idea emphasizes an information-centric architecture to separate the structural aspects of language syntax via normalized schema tables from the operational aspects of language syntax and semantics via programs operating on normalized tables or derived table views. Such tables constitute the basis of a functional information architecture unifying modeling and programming as a radical departure from standardizing APIs in a programming fashion or standardizing serialization interchange in a modeling fashion. This paper focuses on the current API-less serialization-centric modeling paradigm because it is the farthest from a unified functional information architecture compared to functional programming languages where thinking about programs as pure functions and models as pure data is closest to this kind of unification. This paper first deconstructs the multi-level, reflective architecture for modeling languages defined at the Object Management Group (OMG) based on the Meta-Object Facility (MOF) and the Unified Modeling Language (UML) and subsequently reconstructs several normalized schema accounting for the information content and organization of different kinds of resources involved in modeling: libraries of datatypes, metamodels like UML, profiles like the Systems Modeling Language (SysML) that extend metamodels and models that conform to metamodels optionally extended with applied profiles.

1 Introduction

Between 2010 and 2015, the value proposition of OMG's core modeling specifications for the Model-Based Systems Engineering (MBSE) community of tool vendors and users improved dramatically from 2010 with MOF 2.0, UML 2.3, SysML 1.1 and XMI 2.1.1 to 2015 with MOF 2.5, UML 2.5, SysML 1.4, XMI 2.5.1. As NASA's representative at the OMG, the author was a key contributor to improvements made, including simplifying the reflective modeling architecture (UML is a metamodel defined in MOF, which is an extended subset of

© Springer International Publishing AG 2016
T. Margaria and B. Steffen (Eds.): ISoLA 2016, Part II, LNCS 9953, pp. 97–118, 2016.
DOI: 10.1007/978-3-319-47169-3_8

UML), mechanically verifying UML against MOF's well-formedness constraints, support for IEC/ISO 80000 metrology including dimensional analysis of quantity calculus equations, and a simplified serialization scheme where some models can have a predictable Canonical XMI serialization independently of the tool that produced it. In addition to these tactical improvements, the OMG made strategic improvements with programming language inspired specification for a foundational subset for executable UML (FUML) with a Java-like concrete syntax in the Action Language for FUML (ALF). These improvements fueled a growing adoption of UML/SysML based MBSE methodologies in flagship space mission projects at NASA like the missions to Mars and Europa scheduled for 2020. Despite these improvements, there is a considerable gap between the quality of OMG's current modeling specifications and that of state-of-the-art modern programming language specifications. This gap reflects the significant difference between OMG's document-centric processes and the formal methods techniques that are de rigeur in programming language design.

OMG's document-centric processes were sufficient for the 2010 era of modeling specifications since their value proposition was primarily based on using modeling diagrams for communication purposes among human stakeholders. Indeed, OMG's practices for describing the syntax of a language have been widely adopted even for other standards like W3C's OWL2 Structural Specification where the functional syntax of OWL2 is normatively defined in terms of a simplified subset of UML class diagrams. For UML 1.0 and the major revision in UML 2.0, describing the UML in terms of UML class diagrams helped the OMG reach consensus among the competing interests of OMG tool vendors involved. However, the ubiquitousness of UML class diagrams and the familiarity with the core modeling constructs involved (Associations, Classes and Properties) hides significant complexity due to conceptual redundancy (e.g., an association could be modeled as a class with properties), semantic variability (e.g., only binary associations can have composite ends; however, their ends can be owned by associations or classes) and meaning scattered across several specifications including MOF, UML, the Object Constraint Language (OCL) and the XML Metadata Interchange (XMI).

After the 2015 era, the document-centric process is inadequate for addressing in a cost effective manner the strategic issues about the poorly specified syntax and semantics of OMG's modeling specifications. Although the OMG modeling architecture distinguishes between abstract syntax and serialization, the relationship between abstract syntax and serialization is both complicated and incompletely addressed topic in OMG's specifications. For example, the XMI specification describes the rules for serialization in EBNF but there are no rules specified for parsing XMI into an abstract syntax representation. In contrast, W3C's OWL2 Structural Specification includes normative criteria for parsing the serialization of an ontology into an instance of the abstract syntax model and for testing the structural equivalence among arbitrary abstract syntax objects. Given the widespread interoperability of OWL2 ontologies across multiple serialization syntaxes and the poort interoperability of UML/SysML models across tool-specific varians of a single XMI serialization syntax, there is a legitimate basis to revisit the fundamental tenets of OMG's modeling architecture.

To achieve the goal of a simpler metamodeling architecture for modeling languages like UML and SysML, it is important to revisit why MOF-based metamodeling is too complex in Sect. 2. This understanding provides the rational basis for deconstructing the convoluted MOF architecture in Sect. 3 and for reconstructing a parsimonous architecture in Sect. 4.

2   Background: MOF-Based Metamodeling is too Complex

Several factors contribute to the complexity and inadequacy of MOF as architecture for metamodeling and modeling:

1. Poor separation between the abstract syntax of a metamodel in MOF and its serialization mapping to XMI.
2. The reflective MOF architecture lacks a bootstrapping or a fixedpoint foundation for a unified syntax and semantics of all kinds of models in this architecture (e.g., metamodels, profiles, models, queries, transformations).
3. Convoluted semantics for the core metamodeling constructs (Associations, Classes, Generalizations, Properties) due to poor separation of concerns and loose syntax.

Poor separation of concerns between entity and relationship constructs invites significant conceptual redundancy and variability in their use. For example, a relationship among entities may be modeled via several patterns of fundamental constructs: as an association (with association end properties), as properties of the related entities (without an association), as a (relationship) class with properties or as even more redundant combinations of the above. Since the Object Management Group (OMG) uses MOF for defining metamodels, construct redundancy affects all OMG metamodels like the Unified Modeling Language (UML) where redundancy leads to significant variability in the way conceptual relationships are defined in the UML metamodel.

The UML metamodel is defined in terms of MOF classes, associations and properties. A MOF class in a metamodel for a modeling langauge represents a concept in that language. There is no terminology consensus for what MOF associations and properties represent in the modeling language. The metaclasses in the UML metamodel are organized in a classification taxonomy with a single root metaclass, UML Element, which is the toplevel concept in UML for a constituent of a model. All the other metaclasses in the UML metamodel are directly or indirectly classified as a kind of UML Element. For example, a UML Relationship is a kind of UML Element specifying some kind of relationship between other UML Elements. Unfortunately, The UML Relationship metaclass does not classify all of the UML metaclasses that conceptually represent some kind of relationship in the language, for example:

1. In the graph of a UML Interaction, the GeneralOrdering metaclass represents a directed relationship from an OccurrenceSpecification to another.
2. In the graph of a UML Activity, the ActivityEdge metaclass represents a directed relationship from an ActivityNode to another.
3. In the graph of a UML StateMachine, the Transition metaclass represents a directed relationship from a Vertex to another.
4. In the graph of a UML Interaction, the Message metaclass represents a trace relationship between send and receive events.
5. In UML class diagrams, the Dependency metaclass represents a relationship among client/supplier NamedElements.
6. In the graph of a UML StructuredClassifier, the Connector metaclass represents a join relationship among ConnectorEnds.
7. In UML class diagrams, the Association metaclass represents an N-ary relationship among Classifiers.

Table 1. Incoherent modeling of conceptual relationships in the UML metamodel: kind (Rf=Redefinable, Rl = Relationship, Ns = Namespace, Ne = NamedElement, F = Feature, C = Classifier); relationship roles (D = distinct roles vs S = single ordered role), +/−R = has role metaclass, +/−B = has role binding properties, +Op = related metaclasses have opposite role properties, +Od = related metaclasses have derived opposite roles, −O = related metaclasses do not have any opposite role property

Metaclass	Kind	Conceptual Relationship Pattern
Gen.Ordering	Ne	D(before, after), −R, −B, +Op
ActivityEdge	Rf	D(source, target), −R, −B, +Op
Transition	Rf, Ns	D(source, target), −R, −B, +Od
Message	Ne	D(send/receiveEvent), +R(MessageEnd), −B, −O
Dependency	Ne, Rl	D(client, supplier), −R, −B, +Od, +Op
Connector	Rf, F	S(end), +R(ConnectorEnd), +B(ConnectorEnd::role), +Od
Association	Rf, C, Rl	S(memberEnd), +R(Property), +B(Property::type), −O

Table 1 summarizes the characteristics of seven metaclasses intended to represent conceptual relationships in UML. Even though UML defines a Relationship metaclass, some conceptual relationships are not a kind of UML Relationship! (cases 1–4, 6). An intrinsic aspect of a conceptual relationship is to differentiate what it relates; that is, the relationship roles[1]. Such roles are represented in two ways: as a combination of distinct role properties (D) without role binding (−B) (see cases 1–5) or as a combination of a single ordered role (S) with role metaclass (R) and role binding (B) (see cases 6,7). Additionally, there is considerable variation in the way opposite roles are modeled (or not) (see +Op, Od,

---

[1] Without roles, a conceptual relationship would degenerate to a conceptual group of undifferentiated conceptual elements.

−O), even for a single conceptual relationship! (see Dependency which has +Od, +Op).

This analysis of only 7 out of 242 metaclasses highlights significant problems in UML: mismatch between intent and definition; hetereogeneous syntactic pattern representations; and heterogeneous terminological descriptions[2]. Such problems are clearly undesirable characteristics of languages – programming or modeling – because they increase the complexity of the language. Defining programming languages in terms of grammars for their syntax and of type systems for their semantics has been enormously helpful for improving programming languages.

Some problems of conceptual mismatches and syntactical heterogeneity date back to UML 1.0 (e.g., Message, Transition) and persist two decades later in UML 2.5; other problems were introduced in the major UML 2.0 revision a decade ago (e.g. Connector, GeneralOrdering). The fact that these problems involve a relatively small set of syntactic constructs for metamodeling (Class, Property, Association, Generalization) indicates that MOF-based metamodeling (including OCL) has been and remains ineffective for designing metamodels compared to the techniques used for designing programming languages, in particular, language grammars and type systems. Poor choice of syntactic terminology in UML further exacerbates these problems. For example, the conceptual relationship of 'typing' is well understood in programming languages; however, in UML, type is a homonym for two different kinds of relationships with different semantics: the 'type' of a TypedElement (e.g. Property) is a Type (e.g. Class, Association) and the 'type' of a Connector is an Association; however, a Connector is not a kind of TypedElement. The root cause of these problems stems from a small set of metamodeling constructs that can be combined into many syntactic patterns that in turn have been used for similar yet subtly different conceptual or semantic purposes; that is, excessive syntactic complexity. Records of issue resolutions from OMG task forces provide ample historical evidence about this complexity including difficulties encountered with subtle variations in these patterns and with correcting mismatches between intent and definition.

Historically, the cost of finding and correcting these discrepancies has been very high in terms of the man/years of effort by OMG task forces and by tool vendors implementing revisions of OMG specifications. Experience suggests that the current OMG processes for revising OMG specifications incur significant missed opportunity costs because of the lack of pragmatic rigor in exploiting modern computer science techniques for rigorous specification development, in particular:

- Formal methods help ensure that a system behaves according to its specification.

---

[2] A GeneralOrdering represents a binary relation...; An ActivityEdge is an abstract class for directed connections...; A Transition represents and arc....; A Message defines a particular communication between...; A Dependency is a Relationship....; A Connector specifies links...; An Association classifies a set of links... A link is a tuple of values...

OMG modeling specifications define conformance criteria that amount to well-formedness criteria; they do not define any kind of behavior that an implementation must conform to such as parsing or serializing models to/from external representations. Programming languages typically have only one concrete syntax and the grammar specifies the parsing from concrete to abstract syntax. A modeling language can have multiple concrete syntaxes; consequently, parsing & serialization should be specified and tested. This has never been done at the OMG, not even for XMI! However, it has been done for W3C's OWL2 Structural Specification, a descriptive modeling language[3].

– *A type system is a tractable syntactic method for proving the absence of certain program behaviors by classifying phrases according to the kinds of values they compute*[3].

The OMG publishes several modeling specifications with executable semantics such as Alf & fUML and BPMN. Alf is an example of a recently developed specification at the OMG where the Alf modeling language is specified in the same fashion as programming languages are, that is, with an explicitly defined type system. Alf is an exception at the OMG.

The OMG publication process requires every OMG modeling specification to specify criteria of conformance to the specification. Such criteria pertain to notions of abstract and concrete syntax, model interchange, diagram interchange and semantics. Historically, these process requirements have been poorly effective because the OMG modeling architecture provides no standard interoperable way to represent the syntax of an arbitrary model in an arbitrary modeling language and consequently no implementation-neutral way to assess the conformance an implementation to an OMG specification. This paper proposes starting with breaking the reflective language definition paradigm adopted for UML and MOF. This requires a drastic simplification and refactoring of the fundamental constructs for metamodeling.

3   Simplifying MOF

This section explains the rationale of each step involved in simplifying OMG's MOF into a irreducible, ontological, normal form information schema.

3.1   Which of the Three Concepts Is Redundant?

The MOF concepts of Class, Association and Property are redundant for defining metamodels. Which of these three can be eliminated? MOF Class is a first-class concept in metamodels: every element in a model must be an instance of at least one metaclass defined in a metamodel that the model conforms to. It is debatable whether MOF Property or Association needs first-class status. MOF Property is a first-class concept in the Eclipse Modeling Framework (EMF). However, full support for binary MOF Associations requires a suitable EMF code generator

---

[3] See http://preview.tinyurl.com/hx89sxl.

represent them in EMF without loss of information. In terms of OMG's MOF 2.5 and EMF 2.12, there are three variations of binary MOF Associations to consider: (1) metaclass-owned association end properties; (2) one association-owned end and one metaclass-owned end; (3) association-owned ends. EMF directly supports case (1) only: metaclass-owned association end properties are represented as opposite EMF `EReferences` to update the opposite when one end is updated. The other two cases depend on the EMF code generator used. For example, the Eclipse UML code generator adds to each metaclass that is the type of an association-owned end property an EMF annotation that effectively acts as if the association-owned end property were instead owned by that metaclass. Since full association support depends on EMF code generation techniques, navigating models using the EMF `EObject` and `EReference` API is limited to the first case only. For cases (2,3), API-based navigation requires knowledge of the code generation encoding of association-owned ends, if they are represented at all[4] Since EMF is widely accepted as the de-facto open-source reference implementation of OMG's Essential MOF (EMOF) subset [4, Sect. 2.6.2], the above analysis should suffice to claim that EMF is insufficient for code-generation agnostic API-based navigation of models according to all three cases of Complete MOF (CMOF) binary associations. Therefore, one must conclude that EMF's choice of class+property as first-class concepts turns out to be insufficient for CMOF metamodeling.

3.2 Deconstructing the Concept of CMOF Property

MOF Property lacks conceptual unity: a property can play different roles in a CMOF metamodel. In the absence of an official terminology, the terms used in this paper are underlined:

1. An <u>attribute</u> of a metaclass or datatype.
   (`type` is a datatype)
2. A binary association <u>end</u>.
   (`type` is a metaclass; `aggregation=none|composite;isID=false`)
   Since ends are an essential part of the definition of an association, the concept of MOF binary association is augmented to include the relevant characteristics of both ends[5]. Note that the last three characteristics are coupled between the two ends[6]:
   - `aggregation`: Only one end may be `composite`.
   - `subsettedProperty`: must be symmetric.
   - `redefinedProperty`: must be accompanied by corresponding subsetting or redefinition at the other end.

---

[4] The default EMF code generator does not map association-owned end properties [4, See Sect. 6.4].

[5] (i.e., `type`, `lowerValue`, `upperValue`, `isOrdered`, `isUnique`, `isDerived`, `isDerivedUnion`, `isReadOnly`, `aggregation`, `subsettedProperty`, and `redefinedProperty`).

[6] See resolutions of issues 14993 and 14977 in UML 2.4.1 [8] for the last two.

Symmetric subsetting means that link instances of an association with subsetting ends must be also link instances of the other associations with the subsetted ends. This implies that an association with subsetting ends effectively specializes the associations whose ends are subsetted. Like subsetting, redefinition has a semantics of association specialization but with an additional forcing semantics in the contexts of the redefining ends: In such contexts, the redefining ends replace the redefined ends. This means that in such contexts, it is not possible to create link instances of the associations with redefined ends because such links must be instead instances of the association with redefining ends.

3. A metaclass <u>property</u>.

(`type` is a metaclass)

In principle, CMOF constraints allow a metaclass to own a non-association end property typed by a metaclass. Without loss of generality, this paper considers this case to be a degenerate of the previous case that can be refactored accordingly by explicitly defining an association.

3.3   Simplifying Non-union Derived Association End Properties

The UML metamodel adopted a convention where non-union derived association end properties have a corresponding operation query [9, Sect. 6.4.1]. Historically, this redundancy was rationalized on the basis that the operation query enables specifying the derivation rule in OCL while the association end property enables specifying the availability of the derived property. This redundancy also creates confusion: a derived association has both a derived metaclass-owned end (e.g. `Classifier::/inheritedMember`) and a non-derived association-owned end! Since a derived association are intended to provide notation for derived OCL queries, it makes sense to eliminate the redundant derived associations (e.g. `Classifier::/inheritedMember`), keeping only the OCL derived queries. Figure 1 shows the result of carrying out these simplification steps to the fundamental constructs including the two variants of properties described previously.

Whereas the OMG emphasizes the circular definition of UML as a CMOF metamodel which is itself defined as a subset of UML, this paper claims that this is another unecessary source of complexity. To emphasize the strict separation of levels between the CMOF metamodel itself vs. CMOF models (e.g. the UML itself), Class and Association are prefixed 'M' (Meta) to differentiate these CMOF metamodeling constructs from similarly named constructs in the CMOF model of UML. Operation queries corresponding to the ends of deleted derived associations are shown in red. Several metaclass attributes are no longer necessary and were deleted (Association::isDerived, Property::isDerived, StructuralFeature::isReadOnly)

3.4   Deconstructing the Concept of CMOF Association

Although the concept of association is a first-class construct for defining metamodels, the OMG made significant changes to the concept of association end

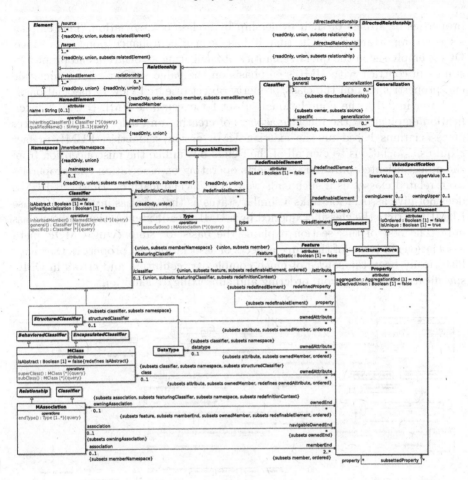

Fig. 1. Simplified CMOF metamodel.

property. The UML 1.x and MOF 1.x specifications used the term 'property' in a general sense for any of three distinct kinds of metaclasses: AssociationEnd (i.e., 2), Attribute (i.e., 1) and TaggedValue (not described in this paper). As part of the major 2.0 revision, these three metaclasses were replaced with a single one, Property. Although a few 1.x distinctions were encoded as MOF constraints, the major revision lost the 1.x separation between AssociationEnd and Attribute. The 2.0 revision added support for the object-oriented paradigm where an association end Property can be owned by a Class or by an Association. Class-owned association end Properties enabled support for Essential MOF metamodels where the semantics of a binary Association is defined in terms of its Class-owned Properties only [4, See Sect. 6.4]. Historically, the 2.0 major revisions of UML and MOF were adopted in 2003 and finalized in 2005; at least a year before the finalization of the 2.0 major revision of OCL was finalized in 2006. OCL 2.0 emphasized the operational aspects of querying association end

properties regardless of their ownership by a class or association. This emphasis is so important for OCL that it has been a compliance point ever since.
OCL's emphasis on the query semantics of navigating association end properties
stands in contrast with UML's emphasis on the value semantics of association
end properties and on the class/property object oriented view of associations.

Later in 2010, the Foundational subset for executable UML (FUML) specification emphasized the lifecycle aspects of creating and deleting link instances
of associations based on the existing UML action semantics. FUML in fact
requires associations to own all of their ends but unlike the misconception from
the object-oriented paradigm, supports operating on association end properties
from related classes as if such ends were class-owned features. However, FUML
does not give association links a similar status as that of class instances because
FUML restricts the classifier queried by a UML ReadExtentAction to be a class
only. The rest of this section explains the basis for simplifying CMOF meta
associations in terms of the three aspects of association end properties that have
historically been the source of much complexity, confusion and errors in OMG
specifications: aggregation, ordering and subsetting/redefinition.

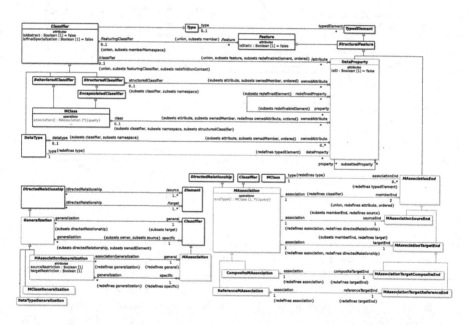

Fig. 2. Refactored CMOF metamodel.

Simplifying and promoting aggregation. Since Property::aggregation has
a significant effect on the semantics of association end properties, the difference
is elevated to the conceptual level instead of being represented in terms of the
Property::aggregation attribute as in current MOF, UML and FUML. Hence,
the refactoring of the relevant subset of the CMOF abstract syntax metamodel

shown in Fig. 2 distinguishes the roles of a CMOF property with respect to typing like UML 1.x and MOF 1.x did (DataProperty corresponds to case 1 and AssociationEnd to case 2) and, in the latter case, further distinguishes the roles of CMOF MetaAssociation and of MetaAssociationEnd with respect to aggregation (this distinction has no counterpart in past & current OMG specifications). Like UML 1.x and FUML, association ends are semantically owned features of their association.

Simplifying association end ordering. Although association ends have always been ordered in UML 1.x and 2.x, this syntactic ordering is independent from all the other characteristics of association ends (aggregation, ownership, navigability and multiplicity). In practice, such characteristics are typically used to explain the intended ordering instead of using the notation for the association end ordering (see [9, Sect. 11.5.4]. The refactored CMOF metamodel is designed to be compatible with current metamodeling practices, in particular, it reflects the practice of infering association end ordering from their characteristics according to the following prioritized criteria:

1. The target end is composite, the source end is not.
2. The source end is owned by the association, the target end by a metaclass.
3. Both ends are owned by the association, the source end is navigable, the target end isn't.
4. Both ends are not composite, the source end is unbounded, the target end has a finite upper bound.
5. The source end (resp. the target end) directly or indirectly subsets or redefines another source end (resp. target end).
6. If none of the above applies, the source and target ends are respectively the first and second properties in the ordered member end collection.

Instead of carrying such complex criteria, the refactored CMOF metamodel explicitly differentiates at the metaclass level the source and target association ends. That is, the ordering of the association ends for a current MOF 2.5 binary association must be determined according to the six criteria above whereas in the refactored CMOF metamodel, the ordering is explicitly represented in differentiated metaclasses, i.e. MetaAssociationSourceEnd and MetaAssociation-TargetEnd. Additional simplifications were possible thanks to the asymmetry of aggregation, which is only relevant for an association target end. Since aggregation has profound semantic implications for the lifecycle semantics of classifiers and their instances, it is an essential characteristic distinguishing MetaAssociationTarget{Composite,Reference}End.

Simplifying subsetting and redefinition. After the UML 2.0 major revision, the relationship between association specialization and association end subsetting or redefinition were poorly understood. This topic was the subject of intense scrutiny in the UML 2.4.1 revision because hundreds of errors were traced to inconsistent and/or incorrect subsets and/or redefinitions. Unfortunately, a clear explanation is missing from the UML 2.5 simplification. Here, the refactored CMOF metamodel reflects a unified ontological view of meta associations as relationships that classify related metaclasses in terms of named roles. In this ontological view, subsetting and redefinition have the semantics of restricting the subsetted or redefined association respectively. More precisely, MAssociationGeneralization with source and target restriction = false corresponds to existential subsetting; that is, the weak restriction that a link classified by the specialized (i.e. subsetting) association must be some link classified by the general (i.e. subsetted) association. MAssociationGeneralization with source or target restriction = true corresponds to a universal redefinition; that is, the strong restriction that all links classified by the general association (i.e., with the redefined source and/or target end) must also be classified by the specific association (i.e. with the redefining source and/or target end.)

4   A Normalized Relational Schema for Ontological Resources

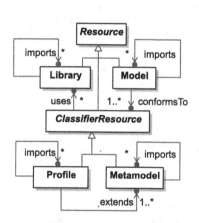

Fig. 3. Ontological resources

From a relational modeling perspective, the refactored CMOF metamodel shown in Fig. 2 would be a materialized view a normalized relational model for metamodeling that has never been defined at the OMG. This section describes normalized relational models for four semantically disjoint categories of resources shown in Fig. 3: libraries (Fig. 4), metamodels (Fig. 5), profiles (Fig. 6) and models (Fig. 7). An explicit concept of Resource is missing from the OMG specifications: Indeed, although MOF defines the concept of Extent (see [6, Sect. 10.2]) and XMI defines the scope of XMI document serialization and deserialization in terms of the unspecified concept of "model or model fragment" (see [6, Sect. 9.2]), the two notions are unrelated. Import relationships shown in Fig. 3 correspond to UML PackageImport and ProfileApplication augmented with programming language-like semantics (cross-references from one resource to another are well-formed if and only if there is a corresponding import relationship) and kinding restrictions (e.g., importation is homogeneous for libraries, models and metamodels; profiles can import either profiles or metamodels). The kinding restrictions induce three layers of resources: (1) libraries that can acyclically import each other; (2) metamodels and profiles that can acyclically import each other and use libraries and (3) models that can acyclically import each other and that must conform to at least one metamodel or profile (ProfileApplication-like semantics) and transitively to any other resource directly or indirectly imported or used. Conformance for a model means that all of the elements, links and values in the model extent must be conforming instances of meta classes, meta associations, stereotypes and datatypes defined in the defined in the metamodels, profiles and libraries that the model directly or indirectly conforms to.

The following explains the notation used for the different kinds of tables in the normalized relational model shown in Figs. 4, 5, 6 and 7:

- An entity table shown in white carries identity criteria, at minimum, a primary key (uuid). Some entities have a name property as a secondary key in accordance to the UML namespace distinguishability contains. AssociationEnd also includes a ternary key, isOrdered, because it is an essential characteristic of the entity. An entity corresponds to a Sortal in OntoClean [10].
- An attribute table shown in yellow class defines a single attribute property typed by a primitive type and relates to a single entity. An attribute table corresponds to an Attribution in OntoClean [10].
- A relation table shown in bold gray has at least one foreign key. Some have an additional property typed by a primitive type (e.g., index, value). Together, the values of all foreign keys and attributes uniquely identify an instance of a relation table. Such a relation table corresponds to an optional MaterialRole in OntoClean [10] of the S.
- A relation table shown in plain gray has at least two foreign keys. Some have an additional property typed by a primitive type (e.g., index). Together, the values of all foreign keys and attributes uniquely identify an instance of a relation table. Such a relation table corresponds to an essential FormalRole in OntoClean [10].

Note that compared with CMOF [6], the normalized relational model provides no support at all for any behavioral feature of any kind. This a deliberate design decision to separate the concerns of managing modeling resources in terms of relational data from the concerns of querying, transforming and reasoning about such resources in terms of functional programs operating on such resources.

4.1   A Library is a Resource of Datatype Classifiers

The MOF extent of a Library resource is exclusively the set of normalized entities, attributes and relationship tables defined in the Library package and those related to the DataTypedFeatures used from the Features package as shown Fig. 4. In contrast to OMG modeling specifications, including variants of MOF and UML, that allow defining datatypes anywhere and that result in significant duplication, the approach described here promotes a clean separation of concerns for entities and relationships pertaining to the definition of conceptual vs. data vocabularies. Conceptual vocabularies are the exclusive province of metamodels and profiles. Data vocabularies are the exclusive province of libraries. These two categories of vocabularies are seldom separated despite having fundamentally very different kinds of semantics: the semantics of conceptual vocabularies is about identified instances of sortal entities and of their relationships via formal roles whereas the semantics of data vocabularies is based on structural equivalence of structured datatype values and equality of atomic datatype values. Note that a StructuredValue carries an identity criteria, uuid. This is a deliberate choice for simplifying change management from the complexity of OMG's XMI tree-based serialization to the simplicity of adding/deleting rows for entity, attribute or relationship tables where a row is comprised of a tuple of key values (uuids) or lexical representations of values of atomic datatypes [12, Sect. 2.3]. For example, the values of the attributes of a StructuredValue entity are specified via separate, essential formal role relations: StructuredValue2{StructuredValueLink, AtomicValue, EnumerationLiteralValue}.

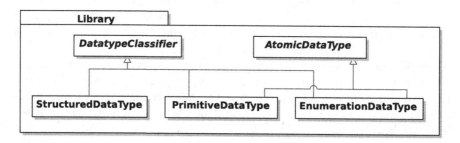

Fig. 4. Libraries

4.2 A Metamodel is a Resource of Meta-classes and Associations

The MOF extent of a Metamodel resource is exclusively the set of normalized entities, attributes and relationship tables defined in the Metamodel package and those used from the Features package as shown in Fig. 5, which is considerably simpler than current CMOF and even the refactored CMOF shown in Fig. 2. Note that the extent of a Metamodel resource also includes all of the Features-based entities, attributes and relations involved in specifying the optional and essential roles of metaclasses and associations. However, the DataTypeClassifiers that are the dataTypes of MetaClass attributes must be directly or indirectly imported from libraries.

4.3 A Profile is a Resource of Stereotypes

The MOF extent of a Profile resource is exclusively the set of normalized entities, attributes and relationship tables defined in the Profile package and those used from the Features package as shown in Fig. 6, which is considerably simpler than current UML Profiles (See [9, Sect. 12.3]). The simplification stems from eliminating associations among stereotypes because these add significant complexity for no demontrated practical value (See the example in UML 2.5 [9, Sect. 12.3.5]),

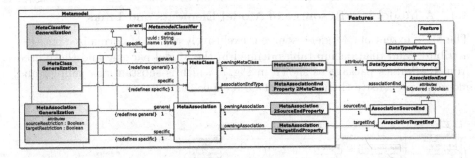

Fig. 5. Normalized relational schema for metamodels

retaining only the AssociationEnds corresponding to the so-called stereotype tag properties. Such AssociationEnds can play two distinct roles according to their type (MetaClass vs. Stereotype). Note that the extent of a Profile resource also includes all of the Features-based entities, attributes and relations involved in specifying the optional and essential roles of stereotypes. The meta classes referenced as targets of Stereotype2ExtendedMetaClass must be directly or indirectly imported. The stereotypes referenced as targets of StereotypeAssociationTargetEndStereotypeProperty or as general/specific of StereotypeGeneralization must be defined in the same resource or must be directly or indirectly imported. Similar to metamodels, the DataTypeClassifiers that are the dataTypes of Stereotype attributes must be directly or indirectly imported from libraries.

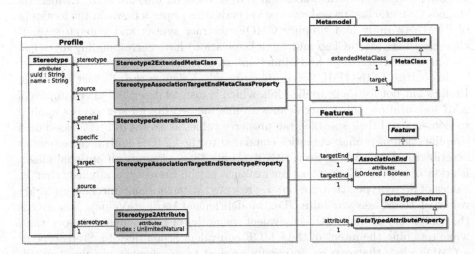

Fig. 6. Normalized relational schema for profiles

4.4   A Model is a Resource of Model Elements and Links

The MOF extent of a Model resource is exclusively the set of normalized entities, attributes and relationship tables defined in the Model package and those used from the Values package as shown in Fig. 7, which is substantially simpler and more comprehensive than in current OMG specifications.

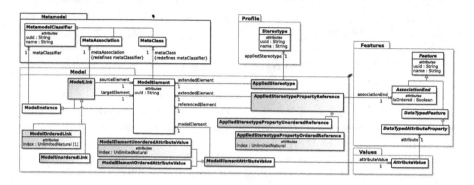

Fig. 7. Normalized relational schema for models

As explained in CMOF Reflection [6, Sect. 13], class and association classify model elements and links respectively. In contrast to the subjective rationale in CMOF Instances Model [6, Sect. 15.3] for a redundant representation of links via CMOF AssociationInstances and CMOF Slots on linked CMOF ElementInstances for metaclass-owned association ends, this paper follows on the footsteps of FUML to unify and simplify CMOF abstract syntax and semantics: first-class classifiers (MetaClass and MetaAssociation) have corresponding first-class instances (ModelElement and ModelLink respectively).

In contrast to the UML 2.x specification which defines the abstract syntax for Profiles but not for their application, which is instead described via examples of XMI serialization, this paper defines an abstract syntax for stereotypes applied to elements and their so-called tag property values as shown in Fig. 7 based on a simplification of profile semantics compared to the CMOF-equivalent semantics described in UML 2.5 [9, Sect. 12.3.3]: AppliedStereotype is an optional classification of a ModelElement as an instance of the Stereotype applied; that is, values of Stereotype attributes are represented with the same mechanism as are values of MetaClass attributes (i.e., ModelElementAttributeValue). This avoids the complexity of the CMOF-equivalent semantics of Extensions as Associations while retaining the intent of the CMOF-equivalent semantics of a Stereotype as a CMOF class that can be optionally applied to an element via the Applied-Stereotype optional role.

ModelLink corresponds to the concept of link in OMG specifications even though this concept is only partially specified in UML, FUML, MOF and SMOF. MOF 2.5 and UML 2.5 state that for ordered association ends, links "carry ordering information in addition to their end values" (see [6, 13.2] and [9, 11.5.3.1]);

however, UML does not explicitly define any abstract syntax for links and although such syntax is defined in MOF, ordering isn't. FUML excludes associations with ordered ends (see [5, Sect. 7.2.2.2.22]). SMOF does not define any syntax or semantics for associations with ordered ends (see [7, Sects. 10.1, 5.6]). Here, support for ordering reflects an implicit assumption in OMG's practice of metamodeling & profiling that at most one association end is ordered.

ModelElement corresponds to the concept of element in FUML [5, Sect. 8.3.2.2.19], MOF [6, Sects. 9.2, 13.5] and SMOF [7, Sect. 9.1.2.3]. SMOF-like multiple classification is supported with multiple ModelElements for the same uuid, one for each classifying metaclass. A Scala implementation of the normalized schemas is available at https://github.com/TIWG/org.omg.oti.mof.schema

5 Serialization and API

UML 1.x revisions were published with an API specification in terms of OMG's Interface Description Language (IDL)[7] The OMG stopped this practice based on the recommendation from the UML 2.0 finalization task force to "retire'Model Interchange Using CORBA IDL' as an adopted technology because of lack of vendor and user interest." As part of the 2.0 major revision, the OMG also switched from XML DTDs to XML Schema to support validating models serialized as XML Documents against their metamodel XML Schemas. Several factors contribute to persistent problems of poor model interchange with XMI: the document production rules specified in English and BNF allowed for many serialization options that increased the complexity of XMI implementations to recognize them when loading XMI documents produced from other tools; since the schema production rules have yet to be applied to UML2.x, tool vendors and user continue to accrue missed opportunity costs due to the inability to validate XMI documents against official XMI schemas. The OMG is keenly aware of these issues. Recent improvements made in Canonical XMI 2.5 minimize but do not eliminate serialization variability and promote but do not ensure serialization reproducibility.

5.1 Normalization Yields Simpler Tabular Serialization

The fundamental source of complexity and poor interchange stems from a design decision in the XMI 2.x specification to represent MOF's exclusive ownership principle in terms of nested XML elements: The resulting tree serialization of a model is a materialized view of the model's ownership structure. XML trees are inherently ill-suited for large-scale model management because comparing trees is computationally expensive even with the state-of-the-art Robust Tree Edit Distance (RTED) algorithm whose cubic worst-case runtime complexity is optimal [2]. This means that comparing serialized models becomes practically unreasonable for models with millions of elements.

---

[7] For UML 1.5's IDL, see http://www.omg.org/spec/UML/1.5.

Switching to a serialization paradigm based on the normalized schemas described in Sect. 4 will provide tangible model interchange benefits for end users compared to the current serialization paradigm based on XMI trees due to the improved efficiency of comparing models serialized as normalized tables vs. trees. Comparing trees is computationally expensive: the Robust Tree Edit Distance (RTED) algorithm has a worst-case cubic runtime complexity [2] that is impractical for large models with millions of elements. Comparing normalized tables reduces is computationally reasonable thanks to a worst-case super-linear runtime complexity that should remain practical even for models with billions of elements (rows) [1] with the added benefit that distributed version control systems like GIT should report precise and accurate changes since differences reduce to additions and deletions of table rows.

This switch has a subtle but important implication on the representation of cross references. Since the 2.0 major revision, the OMG XMI specification has distinguished cross-references within a document vs. across documents. In the former case, a cross reference is represented as an XML idref for the XML id of the locally referenced element. In the latter case, the XMI specification allows for five different representations for a cross reference in terms of XML id, XMI uuid, label or potentially arbitrary XLink and XPointer expressions. Most tools follow OMG's serialization practices that rely on XML idref for local and cross references (the XML idref becomes a fragment for an href). Historically, the multitude of options and technologies involved for representing basic element cross references has been a significant source of poor model interchange across tools. Switching to a normalized serialization strategy eliminates altogether the distinction for local vs. cross references and the options for representing them because all elements are referenced, locally or externally, via their uuid. The fact that cross references are represented uniformly regardless of whether they are local or not means that the representation of the normalized serialization is independent of its organization in one or multiple documents. The fact that the normalized serialization produces tabular data without empty columns means that it is possible to take advantage of modern data analytics frameworks for processing model data because the form and content of normalized tabular data is independent of how it is organized in terms of documents. This is a significant advantage compared to OMG's XMI tree-based serialization where the form and content of the serialized representation depends on its organization in terms of one or more documents and on their location and vice-versa.

5.2   Separating Modeling and Data APIs

The Eclipse Modeling Framework (EMF) established a model-driven development culture for generating the API of a modeling tool from its abstract syntax metamodel [4], that is, a modeling API is generated from a metamodel. Despite its widespread adoption, the EMF-based modeling API generation paradigm does not address the users needs for interoperability of modeling APIs or interchange of model serializations across different tools. For example, Eclipse UML

$5.0.0^8$ and MagicDraw UML 18.0^9 implement the same OMG UML 2.5 meta-model[10]. However, their modeling APIs are incompatible, not only because of differences in EMF code generation techniques used but primarily because these generated modeling APIs are tightly coupled with their generated implementation. This means that for a given OMG UML 2.5 metaclass (e.g., Namespace), there is a corresponding modeling API EClass defined in Eclipse UML 5.0^{11} and MagicDraw 18.0^{12}; however these have nothing in common except for EMF's EObject and Notifier interfaces. In fact, this example illustrates some subtle differences that cause significant API-level interoperability problems when working with EMF-based technologies with these two modeling tools:

- The EMF EModelElement API is important to enable EMF's powerful annotation mechanism [4, Sect. 5.6–7]. However, only the generated Eclipse UML metaclasses inherit from EModelElement, the generated MagicDraw UML metaclasses don't. This difference means that many EMF-based techniques that assume that every model element can be annotated will not work as intended when operating on MagicDraw UML models unlike their Eclipse UML counterparts.
- The MagicDraw UML Namespace metaclass shows that it can own MagicDraw UML Diagrams. This is a MagicDraw-specific implementation of the OMG UML 2.5 metamodel that substantially different than the OMG UML 2.5 Diagram Interchange annex [9, B.2.2].
- Comparing class attributes corresponding to association ends in the Eclipse UML and MagicDraw UML APIs can be difficult; it is particularly helpful to have knowledge of the particular EMF code generation techniques involved to recognize the tool-specific correspondences between CMOF association ends defined in the OMG UML 2.5 metamodel and their corresponding EMF representation in terms of EReferences and/or EOperations in the generated tool-specific APIs.

The root cause of non-existent API-level model interoperability stems from the lack of distinction between two different kinds of APIs: abstract syntax vs. information content schema:

- An abstract syntax API provides support for creating, deleting, updating and navigating across model elements and data according to metaclasses, stereotypes, associations and datatypes defined in metamodels, profiles and libraries. The MOF Abstract Semantics chapter is the closest specification available from the OMG for such APIs, which are the basis for higher-level APIs for model query (e.g. OCL) and transformation (e.g. QVT). The operational nature of MOF Abstract Semantics, OCL and QVT should enable

---

[8] https://wiki.eclipse.org/MDT/UML2/UML2_5.0_Migration_Guide.

[9] http://docs.nomagic.com/display/MD184/UML+2.5+Meta+Model.

[10] http://www.omg.org/spec/UML/20131001/UML.xmi.

[11] http://preview.tinyurl.com/gpfxxxr.

[12] http://preview.tinyurl.com/hj9vhg6.

the OMG to modernize their specification with modern program development techniques for library design, unit testing and integration. Some of this is already underway thanks to the programming-language centric development process used for the Eclipse OCL & QVT implementations.

– A normalized schema data API provides support for internally representing the information content of a model at an API level independently of its external representation in one of possibly multiple serializations (e.g. XMI, RDF, OWL, Json, CSV, ...). The schemas described in Sect. 4 correspond to a 4th normal form normalization of a database schema [13]. Normalization yields tables where each column corresponds to an essential characteristic (a primary key, a foreign key, an attribute); which in turns simplifies serialization matters because there are no optional values and no nulls.

Metamodeling frameworks like EMF provide support for generating abstract syntax APIs (and implementations) from metamodels and profiles (e.g., the Eclipse UML tooling). It is likely that OMG's emphasis on XMI Schemas in the major 2.0 revision of MOF, UML and XMI is responsible for deemphasizing the importance of specifying the information content of models explicitly as is done in this paper. A significant advantage of the normalized schema APIs described in this paper stems from the possibility of leveraging modern data processing frameworks like Apache Spark for scaling up complex model transformation workflows as described in Fig. 8 taking advantage of the relational form of the normalized schemas for query optimization [14] and of the support for specifying complex model query and transformations in terms of graphs of relational data [15]. In contrast to the affinity of the normalized schemas for optimization and parallelization, a conventional approach with an XMI-based or

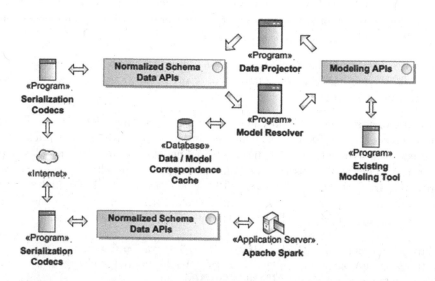

Fig. 8. Proposed architecture to work with existing modeling tools using normalized serialization.

API-based containment tree representation of models would be technically much more difficult to optimize or parallelize.

6 Summary

This paper makes three significant contributions towards addressing significant issues with the current paradigm for developing modeling specifications at the OMG. First, this paper carefully explained the intrinsic sources of complexity in OMG's reflexive metamodeling architecture (MOF) where the notion of a profile does not cleanly fit the multi-layered modeling architecture. It is noteworthy that most of the complexity stems from the multiple roles that the concept of property plays in specifying libraries (datatype attributes), metamodels (association ends) and profiles (stereotype association ends). Second, this paper reconstructs a considerably simpler set of schemas for specifying the information content of all modeling artifacts including models that instantiate metamodels with optionally applied profiles. Focusing on the information content instead of the abstract syntax API is key to a significant simplification compared to the current specification practices where a single abstract syntax is used for both generating an API and for tree-based serialization. Third, the paper only sketched a promising area for future work: leveraging powerful data analytics platforms for scaling up complex modeling workflows thanks to the affinity of normalized schemas for optimization and concurrency.

Acknowledgements. This research was carried out at the Jet Propulsion Laboratory, California Institute of Technology, under a contract with the National Aeronautics and Space Administration.

Reference herein to any specific commercial product, process, or service by trade name, trademark, manufacturer, or otherwise, does not constitute or imply its endorsement by the United States Government or the Jet Propulsion Laboratory, California Institute of Technology.

The author expresses gratitude to many colleagues at the Jet Propulsion Laboratory's Integrated Model-Centric Engineering project and the Laboratory for Reliable Software, in particular, M. Elaasar, K. Havelund, S. Herzig, S. Jenkins and R. Kumar, and to many current and past task force colleagues at the Object Management Group (OMG), in particular, Y. Bernard, C. Bock, R. Burkhart, S. Cook, S. Friedenthal, M. Elaasar, M. Koethe, P. Rivett, E. Seidewitz and B. Selic.

References

1. Skiena, S.S.: The Algorithm Design Manual, 2nd edn. Springer, London (2008)
2. Pawlik, M., Augsten, N.: Efficient computation of the tree edit distance. ACM Trans. Datab. Syst. **40**(1), 1–40 (2015). Article 3
3. Pierce, B.C.: Types and Programming Languages (2002)
4. Steinberg, D., Budinsky, F., Paternostro, M., Merks, E.: EMF Eclipse Modeling Framework, 2nd edn. Addison-Wesley, Boston (2008)
5. Object Management Group: Semantics of a Foundational Subset for Executable UML Models (fUML), version 1.2.1, formal/2016-01-05 (2016)

6. Object Management Group: Meta-Object Facility Core Specification, version 2.5, formal/2015-06-05 (2015)
7. Object Management Group: MOF Support for Semantic Structures, version 1.0 FTF beta 2, ptc/2011-08-22 (2011)
8. Object Management Group: Report of the UML version 2.4.1 Revision Task Force, ptc/2011-01-19 (2010)
9. Object Management Group: Unified Modeling Language version 2.5, formal/2015-03-01 (2015)
10. Guarino, N., Welty, C.: An overview of OntoClean. In: Staab, S., Studer, R. (eds.) The Handbook on Ontologies. International Handbooks on Information Systems, pp. 151–172. Springer, Heidelberg (2004)
11. Procházka, J., Cyganiak, R., Inkster, T., Ferris, B.: The Property Reification Vocabulary 0.11. http://smiy.sourceforge.net/prv/spec/propertyreification.html
12. Biron, P.V., Malhotra, A.: XML Schema Part 2: Datatypes 2nd edn. W3C Recommendation, 28 October 2004. http://www.w3.org/TR/2004/REC-xmlschema-2-20041028/
13. Kent, W.: A simple guide to five normal forms in relational database theory. Commun. ACM **26**(2), 120–125 (1983)
14. Armbrust, M., et al.: Spark SQL: Relational data processing in spark. In: SIGMOD 2015 (2015)
15. Gonzalez, J.E., et al.: GraphX: graph processing in a distributed dataflow framework. In: OSDI 2014 (2014)

Modelling and Testing of Real Systems

Andreas Prinz[1]([⊠]), Birger Møller-Pedersen[2], and Joachim Fischer[3]

[1] Department of ICT, University of Agder, Grimstad, Norway
andreas.prinz@uia.no
[2] Department of Informatics, University of Oslo, Oslo, Norway
birger@ifi.uio.no
[3] Department of Computer Science, Humboldt University, Berlin, Germany
fischer@informatik.hu-berlin.de

Abstract. Modelling and Programming are often used together in system development. However, typically there is a large conceptual gap between modelling and programming. This leads to problems in unified handling and the transition between the two. This way, extra work is required when combining modelling and programming. This paper develops a common understanding that can unify modelling and programming in system development.

1 Introduction

In [6,13] it is emphasized that modelling and programming should be combined in system development. Already now, programming can be used for some kind of modelling, e.g. by including the properties of classes in class hierarchies reflecting the corresponding concepts in the domain. In the other direction, modelling allows some programming in the sense that models can be executable.

In this paper we continue the work of [6] on combined modelling and programming, with focus on correctness of systems. We come back to the definition of what a system is, and explore the importance of runtime in both modelling and programming. We adopt the following definitions of the terms modelling and programming from [6].

Modelling is the activity to *describe* a real or imagined (part of a) system using a language with a semantics. The model does not provide a full match of the real system, but an abstraction.

Programming is the activity to *prescribe* a new (part of a) system using a language with a well-defined execution semantics. The program determines the system.

Those definitions obviously allow programming (prescriptions) in a modelling language and modelling (descriptions) in a programming language. An example for modelling in a programming language are classes and subclasses used to represent domain concepts and specialized concepts and not just for code re-use. Object structures used to represent associations and composition between objects are another example.

© Springer International Publishing AG 2016
T. Margaria and B. Steffen (Eds.): ISoLA 2016, Part II, LNCS 9953, pp. 119–130, 2016.
DOI: 10.1007/978-3-319-47169-3_9

In this paper, we present a common understanding that caters for the unification of modelling and programming. We discuss differences and commonalities between them in relation to reality, executabilty, and correctness.

We discuss models and reality in Sect. 2. Section 3 takes a closer look at the describe and the prescribe relations, and Sect. 4 handles correctness. After having discussed runtime aspects in Sect. 5, we conclude in Sect. 6.

2   Systems, Reality and Discourse

The notion of system is discussed in detail in [6]. The following points from this discussion are important in our context.

- The term 'system' may mean one of three different things: (1) a system to be made, (2) a real world system, and (3) a running system. This paper will subscribe to the idea that 'system' is a running program in terms of object structures and behaviour.
- Programming languages are usually concerned with program executions, and do not consider the executions to be systems.
- Modelling languages are usually not concerned with systems. Many modelling languages do not provide means to express systems.
- Systems are normally composed of existing parts and new parts, see below.

As far as the last item is concerned, computer scientists tend to think of systems as software systems, while in reality very few systems are pure software systems. Almost all systems are either embedded in real hardware, or related to some real entities, e.g. real books, real people, or real money. We use the sample system in Fig. 1 from [6] as an illustration. The figure shows a temperature control system with heating device, cooling device, temperature sensor and temperature controller. In addition, the room provides thermal diffusion between the elements.

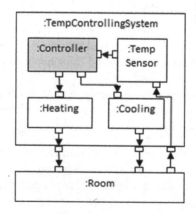

Fig. 1. System with existing and new parts (from [6]).

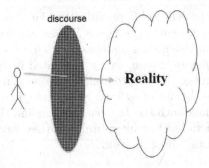

Fig. 2. The discourse determines how we see reality.

This situation is very common and it is a special case when all parts of the systems are to be made. The figure illustrates our understanding that the parts of the system only communicate via the designated ports and connectors according to the related interfaces. Typically, one would think of programming for the new parts, and modelling (and simulation) for the existing parts. There is also another idea of modelling, as for example used in model-driven development [10], which considers modelling to be a high-level way of programming and therefore related to the new parts. In Sect. 4, we come back to this way of modelling which provides a kind of abstraction.

Let us now look into real world systems and identify some characteristics that also apply to other kinds of systems. All modelling and programming starts from a conceptual understanding of the world that influences the way we model and program. This kind of general understanding is usually called discourse, and it entails a way to look at reality. Having a discourse works like a filter onto the world, restricting the things one can see, as depicted in Fig. 2.

The discourse essentially answers the question: In general, what is a possible state of a system (snapshot)? In object-oriented programming, the typical answer is: A system snapshot is an object structure where the objects conform to classes. Formal methods would often answer: A system snapshot is an algebra.

Having a discourse simplifies matters a lot, because we have a restricted view on what is going on in reality. When combining modelling and programming, it is important to agree on the discourse. Still, even with this filter, we need to select the objects we want to consider in our models.

As we cannot relate directly to reality, we consider our view of reality as the real thing. We call this a *referent system*, i.e. an abstraction of reality with respect to the relevant entities based on the purpose of our system.

3   Descriptions and Prescriptions

In Fig. 1, let us consider the white parts, i.e. the existing parts. We can provide descriptions for them taking into account their physical and logical properties, as shown in Fig. 3. Such a description establishes a *describes* relation to the *Referent System*. The relation is provided by the semantics of the description, which leads to the *System* in the figure. The semantics *prescribes* a certain behaviour of the *System*, which then matches the *Referent System*. This way the *System* models the *Referent System*, as e.g. indicated in the language description for the BETA language [12]: 'a program execution is regarded as a physical model simulating the behaviour of either a real or imaginary part of the world'.

With such a definition, both the *Referent System* and the *System* are placed at M0 (in the OMG meta-level architecture) and they have both structure (in terms of object structures) and behaviour.

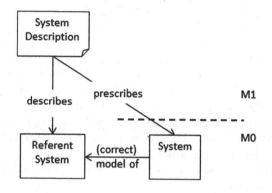

Fig. 3. Describes and prescribes relations (from [6]).

The *describes* relation provides an abstraction of some kind. It does not come with a fixed semantics. The *prescribes* relation, however, has semantics and is central to programming. In some sense, the *prescribes* relation is stronger, such that it implies the *describes* relation, as shown in Fig. 4.

When we look at the grey element of Fig. 1 - a new part that has to be programmed - the situation is slightly different. Now, we do not have an existing *System*, such that the *Referent System* is given as an idea. The relations do not change, but the focus shifts from *describes* (Fig. 3) to *prescribes* (Fig. 4). In both cases, there is a *describes* relation to between *System Description* and *Referent System*, and a *prescribe* relation between *System Description* and *System*. In Fig. 4, it is even more clear, that the semantics of the language *prescribes* (determines) the *System* in structure and behaviour.

We can describe all parts of the system in e.g. UML, maybe even using the same language features (classes, activities, interfaces) for the *Controller* and for the existing parts. The difference is not given in the description, but in the relations to the parts of reality (*Referent System*). The *describes* relation is an observing relation, where the *Referent System* is primary and the *System Description* is secondary. The *prescribes* relation, however, is an active relation, where the *System Description* is primary and the *System* is secondary.

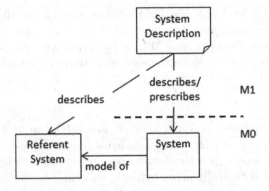

Fig. 4. System being model of Referent System (from [6]).

3.1 Definition and Use

The *prescribes*-relation is closely connected to semantics and follows a general pattern of definition and use (called the meta-relation in [3]) with the *System Description* (prescription) being the definition, and *System* being the use. The prescription is prepared at compile (definition) time, i.e. when the model or program is made. At runtime, the prescription is used to create traces, i.e. sequences of possible runtime object structures. We look closer at runtime structures in Sect. 5.

The definition-use pattern is central to modelling and programming. The definition does not contain the uses in itself, rather it spawns them whenever it is used. Therefore, the relation between definition and use is given by a semantic function, associating the definition with a set of possible uses. This pattern coincides with the physical dimension mentioned in [1], which is now commonly called linguistic instantiation [2].

Definition and use form the underlying distinction that is used to create the levels in OMG's MDA framework [10], in particular the four level architecture, as illustrated in the table below.

OMG level	Examples	Grammar example	OCL example
M3: meta-languages	MOF	EBNF	MOF
M2: languages	UML metamodel	Java grammar	OCL language
M1: models	UML model	a program	a formula
M0: instances	runtime objects	a run	a truth value

Models and programs are placed on level M1 in this architecture. When they are run, their runtime structures appear on level M0 as discussed for Figs. 3 and 4. Models and programs are written in modelling and programming languages, which are placed on level M2. Finally, languages can be described using meta-languages, which are then placed on level M3. The meta-languages are described by meta-languages on the same level M3, i.e. by themselves. The relation between two adjacent levels is always definition-use, sometimes called instantiation.

3.2   Languages

The definition-use pattern becomes very obvious when we look at formal languages, which are on level M2. A language leads to a set of words, which we call specifications. The language is the definition, and the specifications are the uses. A formal language is typically given by three aspects [14], see also Fig. 5.

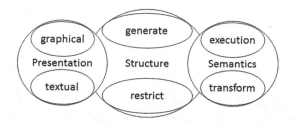

Fig. 5. Language aspects (from [7])

Structure (abstract syntax) identifies the concepts of the language as well as their relations to each other (containment, reference, etc.). In addition, restrictions for the concepts are defined using constraints.

Presentation (concrete syntax) defines how to present the specifications in the language to the user. The presentation can be textual or graphical or a combination.

Semantics (meaning) defines what specifications mean. As we are relating modelling and programming, we will focus on execution semantics, and there are many possibilities for defining semantics.

A language definition on M2 is used for a program in that language on M1. The program as a definition is then used in the execution of the program on M0, where the runtime structure is defined by the language (see Sect. 5). This way, the language bridges three (relative) levels, as already stated in the UML 2.4.1 Infrastructure specification [15]: the language specification (meta-model), the user specification (model), and objects of the model.

4   Correctness

Figure 3 indicates that the *describes* relation is composed of the *prescribes* and the *model of* relations. In this section, we look deeper into this.

4.1   Correct Descriptions

From Fig. 4, which is reproduced as part ① of Fig. 6, it is obvious that a well-defined semantics (meaning) of the *System Description* is essential for the *prescribes* relation. This semantics is provided by the language used for the *System Description*.

The *describes* relation is more difficult to grasp. It is descriptive and is often used for existing parts that are not software. In this case the *Referent System* has behaviour in itself, given by its physical construction and thereby also by the laws of nature. However, we do not have access to the full range of behaviour of such a *Referent System*. We have to rely on running experiments (tests) and comparing the experiment results with the prescribed *System*.

Looking at testing in this way makes it essentially a modelling activity. Then it is natural to ask how well the test cases reflect the reality of the environment of our software, which goes beyond test coverage. The same situation arises for the software parts, where no reality exists. In this situation, there would be some mental reality to match against.

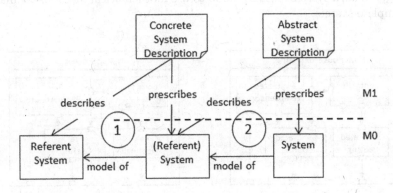

Fig. 6. Abstract and concrete models of the same system.

The comparison of *System* and *Referent System* is often called *validation*. In order to compare systems, we need to compare snapshots and scenarios in terms of traces of the two systems. Traces are sequences of snapshots, and both are more deeply explained in Sect. 5.

For the comparison, we need an equivalence relation between snapshots on both sides. This matching between *System* (model) and *Referent System* (reality) is the core of the scientific method, where we run experiments and check if the outcomes of the tests match in both cases.

4.2   Correct Prescriptions

Sometimes, we have access to the full referent model, and then more detailed analysis is possible. In this case it is not only possible to compare traces, but the whole system can be compared as shown in part ② of Fig. 6. Comparison of whole systems is called *verification*.

This time, there are two system descriptions. As in the previous case, still an equivalence relation between the two systems is needed. That means we need three descriptions: (1) an abstract system description, (2) a concrete system description, and (3) an equivalence relationship between snapshots of the two systems prescribed by the descriptions. When the two descriptions are given in the same language, it is possible to include the description of the equivalence in the same language. This approach is used for example in the B language [11] or in the modelchecker of METAFrame [16]. In contrast, the ASM method [4] only describes one system at a time and handles equivalence outside the ASM language.

4.3   Combined Correctness

A system consisting of existing (white) and new (grey) parts (cyber-physical system) can be handled as one system in a combined modelling and programming language. In such systems it is common to use mathematical methods to analyze the complete system.

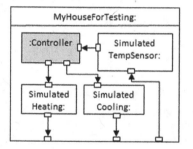 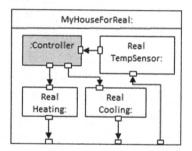

Fig. 7. Simulating or Running the Specification (from [6]).

There are two ways to use such a combined description as shown in Fig. 7. The descriptions of the existing parts can be used to create a simulation of those parts for virtual experiments with the new parts - the controller in our case. This is indicated at the left in Fig. 7. After finishing the tests with the controller, the same controller can be connected to the real devices as shown to the right in Fig. 7. This is the final application scenario.

5   Executable Languages

The run of a program has structure aspects and behaviour aspects. As discussed in Sect. 4, it is important to be able to compare snapshots and traces. Possible snapshots are given by the structure semantics, and traces are given by the behaviour semantics. There may be external inputs to the system influencing the traces. In our example from Fig. 1, the external inputs come from the connections to the room, i.e. heat, cool, and temperature. The rest of the system is self-contained. So the *System* as well as the *Referent System* are given by a set of traces of snapshots including the inputs.

5.1   Snapshots

The execution aspect describes how the programs behave at runtime. It is defined on level M2, and describes the relation between levels M1 and M0 as shown in Fig. 8. The execution aspect is the only language aspect that influences M0, all the other aspects are only relevant at level M1. For describing snapshots, we discuss structure semantics, which is also called instantiation semantics.

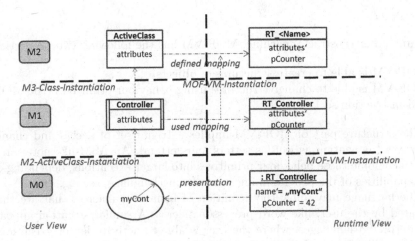

Fig. 8. Snapshots.

Figure 8 shows how instantiation semantics works. First, it is important to note that there is an underlying semantics that is used. This semantics can be given by an underlying (virtual) machine, or by a mathematical construct. As we work with object-oriented modelling and programming, we use objects instantiated from classes as the underlying semantics. Such instantiation semantics is defined by MOF [5], and we call it MOF-VM, see also [8].

The underlying instantiation is shown on the right-hand side of Fig. 8. It is the same for all levels, because it is given by the runtime. On the left-hand side, we see the instantiation as seen by the user. This instantiation is dependent on the language used, in particular the language on the level above. The instantiation from M1 to M0 is defined on M2. The user view depends on a presentation format being available, as the runtime instances get shown using the presentation format. Most often, there is no special presentation defined for runtime elements on M0 – debuggers use an ad-hoc format to show snapshots. Given the importance of runtime, a combined modelling and programming language would provide custom presentation for snapshots similar to *InstanceSpecification* in UML. In our example we assume that there is a presentation for active class objects showing the name in a circle and an arrow to indicate the value of the program counter.

Instantiation semantics is defined in Fig. 8 on level M2 by defining a mapping to MOF-VM classes. In order to show the difference between MOF-VM classes and UML classes, we have shown the instantiation of active classes, which include a program counter at runtime. This M2 mapping is used (instantiated) on level M1 to create real MOF-VM classes out of the elements of the specification (using *Controller* as an example). The MOF-VM classes allow MOF-VM instantiation, which yields objects on level M0. These objects can be presented to the user with a user defined presentation, in our case the circle. Alternatively, some kind of debugger presentation of the object could be used.

5.2   Traces

Like any other (abstract) machine, MOF-VM has the following two properties:

- MOF-VM is able to create structures of objects.
- MOF-VM is able to change structures using behaviour primitives (the MOF-VM instruction set).

The structure part of MOF-VM implies a trivial set of access and change primitives (navigation as well as setters and getters). An ASM-like notation is used to combine those behaviour primitives into larger executions, depending on the capabilities of the programming or modelling language, see e.g. [9].

The language may allow the definition of behaviour macros, that are then activated by the user, like word processor macros. A similar situation appears for interpreted languages, where the user is able to activate larger executions. Languages like Java and C++ allow the definition of complete executions, such that the user only initiates the start of the execution, which is then run to completion.

5.3   Language Categories

Based on the discussion before, we are now in a position to discuss execution properties of languages. Executability of languages in this context means executability of specifications of the language. First of all, any language is defined in its meta-languages, which means that it can be instantiated. This means it is possible to write specifications in this language. This way, the language is just a *presentation language* (first category). The language instances can be presented in a standard MOF-VM way (bottom right of Fig. 8) or in a language-defined presentation (bottom left of Fig. 8).

The second category comprises languages with structure semantics. For these languages it is possible to create specifications of the language itself on M1, and (runtime) instances of these specifications on M0. Trivial state changes of the snapshots are implied, such that we are left with a *purely structural language*.

The next category comprises executable languages, meaning that the language itself allows to define execution sequences. When the language defines a complete execution, then we call it a *fully executable language*, otherwise it is a *partly executable language*.

Finally, as discussed in Sect. 4, there are also languages that allow to define several execution sequences and their equivalence relation to each other. We call those *dually executable languages*.

This leads to the following list of language categories, where the higher categories are subsets of the lower categories, for example Java as a fully executable language (category 4) can also be partly executed (category 3) in a debugger.

1. Presentation language: can create language instances, and may have custom presentation, e.g. XML.
2. Purely structural language: can create language instances and runtime instances. Trivial behaviour primitives are available, e.g. MOF.
3. Partly executable language: can define partial executions, e.g. Word Macros.
4. Fully executable language: allows the definition of complete executions, e.g. executable UML.
5. Dually executable language: allows the definition of several executions and their equivalence, e.g. B.

6   Summary

This paper has discussed the relation between programming and modelling from several points of view.

From a *systems* point of view, it is important to look at systems including existing parts and new parts. These two kinds of elements are related to the *describes* and *prescribes* relations, respectively, which again are closely related to modelling and programming.

From a *correctness* point of view, validation is used for correctness of the *describes* relation, while verification is used for correctness of the *prescribes* relation.

Executability has several levels in relation to languages. We distinguish between presentation languages and purely structural languages, as well as partly, fully, and dually executable languages. Executability beyond purely structural languages is an important precondition for the handling of correctness.

A complete system understanding is the basis for system development, which means to apply a combination of programming and modelling as two ways of relating to reality. In this paper, we have shown that modelling and programming describe a referent system, and prescribe a system at different levels of precision. The focus of programming is on the prescription, while the focus of modelling is on the description. As we have shown, both relations are important.

References

1. Atkinson, C., Kühne, T.: Rearchitecting the UML infrastructure. ACM Trans. Comput. Syst. (TOCS) **12**(4), 290–321 (2002)
2. Atkinson, C., Kühne, T.: Model-driven development: a metamodeling foundation. IEEE Softw. **20**, 36–41 (2003)
3. Bézivin, J., Gerbé, O.: Towards a precise definition of the OMG/MDA framework. In: Proceedings of ASE 2001, Automated Software Engineering (2001)
4. Börger, E., Stärk, R.F.: Abstract State Machines: A Method for High-Level System Design and Analysis. Springer, New York (2003)
5. OMG Editor. OMG Meta Object Facility (MOF) Core Specification Version 2.4.2. Technical report, Object Management Group (2014)
6. Fischer, J., Møller-Pedersen, B., Prinz, A.: Modelling of systems for real. In: Proceedings of the 4th International Conference on Model-Driven Engineering and Software Development, pp. 427–434 (2016)
7. Gjøsæter, T., Prinz, A.: Languagelab 1.1 user manual. Technical report, University of Agder (2013)
8. Gjøsæter, T., Prinz, A., Nytun, J.P.: MOF-VM: instantiation revisited. In: Proceedings of the 4th International Conference on Model-Driven Engineering and Software Development, pp. 137–144 (2016)
9. Glässer, U., Gotzhein, R., Prinz, A.: The formal semantics of SDL-2000: status and perspectives. Comput. Netw. **42**(3), 343–358 (2003)
10. Kleppe, A., Warmer, J.: MDA Explained. Addison-Wesley, Boston (2003)
11. Lano, K.: The B Language and Method: A Guide to Practical Formal Development, 1st edn. Springer, New York (1996)
12. Madsen, O.L., Møller-Pedersen, B., Nygaard, K.: Object-Oriented Programming in the BETA Programming Language. ACM Press/Addison-Wesley Publishing Co., New York (1993)
13. Madsen, O.L., Møller-Pedersen, B.: A unified approach to modeling and programming. In: Petriu, D.C., Rouquette, N., Haugen, Ø. (eds.) MODELS 2010. LNCS, vol. 6394, pp. 1–15. Springer, Heidelberg (2010). doi:10.1007/978-3-642-16145-2_1
14. Mu, L., Gjøsæter, T., Prinz, A., Tveit, M.S.: Specification of modelling languages in a flexible meta-model architecture. In: Software Architecture, 4th European Conference, ECSA 2010, Copenhagen, Denmark, Companion Volume, pp. 302–308, 23–26 August 2010
15. Editor, O.M.G., Language, U.M.: Infrastructure version 2.4.1 (OMG Document formal/2011-08-05). OMG Document. Published by Object Management Group, August 2011. http://www.omg.org
16. Steffen, B., Margaria, T.: Metaframe in practice: design of intelligent network services. In: Olderog, E.R., Steffen, B. (eds.) Correct System Design. LNCS, vol. 1710, pp. 390–415. Springer, Heidelberg (1999)

Unifying Modelling and Programming:
A Systems Biology Perspective

Hillel Kugler[1,2(✉)]

[1] Faculty of Engineering, Bar-Ilan University, Ramat Gan, Israel
hillelk@biu.ac.il
[2] Microsoft Research Cambridge, Cambridge, UK

Abstract. Despite significant research progress made and methodological experience gained over the past few decades, a tight integration between programming and modelling, guided and supported by intuitive yet rigorous formal reasoning and verification methods that ensure high reliability and quality of the developed system remains challenging and is still far from becoming mainstream. We suggest that recent developments in the area of computational systems biology could allow us to gain some new perspectives about the challenges involved in developing pragmatic solutions unifying programming and modelling.

Computational systems biology is gaining momentum as a powerful paradigm in the biological sciences, enabling to derive mechanistic and quantitative understanding of the dynamic behavior of biological systems [1,11,21]. Behavior of cells — the fundamental units of biological systems — can be effectively viewed and described as *biological programs* [24] that determine important functions and decision making that a cell must perform to maintain life [4,20]. Towards elucidating and describing biological programs, and the biological computation they perform, a combination of programming, modelling languages, specification formalisms and methodologies have been adapted and developed to address the challenges in the field, allowing to gainfully develop complex models capable of both explaining known data and mechanisms and allowing to make new predictions, thus supporting a combined mutual synergy with experimental work.

Software and system development shares several of the main challenges that computational systems biology is facing : (1) Effectively integrating specification and verification logics towards making models amendable to formal reasoning and verification [2,5], (2) Scaling up automated reasoning and formal verification methods to effectively deal with real-world systems [7,25,26], (3) Developing and utilizing visual languages and graphical modelling notations to allow effective participation of non-programmers in the development effort [6,10,15,22], and supporting high-level abstraction levels, (4) Seamlessly combining different programming languages and frameworks to construct integrated systems and applications [3,9,13,18,19], (5) Moving towards rapid development life cycles that allow to prototype, implement and deploy changes to the system in much shorter time scales than traditionally common in the past; and (6) Investigating the use

© Springer International Publishing AG 2016
T. Margaria and B. Steffen (Eds.): ISoLA 2016, Part II, LNCS 9953, pp. 131–133, 2016.
DOI: 10.1007/978-3-319-47169-3_10

of synthesis-based methods to build correct-by-construction systems directly from the specification [8,12,14,16,17,23,24], identifying application domains where this is feasible and adds significant value.

Recent research efforts in computational systems biology could allow us to gain some new perspectives about how these challenges can be tackled. This is due to the fact that this domain can provide challenging feasible case studies towards demonstrating proof of concept approaches and tools. An important advantage is that the field is still in an early enough stage where existing methods and tools are not yet well-established and could potentially be replaced by new tools and methodologies once they demonstrate clear advantages. This is in contrast to many of the existing software and systems domains in which often new methods cannot easily gain momentum due to the big investment in existing tools and legacy code. In particular, an approach supporting visual languages for experimental biologists combined with code-based environment allowing to seamlessly integrate modelling and programming is a promising direction. We also believe that synthesis-based approaches may be a key to address some of the other challenges outlined above, and will play a key role in future systems biology applications, thus offering an excellent opportunity to revisit some of the main questions related to unifying programming and modelling.

References

1. Alon, U.: An Introduction to Systems Biology: Design Principles of Biological Circuits. CRC Press, London (2006)
2. Antoniotti, M., Park, F., Policriti, A., Ugel, N., Mishra, B.: Foundations of a query and simulation system for the modeling of biochemical and biological processes. In: Pacific Symposium on Biocomputing (PSB), pp. 116–127 (2003)
3. Atwell, K., Qin, Z., Gavaghan, D., Kugler, H., Hubbard, E., Osborne, J.: Mechano-logical model of C. elegans germ line suggests feedback on the cell cycle. Development **142**(22), 3902–3911 (2015)
4. Brenner, S.: Sequences and consequences. Philos. Trans. R. Soc. B: Biol. Sci. **365**(1537), 207–212 (2010)
5. Chabrier-Rivier, N., Chiaverini, M., Danos, V., Fages, F., Schächter, V.: Modeling and querying biomolecular interaction networks. Theor. Comput. Sci. **325**(1), 25–44 (2004)
6. Chaouiya, C.: Petri net modelling of biological networks. Briefings Bioinform. **8**(4), 210–219 (2007)
7. Cook, B., Fisher, J., Krepska, E., Piterman, N.: Proving stabilization of biological systems. In: Jhala, R., Schmidt, D. (eds.) VMCAI 2011. LNCS, vol. 6538, pp. 134–149. Springer, Heidelberg (2011). doi:10.1007/978-3-642-18275-4_11
8. Guziolowski, C., Videla, S., Eduati, F., Thiele, S., Cokelaer, T., Siegel, A., Saez-Rodriguez, J.: Exhaustively characterizing feasible logic models of a signaling network using answer set programming. Bioinformatics **29**(18), 2320–2326 (2013)
9. Hucka, M., et al.: The systems biology markup language (SBML): a medium for representation and exchange of biochemical network models. Bioinformatics **19**(4), 524–531 (2003)

10. Kam, N., Kugler, H., Marelly, R., Appleby, L., Fisher, J., Pnueli, A., Harel, D., Stern, M., Hubbard, E.: A scenario-based approach to modeling development: a prototype model of C. elegans vulval fate specification. Dev. Biol. **323**(1), 1–5 (2008)

11. Kitano, H.: Computational systems biology. Nature **420**(6912), 206–210 (2002)

12. Koksal, A., Pu, Y., Srivastava, S., Bodik, R., Fisher, J., Piterman, N.: Synthesis of biological models from mutation experimentss. SIGPLAN-SIGACT Symp. Principles Program. Lang. **48**, 469–482 (2013). ACM

13. Kugler, H., Larjo, A., Harel, D.: Biocharts: a visual formalism for complex biological systems. J. R. Soc. interface **7**(48), 1015–1024 (2010)

14. Kugler, H., Plock, C., Pnueli, A.: Controller synthesis from LSC requirements. In: Chechik, M., Wirsing, M. (eds.) FASE 2009. LNCS, vol. 5503, pp. 79–93. Springer, Heidelberg (2009). doi:10.1007/978-3-642-00593-0_6

15. Kugler, H., Plock, C., Roberts, A.: Synthesizing biological theories. In: Gopalakrishnan, G., Qadeer, S. (eds.) CAV 2011. LNCS, vol. 6806, pp. 579–584. Springer, Heidelberg (2011). doi:10.1007/978-3-642-22110-1_46

16. Kugler, H., Pnueli, A., Stern, M.J., Hubbard, E.J.A.: "Don't Care" modeling: a logical framework for developing predictive system models. In: Grumberg, O., Huth, M. (eds.) TACAS 2007. LNCS, vol. 4424, pp. 343–357. Springer, Heidelberg (2007). doi:10.1007/978-3-540-71209-1_27

17. Kugler, H., Segall, I.: Compositional synthesis of reactive systems from live sequence chart specifications. In: Kowalewski, S., Philippou, A. (eds.) TACAS 2009. LNCS, vol. 5505, pp. 77–91. Springer, Heidelberg (2009). doi:10.1007/978-3-642-00768-2_9

18. Lakin, M., Paulevé, L., Phillips, A.: Stochastic simulation of multiple process calculi for biology. Theor. Comput. Sci. **431**, 181–206 (2012)

19. Novère, N.L., et al.: The systems biology graphical notation. Nat. Biotechnol. **27**, 735–741 (2009)

20. Nurse, P.: Life, logic and information. Nature **454**(7203), 424–426 (2008)

21. Palsson, B.: Systems Biology: Constraint-Based Reconstruction and Analysis. Cambridge University Press, Cambridge (2015)

22. Phillips, A., Cardelli, L., Castagna, G.: A graphical representation for biological processes in the stochastic pi-calculus. In: Priami, C., Ingólfsdóttir, A., Mishra, B., Riis Nielson, H. (eds.) Transactions on Computational Systems Biology VII. LNCS, vol. 4230, pp. 123–152. Springer, Heidelberg (2006). doi:10.1007/11905455_7

23. Sharan, R., Karp, R.: Reconstructing boolean models of signaling. J. Comput. Biol. **20**(3), 249–257 (2013)

24. Yordanov, B., Dunn, S.J., Kugler, H., Smith, A., Martello, G., Emmott, S.: A method to identify and analyze biological programs through automated reasoning. NPJ Syst. Biol. Appl. **2**(16010) (2016)

25. Yordanov, B., Wintersteiger, C.M., Hamadi, Y., Kugler, H.: SMT-based analysis of biological computation. In: Brat, G., Rungta, N., Venet, A. (eds.) NFM 2013. LNCS, vol. 7871, pp. 78–92. Springer, Heidelberg (2013). doi:10.1007/978-3-642-38088-4_6

26. Yordanov, B., Wintersteiger, C.M., Hamadi, Y., Phillips, A., Kugler, H.: Functional analysis of large-scale DNA strand displacement circuits. In: Soloveichik, D., Yurke, B. (eds.) DNA 2013. LNCS, vol. 8141, pp. 189–203. Springer, Heidelberg (2013). doi:10.1007/978-3-319-01928-4_14

Formally Unifying Modeling and Design for Embedded Systems - A Personal View

G. Berry[✉]

Collège de France, 11 Place Marcelin Berthelot, 75005 Paris, France
gerard.berry@college-de-france.fr
http://www-sop.inria.fr/members/Gerard.Berry

Abstract. Based on the author's academic and industrial experience, we discuss the smooth relation between model-based design and programming realized by synchronous languages in the embedded systems field. These languages are used to develop high quality embedded software, in particular for safety-critical applications in avionics, railway, etc., subject to the strongest software certification processes in industry. They have also been used for the efficient model-based development of production hardware circuits. One of their main characteristics is their well-defined formal semantics, with is the base of their simulation and compiling processes and is also fundamental for their link to automatic formal verification systems and other tools related to model-based design. We briefly discuss their current limitations and some ideas to lift them.

1 Introduction

A unified and preferably formal path for modeling, design, development and verification of circuits and programs is an old dream of many researchers in the embedded systems community. After years of scientific progress and experimentation, the dream slowly becomes a reality. Formal modeling, design and verification methods are now considered as serious ways to build dependable systems, at least by some part of industry. There are several reasons for this relatively recent change. First, the quest for new formal languages, design methods and verification tools has given positive results in the form of well-founded, well-designed and industry-usable development systems. Second, bugs are really not welcome for safety-critical embedded systems in avionics, railways, etc., nor for mission-critical systems such as rockets and satellites; in some famous cases, the cost induced by a single bug has exceeded the cost of the whole development. This motivates industry to try other solutions than traditional manual coding and testing. Third, the most serious certification processes (e.g., DO-178C avionics certification) have now officially recognized the value of formal modeling and design in the certification process, which used to be mostly administrative.

Nevertheless, except for a few integrated methods, the formal landscape remains quite scattered and difficult to understand for most industry engineers. The community should now recognize that is time to present the subject and the achievements in a more organized way, stressing its strengths and recognizing its weaknesses. This paper is a contribution to this goal, based on the author's

© Springer International Publishing AG 2016
T. Margaria and B. Steffen (Eds.): ISoLA 2016, Part II, LNCS 9953, pp. 134–149, 2016.
DOI: 10.1007/978-3-319-47169-3_11

40 years of research and development in Academia and Industry, notably through the experience of the Esterel [12] and SCADE synchronous languages and their applications in both software and hardware industrial projects.

2   The Modeling and Design Landscape

As an activity, programming is quite easy to define: one write texts or graphics that are compiled into some machine language and executed by some computer. Modeling is not as clear-cut, because it deals with many more concepts and objects. One can model the needs of a customer, an information flow, an architecture, the intended executable application, its execution environment, its users, etc. Here, we restrict our attention to *formal modeling*, based on mathematics and computer science concepts and techniques. Formal (or semi-formal) modeling is often of great help to understand, dimension, design, and verify systems. It actually existed much before computer science, being a standard activity in physics or mechanics. In Informatics, the situation is quite contrasted: model-based design is the rule in some application domains, e.g., avionics, and still quite rare in others, e.g. hardware circuits design.

2.1   Integrated Vs. Toolbox-Based Views

The engineering needs are multiple for embedded hardware and software: architectural and microarchitectural design and modeling, precise specification, program or circuit development, verification, integration in the final system, and maintenance during the system's lifetime. These needs are quite different, use different mindsets and tools, and are usually fulfilled by different people. There are roughly two main views to address them.

In the *integrated view* of model-based design, everything is done in a single formalism to which is applied a number of strongly connected tools. Good examples for embedded software are Abrial's B [2] and Event-B [3] methods, where the modeling, specification and actual programming are all done in the B or Event-B set-theoretical languages. Integrated design and verification tools such as Atelier B and the Rodin platform [1] make it possible to formally verify properties of specifications, refine abstract specifications into concrete ones in a formally verified way, and generate embedable code from the concrete specifications. These methods have been successfully applied to industrial systems, for instance automatic subways in Paris and other towns worldwide, and more generally railway signaling. The advantage is of course the full control and homogeneity of the whole chain. The drawback may be a form of rigidity implied by the unique language and some difficulty to absorb local progress made by other theories and tools.

On the opposite, in the *toolbox* view, each step is done with a specific tool, all tools being linked together by a global IDE (Integrated Development Environment). Then the languages, tools, and verification methods in the toolsets may be developed independently of each other, possibly by several universities and companies. This is by far the dominant model. When the tools are developed and presented in coherent way, preferably using common interchange formats, and when they are well-integrated by the IDE, the development chain is felt by the user as a unified design chain; SCADE Suite by Esterel Technologies is a good example. The advantage is flexibility, the difficulty is to maintain global coherence and correctness of the tools and of their mutual interfaces.

2.2 The Hardware Design Case

In hardware design, the CAD path from ideas to circuits is long and complex. It is a typical toolset-based path. It involves a large number of languages and tools: for specification, mostly text/graphics documents and C/C++/SystemC prototypes; for high-level modeling and simulation-based verification, ISA (Instruction Set Architecture) definitions and simulators for microprocessors, and transaction-level models for SoCs (Systems on Chips) written for instance in SystemC/TLM (Transaction Level Modeling, IEEE standard 1666); for programming, actually called *design* in this field, hardware description languages such as Verilog and VHDL; for design testing, random/directed test generation using hardware verification languages such as e [40]; for design verification, temporal logic formalisms such as PSL (Property Specification Languages, IEEE standard 1850) dealt with by various simulators and model-checkers, or other formal tools dedictated to explicit or symbolic execution trajectory evaluation; for low-level synthesis, gate-level languages with fancy Boolean gate sizing and optimization algorithms based on Binary Decision Diagrams (BDDs) [28,42]. Furthermore, the correctness of most transformations can be formally verified using Boolean satisfiability (SAT) solvers [43], etc. This path is highly complex and uses lots of software tools linked by heavy scripts. Nevertheless, the results are remarkably solid.

A weakness is that most hardware-oriented languages still have informal and sometimes quite fuzzy semantics. In addition, they were designed originally with simulation in mind, not synthesis. This may lead to unexpected difficulties, especially when comparing simulation and synthesis. But formal methods do appear in a growing number of verification steps: property verification of models and designs, verification of all logic optimization steps, equivalence of designs before and after transistor-level synthesis, etc.

2.3 The Safety-Critical Software Case

Safety-critical software plays a major role in several engineering fields: avionics, where it was actually born long ago due to the impossibility for humans to pilot unstable airplanes, the space industry, where satellites vitally depend on software, railways and subways, which have a long tradition of caring with safety, nuclear plants, heavy industry, etc. These domains are submitted to quite stringent certification processes that now recognize the difference between software and mechanics. The most elaborate one is the DO-178C avionics software international standard (see also the DO-254 avionics hardware standard).

Some other domains unfortunately do not yet consider themselves at the same level of criticality. Automotive is a good example, as it seems that the very nature of software is not well understood by many of its actors who still speak of *electronics* and concentrate on cost-reduction more than quality. Development cost is a real economic concern since a certified software is indeed much more expensive than a hastily written one, but it should be compared with the cost of bugs for users and the company. Recent major and lethal problems encountered by a Japanese company with an engine control design that may spontaneously put the engine full speed and by German and American companies with major security flaws allowing to open cars or even to take almost full control of them from the Internet are illustrative examples; for the latter case, it should never be forgotten that security issues most always result from design flaws or apparently innocuous non-functional bugs. Another potential example is medical appliances: I have personally no idea of how and by whom the software of a pacemaker or a robot surgeon is verified, and I have seldom met doctors aware of the problem. And, in several application areas, I have seen companies starting R&D evaluation of safety and security issues by hiring PhD students; they will certainly evaluate the PhD student, but not necessarily the issues.

2.4   Continuous and Discrete Control

Critical embedded software is often related to continuous, discrete or mixed control, and thus on Control Theory. Continuous control is critical to fly an airplane, regulate an engine, or control the brakes and suspension of a car. Any continuous control model must involve a description of a controller at some abstraction level, a model of the physics of the device to control, and a model of the environment. The tools used there are mostly mathematical modelers such as Matlab/Simulink, Modelica, or their competitors, used by engineers trained in Control Theory. Discrete control is critical for airplane cockpits, communication protocols, robot actions control, etc. The typical modeling and implementation tools are based on finite-state machines formalisms that can be simple, hierarchical, concurrent with many possible form of communication, etc. A difficulty is that continuous and discrete control do require quite different skills and thus training. Mixed control appears when both forms of control appear together, for instance when an airplane switches between a number of different flight modes.

Discrete and mixed control are definitely not places where classical mathematical modeling excels, to say the least. Some modelers use hierarchical state machines graphical formalisms with the right drawings but horrendous semantics. And most modelers exhibit strange behaviors when dealing with cascades of discrete events during their basic time-based integration process: they keep relying on incremental integration techniques to handle discrete events, which means that time continues advancing even if causal event cascades should take conceptually no time [8]. It is then possible to see balls traversing walls, for instance.

3   Personal Experience with Formal Modeling and Programming

3.1   The Formal Synchronous Languages

I have worked on formal methods since the beginning of the 1970s and more specifically on embedded systems since 1982. Most of my work has concerned the development of a new way to program embedded systems with *synchronous concurrency* [9,14,37] instead of the asynchronous concurrency that was the mandatory paradigm at that time in Computer Science. Synchronous concurrency simply assumes that computation is defined by a temporal sequence of timeless discrete reactions to external events (or clock ticks, or whatever you like), where computing the reaction to input event and communicating between concurrent processes take no time. Another equivalent way of thinking is that reactions to events are instantaneoulsy computed by a conceptually infinitely fast machine. This idea is not novel: when writing a discretized continuous control equation $z_t = x_t + y_t$ in Control Theory, one always neglects the time it takes to perform + and =. At run-time, one needs of course to check that the physical reaction time is reasonable w.r.t. application constraints, for example by relying on WCET (Worst Case Execution Time) computation tools such as aiT by AbsInt[1]. Similarly, in the Register Transfer Level (RTL) view of a synchronous digital circuit, the cascade of actions that occur during a clock cycle is conceptually seen as instantaneous, while the physical timing closure computation performed by the electronic CAD system ensures that the final voltages of the circuit wires are as defined by the RTL equations at the end of the clock cycle. This greatly simplifies design and verification, since one deals with synchronous discrete Boolean equations instead of asynchronous voltage propagation.

Unlike asynchronous concurrency, synchronous concurrency is deterministic by construction, which makes it very natural for many applications in digital circuit design, continuous and discrete control, robotics, man/machine interface, etc., which are inherently both concurrent and deterministic. An interesting fact is that engineers trained in Control Theory understand and adopt synchrony immediately, which is not the case for most engineers trained in Computer Science with the idea that concurrency is synonym to asynchrony. This clearly shows that modeling and programming are definitely a question of scientific culture.

The three initial synchronous languages were Esterel [12,19,27] for discrete control flow, and Lustre [38] by P. Caspi and N. Halbwachs and Signal [36] by A. Benveniste and P. Le Guernic for continuous control and signal processing. They were developed in interdisciplinary labs gathering researchers in Computer Science and Control Theory, all on fully formal grounds and aimed at industrial applications. They have indeed all become industrial.

At about the same time, the Statecharts [39] graphical formalism was developed for discrete control by D. Harel, with similar ideas but technically quite different semantics. Its great ideas of hierarchical and concurrent graphical state

---

[1] www.absint.com.

machines were soon borrowed by the synchronous community to develop graphical versions of the synchronous languages such as SyncCharts [4] for Esterel, Argos [48] for Lustre, the Sildex IDE developed by the TNI company for Signal, as well as the MARTE UML profile[2]. Statecharts also served as the basis for the Statemate industrial product[3], the various state machine designs of UML, the Mathwork Stateflow product, etc.

The more recent synchronous languages such as SCADE 6 by Esterel Technologies [29] are hybrids of these initial models, with the addition of a bunch of new ideas that appeared later. All their industrial developments have involved developing tools ranging from code generation to automatic test generation and formal verification. The temptation to adopt half-baked constructs with half-baked semantics to please some particular user has always been resisted: it is very easy to kill the mathematical and practical consistency of a language by such constructs. This was felt as bad scientific taste by the authors, and, more importantly definitely unacceptable for safety-critical applications.

Other stable academic synchronous languages are ReactiveC [26] by F. Boussinot, which embeds Esterel's ideas into C, Reactive ML [47] by L. Mandel and M. Pouzet, which does the same for Caml, and Lucid Synchrone [30] by M. Pouzet *et al.*, which is a higher-order functional synchronous language. More recently defined, SCL [62] by R. Van Hanxleden *et al.* is a direct extension of C with constructive synchronous threads that relaxes Esterel constraints, ScCharts [61] is a version of SyncCharts based on SCL, HipHop [20] by M. Serrano and myself is an Esterel-based extension of the Scheme-based HOP system [57] dedicated to Web programming and orchestration, HipHop-js by C. Vidal plays the same role for the Hop-js [58] javascript version of Hop, and the ideas of Esterel have been embedded in the new algorithmic music score definition language of the Antescofo system [31,32] by A. Cont *et al.* for real-time human/computer music based on adaptive score following. From the points of view of modeling and programming, there is actually not much difference between programming an airplane or an electronic orchestra.

3.2   Synchronous Languages : Modeling or Programming?

Conventional programming languages remain mentally close to the structure of the computer. On the contrary, the synchronous languages try to remain as close as possible to the structure of the problem to be solved; they hierarchically describe abstract temporal behaviors instead of concretely specifying machine instructions to execute. Would it be appropriate to also call them modeling languages?

In a sense yes, since their programming style mostly reflects previously existing modeling activities. For instance, to define the Lustre [38] synchronous programming language, the control theorist P. Caspi studied the way control engineers write airplane control models; Lustre was then developed

---

[2] http://www.omg.org/spec/MARTE/1.1/PDF/.

[3] http://www-03.ibm.com/software/products/en/ratistat.

with N. Halbwachs, a computer scientist, precisely with the goal of blurring the distinction between modeling and programming. Because it was both simpler and more powerful, Airbus finally preferred SAGA [10], the industrial graphical version of Lustre, to its own internally developed programming language SAO. This lead to the industrial SCADE (Safety Critical Application Development Environment) product.

In an other sense no, because synchronous languages are deterministic and fully executable, which is not mandatory for other modeling activities and may limit specification power. Technically speaking, to help higher-level modeling, one can introduce non-determinism in synchronous languages by using external "oracle" signals acting as drivers for asynchrony. In some cases, it is quite natural, but it may be artificial in others (but see the Averest project at http://www.averest.org for a formal integration attempt of synchronous and asynchronous behavior). We do not have enough rooms to further analyze this question here.

Statecharts were also explicitly designed as a modeling formalism to help the discussion between airplane engineers and pilots. When designing them, D. Harel was looking for the maximal expressive power, not for direct implementability. But the design was good enough to be also almost directly implementable. In its industrial version and in its appropriation by synchronous languages, several restrictions have been used to make the charts more synchronous without losing much expressivity. Here again, the frontier between modeling and programming is not clear.

Altogether, to classify synchronous languages, I think that it would be fair to view them as model-level programming languages that do generate embedded code - I mean real code that actually pilots many modern airplanes and controls their engines, brakes, displays, etc., or does similar things for many other critical functions in many other critical industrial systems.

4   The Evolution of Esterel and SCADE

4.1   Esterel v5, from Research to Industry (1982–2000)

The Esterel language was developed at Ecole des Mines and Inria Sophia-Antipolis from 1982 to 2000. The language style was initiated by two control theory researchers, J.-P. Rigault and J.-P. Marmorat, again extending and systematizing ideas of time-related discrete control modeling [19]. The first formal semantics was given by L. Cosserat and myself in 1984 [16], and the first Esterel v2 compiler was written by P. Couronné and myself in 1985 based on this semantics. G. Gonthier developed novel ideas in his seminal work on efficient semantics [17] that lead a bigger group to implement the much more efficient compiler Esterel v3 from 1986 on. This academic compiler produced C code and also input for the Auto/Autograph verification system [53] based on process-calculi bisimulation techniques. It was readily used for industrial R&D projects, especially for avionics discrete control modeling and formal verification for the Rafale fighter at Dassault Aviation [15] (testing system, landing gear control, cockpit GUI, etc.), for telecommunication at Bell Labs [50], AT&T [41] and British Telecom, and for robot control at Inria [34]. In the latter case, it is interesting to note that Esterel served as the target language of a robotics domain-specific task description language that provided higher-level modeling based on domain knowledge. The translation to Esterel made it possible to translate robotics models to C and to perform formal verification on them.

But a strong practical limitation was that the Esterel v3 compiler generated deterministic state machines that could and sometimes did explode exponentially in size.

A major progress occurred in 1989–1990, when I worked with J. Vuillemin's hardware group at the Digital Equipment Paris Research Lab. They were developing the Perle programmable FPGA-based board [21] using the first really usable Xilinx FPGAs (programmable circuits). They were very smart in designing fancy data path circuits, but much less at developing the control circuits that drive them. After having tried the well-known one-hot hardware implementation of the automata generated by the v3 compiler, we discovered a much more direct and efficient compiling technique to translate Esterel programs to circuits in a quasi-linear way [11]. The resulting v4 compiler solved once for all the generated code explosion problem. It was readily incorporated in the Agel IDE for Esterel sold by ILOG.

Then, together with H. Touati, J.C. Madre and O. Coudert at Digital Equipment and E. Sentovich and H. Toma at UC Berkeley and Inria, we developed BDD-based optimizers for the generated circuits with excellent practical results [55,56,60], rapidly followed by the Xeve BDD-based formal verifier [24] developed by A. Bouali and R. de Simone at Inria. In practice, our optimized control circuits proved systematically smaller, faster, and easier to verify than human-designed ones. The main reason is that the Esterel modeling style naturally leads to a very efficient, scalable and optimizable state assignment, which is a key for sequential circuits timing and verification efficiency. Another reason is that human beings seem quite incapable of directly designing efficient control circuits with the usual lower-level languages, unlike for data paths.

We could readily adapt the new Esterel v4 hardware compiler to generate C software by simply simulating the circuit in C. Later on, S. Edwards and then D. Potop wrote very different compilers to C [33,51] that generate much more efficient C code that can be either used for circuit simulation or embedded within software systems. The technique and the generated code are quite different, but, thanks to the formal semantics of the language, the results are behaviorally equivalent.

But Esterel v4 did not accept all the programs formerly accepted by Esterel v3, because it was limited to circuits with acyclic combinational structure. This was not a strong limitation for hardware since most circuit CAD tools reject combinational cycles (although S. Malik showed in [46] that cyclic circuits can be more natural and space-efficient than acyclic ones) and since Lustre and most data-flow languages also reject cycles. But our avionics software partners found it natural to program with behaviorally correct combinational cycles; such cycles happen to be cut at some place during each execution step, for instance by an and-gate receiving a 0 from a wire not in the cycle, but not at the same place for all executions steps [15]. The problem was to find which cyclic circuits should be considered as correct, knowing that equations such as "$X = X$" and "$X = $ not X" had to be rejected. Esterel v3 had heuristics for that, but not quite complete ones; we had to solve the problem in a better way. In 1991, extending S. Malik's seminal work [46] with T. Shiple and H. Touati [59], we characterized the circuits that correctly behave for all values of wire and gate delays: they are exactly those whose equations can be solved by Constructive Boolean Logic, i.e., Boolean logic without the excluded middle law "X or not $X = true$" instead of classical logic. The typical counter-example is the amazing *Hamlet* circuit "$ToBe = ToBe$ or not $ToBe$" that cannot be solved without using the excluded middle law, which is not available in constructive logic. This circuit never computes *false*, computes *true* for some wire and gate delays, but does oscillate for some other delays. The initial complicated proof has been recently simplified and made elegant by M. Mendler [49] using a temporal logic of analog stabilization of voltages in circuits, which closes the field at least for Esterel needs.

The Esterel semantics has been unchanged since then, see [13]. More importantly, all the aforementioned semantics remained fully equivalent on the programs they handle in common. We never had to change the language nor the semantic principles.

In 1995, Esterel v5 was also integrated in the Cocentric System Studio tool developed in the US by Synopsys for system-level hardware design, a nascent form of model-based design for circuit design and hardware/software codesign. It was also made part of Cadence's Polis [7] system for hardware/software codesign. But the industry was not yet ready for these design levels and success was meager.

4.2   Esterel v7 for Hardware Design (2001–2009)

At the end of the 1990s, the improved hardware translation of Esterel raised the interest of major actors of the circuit industry, mainly Intel, Xilinx, Texas Instruments, ST micro-electronics, and NXP (formerly Philips). See [18] for instance. But Esterel v5 was weak in data handling. Together with M. Kishinevsky from Intel Strategic CAD Lab in Portland, we developed a much richer version Esterel v7 of the language[4], which enriched the control-flow constructs and added powerful data manipulation constructs. In addition, a novel arithmetic type system allowed us to optimally implement bit-level sizing of variables and communication signals, automatizing a classical headache in data path sizing. The resulting language was very powerful for joint data path and control path handling, both handled at a much higher temporal modeling level than with conventional HDLs.

At the Esterel Technologies company, created in 2000, the Esterel v7 compiler was incorporated into a rich IDE called Esterel Studio that covered design,

---

[4] http://www.inria.fr/members/Gerard.Berry/papers/Esterelv7ReferenceManual7.60.pdf.

simulation with symbolic debugging, formal verification, synthesis, and documentation of circuits. The software compiler generated C and SystemC circuit simulation code and was directly linked with the Prover SL verifier of Prover Technologies to perform SMT (Satisfaction Modulo Theories) formal verification [35,44], test generation, and construction of counter-examples for dissatisfied formulae. A fast-C code generator based on the aforementioned work by S. Edwards and D. Potop [51] was then implemented to improve generated C code performance. The hardware synthesizer and optimizer of Esterel v5 was also improved and coupled with data path circuit generation; it generated standard VHDL or Verilog. Strangely enough, it took us a lot of time to ensure that VHDL/Verilog simulation and logic synthesis of our quite trivial generated code exactly agreed, although this was stated as "obvious for the synthesizable designs" by CAD tools vendors. Finally, circuit synthesis was made modular to improve the optimization of very large designs.

Around 2005, because of the evolution of SoCs (Systems on Chips) towards multiple clock support and dynamic frequency regulation to save power, Esterel v7 was extended to support clock gating (a key to power saving) and multiclock designs [6]. Surprisingly, this did not require any change to the Esterel mathematical semantics, but only the addition of a new *weak suspension* statement previously introduced by K. Schneider in his Quartz language [54]. These extensions provided our users with the first model-level behavioral view of multiclock design and verification.

After various R&D experimentation successes, Esterel v7 entered in production in 2006 at Texas Instruments for the design of various tricky IP blocks such as smart memory controllers, DMAs (Direct Memory Access units), a hardware decoder for full HD TV on smartphones, etc., and for NoC (Network-on-Chip) design at ST Microelectronics. These designs were made at a much higher level than with classical HDLs, verified early in the loop, and did synthesize excellent hardware.

Industrial practice obliged us to deal with something we never heard of in research: *ECOs*, i.e., *Engineering Change Orders* [5]. This strange name depicts the following situation. When the first samples of a circuit come back from factory, bugs are found that have escaped the extensive simulation and verification campaign. These bugs most often concern tricky control paths such as memory access control, functioning mode logic, or communication protocols, exactly where Esterel v7 was beneficial and used. Usually, such bugs were easy to fix on the source Esterel v7 code. But it would be too long and too expensive to completely rebuild the circuit masks: recompiling and resynthesizing the source code as standard for software is not a possibility for hardware. The bugs must be corrected by *patching the masks*, as traditionally done for printed circuit boards; this was non-trivial since the logic out of Esterel v7 program is very heavily optimized. We first had to make our combinational and sequential optimizations *reversible*, i.e., to make it possible to reconstruct any part of the source logic from the mask. Fortunately, this did not affect much optimization quality. Then, using the source-to-circuit traceability mechanism we had put in place for symbolic debugging, we could find ways to appropriately patch the masks and formally prove behavioral equivalence between the source change and the patch. In production integrated circuit design, if you cannot do that, you cannot play.

There were other interesting surprises. For instance, when a design is sufficiently advanced, it is sent to and external test team in charge of comparing it to the paper specification and finding its bugs. Such a team is rated by the number of bugs it finds, according to accumulated experience. External testing teams for the Esterel v7-based projects found almost no bugs in the designs, became misjudged because they were rated by the number of bugs found, and bitterly complained about that new state of affairs! It was not easy to convince program managers that it is a good idea to find bugs *before* testing the designs (we did not try to convince the test team it could be smaller).

Unfortunately, the 2008 financial crisis hit massively the circuit industry and reduced severely the number of designs teams. Esterel Technologies had to abandon the development of Esterel v7 and commit to SCADE for certified software. The Esterel Studio software now belongs to Synopsys, which has put it in the deep freezer, and the ongoing IEEE standardization process with academic and industrial partners has been also abandoned. Sigh...

4.3   From Lustre/SCADE to SCADE 6 for Safety-Critical Software

Since synchronous languages are at ease with both hardware and software because their technical problems are similar enough, our initial plan at Esterel Technologies was to attack both markets with Esterel v7. But this turned out to be difficult since the industrial traditions and thus the selling arguments were completely different in both domains. Fortunately, we could buy SCADE from Telelogic in 2003. We then decided to attack the software market with a new product called SCADE 6 [29], whose language unifies the best features of SCADE for data flow and Esterel/SyncCharts for control, while adding support for functional arrays that had become indispensable in industrial applications. The resulting language is defined by its formal semantics, not by words. As for the previous SCADE systems, the SCADE 6 code generator (written in CAML) is DO-178B qualifiable as a development tool, which greatly simplifies software certification of applications and recertifcation after changes.

SCADE Suite is a complete IDE with simulation, formal verification, a qualifiable display generator, links to mathematical modeling, links with SYSML modeling for architectural engineering, etc. Many other tools are linked to SCADE: a translator of Simulink designs; Astrée [23], a fancy abstract interpretation verifier developed by P. Cousot and his team with Airbus to verify generate code properties, and in particular check absence of possible run-time errors; and the StackAnalyzer and aiT abstract-interpretation based tools developed by the AbsInt company to verify stack size compliance and computer WCET (Worst Case Execution Time).

SCADE Suite is used by more than 250 customers worldwide for all kinds of safety-critical software applications. I think it can be viewed as a good example of technical unification of model-based design and programming within a precise application domain.

5   Open Issues in Model-Based Embedded Systems Design

In theory there is no difference between theory and practice. In practice there is. (Yogi Berra)

Even in the specific domain we discussed, there are many issues to solve to really unify model-based design and programming at both theoretical and practical levels, practical achievements being the real success criterion at the end of the day. I will only cite some of them here, related to currently weak points of the design chain.

Most mathematical modelers for differential equation simulation still lack solid semantics, and, as said before, do not correctly support the mixture of continuous control and discrete event handling. An elegant theoretical solution to continuous/discrete cooperation has been proposed by Benveniste, Bourke, Caillaud, and Pouzet [8]. It is based on non-standard analysis: in addition to progressing by real ϵ's between integration steps, time can progress by *infinitesimal* ϵ's during discrete event cascades. More practically, Pouzet and his team are defining the Zelus simulation language and compiler [25,52], with a type-checker that sorts out continuous and discrete behaviors to ensure that simulation behavior exactly respects the semantics that mathematically defines the expected system behavior. Such a language could advantageously replace the existing ones in mathematical modelers and solve the current continuous/discrete conflicts.

Most code generation tools end up generating C code. But C compilers are not as robust as one usually thinks. For instance, using smart random generation techniques, the CSmith project has generated one million C programs especially triggered to shake C compilers. CSmith found lots of bugs in most tested compilers, be them academic or industrial. These bugs can be compiler crashes or internal errors, which is harmless, but they can also be wrong generated code, which is really harmful and raises questions about the "certification by large usage" often invoked in industry. Only one compiler survived: CompCert [45] by Xavier Leroy and his team. This is not surprising since CompCert has been developed and formally verified with Coq [22], much of its code being automatically extracted from the proof. Such a formally verified and reasonably efficient compiler should definitely be used for safety-critical systems.

Following the same track, L. Rieg and myself are currently feeding Coq with the chain of (Kernel) Esterel semantics up to circuit translation, with the hope of constructing a Coq-verified compiler - and to finally publish my draft book "The Constructive Semantics of Pure Esterel"[5] with all currently unpublished proofs of the theorems done in Coq. Similarly, T. Bourke and others are working on a Coq-verified Lustre compiler.

---

[5] http://www-sop.inria.fr/members/Gerard.Berry/Papers/EsterelConstructiveBook. pdf.

Finally, and most importantly, the models described in this paper correspond to compact 20th-century embedded systems, to which the core synchronous framework is well-suited. But the embedded systems zoo of the 21st century has many more animals, and in particular physically distributed systems mixing signal processing, complex control, fancy GUIs, etc. There have been many attempts to automatically distribute the code generated by synchronous languages (not detailed here), but more general ways to tackle the problem should be investigated.

Ptolemy II[6], developed at UC Berkeley by Edward Lee's team, is an exciting and elegant environment for model-based design of distributed systems. Instead of being based on a single computation paradigm, Ptolemy II supports a variety of computation and communication models, including the synchronous one, and links them quite cleanly within a global graphical framework. I think such a system can play a major role in the unification of model-based design and programming. Other extensions of the synchronous paradigm are the aforementioned SCL approach [62] and the Averest project by K. Schneider *et al.* (http://www.averest.org).

6 Conclusion

We have shown the direct and formal connection between model-based design and programming in the synchronous languages framework, and detailed its industrial tooling and applications developments in the embedded systems application area. By adopting a higher-level model-based way of writing and verifying designs, we could simplify and put closer modeling and programming *in this application domain.* There are many other places where unification of modeling and programming should be performed, probably in a different way. Isola will be an excellent occasion of discussing this.

References

1. Rodin Users Handbook. http://www3.hhu.de/stups/handbook/rodin/current/html/
2. Abrial, J.R.: The B-book: Assigning Programs to Meanings. Cambridge University Press, New York (1996)
3. Abrial, J.R.: Modeling in Event-B: System and Software Engineering. Cambridge University Press, New York (2013)
4. André, C.: Representation, analysis of reactive behaviors: a synchronous approach. In: Proceedings of CESA 1996, IEEE-SMC, Lille, France (1996)
5. Arditi, L., Berry, G., Kishinevsky, M.: Late design changes (ECOs) for sequentially optimized Esterel designs. In: Proceedings of Formal Methods in Computer Aided Design, FMCAD 2004, Austin, Texas (2004)
6. Arditi, L., Berry, G., Kishinevsky, M., Perreaut, M.: Clocking schemes in Esterel. In: Proceedings of Designing Correct Circuits, DCC 2006, Vienna, Austria (2006)

---

[6] http://ptolemy.eecs.berkeley.edu/ptolemyII/.

7. Balarin, F., Chiodo, M., Jurecska, A., Hsieh, H., Lavagno, A.L., Passerone, C., Sangiovanni-Vincentelli, A., Sentovich, E., Suzuki, K., Tabbara, B.: Hardware-Software Co-Design of Embedded Systems: The Polis Approach. Kluwer Academic Press (1997)
8. Benveniste, A., Bourke, T., Caillaud, B., Pouzet, M.: Non-standard semantics of hybrid systems modelers. J. Comput. Syst. Sci. (JCSS) **78**(3), 877–910 (2012). Special issue in honor of Amir Pnueli
9. Benveniste, A., Caspi, P., Edwards, S., Halbwachs, N., Le Guernic, P., de Simone, R.: The synchronous languages 12 years later. Proc. IEEE **91**(1), 64–83 (2003)
10. Bergerand, J.L., Pilaud, E., Saga,: a software development environment for dependability in automatic control. In: Proceedings of Safecomp 1988. Pergamon Press (1988)
11. Berry, G.: A hardware implementation of pure Esterel. Sadhana Acad. Proc. Eng. Sci. Indian Acad. Sci. **17**(1), 95–130 (1992)
12. Berry, G.: The foundations of Esterel. In: Proof, Language and Interaction Essays in Honour of Robin Milner. MIT Press (2000)
13. Berry, G.: The Constructive Semantics of Pure Esterel. Draft book version 3 (without proofs) (2002). http://www-sop.inria.fr/members/Gerard.Berry/Papers/EsterelConstructiveBook.pdf
14. Berry, G., Benveniste, A.: The synchronous approach to reactive and real-time systems. Another Look Real Time Programm. Proc. IEEE **79**, 1270–1282 (1991)
15. Berry, G., Bouali, A., Fornari, X., Nassor, E., Ledinot, E., de Simone, R.: Esterel: a formal method applied to avionic development. Sci. Comput. Program. **36**, 5–25 (2000)
16. Berry, G., Cosserat, L.: The ESTEREL synchronous programming language and its mathematical semantics. In: Brookes, S.D., Roscoe, A.W., Winskel, G. (eds.) CONCURRENCY 1984. LNCS, vol. 197, pp. 389–448. Springer, Heidelberg (1985). doi:10.1007/3-540-15670-4_19
17. Berry, G., Gonthier, G.: The Esterel synchronous programming language: design, semantics, implementation. Sci. Comput. Program. **19**(2), 87–152 (1992)
18. Berry, G., Kishinevsky, M., Singh, S.: System level design and verification using a synchronous language. In: Proceedings of International Conference on Integrated Circuit Design, ICCAD 2003, San Jose, USA (2004)
19. Berry, G., Moisan, S., Rigault, J.-P.: Towards a synchronous and semantically sound high level language for real-time applications. In: IEEE Real Time Systems Symposium, pp. 30–40 (1983). IEEE Catalog 83 CH 1941-4
20. Berry, G., Serrano, M., Hop, H.: Multitier web orchestration. In: Proceedings of the ICDCIT 2014 Conference, pp. 1–13 (2014)
21. Bertin, P., Roncin, D., Vuillemin, J.: Programmable active memories: a performance assessment. In: Borriello, G., Ebeling, C. (eds.) Research on Integrated Systems: Proceedings of the 1993 Symposium, pp. 88–102 (1993)
22. Bertot, Y., Casteran, P.: Interactive Theorem Proving and Program Development-Coq'Art: The Calculus of Inductive Constructions. Springer (2004)
23. Blanchet, B., Cousot, P., Cousot, R., Feret, J., Mauborgne, L., Miné, A., Monniaux, D., Rival, X.: A static analyzer for large safety-critical software. In: PLDI 2003 ACM SIGPLAN SIGSOFT Conference on Programming Language Design and Implementation, San Diego, California, USA, pp. 196–207 (2003)
24. Bouali, A.: Xeve: an Esterel verification environment. In: Proceedings of Computer Aided Verification, CAV 1998, Vancouver, Canada (1998)

25. Bourke, T., Colaço, J.-L., Pagano, B., Pasteur, C., Pouzet, M.: A synchronous-based code generator for explicit hybrid systems languages. In: Franke, B. (ed.) CC 2015. LNCS, vol. 9031, pp. 69–88. Springer, Heidelberg (2015). doi:10.1007/978-3-662-46663-6_4

26. Boussinot, F., Reactive, C.: An extension of C to program reactive systems. Softw. Pract. Exp. **21**(4), 401–428 (1991)

27. Boussinot, F., de Simone, R.: The Esterel language. Another Look Real Time Programm. Proc. IEEE **79**, 1293–1304 (1991)

28. Bryant, R.E.: Graph-based algorithms for Boolean function manipulation. IEEE Trans. Comput. **35**(8), 677–691 (1986)

29. Colaço, J.-L., Pagano, B., Pouzet, M.: A conservative extension of synchronous data-flow with state machines. In: Proceedings of Emsoft 2005, New Jersey, USA (2005)

30. Colaço, J.-L., Girault, A., Hamon, G., Pouzet, M.: Towards a higher-order synchronous data-flow language. In :ACM Fourth International Conference on Embedded Software, EMSOFT 2004, Pisa, Italy, September 2004

31. Cont, A.: A coupled duration-focused architecture for real-time music-to-score alignment. IEEE Trans. Pattern Anal. Mach. Intell. **32**, 974–987 (2010)

32. Echeveste, J., Cont, A., Giavitto, J.-L., Jacquemard, F.: Operational semantics of a domain specific language for real time musician-computer interaction. Discrete Event Dyn. Syst. **23**(4), 343–383 (2013)

33. Edwards, S.: An Esterel compiler for large control-dominated systems. IEEE Trans. Comput. Aided Des. Integr. Circuits Syst. **2**(2), 169–183 (2002)

34. Espiau, B., Coste-Manière, E.: A synchronous approach for control sequencing in robotics applications, pp. 503–508. In: Proceedings of IEEE International Workshop on Intelligent Motion, Istambul (1990)

35. De Moura, L., Bjrner, N.: Satisfiability modulo theories: introduction and applications. Comm. ACM **54**(9), 69–77 (2011)

36. Le Guernic, P., Le Borgne, M., Gauthier, T., Le Maire, C.: Programming real time applications with Signal. Another Look Real Time Programm. Proc. IEEE **79**, 1270–1282 (1991). Special Issue

37. Halbwachs, N.: Synchronous Programming of Reactive Systems. Kluwer, Dordrecht (1993)

38. Halbwachs, N., Caspi, P., Pilaud, D.: The synchronous dataflow programming language Lustre. Another Look Real Time Programm. Proc. IEEE **79**, 1270–1282 (1991). Special Issue

39. Harel, D.: Statecharts: a visual approach to complex systems. Sci. Comput. Program. **8**, 231–274 (1987)

40. Iman, S., Joshi, S.: The e-Hardware Verification Language. Springer, Heidelberg (2004)

41. Jagadeesan, L., Von Olnhausen, J., Puchol, C.: A formal approach to reactive system software: a telecommunications application in Esterel. J. Formal Methods Syst. Des. **8**(2), 132–145 (1996)

42. Knuth, D.: The Art of Computer Programming, Vol. 4: Combinatorial Algorithms, Section 7.1.4: Binary Decision Diagrams. Addison Wesley, Reading (2014)

43. Knuth, D.: The Art of Computer Programming, vol. 4B, 7.2.2.2: Satisfiability. Addison Wesley, Reading (2016)

44. Kroening, D., Strichman, O.: Decision Procedures An Algorithmic Point of View. Springer (2008)

45. Leroy, X.: Formal verification of a realistic compiler. Commun. ACM **52**(7), 107–115 (2009)

46. Malik, S.: Analysis of cyclic combinational circuits. IEEE Trans. Comput. Aided Des. **13**(7), 950–956 (1994)
47. Mandel, L., Pouzet, M.: ReactiveML, a reactive extension to ML. In: Proceedings of Principles and Practice of Declarative Programming, PPDP 2005, Lisbon (2005)
48. Maraninchi, F., Rémond, Y.: Mode automata: a new domain-specific construct for the development of safe critical systems. Sci. Comput. Programm. **46**(3), 219–254 (2003)
49. Mendler, M., Shiple, T., Berry, G.: Constructive Boolean circuits and the exactness of timed ternary simulation. Formal Methods Syst. Des. **40**(3), 283–329 (2012)
50. Murakami, G., Sethi, R.: Terminal call processing in Esterel. In: Proceedings of IFIP 92 World Computer Congress, Madrid, Spain (1992)
51. Potop-Butucaru, D., Edwards, S.A., Berry, G.: Compiling Esterel. Springer, Heidelberg (2007)
52. Pouzet, M.: Building a hybrid systems modeler on synchronous languages principles. In: Proceedings of ACM International Conference on Embedded Software (EMSOFT), Amsterdam (2015)
53. Roy, V., de Simone, R.: Auto and autograph. In: Kurshan, R. (ed.) Proceedings of Workshop on Computer Aided Verification, New-Brunswick, June 1990
54. Schneider, K.: Embedding imperative synchronous languages in interactive theorem provers. In: Proceedings of Conference on Application of Concurrency to System Design (ACSD) (2001)
55. Sentovich, E., Toma, H., Berry, G.: Latch optimization in circuits generated from high-level descriptions. In: Proceedings of International Conference on Computer-Aided Design (ICCAD) (1996)
56. Sentovich, E., Toma, H., Berry, G.: Efficient latch optimization using exclusive sets. In: Proceedings of Digital Automation Conference (DAC) (1997)
57. Serrano, M., Berry, G.: Multitier programming in Hop - a first step toward programming 21st-century applications. Commun. ACM **55**(8), 53–59 (2012)
58. Serrano, M., Prunet, V.: A glimpse of Hopjs. In: 21th Sigplan International Conference on Functional Programming (ICFP), Nara, Japan (2016)
59. Shiple, T., Berry, G., Touati, H.: Constructive analysis of cyclic circuits. In: Proceedings of International Design and Testing Conf (ITDC), Paris (1996)
60. Touati, H., Berry, G.: Optimized controller synthesis using Esterel. In: Proceedings of International Workshop on Logic Synthesis IWLS 1993, Lake Tahoe (1993)
61. von Hanxleden, R., Duderstadt, B., Motika, C., Smyth, S., Mendler, M., Aguado, J., Mercer, S., OBrien, O.: SCCharts: Sequentially constructive statecharts for safety-critical applications. In: Proceedings ACM SIGPLAN Conference on Programming Language Design and Implementation (PLDI14), Edinburgh, UK, (2014)
62. von Hanxleden, R., Mendler, M., Aguado, J., Duderstadt, B., Fuhrmann, I., Motika, C., Mercer, S., O'Brien, O.: Sequentially constructive concurrency - a conservative extension of the synchronous model of computation. In: Proceedings of Design, Automation and Test in Europe Conference, DATE 2013, Grenoble, France (2013)

Interactive Model-Based Compilation Continued – Incremental Hardware Synthesis for SCCharts

Francesca Rybicki, Steven Smyth$^{(\boxtimes)}$, Christian Motika,
Alexander Schulz-Rosengarten, and Reinhard von Hanxleden

Department of Computer Science, Real-Time and Embedded Systems Group,
Christian-Albrechts-Universität zu Kiel, Olshausenstr. 40, 24118 Kiel, Germany
{fry,ssm,cmot,als,rvh}@informatik.uni-kiel.de
http://www.informatik.uni-kiel.de/rtsys

Abstract. The Single-Pass Language-Driven Incremental Compilation (SLIC) strategy uses a series of model-to-model (M2M) transformations to compile a model or program to a specified target. Tool developer and modeler can inspect the result of each transformation step, using a familiar, graphical syntax of the successively transformed model, which is made possible by harnessing automatic layout. Previous work (presented at ISoLA'14) introduced the basics of the SLIC approach and illustrated it with a compiler that translated SCCharts, a synchronous, deterministic statechart language developed for safety-critical systems, to software. The compiler is implemented in the Kiel Integrated Environment for Layout Eclipse Rich Client (KIELER), an open-source development framework based on Eclipse.

This paper proposes two extensions to SLIC. First, we extend the M2M transformation mechanism with a *tracing* capability that keeps track of model elements during transformations. Second, we make use of the tracing capability for an interactive *simulation*, where we not only observe a model's input/output behavior during execution, but can inspect the runtime behavior of each model component, at any transformation stage. We illustrate these concepts by new transformations in the KIELER SCCharts compiler, which allow to synthesize hardware circuits, and a simulator that executes an intermediate-level software model and visualizes the simulation at the high-level model as well as the low-level circuit.

1 Introduction

In an earlier case-study on interactive model-based compilation [12], we investigated possible compilation strategies for *Sequentially Constructive Statecharts* (*SCCharts*). SCCharts [21] is a synchronous statechart modeling language for reactive systems, designed with safety-critical systems in mind. Due to its sequentially constructive model of computation [22] it provides semantic rigor and determinism. At the same time, it permits sequential assignments within a reaction, which is forbidden in classical synchronous languages.

The case-study also introduced *Single-Pass Language-Driven Incremental Compilation* (*SLIC*). The user story is as follows: (i) A user edits a textual

© Springer International Publishing AG 2016
T. Margaria and B. Steffen (Eds.): ISoLA 2016, Part II, LNCS 9953, pp. 150–170, 2016.
DOI: 10.1007/978-3-319-47169-3_12

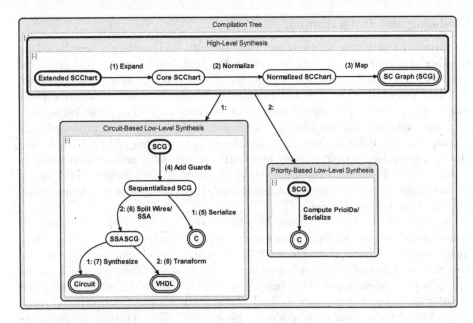

Fig. 1. Full compilation tree from Extended SCCharts to hardware (e.g., VHDL) or software (e.g., C code) splits into a high-level and low-level parts (adapted from [12]).

model. (ii) The user selects a chain of M2M transformations to be applied to the source model. (iii) The selected transformations are applied and the visual representation of the transformed model is updated.

Unlike in traditional compilers, each step of the transformation chain is fully transparent and each intermediate result can be inspected. As long as the M2M transformations are within the same meta model, the same graphical syntax that is already familiar to the user can be used to visualize the transformation results. The tool smith can validate and optimize each step of the compiler. There are no hidden (intermediate) data structures that carry additional information. This is particularly useful for safety-critical systems.

The original introduction of the SLIC approach [12] implemented the compilation tree depicted in Fig. 1, using Statecharts notation, and explained the *high-level synthesis* part in detail. The SCCharts language is split into two parts: Extended SCCharts, the syntactic sugar, and Core SCCharts, the minimal language set. The high-level compilation involves (1) expanding extended features by performing consecutive M2M transformations on Extended SCCharts, (2) normalizing Core SCCharts by using only a small number of allowed Core SCCharts patterns, and (3) straight-forward M2M mapping of these constructs to a *Sequentially Constructive Graph* (*SCG*).

The low-level synthesis strategies involve the code generation for software (e.g., C code) and hardware (e.g., VHDL) as presented earlier [21], with the data-flow approach for software, (4) and (5), explained in detail elsewhere [18].

Modeling and Programming

Traditionally, one way to separate programming and modeling was based on whether the primary concrete syntax of the high-level artifact was graphical ("model") or textual ("program"). However, if that distinction was ever justified, it is now less and less so as textual modeling frameworks such as Xtext become more common place, and these frameworks provide standard compilation services such as parser generation. The SLIC approach and its extensions proposed here is related to the fields of program compilation and modeling alike. We address a classical compilation task, namely translating a high-level artifact developed by a human to a low-level, executable piece of hardware or software. While doing so, we make systematic use of classical modeling concepts and a widely used modeling ecosystem (Eclipse).

We thus see the work presented here as yet another step towards blurring the boundary between modeling and programming. This not only concerns the "technical" aspects of how programs/models are analyzed and synthesized, but also how the programmer/modeler is involved in the process. The choice of concrete syntax is just one example; other examples, which we invite the reader to consider in the remainder of this paper, include the way the compiler is controlled using a "model" of the compilation chain (as illustrated in Fig. 1), how intermediate compilation results are presented, or how a program/model is simulated.

Contributions

In this paper, we present two extensions to the SLIC approach. First, we extend the M2M transformation mechanism with a *tracing* capability that keeps track of model elements during transformations. This allows to map high-level model elements to their low-level counterparts and vice versa. Second, we make use of the tracing capability for an interactive *simulation*. As in source-level debugging familiar from high-level languages, the execution state is reflected in the original model, but here we can inspect the run-time behavior of each model component at any transformation stage as well.

To illustrate these concepts, we further explore the picture given in Fig. 1 by explaining how to create hardware circuits from models written in SCCharts within the SLIC approach. This includes (6) the transformation of the SCG into a Single Static Assignment (SSA) [15] form and (7) the generation of the circuits via M2M transformations as well as the visualization and simulation. The simulation is done based on an intermediate transformation result that determines a *tick function*, which is compiled to C code that is then executed. The bidirectional transformation tracing information not only allows to map simulation results to the original model, but also to the hardware circuit that is the final result of the transformation.

Outline

The next section covers the SCCharts language, as far as required for the remainder of this paper. The section introduces AO, a subset example of ABRO pre-

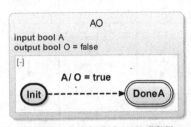

(a) Source model of the AO SCChart

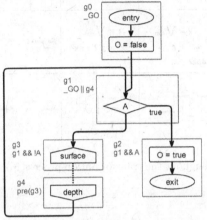

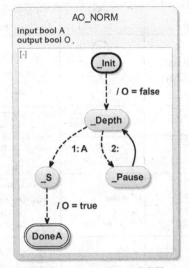

(b) Equivalent Normalized SCChart after high-level compilation (expansion)

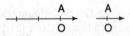

(d) Two possible execution traces with true-valued inputs above the tick time line and true-valued outputs below. The second trace emits O in the first tick because the transition in AO is taken immediately.

(c) SCG of AO depicting the control-flow of AO. The basic blocks (purple boxes) enclose the statements of the program. They are annotated with their name and the expression that determines when a block is active.

Fig. 2. The AO example, illustrating Extended and Normalized SCCharts features and its sequential control-flow (Color figure online)

sented in the previous paper [12]. AO will serve as ongoing example for the circuit synthesis.

Section 3 then discusses the two proposed extensions to the SLIC, tracing and simulation, at a general level. The interactive incremental hardware synthesis that illustrates these extensions follows in Sect. 4. That section explains the transformations that are necessary to create circuits and how to extend the existing toolchain to simulate and validate the generated circuits. The evaluation for the interactive hardware synthesis, showing the practicability of the approach, is discussed in Sect. 5.

We summarize related work in Sect. 6, and conclude in Sect. 7.

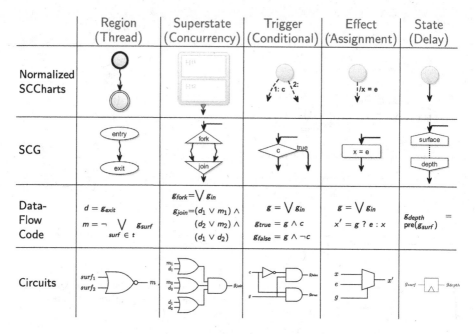

Fig. 3. Matrix showing the entire mapping throughout the transformation process from SCCharts to circuits (adapted from [21])

2   SCCharts

In this section, we will introduce the AO SCChart, see Fig. 2a, a tiny example of SCCharts. We choose AO because of space considerations. Nevertheless, the approach presented here applies any SCChart that is statically schedulable, e. g., ABRO, the "hello world" [1] of synchronous programming, included in the previous case-study [12]. We will explain all used features of SCCharts as far as they are necessary to understand the model. In depth details of the SCCharts language are described in the introductory SCCharts paper [21] and the technical report on the features of the SCCharts language [20].

In general, an SCChart starts with an *interface declaration* at the top that can declare variables and external functions. Variables can be *inputs*, which are read from the environment, and/or *outputs*, which are written to the environment. One may also declare *local variables*. In AO the interface declaration consists out of one input variable A and one output variable O, which will be fed back to the environment at the end of a reaction cycle.

AO has only one (top) level of *hierarchy*. It includes its two *states* Init and DoneA which are connected via a *transition*. Since AO does not comprise any concurrency, only one of these states may be active. At the start of the program AO state Init, the *initial state* (thick border), is the active one. The program ends after DoneA, a *final state* (double border), is reached. If Init is active and the *trigger* of the transition, input A, is true, Init is left and DoneA becomes active.

Simultaneously, the *effect* O = true is executed which sets O to true. If two or more transitions outgoing from the active state are eligible to run, the transition with the higher *priority* is taken (cf. _Depth in Fig. 2b). The transition in AO is an *immediate* transition, indicated by the dashed edge, which means that it is enabled as soon as its source state becomes active. Otherwise, it would have been *delayed* by default, meaning it cannot trigger in the first tick of its source state. This convention prevents instantaneous cycles, which would be problematic for this synthesis.

AO_NORM (Fig. 2b) expresses the exact semantics of AO but uses only language elements of the Core SCCharts subset. The transformation from compact extended SCCharts to Normalized SCCharts and more key features of SCCharts, such as concurrency, hierarchy and preemption, are explained in detail elsewhere [12,20].

According to the compilation strategies presented before [12,18,21] a normalized SCChart is mapped to its corresponding SCG (also see (3) in Fig. 1.). The SCG of the normalized version of AO (cf. Fig. 2b) is shown in Fig. 2c. The basic blocks (purple boxes) determine which part of the program is active in the actual tick. They are annotated with their activation expression, also called *guard*. The specific mapping from normalized SCCharts pattern to SCG elements is depicted in the upper part of Fig. 3. The lower part shows the direct mapping between SCG elements and data-flow code and their corresponding circuits.

The execution of an SCChart is divided into a sequence of logical ticks. Two example traces for AO can be seen in Fig. 2d. The program is terminated as soon as the reaction that emits O occurred. This includes the first tick of the program, in which Init becomes active, because the transition between Init and DoneA is immediate.

3 SLIC Extensions

In this section, we first recall the general SLIC user story [12]. Afterwards, the new extensions, namely tracing and simulation, are introduced. An extended SLIC compiler is able to present every intermediate result and propagate information, such as runtime information about a running simulation, between all intermediate model instances. The models may be instances of different meta models.

SLIC User Story

Figure 4 shows a screenshot of the Kiel Integrated Environment for Layout Eclipse Rich Client (KIELER[1]) modeling tools for SCCharts annotated with a schematic workflow:

---

[1] http://rtsys.informatik.uni-kiel.de/kieler.

(1) A modeler models their model textually.
(2) The model gets displayed graphically. This is done instantly and achieved by using automatic layout techniques, such as KIELER's layouting tools.
(3) At any point in time, the modeler may select one or more transformations in the compiler selection. Subsequently, the model gets transformed and will be displayed as intermediate result. The tooling will only present transformations that match the input model or any model format that is reachable from the input model. As described in the original introduction of SLIC [12], the transformation steps are executed in a statically determined order and each transformation produces an intermediate result. This is depicted as directed chain of arrows in the box at the bottom of Fig. 4. The added tracing technology, explained in Sect. 3.1, allows a bidirectional mapping between all intermediate results.
(4) The results may be simulated. Therefore, an (intermediate) model is compiled to executable code. A simulation engine then runs the program and feeds back runtime information that can be used, e. g., to visualize the model instances.

3.1   SLIC Extension: Tracing

The tracing of model elements creates a map that stores information about the relationships between different model elements w.r.t. intermediate transformation results. Transformation rules, introduced earlier [12], describe how model elements get transformed into different, new model elements. The newly generated model elements may be of the same or a different meta model.

Figure 5 shows a transformation step. Model I with nodes A, B, C, D, and E gets transformed to model II with nodes F, G, H, and I. We observe four kinds of element relations:

(1) Object A transforms to F and G. This depicts a $1:n$ relation.
(2) Node B translates to I in a 1:1 relation.
(3) Element D has no corresponding nodes in the target model.
(4) Nodes C and E both transform to node H, which depicts and $n:1$ relation.

Every transformation produces an intermediate compilation result, which is a fully functional model instance. It can be visualized and used as origin for further transformation steps. The changes that enable tracing capability to SLIC transformations are minimal because the developer must only add tracing information for newly created elements. Elements that are present in both, the source and the target model, are mapped to a 1:1 relation by default. Analogously, model elements without a target are also handled automatically.

For example, the *initialization* transformation of the KIELER SCCharts implementation, see Fig. 6, creates a new *entry action* for every initialization part of a declared variable. Therefore, it retrieves an iterator for objects with initialization part and creates an entry action for each at index 0 in reverse order to preserve the initialization order. The initialValue of the valuedObject will be

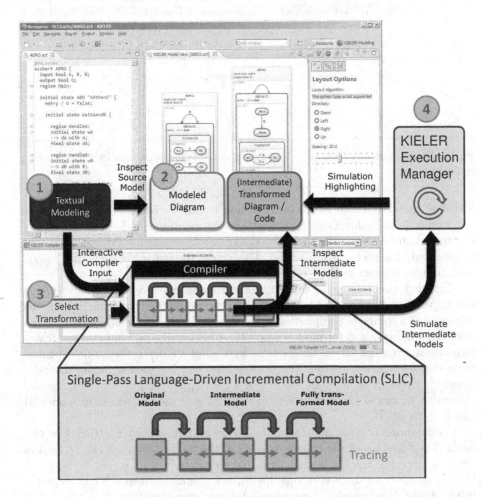

Fig. 4. SLIC extended with tracing and an interactive simulation as implemented in the KIELER SCCharts tools

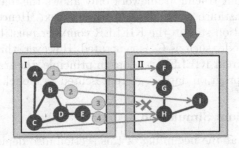

Fig. 5. Transformation step from model I to model II: Model element tracing depicted by arrows

```
1  def transformInitialization(State state) {
2    val valuedObjects = state.valuedObjects.
        filter[initialValue != null].reverseView
3    for(valuedObject : valuedObjects) {
4      state.createEntryAction(0) => [
5        effects +=
           valuedObject.createAssignment(
           valuedObject.initialValue)
6        trace(valuedObject)
7      ]
8    }
9  }
```

Fig. 6. Xtend implementation of transforming variable initializations including tracing command

added to the assignment of the entry action in Line 5. Hence, the expression is removed from the valuedObject containment. As mentioned before, this is implicitly traced and must not be added to the transformation rule explicitly. For the tracing, only Line 6 had to be added. This traces the newly created entry action back to valuedObject in a 1:1 relation.

Applying the tracing to all transformations creates a *tracing tree*, which can be used to trace model information between arbitrary intermediate model instances of a complete compilation chain. Figure 7a shows the application of the rules depicted in Fig. 5 for models I and II. Additionally, four subsequent transformations, creating the instances III, IV, V, and VI, form the model instance hierarchy seen in the figure. The tracing tree can be used to show the relationships between all model elements of a particular compilation. E. g., model element K in model IV corresponds to element A in model I via O in model III and G in model II.

Furthermore, it is not mandatory to always map from source to target or vice versa. The topology of the tracing tree w.r.t. the model instances can be seen in Fig. 7b. Since the tracing is transitive, the elements from, e. g., model instance IV can be used to trace relationships in, e. g., model instance VI as depicted in the figure. Here, model II serves as least common transformation result. For example, as depicted in red in Fig. 7a, elements M and L in model IV both relate to element T in model VI and vice versa.

At the moment our tracing framework only allows the mapping from model instance to model instance and not, e. g., to pure text. Hence, the mapping of the last code generation step in the KIELER compiler must be done explicitly, if textual program code, such as C, is generated. However, this is only a tooling restriction of the current KIELER version. In principle, the tracing tree can also include the textual program data, e. g., represented as model.

3.2   SLIC Extension: Simulation

The user story told at the beginning of this section also depicts the possibility to simulate any intermediate model (cf. (4) in Fig. 4). If using a SLIC compiler equipped with transformation tracing as described in Sect. 3.1, each intermediate result can be simulated to gather runtime information about all other

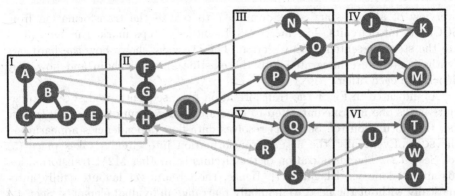

(a) Utilizing the tracing tree to depict model element relationships. Nodes L and M in the model IV correspond to node T in model VI (shown in red). Both tracing paths originate from node I in model II.

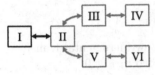

(b) End-to-End mapping depicting the tracing path from model IV to model VI via model II. Information about model elements propagate transitively between the different model instances.

Fig. 7. Resolving model tracing (Color figure online)

model instances. E. g., the model can be compiled down to C code and then be executed by a simulation engine which handles input/output communication. This technique is implemented in the *execution manager* [11] that is part of the KIELER modeling tools. Another way would be the execution of a model by an interpreter on model level. In both cases the runtime information could be propagated throughout the whole tracing tree. The modeler may choose, which model instances they want to inspect (cf. (3) in Fig. 4).

Hence, considering the example depicted in Fig. 7a in Sect. 3.1, any model of models I–VI may be executed to gather runtime information. E. g., if model VI is executed and element T is active, the simulation deduces that elements L and M in model IV would also be active. The granularity of these deductions depends on the structure of the tracing branches of the tracing tree. The simulation sets an element to active as soon as at least one corresponding tracing element is also active. Therefore, while executing model IV, element T would be marked as active if element L or element M is active. Of course, this simulation convention may be changed. Depending on the actual use-case and transformation setup, it is for example conceivable to set an element to active only if all corresponding tracing elements are also active.

4   Interactive Incremental Hardware Synthesis

We used the SLIC approach, including the aforementioned extensions, to implement an interactive incremental hardware synthesis. Figure 8 presents an overview of all necessary steps from 1–7 to realize the transformation from SCCharts into circuits. The incremental synthesis steps marked in blue (3–7) are the steps presented in this section. The overview shows how the hardware synthesis steps are integrated into the existing SLIC toolchain and how they depend on each other.

As indicated in Fig. 1 the transformation from sequentialized SCGs into circuits needs one intermediate step to generate an SSA form of the SCG (3). The SSA transformation (cf. Sect. 4.1) resolves data-flow dependencies appearing in the SCGs. Eventually, the actual transformation into circuits takes place (5) (cf. Sect. 4.2). The visualization of the circuits is another M2M transformation (6) and is done via KLighD [17]. Hence, the circuits get layouted fully automatically without the need to manually rearrange individual elements. Sect. 4.4 explains the mechanics of the simulation. The visualization of the SCG simulation is used to visualize the dynamic behavior of the circuit (7).

User Story for Interactive Hardware Synthesis

Referring to the user story introduced in Sect. 3, the new incremental transformation for hardware synthesis and interaction is depicted in Fig. 9:

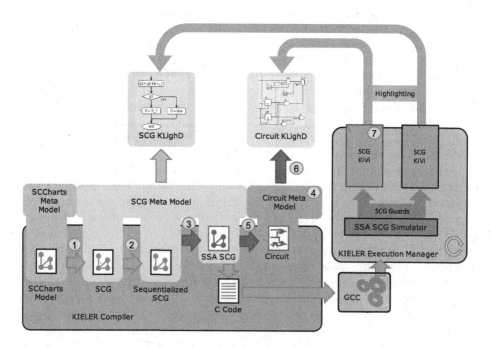

Fig. 8. Interactive Incremental Hardware Synthesis workflow overview. The new steps (3–7, marked in blue) fully integrate into the existing SLIC toolchain. (Color figure online)

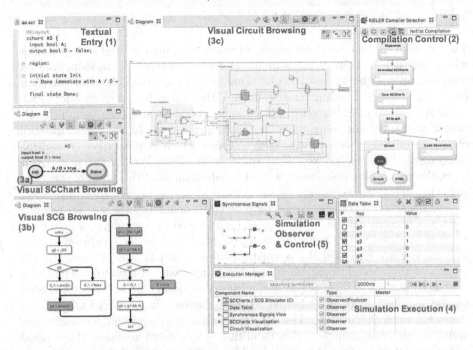

Fig. 9. Screenshot of KIELER SCCharts tool annotated with high-level user story for incremental interactive model-based hardware synthesis

(1) The textual representation of the model is written in SCT, the textual language of SCCharts. In the screenshot, AO is shown.

(2) The interactive compilation control view allows the user to select different M2M transformations. Transformations may depend on each other. The new *feature group* Circuit (lower left part of (2) in Fig. 9) contains the interactive incremental hardware synthesis presented in this paper.

(3) The user may inspect the source model and the results of the transformations, selected in step (2), in the visual browsing windows. (3a) shows the source model, which is AO in this case. Since the user selected the appropriate transformations in (2), (3b) illustrates the SSA version of the SCG corresponding to the source model. (3c) depicts the resulting hardware circuit. If the source model gets modified in the editor (1), all views get updated.

(4) The user may add simulation components in the execution manager view to configure a simulation. The selected transformation (2) serves as input for the simulation. While executing a simulation, for each tick, the active components of the visualized model will be highlighted in all model views. This improves the dynamic comprehensibility of the model instances, and hence, of the circuit.

(5) During the execution of a simulation, the user may set input variables and observe the reaction of the system. This can also be done automatically by loading traces of previous simulations.

4.1 SSA SCG Transformation

The target of the SCCharts data-flow approach is a sequentialized form of an SCG which only consists out of *assignments* and *conditionals* [18]. In sequentialized SCGs multiple writes to one and the same variable are possible. To solve data-flow dependencies if such a variable is read, the SCG is transformed into an SSA form. As defined elsewhere [15] a program is in SSA form if each variable is the target of exactly one assignment in the program text. In the transformation of sequentialized SCGs into SSA, each variable which is the target of multiple assignments becomes indexed. If at some point of execution a variable is read from, the value of the assignment with the highest index at this point of execution is used.

For the SSA SCG transformation only variables defined by the user are relevant w.r.t. SSA because automatically created guard variables are unique by definition. In sequentialized SCGs, assignments to variables depend on conditionals. The assignments are executed if the corresponding guard is true. Hence, the *else branch* of these conditionals does not have any nodes. Figure 10a depicts the sequential SCG of AO. As the first conditional node in this SCG shows, O shall not be modified if g0 is evaluated to false. Instead, it is desired that O still stores the unmodified value. The SSA transformation therefore adds assignment nodes on the *else branches*. If a condition is evaluated to false, those nodes assign the latest version of a variable. This is shown in Fig. 10b. If guard g0 in the first conditional node evaluates to false, O_1 is target of the assignment pre(O). This means the value of O from the previous tick is applied to O_1, which reflects the fact that in SCCharts, variables are static and hence persist across tick boundaries. Otherwise, O_1 is set to false. Analogously, if guard g2 in the second conditional node is evaluated to false, O is set to O_1 which is the latest unmodified instance of O at this point of execution. As observable, the depicted SSA SCG is not in classical SSA form. In general, a ϕ-function decides

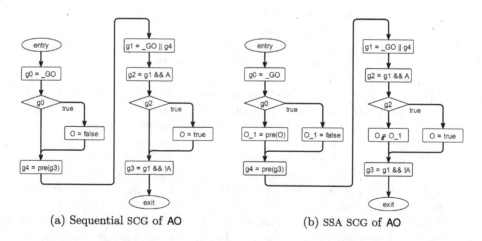

(a) Sequential SCG of AO   (b) SSA SCG of AO

Fig. 10. Transformation of the sequentialized SCG of AO into an SSA form

which version of an SSA variable is used after possible modifications on different instances. However, the ϕ-function that decides which instance of a variable is chosen can directly be resolved in the conditional branches because from both branches always only one is executed exclusively [9,16].

4.2 Circuit Transformation

According to Fig. 8, Step (5), the SSA SCG gets transformed into a circuit representation. SCCharts models are designed for reactive systems. The corresponding circuit is usually meant to be embedded in a reactive environment. Hence, sensor inputs are read from the environment, outputs are computed and then fed back to control the environment. Therefore, for each input (output) in the source model, a corresponding input (output) port is created in the circuit. The structure of the circuit is depicted in Fig. 11. It is divided in two parts. The first part, the Initialization Region, provides the *reset* and *tick* logic. The second part, the Program Logic Region, contains the transformation of the SSA SCG and represents the logic of the program.

The exact translation rules are depicted in Fig. 3. Each SCG node corresponds to data-flow equation which can be translated directly into hardware circuits. For example, an assignment of the form $x = e$ in the SCG gets translated into a Multiplexer (MUX) element. The responsible guard g, which is the composition of its predecessor guards g_{in}, decides whether or not e is assigned to x. Therefore, g is connected to the select pin of the MUX and x and e serve as inputs. x' then becomes the new actual instance of x.

4.3 Traceability

As depicted in the user story at the beginning of Sect. 4, the modeler may inspect the result of every transformation, including the final circuit. The elements of the graphical representation of a model are interactive. Each may be selected to trace its individual transformation history as explained in Sect. 3.1.

Figure 12 illustrates a side-by-side view of selected transformation steps. The modeler may select an arbitrary number of transformations. In the figure, the

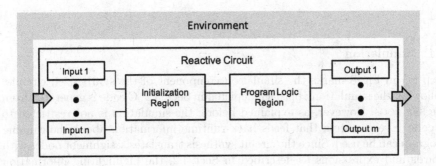

Fig. 11. The circuit and its regions in the context of the controlled environment

source model, the SSA SCG and the final circuit are selected. By selecting the g2 block in the circuit, the modeler sees the origin and transformation history of the g2 block. In this case, the block was created because of the assignment to g2 in the SSA SCG. The guard g2 guards the basic block (cf. Fig. 2c) and hence is indirectly created from the elements which are guarded by g2, namely state _S, the outgoing transition of _S and the assignment O = true.

As can be seen in the middle part of Fig. 12, g2 determines whether or not O is set to true, which is the case when the outgoing transformation from _S is taken (cf. Fig. 12). Otherwise, O is set to O_1, the previous instance of O, meaning the state of O stays unchanged. Inspecting the circuit in Fig. 12 reveals that guard g2 controls the MUX O. Therefore, the aforementioned selection of the O instance is directly visible in the circuit.

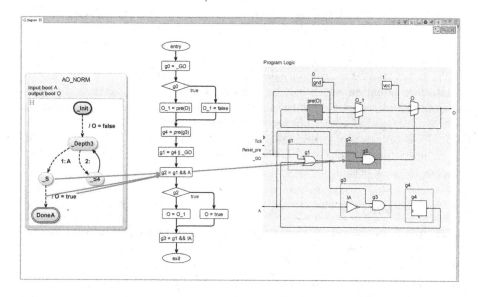

Fig. 12. Tracing of M2M transformations: Selecting the circuit block g2 in the circuit shows the origin in the intermediate and the source model. (Color figure online)

4.4   Simulation

Step (7) in Fig. 8 marks the simulation component of the synthesized circuits. Following the simulation approach depicted in Sect. 3.2, C code is generated from the SSA SCGs. However, as explained before, the simulation is not restricted to C code. Every system that feeds back runtime information about the running program can be used. Since the circuit synthesis translates assignment nodes with guards and expressions as described in Sect. 4.2, the highlighting information gained from the generated C code can be used for the highlighting of circuit components. In each tick, the C code delivers runtime informations of active guards and, hence, their basic blocks. The elements in the SSA SCGs and the circuits are highlighted according to this information. This corresponds to the end-to-end mapping of the tracing tree depicted in Fig. 7b in Sect. 3.1.

Figure 13 shows parts of the simulation of the AO example program. The highlighted nodes in the depicted SCG mark the active guards in two consecutive ticks in Fig. 13a and b. An assignment with orange colored background indicates that this guard is active. Figure 13a shows a non-initial tick in which A is set to false. Therefore, the final state has not been reached yet which is indicated by the highlighting of g3. Furthermore, the highlighting of g4 shows that this tick is non-initial because g4 stores the value of g3 from the last tick. Node g1 is active

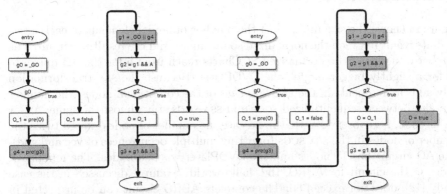

(a) Simulation step of AO with input A set to false

(b) Simulation step of AO with input A set to true

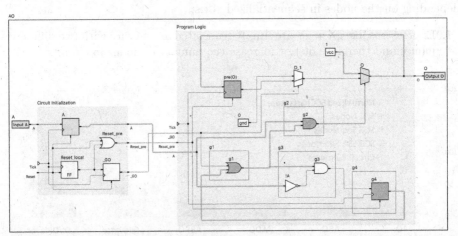

(c) Simulation step of the AO circuit with A set to true: All active elements, analogous to the SSA SCG, are highlighted in orange.

Fig. 13. Simulation visualization of AO (Color figure online)

in every tick. This node describes the guard for the basic block which contains the evaluation of input A. In Fig. 13b, the subsequent tick, A is set to true. Hence, the assignment g2 = g1 && A now evaluates to true. The highlighting of assignment O = true shows that the program reacts as desired.

The simulation of the second tick is also depicted in the circuit in Fig. 13c. All live wires and components are highlighted orange. As described before, g2 is the composition of g1 and A. g1 is either true at the beginning of the program, indicated by the _GO signal, or if register g4 is active. As A is set to true in this tick, guard g2 also becomes true and sets the selection input of MUX O which applies the voltage to the output. Hence, O is set to true.

5   Evaluation

Figure 14 shows the size in terms of the number of model elements of each intermediate result between the normalized source mode and the resulting circuit. The number of nodes of the normalized SCCharts reach from 5 for the AO model to 86 for a slightly bigger model, the DVDPlayer. Because the SSA transformation only adds assignments in the *else branches* of the conditional nodes, the number of nodes between sequentialized SCGs and SSA SCGs stay almost the same. As for the circuits, it is observable that in no case the number of nodes exceed twice the number of nodes in the SSA SCGs (omitting multiple occurrences of vcc and gnd). The AO circuit has 11 nodes and the DVDPlayer has 200 nodes. The number of nodes in the circuit for ABRO, the "hello world" example discussed in the case study [12], does not exceed 50. The complete ABRO circuit can be inspected in the thesis regarding interactive incremental hardware synthesis [16].

There are three different aspects which influence the scaling of circuits depending on the nodes in sequentialized SCGs:

1. Expressions like gX = gY are simply translated as one wire with two different names and therefore do not increase the number of nodes in circuits.

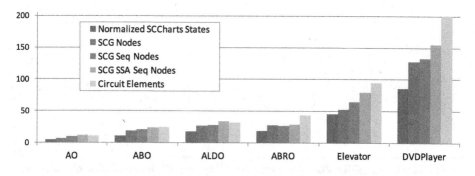

Fig. 14. Scaling of synthesized circuits compared to the corresponding SSA SCG and SCCharts depending on the number of nodes

2. Guard expressions like gX = gY || gZ produce as many logic gates as nested operator expressions exist. Notice that the pre operator results in the creation of a register that stores the value of the previous reaction. Depending on the number of concurrent regions in the SCChart, a *complex guard* [18], which is used for joining threads, may be more complex. For each pause statement per thread, another logic gate is required.

3. New assignment nodes on *else branches* in the SSA SCGs (cf. Sect. 4.1) do not increase the number of logic gates. The conditional still only needs one MUX as each MUX summarizes the assignment nodes from each conditional branch. This is the reason why, e. g., the ALDO circuit has fewer nodes than its sequentialized SCG.

6   Related Work

The close relation between compilation and modeling techniques has been observed quite early, e. g., by Steffen, who proposes to make use of *consistency models* to detect inconsistencies between different model descriptions, and relates this to giving a semantics to a programming language by translation into an intermediate language [19]. Since then, a number of modeling approaches have been developed that also address model compilation. For example, CINCO can automatically construct code generators from a given meta model [13]. Grundy et al. give a good overview of the current state and present MARAMA, which provides a set of mostly visual metatools for language specification and tool building, including synthesis [7]. One difference of these approaches and our proposal here is that we aim to (1) divide the synthesis of the human-authored artifact into the low-level result into rather small, in themselves conceptually simple steps, applied in a single, sequential pass, and to (2) make the intermediate transformation results accessible to the user, by automatically deriving well-readable graphical views of the model stages. Moreover, the separation of model and graphical view starts at the very beginning, as the human works on a textual model description, using all efficiency advantages of a textual editor and frameworks such as Xtext. This is in line with *pragmatic modeling*, which aims to free the user of tedious layout tasks involving a palette and manual place and route [6]. Lopes [10] studies the general specification of mappings and inspired the tracing SLIC extension. However, Lopes's approach considers the mapping specification between two meta models, where we also consider mappings between models of the same meta model.

Concerning our case study, the synthesis of hardware from SCCharts, the hardware synthesis from Statecharts [8] introduced by Drusinsky and Harel [4] uses Statecharts as behavioral HDL. The idea is to use single machines implementing finite state machines (FSMs). Since Statecharts allow non-deterministic behavior this approach is not taken into consideration for the hardware synthesis from SCCharts. Esterel [3] is a synchronous language tailored for the development of embedded reactive applications in hardware and software. Esterel programs can directly be translated into circuits [2]. Since SCCharts' SC MoC is a conservative extension of the classical synchronous MoC [21], the ideas of concurrent regions and the usage of registers to store the system state is adapted from Esterel's hardware synthesis. However, Esterel's hardware synthesis approach is a bit more involved than the synthesis from the SCG we propose here in that preemptions have already been transformed away when the SCG level is reached. Sequentially Constructive Esterel (SCEst), studied by Rathlev et al. [14], can be used to generate hardware circuits with our approach because the hardware synthesis can be directly applied to the SCG. Hence, we also provide a new route for circuit creation for Esterel. Johannsen [9] studied hardware synthesis for SCCharts before and translated SCCharts to VHDL. The ISE tool[2] then visualizes and simulates the circuit. This approach can also be pursued by other tools that are capable of describing FSMs. However, the interactive and incremental approach proposed here has no breaks in the toolchain and is integrated into the KIELER framework and thus uses KIELER layout and visualization. Therefore, no external tool is necessary. The traceability of the circuits behavior is supported since all intermediate transformations are visible. Additionally, SCCharts models can be compiled to software. Nevertheless, a comparison of the synthesis quality of classical hardware design tools with the approach presented here would be interesting future work.

Edwards [5] provides an overview of different approaches for hardware synthesis from C like languages and their limitations. Since SCCharts can be compiled to C or Java code, it is also possible to pursue these routes to generate hardware circuits. This would be particularly useful for *hostcode calls*, which are currently not included in our compiler.

7   Conclusions

The incremental interactive hardware synthesis integrates into the SCCharts SLIC approach. By adding two M2M transformations to the compiler chain, a modeler is able to generate hardware circuits for SCCharts models conveniently. Each transformation step, including the final circuit, can be simulated within the toolchain. During simulation, runtime information is visualized in all selected intermediate transformation results. Additionally, each model element can be traced back to the source model; there are no breaks in the toolchain. Summarized, the convenient creation of source models, automatic generation of hardware circuits, and fully integrated simulation and traceability of model elements are powerful tools for developing integrated circuits. The interactivity between these key component is crucial.

As mentioned in Sect. 3.1, our tracing framework only considers actual model instances. In the future we are going to extend the framework, so that it can handle textual results as well. Additionally, a dedicated simulation interpreter, as proposed in Sect. 3.2, could exemplify the advantages of the combination of SLIC and a tracing framework even further. Concerning synthesis, we plan to reintroduce support for VHDL and hostcode calls. Simulation and visualization

---

[2] http://www.xilinx.com.

of dedicated tools, such as the ISE tool, could be compared to the KIELER results and hence represent a new resource for validation.

References

1. André, C.: Semantics of SyncCharts. Technical Report ISRN I3S/RR-2003-24-FR, I3S Laboratory, Sophia-Antipolis, France April 2003
2. Berry, G.: Esterel on hardware. Philos. Trans. R..Soc. Lond. **339**, 87–104 (1992)
3. Berry, G.: The foundations of Esterel. In: Plotkin, G., Stirling, C., Tofte, M. (eds.) Proof, Language, and Interaction: Essays in Honour of Robin Milner, pp. 425–454. MIT Press, Cambridge (2000)
4. Drusinsky, D., Harel, D.: Using Statecharts for hardware description and synthesis. IEEE Trans. Comput. Aided Des. Integr. Circuits Syst. **8**(7), 798–807 (1989)
5. Edwards, S.A.: The challenges of hardware synthesis from c-like languages. In: Proceedings of the Conference on Design, Automation and Testin Europe, vol. 1, DATE 2005, pp. 66–67, Washington, DC, USA. IEEE Computer Society (2005)
6. Fuhrmann, H., Hanxleden, R.: On the pragmatics of model-based design. In: Choppy, C., Sokolsky, O. (eds.) Monterey Workshop 2008. LNCS, vol. 6028, pp. 116–140. Springer, Heidelberg (2010). doi:10.1007/978-3-642-12566-9_7
7. Grundy, J.C., Hosking, J., Li, K.N., Ali, N.M., Huh, J., Li, R.L.: Generating domain-specific visual language tools from abstract visual specifications. IEEE Trans. Softw. Eng. **39**(4), 487–515 (2013)
8. Harel, D.: Statecharts: A visual formalism for complex systems. Sci. Comput. Program. **8**(3), 231–274 (1987)
9. Johannsen, G.: Hardwaresynthese aus SCCharts. Master thesis, Kiel University, Department of Computer Science. http://rtsys.informatik.uni-kiel.de/biblio/downloads/theses/gjo-mt.pdf
10. Lopes, D., Hammoudi, S., Bézivin, J., Jouault, F.: Mapping specification in MDA: from theory to practice. In: Konstantas, D., Bourrières, J.-P., Léonard, M., Boudjlida, N. (eds). Interoperability of Enterprise Software and Applications - INTEROP-ESA, pp. 253–264. Springer, New York (2006)
11. Motika, C., Fuhrmann, H., von Hanxleden, R.: Semantics and execution of domain specific models. In: 2nd Workshop Methodische Entwicklung von Modellierungswerkzeugen (MEMWe 2010) INFORMATIK 2010, GI-Edition - Lecture Notes in Informatics (LNI), pp. 891–896, Leipzig, Germany, September 2010. Bonner Köllen Verlag (2010)
12. Motika, C., Smyth, S., Hanxleden, R.: Compiling SCCharts — a case-study on interactive model-based compilation. In: Margaria, T., Steffen, B. (eds.) ISoLA 2014. LNCS, vol. 8802, pp. 461–480. Springer, Heidelberg (2014). doi:10.1007/978-3-662-45234-9_32
13. Naujokat, S., Traonouez, L.-M., Isberner, M., Steffen, B., Legay, A.: Leveraging applications of formal methods, verification and validation. In: Technologies for Mastering Change: 6th International Symposium, ISoLA 2014, Imperial, Corfu, Greece, 8–11 October 2014, Proceedings, Part I, chapter Domain-Specific Code Generator Modeling: A Case Study for Multi-faceted Concurrent Systems, pp. 481–498. Springer, Heidelberg (2014)
14. Rathlev, K., Smyth, S., Motika, C., von Hanxleden, R., Mendler, M.: SCEst: sequentially constructive Esterel. In: Proceedings of the 13th ACM-IEEE International Conference on Formal Methods and Models for System Design, MEMOCODE 2015, Austin, TX, USA, September 2015

15. Rosen, B.K., Wegman, M.N., Zadeck, F.K.: Global value numbers and redundant computations. In: Proceedings of the 15th ACM SIGPLAN-SIGACT Symposium on Principles of Programming Languages, POPL 1988, pp. 12–27. ACM, New York (1988)
16. Rybicki, F.: Interactive incremental hardware synthesis for SCCharts. Bachelor thesis, Kiel University, Department of Computer Science. http://rtsys.informatik. uni-kiel.de/~biblio/downloads/theses/fry-bt.pdf
17. Schneider, C., Spönemann, M., von Hanxleden, R.: Just model! - Putting automatic synthesis of node-link-diagrams into practice. In: Proceedings of the IEEE Symposium on Visual Languages and Human-Centric Computing, VL/HCC 2013, San Jose, CA, USA, pp. 75–82, 15–19 September 2013
18. Smyth, S., Motika, C., von Hanxleden, R.: A data-flow approach for compiling the sequentially constructive language (SCL). In: 18. Kolloquium Programmiersprachen und Grundlagen der Programmierung (KPS 2015), Pörtschach, Austria, 5–7 October 2015
19. Steffen, B.: Unifying models. In: Reischuk, R., Morvan, M. (eds.) STACS 1997. LNCS, vol. 1200, pp. 1–20. Springer, Heidelberg (1997). doi:10.1007/BFb0023444
20. von Hanxleden, R., Duderstadt, B., Motika, C., Smyth, S., Mendler, M., Aguado, J., Mercer, S., O'Brien, O.: SCCharts: Sequentially Constructive Statecharts for safety-critical applications. Technical Report 1311, Christian-Albrechts-Universität zu Kiel, Department of Computer Science, ISSN 2192–6247, December 2013
21. von Hanxleden, R., Duderstadt, B., Motika, C., Smyth, S., Mendler, M., Aguado, J., Mercer, S., O'Brien, O.: SCCharts: Sequentially Constructive Statecharts for safety-critical applications. In: Proceedings of ACM SIGPLAN Conference on Programming Language Design and Implementation, PLDI 2014, Edinburgh, UK, June 2014. ACM (2014)
22. von Hanxleden, R., Mendler, M., Aguado, J., Duderstadt, B., Fuhrmann, I., Motika, C., Mercer, S., O'Brien, O., Roop, P.: Sequentially Constructive Concurrency–a conservative extension of the synchronous model of computation. ACM Trans. Embedded Comput. Syst. 13(4s), 144:1–144:26 (2014). Special Issue on Applications of Concurrency to System Design

Towards Semantically Integrated Models and Tools for Cyber-Physical Systems Design

Peter Gorm Larsen[1]([⊠]), John Fitzgerald[2], Jim Woodcock[3], René Nilsson[1], Carl Gamble[2], and Simon Foster[3]

[1] Department of Engineering, Aarhus University, Aarhus, Denmark
{pgl,rn}@eng.au.dk
[2] School of Computing Science, Newcastle University, Newcastle upon Tyne, UK
{john.fitzgerald,carl.gamble}@ncl.ac.uk
[3] Department of Computer Science, University of York, York, UK
{jim.woodcock,simon.foster}@york.ac.uk

Abstract. We describe an approach to the model-based engineering of embedded and cyber-physical systems, based on the semantic integration of diverse discipline-specific notations and tools. Using the example of a small unmanned aerial vehicle, we explain the need for multiple notations and collaborative modelling. Learning from experience with binary co-modelling based on a bespoke operational semantics, we describe current work delivering an extended approach that enables integration of multiple models and tools in a consistent tool chain, founded on an extensible semantic framework exploiting the Unifying Theories of Programming.

1 Introduction

In Cyber-Physical Systems (CPSs), computing processes interact closely with physical systems and humans. Examples range from networked embedded systems to large-scale applications such as distributed transport systems. The effective design of dependable CPSs requires methods and tools that bring together diverse engineering disciplines. Without these it would be difficult to gain confidence in the system-level consequences of design decisions made in any one domain, and it would be challenging to manage trade-offs between them. How, then, can we support such multidisciplinary design with semantically well-founded approaches?

We start from the view that disciplines such as software, mechatronic and control engineering have evolved notations and theories that are tailored to their needs, and that it is undesirable to suppress this diversity by enforcing uniform general-purpose models. Our goal is to achieve a practical integration of diverse formalisms at the semantic level, and to realise the benefits in integrated tool chains. To the CPS engineer, the system of interest includes both computational and physical elements, so the foundations, methods and tools of CPS engineering should incorporate both the discrete-event (DE) models of computational processes, and the continuous-value and continuous-time (CT) formalisms of physical engineering.

T. Margaria and B. Steffen (Eds.): ISoLA 2016, Part II, LNCS 9953, pp. 171–186, 2016.
DOI: 10.1007/978-3-319-47169-3_13

Our initial approach is to support the development of collaborative models (*co-models*) containing DE and CT elements expressed in diverse notations, and to support their analysis by means of co-simulation based on a reconciled operational semantics of the individual notations' simulators. This enables exploration of the design space and allows relatively straightforward adoption in businesses that are unfamiliar with formal methods. Our current work extends this approach with co-simulation of extensible groups of semantically diverse models, and at the same time the semantic foundations are extended using Unifying Theories of Programming (UTP) to permit analysis using advanced tools.

We are not unique in proposing co-models as a solution to the problem of modelling multi-domain systems, the HybridSim [29] tool chain, supports importing existing system components from multi-domains into SysML blocks [27], where Functional Mock-up Units (FMUs) and configuration scripts can be generated and co-simulated. CPSs are also modelled as hybrid systems, including techniques such as hybrid statecharts [20] and hybrid automata [1], where finite control graphs describe discrete behaviours and differential equations describe continuous behaviours. More recently, several languages have been proposed to describe hybrid systems and to support simulation and verification and a survey of these is presented by Carloni et al. [6].

The challenge of providing semantic foundations for CPSs that allow the development of comprehensive and integrated formal models is widely acknowledged [4,23]. The need for rigorous modelling foundations to ensure safe CPSs and the importance of well-founded semantic meta-models for CPSs with the ability to model and compare heterogeneous computational models have been identified [7], and the Ptolemy framework, with its actor-based model, proposed as a solution. Our UTP approach similarly provides a uniform notation for computational models in the hybrid relational calculus, with *CyPhyCircus* providing actor-style concurrency. Other semantic approaches to CPS modelling include MontiArc, which is given a denotational semantics in [16] and a semantic agent framework for CPS.

We first introduce a small case study based on the control of a quadrotor Unmanned Aerial Vehicle (UAV) in Sect. 2, demonstrating the merits of specialist notations for DE and CT modelling of system elements. Using this as a running example, we show how a single DE model in the notation VDM-RT and a CT model in the 20-sim tool can be successfully integrated in a co-model (Sect. 3). We then describe our current work extending this approach to accommodate more diverse component models, and to better integrate co-modelling in the full development toolchain (Sect. 4). We discuss our approach to providing integrated semantic foundations needed to underpin such co-modelling (Sect. 5) before reviewing related work and looking forward (Sect. 6).

2   Example: UAV Control

We consider the model of a small quadrotor UAV, which involves software, electrical and mechanical domains [15]. The controller is implemented on an embedded device with discrete logic, while the electronics and physical dynamics are

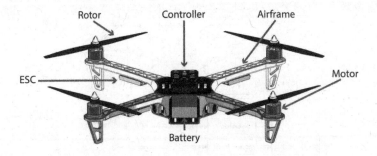

Fig. 1. Main components of a quadrotor UAV

described in terms of differential equations over continuous values. We would thus expect to have a CT model of the physical dynamics and a DE model of the control application. We use VDM-RT as the DE notation and 20-sim as the CT notation; both are described in [9]. VDM-RT is an extension of the Vienna Development Method's modelling language with features for object-orientation, concurrency and real-time computation, including the distribution of processes to virtual CPUs [28]. 20-sim is a package for modelling and simulating complex physical systems [2,21], which provides an abstract representation of differential equations. Iconic diagrams with flow ports, adopted from bond graphs, are used to describe both the electronics and mechanics of the propulsion system, whereas rigid body dynamics are modelled directly with differential equations.

Our UAV (Fig. 1) consists of an airframe, sensors, actuators, controller and battery. Sensors include accelerometers, gyroscopes and GPS. The actuators are four Electronic Speed Controllers (ESCs), motors and rotors. The overall system controller reads sensor data and steers the UAV to a desired state by adjusting the set points of each motor. The desired state is usually given by a pilot and retrieved through telemetry.

2.1   Modelling the Physical Components

The CT model of the UAV, Fig. 2, shows the main components of the model along with their relationships. From the diagram we can trace a loop formed by the controller → motor controllers → motors → rotors → rigid body dynamics → sensors → controller. The controller itself is modelled in the DE environment, so the purpose of the controller block here is to contain the declarations defining the variables we expect the DE controller to set and also those monitored variables we want to expose to the DE controller.

Following the loop round from the controller first we arrive at the motor controllers and Fig. 3 depicts expanded 20-sim models of the ESC, motor and rotor using iconic diagrams. The ESC is represented by a controlled voltage source and the motor is modelled as an ideal DC motor with electrical parasitic components, mechanical losses and inertia. This construction allows the modeller to specify relatively simple equations for each subcomponent, such as Ohm's law for a resistor: $U = R * I$. By assigning indifferent causality to all flow ports, an

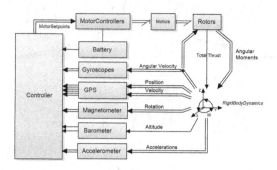

Fig. 2. Top level of the CT model showing connections of the main model elements

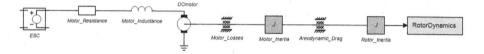

Fig. 3. Part of the CT model of quadrotor UAV propulsion system

explicit model is achieved, enabling the 20-sim tool to calculate the resulting differential equations.

In cases where the dynamics are not easily described by composition of simple components such as in the rigid body model of the UAV, differential equations are recorded directly. For example, angular acceleration is calculated with a differential equation, since it incorporates gyroscopic effects (Eqs. 1 and 2):

$$\mathbf{a}_{ang} = \mathbf{I}^{-1} * (-\mathbf{v}_{ang} \times (\mathbf{I} * \mathbf{v}_{ang})) + \mathbf{t} \tag{1}$$

$$\mathbf{v}_{ang} = \int \mathbf{a}_{ang} \tag{2}$$

where $\mathbf{a}_{ang}$ and $\mathbf{v}_{ang}$ are angular accelerations and velocities respectively (three-dimensional); $\mathbf{t}$ is the angular moments and $\mathbf{I}$ is the rotational inertia matrix. These equations are easily represented in 20-sim's textual notation as follows:

$$a = \text{inverse}(I) * (-\text{cross}(v,(I*v)) + t);$$
$$v = \text{int}(a);$$

The output from the rigid body dynamics is processed by five blocks, each representing one of the sensor components possessed by the UAV. The function of these blocks is to take the raw dynamic properties of the UAV body, such as linear and rotational acceleration, velocities and positions and to process them to give sensors outputs that are consistent with those of the real hardware sensors on the UAV. The sensor models here, such as the magnetometer shown in Fig. 4, are ideal in the sense that their outputs do not contain error or exhibit fault behaviour as described in [9].

Iconic diagrams let the engineer build a model by connecting blocks that represent dominant physical elements; blocks contain equations representing how

```
parameters
  // Magnetic Sensitivity, default for the HMC5883L Digital Compass (gauss/LSB)
  real magSens = 1090;
  // Earths magnetic field at Aarhus, DK: {North + | South - , East + | West - , Down + | Up -}
  // From http://www.ngdc.noaa.gov/geomag-web/#igrfwmm
  real earthMagField [3] = [16900.1; 740.9; 47304.5] {nT};
variables
  real quadMagField [3];
equations
  // Effect of the magnetic field converted to the body frame
  quadMagField = Rotation*earthMagField;
  // Scaling and sensitivity
  MagnetometerOut = quadMagField/100000*magSens;
```

Fig. 4. Magnetometer component of the CT model

those elements affect the effort and flow. This is "what we want to model". The above equations are not, however, suitable for simulation and 20-sim manipulates them, according to the connections between their flow ports, into a form that can be simulated using one of the integration methods offered by the tool. Importantly, all elements connected by power bonds are considered when generating the new set of equations and so interactions and feedback between components that may be on opposite corners of the model are included; so we arrive at a set of equations that represent the "dynamic behaviour of what we want to model".

If the engineer were to attempt to model this system using a DE environment such as VDM-RT then they are obliged to do two things. First, instead of being able to think about the behaviour of individual elements, they must generate the equations that represent the dynamic behaviour of the whole system, including feedback, manually. This dynamic system would change each time a component is introduced or removed from the system they are modelling. Second, the engineer is obliged to construct numerical solvers that implement one or more of the integration methods required to generate continuous results. Thus, while it is not impossible to model such a dynamic system using a DE environment it is much more practical to do so using a CT tool. The iconic diagrams help manage the complexity of generating suitable dynamic models by allowing the engineer to only have to think about the dominant elements and their connections.

2.2   Modelling the Controller

The control application on a quadrotor UAV has two major objectives: first it must keep the UAV stable in the air and second it must react to pilot input. Figure 5 shows a block diagram of the control application model. Here the control loop from Fig. 2 is completed with the DE blocks sensor data processing → control architecture → motor control. Sensor fusion and filtering are performed on the input data from the sensors to obtain accurate estimates of angular and translational acceleration, velocity and position. These estimates are used in the control architecture along with processed pilot inputs to calculate control signals for the motor control block. These control signals are expressions of angular accelerations and total thrust, which decouples the control architecture from the motor/rotor configuration. A UAV can have from 3 to 16 rotors and,

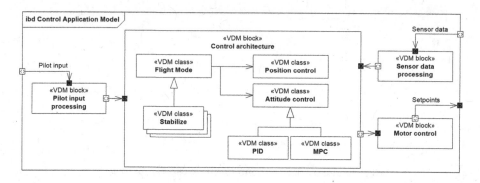

Fig. 5. High level block diagram of the control application model

with proper transformations in the motor control block, the control architecture can be reused for any number of rotors.

The control architecture block is shown inside a small class diagram, including flight modes and position and attitude controllers. The flight modes are used with a strategy design pattern, such that the pilot is able to change flight mode in-flight. Each of the flight mode implementations may use both the position and an attitude controller. The position controller is based on Proportional Integral Derivative (PID) control, whereas two alternative attitude controllers are modelled (and subsequently implemented): a PID-based and a Model Predictive Control (MPC) [5] based controller. With the use of inheritance the two controllers are made interchangeable, enabling comparison through co-simulations by comparing the overall system performance.

Figure 6 shows a code snippet, from the position controller, with a type declaration and an operation, which calculates the bearing between two vector positions. This illustrates the use of type invariants and operation pre-conditions in VDM. A type invariant is a condition that must be true for all instances of that particular type throughout the entire model execution, whereas a precondition needs only to be true when the given operation is called. Similarly post-conditions can be added to operations to further improve the documentation of the precise properties of the model. If either an invariant or a pre- or post-condition is violated a runtime error is thrown, enabling the developer to correct the faulty behaviour of the model.

One of the advantages of using VDM-RT with the Overture tool compared to other formal modelling tools is the support for calling external Java and native C++ libraries. This is exploited in the modelling of the MPC controller, where an external C++ optimisation library is used. This library is also used in the realisation code, which is deployed to the real UAV. An increase in model fidelity is thereby achieved. VDM-RT's built-in notion of time makes it easy to create a soft real-time scheduling mechanism. In the control application model the main control loop and sensor readings are scheduled. Sensor readings are scheduled based on the availability of data from the different types of sensor. Figure 7 shows the controller model being deployed onto a user defined CPU, this allows the

```
values
  MAX_BEARING_CD = 36000;

types
  public Bearing = real
    inv b == b >= 0 and b < MAX_BEARING_CD;

operations
  public getBearingCd: Vector`Vector3 * Vector`Vector3 ==> Bearing
  getBearingCd(origin,destination) ==
    let bearing = Vector`atan2(destination.y - origin.y, destination.x - origin.x) in
      return AP_Math`wrap(AP_Math`radToCentiDegrees(bearing), 0, MAX_BEARING_CD)
  pre origin <> destination;
```

Fig. 6. Pre condition and type invariant in VDM-RT

```
instance variables
  public static arduCopter: ArduCopter := new ArduCopter();
  cpu : CPU := new CPU(<FP>, 168E6); -- PixHawk: 168MHz Cortex M4F CPU

operations
  public ArduPilot: () ==> ArduPilot
  ArduPilot() ==
    cpu.deploy(arduCopter, "ArduCopter");
```

Fig. 7. Defining CPU and deploying a controller model in VDM-RT

execution time of each instruction to be simulated. The main control loop is run at 400 Hz for the PID-based attitude control, while the MPC controller could only be run at 100 Hz in the realisation, as it requires far more computation.

The DE model architecture is presented here using SysML[1], reflecting the object-oriented class structure of the VDM-RT model. This structure also lends itself to the generation of product source code. Apart from the structure, there are several reasons why constructing the controller in DE is preferable to a CT model. 20-sim does support the definition of *code* blocks with models, there are no language differences between these block and the normal *equation* blocks, the only different being that the statements are not reordered to improve simulation speed, and so the order of equation execution and branching statement evaluation is explicit. This permits the definition of "simple" controllers, but there are limitations that make more complex controllers challenging.

The argument for a DE model of a controller mirrors that for using a CT formalism to model the physics. The UAV operating modes are described in VDM-RT using a *modal controller pattern* [14], and standard inheritance allows the alternate PID and MPC motor controller implementations to be easily described. Both are much more complex in 20-sim, which lacks explicit support for these features. Similarly, VDM-RT's support for rich data structures such as mappings, sets and sequences allows the description of more sophisticated control than the CT formalism of 20-sim with its basic boolean, numeric and matrix data types. The CT formalism lacks a method or function call concept, requiring calculations at the call point, increasing the cognitive workload in understanding and maintaining the controller. Finally, the explicit time budget for each instruction in the DE model allows us to offer evidence regarding the real-time performance of the controller.

---

[1] Figure 5 is not a well-formed SysML block diagram: we have condensed the presentation for reasons of space.

3   Binary Co-modelling and Co-simulation: The Crescendo Tool

In this section we describe co-modelling and co-simulation in which DE models are developed in VDM-RT supported by the Overture/VDM simulator [22] and CT models are developed in the 20-sim tool [21].

3.1   Crescendo Framework

The DESTECS project[2] developed methods and tools for co-modelling and co-simulation, based on co-models consisting DE models in VDM-RT and CT models in 20-sim [3]. These were embodied in the Crescendo tool[3] based on a master-slave architecture with the Overture and 20-sim simulators acting as slaves. Co-simulation was defined by a reconciled operational semantics [8]. The technology and industry experience are described in [9].

In a Crescendo co-model the interface between DE and CT models (here called a *contract*) identifies the shared features of the two constituent models. These are: *design parameters* that are kept constant in one simulation; *events* which are typically zero crossings[4]; and *variables* that are passed between models as they run in their respective simulators during a co-simulation.

The Crescendo tool is structured as in Fig. 8, where the master co-simulation engine coordinates the DE simulator (realised in the Overture/VDM tool [22]) and the CT simulator (realised by the 20-sim solvers). Based on the contract, the co-simulation engine exchanges data between the simulators and produce logs of results. In order to explore potential fault scenarios it is possible also to include scripts that can activate latent errors in the constituent models.

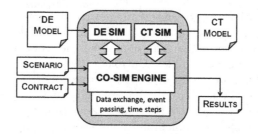

Fig. 8. Tool-oriented perspective of a co-model.

3.2   UAV Co-model

The UAV co-model is connected via a contract that in reality would fall inside the embedded controller. On the CT side we find the elements of the physical world including the motors, framework, battery and sensors, and on the DE side we find the model of the controller. The monitored variables in this case are the outputs of the sensor devices (gyroscopes, accelerometers and GPS) and the controlled variables are the set points for each motor. The contract and models abstract the details of how physical sensors compute their values and also how the ESC senses motor motion and controls the power it feeds to them.

Model-based design will be ineffective if model and realisation behaviour do not align; effort is therefore directed into achieving a known level of model fidelity. For example, by comparing co-simulations and real-time test, an average deviation of 2 degrees has been achieved for the attitude angles; in practice dynamic response is at least as important as such static measures. Crescendo's scripting feature allows emulation of predefined user input. Figure 9 shows both the co-simulated and measured (test) response of the UAV to scripted reference angle changes.

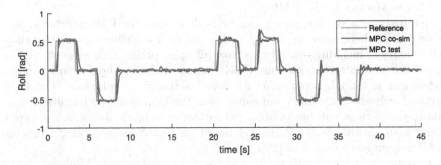

Fig. 9. Graph comparing of the modelled and actual roll response of the UAV to a reference input.

3.3   Evaluation of Crescendo

Crescendo has been successfully used to model embedded systems ranging from line following robots through to dredging excavators, and demonstrable gains in development effort have been seen through a reduction in the number of physical prototypes needed to converge to a final design [9]. However, this co-simulation technology is deficient in two significant areas. First, it only supports bipartite co-models using a single DE model in VDM-RT and a single CT model in 20-sim. The semantic foundations are limited to an operational semantics developed for these two formalisms, and so there is significant effort in modelling larger and more complex CPSs that may have a greater variety of constituent models. Second, it stands alone in a development process and assumes the engineer both understands what they wish to model before starting, and has external means to analyse the results of simulation. These concerns formed the basis for developing an integrated tool chain in the ongoing INTO-CPS project[5].

4   N-ary Multi-modelling: The INTO-CPS Tool Chain

In order to address the limitations of the binary co-modelling approach based on bespoke operational semantics, as embodied in Crescendo, we are developing a more open *integrated tool chain* to allow n-ary co-simulation of a wider range of model types. In order to facilitate this, we develop an extensible semantic foundation using UTP. Figure 10 gives a graphic overview of the toolchain, which is being developed in INTO-CPS.

In the INTO-CPS tool chain, requirements and CPS architectures may be expressed using SysML. We define an architectural profile that allows cyber and physical system elements to be identified such that each of these elements corresponds to a constituent model. From each element, we generate an interface following the Functional Mockup Interface (FMI) standard[6]. In our approach, which is inspired by HybridSim, the tools in which the constituent models are developed can then import these interfaces and export conformant executable *Functional Mockup Units (FMUs)*.

Heterogeneous system models can be built around the FMI interfaces, permitting these heterogeneous *multi-models* to be co-simulated, and to allow static analysis, including model checking (of appropriate abstractions). A Co-simulation Orchestration Engine (COE) manages the co-simulation of multi-models and is built by combining existing co-simulation solutions. The COE permits hardware-in-the-loop and software-in-the-loop analysis. Results of multiple co-simulations can be collated, permitting systematic design space exploration, and allowing test automation based on test cases generated from the SysML requirement diagrams [25].

To date, the CPS SysML profile has been demonstrated in Modelio[7]. FMI-conformant constituent models have been produced from VDM-RT, and the CT formalisms 20-sim and OpenModelica [13][8].

Returning to the UAV case study, the INTO-CPS tool chain will support multiple improvements over the Crescendo version of the model. The first of these is the support for more than two FMUs in a single co-model. This greatly reduces the workload when constructing a model of a swarm of identical UAVs as it is possible to create multiple instances of the UAV controller and physics models. The resulting swarm of UAVs then interact via one or more FMUs representing communications and the physical world. The second benefit is that FMUs can be created using any tool that exports a compatible FMU and so could allow the generation of a terrain model from a mapping tool. The final benefit is the possibility to use third party or proprietary FMUs as part of the

---

[5] http://into-cps.au.dk/.

[6] FMI essentially defines a standardised interface to be used in computer simulations to develop complex CPSs.

[7] http://www.modelio.org/.

[8] https://www.openmodelica.org/.

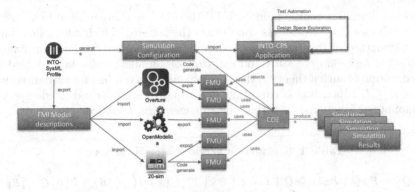

Fig. 10. The current INTO-CPS Tool Chain

simulation, in an industrial context this would allow competing organisations to share models to develop the UAV swarm without revealing sensitive details of, for example, how their controller performs key tasks such as route finding.

5   A Unified Semantic Approach

We are developing unified foundations for the INTO-CPS languages using a framework called Unifying Theories of Programming (UTP) [19], that supports the description and unification of formal semantics for heterogeneous modelling languages. The core notation of the UTP is the alphabetised predicate calculus, that consists of the usual operators of a first-order logic, ranging over the variables of a particular model. UTP is then based around the idea that any program or model can be represented by such a predicate. For example, the operators of an imperative program can be denoted by dividing the alphabet $\alpha(P)$ of a predicate P into input variables x and output variables x'. Imperative programming operators can then be given predicative interpretations, for example assignment $x := v$ can be formally denoted by predicate $x' = v \land y' = y$ where y represents all other variables in the alphabet.

Unification of semantic models is achieved through isolation of "UTP theories" that describe the foundational paradigms, such as real-time, object orientation, or concurrency, and thus act as semantic "building blocks" [10]. Describing various language semantics in terms of these building blocks, also allows one to link them through the common theoretical factors. For example, we could link theories of discrete and continuous real-time through an appropriate discretisation. Combination of several UTP theories then allows production of denotational semantics for a particular language. Then we can derive other semantic models, such as operational or algebraic semantics, which can be used as input for the development of tools. This will then ensure the well-foundedness of the INTO-CPS tool-chain, by allowing the evidence of several tools to be soundly composed. Our overall approach to semantics in INTO-CPS is thus to develop UTP theories that will provide the semantic building blocks, and then use these to produce formal semantic models. UTP theories are characterised by observational variables and healthiness conditions, the latter of which act as invariants on the structure of the theory. For example we have observational variables ti and ti' that represent the start and end time of a model's behaviour. A healthiness condition of such a theory is that time should proceed in a forward direction, that is $ti \leq ti'$. Healthiness conditions are usually characterised as idempotent and monotone functions, such that their images form a lattice.

Table 1. Signature of hybrid relational calculus

$$P, Q ::= P \mathbin{;} Q \mid P \lhd B \rhd Q \mid x := e \mid P^* \mid P^\omega \mid \langle \dot{\underline{x}} = f(t, \underline{x}) \mid B \rangle \mid P[B]Q \mid \llbracket P \rrbracket$$

CPSs are usually represented by hybrid computational models consisting of both discrete and continuous variables, and thus we first develop a UTP theory of hybrid relations [11]. In addition to discrete input and output variables this theory also provides support for continuous variable trajectories $\underline{x} : \mathbb{R} \to \mathbb{R}$. The healthiness condition for this theory is called **HCT**: it ensures that variables are piecewise continuous over a particular interval of time. The signature of the theory is shown in Table 1. It includes the standard operators of the relational calculus like sequential composition $P \mathbin{;} Q$, if-then-else conditional $P \lhd b \rhd Q$, assignment $x := v$, finite iteration P^*, and infinite iteration P^ω. Additionally it has three operators for continuous modelling. $\langle F_n \mid B \rangle$ allows the behaviour of a continuous variables to be described by a system of differential and algebraic equations. $P[B]Q$ represents the evolution of a continuous system P which is preempted when condition B is satisfied by the continuous variable valuations, following which Q is activated. Finally, $\llbracket P \rrbracket$ is adapted from Duration Calculus [33], and states that the predicate P holds continuously over the present time interval. The final operator can be used to logically specify the behaviour of a continuous system. We exemplify the calculus with a simple example based on the classic bouncing ball.

$$h, v := 2, 0 \mathbin{;} \left(\left\langle \dot{\underline{h}} = \underline{v}; \dot{\underline{v}} = -9.81 \right\rangle [\underline{h} < 0] \, v := -v' \cdot 0.8) \right)^\omega$$

The height and velocity, h and v, are initially set to 2 and 0 respectively and the evolution of the differential equations begin. When the condition $\underline{h} < 0$ becomes true, then the evolution is preempted and an assignment is executed that reverses the velocity and applies a dampening factor. Finally the whole system iterates. We have used our hybrid relational calculus to give a semantics to a subset of Modelica, which elaborates the latter's event handling system [11]. Moreover we have mechanised the calculus in our Isabelle based theorem prover for UTP [12], which enables automated proof about hybrid relations.

Ultimately we will use this hybrid relational calculus to produce a formal language into which the various notations used on this project can be soundly converted, and appropriate analysis performed. This will then allow the integration of the heterogeneous models and a formal description of their co-simulation in FMI. Real-time, concurrency, and rich-state modelling have already been given substantial study in the UTP within the context of the *Circus* language family [24]. *Circus* is a formal modelling language that combines the constructs of the CSP process specification language [18] for modelling concurrent systems with rich-state as provided by the Z notation [32]. *Circus* has been extended to enable specification of discrete real-time systems by adding constructs for modelling waiting states, timeouts, and deadlines in languages *CircusTime* [30] and *CML* [31].

The semantic model of *CML* will be applied to give a semantics to the real-time CPUs and threads of VDM-RT. We will model each thread, object, CPU, and bus from VDM-RT as different types of *Circus* processes. A thread, for example, will have a collection of local state variables to be synchronised with the corresponding object process variable store, by the CPU process, when sufficient time has passed. However, the existing variants of *Circus* provide only discrete time modelling, and so for INTO-CPS we are creating a further extension of *Circus* to enable modelling of CPSs in a language called *CyPhyCircus* based on our hybrid relational calculus. This will enable the description of concurrent interacting systems, as in FMI. Moreover, we will allow the modelling of the real-time language aspects by taking direction from Timed CSP [26], and the system dynamics aspects from Hybrid CSP [17].

Figure 11 illustrates the approach, whereby models described in VDM-RT, Modelica, and 20-sim can be soundly mapped to *CyPhyCircus* processes that represent the individual FMUs. The composition of these different models, as described by FMI, is given a semantics in terms of CSP processes that provide channels to represent stepping forward and otherwise manipulating an FMU. In addition to enabling their sound unification, the use of *CyPhyCircus* as a lingua franca also enables application of various verification technologies, such as Isabelle for theorem proving.

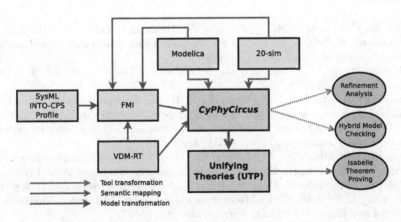

Fig. 11. INTO-CPS foundations through *CyPhyCircus*

6 Conclusions

We have presented an argument for formal model-based CPS engineering to allow the use of diverse notations, unifying them at a semantic level. The DE and CT environments have appropriate abstractions for modelling software and physical systems respectively that allow the engineer to think about what they want to model more than what form it needs for simulation. We have also shown that such a co-model can produce a result that is close to the response of the physical device. Semantic integration of diverse notations has been shown to be beneficial even for binary co-modelling with only an operational semantics for co-simulation. However, we have identified the need to scale to n-ary multi-models, and to provide the corresponding extensible semantic framework. We have shown how these features may be delivered through the use of FMI-based co-simulation in an integrated tool chain, and through the use of UTP as a vehicle for supporting theory development, enabling a range of analytic tools.

We also observe that while semantically sound co-modelling is vital for the development of dependable CPSs, it is certainly not enough on its own. There is a need for integrated development methods and tools that span from requirements through to the analysis of simulation results and the generation of software source code and test automation. Critically in this complex multi-model environment, there is a need for efficiently managing the traceability of design artefacts, both for the change impact analysis and for the managing of the evidence on which the dependability cases for CPSs will rely.

Acknowledgments. Crescendo and Symphony were developed in DESTECS (FP7, 248134), and COMPASS (FP7, 287829). Our current work is partially supported by the INTO-CPS project (Horizon 2020, 664047). We would like to thank all the participants of those projects for their efforts making this a reality.

References

1. Alur, R., Courcoubetis, C., Halbwachs, N., Henzinger, T.A., Ho, P.H., Nicollin, X., Olivero, A., Sifakis, J., Yovine, S.: The algorithmic analysis of hybrid systems. Theoret. Comput. Sci. **138**, 3–34 (1995)
2. van Amerongen, J.: Dynamical Systems for Creative Technology. Controllab Products, Enschede (2010)
3. Broenink, J.F., Larsen, P.G., Verhoef, M., Kleijn, C., Jovanovic, D., Pierce, K., Wouters, F.: Design support and tooling for dependable embedded control software. In: Proceedings of Serene 2010 International Workshop on Software Engineering for Resilient Systems, pp. 77–82. ACM, April 2010
4. Broy, M., Cengarle, M.V., Geisberger, E.: Cyber-physical systems: imminent challenges. In: Calinescu, R., Garlan, D. (eds.) Monterey Workshop 2012. LNCS, vol. 7539, pp. 1–28. Springer, Heidelberg (2012). doi:10.1007/978-3-642-34059-8_1
5. Camacho, E.F., Alba, C.B.: Model Predictive Control. Advanced Textbooks in Control and Signal Processing. Springer, London (2007)
6. Carloni, L.P., Passerone, R., Pinto, A., Sangiovanni-Vincentelli, A.L.: Languages and tools for hybrid systems design. Found. Trends Electron. Des. Autom. **1**(1/2) (2006)

7. Derler, P., Lee, E.A., Sangiovanni-Vincentelli, A.: Modeling cyber-physical systems. Proc. IEEE (special issue on CPS) **100**(1), 13–28 (2012)
8. Fitzgerald, J., Larsen, P.G., Pierce, K., Verhoef, M.: A formal approach to collaborative modelling and co-simulation for embedded systems. Math. Struct. Comput. Sci. **23**(4), 726–750 (2013)
9. Fitzgerald, J., Larsen, P.G., Verhoef, M. (eds.): Collaborative Design for Embedded Systems - Co-modelling and Co-simulation. Springer, Heidelberg (2014)
10. Foster, S., Miyazawa, A., Woodcock, J., Cavalcanti, A., Fitzgerald, J., Larsen, P.: An approach for managing semantic heterogeneity in systems of systems engineering. In: Proceedings of the 9th International Conference on Systems of Systems Engineering. IEEE (2014)
11. Foster, S., Thiele, B., Cavalcanti, A., Woodcock, J.: Towards a UTP semantics for Modelica. In: 6th International Symposium on Unifying Theories of Programming (2016)
12. Foster, S., Zeyda, F., Woodcock, J.: Isabelle/UTP: a mechanised theory engineering framework. In: Naumann, D. (ed.) UTP 2014. LNCS, vol. 8963, pp. 21–41. Springer, Heidelberg (2015). doi:10.1007/978-3-319-14806-9_2
13. Fritzson, P.: Principles of Object-Oriented Modeling and Simulation with Modelica 2.1. Wiley-IEEE Press, Chichester (2004)
14. Gamble, C., Pierce, K.: Design patterns for use in co-modelling. In: Fitzgerald, J., Larsen, P.G., Verhoef, M. (eds.) Collaborative Design for Embedded Systems, pp. 319–356. Springer, Heidelberg (2014)
15. Grujic, I., Nilsson, R.: Model-based development and evaluation of control for complex multi-domain systems: attitude control for a quadrotor UAV. Technical report 23, Department of Engineering, Aarhus University, January 2016
16. Haber, A., Ringert, J.O., Rumpe, B.: MontiArc - Architectural Modeling of Interactive Distributed and Cyber-Physical Systems. Technical report AIB-2012-03, RWTH Aachen, February 2012
17. He, J.: From CSP to hybrid systems. In: Roscoe, A.W. (ed.) A Classical Mind: Essays in Honour of C.A.R. Hoare, pp. 171–189. Prentice Hall (1994)
18. Hoare, T.: Communication Sequential Processes. Prentice-Hall International, Englewood Cliffs (1985)
19. Hoare, T., Jifeng, H.: Unifying Theories of Programming. Prentice Hall, Englewood Cliffs (1998)
20. Kesten, Y., Pnueli, A.: Timed and hybrid statecharts and their textual representation. In: Vytopil, J. (ed.) FTRTFT 1992. LNCS, vol. 571, pp. 591–620. Springer, Heidelberg (1992). doi:10.1007/3-540-55092-5_32
21. Kleijn, C.: Modelling and simulation of fluid power systems with 20-sim. Int. J. Fluid Power **7**(3), November 2006
22. Larsen, P.G., Battle, N., Ferreira, M., Fitzgerald, J., Lausdahl, K., Verhoef, M.: The overture initiative - integrating tools for VDM. SIGSOFT Softw. Eng. Notes **35**(1), 1–6 (2010). http://doi.acm.org/10.1145/1668862.1668864
23. Lee, E.A.: Computing needs time. Commun. ACM **52**(5), 70–79 (2009)
24. Oliveira, M., Cavalcanti, A., Woodcock, J.: A UTP semantics for circus. Formal Aspects Comput. **21**, 3–32 (2009)
25. Peleska, J.: Industrial-Strength Model-Based Testing - State of the Art and Current Challenges. Electronic Proceedings in Theoretical Computer Science abs/1303.1006, 3–28 (2013)
26. Reed, G., Roscoe, A., et al.: Timed CSP: theory and practice. In: Bakker, J.W., Huizing, C., Roever, W.P., Rozenberg, G. (eds.) REX 1991. LNCS, vol. 600, pp. 640–675. Springer, Heidelberg (1992). doi:10.1007/BFb0032011

27. OMG Systems Modeling Language (OMG SysML^{TM}): Technical report Version 1.4, Object Management Group, September 2015. http://www.omg.org/spec/SysML/1.4/

28. Verhoef, M., Larsen, P.G., Hooman, J.: Modeling and validating distributed embedded real-time systems with VDM++. In: Misra, J., Nipkow, T., Sekerinski, E. (eds.) FM 2006. LNCS, vol. 4085, pp. 147–162. Springer, Heidelberg (2006). doi:10.1007/11813040_11

29. Wang, B., Baras, J.S.: HybridSim: a modeling and co-simulation toolchain for cyber-physical systems. In: 17th IEEE/ACM International Symposium on Distributed Simulation and Real Time Applications, DS-RT 2013, Delft, The Netherlands, 30 October–1 November 2013, pp. 33–40. IEEE Computer Society (2013)

30. Wei, K., Woodcock, J., Cavalcanti, A.: Circus Time with reactive designs. In: Wolff, B., Gaudel, M.-C., Feliachi, A. (eds.) UTP 2012. LNCS, vol. 7681, pp. 68–87. Springer, Heidelberg (2013). doi:10.1007/978-3-642-35705-3_3

31. Woodcock, J.: Engineering UToPiA - formal semantics for CML. In: Jones, C., Pihlajasaari, P., Sun, J. (eds.) FM 2014. LNCS, vol. 8442, pp. 22–41. Springer, Heidelberg (2014). doi:10.1007/978-3-319-06410-9_3

32. Woodcock, J., Davies, J.: Using Z - Specification, Refinement, and Proof. Series in Computer Science. Prentice Hall International, Englewood Cliffs (1996)

33. Zhou, C., Hoare, C.A.R., Ravn, A.P.: A calculus of durations. Inf. Process. Lett. **40**(5), 269–276 (1991)

Merging Modeling and Programming
Using Umple

Timothy C. Lethbridge[✉], Vahdat Abdelzad,
Mahmoud Husseini Orabi, Ahmed Husseini Orabi,
and Opeyemi Adesina

University of Ottawa, Ottawa, Canada
{tcltcl,vabde040,mhuss092,
ahuss045,oades013}@uottawa.ca

Abstract. We discuss how Umple merges modeling and programming by adding modeling constructs to programming languages and vice-versa. Umple has what we call model-code duality; we show how it fulfills key attributes of being both a programming language and a modeling technology. Umple also has what we call text-diagram duality in that the model or code can be updated by editing the textual or diagram form. We give an example of Umple, and explain how key benefits of textual programming languages are found in Umple, as are important features of modeling technology.

Keywords: Modeling · Programming languages · Duality · State machines · Associations

1 Introduction

Umple is an open-source software development technology designed to fully merge modeling and programming [1]. Umple is motivated by the vision that model-driven development will become ubiquitous in the not-too-distant future, but that this can only be realized if the best capabilities of modeling and programming are blended, while eliminating the biggest drawbacks of each.

Section 2 of this paper gives an overview of how Umple implements a duality between modeling and code, and between diagrams and text. It also briefly discusses various features of Umple and the uses to which it has been put. Section 3 gives an example of Umple to help the reader understand the concepts explained in the paper. Section 4 gives an overview of the strengths obtained by being able to operate on an Umple system in its programming-language perspective; we suggest that modeling tools in general should have a programming-language perspective in order to benefit from these sorts of strengths. Section 5 overviews the capabilities Umple exhibits as a modeling tool. Section 6 highlights the evidence for Umple's effectiveness, while Sect. 7 provides the conclusion.

© Springer International Publishing AG 2016
T. Margaria and B. Steffen (Eds.): ISoLA 2016, Part II, LNCS 9953, pp. 187–197, 2016.
DOI: 10.1007/978-3-319-47169-3_14

2 Perspectives of Umple

2.1 Duality: Model-Code and Text-Diagram

Umple, which has been under development since 2007. incorporates what we call *model-code duality*: An Umple system looks and feels like code when viewed in a programming environment, but looks and feels like a model when viewed in a modeling environment.

By *looking and feeling like code*, we mean that,

(c1) The system, or parts of it, are composed of a set of units (files in the case of Umple), which can be edited using a text editor supporting syntax highlighting.
(c2) The textual syntax is designed to be usable by programmers.
(c3) When it is processed (compiled in the case of Umple), feedback such as warnings and errors is produced, highlighting issues on specific lines.

By *looking and feeling like a model*, we adopt Ludewig's criteria [2]. We summarize these as follows:

(m1) There is a *mapping* between the model and the system being modeled, or part of it. The system is called the 'original' by Ludewig.
(m2) This mapping *abstracts* some properties of the system, hence providing a simplified view. Typical abstractions focus on behavioural properties or structural properties, but the same model may include both, as well as other types of abstractions.
(m3) The model is *useful* in that it one can do things with the model instead of having to have access to the full (executable) system. Key things one can do with a model under m3 include analyzing it to measure it or to find defects, and transforming it into other forms. Models are therefore useful in early stages of design, but in some cases can also be used to generate some or all of the system.

Model-code duality applies to a technology when all six of the above criteria apply simultaneously. It can be argued that all programming languages to some extent meet criteria m1 to m3; for example, a C++ program abstracts from the much more complex machine code and can be analyzed to find various kinds of defects. The more abstract and non-procedural (declarative) an abstraction is, however, the more strongly it would seem that model-code duality applies.

Umple is designed so it can be treated exactly like any programming language, with a syntax that follows characteristics of C-family languages. Criteria c1 to c3 clearly apply [7]. Umple also incorporates abstractions commonly considered to be at the modeling level such as UML associations, state machines and patterns; it also provides measurement, defect-analysis and transformation capabilities for these. Thus, m1 to m3 also clearly apply. We argue in this paper that in the long term, model-code duality should apply increasingly strongly to all software development technologies, and part of the objective of Umple is to show a possible path towards this future vision.

Nothing in Ludewig's criteria states what the concrete syntax of a model has to look like; therefore text should be just as good as diagrams. In fact, Umple is designed such that various diagram views (e.g. class diagrams, state diagrams, composite structure diagrams) can be used as the concrete syntax by which the developer explores and edits the system. We call this *text-diagram duality*.

Umple therefore goes beyond what typical software development technology provides: It is common to be able to extract a diagram from textual code (as a reverse-engineering operation), or to generate code from a UML diagram. *Round-tripping* may also often be employed in various other technologies, wherein extraction and regeneration cycles occur. However, for true text-diagram duality, there should be no need for round-tripping. This is the case in Umple: its model/code abstract syntax can simultaneously be viewed and edited in textual or diagram form.

Model-diagram duality does not preclude the possibility that not all aspects of the model have or routinely use a diagram representation: For example, Umple embeds pure algorithmic methods; it does not provide equivalent flowcharts as their usefulness is questionable. In Umple, therefore, while much of the model/code can be viewed or edited diagrammatically or textually, there are portions (algorithms, constraints, identifier labels) that require textual editing.

2.2   Components and Functions of the Umple Technology

A key component of Umple is its compiler whose input language consists of a blend of textual modeling constructs (including associations [3, 4], state machines [5], patterns and many more) and code in programming languages such as Java, PhP and C++. The compiler analyses the model, giving feedback to the software engineer as to correctness, as would any compiler. It then generates complete systems in any of its input programming languages (i.e. Java, PhP, C++). A developer used to any of these languages would therefore see Umple just like any other programming language – in fact, she or he might perceive of Umple as a pre-processor, simply extending these programming languages with additional abstractions.

In addition to generating an executable system, Umple also can generate SQL database code, Formal methods code (e.g. Alloy) [6], and other modeling syntaxes such as XMI. Umple can also generate metrics and various forms of analysis.

In addition to being a transform engine, Umple also has development environment components, allowing its model diagrams or text to be edited. UmpleOnline [7] is its web-based environment, principally useful for small-scale systems – theoretically unlimited, but practically up to about 1000 lines of Umple code. Larger Umple systems are better manipulated using IDEs like Eclipse or else command-line technology.

2.3   Uses of Umple

Umple has been put to use in two contexts: The first is model-driven development of significantly-sized software, and the second is the teaching of software engineering in general, and modeling specifically.

It is being used in several universities for teaching modeling. Students, who are typically adept at programming, come to see the value of modeling, and develop deeper skills in modeling, when they can work with a tool that allows them to see a system from either a modeling or programming perspective [8, 9].

The largest system so far build in Umple (that we are aware of) is Umple itself. After a bootstrapping period, the initial Java version of Umple was re-written in Umple. Until 2016, there remained a few non-Umple component in Umple; most notably Jet was used in code generation. However as of early 2016 even the Jet code was replaced with Umple's native UmpleTL templating code.

The use of Umple to develop itself serves as a proof that the vision of blending modeling and programming is indeed possible; it also provides a large case study and research testbed to explore how to move this vision forward into practical use.

3   A Small Executable Example of Umple

An extensive set of examples of Umple can be found online, including in UmpleOnline [7], and in the Umple GitHub site [10]. Examples can also be found in many of the papers we will cite in this paper.

However, to aid understanding we present a small sample of Umple code below:

```
1   class VehicleModel {
2      name;  // attribute, defaults to String
3      Integer modelYear;
4   }
5
6   class CityVehicle {
7      * -- 1 VehicleModel; // association
8      vin;
9      trace vState record vin; // umple trace sublanguage
10     vState { // start of state machine
11        Active { // first state
12           sell -> Sold; // transition
13           scrap -> Scrapped;
14           confirmStolen -> Stolen;
15           BeingAcceptanceTested { // substate of Active
16              accepted -> InService;
17              unacceptable -> Returned;
18           }
19           InService {
20              InUse {
21                 routineMaintenaceDue -> UnderMaintenance;
22                 accident -> UnderMaintenance;
23              }
24              UnderMaintenance {
25                 maintenanceComplete -> InUse;
26              }
27           }
28        }
29        Retired {
```

```
30          Sold {}
31          Scrapped {}
32        }
33        Returned {} // one of several end states
34        Stolen {}
35      }
36
37    public static void main (String[] args) { // standard Java
38        VehicleModel m1 = new VehicleModel("AX7 Digger", 2015);
39        VehicleModel m2 = new VehicleModel("E25 Truck", 2016);
40        CityVehicle v1 = new CityVehicle("AD13743",m1);
41        CityVehicle v2 = new CityVehicle("GT29754",m2);
42        CityVehicle v3 = new CityVehicle("GT31974",m2);
43        v1.unacceptable();
44        v2.accepted();
45        v3.accepted();
46        v2.accident();
47        v3.sell();
48        v2.maintenanceComplete();
49        v2.confirmStolen();
50      }
51 }
```

We assume the reader has some understanding of UML, the widely used modeling language, but for clarity: an *association* is a UML abstraction that expresses the fact that there is to be a run-time relationship between instances of particular classes. Notations called *multiplicities* constrain how many instances of the class at one end of the association can be related to an instance at the other end, and vice-versa. The multiplicity '*' means 'many' or 'any number.' Umple enforces *referential integrity* in associations: If class A has an association with class B, and if an instance of A is linked to an instance of B, then that instance of B is also linked to the instance of A.

State machines in Umple follow standard UML semantics, each describing the state of instances of a particular class. The state machine can be considered an attribute whose values are the states. *Events* (method calls) are the only way to cause changes in the state of the machine.

The above code shows two classes (lines 1–4 and 6–51 respectively). The classes are linked by an association (line 7). CityVehicles go through a lifecycle represented using a state machine (lines 10–35). Lines 37–50 are ordinary Java, embedded in the Umple, used to instantiate objects and take the objects through their lifecycles. Line 9 is a sample of Umple's tracing capability [11], instructing Umple to output details as the system executes; the output is in Fig. 3.

When loaded into UmpleOnline, various diagrams appear: a class diagram in Fig. 1 and a state diagram in Fig. 2. These diagrams will change as the code is edited. The system can be compiled using Eclipse or the command line. The resulting Java, which amounts to about 800 lines, is designed to be readable for teaching and inspection purposes, but never needs to be edited or read since the original Umple is the 'gold master' of the system, and any modifications can be applied there.

An Umple system is compiled and executed just like one might compile and execute a Java system or C++. Umple generates Java (or other programming languages) as intermediate languages. But the Umple compiler is designed to hide this

Fig. 1. Class diagram of the example system; in UmpleOnline this diagram can be edited, with changes reflected in the Umple code, or the text can be edited with changes reflected in this diagram. Other presentation friendly views are available too.

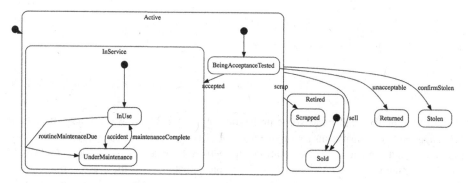

Fig. 2. State diagram of the example system that Umple dynamically updates.

Time,Thread,UmpleFile,LineNumber,Class,Object,Operation,Name,Value
87,1,CityVehicle.ump,9,CityVehicle,54,sm_t,BeingAcceptanceTested,exitActive,Null,AD13743
88,1,CityVehicle.ump,9,CityVehicle,54,sm_t,BeingAcceptanceTested,unacceptable,Returned,AD13743
89,1,CityVehicle.ump,9,CityVehicle,35,sm_t,BeingAcceptanceTested,accepted,InService,GT29754
89,1,CityVehicle.ump,9,CityVehicle,62,sm_t,BeingAcceptanceTested,accepted,InService,GT31974
89,1,CityVehicle.ump,9,CityVehicle,35,sm_t,InUse,accident,UnderMaintenance,GT29754
89,1,CityVehicle.ump,9,CityVehicle,62,sm_t,InService,exitActive,Null,GT31974
89,1,CityVehicle.ump,9,CityVehicle,62,sm_t,InUse,exitActive,Null,GT31974
89,1,CityVehicle.ump,9,CityVehicle,62,sm_t,Active,sell,Sold,GT31974
89,1,CityVehicle.ump,9,CityVehicle,35,sm_t,UnderMaintenance,maintenanceComplete,InUse,GT29754
89,1,CityVehicle.ump,9,CityVehicle,35,sm_t,InService,exitActive,Null,GT29754
89,1,CityVehicle.ump,9,CityVehicle,35,sm_t,InUse,exitActive,Null,GT29754
89,1,CityVehicle.ump,9,CityVehicle,35,sm_t,Active,confirmStolen,Stolen,GT29754

Fig. 3. Trace of state transitions of the example system

from the developer, in the same manner as the developer does not need to be involved with the Java bytecode files (.class files).

When the above system is executed, the output shown in Fig. 3 is produced by the tracing mechanism (to save space in the paper, only the last 2 digits of the time and object identifiers have been kept). These lines describe the various state transitions of the various objects.

4 The Programming Language Perspective of Umple

Part of Umple's vision is to incorporate a set of strengths, listed below, that are generally attributable to modern programming languages. We highlight places where Umple's incorporation of these, provides advantages over other modeling tools.

Flexible textual IDE support: As with any other mainline programming language, developers using Umple have the ability to use powerful IDEs such as Eclipse or Microsoft Visual Studio, or any of the wide variety of standalone text editors, for tasks like syntax-directed editing and debugging. Umple has an Eclipse plugin, but does not have any dependencies on Eclipse, unlike most competing modeling platforms – this allows potentially greater scope of use. Plugins for various other tools are also available for Umple.

Configuration management: Umple gives the ability to take full advantage of the power of Git and tools like GitHub for versioning, code inspection and differencing. Umple is open-source and hosted on GitHub. Unlike other modeling tools, Umple's programming-language nature makes versioning and merging of models transparent. Competing modeling tools either use awkward XML-based differencing and versioning, or require complex special-purpose algorithms [12].

Manipulability of text: As a language that looks like any other programming language, Umple gives programmers the ability to work fluidly with command-line tools of the developer's choice, including Vim, Grep, AWK, and many others.

Separation and combination of concerns: Researchers have evolved several technologies designed to help separate concerns or weave concerns or features together in textual languages. Umple natively supports three of these:

- **Mixins:** Mixins in Umple allow files to be combined in a variety of ways, to build various different products from the same source code base. Different mixins can contribute elements to a given class or state machine.
- **Traits:** Traits are a powerful capability finding their way into various languages [13]. A trait can be seen as building on the power of the interface, in that implementation can be injected into multiple classes. Traits are fundamentally a textual construct. Umple is the first technology to allow traits to work at the modeling level, injecting pieces of model (such as state machine fragments) into other models. More details on Umple traits can be found here [14].
- **Aspects:** Umple has a basic aspect technology for injecting code before or after various join points using pattern-matching pointcuts.

    All three of the above work together with each other.

Text-generation templates: Umple incorporates text-generation template technology as found in languages such as PhP and technologies such as Xpand [15]. Umple has its own best-of-breed sublanguage for this called UmpleTL, which is central to Umple's own generation of itself. This replaced Jet, a now-deprecated Eclipse technology, which was the original template language in which Umple was bootstrapped. In fact any user of Jet can make use of an application written in Umple to convert Jet to Umple [16].

Legacy and libraries: Umple, as with many other programming languages, gives the ability to work with legacy code frameworks. Umple, in fact works fluidly with legacy or library code in Java, C++ and PhP. It can embed or call APIs in any of these languages, and its modeling constructs generate these languages. In fact, Umple can serve as a medium for cross-language development, since Umple code can simultaneously blend with more than one of these languages.

Testing: Fundamental to modern programming methods is the ability employ test-driven development, including use of xUnit tools such as Junit and CppUnit. The Umple system has an extensive multi-level test suite and is developed using test-driven development [17].

Compatibility with open source methods: Umple gives accessibility to programmers worldwide as it enables adoption of tools and techniques standard in the open-source community, including those listed above [18].

5   The Modeling Perspective of Umple

The other side of Umple's code-model duality vision is to leverage the following strengths of modern model-driven development:

High-level abstractions. The abstractions below supported by Umple have long been a part of requirements and design methods, but have required translation into code. Umple brings these directly to the programming language level. The abstractions provide concise ways of expressing design concepts that would be much more complex and repetitive if written using classic code. Additionally, the presence of these in the source allows the compiler to do high-level analysis to find defects that otherwise might be hidden. Examples of the latter include detecting violations of constraints, and unreachable states.

- **UML attributes:** Attributes in Umple are more than just variable declarations; they have richer semantics including being subject to constraints, and patterns such as immutability. More details can be found here [19].
- **UML associations:** Umple's supports the rich feature set of UML associations; multiplicity and referential integrity are enforced in the running system. More details can be found here [3] and an example is found in Sect. 3.
- **State machines:** Umple supports the sophisticated semantics of state machines, including nesting, orthogonal regions, concurrent activities in separate threads, and so on. More details are here [5].
- **Constraints:** Umple supports a core subset of OCL constraints, service as class invariants, method preconditions and transition guards.

- **Components and structural modeling:** Umple has been extended to incorporate distributed features such as components, ports, and connectors [20]. It supports the core features of UML related to composite and component structural modeling.
- **Patterns:** Umple has various built-in notions such as immutable and singleton that provide capabilities which in a programming environment would require following a formulaic 'pattern'.

Diagrams: As discussed earlier, Umple provides class diagrams, state diagrams and composite structure diagrams that are always in full agreement with the source code view, with and the diagrams can be edited to update the textual source. In our experience developers most often find it easier to edit text, and sometimes easier to edit diagrams. Likewise developers most often find it easier to inspect diagrams for defects, but also find different kinds of defects by inspecting the textual form.

Transformations. Model transformations have been central to the modeling community. Umple has numerous built-in model transformations [6], such as from Umple to formal languages Alloy and nuXmv; to programming languages, and to diagrams and tables of various kinds. Since there is a built-in transformation to Ecore, transformations designed to work with Ecore can also be used. Some of the transformations represent ongoing research and are thus still under development, with various limitations. For example, the transformation to nuXmv [26] currently transforms only state machines, simple attributes and simple Boolean expressions.

6 Evidence for Umple's Effectiveness

Umple is, first and foremost, proof of its own effectiveness. Essentially every feature of Umple, as it has been developed, as been rolled into improvements to the Umple compiler and supporting tools.

Over 60 developers (full list with the Umple MIT license [21]), mostly 4th-year undergraduates working for 4 months at a time, plus 8 Ph.D. students and a few masters students, have been able to rapidly develop the technology. Its maintainability is witnessed by the ability of students to rapidly understand the system, and make contributions within 4-month semester windows. Developers have been able to not only use the best capabilities of textual tools, but have also been able to navigate Umple's self-descriptive metamodel, which is available online and is hyperlinked to online code [22]. Umple's quality has been maintained, as proven by the fact that it is always been required that it compiles itself, and that over 6000 tests always execute with 100 % pass rate.

Studies have shown that the Umple language is usable by developers [23–25] – moreover it is more usable than plain traditional code, and models in Umple's textual form are as usable as in the UML diagrammatic form.

Umple has also proved beneficial at teaching modeling in the classroom [9]. Studies have shown that grades and comprehension improve after Umple is introduced.

7 Conclusions

In this paper, we have described the Umple technology and demonstrated that it has what we call model-code duality. This means that it has the advantages of both code (being textual in addition to diagrammatic) and model (incorporating declarative abstractions for views of a system), and can be used as a programming or modeling language interchangeably.

We anticipate that tools like Umple will become the norm. Our experience is that Umple helps developers develop systems more effectively, since they can work at the abstract level and always see diagrammatic representations of their code without reverse engineering. Also Umple helps students learn to model and to develop systems faster.

Acknowledgements. We would like to thank the following for supporting the development of Umple over the years: NSERC through Discovery Grants, the Ontario Research Fund (ORF), and IBM who supported much of the early development of Umple. We would also like to acknowledge the over-60 open-source developers of Umple.

References

1. Umple.org, Model-Oriented Programming. http://www.umple.org
2. Ludewig, J.: Models in software engineering – an introduction. Softw. Syst. Model **2**, 5–14 (2003)
3. Forward, A.: The convergence of modeling and programming: facilitating the representation of attributes and associations in the Umple model-oriented programming language, Ph.D. thesis, University of Ottawa (2010). http://www.site.uottawa.ca/ ~ tcl/gradtheses/aforwardphd/
4. Badreddin, O., Forward, A., Lethbridge, T.C.: Improving code generation for associations: enforcing multiplicity constraints and ensuring referential integrity. In: Lee, R. (ed.) SERA 2013. SCI, vol. 496, pp. 129–149. Springer, Heidelberg (2013). http://dx.doi.org/10.1007/978-3-319-00948-3_9
5. Badreddin, O., Lethbridge, T.C., Forward, A., Elasaar, M. Aljamaan, H., Garzon, M.: Enhanced code generation from UML composite state machines. In: MODELSWARD 2013, Portugal (2014)
6. Adesina, O.: integrating formal methods with model-driven engineering. In: Models 2015 Doctoral Symposium (2015). http://ceur-ws.org/Vol-1531/paper2.pdf
7. UmpleOnline. http://try.umple.org
8. Lethbridge, T.C.: Teaching modeling using umple: principles for the development of an effective tool. In: CSEET 2014, Klagenfurt Austria. IEEE Computer Society (2014)
9. Lethbridge, T., Mussbacher, G., Forward, A., Badreddin, O.: Teaching UML using umple: applying model-oriented programming in the classroom. In: CSEE&T 2011, pp. 421–428 (2011). doi:10.1109/CSEET.2011.5876118
10. Github Umple. https://github.com/umple/umple
11. Aljamaan, H., Lethbridge T.C.: MOTL: a textual language for trace specification of state machines and associations. In: CASCON 2015. ACM (2015)
12. Badreddin, O., Lethbridge, T.C., Forward, A.: A novel approach to versioning and merging model and code uniformly. In: MODELSWARD 2014, Portugal (2014)

13. Ducasse, S., Nierstrasz, O., Schärli, N., Wuyts, R., Black, A.P.: Traits: a mechanism for fine-grained reuse. ACM Trans. Program. Lang. Syst. **28**(2), 331–388 (2006)
14. Abdelzad, V., Lethbridge, T.C.: Promoting traits into model-driven development. Softw. Syst. Model. (2015). doi:10.1007/s10270-015-0505-x. Springer
15. Xpand. https://eclipse.org/modeling/m2t/?project=xpand
16. JetToUmpleTL. https://github.com/umple/JETToUmpleTL
17. Badreddin, O., Forward, A., Lethbridge, T.C.: A test-driven approach for developing software languages. In: MODELSWARD 2014, Portugal (2014)
18. Badreddin, O., Lethbridge, T.C., Elassar, M.: Modeling practices in open source software. In: Petrinja, E., Succi, G., Ioini, N., Sillitti, A. (eds.) OSS 2013. IFIP AICT, vol. 404, pp. 127–139. Springer, Heidelberg (2013). doi:10.1007/978-3-642-38928-3_9
19. Badreddin, O., Forward, A., Lethbridge, T.C.: Exploring a model-oriented and executable syntax for UML attributes. In: Lee, R. (ed.) SERA 2013. SCI, vol. 496, pp. 33–53. Springer, Heidelberg (2013). http://dx.doi.org/10.1007/978-3-319-00948-3_3
20. Husseini Orabi, M., Husseini Orabi, A., Lethbridge, T.C.: Umple as a component-based language for the development of real-time and embedded applications. In: MODELSWARD 2016 (2016)
21. Github Umple: Open-Source License for the Umple Model-Oriented Software Technology. https://github.com/umple/umple/blob/master/LICENSE.md
22. Github Umple: Umple Metamodel. http://metamodel.umple.org
23. Badreddin, O., Forward, A., Lethbridge, T.: Model oriented programming: an empirical study of comprehension. In: CASCON. ACM (2012)
24. Badreddin, O., Lethbridge, T.: Combining experiments and grounded theory to evaluate a research prototype: lessons from the umple model-oriented programming technology. In: 2012 First International Workshop on User evaluation for Software Engineering Researchers (USER 2012), in conjunction with ICSE 2012, pp. 1–4 (2012). doi:10.1109/USER.2012. 6226575
25. Aljamaan, H.: Model-oriented tracing language: producing execution traces from tracepoints injected into code generated from uml models, Ph.D. thesis, University of Ottawa (2015). https://www.ruor.uottawa.ca/handle/10393/33419
26. Adesina, O., Lethbridge, T., Somé, S.: A fully automated approach to discovering non-determinism in state machine diagrams. In: 10th International Conference on the Quality of Information and Communications Technology, Portugal (2016)

Systems Modeling and Programming in a Unified Environment Based on Julia

Hilding Elmqvist[1(✉)], Toivo Henningsson[2], and Martin Otter[3]

[1] Mogram AB, Magle Lilla Kyrkogata 24, 223 51 Lund, Sweden
hilding.elmqvist@mogram.net
[2] Lund, Sweden
toivo.h.h@gmail.com
[3] Institute of System Dynamics and Control, DLR,
Oberpfaffenhofen, Germany
martin.otter@dlr.de

Abstract. A new approach for modeling of cyber-physical systems is proposed that combines the modeling power of a Modelica-like equation-based language with the powerful features of Julia; a programming language with strong focus on scientific computing, meta-programming and just-in-time compilation. The modeling language is directly defined and implemented with Julia's meta-programming constructs and is designed tightly together with the symbolic and numeric algorithms. This approach is very well suited for experimenting with evolutions of modeling capabilities.

Keywords: Modelica · Julia · Modeling · Simulation

1 Introduction

The object- and equation-oriented modeling language Modelica [1] is successfully utilized in industry for modeling, simulating and optimizing complex systems such as automobiles, aircraft, power systems, etc. The dynamic behavior of system components is modelled by equations, for example, mass- and energy-balances. Modelica is quite different from ordinary programming languages since equations with mathematical expressions on both sides of the equals sign are allowed. Structural and symbolic methods are used to compile such equations into efficient executable code.

In addition, Modelica also has a function concept for procedural programming of tasks, such as table look-up, media calculations and control system implementations. The function part of Modelica is, however, not rich enough. There are no advanced data structures such as union types, no matching construct, no type inference, etc. For example, there are presently separate blocks for adding Reals, Integers and Complex numbers. The evolution of Modelica has slowed down since it's a too large task to make a full algorithmic language. Instead of inventing all such features and forcing all Modelica tool vendors to adapt, it makes sense to use another language as a base.

Julia [2] is a very promising language design effort with focus on scientific computing and has many of the properties needed to complement the equational style for modeling. Julia also allows definition of real equations (expression = expression) and handles

T. Margaria and B. Steffen (Eds.): ISoLA 2016, Part II, LNCS 9953, pp. 198–217, 2016.
DOI: 10.1007/978-3-319-47169-3_15

matrices in a mathematical way with indices starting at 1. Furthermore, advanced meta-programming features are available which are suitable for symbolic treatment of equations before just-in-time compilation.

Julia would allow developing a modeling language together with a public reference implementation so that language features and symbolic/numeric algorithms are designed tightly together.

Examples of other research oriented language designs for modeling are: SOL [3], Hydra [4] and Modelyze [5]. There is also one experimental simulation package for Julia called Sims [6]. Sims does not make any structural and symbolic processing though, but has event handling. It is based on ideas from Modelyze and Hydra.

As an example showing the economic function notation used in Julia, consider the following Modelica function from the Modelica Standard Library [7].

```
function planarRotation "Return orientation object of a planar rotation"
  import Modelica.Math;
  extends Modelica.Icons.Function;
  input Real e[3](eachfinal unit="1") "Normalized axis of rotation (must have length=1)";
  input Modelica.SIunits.Angle angle "Rotation angle to rotate frame 1 into 2 along axis e";
  outputTransformationMatrices.Orientation T "Orientation object to rotate frame 1 into 2";
  algorithm
    T := [e]*transpose([e]) + (identity(3) - [e]*transpose([e]))*Math.cos(angle) -
      skew(e)*Math.sin(angle);
    annotation(Inline=true);
  end planarRotation;
```

This function can be much more conveniently expressed using Julia (although without the description texts of the variables):

```
planarRotation(e, angle) =
  e*e' + (eye(3) - e*e')*cos(angle) - skew(e)*sin(angle)
```

Julia has type inference, that is, declaring variables types is optional. Also vector dimensions are inferred.

This paper introduces a Julia macro set called Modia that enables modeling and simulation of systems. Details of Modia will be given in Sect. 4. Section 2 discusses needs for model based systems engineering. Section 3 summarizes important Julia properties. Section 5 describes the current status of the prototype implementation.

2   Model Based Systems Engineering Needs

This section summarizes the fundamental needs for modeling the behavior of systems.

- **Modeling continuous behavior using differential and algebraic equations.** The behavior of the physical part of a system is captured by equations such as mass- and energy-balances. The rate of change of positions, velocities, temperature, etc. may be included in the equations by using time derivative notation such as the operator der(...). Such equations are called ordinary differential equations. Engineering text books, articles and papers dealing with mathematical modeling uses equations, that is, equality between the expression on the left and right hand side of the equals sign. In general, a special DAE-solver is used to solve the Differential-Algebraic set of Equations.

- **System composition using graphs.** Basic component models are described by equations. Reuse of modeling know-how is accomplished by instantiating model components, setting their parameters and connecting them together in the same way as the physical systems is connected. Special terminal definitions are needed that describe which variables are involved in the interaction between components.
- **Graphical user experience.** In addition to the modeling language, a convenient user interface is needed to define the system topology, that is, how components are connected.
- **Generic model parameters and templates.** It is important to allow flexibility with regards to, for example, level of detail of models, so that it's possible to easily change the model representation of a physical component. Such features enable the use of high-level templates defining, for example, the architecture of an automobile.
- **Problem solving using advanced scripting.** The systems engineer needs a flexible environment for performing simulation studies, such as, changing parameters of a model, simulating, plotting, animating and optimizing. A scripting environment is typically used.
- **Events and safe controllers using synchronous semantics.** Features for describing model discontinuities are needed in addition to continuous time equations. Furthermore, special handling is needed for idealized contact, that is, Dirac pulses are desired. For safe control systems implementation, synchronous clock semantics should be utilized.

3   Julia Programming Language

As stated on the Julia web page www.Julialang.org, "*Julia is a high-level, high-performance dynamic programming language for technical computing, with syntax that is familiar to users of other technical computing environments. It provides a sophisticated compiler, distributed parallel execution, numerical accuracy, and an extensive mathematical function library.*"

Some of the properties which are essential for mathematical modeling are summarized below.

3.1   Basic Features of Julia

- Julia combines features of imperative, functional, and object-oriented programming.
- Multiple dispatch: providing the ability to define function behavior across many combinations of argument types. Dispatching is made to the function with the most specific matching definition. This is especially useful to implement mathematical operators.

- Designed for linear algebra from the beginning, with a built-in multidimensional `Array` type.
- Array indices start with 1, which is standard mathematical definition contrary to most programming language arrays (C, etc.) which start with index 0.
- Allows literal coefficient expressions to be written without `*`: $2x == 2*x$. This enables a compact notation for complex numbers: $2 + 3im == complex(2,3)$. It also enables unit handling, that is, the possibility to write: $2kg$, $5m/s$, etc. There is a special `SIUnits.jl` package that can be used for this.
- Comparisons can be chained: $1 < x < 2$, instead of: $1 < x \&\& x < 2$
- Statements do not need to be terminated with `;` if ended with a newline.
- Optional typing: Types may be annotated where desirable but can often be left out.
- Julia performs type inference to be able to create efficient Just-In-Time (JIT) compiled code even if there are no type annotations.
- Unions are available: `Union(Rec1, Rec2)` describes a value that may be of either type `Rec1` or `Rec2`.
- The value `nothing` can be used to stand for an unspecified value.
- Large set of function packages is available.

3.2 Advanced Features

- In function calls, immutable scalars are passed *by value* and data structures *by reference*. This means that values of an input array or another data structure can be changed in a function and this is visible in the calling environment. Julia uses the convention to have an exclamation mark `!` in the function name in such a case. It is therefore possible to operate efficiently on large and complex data structures.
- Quoted expressions (prefix `:` and enclosed in parenthesis) return the Abstract Syntax Tree (AST) for an expression, built of terminals and nodes of type `Expr` with head, arguments, and a type field that can be used to store the inferred type.

```
julia> equ = :(0=x+y)
:(0 = x + y)
julia> dump(equ)
Expr
  head: Symbol =
  args: Array(Any,(2,))
    1: Int64 0
    2: Expr
      head: Symbol call
      args: Array(Any,(3,))
        1: Symbol +
        2: Symbol x
        3: Symbol y
      typ: Any
```

- ASTs can be traversed and new ASTs built. Packages `Match.jl` or `PatternDispach.jl` can be used for pattern matching.
- Macros are user defined functions that rewrite the AST given to them when invoked; the returned AST is used in place of the macro invocation.
- The `eval` function applied to the AST uses just-in-time compilation before execution.

3.3   Missing Features and Drawbacks

- Inheritance of fields is not available (at least not yet, discussed in "Julia issues").
- Not possible to give default values for fields in composite types (at least not yet, discussed in "Julia issues").
- Diagnostics are often hard to interpret and often just one error is reported.

4   A New Modeling Language - Modia

The goal is to design a new modeling language which is both simpler and more powerful than Modelica 3.3 and takes into account the experienced gained with Modelica in the last 20 years. Native Julia functions will be used instead of a new function concept and equations will use Julia syntax. The new language will be called Modia in this paper. The present status is described below.

In order to migrate the huge number of Modelica libraries and models to Modia, utilities for automatic translation to Modia are needed. A semi-automatic utility has so far been developed using the Julia PEGparser module.

4.1   Modia Design

Model with differential equations. Modia is a domain specific language extension of Julia by means of macros, that is, the Julia parser is used to parse Modia models.

A simple first order example model is shown below:

```
@model FirstOrder begin
  x=Variable(start=1)
  T=Parameter(0.5, "Time constant")
  u=2.0
@equations begin
  T*der(x) + x = u
  end
end
```

@model is a call to the Modia macro called model. The first part after begin is used for variable and component declarations by means of calling constructors. The second part inside the @**equations** macro contains differential and algebraic equations as well as connections. # starts a Julia comment.

The constructor Variable is used to declare x with a start value of 1. In general it constructs instances of ordinary variable types and arrays of those. It is a Julia composite type which in addition to its value also allows specifying type, min, max, variability, start value, unit, description, etc. The constructor Parameter is a specialization of the Variable constructor which sets the variability to parameter, that is, a quantity that is changeable before simulation starts but constant during simulation. There is also a special short hand notation to define parameters by just giving a default value. This notation is used to define the parameter u. Float is another constructor specializing the Variable to be of Float64 type. The operator der() denotes the time derivative of its argument.

The corresponding Modelica model is:

```
model FirstOrder
  Real x(start=1);
  parameter Real T=0.5 "Time constant";
  parameter Real u = 2.0;
equation
  T*der(x) + x = u;
end FirstOrder;
```

It can be noted that Modia has a simpler syntax since value, variability, description, etc. are all given in the constructor calls. Variable type can be omitted since Julia infers type and matrix dimensions. Semicolons can also be omitted in Julia. On the other hand the @-sign has to be used in order to utilize the macros and the scope of the macros is given by begin-end.

Hierarchical models. A model can be instantiated with a constructor taking new parameter values and new declarations of other variables, for example:

```
@model Models begin
  m1=FirstOrder()
  m2=FirstOrder(x=Float(start=2),T=2,u=5)
end
```

It can be noted that all declarations can be redeclared, that is, replaced in a higher model level by other model components (e.g. exchanging a simple motor model by a detailed motor model). There is no need, as in Modelica, to specially mark which declarations that may be redeclared (replaceable keyword in Modelica). However, the original declaration and the new one must be compatible.

Coupled models. In order to couple models, the interfaces need to be defined. For example, for electrical coupling, potential and current at the terminals are considered. In Modia, this is described by a model:

```
@model Pin begin
  v=Float()
  i=Float(flow=true)
end
```

The current variable, i, is marked with an attribute flow=true. This means that when several pins are connected together, the currents are automatically summed to zero according to Kirchhoff's current law (KCL).

Such a Pin can be used to define the terminals p and n of an electrical resistor:

```
@model Resistor begin
    p=Pin()
    n=Pin()
    v=Float()
    i=Float()
    R=Parameter(info="Resistance")
@equations begin
    v = p.v - n.v # Voltage drop
    0 = p.i + n.i # KCL within component
    i = p.i
    R*i = v # Ohm's law
    end
end
```

An electrical component library has been developed containing also Capacitor, Inductor, VoltageSource, etc. A low-pass filter can then be defined as a set of connected components (the diagram of a corresponding Modelica model is shown in Fig. 1):

```
@model LPfilter begin
    R=Resistor(R=100)
    C=Capacitor(C=0.001)
    V=ConstantVoltage(V=12)
    ground=Ground()
@equations begin
    connect(V.n, ground.p)
    connect(V.p, R.p)
    connect(R.n, C.p)
    connect(C.n, V.n)
    end
end
```

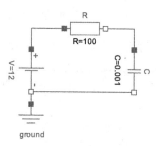

Fig. 1. Low pass filter

The function connect has a special meaning. It creates equations setting the potential variables (v) of all connected pins equal and generating an equation summing all flow variables (i) to zero.

Inheritance. There are several electrical components that share the property of having two Pins. Such components are called OnePorts. It is possible to describe the common properties once and inherit them. The common properties are:

```
@model OnePort begin
  p=Pin()
  n=Pin()
  v=Float()
  i=Float()
@equations begin
  v = p.v - n.v # Voltage drop
  0 = p.i + n.i # KCL within component
  i = p.i
  end
end
```

The Resistor model can then be simplified:

```
@model Resistor begin
  @extends OnePort()
  @inherits i, v
  R=Parameter(info="Resistance")
@equations begin
  R*i = v # Ohm's law
  end
end
```

The @**extends** macro incorporates all declarations and all equations from OnePort. The @**inherits** macro enables use of the variables i and v in the equations of the Resistor.

Equations. Equations are defined as the equality of two Julia expressions, that is, the power of Julia can be utilized as is shown in the example below:

```
@model Test begin
  a = -1; b = 1; c = 1
  n=10; M=Float()
  u=Float(); x=Float()
  on=Variable(); s=Variable()
  QR=Float(); Q=Float(); R=Float()
  dummy=Variable()
@equations begin
  u = if s == "on"; 10 else M end
  der(x) - a*x = b*(s == "on" ? u : 10*u[1,1])
  on := time>1 && time<3
  s = on ? "on" : "off"
  dummy = println("Size of u: ", size(u))
  ((time+1)*diagm(1:n)+ones(n,n))^3*M*diagm(1:n)=eye(n)
  QR = qr(M)
  Q=QR[1]; R=QR[2]
  end
end
```

The independent variable is denoted `time`. Conditional expressions can either use an `if-else-end` construct or `? :` construct. The assignment operator `:=` can be used when the causality is known. This information might also enable the translator to introduce fewer iteration variables for systems of equations. String variables can be used. Variables can have varying dimensions: u is either scalar or a 10×10 matrix depending on time. The size of u is printed by `println()`. The current implementation only allows equations, that is, not just a function call. Therefore, the result of `println()` is assigned to dummy. Matrix equations are allowed. The matrix M is solved by using both divide (`/`) and inverse divide (`\`) operators on matrices. Julia functions such as `qr` can be utilized. It returns a tuple `(Q, R)`. The current implementation does not allow multiple outputs, so a tuple variable QR is used.

Type and size inference. The Modelica Standard Library [7] contains similar models operating on different data types. One example is switches, which based on a Boolean signal select between two real, two Booleans, or two Complex numbers. There is a desire in the Modelica community to unify this situation by means of type inference. In Modia, one can write a generic switch which can be applied to matrices and strings as well:

```
@model Switch begin
  sw=Boolean()
  u1=Variable(); u2=Variable()
  y=Variable()
@equations begin
  y = if sw; u1 else u2 end
  end
end
```

A linear continuous time model is described by one differential equation for the state x depending on inputs u and one algebraic equation defining the outputs y:

```
@model ABCD begin
  A=-1; B=1; C=1; D=0
  u=Float(); y=Float()
  x=Float(start=0)
@equations begin
  der(x) = A*x + B*u
  y = C*x + D*u
  end
end
```

This model has one input, one state and one output since the parameters A, B, C, and D are all scalar. A single input, single output model (SISO) with non-scalar state can be defined as:

```
@model MySISOABCD begin
  @extends ABCD(x=Float(start=[0; 0]),
    A=[-1 0; 0.5 -2],
    B=[1; 1], C=[1 1])
  end
```

In this case, the A matrix is square, B is a column vector and C is a row vector. Correspondingly, a multiple input, multiple output system (MIMO) can be defined as:

```
@model MyMIMOABCD begin
  @extends ABCD(x=Float(start=[0; 0]),
    A=[-1 0; 0.5 -2],
    B=[1 0; 0 1], C=[1 0; 0 1], D=zeros(2,2))
end
```

The example demonstrates the powerful type and size inference mechanism of Julia.

Redeclaration of models. Components can be re-constructed by using constructors in higher level constructors. This, for example, allows making a high pass filter from the low pass filter by interchanging capacitor and resistor:

```
@model HPfilter begin
  @extends LPfilter(R=Capacitor(C=2), C=Resistor(R=3))
end
```

There is a requirement in the Modelica community to be able to select component models (make redeclarations) based on parameters. This is already possible in Modia:

```
@model CondFilter begin
  high = true
  @extends LPfilter(
    R=if high; Capacitor(C=2) else Resistor(R=3) end,
    C=if high; Resistor(R=1) else Capacitor(C=1) end)
end
```

Time events and synchronous controllers. Modelica 3.3 introduced synchronous features for implementation of sampled data systems [13], that is, discrete controllers that run at a periodic rate. Modia presently contains a subset of such features. A discrete PI controller can be modelled as follows:

```
@model DiscretePIController begin
  K=1 # Gain
  Ti=1E10 # Integral time
  dt=0.1 # sampling interval
  ref=1 # set point
  u=Float(); ud=Float()
  y=Float(); yd=Float()
  e=Float(); i=Float(start=0)
@equations begin
  # sensor:
  ud = sample(u, Clock(dt))
  # PI controller:
  e = ref-ud
  i = previous(i, Clock(dt)) + e
  yd = K*(e + i/Ti)
  # actuator:
  y = hold(yd)
  end
end
```

The `sample` operator samples a continuous signal at a certain rate defined by a `Clock`. It is possible to introduce discrete state variables such as the integral part, `i`, using the operator `previous` to access old values of a variable at the previous clock tick. When the discrete control signal has been determined, it is converted to a continuous time signal by means of the `hold` operator.

This controller is coupled to a physical system consisting of a rotating mass with viscous friction. The resulting speed is shown in Fig. 2 to the left and the applied torque as determined by the PI controller is shown to the right.

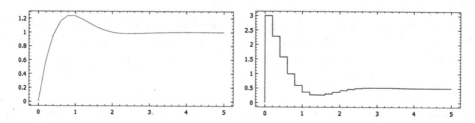

Fig. 2. Speed (left), torque (right)

State events. In order to achieve robust simulations it is important that the numerical solver gets information about discontinuities by means of zero crossing functions. Events which depend on the state of the system are called state events. The semantics of Modelica specifies that all relational operators, such as x > y give rise to a crossing function x-y unless enclosed within noEvent().

Modia has an experimental construct `positive(c)`, which signals that a state event occurs when c becomes positive or becomes negative and returns true when c > 0.

Using this construct it is possible to model an ideal diode. The i versus u characteristic is described as a parametric curve with a curve parameter s: (v(s), i(s)), since the characteristic is vertical for non-negative voltage. The Modia model of the ideal diode is:

```
@model IdealDiode begin
  @extends OnePort()
  @inherits v, i
  s = Float(start=0.0)
@equations begin
  v = if positive(s); 0 else s end
  i = if positive(s); s else 0 end
  end
end
```

A capacitor is connected in parallel to the load resistor. The simulation result is shown in Fig. 3.

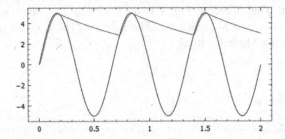

Fig. 3. Input voltage and load voltage for rectifier

Media propagation. A common problem for fluid systems is how to represent and propagate the media properties. Julia has functions as first class objects. This makes it possible to set up equations relating functions themselves.

The density of water as a function of pressure can, for example, be modelled by the following function:

```
const ρ0 = 999.8 # density of water at 0 deg (kg/m3)
const p0 = 1E5
const E = 2.15E9 # bulk modulus of water(N/m2)
ρ(p) = ρ0 / (1 - (p - p0) / E)
```

Note that the function name is ρ. Julia allows a subset of Unicode characters in identifiers. A FluidPort would in addition to pressure and mass flow rate also have a function variable declared as: density=Anonymous():

```
@model FluidPort begin
  p=Float()
  m_flow=Float(flow=true)
  density=Anonymous()
end
```

A pipe model just states that the density function is the same in both ports: b.density = a.density.

A pressure source could use the provided density function in its port to calculate the density: d = a.density(a.p).

The pipe system needs to define the property of the media by giving the density function at least once for each circuit: a=FluidPort(density=ρ).

Depending on the circuit, the density function equations is solved as: a.density = b.density or vice versa. For fluid systems with loops and for redundant media specifications, the redundant equations need to be removed and consistency checked. A complete medium specification could be a composite type with several functions for different properties.

4.2 Application Examples

Some application examples are shown below that have been used, besides others, to test the Modia prototype.

Electrical circuit. The circuit in Fig. 4 is a Cauer low pass filter with operational amplifiers adapted from the Modelica Standard Library. (The graphics have been made from a corresponding Modelica model.)

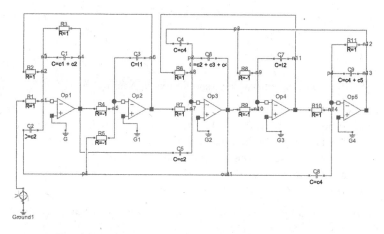

Fig. 4. Cauer low pass filter with operational amplifiers

The model has 207 equations and 5 states. DAE index reduction is needed since the capacitors are tightly coupled. Parameter expressions and parameter propagation is used in this model. The connections for this model are defined with the help of nodes, n1, n2, n3, etc., which are Pins. The components are then connected between these nodes.

Multi domain model. A small library for rotational mechanics (inertia, gearbox, spring, etc.) and for input/output block diagram modeling (step input, PI-controller, filter, etc.) has been built-up allowing to define multi-domain models, such as the current controller of a servo system coupled to rotating mechanical components shown in Fig. 5.

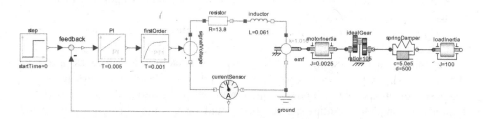

Fig. 5. Multi domain model: current controller and rotational system

The model has 85 equations and 7 states. DAE index reduction is needed since the electromotive force (emf) model and the spring damper needs the angular velocity, but only angle and torque are available in the terminals for rotational mechanics.

The current response due to a step change in the reference input is shown in Fig. 6.

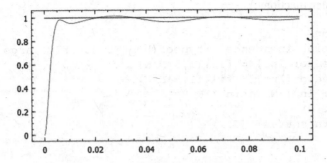

Fig. 6. Current response due to step reference change.

2-dimensional heat transfer. The left part of Fig. 7 shows the discretization of a 2-dimensional area in N^2 temperature nodes. The boxes and the temperature nodes describe the heat capacitors (elements that only store heat) and the resistor-like elements describe the heat conductances (elements that only transport heat). In the right part of the figure the Modia model is sketched that models this system.

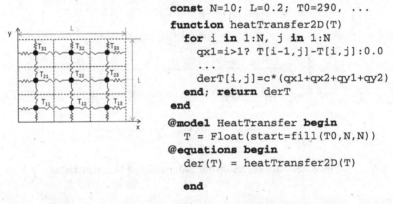

```
const N=10; L=0.2; T0=290, ...
function heatTransfer2D(T)
    for i in 1:N, j in 1:N
        qx1=i>1? T[i-1,j]-T[i,j]:0.0
        ...
        derT[i,j]=c*(qx1+qx2+qy1+qy2)
    end; return derT
end

@model HeatTransfer begin
    T = Float(start=fill(T0,N,N))
@equations begin
    der(T) = heatTransfer2D(T)

    end
```

Fig. 7. Heat transfer discretization and Modia/Julia model

The discretization of the 2-dimensional heat transfer is performed in the Julia function heatTransfer2D(..). From the point of view of the symbolic engine, only two symbols (T, der(T)) have to be handled, independently of the dimension N, so symbolic processing and translation is very fast. On the other hand, the simulation engine has to integrate a system of N^2 differential equations. Without further information this becomes slow for N greater than fifty, since in every integration step a dense linear system of size N^2 has to be solved. It is planned to enhance the symbolic engine to take the incidence matrix of the function output argument with respect to its input arguments into account. This incidence matrix has to be provided in form of a sparse matrix that is returned by a function with a predefined name where the first argument is the type of the heat transfer function.

```
function
  jacobian_incidence(::typeof(heatTransfer2D),args...)
  I::Vector{Int} = fill(1,5*N*N)
  J::Vector{Int} = fill(1,5*N*N)
  for i in 1:N, j in 1:N
    ...
  return sparse(I,J,1)
end
```

The symbolic engine is then able to inquire whether an incidence function is defined for function heatTransfer2D and can call it if this is the case. Although this is not yet supported in Modia's symbolic engine, tests have been performed where this incidence matrix was manually given to the simulation engine. Simulation tests up to N = 1000 have been performed, so up to *1 million differential equations*. Simulating for 30 s needs about 10 min on a standard notebook. Simulation results are shown in Fig. 8 with boundary conditions: y = 0 and x = 0 are completely isolated; T(x = L) = 310 K, T(y = L) = 330 K.

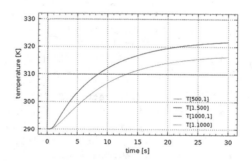

Fig. 8. Simulation results for 2-dimensional heat transfer

This example demonstrates that Modia offers completely new possibilities to combine physical components described by differential-algebraic equations with components described by partial differential equations that are discretized with the method-of-lines approach.

5   Prototype Implementation

Models defined with the @**model** macro are represented using the Model type. A Model object holds instructions for how to fill out an Instance object, which contains a list of variables and equations.

To simulate a model, it is first instantiated into an instance tree, which is then flattened into a flat model represented by a single `Instance` object. Symbolic analysis transforms the flat instance into another flat instance. The final instance is used to generate code for a callback function, which is Just-in-Time (JIT) compiled and passed to a numeric solver.

5.1 Embedding Modia into Julia

Care has been taken to allow Modia to interoperate with and reuse functionality from Julia as much as possible.

Name lookup is handled mostly through Julia itself:

- The model defined by a `@model` macro is stored into a Julia constant variable with the same name as the model, making it available to both Modia and Julia code.
- Identifiers used in a model definition are looked up as Julia names.
- Identifiers that are known to be local to the model itself are bound as Julia variables in the scope where the model's identifiers are evaluated.

This setup makes sure that scoping rules are consistent between Julia and Modia, and that Julia and Modia names share the same name space.

The `@model` macro accepts any valid Julia expression as a model equation, binding expression, etc., so that valid Julia code is generally valid Modia code. As far as possible, Modia constructs are also valid Julia code. For instance, instantiation is done by overloading the function call operator on models, supplying modifiers as keyword arguments.

There are some exceptions, though:

- Dotted access such as `component.field` is used in Modia code to access fields of model instances. The `.` operator is so far not overloadable in Julia, so the `@model` macro converts dotted access to call an internal function that is overloaded to signify access of the corresponding field.
- The `der()` and `connect()` operators are recognized and represented in a special way.

When the `@model` macro receives the AST for an equation, it contains names that need to be resolved in the scope where the model is defined. This name lookup is carried out while otherwise preserving the structure of the AST, by letting the `@model` macro emit code that builds a syntax tree with the same structure as the input, but using identifiers verbatim.

Macros that are used specifically inside of `@model`, such as `@extends` and `@equations`, are used as a way to create custom keywords. They are never actually processed as macro invocations by Julia, but recognized directly in the `@model` macro's implementation.

The tight integration between Modia and Julia allows Modia to take advantage of much of the power of Julia, but also places some constraints on Modia's semantics. The `@model` macro only sees the AST of the code block given to it. It cannot do any name lookup itself, but must emit code that will produce the desired effect (including name lookup) when executed.

Thus, the macro's implementation itself cannot look up the definition of a base class to see which variable names are defined in it. Instead, the user has to supply an @**inherits** statement to tell which names are expected to be inherited from a base class, or explicitly qualify an inherited name as this.name.

5.2   Instantiation of Modia Models

When a Model is instantiated, its variables, @**extends** clauses, and equations are used to fill out an Instance. Filling out variables will cause components to be instantiated in recursive fashion, resulting in an instance tree. Equations are copied verbatim into the instance, while variables and @**extends** clauses cause evaluation of expressions to initialize the variable or base model.

Binding expressions given to model variables in a model declaration are taken as defaults, but can be overriden by supplying a modifier to the instantiation. If no binding expression is given, the default is a binding expression that reports an error telling that the value must be specified with a modifier.

When processing an @**extends** clause, the base model is first instantiated, passing along the modifiers applied to the current model. The content of the base instance are then transferred into the current instance.

5.3   Flattening of Modia Models

Flattening creates a single Instance from an instance tree by gathering all the primitive variables and equations. Starting from the root instance, all variables that are bound to Instance objects are considered as components to be recursively flattened.

When flattening, variables are renamed based on their path from the root instance, so that a variable accessed from the root as component.x will get the actual name component.x (with a dot in the name). Corresponding substitutions are carried out in the equations before adding them to the flat instance.

Connection sets are gathered during flattening and then used to create the appropriate equations for potential and flow variables, respectively, which are added to the flat model. Flow variables that are unconnected from the outside are set to zero.

5.4   Structural and Symbolic Treatment of Equations

The equations are first analyzed structurally, concerning which variables appear or not in each equation. This is done by graph theoretical algorithms. The analysis is made on the original scalar and *matrix* equations, that is, expansion of matrix equations is not done contrary to what Modelica tools do.

The first problem is called *Assignment* and associates a unique variable with each equation. This is not possible if there are constraints between state variables, since the DAE index is larger than 1. Index reduction is then performed, that is certain equations are differentiated. Which equations to differentiate are determined by the algorithm of Pantelides [8].

The next step is to sort the equations into executable order. If there are mutual dependencies, that is loops, minimal loops are determined. The structure of the Jacobian becomes block lower triangular (*BLT*). For the Assignment and BLT operations, the algorithms used in [9] have been re-coded in Julia.

The final step is to symbolically solve each equation in blocks of size one for the unknown which was determined by Assignment. A new method has been designed which allows for also solving matrix equations. Equations in blocks of size larger than one are solved by the DAE solver.

5.5 Code Generation

Numerical solvers typically require a callback function to evaluate e.g. the right hand side of an ODE or the residuals of a DAE. Once the symbolic treatment is finished, the resulting flat instance is used to generate code for the callback function, which is then compiled using Julia's just-in-time compilation:

- Space is allocated for states and residuals in the solver's state and residual vectors. Solved variables, represented with $:=$ equations, are kept internal to the callback's computations.
- Equations are evaluated in order and may use results computed in previous $:=$ equations.
- A unique Julia variable is used to store each intermediate result, to allow type inference on the generated code.

The residuals are evaluated at the initial point to infer their array dimensions (if any), which are then assumed to be fixed.

5.6 Numerical Solution of Equations

Modelica tools are primarily designed to generate Ordinary Differential Equations (ODEs) in state space form, $\dot{x} = f(x, t)$, in particular to allow the import of such models in to other simulation environments and the usage of a large class of integration methods. Typically, this means that for physical system models linear and/or nonlinear algebraic equations have to be solved inside of $f(x, t)$. This complicates the code generation and the numerical treatment significantly. Furthermore, typically Modelica tools generate C code that is compiled and linked before the simulation can start.

Since Modia is starting fresh from scratch and it is based on Julia a different approach can be used: The primary target of the current prototype is no longer an ODE but a DAE description: $0 = f(\dot{x}, x, w, t)$, where $x(t)$ are variables that appear differentiated and $w(t)$ are pure algebraic variables. With the BLT transformation mentioned in the previous section and the symbolic solution of the scalar blocks in the BLT form, many algebraic variables are eliminated and do not show up in the DAE form above. The resulting DAE is solved with DAE integrator IDA from the Sundials integrator suite, version 2.6.2 [10], utilizing the KLU sparse matrix package [11] if the sparsity of the Jacobian is larger as a given threshold. For this, the existing Sundials Julia package [12] was adapted to utilize version 2.6.2 (with KLU) instead of 2.5.0. Sparse matrix handling in the DAE solver also allows treating models with a large number of differential equations, which is currently a limiting factor for most Modelica tools. Sparse DAEs with up to 1 million differential equations have been tested in the prototype as demonstrated with the 2-dimensional heat transfer model in Sect. 4. It is well known that direct methods (including the KLU sparse matrix package) have limitations for 3-dimensional problems and for very large systems. For example, simulating 3-dimensional heat transfer in a cube with N = 50 nodes in every direction leads to 125000 differential equations. Modia's simulation engine needs about 1 h cpu-time for a similar scenario as in Fig. 7 but in 3D. Sundials also provides iterative solvers with pre-conditioners and in the future they could be used if needed. Note, transforming to ODE form often destroys the sparsity structure and therefore it is important to use the DAE form for large scale models.

6   Conclusions

An analysis was started in January 2016 whether Julia would be suited as a basis for a domain specific language for modeling with at least the modeling power of Modelica. The answer was *yes* and the project was changed to actually design such a language and implement a translator and simulation environment for it. The status after six months work is that a substantial part of the needed functionality for systems modeling is prototyped. The Julia implementation also shows good scalability both with regards to translating and compiling a model as well as numerically solving the equations.

Acknowledgments. We would like to thank Klaus Schnepper from DLR for generating the dynamic link libraries of the Sundials Suite 2.6.2 with KLU for Windows.

References

1. Modelica Association: The Modelica Language Specification, Version 3.3 Revision 1, (2014). https://www.modelica.org/documents/ModelicaSpec33Revision1.pdf
2. Bezanson, J., Edelman, A., Karpinski, S., Shah, V.B.: Julia: a fresh approach to numerical computing (2015). http://arxiv.org/abs/1411.1607
3. Zimmer, D.: Equation-Based Modeling of Variable Structure Systems, Ph.D. Dissertation, ETH Zürich (2010). http://e-collection.library.ethz.ch/eserv/eth:1512/eth-1512-02.pdf
4. Giorgidze, G., Nilsson, H.: Higher-order non-causal modelling and simulation of structurally dynamic systems. In: Proceedings of the 7th International Modelica Conference, Como, Italy, pp. 208–218. Linköping University Electronic Press, September 2009. http://www.ep.liu.se/ecp/043/022/ecp09430137.pdf

5. Broman, D., Siek, J.G.: Modelyze: a Gradually Typed Host Language for Embedding Equation-Based Modeling Languages, University of California at Berkeley, No. UCB/EECS-2012-173 (2012). www.eecs.berkeley.edu/Pubs/TechRpts/2012/EECS-2012-173.html

6. Short, T.: Sims - A Julia package for equation-based modeling and simulations. https://github.com/tshort/Sims.jl

7. Modelica Association: The Modelica Standard Library, Version 3.3.2 (2016). https://github.com/modelica/Modelica

8. Pantelides, C.: The consistent initialization of differential-algebraic systems. SIAM J. Sci. Stat. Comput. **9**(2), 213–231 (1988)

9. Elmqvist, H.: A Structured Model Language for Large Continuous Systems. Ph.D. thesis ISRN LUTFD2/TFRT–1015–SE, Department of Automatic Control, Lund University, Sweden (1978). http://www.control.lth.se/documents/1978/elm78dis.pdf

10. Hindmarsh, A.C., Serban, R., Collier, A.: User Documentation for IDA v2.8.2 (Sundials v2.6.2). UCRL-SM-208112 (2015). http://computation.llnl.gov/projects/sundials-suite-nonlinear-differential-algebraic-equation-solvers

11. Davis, T.A., Ekanathan, P.N.: Algorithm 907: KLU, a direct sparse solver for circuit simulation problems. ACM Trans. Math. Soft. **37**(3), 36:1–36:17 (2010). http://faculty.cse.tamu.edu/davis/suitesparse.html. (KLU is part of SuiteSparse)

12. Short, T.: Julia interface to Sundials 2.5.0. https://github.com/JuliaLang/Sundials.jl

13. Elmqvist, H., Otter, M., Mattsson, S.E.: Fundamentals of synchronous control in Modelica. In: Proceedings of 9th International Modelica Conference, Munich, Germany, 3–5 September 2012

Meta-Level Reuse for Mastering Domain Specialization

Stefan Naujokat[1]([✉]), Johannes Neubauer[1], Tiziana Margaria[2],
and Bernhard Steffen[1]

[1] Chair for Programming Systems, TU Dortmund University, Dortmund, Germany
{stefan.naujokat,johannes.neubauer,steffen}@cs.tu-dortmund.de
[2] Chair of Software Systems, University of Limerick and Lero,
The Irish Software Research Centre, Limerick, Ireland
tiziana.margaria@lero.ie

Abstract. We reflect on the distinction between modeling and programming in terms of WHAT and HOW and emphasize the importance of perspectives: what is a model (a WHAT) for the one, may well be a program (a HOW) for the other. In fact, attempts to pinpoint technical criteria like executability or abstraction for clearly separating modeling from programming seem not to survive modern technical developments. Rather, the underlying conceptual cores continuously converge. What remains is the distinction of WHAT and HOW separating true purpose from its realization, i.e. providing the possibility of formulating the primary intent without being forced to over-specify. We argue that no unified general-purpose language can adequately support this distinction in general, and propose a meta-level framework for mastering the wealth of required domain-specific languages in a bootstrapping fashion.

Keywords: Simplicity · Abstract tool specification · Full code generation · Metamodeling · Domain-specific tools · Hierarchy · Service-orientation · Modularity

1 Motivation and Background

At a conceptual level, modeling and programming can be regarded as two sides of the same medal: the WHAT and the HOW descriptions of a certain artefact. This duality of WHAT and HOW has a long tradition in engineering, where models were built to predict certain WHATs, like the aerodynamics of an envisioned car or its visual appearance, in order to optimize vital aspects, before entering the costly HOW-driven production phase, where modifications become extremely expensive. Because of their purpose-specific nature, there are usually many WHAT descriptions that together describe one artefact with only one HOW description.

In classical engineering, there is typically a very clear and agreed upon distinction between a model (a WHAT) and an implementation (the HOW), frequently connected to distinct abstraction layers and different natures of the respective description means. For example, in hardware design there are agreed

© Springer International Publishing AG 2016
T. Margaria and B. Steffen (Eds.): ISoLA 2016, Part II, LNCS 9953, pp. 218–237, 2016.
DOI: 10.1007/978-3-319-47169-3_16

and standardized abstractions in terms of chip layout, transistor level, gate level, register transfer level, etc. This clarity of distinction is, however, lost in computer science, where the viewpoints changed quite a bit over time: 60 years ago, assembler was considered a WHAT for the HOW descriptions at the processor's instruction set level and this has been considered in turn a WHAT for lower levels. Assembler then became itself the HOW for WHAT descriptions in terms of 'higher' programming languages like Fortran and ALGOL and so on. In fact, the understanding of what is a HOW (an implementation or a program) and what a WHAT (a model or a specification) in software becomes quite situation dependent. This distinction hinges on the purpose as well as the community, and it steadily changes over time. How can it be that the same language, e.g. ML by Robin Milner [19], was designed as a modeling language[1] and later on considered a programming language by its inventor? In fact, today few will remember that ML was originally not intended to be a programming language!

This development suggests that this phenomenon has to do with a certain understanding of maturity: a modeling language becomes a programming language as soon as one can 'program' with it. This self-referential definition requires a convention of what it means to program, or what is the 'essence' of programming. Are, for instance, executable specifications (models) already programs, or do we have certain performance requirements to the 'program' or 'program-like' artefacts? In the ML case, the growing quality of the ML compiler was certainly important for its change of status. However, we are very distant from reaching a global agreement about the distinction between modeling and programming. For example, many would consider writing a class diagram in UML as modeling, whereas they would consider the same as programming if done directly in Java.

Independently of this discussion, there is no doubt that modeling and programming converge at the conceptual level [7]. A lot of concepts and techniques have been transferred between them, making e.g. modeling languages executable or adding powerful concepts of abstraction to the programming level. They have also been sharing numerous concerns for a long time, like modularity, comprehensibility, variability, or versioning. Further on, in numerous scenarios unifying efforts in terms of integrating features into a single language seems to have the intended effect. For example, general-purpose languages like *Kotlin*[2] and frameworks like *GWT*[3] (Google Web Toolkit) offer to transpile to JavaScript (another general-purpose language), in order to lower the overall complexity of the software stack as well as the learning curve for developers. However, this does not (necessarily) mean that there is a convergence in the direction of a concrete universal language. In most scenarios, integrating additional abstractions into programming languages via *internal DSLs* [17], libraries, or frameworks seems to be at first sight a good tradeoff. It leads however to WHAT-descriptions embedded in a more or less hidden fashion in the syntax of HOW-descriptions in the universal host language. Another path is to add more and more *native language*

---

[1] Originally ML was designed to describe proof tactics of the LCF theorem prover [34].
[2] http://kotlinlang.org.
[3] http://www.gwtproject.org.

constructs, resulting in increasingly complex *multi-paradigm languages*. Such heterogeneity makes it hard to reason about their WHAT, and raises the knowledge bar for developers: adopters must now learn a multi-paradigm general-purpose language, the semantics of internal DSLs and *APIs* (the WHAT), and how to use them in the host language (the HOW).

Due to these observations, we do not believe in a single universal language, and consider rather the opposite path as viable: in addition to powerful general-purpose languages, there will be a plethora of domain-specific programming and modeling languages, all conceptually based on a *growing common conceptual core*. Accordingly, we envision development frameworks that allow one to master the inherent diversity of modeling and programming, and support the conceptual common core via meta-level functionality. The common core and the sharing establish a new kind of invariants (called Archimedean Points in [51]) spanning whole landscapes of domain-specific modeling languages and tools. The envisioned metamodeling-based software development paradigm aims at simplifying the adopter's experience by strongly exploiting domain-specific characteristics after a rapid model-driven development of the corresponding domain-specific modeling tools. The success of this approach depends on the ease of this development process, which is envisioned to already pay off even for one time use via meta-level reuse.

In the following, we will first argue in Sect. 2 whether a universal language comprising both modeling and programming is desirable. Then Sect. 3 discusses domain-specific modeling and sketches an approach aimed at mastering or even exploiting heterogeneity. Key to this approach is continuous improvement in a bootstrapping-like modeling style, where generated artefacts are fed back into the generation framework itself, and thereby enable a new level of reuse. We then present in Sect. 4 how to achieve this meta-level reuse using the CINCO Meta Tooling Suite. The paper closes with our conclusions and some concrete proposal for future work.

2   Inherent Limitations of Universality

History provides some evidence supporting both the doubts concerning unified approaches to programming and modeling, and the hopes concerning the usefulness of meta-level approaches to master a growing landscape of domain-specific solutions in a unified and holistic fashion.

Originally, the formal methods community started developing universal proposals for modeling and specification languages, to serve as a means for documentation and manual reasoning. Later on such languages became a target of automated analysis tools. In the nineties, Pierre Wolper coined the term *strong formal methods* to classify this new tool-oriented direction [53]. Whereas Wolper and others focused on behavioral models and technologies like model checking [11], the software community originally elaborated on Entity/Relation models so successful in the database community [10] and thereby on static aspects of software. This resulted, in particular, in the static diagrams core of UML, the arguably most popular modeling landscape, which claims to comprise or even unify essentially all aspects of software. In particular, UML covers also behaviors, typically modeled in terms of state diagrams, activity diagrams or message sequence charts [43].

The formal methods community embraced the challenges posed by UML and provided various approaches to its semantic foundation [13], consistency checking [41], and (partial) code generation [48]. Despite all these efforts, the common usage of UML and most of its impact concerns static models: they provide the basis for generating code stubs to be subsequently manually refined. They also provide the foundation for the EMF [52] and MOF [40] metamodeling frameworks. UML therefore clearly establishes a level of description and modeling above the programming level, and requires modelers to pay special attention to keep models and the corresponding programs aligned and consistent. Most popular here is the round trip engineering approach [50], which, however, hardly lives up to its promises, especially when including behavioral aspects and not only classes and packages, and therefore found only marginal attention in practice [16].

In practice, accordingly, UML seems far from being a good candidate for unifying modeling and programming. This impression is also supported by its conceptual heterogeneity which clearly indicates that the intended meaning of 'unified' in its name is 'comprehensive' rather than 'holistic' or 'consistent'.

The remainder of this section sketches recent developments for enhancing the classical concept of programming language in order to provide a background for the subsequent discussion of inherent limitations of universality.

2.1   Extensions, Internal DSLs, Libraries, and Frameworks

Over the last decades significant effort was poured into integrating complex functionality into general-purpose languages via language extensions, internal DSLs, libraries, and frameworks. Prominent examples are *graphical user interface* (GUI) frameworks, *Java EE* (Java Enterprise Edition) and application servers, the *Document Object Model* (DOM) for representing *Extended Markup Language* (XML) documents in memory, and *object relational mapper* (ORM). These approaches offer powerful abstractions and in some cases even seem to be valid WHAT descriptions. In the following we will take a deeper look at examples of the different variants and their pros and cons.

The most invasive approach is to extend the syntax of a language to comprise another (domain-specific) language. Scala, e.g., allows writing XML code directly in the Scala code: the Scala language designer assumed that XML would be the long term standard way to represent structured data. However, the growing significance of *JavaScript Object Notation* (JSON) challenges this early decision. A major disadvantage of such hardwired language extensions is that it is hard to change them. Because universal languages should have a long life cycle, they must give hard guarantees regarding backward compatibility also in the long term. If removing support for XML at some point is unlikely, since it would break existing code, one could instead add more and more language extensions at need. However, this universality path leads to an overly complex and hard to learn language, and makes its compiler and auxiliary tools harder to maintain.

The least invasive approach is to integrate text blobs of a domain-specific language (in form of string literals or files loaded from disc) into the host language, and interpret them at runtime. Script engines allow to load code of scripting languages into the host language and execute them. For example the *Oracle Nashorn* project enables integrating JavaScript into Java via an interpreter. However, the interaction between host and guest language is very generic, similar to spawning new processes and collecting their results after termination. Further on, *SQL* queries – or, in case of an ORM language like *JPQL* (Java Persistence Query Language) – are often represented as string literals. They are hard to validate, since the compiler cannot distinguish literals that are queries from others of different nature. Some *IDEs* (Integrated Development Environments) try to guess whether a string is a query or not and validate it. But these approaches are stretched to their limits if the string (i.e. the DSL code) is constructed dynamically in the host language via string interpolation or template processing. Hence, this approach towards a universal language inherently lacks referential integrity. Because whatever is not captured by the language itself has to be captured via language constructs, integrations tend to be too loose.

The issue of striking the 'right' balance is a central motivation behind the emergence of internal DSLs. For example, *Criteria* facilitates the type-safe implementation of JPQL queries directly in Java by making heavy use of *Generics*, i.e., parametric polymorphy. As a result, the internal DSL *Criteria* is closely related to the external DSL *JPQL* by modeling basic components like SELECT, FROM, JOIN, and WHERE clauses via corresponding generic classes, so that they appear to be WHAT descriptions. But a Criteria query is an object tree of these generic components, constructed via slotting the objects together in Java code. At runtime, the object tree is constructed and used to generate a database query. So, the WHAT description of JPQL is hidden in a HOW description in the host language Java. In contrast to using a text blob, the Java compiler is now able to check whether the internal DSL has been used syntactically correctly. The 'knowledge' of the semantics is however very limited.

Languages like *Ruby* or *Python* try to compensate this limitation by allowing a high degree of language adaptation, so that internal DSLs can express WHAT descriptions more naturally. This is realized by relaxing the type system to be dynamic, i.e., checked at runtime. Runtime typing makes it much harder to reason about types, and prevent errors, so it ends up generating the need for highly skilled and disciplined developers. The increased level of programming discipline has two reasons. Firstly, many problems a type checker would identify and prevent in a statically typed language are now left under the responsibility of the developer. Secondly, the more a language changes, the less predictability a developer can expect.

2.2   The Power of Domain-Specificity

Modern programming languages free programmers from memory management; automatic clustering software takes care of scalability; version management systems support the development process; application servers ease the mastering of the web stack; security frameworks deal with authentication and authorization; technologies like *SSL/TLS* (secure socket layer/transport layer security) provide transparent encryption and decryption of network connections etc. In turn, e.g., the development of version management systems is certainly a very specific domain and could benefit from a domain-specific development framework. However, future challenges will not be limited to this kind of *horizontal* separation of concerns, which is typically addressed with technologies like aspect-oriented programming, but also *vertical* separation of concerns as classically provided by compilation (or transformation) technologies.

The example of program analysis is a good illustration. Dataflow analysis (DFA) frameworks provide a domain-specific language for specifying program analysis problems in terms of minimal or maximal solutions of (boolean) equation systems. The corresponding solutions can be typically computed via fixpoint iteration, so the user's task is essentially reduced to the specification of an equation system. Compared to a traditional program for the analysis algorithm, equation systems can be certainly regarded as WHAT-style descriptions. However, this WHAT is the implied fixpoint computation and not the original analysis problem. In the implied fixpoint computation, for example, live variable analysis amounts to a backward propagation of information about variable usage: a variable is considered live at each program point where such usage information can be propagated. This means that one has to understand the fixpoint computation, which itself is a HOW, in order to understand what the equation system means. The situation dramatically improves when one specifies the program analysis in terms of temporal logic properties. The property of liveness of a variable or, as one could say, the "true" WHAT specification becomes

> *there is a path that passes through a variable* use *before its* modification
> *or* termination

which is a simple *unless* property in temporal logic.

This gain in abstraction may not seem very impressive. However, it is crucial when it comes to verifying properties about the program analyses. This impact became apparent during our construction of the lazy code motion algorithm [27,28]. The possibility to refine the WHAT specification by conjunction of other WHAT specifications, which is typically impossible for HOW specifications, let us elegantly and efficiently solve a 15 year old problem (see e.g. [14]) in dataflow analysis. In fact, our corresponding temporal specification runs faster on a classical iterative model checker [47] than the weaker original handwritten algorithm. Conceptually more intriguing is, however, the elegance of the corresponding correctness and optimality proofs: this comparison is particularly striking with respect to the required argumentation in the original paper on partial redundancy elimination [35]. There was yet another benefit: the algorithms specified in terms of temporal formulas worked directly also for an interprocedural setting when using a model checker for context-free systems [8,9,47], demonstrating this way the superiority of WHAT descriptions when it comes to adaptation and migration.

Another striking example are BNF grammars [4], which form an (even reflexive) (meta)modeling language for extremely concise definition of the syntax of languages. E.g., the BNF

$$N ::= 0 \mid succ(N)$$

defines a language that syntactically represents the natural numbers and reflects faithfully all five Peano Axioms.

How can this be? The first Peano Axiom requires 0 to be a natural number and is explicitely covered. So is the required existence of a (unique) successor $succ(N)$ for each natural number (the second Peano Axiom). The other three Peano Axioms are consequences of two essential conventions of BNFs:

- the syntactic (free) interpretation[4] of terms or two different strings also means different things, and
- the minimality requirement of the sets defined via BFN, i.e., everything must be constructible in finitely many steps by applying the BNF rules.

In particular the fifth Peano Axiom, the foundation for natural induction, is nothing more than an elegant formulation of the minimality requirement.

Thus, in contrast to the Peano Axioms, which specify natural numbers from scratch, the BNF formulation is based on two powerful conventions: the term interpretation and the minimality requirement.

It is the power of such conventions that imposes the lever of the resulting domain-specific scenario. E.g., if we are interested in parsing, BNF specifications are sufficient to entirely generate the corresponding parser code[5]. This impressively shows the leverage of the distinction between WHAT and HOW: the BNF describes only the syntax of the envisioned language, whereas the parser generated from it is a complex program that automatically reads a string from a file, tokenizes it, and builds an abstract syntax tree (AST), all along checking for syntax correctness. This lever impact depends on domain knowledge about parser generation, and reaches far beyond what is reachable with what we traditionally would call code generation (cf. also [22]).

Many striking examples work along these lines, like (hardware and software) synthesis environments, planners, the generation of language interpreters via SOS rules [42], the generation of dataflow analysis algorithms from temporal logic specifications [44–46], or even the (interactive) theorem-prover-based proof generation directly from problem descriptions, even to the point that it comprises program and hardware synthesis [12,20].

---

[4] One sometimes speaks of term or Herbrand interpretation.

[5] ANTLR: http://www.antlr.org/
Yacc: http://dinosaur.compilertools.net/yacc/
JavaCC: https://javacc.java.net/.

In particular the last example illustrates the extreme power of domain specificity: the entire theorem prover is considered 'domain knowledge' allowing to reduce a proof construction language to simply describe the problem (a WHAT) and not the solution (a HOW). This way, the hard part is moved to *the few* designers of the theorem prover, while making life easy for *the many* users. As a rule of thumb, the more specific is the knowledge about a domain, the more tool support can be given.

The described domain-specific scenarios are clearly far beyond what can be adequately covered by traditional programming. Of course, one may argue that the enhancements discussed in Sect. 2.1 are well capable of treating each of these individual domains in some satisfactory way. However, the approaches described in Sect. 2.1 do not scale to support a significant number of domain-specific settings. In particular, it does not scale to the envisioned scenario where the support for the developer should not only be domain-specific, but problem-specific, or even specific to a particular new requirement for a system already in operation [51].

3   Mastering Domain-Specific Diversity

A number of approaches aim at trading generality for systematic development support and, in particular, full code generation [5, 6, 21, 26, 29]. In essence, they advocate domain-specificity as a key for turning generic modeling environments into so-called domain-specific modeling (DSM) frameworks[6] where traditional programming becomes obsolete. In contrast to common UML frameworks, these approaches constrain the addressed (domain-specific) modeling scenario so much that all the running code can be generated fully automatically. Manually filling gaps in generated code stubs is not required, avoiding the need for round trip engineering.

In a comprehensive framework, modeling of a system splits into a number of modeling activities to address individual aspects. These many (aspect) models need to be aggregated during code generation in a consistent fashion. This is a change of mindset from usual programming: instead of taking source files of the same type and generate from each a single artefact of the same target format, here many source files of different types specify different aspects of the target artefacts, which can be themselves of multiple types (cf. Fig. 1).

This multi-dimensional approach is similar to classical mechanical engineering design where, e.g., models for evaluating the wind resistance and models used in crash tests are completely different in nature. On the one hand this tendency to heterogeneity (also) explains the wealth of model types in UML. On the other hand it emphasizes the impact of the *One-Thing Approach* (OTA) [30], whose consistency requirement is a key prerequisite for enabling full code generation. In the following, we first sketch these aspects along a concrete case study: a tool for modeling and fully generating web applications. We then discuss the concepts

---

[6] The term DSM is often correlated to Kelly and Tolvanen's book [26] and the corresponding MetaEdit framework. However, we broaden the term to all approaches aiming at a similar purpose.

that make us confident to master the challenge of developing and maintaining the wealth of such domain-specific tools.

3.1   Case Study: Full Modeling of Web Applications

The *DyWA Integrated Modeling Environment* (DIME) [5,6] is a model-driven development framework for web applications that puts the application expert (potentially, non-programmers) in the center of the web application development process. DIME is developed with Cinco (cf. Sect. 4) and follows the *One-Thing Approach*. In OTA, multiple models of different types, specialized to certain areas of development, are interdependently connected yielding by construction a much higher traceability than what is common in today's model-driven approaches. This model collective consistently shapes the *one thing*, to the extent of completeness that the described artefact (e.g., a tool, or a web application) can be one-click-generated from that model collective and deployed as a running application. This way, the user is provided with an early prototype of an up-and-running web application right from the beginning. DIME generates entire web applications which run within the Dynamic Web Application (DyWA) [38], a framework that fosters prototype-driven development of web applications throughout the whole application life-cycle in a service-oriented manner [32].

A web application is specified in DIME using three different modeling languages: for data, processes, and GUI. While *data models* define the target domain model in terms of types (including inheritance, attributes, and relations), the business logic is modeled with *processes*. Processes are conceptually based on the service logic graphs (SLGs) already used in jABC4 [39] and its predecessors [31,49], but provide different – more specialized yet similarly structured and handled – types for dedicated behavioral aspects of the application[7]. Finally, *GUI models* reflect the structure of the individual web pages and are primarily used as interaction points within sitemap processes.

In combination, those three model types allow to specify the complete application. As introduced before, a model influences multiple generated artefacts. For example, domain concepts defined in a data model are represented by corresponding types on all layers of the running application (cf. Fig. 1):

- At the lowest layer, data is persisted using the *Java Persistence API* (JPA).
- Processes executed within the DyWA (backend business logic) use dedicated DyWA types implemented in Java.
- During communication between frontend and backend via REST [15], data is represented with JSON objects.
- Finally, for use in the interaction processes of the frontend business logic and in the GUI models for the user interface, DIME data models are generated to dedicated Dart types [1].

---

[7] A detailed introduction to the available process model types is given in [5,6] and DIME's web site: http://dime.scce.info.

DIME High-Level Specification   Running Web Application
(Models)   (Source Code)

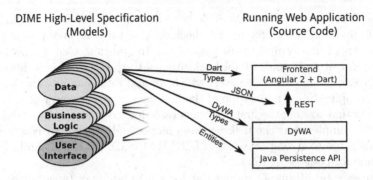

Fig. 1. Examples for Data Model targets

The required management happens in the corresponding code generators and in the running application, without any need for the modeling user, i.e. the application expert who develops the system, to actually know this structure. A more detailed explanation can be found in [5].

3.2 The Continuous Improvement Process

A major challenge and clear bottleneck for DSM approaches is how to provide the required code generators. Today this is mainly treated manually, while the DSM approach we envisage addresses this problem in a framework-bootstrapping fashion. Starting from simple core capabilities, framework bootstrapping enriches this core by successively integrating and then improving tools for modeling very specific kinds of code generators dedicated to specific scenarios like process modeling, parser generation, theorem proving, model checking, planning, synthesis, and SMT solving.

The idea is to use state-of-the-art functionalities and integrate them into dedicated domain-specific modeling environments for enhancing, adapting, and combining these functionalities into increasingly sophisticated solutions. These solutions are then themselves integrated into the overall framework,

- as basic functional building blocks to be (re-)used during subsequent modeling, or
- as extensions enhancing the framework's conceptual support for the development of more or less specialized modeling environments itself.

Whereas the integration of functional building blocks simply supports some higher-level concept of hierarchical design, the extensions introduce a continuous improvement process in a bootstrapping fashion for the entire framework. First results of this approach have been presented in [21,23,24,37] with the Genesys framework. Being a generator of code generators, Genesys' required building blocks concern the basic functionality for writing code generators. These blocks were automatically generated from metamodels of the considered (source) modeling languages, turning the actual code generator development into a modeling discipline. This approach frees the code generator developers from dealing with tedious syntax, and allows for model checking-based consistency proofs [23] of the properties of the resulting code generators. In addition, Genesys provides a model-driven testing framework for back-to-back testing [25]. This technology is based on Genesys' model interpreter, which, in addition, was also the basis for the bootstrapping-based realization of the first Java code generator [21]. Experience showed that writing the first code generator for a certain family of scenarios is still quite complex, but the task becomes increasingly simple for new variants or languages due to strong reuse effects [21] that make it behave similarly to a product line for code generators.

Of course, establishing a product line for a new family of (generalized code) generators, like parser generators, theorem provers, planners etc., is a non-trivial effort and it requires to establish dedicated domain-specific modeling languages. Such languages may require their own analysis and generation technologies, but they profit from a common conceptual core for model checking, simulation, constraint solving, abstraction, view generation etc. Many of these technologies can be applied and reused elsewhere as long as the domain-specific modeling obeys certain rules. Important is here that these rules can be enforced, if required, already at the metamodeling level, in order to guide the domain expert at domain definition time [51]. Many such rules are part of today's implicitly existing common conceptual core. They concern

- The use of BNF for syntax definition as a basis for inductive definition and reasoning
- The use of some kind of typing to enforce consistency at some abstract level
- The use of relational modeling (taxonomies and ontologies) as a basis for defining domains
- The use of structured operational semantics [42] for behavioral semantic definition as the basis for simulation, code generation, and the generation of transition graphs
- The use of transition graphs as a basis for some kind of abstract model checking

However, specific domains allow for stronger constraints and therefore provide better support. E.g., in the context of DIME a lot more is set up upfront for the development of web applications:

- The use of a browser as the GUI technology
- The use of databases for persisting data
- The treatment of events
- User log-in and session handling
- Asynchronous communication between frontend and backend
- Suspending and resuming long-running processes

In fact, in a typical DIME application scenario, the entire web technology stack consisting of database servers, application servers, etc. will be already installed and set up, taking away the burden of technology choice and installation.

Altogether we envision a future design and development technology landscape where hierarchies of (application) domains will be directly linked to product lines of corresponding modeling frameworks, and these hierarchies will be mutually supporting each other in a bootstrapping fashion, inheriting corresponding common conceptual cores. We are therefore convinced that what will increasingly be unified are meta-level patterns rather than concrete languages, and that future tools will be fit to directly deal with these patterns and not just with specific instances.

4 Meta-Level Reuse with the Cinco Framework

The CINCO Meta Tooling Suite [36] provides an initial implementation framework designed to serve as a platform for adoption and use of the concepts on continuous meta-level improvement envisioned in this paper. CINCO is a metamodeling-based tool for creating domain-specific modeling environments. It follows a fully generative approach insofar as it generates complete modeling solutions (which we call CINCO Products) from high-level specifications. CINCO is built upon the Eclipse ecosystem, using the metamodeling framework EMF [52] and the *Rich Client Platform* [33]. Basically, CINCO and all modeling tools it generates comprise of a set of bundles[8] added to the standard Eclipse Modeling Tools release [2].

Framework enhancements leading towards our envisioned unified conceptual core can happen on two levels:

1. CINCO is built to ease the development of highly specialized modeling tools. We thus intend to use CINCO to build modeling tools for the target domain "modeling tool development", and then integrate these tools into CINCO itself in a bootstrapping fashion. This way, certain tool development tasks are designed the first time, but are incorporated in the platform and ready to use from then on. Tools that lend themselves may concern, e.g., checking the syntax of some input string, and obtain their specific DSL, perhaps BNFs. They can arise at the level of the individual modeling tools, the CINCO products, to ease the domain-specific modeling task (in the DIME example, a web application), which may comprise parsing a certain string, and be successively lifted to the CINCO-level, to ease the development of modeling tools (in the DIME example, DIME itself).

2. More general concepts required in many domains (and thus in many tools developed with CINCO) will be 'lifted to the meta level', i.e. they are adequately generalized and abstracted to be integrated as a meta plug-in into CINCO. This way, they can be configured on the meta level with WHAT-driven specifications, resulting in complete sophisticated realizations in the generated modeling tool. Examples range from commonly required 'flavors' of model types (such as data, processes, etc.) to various features found in programming languages (execution semantics, type systems, error handling, scoping, higher order, etc.).

---

[8] Bundle is the term used by Eclipse's underlying OSGi architecture. The term plug-in is probably more commonly understood for non-Eclipse developers.

The following two subsections individually sketch each of these levels along the example of specifying model semantics, in particular with code generation. A detailed introduction of CINCO can be found in [36] and on the CINCO website[9].

4.1 Framework Evolution in a Bootstrapping Fashion

The formalisms used by CINCO to fully specify and automatically generate a modeling tool can be regarded under four orthogonal aspects (cf. Fig. 2 (left)):

Metamodels of a CINCO product are defined in the Meta Graph Language (MGL), a specialized textual meta-level DSL for the definition of graph structures built from *nodes* and *edges*. The metamodel of each modeling language in a CINCO Product is defined by its own MGL specification.

The visual appearance of nodes and edges is defined with a Meta Style Language (MSL) model, which is also a CINCO-specific textual DSL. It allows for the simple definition of rendering styles in form of shapes and their appearance and is designed to specifically support metamodels defined in MGL.

The semantics in a modeling tool is often defined in a translational way, i.e. the semantics of a model is given by a translation (i.e. code generator or model to model transformation), and the inherent semantics of the target structure. The semantics of a CINCO product's model type can be defined either with modeled code generators based on the jABC and Genesys frameworks, or be implemented programmatically with Java or Xtend [3].

Validation covers aspects of static semantics, i.e. properties of models that can not directly be reflected by the metamodel defined with MGL. It requires similar constructs as translational semantics, e.g. regarding model traversal, but it checks for properties instead of generating a target artefact. Thus, validation can also be realized with jABC models, or implemented programmatically.

CINCO already simplifies the development of modeling tools by providing strong domain-specific support, but improvements are still possible: MGL and MSL are specifically designed for CINCO as textual formats, but some users might prefer graphical representations. Moreover, modeling code generators, transformations, and validation checks as supported by the Genesys framework is still based on jABC, which is not specialized to any of those tasks. As CINCO is developed for defining modeling languages, we intend to enhance all the aspects of this specification activity with more specialized variants realized with CINCO itself. This does, of course, not necessarily mean that there will be exactly four new languages, as certain parts of aspects might be better supported with even more specialized model types. For instance, separate formalisms for semantics definitions – one specialized on code generation, the other on transformations – would further focus the development.

Figure 2 illustrates this idea. The CINCO side (left) shows the four aspects of modeling tool specification, each of which is required for the generation of

---

[9] http://cinco.scce.info.

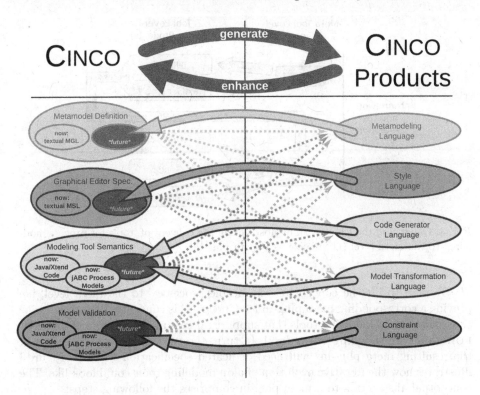

Fig. 2. Extending CINCO's specification formats in a bootstrapping fashion with specialized modeling tools generated with CINCO.

each CINCO Product on the right side (depicted with the dashed arrows in the background). The CINCO Products on the right side specialize on individual aspects of modeling tools and are integrated into future versions of CINCO to enhance the pool of available meta-level languages.

4.2   Enhancing the Conceptual Core with Meta Plug-Ins

A first step in the evolution of CINCO will be to develop a successor of the Genesys framework to free the CINCO ecosystem from jABC's legacy technology[10], to replace the jABC-based definition of code generators for CINCO Products. Such a new CINCO-Genesys will have considerable similarities with process models in DIME, as both are spiritual successors of jABC-based processes[11]. However, they will come with certain characteristics of their domains.

---

[10] This is the main reason why we developed DIME's initial code generators using Xtend.

[11] Prior to DIME, processes for DyWA-based web applications were modeled in jABC with dedicated components generated from the application's data schema, in turn modeled in DyWA.

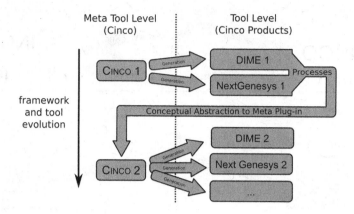

Fig. 3. Enhancing the framework by abstracting the concept of 'tools for process modeling' to the meta level (i.e. realize as a meta plug-in).

We plan to lift the concept of 'executable processes' to the meta level, i.e. provide a corresponding meta plug-in for CINCO. This conceptual uplift will take the realization of modeling tools that support process modeling from the current HOW to a corresponding WHAT level. In turn, the WHAT-level configurations of the resulting meta plug-ins will need dedicated specification formats. Figure 3 illustrates how the iterative evolution of akin modeling tools could look like. The conceptual abstraction to a meta plug-in comprises the following steps:

- Certain structural and visual design decisions (i.e. portions of MGL and MSL specifications) will be shared.
- Parts of the semantics will essentially be the same, only with several basic modeling components then specialized to the modeling of code generators (for instance, the efficient inclusion of templates, and structures supporting the traversal of models), and of web applications (e.g., long-running processes, and interaction with the database).
- Other future tools realizing more specialized variants of jABC will benefit from them too, if they require similar (structural as well as semantical) aspects.

The general structure of processes just served as one example. We envision other concepts to be abstracted as meta plug-ins that handle how to design, manipulate and check them, for instance type systems, error handling, scoping, and higher order.

Integrating those into a common conceptual core aims at evolving language creation to a "shopping experience", where one just selects what aspects the domain-specific language requires, finds predesigned off-the-shelf specialized and well-fitting tools to handle them, and just needs to apply some configuration and fine-tuning in order to tailor the concept and its tooling annex to the specific domain.

5 Summary and Discussion

We have sketched a scenario where application programming gradually evolves into the discipline of using highly specialized domain-specific (modeling) languages, and where the art of mastering the required construction of languages and development tools becomes a commodity. In our terminology, this means that there will be an increasing number of dedicated WHAT-style languages, whose corresponding tool frameworks profit from a growing unified conceptual core on the HOW level. It does, however, not mean that there will be a uniform general-purpose HOW language. Rather, because the distinction between WHAT and HOW very much depends on the beholder's perspective, there will also be domain-specific HOW languages. For example, BNF grammars are very domain-specific and they are certainly considered to be at the HOW level by many people. In fact, we envision a bootstrapping effect where the results of dedicated WHAT-level developments (e.g. for certain analyses) are integrated into development frameworks, rendering these tasks from then on for the bulk of the enhanced framework's users. With this change, we believe that domain-specific tool development will evolve and be simplified to a point where domain-specific frameworks are designed even for individual projects as discussed in [51].

Domain-specific languages do not necessarily describe an application[12] entirely. Therefore, some programming languages already offer an interoperability or bridging layer. Java needs this capabiliy, e.g., in order to call system dependent functions. Although Java processes live in a virtual machine (i.e., the JVM) they have to interact with the concrete system when it accesses devices, e.g., for reading files from disc or communicating over the network. Java offers JNI in order to bind constructs from the underlying system directly to Java components with a well-defined and configurable transformation of data for parameters and return value. Apple's language *Swift* has a sophisticated interoperation layer to *Objective-C* and *C* code, too. The focus in Swift does not lie on accessing system dependent functions, but in code reuse for existing frameworks and libraries, as the underlying *LLVM* compiler framework is not based on a virtual machine.

These interoperability layers offer a well-defined mapping from language constructs between the participating languages, so they allow to introduce referential integrity. Until now this has been used for enabling platform independence (Java) and reuse (Swift), only. We believe that the trend will be to transfer this pattern to realize interdependent families of domain-specific languages quite similar to the envisioned scenario proposed in this paper.

This trend will not help to overcome the difference between modeling and programming. Rather, what we call programming today will appear in special sub-disciplines in the future landscape of system development: a special art, mastered by a few experts, who are, in particular, required to evolve the overall scenario. They will e.g. be responsible for all the required meta tooling and development frameworks, apply bootstrapping technology, aggregate purpose-specific models to a whole, provide automatic deployment and quality assurance,

---

[12] This can be very different artefacts, not just classic desktop applications.

and guarantee security. The bulk of the development, however, will concern application development, and be in the hands of the application experts who do not need to have any dedicated programming knowledge, just as today one does not need to be a web designer with special knowledge in HTML, CSS, or JavaScript to set up a website [18]. Thus programming experts will turn into a kind of generalized infrastructure providers, enabling the application experts to solve their customer-specific tasks themselves.

From a wider perspective, programming and modeling will be quite similar in this new setting. Both will serve very specific purposes while abstracting from many other issues. For example, the purpose of programming may, depending on the actual sub-discipline, just concern the code generation, security aspects, performance issues, scalability, etc., i.e. issues that can be treated independently of the actual primary customer concern, while the application experts can fully focus on the functionality of the application. The underlying domain-specific frameworks are intended to support a clean separation of concerns by providing required but purpose-specific functionality as built-in commodity.

This future scenario illustrates the impact an underlying framework or domain-specific setting can have on the mindset. Rather than trying to establish a universal language, we consider the identification, design, realization, and the evolution of conceptually new domain-specific languages as a driver for innovation. Of course, the unification of modeling and programming, and in particular the steadily growing underlying conceptual common core, are essential for mastering this challenge.

Acknowledgments. This work was supported, in part, by Science Foundation Ireland grant 13/RC/2094 and co-funded under the European Regional Development Fund through the Southern & Eastern Regional Operational Programme to Lero - the Irish Software Research Centre (www.lero.ie).

References

1. Dart programming language. https://www.dartlang.org/. Online; last accessed 26 Jul 2016
2. Eclipse Modeling Tools. http://www.eclipse.org/downloads/packages/eclipse-modeling-tools/lunasr2. Online; last accessed 30 Jul 2016
3. Xtend - Modernized Java. https://www.eclipse.org/xtend/. Online; last accessed 30 Jul 2016
4. Backus, J.W.: The syntax and semantics of the proposed international algebraic language of the Zurich ACM-GAMM Conference. In: IFIP Congress, pp. 125–131 (1959)
5. Boßelmann, S., Frohme, M., Kopetzki, D., Lybecait, M., Naujokat, S., Neubauer, J., Wirkner, D., Zweihoff, P., Steffen, B.: DIME: a programming-less modeling environment for web applications. In: Margaria, T., Steffen, B. (eds.) ISoLA 2016, Part II. LNCS, vol. 9953, pp. 809–832. Springer, Cham (2016)

6. Boßelmann, S., Neubauer, J., Naujokat, S., Steffen, B.: Model-driven design of secure high assurance systems: an introduction to the open platform from the user perspective. In: Margaria, T., Solo, A.M.G. (eds.) The 2016 International Conference on Security and Management (SAM 2016). Special Track "End-to-end Security and Cybersecurity: from the Hardware to Application", pp. 145–151. CREA Press (2016)

7. Broy, M., Havelund, K., Kumar, R.: Towards a unified view of modeling and programming. In: Margaria, T., Steffen, B. (eds.) ISoLA 2016, Part II. LNCS, vol. 9953, pp. 238–257. Springer, Cham (2016)

8. Burkart, O., Steffen, B.: Model checking for context-free processes. In: Cleaveland, W. (ed.) CONCUR 1992. LNCS, vol. 630, pp. 123–137. Springer, Heidelberg (1992)

9. Burkart, O., Steffen, B.: Model checking the full modal mu-calculus for infinite sequential processes. Theoret. Comput. Sci. 221(1–2), 251–270 (1999)

10. Chen, P.P.S.: The entity-relationship model - toward a unified view of data. Trans. Database Syst. (TODS) 1(1), 9–36 (1975)

11. Clarke, E.M., Grumberg, O., Peled, D.A.: Model Checking. The MIT Press, Cambridge (1999)

12. Constable, R., Allen, S., Bromley, H., Cleaveland, W., Cremer, J., Harper, R., Howe, D., Knoblock, T., Mendler, N., Panangaden, P., Sasaki, J., Smith, S.: Implementing Mathematics with the Nuprl Proof Development System. Prentice-Hall, Upper Saddle River (1986)

13. Damm, W., Harel, D.: LSCs: breathing life into message sequence charts. Formal Methods Syst. Des. 19(1), 45–80 (2001)

14. Dhamdhere, D.M.: A new algorithm for composite hoisting and strength reduction optimisation (+ Corrigendum). Int. J. Comp. Math. 27, 1–14 (1989)

15. Fielding, R.T.: Architectural styles and the design of network-based software architectures. Ph.D. thesis, University of California, Irvine (2000)

16. Filev, A., Loton, T., McNeish, K., Schoellmann, B., Slater, J., Wu, C.G.: Professional UML Using Visual Studio .Net. Wiley Publishing Inc., Indianapolis (2003)

17. Fowler, M., Parsons, R.: Domain-specific languages. Addison-Wesley/ACM Press (2011)

18. Gelbmann, M.: WordPress powers 25% of all websites (2015). https://w3techs.com/blog/entry/wordpress-powers-25-percent-of-all-websites.   Online;   last accessed 19 Jul 2016

19. Gordon, M., Milner, R., Morris, L., Newey, M., Wadsworth, C.: A metalanguage for interactive proof in LCF. In: Proceedings of the 5th Symposium on Principles of Programming Languages (POPL 1978) (1978)

20. Jackson, P.B.: Nuprl and its use in circuit design. In: Stavridou, V., Melham, T., Boute, R. (eds.) Proceedings of the IFIP TC10/WG10.2 International Conference on Theorem Provers in Circuit Design: Theory, Practice and Experience, pp. 311–336 (1992)

21. Jörges, S. (ed.): Construction and Evolution of Code Generators. LNCS, vol. 7747. Springer, Heidelberg (2013)

22. Jörges, S., Lamprecht, A.L., Margaria, T., Naujokat, S., Steffen, B.: Synthesis from a practical perspective. In: Margaria, T., Steffen, B. (eds.) ISoLA 2016, Part I. LNCS, vol. 9952, pp. 282–302. Springer, Cham (2016)

23. Jörges, S., Margaria, T., Steffen, B.: Genesys: service-oriented construction of property conform code generators. Innov. Syst. Softw. Eng. 4(4), 361–384 (2008)

24. Jörges, S., Steffen, B.: Exploiting ecore's reflexivity for bootstrapping domain-specific code-generators. In: Proceedings of 35th Software Engineering Workshop (SEW 2012), pp. 72–81. IEEE (2012)

25. Jörges, S., Steffen, B.: Back-to-back testing of model-based code generators. In: Margaria, T., Steffen, B. (eds.) ISoLA 2014. LNCS, vol. 8802, pp. 425–444. Springer, Heidelberg (2014). doi:10.1007/978-3-662-45234-9_30
26. Kelly, S., Tolvanen, J.P.: Domain-Specific Modeling: Enabling Full Code Generation. Wiley-IEEE Computer Society Press, Hoboken (2008)
27. Knoop, J., Rüthing, O., Steffen, B.: Lazy code motion. In: Proceedings of the ACM SIGPLAN 1992 Conference on Programming Language Design and Implementation (PLDI), pp. 224–234. ACM (1992)
28. Knoop, J., Rüthing, O., Steffen, B.: Optimal Code Motion: Theory and Practice. ACM Trans. Program. Lang. Syst. **16**(4), 1117–1155 (1994)
29. Ledeczi, A., Maroti, M., Bakay, A., Karsai, G., Garrett, J., Thomasson, C., Nordstrom, G., Sprinkle, J., Volgyesi, P.: The generic modeling environment. In: Workshop on Intelligent Signal Processing (WISP 2001) (2001)
30. Margaria, T., Steffen, B.: Business process modelling in the jABC: the one-thing-approach. In: Cardoso, J., van der Aalst, W. (eds.) Handbook of Research on Business Process Modeling. IGI Global (2009)
31. Margaria, T., Steffen, B., Reitenspieß, M.: Service-oriented design: the jABC approach. In: Cubera, F., Krämer, B.J., Papazoglou, M.P.(eds.) Service Oriented Computing (SOC). No. 05462 in Dagstuhl Seminar Proceedings. Internationales Begegnungs- und Forschungszentrum für Informatik (IBFI), Schloss Dagstuhl, Germany (2006)
32. Margaria, T., Steffen, B., Reitenspieß, M.: Service-oriented design: the roots. In: Benatallah, B., Casati, F., Traverso, P. (eds.) ICSOC 2005. LNCS, vol. 3826, pp. 450–464. Springer, Heidelberg (2005). doi:10.1007/11596141_34
33. McAffer, J., Lemieux, J.M., Aniszczyk, C.: Eclipse Rich Client Platform, 2nd edn. Addison-Wesley Professional (2010)
34. Milner, R.: LCF: a way of doing proofs with a machine. In: Bečvář, J. (ed.) MFCS 1979. LNCS, vol. 74, pp. 146–159. Springer, Heidelberg (1979). doi:10.1007/3-540-09526-8_11
35. Morel, E., Renvoise, C.: Global optimization by suppression of partial redundancies. Comm. ACM **22**(2), 96–103 (1979)
36. Naujokat, S., Lybecait, M., Kopetzki, D., Steffen, B.: CINCO: A Simplicity-Driven Approach to Full Generation of Domain-Specific Graphical Modeling Tools (to appear, 2016)
37. Naujokat, S., Neubauer, J., Lamprecht, A.L., Steffen, B., Jörges, S., Margaria, T.: Simplicity-first model-based plug-in development. Softw. Pract. Exp. **44**(3), 277–297 (2013)
38. Neubauer, J., Frohme, M., Steffen, B., Margaria, T.: Prototype-driven development of web applications with DyWA. In: Margaria, T., Steffen, B. (eds.) ISoLA 2014. LNCS, vol. 8802, pp. 56–72. Springer, Heidelberg (2014). doi:10.1007/978-3-662-45234-9_5
39. Neubauer, J., Steffen, B., Margaria, T.: Higher-order process modeling: product-lining, variability modeling and beyond. Electron. Proc. Theoret. Comput. Sci. **129**, 259–283 (2013)
40. Object Management Group (OMG): OMG Meta Object Facility (MOF) Core Specification Version 2.4.1, http://www.omg.org/spec/MOF/2.4.1/PDF. Online; last accessed 23 Apr 2014
41. Object Management Group (OMG): Documents associated with Object Constraint Language (OCL), Version 2.4, February 2014. http://www.omg.org/spec/OCL/2.4/

42. Plotkin, G.D.: A Structural Approach to Operational Semantics. Tech. rep., University of Aarhus, dAIMI FN-19 (1981)
43. Rumbaugh, J., Jacobsen, I., Booch, G.: The Unified Modeling Language Reference Manual. The Addison-Wesley Object Technology Series, 2 edn. Addison-Wesley Professional, July 2004
44. Schmidt, D., Steffen, B.: Program analysis *as* model checking of abstract interpretations. In: Levi, G. (ed.) SAS 1998. LNCS, vol. 1503, pp. 351–380. Springer, Heidelberg (1998). doi:10.1007/3-540-49727-7_22
45. Steffen, B.: Data flow analysis as model checking. In: Ito, T., Meyer, A.R. (eds.) TACS 1991. LNCS, vol. 526, pp. 346–364. Springer, Heidelberg (1991). doi:10.1007/3-540-54415-1_54
46. Steffen, B.: Generating data flow analysis algorithms from modal specifications. Sci. Comput. Program. **21**(2), 115–139 (1993)
47. Steffen, B., Claßen, A., Klein, M., Knoop, J., Margaria, T.: The fixpoint-analysis machine. In: Lee, I., Smolka, S. (eds.) CONCUR 1995. LNCS, vol. 962, pp. 72–87. Springer, Berlin Heidelberg (1995)
48. Steffen, B., Jörges, S., Wagner, C., Margaria, T.: Maintenance, or the 3rd dimension of eXtreme model-driven design. In: IEEE International Conference on Software Maintenance 2009 (ICSM 2009), pp. 483–486 (2009)
49. Steffen, B., Margaria, T., Nagel, R., Jörges, S., Kubczak, C.: Model-driven development with the jABC. In: Bin, E., Ziv, A., Ur, S. (eds.) HVC 2006. LNCS, vol. 4383, pp. 92–108. Springer, Heidelberg (2007)
50. Steffen, B., Margaria, T., Wagner, C.: Round-Trip Engineering, chap. 94, pp. 1044–1055. Taylor & Francis (2010)
51. Steffen, B., Naujokat, S.: Archimedean points: the essence for mastering change. LNCS Trans. Found. for Mastering Change (FoMaC) **1**(1) (2016)
52. Steinberg, D., Budinsky, F., Paternostro, M., Merks, E.: EMF: Eclipse Modeling Framework, 2nd edn. Addison-Wesley, Boston (2008)
53. Wolper, P.: The meaning of "formal": from weak to strong formal methods. Int. J. Softw. Tools Technol. Transf. (STTT) **1**(1), 6–8 (1997)

Towards a Unified View of Modeling and Programming

Manfred Broy[1], Klaus Havelund[2(✉)], and Rahul Kumar[3]

[1] Technische Universität München, Munich, Germany
[2] Jet Propulsion Laboratory, California Institute of Technology, Pasadena, USA
klaus.havelund@jpl.nasa.gov
[3] Microsoft Research, Redmond, USA

Abstract. In this paper we argue that there is a value in providing a unified view of modeling and programming. Models are meant to describe a system at a high level of abstraction for the purpose of human understanding and analysis. Programs, on the other hand, are meant for execution. However, programming languages are becoming increasingly higher-level, with convenient notation for concepts that in the past would only be reserved formal specification languages. This leads to the observation, that programming languages could be used for modeling, if only appropriate modifications were made to these languages. At the same time, model-based engineering formalisms such as UML and SysML are highly popular in engineering communities due to their graphical nature. However, these communities are, due to the complex nature of these formalisms, struggling to find grounds in textual formalisms with proper semantics. A unified view of modeling and programming may provide a common ground. The paper illustrates these points with selected examples comparing models and programs.

1 Introduction

Over the last several decades we have observed the development of a large collection of specification and modeling languages and associated methodologies, and tools. Their purpose is to support formulation of requirements and high-level designs before programming is initiated. Agile approaches advocate to avoid explicit modeling entirely and suggest to go directly to coding. Other approaches advocate avoiding manual coding in a programming language entirely and suggest instead the generation of code directly from the models. This way modeling languages replace programming languages. We can divide modeling languages into formal specification languages (formal methods), usually focusing on textual languages based on mathematical logic and set theory, and associated proof tools (theorem provers, model checkers, etc.), and on the other hand model-based engineering languages (UML, SysML, Modelica, Mathematica, ...), focusing more

K. Havelund—The research performed by this author was carried out at Jet Propulsion Laboratory, California Institute of Technology, under a contract with the National Aeronautics and Space Administration.

T. Margaria and B. Steffen (Eds.): ISoLA 2016, Part II, LNCS 9953, pp. 238–257, 2016.
DOI: 10.1007/978-3-319-47169-3_17

on visual descriptions, code generation, and simulation. Many of these languages have similarities with programming languages.

In parallel, and frankly seemingly independent, we have seen the development of numerous new programming languages. Few languages have had the success of C, which still today is the main programming language for embedded systems. The success is so outstanding that nearly no progress wrt. praxis has been made in this domain (embedded programming) since the 1970ties, although some richer languages appeared soon after C in this domain, such as C++, Ada, and Eiffel. These later languages for example all have module systems, which C does not. We have seen several high-level languages appear that target the softer side of software engineering (such as web-programming, user interfaces, scripting), including languages such as Java, JavaScript, Ruby, Python and Scala. More academic languages include Haskell and the ML family, including OCaml.

There is seemingly a strict difference between a modeling language and a programing language. For a programming language we always assume a notion of *executability* and *computability*. Programming languages are restricted to concepts that can be executed. Put differently, programming languages put emphasis on the *"how"*, the algorithms for solving problems. A specification and modeling language in principle should rather focus on the *"what"*. A mathematical way of phrasing this is that specifications should ideally be *predicates* on solutions (executions for example). Intuitively, one may also argue that there are modeling tasks which do not directly aim at programing, for instance if we model a business process independent of the question which parts should be carried out by machines. This is modeling, which seems far away from programming. It might be interesting to bring it into a form which is closer to programming if we want to simulate or automatically analyze such models. But here there seems to be a boundary. Programming means computability. Modeling can be more general. Finally, at a more technical level, in programming, at least when we work in general purpose programming languages, we have to deal with non termination and the concept of undefined [15]. In a number of modeling approaches such concepts like undefined are avoided. Here again there is an interesting challenge in a unifying view of modeling and programming. We would have to manage to introduce the concepts of undefined into modeling, representing nonterminating expressions in programming. Some attempts have been made in this direction though, for example 3-valued logic as found in VDM [31].

In spite of these perceived differences, the similarities between modeling languages and programming languages are obvious, which suggests a unifying view. For example, many logics support the notions of local variables with bounded scopes and syntactic expressions similar to programming languages. Many modeling languages even offer programming constructs, such as mutable variables, assignment statements, and looping (while) statements, and of course recursion. Furthermore, some of the modeling languages, such as UML, are deeply influenced by programming languages wrt. how models are structured. In particular, the idea of object-oriented modeling is taken from the concept of object-oriented programming. It is even considered one of the strong sides of object-orientation, that one can have a unified view of object-oriented specification, object-oriented design, and object-oriented programming. In summary, the concepts that are used in modeling and the concepts that are used in programming are so closely related that it is beneficial to attempt a unified view.

In this paper we attempt to argue for such a unified view of modeling and programming. This view can in the extreme be considered a call for a single universal formalism for modeling and programming any form of system. This is done by high-lighting some trends in modeling and programming, and by programming some example models in the Scala programming language, a high-level formalism suited for this purpose. However, we fully understand that such a unification faces many obstacles, some of which are non-technical. What we intend is to fuel an *effort* to at least consider merging efforts to the extent feasible. We believe that the model-based engineering community can learn from the formal methods and programming language communities, and vice versa. Note that even if a single formalism would appear, there will always be alternatives, just like there are multiple programming languages (evolution continues).

The paper is organized as follows. In Sect. 2 we give a brief overview of some of the trends in modeling and programming, that we consider important. In Sect. 3 we illustrate with examples how modeling can be perceived as programming. Finally Sect. 4 outlines brief discussion points to be reflected on when considering a unified approach, as well as a conclusion.

2   Trends in Modeling and Programming

In this section we briefly survey some trends in the fields of formal methods, model-based engineering, and programming, that we find worthwhile highlighting.

2.1   Formal Methods

Early work on formal methods include the work of John McCarthy (*Recursive Functions of Symbolic Expressions and Their Computation by Machines* [34] and *Towards a Mathematical Science of Computation* [35]), Robert Floyd (*Assigning Meanings to Programs* [19]), Edsger Dijkstra (*A Discipline of Programming* [16]), Tony Hoare (*An Axiomatic Basis for Computer Programming* [29]), and Dana Scott and Christopher Strachey (*Towards a Mathematical Semantics for Computer Languages* [36]), to mention a few. These ideas were theoretic in nature and deeply influential. They brought us the ideas of annotating programs with assertions, such as pre- and post-conditions, and invariants, correct by construction development (refinement), and giving semantics to programming languages.

These ideas were subsequently the basis for several, what we could call, second generation formal specification languages such as VDM [13,14,31], VDM++ [18], Z [37], B and Event-B [12], CIP [38], TLA [32], RAISE [22], and OBJ [21], to mention just a few. Each of these languages are full specification languages, most with rich type systems and detailed rules (grammars) for what constitutes a valid specification. These languages were ahead of their time wrt. language features in the sense that many of these features have found their way into modern programming languages of today. A particular example of this is collections (sets, lists, and maps).

The VDM language for example is a wide-spectrum specification language offering a combination of high-level specification constructs and low level programming like constructs. The methodology consists in part, as in CIP, of refining a high-level specification into a low-level program like specification in a stepwise manner. The language offers concepts such as the combination of imperative (procedural and later object-oriented in VDM^{++}) and functional programming; exceptions; algebraic data types and pattern matching; functions as values and lambda abstractions; built-in collection types such as sets, lists and maps, with mathematical notation for creating values of these types, such as for example set comprehension; design-by-contract through pre- and post conditions and invariants; predicate subtypes (so one for example can define natural numbers as a subset of the integers); and predicate logic including universal and existential quantification over any type as Boolean expressions. VDM and Z are so-called *model oriented* specification languages, meaning that a specification is an example model of the desired system. This means that such specifications are somewhat close to high-level programs. This is in contrast to so-called *property oriented* (algebraic) specification languages, such as OBJ, where a specification denotes a set of models[1].

A different branch of formal methods includes theorem proving and model checking. In theorem proving we have seen specification languages, which resemble functional programming languages, including for example Isabelle [10], PVS [11], and Coq [9]. In model checking, early work, such as Spin [30], focused on modeling notations. However, recent research has focused on software model checking, where the target of model checking is code, as for example seen in the Java PathFinder model checker (JPF) [27,28], and in Modex [30] (for C). JPF was created due to the observation that a powerful programming language might be a more convenient modeling language than the traditional model checker input languages. Numerous model checkers now target C.

As can be seen from the above discussion, formal specification languages have for a long time been flirting with programming language like notations, and vice versa. However, the two classes of languages have by tradition been considered as belonging to strictly separate categories. VDM for example was always, and still is, considered a specification language, albeit with code generation capabilities. It has never, in spite of the possibility, been named a programming language, which one may consider being as one of the reasons it is not more wide spread. Writing specifications in VDM and generating code in Java, for example, has not become popular. Programmers feel uncomfortable working with two languages (a specification language and a programming language) when the two languages

---

[1] This characteristic of the difference is somewhat simplified since a VDM specification in fact also can denote more than one model.

are too similar. This is an argument for merging the concepts into a specification, design and implementation language.

2.2 Model-Based Engineering

Model-based engineering includes modeling frameworks that are usually visual/-graphical of nature. One of the main contributions in this field is UML [8] for software development, and its derivatives, such as SysML [7] for systems development. The graphical nature of the UML family of languages has caused it to become rather popular and wide-spread in engineering communities. Engineers are more willing to work with graphical notations, such as class diagrams and state machines, than they are working with sets, lists and maps and function definitions. It seems clearly more accepted than formal methods as described in the previous section.

One of the important notations in UML/SysML is class diagrams. Class diagrams are, just like E/R-diagrams, really a simple way of defining data, an alternative to working with sets, lists and maps as found in VDM and modern programming languages. For example, to state that a person can own zero or more cars one draws a box for Person, and a box for Car, and draws a line between them. It is an idea that quickly can be picked up by a systems engineer, quicker than learning to use programming language data structures. Another notation is that of state machines, a concept that interestingly enough has not found its way into programming languages, in spite of its usefulness in especially embedded programming. UML and SysML also support requirements (as special comments), a concept that usually is not embedded as a first citizen in programming.

The above observations are rather positive. However, UML and SysML are very complexly and weakly defined formalisms. For example, the (human unreadable) abstract syntax for UML (including OCL, in a different document) is 11605 lines of XML, whereas the typical (human readable) concrete syntax (grammar) for a programming language is between 500 and 2500 lines. The UML/SysML standards are long and complex documents. Furthermore, the connection between models and code is fragile, relying on the correctness of translators from for example UML state machines to code. Finally, a discussion about semantics (what do two boxes with a line in between mean?) can turn a project meeting into chaos.

2.3 Programming

Several new programming languages have emerged over the last decades, which include abstraction mechanisms known from the formal specification languages mentioned above. Such languages include SPARK Ada, Eiffel, Java, Python, Scala, Julia, Fortress, C#, Spec#, F#, D, RUST, Swift, Go, Dafny, and Agda. Some languages support design-by-contract with pre-post conditions, and in some cases with invariants. These languages include for example SPARK Ada, Eiffel, Spec#, Dafny, and to some limited extent Scala. Java supports contracts through JML, which, however, is not integrated with Java, but an add-on comment language (JML specifications are comments in a Java program). Most of the languages above support abstract collections such as sets, lists and maps. It is interesting to observe that SUNs Fortress language (which unfortunately was not finished due to lack of funding) supports a mathematical notation for collections very similar to VDM. The systems Dafny and Why3 are amongst the newest branches of work, interesting since these languages are developed specifically with verification in mind.

A trend on the rise is the combination of object-oriented and functional programming, as seen perhaps most prominently in Scala, but also in the earlier Python, and now in Java which got closures in version 1.8. Ocaml is a similar earlier attempt to integrate object-oriented and functional programming, although in a layered manner, and not integrated with the standard module system. As in many other aspects, Lisp was early out with this combination with the Common Lisp Object System (CLOS). Some interesting new directions of research include dependent types as found in Agda (to some extent related to predicate subtypes in VDM) and session types. Session types are temporal patterns that can be checked at compile time. They are much related to temporal logic as used within the formal methods community to express properties of concurrent programs. At the same time there are also attempts to move away from C, but without losing too much efficiency. Examples include the languages Go, D and RUST. However, as stated earlier, C has an impressive staying power, and none of such attempts have yet become main stream.

3   Modeling as Programming

In this section we shall attempt to explore the argument that modeling can be perceived as programming. We will do this through a small collection of examples, illustrating how what is normally considered as modeling can be perceived as programming. Models are encoded in the Scala programming language, which is sufficiently high-level to illustrate the point. We start with class diagrams, as found in UML and SysML, then move on to a classical formal specification language such as VDM^{++}, and finally discuss Domain-Specific Languages (DSLs).

3.1   Modeling of Class Diagrams

A commonly used part of UML and SysML is the class diagram. The class diagram is a visualization of data structures as nodes and edges. Nodes represent data elements and edges represent the relationships between data elements. To take an example, consider the class diagram in Fig. 1 (the example is adopted from [6]). This diagram models libraries of books. In this diagram a box (node) denotes a type, a set of objects of that type. Hence for example the top node ⌊Library⌋ (references to text, for example names, in models are enclosed in ⌊...⌋) denotes the type of libraries: a set of library objects each representing a library. A library has a name, which is a string. Note that such data of primitive types

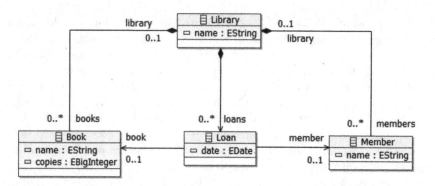

Fig. 1. The book library (from [6])

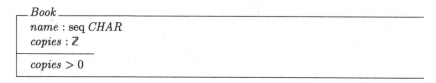

Fig. 2. Z model of books in a library

(strings, integers, reals, Booleans, ...) are represented as so-called *attributes* and are declared inside the boxes instead of as edges, although in principle they can be perceived edges to boxes representing primitive types[2]. A library consists of (left arrow) a collection of books (zero or more represented by the *multiplicity* 0..*), reachable from a library object via the field ⌊books⌋. In the other direction: a book is related to zero or one (0..1) libraries. Similarly, a library (right arrow) has associated a collection of members. Books and members have names. In addition each book has as attribute the number of books on shelf. Finally, a loan is a connection between a book and a member, and a library has associated a collection of (current) loans.

In many modeling situations such diagrams form the core of the modeling effort. Constraints can be added to such diagrams. For example one constraint could be that the number of copies of a book should be positive. Such a constraint (not shown) can be added inside a special constraint box on the diagram in Fig. 1, attached to the ⌊Book⌋ box with a dotted line. It is interesting to note, that a box with an associated constraint (written in another box and linked with a line) conceptually is very similar to the idea of a Z schema [37], as shown in Fig. 2[3]. This schema represents the fundamental concept of a model: a signature (the declaration of ⌊name⌋ and ⌊copies⌋ above the line with their types) and

---

[2] This is an example of a discussion about semantics that can throw a project meeting off its course.

[3] Note that the constraint can actually be avoided in Z by defining the type of ⌊copies⌋ to be $\mathbb{N}_1$, the natural numbers starting from 1.

then zero or more axioms (below the line). Attempts have been made to provide textual versions of UML and SysML diagrams. An example is the K specification language [26], that was developed at JPL. The expression language of K as well as Z (what is written in constraints) is predicate logic. Both languages support datatypes such as sets, including advanced set expressions such as set comprehension. K is object-oriented and is inspired by Z, as well as by other languages, such as VDM [13,14,18,31] and RAISE [22].

Another textual notation coming out of the model-based engineering community itself is OCLInEcore [5], which is an attempt to define a textual language combining the structure oriented Ecore meta-model of the Eclipse Modeling Framework (EMF) [2] with the OCL constraint language (Object Constraint Language) [1]. OCL is a declarative expression language that is now part of the UML standard. OCL descended from Z, but is based on chained method calls read from left to right, starting from *finite* collections, in contrast to predicate logic. For example OCL does not have general universal and existential quantification over infinite sets. In predicate logic we would write a universal quantification over a set/type S as follows: $\forall x : S \bullet P(x)$, meaning: for all x in the set S, $P(x)$ is true. In OCL one would write this as: $\lfloor S \rightarrow \textbf{forAll}(x \mid P(x)) \rfloor$. However, OCL requires S to be finite, in contrast to predicate logic, where S can be infinite. This is the major distinction between OCL and predicate logic, in addition to the alternative syntax. OCL is executable, given a model instance.

In order to illustrate OCLInEcore we expand our example by adding the following requirement: "*The number of loans that a book is part of should be less than or equal to the number of copies of the book*". The OCLInEcore model in Fig. 3 formalizes this requirement. For this purpose, in addition to the two attributes $\lfloor$name$\rfloor$ and $\lfloor$copies$\rfloor$, two *properties* are defined. In contrast to an attribute, which has a primitive type, a property is linked to one or more objects of another user-defined type (those drawn as boxes in class diagrams). The property $\lfloor$library$\rfloor$ links a book to the library it is part of, and is the "*opposite property*" of the $\lfloor$books$\rfloor$ property of the $\lfloor$Library$\rfloor$ (expressed using the $\lfloor$#$\rfloor$-notation), meaning that if a book is in the $\lfloor$books$\rfloor$ set (technically a bag) of a library, then the library is also in the $\lfloor$library$\rfloor$ of the book. The '$\lfloor$?$\rfloor$' represents 0 or 1.

The property $\lfloor$loans$\rfloor$ denotes a collection of $\lfloor$Loan$\rfloor$ objects and is derived (meaning its value depends on other values), with the formula defining its value provided as an OCL expression. The expression reads as follows: from this book (referred to as $\lfloor$self$\rfloor$ later in the expression), retrieve the library it is part of, retrieve the loans of this library, and select those for which the book is equal to $\lfloor$self$\rfloor$. For a given collection $\lfloor S \rfloor$, the notation $\lfloor S \rightarrow M(...) \rfloor$ means calling the method $\lfloor M \rfloor$ on the set $\lfloor S \rfloor$. Hence in this case the $\lfloor \textbf{select}(\text{predicate}) \rfloor$ method is defined on sets and returns the subset of elements of the set satisfying the predicate. The two invariants can now be formulated, and their explanation should at this point be straight forward. The *operation* $\lfloor$isAvailable$\rfloor$ is defined to illustrate that one can also define such, here with an OCL expression as body. One can also define operations with side-effects specified with pre/post

```
class Book {
  attribute name : String;
  attribute copies : Integer;

  property library#books : Library[?];

  property loans : Loan[*] { derived }
  {
    derivation: library.loans→ select(book=self);
  }

  operation isAvailable() : Boolean[?]
  {
    body: loans→ size() < copies;
  }

  invariant CopiesPositive:
    copies > 0;

  invariant SufficientCopies:
    loans→ size() ≤ copies;
}
```

Fig. 3. OCLInEcore model of books in a library (from [6], modified)

conditions. No code with side-effects, however, is allowed in bodies of operations, which seems to be a limitation, and a sign of an attempt to move towards a programming language, but not all the way.

The main point we are trying to make here is that the OCLInEcore model, which in reality is very similar to a Z specification (signature + axioms), can (for the most part) be elegantly expressed in the Scala programming language. This is shown in Fig. 4. The class ⌊Book⌋ extends the class ⌊Model⌋, which we have programmed to offer various methods for writing models, including the ⌊invariant⌋ method used to define invariants. What in the OCLInEcore model was the property ⌊loans⌋ and the operation ⌊isAvailable⌋, are here modeled as methods (using the ⌊**def**⌋ keyword). Multiplicities such as ⌊Loan[*]⌋ are modeled using Scala's collection libraries, in this case ⌊Set[Loan]⌋. The Scala definitions should be somewhat obvious. It is clear that Scala in this case can model this problem in a manner comparable to OCLInEcore. In addition, Scala offers so much more than OCLInEcore, such as an actual programming language.

The only code that has to be written to provide support for writing class invariants is the definition of the class ⌊Model⌋, which is shown in Fig. 5. Without going into details, the class defines a method ⌊invariant⌋, which as argument takes a Boolean call-by-name argument. The argument is not evaluated before the method body is executed, rather, it is only evaluated whenever referred to. In this case it is stored, still unevaluated, in a list of invariants, all of which can

```
trait Book extends Model {
  var name: String
  var copies: Int
  var library: Library

  def loans: Set[Loan] =
    library.loans.filter (_.book eq this)

  def isAvailable (): Boolean =
    loans.size < copies

  invariant("CopiesPositive") {
    copies > 0
  }

  invariant("SufficientCopies") {
    loans.size <= copies
  }
}
```

Fig. 4. Scala program modeling books in a library

then be verified on an object of this class with a call of ⌊verify⌋. Note that such invariants (specifications) in addition can be the target of more formal analysis, just as they can in a formal specification language.

3.2 VDM++ Specifications

As another example, we shall consider a chemical plant alarm management system, first modeled in VDM++ in [18] and also later modeled in Scala in [23], which goes into further detail comparing VDM++ and Scala. We show here a slight modification of the VDM++ specification as well as the corresponding Scala program. In [18] the example specification was associated with a corresponding UML class diagram to illustrate how the two techniques can co-exist. Here we shall put emphasis on VDM++ and its relationship to Scala.

The system shall manage the calling out of experts to deal with operational faults discovered in a chemical plant. Two operations must be provided. ⌊ExpertToPage⌋: Upon detection of a faulty condition, an alarm is raised, and this operation must find an expert on duty able to handle the alarm. Each alarm is associated with a specific qualification required to fix the causing problem, and each expert is associated with a set of qualifications. Upon an alarm, an expert must be found, and paged, that is on duty during the corresponding period and with the right qualification. ⌊ExpertIsOnDuty⌋: returns the periods during which an expert is on duty. In addition to providing these two operations, the state of the system must satisfy the following *invariant*: (i) There must be experts on duty during all periods allocated in the system. (ii) For any alarm and for

```scala
trait Model {
  type Constraint = Unit ⇒ Boolean

  var constraints: List [(String, Constraint)] = Nil

  def invariant (name: String)(c: ⇒ Boolean) {
    constraints ::= (name, (Unit ⇒ c))
  }

  def verify () {
    for ((n, c) <- constraints) assert(c (), n)
  }
}
```

Fig. 5. Support for defining invariants in Scala

any period, there should exist an expert assigned to that period that has the qualification required to fix the source problem of the alarm.

The VDM++ class ⌊Plant⌋ in Fig. 6 is part of the model of this system (other classes/types shown in [18] have been left out here: ⌊Alarm⌋, ⌊Period⌋, and ⌊Expert⌋). The body of this class is divided into three sections: *instance variables* (mutable variables), *functions* (with no side-effects), and *operations* (with side-effects). An invariant defined by the function ⌊PlantInv⌋ is imposed on the instance variables. The corresponding Scala program modeling the plant is shown in Fig. 7. We shall not go into the further details, except for mentioning the use of the ⌊suchthat⌋ method in the Scala program, defined in the ⌊Model⌋ class, which from a finite set selects an element satisfying a predicate provided as argument.

3.3   Domain-Specific Languages

We consider the ability to define domain-specific languages (DSLs) an essential part of a modeling/programming framework. This form of activity is supported within the UML/SysML community through meta-modeling and profiles. Programming languages have been slower to pick up this concept, although an early language such as Lisp supported macros from its birth. A modern programming language such as Scala supports definition of so-called *internal* DSLs with a collection of a few elegant language features. In this section we shall illustrate this with an example DSL for monitoring event sequences. The example was also listed in [25]. An *internal* DSL is an extension of the programming language, in this case effectively an API, however, expressed in such a way that use of this API has the flavor of new syntax added to the language.

The DSL illustrated here is LogFire [24], created for rule-based programming, and specifically for writing temporal trace properties. We shall not go into the details of LogFire (the reader is referred to [24]), but only show a model written

```
class Plant
  instance variables
    alarms : set of Alarm;
    schedule : map Period to set of Expert;

    inv PlantInv(alarms,schedule);

  functions
    PlantInv: set of Alarm * map Period to set of Expert → bool
    PlantInv(as,sch) ==
      (forall p in set dom sch & sch(p) <> {})
        and
      (forall a in set as &
          forall p in set dom sch &
            exists expert in set sch(p) &
              a.GetReqQuali() in set expert.GetQuali());

  operations
    public ExpertToPage: Alarm * Period ⇒Expert
    ExpertToPage(a, p) ==
      let expert in set schedule(p) be st
        a.GetReqQuali() in set expert.GetQuali()
      in
        return expert
    pre a in set alarms and p in set dom schedule
    post let expert = RESULT in
      expert in set schedule(p) and
      a.GetReqQuali() in set expert.GetQuali();


    public ExpertIsOnDuty: Expert ⇒set of Period
    ExpertIsOnDuty(ex) ==
      return {p | p in set dom schedule & ex in set schedule(p)};
end Plant
```

Fig. 6. VDM^{++} model of plant

in this DSL, and briefly explain how the DSL is defined. A monitor is specified as a set of rules, each of the form:

$$name \; -- \; condition_1 \; \& \ldots \& \; condition_n \; \longmapsto \; action$$

A rule consists of a left-hand side: a list of conditions, and a right-hand side: an action. The rules operate on a set of facts, the *fact memory* (implemented as a Rete network [20]) where conditions check the presence or absence of certain facts, and the action adds or deletes facts, or executes any Scala code inserted as part of the action. Figure 8 illustrates a monitor, which monitors *acquire(thread, lock)* and *release(thread, lock)* events emitted from an instrumented multi-threaded application, that uses locks to protect against data races.

```
trait Plant extends Model {
  var alarms: Set[Alarm]
  var schedule: Map[Period, Set[Expert]]

  invariant{PlantInv(alarms, schedule)}

  def PlantInv(alarms: Set[Alarm], schedule: Map[Period, Set[Expert]]): Boolean =
    (schedule.keySet forall {p ⇒ schedule(p) != Set()})
      &&
    (alarms forall { a ⇒
      schedule.keySet forall { p ⇒
        schedule(p) exists { expert ⇒
          a.reqQuali in expert.quali
        }
      }
    })

  def ExpertToPage(a: Alarm, p: Period): Expert = {
    require((a in alarms) && (p in schedule.keySet))
    schedule(p) suchthat { expert ⇒
      a.reqQuali in expert.quali
    }
  } ensuring { expert ⇒
    (a.reqQuali in expert.quali) &&
      (expert in schedule(p))
  }

  def ExpertIsOnDuty(ex: Expert): Set[Period] =
    schedule.keySet filter { p ⇒ ex in schedule(p) }
}
```

Fig. 7. Scala program modeling plant

```
class NoLockCycles extends Monitor {
  "r1" -- 'acquire('t,'l) |-> 'Locked('t,'l)
  "r2" -- 'Locked('t,'l) & 'release('t,'l) |-> remove('Locked)
  "r3" -- 'Locked('t,'l1) & 'acquire('t,'l2) |-> 'Edge('l1,'l2)
  "r4" -- 'Edge('l1,'l2) & 'Edge('l2,'l3) & not('Edge('l1,'l3)) |-> 'Edge('l1,'l3)
  "r5" -- 'Edge('l1,'l2) |-> { if (get('l1) == get('l2)) fail () }
}
```

Fig. 8. Scala program written in the rule DSL, monitoring lock operations

The monitor attempts to determine whether any group of threads access locks in a cyclic manner, which potentially can lead to deadlocks (the classical dining philosopher problem). A cycle is detected if for any lock l there is an edge from l back to itself.

```
implicit def liftRuleName(name: String) =
  new {
    def ––(c: Condition) = new RuleDef(name, List(c))
  }

class RuleDef(name: String, conditions: List[Condition]) {
  def &(c: Condition) = new RuleDef(name, c :: conditions)

  def |->(stmt: ⇒ Unit) {
    addRule(Rule(name, conditions.reverse, Action((x: Unit) ⇒ stmt)))
  }
}
```

Fig. 9. Scala rule DSL implementation

The class contains five rules. Beyond the monitored events ⌊acquire⌋ and ⌊release⌋, the monitor adds and deletes ⌊Locked(thread,lock)⌋ facts (the thread holds the lock), and adds ⌊Edge(lock1,lock2)⌋ facts, representing that there is an edge from ⌊lock1⌋ to ⌊lock2⌋, indicating that a thread holds ⌊lock1⌋ while acquiring ⌊lock2⌋. The class extends the ⌊Monitor⌋ class which contains the DSL definitions that allow us to write rules in this manner. Specifically the functions: ⌊––⌋, ⌊&⌋, ⌊|->⌋, ⌊remove⌋, and ⌊fail⌋.

The implementation of this DSL relies on Scala's (1) allowance for methods having symbol names, such as ⌊––⌋ and ⌊|->⌋, (2) allowance for method calls of the form ⌊obj.method(arg)⌋ to be written as ⌊obj method arg⌋, and (3) automated insertion (by the compiler) of user-defined *implicit* functions that can lift a value of one type to a value of another type in places where the compiler's type checker fails to type check an expression. For example part of the DSL implementation are the definitions shown in Fig. 9. The implicit function ⌊liftRuleName⌋ gets invoked by the compiler automatically when a string is followed by the symbol ⌊––⌋. It lifts the string (rule name) to an anonymous object, which provides the method ⌊––⌋, which when applied to a condition returns an ⌊RuleDef⌋ object, which provides the methods ⌊&⌋ and ⌊|->⌋. This way method calls can be chained together.

We do notice, however, some drawbacks of the Scala DSL. Notice the quoted names: ⌊'acquire⌋, ⌊'Locked⌋, ⌊'t⌋, etc. These are Scala symbols (elements of the type ⌊Symbol⌋). It is not possible in this form of DSL to avoid these quotes. Likewise, the name of the rule is a string. Furthermore, a monitor in this DSL cannot be type checked without actually running the monitor. That is to say, Scala's DSL defining features are not optimal, although they do make defining internal DSLs somewhat easier.

4   Discussion and Conclusion

A unified modeling and programming framework has to satisfy quite different and contradicting goals. First of all, it has to represent the concepts of the application domain at an adequate level of abstraction such that the specialities of the applications are directly represented and not covered by awkward implementation concepts. Second it has to address the structuring of algorithms and data structures in a way such that programs stay understandable, modular and support the most important methods of structured program development. And finally it has to allow addressing specific implementation properties of execution machines including their operating systems, such that it can be controlled how the implementation uses resources and exploits the possibilities of the execution platform and its hardware. An obvious problem here of course is to what extent the particular application domain influences the programming language, and to what extent this is true for the execution platform and efficiency concerns as well. In the following we shall briefly mention some of the elements to consider when imagining a unified approach to modeling and programming.

Target domains: We can observe three major domains of interest, namely modeling; programming of non-embedded systems, such as web applications, including scripting; and finally programming of embedded and cyber-physical systems. It is clear that these three domains till date have been addressed by different communities and different languages. The question is to what extent these quite different domains could be targeted with the same formalism. Note that the different modeling and programming languages used on different targets have an overwhelming number of language constructs in common, to an extent where this question at least needs to be answered in a scientific manner rather than in an opinionated emotional manner.

Predicate specifications: A formalism must generally support specifying properties as predicates rather than only as algorithms. Predicate-oriented techniques include design-by-contract, including pre- and post-conditions, as well as state invariants. Such can for example be found in Eiffel as well as in SPARK. This concept can be carried further to for example include behavioral sequence specification, such as temporal logics, sequence diagrams, etc. Note, however, that many models are very operational in nature, and hence can very well best be formulated as state machines, or programs (data structures and algorithms).

Programming in the large: A formalism must support programming in the large, and in general provide good modularization and component-based development. One cannot discuss components without discussing concurrency. Concurrency is an essential part of modern programming, especially considering the emergence of multi-core computers. However, concurrency is important at the modeling level as well, where it can serve as a natural way to describe interacting agents. Important concepts include agent systems, message passing based communication, parallel data structures (programming concurrent without knowing it), and distributed programming.

High-level programming: A formalism must support high-level programming as found in modern programming languages. The elegance of functional programming has been praised many times. Nevertheless its breakthrough is only recent. In contrast, object-oriented programming, which in particular addresses encapsulation and reuse, has been very popular for decades now. A language such as Scala integrates the two paradigms nicely, as even early versions of Lisp (CLOS) did. Functional programming means for example functions as values (lambda abstractions) and pattern matching, and of course reliance on recursion. Functional programming is by some considered the best approach to use multi-core systems due to no shared state updates. A key feature of VDM was the introduction of elegant syntax for collections, such as sets, lists and maps. These days such concepts are introduced in languages mostly as libraries. Fortress has built-in syntax for these very similar to VDM. There should be easy ways of iterating through collections to avoid indexing problems, as well as support for parallel computation over such. A formalism should be statically typed, although with type inference, and with allowance for going type less in clearly defined regions to support scripting. Decades of experience in strong type systems should be harvested, including more recent topics such as dependent types, session types, and units.

Low-level programming: A formalism must support low-level programming. Embedded programing often means: no dynamic memory allocation after initialization, no garbage collection, some knowledge of memory layout, even to the point where computation with addresses is used to improve speed. This again means use of low level programming languages such as C. C, however, allows for memory errors and makes programmers less effective as they would otherwise be were they allowed to program in higher-level languages. We need to satisfy the needs encountered by typical C programmers, including offering comparable speed and memory control. This includes support for hardware control and targeting specific execution platforms.

Continuous mathematics: A formalism can support modeling of cyber-physical systems. That is: physical systems controlled by computer programs. To model (not program) a cyber-physical system, there is a need for describing continuous behavior using continuous mathematics, including for example differential equations, as supported by for example Modelica [4,17] and Mathematica [3]. Modelica is an object-oriented language for modeling systems containing mechanical, electrical, electronic, hydraulic, thermal, control, electric power or process-oriented subcomponents. Models can be simulated. Mathematica is a more broadly scoped symbolic mathematical computation program. A closely related continuous mathematics topic is real-time analysis, as for example performed by real-time model checkers such as UPPAAL [33]. Whether continuous mathematics should be part of a programming solution is a controversial topic.

Domain-specific languages: A formalism must support definition of domain-specific languages. A key to modeling and programming is to capture the relevant concepts of the application domain. UML for example supports meta-modeling and profiles, used for defining (graphical) domain-specific languages. The programming language community is still somewhat behind in this respect. It should be easy for developers to define new domain-specific languages, either external stand-alone, or internal extending the modeling/programming formalism.

Visualization: A formalism must be visualizable. Visualization is of extreme importance, as demonstrated by the relative success of formalisms such as UML and SysML in the engineering community, when compared to formal methods textual notations. People generally are more at ease looking at a two-dimensional illustration when they encounter a problem specification for the first time, and it eases communication. Whether visualization is useful as well for entering and maintaining specifications is another matter. We do believe that visualization and text should match up, such that modification of one leads to immediate change in the other. Visualization is normally static, rendering static models as pictures. However, visualization can also be dynamic, of program executions, illustrating how behavior evolves.

Analysis: A formalism must be analyzable. A key concept in a combined modeling and programming environment is the support for advanced analysis of models/programs, including, but also beyond, what is normally supported in standard programming environments. This ranges from basic built-in support for unit testing, over advanced testing capabilities, including test input generation and monitoring, to concepts such as static analysis, model checking, theorem proving and symbolic execution. A core requirement, however, must be the practicality of these solutions. The main emphasis should be put on automation. The average user should be able to benefit from automated verification, without having to do manual proofs. However, support for manual theorem proving should also be possible, for example for core critical algorithms. Integration of static and dynamic analysis will be desirable: verify what is practically feasible, and test (monitor) the remaining proof obligations.

What modelers do that programmers don't: A central question is how a model/program is represented. Within the formal methods and programming communities this is simple: specifications/programs are represented as text, exactly as typed in by a user. Any tools such as analyzers and compilers read in the text and produce results. The specification language or programming language is defined by a grammar, which succinctly formalizes what is the language of syntax correct texts. In the case of a compiler it produces binary code/byte code, which of course can be stored and used by other programs. However, at the core, the program text is the main reference, from which other formats can be generated. A compiler will produce an abstract syntax tree (AST) from the text, but it only lives as long as the compiler runs. The situation is different in the model-based engineering community. Here the syntax is mostly graphical, and it is not the main representation (and not of main importance). Instead, abstract syntax is the key representation, often stored in XML, from which everything else is generated. In support of collaborative environments there is even a push for storing models in databases, which can be accessed by multiple users simultaneously, hence a more sophisticated approach than the text-based source code repositories often used by programmers. Modelers furthermore have the habits of querying models, transforming models, and generally consider models as data, in contrast to the programming community where data usually are separated from programs. That is, from within a program one can usually not get access to the entire AST of the program itself, although often limited forms of reflection are possible. These different views of representations are worthwhile investigating.

Conclusion We have in this paper outlined some views on the potential in combining modeling and programming, supported by analysis capabilities such as static analysis, model checking, theorem proving, monitoring, and testing. We believe that the time is right for the formal methods/modeling and programming language communities to join forces. To some extent this is already happening in the small. However, we believe that we are standing in front of a major wave of research creating a united foundation for modeling, programming and verification. A cynical argument is that this is all obvious, which may very well be true.

References

1. Documents associated with Object Constraint Language (OCL), Version 2.4. http://www.omg.org/spec/OCL/2.4. Accessed 29 June 2016
2. EMF. http://www.eclipse.org/modeling/emf/. Accessed 6 July 2016
3. Mathematica. https://www.wolfram.com/mathematica. Accessed 29 June 2016
4. Modelica - A Unified Object-Oriented Language for Systems Modeling. Language Specification Version 3.3. https://www.modelica.org/documents/ModelicaSpec33.pdf. Accessed 29 June 2016
5. OCLInEcore. https://wiki.eclipse.org/OCL/OCLinEcore. Accessed 28 June 2016
6. OCLInEcore online tutorial. http://goo.gl/wR2HvP. Accessed 28 June 2016
7. OMG Systems Modeling Language (SysML). http://www.omgsysml.org. Accessed 12 July 2016
8. OMG Unified Modeling Language (UML). http://www.omg.org/spec/UML. Accessed: 12 July 2016
9. The Coq Theorem Prover. https://coq.inria.fr. Accessed: 12 July 2016
10. The Isabelle Theorem Prover. https://isabelle.in.tum.de. Accessed 12 July 2016
11. The PVS Theorem prover. http://pvs.csl.sri.com. Accessed 12 July 2016
12. Abrial, J.-R.: Modeling in Event-B. Cambridge University Press, New York (2010)
13. Bjørner, D., Jones, C.B.: The Vienna Development Method: The Meta-Language. Lecture Notes in Computer Science, vol. 61. Springer, Heidelberg (1978)
14. Bjørner, D., Jones, C.B.: Formal Specification and Software Development. Prentice Hall International, Upper Saddle River (1982). ISBN: 0-13-880733-7

15. Broy, M.: From chaos to undefinedness. In: Futatsugi, K., Jouannaud, J.-P., Meseguer, J. (eds.) Algebra, Meaning, and Computation. LNCS, vol. 4060, pp. 476–496. Springer, Heidelberg (2006). doi:10.1007/11780274_25

16. Dijkstra, E.W.: A Discipline of Programming. Prentice-Hall, Upper Saddle River (1976)

17. Elmqvist, H., Otter, M., Henriksson, D., Thiele, B., Mattsson, S.E.: Modelica for embedded systems. In: Proceedings of the 7th Modelica Conference, Como, Italy, pp. 354–363, September 2009

18. Fitzgerald, J., Larsen, P.G., Mukherjee, P., Plat, N., Verhoef, M.: Validated Designs For Object-Oriented Systems. Springer, Santa Clara (2005)

19. Floyd, R.W.: Assigning meanings to programs. In: Schwartz, J. (ed.) Mathematical Aspects of Computer Science, Proceedings of Symposium in Applied Mathematics, pp. 19–32. American Mathematical Society, Rhode Island (1967)

20. Forgy, C.: Rete: a fast algorithm for the many pattern/many object pattern match problem. Artif. Intell. **19**, 17–37 (1982)

21. Futatsugi, K., Goguen, J.A., Jouannaud, J.-P., Meseguer, J.: Principles of OBJ2. In: POPL (1985)

22. George, C., Haff, P., Havelund, K., Haxthausen, A., Milne, R., Nielsen, C.B., Prehn, S., Wagner, K.R.: The RAISE Specification Language. The BCS Practitioner Series. Prentice-Hall, Hemel Hampstead (1992)

23. Havelund, K.: Closing the gap between specification and programming: VDM^{++} and Scala. In: Korovina, M., Voronkov, A. (eds.) HOWARD-60: Higher-Order Workshop on Automated Runtime Verification and Debugging, EasyChair Proceedings, vol. 1, Manchester, UK, December 2011

24. Havelund, K.: Rule-based runtime verification revisited. Softw. Tools Technol. Transf. (STTT) **17**, 143–170 (2015)

25. Havelund, K., Joshi, R.: Experience with rule-based analysis of spacecraft logs. In: Artho, C., Ölveczky, P.C. (eds.) Formal Techniques for Safety-Critical Systems. Communications in Computer and Information Science, vol. 476. Springer, Switzerland (2015)

26. Havelund, K., Kumar, R., Delp, C., Clement, B., K: a wide spectrum language for modeling, programming and analysis. In: Proceedings of the 4th International Conference on Model-Driven Engineering and Software Development (MODEL-SWARD), Rome, Italy, pp. 111–122. Scitepress Digital Library, February 2016

27. Havelund, K., Pressburger, T.: Model checking Java programs using Java PathFinder. Int. J. Softw. Tools Technol. Transf. STTT **2**(4), 366–381 (2000)

28. Havelund, K., Visser, W.: Program model checking as a new trend. STTT **4**(1), 8–20 (2002)

29. Hoare, C.A.R.: An axiomatic basis of computer programming. Commun. ACM **12**, 567–583 (1969)

30. Holzmann, G.J.: The Spin Model Checker - Primer and Reference Manual. Addison-Wesley, Boston (2004)

31. Jones, C.B.: Systematic Software Development using VDM. Prentice Hall, Englewood Cliffs (1990). ISBN: 0-13-880733-7

32. Lamport, L.: The temporal logic of actions. ACM Trans. Program. Lang. Syst. **16**, 872–923 (1994)

33. Larsen, K.G., Pettersson, P., Yi, W.: Uppaal in a nutshell. STTT **1**, 134–152 (1997)

34. McCarthy, J.: Recursive functions of symbolic expressions and their computation by machines, part I. Commun. ACM **3**, 184–195 (1960)

35. McCarthy, J.: Towards a mathematical science of computation. In: Popplewell, C. (ed.) IFIP World Congress Proceedings, pp. 21–28 (1962)

36. Scott, D., Strachey, C.: Towards a mathematical semantics for computer languages. Comput. Automata Microwave Res. Inst. Symp. **21**, 19–46 (1971)
37. Spivey, J.M.: The Z Notation - a Reference Manual. International Series in Computer Science, 2nd edn. Prentice Hall, Hemel Hempstead (1992)
38. The CIP Language Group. The Munich Project CIP Volume I: The Wide Spectrum Language CIP-L. LNCS, vol. 183. Springer (1985)

Formal Methods and Safety Certification: Challenges in the Railways Domain

Formal Methods and Safety Certification: Challenges in the Railways Domain

Alessandro Fantechi[1,2,3]($\boxtimes$), Alessio Ferrari[2], and Stefania Gnesi[2]

[1] DINFO, Università degli Studi di Firenze, Via S. Marta 3, Florence, Italy
fantechi@dsi.unifi.it
[2] Istituto di Scienza e Tecnologie dell'Informazione
"A. Faedo" CNR, Via Moruzzi 1, Pisa, Italy
{alessio.ferrari,stefania.gnesi}@isti.cnr.it
[3] DTU Compute, Technical University of Denmark, Kongens Lyngby, Denmark

1 Motivation

The railway signalling sector has historically been a source of success stories about the adoption of formal methods in the certification of software safety of computer-based control equipment. Although it is not possible to exhaustively cite such stories here, we can refer to some witnesses in the two main classes in which we can roughly divide railway signalling systems:

- *ATP/ATC (Automatic Train Protection/Control)* systems guarantee safe speed and braking control for trains, along the line, where the main safety criterion is to guarantee that two trains travelling at speed in the same direction stay a safe distance apart. The basic concept in ATP/ATC is the *braking curve*: safety is guaranteed if the speed is always below the line of the braking curve; should the speed go above the line, emergency braking is enforced.
These systems accommodate both train distancing and protection of singular points of the line: for the first purpose a line is divided in sections of which appropriate sensors detect occupancy by a train. Distancing is obtained by ensuring that at any moment the speed of the train is such that the train can be brought to a halt before entering in an occupied section, that is, the braking curve is at zero at the entrance of the occupied section: the value of allowed speed given by the braking curve depend on the number of free sections in front of the train. Protection of singular points of the line (e.g., an open level crossing) is obtained by setting the braking curve at zero at the protected point.
ATP/ATC systems are constituted by on-board components that receive information from wayside components. In the early computer-based systems of this kind, this communication is rather simple and occurs at specific points of the line. As a consequence, the safety enforcing algorithms were not excessively complex and were directly amenable to formal specification [4].
- *Interlocking* systems establish safe routes through the intricate layout of tracks and points. Interlocking systems have since many years called for a direct application of model checking, due to the fact that their safety properties can

T. Margaria and B. Steffen (Eds.): ISoLA 2016, Part II, LNCS 9953, pp. 261–265, 2016.
DOI: 10.1007/978-3-319-47169-3_18

be expressed in temporal logic, and that their specifications by means of control tables can be directly formalized [3,11,13,14]. Typical of these verification tasks is the combinatorial state space explosion problem, due to the high number of boolean variables involved: the first applications of model checking have therefore addressed portions of an interlocking system (e.g., [2,8]); but even recent works [7,15,18] show that routine verification of interlocking designs for large stations is still a challenge for model checkers.

The latest technological evolutions of signalling systems promise a significant improvement on transport capacity, on the regularity of the service, on the very quality and safety of the offered service. These solutions are increasingly based on the presence, on board trains and at ground, of processors that deal with more and more complex real-time information, and on the adoption of wireless communication links between trains and ground.

Examples of this trend are the roll-out of ERTMS/ETCS (European Rail Traffic Management System/European Train Control System) to improve capacity and enhance cross-border operation within Europe, and the CBTC (Communication Based Train Control) systems deployed in metro and suburban railways to improve capacity and to add automated driving capabilities.

This evolution poses big challenges to the consolidated safety certification processes, and raises concerns about the guarantees to maintain the typically high standards of safety in railway operation whilst being able to satisfy availability, capacity and interoperability requirements. The actual achievement of capacity, availability and interoperability improvements prospected for the future is still a challenge, also in view of the necessary economic investment that these new technologies require. In addition, given the heavy presence of wireless communication links in novel railway systems, security has become a central issue to cope with. Finally, railway systems are by nature *green* transportation systems, which have to keep this desirable attribute even in presence of increasing capacity requirements. Hence, energy consumption is also a primary aspect to consider.

New visionary systems are also beginning to be proposed within the railway signalling community [5]. These have in common the removal of historic assumptions and constraints that have ruled railway safety so far, by resorting to the possibilities offered by technological advances. In particular, moving and distributing the intelligence, that is so far concentrated in a few control centres, is seen as a step towards more efficient, less expensive, more easily maintainable control and management systems. Although distribution makes safety certification much more complex, it promises a more flexible operation and reconfiguration to address planned and emergency changes. These ideas will be the basis for future innovative system architectures. Analysing their safety will be vital to ensure that such innovations will be fit for purpose.

Coping with the challenges posed by the increasing scale and complexity of railway systems, and by the novel technologies available, require the formal methods community to extend and customise the modelling and verification methodologies that showed their effectiveness in earlier computer-based railway systems.

In particular, the community is asked to provide formal solutions that: (a) can deal with *systems-of-systems* that, besides interoperability, have to guarantee high safety and capacity standards; (b) are able to enforce system dependability aspects that go beyond safety – especially security and availability; (c) take into account the *cyber-physical*, hybrid, nature of railway systems to cope, e.g., with the issue of energy consumption.

Addressing these challenges requires an effort from the formal methods research community as well as a stronger cross-fertilisation with railway systems developers, operators, and certification authorities. On the one hand, this will enable the research community to have a proper in-depth understanding of the railway domain, and to focus on solutions to real-world needs of the domain. On the other hand, this will ensure that solutions proposed within the academic world will be properly tailored to be usable, and acceptable, for practitioners.

2   Goals and Contributions

Inspired by the track on "Formal Methods for Intelligent Transportation Systems" held at ISOLA 2012 [6], which actually focused mostly on railway applications, the track "Formal Methods and Safety Certification: Challenges in the Railways Domain" of this year edition aims to present some advanced results addressing the challenges discussed above, in order to show how existing modelling techniques are extended and customized to cope with such challenges. Although addressing different aspects of the domain, the contributions to the track share the approach of basing their specific analysis of different dependability characteristic on a rigorous formal modelling approach.

Three contributions to this track concentrate on the big challenge of verifying large railway interlocking systems, proposing different verification strategies to attack their complexity, in order to decrease the cost of their safety certification. While [10] proposes the adoption of static analysis for the early detection of defects in the specification of the interlocking logics, [12] exploits a compositional approach for attacking large systems of this class. The short contribution [17] describes an open integrated toolset for interlocking verification. The interest of the research community to this challenge is witnessed also by a contribution to the track on "Variability Modelling for Scalable Software Evolution" [9], which proposes an incremental approach based on techniques from the Software Product Lines discipline in order to reduce the time and cost for certification at system updates and layout changes of an interlocking system.

Not only safety contributes to the dependability of nowadays signalling systems: in the railway domain, safety is typically obtained at the cost of reducing service, by halting trains in case of adverse situations; in the current quest of gaining more and more capacity from existing rail lines, availability is indeed of paramount importance. Contribution [16] shows how modelling and model checking techniques used for safety verification can be employed as well, although at a different abstraction level, to establish liveness of a railway line by the detection of possible deadlocks.

Contribution [1] shows how formal modelling can be exploited as well for analysing particular aspects of physical components of the railway system: a precise analysis of energy consumption of switch heaters, although a very localized and apparently minor issue, contributes to the overall safety and availability assessment of a railway system in an important way. In addition, the contribution shows how formal techniques can be used to deal with cyber-physical aspects related to energy consumption.

It is our opinion that, notwithstanding the limited space available, the contributions to the track succeed to give a glance of the state of the art and of the opportunities offered by up-to-date formal modelling and verification techniques and tools in the railway domain. In the future, we foresee a stronger effort towards refining the proposed solutions, and towards a major focus on the issues related to *security*, and to the interplay between security and the other dependability attributes.

References

1. Basile, D., Di Giandomenico, F., Gnesi, S.: Tuning energy consumption strategies in the railway domain: a model-based approach. In: Margaria, T., Steffen, B. (eds.) ISoLA 2016, Part II. LNCS, vol. 9953, pp. 315–330. Springer, Heidelberg (2016)
2. Bernardeschi, C., Fantechi, A., Gnesi, S., Larosa, S., Mongardi, G., Romano, D.: A formal verification environment for railway signaling system design. Formal Methods Syst. Des. **12**(2), 139–161 (1998)
3. Bonacchi, A., Fantechi, A., Bacherini, S., Tempestini, M., Cipriani, L.: Validation of railway interlocking systems by formal verification, a case study. In: Counsell, S., Núñez, M. (eds.) SEFM 2013. LNCS, vol. 8368, pp. 237–252. Springer, Heidelberg (2014). doi:10.1007/978-3-319-05032-4_18
4. Da Silva, C., Dehbonei, B., Mejia, F.: Formal specification in the development of industrial applications: subway speed control system. In: Proceedings 5th IFIP Conference on Formal Description Techniques for Distributed Systems and Communication Protocols (FORTE 1992), Perros-Guirec, pp. 199–213. North-Holland (1993)
5. Fantechi, A.: Formal techniques for a data-driven certification of advanced railway signalling systems. In: ter Beek, M.H., Gnesi, S., Knapp, A. (eds.) FMICS-AVoCS 2016. LNCS, vol. 9933, pp. 231–245. Springer, Heidelberg (2016). doi:10.1007/978-3-319-45943-1_16
6. Fantechi, A., Flammini, F., Gnesi, S.: Formal methods for intelligent transportation systems. In: Margaria, T., Steffen, B. (eds.) ISoLA 2012. LNCS, vol. 7610, pp. 187–189. Springer, Heidelberg (2012). doi:10.1007/978-3-642-34032-1_19
7. Ferrari, A., Magnani, G., Grasso, D., Fantechi, A.: Model checking interlocking control tables. In: Schnieder, E., Tarnai, G. (eds.) FORMS/FORMAT 2010, pp. 107–115. Springer, Heidelbreg (2010). doi:10.1007/978-3-642-14261-1_11
8. Groote, J.F., van Vlijmen, S., Koorn, J.: The safety guaranteeing system at station Hoorn-Kersenboogerd. In: Logic Group Preprint Series 121. Utrecht University (1995)
9. Hähnle, R., Muschevici, R.: Towards incremental validation of railway systems. In: Margaria, T., Steffen, B. (eds.) ISoLA 2016, Part II. LNCS, vol. 9953, pp. 433–446. Springer, Heidelberg (2016)

10. Haxthausen, A.E., Østergaard, P.H.: On the use of static checking in the verification of interlocking systems. In: Margaria, T., Steffen, B. (eds.) ISoLA 2016, Part II. LNCS, vol. 9953, pp. 266–278. Springer, Heidelberg (2016)

11. Haxthausen, A.E., Peleska, J., Pinger, R.: Applied bounded model checking for interlocking system designs. In: Counsell, S., Núñez, M. (eds.) SEFM 2013. LNCS, vol. 8368, pp. 205–220. Springer, Heidelberg (2014). doi:10.1007/978-3-319-05032-4_16

12. Macedo, H.D., Fantechi, A., Haxthausen, A.E.: Compositional verification of multistation interlocking systems. In: Margaria, T., Steffen, B. (eds.) ISoLA 2016, Part II. LNCS, vol. 9953, pp. 279–293. Springer, Heidelberg (2016)

13. James, P., Lawrence, A., Moller, F., Roggenbach, M., Seisenberger, M., Setzer, A., Kanso, K., Chadwick, S.: Verification of solid state interlocking programs. In: Counsell, S., Núñez, M. (eds.) SEFM 2013. LNCS, vol. 8368, pp. 253–268. Springer, Heidelberg (2014). doi:10.1007/978-3-319-05032-4_19

14. James, P., Moller, F., Nguyen, H.N., Roggenbach, M., Schneider, S., Treharne, H., Trumble, M., Williams, D.: Verification of scheme plans using CSP||B. In: Counsell, S., Núñez, M. (eds.) SEFM 2013. LNCS, vol. 8368, pp. 189–204. Springer, Heidelberg (2014). doi:10.1007/978-3-319-05032-4_15

15. Limbrée, C., Cappart, Q., Pecheur, C., Tonetta, S.: Verification of railway interlocking - compositional approach with OCRA. In: Lecomte, T., Pinger, R., Romanovsky, A. (eds.) RSSRail 2016. LNCS, vol. 9707, pp. 134–149. Springer, Heidelberg (2016). doi:10.1007/978-3-319-33951-1_10

16. Mazzanti, F., Ferrari, A., Spagnolo, G.O.: Experiments in formal modelling of a deadlock avoidance algorithm for a CBTC system. In: Margaria, T., Steffen, B. (eds.) ISoLA 2016, Part II. LNCS, vol. 9953, pp. 297–314. Springer, Heidelberg (2016)

17. Nguyen, H.N., Roggenbach, M., Wang, X., Treharne, H.: The railway verification toolset OnTrack. In: Margaria, T., Steffen, B. (eds.) ISoLA 2016, Part II. LNCS, vol. 9953, pp. 294–296. Springer, Heidelberg (2016)

18. Vu, L.H., Haxthausen, A.E., Peleska, J.: Formal modeling and verification of interlocking systems featuring sequential release. In: Artho, C., Ölveczky, P.C. (eds.) FTSCS 2014. CCIS, vol. 476, pp. 223–238. Springer, Heidelberg (2015). doi:10.1007/978-3-319-17581-2_15

On the Use of Static Checking
in the Verification of Interlocking Systems

Anne E. Haxthausen[✉] and Peter H. Østergaard

DTU Compute, Technical University of Denmark, Kongens Lyngby, Denmark
aeha@dtu.dk

Abstract. In the formal methods community, the correctness of interlocking tables is typically verified by model checking. This paper suggests
to use a static checker for this purpose and it demonstrates for the RobustRailS verification tool set that the execution time and memory usage of
its static checker are much less than of its model checker. Furthermore,
the error messages of the static checker are much more informative than
the counter examples produced by classical model checkers.

1   Introduction

An *interlocking system* is one of the central components of any railway signalling
system. It is responsible for guiding trains safely through a given railway network
such that train collisions and derailments are avoided. Therefore interlocking systems have the highest safety integrity level (SIL4) according to the CENELEC
50128 standard [3] for railway applications. The safety verification of interlocking systems represents a considerable challenge and for such SIL4 applications
CENELEC 50128 strongly recommends the use of formal methods. Therefore,
formal verification of interlocking systems is an active research topic investigated by several research groups, e.g. in [1,2,5,6,9–13,17,21,23]. An overview
of the trends in this research field can be found in [4]. In this paper we will
consider how static checking can be used as a part of the formal verification of
interlocking system designs.

Conventional development and verification of interlocking systems. Typically
for a product line of interlocking systems, each interlocking system consists of
(1) a generic part that is the same for all instances of the product line and
(2) a part which depends on the network under control and the routes through
this and therefore is specific for that system. The generic part is developed and
verified once-and-for-all. For an interlocking instance of a product family, first
the layout of the network under control is specified and then the specific part
is specified by a so-called *interlocking table*[1]. The interlocking table describes
the allowed train routes in the network and the specific control rules that the

---

A.E. Haxthausen and P.H. Østergaard—The authors' research has been funded by
the RobustRailS project granted by Innovation Fund Denmark.

[1] Interlocking tables are also sometimes called *control tables*.

© Springer International Publishing AG 2016
T. Margaria and B. Steffen (Eds.): ISoLA 2016, Part II, LNCS 9953, pp. 266–278, 2016.
DOI: 10.1007/978-3-319-47169-3_19

interlocking instance must obey. Later the specific part is developed according to the specification expressed by the interlocking table and then integrated with the generic part. One of the verification tasks in this development is to verify that the interlocking table does not contain errors, while another verification task is to verify that the instantiated system is safe. The first verification task is conventionally manual and informal, while the second task is conventionally done by testing.

Automated, formal verification of interlocking systems. As manual, informal verification is time-consuming and error-prone, and testing first can be done after implementation, automated, formal verification of these tasks in the design phase is an active research topic. Some research groups, e.g. [2,5,11,13,17], verify the interlocking tables by translating these into interlocking design models and then formally verify by model checking that these models are safe. However, there might be errors in the interlocking tables that can't be found by model checking as they do not lead to safety violations. Also it is a well-known problem that for large networks model checking takes long time and uses much memory (and in worst case fails due to the state-space-explosion problem).

Instead of verifying interlocking tables by means of model checking, we suggest to use a static checker that is able to catch all kinds of data errors in interlocking tables, also those that do not lead to safety violations and therefore can't be found by model checking. The use of a static checker not only has the advantage that it can find more kinds of errors, it is also faster and uses less memory than model checking (as experiments in this paper will show). Time is especially saved, if there are several errors in the interlocking table, as a static checker in contrast to a model checker typically can find all of the errors in one run. In a second step, after having verified the correctness of an interlocking table, we suggest to use a model checker to catch errors in the designed control algorithms of the interlocking model instance that can be derived from the control table. An example of the latter kind of error could be a missing check for the status of conflicting routes in the route allocating protocol. This could lead to a safety violation even the interlocking table were correct. So to detect this kind of error the model checking step is needed. The static checking in the first step is needed as the table can contain errors that do not lead to safety violations and therefore can't be caught by model checking. Hence, the two steps complement each other.

We have previously [7,8] used this idea for the old relay-based Danish interlocking systems and recently [21] in the RobustRailS[2] project for the interlocking systems of the new Danish ERTMS/ETCS level 2 based signalling systems which are currently being developed. In this paper we will analyse the advantages of using a static checker, and for the RobustRailS tool suite we will make some experiments comparing the execution time and memory usage when using the static checker and the model checker of the RobustRailS tool suite, respectively, to catch errors in interlocking tables. Note that in this comparison we use the

---

[2] http://robustrails.man.dtu.dk.

model checker in a way for which it is not intended. We compare with this use of the model checker as this use is the way other research groups usually catch errors in interlocking tables. To our best knowledge such an analysis and comparison has not been made before.

Paper overview. The remainder of the article is organised as follows: First, in Sect. 2, we introduce the RobustRailS verification tools and basic notions of the railway domain, including the notions of track plans and interlocking tables. Next, in Sects. 3 and 4, we describe the static checker and report on experimental results comparing the execution time and memory usage of the static checker and the model checker for the RobustRailS tool suite. Finally, in Sect. 5, we make a conclusion.

2 Background

This section gives a brief introduction to (1) the new Danish railway networks, (2) interlocking tables, and the (3) RobustRailS verification method and tools.

2.1 Railway Networks

A railway network in ETCS Level 2 consists of a number of track-side elements like linear sections, points, and marker boards. Figure 1 shows an example layout of a railway network having six linear sections (b10, t10, t12, t14, t20, b14), two points (t11, t13), and eight marker boards (mb10, ..., mb21). These terms, as well as their functionality within the railway network, will be explained in more detail in the next paragraphs.

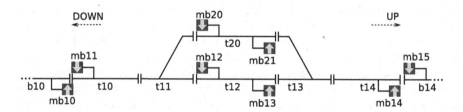

Fig. 1. An example railway network layout.

A *linear section* is a section with up to two neighbours. For example, the linear section t12 in Fig. 1 has t13 and t11 as neighbours. A *point* can have up to three neighbours: one at the *stem*, one at the *plus* end, and one at the *minus* end, e.g., point t11 in Fig. 1 has t10, t12, and t20 as neighbours at its stem, plus, and minus ends, respectively. The ends of a point are named so that the *stem* and *plus* ends form the straight (main) path, and the *stem* and *minus* ends form the branching (siding) path. A point can be switched between two positions: PLUS and MINUS. When a point is in the PLUS (MINUS) position, its *stem* end is connected to its *plus* (*minus*) end, so traffic can run from its *stem* end to its *plus* (*minus*) end and vice versa. It is not possible for traffic to run from *plus* end to *minus* end and vice versa. Linear sections and points are collectively called *(train detection) sections*, as they are provided with train detection equipments used by the interlocking system to detect the presence of trains on the sections.

Along each linear section, up to two *marker boards* (one for each direction) can be installed. A marker board can only be seen in one direction and is used as reference location (for the start and end of routes) for trains going in that direction. For example, in Fig. 1, marker board `mb13` is installed along section `t12` for travel direction up. Contrary to legacy systems, there are no physical signals in ETCS Level 2, but interlocking systems have a *virtual signal* associated with each marker board. Virtual signals play a similar role as physical signals in legacy systems: a virtual signal can be OPEN or CLOSED, respectively, allowing or disallowing traffic to pass the associated marker board. However, trains (more precisely train drivers) do not see the virtual signals, as opposed to physical signals. Instead, the aspect of virtual signals (OPEN or CLOSED) are communicated to the onboard computer in the train via a radio network. For simplicity, the terms *virtual signals*, *signals*, and *marker boards* are used interchangeably throughout this paper.

2.2 Interlocking Tables

An interlocking system monitors constantly the status of track-side elements, and sets them to appropriate states in order to allow trains travelling safely through the railway network under control. A common approach of interlocking systems is to use the concept of train routes, where a *(train) route* is a path from a *source (entry)* signal to a *destination (exit)* signal in the given railway network. The idea is that trains should travel along predefined routes in the network. Before a train can enter a route, the route must first be *set*, i.e. resources such as sections, points, and signals must be allocated (set to appropriate states) for the route and then *locked* exclusively for that train. For more details on the interlocking principles for the new Danish systems, see [19–22].

An *interlocking table* specifies routes in the railway network under control and the conditions for setting these routes. The specification of a route r and conditions for setting r include the following information:

- $id(r)$ – the route's unique identifier,
- $src(r)$ – the source/entry signal of r,
- $dst(r)$ – the destination/exit signal of r,
- $path(r)$ – the list of sections constituting r's path from $src(r)$ to $dst(r)$,
- $overlap(r)$ – a list of the sections in r's overlap, i.e., the buffer space after $dst(r)$ that would be used in case trains overshoot the route's path,
- $points(r)$ – a map from points[3] used by r to their required positions,

---

[3] These include points in the path and overlap, and points used for flank and front protection. For detail about flank and front protection, see [16].

Table 1. Interlocking table generated for the network layout in Fig. 1. The overlap column is omitted as it is empty for all of the routes. (p means PLUS, m means MINUS.)

id	src	dst	path	points	signals	conflicts
1a	mb10	mb13	t10;t11;t12	t11:p;t13:m	mb11;mb12;mb20	1b;2a;2b;3;4;5a;5b;6b;7
1b	mb10	mb13	t10;t11;t12	t11:p	mb11;mb12;mb15;mb20;mb21	1a;2a;2b;3;5a;5b;6a;6b;7;8
2a	mb10	mb21	t10;t11;t20	t11:m;t13:p	mb11;mb12;mb20	1a;1b;2b;3;5b;6a;6b;7;8
2b	mb10	mb21	t10;t11;t20	t11:m	mb11;mb12;mb13;mb15;mb20	1a;1b;2a;3;4;5a;5b;6a;6b;7
3	mb12	mb11	t11;t10	t11:p	mb10;mb20	1a;1b;2a;2b;5a;6b;7
4	mb13	mb14	t13;t14	t13:p	mb15;mb21	1a;2b;5a;5b;6a;6b;8
5a	mb15	mb12	t14;t13;t12	t11:m;t13:p	mb13;mb14;mb21	1a;1b;2b;3;4;5b;6a;6b;8
5b	mb15	mb12	t14;t13;t12	t13:p	mb10;mb13;mb14;mb20;mb21	1a;1b;2a;2b;4;5a;6a;6b;7;8
6a	mb15	mb20	t14;t13;t20	t11:p;t13:m	mb13;mb14;mb21	1b;2a;2b;4;5a;5b;6b;7;8
6b	mb15	mb20	t14;t13;t20	t13:m	mb10;mb12;mb13;mb14;mb21	1a;1b;2a;2b;3;4;5a;5b;6a;8
7	mb20	mb11	t11;t10	t11:m	mb10;mb12	1a;1b;2a;2b;3;5b;6a
8	mb21	mb14	t13;t14	t13:m	mb13;mb15	1b;2a;4;5a;5b;6a;6b

- *signals*(*r*) – a set of protecting signals used for flank or front protection [16] for the route, and
- *conflicts*(*r*) – a set of conflicting routes which must not be set while *r* is set.

Table 1 shows an example of an interlocking table for the network shown in Fig. 1. Each row of the table corresponds to a route specification. The column names indicate the information of the route specifications that these columns contain. As can be seen, one of the routes has id 1a, goes from mb10 to mb13 via three sections t10, t11 and t12 on its path, and has no overlap. It requires point t11 (on its path) to be in PLUS position, and point t13 (outside its path) to be in MINUS position (as a protecting point). The route has mb11, mb12 and mb20 as protecting signals, and it is in conflict with routes 1b, 2a, 2b, 3, 4, 5a, 5b, 6b, and 7.

2.3   The RobustRailS Verification Method and Tool Set

This section describes shortly the RobustRailS verification method and tool set. For more information, see [19–22].

The tools are centred around a domain-specific language (DSL) for representations of network diagrams and interlocking tables as described in the preceding subsections. The tools comprise among others:

- *A static checker* for checking that a DSL specification follows certain general wellformedness rules.
- The bounded *model checker* of RT-Tester [14,18] which is set up such that it can make a k-induction proof.
- *Generators* which from a DSL specification produce input to the model checker: (1) a formal, behavioural model of interlocking system and its environment and (2) required safety properties expressed as formulae in the temporal logic LTL.

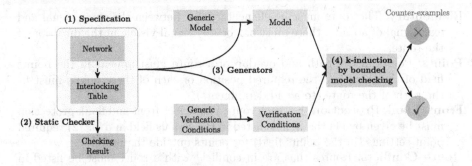

Fig. 2. The RobustRailS verification process.

There are additional tools supporting automated, model-based testing of implemented interlocking systems, see [19].

The tools can be used to verify the design of an interlocking system in the following number of steps, as illustrated in Fig. 2:

1. Write a DSL specification of the interlocking system:
   (a) first the network layout,
   (b) and then the interlocking table (this is either done manually or generated automatically from the network layout)
2. Validate the specification using the static checker.
3. Apply the generators to generate input to a model checker.
4. Apply the model checker to that input to investigate whether the model satisfies the required safety properties.

The static checking in step (2) is intended to catch errors in the network layout and interlocking table, while the model checking in step (4) is intended to catch safety violations in the control algorithm of the instantiated model.

3   Static Checker

This section describes the static checker of the RobustRailS tool set.

The static checker takes as input a network layout and an associated interlocking table and checks whether these are well-formed. In case there are errors, it suggests what might be wrong and in some cases also how this can be fixed. It checks for instance that the network layout represents a legal railway network of track elements and that the interlocking table satisfies the following conditions:

Elements Exist. It refers only to existing track elements in the network layout.
Path. The path of a route is a connected path in the network layout.
Overlap. The overlap of a route must be a connected path that continues right after the last section of the route path itself.
Entry/Exit. The entry/exit signal of a route must be at the start/end of the path of the route and be visible in the direction of the route.

Elementary. The route must be elementary, i.e. between the entry signal and exit signal of a route, there must not be any signal visible in the direction of the route.

Points. Points in the path and overlap of a route must appear in the points field of the route and the required position of each of these points must fit the path of the route (to avoid derailments).

Front/Flank Protection. For each route a sufficient front and flank protection must be given by (1) the signals listed in the signals field and/or (2) required point settings (in the points field) for points outside the route.

Route Conflicts. Routes that are in conflict[4] with a route must be listed in the conflicts field of the route.

The checker has been formally specified in the RAISE Specification Language, RSL [15], as described in [19,20], and implemented in C++.

3.1   Examples of Error Messages from the Static Checker

Below we give examples of some illegal interlocking tables for the network layout given in Fig. 1 and show the error messages that the static checker gives for these tables. In each case it is explained how the illegal interlocking table is obtained from Table 1 by modifying some of the fields for route 1a.

If a table contains several errors, the static checker will provide error messages for each of these.

Example breaking the **Path** *condition:* Remove t10 in the path field. For this the static checker provides the error message:

```
In route 1a, two consecutive segments, b10 and t11, are not
connected.
```

Example breaking the **Point** *condition:* Remove t11 in the points field. For this the static checker provides the error message:

```
For route 1a, point t11 is not given a point position.
```

Example breaking the **Point** *condition:* Require point t11 to be in a wrong position (m rather than p). Note that this change means that route 1a now also becomes in conflict with route 6a, as these two routes require t11 to be in different positions, but in the interlocking table we have not listed them as being in conflict. Therefore, the static checker provides the error message:

```
For route 1a, point t11 is set to MINUS,
but it should have been set to PLUS.

Routes 1a and 6a are in conflict, but are not listed as being in
conflict. Reasons to be in conflict:
- Shared point required in different positions: t11
```

---

[4] This essentially means that they use the same track elements. For a complete definition, see [19].

Example breaking the **Route Conflicts** *condition:* Remove route 7 in the conflicts field (and remove 1a from the conflicts field of route 7). For this the static checker provides the error message:

```
Routes 1a and 7 are in conflict, but not listed as being in
conflict. Reasons to be in conflict:
- Non-concatenated routes with shared elements: {t10, t11}.
- Entry signal of one route used as protecting signal for the
  other route.
```

Example breaking the **Flank Protection** *condition:* Remove protecting point t13 in the points field. Note with this change, routes 1a and 4 are not anymore in conflict. For this the static checker provides the error message:

```
Routes 1a and 4 are listed as being in conflict, but they are not.

Improper protection of section t12 in route 1a.
Possible protections:
----------------------------
Signals: {}
Points: {t13:m}
----------------------------
Signals: {mb15, mb21}
Points: {}
```

As it can be seen, two alternative ways of obtaining a flank protection for section t12 are suggested. The first one corresponds to re-introducing what was removed, while the second one corresponds to the protection in route 1b.

4   Experiments

This section compares for a selection of railway networks the execution time and memory usage of the static checking and the model checking of these.

4.1   Selection of Networks

Ten cases of networks from [19] have been selected. The layout of the seven smallest cases are shown in Fig. 3. These seven networks are inspired by the typical examples used in other studies about formal verification of railway interlocking systems. The three last networks are some real examples from Denmark: Gadstrup-Havdrup and Køge are extracted from the Early Deployment Line (EDL) in the Danish Signalling Programme. The EDL is the first regional line in Denmark to be commissioned in the Danish Signalling Programme. The line goes from Roskilde station to Næstved station and is over 55 kms long. It includes eight stations ranging from simple stations similar to the one shown in Fig. 1, to complex stations such as Køge. The network descriptions

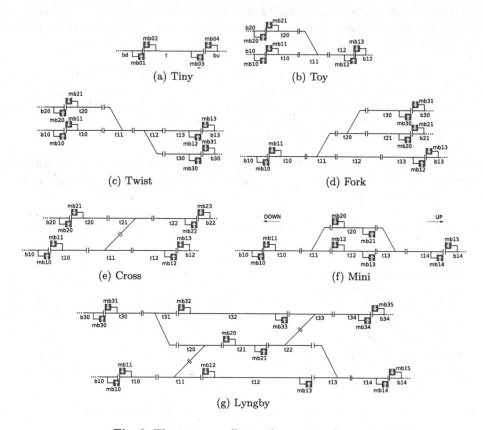

Fig. 3. The seven smallest railway network cases.

Table 2. Metrics of network cases.

	Linears	Points	Signals	Routes	States
Tiny	3	0	4	2	10^{11}
Toy	6	1	6	4	10^{26}
Twist	8	2	8	8	10^{39}
Fork	9	2	8	6	10^{40}
Cross	8	2	8	10	10^{41}
Mini	6	2	8	12	10^{37}
Lyngby	11	6	14	24	10^{79}
Gadstrup-Havdrup	21	5	24	33	10^{113}
Køge	57	23	60	73	10^{332}
EDL	110	39	126	179	10^{651}

(in XML representation) and the corresponding generated properties and model instances for the first seven cases can be found at http://www.imm.dtu.dk/~aeha/RobustRailS/data/casestudy.

Table 2 lists the following metrics for each of the selected networks: The number of linear sections, points, and signals, the number of routes in the interlocking table that can be generated from the network, and the number of states in the model that can be generated from the network and the interlocking table.

4.2 Experiments with Correct Networks and Interlocking Tables

For each of the networks we first used the interlocking table generator to generate an interlocking table for that network. Then for each case we used

1. the static checker to verify correctness conditions for the network and interlocking table and
2. the generator tools to generate a model and safety conditions, whereupon we used the model checker to check the model against the safety conditions.

In all cases the static check and the model check confirmed that there were no static errors in the network layout or interlocking table and that the instantiated model was safe, respectively. All experiments have been performed on a machine with Intel(R) Xeon(R) CPU E5-2667 @ 2.90 GHz, 64 GB RAM, CentOS 6.6, Linux 2.6.32-504.8.1.el6.x86_64 kernel.

Table 3. Execution times and memory usage.

| | Static checker | | Model checker | | Time ratio |
	Time	Memory	Time	Memory	
Tiny	0.20	–	0.74	18.4	3.7
Toy	0.52	–	2.78	86.3	5.4
Twist	0.24	–	9.76	170.4	41
Fork	0.22	–	8.80	168.8	40
Cross	0.28	–	14.48	191.8	52
Mini	0.26	–	17.56	197.4	68
Lyngby	0.30	–	254.3	868.1	848
Gadstrup-Havdrup	0.36	–	230.1	1146	639
Køge	0.34	–	5528.5	8471.6	16260
EDL	0.43	–	19358.9	23389.4	45020

Table 3 shows for each of the network cases, the approximate real execution time (in seconds) and memory usage (in MB) for the static checking and the model checking (incl. model generation), respectively. Furthermore, the last column shows the ratio between the execution time of the model check and the execution time of the static check. As it can be seen the static checking is much faster than the model checking. For the smallest network it is a factor 3.7 faster, and then it increases up to a factor 45020 for the largest network. The static checker ran too quick for the profiler tool (*runlim*) to measure the memory usage.

4.3 Experiments with Illegal Interlocking Tables

We also tried to inject some errors in the interlocking tables. Also in this case the static checker was much faster to catch errors than the model checker. For instance, if we for route 1a in Table 1 require t11 to be m instead of p in the points field, then the static checker detects this in 0.14 s, while it takes the model checker 20.54 s, i.e. the static checker is a factor 146.7 faster.

In some cases the errors are even not caught by the model checker, as the wrong data does not lead to a safety violation in the instantiated model. The reason for this is that the interlocking system (and thereby also the model) contains redundant checks to make the system more fault tolerant. This fact also indicates the advantage of using a static checker.

Furthermore, the error messages provided by the static checker are much more informative. They explain exactly what the problem is and in some cases suggest how to fix it. In contrast to that, when the model checker gives a counter example, this has to be analysed to find out what the problem is: first it has to be determined whether the unsafe situation is due an error in the interlocking table or in the model.

5 Conclusion

In the formal methods community, the correctness of interlocking tables are typically verified by model checking. While this is a good method, it suffers from the state space explosion problem for larger networks. This paper has suggested to use a static checker to verify the correctness of interlocking tables. Experiments using the RobustRailS interlocking verification tool set showed for a selection of railway networks with associated interlocking tables that the execution time and memory usage of verifying the interlocking tables using the static checker was much less than of using the model checker[5]. Furthermore, the error messages of the static checker are more informative and do not need an analysis to find out what the error is, as it is the case of the counter examples of the model checker. The static checker can also in contrast to the model checker catch several errors in the same execution. So our conclusion is that for the checking of interlocking tables it is worth to provide such a user-friendly static checker.

---

[5] It should here be noted that using this model checker in a second step for verifying the safety of the model of the instantiated interlocking system has actually turned out to be very efficient. For instance, it succeeded to verify the EDL line, where other model checkers failed within some given resources, cf. [22].

Acknowledgements. The authors would like to express their gratitude to (1) Jan Peleska and Linh Hong Vu for the excellent contribution to the development of the RobustRailS interlocking verification method and tool set (including the static checker discussed in this paper) and for an always very enjoyable collaboration, (2) Ross Edwin Gammon and Nikhil Mohan Pande from Banedanmark and Jan Bertelsen from Thales for helping with their expertise about Danish interlocking systems, and (3) Uwe Schulze and Florian Lapschies from the University of Bremen for their help with the implementation in the RT-Tester toolchain.

References

1. Banci, M., Fantechi, A., Gnesi, S.: Some Experiences on Formal Specification of Railway Interlocking Systems Using Statecharts (2005)
2. Cao, Y., Xu, T., Tang, T., Wang, H., Zhao, L.: Automatic generation and verification of interlocking tables based on domain specific language for computer based interlocking systems (DSL-CBI). In: Proceedings of the IEEE International Conference on Computer Science and Automation Engineering (CSAE 2011), pp. 511–515. IEEE (2011)
3. C. European Committee for Electrotechnical Standardization. EN 50128:2011 - Railway applications - Communications, signalling and processing systems - Software for railway control and protection systems (2011)
4. Fantechi, A.: Twenty-five years of formal methods and railways: what next? In: Counsell, S., Núñez, M. (eds.) SEFM 2013. LNCS, vol. 8368, pp. 167–183. Springer, Heidelberg (2014). doi:10.1007/978-3-319-05032-4_13
5. Ferrari, A., Magnani, G., Grasso, D., Fantechi, A.: Model checking interlocking control tables. In: Schnieder, E., Tarnai, G. (eds.) FORMS/FORMAT 2010 – Formal Methods for Automation and Safety in Railway and Automotive Systems, pp. 107–115. Springer, Heidelberg (2010)
6. Hvid Hansen, H., Ketema, J., Luttik, B., Mousavi, M.R., Pol, J., Santos, O.M.: Automated verification of executable UML models. In: Aichernig, B.K., Boer, F.S., Bonsangue, M.M. (eds.) FMCO 2010. LNCS, vol. 6957, pp. 225–250. Springer, Heidelberg (2011). doi:10.1007/978-3-642-25271-6_12
7. Haxthausen, A.E.: Towards a framework for modelling and verification of relay interlocking systems. In: Calinescu, R., Jackson, E. (eds.) Monterey Workshop 2010. LNCS, vol. 6662, pp. 176–192. Springer, Heidelberg (2011). doi:10.1007/978-3-642-21292-5_10
8. Haxthausen, A.E.: Automated generation of formal safety conditions from railway interlocking tables. Int. J. Softw. Tools Technol. Transf. (STTT) **16**(6), 713–726 (2014). Special Issue on Formal Methods for Railway Control Systems
9. Haxthausen, A.E., Bliguet, M., Kjær, A.A.: Modelling and verification of relay interlocking systems. In: Choppy, C., Sokolsky, O. (eds.) Monterey Workshop 2008. LNCS, vol. 6028, pp. 141–153. Springer, Heidelberg (2010). doi:10.1007/978-3-642-12566-9_8
10. Haxthausen, A.E., Peleska, J., Kinder, S.: A formal approach for the construction and verification of railway control systems. Formal Aspects Comput. **23**(2), 191–219 (2011)
11. James, P., Moller, F., Nguyen, H.N., Roggenbach, M., Schneider, S., Treharne, H., Trumble, M., Williams, D.: Verification of scheme plans using CSP∥B. In: Counsell, S., Núñez, M. (eds.) SEFM 2013. LNCS, vol. 8368, pp. 189–204. Springer, Heidelberg (2014). doi:10.1007/978-3-319-05032-4_15

12. Limbrée, C., Cappart, Q., Pecheur, C., Tonetta, S.: Verification of railway interlocking - compositional approach with OCRA. In: Lecomte, T., Pinger, R., Romanovsky, A. (eds.) RSSRail 2016. LNCS, vol. 9707, pp. 134–149. Springer, Heidelberg (2016). doi:10.1007/978-3-319-33951-1_10

13. Mirabadi, A., Yazdi, M.B.: Automatic generation and verification of railway interlocking control tables using FSM and NuSMV. Transp. Probl. **4**, 103–110 (2009)

14. Peleska, J.: Industrial-strength model-based testing - state of the art and current challenges. In: Petrenko, A.K., Schlingloff, H. (eds.) Proceedings 8th Workshop on Model-Based Testing. Electronic Proceedings in Theoretical Computer Science, vol. 111, pp. 3–28. Open Publishing Association, Rome (2013)

15. George, C., Haff, P., Havelund, K., Haxthausen, A.E., Milne, R., Nielsen, C.b., Prehn, S., Wagner, K.R: The RAISE Language Group: The RAISE Specification Language. The BCS Practitioners Series. Prentice Hall Int. (1992)

16. Theeg, G., Vlasenko, S.V., Anders, E.: Railway Signalling & Interlocking: International Compendium. Eurailpress, Germany (2009)

17. Tombs, D., Robinson, N., Nikandros, G.: Signalling control table generation and verification. In: CORE 2002: Cost Efficient Railways through Engineering, p. 415. Railway Technical Society of Australasia/Rail Track Association of Australia (2002)

18. Verified Systems International GmbH. RT-Tester Model-Based Test Case and Test Data Generator - RTT-MBT - User Manual (2013). Available on request from http://www.verified.de

19. Vu, L.H.: Formal Development and Verification of Railway Control Systems - In the context of ERTMS/ETCS Level 2. Ph.D. thesis, Technical University of Denmark, DTU Compute (2015)

20. Vu, L.H., Haxthausen, A.E., Peleska, J.: A domain-specific language for railway interlocking systems. In: Schnieder, E., Tarnai, G. (eds.) FORMS/FORMAT 2014–10th Symposium on Formal Methods for Automation and Safety in Railway and Automotive Systems, Institute for Traffic Safety and Automation Engineerin, pp. 200–209. Technische Universität Braunschweig (2014)

21. Vu, L.H., Haxthausen, A.E., Peleska, J.: Formal modeling and verification of interlocking systems featuring sequential release. In: Artho, C., Ölveczky, P.C. (eds.) Formal Techniques for Safety-Critical Systems. Communications in Computer and Information Science, vol. 476, pp. 223–238. Springer, Heidelberg (2015)

22. Vu, L.H., Haxthausen, A.E., Peleska, J.: Formal modeling and verification of interlocking systems featuring sequential release. Sci. Comput. Program. (2016). http://dx.doi.org/10.1016/j.scico.2016.05.010

23. Winter, K., Johnston, W., Robinson, P., Strooper, P., van den Berg, L.: Tool support for checking railway interlocking designs. In: Proceedings of the 10th Australian Workshop on Safety Critical Systems and Software, SCS 2005, vol. 55, pp. 101–107. Australian Computer Society, Inc., Darlinghurst (2006)

Compositional Verification of Multi-station Interlocking Systems

Hugo D. Macedo[1]([✉]), Alessandro Fantechi[1,2], and Anne E. Haxthausen[1]

[1] DTU Compute, Technical University of Denmark, Kongens Lyngby, Denmark
{hudo,aeha}@dtu.dk
[2] DINFO, University of Florence, Via S. Marta 3, Florence, Italy
alessandro.fantechi@unifi.it

Abstract. Because interlocking systems are highly safety-critical complex systems, their automated safety verification is an active research topic investigated by several groups, employing verification techniques to produce important cost and time savings in their certification. However, such systems also pose a big challenge to current verification methodologies, due to the explosion of state space size as soon as large, if not medium sized, multi-station systems have to be controlled.

For these reasons, verification techniques that exploit *locality* principles related to the topological layout of the controlled system to split in different ways the state space have been investigated. In particular, compositional approaches divide the controlled track network in regions that can be verified separately, once proper assumptions are considered on the way the pieces are glued together.

Basing on a successful method to verify the size of rather large networks, we propose a compositional approach that is particularly suitable to address multi-station interlocking systems which control a whole line composed of stations linked by mainline tracks. Indeed, it turns out that for such networks, and for the adopted verification approach, the verification effort amounts just to the sum of the verification efforts for each intermediate station and for each connecting line.

1 Introduction

An interlocking system is responsible for guiding trains safely through a given railway network. It is a vital part of any railway signalling system and has the highest safety integrity level (SIL4) according to the CENELEC 50128 standard [1]. Automated safety verification of interlocking systems is hence an important issue and an active research topic, investigated by several research groups, see e.g., [3–5,9,21]. Model-checking techniques are considered for this purpose, but, notwithstanding the important advancements witnessed for these techniques, they fail to give results on large interlocking systems due to the state space explosion problem.

© Springer International Publishing AG 2016
T. Margaria and B. Steffen (Eds.): ISoLA 2016, Part II, LNCS 9953, pp. 279–293, 2016.
DOI: 10.1007/978-3-319-47169-3_20

In this paper we elaborate on previous results of the RobustRailS research project[1], in which an automatic method for the formal verification of interlocking systems was developed [18–20]. Using a combination of SMT based bounded model checking (BMC) and inductive reasoning, the method succeeded to verify interlocking systems of large sizes. Indeed, in a comparison with other model checkers, the proposed method succeeded to verify a multi-station interlocking controlling a whole line, while the other tools failed to conclude the verification with the given time and resources available. Nevertheless, the verification of the considered systems just reached the limits of time and memory showing that larger systems cannot be addressed any more, and hence these verification methods need to be further improved.

Interlocking systems typically exhibit a high degree of *locality*: if we consider a typical safety property desired for an interlocking system, e.g. that the same track element shall not be reserved by more than one train at a time, it is likely that this property is not influenced by a train moving on a distant, or parallel, track element. Locality of a safety property can be exploited for verification purposes, by limiting the state space on which to verify it.

This principle has been exploited in [22] to define domain-oriented optimizations of the variable ordering in a BDD-based verification. Locality can be used also for slicing, as suggested in [3,8,10]. The idea is to consider only the portion of the model that has influence on the property to be verified, by a topological selection of interested track elements (therefore closely related to the *cone of influence* of the property): this allows for a much more efficient verification of the single property, but comes at the price of repeating the verification for every property (in principle a single verification of the conjunction of all safety properties on the whole model would otherwise suffice), and of separately checking that verifying slices does actually imply the satisfaction of desired properties for the whole system. Nevertheless, it appears that when automated, this process can offer significant time and memory savings.

A compositional approach that also exploits locality is the one used in [11], where the interlocking of a quasi-symmetrical station is divided in two halves, and the verification of one half takes into account assume/guarantee conditions at the interface with the other half. The verification effort is hence repeated for the two halves, with the extra effort of proving that assume/guarantee conditions do hold at the interface: locality allows such conditions to be rather simple so that they do not add much time to the verification.

In this paper we adopt a similar compositional approach to chop a large interlocking system into smaller fragments, but by considering a different way of dividing the network in fragments. The presented approach is particularly

---

[1] In Denmark, in the years 2009–2021, new interlocking systems that are compatible with the standardised European Train Control System (ETCS) Level 2 [2] will be deployed in the entire country within the context of the Danish Signalling Programme. In the context of the RobustRailS project accompanying the signalling programme on a scientific level, the proposed method will be applied to these new systems.

suitable to address multi-station interlocking systems, which control a whole line composed of stations linked by mainline tracks. Indeed, it turns out that for such networks, and for the adopted verification approach, the verification effort amounts just to the sum of verification efforts for each intermediate station and for each connecting line. Since in reality the intermediate stations often share an identical layout, the gain in verification is made even larger by factoring out the identical stations.

The paper is structured as follows: in Sect. 2 we present the verification approach on which we have built our compositional approach; in Sect. 3 we show how a network can be divided in smaller fragments, and how the verification of the whole network is obtained from the verification of the single elements, using as running example a simple network. In Sect. 4 we report on the results given by the application of our decomposition approach to a small example and to the EDL line that nearly reached the capacity bounds of the adopted tools when proved as a whole. In both cases the results show significant gains in verification effort can be achieved. Section 5 summarizes the achieved results and discusses possible future extensions and improvements of the work presented here, especially in the direction of addressing interlocking systems that control large stations.

2   The New Danish Route-Based Interlocking Systems

In this section we introduce briefly the new Danish interlocking systems and the domain terminology. The subsequent subsections explain (Sect. 2.1) different components of a specification of an interlocking system which is compatible with ERTMS/ETCS Level 2 [2], and (Sect. 2.2) how the safety properties are verified, respectively.

2.1   Specification of Interlocking Systems

The specification of a given route-based interlocking system consists of two main components: (1) a railway network, and (2) a corresponding interlocking table.

Railway Networks. A railway network in ETCS Level 2 consists of a number of track and track-side elements of different types[2]: linear sections, points, and marker boards. Figure 1 shows an example layout of a railway network having six linear sections (b10, t10, t12, t14, t20, b14), two points (t11, t13), and eight marker boards (mb10, ..., mb21). These terms, and their functionality within the railway network, will be explained in more detail in the next paragraphs.

A *linear section* is a section with up to two neighbours: one in the *up* end, and one in the *down* end. For example, the linear section t12 in Fig. 1 has t13 and t11 as neighbours at its up end and down end, respectively. In Danish railway's terminology, *up* and *down* denote the directions in which the distance

---

[2] Here we only show types that are relevant for the work presented in this article.

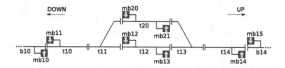

Fig. 1. An example railway network layout.

from a reference location is *increasing* and *decreasing*, respectively. The reference location is the same for both up and down, e.g., an end of a line. For simplicity, in the examples and figures in the rest of this article, the *up* (*down*) direction is assumed to be the left-to-right (right-to-left) direction.

A *point* can have up to three neighbours: one at the *stem*, one at the *plus* end, and one at the *minus* end, e.g., point t11 in Fig. 1 has t10, t12, and t20 as neighbours at its stem, plus, and minus ends, respectively. The ends of a point are named so that the *stem* and *plus* ends form the straight (main) path, and the *stem* and *minus* ends form the branching (siding) path. A point can be switched between two positions: PLUS and MINUS. When a point is in the PLUS (MINUS) position, its *stem* end is connected to its *plus* (*minus*) end, thus traffic can run from its *stem* end to its *plus* (*minus*) end and vice versa. It is not possible for traffic to run from *plus* end to *minus* end and vice versa.

Linear sections and points are collectively called (train detection) sections, as they are provided with train detection equipment used by the interlocking system to detect the presence of trains. Note that sections are bidirectional, i.e., trains are allowed to travel in both directions (but not at the same time).

Along each linear section, up to two *marker boards* (one for each direction) can be installed. A marker board can only be seen in one direction and is used as reference location (for the start and end of routes) for trains going in that direction. For example, in Fig. 1, marker board mb13 is installed along section t12 for travel direction up. Contrary to legacy systems, there are no physical signals in ETCS Level 2, but interlocking systems have a *virtual signal* associated with each marker board. Virtual signals play a similar role as physical signals in legacy systems: a virtual signal can be OPEN or CLOSED, respectively, allowing or disallowing traffic to pass the associated marker board. However, trains (more precisely train drivers) do not see the virtual signals, as opposed to physical signals. Instead, the aspect of virtual signals (OPEN or CLOSED) is communicated to the onboard computer in the train via a radio network. For simplicity, the terms *virtual signals*, *signals*, and *marker boards* are used interchangeably throughout this paper.

Interlocking Tables. An interlocking system monitors constantly the status of track-side elements, and sets them to appropriate states in order to allow trains traveling safely through the railway network under control. The new Danish interlocking systems are route-based. A *route* is a path from a *source* signal to a *destination* signal in the given railway network. A route is called an *elementary route* if there are no signals that are located between its source signal and its destination signal, and that are intended for the same direction as the route.

In railway signalling terminology, *setting* a route denotes the process of allocating the resources – i.e., sections, points, and signals – for the route, and then *locking* it exclusively for only one train when the resources are allocated.

An *interlocking table* specifies the elementary routes in the given railway network and the conditions for setting these routes. The specification of a route r and conditions for setting r include the following information:

- src(r) – the source signal of r,
- dst(r) – the destination signal of r,
- path(r) – the list of sections constituting r's path from src(r) to dst(r),
- overlap(r) – a list of the sections in r's *overlap*[3], i.e., the buffer space after dst(r) that would be used in case trains overshoot the route's path,
- points(r) – a map from points[4] used by r to their required positions,
- signals(r) – a set of protecting signals used for flank or front protection [15] for the route, and
- conflicts(r) – a set of conflicting routes which must not be set while r is set.

that is needed while verifying the expected properties.

2.2   The RobustRailS Verification Approach and Toolkit

This section describes shortly the RobustRailS verification method and tool set that we use as verification technology. For detailed information, see [17–20].

The method for modelling and verifying railway interlocking systems is a combination of formal methods and a domain-specific language (DSL) to express network diagrams and interlocking tables. According to this, an environment consisting of the following components is provided.

- *An editor and static checker* [6] for editing and checking that a DSL specification (describing an interlocking system) follows certain well-formedness rules.
- The bounded *model checker* of RT-Tester [12,16] which we use for making *k*-induction proofs as described in [20].
- *Generators* transforming a DSL specification into inputs to the model checker:
  - a behavioural model of the interlocking system and its environment, and
  - the required safety properties given as linear temporal logic formulae.

The tools can be used to verify the design of an interlocking system in the following steps:

---

[3] An overlap section is needed when, for the short distance of a marker board to the end of the section, there is the concrete danger that a braking train stops after the end of the section, e.g. in adverse atmospheric conditions.

[4] These points include points in the path and overlap, and points used for flank and front protection. Sometimes it is required to protect tracks occupied by a train from another train not succeeding to brake in due space. For details about flank and front protection, see [15].

1. A DSL specification of the configuration data (a network layout and its corresponding interlocking table) is constructed in the following order:
   (a) first the network layout,
   (b) and then the interlocking table (this is either done manually or generated automatically from the network layout).
2. The static checker verifies whether the configuration data is statically well-formed according to the static semantics [19] of the DSL.
3. The generators instantiate a generic behavioural model and generic safety properties with the well-formed configuration data to generate the model input of the model checker and the safety properties.
4. The generated model instance is then checked against the generated properties by the bounded model checker performing a k-induction proof.

The static checking in step (2) is intended to catch errors in the network layout and interlocking table, while the model checking in step (4) is intended to catch safety violations in the control algorithm of the instantiated model.

The toolchain associated with the method has been implemented using the RT-tester framework [12,16]. The bounded model checker in RT-tester uses the SONOLAR SMT solver [13] to compute counterexamples showing the violations of the base case or induction step.

3   Method

We now proceed to describe the details of how we use the locality features of railway networks to verify large interlocking systems in a compositional approach. The idea is to decompose the networks in chunks that are separately verified for safety properties, and to show how under given conditions such separate verifications are enough to guarantee that the whole network satisfies the safety properties as well. We show that a multi-station interlocking system satisfies such conditions if a suitable (and natural) divide strategy is applied. Indeed, the strategy can be easily automated, providing a completely automated method to verify this kind of interlocking systems.

3.1   Border Assumptions

The approach of Sect. 2 is able to verify an interlocking system when immersed in an *environment* that satisfies some assumptions on the borders of the system network. The borders of the network (in the diagram of Fig. 1, they are partially dotted) are defined as track elements which are not under control of the interlocking system for the network under consideration. Thus our method assumes the following:

- *assumptions on the network*
  1. the border elements include a marker board (signal), controlled by the interlocking that protects the entrance to the network;

2. the routes of the network are elementary: start at one and end at another of the marker boards of the network (including the border ones), and do not include intermediate marker boards;

– *assumptions on the trains' behaviour*

3. trains can "materialize" on a border element at any time, unless a train has already materialized on it and has not yet moved away;
4. trains on a border track element can enter the network if they are allowed to do (that is, if the border virtual entry signal is OPEN);
5. trains cannot enter in the middle of the network;
6. trains that pass from an adjacent track element to a border one can "dematerialize" at any moment.

The assumptions on the status of the border track elements are an abstraction of the real environment in which the network is immersed: since the real environment puts restrictions on the actual behaviour of trains (for example, it introduces minimum time intervals between two incoming trains), these assumptions give actually an *over-approximation* of its behaviour. Hence, if safety is verified for every behaviour of the network and of its environment, it is verified also in the case the environment is substituted by a more constrained behaviour, which is the case when the network is connected to another one.

3.2 Divide Strategy

We exploit the border assumptions to divide a network controlled by a single interlocking into several sub-networks, each to be controlled by its own interlocking system, such that the verification of the original interlocking system can be done by verifying the interlocking systems of the sub-networks. For the purpose of this paper, we consider that a division produces two sub-networks (a down and an up sub-network) by making one or several cuts each respecting the conditions defined below:

A network cut satisfies the *border cut conditions (BCCs)* if:

1. it separates two consecutive linear sections such that in the joint between the two there is an up markerboard on the upper part of the down section and a down markerboard on the down part of the upper section;
2. no *overlap* section for the up sub-network includes elements in the down sub-network, and vice-versa;
3. no *flank/front protection* requirement on the up sub-network depends on elements of the down sub-network, and vice-versa.

The conditions above assure that the setting (reservation) of any route depends only on the status of the elements belonging to one of the sub-networks.

A network with a cut (between the sections t14 and b14) satisfying the BCCs is illustrated in Fig. 2. In such a figure one can identify two sub-networks one on the left-hand side and one on the right-hand side, thus allowing the monolithic interlocking system controlling the whole network to be safely divided into two interlocking systems controlling two networks.

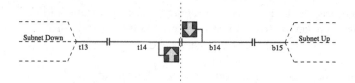

Fig. 2. A cut between sections t14 and b14 satisfies the border cut conditions.

Such a situation can be found when considering a multi-station interlocking, which controls several stations on a line: the long sections of track between two stations, according to the Danish signalling rules, do not carry over route information and present specific joints of the form described in Fig. 2, and are hence natural places in which to cut the overall network.

In the division process a network is inspected in search for regions that present candidate patterns to be cut, that is, joints of the form of Fig. 2. Once such a joint has been pointed out, the cut is operated forming two sub-networks as illustrated in Figs. 3 and 4, where the down section of the joint (t14) will be kept as the down border element of the Up sub-network, and up section of the joint (b14) is kept as the up border element of the Down sub-network. The search is then recursively applied to the created sub-networks, until no more suitable cut points can be found.

Fig. 3. Resulting sub-network Down.

Fig. 4. Resulting sub-network Up.

On more complex network layouts, our division process would require refinements to cope with richer interfaces between the two sub-networks, that would have, anyway, to respect the BCCs.

The concepts described above allow to automate the compositional verification of multi-station interlocking systems by dividing the network in sub-networks by means of a three steps algorithm:

1. Search the network for cuts satisfying the BCCs, and divide the network into sub-networks.
2. For each of the resulting sub-networks, complete the specification of a sub-interlocking system using the generator mentioned in item 1 of Sect. 2.2.
3. Verify a model of each sub-interlocking system by following the steps in item 2, 3, and 4 of Sect. 2.2.

3.3   Soundness of the Approach

Building upon the assumptions on the model and verification process we sketch an induction argument for the soundness of the compositional approach focusing on the case where we divide a network into two. First we prove that the resulting sub-networks satisfy the required network assumptions 1 and 2. Then we argue that the disjoint union of the interlocking tables generated for the sub-networks constitute the whole interlocking table for the monolithic network. Then we proceed to guarantee that from the verification results of the local sub-interlocking systems it is possible to infer the global verification result.

When dividing a monolithic network into sub-networks at joints satisfying BCC 1, it follows that the resulting sub-networks satisfy the required assumption 1 for network borders also at their new borders.

When dividing a monolithic network satisfying network assumption 2 (that routes are elementary) into sub-networks at joints satisfying BCC 1, the generated routes for the sub-networks will be disjoint and "internal" either to one or to the other sub-networks, and they will also satisfy network assumption 2 for the sub-networks. Furthermore, the union of the routes generated for the sub-networks is the set of routes of the original monolithic interlocking system.

When the cutting interfaces also satisfy conditions BCC 2 and BCC 3, the conditions for setting any route depends only on the status of the sole elements belonging to the sub-network to which the route belongs, and therefore the disjoint union of the interlocking tables generated for the sub-networks constitutes the whole interlocking table for the monolithic network.

Due to the above conclusions, the behaviour of the interlocking for the big network is the sum of the behaviours of the interlocking systems for the sub-networks. Only the train behaviour at the new borders is different. Due to the fact that trains' behaviour assumption 3 allows the materialization of trains in the border elements of the interlocking systems for the sub-networks, our compositional approach to the monolithic network over-approximates the verification of the safety property by allowing more trains to "materialize" in sections that are not border of the monolithic network. Thus terminating our argument.

4   Experiments

In this section we present the results of applying our approach to a case study invented for the sake of explanation and to a real world case study we adapted from our group's previous work: the Early Deployment Line (**EDL**) in the Danish Signalling Programme. In Sect. 4.1 we describe our experimental approach, then in Sect. 4.2 we describe and summarize the results obtained in the invented case study, and the results for the (**EDL**) example are shown in Sect. 4.3.

4.1   Experimental Approach

For each of the case studies, we put the method described in Sect. 3 in practice by first obtaining sub-networks (in XML format) according to the divide strategy explained in Sect. 3.2. Then for each sub-network, we use the RobustRailS verification tool described in [18–20] and Sect. 2.2 to generate a model instance and safety properties, and then to verify that the generated safety properties hold in the model.

We also use the RobustRailS verification tool to monolithically verify the railway network (without decomposing it) such that we can compare verification metrics for the compositional approach with verification metrics for the monolithic approach.

While verifying each instance we measure (in seconds) the real time taken to obtain the verification result and what was the total memory (in MB) used by the verification tool. In addition we collect some statistics about the model instances as presented in Tables 1 and 2. Such statistics provide a basis for complexity comparison and include: the number of linear and point sections for each instance, the number of marker boards, routes, and the state space dimension (in logarithmic scale).

All the experiments for both case studies have been performed on a machine with an Intel(R) Xeon(R) CPU E5-2667 @ 2.90 Gz, 64 GB RAM, and running CentOS 6.6, Linux 2.6.32-504.8.1.el6.x86_64 kernels.

4.2   Mini-Tiny-Fork: A Small Case Study

To illustrate and evaluate our approach we have devised a case study based on existing networks from [18,19] inspired by the typical examples from real world used in other studies about formal verification of railway interlocking systems [5,7,9,22]. The used network, although invented, represents a realistic case.

The case study is based on three networks: Mini, Tiny, and Fork. Mini is the network shown in Fig. 1 and it represents a typical pattern of a station found on lines with small stations. Tiny, a network expressing a typical line pattern between stations, is depicted in Fig. 5, and Fork, a common network shape for a terminal station, is depicted in Fig. 6.

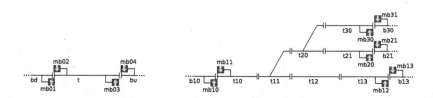

Fig. 5. Tiny network.   **Fig. 6.** Fork network.

These networks, when connected left to right in the respective order, form an example of a monolithic network of a line with two stations: Mini and Fork, connected by a single track: Tiny. We designate this network by the acronym **M · T · F** and show it (without labels) in Fig. 7.

The **M · T · F** network can be used to compare the monolithic approach described in Sect. 2 with the compositional approach described in Sect. 3 because the border (bd,t) between **Mini** and **Tiny**, and the border (t,bu) between **Tiny** and **Fork** are both satisfying the BCCs. Therefore, the **M · T · F** network can be naturally divided into the three networks Mini, Tiny, and Fork according to the method described in Sect. 3, hence allowing for a compositional analysis that we will refer to as **M + T + F**.

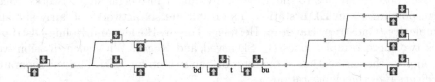

Fig. 7. **M · T · F** network.

Table 1 shows the verification metrics for the compositional analysis **M + T + F**: all metrics are obtained by summing the corresponding metrics for the sub-networks, except for the memory usage, which is calculated as the maximum memory usage of the sub-networks. The table also shows the verification metrics for the monolithic analysis of the monolithic network **M · T · F**. In all cases the verification tool succeeded to verify the safety properties using simple induction (k-induction with $k = 1$). As it can be observed the verification time and memory usage of the compositional analysis **M + T + F** is, as expected, much better than for the monolithic analysis of **M · T · F**: The verification time is five times faster and the memory usage (204 MB) is more than three times less. Moreover, if the verification for the sub-networks were run in parallel, our compositional approach would achieve a running time of just 18 s. Even though memory consumption would increase in this case, the parallelization would still use less memory resources (the sum of individual memory usages: 391 MB) than the monolithic case (759 MB).

Table 1. Verification metrics for the Mini-Tiny-Fork case study.

	Linears	Points	Signals	Routes	$log_{10}(|S|)$	Time	Memory
Tiny	3	0	4	2	11	1	13
Fork	9	2	8	6	40	10	174
Mini	6	2	8	12	37	18	204
M + T + F	18	4	20	20	76	29	204
M · T · F	14	4	16	20	76	145	759

We introduced faults in the model and ran the tool to find a counterexample witnessing a safety violation. As expected the time taken to find the witness was improved by the compositional analysis. Whereas **M · T · F** takes 6.6 h using 20.7 GB, the compositional approach takes 40 min using 7.2 GB.

4.3   EDL: A Real World Case Study

The **EDL** is the first regional line in Denmark to be commissioned in the Danish Signalling Programme. The line spreads over 55 km from the station in Roskilde to Næstved's station, and the statistics shown in Table 2 gives insight on its composition.

We apply seven cuts to the network dividing it into eight sub-networks, each corresponding to an **EDL** station. The result are six networks of fairly similar complexity (Gadstrup, Havdrup, Herfølge, Tureby, Haslev, and Holme-Olstrup) plus two more complex ones (L. Skensved and Køge). With such division we decompose the verification of the interlocking system for **EDL** into the separate verification of the eight stations.

Table 2. Verification metrics for the EDL line.

	Linears	Points	Signals	Routes	$log_{10}(|S|)$	Time	Memory
Gadstrup	14	3	16	21	73	86	513
Havdrup	10	2	12	14	51	20	263
L. Skensved	20	4	22	28	101	223	1212
Køge	52	22	54	66	306	6581	9393
Herfølge	6	2	10	14	39	13	191
Tureby	6	2	10	14	39	12	180
Haslev	10	2	12	14	51	22	261
Holme-Olstrup	12	2	16	20	63	27	350
Compositional	130	39	152	191	682	6984	9393
EDL	116	39	138	191	682	22793	26484

As in the Mini-Tiny-Fork case study, the verification tool succeeded to verify the safety properties for the eight sub-interlocking systems using simple induction (k-induction with $k = 1$) and the verification metrics show that for the compositional analysis (see the table entry Compositional) the verification time is approximately a third (taking approx. 2 h) than for the monolithic analysis (taking aprox. 6 h).

Furthermore, the compositional analysis uses less than half of the memory resources (9393 MB) because we only need as much as the maximum value of memory used to verify each sub-interlocking. Such memory reduction is important when checking real world interlocking systems where a single station with a complex network may quickly exhaust the amount of memory available. As already discussed, if run in parallel our compositional approach would achieve a much better running time. Even though memory consumption would increase, the parallelization would only use roughly half (the sum of the individual memory usages: 12363 MB) of the memory resources than the monolithic case.

5   Conclusions

We have presented a compositional method to address the safety verification of railway interlocking systems of large size by means of formal verification techniques. The method, built on top of tools providing support for efficient verification of this kind of systems, is tailored to the characteristics of multi-station interlocking systems, that is, systems that control a line connecting several stations.

The idea of our method is as follows: Multi-station interlocking systems exhibit a good deal of topological locality, which is exploited to easily, and automatically, decompose the layout in smaller chunks, easier to verify. Figures on the time and memory consumption gains obtained have been given for a simple example and for a large, real world case study, the **EDL** line in Denmark, showing that this approach is a good first step in the direction of defining a general compositional approach able to exploit as better as possible the inherent locality present in models of the interlocking logics of large networks.

The presented method assumes some Border Cut Conditions to be fulfilled in order to guarantee soundness. These conditions require that the cuts are made such that each route of the full network and the overlap and flank protection of that route are completely within one of the sub-networks after the decomposition. More work is needed to identify other patterns and conditions that identify a safe place to cut a network employing these features in sub-networks, maintaining some possibility of compositional verification.

As evidenced in the results for the **EDL** line, and expected from the parallelization theory, the gains of the method depend on the running time for the largest sub-interlocking system resulting from the division step. Future works should take into account such bottleneck either by applying it to suitable lines (for instance big lines with stations with relative simple complexity), or by finding better strategies to divide the interlocking systems, or both.

- In general, a more systematic study is needed on which ways to cut a network allow for compositional safety verification and which do not. We are currently exploring the challenge to find a way to cut into sub-networks the layout of very large stations, which tend to appear in terminal stations. In such case, due to the intricacy of the routes allowing trains to traverse the many tracks of the station, it is likely that finding a generic, automated, way to divide the network in sub-networks will be difficult, but future solutions to such problem would benefit from compositional approaches like ours.

Acknowledgments. The authors would like to express their gratitude to Jan Peleska and Linh Hong Vu for their excellent contribution to the development of the RobustRailS interlocking verification method and tool set and for an always very enjoyable collaboration. Furthermore, the authors would like to express their gratitude to Peter Holm Østergaard for helping us with some practical work, and to Ross Edwin Gammon and Nikhil Mohan Pande from Banedanmark (Railnet Denmark) and Jan Bertelsen from Thales for helping us with their expertise about Danish interlocking systems.

The research presented in this paper has been funded by Villum Fonden and the RobustRailS project granted by Innovation Fund Denmark.

References

1. CENELEC European Committee for Electrotechnical Standardization: EN 50128:2011 – Railway applications – Communications, signalling and processing systems – Software for railway control and protection systems (2011)
2. European Railway Agency: ERTMS - System Requirements Specification - UNISIG SUBSET-026, April 2014. http://www.era.europa.eu/Document-Register/Pages/Set-2-System-Requirements-Specification.aspx
3. Ferrari, A., Magnani, G., Grasso, D., Fantechi, A.: Model checking interlocking control tables. In: Schnieder, E., Tarnai, G. (eds.) FORMS/FORMAT 2010, pp. 107–115. Springer, Heidelberg (2010). doi:10.1007/978-3-642-14261-1_11
4. Hvid Hansen, H., Ketema, J., Luttik, B., Mousavi, M.R., Pol, J., Santos, O.M.: Automated verification of executable UML models. In: Aichernig, B.K., Boer, F.S., Bonsangue, M.M. (eds.) FMCO 2010. LNCS, vol. 6957, pp. 225–250. Springer, Heidelberg (2011). doi:10.1007/978-3-642-25271-6_12
5. Haxthausen, A.E., Bliguet, M., Kjær, A.A.: Modelling and verification of relay interlocking systems. In: Choppy, C., Sokolsky, O. (eds.) Monterey Workshop 2008. LNCS, vol. 6028, pp. 141–153. Springer, Heidelberg (2010). doi:10.1007/978-3-642-12566-9_8
6. Haxthausen, A.E., Østergaard, P.H.: On the use of static checking in the verification of interlocking systems. In: Margaria, T., Steffen, B. (eds.) ISoLA 2016, Part II. LNCS, vol. 9953, pp. 266–278. Springer, Heidelberg (2016)
7. Haxthausen, A.E., Peleska, J., Pinger, R.: Applied bounded model checking for interlocking system designs. In: Counsell, S., Núñez, M. (eds.) SEFM 2013. LNCS, vol. 8368, pp. 205–220. Springer, Heidelberg (2014). doi:10.1007/978-3-319-05032-4_16
8. James, P., Möller, F., Nguyen, H.N., Roggenbach, M., Schneider, S., Treharne, H.: Decomposing scheme plans to manage verification complexity. In: Schnieder and Tarnai [14], pp. 210–220
9. James, P., Möller, F., Nguyen, H.N., Roggenbach, M., Schneider, S., Treharne, H., Trumble, M., Williams, D.: Verification of scheme plans using CSP||B. In: Counsell, S., Núñez, M. (eds.) SEFM 2013. LNCS, vol. 8368, pp. 189–204. Springer, Heidelberg (2014). doi:10.1007/978-3-319-05032-4_15
10. James, P., Lawrence, A., Möller, F., Roggenbach, M., Seisenberger, M., Setzer, A., Kanso, K., Chadwick, S.: Verification of solid state interlocking programs. In: Counsell, S., Núñez, M. (eds.) SEFM 2013. LNCS, vol. 8368, pp. 253–268. Springer, Heidelberg (2014). doi:10.1007/978-3-319-05032-4_19
11. Limbrée, C., Cappart, Q., Pecheur, C., Tonetta, S.: Verification of railway interlocking - compositional approach with OCRA. In: Lecomte, T., Pinger, R., Romanovsky, A. (eds.) RSSRail 2016. LNCS, vol. 9707, pp. 134–149. Springer, Heidelberg (2016). doi:10.1007/978-3-319-33951-1_10
12. Peleska, J.: Industrial-strength model-based testing - state of the art and current challenges. In: Petrenko, A.K., Schlingloff, H. (eds.) 8th Workshop on Model-Based Testing. Electronic Proceedings in Theoretical Computer Science, Rome, Italy, vol. 111, pp. 3–28. Open Publishing Association (2013)
13. Peleska, J., Vorobev, E., Lapschies, F.: Automated test case generation with SMT-solving and abstract interpretation. In: Bobaru, M., Havelund, K., Holzmann, G.J., Joshi, R. (eds.) NFM 2011. LNCS, vol. 6617, pp. 298–312. Springer, Heidelberg (2011). doi:10.1007/978-3-642-20398-5_22

14. Schnieder, E., Tarnai, G. (eds.) FORMS/FORMAT 2014 - Formal Methods for Automation and Safety in Railway and Automotive Systems. Institute for Traffic Safety and Automation Engineering, Technische Universität Braunschweig (2014)
15. Theeg, G., Vlasenko, S.V., Anders, E.: Railway Signalling & Interlocking: International Compendium. Eurailpress, Germany (2009)
16. Verified Systems International GmbH: RT-Tester Model-Based Test Case and Test Data Generator - RTT-MBT - User Manual (2013). http://www.verified.de
17. Vu, L.H., Haxthausen, A.E., Peleska, J.: A domain-specific language for railway interlocking systems. In: Schnieder and Tarnai [14], pp. 200–209
18. Vu, L.H., Haxthausen, A.E., Peleska, J.: Formal modeling and verification of interlocking systems featuring sequential release. In: Artho, C., Ölveczky, P.C. (eds.) FTSCS 2014. CCIS, vol. 476, pp. 223–238. Springer, Heidelberg (2015). doi:10. 1007/978-3-319-17581-2_15
19. Vu, L.H.: Formal development and verification of railway control systems. In: The Context of ERTMS/ETCS Level 2. Ph.D. thesis, Technical University of Denmark, DTU Compute (2015)
20. Vu, L.H., Haxthausen, A.E., Peleska, J.: Formal modelling and verification of interlocking systems featuring sequential release. Science of Computer Programming (2016)
21. Winter, K.: Symbolic model checking for interlocking systems. In: Flammini, F. (ed.) Railway Safety, Reliability, and Security: Technologies and Systems Engineering. IGI Global (2012)
22. Winter, K.: Optimising ordering strategies for symbolic model checking of railway interlockings. In: Margaria, T., Steffen, B. (eds.) ISoLA 2012. LNCS, vol. 7610, pp. 246–260. Springer, Heidelberg (2012). doi:10.1007/978-3-642-34032-1_24

OnTrack: The Railway Verification Toolset
Extended Abstract

Phillip James[1(✉)], Faron Moller[1], Hoang Nga Nguyen[2], Markus Roggenbach[1], Helen Treharne[3], and Xu Wang[1]

[1] Swansea University, Swansea, Wales
{p.d.james,f.g.moller,m.roggenbach}@swansea.ac.uk,
xu.wang.comp@gmail.com
[2] University of Coventry, Coventry, England
hoang.nguyen@coventry.ac.uk
[3] University of Surrey, Guildford, England
h.treharne@surrey.ac.uk

Abstract. The verification of railway interlocking systems is a challenging task for which a number of different modelling, simulation and verification approaches have been proposed. In this paper, we present the OnTrack toolset. In OnTrack, application data for the railway domain is represented using a domain specific language. This data can be entered manually or imported from standard data formats. OnTrack then comprises of a number of different model transformations that allow the user to automatically generate formal models for a specific approach, e.g., in CASL, CSP, or CSP$||B$. Other transformations offer abstractions on the application data to address scalability.

OnTrack [3] is an open toolset for railway verification developed in collaboration between Swansea University and Surrey University. It has been created using the GMF framework [5] and multiple associated Epsilon [4] model transformations.

Figure 1 shows the workflow that OnTrack currently provides. Firstly, given a CAD track plan and associated control tables, a user draws a scheme plan using the OnTrack graphical front end (centre path). Scheme plans are models formulated relative to the metamodel of OnTrack's Domain Specific Language (DSL). One can also read models described in the BRaVE [1] tool format (right path), whilst reading in RailML representations (left path, dashed) is work in progress. A scheme plan is then the basis for workflows that support its abstraction or analysis. For example, a covering construction [2] is implemented as an *abstraction transformation* on the DSL level.

Scheme plans can be translated to formal specifications in various (specification) formalisms. This can be achieved in two ways. The first approach is to use a metamodel describing the formal specification language. A *represent transformation* translates a scheme plan over the DSL into an equivalent formal scheme plan over the metamodel. Various *model-to-text transformations* then turn a formal scheme plan into formal specification text ready for verification. The advantage

© Springer International Publishing AG 2016
T. Margaria and B. Steffen (Eds.): ISoLA 2016, Part II, LNCS 9953, pp. 294–296, 2016.
DOI: 10.1007/978-3-319-47169-3_21

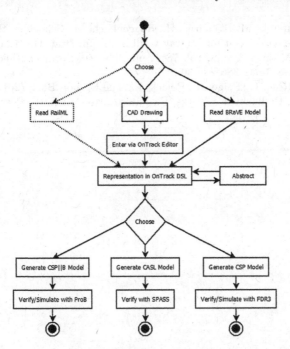

Fig. 1. The OnTrack workflow.

of this approach is that all transformations involved can be defined relative to the specification language's metamodel. The second approach is to directly generate a formal specification. Here, transformations turn a scheme plan over the DSL directly into formal specification text ready for verification.

Once a formal model has been generated, it can then be simulated or verified using the tools associated with the chosen approach. For example, ProB and FDR3 can be used for simulating and verifying CSP||B and CSP models (resp.) for safety, whereas the SPASS theorem prover can be used for verifying CASL models for safety.

Finally, OnTrack is extendable, e.g., other models from various contexts can be generated and analysed through the implementation of new model transformations. For example, the generation of Real Time Maude models is currently planned.

References

1. Douglas, H., Weston, P., Kirkwood, D., Hillmansen, S., Roberts, C.: Method for validating the train motion equations used for passenger rail vehicle simulation. J. Rail Rapid Transit (2016)
2. James, P., Moller, F., Nguyen, H., Roggenbach, M., Schneider, S., Treharne, H.: Techniques for modelling and verifying railway interlockings. STTT **16**(6), 685–711 (2014)

3. James, P., Trumble, M., Treharne, H., Roggenbach, M., Schneider, S.: OnTrack: an open tooling environment for railway verification. In: Brat, G., Rungta, N., Venet, A. (eds.) NFM 2013. LNCS, vol. 7871, pp. 435–440. Springer, Heidelberg (2013). doi:10.1007/978-3-642-38088-4_30
4. Kolovos, D., Rose, L., Paige, R., Polack, F.: The Epsilon Book (2013)
5. Steinberg, D., Budinsky, F., Merks, E., Paternostro, M.: EMF. Pearson (2008)

Experiments in Formal Modelling of a Deadlock Avoidance Algorithm for a CBTC System

Franco Mazzanti, Alessio Ferrari[✉], and Giorgio O. Spagnolo

Istituto di Scienza e Tecnologie dell'Informazione "A. Faedo",
Consiglio Nazionale delle Ricerche, ISTI-CNR, Pisa, Italy
alessio.ferrari@isti.cnr.it

Abstract. This paper presents a set of experiments in formal modelling and verification of a deadlock avoidance algorithm of an Automatic Train Supervision System (ATS). The algorithm is modelled and verified using four formal environment, namely UMC, Promela/SPIN, NuSMV, and mCRL2. The experience gained in this multiple modelling/verification experiments is described. We show that the algorithm design, structured as a set of concurrent activities cooperating through a shared memory, can be replicated in all the formal frameworks taken into consideration with relative effort. In addition, we highlight specific peculiarities of the various tools and languages, which emerged along our experience.

Keywords: Model checking · Formal design · NuSMV · SPIN · UMC · mCRL2 · Comparison of model checkers · CBTC · Deadlock avoidance · Railways

1 Introduction

In this paper, we show that a representative railway problem can be modelled and verified with limited effort using four different tools, namely: UMC, Promela/SPIN, NuSMV, and mCRL2. In particular, we modelled an algorithm for deadlock avoidance in train scheduling. The algorithm was previously implemented as part of an Automatic Train Supervision (ATS) system [8,9] of a Communications-based Train Control System (CBTC) [17]. Such system controls the movements of driverless trains inside a given yard. The deadlock avoidance algorithm takes care of avoiding situations in which a train cannot move because its route is blocked by another train. Equipped with this algorithm, the ATS is able to dispatch the trains without ever causing situations of deadlock, even in presence of arbitrary delays with respect to the planned timetable. This kind of problem is a rather typical one – not only for the railway domain – which can be modelled as a set of global data that is concurrently and atomically updated by a set of concurrent guarded agents – i.e., agents that, when certain global conditions are met, are allowed to atomically change the global status. In the paper, we show relevant excerpts of the models and the verification results.

From our experience, we saw that small choices in the specification of the models, or in the verification options, can greatly impact on the verification

© Springer International Publishing AG 2016
T. Margaria and B. Steffen (Eds.): ISoLA 2016, Part II, LNCS 9953, pp. 297–314, 2016.
DOI: 10.1007/978-3-319-47169-3_22

time. With some differences, this observation holds for all the modelling frameworks considered. Hence, we argue that a deep proficiency with each one of the frameworks is required to effectively exploit their verification capabilities.

The rest of the paper is structured as follows. In Sect. 2 we describe the deadlock avoidance algorithm that we modelled. In Sects. 3–6, we show our models and the verification results for UMC, NuSMV, Promela/SPIN and mCRL2, respectively[1], and, within the descriptions of the models, we highlight the peculiarities of the different languages and environments. Finally, Sect. 7 concludes the paper and provides general observations on the experience.

2   The Deadlock Avoidance Algorithm

This section describes basic elements of the modelled algorithm, which was defined in our previous works [8,9]. Figure 1 shows the structure of the railway layout considered in this study. Nodes in the yard correspond to itinerary endpoints, and the connecting lines correspond to the entry/exit itineraries to/from those endpoints. Eight trains are placed in the layout. Each train has its own mission to execute, defined as a sequence of itinerary endpoints. For example, the mission of train0, which traverses the layout from left to right along top side of the yard, is defined by the mission vector: $T_0 = [1, 9, 10, 13, 15, 20, 23]$. The mission of train7, which instead traverses the layout from right to left, is defined by the vector: $T_7 = [26, 22, 17, 18, 12, 27, 8]$. The progress status of each train is represented by the index, in the mission vector, which allows to identify the endpoint in which the train is at a certain moment. We will have 8 variables $P_0, \ldots, P_7$, one for each train, which store the current index for the train. For example, at the beginning, we have $P_0 = 0, \ldots, P_7 = 0$, since all the trains occupy the initial endpoints of their missions – at index 0 in the vector.

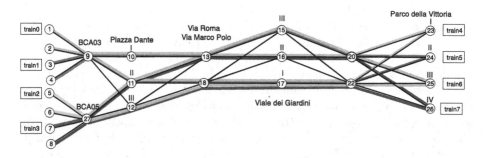

Fig. 1. A fragment of the yard layout and the 8 missions of the trains

[1] All the verification experiments have been conducted on a Mac Pro (late 2013) workstation with *Quad-core 3,7Ghz Intel Xeon E5, 64 GB RAM* running OS X 10.11 (El Capitan). All the models referred in this paper can be retrieved from the URL http://fmt.isti.cnr.it/WEBPAPER/ISOLA2016data.zip.

If the 8 trains are allowed to move freely, i.e., if their next endpoint is free, there is the possibility of creating deadlocks, i.e., a situation in which the 8 trains block each other in their expected progression. To solve this problem the scheduling algorithm of the ATS must take into consideration two *critical sections* A and B – i.e., zones of the layout in which a deadlock might occur, – which have the form of a ring of length 8 (see Fig. 2), and guarantee that these rings are never saturated with 8 trains – further information on how critical sections are identified can be found in our previous work [8,9]. This can be modelled by using two global counters RA and RB, which record the current number of trains inside these critical sections, and by updating them whenever a train enters or exits these sections. For this purpose, each train mission T_i, with $i = 0 \ldots 7$, is associated with: a vector of increments/decrements A_i to be applied to counter RA at each step of progression; a vector B_i of increments/decrements to be applied to counter RB.

For example, given $T_0 = [1, 9, 10, 13, 15, 20, 23]$, and $A_0 = [0, 0, 0, 1, 0, -1, 0]$, when train0 moves from endpoint 10 to endpoint 13 ($P_0 = 3$) we must check that the $+1$ increment of RA does not saturate the critical section A, i.e., $RA + A_0[P_0] \leq 7$; if the check passes then the train can proceed and safely update the counter $RA := RA + A_0[P_0]$. The maximum number of trains allowed in each critical section (i.e., 7), will be expressed as LA and LB in the rest of the paper.

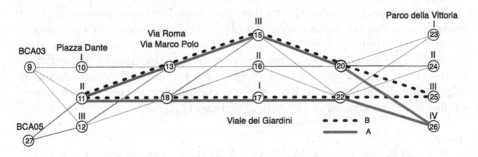

Fig. 2. The critical section A and B which must not be saturated by 8 trains

The models presented in the following sections, which implement the algorithm described above, are deadlock-free, since the verification is being carried on as a final validation of a correct design. The actual possibility of having deadlocks, if the critical sections management were not supported or incorrectly implemented, can easily be observed by raising from 7 to 8 the values of the variables LA and LB.

The current design, in which each train movement logically corresponds to an atomic system evolution step, leads to a state-space of 1,636,537 configurations.

3   The UMC Model

UMC [4] is a model checker that belongs to the KandISTI [2,3] family. Its development started at ISTI in 2003 and has been since then used in several research projects. So far UMC is not really an industrial scale project but more an (open source) experimental research framework. It is actively maintained and is publicly usable through its web interface [5].

The KandISTI family comprises four model checkers, each of which is oriented to a particular system design approach, but all of which share the same underlying abstract model and verification engine. The basic underlying idea behind KandISTI is that the evolution in time of the system behaviour can be seen as a graph where both edges and states are associated with sets of (composite) labels [7]. Labels on the states represent basic state properties, and labels on the edges represent properties of system transitions. The logic supported by the KandISTI framework uses the evolution graph as semantic model and allows to specify abstract properties in a way that is rather independent from the internal implementation details of the system [6].

The different flavours of the various KandISTI tools have to do with the choice of one of the supported specifications languages, which range from process algebras to sets of UML-like statecharts. In our case, we will use the UMC tool, since we considered it the most adequate to model our algorithm. In UMC, a system is described as a set of communicating UML-like state machines. In our particular case, the system is composed of a unique state machine, in which we have a Vars part – including the global state – and a Behavior part – specifying the state machine behavior.

The Vars part contains the vectors describing the train missions (T_i), the indexes recording the train progresses (P_i) – i.e., the indexes in the previous vectors –, the occupancy counters RA and RB of the two critical sections, and the vectors A_i, B_i including the increments/decrements that should be performed by the trains at each step of their progress for the critical sections A and B, respectively. In addition, we have the two constants indicating the maximum number of trains allowed in the critical sections (LA, LB).

```
Vars:
  T0: int[] := [ 1, 9,10,13,15,20,23];  -- mission steps for train0
      . . .
  T7: int[] := [26,22,17,18,12,27, 8];  -- mission steps for train7
  LA: int :=7;                          -- limit value for region RA
  A0: int[] := [0, 0, 0, 1, 0,-1, 0];  -- RA updates steps for train0
      . . .
  A7: int[] := [1, 0, 0, 0,-1, 0, 0];  -- RA updates steps for train7
  RA: int :=1;                          -- occupancy of region RA
  LB: int :=7;                          -- limit value for region RB
  B0: int[] := [0, 0, 0, 1, 0,-1, 0];  -- RB updates steps for train0
      . . .
  B7: int[] := [1, 0, 0, 0,-1, 0, 0];  -- RB updates steps for train7
  RB: int :=1;                          -- occupancy of region RA
  P0,P1,P2,...,P7:int :=0;              -- train progresses
```

In this particular case the size of a state is fixed and static. However, this is not a requirement for UMC, since we can have variables representing unbounded vectors, queues, unbounded integers, which together with the (potentially unbounded) events queues can contribute to make the actual size of a state highly dynamic. This dynamism might lead to potentially infinite state systems.

In the `Behavior` part of our class definition we will have one transition rule for each train, which describes the conditions and the effects of the advancement of the train. A generic transition rule is expressed as follows:

`<SourceState> -> <TargetState>{<EventTrigger>[<Guard>]/<Actions>}`

A transition rule expressed as above intuitively states that when the system is in the state `SourceState`, the specified `EventTrigger` is available, and all the `Guards` are satisfied, then all the `Actions` of the transition are executed and the system state passes from `SourceState` to `TargetState`.

The interleaving of the progress of the various trains is therefore modelled by the internal non-determinism of the possible applications of state machine transitions. In our case there is no external event that triggers the system transitions, therefore the transitions will be controlled only by their guards.

In the case of `train0`, for example, we will have the transition rule:

```
s1 -> s1
  {- P0 <6 &                     -- train0 has not yet completed its mission
     T0[P0+1] != T1[P0]&         -- next position not occupied by train1
     . . .                       -- next position not occupied by ...
     T0[P0+1] != T7[P7]&         -- next position not occupied by train7
     RA + A0[P0+1] <= LA &       -- A is not saturated by arrival of train0
     RB + B0[P0+1] <= LB]/       -- B is not saturated by arrival of train0
   RA = RA + A0[P0+1];           -- update occupancy of critical section A
   RB = RB + B0[P0+1];           -- update occupancy of critical section B
   P0 := P0 +1;                  -- update train progress
  }
```

As a last step we have to define what we want to see on the abstract L2TS associated to the system evolutions. Indeed, the overall behaviour of a system is formalised as an abstract doubly labelled transition system (L2TS), and abstraction rules allow to define what we want to see as labels of the states and edges of the L2TS. The abstraction rules are expressed in the `Abstraction` part of the specification, in which we define which labels should appear on the edges and states of the abstract evolution graph. In our case, we are interested to observe the existence of a certain state where all trains have completed all their missions. This can be done assigning a state label, e.g. ARRIVED, to all the system configurations in which each train is in its final position.

```
Abstractions {
State SYS.P0=6 and
      SYS.P1=6 and
          . . .
      SYS.P7=6 -> ARRIVED    -- abstract label on final node
}
```

At this point, the L2TS associated to our model will be a directed graph that will converge to a final state labelled ARRIVED in the case that no deadlock occurs in the system. The branching-time, state/event based temporal logic supported by UMC has the power of full μ-calculus but also supports the more high level operators of Computation Tree Logic (CTL). The property that for all executions all the trains eventually reach their destinations be easily checked by verifying the CTL-like formula:

AF ARRIVED

The **AF** operator inside the above CTL formula specifies that for all execution paths (**A**) of the system, eventually in the future (**F**), we should reach a state in which the state predicate ARRIVED holds.

If this property does not hold, UMC allows to interactively explore the set of system evolution steps which led to a failure (which in this case do have the shape of a single path but which in general may have the shape of a graph), and view all the internal details of the traversed states. One of the design goals of UMC is indeed the one of helping the user to easily understand the defects in its early designs, by exploiting an interactive explanation of the obtained evaluation results – not just a state-space fragment acting as counter-example.

In our case the formula is *true* and UMC completes the evaluation in a time which ranges from 28 s to 106 s depending on how the tool is used. The fastest results of 28 s is obtained by exploiting a prototypal parallel version of UMC [10], by adopting a depth-first exploration strategy, and letting the evaluation to proceed in a non-interactive way which does not collect the data necessary for a subsequent explanation of the results.

As an alternative modelling approach, we might have modelled the successful completion of all the train missions as an observable *event* on the graph. To achieve this we should introduce an additional evolution to the state machine, which generates the Arrived signal after all trains have completed their missions.

```
s1 -> s2 {- [P0=6 & P1=6 & ... & P7=6] / Arrived}
```

Furthermore, in this case we should associate an observable label in the abstract evolution graph, corresponding to the internal event of signal generation.

```
Abstractions {
Action : Arrived -> arrived    -- abstract label on final edge
}
```

At this point the property to be verified becomes:

AF {arrived} true

The **AF** { } operator inside the above CTL formula specifies that for all execution paths (**A**) of the system, eventually in the future (**F**), we should reach a transition whose labels satisfy the action predicate arrived, and whose target state satisfies the formula true.

4   The NuSMV Model

NuSMV [13,14] is a software tool for the formal verification of finite state systems. NuSMV was jointly developed by FBK-IRST and by Carnegie Mellon University. NuSMV allows to check finite state systems against specifications in the Computation Tree Logic (CTL), Linear Temporal Logic (LTL) and in the Property Specification Language (PSL) [1].

Since NuSMV is intended to describe finite state machines, the only data types in the language are finite ones, i.e. boolean, scalar, bit vectors and fixed arrays of basic data types. A state of the system is represented by a set of variables. Assignment rules in the language allow to specify *total* functions, which define all the possible values that a state variable can assume in the next state.

NuSMV distinguishes between system constants (DEFINE construct), and variables (VAR construct). The system constants are represented by the T_i, A_i, B_i and LA, LB data values:

```
DEFINE
    T0  := [ 1,  9,10,13,15,20,23];
    . . .
    T7  := [26,22,17,18,12,27, 8];
    LA  := 7;
    A0  := [0,  0,  0,  1,  0,-1,  0];
    . . .
    A7  := [0,  1,  0,  0,-1,  0,  0];
    LB  := 7;
    B0  := [0,  0,  0,  1,  0,-1,  0];
    . . .
    B7  := [1,  0,  0,  0,-1,  0,  0];
```

The state variables consist of the different P_i of the various train progresses, and of the occupancy status of RA and RB of the two critical sections. Furthermore, we will need an additional RUNNING state variable for modelling the non-determinism in the choice of the potentially moving train and consistently synchronise the updates of the P_i, RA, and RB variables.

```
VAR
    RUNNING: 0..7;
    P0:  0..6;
    . . .
    P7:  0..6;
    RA:  0..8;
    RB:  0..8;
```

The initial state, and the state transitions specifying the behaviour are expressed under the ASSIGN construct of a NuSMV mudule. The definition of the initial state is specified making use of the init operator:

```
ASSIGN
  init(P0) := 0;
    . . .
  init(P7) := 0;
  init(RA) := 1;
  init(RB) := 1;
```

The evolutions corresponding to the train movements, i.e., the system transitions, are specified making use of the next operator. For example, the evolution of train0 is now described by the following rule:

```
next(P0) :=
    case
        RUNNING =0 &      -- train0 selected for possible movement
        P0 < 6 &          -- train0 has not yet completed its mission
        T0[P0+1] != T1[P1] &
          . . .           -- next place not occupied by other trains
        T0[P0+1] != T7[P7] &
        RA + A0[P0+1] <= LA &   -- critical section constraints satisfied
        RB + B0[P0+1] <= LB &
        RA + A0[P0+1] >= 0 &
        RB + B0[P0+1] >= 0
        :    P0+1;
        TRUE              -- train0 not selected or not allowed to move
        :    P0;
    esac;
```

We must observe that the definition of the next value for the P_0 variable is now total. If the train can move, the value of P_0 is incremented, while if the train is not allowed to move, the value of P_0 in the next state remains the same. Notice that in this way we are introducing loops, in each node of the graph, corresponding to the dummy evolutions of trains which cannot actually move.

The definition of the next values of the RA variable should take into consideration again which train is selected for possible movements, and whether or not the train is actually allowed to move. Therefore, the transition definition for the RA variable now becomes:

```
next(RA) :=
    case
        RUNNING =0 &           -- train0 selected for possible evolution
        P0 < 6 &               -- train0 actually allowed to move
        T0[P0+1] != T1[P1] & --
          . . .                -- next place not occupied by other trains
        T0[P0+1] != T7[P7] & --
        RA + A0[P0+1] <= LA &  -- critical section constraints satisfied
        RB + B0[P0+1] <= LB &  --
        RA + A0[P0+1] >= 0 &   --
        RB + B0[P0+1] >= 0     --
        : RA + A0[P0+1];  -- RA updated according to movement of train0
```

```
           --
     RUNNING =1 &              -- train1 selected for possible evolution
        . . .                  -- train1 actually allowed to move
        : RA + A1[P1+1];   -- RA updated according to movement of train1
        . . .
        TRUE     -- no train can move (deadlock or all trains arrived)
        : RA;   -- RA remains the same
     esac;
```

The description of the properties to be verified is expressed within the
CTLSPEC/LTLSPEC constructs of a NuSMV module. The property that all
trains eventually complete their mission is encoded in the following way:

```
CTLSPEC      -- all trains eventually complete their mission
   AF ((P0=6) & (P1=6) & (P2=6) & (P3]=6) &
       (P4=6) & (P5=6) & (P6=6) & (P7=6))

LTLSPEC      -- all trains eventually complete their mission
   F ((P0=6) & (P1=6) & (P2=6) & (P3=6) &
       (P4=6) & (P5=6) & (P6=6) & (P7=6))
```

The NuSMV version of CTL formula makes use of the same **AF** operator
already seen in the previous Section. The only difference with respect to the
UMC version is that now the state predicate to be verified is directly expressed in
terms of values on internal variables of the model. The LTL version of the formula
contains only the **F** operator applied to the same state predicate, because LTL
formulas by definition must be satisfied by all the execution paths of the system
(and cannot therefore contain further existential or universal quantifiers over the
branches outgoing from the states). In this simple case it is quite immediate to
see that the two CTL and LTL formulas describe the same behavioural property.

Unfortunately, unless we introduce appropriate fairness constraints the above
formulas would result to be *false*. Indeed, since the next(P0) function is total,
a possible, infinite system evolution is the one in which only train0 is selected
for possible movement, i.e., during this evolution path the variable RUNNING is
always equal to 0. In order to discard these uninteresting paths, and to make
inisgnficant the dummy transitions corresponding to trains that are not moving,
we must introduce a set of FAIRNESS constraints of the form:

```
FAIRNESS  RUNNING = 0;
   . . .
FAIRNESS  RUNNING = 7;
```

In this way, NuSMV limits its evaluations to the fair paths of the system
evolutions, i.e. those infinite paths for which the fairness constraints are true
for an infinite number of times. With the above constraints, an infinite path in
which only train0 is selected is discarded, because it violates the fairness rules
RUNNING=1,...,RUNNING=7.

If a logical formula is found to be false, NuSMV automatically returns a path as counterexample of the formula, and it is possible to check in detail the internal state of the variables for the states in the path. This approach works well for counterexamples of LTL formulas, which are just linear paths, but it does not work very well for counterexamples of CTL formulas which in general might have the form of a sub-graph of the system evolution graph. The task of understanding why a given counterexample path does not satisfy the expected property is left completely to user, i.e. no help is provided from the tool in understanding precisely why the evaluation failed. This does not constitute a problem in most cases, like our case, where the formula is rather simple and intuitive.

In our case, NuSMV found the formula to be true in about 413 s in the case of the CTL formula, and in about 166 s in the case of the LTL formula. However if the RUNNNING variable is declared as an *Input Variable* (**IVAR**) instead that as a *State Variable* (**VAR**), the execution times immediately decrease to 140 and 153 s respectively, and the CTL version not only recovers the original penality w.r.t. the LTL case, but even overtakes it.

Up to version 2.4 of NuSMV, a specific `process` construct was allowed to specify asynchronous systems. From version 2.5, this operator has been deprecated and it might be no longer supported in future versions of the tool. We have experimented also a specification of the model using the deprecated `process` construct. This alternative version is very similar the the current one, and essentially encloses the progression statements of the trains inside specific `process` modules. The evaluation time of this alternative version decreases to about 91 s in the CTL case and to about 88 s in the LTL case. This discrepancy in execution times is probably a sign of our relative inexperience in correctly using the tool and suggests that a deeper knowledge of the verification environment is needed for an actual mastering of the framework.

5   The Promela/SPIN Model

SPIN [11,12] is an advanced and very efficient tool specifically targeted for the verification of multi-threaded software. The tool was developed at Bell Labs in the Unix group of the Computing Sciences Research Center, starting in 1980. In April 2002 the tool was awarded the ACM System Software Award. The language supported for the system specification is called Promela (PROcess MEta LAnguage). Promela is a non-deterministic language, loosely based on Dijkstra's guarded command language notation, and borrowing the notation for I/O operations from Hoare's CSP language. Once a model is formalised in Promela, a corresponding analyser in generated as a source C program (`pan.c`). The compilation and execution of the analyser performs all the needed on-the-fly state generations and verification steps. The properties to be verified can be expressed in LTL, and a violation of a property can be explained by observing the generated counterexample trail path.

In our case, a Promela model consists of (a) state variable declarations, (b) property specifications, and (c) system initialisation/execution code.

The state variables declarations (a) in our case consist in the definition of T_i, A_i, B_i vectors, plus the numeric variables P_i, RA, RB, LA, LB, as shown below.

```
byte   T0[7];        //  mission data for train0
...
byte   T7[7];        //  mission data for train7
byte   P0,...,P7;    //  progress data for train0,...train7
byte   RA;           //  occupancy of region A
byte   RB;           //  occupancy of region B
byte   LA;           //  limit of region A
byte   LB;           //  limit if region B
short A0[7];         //  increments/decrements of train 0 for Region A
...
short A7[7];         //  increments/decrements of train 1 for Region B
short B0[7];         //  increments/decrements of train 0 for Region B
...
short B7[7];         //  increments/decrements of train 7 for Region B
```

The property (b) we are interested in is the classical property that all trains eventually complete their missions:

```
ltl p1 { <> ((P0==6) && (P1==6) && (P2==6) && (P3==6) &&
             (P4==6) && (P5==6) && (P6==6) && (P7==6)) }
```

The above LTL formula is equivalent to the one already seen in the NuSMV example. The only difference is in the syntax of the *eventually* operator which is in this case encoded as <> instead of F.

The system initialisation/execution code (c) consists of: (1) the setting of the initial value for the state variables; (2) the possible activation of concurrent, communicating, asynchronous subprocesses (sharing the same global memory); the main execution of a sequence of statements. In Promela, sequences of statements, when included inside an atomic {...} construct, are executed as part of a single system (or process) transition.

The setting of the initial value for the state variables (1) has to assign a single numeric value to each vector component, as shown below:

```
init {
  atomic {   //  initializations of state variable
  // T0:[1,9,10,13,15,20,23]
  T0[0]=1;   T0[1]=9;   T0[2]=10; T0[3]=13; T0[4]=15;
  T0[5]=20; T0[6]=23;
  ...
  // T7:[26,22,17,18,12,27,8]
  T7[0]=26; T7[1]=22; T7[2]=17; T7[3]=18; T7[4]=12;
  T7[5]=27; T7[6]=8;
  A0[3]= 1; A0[5]= -1;              // A0:[0,0,0,1,0,-1,0]
  ...
```

```
A7[1]=1;   A7[4]=-1;                  // A7:[0,1,0,0,-1,0,0]
B0[3]=1;   B0[5]=-1;                  // B0:[0,0,0,1,0,-1,0]
 . . .
B7[0]=1;   B7[4]=-1;                  // B7:[1,0,0,0,-1,0,0]
RA=1;      RB=1;        LA=7;     LB=7;
}        . . .// end of initializations of state variables
    . . . // activation of subprocesses
    . . . // main sequence of statement
```

In our case, we can avoid the definition and activation of subprocesses (2) – i.e. not modelling each train as a subprocess. Indeed, the non-determinism of the system can be modelled, as already done in the UMC and SMV case, by the non-determinism of the main process evolutions.

The main sequence of statements (3), in our case, is a loop of atomic guarded transitions, in which each transition models the progresses of a train.

```
init {
    . . .   //  initializations of state variables
    do       // main loop
    :: atomic {       // guarded progress of train0
      (P0 < 6 &&       // train0 has not yet completed its mission
      T0[P0+1] != T1[P1] &&
         . . .          // next place not occupied by other trains
      T0[P0+1] != T7[P7] &&
      RA+A0[P0+1] <= LA && // critical sections constraints satisfied
      RB+B0[P0+1] <= LB
      ) ->
      RA = RA + A0[P0+1];   // update the status of critical section A
      RB = RB + B0[P0+1];   // update the status of critical section B
      P0++; };             // update the progress of train0
    . . .
    :: atomic { . . . };  // guarded progress of train1
    . . .
    // successful loop exit when all missions are completed
    :: (P0==6) && (P1==6) && (P2==6) && (P3==6) &&
       (P4==6) && (P5==6) && (P6==6) && (P7==6)
       -> break;
    od;
```

The evaluation of the formula is carried over by the process analyser (pan.c) in about 25 s, which decrease to 10 s when the process analyser is compiled with all gcc optimisations turned on (-O3 flag). We have also experimented the version of this specification in which each train was represented by an explicit process, whose activity consists in just executing the loop of its own atomic progress transition. This architecture, indeed, is the one which more precisely reflects our logical system design. In this case, the evaluation time raises to about 126 s (which decrease to about 47 s with gcc optimisations turned on).

Like in the case of NuSMV, when a formula does not hold it is possible to obtain a counter-example path to be analysed. Several features are explicitly provided for this purpose but we have experienced major difficulties in their use in terms of usability from the point of view of a non-experienced user.

6   The mCRL2 Model

mCRL2 [15,16] is a formal specification language with an associated toolset. The toolset can be used for modelling, validation and verification of concurrent systems and protocols. The mCRL2 toolset is developed at the department of Mathematics and Computer Science of the Technische Universiteit Eindhoven, in collaboration with LaQuSo, CWI and the University of Twente. The mCRL2 language is based on the Algebra of Communicating Processes (ACP) which is extended to include data and time. Processes can perform actions and can be composed to form new processes using algebraic operators. A system usually consists of several processes, or components, running in parallel. A process can carry data as its parameters. The state of a process is a specific combination of parameter values. In our case, we need to model the existence of a global status shared among the various trains, and this can be represented in mCRL2 by a single, recursive, non-deterministic process, whose parameters precisely model the global system state. Also in this case, the non-determinism of the system evolutions is modelled through the non-determinism of the main process behaviour.

In our case the mCRL2 specification includes (a) a data types specification; (b) actions specifications; (c) process definitions; (d) main process specification.

The data types specifications (a) in our case can be used to define the global constant data of our model. For example, we can model the vector of a train mission T_i as a map, i.e., a function from natural numbers (Nat) to natural numbers. The values returned by the function are expressed by means of the eqn construct.

```
map T0: Nat -> Nat;      %% T0 [ 1, 9,10,13,15,20,23]
    eqn T0(0)=1;  T0(1)=9;  T0(2)=10;...;T0(5)=20;  T0(6)=23;
    . . .
map T7: Nat -> Nat;      %% T7[26,22,17,18,12,27, 8]
    eqn T7(0)=26; T7(1)=22; T7(2)=17;...; T7(5)=27; T7(6)=8;
```

Similarly, we can use the map construct for the critical sections limits (LA, LB), and for the vectors of increments A_i, B_i that trains should apply, with respect to critical sections, during their progress in the mission:

```
map  LA: Nat;            %% limit for region A
    eqn  LA = 7;
map A0: Nat -> Int;      %% A0 [0, 0, 0, 1, 0,-1, 0]
    eqn A0(0)=0; A0(1)=0; A0(2)=0;...; A0(5)=-1; A0(6)=0;
    . . .
map B0: Nat -> Int;      %% B0 [ 0, 0, 0, 1, 0,-1, 0]
    eqn B0(0)=0; B0(1)=0; B0(2)=0;...; B0(5)=-1; B0(6)=0;
```

The actions specification (b) should define the structure of the possible actions (act) appearing inside processes. In our case, we define an action move, to represent the movement of the train at each progress step, and a final arrived action, which is performed when all trains have completed their missions:

```
act arrived; move: Nat;
```

The set of process definitions (c) consists in one unique recursive process, which we name AllTrains, whose parameters represent: (1) the progress indexes P_i of all the train missions, and (2) the occupancy counters of the two critical sections RA and RB.

```
proc AllTrains(P0:Nat, P1:Nat, P2:Nat, P3:Nat, P4:Nat,
               P5:Nat, P6:Nat, P7:Nat, RA:Int, RB: Int) =
    (P0 < 6                 &&    % progress of train0
     T0(P0+1) != T1(P1)     &&
     . . .
     T0(P0+1) != T7(P7)     &&
     RA + A0(P0+1) < LA     &&
     RB + B0(P0+1) < LB
    )  -> move(0).
    AllTrains(P0+1,P1,P2,P3,P4,P5,P6,P7,RA+A0(P0+1),RB+B0(P0+1))
    +

    . . .

    +
    (P7 < 6                 &&    % progress of train7
     T7(P7+1) != T0(P0)     &&
     . . .
     T7(P7+1) != T6(P6)     &&
     RA + A7(P7+1) < LA     &&
     RB + B7(P7+1) < LB
    )  -> move(7).
    AllTrains(P0,P1,P2,P3,P4,P5,P6,P7+1,RA+A7(P7+1),RB+B7(P7+1))

    +    % all trains have completed their missions
    ((P0 ==6) && (P1 ==6) && (P2 ==6) && (P3 ==6)   &&
     (P4 ==6) && (P5 ==6) && (P6 ==6) && (P7 ==6)
    ) ->
    arrived . AllTrains(P0,P1,P2,P3,P4,P5,P6,P7,RA,RB);
```

Finally, the main process specification (d) consists in the call of our AllTrains process with the appropriate initial data:

```
init   AllTrains(0,0,0,0,0,0,0,0, 1,1);
```

The mCRL2 toolset allows first to linearise the mCRL2 specification, and then to convert it into a linear process. Given a linear process and a formula that expresses some desired behaviour of the process, a PBES (Parametrised Boolean Equation System) can be generated. The tool `pbes2bool` executes the PBES and returns the evaluation status of the formula. The formulas supported by the mCRL2 toolset are based on full μ-calculus with parametric fix points, and with the introduction of regular expressions inside the basic *box* (`[]`) and *diamond* `<>` operators.

The property that the system will eventually always reach a state in which all trains have completed their mission can be expressed as:

mu X.((`[arrived]` true) && (`[!arrived]`X) && (`<true>` true))

The above formula is just a translation in μ-calculus of action-based CTL-like formula **AF** {arrived} true used with UMC. We refer to [6,15] for detailed description of the semantics of these two logics.

The evaluation of this formula takes from 1 to about 19 min before returning the *true* value, depending on the options selected during the various evaluation steps. The greatest impact, which reduces the evaluation time from 19 min to about 1 min and 40 s, is obtained with the selection of the `jittyc` data rewriting mode.

When an unexpected *false* value is returned by the evaluation, the user can request the generation of a counter example. This counterexample, however, is based on the structure of the evaluation process, and shows the occurred nested evaluations of the fixpoint formulas, without any link to the actual structure of the model or the details of its possible evolutions. The tool `lpsxsim` allows to explore the possible evolutions of the model under analysis. However, it does not seems that this exploration can be directly connected to a counterexample generated by a previous unsuccessful evaluation.

7   Discussion and Conclusion

The pattern of having a set of global data that is concurrently and atomically updated by a set of concurrent guarded agents is a formalisation pattern often encountered also in the railway field. In our case, we met this pattern during the verification of the deadlock avoidance kernel inside the ground scheduling system that controls the movements of driverless trains inside a given yard. This pattern can be rather easily formalised and verified using different languages and frameworks. We have experimented with four possible alternatives, i.e., UMC, NuSMV, Promela/SPIN, mCRL2, which differ greatly in maturity, support alternative verification logics, and provide different degrees of friendliness and flexibility in the user support during the formalisation and verification steps.

The activity is still in progress, since, on the one hand, we plan to extend our experiments to several other well known toolsets, and, from the other hand, there are still many aspects of the currently explored four frameworks that need a deeper understanding and evaluation.

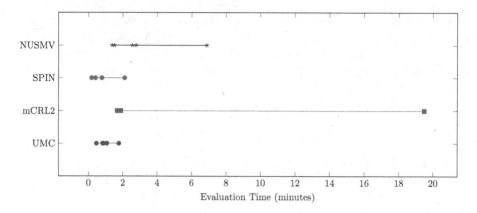

Fig. 3. Summary of evaluation time ranges for the 4 frameworks

Figure 3 summarises the execution time for each model configuration adopted in our experiments[2]. Already from the data that we have collected we can observe that apparently small choices in the construction of the models, or in the selection of the best options for the evaluations, can greatly affect the performance of the verification. Almost all the tools show extremely great differences in terms of execution times depending on the choices done by the user. In our case, we obtained the best performances from NuSMV by declaring the RUNNING variable as **IVAR**. For SPIN, the usage of the -O3 flag (i.e., all `gcc` optimisations turned on) was the factor determining the major decrease in terms of verification time. For mCRL2, the selection of the `jittyc` data rewriting mode was crucial in increasing the performance. Finally, with UMC, the lower verification time was obtained with a parallel version of the tool, and selecting the non-interactive evaluation mode. The differences in terms of verification times obtained, and the different solutions adopted for each tool to minimise the verification time, indicate that a deep mastering of the tools is required to exploit at their best the capabilities of the various frameworks.

Another observation arising from our experiment, is that almost all platforms seem to be mainly tailored to the (successful) validation of a (correct) system design. When it comes to providing the user with an easy-to-understand description of why a given system design does not behave as expected, almost all the tools show great losses in terms of usability. One of the driving long term goals of the UMC/KandISTI project is precisely that one of supporting the user in a friendly way during the early steps of the system design, when the ideas might not yet be perfectly clear and the generated models still contain errors. The model checkers of the KandISTI framework are still far from a successful solution to this problem, however they seems to be moving in the correct direction towards a more easily usable early-designs verification environment. mCRL2 is

---

[2] Each configuration corresponding to a point in Fig. 3, with associated verification time, is available at http://fmt.isti.cnr.it/WEBPAPER/ISOLA2016data.zip.

probably the framework which currently suffers most from this point of view, probably because it is also the most powerful framework in terms of specification language and verification logic, and this makes particularly hard the construction of a user friendly explanation of the link between the property evaluation results and the operational system behaviour.

A final consideration which has been stimulated by our experimentation is that modelling and verifying a system using different approaches can really give a plus in the reliability of the verification results. We have actually experienced that the effort of modelling and checking a system design in several variants is essential for identifying the errors introduced in the construction of the formal specification or in the verification process. The possibility to model and verify a certain design with completely different verification frameworks can be an interesting solution also from the point of view of the *validation* of critical systems. Indeed, while none of the verification tools considered is designed and validated at the greatest safety integrity levels by itself, the existence of different, non validated, tools producing the same result might increase the overall confidence on the verification results.

References

1. Accellera, Property Specification Language - Reference Manual - Version 1.01, April 2003. http://www.eda.org/vfv/docs/psllrm-1.01.pdf
2. ter Beek, M.H., Gnesi, S., Mazzanti, F.: From EU projects to a family of model checkers. In: Nicola, R., Hennicker, R. (eds.) Software, Services, and Systems. LNCS, vol. 8950, pp. 312–328. Springer, Heidelberg (2015). doi:10.1007/978-3-319-15545-6_20
3. http://fmt.isti.cnr.it/kandisti
4. ter Beek, M.H., Fantechi, A., Gnesi, S., Mazzanti, F.: A state/event-based model-checking approach for the analysis of abstract system properties. Sci. Comput. Program. **76**(2), 119–135 (2011)
5. UMC home site. http://fmt.isti.cnr.it/umc
6. Fantechi, A., Gnesi, S., Lapadula, A., Mazzanti, F., Pugliese, R., Tiezzi, F.: A logical verification methodology for service-oriented computing. ACM Trans. Softw. Eng. Methodol. **21**(3), 16:01–16:46 (2012)
7. Gnesi, S., Mazzanti, F.: An abstract, on the fly framework for the verification of service-oriented systems. In: Wirsing, M., Hölzl, M. (eds.) SENSORIA Project. LNCS, vol. 6582, pp. 390–407. Springer, Heidelberg (2011). doi:10.1007/978-3-642-20401-2_18
8. Mazzanti, F., Spagnolo, G.O., Della Longa, S., Ferrari, A.: Deadlock avoidance in train scheduling: a model checking approach. In: Lang, F., Flammini, F. (eds.) FMICS 2014. LNCS, vol. 8718, pp. 109–123. Springer, Heidelberg (2014). doi:10.1007/978-3-319-10702-8_8
9. Mazzanti, F., Spagnolo, G.O., Ferrari, A.: Designing a deadlock-free train scheduler: a model checking approach. In: Badger, J.M., Rozier, K.Y. (eds.) NFM 2014. LNCS, vol. 8430, pp. 264–269. Springer, Heidelberg (2014). doi:10.1007/978-3-319-06200-6_22

10. Mazzanti, F.: An experience in ada multicore programming: parallelisation of a model checking engine. In: Bertogna, M., Pinho, L.M., Quiñones, E. (eds.) Ada-Europe 2016. LNCS, vol. 9695, pp. 94–109. Springer, Heidelberg (2016). doi:10.1007/978-3-319-39083-3_7

11. Holzmann, G.H.: The SPIN Model Checker. Addison-Wesley Pearson Education (2003). ISBN 0-321-22862-6

12. Verifying Multi-threaded Software with Spin. http://spinroot.com

13. Cimatti, A., Clarke, E., Giunchiglia, E., Giunchiglia, F., Pistore, M., Roveri, M., Sebastiani, R., Tacchella, A.: NuSMV 2: an opensource tool for symbolic model checking. In: Proceedings of Computer Aided Verification (CAV 2002) (2002)

14. NuSMV: a new symbolic model checker. http://nusmv.fbk.eu/

15. Groote, J.F., Mousavi, M.R.: Modeling and Analysis of Communicating Systems. MIT Press, Cambridge (2014). ISBN: 9780262027717

16. MCRL2 analysing system behavior. http://www.mcrl2.org/

17. Ferrari, A., Spagnolo, G.O., Martelli, G., Menabeni, S.: From commercial documents to system requirements: an approach for the engineering of novel CBTC solutions. STTT 16(6), 647–667 (2014)

Tuning Energy Consumption Strategies in the Railway Domain: A Model-Based Approach

Davide Basile[(✉)], Felicita Di Giandomenico, and Stefania Gnesi

Istituto di Scienza e Tecnologia dell'Informazione "A. Faedo",
Consiglio Nazionale delle Ricerche, ISTI-CNR, Pisa, Italy
davide.basile@isti.cnr.it

Abstract. Cautious usage of energy resources is gaining great attention nowadays, both from environmental and economical point of view. Therefore, studies devoted to analyze and predict energy consumption in a variety of application sectors are becoming increasingly important, especially in combination with other non-functional properties, such as reliability, safety and availability.

This paper focuses on energy consumption strategies in the railway sector, addressing in particular rail road switches through which trains are guided from one track to another. Given the criticality of their task, the temperature of these devices needs to be kept above certain levels to assure their correct functioning. By applying a stochastic model-based approach, we analyse a family of energy consumption strategies based on thresholds to trigger the activation/deactivation of energy supply. The goal is to offer an assessment framework through which appropriate tuning of threshold-based energy supply solutions can be achieved, so to select the most appropriate one, resulting in a good compromise between energy consumption and reliability level.

1 Introduction

Nowadays studies devoted to analyze and predict energy consumption in a variety of application sectors are receiving increasing importance, both from environmental and economical point of view. When the application domain is a dependability-critical one, such as the transportation sector, energy saving needs to be considered in conjunction with other properties requested to the system, including reliability, safety and availability. Therefore, the interplay of energy consumption and dependability-related measures needs to be analysed. This is a rather new research activity. Dependability analysis has been pursued for a long time, while energy consumption evaluation is becoming rather popular only in recent years. However, the research effort in these topics have been mainly conducted in isolation and not in combination, as addressed in this paper.

A research line by the authors in this direction has been developed over the last year [3,4], by applying a stochastic model-based approach to evaluate energy consumption strategies in the railway sector, addressing in particular

© Springer International Publishing AG 2016
T. Margaria and B. Steffen (Eds.): ISoLA 2016, Part II, LNCS 9953, pp. 315–330, 2016.
DOI: 10.1007/978-3-319-47169-3_23

rail road switches through which trains are guided from one track to another. Such switches are critical components in the railway domain, since reliability of the railway transportation system highly depends on their correct operation, in absence of which potentially catastrophic consequences may be generated. Low temperature, especially during winter, can put in danger their correct operation. To deal with this problem, nowadays heaters are used so that the temperature of the rail road switches can be kept above freezing.

The referred previous studies developed a modeling and analysis framework suited to analyze a variety of policies for heating rail road switches, to assess the degree of their ability to optimise the energy consumption and at the same time to ensure reliability. In line with such previous studies and resorting to the same modelling framework, this paper provides as original contribution the analysis of a family of energy consumption strategies tailored to rail road switch heaters, based on thresholds to trigger the activation/deactivation of energy supply. In particular, we consider an *adaptive* strategy which changes the behaviour of the policy of energy-saving based on the environment temperature, and a *static policy* which does not.

We show how the adaptive strategy improves the reliability indicators, by saving 25 % of supplied energy while guaranteeing acceptable reliability levels. The goal is to offer an assessment framework through which appropriate tuning of threshold-based energy supply solutions can be achieved, so to select the most appropriate one, resulting in a good compromise between energy consumption and reliability level. A prioritized approach has been considered, where the heaters are categorized according to their importance inside the analysed railway station. Note that a failure of the heating system is accounted for by other components of the railway system, namely interlocking mechanisms which guarantee safety; however we do not include them in our analysis.

Structure of the Paper. Stochastic model-based analysis is introduced in Sect. 2. We present the models of the rail road switch heating system in Sect. 3, which are then instantiated to a real scenario in Sect. 4. The results of our experiments are discussed in Sect. 5, while related work and conclusions are in Sects. 6 and 7, respectively.

2   Stochastic Model-Based Analysis

For evaluating the selected case study, a stochastic model-based approach has been adopted [6,12]. Indeed, stochastic phenomena are involved in our analysis, namely the failure occurrence and weather forecast. Stochastic model-based methods are useful to support the development of systems, in all the phases of their life cycle.

In the early design phases they provide indications in several directions, leading to better efficiency in time and resources in the development phase. Typically, starting from the properties and the requirements that the system under development must satisfy, which can be both non-functional properties such as dependability and performability, a model of the system under analysis is built, to represent its behaviour. The developed model can be exploited to: (i) highlight problems in the design of the system, such as criticality of the system components with respect to stated requirements; (ii) compare different alternatives for the same system, and select the one that better suits the requirements; (iii) conduct sensitivity analysis to varying system parameters, to find the best tuning in accordance with system relevant criteria. In this work, model-based analysis is applied to obtain support in tuning the parameters of the considered heating strategy.

When the design phase is completed, a model allows predicting the overall behaviour of the system, fostering an analysis for the fulfilment of constraints in the design phase and the acceptance cases.

For an already existing system, an a-posteriori analysis of properties such as dependability or performance is useful in order to improve the system in its future releases.

Moreover, with a model-based analysis it is possible to predict future behaviours to plan the maintenance and the upgrading of the system [19].

Stochastic Activity Network. In the literature a vast number of stochastic modelling techniques and methods have been proposed [1,2,5,10,18]. SAN [18] is a formalism widely used for performance, dependability and performability evaluation of complex systems, given its high expressiveness and the powerful tools for modelling and evaluating them [9]. The SAN formalism is a variant of Stochastic Petri Nets [5], and has similarities with Generalised Stochastic Petri Nets [2].

Möbius [9] is a multi-formalism multi-solver tool that can be used for defining and solving SAN models. Möbius supports various formalisms and different analytical and simulative solvers, and can be used for studying the reliability, availability, and performability of systems. It follows a modular modelling approach, where atomic models are building blocks that can be composed with proper operators *Rep* and *Join* to generate a composed model.

3   Description of the Model

The considered case study is a rail road switch heating system. A rail road switch is a mechanism enabling trains to be guided from one track to another. It works with a pair of linked tapering rails, known as points. These points can be moved laterally into different positions, in order to direct a train into the straight path or the diverging path. Such switches are therefore critical components in the railway domain, since reliability of the railway transportation system highly depends on their correct operation.

During winter, snow and ice can prevent the switches from working properly, hence heaters are used so that the temperature of the rail road switches can be kept above freezing. Different policies may be adopted to power the heaters (by electricity), as for example to heat a selection of switches for a given amount of time or to heat all the switches together.

Stochastic Model. We briefly outline the models of the system of (remotely controlled) rail road switch heaters, which will be used for evaluating energy and reliability indicators. A more detailed description of the proposed models can be found in [3]. We will consider an on-off policy for heating the switches, with parametric thresholds representing the temperatures triggering the activation/deactivation of the heating. We will also consider a prioritized approach. Indeed, in a railway station there are tracks which are less important than others, and it is important to distinguish between those switches that must be primarily heated and those that may be heated later on. The switches whose temperature cannot be kept above the freezing threshold may experience a failure.

The two main logical components describing the system are the *heater* and the *central coordinator*. The network of heaters is realised by replicating the heater component. The central coordinator manages the activation/deactivation of each heater. We discuss these two main components.

- *Heater*: we have based the policy employed for activating and deactivating the heating on two threshold temperatures:
  - *warning threshold* (T_{wa}): this temperature represents the lower temperature that the track should not trespass. If the temperature is lower than T_{wa}, then the risk of ice or snow can lead to a failure of the rail road switch and therefore the heating system needs to be activated;
  - *working threshold* (T_{wo}): this is the working temperature of the heating system. Once this temperature is reached, the heating system can be safely turned off in order to avoid an excessive waste of energy.

  In [3] we have considered *fixed values* of T_{wa} and T_{wo}. Here we will consider a *fine-grained* warning threshold, which is *flexible* and adapts to the different temperatures during the day, which corresponds to different hours. Indeed, as shown in Fig. 1, we have partitioned the day in three intervals. In the analysis, we assume that during a day the *higher* temperatures are from 2 *pm* to 10 *pm*, the *medium* temperatures are from 10 *pm* to 2 *am* and from 10 *am* to 2 *pm*, while the *lower* temperatures are from 2 *am* to 10 *am*. Of course, different intervals can be accommodated in the developed model. Accordingly we will adopt *three warning thresholds*: T_{wa_h}, T_{wa_m} and T_{wa_l}, which will be used during respectively the higher, the medium and the lower temperatures of the day. In Sect. 5 we will show how the flexible warning threshold improves the reliability and energy consumption of the system. In the following, if not stated otherwise, T_{wa} will refer to the tuple (T_{wa_h}; T_{wa_m}; T_{wa_l}), also called *flexible* warning threshold.
- *Coordinator*: the coordinator collects the requests of activation from the pending heaters, and it manages the energy supply according to a prioritized FIFO order, i.e. the first heater which asks to be turned on will be the first to be activated. The percentage of heaters that can be turned on at the same time is called NH_{max}. This value represents the maximum amount of energy deliverable by the system, and cannot be exceeded. If there is no energy available, each request will be enqueued in the queue of pending heaters.

The overall model is obtained by the composition of the atomic models, using the *Join* and *Rep* operators of the Möbius tool, as shown in Fig. 2. Basically, with the *Join* operator different models are linked by sharing some places, called *shared places*, through which they interact. The *Rep* operator generates several instances of the same model, which can be uniquely identified using a tailored SAN model (*SwitchIDSelector* in our case).

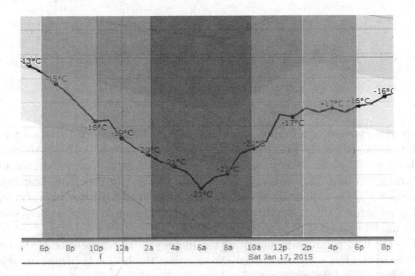

Fig. 1. The temperatures for coldest winter nights in the city Montreal, retrieved from [22]. Different areas represent different warning threshold levels.

The atomic model *Coordinator* represents the central coordinator. The submodel *HeatherModuleM* corresponds to an instance of a single heater module, obtained by the composition, using the join operator, of the four atomic SAN models *ProfileSelector*, *LocalitySelector*, *SwitchIDSelector* and *RailRoadSwitchHeater*, which share different parameters concerning a single rail road switch heater. The submodel *HeatersNetM*, obtained by replicating *numRep* times the model *HeatherModuleM*, models the network of heaters, where the parameter *numRep* identifies the number of devices composing the network. Finally, the model *SwitchHeatingSysM*, obtained using the join operator, represents the overall system. Indeed, all the submodels share the same coordinator.

The SAN model *RailRoadSwitchHeater* models an instance of a rail road switch heater. It is used for evaluating the energy consumption and the probability of failure of the modelled heater. Indeed, according to the heating policy, once the system temperature goes below a pre-defined warning threshold (T_{wa}), the heating needs to be activated, otherwise the associated switch fails. Then, once the temperature rises and reaches the working threshold (T_{wo}), the heating system can be safely turned off. If the temperature goes below 0°C then the

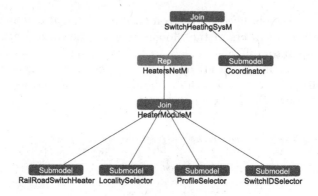

Fig. 2. The composed model.

switch may experience a failure, according to an exponential distribution where the rate is based on the internal temperature of the switches. This SAN model has been modified as follows: the input and output gates that are responsible for turning on and off the heater are updated with two functions that select the proper T_{wa} according to the current time. The heater sub-net interacts with the Coordinator SAN model through places shared among all the replicas of the heater model and the Coordinator model.

The physical behaviour concerning the increment and decrement of the temperature of the rail road track, respectively when the heater is turned on or off, is modelled by a differential equation representing the balance of energy, see [3] for more details. Assuming that the values of the temperature of the surrounding area T_e and the previous internal temperature T are known, the updated internal temperature T after time t is computed by solving the following differential equation:

$$mc\frac{\partial T}{\partial t} = -uA(T - T_e) + \dot{Q}$$

where u is the coefficient of convective exchange; c, the heat capacity of iron; A, the surface area exposed to the external temperature; m, the mass of the iron bar; $\dot{Q}$, the power used when the heater is turned on, if the heater is turned off this value will be zero.

4   Scenarios and Settings

The scenarios and settings that we have considered for our analysis are described in the following, where we have used real world data for guaranteeing that our evaluation is realistic. Indeed, we have considered an average medium-size railway station of a northern city [8], with cold winter days. The instantiation of the physical model is based on real devices data [7].

The chosen railway station is composed of 41 switches that we have divided into three different classes of priority depending on the criticality of the service offered by the switches. In the considered case study, we have 23 high priority switches, 6 medium priority switches and 12 low priority switches [3].

Concerning the weather data, we have used environment temperatures based on those of mid-January 2015 in the city of Montreal [22]. The temperatures for the considered days are displayed in Fig. 1, where we emphasize the partitioning of the day into three portions corresponding to T_{wa_h}, T_{wa_m} and T_{wa_l}. In our experiments, the environment temperatures are selected according to a uniform distribution.

The setting of parameters representing the best compromise between energy consumption and reliability in [3] is $T_{wa} = 7°C$, $T_{wo} = 8°C$ and for high priority switches $NH_{max} = 50\%$, while for medium and low priority switches $NH_{max} = 75\%$. By comparing the above values with the results of the experiments we have conducted, we will show that by adopting a fine-grained warning threshold an improvement in the overall reliability of the system and its energy consumption can be obtained.

We will analyse two different strategies of deactivation of the heating system, by considering a fixed value of:

1. $T_{wa} - T_{wo}$, that is a fixed gap between T_{wa} and T_{wo}. For different values of T_{wa_h}, T_{wa_m} and T_{wa_l} the value of T_{wo} will change accordingly. For example, for a fixed value of $T_{wa} - T_{wo} = 1°C$, if $T_{wa} = (7; 8; 9)$ then $T_{wo} = (8; 9; 10)$;
2. T_{wo}, hence for different values of T_{wa_h}, T_{wa_m} and T_{wa_l} we will obtain different gaps between T_{wa} and T_{wo}.

In all the experiments we have performed, we only have considered an amount of energy that suffices for charging contemporary 50% of all the switches in the network, i.e. $NH_{max} = 50\%$. Indeed, for $NH_{max} = 75\%$ we have shown in [3] that a higher level of reliability is obtained, which is not the case for $NH_{max} = 50\%$. Conversely, by adopting $NH_{max} = 25\%$ the energy consumption is too low to guarantee acceptable reliability levels. In the following analysis we will show that the supplied energy can be reduced to $NH_{max} = 50\%$ while guaranteeing levels of reliability similar to $NH_{max} = 75\%$ for the low priority switches. This is important because we are able to save 25% of supplied energy per time. The values for T_{wa_h}, T_{wa_m} and T_{wa_l} range from 6°C to 10°C, with an increment of 0.25°C. For item 1, in our experiments we considered $T_{wa} - T_{wo} = 1°C$, which is the optimal value according to [3]; while for item 2 the values of T_{wo} range from 8°C to 10°C, with an increment of 0.25°C.

In all the considered evaluations, we assume that at starting time the system is in a safe condition, that is the internal temperature of all switches is equal to its working temperature. This assumption is useful for avoiding instantaneous failure.

We have considered all the combinations of those parameters, and in the following we will discuss the evidence of our experiments, emphasizing the most significant results.

Measures of Interest. We borrow the two considered measures of interest from [3]. The first concerns the energy consumption while the second addresses reliability.

1 $CE(t,l)$: the time (in hours) a heater is activated in the time interval $[t, t+l]$. This measure is defined by accumulating the time that each replica of the SAN model *RailRoadSwitchHeater* spends in the marking m, where m represents the heating phase. Hence $CE(t,l)$ is the amount of time (expressed in hours) that a heater is active. By multiplying $CE(t,l)$ for the power consumed (kilowatt per hour) it is possible to derive the energy consumed by the system;
2 $PFAIL(t,l)$: the probability that at least a switch fails (becomes frozen) within time $t+l$, given that at time t is not failed. This measure is defined as the probability that within time $t+l$ the switch has failed.

We remark that reliability is computed as the probability that no failure occurs in the interval of time under analysis [20], that is $1 - PFAIL(t,l)$. Note that the measures of interest are priority-wise.

5 Discussion of Results

We now describe the results of the evaluations we have performed in order to compare the two strategies of energy saving based on a fixed and a flexible warning threshold. We have plotted the outcome of our results in different graphs, to show how the measures of interest are affected by the relevant parameters.

Concerning the fixed value of $T_{wa} - T_{wo} = 1°C$, in Fig. 3 we compare a fixed T_{wa} with a flexible T_{wa}, focussing on values of T_{wa} through which the best results are obtained. Note that the values on the x axis concern both flexible and fixed T_{wa}, and their order is immaterial. The probability of failure is analysed in Fig. 3b and a, the energy consumption in Fig. 3d and c, with medium priority in Fig. 3c and a and low priority in Fig. 3d and b. The high priority switches are not displayed because their probability of failure is neglectable.

In Figs. 4 and 5 we evaluate the measures of interest with "bad" values of T_{wa} considering all the priority classes, to better understand how the different values of T_{wa_h}, T_{wa_m} and T_{wa_l} affect the reliability of the switches with different priorities. The probability of failure is analysed in Figs. 4a and 5a while the energy consumption is in Figs. 4b and 5b.

The case of fixed T_{wo} is displayed in Fig. 6, where we focus on the probability of failure at varying T_{wa} and T_{wo}.

Fixed Gap Between Thresholds. We will analyse $PFAIL(t,l)$ and $CE(t,l)$, observing that in general $CE(t,l)$ is affected by $PFAIL(t,l)$, i.e. if a heater fails then it will no longer consume energy.

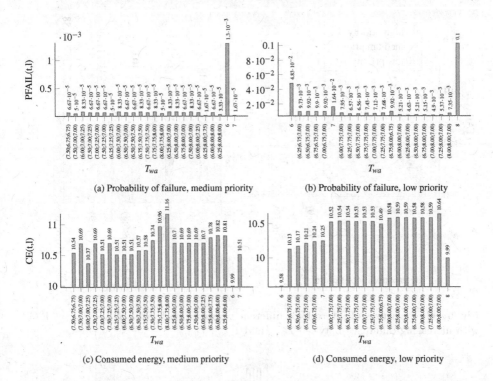

Fig. 3. The measures of interest of the heaters with fixed $T_{wo} - T_{wa} = 1°C$ and optimal values of T_{wa}

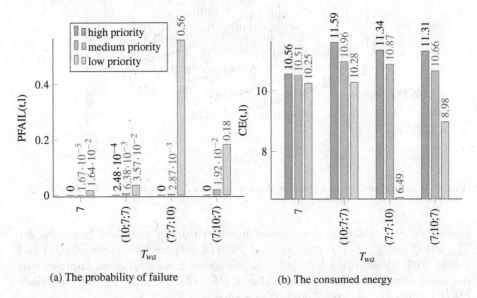

Fig. 4. The measures of interest for different priorities with fixed $T_{wo} - T_{wa} = 1°C$, with fixed $T_{wa} = 7°C$ and "bad" values for respectively $T_{wa(h)}, T_{wa(l)}$ and $T_{wa(m)}$

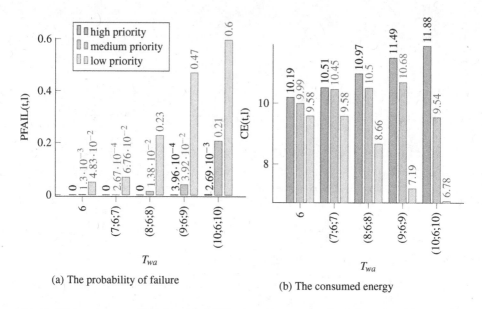

(a) The probability of failure

(b) The consumed energy

Fig. 5. The measures of interest for different priorities with fixed $T_{wo} - T_{wa} = 1°C$, with increasing difference between T_{wa_m} and T_{wa_h}, T_{wa_l}

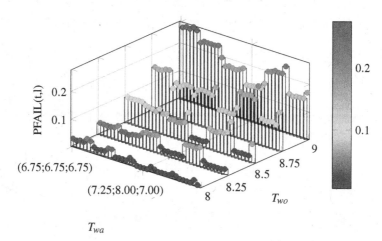

Fig. 6. The probability of failure of the low priority heaters with fixed values of T_{wo}

Improving the reliability. Concerning medium priority switches, in Fig. 3a for $T_{wa} = 6°C$ and $T_{wa} = 7°C$ the values of $PFAIL(t, l)$ are respectively 0.0013 and $1.667e - 05$. By adopting a flexible T_{wa} we do not have neither an improvement nor a deterioration of the optimal value of $PFAIL(t, l)$, while we slightly reduce $CE(t, l)$ with $T_{wa} = (6.00; 7.00; 7.25)$, as shown in Fig. 3c.

The results for the low priority switches are more interesting. In this case, as shown in Fig. 3b, with fixed T_{wa} the lower value of $PFAIL(t,l)$ is 0.0164 (for $T_{wa} = 7$). Remarkably, by considering the flexible $T_{wa} = (6.25; 8.00; 7.00)$, we reduce $PFAIL(t,l)$ of one order of magnitude, i.e. $PFAIL(t,l) = 0.004625$. Moreover, we register an improvement in $PFAIL(t,l)$ by also considering the other values of T_{wa} closer to the optimum. In Fig. 3d we observe that the energy consumption $CE(t,l)$ is affected marginally, which is due to the reduced probability of failure.

An explanation of these results follows. We note that the values of T_{wa_h}, T_{wa_m} and T_{wa_l} are correlated with the different priorities. Indeed, since our experiments start at $6pm$ and the high priority switches are the first to be activated, they are mostly affected by T_{wa_h}, that is the warning threshold adopted from $6pm$ to $10pm$. In Fig. 3b (low priority switches) we note that by increasing T_{wa_h}, $PFAIL(t,l)$ is affected marginally; this is because those are not the coldest hours of the day. Conversely, with higher values of T_{wa_m}, $PFAIL(t,l)$ decreases. This is because the heaters are approaching the coldest hours of the day, and it is important to raise to a higher level of temperature for getting prepared to the minimum temperatures. In the coldest hours T_{wa_l} is adopted, and the optimal value corresponds to the one with fixed T_{wa}, i.e. 7°C. This is because T_{wa_l} is the threshold which mostly affects $PFAIL(t,l)$, as explained below.

Impact of T_{wa_l} on the reliability. In Fig. 4 we emphasise the impact of T_{wa_h}, T_{wa_m} and T_{wa_l} in $PFAIL(t,l)$ and $CE(t,l)$, considering all the priorities. This is done by analysing the warning thresholds $(10; 7; 7)°C$, $(7; 10; 7)°C$ and $(7; 7; 10)°C$. Indeed, from the previous analysis we know that 7°C is a "good" value while 10°C is a "bad" value.

In Fig. 4a we note that, starting from the fixed $T_{wa} = 7°C$, the worst value of $PFAIL(t,l)$ for the high priority switches is $T_{wa} = (10; 7; 7)°C$, that is $PFAIL(t,l) = 2.40e - 04$. In this case an increment in the energy consumed is also registered, as shown in Fig. 4b, even though $PFAIL(t,l)$ has increased too.

For the medium priority switches, with $T_{wa} = (7; 10; 7)°C$ we obtain $PFAIL(t,l) = 1.92e - 2$, while $CE(t,l)$ is marginally affected.

For the low priority switches, with $T_{wa} = (7; 7; 10)°C$ we obtain $PFAIL(t,l) = 0.56$ as the worst value, which is unacceptable. In this case, $CE(t,l)$ is highly affected, since almost half of the heaters with low priority have failed.

Hence, Fig. 4 has shown that the worst case scenario is $T_{wa} = (7; 7; 10)°C$. This means that $PFAIL(t,l)$ for low priority switches is the one which is mostly affected by the corresponding T_{wa_l}. Intuitively, the coldest hours are the most critical for the reliability of the system, and the low priority switches are the most failure-prone.

Worst scenario for medium priority switches. From the experiments we have conducted, we observed that by adopting particular values of the flexible T_{wa}, an important increment in $PFAIL(t,l)$ for the medium priority switches is registered, which was not evaluated in the previous experiments. We discuss this phenomenon in Fig. 5, in order to better understand the behaviour of the system. We considered $PFAIL(t,l)$ and $CE(t,l)$ for an increasing difference of T_{wa_m} from both T_{wa_h} and T_{wa_l}, that is $(7;6;7)°C$, $(8;6;8)°C$, $(9;6;9)°C$ and $(10;6;10)°C$.

While in Fig. 4a for the medium priority switches with $T_{wa} = (7;10;7)°C$ we obtained the worst value of $PFAIL(t,l)$ (i.e. $PFAIL(t,l) = 1.92e-2$), in Fig. 5a with $T_{wa} = (10;6;10)°C$ we obtain $PFAIL(t,l) = 0.21$, which is surprisingly higher than the previous values, and represents the worst reliability value of our analysis for all priorities. We note that this result is not generated by the higher value of T_{wa_h}, for example for $T_{wa} = (10;6;6)°C$, we have $PFAIL(t,l) = 1.74E-02$ for the medium priority switches. On the converse, the higher value of T_{wa_l} highly affects $PFAIL(t,l)$, as explained above, and for example for $T_{wa} = (6;6;10)°C$ we obtain $PFAIL(t,l) = 1.39E-01$ for the medium priority switches; while for $T_{wa} = (10;10;6)°C$, we have $PFAIL(t,l) = 5.33E-04$.

We explain this phenomenon as follows: with $T_{wa_h} = 10°C$, the high priority switches jeopardize all the energy for reaching a higher temperature, then during $T_{wa_m} = 6°C$ the medium priority switches are heated, but their temperature does not rise to a sufficient level. Finally, with $T_{wa_l} = 10°C$, all the energy is once again jeopardized by the high priority switches, thus leaving the medium and low priority switches with a low temperature and no energy, so maximising their probability of failure.

Fixed Working Threshold. We analyse the second strategy presented in Sect. 4, that is a fixed value of T_{wo}. We only focus on the low priorities switches, and the values of $PFAIL(t,l)$ for varying values of the fixed T_{wo} are shown in Fig. 6. When $T_{wo} = 8°C$ we observe the lower values for $PFAIL(t,l)$, in particular for $T_{wa} = (6.50;7.75;7.00)°C$, we obtain $PFAIL(t,l) = 0.0056$, which is the best reliability level of this strategy. By adopting higher values of fixed T_{wo}, we observe in Fig. 6 that $PFAIL(t,l)$ gradually increases.

Comparisons. We compare the two strategies described in Sect. 4, focussing on the low priority switches. We note that in the fixed T_{wo} strategy, when $T_{wo} = 8°C$ we have approximatively $T_{wa} - T_{wo} = 1°C$, that is the two strategies are similar. This is also the optimal value for the fixed T_{wo}, that is $PFAIL(t,l) = 0.0056$. A similar value is obtained for the case of fixed $T_{wa} - T_{wo}$, that is $PFAIL(t,l) = 0.0046$. However, the strategy of maintaining a fixed gap between T_{wa} and T_{wo} has shown to be more reliable also for other combinations of T_{wa_h}, T_{wa_m} and T_{wa_l}.

Summary of results. Concluding, we have shown that by adopting a flexible warning threshold, which adapts to the different temperatures during the day, we improve the overall reliability of the system. Remarkably, the probability of failure for the low priority switches has reduced of one order of magnitude, so passing from 0.0164 with fixed T_{wa} to 0.0046 with a flexible T_{wa}. Hence, the overall energy supplied to the system can be reduced from $NH_{max} = 75\%$ to $NH_{max} = 50\%$ while guaranteeing similar reliability levels. Moreover, by comparing the two strategies of energy management, we have obtained better results with a fixed gap between T_{wo} and T_{wa}, while considering a fixed T_{wo} we observed a deterioration in the reliability of the system.

Experiments Performance. Simulation-based evaluations have been performed using the Möbius tool [9], considering from a minimum of 1000 batches to a maximum of 10000 batches. The measures of interest were estimated within an interval of confidence of 0.95 using simulations. For computing the results of $PFAIL(t, l)$ and $CE(t, l)$, considering all three levels of priorities and the set-up of parameters discussed in Sect. 4 we have performed 1500 experiments (only a portion of the overall results has been discussed in this paper) with an average time of 30 s per experiment. It has been used a machine with CPU Intel Core i5-4570 at 3.20 GHZ with 8 GB of RAM, running 64-bit Windows 10.

6 Related Work

In the literature there are several works that analyse and optimise the energy consumption in several application domains using formal approaches, even though they do not analyse rail road switch heating systems. We recall some of them in the following. Services negotiation of energy and reliability requirements is the selected case study in [21], where an energy provider, an energy consumer and a mediator try to find an agreement on the amount of energy delivered, its reliability and price. Their reliability and energy requirements are given parameters that are negotiated between the parties; instead in our approach we are interested in computing their optimal values at the varying of prescribed parametric policies.

In [16] Generalized Stochastic Petri Nets [2] are used to solve the dynamic power management problem for systems with complex behaviour. Dynamic power management addresses reduction of power dissipation in embedded systems with a selective shut-off or slow-down of system components that are idle or underutilized. In our case complex behaviours are modelled with SAN models, which are a generalization of Generalised Stochastic Petri Nets. We also consider a policy of switching on/off the heater when a given temperature threshold is reached.

The dynamic power management problem is interpreted as a hybrid automaton control problem and integrated stochastic control in [13], where Hybrid automata mixed both a discrete state, representing the power mode of the system, and a continuous one, representing the consumed power. Two strategies are compared: on demand wake-up of a component (that was previously turned off) and pre-emptive wake-up. The former provides better results for the conservation of energy and prevention of latency. It would be interesting to implement in our work a power adjustment mechanism.

The survivability of a smart house is analysed in [14], that is the probability that a house with locally generated energy (photovoltaic) and a battery storage can continuously be powered in case of a grid failure. Hybrid Petri Nets [10] are used for modelling this scenario. The authors consider a randomly chosen probability of failure and fixed thresholds, while in our case the probability of failure is derived from the model and we consider flexible thresholds. The trade-off between energy saving and reliability is studied in [23], by managing frequencies and voltage of the delivered energy. In our approach the energy consumption is managed by changing the power consumed by the system.

Concerning the analysis and optimization of a railway station using formal techniques, in [11] Stochastic Activity Networks are used to improve timetable and delay minimization of the traffic in a station. In [15] an Automatic Train Supervision is designed that prevents the occurrence of deadlocks. It would be interesting to integrate such studies with the possible failure of switches studied here, in order to analyse how a failure in a switch impacts on possible delays of trains, and deadlocks.

7   Conclusion and Future Work

The paper addressed analysis for a rail road switch heating system through a model-based approach, using Stochastic Activity Networks and the Möbius tool [9]. In previous work [3,4], a SAN modelling framework has been developed to represent (i) the behaviour of the physical system and (ii) the strategies of energy management of the switch heaters. Building on that, a study devoted to explore the tuning of such heating strategies has been carried out here. In particular, we have studied the sensitivity of energy consumption and reliability indicators at varying the thresholds temperatures adopted by the heating strategies. To make the analysis more realistic, the adaptation of thresholds to different time intervals characterized by different temperatures during the day has been performed.

We have considered a realistic scenario for our case study. The data concerning the layout of the railway station were taken from a real case [8], and the data for the temperatures in extremely cold conditions were retrieved from [22]. The physical model for the heater has been instantiated by taking values available at [7,17].

The results have shown that by adopting thresholds that adapt to different temperatures during the day, we have improved the overall reliability of the system, especially for the low priority switch heaters. It is then possible to safely save almost 25 % of the overall energy supplied to the system.

An interesting direction for extending this study would be considering different layouts of railway stations. Indeed, in this analysis only a fixed percentage of higher, medium and low level priority switches have been evaluated. Even though these values represent a "standard" layout for a middle-size railway station, it would be valuable to study how the reliability and energy consumption indicators are affected by different distributions of priorities, and how to tune the thresholds accordingly.

References

1. Alur, R., Dill, D.L.: A theory of timed automata. Theoret. Comput. Sci. **126**(2), 183–235 (1994)
2. Balbo, G.: Introduction to generalized stochastic petri nets. In: Bernardo, M., Hillston, J. (eds.) SFM 2007. LNCS, vol. 4486, pp. 83–131. Springer, Heidelberg (2007). doi:10.1007/978-3-540-72522-0_3
3. Basile, D., Chiaradonna, S., Giandomenico, F.D., Gnesi, S.: A stochastic model-based approach to analyse reliable energy-saving rail road switch heating systems. J. Rail Transp. Plan. Manag. (2016). http://www.sciencedirect.com/science/article/pii/S2210970616300051
4. Basile, D., Chiaradonna, S., Giandomenico, F., Gnesi, S., Mazzanti, F.: Stochastic model-based analysis of energy consumption in a rail road switch heating system. In: Fantechi, A., Pelliccione, P. (eds.) SERENE 2015. LNCS, vol. 9274, pp. 82–98. Springer, Heidelberg (2015). doi:10.1007/978-3-319-23129-7_7
5. Bause, F., Kritzinger, P.S.: Stochastic petri nets: an introduction to the theory. SIGMETRICS Perform. Eval. Rev. **26**(2), 2–3 (1998)
6. Bernardi, S., Merseguer, J., Petriu, D.C.: Model-Driven Dependability Assessment of Software Systems. Springer, Heidelberg (2013)
7. Brodowski, D., Komosa, K.: A railroad switch and a method of melting snow and ice in rail road switches (2013). https://data.epo.org/publication-server/rest/v1.0/publication-dates/20131225/patents/EP2677079NWA1/document.html
8. https://en.wikipedia.org/wiki/Carlisle_railway_station
9. Clark, G., Courtney, T., Daly, D., Deavours, D., Derisavi, S., Doyle, J.M., Sanders, W.H., Webster, P.: The möbius modeling tool. In: Proceedings of the 9th International Workshop on Petri Nets and Performance Models, pp. 241–250 (2001)
10. David, R., Alla, H.: On hybrid petri nets. Discrete Event Dyn. Syst. **11**(1–2), 9–40 (2001)
11. Di Giandomenico, F., Fantechi, A., Gnesi, S., Itria, M.L.: Stochastic model-based analysis of railway operation to support traffic planning. In: Gorbenko, A., Romanovsky, A., Kharchenko, V. (eds.) SERENE 2013. LNCS, vol. 8166, pp. 184–198. Springer, Heidelberg (2013). doi:10.1007/978-3-642-40894-6_15
12. Diab, H.B., Zomaya, A.Y.: Dependable Computing Systems: Paradigms, Performance Issues and Applications. Wiley (2005)
13. Erbes, T., Shukla, S.K., Kachroo, P.: Stochastic learning feedback hybrid automata for dynamic power management in embedded systems. In: SMCia/05, IEEE Mid-Summer Workshop on Soft Computing in Industrial Applications, June 2005
14. Ghasemieh, H., Haverkort, B.R., Jongerden, M.R., Remke, A.: Energy resilience modelling for smart houses. In: 45th Annual IEEE/IFIP International Conference on Dependable Systems and Networks, DSN 2015, pp. 275–286. IEEE (2015)
15. Mazzanti, F., Spagnolo, G.O., Longa, S., Ferrari, A.: Deadlock avoidance in train scheduling: a model checking approach. In: Lang, F., Flammini, F. (eds.) FMICS 2014. LNCS, vol. 8718, pp. 109–123. Springer, Heidelberg (2014). doi:10.1007/978-3-319-10702-8_8
16. Qiu, Q., Wu, Q., Pedram, M.: Dynamic power management of complex systems using generalized stochastic petri nets. In: DAC, pp. 352–356 (2000)
17. http://www.railsco.com/~electric_switch_heater_controls.htm. Accessed on June 2016

18. Sanders, W.H., Meyer, J.F.: Stochastic activity networks: formal definitions and concepts. In: Brinksma, E., Hermanns, H., Katoen, J.-P. (eds.) EEF School 2000. LNCS, vol. 2090, pp. 315–343. Springer, Heidelberg (2001). doi:10.1007/3-540-44667-2_9
19. Karlin, H.M.T. (ed.) An Introduction to Stochastic Modeling (Revised Edition), p. iii. Academic Press, revised edn. (1994). http://www.sciencedirect.com/science/article/pii/B978012684885450001X
20. Trivedi, K.S.: Probability & Statistics With Reliability, Queuing and Computer Science Applications. Wiley (2008)
21. Čaušević, A., Seceleanu, C., Pettersson, P.: Distributed energy management case study: a formal approach to analyzing utility functions. In: Margaria, T., Steffen, B. (eds.) ISoLA 2014. LNCS, vol. 8803, pp. 74–87. Springer, Heidelberg (2014). doi:10.1007/978-3-662-45231-8_6
22. https://weatherspark.com/#!graphs;ws=27985. Accessed on March 2016
23. Zhu, D., Melhem, R., Mossè, D.: The effects of energy management on reliability in real-time embedded systems. In: IEEE/ACM International Conference on Computer Aided Design, ICCAD 2004, pp. 35–40, November 2004

RVE: Runtime Verification and Enforcement, the (Industrial) Application Perspective

Runtime Verification and Enforcement, the (Industrial) Application Perspective (Track Introduction)

Ezio Bartocci[1(✉)] and Ylies Falcone[2]

[1] Vienna University of Technology, Vienna, Austria
`ezio.bartocci@tuwien.ac.at`
[2] Univ. Grenoble Alpes, Inria, LIG, 38000 Grenoble, France

Abstract. During the last decade, the runtime verification and enforcement (RVE) community has been incredibly prolific in producing many theories, tools and techniques aiming towards the efficient analysis of systems' executions and guaranteeing their correctness w.r.t. some desired properties. With the major strides made in recent years, much effort is still needed to make RVE attractive and viable methodologies for industrial use. In addition to industry, numerous other domains, such as security, bio-health monitoring, etc., can gain from RVE. The purpose of the " Runtime Verification and Enforcement: the (industrial) application perspective" track at ISoLA'16 is to bring together RVE experts and potential application domains to try and advance the state-of-the-art on how to make RVE more useable and attractive to industry and other disciplines.

1 Introduction

Runtime verification (RV) and *runtime enforcement* (RE) refer to a class of lightweight yet powerful formal techniques aiming towards the efficient analysis of systems' executions and guaranteeing their correctness w.r.t. some desired properties.

RV [12] is concerned with monitoring of software or hardware at execution time. RV is based on extracting information from a running system (*instrumentation*) and monitoring if the observed behaviors satisfy or violate the properties of interest. These techniques are very important for system correctness, safety, reliability, security, and robustness. Monitoring is generally used when the state-space of the system model is impractical to handle using model checking [8,30] due to the state-explosion problem, or when the system model is not available and the system appears as a black-box where only outputs are observable.

During the last decade, the RV community has been incredibly prolific in producing many theories, tools and techniques that are now successfully employed in several application domains that go beyond the program verification: streaming processing applications [9,22], checking interoperability of medical devices [25],

© Springer International Publishing AG 2016
T. Margaria and B. Steffen (Eds.): ISoLA 2016, Part II, LNCS 9953, pp. 333–338, 2016.
DOI: 10.1007/978-3-319-47169-3_24

mixed-signal circuit analysis [20,21,27,35], analysis of cyber-physical [19] and biological systems [1,3,5,17], signal processing [4,7] and music detection [10].

RV can be employed before the deployment, for testing, verification, and debugging purposes or after deployment to trigger some system recovery actions when a safety property is violated and for ensuring reliability, safety, and security and for providing fault containment and recovery as well as online system repair.

For example, RV can be used in combination with RE [13–15,28,32], a powerful technique to ensure that a program conforms to a given set of properties. For example, one of the pioneer work on RE is the paper on *security automata* [33] where monitors can decide to halt the underlying program whenever its behavior deviates from the desired property. More recently in [28,32], RE mechanisms have been extended to ensure timed properties.

One of the major challenges in RV and RE is characterising and formally expressing requirements that can be efficiently verified and enforced [11,29,33]. With the major strides made in recent years, much effort is still needed to make RV and RE attractive and viable methodologies for industrial use. In addition to industry, numerous other domains, such as security, bio-health monitoring, etc., can gain from RV and RE. The purpose of the "Runtime Verification and Enforcement: the (industrial) application perspective" track at ISoLA'16 is to bring together experts on runtime verification and runtime enforcement and potential application domains to try and advance the state-of-the-art on how to make RV and RE more useable and attractive to industry and other disciplines.

2   Overview of the Track's Sessions

The track consists of 10 contributed papers presented during three sessions. In the following we provide an overview of the topics discussed during each session.

2.1   Session 1 - RV Core: Reasoning About Traces and Distributed Monitoring

The first session is dedicated to RV foundational problems concerned with the notion of *trace* and the open challenges on *fault-tolerant monitoring of distributed systems*.

The first session paper [31] by Reger et al. provides an important overview on different notions of *system's execution trace* used in RV. This study is motivated by the need of a standard representation of system's execution traces. The paper aims at improving the development and the performance evaluation of offline monitoring tools [2,16].

Traces are useful models for several types of program analysis, including debugging and performance analysis. For example, assembly traces provide a detailed information about the target program's behavior, and they can be used to detect the violation of security properties at low-level code execution. The second paper [23] by Khoury et al. explores the BeepBeep tool, a monitor for the first-order extension of Linear Temporal Logic LTL-FO+, interpreting security properties over assembly traces.

The third session paper [6] by Bonakdarpour et al. provides an interesting and useful insight on the current open research problems on RV techniques for distributed systems, where a set of monitors have only a partial view of a large system and may be exposed to different types of faults.

2.2 Session 2 - an Application Perspective of Runtime Verification

The second session provides an application perspective of RV tools and techniques used in industrial case studies and within recent national and European projects.

The first session paper [27] by Nguyen et al. focuses on the problem of verification and validation (V & V) of complex mixed-analog integrated circuit that in industrial practice accounts for 60–70% of project development time. Simulation, which is the dominant method for pre-silicon verification, is the main bottleneck in this process because immense computing requirements prevents scaling. The increasing trend to overcome this issue is to complement simulation techniques with an emulation-based approach where the designed system is replaced by an early prototype implemented on Field Programmable Gate Array (FPGA) allowing long-term/stress testing and whole-range parameter variations, which are impractical with simulation-based verification. The authors provide an overview about their experience in the Austrian FFG-funded HARMONIA project whose goal is to improve the verification techniques of the emulation-based approach by combining RV with design emulation.

The second session paper [26] by Pastore et al. focuses on important problems in software engineering such as the dynamic analysis of *regression problems*, where software upgrades, may introduce also side-effects that break existing functionalities. *Localizing* and *understanding* the causes of regression failures are extremely challenging. The authors show how they address automatic detection of regression problems by integrating *runtime verification, testing* and *static analysis*.

The third session paper [25] by Leucker et al. shows the relevance of RV techniques application on ensuring the interoperability among interconnected medical devices. The authors present a software development kit (SDK) for the *Open Surgical Communication Protocol* (OSCP) supporting the development of interconnected medical devices according to the IEEE 11073 standards for interoperable medical communication.

2.3 Session 3 - Stream Processing and Runtime Enforcement Applications

The third session is dedicated to stream processing and RE techniques with a special focus on online social networks as potential application domain.

Online social networks are nowadays so popular that according to a recent survey [24] almost 70 % of the internet users are active on them. In this scenario, ensuring the desired privacy is one key challenges of these nowadays so pervasive technologies. One common problem is that the current state-of-the-art in privacy settings do not take in consideration the fact the networks evolve as well as the privacy preferences of the users. The first session paper [18] by Pace et al. proposes an automata-based approach to define and to enforce such policies using runtime verification techniques.

Another important issue is to enable the user to verify that his/her own privacy policy conforms to the *terms of service* of a certain social network or smart phone app that generally a user must agree before getting the right to install and/or use their services. The second session paper [34] by Schneider presents such challenge by providing an interesting perspective of how to combine RV with RE in this application domain.

With the ever growing information available in online social network, the number of businesses that would like to exploit this huge stream of data available (i.e. the post and the likes on social media) is dramatically increasing. The third session paper [9] by Colombo et al. show how RV technology can be used not only for verification, but also to easily develop stream-processing applications using monitor-oriented programming.

On the same line of research on stream processing applications is also the fourth session paper by Kaufmann et al. [22] addressing the problem of *software comprehension*, where a user provides a formal specification to annotate a given event stream with contextual information that enables to build tools for visualizing and analyzing the trace. This work is motivated by the need to quickly process on the ground event streams with millions of events that are generated by a spacecraft.

Acknowledgements. The authors acknowledge the support of the ICT COST Action IC1402 Runtime Verification beyond Monitoring (ARVI). Ezio Bartocci acknowledges also the partial support of the Austrian Science Fund (FWF) and the IKT der Zukunft of Austrian FFG project HARMONIA (nr. 845631).

References

1. Bartocci, E., Bortolussi, L., Nenzi, L.: A temporal logic approach to modular design of synthetic biological circuits. In: Gupta, A., Henzinger, T.A. (eds.) CMSB 2013. LNCS, vol. 8130, pp. 164–177. Springer, Heidelberg (2013). doi:10.1007/978-3-642-40708-6_13

2. Bartocci, E., Bonakdarpour, B., Falcone, Y.: First international competition on software for runtime verification. In: Bonakdarpour, B., Smolka, S.A. (eds.) RV 2014. LNCS, vol. 8734, pp. 1–9. Springer, Heidelberg (2014). doi:10.1007/978-3-319-11164-3_1

3. Bartocci, E., Bortolussi, L., Nenzi, L., Sanguinetti, G.: System design of stochastic models using robustness of temporal properties. Theor. Comput. Sci. **587**, 3–25 (2015)

4. Bartocci, E., Bortolussi, L., Sanguinetti, G.: Data-driven statistical learning of temporal logic properties. In: Legay, A., Bozga, M. (eds.) FORMATS 2014. LNCS, vol. 8711, pp. 23–37. Springer, Heidelberg (2014). doi:10.1007/978-3-319-10512-3_3

5. Bartocci, E., Liò, P.: Computational modeling, formal analysis, and tools for systems biology. PLoS Comput. Biol. 12(1) (2016)

6. Bonakdarpour, B., Rajsbaum, S., Fraigniaud, P., Travers, C.: Challenges in fault-tolerant distributed runtime verification. In: Margaria, T., Steffen, B. (eds.) ISoLA 2016, Part II. LNCS, vol. 9953, pp. 363–370. Springer, Cham (2016)

7. Bufo, S., Bartocci, E., Sanguinetti, G., Borelli, M., Lucangelo, U., Bortolussi, L.: Temporal logic based monitoring of assisted ventilation in intensive care patients. In: Margaria, T., Steffen, B. (eds.) ISoLA 2014. LNCS, vol. 8803, pp. 391–403. Springer, Heidelberg (2014). doi:10.1007/978-3-662-45231-8_30

8. Clarke, E.M., Emerson, E.A.: Design and synthesis of synchronization skeletons using branching time temporal logic. In: Kozen, D. (ed.) Logic of Programs 1981. LNCS, vol. 131, pp. 52–71. Springer, Heidelberg (1982). doi:10.1007/BFb0025774

9. Colombo, C., Pace, G., Camilleri, L., Dimech, C.F.R., Grech, J.P., Magro, A., Sammut, A.C., Adami, K.Z.: Runtime verification for stream processing applications. In: Margaria, T., Steffen, B. (eds.) ISoLA 2016, Part II. LNCS, vol. 9953, pp. 400–406. Springer, Cham (2016)

10. Donzé, A., Maler, O., Bartocci, E., Nickovic, D., Grosu, R., Smolka, S.A.: On temporal logic and signal processing. In: Chakraborty, S., Mukund, M. (eds.) ATVA 2012. LNCS, vol. 7561, pp. 92–106. Springer, Heidelberg (2012)

11. Falcone, Y., Fernandez, J., Mounier, L.: What can you verify and enforce at runtime? STTT 14(3), 349–382 (2012)

12. Falcone, Y., Havelund, K., Reger, G.: A tutorial on runtime verification. In: Broy, M., Peled, D., Kalus, G. (eds.) Engineering Dependable Software Systems, NATO Science for Peace and Security Series, D: Information and Communication Security, vol. 34, pp. 141–175. IOS Press (2013)

13. Falcone, Y., Jéron, T., Marchand, H., Pinisetty, S.: Runtime enforcement of regular timed properties by suppressing and delaying events. Syst. Control Lett. 123, 2–41 (2016)

14. Falcone, Y., Marchand, H.: Enforcement and validation (at runtime) of various notions of opacity. Discrete Event Dyn. Syst. 25(4), 531–570 (2015)

15. Falcone, Y., Mounier, L., Fernandez, J., Richier, J.: Runtime enforcement monitors: composition, synthesis, and enforcement abilities. Formal Methods Syst. Des. 38(3), 223–262 (2011)

16. Falcone, Y., Ničković, D., Reger, G., Thoma, D.: Second international competition on runtime verification. In: Bartocci, E., Majumdar, R. (eds.) RV 2015. LNCS, vol. 9333, pp. 405–422. Springer, Heidelberg (2015). doi:10.1007/978-3-319-23820-3_27

17. Gol, E.A., Bartocci, E., Belta, C.: A formal methods approach to pattern synthesis in reaction diffusion systems. In: Proceedings of 53rd IEEE Conference on Decision and Control, CDC 2014, Los Angeles, CA, USA, 15–17 December 2014, pp. 108–113. IEEE (2014)

18. Gordon, P., Pardo, R., Schneider, G.: On the runtime enforcement of evolving privacy policies in online social networks. In: Margaria, T., Steffen, B. (eds.) ISoLA 2016, Part II. LNCS, vol. 9953, pp. 407–412. Springer, Cham (2016)

19. Haghighi, I., Jones, A., Kong, Z., Bartocci, E., Grosu, R., Belta, C.: Spatel: a novel spatial-temporal logic and its applications to networked systems. In: Proceedings of HSCC 2015: The 18th International Conference on Hybrid Systems: Computation and Control, pp. 189–198. ACM (2015)

20. Jaksic, S., Bartocci, E., Grosu, R., Kloibhofer, R., Nguyen, T., Ničković, D.: From signal temporal logic to FPGA monitors. In: Proceedings of MEMOCODE 2015: The ACM/IEEE International Conference on Formal Methods and Models for Codesign, pp. 218–227. IEEE (2015)

21. Jaksic, S., Bartocci, E., Grosu, R., Ničković, D.: Quantitative monitoring of STL with edit distance. In: Falcone, Y., Sánchez, C. (eds.) RV 2016. LNCS, vol. 10012, pp. 201–218. Springer, Heidelberg (2016). doi:10.1007/978-3-319-46982-9_13

22. Joshi, R., Kauffman, S., Havelund, K.: Towards a logic for inferring properties of event streams. In: Margaria, T., Steffen, B. (eds.) ISoLA 2016, Part II. LNCS, vol. 9953, pp. 394–399. Springer, Cham (2016)

23. Khoury, R., Hallé, S., Waldmann, O.: Execution trace analysis using LTL-FO+. In: Margaria, T., Steffen, B. (eds.) ISoLA 2016, Part II. LNCS, vol. 9953, pp. 356–362. Springer, Cham (2016)

24. Lenhart, A., Purcell, K., Smith, A., Zickur, K.: Social media & mobile internet use among teens and young adults. Pew Internet & American Life Project (2010)

25. Leucker, M., Schmitz, M., Tellinghusen, D.A.: Runtime verification for interconnected medical devices. In: Margaria, T., Steffen, B. (eds.) ISoLA 2016, Part II. LNCS, vol. 9953, pp. 380–387. Springer, Cham (2016)

26. Mariani, L., Pastore, F.: Dynamic analysis of regression problems in industrial systems: challenges and solutions. In: Margaria, T., Steffen, B. (eds.) ISoLA 2016, Part II. LNCS, vol. 9953, pp. 388–393. Springer, Cham (2016)

27. Nguyen, T., Bartocci, E., Ničković, D., Grosu, R., Jaksic, S., Selyunin, K.: The HARMONIA project: hardware monitoring for automotive systems-of-systems. In: Margaria, T., Steffen, B. (eds.) ISoLA 2016, Part II. LNCS, vol. 9953, pp. 371–379. Springer, Cham (2016)

28. Pinisetty, S., Falcone, Y., Jéron, T., Marchand, H., Rollet, A., Nguena-Timo, O.: Runtime enforcement of timed properties revisited. Formal Methods Syst. Des. **45**(3), 381–422 (2014)

29. Pnueli, A., Zaks, A.: PSL model checking and run-time verification via testers. In: Misra, J., Nipkow, T., Sekerinski, E. (eds.) FM 2006. LNCS, vol. 4085, pp. 573–586. Springer, Heidelberg (2006). doi:10.1007/11813040_38

30. Queille, J.P., Sifakis, J.: Specification and verification of concurrent systems in CESAR. In: Dezani-Ciancaglini, M., Montanari, U. (eds.) Programming 1982. LNCS, vol. 137, pp. 337–351. Springer, Heidelberg (1982). doi:10.1007/3-540-11494-7_22

31. Reger, G., Havelund, K.: What is a trace? A runtime verification perspective. In: Margaria, T., Steffen, B. (eds.) ISoLA 2016, Part II. LNCS, vol. 9953, pp. 339–355. Springer, Cham (2016)

32. Renard, M., Falcone, Y., Rollet, A., Pinisetty, S., Jéron, T., Marchand, H.: Enforcement of (Timed) properties with uncontrollable events. In: Leucker, M., Rueda, C., Valencia, F.D. (eds.) ICTAC 2015. LNCS, vol. 9399, pp. 542–560. Springer, Heidelberg (2015). doi:10.1007/978-3-319-25150-9_31

33. Schneider, F.B.: Enforceable security policies. ACM Trans. Inf. Syst. Secur. **3**(1), 30–50 (2000)

34. Schneider, G.: On the specification and enforcement of privacy-preserving contractual agreements. In: Steffen, B., Margaria, T. (eds.) ISoLA 2016, Part II. LNCS, vol. 9953, pp. 413–419. Springer, Cham (2016)

35. Selyunin, K., Nguyen, T., Bartocci, E., Ničković, D., Grosu, R.: Monitoring of MTL specifications with IBM's spiking-neuron model. In: Proceedings of DATE 2016: The 19th Design, Automation and Test in Europe Conference and Exhibition, pp. 924–929. IEEE (2016)

What Is a Trace? A Runtime Verification Perspective

Giles Reger[1(✉)] and Klaus Havelund[2]

[1] University of Manchester, Manchester, UK
giles.reger@manchester.ac.uk
[2] Jet Propulsion Laboratory, California Institute of Technology, Pasadena, USA

Abstract. Runtime Monitoring or Verification deals with *traces*. In its most simple form a monitoring system takes a trace produced by a system and a specification of correct behaviour and checks if the trace conforms to the specification. More complex applications may introduce notions of feedback and reaction. The notion that unifies the field is that we can abstract the runtime behaviour of a system by an execution trace and check this for conformance. However, there is little uniform understanding of what a trace is. This is most keenly seen when comparing theoretical and practical work. This paper surveys the different notions of trace and reflects on the related issues.

1 Introduction

Runtime Monitoring or Verification [29,45] is a form of dynamic analysis where a system of interest is abstracted as an execution trace. The most common notion of runtime verification is to take a specification of correct behaviour ϕ and a trace τ and check for language inclusion i.e. $\tau \overset{?}{\in} \mathcal{L}(\phi)$. This can be applied *offline* by collecting a trace as a log file or *online* by monitoring the system whilst it is running.

How the trace τ is captured from the system and described for the monitoring process is important. We observe that currently (i) there is no general notion of what should be recorded in a trace, and (ii) there is no general format for recording traces as log files. This state of affairs hinders interoperability of runtime verification tools, sharing of case studies and benchmarks, and application of runtime verification techniques (as time must be spent deciding how to generate traces).

A solution would be to develop a general trace format to be used in runtime verification that is optimal from the perspective of runtime verification tools.

G. Reger—The contribution of this author is based upon work from COST Action ARVI IC1402, supported by COST (European Cooperation in Science and Technology).
K. Havelund—The research performed by this author was carried out at Jet Propulsion Laboratory, California Institute of Technology, under a contract with the National Aeronautics and Space Administration.

© Springer International Publishing AG 2016
T. Margaria and B. Steffen (Eds.): ISoLA 2016, Part II, LNCS 9953, pp. 339–355, 2016.
DOI: 10.1007/978-3-319-47169-3_25

However, we also observe that recording log files or execution traces is common in many areas of software engineering where runtime verification is not used. To encourage use of (formal) monitoring techniques in such areas it is important to understand the kinds of traces they deal with.

Therefore, we begin in Sects. 2 and 3 by reviewing existing notions of trace, both within and outside the runtime verification community. Then we discuss two important points. In Sect. 4 we discuss what should appear in a trace, and in Sect. 5 we discuss what format a trace file should take. Finally, Sect. 6 concludes with a discussion of what further issues to take into account when considering general trace formats.

2   Traces in Runtime Verification

We briefly review the role and occurrence of different notions of trace within the field of runtime verification.

2.1   Traces as Models

Traces are typically introduced as models of specifications written in a specification language. It is common to say that a specification φ denotes a (usually infinite) set of *traces*. More precisely one would normally define a signature Σ which induces a set of possible interpretations or traces $\mathcal{T}$, and define a denotation $|\varphi| \subseteq \mathcal{T}$, i.e. the conditions for the trace to be a *model* for φ. As discussed below, the signature and the form of traces built from it can vary. But in general the signature will capture a notion of *event* and traces will be (finite) sequences of events.

Propositional Traces. The most simple case of this is when regular expressions or state machines are used as specifications and traces are taken as finite traces of propositional symbols. For example, the regular expression specification $(ab)^*$ has the trace $abab$ in its language but not the trace $abbab$. Another popular language for runtime verification is Linear Temporal Logic (LTL). In the propositional case it is common to have a one-event-at-a-time assumption. This makes the traces similar to those above. However, in contrast to model checking, traces are usually considered finite, and there have been various proposals for finite-trace versions of LTL. Relaxing the one-event-at-a-time assumption means that multiple events may occur at each time point, leading to a sequence of sets presentation. For example, assuming some appropriate finite-trace semantics, the LTL specification $\Box(a \rightarrow \Diamond(b \wedge c))$ has the trace $\{a\}.\{\}.\{b\}.\{b, c\}$ in its language. More complicated notions of trace tend to build on these ideas and we briefly cover some of these in the following.

Adding Time. The traces above introduce a *qualitative* notion of time i.e. give an ordering of events. However, they do not capture the *quantitative* distance (in time) between events. There have been various extensions of specification languages to deal with this. We can add clocks to automata to get timed automata [2,17] and add intervals to get timed regular expressions [4]. Intervals can also be added to LTL to get extensions such as Metric Temporal Logic (MTL) [44,54] and Timed Propositional Temporal Logic (TPTL) [3].

Such specifications often come with two alternative notions of trace or variations on their semantics. The first is to take a *pointwise semantics* as before where specifications denote (possibly infinite) *timed words* that add (strictly increasing) real-valued timestamps to events (or sets of events). For example, the MTL specification $\Box(a \rightarrow \Diamond_{(1,3)} b)$ has the trace $(1, a)(1.5, a)(3.5, b)$ in its language but not $(1, a)(1.5, a)(2.4, b)$ (again assuming an appropriate finite trace semantics). The second is to consider a *continuous semantics* where the trace is captured by a signal function $f : \mathbb{R}_+ \rightarrow 2^\Sigma$ mapping time t to a set of events $f(t)$ holding at time t. A signal function can be transformed into a timed word and a timed word can be transformed into a signal function if they satisfy properties that mean that an infinite number of events cannot occur in a finite amount of time. For signal functions this is called the *finite variability* property and for timed words this is called the *non-Zeno* property. Pragmatically, the difference between the pointwise and continuous view is that the former has an event-driven quality, and the second more intuitively reflects a setting where a system is periodically sampled.

Adding Data. Relatively early on in the history of runtime verification it was noted that it was useful to add a notion of data to specification languages, in order to capture traces with data carrying events. There is a wide range of different approaches to specification but the underlying traces are similar although the context of the specification language often leads to differing terminology when talking about traces.

There is a large body of work [1,7–9,20,49] dealing with traces as (finite) sequences of so-called *parametric events* of the form $e(a, b, c)$, where e is an event name and a, b, c are data values. We note that not all of these work uses the term *parametric event*, but the overall concept remains the same. A separate effort is built on the existing theory of *data words* captured by *register automata* [26,32]. The notion of trace is the same i.e. a trace is a sequence of letters from a finite alphabet paired with a data value from some infinite set. We mention this work separately as it is associated with a large body of theoretical work from outside of runtime verification [41,52,61].

A few extensions naturally lift propositional temporal logic to first-order, introducing functions, predicates, and quantification. As per the standard lifting, interpretations must be extended to interpret function and predicate symbols, thus leading to additional information being added to the trace as in [15,25]. Although we note that it is unusual to do this in practice. It is common [15] for specifications to restrict functions and predicates to some well-defined *theory* such as arithmetic. In this case the interpretation of such symbols is implicitly defined by the theory. An approach to monitoring called *monitoring modulo theories* [25] (following satisfiability modulo theories) considers traces mixing theory symbols and so-called *observation* symbols capturing system events.

In cases where specification languages include a notion of *quantification*, the domain of quantification must be captured in some way. In some situations it would be reasonable for this to be captured in the specification (e.g. if quantifying over some fixed set of values) but more typically it is considered part of the trace. Whilst it would be reasonable to define this domain separately it is most common [7,20,58] for it to be defined exactly as values extracted from the trace. Independently of how the quantification domain is captured there is also the consideration of whether it should be fixed throughout the trace. For example, some approaches [68] quantify over values seen in the trace *so far* rather than the whole trace. Such decisions can significantly alter the interpretation of the specifications.

As a final note, once the notion of event is no longer propositional it is possible to introduce the notion of events with complex *structure*. So far, in our discussion, events have had a flat form consisting of a name and a sequence of data values. This may not reflect real-world scenarios where data structures often encapsulate other nested structures, and recorded observations therefore may have structured fields. However, it is not common to consider structured events, although such efforts have been seen. For example, in [35] a first-order temporal logic is defined over XML documents where events are structured XML records.

Data and Time. One can add both data and time to produce a language that has more complex traces. One can, of course, treat time as just another element of data, and this is often sufficient. However, approaches that do this do not lend particular support for special metric operators as the specification language is not aware of the special status of this data.

One example of a language that combines data and time is Metric First Order Temporal Logic (MFOTL) [16] defined over traces consisting of timestamped parametric events. Another example is Signal Temporal Logic (STL) [48] where (continuous semantics) MTL is extended so that signals are real-valued (rather than boolean-valued). Implicitly this means that each propositional event has a real-valued parameter. Properties can then place conditions on functions of signals over time. There is also an extension of STL that deals with time-frequency analysis where traces are represented by a spectogram (a two-dimensional representation of time versus frequency) [27].

We would also like to mention a specific form of structured data in traces coming from the related field of statistical model checking. Spatial-Temporal logics [12,31,33,34] are defined over sequences of spatial structures, for example quarternary tree structures [34]. This is an example of an application domain where the structure of data is well-defined and the specification language is interpreted over this structure.

2.2 Instrumentation Techniques

Another way of viewing what traces are, from a runtime verification perspective, is to consider the different instrumentation techniques commonly used in runtime verification as these reflect what is being observed.

Instrumenting Java. The most common approach in the literature for observing events in Java programs is to use AspectJ [6]. This approach tends to be used for intercepting method calls and their parameters. Therefore, event names typically relate to method calls with a few exceptions, for example taking and releasing locks. However, early work on Java instrumentation was more general. The Java-MaC [42] tool introduces a low-level language for identifying events in terms of program variables and fields in objects. Alternative approaches to Java instrumentation include JVM agents (used by RV-Monitor [47]) and Java Reflection (used by JUnitRV [24]). Again these techniques tend to focus on method invocations, but are not restricted to these.

Instrumenting C. Instrumentation techniques for the runtime verification of C (and C++) programs are less well established. There exists some work on extending the AOP approach to C, but with relatively little uptake compared to AspectJ. RMOR [36] is a framework for monitoring the execution of C programs against state machines using an aspect-oriented pointcut language similar to AspectJ's. The system is implemented in the C analysis and transformation package CIL [22], which itself is programmed in Ocaml. AspectC++ [5] is a mature framework for aspect-oriented programming in C++. InterAspect [66] provides a GCC-plugin that supports pointcut definitions for the GIMPLE intermediate language. Finally, [21] reports on recent promising work and gives a good overview of previous efforts. The two main other approaches are manual instrumentation and code rewriting (as done by E-ACSL [43] and RiTHM [51]). For C programs it is more common to take changes in variable values as events. Another large consideration for C programs is that of memory safety, and this is a common behaviour to observe.

Other Languages. Whilst Java and C remain the two most common languages considered for monitoring, there exists some work on monitoring other languages. There is a recent body of work monitoring Erlang programs (ELARVA [23] and detectEr[1]). Initially, this work took advantage of Erlang's tracing mechanism to hook into Erlang's virtual machine to receive events as messages [23]. More recent work [18,19] employs an Aspect-Oriented Programming framework to inject instrumentation as in AspectJ. It should be noted that when monitoring Erlang programs there is an additional issue of distributed (asynchronous) computation to contend with. There is also some work on monitoring Python programs [59] which employs function decorators to modify functions with additional instrumentation.

---

[1] http://www.cs.um.edu.mt/svrg/Tools/detectEr.

Hardware Instrumentation. For hardware monitoring there appears to be two main approaches [70]. The first is to add a passive device to the system bus and "sniff" ongoing activities. For example, BusMOP [56] uses this approach to detect I/O accesses, memory accesses and interrupts. The second approach is to directly access relevant signals and registers and compile the property to be monitored directly to a circuit [39,46,62,69]. The former approach is event-triggered whilst the second samples a continuous signal on clock cycles.

3   Traces Elsewhere

In this section we briefly discuss sources of traces in areas that have received a mixed level of attention from the runtime verification. Understanding what traces are available here could be useful in understanding what kinds of traces we should be dealing with.

Web Servers. Web servers typically log accesses and errors. There are a number of standards for access logs supported by the main web server technologies. For example, the Common Log Format[2] logs each access as a single line consisting of the host, an identity, the user, a date, the request, the status and the number of bytes. Within this the identity, timestamps and statuses are also standardised. Whilst this format is quite straightforward, and looks similar to what we discussed above, the more complex (draft) Extended Log Format[3] uses a header to specify the data types in each field.

Databases. Database systems typically log transactions to guarantee durability of data. As these logs are meant for internal consumption there is little available about the format of such logs. The information stored would typically involve the query type and any arguments. As these logs are used to ensure durability they are typically circular i.e. older records are overwritten by newer records once the changes in older records have been flushed to main storage.

System Logging in Unix. When exploring security related issues it is common to observe the system calls made to the Unix kernel. Tools for this task include strace and ltrace. strace[4] attaches to a process and records system calls and signals. Each line of the log file records the system call name followed by its arguments in parenthesis and its return value. For example,

```
open("/dev/null", O_RDONLY) = 3
```

records open being called with a pathname and flag. Errors include the relevant error number and string, for example

---

[2] https://www.w3.org/Daemon/User/Config/Logging.html#common-logfile-format.
[3] https://www.w3.org/TR/WD-logfile.html.
[4] This information is based on that found in man strace.

```
open("/foo/bar", O_RDONLY) = -1 ENOENT (No such file or directory)
```

Additionally, signals are printed as signal symbol and decoded siginfo structure. For example,

```
sigsuspend([] <unfinished ...>
--- SIGINT {si_signo=SIGINT,si_code=SI_USER,si_pid=...}
+++ killed by SIGINT +++
```

is an excerpt from stracing and interrupting the command "sleep 666". ltrace is very similar to strace but intercepts calls to dynamic libraries. This could be used to detect calls to the standard C library (for example).

System Logging in Windows. As expected, Windows systems have more propriety logging facilities than Unix-based systems. However, one can access *Windows Event Logs*, which record a range of different events occurring in the system. Recorded events contain a source, category, identifier and an event-specific string such as a filename or username. Events can be of a number of kinds, e.g. application events, system events, security events. There has been some work filtering and extracting well-defined events to perform log checking [60] but it seems that this is not well-supported.

4 What Should Go into the Trace

Let us attempt to summarise the previous review to draw some conclusions about the kinds of things that should be supported in traces (ignoring the format of such things for now). Firstly, it is clear that we need good support for *Data* and *Time* as these are fundamental. In addition, we note that separate support for time is beneficial as it may have special requirements (e.g. is strictly increasing) not shared by normal data parameters. Beyond this there are a number of ideas to discuss.

Assumptions About Relevance. The main observation from Sect. 2.2 is that RV activities tend to specify the required events, record such events in a trace, and perform monitoring on that trace. However, many log files produced for other purposes will attempt to record as much relevant information as possible. Any useful system for recording and using traces would likely need to support traces containing more information than is relevant to the task in hand.

Do We Need Event Names? It would seem that each event should be given a name. However, this could be an overly rigid requirement coming from a particular view of monitoring. In the setting of hardware monitoring where one has a number of signals one is observing, there is no notion of event name, as each event contains the same information i.e. a vector of values. Perhaps forcing an event to have a name is therefore restrictive.

Ordered or Named Parameters? Previously we assumed events had a fixed number of parameters and the values for each parameter was included in events. However, this does not allow for two scenarios. Firstly, where there are a large number of parameters and only a few are relevant. Secondly, where there may be a variable number of parameters but we know that the particular parameter of interest will be present. These cases can be addressed by identifying parameters by a *name* rather than a position. Supporting these alternative presentations would extend applicability to these scenarios.

Structured Events. Most observations mentioned in the previous section are flat e.g. system calls have a flat list of parameters. However, there are some notable contexts where data values may have structure that should be recorded. A simple case is where the data value is a collection of other data values i.e. has variable non-fixed size. Two places where this issue is likely to occur is when serialising data structures and in Web Services, where structured data is common-place.

Notions of Equality and Other Types. There is often an implicit direct notion of equality i.e. that one can compare data values in the trace directly. However, this may be too simplistic. For example, if one were to record memory addresses to identify data structures then equality should be interpreted within the context of memory management or garbage collection, which indicates the lifetime of that identity[5]. When richer data values appear in the trace there may be non-standard interpretations for equality operations on them. In either case, additional information may be required to interpret the trace.

The MetaData. One may need more information to understand the trace than is described in the events. For example, domains of quantification, the relevant signature/alphabet, sampling information, units for certain measurements etc. It would be useful for a trace format to support additional (structured) metadata of this kind. Otherwise a separate file will be required.

Capturing Context. For some monitoring activities there is a wider context that may be relevant. For example, when monitoring Java applications it may be relevant when a certain (monitored) object is garbage collected. This could be encoded as events.

5   What Format Should a Trace File Take?

It seems clear that traces should follow a well-defined common format. This allows parsing and printing tools, as well as libraries to be easily reused. This was

---

[5] The issue here is that over the lifetime of a program the same memory address could refer to different data structures if some structures are deleted.

the approach taken by the RV competition [10, 11, 30], and we here review the file formats used for this competition, highlight their advantages and disadvantages, and point out some alternative uses of these formats.

Comma Separated Values (CSV). This standardised[6] format is often used for the storage and transport of simply structured data. It would be difficult to represent complexly structured events in this format. Parsing of CSV files is, however, very efficient due to its simple format. Each data record in a CSV file occupies one line. Values on the line are separated by commas. An optional initial header line can contain column names, allowing CSV processing software to access values by name. It is important to note that whitespace is taken as part of values.

In the case where all events have the same number of arguments, and each position has the same interpretation across lines, the CSV format is optimal. As an example consider the CSV file containing drawing commands taking x- and y-coordinates as arguments:

```
command, x, y
move, 3, 4
draw, 0, 4
move, 0, 0
draw, 3, 4
```

However, the typical case is that different commands take different numbers and kinds of arguments, with different interpretations. During the latest RV competition CSV files were for example generated for keeping track of Java operations on maps (update map, create the collection of keys of the map, create a derived iterator from this key set, use the iterator - and check that after an update to a map no such derived iterator is further used). The CSV files used a header as in the following example:

```
event, map, collection, iterator
updateMap, 6750210, ,
createColl,6750210, 2081191879,
createIter, , 2081191879, 910091170
useIter, , , 910091170
updateMap, 1183888521, ,
```

Note that in order to match the header, empty fields are required when a particular column is not relevant to an event. A CSV file can also be constructed without using a header, in which case the CSV file reading software must know and interpret the postions of the arguments correctly. Here arguments are just listed sequentially without blank fields in between. Positions here have different interpretations for different commands, for example argument number 1 in a updateMap command is a map while argument number 1 in a createIter command is a collection:

---

[6] See http://www.ietf.org/rfc/rfc4180.txt.

```
updateMap, 6750210
createColl, 6750210, 2081191879
createIter, 2081191879, 910091170
useIter, 910091170
updateMap, 6750210
```

Finally one can consider a format where there is also no header, but where fields are named in each row (every second position in a line is the name of a value, which then follows in the next position):

```
updateMap, map, 6750210
createColl, map, 6750210, collection, 2081191879
createIter, collection, 2081191879, iterator, 910091170
useIter, iterator, 910091170
updateMap, map, 6750210
```

eXtended Markup Language (XML). This standardised[7] format associated with web services is a markup language where data are tagged. In the RV competition five tags were introduced: log, event, name, field, and value. The following gives a log consisting only of the second event in the previous log.

```
<log>
  <event>
    <name>createColl</name>
    <field>
      <name>map</name>
      <value>6750210</value>
    </field>
    <field>
      <name>collection</name>
      <value>2081191879</value>
    </field>
  </event>
</log>
```

This format clearly supports structured data and also metadata, for example an event could be further tagged with additional time information:

```
<event timestamp="1462810918">
```

Although this does not add much functionality as the same information could be represented as data (e.g. in CSV); the role of metadata is to separate data from information that describes it.

However, the above representation is verbose. Similar to the CSV format, the XML format can be simplified, not mentioning names of fields, but rather giving them just by position. The above one-event log would in such a solution become simpler, although still somewhat verbose:

---

[7] See https://www.w3.org/TR/REC-xml.

```
<log>
  <event>
    <name>createColl</name>
    <value>6750210</value>
    <value>2081191879</value>
  </event>
</log>
```

Finally, XML supports the notion of *schema* that defines the expected structure and can be used to validate XML documents.

JavaScript Object Notation (JSON). This standardised[8] format stores structured attribute-value pairs as well as arrays. The first one-event log presented as XML above can be captured in JSON as follows.

```
[
  {
    "createColl" : {
      "map" : "6750210",
      "collection" : "2081191879"
    }
  }
]
```

This seems to have the advantages of XML but is relatively more concise. Similar to the cases of CSV and XML, JSON can be made more succinct by using arrays to model positional arguments, as in the following where we have listed all the events in the original CSV file:

```
[
  {"updateMap" : ["6750210"]},
  {"createColl" : ["6750210", "2081191879"]},
  {"createIter" : ["2081191879", "910091170"]},
  {"useIter" : ["910091170"]},
  {"updateMap" : ["6750210"]}
]
```

Tool Formats. Finally, we note that some tools have their own propriety trace file format. Monpoly [14] has a plain text format with an event per-line where each line contains a timestamp, event name and then (optionally) some data parameters. Both OCLR-Check [28] and BeepBeep [35] make use of custom XML formats.

---

[8] See https://tools.ietf.org/html/rfc7159.

6   Discussion and Conclusion

The aim of this paper was to review various notions of trace from a runtime verification perspective, and beyond. This review has been relatively lightweight but hopefully provides some discussion points and useful references. We finish with a few discussion points relevant to the topic of traces, which we have not yet touched.

Rolling Logs. Something that is rarely dealt with in runtime verification is the issue of monitoring logs from systems that have been running for a long time. The first problem is that one will not want to repeatedly analyze all logs from the beginning of time. Approaches will be needed for *accumulating* monitoring results from past analyses. The second problem is that of *bootstrapping*, if one has not been recording logs so far, but wants to start monitoring, then it may be necessary to make some assumptions about the unseen logs.

Uncertainty. A common issue is where a trace contains partial information. This can either be partial by construction and therefore known to be partial, for example where a system's execution is sampled only periodically for efficiency reasons [13,40,67]. Or it may be partial due to unreliability in the recording process. In either case it may be necessary to either estimate or predict what has been omitted, or provide some confidence in the computed verdict. An alternative approach is to compute the *distance* between the observed behaviour and expected behaviour [55,57].

Concurrency. We have ignored the issue of concurrent or distributed systems. Such systems can be abstracted as a set of separate but related execution traces with a single trace per concurrent or distributed process. A notable property of such systems is that there is (generally) no notion of a *global clock*. If the behaviour of each process is independent then it may be sufficient to consider the behaviour of the system as a set of independent sequential traces. However, it is more common for there to be dependencies between processes. In such a case there is a choice: one can enforce a *total ordering* of events or record the observed *partial order*.

The first case equates to flattening the set of traces into a single trace, for example serialising the trace by selecting an arbitrary ordering. But unless this ordering is enforced (via synchronization) the trace may not reflect actual behaviour, possibly leading to false positives or false negatives in monitoring. If the ordering is enforced by synchronization this can have a large impact on performance.

In the second case it is typical [50,53,63,64] to consider a *distributed computation* as a *partial order* $\langle E, \rightarrow \rangle$ on a set of events E based on the *happens-before* relation $\rightarrow$. The happens-before relation necessarily totally orders events from the same process and represents synchronisation (e.g. message passing) between different processes. In such a setting a *global state* (or *consistent cut*) is a tuple of events (one from each process) representing a frontier in the distributed computation that satisfies the happens-before relation. These global states can then be formed into a *computation lattice* or *state lattice* where one global state is above another global state if it occurs strictly later in the computation. This differs from the previous structure as the nodes now represent global states rather than individual events. A path through the computation lattice is one possible global trace of the system and it is typical to consider all such traces. In the context of multithreaded programs there exist methods generalising the happens-before relationship by considering additional causal relationships [38,65]. This can lead to more possible global traces being explored, increasing the chances of finding buggy behaviour even if this behaviour was not observed at runtime. Such exploration of all possible global traces in the partial order has similarities to model checking [37]. However, a model checker will explore all possible traces of the program, whereas the above described method will not.

As a concluding remark, it is clear that any efforts to unify notions of trace and standardise how runtime verification tools record and process events will be beneficial to both the developers and users of such tools.

References

1. Allan, C., Avgustinov, P., Christensen, A.S., Hendren, L., Kuzins, S., Lhoták, O., de Moor, O., Sereni, D., Sittampalam, G., Tibble, J.: Adding trace matching with free variables to AspectJ. SIGPLAN Not. **40**, 345–364 (2005)
2. Alur, R., Dill, D.: Automata for modeling real-time systems. In: Paterson, M.S. (ed.) ICALP 1990. LNCS, vol. 443, pp. 322–335. Springer, Heidelberg (1990). doi:10.1007/BFb0032042
3. Alur, R., Henzinger, T.A.: A really temporal logic. J. ACM **41**(1), 181–203 (1994)
4. Asarin, E., Caspi, P., Maler, O.: Timed regular expressions. J. ACM **49**(2), 172–206 (2002)
5. AspectC++. Aspect oriented programming for C++ (2016). http://www.aspectc.org
6. AspectJ. Aspect oriented programming for Java (2016). https://eclipse.org/aspectj/
7. Barringer, H., Falcone, Y., Havelund, K., Reger, G., Rydeheard, D.: Quantified event automata: towards expressive and efficient runtime monitors. In: Giannakopoulou, D., Méry, D. (eds.) FM 2012. LNCS, vol. 7436, pp. 68–84. Springer, Heidelberg (2012). doi:10.1007/978-3-642-32759-9_9
8. Barringer, H., Goldberg, A., Havelund, K., Sen, K.: Rule-based runtime verification. In: VMCAI, pp. 44–57 (2004)
9. Barringer, H., Havelund, K.: TRACECONTRACT: a scala DSL for trace analysis. In: Butler, M., Schulte, W. (eds.) FM 2011. LNCS, vol. 6664, pp. 57–72. Springer, Heidelberg (2011). doi:10.1007/978-3-642-21437-0_7
10. Bartocci, E., Bonakdarpour, B., Falcone, Y.: First international competition on software for runtime verification. In: Bonakdarpour, B., Smolka, S.A. (eds.) RV 2014. LNCS, vol. 8734, pp. 1–9. Springer, Heidelberg (2014). doi:10.1007/978-3-319-11164-3_1

11. Bartocci, E., Bonakdarpour, B., Falcone, Y., Colombo, C., Decker, N., Klaedtke, F., Havelund, K., Joshi, Y., Milewicz, R., Reger, G., Rosu, G., Signoles, J., Thoma, D., Zalinescu, E., Zhang, Y.: First international competition on runtime verification. Int. J. Softw. Tools Technol. Transf. (STTT) (to appear, 2016)

12. Bartocci, E., Bortolussi, L., Milios, D., Nenzi, L., Sanguinetti, G.: Studying emergent behaviours in morphogenesis using signal spatio-temporal logic. In: Abate, A., Šafránek, D. (eds.) HSB 2015. LNCS, vol. 9271, pp. 156–172. Springer, Heidelberg (2015). doi:10.1007/978-3-319-26916-0_9

13. Bartocci, E., Grosu, R., Karmarkar, A., Smolka, S.A., Stoller, S.D., Zadok, E., Seyster, J.: Adaptive runtime verification. In: Qadeer, S., Tasiran, S. (eds.) RV 2012. LNCS, vol. 7687, pp. 168–182. Springer, Heidelberg (2013). doi:10.1007/978-3-642-35632-2_18

14. Basin, D., Harvan, M., Klaedtke, F., Zălinescu, E.: Monpoly: monitoring usage-control policies. In: Khurshid, S., Sen, K. (eds.) RV 2012. LNCS, vol. 7186, pp. 360–364. Springer, Berlin Heidelberg (2012)

15. Basin, D., Klaedtke, F., Marinovic, S., Zălinescu, E.: Monitoring of temporal first-order properties with aggregations. Formal Methods Syst. Des. **46**(3), 262–285 (2015)

16. Basin, D., Klaedtke, F., Müller, S., Zălinescu, E.: Monitoring metric first-order temporal properties. J. ACM **62**(2), 15:1–15:45 (2015)

17. Bengtsson, J., Yi, W.: Timed automata: semantics, algorithms and tools. In: Desel, J., Reisig, W., Rozenberg, G. (eds.) ACPN 2003. LNCS, vol. 3098, pp. 87–124. Springer, Heidelberg (2004). doi:10.1007/978-3-540-27755-2_3

18. Cassar, I., Francalanza, A.: On synchronous and asynchronous monitor instrumentation for actor-based systems. In: Proceedings of the 13th International Workshop on Foundations of Coordination Languages and Self-Adaptive Systems, FOCLASA 2014, Rome, Italy, 6th September 2014, pp. 54–68, 2014 (2014)

19. Cassar, I., Francalanza, A.: On implementing a monitor-oriented programming framework for actor systems. In: Ábrahám, E., Huisman, M. (eds.) IFM 2016. LNCS, vol. 9681, pp. 176–192. Springer, Heidelberg (2016). doi:10.1007/978-3-319-33693-0_12

20. Chen, F., Roşu, G.: Parametric trace slicing and monitoring. In: Kowalewski, S., Philippou, A. (eds.) TACAS 2009. LNCS, vol. 5505, pp. 246–261. Springer, Heidelberg (2009). doi:10.1007/978-3-642-00768-2_23

21. Chen, Z., Wang, Z., Zhu, Y., Xi, H., Yang, Z.: Parametric runtime verification of C programs. In: Chechik, M., Raskin, J.-F. (eds.) TACAS 2016. LNCS, vol. 9636, pp. 299–315. Springer, Heidelberg (2016). doi:10.1007/978-3-662-49674-9_17

22. CIL. C Intermediate Language (2016). https://www.cs.berkeley.edu/~necula/cil/

23. Colombo, C., Francalanza, A., Gatt, R.: Elarva: a monitoring tool for Erlang. In: Khurshid, S., Sen, K. (eds.) RV 2011. LNCS, vol. 7186, pp. 370–374. Springer, Heidelberg (2012). doi:10.1007/978-3-642-29860-8_29

24. Decker, N., Leucker, M., Thoma, D.: jUnit^{RV}–adding runtime verification to jUnit. In: Brat, G., Rungta, N., Venet, A. (eds.) NFM 2013. LNCS, vol. 7871, pp. 459–464. Springer, Heidelberg (2013). doi:10.1007/978-3-642-38088-4_34

25. Decker, N., Leucker, M., Thoma, D.: Monitoring modulo theories. In: Ábrahám, E., Havelund, K. (eds.) TACAS 2014. LNCS, vol. 8413, pp. 341–356. Springer, Heidelberg (2014). doi:10.1007/978-3-642-54862-8_23

26. Demri, S., Lazić, R.: LTL with the freeze quantifier, register automata. ACM Trans. Comput. Logic **10**(3), 1–30 (2009)

27. Donzé, A., Maler, O., Bartocci, E., Nickovic, D., Grosu, R., Smolka, S.: On temporal logic and signal processing. In: Chakraborty, S., Mukund, M. (eds.) ATVA 2012. LNCS, vol. 7561, pp. 92–106. Springer, Heidelberg (2012)
28. Dou, W., Bianculli, D., Briand, L.: *OCLR*: a more expressive, pattern-based temporal extension of OCL. In: Cabot, J., Rubin, J. (eds.) ECMFA 2014. LNCS, vol. 8569, pp. 51–66. Springer, Heidelberg (2014). doi:10.1007/978-3-319-09195-2_4
29. Falcone, Y., Havelund, K., Reger, G.: A tutorial on runtime verification. In: Broy, M., Peled, D. (eds.) Summer School Marktoberdorf 2012 - Engineering Dependable Software Systems. IOS Press (2013). to appear
30. Falcone, Y., Ničković, D., Reger, G., Thoma, D.: Second international competition on runtime verification. In: Bartocci, E., Majumdar, R. (eds.) RV 2015. LNCS, vol. 9333, pp. 405–422. Springer, Heidelberg (2015). doi:10.1007/978-3-319-23820-3_27
31. Gol, E.A., Bartocci, E., Belta, C.: A formal methods approach to pattern synthesis in reaction diffusion systems. In: 53rd IEEE Conference on Decision and Control, pp. 108–113, December 2014
32. Grigore, R., Distefano, D., Petersen, R.L., Tzevelekos, N.: Runtime verification based on register automata. In: Piterman, N., Smolka, S.A. (eds.) TACAS 2013. LNCS, vol. 7795, pp. 260–276. Springer, Heidelberg (2013). doi:10.1007/978-3-642-36742-7_19
33. Grosu, R., Smolka, S.A., Corradini, F., Wasilewska, A., Entcheva, E., Bartocci, E.: Learning and detecting emergent behavior in networks of cardiac myocytes. Commun. ACM **52**(3), 97–105 (2009)
34. Haghighi, I., Jones, A., Kong, Z., Bartocci, E., Gros, R., Belta, C.: Spatel: a novel spatial-temporal logic and its applications to networked systems. In: Proceedings of the 18th International Conference on Hybrid Systems: Computation and Control, HSCC 2015, pp. 189–198. ACM, New York (2015)
35. Halle, S., Villemaire, R.: Runtime enforcement of web service message contracts with data. IEEE Trans. Serv. Comput. **5**(2), 192–206 (2012)
36. Havelund, K.: Runtime verification of C programs. In: Suzuki, K., Higashino, T., Ulrich, A., Hasegawa, T. (eds.) FATES/TestCom 2008. LNCS, vol. 5047, pp. 7–22. Springer, Heidelberg (2008). doi:10.1007/978-3-540-68524-1_3
37. Holzmann, G.: Spin Model Checker, The: Primer and Reference Manual, 1st edn. Addison-Wesley Professional (2003)
38. Huang, J., Meredith, P.O., Rosu, G.: Maximal sound predictive race detection with control flow abstraction. SIGPLAN Not. **49**(6), 337–348 (2014)
39. Jakšić, S., Bartocci, E., Grosu, R., Kloibhofer, R., Nguyen, T., Ničkovié, D.: From signal temporal logic to FPGA monitors. In: 2015 ACM/IEEE International Conference on Formal Methods and Models for Codesign (MEMOCODE), pp. 218–227, September 2015
40. Kalajdzic, K., Bartocci, E., Smolka, S.A., Stoller, S.D., Grosu, R.: Runtime verification with particle filtering. In: Legay, A., Bensalem, S. (eds.) RV 2013. LNCS, vol. 8174, pp. 149–166. Springer, Heidelberg (2013). doi:10.1007/978-3-642-40787-1_9
41. Kaminski, M., Francez, N.: Finite-memory automata. Theor. Comput. Sci. **134**(2), 329–363 (1994)
42. Kim, M.Z., Viswanathan, M., Kannan, S., Lee, I., Sokolsky, O.: Java-MaC: a runtime assurance approach for java programs. Formal Methods Syst. Des. **24**(2), 129–155 (2004)
43. Kosmatov, N., Petiot, G., Signoles, J.: An Optimized Memory Monitoring for Runtime Assertion Checking of C Programs. In: Legay, A., Bensalem, S. (eds.) RV 2013. LNCS, vol. 8174, pp. 167–182. Springer, Heidelberg (2013). doi:10.1007/978-3-642-40787-1_10

44. Koymans, R.: Specifying real-time properties with metric temporal logic. Real-Time Syst. **2**(4), 255–299 (1990)
45. Leucker, M., Schallhart, C.: A brief account of runtime verification. J. Logic, Algebr. Program. **78**(5), 293–303 (2008)
46. Lu, H., Forin, A.: The design and implementation of P2V, an architecture for zero-overhead online verification of software programs. Technical Report MSR-TR-2007-99, Microsoft Research, August 2007
47. Luo, Q., Zhang, Y., Lee, C., Jin, D., Meredith, P.O.N., Şerbănuţă, T.F., Roşu, G.: RV-Monitor: efficient parametric runtime verification with simultaneous properties. In: Bonakdarpour, B., Smolka, S.A. (eds.) RV 2014. LNCS, vol. 8734, pp. 285–300. Springer, Heidelberg (2014). doi:10.1007/978-3-319-11164-3_24
48. Maler, O., Nickovic, D.: Monitoring temporal properties of continuous signals. In: Lakhnech, Y., Yovine, S. (eds.) FORMATS/FTRTFT -2004. LNCS, vol. 3253, pp. 152–166. Springer, Heidelberg (2004). doi:10.1007/978-3-540-30206-3_12
49. Meredith, P., Jin, D., Griffith, D., Chen, F., Roşu, G.: An overview of the MOP runtime verification framework. J. Softw. Tools Technol. Transf., 1–41 (2011)
50. Mostafa, M., Bonakdarpour, B.: Decentralized runtime verification of LTL specifications in distributed systems. In: 2015 IEEE International Parallel and Distributed Processing Symposium (IPDPS), pp. 494–503, May 2015
51. Navabpour, S., Joshi, Y., Wu, C.W.W., Berkovich, S., Medhat, R., Bonakdarpour, B., Fischmeister, S.: RiTHM: a tool for enabling time-triggered runtime verification for c programs. In: ACM Symposium on the Foundations of Software Engineering (FSE), pp. 603–606 (2013)
52. Neven, F., Schwentick, T., Vianu, V.: Finite state machines for strings over infinite alphabets. ACM Trans. Comput. Logic **5**(3), 403–435 (2004)
53. Ogale, V.A., Garg, V.K.: Detecting temporal logic predicates on distributed computations. In: Pelc, A. (ed.) DISC 2007. LNCS, vol. 4731, pp. 420–434. Springer, Heidelberg (2007). doi:10.1007/978-3-540-75142-7_32
54. Ouaknine, J., Worrell, J.: Some recent results in metric temporal logic. In: Cassez, F., Jard, C. (eds.) FORMATS 2008. LNCS, vol. 5215, pp. 1–13. Springer, Heidelberg (2008). doi:10.1007/978-3-540-85778-5_1
55. Pastore, F., Mariani, L.: AVA: supporting debugging with failure interpretations. In: Sixth IEEE International Conference on Software Testing, Verification and Validation, ICST 2013, Luxembourg, 18–22 March 2013, pp. 416–421 (2013)
56. Pellizzoni, R., Meredith, P., Caccamo, M., Rosu, G.: Hardware runtime monitoring for dependable COTS-based real-time embedded systems. In: Real-Time Systems Symposium 2008, pp. 481–491, November 2008
57. Reger, G.: Suggesting edits to explain failing traces. In: Bartocci, E., Majumdar, R. (eds.) RV 2015. LNCS, vol. 9333, pp. 287–293. Springer, Heidelberg (2015). doi:10.1007/978-3-319-23820-3_20
58. Reger, G., Rydeheard, D.: From first-order temporal logic to parametric trace slicing. In: Bartocci, E., Majumdar, R. (eds.) RV 2015. LNCS, vol. 9333, pp. 216–232. Springer, Heidelberg (2015). doi:10.1007/978-3-319-23820-3_14
59. Renberg, A.: Test-inspired runtime verification. Master's thesis, Royal Institute of Technology (KTH), Stockholm (2014)
60. Russ, A.: Detecting security incidents using windows workstation event logs. Technical report, Sans Institute InfoSec Reading Room (2013)
61. Segoufin, L.: Automata and logics for words and trees over an infinite alphabet. In: Ésik, Z. (ed.) CSL 2006. LNCS, vol. 4207, pp. 41–57. Springer, Heidelberg (2006). doi:10.1007/11874683_3

62. Selyunin, K., Nguyen, T., Bartocci, E., Nickovic, D., Grosu, R.: Monitoring of MTL specifications with IBM's spiking-neuron model. In: 2016 Design, Automation Test in Europe Conference Exhibition (DATE), pp. 924–929, March 2016

63. Sen, A., Garg, V.K.: Rv '2003, run-time verification (satellite workshop of cav '03) partial order trace analyzer (pota) for distributed programs. Electron. Not. Theoret. Comput. Sci. **89**(2), 22–43 (2003)

64. Sen, A., Garg, V.K.: Detecting temporal logic predicates in distributed programs using computation slicing. In: Papatriantafilou, M., Hunel, P. (eds.) OPODIS 2003. LNCS, vol. 3144, pp. 171–183. Springer, Heidelberg (2004). doi:10.1007/978-3-540-27860-3_17

65. Şerbănuţă, T.F., Chen, F., Roşu, G.: Maximal causal models for sequentially consistent systems. In: Qadeer, S., Tasiran, S. (eds.) RV 2012. LNCS, vol. 7687, pp. 136–150. Springer, Heidelberg (2013). doi:10.1007/978-3-642-35632-2_16

66. Seyster, J., Dixit, K., Huang, X., Grosu, R., Havelund, K., Smolka, S.A., Stoller, S.D., Zadok, E.: Interaspect: aspect-oriented instrumentation with GCC. Formal Methods Syst. Des. **41**(3), 295–320 (2012)

67. Stoller, S.D., Bartocci, E., Seyster, J., Grosu, R., Havelund, K., Smolka, S.A., Zadok, E.: Runtime verification with state estimation. In: Khurshid, S., Sen, K. (eds.) RV 2011. LNCS, vol. 7186, pp. 193–207. Springer, Heidelberg (2012). doi:10.1007/978-3-642-29860-8_15

68. Stolz, V.: Temporal assertions with parametrized propositions*. J. Log. Comput. **20**, 743–757 (2010)

69. Todman, T., Stilkerich, S., Luk, W.: In-circuit temporal monitors for runtime verification of reconfigurable designs. In: Proceedings of the 52nd Annual Design Automation Conference, DAC 2015, pp. 50:1–50:6. ACM, New York (2015)

70. Watterson, C., Heffernan, D.: Runtime verification and monitoring of embedded systems. IET Softw. **1**(5), 172–179 (2007)

Execution Trace Analysis Using LTL-FO$^+$

Raphaël Khoury$^{(\boxtimes)}$, Sylvain Hallé, and Omar Waldmann

Laboratoire d'informatique formelle,
Université du Québec à Chicoutimi, Chicoutimi, Canada
`raphael.khoury@uqac.ca`

Abstract. We explore of use of the tool BeepBeep, a monitor for the temporal logic LTL-FO$^+$, in interpreting assembly traces, focusing on security-related applications. LTL-FO$^+$ is an extension of LTL, which includes first order quantification. We show that LTL-FO$^+$ is a sufficiently expressive formalism to state a number of interesting program behaviors, and demonstrate experimentally that BeepBeep can efficiently verify the validity of the properties on assembly traces in tractable time.

1 Introduction

Traces are a useful basis for several types of program analysis when the source code may be unavailable, including notably debugging [7], performance analysis [1], and feature enhancement. Assembly traces are particularly interesting since they provide a detailed picture of the target program's runtime behavior, and can thus be used to detect the occurrence of behaviors that would otherwise not be observable if we relied only on higher level information traces such as system calls or program functions calls. However, the large volume of information present in assembly traces raises several challenges, especially with regards to scalability and pattern detection.

Assembly traces have often been eschewed by security researchers, perhaps because of tractability problems related to their size. Recently, Roşu et al. [8] proposed an extension of past time LTL in which matching function calls and returns are explicitly stated. Ghiasi et al. [4] propose a method that relies upon the register values at the moment when critical library functions are called and return to detect a wide variety of malware.

In this study, we propose a new approach for the verification of assembly traces through runtime monitoring. Security properties are expressed in a first-order extension of Linear Temporal Logic, called LTL-FO$^+$, and are verified using the BeepBeep monitor [5]. We focus on the detection of potential error conditions in the trace, call sequence profiling as well as the detection of specific, potentially malicious patterns in the trace. What distinguishes our study from previous ones is the ease with which properties of any kind can be stated over the relationship between any values present in the trace. The properties we check encompass that of previous related work, and as we will show, most of them could not have been stated in a formalism less expressive than LTL-FO$^+$.

T. Margaria and B. Steffen (Eds.): ISoLA 2016, Part II, LNCS 9953, pp. 356–362, 2016.
DOI: 10.1007/978-3-319-47169-3_26

Previous work on enforcing security policies on assembly traces focused on developing heuristics to allows the detection of malware. For example, Ghiasi et al. [4] extract from the trace a model that captures the target program's register values before and after each system call, and raises an alarm if the observed values diverge sufficiently from expected values. Likewise, Storlie et al. [10] build a Markov chain model from the program's assembly trace. While these methods have high accuracy rate (in the 90 %–98 % range), we believe we are the first to capture the specific behavior of malware using temporal logic and detecting it over assembly traces. This detection method is even more accurate and avoid the possibility of false positives. Our study further shows that LTL-FO$^+$ is sufficiently expressive to state the properties of interest and that the BeepBeep monitor is capable of handling the considerable size of assembly traces.

2   Temporal Properties over Assembly Traces

In this section, we give examples of some of the type of properties that we have been able to verify by applying LTL-FO$^+$ to assembly traces. The traces we use are assembly-level generated by a proprietary tracer for Intel 64 developed at the center of Research and Development for Defence Canada (RDDC) based in Valcartier, Québec. Each line of these files corresponds to a single assembly-level instruction performed by the system being monitored or to a system call. While none of the properties used in this paper contains a system call, they are present in the trace and could be a component of the property.

```
06bb5c  mov esp, ebp | EBP=001bfbf4 | ESP=001bfbf4
06bb5d  pop ebp | ESP=001bfbf4 [001bfbf4]=001bfc24 | EBP=001bfc24 ESP=001bfbf8
06bb5e  push ecx | ECX=71f1a8b9 ESP=001bfbf8 | ESP=001bfbf4 [001bfbf4]=71f1a8b9
06bb5f  ret | ESP=001bfbf4 [001bfbf4]=71f1a8b9 | ESP=001bfbf8
06bb60  ret | ESP=001bfbf8 [001bfbf8]=01391036 | ESP=001bfbfc
06bb61  add esp, 0x20 | ESP=001bfbfc | ESP=001bfc1c EFLAGS=
06bb62  cmp  [ebp-0x4], 0x3e8 | [001bfc20]=000003e8 EBP=001bfc24 | EFLAGS=ZP
06bb63  jnz 0x1391057 | EFLAGS=ZP |
06bb64  push 0x1392144 | ESP=001bfc1c | ESP=001bfc18 [001bfc18]=01392144
```

Fig. 1. A fragment of assembly trace

A short fragment of a trace is shown in Fig. 1. Each line begins with a sequential number, and then contains three sets of information, separated by |. The first is the assembly instruction that occurred, with its parameters. This is followed by the initial values present in each relevant register or memory location before this instruction is executed. Finally, the tracer records the values of registers, memory locations or flags that were modified by the instruction. In this example, the trace is that of a simple C program that reads an integer value from a file, checks whether or not the value that has been read equals 1000 (which is the case in our example) and branches accordingly. The relevant assembly instructions are on lines 06bb62 and 06bb63 of the trace file. The complete trace file contains about 470,000 lines.

We focus on five types of properties of assembly traces, which we describe below. These examples do not exhaust the possible uses of temporal logic verification over assembly traces. Rather, they illustrate the diversity of behavior that can be stated in LTL-FO$^+$ and verified over assembly traces using BeepBeep. The properties are reproduced in the Appendix.

Property 1: Integer overflow detection. Integer overflow is a potential source of abnormal program behavior if its occurrence was unanticipated by the program developer or if it is unsupported or undefined by the programming environment. For example, integer overflow of signed integers is undefined behavior in C and C++, despite being widely relayed upon by programmers [3]. Integer overflow is also a know source of vulnerabilities in programs. For example, the "jpeg of death" vulnerability was caused by an integer overflow [6].

Property 2: Call sequence profiling is a program analysis that serves to reconstitute the call-chain occurring in the target program during its execution. It has applications notably in program comprehension, software maintenance and software re-engineering, amongst other. In this paper, we consider two properties, namely determining if it is possible for a given function to be called by a specific caller, and if a caller function always calls a given callee before returning.

Property 3: Return address protection. One of the main classes of malicious code functions by overriding the return address on the stack before the executing function returns. Buffer overflow vulnerabilities, return-to-LibC and return oriented programming are all examples or malware that exploit this type of vulnerability.

Property 4: Pointer subterfuge detection. A pointer subterfuge is a potentially malicious behavior in which a value is written to memory through a buffer-copy or a string manipulation operation, and then used as the target of a function call [9].

Property 5: Malicious Pattern detection. Christodorescu et al. [2] showed how logical expressions can be used to describe specific malicious patterns of assembly code. Such patterns can be used to detect the presence of malicious code even when obfuscation techniques have been used to hide their presence. In our final example we wrote an LTL-FO$^+$ formula that detects the presence of this pattern in the trace.

It is important to stress that these properties simply could not have been stated in a formalism less expressive than LTL-FO$^+$, which includes quantified variables over complex events. This is because the interpretation of the property requires that we reason about the relationship between the different elements present in the trace. For instance, to determine if a return address on the stack is overwritten, we check that whenever a call event occurs, the return address it places on the stack is not overwritten until the occurrence of the *corresponding* ret instruction (regardless of how many call-ret pairs occur in the interim). In this absence of quantified variable in the formula, the same effect could only be achieved by including in the formula every possible pairing of call-ret values—in our case, every virtual memory location in use in the execution environment. The size of the automaton representing this property would be exponential in the number of such locations.

Other properties would be even harder to state. Pointer subterfuge detection involves verifying if a given write, occurring in a buffer, is later used as the destination for of a call. A simple LTL-FO$^+$ formula achieves this by quantifying over the location and value of mov instruction, and then verifying that these same values never occur as the location and destination of a call instruction. (see property in Appendix 1). A flag indicating that the write instruction occurred as part of a buffer write (the rep flag was set) helps constraint the search for optimization purposes. Absent quantified variable int he formula, it is not clear how such a property could be checked, short checking every mov instruction in the trace against every single call instruction (Up to 30 % of all events occurring in each sample trace where movs).

3   Experimental Results

We tested the five properties described above using traces of varying length, up to 500,000 assembly instructions. A preprocessing script was run over each trace file beforehand in order to format them into an XML structure suitable for verification with BeepBeep. The tests were generated using the ParkBench test suite.[1] The results are summarized in Table 1.

Table 1. Experimental results

	Number of lines	Number of quant.	Number of connectives	Nesting depth	Total exec. time (ms)	Max heap (MB)	Avg time per event (ms)
Property 1	500,000	0	2	2	175611	593	0.35
Property 2	500,000	1	9	8	6245	481	0.12
Property 3	500,000	2	6	7	30996224	1331	61.99
Property 4	500,000	2	6	8	6360461	739	12.72
Property 5	381,583	5	20	19	293033440	1969	767.94

Figure 2a and b show the detailed execution time of the monitor for each property. With the exception of Property 5, the execution times grow linearly with the size of the execution trace at a very tractable rate. Properties 1 and 3

---

[1] http://github.com/sylvainhalle/ParkBench.

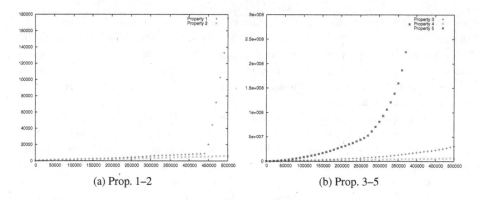

(a) Prop. 1–2   (b) Prop. 3–5

Fig. 2. Experimental results: execution time

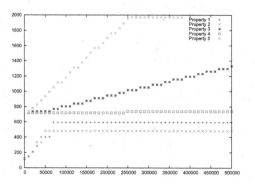

Fig. 3. Experimental results: heap usage

both exhibit sudden increases in their execution time. This seems to be related to the functioning of the Java garbage collection. The execution time is generally proportional to the size of the size of the property under consideration. Fig. 3 shows the heap usage for each property. Most properties require a constant amount of memory regardless of of the size of the execution trace.

4 Conclusion

In this paper, we showed that the BeepBeep monitor is an effective tool to verify LTL-FO$^+$ properties over assembly traces. The expressive power of LTL-FO$^+$ permits users to state fine-grained properties, drawing on the specific values present in the trace, thus allows users to harness the detailed content of assembly-level traces. Furthermore, we showed that the BeepBeep monitor is sufficiently powerful to verify these properties on real traces, despite the considerable size of these traces.

We are currently exploring other uses of LTL-FO$^+$ and of the BeepBeep monitor. The LTL-FO$^+$ language is sufficiently expressive to state interesting properties for several types of program traces, in addition tot he assembly-level traces discussed in this paper. Likewise, the BeepBeep monitor is capable of verifying such properties in tractable time over traces of considerable size. We are especially interested in applying these tools to the problems associated with program comprehension and program re-engineering, which require a thorough understanding of method call and system call traces.

Appendix 1: LTL-FO+ Properties

Property 1: Integer Overflow Detection

```
G ((./instruction=add) → (./overflow-flag=False) )
```

Property 2: Call Sequence Profiling

```
F (∃ Address1 ∈ ./return-address : (( ((((./instruction)= call)
   ∧ ((./destination)= 71f1acdc) ) ∧ (¬ (((./instruction) = ret) ∧
     (X ((./location) = Address1) ) ) ))
     U ( ((./instruction) = call) ∧ ((./destination)= 71f1a42e))))
```

Property 3: Return Address Protection

```
G ( (./instruction = call ) → (∀ eip ∈ ./locOnStack :
(∀ retAddrVal ∈ ./return-address :((¬ ((./instruction = mov)
∧(./output/value =    eip)) )U
((message/instruction = return )∧ (
message/fonction-returned = retAddrVal ))))))
```

Property 4: Pointer Subterfuge Detection

```
G ( (./rep-Flag=True) →( ∀ addr ∈ ./destination :
( ∀ val ∈ ./value :(¬ (F((./instruction = call)∧
((./locOnStack =    addr) ∧ (./destination =   val)) ))))))
```

Property 5: Malicious Pattern Detection

```
G (∃ retAddrVal ∈ ./return-address : (
    (./instruction = call)∧ (¬ ((F( ((./instruction = mov)
∧ (./output/type = general-register)) →
 (∃ regA ∈ ./output/name : (F (( ((./instruction = mov)
∧ (./output/type = general-register))
∧ (./input/type = litteral) ) →
           (∃ regB ∈ ./output/name :
              ( ∃ constAddr ∈ ./input/value :
                 (F (((./instruction = cmp ) ∧
```

```
           (./output/type = regA))   →
              (∃ loc  ∈ ./location : (F((
((./instruction = mov )  ∧
(./output/type = general-register))  ∧
(./output/name = regA ) ) ∧
((./input/name = regB )  ∧ (./input/type = ptr)))))) ))))) )))
        U((./instruction = return)
          ∧(./fonction-returned = retAddrVal)) )) ))
```

References

1. Becker, D., Wolf, F., Frings, W., Geimer, M., Wylie, B., Mohr, B.: Automatic trace-based performance analysis of metacomputing applications. In: 2007 Parallel and Distributed Processing Symposium, pp. 1–10 (2007)
2. Christodorescu, M., Jha, S., Seshia, S.A., Song, D., Bryant, R.E.: Semantics-aware malware detection. In: Proceedings of the 2005 IEEE Symposium on Security and Privacy, SP 2005, pp. 32–46. IEEE Computer Society, Washington, DC (2005)
3. Dietz, W., Li, P., Regehr, J., Adve, V.: Understanding integer overflow in C/C++. In: Proceedings of the 34th International Conference on Software Engineering, ICSE 2012, pp. 760–770. IEEE Press, Piscataway (2012)
4. Ghiasi, M., Sami, A., Salehi, Z.: Dynamic VSA: a framework for malware detection based on register contents. Eng. Appl. Artif. Intell. **44**, 111–122 (2015)
5. Hallé, S., Villemaire, R.: Runtime enforcement of web service message contracts with data. IEEE Trans. Serv. Comput. **5**(2), 192–206 (2012)
6. Hornat, C.: JPEG vulnerability: a day in the life of the JPEG vulnerability. Technical report, Info Security Writers (2004)
7. Jerding, D., Stasko, J.: The information mural: a technique for displaying and navigating large information spaces. IEEE Trans. Visual. Comput. Graphics **4**(3), 257–271 (1998)
8. Roşu, G., Chen, F., Ball, T.: Synthesizing monitors for safety properties: this time with calls and returns. In: Leucker, M. (ed.) RV 2008. LNCS, vol. 5289, pp. 51–68. Springer, Heidelberg (2008). doi:10.1007/978-3-540-89247-2_4
9. Seacord, R.C.: Secure Coding in C and C++, 2nd edn. Addison-Wesley Professional, Upper Saddle River (2013)
10. Storlie, C., Anderson, B., Wiel, S.V., Quist, D., Hash, C., Brown, N.: Stochastic identification of malware with dynamic traces. Ann. Appl. Stat. **8**(1), 1–18 (2014)

Challenges in Fault-Tolerant Distributed Runtime Verification

Borzoo Bonakdarpour[1]([⊠]), Pierre Fraigniaud[2], Sergio Rajsbaum[3], and Corentin Travers[4]

[1] McMaster University, Hamilton, Canada
borzoo@mcmaster.ca
[2] LIAFA, Paris, France
Pierre.Fraigniaud@liafa.univ-paris-diderot.fr
[3] Instituto de Matemáticas, UNAM, Mexico D.F., Mexico
rajsbaum@im.unam.mx
[4] University of Bordeaux, Bordeaux, France
travers@labri.fr

Abstract. *Runtime Verification* is a lightweight method for monitoring the formal specification of a system (usually in some form of temporal logics) at execution time. In a setting, where a set of distributed monitors have only a partial view of a large system and may be subject to different types of faults, the literature of runtime verification falls short in answering many fundamental questions. Examples include techniques to reason about the soundness and consistency of the collective set of verdicts computed by the set of distributed monitors. In this paper, we discuss open research problems on fault-tolerant distributed monitoring that stem from different design choices and implementation platforms.

1 Introduction

Runtime verification (RV) is concerned with monitoring software and hardware system executions. It is used after deployment of the system for ensuring reliability, safety, and security, and for providing fault containment and recovery. Its essential objective is to determine at run time, whether the system is in a legal or illegal state, with respect to some specification.

1.1 The RV Framework

An RV framework is essentially a two-layered system: the *underlying system*, and the *monitoring system*, interacting through two components. First, a *correctness specification* ϕ, which defines, at any moment during run time, if the underlying system is behaving correctly. Second, a *communication interface*, which is the subsystem stating how both layers communicate with each other. The communication is mainly one way, the monitoring system continuously gets information about the state of the underlying system. Although eventually there should be some way of getting feedback into the underlying system, for the whole setting

© Springer International Publishing AG 2016
T. Margaria and B. Steffen (Eds.): ISoLA 2016, Part II, LNCS 9953, pp. 363–370, 2016.
DOI: 10.1007/978-3-319-47169-3_27

to be useful. As soon as a violation of the legality of the execution is revealed recovery code can be executed for bringing the system back to a legal state, for runtime enforcement. For example, the recovery code can reboot the system, or release its resources. Runtime enforcement aims at guaranteeing desired behaviors, e.g. [8]. The main communication is nevertheless upwards, and it defines what can be observed about the underlying system, by which means, how frequently and how reliably.

One source of difficulties in RV is the *decoupled design* of its two layers. The whole RV system is designed and built by two different parties, one of which does not know about the other. The underlying system is designed, and deployed, perhaps without even considering the possibility that a monitoring system will be built later on. Thus, with no concerns about the communication interface; no provisions for exporting data to a monitoring layer and neither for receiving feedback from it. Also, the correctness specification is not designed with a monitoring system in mind. It may be stated for infinite traces, while at run time, only finite traces are available. There may not exist at all a specification of whether a finite trace is correct or not. In addition, classic specification languages such as LTL are designed for infinite traces. Thus, a main concern in RV is to design finite trace semantics for RV, often based on LTL, and to study which properties are monitorable at run time.

In the simplest scenario, both the underlying system and the monitoring system are considered to be centralized, sequential processes. The underlying system produces *runtime traces*, which are finite sequences of *samples*, where each sample contains relevant information for the monitor about the current underlying system state. The monitoring system receives the sequence of samples as input. Perhaps each sample is triggered by an event in the underlying system or it is requested by demand of the monitoring system. In any case, the monitoring system uses the sequence of samples to successively expand a runtime trace. The goal of the monitoring system is, for each such trace, to emit a *verdict* about the valuation of ϕ. It maybe that a clear violation of correctness is observed on a trace α, or that no violation is seen and cannot happen in the future. But in general, without knowing the future, the problem of what verdict to emit arises. The three-valued logic LTL$_3$ [4] suggests to use the value '?' as a verdict in such a situation, while RV-LTL [3] refines this inconclusive verdict in two, possibly true $\top_p$ and possibly false $\bot_p$ verdicts, and more generally, LTL$_K$ is a family of $(2k+4)$-valued logics, for $k \geq 0$ [7]. For each $k \geq 0$, the kth instance of the family has $2k+4$ truth values, that intuitively represent a *degree of certainty* that the formula is satisfied [7].

1.2   Decentralized RV

In this paper, we are concerned with RV when the underlying system is distributed. It could consist of computer hardware or other interacting machines, or a set of collaborating software components or a mix of both, for example, an aircraft. In this case, it makes sense to deploy monitors at different locations of the underlaying system. Passing messages to a *central* monitor at every event leads to communication bottlenecks, a single point of failure, and delays from far away components of the underlying system to the central monitor. Therefore, recent contributions e.g., [5,6,17,18] on RV of distributed systems assume a set of n monitors observing the behavior of the underlying system, with benefits such as replication (e.g. tolerate failures of the monitors themselves, or failures of sensors) or locality (e.g. a monitor observing some region or component of the underlying system). The monitors communicate with each other, to be able to tolerate failures of the monitors themselves. Also, to be able to evaluate a correctness condition that may depend on samples by several monitors. In short, in *decentralised RV*, both the underlying and the monitoring system are distributed systems.

The specific distributed RV setting depends first of all on which type of distributed system each one of its two layers is. A distributed system is defined by the asynchrony of processes, how they communicate with each other, and by the types of failures that may happen. One may divide them in two classes. Those where the processes can solve consensus, and those where they cannot. When the monitoring system is reliable enough to be able to solve consensus, monitors can exchange samples, and compute a snapshot representing the underlying system state. Then, each one locally can evaluate ϕ on this global state, and emit a verdict. Many papers exists on this scenario, where the concerns are about efficiency, perhaps distribution of the correctness formula, snapshot computation, reaching consensus on the snapshot as fast as possible, and so on, to build a monitoring layer that is as lightweight and quick as possible.

1.3   Distributed RV

In this paper we focus on the issues that arise when the monitoring system itself is distributed, unreliable, and unable to solve consensus. We call this setting *distributed RV*, to distinguish it from the more general decentralised RV. Instead of efficiency considerations, we discuss modeling and computability difficulties that arise in distributed RV. Many other issues related to efficiency in reliable decentralised RV, although they are challenging and important, they are somewhat better understood.

The purpose of this note is to discuss some of the new, fascinating issues that arise in distributed RV, and to discuss some of the existing work, which is far less than the work done on centralized RV. For some of the issues we discuss some possible solutions, for others we leave them open for discussion.

1. How to model an unreliable distributed RV system?
2. How is the correctness of the underlying system specified?
3. How many different verdicts are needed, and what is their meaning?
4. What is the meaning of a set of verdicts emitted by the monitors?
5. What is the process of giving feedback to the underlying system?

2   Challenges in Distributed Monitoring

We present a concrete distributed RV setting, very simple, but that serves as
a basis to discuss the issues mentioned above. There are many other possible
settings, but even in this very ideal setting already interesting difficulties appear.

2.1   A Distributed RV System

*Challenge: how to make sure the monitors take samples about the same global
state of the underlying system?*

We now describe a distributed monitor system with two properties: monitors
are unable to solve consensus, and it is simple. This system is very weak, but
computability issues here extrapolate to other, stronger models, such as message-
passing where at most t monitors may fail by crashing, Byzantine failures and
others [14]. In particular, the following shared-memory model can be simulated
in a message passing system if less than half of the monitors can fail[1] [1].

Assume that the system under inspection produces a finite trace $\alpha =
s_0 s_1 \cdots s_k$ of global states. The trace is inspected with respect to some cor-
rectness specification expressed by a formula φ and a set of monitors $\mathcal{M} =
\{M_1, M_2, \ldots, M_n\}$. The monitors communicate with each other by writing and
reading shared memory registers. They execute the following algorithm.

For every $j \in [0, k-1]$, between each s_j and s_{j+1}, each monitor M_i:

1. takes a sample which results in a *partial* observation of s_j, denoted $\mathcal{S}_i(s_j)$;
2. repeatedly communicates with other monitors through a shared memory, and
3. emits a verdict about the correctness of $\alpha = s_0 s_1 \cdots s_j$.

If the samples $\mathcal{S}_i(s_j)$ *cover* s_j, i.e. collectively have all the information about
s_j, then if the monitors could gather all their samples, they could locally evaluate φ. Instead, we assume each monitor $M_i \in \mathcal{M}$ is a sequential asynchronous
process. It runs at its own speed, that may vary along with time. In step 2,
monitors communicate with each other as much as they want, but a fixed, finite
number of times. Namely, the code that each monitor executes in step 2 consists
of N write and read instructions (no waiting for events in other monitors). We
assume the monitors can communicate fast enough so that the underlying system changes to its new state s_{j+1} only once each monitor has executed its N
instructions.

The monitor system corresponds to a *layered asynchronous wait-free
read/write shared memory* model [16]. In such a model, monitors cannot agree
on a common view about s_j, due to the impossibility of solving consensus [13].
Additional details about fault-tolerant distributed computing appear in standard
textbooks e.g. [2].

---

[1] We work in shared memory because then we can consider runs composed of *any* interleaving of monitor operations, facilitating analysis. Also to including the extreme case
where any number of monitors may fail. In message passing partitions may happen
if half of the monitors can fail.

2.2   Distributed Correctness Specifications

Challenge: how to define a correctness specification in a way that can be evaluated on partial views of the global underlying system state?

An execution of the monitoring system starting in state s_j (step 2 above), consists of an interleaving of the N operations of each one of the n monitors, and furthermore, any interleaving is possible (thus, it is as if monitors may crash, but technically it is not necessary to assume crashes). Consider a monitor M_i, and such an execution α. There is a subset of monitors from which M_i learns their samples: all of the monitors that write their samples to shared registers before M_i reads those registers. Therefore, M_i has to be able to emit its verdict based only on a partial view about s_j. Given that the code executed by the monitors is wait-free, in an extreme case, it is possible that M_i finishes its code before all the other monitors, and its partial view could consists of only its own sample.

It follows from the above discussion there has to be a way for a monitor to emit a verdict based on a partial view of the state. One approach is to assume a list of all possible partial views is given, including a predicate stating if the partial view is correct or not. This type of specification is called a *distributed language* in [10–12], and is used without any formal semantics.

Another approach is to assume that the specification φ was designed for (full) global states of the underlying system only, and use an *extension function* which somehow completes the partial view to a full state that *could* have occurred in the underlying system, as in [7,9]. Care must be taken to ensure that different monitors use extensions on their own partial views that are somehow compatible.

Also, the difficulty remains even in the case that the monitors are much more synchronous and reliable. The partial views will be much more complete, but still consensus is impossible if the monitors may miss at least one sample. Notice that even if monitors are fully synchronous, there are lower bounds on how many rounds of communication are needed to solve consensus [2,16], and thus there may not be enough time to reach consensus in between s_j and s_{j+1}.

2.3   Different Verdicts

Challenge: given that different perspectives about the underlying system state are unavoidable, how should they be used?

Given that in a wait-free distributed monitoring system it is impossible for the monitors to solve consensus, it is unavoidable that different verdicts are emitted. It was shown in [12], that as φ gets more and more "complex," more and more different verdicts have to be used.

Let us consider the following motivating example e.g. [3], of a system in which *requests* are sent by clients, and *acknowledged* by servers. The system is in a legal state if and only if (1) all requests have been acknowledged, and (2) every received acknowledgment corresponds to a previously sent request. Each monitor i is aware of a subset R_i of requests that has been received by the servers, and a subset A_i of acknowledgments that has been sent by the servers. To verify legality of the system, each monitor M_i communicates with other monitors in order to produce some verdict o_i. In a traditional setting of decentralized monitoring, it may be required that the monitors produce opinions $o_i \in \{\text{true}, \text{false}\}$ such that, whenever the system is not in a legal state, at least one monitor produces the opinion false. It was shown in [12] that even if there is only one possible request and one possible acknowledgment, already three different verdicts are needed (with wait-free monitors).

To prove the lower bound on the number of verdicts required, a minimal *consistency* requirement is assumed in [12], stating that the set of verdicts should distinguish correct from incorrect traces. Namely, if a set of verdicts S is emitted on a correct trace, the same set should never be emitted on an incorrect trace.

2.4 Semantics of Verdicts

Challenge: which logic, which semantics should be assigned to an opinion, and which formulas are monitorable under a given distributed model?

Even in centralized RV, it has been observed that we need more than binary verdicts (i.e., true/false) to evaluate a finite trace. In Rv-Ltl [3] four truth values $\mathbb{B}_4 = \{\top, \bot, \top_p, \bot_p\}$ are used. These values identify cases where a finite execution (1) permanently satisfies, (2) permanently violates, (3) presumably satisfies, or (4) presumably violates an Ltl formula. A multi-valued family of temporal logics refining Rv-Ltl was proposed in [7], each one with $2k + 4$ values, denoted Ltl_K, for $k \geq 0$. In particular, Ltl_K coincides with Rv-Ltl when $k = 0$. The syntax of Ltl_K is identical to that of Ltl. Its semantics is based on Fltl [15] and Ltl_3 [4], two Ltl-based finite trace semantics for RV. For each $k \geq 0$, the kth instance of the family has $2k + 4$ truth values, that intuitively represent a *degree of certainty* that the formula is satisfied. In particular, when $t = 2$, the set of truth values $\mathbb{B}_6 = \{\top, \bot, \top_0, \bot_0, \top_1, \bot_1\}$, can be used to monitor a request/acknowledgment formula with two types of requests and acknowledgments. It evaluates to: $\bot_0$ (presumably false with low degree of certainty) in a finite execution that only contains r_1, to $\top_0$ (presumably true with the same degree of certainty) in an execution that includes r_1 and a_1, to $\bot_1$ (presumably false with higher degree of certainty) in an execution that contains r_1, a_1, and r_2, and to $\top_1$ (presumably true with higher degree of certainty) in an execution that contains r_1, a_1, r_2, and a_2.

The Ltl_K logic gives a formal semantics for the verdict of each monitor. It remains an open question how to get a formal semantics for *collections* of opinions emitted by the monitors of a decentralized system.

3   Conclusion

In this short note we are unable to discuss many other interesting issues related to distributed RV. The mechanisms of giving feedback from the monitors to the underlying system have not been studied. Given that each monitor emits a verdict, how and when are the collective verdicts used to give feedback to the underlying system? The simplest approach it to send all the verdicts to a human or machine control center, that decides what to do, but other, more distributed approaches should be studied. The work on wait-free distributed RV [10–12] has focused on studying only one iteration of the algorithm discussed above, namely, where monitors take only one sample, and emit a verdict only once. Many technical issues arise in the general case of repeatedly taking samples.

There are already quite a few papers studying situations where more than one monitor is used, from different angles and using different techniques, and the *Bertinoro Seminar on Distributed Runtime Verification*, May 2016, was devoted to discuss these ideas.

Acknowledgment. This work was partially sponsored by Canada NSERC Discovery Grant 418396-2012 and NSERC Strategic Grants 430575-2012 and 463324-2014, Mexico UNAM-PAPIIT IN107714 and CONACYT-ECOS-NORD grants, as well as the French State, managed by the French National Research Agency (ANR) in the frame of the "Investments for the future" Programme IdEx Bordeaux - CPU (ANR-10-IDEX-03-02).

References

1. Attiya, H., Bar-Noy, A., Dolev, D.: Sharing memory robustly in message-passing systems. J. ACM **42**(1), 124–142 (1995)
2. Attiya, H., Welch, J.: Distributed Computing: Fundamentals, Simulations, and Advanced Topics. Wiley, Chichester (2004)
3. Bauer, A., Leucker, M., Schallhart, C.: Comparing LTL semantics for runtime verification. J. Logic Comput. **20**(3), 651–674 (2010)
4. Bauer, A., Leucker, M., Schallhart, C.: Runtime verification for LTL and TLTL. ACM Trans. Softw. Eng. Methodol. (TOSEM) **20**(4), 14 (2011)
5. Bauer, A., Falcone, Y.: Decentralised LTL monitoring. In: Giannakopoulou, D., Méry, D. (eds.) FM 2012. LNCS, vol. 7436, pp. 85–100. Springer, Heidelberg (2012). doi:10.1007/978-3-642-32759-9_10
6. Berkovich, S., Bonakdarpour, B., Fischmeister, S.: Runtime verification with minimal intrusion through parallelism. Formal Methods Syst. Des. (FMSD) **46**(3), 317–348 (2015)
7. Bonakdarpour, B., Fraigniaud, P., Rajsbaum, S., Rosenblueth, D.A., Travers, C.: Decentralized asynchronous crash-resilient runtime verification. In: Proceedings of the 27th International Conference on Concurrency Theory (CONCUR) (2016, to appear)
8. Falcone, Y.: You should better enforce than verify. In: Barringer, H., Falcone, Y., Finkbeiner, B., Havelund, K., Lee, I., Pace, G., Roşu, G., Sokolsky, O., Tillmann, N. (eds.) RV 2010. LNCS, vol. 6418, pp. 89–105. Springer, Heidelberg (2010). doi:10.1007/978-3-642-16612-9_9
9. Falcone, Y., Cornebize, T., Fernandez, J.-C.: Efficient and generalized decentralized monitoring of regular languages. In: Ábrahám, E., Palamidessi, C. (eds.) FORTE 2014. LNCS, vol. 8461, pp. 66–83. Springer, Heidelberg (2014). doi:10.1007/978-3-662-43613-4_5

10. Fraigniaud, P., Rajsbaum, S., Roy, M., Travers, C.: The opinion number of set-agreement. In: Aguilera, M.K., Querzoni, L., Shapiro, M. (eds.) OPODIS 2014. LNCS, vol. 8878, pp. 155–170. Springer, Heidelberg (2014). doi:10.1007/978-3-319-14472-6_11

11. Fraigniaud, P., Rajsbaum, S., Travers, C.: Locality and checkability in wait-free computing. Distrib. Comput. **26**(4), 223–242 (2013)

12. Fraigniaud, P., Rajsbaum, S., Travers, C.: On the number of opinions needed for fault-tolerant run-time monitoring in distributed systems. In: Bonakdarpour, B., Smolka, S.A. (eds.) RV 2014. LNCS, vol. 8734, pp. 92–107. Springer, Heidelberg (2014). doi:10.1007/978-3-319-11164-3_9

13. Herlihy, M.: Wait-free synchronization. ACM Trans. Program. Lang. Syst. **13**(1), 124–149 (1991)

14. Herlihy, M., Kozlov, D., Rajsbaum, S.: Distributed Computing Through Combinatorial Topology. Morgan Kaufmann-Elsevier, Boston (2013)

15. Manna, Z., Pnueli, A.: Temporal Verification of Reactive Systems - Safety. Springer, New York (1995)

16. Moses, Y., Rajsbaum, S.: A layered analysis of consensus. SIAM J. Comput. **31**(4), 989–1021 (2002)

17. Mostafa, M., Bonakdarpour, B.: Decentralized runtime verification of LTL specifications in distributed systems. In: International Parallel and Distributed Processing Symposium (IPDPS) (2015)

18. Sen, K., Vardhan, A., Agha, G., Rosu, G.: Decentralized runtime analysis of multi-threaded applications. In: International Parallel and Distributed Processing Symposium (IPDPS) (2006)

The HARMONIA Project: Hardware Monitoring for Automotive Systems-of-Systems

Thang Nguyen[3], Ezio Bartocci[1(✉)], Dejan Ničković[2], Radu Grosu[1],
Stefan Jaksic[1,2], and Konstantin Selyunin[1]

[1] Technische Universität Wien, Treitlstrasse 3, Vienna, Austria
{ezio.bartocci,radu.grosu,konstantin.selyunin}@tuwien.ac.at
[2] Austrian Institute of Technology (AIT), Donau-City-Strasse 1, Vienna, Austria
{dejan.nickovic,stefan.jaksic.fl}@ait.ac.at
[3] Infineon Technologies Austria AG, Siemenstrasse 2, Villach, Austria
thang.nguyen@infineon.com

Abstract. The verification of complex mixed-signal integrated circuit products in the automotive industry accounts for around 60%–70% of the total development time. In such scenario, any effort to reduce the design and verification costs and to improve the time-to-market and the product quality will play an important role to boost up the competitiveness of the automotive industry.

The aim of the HARMONIA project is to provide a framework for assertion-based monitoring of automotive systems-of-systems with mixed criticality. It will enable a uniform way to reason about both safety-critical correctness and non-critical robustness properties of such systems. Observers embedded on FPGA hardware will be generated from assertions, and used for monitoring automotive designs emulated on hardware. The project outcome will improve the competitiveness of the automotive application oriented nano and microelectronics industry by reducing verification time and cost in the development process.

1 Introduction

Verification & Validation of complex mixed-signal integrated circuit products in industrial practice accounts for 60–70% of project development time. Our work aims to reduce verification time and effort. It is known that simulation, which is the dominant method for pre-silicon verification, does not scale due to immense computing requirements. The increasing trend to overcome the simulation bottleneck is to complement it with the emulation based approach: the designed system is replaced by an early prototype implemented using Field Programmable Gate Array (FPGA) allowing long-term/stress testing and whole-range parameter variations, which is usually limited to small examples with simulation-based verification [1–4]. Design emulation techniques also allow one to approximate an analog component with discretized behavioral model, therefore enabling end-to-end testing early on. However, verification techniques used with the emulation-based approach involve manual tasks, making them error-prone and time consuming.

© Springer International Publishing AG 2016
T. Margaria and B. Steffen (Eds.): ISoLA 2016, Part II, LNCS 9953, pp. 371–379, 2016.
DOI: 10.1007/978-3-319-47169-3_28

In this scenario, the goal of the Austrian FFG-funded HARMONIA project is to improve the verification techniques of the emulation-based approach by combining assertion-based runtime verification with design emulation. In this framework we employ *Signal Temporal Logic* (STL) [5] as specification language to express the desired requirements. STL has a rigorous syntax and semantics supporting the specification in a concise and intuitive way of complex timing relations between analog and digital signals. In [6], we introduce novel algorithms for translating STL specifications to hardware runtime monitors implemented in FPGA. Our recent finding in [7] shows also a direct connection between temporal logic and filtering, which allows to freely navigate between realms of logic and signal processing [8–10].

The STL qualitative semantics decides whether a signal satisfies or violates a given requirement by providing a true/false verdict. However, in case of analog signals, noise and jitter may affect the correctness verdict based on hard satisfaction threshold. Indeed, the qualitative semantics is not always enough informative. For this reason, we also consider the problem of quantifying the satisfaction or violation of an analog signal w.r.t. STL specifications. In the last decade, several STL quantitative semantics [3,7,11–13] have been introduced to provide suitable measures of satisfaction or violation. In particular, in [11,12] the classic satisfaction relation between a signal and an STL formula is replaced with the notion of *robustness degree* which shows precisely how far is the behavior from satisfying a requirement in STL. Conversely, if the behavior satisfies the formula then the robustness degree will quantify the distance from the nearest incorrect behavior [11]. The robustness degree can be used to automatically guide the input and the parameter space exploration enabling the *falsification analysis* [3,4] or the *parameter synthesis* [1,2,14] of the emulated or simulated *system under test* (SUT). In a recent work [13], we tackle this problem by adopting a novel quantitative semantics for STL formulas and by introducing an effective online algorithm for computing the robustness degree using FPGA.

In this project we also explore how novel hardware architectures based on spiking neural networks can be used to monitor a temporal specification. IBM recently revealed such an architecture called TrueNorth. In [15] we show how to apply the underlying TrueNorth model for runtime monitoring of Metric Temporal Logic (MTL) properties. Having identified how to recognize MTL operators with TrueNorth, we are able to build neural monitors from MTL formulae. Since our ultimate goal is to build hardware monitors that provide both qualitative and quantitative information we see TrueNorth as a perfect candidate for our framework. In [16] we have also shown how one can employ smooth neuronal behavior in programming constructs to make robust decisions.

In this paper we provide an overview of our experience in the HARMONIA project with the application of assertion-based runtime verification techniques combined with design emulation. The paper is organised as follows: Sect. 2 presents the assertion-based monitoring framework employed in HARMONIA, Sect. 3 shows the complete flow from an STL specification to hardware monitor synthesis, Sect. 4 introduces a recent novel technique to online monitor the robustness degree using *edit distance*, Sect. 5 presents an industrial case study that would benefit from the application of the techniques developed within the HARMONIA project and in Sect. 6 we conclude.

2   Assertion Based Monitoring

HARMONIA aims at advancing the state-of-the-art in design and verification of heterogeneous *systems-of-systems* (SoS) with mixed-criticality, involving complex interaction of digital and analogue elements.

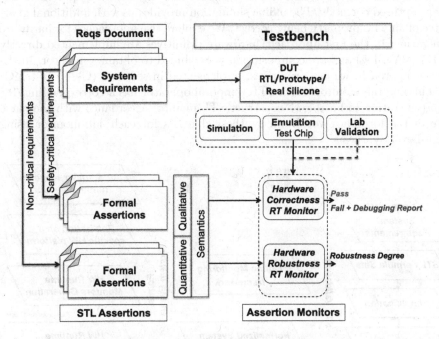

Fig. 1. HARMONIA assertion-based monitoring framework

The goal of the project is to provide an assertion-based formal framework for assessing correctness and robustness of heterogeneous SoS, emulated on hardware test chips. This framework, illustrated in Fig. 1, targets the problems and challenges and results in:

- Enabling formal specification of rich mixed-signal mixed-criticality properties involving complex logical and timing relations between events in digital and analogue signals;
- Providing a qualitative and quantitative interpretations of STL assertions over mixed-analog signals;
- Enabling automatic generation of hardware online monitors from formal assertions that will observe emulated data in real-time and assess their correctness and/or robustness with respect to the design specification.

3   Hardware Monitors Generation

In Fig. 2 we provide an overview of the *complete flow* for the hardware monitor generation, from natural language requirements to a synthesizable HDL code using STL as a specification language and two approaches for hardware generation. First, time invariant system requirements must be formalized to obtain a set of STL formulae which are used for hardware monitor generation. The formulae to be hardware-synthesizable need to be converted in a specific format (containing only past temporal operators i.e. pastified) and simplified. We use these formulae after the conversion step to simulate and check if the requirement has been captured correctly. The offline simulation provides us with additional guarantee of an STL property being correct. We explore two approaches for hardware generation. In the first approach, hardware primitives are implemented directly in HDL (Verilog) and are compositionally combined to obtain a monitor. In the second approach, we use primitives, implemented in software (C++/SystemC) for building the monitor. Each STL temporal operator has a corresponding C++ implementation to be able to construct STL monitor accordance with the parse tree of the formula. We obtain synthesizable IPs for each sub-monitor using High-Level Synthesis.

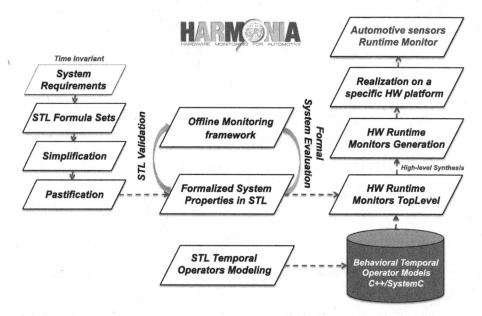

Fig. 2. Hardware runtime STL monitor generation flow using high-level synthesis at Infineon Technologies Austria AG

3.1   From Signal Temporal Logic to FPGA Monitors

In [6] we show in detail how to automatically generate a hardware monitor from an arbitrary STL formula with past and bounded future timing operators.

We do not allow unbounded future operators because our monitors are based on deterministic temporal testers [17]. Formulas with bounded future operators are transformed into equisatisfiable formulas using only past temporal operators according to the procedure from [18]. In this case, the verdict will be delayed to the max interval of time needed to decide whether the formula is satisfied or violated. We use the compositional approach to build complex testers from basic ones which relate to specific timing operators. Furthermore, we introduce an algorithm for evaluating specific temporal operators efficiently [6]. For the testers that are difficult to implement directly (e.g. bounded until or bounded since require significant hardware resources), we use rewriting rules to express them as a combination of simple temporal operator testers. Analog signals of STL are handled by analog-to-digital (ADC) converters and comparators inside FPGA logic. In [6] we also present evaluation results which expose resource consumption of specific types of formulas.

3.2 Monitoring of MTL Specifications with IBM's Spiking-Neuron Model

In [15] we implement monitors for MTL specifications on top of our hardware implementation of the IBM's TrueNorth model. IBM in a series of papers [19] revealed a purely digital spiking neuron model, which is suitable for the hardware implementation. In [15] we show how to build hardware monitors using this model for a past fragment of MTL.

A monitor for an MTL formula is seen as a neural circuit, which we construct compositionally from sub-parts that recognize logical and temporal operators. To obtain the behaviour which corresponds to MTL operators we need to instantiate parameters of neurons. We formulate a set of constraints that restrict the behaviour and use integer linear programming to find the parameters of neurons.

In this work we also explore how High Level Synthesis (HLS) from C/C++ can be applied for synthesizing hardware monitors. Given an MTL specification that describes a missile launch from a battle ship we show how one can obtain a hardware neural monitor using HLS and our C++ implementation.

4   Quantitative Monitoring of STL with Edit Distance

In [13] we introduce a novel quantitative semantics for STL which computes the robustness degree w.r.t. an analog signal taking in consideration both the *amplitude noise* and the *timing jitter*. We interpret STL over discrete time digitized behaviors because continuous real-valued signals are discretized in time and value domain by an ADC. As a distance measure for quantifying the amplitude noise and timing jitter differences, we adopt *weighted edit distance* (WED) which can be defined as the total cost of all the insert, delete and substitution operations necessary to transform one signal into another. Conversely to Hamming and edit distance, the WED takes into account the actual difference between the signals' values, rather than assigning fixed cost for substitutions. This way the WED expresses the amplitude difference more precisely. Since weighted edit distance includes insert and delete operations it exactly reflects signal similarity in case where other point-wise based distances such as Hamming distance fail: i.e. in case of same signals are shifted by a constant time.

In [13] we develop an efficient on-line algorithm for computing the robustness degree of a STL formula w.r.t. to a discretized signal. We create a structure called *weighted symbolic automaton* (WSA) by adding additional transitions for delete, insert and substitute operations to a regular language acceptor for specified STL formula. The algorithm calculates WED by searching for the shortest paths to any of the accepting states in WSA.

5 Automotive Sensor Interface Runtime Monitor Case Study

As case study within HARMONIA, we would like to evaluate the new developed assertion-based monitoring methodology on the modern automotive system application such as airbag application, electronic power steering or electronic throttle control for engine management with a special focus on the sensor interface using PSI5, SPC or SENT communication protocol. Figure 3 illustrates an electronic throttle control system for engine management application while Fig. 4 illustrates the Infineon Technologies Chipset solution for Engine Management, including Electronic Throttle Control. These sensors constantly measure different information happening during the system runtime (such as deceleration force, pressure, steering wheel angle or the position of the accelerator pedal) and provide them to the main micro-controller for further data processing and actualization of the application.

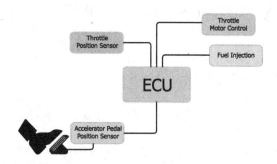

Fig. 3. Electronic throttle control for engine management

According to the state-of-practice, verification (computer-based simulation) and validation (lab evaluation) of such sensor interfaces become challenging tasks for the following reasons:

- Verification for the sensor interfaces has to cover real-time embedded mixed signal domains.

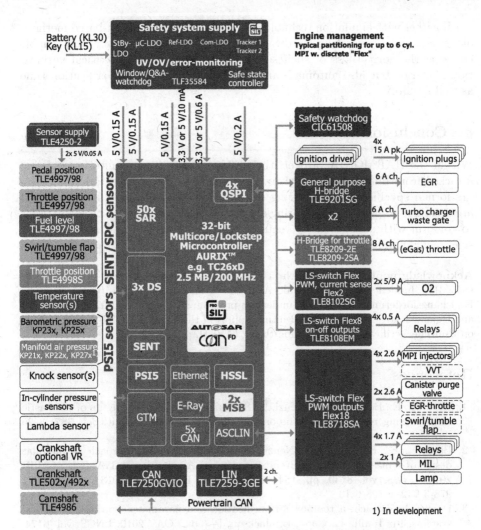

Fig. 4. Infineon Technologies engine management chipset solution

- Failure during the reception, decoding and processing of sensor data in system electronic controller can lead to unexpected or false events which might put human safety in violation.
- Most of the functionalities of sensor interfaces can only be verified at the system level of the chip and at the system application level. Only using classical mixed-signal simulation approach becomes a bottle neck.
- Many verification scenarios of the sensor interfaces such as long-term verification run with checking of millions sensor data frames are not suitable using computer-based simulation as well as manual sensor data evaluation/checking method.

Together with emulation technologies, HARMONIA assertion-based methodology including generating hardware runtime monitor shall not only enable checking the correctness of such sensor interfaces over those critical verification scenarios but also automate and significantly reduce the verification time as well as effort.

6   Conclusion

Within the HARMONIA project, the problem of runtime monitoring is being attacked from different perspectives. Generating hardware monitors, interpreting formal specification, measuring distance between signals and using neural architectures to perform monitoring are the research questions to tackle in order to conform with stricter safety requirements in automotive and make systems safe, reliable and robust.

Acknowledgment. This research is supported by the project HARMONIA (845631), funded by a national Austrian grant from FFG (Österreichische Forschungsförderungsgesellschaft) under the program IKT der Zukunft. Ezio Bartocci and Dejan Ničković acknowledge also the support of the EU ICT COST Action IC1402 on Runtime Verification beyond Monitoring (ARVI).

References

1. Bartocci, E., Bortolussi, L., Nenzi, L., Sanguinetti, G.: System design of stochastic models using robustness of temporal properties. Theor. Comput. Sci. **587**, 3–25 (2015)
2. Bartocci, E., Bortolussi, L., Nenzi, L.: A temporal logic approach to modular design of synthetic biological circuits. In: Gupta, A., Henzinger, T.A. (eds.) CMSB 2013. LNCS, vol. 8130, pp. 164–177. Springer, Heidelberg (2013). doi:10.1007/978-3-642-40708-6_13
3. Donzé, A.: Breach, a toolbox for verification and parameter synthesis of hybrid systems. In: Touili, T., Cook, B., Jackson, P. (eds.) CAV 2010. LNCS, vol. 6174, pp. 167–170. Springer, Heidelberg (2010). doi:10.1007/978-3-642-14295-6_17
4. Annpureddy, Y., Liu, C., Fainekos, G., Sankaranarayanan, S.: S-TaLiRo: a tool for temporal logic falsification for hybrid systems. In: Abdulla, P.A., Leino, K.R.M. (eds.) TACAS 2011. LNCS, vol. 6605, pp. 254–257. Springer, Heidelberg (2011). doi:10.1007/978-3-642-19835-9_21
5. Maler, O., Nickovic, D.: Monitoring properties of analog and mixed-signal circuits. Int. J. Softw. Tools Technol. Transfer **15**(3), 247–268 (2013)
6. Jaksic, S., Bartocci, E., Grosu, R., Kloibhofer, R., Nguyen, T., Ničković, D.: From signal temporal logic to FPGA monitors. In: Proceedings of MEMOCODE 2015: The ACM/IEEE International Conference on Formal Methods and Models for Codesign, pp. 218–227. IEEE (2015)
7. Rodionova, A., Bartocci, E., Ničković, D., Grosu, R.: Temporal logic as filtering. In: Proceedings of HSCC 2016: The 19th ACM International Conference on Hybrid Systems: Computation and Control, pp. 11–20. ACM (2016)

8. Donzé, A., Maler, O., Bartocci, E., Nickovic, D., Grosu, R., Smolka, S.: On temporal logic and signal processing. In: Chakraborty, S., Mukund, M. (eds.) ATVA 2012. LNCS, vol. 7561, pp. 92–106. Springer, Heidelberg (2012). doi:10.1007/978-3-642-33386-6_9

9. Bartocci, E., Bortolussi, L., Sanguinetti, G.: Data-driven statistical learning of temporal logic properties. In: Legay, A., Bozga, M. (eds.) FORMATS 2014. LNCS, vol. 8711, pp. 23–37. Springer, Heidelberg (2014). doi:10.1007/978-3-319-10512-3_3

10. Bufo, S., Bartocci, E., Sanguinetti, G., Borelli, M., Lucangelo, U., Bortolussi, L.: Temporal logic based monitoring of assisted ventilation in intensive care patients. In: Margaria, T., Steffen, B. (eds.) ISoLA 2014. LNCS, vol. 8803, pp. 391–403. Springer, Heidelberg (2014). doi:10.1007/978-3-662-45231-8_30

11. Fainekos, G.E., Pappas, G.J.: Robust sampling for MITL specifications. In: Raskin, J.-F., Thiagarajan, P.S. (eds.) FORMATS 2007. LNCS, vol. 4763, pp. 147–162. Springer, Heidelberg (2007). doi:10.1007/978-3-540-75454-1_12

12. Donzé, A., Maler, O.: Robust satisfaction of temporal logic over real-valued signals. In: Chatterjee, K., Henzinger, T.A. (eds.) FORMATS 2010. LNCS, vol. 6246, pp. 92–106. Springer, Heidelberg (2010). doi:10.1007/978-3-642-15297-9_9

13. Jaksic, S., Bartocci, E., Grosu, R., Ničković, D.: Quantitative monitoring of stl with edit distance. In: Proceedings of RV 2016: The 16th International Conference on Runtime Verification. LNCS (2016, to appear)

14. Bartocci, E., Bortolussi, L., Nenzi, L., Sanguinetti, G.: On the robustness of temporal properties for stochastic models. In: Proceedings of HSB 2013: The Second International Workshop on Hybrid Systems and Biology. EPTCS, vol. 125, pp. 3–19 (2013)

15. Selyunin, K., Nguyen, T., Bartocci, E., Ničković, D., Grosu, R.: Monitoring of MTL specifications with IBM's spiking-neuron model. In: Proceedings of DATE 2016: The 19th Design, Automation and Test in Europe Conference and Exhibition, pp. 924–929. IEEE (2016)

16. Selyunin, K., Ratasich, D., Bartocci, E., Islam, M.A., Smolka, S.A., Grosu, R.: Neural programming: towards adaptive control in cyber-physical systems. In: Proceedings of CDC 2015: The 54th IEEE Conference on Decision and Control, pp. 6978–6985. IEEE (2015)

17. Pnueli, A., Zaks, A.: On the merits of temporal testers. In: Grumberg, O., Veith, H. (eds.) 25MC Festschrift. LNCS, vol. 5000, pp. 172–195. Springer, Heidelberg (2008). doi:10.1007/978-3-540-69850-0_11

18. Maler, O., Nickovic, D., Pnueli, A.: On synthesizing controllers from bounded-response properties. In: Damm, W., Hermanns, H. (eds.) CAV 2007. LNCS, vol. 4590, pp. 95–107. Springer, Heidelberg (2007). doi:10.1007/978-3-540-73368-3_12

19. Cassidy, A.S., Merolla, P., Arthur, J.V., Esser, S.K., Jackson, B., Alvarez-icaza, R., Datta, P., Sawada, J., Wong, T.M., Feldman, V., Amir, A., dayan Rubin, D.B., Mcquinn, E., Risk, W.P., Modha, D.S.: Cognitive computing building block: a versatile and efficient digital neuron model for neurosynaptic cores. In: Proceedings of IJCNN 2013: The IEEE International Joint Conference on Neural Networks. IEEE (2013)

Runtime Verification for Interconnected Medical Devices

Martin Leucker, Malte Schmitz[✉], and Danilo à Tellinghusen

Institute for Software Engineering and Programming Languages,
Universität zu Lübeck, Lübeck, Germany
{leucker,schmitz,tellinghusen}@isp.uni-luebeck.de

Abstract. In this tool paper we present a software development kit (SDK) for the Open Surgical Communication Protocol (OSCP) that supports the development of interconnected medical devices according to the recent IEEE 11073 standards for interoperable medical device communication. Building on service-oriented architecture (SOA), dynamically interconnected medical devices publish their connectivity interface, via which these systems provide data and can be controlled. To achieve the safety requirements necessary for medical devices, our tool, the OSCP Device Modeler, allows the specification of temporal assertions for the respective data streams of the systems and generates automatically corresponding monitors that may be used during testing, but also during the application in field to ensure adherence to the interface specification. A further tool, the OSCP Swiss Army Knife, allows subscribing to the services provided via the interfaces of the system under development and thereby supports its debugging. The whole OSCP SDK makes heavy use of runtime verification techniques and shows their advantages in this application area.

1 Introduction

To enhance the overall functionality of medical devices, their interconnection is a current trend. Within the OR.NET project[1], an open protocol for the interconnection of medical devices has been developed and standardized and is expected to become a typical solution for the communication among medical devices [3].

As in many cases whenever humans' life may depend on the correct functionality of a device, there are strict rules for its development and most medical devices have to be certified before their operation in the field is allowed.[2]

This work is supported in part by the European Cooperation in Science and Technology (COST Action ARVI), the BMBF project CONIRAS under number 01IS13029, and the BMBF project OR.NET under number 16KT1231.

[1] www.ornet.org.

[2] Strictly speaking, a medical device with high criticality level has to be declared as conformant to the underlying medical device by its manufacturer with consultation of a so-called notified body checking that the conformance declaration follows the rules. For simplicity, we use the term *certification* here anyway.

T. Margaria and B. Steffen (Eds.): ISoLA 2016, Part II, LNCS 9953, pp. 380–387, 2016.
DOI: 10.1007/978-3-319-47169-3_29

In this paper we present a software development kit (SDK) comprising two tools simplifying the development of safe and reliable medical devices. The first tool, called MD Modeler, helps in defining a clear and precise (network) interface of the system under development as well as giving evidence that it adheres to given correctness properties. The second tool, called OSCP Swiss Army Knife, helps in debugging the medical devices via its network interface.

The communication solution developed within OR.NET is called the *Open Surgical Communication Protocol (OSCP)*, comes in three different layers and basically builds on top of a service-oriented architecture (SOA) with an implementation in terms of web services. The main idea is that devices within the network of the medical units publish their services and clients may connect via well-defined interfaces. Via these interfaces the corresponding devices can also be controlled. As for any interface – let it be human or let it be device-driven – a risk analysis has to be performed when developing medical devices. The risk analysis together with corresponding risk control measures ensures that the corresponding device is most likely only used in the intended fashion [6].

To ensure such a controlled usage of the medical device, we have proposed

1. that the interface for medical devices is formalized in a precise manner together with (temporal) constraints putting additional restrictions on its usage and
2. a monitoring layer ensuring the adherence to the given constraints plus fallback mechanisms whenever a mismatch between the actual usage at runtime and the constraints is detected [9,13].

The first tool of our SDK, the OSCP Device Modeler, helps in realizing this concept. Its web-based interface allows the specification of both the interface definition as well as the additional constraints. Moreover, a Java skeleton for the interface plus corresponding monitoring code can be synthesized automatically simplifying both the development of connective medical devices as well as the monitoring layer considerably. As the monitoring layer is synthesized automatically from high-level specifications it is expected that a certification of the resulting system is simplified a lot, since we realized a clear separation of concerns: the concern of checking the right properties as well as having the right code for checking the properties. To the best of our knowledge no such tool has existed before. Moreover we believe that our tool is the first targeting the simplification of certification by using runtime verification techniques.

The second tool in our SDK, the OSCP Swiss Army Knife, is a network-based debugging tool. It allows to join an existing connected set of medical devices and to show their interfaces as well as the current values of the systems participating in the network. Using the published information about the methods for changing the system's parameters it also allows to steer the corresponding devices. The distinguishing feature of our debugging tool, however, is its ability to check for temporal correctness properties. Interconnected devices, such as medical devices, often follow a sequence of protocol steps for the exchange of data. Likewise a debugging tool should support checking for the correctness of such execution sequences. The OSCP Swiss Army Knife allows the formulation of such correctness properties in temporal logic at runtime and to synthesize monitors that are deployed in the network consisting of the connected medical devices and will then check corresponding properties.

Such monitors may be used to find bugs in the system but may also be used to identify points of interests in the execution sequence of the systems. We are not aware of any similar tool that allows the specification of temporal patterns to identify these points of interest at runtime. While on the one hand it is limited to examining the system via its network interface, on the other hand our method does – in contrast to many existing runtime verification approaches – not require the re-compilation of the system under test and does not interfere with its main functionality or its timing behavior.

The paper is organized as follows:

- Section 2 describes the communication protocol and the basics of our runtime verification approach and
- Sections 3 and 4 introduce the two main tools of our SDK.

2   Preliminaries

OSCP consists of the data transmission technology Medical Device Profile for Web Services (MDPWS), standardized as IEEE 11073-20702 (see [7]), and the domain information and service model, standardized as IEEE 11073-10207 (see [8]). MDPWS is based on a SOA and allows devices to find each other in a local network using WS-Discovery.

The domain information provides a generic framework which is used to describe configuration parameters and measured values of a medical device in terms of physical quantities and units. A medical device publishes this description along with the current values in the network. Clients can subscribe to changes of these values and are notified either periodically after a specific amount of time or episodically for every change. Furthermore the service model is used to describe how clients can control a medical device through its public interface.

As already stated in the introduction, we want to assert the correct temporal behavior of the medical devices regarding their network interfaces. The devices' state changes over time can be seen as a sequence of states. We call such a sequence the run of a medical device. We want to express correctness properties regarding the run of a medical device and monitor at runtime whether the interface of a medical device fulfills this correctness property. We call a finite prefix of the run an execution of the medical device, which grows with every new state. Doing runtime monitoring means we want to create a monitor which tells us at every step whether the current execution satisfies the property [10,12].

Our tools support several temporal logics for the specification of the correctness properties:

- ω-regular expressions,
- Linear Temporal Logic (LTL, [14]),

– Smart Assertion Logic for Temporal Logic (SALT, [1]), which adds syntactic sugar to LTL and
– regular LTL (RLTL, [11,15]), which offers the expressiveness of regular expressions while being as applicable to the domain of temporal specifications as LTL.

In order to evaluate the properties on executions, we adopt the LTL_3 semantics [2] to all the logics mentioned before. Hence our monitors report fulfillment or violation of the correctness properties as soon as possible while the execution continuously grows.

Each of the available logics uses atomic propositions as basic building blocks. Our tools allow the specification of these propositions as comparison of variables published by the medical device either with constants or other variables of the same or another medical device. New states of the execution are created based on variables changing their values. Hence along with a specification formula we need to define the list of its change-inducing variables.

3   OSCP Device Modeler

The OSCP device description provides a generic formalism to describe the (network) interface of a medical device. We enrich this description with (temporal) constraints putting additional restrictions on its usage. At runtime the device needs to check the adherence to these constraints.

The Device Modeler supports the process of developing network interfaces for medical devices: It provides a graphical user interface to design a MD description and it generates source code which publishes the interface description and the current values to the network. The generated code is also capable of handling incoming requests changing the devices parameters and controlling the device and contains synthesized monitors continuously enforcing the (temporal) constraints by rejecting requests which would lead to invalid states. The generated code can either be used as network interface for a real medical device or without further need of writing any code as a stand-alone simulator.

The Device Modeler is a web application written in Ruby on Rails. It is equipped with a modern HTML5 front end guiding the user through the definition of the device description (see Fig. 1, left). Users can create new devices from scratch or import existing XML serializations of device descriptions. The user input is stored in an internal database, which allows users to store and maintain their device modelings. The back end uses Rails' default template engine ERB to generate Java code using the OSCP library OpenSDC[3], which is the reference implementation for the OSCP standard [4,5].

Along with the device description, the user can specify (temporal) correctness properties for the device in the front end of the Device Modeler. These correctness properties are synthesized in monitors: We use our library LamaConv[4] to

---

[3] sf.net/projects/opensdc/.
[4] www.isp.uni-luebeck.de/lamaconv.

translate the specified formula into a deterministic Moore machine using an adopted LTL$_3$ monitor synthesis [2]. The current valuation for all propositions used in the formula serves as input for the monitor.

In case of any change of the devices values, the monitor compares the updated values with the change-inducing variables of its formula. If the change induces a new state as described in the previous section, the monitor computes the valuations for all its propositions using the current properties of the model. These valuations are then used as input for the Moore machine. The output of the monitor can naturally be used for debugging and logging purposes, but furthermore the user of the Device Modeler can also demand that the value changes of the defined metrics must fulfill the specified correctness properties. Any change either through the local UI or the network layer that would break the correctness property will be rejected in this case.

4   OSCP Swiss Army Knife

While the Device Modeler allows us to automatically synthesize monitors when generating the code for the network interface of the device, it is also desirable for debugging purposes to synthesize monitors checking the correct behavior of the interconnected devices at runtime without restarting the system. The Swiss Army Knife is a generic client which can connect to all available medical devices in an OSCP network. It allows the user to inspect the devices' descriptions and current states as well as watch the state changes over time, either manually or with synthesized monitors checking the adherence of the system to user defined correctness properties.

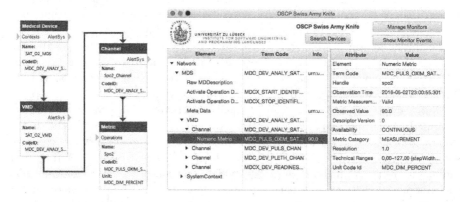

Fig. 1. Screenshot of modeling a pulse oximeter in the Device Modeler's GUI (left) and inspecting the running pulse oximeter with the Swiss Army Knife (right).

In order to do this, the Swiss Army Knife subscribes to all devices available in the local network using the OSCP library OSCLib[5]. It is written in Scala and uses

---

[5] www.surgitaix.com/cms/osclib.

the C++ library OSCLib through Java SWIG[6] wrappers. The GUI is written
in ScalaFX[7] and consists of a tree table view displaying the hierarchical device
descriptions of all available devices (see Fig. 1, right). The values of the devices
are automatically updated in the GUI by callbacks registered with the OSCLib.
Attributes of interest for the monitoring are stored in JavaFX properties which
are updated along with the GUI in the OSCLib callbacks. This way multiple
monitors can easily observe the same property and receive its values in case of
any change.

A monitor observes the JavaFX properties of its change-inducing variables in
order to generate a new execution state every time any of them change. Then the
monitors behave the same as the one generated by the Device Modeler described
in the last section. They evaluate the propositions based on the current values
of the involved properties. Each event handled by a monitor is displayed on the
GUI in the event log together with the current valuation of the watched variables
and the current output of the monitor is displayed in the list of monitors.

As an example consider a foot switch controlling a pump. If the foot switch's
value changes from OPEN to PRESSED, the pump's state must either change from
ON to OFF or from OFF to ON. Note the usage of the SALT operator nextn[2]
which translates to two nested next operators in LTL.

```
assert always (("@switch.value = OPEN" and next "@switch.value = PRESSED") implies
  ((next "@pump.value = ON" and nextn[2] "@pump.value = OFF") or
   (next "@pump.value = OFF" and nextn[2] "@pump.value = ON")))
-- on change of switch.value and pump.value
```

The above example shows how the Swiss Army Knife can be used as a non-
invasive inspection tool in order to monitor the correct behavior of the connected
medical devices. Furthermore this generic client is able to manipulate the configuration parameters and take control over the available devices. Such invocations
trigger changes of the published values of the devices as well, which are again
recognized by the monitors. This way one does not have to wait for edge cases
to occur in order to monitor them, but can induce them manually.

The defined monitors can be edited at any time and can be activated and
paused independently. As described in the section on runtime verification above
the monitors can be defined in regular expressions, LTL, RLTL and SALT. The
editor supports syntax highlighting, auto-completion and in-place error annotations. All defined monitors are automatically stored in a simple XML serialization and restored with every program start.

The Swiss Army Knife will be made available for evaluation, education and
teaching purpose[8].

---

[6] www.swig.org.

[7] www.scalafx.org.

[8] www.isp.uni-luebeck.de/oscp.

5 Conclusion

In this paper we have presented the OSCP SDK that simplifies implementation and testing of medical devices using communication libraries OpenSDC and OSCLib. Its two tools, the OSCP Device Modeler and the OSCP Swiss Army Knife, allow the specification of correctness properties using benefits of the well-known established techniques of LTL_3 and SALT and make use of runtime verification to ensure safe interconnection of medical devices. The OSCP Swiss Army Knife allows the user to synthesize and use monitors for debugging at runtime while the OSCP Device Modeler adds monitors to the devices which adds an additional safety layer to their network interface. Thus, both tools use runtime verification in practical applications adding value for industrial users.

References

1. Bauer, A., Leucker, M.: The theory and practice of SALT. In: Bobaru, M., Havelund, K., Holzmann, G.J., Joshi, R. (eds.) NFM 2011. LNCS, vol. 6617, pp. 13–40. Springer, Heidelberg (2011). doi:10.1007/978-3-642-20398-5_3
2. Bauer, A., Leucker, M., Schallhart, C.: Runtime verification for LTL and TLTL. ACM Trans. Softw. Eng. Methodol. **20**(4), 14:1–14:64 (2011)
3. Birkle, M., Bergh, B.: OR.NET: Ein Projekt auf dem Weg zur sicheren dynamischen Vernetzung in OP und Klinik. In: Jahrestagung der Gesellschaft für Informatik e.V. (GI), vol. 208, pp. 1235–1236. GI (2012)
4. Gregorczyk, D., Bußhaus, T., Fischer, S.: Systems, signals and devices (SSD). In: SDD, pp. 1–6. IEEE (2012)
5. Gregorczyk, D., Fischer, S., Busshaus, T., Schlichting, S., Pöhlsen, S.: Workshop on medical cyber-physical systems. In: MedCPS. OASIcs, vol. 36, pp. 15–27. Dagstuhl (2014)
6. Johner, C., Wittorf, S., Hölzer-Klüpfel, M.: Basiswissen Medizinische Software. dpunkt.verlag, Heidelberg (2011)
7. Kasparick, M., Schlichting, S., Golatowski, F., Timmermann, D.: Medical DPWS: new IEEE 11073 standard for safe and interoperable medical device communication. In: Standards for Communications and Networking (CSCN), pp. 212–217, October 2015
8. Kasparick, M., Schlichting, S., Golatowski, F., Timmermann, D.: New IEEE 11073 standards for interoperable, networked point-of-care medical devices. In: IEEE Engineering in Medicine and Biology Society (EMBC), pp. 1721–1724, August 2015
9. Kühn, F., Leucker, M.: OR.NET: safe interconnection of medical devices. In: Gibbons, J., MacCaull, W. (eds.) FHIES 2013. LNCS, vol. 8315, pp. 188–198. Springer, Heidelberg (2014). doi:10.1007/978-3-642-53956-5_13
10. Leucker, M.: Teaching runtime verification. In: Khurshid, S., Sen, K. (eds.) RV 2011. LNCS, vol. 7186, pp. 34–48. Springer, Heidelberg (2012). doi:10.1007/978-3-642-29860-8_4
11. Leucker, M., Sánchez, C.: Regular linear temporal logic. In: Jones, C.B., Liu, Z., Woodcock, J. (eds.) ICTAC 2007. LNCS, vol. 4711, pp. 291–305. Springer, Heidelberg (2007). doi:10.1007/978-3-540-75292-9_20
12. Leucker, M., Schallhart, C.: A brief account of runtime verification. J. Logic Algebraic Program. **78**(5), 293–303 (2009)

13. Leucker, M., Schmitz, M.: Secured SOA for the safe interconnection of medical devices (position paper). In: CEUR Workshop Proceedings Software Engineering (SE), vol. 1337, pp. 11–14 (2015). CEUR-WS.org
14. Pnueli, A.: The temporal logic of programs. In: Foundations of Computer Science (FOCS), pp. 46–57. IEEE Computer Society (1977)
15. Sánchez, C., Samborski-Forlese, J.: Efficient regular linear temporal logic using dualization and stratification. In: Temporal Representation and Reasoning (TIME), pp. 13–20. IEEE Computer Society (2012)

Dynamic Analysis of Regression Problems in Industrial Systems: Challenges and Solutions

Fabrizio Pastore[✉] and Leonardo Mariani

Department of Informatics, Systems and Communication,
University of Milano - Bicocca, Milan, Italy
{pastore,mariani}@disco.unimib.it

Abstract. This paper presents the result of our experience with the application of runtime verification, testing and static analysis techniques to several industrial projects. We discuss the eight most relevant challenges that we experienced, and the strategies that we elaborated to face them.

1 Dynamic Analysis of Regression Problems

Industrial software systems are complex systems that must evolve quickly to remain competitive. Consider for instance the case of unmanned airborne vehicles, which might be upgraded to extend the set of missions that can be performed, to support new devices that might be installed on the vehicles, to fix bugs, and to eliminate inefficiencies. Although upgrades are designed to improve software systems, they may also expose systems to *regression problems*, that is the changes may introduce unwanted side-effects that break existing functionalities.

Regression problems are known to be tricky to detect and expensive to fix because they are the result of unexpected interactions between the changes and the existing functionalities. In particular, *localizing* and *understanding* the causes of regression failures can be extremely challenging [16,18].

In the context of the European project PINCETTE [3], we addressed the automatic detection of regression problems by integrating *runtime verification*, *testing*, and *static analysis*, as shown in Fig. 1. The analysis starts from a *base* software version and an *upgraded* software version; the latter extending the base version with new features while introducing some regression faults. Our approach first *automatically discovers relevant behavioral properties for the base version* of the software by collecting *traces* (Step 1, Fig. 1) and mining *properties* from traces (Step 2) [14,15]. Since mined properties might be imprecise, it uses *static analysis* (e.g., model checking) to eliminate inaccurate properties and keep only the *true properties* that have been proved to be correct for the base version (Step 3) [15]. For example, this approach may automatically discover that the speed of a vehicle cannot be negative and discard a property that allows for negative speed values.

Our approach continues by *automatically determining the obsolete properties, that is the properties that have been intentionally invalidated by the change.*

T. Margaria and B. Steffen (Eds.): ISoLA 2016, Part II, LNCS 9953, pp. 388–393, 2016.
DOI: 10.1007/978-3-319-47169-3_30

This is done by executing the passing test cases designed for the upgraded system (Step 4) while verifying the true properties at runtime (Step 5) [15]. Since property violations are detected by running passing test cases, the violations indicate behaviors that have been intentionally changed by the upgrade. For example, a vehicle may allow for negative speeds once the capability to move backward has been introduced, intentionally violating properties that state that the speed must be positive or 0. The remaining properties are the *up-to-date properties*, that is the properties that hold on the base version and have not been intentionally invalidated by the upgrade.

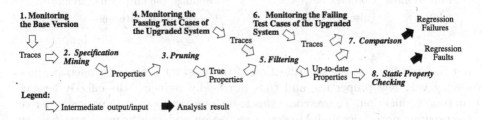

Fig. 1. Detection and analysis of regression faults.

Finally, if there is any failing test case designed for the upgraded system, the up-to-date properties can be *verified at runtime* while executing the failing tests (Step 6) to discover the anomalous events that may explain the causes of *regression failures* (Step 7) [2,11–14,19]. In addition, the up-to-date properties can be *verified statically* to discover the *regression faults* that have not been revealed by any test case (Step 8) [15].

We applied this solution to multiple industrial systems, including a trajectory controller for robotic arms used in experimental nuclear reactors developed by VTT [17], a control system to detect spikes in large-scale power distribution networks developed by ABB [1], a real-time software framework for distributed control systems developed by ABB, and a controller for unmanned airborne vehicles developed by IAI [6]. Our experience with these systems revealed the presence of several important challenges that must be addressed to make runtime verification, and more specifically the analysis of regression problems, effective.

2   Challenges

This section presents the main challenges that we experienced when applying runtime verification to industrial software systems and describes the solutions that we experimented, as indicated in Table 1.

Properties. We faced two main challenges related to properties: the lack of properties and the presence of inaccurate properties.

Lack of Properties. The manual specification of the properties that can be verified at runtime is an *expensive* and *error-prone* activity. Engineers may deliberately

Table 1. Runtime verification challenges and possible solutions

Context	Challenge	Applied solution
Properties	Lack of properties	Derive properties automatically
	Inaccurate properties	Prune inaccurate properties
Monitoring	Impact of monitoring	Goal-driven monitoring
	Seamless integration	Avoid code instrumentation
Applicability	Scalability of the analysis	Reduce the scope of the analysis
	Integration with the process	Exploit continuous integration
Effectiveness	Complex output	Organize the output hierarchically
	False positives	Priority-based filtering

put limited effort on the identification of the relevant program properties, producing very few properties, and thus drastically reducing the effectiveness of runtime verification. To overcome this issue, our idea is to automatically derive the program properties useful to detect regression problems by using *specification mining* techniques (Step 2 in Fig. 1).

So far we focused on the functional behaviour of the programs considering properties that capture the values of program variables (e.g., method pre- and post-conditions) [4] and the sequences of operations executed by a program (e.g., finite state machines) [9–11]. Results showed that mined properties could be a valid replacement of manually specified properties [11,14,15].

Inaccurate Properties. Mined properties may overfit the data used for the mining, that is they capture properties that hold for the collected data but not for the program. Furthermore, in the presence of software changes, properties may become obsolete and be valid for the base version only. Overfitting and obsolete properties may generate false alarms, thus limiting the effectiveness of runtime verification and reducing the chance of its industrial adoption.

In order to be effective, our approach formally checks the correctness of mined properties (Step 3 in Fig. 1), and removes the properties that are intentionally invalidated by the changes (Step 5 in Fig. 1), thus *guaranteeing to work with up-to-date precise properties* when revealing failures and detecting faults [15].

Monitoring. When monitoring industrial software systems, we faced two main challenges: keeping the impact of monitoring small and building a monitoring infrastructure easy to integrate with target systems.

Impact of Monitoring. Monitoring slows down software systems, sometimes significantly altering the performance of an application and the outcome of the test cases. To address these issues we elaborated a *goal-driven monitoring* strategy that captures the strictly relevant events only.

Since it is intuitively true that incorrect changes are likely to affect the functionalities that directly depend on the changed code, we specifically restrict the monitoring to the neighbourhood of the changes [14]. At the same time we do not want to monitor the modified lines of code, because data collected from different software versions might be incomparable. Results show that the combination of these two criteria produces a focused monitoring strategy that may scale to industrial systems [14,15].

Seamless Monitoring Infrastructure. Monitoring code is often injected into applications using code transformation tools, which may require changes to the build process, such as changes to makefiles. These changes are hardly tolerated by developers, who are not happy to change program artefacts to enable specific analyses. We addressed this issue by only *using monitoring techniques that work with either the executables or the runtime environment.*

In particular, we implemented a monitoring tool that can generate GDB scripts [5] and PIN tools [7] with the capability to collect runtime data from the program functions that depend on the changes under analysis without requiring modifications to the build process. According to our experience, this approach is highly appreciated by software developers.

Applicability. To make runtime verification easily applicable, it is important to define analysis strategies that both scale well with the complexity and size of industrial software systems and suitably integrate with tools for automation commonly available within professional organizations.

Scalability of the Analysis. In presence of complex and large software systems, program analysis might not scale well. In our experience, this happened when using formal static analysis to prune the inaccurate properties mined from traces.

To deal with this issue, we had to find a *compromise between the soundness and the completeness* of the analysis. We thus decided to prune properties by running model checking on a *restricted scope* [15]. This might incidentally drop some true properties, but scales to large industrial systems. Findings compromises like this one is of crucial importance to address industrial systems.

Integration with the Process. Industry people do not want to invest major effort on the configuration and the execution of tools. The adoption of novel analysis solutions, including runtime verification, might be facilitated if tools are implemented as components pluggable into *the environments commonly used in industry for automation.* In our experience, it has been a successful choice to develop our analysis technique as a Jenkins plugin [8] that can be simply installed in a continuous integration server.

Effectiveness. To make runtime verification effective, it is important to produce outputs that can be easily inspected by the developers and to limit the number of false positives that can be generated.

Complex Output. The explanation of a regression failure might depend on a number of mutually related events. In addition to identifying these events, it is important to present the information in a form that facilitates the inspection and the understanding of the failure.

We addressed this challenge by defining proper *views that show the cause-effect chains that relate anomalous events, and the hierarchical organization of the data* [2]. Compared to a plain list of apparently unrelated events, structured views are extremely easy to inspect.

False Positives. Techniques that generate *many false positives* are usually perceived as useless techniques by industry people. It is thus a priority of any analysis technique to limit the number of false positives that might be generated.

Since an analysis based on mined properties might produce false positives, we mitigated this issue by using *statically verified mined properties* [15] and by generating *structured views* that prioritize correct failure information to false positives, which usually are not inspected at all [2].

3   Conclusion

Our experience with industrial projects revealed the presence of several challenges that have to be faced to make runtime verification easily applicable to large and complex systems. In the context of evolving software, we identified strategies that can be used to face these challenges, specifically referring to functional faults. More work is needed to address a broader set of faults, (e.g. performance problems), and industrial systems, (e.g. low-power devices).

Acknowledgments. This work has been partially supported by the H2020 Learn project, which has been funded under the ERC Consolidator Grant 2014 program (ERC Grant Agreement no. 646867).

References

1. ABB: Power and automation company (2016). http://www.abb.com/
2. Babenko, A., Mariani, L., Pastore, F.: AVA: automated interpretation of dynamically detected anomalies. In: ISSTA. ACM (2009)
3. Chockler, H., Denaro, G., Ling, M., Fedyukovich, G., Hyvrinen, A.E.J., Mariani, L., Muhammad, A., Oriol, M., Rajan, A., Sery, O., Sharygina, N., Tautsching, M.: Pincette - validating changes and upgrades in networked software. In: CSMR - EU Projects Track. IEEE (2013)
4. Ernst, M.D., Cockrell, J., Griswold, W.G., Notkin, D.: Dynamically discovering likely program invariants to support program evolution. TSE **27**(2), 99–123 (2001)
5. FSF: GDB debugger (2016). http://sources.redhat.com/gdb/
6. IAI: Israel aerospace industry (2016). http://www.iai.co.il
7. Intel: Pin - a dynamic binary instrumentation tool (2016). https://software.intel.com/en-us/articles/pintool
8. Jenkis: Continuous integration server (2016). https://jenkins-ci.org/
9. Lorenzoli, D., Mariani, L., Pezzè, M.: Automatic generation of software behavioral models. In: ICSE. IEEE (2008)
10. Mariani, L., Pastore, F.: Automated identification of failure causes in system logs. In: ISSRE. IEEE (2008)
11. Mariani, L., Pastore, F., Pezzè, M.: Dynamic analysis for diagnosing integration faults. IEEE TSE **37**(4), 486–508 (2011)
12. Pastore, F., Mariani, L.: AVA: supporting debugging with failure interpretations. In: ICST - Tool Demo Track. IEEE (2013)

13. Pastore, F., Mariani, L., Goffi, A.: Radar: a tool for debugging regression problems in C/C++ software. In: ICSE - Tool Demo Track. IEEE (2013)
14. Pastore, F., Mariani, L., Goffi, A., Oriol, M., Wahler, M.: Dynamic analysis of upgrades in C/C++ software. In: ISSRE. IEEE (2012)
15. Pastore, F., Mariani, L., Hyvärinen, A.E.J., Fedyukovich, G., Sharygina, N., Sehestedt, S., Muhammad, A.: Verification-aided regression testing. In: ISSTA. ACM (2014)
16. Rothermel, G., Harrold, M.J.: A safe, efficient regression test selection technique. ACM TOSEM 6(2), 173–210 (1997)
17. VTT: Research center (2016). http://www.vtt.fi/
18. Yu, K., Lin, M., Chen, J., Zhang, X.: Practical isolation of failure-inducing changes for debugging regression faults. In: ASE. IEEE (2012)
19. Zuddas, D., Jin, W., Pastore, F., Mariani, L., Orso, A.: Mimic: locating and understanding bugs by analyzing mimicked executions. In: ASE. ACM (2014)

Towards a Logic for Inferring Properties of Event Streams

Sean Kauffman[1], Rajeev Joshi[2], and Klaus Havelund[2(✉)]

[1] University of Waterloo, Waterloo, Canada
[2] Jet Propulsion Laboratory, California Institute of Technology, Pasadena, USA
klaus.havelund@jpl.nasa.gov

Abstract. We outline the background, motivation, and requirements of an approach to create abstractions of event streams, which are time-tagged sequences of events generated by an executing software system. Our work is motivated by the need to process event streams with millions of events that are generated by a spacecraft, that must be processed quickly after they are received on the ground. Our approach involves building a tool that adds hierarchical labels to a received event stream. The labels add contextual information to the event stream, and thus make it easier to build tools for visualizing and analyzing telemetry. We describe a notation for writing hierarchical labeling rules; the notation is based on a modification of Allen Temporal Logic, augmented with rule-definitions and features for referring to data in data parameterized events. We illustrate our notation and its use with an example.

1 Introduction

The most broadly applied approach to ensure functional correctness of software systems is testing. That is, executing the software in a finite number of scenarios and verifying the correct behavior. Various techniques have been developed to improve the testing experience, including Runtime Verification (RV). RV is a method for verifying that a program execution satisfies a user-provided formal specification. Such specifications are typically expressed in some form of temporal logic, regular expressions, or state machines. Occasionally, but more rarely, they are expressed as rule systems and grammars. RV usually results in a binary decision (true/false) as to whether the execution trace satisfies the specification, although variations on this theme have been developed. Logics have, furthermore, been developed which aggregate data as part of the verification [2–4].

In this paper, we outline an approach to *software comprehension*. A user provides a specification that is used to annotate a given event stream with contextual information that makes it easier to build tools for visualizing and analyzing the trace. The proposed specification logic is a modification of Allen's Temporal Logic (ATL) [1], well known from AI, which turns out to be suitable

---

The research performed by the last two authors was carried out at Jet Propulsion Laboratory, California Institute of Technology, under a contract with the National Aeronautics and Space Administration.

T. Margaria and B. Steffen (Eds.): ISoLA 2016, Part II, LNCS 9953, pp. 394–399, 2016.
DOI: 10.1007/978-3-319-47169-3_31

for expressing hierarchical specifications of spacecraft behavior. We have implemented our ideas in a system named nfer (a tool for "telemetry inference"). The design of this logic is driven by the challenges faced in operating spacecraft, where the only knowledge ground personnel have of the remote behavior is from telemetry sent down to Earth. The nfer system provides both a declarative notation that allows engineers to write hierarchical specifications of spacecraft behavior, and a tool that uses these specifications to automatically label a received telemetry stream. The labels are used both in visualizing telemetry in real-time as it is received, as well as for building tools that make it easier to query past telemetry. The tool is being applied for analyzing telemetry received from the Curiosity rover currently on Mars [6].

The work is a continuation and refinement of previous work described in [5]. Roşu and Bensalem [7] define a translation of a modified modified ATL to Linear Temporal Logic (LTL) for monitoring, realizing, however, that a specialized monitoring algorithm is more efficient. Our work differs in a number of respects: (i) instead of monitoring ATL relationships for verification, we generate a relationship hierarchy for program understanding, (ii) we handle data parameterized intervals, (iii) we allow any constraints on time and parameter values, not just the 13 ATL constraints, (iv) in their system, an interval is unique, while in nfer it can occur multiple times. Our work has strong similarities to data-flow (data streaming) languages. A very recent example is QRE [2], which is based on regular expressions, and offers a solution for computing numeric results from traces. QRE allows the use of regular programming to break up the stream for modular processing, but is limited in that the resulting sub-streams may only be used for computing a single quantitative result, and only using a limited set of numeric operations, such as sum, difference, minimum, maximum, and average, in order to achieve linear time (in the length of the trace) performance. Our approach is based on Allen logic, and instead of a numeric result produces a set of named intervals, useful for visualization (and thereby systems comprehension). Furthermore, data arguments to intervals can be computed using arbitrary functions.

The remainder of the paper is organized as follows. Section 2 outlines the background as well as requirements for this effort, including an example. Section 3 suggests a solution and uses it to formalize the provided example. Finally, Sect. 4 concludes the paper.

2   Requirements

In this section we briefly outline the requirements to our specification language. We first illustrate a concrete problem with an example. Subsequently we outline the specific requirements.

2.1   Illustrating Example

Consider the trace shown in Fig. 1(a), that we assume has been generated by a spacecraft[1]. The trace consists of a sequence of events, or Event Verification

---

[1] The trace is artificially constructed to have no resemblance to real artifacts.

Records (EVRs), each with a name, and list of arguments, including a time stamp. This sequence of 15 events is already too long for human comprehension, even if we provide the following informal description of how to read the trace:

- A session interval consists of a *boot* interval followed by a *window* interval.
- A *boot* interval starts with a VERSION event, ends with a DEACTIVATE event, and must contain a BOOT_COUNT event.
- A *window* interval starts with a *prep* interval, followed by an *active* interval, followed by a *cleanup* interval, and must contain an ACTIVATE_SEQ event.
- A *prep* interval starts with a WINDOW_PREP event and ends with a DUR1 event.
- An *active* interval starts with a *task1* interval, followed by a *task2* interval, followed by a *task3* interval.
- A *task1* interval starts with a DUR1 event and ends with a DUR2 event.
- A *task2* interval starts with a DUR2 event and ends with a DUR3 event.
- A *task3* interval starts with a DUR3 event and ends with a FINISHED event.
- A *cleanup* interval starts with a FINISHED event and ends with a CLEANUP event.

Our objective is to formalize the above information in a specification, match the specification against the trace, and convey the actual matches in a visually appealing manner. We are not interested in whether the trace satisfies the above information exactly, but rather to what extent it matches. The result could for example be the visualization shown in Fig. 1(b). As can be seen, the visualization clearly shows how a *session* consists of a *boot* and a *window*, which itself consist of a *prep*, *active* and *cleanup*, and where an *active* consists of the three tasks executed in sequence.

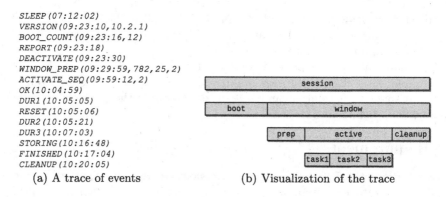

```
SLEEP (07:12:02)
VERSION (09:23:10, 10.2.1)
BOOT_COUNT (09:23:16, 12)
REPORT (09:23:18)
DEACTIVATE (09:23:30)
WINDOW_PREP (09:29:59, 782, 25, 2)
ACTIVATE_SEQ (09:59:12, 2)
OK (10:04:59)
DUR1 (10:05:05)
RESET (10:05:06)
DUR2 (10:05:21)
DUR3 (10:07:03)
STORING (10:16:48)
FINISHED (10:17:04)
CLEANUP (10:20:05)
```

(a) A trace of events   (b) Visualization of the trace

Fig. 1. An event trace and its visualization. (a) A trace of events (b) Visualization of the trace

2.2 Desired Features

The specification language should allow a user to:

1. label event relations in the trace, for example to define the label *task1* to represent an interval delimited by the events DUR1 and DUR2.
2. define higher-level labels as a composition of lower-level labels. For example, a *session* is composed of a *boot* and a *window* in sequence.
3. refer to time stamps associated to events in the trace, as well as generate and read start and end times of generated labels.
4. refer to other data associated with events, as well as generate and read data of generated labels using arbitrary expressions. For example, a label can have a datum value defined as the sum of two lower-level event data.
5. specify other relationships than one event/labeling occurs before another. For example it should be possible to specify that one label contains another, that two labels overlap, etc.

3 Outline of a Logic

Our logic is inspired by ATL [1], specifically its operators for expressing temporal constraints on time intervals. In ATL, a time interval represents an action taking place over a time period (e.g. "Drive"), or a system state over a time period (e.g. "Overheated"). A time interval has a name, a start time, and an end time.

ATL offers 13 mutually exclusive binary relations. Examples are: $Before(i, j)$ which holds iff interval i ends before interval j starts, and $During(i, j)$ which holds iff i starts strictly after j starts and ends before or when j ends (or vice versa). An ATL formula is a conjunction[2] of such relationships, for example, $Before(A, B) \land Contains(B, C)$. A model is a set of intervals satisfying such a conjunction of constraints. ATL is typically used for generating a model (plan) from a formula (planning), but can also be used for checking a model against a formula, as described in [7].

Our objective is different from planning and verification. Given a trace, we want to generate a model (a set of intervals), guided by a specification that we provide, that represents a layered view of the trace. Let an interval be defined as a 4-tuple (η, t_1, t_2, m) consisting of a name η, and a start time t_1, an end time t_2, and a map $m : Id \to V$ from identifiers to values, the arguments of the interval. The input to our system is a trace σ: a sequence of named events of the form $\eta(t, m)$ consisting of a name η, a unique time stamp t, and a map m (the arguments to the event). The trace is converted into an initial model, which is the set $\{(\eta, t, t, m) \mid N(t, m) \in \sigma\}$. The specification defining the transformation of this initial model is a set of rules of the form:

$$\eta \doteq \eta_1(m_1) \oplus \eta_2(m_2) \text{ if } C \text{ map } M$$

---

[2] A limited form of disjunction is also allowed but not described here.

Table 1. `nfer` operators

Operator $\oplus$	Name	Explanation
$A \, ; B$	A before B	A ends before B starts
$A \, : B$	A meet B	A ends where B starts
$A \sqsubseteq B$	A during B	All of A occurs during B
$A = B$	A coincide B	A and B occur at the exact same time
$A \vdash B$	A start B	A starts at the same time as B
$A \dashv B$	A finish B	A finishes at the same time as B
$A + B$	A join B	An A and a B with no constraint
$A \mid B$	A overlap B	A and B overlap in time
$A \sqcap B$	A slice B	A and B overlap in time and only overlap is returned

The rule states that: if there are two intervals named η_1 respectively η_2 already generated, with maps specified by m_1 and m_2 respectively, that are related time-wise with the temporal operator $\oplus$, and if the condition C holds on the maps of the respective intervals (true if left out in abbreviated form)[3], then an interval named η is generated, with the map described by the map expression M (the empty map if left out in abbreviated form). The operators are those presented informally in Table 1, which are inspired by ATL, although not identical, since

```
session ← boot ; window .

boot ←  VERSION ; BOOT_COUNT(2 : count) ; DEACTIVATE
    if count > 10 map {boot_count : count} .

window ← ACTIVATE_SEQ(2 : x) ⊑(prep(m) ; active ; cleanup)
    map m † {seq : x} .

prep ← WINDOW_PREP(3 :wi, 4 : ty) ; DUR₁
    map {wid : wi, type : ty} .

active   ← task₁; task₂; task₃.
task₁← DUR₁; DUR₂.
task₂← DUR₂; DUR₃.
task₃← DUR₃; FINISHED .
cleanup ← FINISHED ; CLEANUP .
```

Fig. 2. Example specification

---

[3] In the fully generic form the user can define his/her own operators as arbitrary predicates on time stamps.

our needs are slightly different. Each operator on two intervals A and B returns an interval that time wise spans both intervals in their entirety (the maximal view), except for the last *slice* operator $A \sqcap B$, which returns only the interval (slice) which A and B have in common (the minimal view).

As convenient syntax we allow expressions containing several operators on the right hand side of a rule, but such derived rules map to the simple form above. The specification of our trace abstraction outlined in Sect. 2 is shown in Fig. 2 (with a condition and map functions added for illustration). A term such as $BOOT\_COUNT(2 : count)$ means matching a $BOOT\_COUNT$ event where the second map argument is bound to the free variable $count$, and the expression $m \dagger \{seq : x\}$ is the map m overridden by seq being mapped to x.

4 Conclusion

We have introduced the problem of inferring a model from an event stream, guided by a formal specification, for the purpose of system comprehension. We have outlined a rule-based logic, nfer, influenced by Allen Temporal Logic (ATL), for writing specifications. ATL itself is an attractive logic due to its simplicity, as well as naturalness for visualization, and is normally used for planning purposes. nfer adds rule-definitions as well as data parameterization to a variant of this logical system. A prototype of nfer has been implemented in Scala as an internal DSL (API), and is built on a publish and subscribe framework, for processing telemetry data from the Mars Curiosity rover. Future work includes refining the implementation, including optimizing time and space; improving the internal rule DSL; creating an external DSL; and allowing rules to be written in other languages, such as Python, commonly used by flight mission engineers.

References

1. Allen, J.F.: Maintaining knowledge about temporal intervals. Commun. ACM **26**(11), 832–843 (1983)
2. Alur, R., Fisman, D., Raghothaman, M.: Regular programming for quantitative properties of data streams. In: Thiemann, P. (ed.) ESOP 2016. LNCS, vol. 9632, pp. 15–40. Springer, Heidelberg (2016). doi:10.1007/978-3-662-49498-1_2
3. Basin, D., Harvan, M., Klaedtke, F., Zălinescu, E.: MONPOLY: monitoring usage-control policies. In: Khurshid, S., Sen, K. (eds.) RV 2011. LNCS, vol. 7186, pp. 360–364. Springer, Heidelberg (2012). doi:10.1007/978-3-642-29860-8_27
4. Finkbeiner, B., Manna, Z., Sipma, H.B.: Deductive verification of modular systems. In: de Roever, W.-P., Langmaack, H., Pnueli, A. (eds.) COMPOS 1997. LNCS, vol. 1536, pp. 239–275. Springer, Heidelberg (1998)
5. Havelund, K., Joshi, R.: Comprehension of spacecraft telemetry using hierarchical specifications of behavior. In: Merz, S., Pang, J. (eds.) ICFEM 2014. LNCS, vol. 8829, pp. 187–202. Springer, Heidelberg (2014)
6. Mars Science Laboratory (MSL). http://mars.jpl.nasa.gov/msl
7. Roşu, G., Bensalem, S.: Allen linear (Interval) temporal logic – translation to LTL and monitor synthesis. In: Ball, T., Jones, R.B. (eds.) CAV 2006. LNCS, vol. 4144, pp. 263–277. Springer, Heidelberg (2006)

Runtime Verification for Stream Processing Applications

Christian Colombo[1]([✉]), Gordon J. Pace[1], Luke Camilleri[2], Claire Dimech[1],
Reuben Farrugia[3], Jean Paul Grech[1], Alessio Magro[4], Andrew C. Sammut[3],
and Kristian Zarb Adami[4]

[1] Department of Computer Science, University of Malta, Msida, Malta
christian.colombo@um.edu.mt
[2] Ixaris System Ltd, San Ġwann, Malta
[3] Department of Communications and Computer Engineering,
University of Malta, Msida, Malta
[4] Institute of Space Sciences and Astronomy, University of Malta, Msida, Malta

Abstract. Runtime verification (RV) has long been applied beyond its
strict delineation of *verification*, through the notion of monitor-oriented
programming. In this paper we present a portfolio of real-life case studies
where RV is used to program stream-processing systems directly —
where all the logic of the implemented system is defined in terms of monitors. The systems include the processing of Facebook events for business
intelligence, analysing users' activity log for detecting UI usability issues,
video frame analysis for human movement detection, and telescope signals processing for pulsar identification.

1 Introduction

Runtime verification (RV) [1] is a lightweight formal methods technique which
allows users to specify formal properties and through instrumentation and automatically synthesised monitors, check that a system's behaviour adheres to the
properties. However, RV has long been applied beyond this strict definition. In
particular, the notion of verification is not the sole application of monitoring,
especially with the rise of the notion of Monitor-Oriented Programming (MOP)
[9] which takes the approach further — advocating how a system's functionality can be extended through the use of monitors. The architecture of a system
built in such a manner is shown in Fig. 1(a): The system, interacting with the
real world, generates events which are captured by the specification-synthesised
monitor, which in turn reacts to particular traces of events according to the
specification. However, the use of runtime monitoring techniques and tools has
been pushed even further by programming stream processing systems directly
as monitors, thus having the monitors generated from the specifications interact
directly with events generated from a real-world event sensor or event generator
(which might also be a computer system). The architecture of such a system is
shown in Fig. 1(b), with the monitor processing the stream of events directly.
The key feature of this approach is that if we see a stream as a total function

© Springer International Publishing AG 2016
T. Margaria and B. Steffen (Eds.): ISoLA 2016, Part II, LNCS 9953, pp. 400–406, 2016.
DOI: 10.1007/978-3-319-47169-3_32

from the discrete time domain ℕ to the type of values carried on the stream, a stream processing system is one which takes an input stream, and produces an output stream[1]. In general, while the output stream does not need to be produced in sync with the input stream, we expect that the values are produced in sequence and not out of order[2].

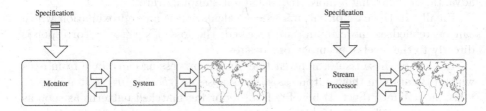

Fig. 1. (a) MOP architecture; (b) Stream-processing architecture

While RV can be seen as providing a convenient layer of abstraction for stream processing applications, stream processing techniques can provide support in two challenging aspects of RV: *reactivity* and *efficient computability*.

Reactivity. Stream processing applications, such as sound or video processing, frequently tolerate little delay between the input stream and the corresponding points in the output stream. This is also a desirable property in several RV applications. The problem, however, is that not all stream processors can have the output corresponding to a particular point in time to be produced at that same time instant. Consider a processor which encodes: $o(t) = i(t + 2)$ — the output at time t is the input at time $t+2$. Clearly, without some form of temporal look-ahead, the output can only be produced two time units late. This is an issue when future time logics are used to specify properties or behaviour of stream processors. For example, the interpretation of the LTL formula XXa on a stream starting at time t, can only be known when the value of a at time $t+2$ is known. Similarly, when matching a pattern such as a fraudulent set of transactions, the pattern may only be detectable after a significant part of fraudulent action has been observed. This is the case with the intelligent video surveillance as well as the radio telescope signal processing applications presented in the paper (Sects. 4 and 5). Conversely in the Facebook event processing application (Sect. 2), we consciously choose a specification language which enables reactivity, since we would like to have notifications triggered immediately.

Even if the specification language or logic allows for full reactivity (being able to calculate the value of $o(t)$ knowing the values of $i(0)$ till $i(t)$), one may still

---

[1] A tuple of streams can be converted into a stream of tuples, which allows this view to cater for multiple inputs and outputs.

[2] Out of order generation can still be catered for, by caching the calculated outputs but outputting them only once their turn comes. Needless to say, this might induce additional space requirements, though.

adopt an implementation which is not reactive. For instance, if we are given the specification $o(t) = E(i(t))$, where E is a calculation increasingly expensive as the input parameter grows, and also that large values of the input are statistically rare, we might adopt a solution which, upon receiving a large input, will continue reading inputs while computing the output in the background. This would result in a non-reactive implementation even if a reactive one was possible — with the advantage of allowing a more frequent input sampling rate.

Finally, in the case of outputs whose calculation is an approximation which can be refined as more inputs are received, the loss of reactivity corresponds directly to the level of accuracy one desires.

In view of these issues, non-reactive stream processing can range from ones which (a) compute their output as soon as possible (*'best effort'* systems), e.g., video surveillance (Sect. 4) benefits from reporting matched patterns as soon as it is possible; and ones which (b) can take even longer than strictly required by the specification language (*'late'* systems) e.g., telescope signal processing and user profiling (Sect. 3) do not require the verdict with particular urgency.

Efficient Computability. In the context of stream processing, we say an application is *efficiently computable* if computing the output stream never requires more than a fixed length of history to be recorded. Contrast the stream processor $o(t) = i(t - 1) + i(t)$ which requires a history buffer of size 1, with the stream processor $o(t) = i(t \text{ div } 2)$ which requires increasing memory as time progresses. This is crucial given the amount of data one would expect to process in the applications presented below, particularly if reactivity is required without slowing down input reading rates. In the case of the telescope signal processing system (Sect. 5), we used statistical methods which do not need to store history. For the Facebook event processing application (Sect. 2), the length of the history depends on the user-defined properties being monitored, but with the guarantee that for any given property, one can statically decide the (maximum) buffer size required. Finally, in the case of the video surveillance system (Sect. 4), the history bound depends on the maximum size of a continuous video sequence. In our implementation, the video sequence resets whenever no persons are observed for a number of frames, or if the number of frames exceed a user-specified bound. While ideal, efficient computability might not be necessary for a number of RV applications: e.g., the user web interface profiling system (Sect. 3). This is particularly so, given that it is effectively creating a statistics database based on the observed input.

2   Facebook Events Processing

With ever increasing information available in social networks, the number of businesses attempting to exploit it is on the rise, particularly by keeping track of their customers' posts and likes on social media sites like Facebook. Whilst APIs can be used to automate the tracking process, writing scripts to extract information and processing it requires considerable technical skill and is thus not an option for non-technical business analysts. On the other hand, off-the-shelf business intelligence solutions do not provide the desired flexibility for the specific needs of particular businesses.

One way of allowing a high degree of flexibility while providing an off-the-shelf solution would be to present a simple interface based on a controlled natural language (CNL) [8] which would allow a business intelligence analyst the flexibility to express the desired events for notification. These would in turn be automatically compiled into Facebook monitors without further human intervention.

Based on interviews with two business analysts, such a CNL should allow the user to specify patterns such as: (i) *Create an alert when the service page has a post and the post contains the keywords fridge, heater, or freezer.* (ii) *Create an alert when my page has a post and the post is negative and the post has 10 likes.*

Once a prototype CNL was designed, it could have potentially been compiled into any executable programming language. With the aim of keeping the translation as simple as possible, we translated the CNL into an intermediary specification from the RV domain. Translating our CNL into the formal specification accepted by the RV tool Larva [5] and using a simple adapter to present relevant Facebook events as method calls in the control flow of a program, we were able to detect Facebook behaviour through RV software. Results [4] suggest that users indeed found the CNL manageable although UI support could facilitate writing CNL sentences further.

3 Profiling User Web Interfaces

User interface designers try their best to improve the user experience to facilitate user productivity. However, the ways in which users end up using the product (e.g., the sequence in which a number of features are used) might be difficult to predict in practice. Furthermore, new features are regularly deployed with the possibility of unforeseen effects such as performance degradation. Adding profiling logic within the system code to gather such statistics would typically lead to cluttered code. In such a scenario, RV was convenient due to its separation of concerns: having the profiling logic handled by the monitor without affecting the live system.

This approach has been successfully used in the context of Ixaris System Ltd[3], a transaction processing software company, where the effectiveness with which the users were able to use the interface needed to be evaluated. A database was available with several months of logs of user activity: which users are logged in, which activities are being carried out, which currency is being used, whether the user is a first time visitor (and if so whether through a referral or a particular campaign), etc. Subsequently, we defined the possible paths of user activities in terms of a finite state machine (FSM) and by running the FSM over the logs, statistics and information could be gathered that otherwise would have had to be implemented into the production code.

---

[3] http://www.ixaris.com.

The statistics gathered through RV help us identify paths in the system that need performance improvements before clients do and RV reports serve as proof that service level agreements are met. In the future, we aim to investigate ways of processing and presenting statistics in real-time without compromising performance.

4 Intelligent Video Surveillance

Video analytics has become an important feature in security systems particularly in public areas or buildings with controlled entry or exit, or where disturbances can be caused. For example motion tracking of a crowd in a football stadium may detect the start of a commotion, enabling the security personnel to act fast.

For these purposes, image processing and computer vision techniques [2,11] have been developed with success, typically starting by identifying human body parts such as the head, the hands, the legs and so on, then tracking these parts, and subsequently attempting to identify human activity based on the movement of the individual parts. However, these techniques do not perform well in low frame rate which is the case in our case study — a prominent public building in Malta (which cannot be named). In this context, we are employing RV to specify high-level rules complementing the information provided by low-level features to suppress false positives: In the area of image processing, it is well known that it is virtually impossible to correctly identify body parts at 100 % accuracy — particularly, if images are taken from poor-quality videos. RV has thus been used to specify high level rules which consider multiple subsequent frames at a time: filtering out any detections which are not found in more than one frame or propagating detections within a frame which would otherwise have been missed. This has been achieved by specifying a number of rules such as *"humans can only start or stop appearing near one of the doors"* or a *"human can only move a limited distance from one frame to the next"* and applying them on frames through an RV-synthesised monitor.

The work is still ongoing but the results achieved so far are promising: when applying the monitor to remove false positives, we obtained a 100 % recall and 91 % precision. In the future we hope to specify a domain-specific language to enable non-technical end users to express custom surveillance rules.

5 Radio Telescope Signal Processing

Whilst for many years the visible light was the only source of information used to discover the universe through optic telescopes, the discovery of the electromagnetic spectrum has provided a wide range of waves which can shed more light about our universe. Amongst these are the radio waves, which through the use of radio telescopes have enabled us to learn more about the universe.

The LOw Frequency ARay (LOFAR) is a radio telescope built and operated by the Netherlands Institute for Radio Astronomy (ASTRON) To detect pulsars[4]

---

[4] Pulsars are rapidly spinning neutron stars which emit regular electromagnetic radiation beams.

within this data on-the-fly, we have employed RV to process radio telescope signals. Due to the pulsars' periodic nature, we could detect the beam of light by keeping track of the standard deviation of the signal. The monitoring tool used was LarvaStat [3], since it provides direct support for gathering statistics. In particular, we made extensive use of LarvaStat's notion of *point statistics* to provide a context, maintain the running standard deviation while simultaneously evaluating the next value.

To evaluate the precision of our approach, we compared our results to those of a standard Fast Fourier Transform (FFT) [10] technique. We observed that our approach is not as precise: 1.01 % error as opposed to 0.02 %. However, the advantage of using the runtime monitoring technique is that while the time complexity of the FFT is $O(n \cdot log_2(n))$, ours is $O(n)$. Furthermore, the FFT processes data in chunks, requiring a suitably-sized buffer and a corresponding delay for detection. This is not the case with our approach which is able to process the data on-the-fly. In terms of performance, the monitoring approach did one order of magnitude worse than the FFT but this may be mainly due to the fact that the former is implemented in Java while the latter is in C.

6   Conclusion

This is not the first time that the connection between stream processing and RV has been shown with tools such as LOLA [7] and a Larva flavour [6] which accepts Lustre as a property specification language. The contribution of this paper is to highlight different case studies in which RV has proved useful in alleviating the challenges of the domain through the abstraction it provides. Returning to the stream processing categories introduced in Sect. 1, the presented applications are categorised below:

	Reactivity	Non-reactive	
		Best effort	Late
Efficient	Facebook	Surveillance	Telescope
Non-efficient			Profiling

We note that with the exception of profiling where the monitor is used to essentially populate a database, efficiency is a common property of monitoring applications dealing with large volumes of data. Another observation is that if monitoring is to be reactive, then it would be undesirable to have non-efficiency. Therefore, one would not typically expect to have applications which fall in the bottom-left quadrant.

We hope that this study serves as an inspiration to the wide ranging usefulness of RV techniques and, consequently, further take-up in industrial settings.

References

1. Runtime Verification Conference, Yearly LNCS Proceedings Since (2010)
2. Benfold, B., Reid, I.: Stable multi-target tracking in real-time surveillance video. In: Computer Vision and Pattern Recognition (CVPR), pp. 3457–3464. IEEE (2011)
3. Colombo, C., Gauci, A., Pace, G.J.: LarvaStat: monitoring of statistical properties. In: Barringer, H., Falcone, Y., Finkbeiner, B., Havelund, K., Lee, I., Pace, G., Roşu, G., Sokolsky, O., Tillmann, N. (eds.) RV 2010. LNCS, vol. 6418, pp. 480–484. Springer, Heidelberg (2010)
4. Colombo, C., Grech, J.-P., Pace, G.: A controlled natural language for business intelligence monitoring. In: Biemann, C., Handschuh, S., Freitas, A., Meziane, F., Métais, E. (eds.) NLDB 2015. LNCS, vol. 9103, pp. 300–306. Springer, Heidelberg (2015) (to appear)
5. Colombo, C., Pace, G.J., Schneider, G.: Larva – safer monitoring of real-time java programs (tool paper). In: Seventh IEEE International Conference on Software Engineering and Formal Methods (SEFM), pp. 33–37. IEEE (2009)
6. Colombo, C., Pace, G.J., Schneider, G.: Resource-bounded runtime verification of java programs with real-time properties. Technical report CS2009-01, Department of Computer Science, University of Malta (2009). http://www.cs.um.edu.mt/~reports
7. D'Angelo, B., Sankaranarayanan, S., Sánchez, C., Robinson, W., Finkbeiner, B., Sipma, H.B., Mehrotra, S., Manna, Z.: LOLA: runtime monitoring of synchronous systems. In: TIME, pp. 166–174. IEEE (2005)
8. Kuhn, T.: A survey and classification of controlled natural languages. Comput. Linguist. 40(1), 121–170 (2014)
9. Meredith, P.O., Jin, D., Griffith, D., Chen, F., Roşu, G.: An overview of the MOP runtime verification framework. STTT 14, 249–289 (2012)
10. Rao, K.R., Kim, D.N., Hwang, J.J.: Fast Fourier Transform - Algorithms and Applications, 1st edn. Springer, Netherlands (2010)
11. Rodriguez, M., Laptev, I., Sivic, J., Audibert, J.Y.: Density-aware person detection and tracking in crowds. In: Computer Vision (ICCV), pp. 2423–2430. IEEE (2011)

On the Runtime Enforcement of Evolving Privacy Policies in Online Social Networks

Gordon J. Pace[1], Raúl Pardo[2], and Gerardo Schneider[3(✉)]

[1] Department of Computer Science, University of Malta, Msida, Malta
gordon.pace@um.edu.mt
[2] Department of Computer Science and Engineering, Chalmers University of Technology, Gothenburg, Sweden
pardo@chalmers.se
[3] Department of Computer Science and Engineering, University of Gothenburg, Gothenburg, Sweden
gersch@chalmers.se

Abstract. Online Social Networks have increased the need to understand well and extend the expressiveness of privacy policies. In particular, the need to be able to define and enforce *dynamic* (and *recurrent*) policies that are activated or deactivated by context (events) or timeouts. We propose an automaton-based approach to define and enforce such policies using runtime verification techniques. In this paper we discuss how our proposed solution addresses this problem without focussing on concrete technical details.

1 Introduction

Online Social Networks (OSNs) are not only a way to keep in touch and socialise but a way of life. Nearly 70 % of the Internet users are active on OSNs as shown by a recent survey [5], and this number keeps increasing. New technologies usually comes with a lot of opportunities, but also with new sometimes unexpected threats and challenges. One of such problems in OSNs is that of privacy. Very often users' requirements are far from the privacy guarantees offered by OSNs which do not meet their expectations [6].

OSN privacy policies can typically enforce many desirable policies; for instance, in Facebook users can state polices like: *'Only my friends can see a post on my timeline'* or *'Whenever I am tagged, the picture should not be shown on my timeline unless I approve it'*. Many other policies, however, are not possible to enforce, although they might be important from a user's privacy perspective. For instance, users cannot specify privacy policies such as *'I do not want to be tagged in pictures by anyone other than myself'*, nor *'Nobody apart from myself can know my child's location'*. These limitations to what current privacy control settings can describe and enforce might be limiting user adoption and use of effective privacy policies.

Besides, the current state of the art in privacy settings do not take into account the *dynamic* aspect of privacy policies. That is, privacy policies should

T. Margaria and B. Steffen (Eds.): ISoLA 2016, Part II, LNCS 9953, pp. 407–412, 2016.
DOI: 10.1007/978-3-319-47169-3_33

consider the fact that the networks *evolve*, as well as the privacy preferences of the users. An OSN may evolve in different ways, by introducing new users, by sending posts and invitations to participate in events, by accepting such invitations, liking pictures and posts, etc.

The privacy policy may also evolve due to explicit changes done by the users (e.g., a user may change the audience of an intended post to make it more restrictive), or because the privacy policy is dynamic *per se*. Examples of the latter, are for instance: *'My boss cannot know my location between 20:00–23:59 every day'*, *'Only my friends can know my location from Fridays at 20.00 till Mondays at 08:00'*, and *'Co-workers cannot see my posts while I am not at work, and only family can see my location while I am at home.'* These are recurrent policies triggered by some time events ("every day between 20:00 and 23:59", and "every week from Friday at 20.00 till Monday at 08:00"), or location-based ("not at work [...] at home"). Other policies may be activated or deactivated by certain events: *'Only up to 3 posts, disclosing my location, are allowed per day in my timeline'.*

In this paper, we are concerned with evolving privacy policies of the latter kind: how to define and enforce dynamic (possible *recurrent*) privacy policies that are activated or deactivated by context (events or location) or timeouts. In particular, we aim at proposing one approach on how to define such policies and discuss how to guarantee at runtime their enforcement. We do not develop in this paper a concrete technical solution but rather outline an automata-based approach, and discuss how it could be implemented.

2   An Approach to Represent Evolving Privacy Policies

An evolving policy effectively corresponds to temporal modalities sitting above predicates in a static policy logic. Given that much work has been done in the area of representing and enforcing static policies, with different approaches being proposed to address different contexts, we have chosen to keep the approach policy logic agnostic and have a description of which policies are triggered as time progresses.

The formalism we propose to describe the evolving behaviour of policies is to use deterministic automata with transitions labelled by events which the policy's environment — in our case the online social network — can perform. By tagging each state with a static policy which expresses what is and what is not allowed, we automatically obtain an operational view of which policies are switched on and off during the system's lifetime. By synchronising the policy automaton's state with the events from the social network, other users and the general policy environment, we can add and remove policies appropriately.

For example, consider the policy *'Co-workers cannot see my posts while I am not at work, and only family can see my location while I am at home'* (P1). If we use the static policy operator $\mathcal{F}_g(x)$ to denote that anyone in group g is forbidden from performing action x (x can refer to posting, viewing a post, liking a post, etc.) we can express the policy while not being at work to be $\mathcal{F}_{co\text{-}workers}(read\text{-}post)$, and the policy when not at home to be $\mathcal{F}_{\overline{family}}(see\text{-}location)$ (we use $\bar{g}$ to denote the complement of a group of users g). By synchronising with the actions of our social network application registering our arriving at and leaving a location ($enter(l)$ and $leave(l)$ respectively), we can express the evolving policy in the following manner:

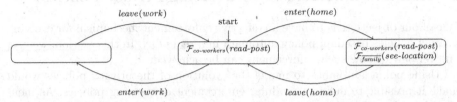

This approach allows the adoption of any static policy language and allow its dynamic extension. In addition, we can easily extend definitions of concepts such as policy refinement and policy conflicts already defined on static policies to the policy automaton level — for instance, an evolving policy represented as a policy automaton P is a refinement of another evolving policy P' if, for any trace t, the policy in the state of P reachable after following trace t is a refinement of the policy in the state of P' reachable from following trace t.

In practice, when specifying these policy automata, we allow for symbolic states to be used by using variables which can be checked and updated on the transitions. For instance, consider the policy *'Only up to 3 posts, disclosing my location, are allowed per day in my timeline'* (P2), which can be encoded as the following automaton:

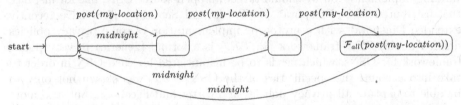

If the maximum number of posts were to be increased, specifying this as an explicit automaton can quickly become unwieldy, and using a symbolic state variable can simplify specifying the automaton in a more concise way. In the representation below, each transition is labelled as: *event/ condition/ state-update* — triggering when the specified event happens and the condition holds, performing the state update before proceeding. The property allowing for 10 location posts can be expressed in this notation in the following manner:

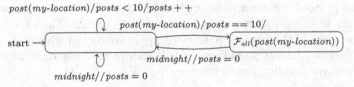

Note that this can be reduced to an infinite state explicit automaton with the state consisting of a tuple (q, n) where $q \in \{1, 2\}$ represents the two states, while $n \in \mathbb{N}$ represents the value of the variable *posts*.

3   Runtime Enforcement of Evolving Privacy Policies

One of our objectives is to have an effective enforcement mechanism for evolving privacy policies based on policy automata in a real OSN. In this section, we give an overview of how such enforcement can be achieved.

Using policy automata to model the evolution of the privacy policies would make it possible to define a modular enforcement of evolving policies. As mentioned in the previous section, policy automata are independent of the static policy language of the OSN, and consequently, they are also independent of the underlying enforcement of each particular static policy. Therefore, the two main required ingredients for an enforcement of evolving privacy policies are:

(i) An OSN with a built-in enforcement for static privacy policies,
(ii) A tool which monitors the evolution of the OSN and controls the state of the policies at each moment in time.

All the popular OSNs such as Facebook, Twitter, Google+, Instagram, etc. have a built-in mechanism for enforcing static policies. However, monitoring the events occurring in the OSN requires full access to the internals of the system, which is normally not publicly available for those OSNs. Thus, in order to have a working implementation we should target an open-source OSN, like for instance the distributed OSN Diaspora* [3]. Pardo and Schneider [7,8] have recently extended Diaspora* with a prototype implementation of some privacy policies defined in the $\mathcal{PPF}$ framework [4]. $\mathcal{PPF}$ is a formal (generic) privacy policy framework for OSNs, which needs to be instantiated for each OSN in order to take into account the specificities of the OSN. $\mathcal{PPF}$ was shown not only to be able to capture all privacy policies of Twitter and Facebook, but also more complex ones involving implicit disclosure of information.

The remaining element of the enforcement is a tool which is able to model policy automata (cf. (ii)). In previous work Colombo *et al.* introduced LARVA [2], a tool to automatically generate a monitor from properties expressed in DATEs (*Dynamic Automata with Events and Timers*). Though the expressiveness of DATEs is not sufficient to encode policy automata, we believe they can be extended in order to reach the intended expressiveness.[1]

In order for the runtime enforcement to work we would need to use a communication protocol between Diaspora* and LARVA. Every time that a relevant event occurs in Diaspora* it should be reported to LARVA. Then LARVA would update the state of the privacy policies (if applicable), and whenever a privacy policy is updated LARVA would report this change to Diaspora*, which would update the corresponding (static) privacy policy (see Fig. 1).

---

[1] All the behaviour and information in DATEs are carried on the transitions: states are only used as a way to define transitions.

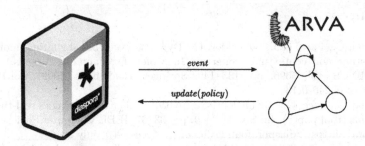

Fig. 1. High-level representation of the Diaspora*-LARVA communication

One possibility is to implement the communication protocol using sockets. Imagine we were to implement the policy (P2) described in the previous section, which states that at most 3 times per day posts containing a user's location are allowed. Every time that a user publishes a post including a location, a message would be sent to the LARVA monitor. This message must include the information of which users are included in the post, since their location is (potentially) going to be disclosed. At this moment, LARVA would update the state of the policy automaton by either increasing the variable controlling the number of posts including a location (for each user) and/or updating the state of the automaton. Finally, if the automaton goes to a state in which no further user location disclosures are allowed, then LARVA would communicate with Diaspora* updating the relevant privacy settings for the user, and Diaspora's built-in mechanism for enforcing static policies would then take care of the rest. At midnight, the automaton returns to the initial state, updating the static policy in Diaspora* accordingly, i.e., permitting location disclosure once again.

4 Conclusions

We have sketched an approach to formally represent evolving privacy policies, and a practical solution enabling the synthesis of monitors to enforce such policies. Our objective here is not to provide a technical solution, but rather to give some initial ideas on how to address it and to pave the way to further research on the topic.

We are currently looking into the formal definition of policy automata, and a translation into LARVA monitors [1,2] instantiated for Diaspora*. In particular, we would like to apply the approach by using privacy policies using an instantiation of the $\mathcal{PPF}$ privacy framework [8].

Acknowledgements. This research has been supported by: the Swedish funding agency SSF under the grant *Data Driven Secure Business Intelligence*, the Swedish Research Council (*Vetenskapsrådet*) under grant Nr. 2015-04154 (*PolUser: Rich User-Controlled Privacy Policies*), and the European ICT COST Action IC1402 (*Runtime Verification beyond Monitoring (ARVI)*).

References

1. Colombo, C., Pace, G.J., Schneider, G.: Dynamic event-based runtime monitoring of real-time and contextual properties. In: Cofer, D., Fantechi, A. (eds.) FMICS 2008. LNCS, vol. 5596, pp. 135–149. Springer, Heidelberg (2009). doi:10.1007/978-3-642-03240-0_13

2. Colombo, C., Pace, G.J., Schneider, G.: LARVA – safer monitoring of real-time Java programs (tool paper). In: SEFM 2009, pp. 33–37. IEEE Computer Society (2009)

3. Diaspora*. https://diasporafoundation.org/. Accessed 1 July 2016

4. $\mathcal{PPF}$ Diaspora*. Test pod (2016). https://ppf-diaspora.raulpardo.org, Code. https://github.com/raulpardo/ppf-diaspora

5. Lenhart, A., Purcell, K., Smith, A., Zickuhr, K.: Social media & mobile internet use among teens and young adults. millennials. Pew Internet & American Life Project (2010)

6. Liu, Y., Gummadi, K.P., Krishnamurthy, B., Mislove, A.: Analyzing facebook privacy settings: User expectations vs. reality. In: ACM SIGCOMM IMC 2011, pp. 61–70. ACM (2011)

7. Pardo, R.: Formalising Privacy Policies for Social Networks. Department of Computer Science and Engineering, Chalmers University of Technology, Licentiate thesis (2015)

8. Pardo, R., Schneider, G.: A formal privacy policy framework for social networks. In: Giannakopoulou, D., Salaün, G. (eds.) SEFM 2014. LNCS, vol. 8702, pp. 378–392. Springer, Heidelberg (2014). doi:10.1007/978-3-319-10431-7_30

On the Specification and Enforcement of Privacy-Preserving Contractual Agreements

Gerardo Schneider[✉]

Department of Computer Science and Engineering, University of Gothenburg,
Gothenburg, Sweden
gerardo@cse.gu.se

Abstract. We are here concerned with the enforcement at runtime of contractual agreements (e.g., Terms of Service) that respect users' privacy policies. We do not provide a technical solution to the problem but rather give an overview of a framework for such an enforcement, and briefly discuss related work and ideas on how to address part of the framework.

1 Introduction

Each time we download an app in our smart phone or access certain webpages we need to deal with *contractual agreements* (e.g. *Terms of Service* —ToS) and *privacy policies*. These are usually written in *legalese*, a somehow obscure language, motivating people to click the *I agree* button without reading the text, eventually having unexpected consequences. The situation is even more complex given that in many cases the applications may interact with each other in complex ways, most of the time without our knowledge nor consent.

As an example, let us consider the following scenario. Facebook and Spotify have their own ToS which users must agree on before getting the right to install and use their services. It could happen that when listening to a song in Spotify, a message in your wall is posted showing what the user is listening to. This might no be wanted by most users, compromising their privacy. It could be desirable to have the possibility to statically check whether the ToS conforms with the user's privacy policies. In case a potential breach of privacy is found statically, if the user still want to install and use the application, it could be desirable to have a monitor that warns the user when Facebook is going to post about what you are listening to (even better, the monitor could prevent Spotify and Facebook to make the post public if this is not allowed by the user's privacy policy).

Two crucial observations: (i) Privacy is an important concern as personal information may be collected without our (explicit, or informed) consent from online social networks, search engines, mobile devices, etc., and used and shared by private and governmental agencies for different purposes (e.g., see the series of articles in the Wall Street Journal[1]); (ii) Normal citizens do not have the knowledge

---

[1] "What they know", *Wall Street Journal*. Accessed on March 10, 2014 (http://online.wsj.com/public/page/what-they-know-digital-privacy.html).

© Springer International Publishing AG 2016
T. Margaria and B. Steffen (Eds.): ISoLA 2016, Part II, LNCS 9953, pp. 413–419, 2016.
DOI: 10.1007/978-3-319-47169-3_34

(nor the time) to go through the details of contractual agreements (e.g., ToS), accepting them with the naive expectation that they are to be trusted.

Our ultimate goal is to make the hard task of analyzing contractual agreements easier for normal users. Besides, we want to empower users with the possibility to be in control of *what* may be seen by *whom*, and *when*. For that we envision a framework allowing users to: (i) Define their own privacy policies, at different levels and for general or specific applications, using a user-friendly environment; (ii) Perform some simple queries on contractual agreements to ensure they are satisfied with the terms, before accepting them; (iii) Check the contractual agreements do not violate the user's privacy policies (offline, static checking); (iv) Get a warning in case the application is going to perform an action not allowed by the contractual agreement, or that might violate their privacy policies (online, at runtime).

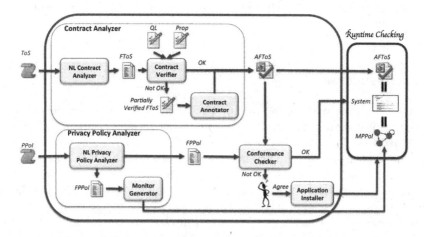

Fig. 1. Conceptual view of our framework

In order to achieve the above, there is a need for a multi-disciplinary approach combining expertise from natural language processing (NLP), machine learning (ML), formal methods (formal semantics, specification and verification), logics, security, and legal analysis and formalization of law. More concretely, we aim at a framework (*cf.* Fig. 1) where policies are written in natural language and translated into a formal language (*cf. NL Privacy Policy Analyzer*), and a monitor is automatically generated to ensure that the policies are not violated at runtime (*cf. Monitor Generator*). Contractual agreements written in natural language, e.g. ToS, are also transformed into a formal language (*cf. NL Contract Analyzer*) so they are verified against properties (*cf. Contract Verifier*) and statically checked for conformance with the privacy policies (*cf. Conformance Checker*). These formal languages will be used during the execution of the application to ensure that the privacy policies are respected (*cf. Runtime Checking*).

We give an overview of the framework in Sect. 2, and discuss some of its components in more detail in Sect. 3 putting them into context w.r.t. the state-of-the-art.

2   Description of the PPCA Framework

We describe below a prototypical scenario of our framework (*cf.* Fig. 1).

1. The user will define her privacy policies interacting with a user-friendly interface. The policies will be translated by the module *NL Privacy Policy Analyzer* into the formal language *FPPol*.
2. The *Monitor Generator* will generate a monitor for the privacy policies.
3. When an application is uploaded, the user will be asked to approve the ToS (*ToS*). Before agreeing to upload the application, the ToS will be translated into a formal contract language (*FToS*) by the *NL Contract Analyzer*.
4. *FToS* will be analyzed by using the *Contract Verifier* module, allowing the verification of the contract against user-defined properties (*Prop*), or queries defined in the query language *QL*. The results of the the analysis (and queries) will be shown to the user, who will decide whether to accept it or not. If not accepted, *FToS* will be annotated with additional information by the *Contract Annotator* module.
5. The *Conformance Checker* module will statically check whether the contract *might* violate the policies specified by the user. If so, the user will get to know what clauses are to be analyzed in detail. In case of uncertainty the ambiguous sentences will be highlighted to be further analyzed interactively. The user will decide whether to agree to upload the application or not.
6. The user may decide to modify her privacy policies, by relaxing or constraining the policies for this particular application. This is done by the module *Privacy Policy Updater* (*not shown in the picture*). This is fed into the corresponding modules to obtain a runtime monitor for the new privacy policies.
7. If the user agrees to upload the application (or automatically done by the *Conformance Checker*), the monitor *MPPol* will run in parallel with the underlying system, checking that the privacy polices are respected at runtime.
8. The *Runtime Violation Analyzer* (*not shown in the picture*) detects when the contract is violated and uses the history of the transaction to analyze it at runtime (and eventually acting accordingly by canceling the transaction, or giving a warning). In case of non-conformance with respect to the privacy policies, the user is notified and the application temporary blocked.
9. The result provided by the *Runtime Violation Analyzer* (a *Log* file) will be passed to the *Static Violation Analyzer* so the end-user (or a specialist in case of litigation) can analyze it off-line to further determine what where the causes and who was responsible for the contract violation (*not depicted*).

3   On the Specification and Enforcement of Contractual Agreements and Privacy Policies

We only focus here on three main parts of the framework: (i) The formal specification of contractual agreements; (ii) The formal specification of privacy policies; (iii) The static and runtime conformance checking.

Formalization and analysis of contractual agreements. Since its modern conception in the 1950's *deontic logic* [19] has been the base of almost all the attempts to formalize normative systems. Most of the work have been dedicated to the study of properties of normative operators, e.g., obligations, permissions and prohibitions, and how to handle their violations (e.g. [13]), but few attempts have been made in order to obtain a usable formal language for the specification and analysis of contractual agreements. One of such languages is $\mathcal{CL}$ [16,17], based on deontic, temporal and dynamic logic. $\mathcal{CL}$ has been shown to be insufficient to handle rich contractual documents; besides it does not have many of the desirable properties of contract specification languages [12]: does not allow to determine liabilities nor causalities, it is not compositional, and it cannot express real-time constraints. Some of these issues have been partially solved by *C-O Diagrams* [10] but the language is still not expressive enough as to capture real contractual agreements. Another language, FLAVOR [18], allows to distinguish between different "instances" of a contract, but reasoning about permissions is not possible. Besides, there are no analysis algorithms/tools associated with the language. In what concerns the formal analysis of contractual agreements, there is not much work. For instance for $\mathcal{CL}$ a complex translation into an existing model checker has been provided [11] by abstracting away some of the features of the language losing expressivity in what can be proven. The translation of C-O Diagrams into timed automata is promising as it opens the possibility to use verification tools like UPPAAL [4].

In order to ensure the fulfillment of the contractual clauses, the contract needs to be monitored at runtime. An interesting work along these lines is based on the event calculus [8]. However, this and other up-to-date approaches can only partially monitor a contract fulfillment, and more powerful monitoring techniques are needed. A complete automatic generation of a monitor from a formal contract is in general impossible, because most contracts contain prescriptions and descriptions at a high level, not specifying the underlying (algorithmic) procedures. This is the case for instance if the contract talks about average or percentages within a given period of time. We are not aware of any work providing (semi-)automatic monitor extraction techniques for such complex contracts.

Formalization and analysis of privacy policies. As for contractual agreements, privacy policies would need to be expressed in a formal language, for instance based on real-time, epistemic and deontic logics. Epistemic logic is needed to specify and reason about *who* knows *what*, deontic operators are needed to describe for instance who is (not) *allowed* to perform certain actions, and real-time is obviously needed as policies may have deadlines or durations, and to describe and reason about the evolution of the system and the policies themselves.

One approach to formally define privacy policies is to use some variant of *epistemic logic* [7], where it is possible to express the knowledge of *multi-agent systems*. Other approach for privacy, not based on epistemic logic, is *Relationship-based access control* (REBAC) [9], where the reasoning is focused on the resources owned by the agents. This approach is highly suitable for a practical implementation of a policy checking algorithm. On the other hand, it is mostly suitable for controlling access to resources, not for detecting certain kinds of implicit knowledge flow. Datta *et al.* present in [6] the logic PrivacyLFP for defining privacy policies based on a restricted version of first-order logic (the restriction concerns quantification over infinite values is avoided by considering only relevant instances of variables). The logic is quite expressive though it is not clear how it could be used for the kind of polices we are aiming here.

Though not directly concerned with privacy policies, the work by Basin and colleagues on different aspects of *usage control* is quite relevant. These include works on the definition of formal models for mechanisms to enforce usage control policies on the consumer side [15], and the use of temporal logics to express usage policies and runtime monitoring to check system compliance e.g. [2,3].

A starting point for defining a rich formal language for privacy policies could be the recent work on the definition of the $\mathcal{PPF}$ framework [14].

Static and runtime conformance checking. Our aim is to develop static verification techniques and algorithms for determining whether a given contract might compromise the parties' privacy policies. The static verification would be done with respect to a compliance relation between the formal term representing the contract and the formal privacy policy. The techniques behind this kind of proofs are quite standard, the challenge being in specializing them into our particular formal languages. One challenge is to obtain algorithms to extract a monitor from the formal policy language in order to check that the contracts do not violate the parties' privacy policies at runtime. An idea would be to apply techniques based on the *sub-formula construction*. However, this approach cannot capture clauses having *algorithmic content*. A possible solution to that would be to enhance the monitor with a library computing such clauses, and combine it with a *rule-based* approach to consider in more detail the specific events that might violate the policy. Besides, there might be a need to provide a full operational semantics of the system under test in order to consider what are the side effects of every event. We are not aware of any work checking conformance between contractual agreements and privacy policies.

An interesting promising approach would be to combine static and runtime verification as done in the StaRVOOrS framework [1,5].

4   Conclusion

We believe the benefits of the PPCA framework are many, as well as the challenges to achieve it. A specific challenge for the runtime verification community is how to automatically obtain and deploy runtime monitors from formal contractual agreements and privacy policies, in order to enforce their satisfaction as well as the compliance of the former w.r.t. the latter.

Acknowledgements. Partially supported by: the Swedish Research Council (*Vetenskapsrådet*) under grants Nr. 2015-04154 (*PolUser: Rich User-Controlled Privacy Policies*) and Nr. 2012-5746 (*Remu: Reliable Multilingual Digital Communication*), and the European ICT COST Action IC1402 (*ARVI: Runtime Verification beyond Monitoring*).

References

1. Ahrendt, W., Chimento, J.M., Pace, G.J., Schneider, G.: A specification language for static and runtime verification of data and control properties. In: Bjørner, N., de Boer, F. (eds.) FM 2015. LNCS, vol. 9109, pp. 108–125. Springer, Heidelberg (2015). doi:10.1007/978-3-319-19249-9_8

2. Basin, D., Harvan, M., Klaedtke, F., Zalinescu, E.: Monitoring data usage in distributed systems. IEEE Trans. Soft. Eng. **39**(10), 1403–1426 (2013)

3. Basin, D., Harvan, M., Klaedtke, F., Zălinescu, E.: MONPOLY: monitoring usage-control policies. In: Khurshid, S., Sen, K. (eds.) RV 2011. LNCS, vol. 7186, pp. 360–364. Springer, Heidelberg (2012)

4. Bengtsson, J., Larsen, K., Larsson, F., Pettersson, P., Yi, W.: UPPAAL — a tool suite for automatic verification of real-time systems. In: Alur, R., Henzinger, T.A., Sontag, E.D. (eds.) HS 1995. LNCS, vol. 1066, pp. 232–243. Springer, Heidelberg (1996). doi:10.1007/BFb0020949

5. Chimento, J.M., Ahrendt, W., Pace, G.J., Schneider, G.: STARVOORS: a tool for combined static and runtime verification of java. In: Bartocci, E., Majumdar, R. (eds.) RV 2015. LNCS, vol. 9333, pp. 297–305. Springer, Heidelberg (2015). doi:10.1007/978-3-319-23820-3_21

6. Datta, A., Blocki, J., Christin, N., DeYoung, H., Garg, D., Jia, L., Kaynar, D., Sinha, A.: Understanding and protecting privacy: formal semantics and principled audit mechanisms. In: Jajodia, S., Mazumdar, C. (eds.) ICISS 2011. LNCS, vol. 7093, pp. 1–27. Springer, Heidelberg (2011). doi:10.1007/978-3-642-25560-1_1

7. Fagin, R., Halpern, J.Y., Moses, Y., Vardi, M.Y.: Reasoning About Knowledge, vol. 4. MIT Press, Cambridge (1995)

8. Farrell, A., Sergot, M., Sallé, M., Bartolini, C.: Using the event calculus for tracking the normative state of contracts. Int. J. Coop. Inf. Syst. **14**(2–3), 99–129 (2005)

9. Fong, P.W.: Relationship-based access control: protection model and policy language. In: CODASPY 2011, pp. 191–202. ACM (2011)

10. Martínez, E., Cambronero, E., Diaz, G., Schneider, G.: A model for visual specification of e-contracts. In: IEEE SCC 2010, pp. 1–8. IEEE Computer Society (2010)

11. Pace, G.J., Prisacariu, C., Schneider, G.: Model checking contracts – a case study. In: Namjoshi, K.S., Yoneda, T., Higashino, T., Okamura, Y. (eds.) ATVA 2007. LNCS, vol. 4762, pp. 82–97. Springer, Heidelberg (2007). doi:10.1007/978-3-540-75596-8_8

12. Pace, G.J., Schneider, G.: Challenges in the specification of full contracts. In: Leuschel, M., Wehrheim, H. (eds.) IFM 2009. LNCS, vol. 5423, pp. 292–306. Springer, Heidelberg (2009). doi:10.1007/978-3-642-00255-7_20

13. Palmirani, M., Governatori, G., Rotolo, A., Tabet, S., Boley, H., Paschke, A.: LegalRuleML: XML-based rules and norms. In: Olken, F., Palmirani, M., Sottara, D. (eds.) RuleML 2011. LNCS, vol. 7018, pp. 298–312. Springer, Heidelberg (2011). doi:10.1007/978-3-642-24908-2_30

14. Pardo, R., Schneider, G.: A formal privacy policy framework for social networks. In: Giannakopoulou, D., Salaün, G. (eds.) SEFM 2014. LNCS, vol. 8702, pp. 378–392. Springer, Heidelberg (2014). doi:10.1007/978-3-319-10431-7_30

15. Pretschner, A., Hilty, M., Basin, D.A., Schaefer, C., Walter, T.: Mechanisms for usage control. In: ASIACCS, pp. 240–244. ACM (2008)

16. Prisacariu, C., Schneider, G.: A formal language for electronic contracts. In: Bonsangue, M.M., Johnsen, E.B. (eds.) FMOODS 2007. LNCS, vol. 4468, pp. 174–189. Springer, Heidelberg (2007). doi:10.1007/978-3-540-72952-5_11

17. Prisacariu, C., Schneider, G.: $\mathcal{CL}$: an action-based logic for reasoning about contracts. In: Ono, H., Kanazawa, M., Queiroz, R. (eds.) WoLLIC 2009. LNCS (LNAI), vol. 5514, pp. 335–349. Springer, Heidelberg (2009). doi:10.1007/978-3-642-02261-6_27

18. Thion, R., Métayer, D.L.: Flavor: a formal language for a posteriori verification of legal rules. In: POLICY 2011, pp. 1–8. IEEE Computer Society (2011)

19. Wright, G.H.V.: Deontic logic. Mind **60**, 1–15 (1951)

Variability Modeling for Scalable Software Evolution

Introduction to the Track on Variability Modeling for Scalable Software Evolution

Ferruccio Damiani[1], Christoph Seidl[2(✉)], and Ingrid Chieh Yu[3]

[1] University of Torino, Turin, Italy
`ferruccio.damiani@unito.it`
[2] Technische Universität Braunschweig, Braunschweig, Germany
`c.seidl@tu-braunschweig.de`
[3] University of Oslo, Oslo, Norway
`ingridcy@ifi.uio.no`

Abstract. Information and communication technology today is increasingly integrated into the environment we live in, distributed on cars, appliances and smart infrastructures. The software running on these devices is increasingly individualized, adapted to the preferences and needs of the specific customer and must be able to evolve after deployment by means of software patches. Upgrades are becoming individualized; software patches used to upgrade the software are selected and adapted depending on the configuration and external constraints of the host device. The objective of the European project HyVar is to develop techniques and tools for fast and customizable software design, for the management of highly distributed applications, for continuous software evolution of remote devices, and scalable infrastructure to accommodate a large number of devices. The track *Variability Modeling for Scalable Software Evolution* aims to foster cooperation opportunities and create synergies between related research directions to address challenges stemming from software variability, evolution, and cloud technology for highly distributed applications in heterogeneous environments. This paper introduces the track and its individual contributions.

1 Context and Background

Software is an essential part of information and communication technology so that it is becoming increasingly integrated into our everyday environment, distributed on cars, appliances and a wide variety of devices. The struggle between the ideal fit of software resulting from individual development and the low cost of off-the-shelf software creates tension for developers and customers of software products alike. With the advent and rise of the Internet of Things (IoT) [2] and its devices (e.g., smartphones, tablets), the need for software that can be used on many similar yet slightly different devices and that can be individualized in

---

This paper contains an introduction to the ISoLA'16 track organized in the context of the EU H2020 project 644298 HyVar: Scalable Hybrid Variability for Distributed Evolving Software Systems (http://www.hyvar-project.eu).

T. Margaria and B. Steffen (Eds.): ISoLA 2016, Part II, LNCS 9953, pp. 423–432, 2016.
DOI: 10.1007/978-3-319-47169-3_35

functionality has further increased this tension towards favoring customizable software but still having to keep development costs at a reasonably low level. Furthermore, highly configurable software systems are a major asset in a wide range of areas from business software (e.g., SAP ERP[1] with its configurable modules for enterprise resource planning) to the transportation domain (e.g., cars with different on board electronics and specific integrated navigation systems desired by customers). Due to the sheer number of variants resulting from the configuration options, it is infeasible to develop, maintain or test all individual variations of the respective *software families* independent of one another and in isolation.

A Software Product Line (SPL) [18, 21, 22] is an approach to software reuse in the large where a set of related software systems is perceived as a software family consisting of a common core and variable parts often referred to as *features* [14]. A *product* or *variant* of the SPL is created by combining the common core with the functionality associated with a set of selected features. However, not all combinations of features form valid products, e.g., due to technical incompatibilities of the features' realization or due to business constraints that do not allow combining certain features. To define the principally valid constellations of features, a *variability model*, such as a *feature model* [14] is employed, which represents all valid *configurations* (sets of selected features) in a compact representation on a conceptual level. To create executable software system from this selection of conceptual features, a *variability realization mechanism* collects the realizations associated with each feature (e.g., source code or design models) and assembles them with the common core. Delta modeling [4, 20] is a transformational variability realization mechanism that realizes variation of a software artifact by adding, modifying or removing parts of a software artifact in accordance with a feature's functionality, e.g., a feature might add certain methods to a class written in Java to realize additional functionality.

Modern software systems outgrow the scope of a traditional SPLs. When a software family consists of multiple SPLs, the software family may be managed by a Multi-software Product Line (MSPL) [10, 12]. In a MSPL, several SPLs are composed in order to build a larger system of configurable components. These variable components need to be configured together to build a common system configuration but still depend on a common notation for a variability model. A Software Ecosystem (SECO) [5, 26] is similar to an SPL or even a MSPL in the sense that it also manages a set of closely related software systems. However, a SECO is different from an SPL, in the sense that it does not have a variability model as central configuration knowledge and that multiple independent developers create and maintain the variable parts of the SECO.

SPLs, MSPLs and SECOs are subject to change over the course of time when their products have to adapt to altered or new requirements. This procedure is called *software evolution* [16] and poses a major challenge for SPLs, MSPLs and SECOs as not only single software systems but entire families of software systems have to be evolved [23, 24]. Software evolution is especially difficult for SECOs

---

[1] http://go.sap.com/product/enterprise-management/erp.html.

where independent developers release new features or versions thereof in unsynchronized intervals and, possibly, without explicitly notifying other developers or users so that awareness of the current state of evolution of a SECO becomes a further challenge. As both configuration and evolution are sources of variability within the set of related software systems, it is also customary to denote them as *variability in space* and *variability in time*, respectively [18].

Due to the level of maturity of cloud technology and the wide variety of offered services, SPLs, MSPLs and SECOs become heavily based on cloud technology. Features may be realized as webservices [1] accessible by customers over the web and end-users may contribute features to shared platforms for various domains similar to apps for smartphones. In the automotive domain, utilizing the web for over-the-air update of entire products as well as individual features receives increasing attention.[2]

This combination of challenges stemming from configuration, evolution and cloud technology is at the center of the research conducted within the European Union H2020 project HyVar. To foster opportunities for cooperation on the topics of HyVar and to capitalize on synergies of related research directions, we organized the special track *Variability Modeling for Scalable Software Evolution* at the *International Symposium on Leveraging Applications of Formal Methods, Verification and Validation (ISoLA)*. This paper introduces the track and provides and overview of its sessions and their respective contributions.

2   The European Union H2020 Project HyVar

The EU H2020 project *HyVar* plans to integrate and enhance state-of-the-art techniques for the management of complex software systems from software product lines with cutting edge technology for over-the-air software upgrades and scalable cloud solutions from European industry to support highly individualized and reconfigurable distributed applications. HyVar's objectives are:

1. To develop a Domain Specific Variability Language (DSVL) and a tool chain to support software variability of highly distributed applications in heterogeneous environments, which allows developers to encompass unanticipated evolution as a standard feature of software systems in production.
2. To develop a cloud infrastructure that exploits the software variability supported by the DSVL and a tool chain to track the exact software configurations deployed on remote devices to enable the collection of data from the devices to monitor their behavior and perform statistical analyses.
3. To develop a technology for supporting over-the-air updates of distributed applications in heterogeneous environments and enabling continuous software evolution after deployment on complex remote devices that incorporate a system of systems.
4. To test HyVar's approach as described in the above objectives in an industry-led demonstrator in the automotive domain to assess in quantifiable ways the benefits of the approach.

---

[2] http://www.wired.com/2014/02/teslas-air-fix-best-example-yet-internet-things/.

HyVar aims to create a development framework for continuous and highly individualized evolution of distributed software applications, which can be integrated into existing software development processes. The framework, which is currently under development, will consist of advanced methods and tools that support

- modeling of both variability in space and time in all phases of the software lifecycle,
- scalable, elastic solutions to accommodate numerous individualized application instances, and
- secure and efficient over-the-air software update on remote devices.

This framework will be realized by combining variability modeling from SPL engineering with formal methods and software upgrades for distributed applications. HyVar goes beyond the state-of-the-art in devising and assessing the feasibility of the notion of *hybrid variability*, i.e., the automatic generation and deployment of software updates by relying on both

1. the variability model that describes the possible software variants that may be deployed to a remote device; and
2. the sensor data collected from that device.

The selection of features (and parameters) that will trigger the automatic generation and deployment of the most appropriate upgrades to a specific remote device depends on sensor data from that device (e.g., its location, and/or other things).

3 Track Papers

The ISoLA track *Variability Modeling for Scalable Software Evolution*, organized in the context of the EU H2020 project HyVar, is aimed at disseminating the results of the HyVar project and at promoting fruitful collaborations on its topics between researchers from academia and industry. Topics of special interest within the track are:

- Mobility, mobile and cloud.
- Methodologies, languages and tools.
- Research on variability retrieval, reconfiguration and refactoring.

The track consists of papers that directly relate to the core challenges of HyVar written by the consortium members [6,9,13,17,27] as well as papers addressing issues extending beyond the scope of HyVar written by other researchers [7,11,15,19,25] that contribute their insights to a joint effort of combining highly configurable software with customizable upgrades and flexible cloud technology for over-the-air distribution.

3.1   Keynote

Hähnle and Muschevici [11] outline an approach for formal modeling, simulation, and analysis of railway systems together with their requirements and interoperability constraints. The approach is based on the Abstract Behavioral Specification (ABS) language, which permits precise, executable specifications as basis for efficient code generation. ABS permits to trace system updates from requirements down to the implementation via delta modeling, thus allowing to analyse functional and non-functional properties that may have have changed. The specification of system updates in terms of SPL in ABS permits traceability of features down to code. Together with the analysis tool suite of ABS, this forms a feasible technological basis for an incremental verification and certification process.

3.2   Session 1: Mobility, Mobile and Cloud

Mobile systems, such as smartphones or the electronic devices found in cars, pose extensive challenges on software configuration and evolution. For one, this class of systems is usually characterized by a large degree of hardware heterogeneity that has to be addressed through software configurability for drivers and applications building upon the respective hardware, e.g., smarthpones by various vendors may have a different screen size and cars may have different engines or multimedia systems due to customer preferences, which the respective software has to respect. Moreover, this class of systems poses significant challenges in software evolution not only to frequent changes (e.g., updates to apps in smartphones) but also be the means of transporting respective software updates without having to call devices to service stations (e.g., performing updates to a car's software only in the garage). A cloud infrastructure is suitable for providing solutions to these challenges as mass-customized products may be supplied by scalable online servers and individualized updates from a version installed for one user's configuration to a newer version may be assembled and provided via over-the-air updates. The contributions of Session 1 deal with variability-aware design of services, designing and analyzing the architecture of highly configurable software systems as well as the conscious choice of cloud technology regarding the tradeoff between cost and performance, e.g., to create scalable cloud infrastructures for assembling and deploying updates of configurable software systems.

    Ter Beek et al. [25] present a variability-based design of services for smart transportation systems. The addressed research topic is at the intersection of SPL engineering and machine learning. The key idea is to guide the design and implementation of an SPL by measuring the effectiveness of certain features in practice. The considered application domain is bike sharing, where the features correspond to various user-assisting prediction services that improve over time through machine learning. The investigation is based on concrete experiments with data concerning the bike-sharing system of the city of Pisa.

    Khalilov et al. [15] model and optimize automotive electric/electronic architectures by making the variability-aware modeling language Clafer [3] more accessible to practitioners. At present, software architectures, e.g., as used in the automotive domain, are nearing the point where the size and complexity of the design prevent software architects from making assessments on the impact of proposed changes. Tools of the variability-aware modeling language Clafer may, principally, be used to evaluate effects of design decisions but the Clafer language offers no dedicated support for modeling architectures. The authors present a Domain-Specific Language (DSL) on top of Clafer to model architectures, which embodies a reference architecture model and ensures that practitioners apply it adequately so that typical errors in the specification process can be caught early.

Johnsen et al. [13] compare different deployments on Amazon Web Services (AWSs) using model-based predictions. With the plethora of cloud services offered on the market today, it is challenging for a user to select a solution which best balances performance and incurred cost for a particular application. This paper builds upon ABS and Yet Another Resource Negotiator (YARN) by showing how the ABS-YARN framework enables users to assess the impact of different deployment decisions on the performance, operational cost, and workload completion of their software. Several workload scenarios are used to compare the cost-performance tradeoffs between different AWS on-demand resource purchasing options. The presented AWS instance study is based on MapReduce benchmarks of varied length, time requirements and distribution. Based on the simulation results, one may identify non-trivial tradeoffs early at the design phase of a software development process.

3.3   Session 2: Methodologies, Languages and Tools

To successfully employ, foster and maintain an SPL or a SECO of highly configurable software systems, a variety of methodologies, languages and tools are required. For both SPLs and SECOs, a tool chain is required that allows structured reuse within a family of related software systems by supporting the specification of a variability model, the derivation of variants according to selected configurations as well as the assembly and distribution of updates for the variants. For SECOs, a major challenge is to obtain on overview of the ongoing development efforts of loosely coupled contributors of extensions. For deployed variants running as individual software systems, runtime monitoring is a prerequisite to allow runtime adaptation for dynamic reconfiguration. The contributions of Session 2 introduce methodologies, languages and tools to cope with these challenges.

Chesta et al. [6] present a tool chain for delta-oriented modeling of SPLs. The paper addresses the challenge associated with large-scale reuse of software intensive systems by proposing an architecture and tool chain for customizing and managing variability modeling, derivation of product variants and scalable software repositories for distributed applications. The authors present a component-based architecture including a model variant generator, a state-diagram code generator, a source-code packager and a cross compiler as the main components. The paper demonstrates the overall approach through an industrial use case taken form the automotive domain.

Stănciulescu et al. [7] present a technology-neutral role-based collaboration model for Software Ecosystems (SECOs). Due to the independent development efforts and the lack of a central steering mechanism in SECOs, largely similar features may be developed multiple times by different developers, which increases effort and creates redundancy. The authors present remedy to this problem by contributing a role-based collaboration model for SECOs to make such implicit similarities explicit and to raise awareness among developers during their ongoing efforts, which fosters overview of the software ecosystem, analyses of duplicated development efforts and information of ongoing development efforts.

Rosà et al. [19] applies the DiSL framework for runtime monitoring on the Java Virtual Machine (JVM). DiSL is an aspect-oriented programming system specialized for dynamic program analysis which offers additional join points, pointcuts and advices. DiSL also uses partial evaluation in weaving and adaptive runtime instrumentation. The paper explains how runtime adaptation can be used for runtime monitoring and demonstrates the approach on an example using stationary field analysis. Benchmarks from the Da Capo suite[3] are used to evaluate the approach.

3.4   Session 3: Variability Retrieval, Reconfiguration and Refactoring

Choosing SPLs as a reuse strategy yields benefits in terms of reduced effort for creating products and increased product quality. However, adopting and maintaining an SPL strategy requires maintenance effort: *(i)* For adopting an SPL strategy, the product line has to be created, e.g., by retrieving it from a set of similar products that resulted from copying and then modifying an individual software system; *(ii)* For maintaining an SPL strategy, individual customer concerns regarding product functionality have to be addressed through flexible means of reconfiguration. Through the course of adapting an SPL to new or altered requirements, specific properties of the SPL have to be maintained, e.g., through refactoring. The contributions to Session 3 deal with retrieval, reconfiguration and refactoring of SPLs.

Wille et al. [27] identify variability in object-oriented code using model-based code mining. Companies often employ Object-Oriented Programming (OOP) languages to create variants of their existing software by copying and modifying individual products to changed requirements. While these so-called *clone-and-own* approaches allow to save money in short-term, they expose the company to severe risks regarding long-term evolution and product quality. The authors introduce a model-based approach to identify variability information for OOP code, which allows companies to better understand and manage variability between their variants. This information allows to improve maintenance of the variants and to transition from single variant development to the more elaborate reuse strategy of an SPL.

---

[3] http://www.dacapobench.org/.

Nieke et al. [17] incorporate user-preferences into the reconfiguration process for products of an SPL by presenting user profiles for context-aware reconfiguration in SPLs. Although user customization has a growing importance in software systems and is a vital sales argument, SPLs currently only allow user customization at deploy-time. The authors extend the notion of context-aware SPLs by means of user profiles, containing a linearly ordered set of preferences with priorities. Furthermore, they present a reconfiguration engine that checks the validity of the current configuration and, if necessary, reconfigures the SPL while trying to fulfill the preferences of the active user profile to provide the most suitable configuration.

Damiani and Lienhardt [9] refactor delta-oriented product lines to enforce guidelines for efficient type-checking. Ensuring type safety in an SPL (i.e., ensuring that all programs of the SPL are well-typed) is a computationally expensive task. Recently, five guidelines to address the complexity of type checking delta-oriented SPLs have been proposed by the same authors [8]. In this paper, the authors present algorithms to refactor delta-oriented SPLs to follow the five guidelines. Individual steps, complexity and correctness of the refactoring algorithms are stated.

References

1. Armbrust, M., Fox, A., Griffith, R., Joseph, A.D., Katz, R., Konwinski, A., Lee, G., Patterson, D., Rabkin, A., Stoica, I., Zaharia, M.: A view of cloud computing. Commun. ACM **53**(4), 50–58 (2010)
2. Atzori, L., Lera, A., Morabito, G.: The internet of things: a survey. Comput. Netw. **54**(15), 2787–2805 (2010)
3. Bak, K., Diskin, Z., Antkiewicz, M., Czarnecki, K., Wasowski, A.: Clafer: unifying class and feature modeling. In: Software and Systems Modeling, pp. 1–35 (2014)
4. Bettini, L., Damiani, F., Schaefer, I.: Compositional type checking of delta-oriented software product lines. Acta Informatica **50**, 77–122 (2013). doi:10.1007/s00236-012-0173-z
5. Bosch, J.: From software product lines to software ecosystems. In: Proceedings of the 13th International Software Product Line Conference, SPLC (2009)
6. Chesta, C., Damiani, F., Dobriakova, L., Guernieri, M., Martini, S., Nieke, M., Rodrigues, V., Schuster, S.: A toolchain for delta-oriented modeling of software product lines. In: Proceedings of the International Symposium on Leveraging Applications of Formal Methods, Verification and Validation (ISoLA), ISoLA 2016, Heidelberg (2016)
7. Stănciulescu, Ş., Rabiser, D., Seidl, C.: A technology-neutral role-based collaboration model for software ecosystems. In: Proceedings of the International Symposium on Leveraging Applications of Formal Methods, Verification and Validation (ISoLA), ISoLA 2016, Heidelberg (2016)
8. Damiani, F., Lienhardt, M.: On type checking delta-oriented product lines. In: Ábrahám, E., Huisman, M. (eds.) IFM 2016. LNCS, vol. 9681, pp. 47–62. Springer, Heidelberg (2016). doi:10.1007/978-3-319-33693-0_4
9. Damiani, F., Lienhardt, M.: Refactoring delta oriented product lines to enforce guidelines for efficient type-checking. In: Proceedings of the International Symposium on Leveraging Applications of Formal Methods, Verification and Validation (ISoLA), ISoLA 2016, Heidelberg (2016)

10. Damiani, F., Schaefer, I., Winkelmann, T.: Delta-oriented multi software product lines. In: 18th International Software Product Line Conference, SPLC 2014, pp. 232–236 (2014)
11. Hähnle, R., Muschevici, R.: Towards incremental validation of railway systems. In: Proceedings of the International Symposium on Leveraging Applications of Formal Methods, Verification and Validation (ISoLA), ISoLA 2016, Heidelberg (2016)
12. Holl, G., Grünbacher, P., Rabiser, R.: A systematic review and an expert survey on capabilities supporting multi product lines. Inf. Soft. Technol. **54**, 828–852 (2012)
13. Johnsen, E.B., Lin, J.-C., Yu, I.C.: Comparing AWS deployments using model-based predictions. In: Proceedings of the International Symposium on Leveraging Applications of Formal Methods, Verification and Validation (ISoLA), ISoLA 2016, Heidelberg (2016)
14. Kang, K., Cohen, S., Hess, J., Novak, W., Peterson, A.: Feature-oriented domain analysis (FODA) feasibility study. Technical report, DTIC document (1990)
15. Khalilov, E., Ross, J., Antkiewicz, M., Markus Völter, K.C.: Modeling and optimizing automotive electric/electronic (E/E) architectures: towards makingclafer accessible to practitioners. In: Proceedings of the International Symposium on Leveraging Applications of Formal Methods, Verification and Validation (ISoLA), ISoLA 2016, Heidelberg (2016)
16. Lehman, M.M.: Programs, life cycles, and laws of software evolution. In: Proceedings of the IEEE (1980)
17. Nieke, M., Mauro, J., Seidl, C., Yu, I.C.: User profiles for context-aware reconfiguration in software product lines. In: Proceedings of the International Symposium on Leveraging Applications of Formal Methods, Verification and Validation (ISoLA), ISoLA 2016, Heidelberg (2016)
18. Pohl, K., Böckle, G., van der Linden, F.J.: Software Product Line Engineering - Foundations Principles and Techniques. Springer, Berlin/Heidelberg (2005)
19. Rosà, A., Zheng, Y., Sun, H., Javed, O., Binder, W.: Adaptable runtime monitoring for the java virtual machine. In: Proceedings of the International Symposium on Leveraging Applications of Formal Methods, Verification and Validation (ISoLA), ISoLA 2016, Heidelberg (2016)
20. Schaefer, I., Bettini, L., Bono, V., Damiani, F., Tanzarella, N.: Delta-oriented programming of software product lines. In: Bosch, J., Lee, J. (eds.) Software Product Lines: Going Beyond. LNCS, vol. 6287, pp. 77–91. Springer, Heidelberg (2010)
21. Schaefer, I., Rabiser, R., Clarke, D., Bettini, L., Benavides, D., Botterweck, G., Pathak, A., Trujillo, S., Villela, K.: Software diversity: state of the art and perspectives. STTT **14**(5), 477–495 (2012)
22. Schmid, K., Santana de Almeida, E.: Product line engineering. IEEE Softw. **4**, 24–30 (2013)
23. Seidl, C., Schaefer, I., Aßmann, U.: Integrated management of variability in space and time in software families. In Proceedings of the 18th International Software Product Line Conference (SPLC), SPLC 2014 (2014)
24. Svahnberg, M., Bosch, J.: Evolution in software product lines. J. Softw. Maint. Res. Pract. **11**(6), 391–422 (1999)
25. ter Beek, M., Fantechi, A., Gnesi, S., Semini, L.: Variability-based design of services for smart transportation systems. In: Proceedings of the International Symposium on Leveraging Applications of Formal Methods, Verification and Validation (ISoLA), ISoLA 2016, Heidelberg (2016)
26. van den Berk, I., Jansen, S., Luinenburg, L., Ecosystems, S.: A software ecosystem strategy assessment model. In: Proceedings of the Fourth European Conference on Software Architecture: Companion Volume, pp. 127–134. ACM (2010)

27. Wille, D., Tiede, M., Schulze, S., Seidl, C., Schaefer, I.: Identifying variability in object-oriented code using model-based code mining. In: Proceedings of the International Symposium on Leveraging Applications of Formal Methods, Verification and Validation (ISoLA), ISoLA 2016, Heidelberg (2016)

Towards Incremental Validation of Railway Systems

Reiner Hähnle[1,2](✉) and Radu Muschevici[1](✉)

[1] Department of Computer Science, Technische Universität Darmstadt,
Darmstadt, Germany
{haehnle,radu}@cs.tu-darmstadt.de
[2] Department of Computer Science, Università degli Studi di Torino, Torino, Italy

Abstract. We propose to formally model requirements and interoperability constraints among components of a railway system to enable automated, incremental analysis and validation mechanisms. The goal is to provide the basis for a technology that can drastically reduce the time and cost for certification by making it possible to trace changes from requirements via design to implementation.

1 Introduction

Railway systems have stringent safety, reliability and availability requirements. Verification and certification are central aspects of system development in the railway domain.

The ongoing *digitalization* of all technical systems affects the railway domain in a manner similar to other systems: an increasing number of functionalities that used to be realized by dedicated hardware are now implemented in software on standard platforms; in addition, these software systems become connected, raising completely new demands regarding usability and security. As a consequence, technical systems become affected by changes in the technological infrastructure, legal regulations and user behavior. While this global trend affects most technical domains, the railway domain is particularly sensitive because of its high quality and safety requirements, which necessitate certification.

It has been pointed out by railway technology suppliers [28] that the expected increase in effort for frequent (re-)certification is about to become a major problem for the railway industry. The reason is that, while railway systems evolve incrementally throughout their lifetime, their validation typically involves re-verifying the whole system. That is, whenever a part of the system changes, the entire system is again subjected to full verification to renew its authorisation for

The research reported here was partially supported by project FORMBAR "Formalisierung von betrieblichen und anderen Regelwerken", part of AG Signalling/DB RailLab within the Innovation Alliance between Deutschen Bahn AG and TU Darmstadt. Parts of this paper were written during a research stay of the first author at and supported by University of Torino. All support is gratefully acknowledged.

T. Margaria and B. Steffen (Eds.): ISoLA 2016, Part II, LNCS 9953, pp. 433–446, 2016.
DOI: 10.1007/978-3-319-47169-3_36

placing it in service. An *incremental* verification approach would substantially decrease the cost and effort of renewing this authorisation.

In this paper, we propose an incremental certification approach based on a formal modeling language. It consists of the following components:

- *Modeling* of the railway domain, its operative constraints, and its safety regulations in a formal, executable language that allows to represent system variability in an explicit, traceable manner.
- The model is sufficiently precise to permit *code generation* for the intended implementation platform. The code generator needs to be certified only once and for all.
- System *updates* are modeled as new system variants that change or extend some of the existing features. Updates are *traced* from requirements via a feature model to the executable model. The difference between the given model and the updated model is captured in a structured manner in terms of so-called "deltas".
- A structured description of a system update in a formalized language is the basis for advanced *formal methods tools* support: behavioral regression analysis, automated test generation, resource analysis, correctness checks such as deadlock freedom, are available to speed up certification and decrease workload.

The viability of the process sketched above hinges on the availability of a suitable modeling language and tool suite. Such a language is presented in the following section.

2   The Abstract Behavioral Specification (ABS) Language

The Abstract Behavioral Specification (ABS) language [24] is a formal, executable modeling language that has been developed in a series of EU projects since 2009. It comes with a comprehensive tool suite [9,35] that is integrated into a web-based IDE and also available as an Eclipse plugin. ABS was used successfully in industrial projects [7]. In particular, it is currently used in a joint project[1] between Deutsche Bahn Netz AG and TU Darmstadt to formally model and analyze the operation of trains.

In contrast to general purpose formal specification languages such as B [1] or Event-B [2] that are based on set theory, ABS can be seen as a modern programming language based on an ADT—functional—OO—actor paradigm. The core of ABS appears somewhat like a light version of the Scala language but with a less complex syntax. ABS is type-safe, free of data races, and has a formal semantics [3]. It has been carefully designed to admit scalable static analyses of various kinds. As ABS is not based on a mathematical notation but on mainstream programming language idioms, it is easy to learn for anyone with programming knowledge. In this paper, we introduce ABS by example. We refer to the ABS language specification [4] and a tutorial [20] for details.

---

[1] http://www.formbar.raillab.de.

3   Modelling the Railway Domain in ABS

The operative rules of the German Railways for running trains [13] contain a very thorough domain analysis with highly precise definitions of all relevant elements of the railway domain: points, track, signal, train, station, etc. Thanks to the object-oriented modeling capabilities of ABS, these can be rendered in a rather natural OO model almost one-to-one. The ABS snippet in Fig. 1, which models a tiny part of *Fahrdienstvorschrift Richtlinie 408*[2] [13], is nearly self-explanatory.

```
1 module DomainElements;
2 data PointsPosition = Left | Right;
3
4 interface Points {
5   Unit change(PointPosition setting);
6 }
7
8 class Points implements Points {
9   PointsPosition position = Left; // default setting
10  Unit change(PointsPosition setting) { this.position = setting; }
11 }
```

Fig. 1. ABS implementation of railway points

As can be seen, classes and interfaces may have the same name. ABS enforces a strict "programming-to-interfaces" discipline where only interfaces define types, so that no ambiguity arises.

ABS is a concurrent language supporting both shared-memory as well as distributed (actor-based) concurrency. Inter-object communication is realized with messages (i.e., method calls). This is a good fit to the train domain where all safety-relevant events are triggered by explicit communication that happens at precisely defined points.

In contrast to thread-based concurrency with interleaving semantics, as found in languages such as Java or C, ABS is based on *cooperative scheduling*. This means that an ABS process cannot be preempted unless its designer explicitly states it. This is a good match with the kind of concurrency encountered in the railway domain: trains, controllers, track elements are modeled naturally as different actors that do not communicate by shared resources, but with explicit messaging events. In addition, there is at most one train at each position of a track; trains can enter block sections only at explicit locations marked by signaling elements, etc.

We explain the ABS concurrency model with an example, shown in Fig. 2, that gives a fragment of a model of train runs. It is encapsulated in an interface TrainRun, of which we give an implementation in an identically named class.

---

[2] Richtlinie 408 is the official document that regulates in detail how trains are to be operated in Germany. Similar documents exist in other countries.

```
1 class TrainRun(Int trainNr, Route route) implements TrainRun {
2
3   BlockPost position; // end of current block section
4
5   Unit run() {
6     BlockPost position = route.getStart();
7     Fut<Unit> entered = position!enterTrain(this);
8     BlockPost destination = route.getDestination();
9     await entered?;
10     while (position != destination) {
11       BlockPost next = route.getNext();
12       ...
13       position = next;
14     }
15   }
16 }
```

Fig. 2. An ABS model of train runs

Each train run is parametrized with a unique identification number and the route it is supposed to take. How routes are modeled is not of interest here and is encapsulated in the Route interface. If the implementation of routes is ever changed, then the rest of the model is not affected. For simplicity of presentation, we also do not model elapsed time, schedules, delays, and many other elements.

At each time a train run has a position, by definition the block post (signaling element) that marks the end of the block section it occupies. The method run models how a train is run along a given route.

In line 6, a synchronous (i.e., sequential and blocking) method call obtains the initial position of the train. However, the train might still be elsewhere (e.g., in the previous block section), so we must ensure that it has arrived at the current position before it is dispatched further. We do not know exactly how long this takes. Therefore, it is appropriate to model the action with an asynchronous call to enterTrain. This call encapsulates a number of complex actions including updating several tables, logging events, etc. In ABS, this asynchronous call *does not* interrupt the execution of run, which directly proceeds with line 8. The type of the result variable entered is annotated as a *future* value that is not immediately available. If the call to enterTrain is executed on a different processor, then it can run concurrently to the run process.

Before the loop is entered, where the train is advanced along the route, we must ensure that it has arrived at the current position. This is achieved by the **await** statement in line 9 which suspends execution of run until its guard becomes true. An expression of the form f?, where f is a future, becomes true once the call associated with it has completed. Observe that we are not interested in the return value of the call, only in the fact that it has finished.[3]

---

[3] Of course, it is also possible to retrieve the value of a finished call by accessing a future with f.get.

Cooperative scheduling with explicit **await**s avoids data races. In particular, it is sufficient that a method reestablishes the class invariant before suspension and upon termination—these are the only opportunities for other methods to modify the state of a process. As a consequence, it was possible to design a *modular* proof system for functional verification of ABS models [15], where global invariants are decomposed into locally sequential properties. This is the prerequisite to formally prove safety properties of ABS models for an *unbounded* number of objects and *unbounded* data [16].

It is possible in ABS to model the passing of time, making it suitable for real-time simulation. For example, if we want to model that a train spends a certain amount of time within each block section, we could insert a statement of the form `duration(t,t')` at the beginning of the while loop before line 11. It has the effect to block the current process for at least t and at most t' time units. If we want the processor not to be idle during this period, then we could write **await** `duration(t,t')` to allow suspension of control. Time parameters such as t might be computed by complex expressions. Assume that expression e computes the minimum time it takes a train to pass through the current block section. Then we could set t = e; before the duration statement. The current system time can be queried with the built-in function `now()` in ABS. This makes it possible, for example, to model in a natural manner that a train waits at least until its scheduled departure time, etc. A global clock, which tends to clutter models and render simulation expensive, is not required.

To finish with the example, the while loop (without giving details) steps through the **route** until the destination is reached. Each loop body contains various asynchronous calls that implement the protocol governing how a train passes from one block section to the next.

As mentioned above, the concurrency model of ABS is a good match for the kind of concurrency encountered in railway systems: in either, actions are asynchronous (e.g., time passes between the signal going green and the train starting to move) and scheduling points are explicit (e.g., signals). It is tedious and complex to model concurrency in general purpose specification languages. This motivated, for example, CSP||B [30] that combines stateful and event-based modeling and is used to formalize railway interlocking [23]. But while CSP||B is a combination of two different formalisms, in ABS data modelling, imperative-OO stateful programming, and asynchronous events are tightly integrated into a uniform high-level language that nonetheless stays formally analyzable.

4 Variability Modelling with ABS

The ABS language can model system updates as new system variants that change or extend existing variants. Following a *feature-oriented software development (FOSD)* approach [8], variants are described as sets of *features*. Each feature has its corresponding ABS implementation. A feature's implementation is specified in terms of the code modifications (i.e., additions and removals) that need to be performed to a variant of the system that does not include that feature in order to add it. As the modeler needs to specify differences between system variants, this style of programming is called *delta-oriented programming* [29]. The ABS code modules that encapsulate feature implementations are called *delta modules*, or *deltas* for short. Deltas can modify a given ABS program extensively and comprehensively by adding, removing or modifying program elements, including interfaces, classes, algebraic data types and functions.

The ABS code in Fig. 3 shows a delta that extends points with a configurable maximal traversal speed. Historically, points were designed to be safely traversed at low speeds of around 40–100 km/h. Contemporary point designs embrace the demands of high speed railways and allow trains to pass them at higher speeds of 200 km/h or above.

```
1  delta ConfigurableSpeedPoints(Int maxPointsSpeed);
2  uses DomainElements;
3
4  modifies interface Points {
5      adds Unit setMaxSpeed(Int s);
6  }
7
8  modifies class Points {
9      adds Int   maxSpeed = maxPointsSpeed;
10     adds Unit setMaxSpeed(Int s) { maxSpeed = s; }
11 }
```

Fig. 3. An ABS delta implementing the feature "points with a configurable speed"

The delta ConfigurableSpeedPoints modifies the Points class by adding a private[4] field speed and a setter method to change its value. It also adds the setSpeed method to the points' public interface; otherwise the method would be private to its class (because of ABS' "programming-to interfaces" discipline). The points' default maximal speed value is assigned based on the delta's maxPointsSpeed parameter. To understand how this delta parameter is configured we need to introduce the feature modelling facility of ABS.

A *feature* is a familiar but informal notion in software engineering—it is quite common to describe a software system in terms of the features that it offers. FOSD uses features in a more rigorous sense: features are derived from software requirements and their relationships are formally captured in a *feature model* [25]. ABS feature models define features as names (labels) and also allow feature attributes, which are name-value pairs that make features parametrizable.

A feature model describes a system at a high level of abstraction: its specification relates to the requirements engineering phase in a software development

---

[4] ABS enforces strong encapsulation of object states. All fields are strictly private and the only way to access them from other objects is by getter and setter methods.

process. Delta modeling, that is, the declaration of deltas and their relationships, is part of the design and implementation phase.

The crucial point is that feature model and delta model are *connected*: a feature is implemented using a series of one or more deltas while a delta supplies the (partial) implementation for one or multiple features. Hence, there is a many-to-many relation between features and deltas.[5] This flexibility makes it possible, on the one hand, to avoid pollution of the feature model with implementation aspects and helps to realize a modularization among deltas, on the other.

Importantly, the connection between features and deltas in ABS is *explicit*: we can trace a feature to its delta-based implementation, and we can trace deltas back to the features that they implement. Traceability between feature and delta model allows *automatic generation* of system variants: upon selecting a set of features, the corresponding software product can be generated automatically by tracing the corresponding delta modules and composing them. This is explained in the next section.

5   Modeling Railway Systems Evolution with ABS

To specify variability in the railway domain, we introduce a feature model. This model reflects an evolution scenario: the system model described in Sect. 3 evolves over time to reflect actual developments in the railway domain, such as the introduction of points traversable at higher speeds. Instead of changing the point's implementation (see Fig. 1) directly, we associate the capability of traversing points at variable maximum speeds with a new *feature* `ConfigurableSpeedPoints`. Then we specify the difference in terms of implementations between historical points and modern points by providing the delta shown in Fig. 3.

The advantage of this approach from a validation/certification standpoint is that the old system continues to exist in its *original form* and therefore does not need to be re-validated. Merely the changes applied to the old system, which are encapsulated in the new features and deltas, need to be re-validated/certified. This is the basis for an *incremental* approach to system validation. By implementing system evolution in this way, we effectively turn our railway system specification into a software product line (SPL) [27]—a *set* of system specifications that are developed together from a collection of common software assets.

Figure 4 illustrates the fragment of an ABS feature model associated with the evolution scenario described above. On the left is a textual description and on the right an equivalent, diagrammatic one.

A feature model consists of a hierarchy of features, with the most general feature that describes the overall concept (here: `RailwayDomain`) at the top. Below the top feature, an arbitrary number of sub-features can be declared;

---

[5] Due to the many-to-many association of features and deltas, it is generally not feasible to rely on feature models to abstractly describe delta composition – other modeling tools, such as an extended UML [32] are preferable for this purpose.

```
1 root RailwayDomain {
2   group allof {
3     opt ConfigurableSpeedPoints {
4       Int max;
5     }
6   }
7 }
```

Fig. 4. A simple feature model for the railway domain model

these are specified as a **group**. Sub-features can in turn have their own sub-features and so on. In our example, the only sub-feature of RailwayDomain is ConfigurableSpeedPoints. Moreover, this feature is declared **opt**ional to reflect that it does not have to be part of all variants of the railway domain system (in the graphical representation optional sub-features are marked with a hollow circle). The feature has an attribute max that represents the maximum traversal speed of points in the domain. By designing system variants that assign specific concrete values to this attribute, the points in our system will have different capabilities.

To specify different system variants, the ABS language provides **product** declarations. A product is simply a set of features and feature attribute assignments that are given a name. Figure 5 shows the declaration of four products.

```
1 product Legacy(RailwayDomain);
2 product LowSpeed(RailwayDomain, ConfigurableSpeedPoints{max=40});
3 product MedSpeed(RailwayDomain, ConfigurableSpeedPoints{max=130});
4 product HighSpeed(RailwayDomain, ConfigurableSpeedPoints{max=230});
```

Fig. 5. A set of products (variants) of the railway domain system

The Legacy product includes only the RailwayDomain feature while the other three also include the ConfigurableSpeedPoints feature specifying different values for the maximum traversal speed attribute.

So far we have shown how to declare deltas that specify modifications to an ABS program without deltas. We have also shown how to specify feature models that model system variability abstractly, using features and attributes. We still lack the connection between both, a component that is essential in establishing the desired traceability between features and delta models. The construct that provides this link in ABS is called *software product line (SPL) configuration*. An SPL configuration specifies the (many-to-many) relation between the features in a feature model and the deltas in a delta model. Based on the set of features in a specific product, the configuration defines which delta modules should be applied to build the corresponding system variant.

```
1 productline RailwayDomain;
2 features RailwayDomain, ConfigurableSpeedPoints;
3 delta ConfigurableSpeedPoints(ConfigurableSpeedPoints.max)
4     when ConfigurableSpeedPoints;
```

Fig. 6. An SPL configuration for the railway domain SPL

Figure 6 shows the SPL configuration for our running example. In lines 3–4, it is specified that the *delta* ConfigurableSpeedPoints should be applied whenever the *feature* ConfigurableSpeedPoints is selected. As a consequence, we are able to trace the ConfigurableSpeedPoints feature to its implementation by the ConfigurableSpeedPoints delta and vice versa.[6]

Looking at the product declarations in Fig. 5, we can see that the bottom three products include the feature ConfigurableSpeedPoints. Each of these products assigns a specific value to the feature's max attribute. Thanks to the SPL configuration, the delta's maxPointsSpeed parameter is initialized using that value, which then becomes the default value for the maxSpeed field introduced in the Points class by the very same delta (cf. Fig. 3).

6   Towards Automated and Incremental Certification

The example in Fig. 6 demonstrates how ABS supports traceable connections between features and their implementation in terms of deltas, where the latter describe code modifications in a precise and structured manner. This capability can be used to make certification after updates more cost efficient.

Updating and renewal of railways equipment is costly, partly due to the necessity to ensure continuing safety and interoperability of systems throughout their lifespan. Renewal or updating can lead to the loss of the "authorisation for placing in service", which subsequently has to be renewed by following a verification procedure.[7] That verification procedure, i.e., the effort required to ensure that the equipment continues to conform to the requirements (safety, performance, interoperability, etc.) is a major cost factor due to its manual nature. The decision whether and to what extent a verification procedure is necessary is taken on a case by case basis, based on manual assessment of the impact of each change.

The model-centric approach to specification of railway systems with ABS sketched in the previous sections has the potential to substantially reduce the cost of updates, with respect to both assessment and verification. This expectation is based on the capabilities of our approach in terms of *traceability*,

---

[6] For sake of simplicity, our example constitutes a one-to-one relation between a feature and a delta but in general it is many-to-many.

[7] See Directive 2008/57/EC, specifically Annex III which spells out essential requirements relating to safety, reliability, availability, etc.

code generation, and *automated analysis*. For each of these, we now describe its detailed role within the overall picture.

Traceability. Subsequent stages of system evolution are specified in terms of a software product line defined on the basis of a feature model. As the definition of SPLs in ABS permits traceability of features through to code deltas, one can precisely pin down the differences between two product variants (i.e., a legacy system and its update) in terms of implementation within an SPL as illustrated by the `ConfigurableSpeedPoints` update in the previous section.

The ability to present the changes between two system variants in a precise and structured manner not only simplifies the assessment of the impact of a change, but, importantly, even narrows down the scope of assessment to the exact *increment* embodied in the change.

Code generation. ABS code is executable and highly precise, which not only permits code generation, but results in *efficiently* executable code. At this time, ABS supports code generation backends to Java 8 [31], Haskell, Erlang, and ProActive [21]. All these code backends are highly optimized for concurrent execution on multi-processor systems.

To test this claim, we created a prototypic ABS model of railway operations based on [13] for a simple track layout that corresponds to a typical medium-sized station with 5–10 trains running in parallel. We chose 5 m as its spatial resolution and 50 ms as temporal resolution (corresponding to a maximum of 360 km/h). We were able to simulate several hours of operation with dozens of train runs within a few seconds on a standard laptop.

In addition to simulation, a major advantage of code generation is that verification and certification of code generators can be performed completely independent from system modeling. As a consequence, certification of code generation needs to be done only once and then can be re-used for all subsequent system updates.

Automated analysis. Verification of a system update requires to ensure that (i) existing system properties are preserved, (ii) the new features work as intended, and (iii) no undesired properties are introduced by the update. This is a highly complex and time consuming, therefore, expensive task. It is here that the model-centric approach to system validation sketched in this paper offers its greatest potential. The reason is that the ABS language was explicitly designed to be analysable by highly automated tools [9] and is delivered with a comprehensive tool suite [35].

Regarding verification of system updates we distinguish between functional ("behavior") and non-functional ("performance") properties. In addition, we look at global correctness properties of ABS code, such as deadlock-freedom, uncaught exceptions, etc.

Functional properties are established by two complementary approaches: symbolic execution and automated test generation. Symbolic execution [22] of the legacy and the updated system is useful to compare control flows, which can then be checked for inaccurate modeling or hidden assumptions. In addition, test cases can be automatically generated from ABS code [6]. With regard to non-functional properties, we rely on automated *resource analysis* of ABS models [5]. Finally, it is important to ensure that the updated system does not introduce unwanted behavior in the form of deadlocks, uncaught exceptions, etc. To this end, it is important to ensure *correctness* of ABS code which is done either by deductive verification [14] or by type-based inference systems [19]. Importantly, these verification methods also support incremental changes [10] and, specifically, deltas [34].

Limitations. Like any modeling framework, also the approach based on SPL and ABS, has the limitation to cover merely those parts of the real world that have been modeled. Not all aspects of the train domain are suitable for modeling in ABS. This is the case, for example, with respect to usability/UIs, optimization, or continously evolving states. Some aspects, such as usability, are inherently difficult to formalize and our approach does not extend to them. Other aspects, such as optimization, are not the focus of (re-)certification and need not to be modeled. Or they could be modeled in a different, more suitable formal framework. For example, the system KeYmaera [18] is able to prove safety properties [26] of a hybrid model of the European Train Control System. These properties, for example, maximum break distance, can then be assumed and trusted in the ABS model.

7   Related Work

Refinement calculi such as Z, B, and Event-B are frequently used in the railway domain [28] because one can refine a declarative specification into a provably correct, executable program. This may involve a high number of refinement steps which typically results in considerable verification effort. Refinement-based approaches support a limited number of target languages (e.g., OCaML in the case of Event-B). While it is possible to model distributed concurrency [11,23], shared memory access, such as in ABS, seems problematic. The largest drawback of refinement-based approaches we see is that they do not support incremental system updates. The term *incremental* in connection with refinement-based models (e.g., [11,12]) refers to refinement steps. General system updates, however, are often not strictly refinements of data or behavior but modifications or extensions.

There is considerable work on formalization of different aspects of railway systems (see [17] for a recent collection). Unsurprisingly, much of it is concerned with safety-critical aspects such as interlocking systems. In addition to B and Event-B, Petri nets are commonly used [33]. These have the limitation that it is not feasible to model and analyze a large or unbounded number of objects (e.g., train runs).

We are not aware of a formal model that attempts to formalize signaling as well as operational aspects of railways at the same time. We are also not aware of a formal model that supports incremental system updates that are not refinements.

8 Conclusion

In this paper, we sketched an approach for formal modeling, simulation, and analysis of railway systems, their requirements, and their interoperability constraints. It is based on the modeling language ABS that permits precise, executable specifications from which efficient code generation is possible. ABS permits to trace system updates from requirements down to the implementation via delta modeling, thus allowing to analyse functional and non-functional properties that may have changed. We showed that the specification of system updates in terms of software product lines in ABS permits traceability of features down to code. Together with the analysis tool suite of ABS, this forms a feasible technological basis for an incremental verification and certification process.

References

1. Abrial, J.R.: The B Book: Assigning Programs to Meanings. Cambridge University Press, Cambridge (1996)
2. Abrial, J.: Modeling in Event-B — System and Software Engineering. Cambridge University Press, Cambridge (2010)
3. Deliverable 1.2 of project FP7-231620 (HATS): Full ABS Modeling Framework, March 2011. http://www.hats-project.eu
4. The ABS Language Specification (2016). http://abs-models.org/documentation/manual/
5. Albert, E., Arenas, P., Flores-Montoya, A., Genaim, S., Gómez-Zamalloa, M., Martin-Martin, E., Puebla, G., Román-Díez, G.: SACO: static analyzer for concurrent objects. In: Ábrahám, E., Havelund, K. (eds.) TACAS 2014 (ETAPS). LNCS, vol. 8413, pp. 562–567. Springer, Heidelberg (2014). doi:10.1007/978-3-642-54862-8_46
6. Albert, E., Arenas, P., Gómez-Zamalloa, M., Wong, P.Y.H.: aPET: a test case generation tool for concurrent objects. In: Meyer, B., Baresi, L., Mezini, M. (eds.) Joint Meeting European Software Engineering Conference and ACM SIGSOFT Symposium on Foundations of Software Engineering, ESEC/FSE, St Petersburg, pp. 595–598. ACM (2013)
7. Albert, E., de Boer, F.S., Hähnle, R., Johnsen, E.B., Schlatte, R., Tapia Tarifa, S.L., Wong, P.Y.H.: Formal modeling of resource management for cloud architectures: an industrial case study using Real-Time ABS. J. Service-Oriented Comput. Appl. 8(4), 323–339 (2014)
8. Apel, S., Kästner, C.: An overview of feature-oriented software development. J. Object Technol. 8(5), 49–84 (2009)
9. Bubel, R., Montoya, A.F., Hähnle, R.: Analysis of executable software models. In: Bernardo, M., Damiani, F., Hähnle, R., Johnsen, E.B., Schaefer, I. (eds.) SFM 2014. LNCS, vol. 8483, pp. 1–25. Springer, Heidelberg (2014). doi:10.1007/978-3-319-07317-0_1
10. Bubel, R., Hähnle, R., Pelevina, M.: Fully abstract operation contracts. In: Margaria, T., Steffen, B. (eds.) ISoLA 2014, Part II. LNCS, vol. 8803, pp. 120–134. Springer, Heidelberg (2014). doi:10.1007/978-3-662-45231-8_9

11. Butler, M.: Incremental design of distributed systems with event-b. In: Broy, M., Sitou, W., Hoare, T. (eds.) Engineering Methods and Tools for Software Safety and Security: Marktoberdorf Summer School 2008, pp. 131–160. IOS Press (2009). http://eprints.soton.ac.uk/266910/. Chap. 4
12. Butler, M.J., Yadav, D.: An incremental development of the Mondex system in Event-B. Formal Aspects Comput. **20**(1), 61–77 (2008)
13. Deutsche Bahn Netz AG, Frankfurt, Germany: Fahrdienstvorschrift Richtlinie 408, December 2015. http://fahrweg.dbnetze.com/fahrweg-de/nutzungsbedingungen/regelwerke/betriebl_technisch/eiu_interne_regeln_ril_408.html
14. Din, C.C., Bubel, R., Hähnle, R.: KeY-ABS: a deductive verification tool for the concurrent modelling language ABS. In: Felty, A.P., Middeldorp, A. (eds.) CADE 2015. LNCS (LNAI), vol. 9195, pp. 517–526. Springer, Heidelberg (2015). doi:10.1007/978-3-319-21401-6_35
15. Din, C.C., Owe, O.: Compositional reasoning about active objects with shared futures. Formal Aspects Comput. **27**(3), 551–572 (2015)
16. Din, C.C., Tapia Tarifa, S.L., Hähnle, R., Johnsen, E.B.: History-based specification and verification of scalable concurrent and distributed systems. In: Butler, M., Conchon, S., Zaïdi, F. (eds.) ICFEM 2015. LNCS, vol. 9407, pp. 217–233. Springer, Heidelberg (2015). doi:10.1007/978-3-319-25423-4_14
17. Fantechi, A., Flammini, F., Gnesi, S.: Formal methods for railway control systems. STTT **16**(6), 643–646 (2014)
18. Fulton, N., Mitsch, S., Quesel, J.-D., Völp, M., Platzer, A.: KeYmaera X: an axiomatic tactical theorem prover for hybrid systems. In: Felty, A.P., Middeldorp, A. (eds.) CADE 2015. LNCS (LNAI), vol. 9195, pp. 527–538. Springer, Heidelberg (2015). doi:10.1007/978-3-319-21401-6_36
19. Giachino, E., Laneve, C., Lienhardt, M.: A framework for deadlock detection in core abs. Softw. Syst. Model. 1–36 (2015)
20. Hähnle, R.: The abstract behavioral specification language: a tutorial introduction. In: Giachino, E., Hähnle, R., de Boer, F.S., Bonsangue, M.M. (eds.) Formal Methods for Components and Objects. LNCS, vol. 7866, pp. 1–37. Springer, Heidelberg (2013). doi:10.1007/978-3-642-40615-7_1
21. Henrio, L., Rochas, J.: From modelling to systematic deployment of distributed active objects–extended version. Research Report <hal-01299817>, I3S, April 2016
22. Hentschel, M., Bubel, R., Hähnle, R.: Symbolic execution debugger (SED). In: Bonakdarpour, B., Smolka, S.A. (eds.) RV 2014. LNCS, vol. 8734, pp. 255–262. Springer, Heidelberg (2014). doi:10.1007/978-3-319-11164-3_21
23. James, P., Moller, F., Nga, N.H., Roggenbach, M., Schneider, S.A., Treharne, H.: Techniques for modelling and verifying railway interlockings. STTT **16**(6), 685–711 (2014)
24. Johnsen, E.B., Hähnle, R., Schäfer, J., Schlatte, R., Steffen, M.: ABS: a core language for abstract behavioral specification. In: Aichernig, B.K., de Boer, F.S., Bonsangue, M.M. (eds.) Formal Methods for Components and Objects. LNCS, vol. 6957, pp. 142–164. Springer, Heidelberg (2011). doi:10.1007/978-3-642-25271-6_8
25. Kang, K.C., Cohen, S., Hess, J., Nowak, W., Peterson, S.: Feature-Oriented domain analysis (FODA) feasibility study. Technical report, CMU/SEI-90-TR-021, Carnegie Mellon University Software Engineering Institute (1990)
26. Platzer, A., Quesel, J.-D.: European train control system: a case study in formal verification. In: Breitman, K., Cavalcanti, A. (eds.) ICFEM 2009. LNCS, vol. 5885, pp. 246–265. Springer, Heidelberg (2009). doi:10.1007/978-3-642-10373-5_13
27. Pohl, K., Böckle, G., van der Linden, F.: Software Product Line Engineering. Springer, Heidelberg (2005)

28. Reichl, K., Fischer, T., Tummeltshammer, P.: Using formal methods for verification and validation in railway. In: Aichernig, B.K., Furia, C.A. (eds.) Tests and Proofs. LNCS, vol. 9762, pp. 3–13. Springer, Heidelberg (2016). doi:10.1007/978-3-319-41135-4_1

29. Schaefer, I., Bettini, L., Bono, V., Damiani, F., Tanzarella, N.: Delta-oriented programming of software product lines. In: Bosch, J., Lee, J. (eds.) SPLC 2010. LNCS, vol. 6287, pp. 77–91. Springer, Heidelberg (2010). doi:10.1007/978-3-642-15579-6_6

30. Schneider, S., Treharne, H.: CSP theorems for communicating B machines. Formal Aspects Comput. **17**(4), 390–422 (2005)

31. Serbanescu, V., Azadbakht, K., de Boer, F.S., Nagarajagowda, C., Nobakht, B.: A design pattern for optimizations in data intensive applications using ABS and JAVA 8. Concurrency Comput. Pract. Experience **28**(2), 374–385 (2016)

32. Setyautami, M.R.A., Azurat, A., Hähnle, R., Muschevici, R.: A UML profile for delta-oriented programming to support software product line engineering. In: International Software Product Line Conference. ACM Press (2016)

33. Sun, P., Dutilleul, S.C., Bon, P.: A model pattern of railway interlocking system by Petri nets. In: International Conference on Models and Technologies for Intelligent Transportation Systems (MT-ITS), Budapest, Hungary, pp. 442–449. IEEE (2015)

34. Thüm, T., Schaefer, I., Hentschel, M., Apel, S.: Family-based deductive verification of software product lines. In: Ostermann, K., Binder, W. (eds.) Generative Programming and Component Engineering, GPCE 2012, Dresden, Germany, pp. 11–20. ACM (2012)

35. Wong, P.Y.H., Albert, E., Muschevici, R., Proença, J., Schäfer, J., Schlatte, R.: The ABS tool suite: modelling, executing and analysing distributed adaptable object-oriented systems. STTT **14**(5), 567–588 (2012)

Modeling and Optimizing Automotive Electric/Electronic (E/E) Architectures: Towards Making Clafer Accessible to Practitioners

Eldar Khalilov[1]([⊠]), Jordan Ross[1], Michał Antkiewicz[1], Markus Völter[2], and Krzysztof Czarnecki[1]

[1] University of Waterloo, Waterloo, Canada
ekhalilov@gsd.uwaterloo.ca
[2] Independent/ITEMIS, Stuttgart, Germany

Abstract. Modern automotive electric/electronic (E/E) architectures are growing to the point where architects can no longer manually predict the effects of their design decisions. Thus, in addition to applying an architecture reference model to decompose their architectures, they also require tools for synthesizing and evaluating candidate architectures during the design process. Clafer is a modeling language, which has been used to model variable multi-layer, multi-perspective automotive system architectures according to an architecture reference model. Clafer tools allow architects to synthesize optimal candidates and evaluate effects of their design decisions. However, since Clafer is a general-purpose structural modeling language, it does not help the architects in building models conforming to the given architecture reference model. In this paper, we present an E/E architecture domain-specific language (DSL) built on top of Clafer, which embodies the reference model and which guides the architects in correctly applying it. We evaluate the DSL and its implementation by modeling two existing automotive systems, which were originally modeled in plain Clafer. The evaluation showed that by using the DSL, an evaluator obtained correct models by construction because the DSL helped prevent typical errors that are easy to make in plain Clafer. The evaluator was also able to synthesize and evaluate candidate architectures as with plain Clafer.

Keywords: Architecture · Modeling · Optimization · Synthesis · Language engineering · Domain-specific language · DSL · Clafer · Metaprogramming system · MPS

1 Introduction

With the increasing number of intelligent automotive features and the push towards autonomous cars, modern automotive electric/electronic (E/E) architectures are becoming increasingly complex. The architects can no longer create

© Springer International Publishing AG 2016
T. Margaria and B. Steffen (Eds.): ISoLA 2016, Part II, LNCS 9953, pp. 447–464, 2016.
DOI: 10.1007/978-3-319-47169-3_37

and evaluate candidate architectures manually to understand the effects of their design decisions. Thus, architects require powerful modeling and reasoning tools to allow them to synthesize candidate architectures given some design decisions and discover the correct and optimal ones automatically.

One approach to conquering the complexity is using a *reference model* which prescribes a certain way of decomposing the overall architecture into layers and capturing the crosscutting concerns, including variability and quality. We present such a reference model in Sect. 2. Furthermore, in order to be able to automatically reason about an E/E architecture (evaluate the effect of design decisions), the architecture must be represented using a formal modeling language which is supported by a scalable automated reasoner. One such language is Clafer [1], and we introduce architectural modeling using Clafer in Sect. 3. However, Clafer is a general-purpose structural modeling language which does not provide the architectural concepts from the reference model as first-class language constructs. Thus, to make the modeling and reasoning power of Clafer available to practitioners who are not Clafer experts, we implemented an architecture domain-specific language (DSL) based on the reference model to guide users in correctly and consistently applying the reference model (Sect. 4). Our implementation relies on the JetBrains MPS language workbench [2], whereby we implemented Clafer as an MPS language and the Architecture DSL as an extension of Clafer in MPS.

We present the design of the Architecture DSL and how it addresses the challenges of applying plain Clafer to architectural modeling in Sect. 5. We evaluate our work by using the DSL to model two existing architectures of two automotive subsystems which were previously modeled in plain Clafer [3]. The goal of the evaluation is to see whether the DSL improves the modeling experience compared to plain Clafer while still supporting the reasoning capabilities. We present the key observations and discussion in Sect. 6. We briefly summarize the related work in Sect. 7, and conclude the paper in Sect. 8.

2   A Reference Model for E/E Architecture Modeling

In this work, we use the reference model illustrated in Fig. 1, which is an adaptation of the EAST-ADL [4] (details in [3]). The model is *multi-layer* and it prescribes dividing the architecture into a feature model, a functional architecture, and a hardware architecture. The feature model contains *user-facing features*, such as *express up* and *pinch protection* in a power window system. These features are then implemented using functions, which are subsequently deployed onto hardware (the block arrow).

The model is also *multi-perspective*: it supports multiple cross-cutting concerns, including variability and quality. Variability crosscuts all layers of the architecture. For example, an optional feature (e.g., *express up*) is implemented by functions and hardware which also have to be optional as they are not needed when the feature is not selected. Furthermore, there may exist alternative ways of realizing the feature as different functions (e.g., different techniques of pinch

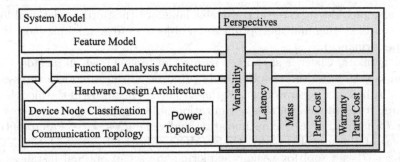

Fig. 1. An automotive E/E system architecture reference model. The block arrow denotes the deployment of the functional analysis architecture to the hardware design architecture.

detection), as well as alternative ways of deploying the functions onto hardware. Similarly, the quality perspectives may crosscut each layer of the architecture. For example, the latency of end-to-end flows (from sensors to actuators) depends on the functional connectors among the functions and functional devices, as well as on the particular deployment of these connectors onto the communication media (e.g., shared memory communication within an ECU vs. network communication between ECUs). Some qualities may also be confined to a particular layer, for example, hardware part cost only applies to the hardware design architecture.

3   E/E Architecture Modeling in Clafer

Clafer [1] has been successfully applied in several automotive architecture case studies [3,5]. Here, we first briefly introduce the modeling and reasoning workflow when using Clafer and next, we summarize the main challenges of using plain Clafer.

Clafer is a lightweight, general-purpose, textual, structural modeling language. In Clafer, a model consists of *clafers*[1]. The name "clafer" comes from the words <u>cl</u>ass, <u>fea</u>ture, and <u>ref</u>erence because a clafer provides modeling capabilities of all these language constructs. A clafer is like a *class* in that it can have instances, it can contain other clafers which represent attributes, references, and contained classes, and it can inherit the children from other clafers. A clafer is like an *attribute* and a *reference* in that its instances can point to primitive values (e.g., integers) or instances of clafers. A clafer is like a *feature* in that it has multiplicity restricting how many instances of that clafer are allowed per instance of its parent (1 - exactly one, ? - at most one, * - any number, etc.). A clafer is like a *feature group* in that it has group cardinality restricting how many instances of its children are allowed (mux - at most one, xor - exactly one, or - at least one, etc.).

---

[1] Throughout this paper if the word Clafer begins with an uppercase letter it refers to the language while a lowercase one refers to the language construct.

Clafer also provides a powerful constraint language (first-order relational logic) and means of stating multiple optimization objectives (e.g., minimize cost, maximize performance).

Furthermore, Clafer is supported by a set of tools [6], which include a scalable and exact instance generator and optimizer. Given a model expressed in Clafer, the instance generator can synthesize correct instances of the model. Furthermore, if the model contains optimization objectives, the instance generator can perform multi-objective optimization and generate a set of Pareto-optimal instances of the model. Finally, Clafer MOO (Multi Objective Optimization) Visualizer [7] is a tool for visually exploring the set of optimal instances and performing trade-off analysis.

All these capabilities make Clafer suitable for expressing architectural models, which include representing variability and quality attributes, stating optimization objectives, synthesizing (optimal and non-optimal) candidate architectures, and evaluating the impact of design decisions, and performing design space exploration [3,5].

Challenges with E/E Architecture Modeling using Plain Clafer. Clafer is not domain-specific for the E/E modeling domain: it does not provide the architectural concepts from the reference model as first-class language constructs. Furthermore, Clafer can only express the structure (metamodel) of the architectural concepts from the reference model; Clafer and its general-purpose tools (compiler, instance generator, visualizer) cannot guide users in correctly applying the reference model rules. For example, Clafer will allow a user to leave references unconstrained and the instance generator will produce instances not intended by the modeler.

This causes some challenges for model creators and model readers related to applying and recognizing the modeling idioms needed for architectural modeling. Thus, to make the modeling and reasoning power of Clafer available to practitioners who are not Clafer experts, we implemented an Architecture DSL [8] which encodes the reference model concepts and which guides the users in correctly and consistently applying the reference model rules. We first present the overview of the implementation of the DSL in Sect. 4 followed by detailed design which addresses the challenges of using plain Clafer in Sect. 5.

4   Overview of ClaferMPS

Instead of writing user manuals and relying on modeling idioms, we decided to formally encode the reference model and its rules as an Architecture DSL. We implemented the DSL using the Meta Programming System (MPS) [2] language workbench.

Meta Programming System (MPS). As a language workbench [9], MPS is a tool which allows for efficiently developing domain-specific and general-purpose languages. MPS supports the definition of abstract syntax, textual, visual or tabular concrete syntax, type system, various rules and constraints, transformations, and code generators. All ingredients of powerful IDEs are also supported.

MPS relies on *projectional editing*, where users directly modify the abstract syntax through a projected concrete syntax; no parsing is involved. This allows MPS to support a wide range of notations [10] and various ways of language composition [11]. In particular, it supports language extension, where additional language concepts are added to a base language without invasively modifying this base language. MPS has been used to build ecosystems of integrated languages in various domains including embedded software, system specification, requirements engineering, safety and security analysis, insurance contract specification, medical software and public benefits calculations [2, 12].

Components of ClaferMPS. Fig. 2 shows the components of our implementation. The boxes with gray background represent existing tools. On the plain Clafer side (right), we are using the Clafer compiler, which works with plain-text files, the instance generator, and the visualizer [6, 7].

On the MPS side (left), we build on top of MPS and use some utilities of mbeddr [12] such as the module system and graphical notation. The boxes with a pattern background represent the new components we developed: Clafer language, which implements full Clafer and provides a textual syntax; and Architecture DSL, which provides textual and graphical syntaxes. A model created in Architecture DSL is first transformed into a model expressed in the Clafer language in MPS, from which a plain-text Clafer model is generated. Generating a plain-text Clafer model allows us to leverage the existing Clafer toolchain. We refer to both the Clafer implementation in MPS and the Architecture DSL collectively as "ClaferMPS".

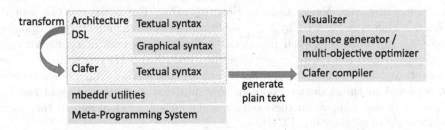

Fig. 2. ClaferMPS (left) and plain Clafer (right) tool stacks

5   E/E Architecture Modeling: Clafer vs. ClaferMPS

In this section, we demonstrate how the challenges of using plain Clafer for E/E architectural modeling are solved with ClaferMPS by comparing both approaches.

5.1 Applying E/E Reference Model Concepts

Since Clafer does not have first-class support for the E/E reference model concepts, we must define these abstractions first. In addition, both the reference model concepts and the concrete model must be contained in the same file, because Clafer currently lacks a module system. Listing 1.1 shows the feature modeling concepts *feature model* and *feature* encoded as abstract clafers.

Listing 1.1. Feature modeling concepts defined in plain Clafer

```
abstract FeatureModel
abstract Feature
```

Listing 1.2. Feature modeling (Clafer)

```
DWinSysFM : FeatureModel
  manualUpDown : Feature
  express : Feature ?
  expressUp : Feature ?
```

Concrete feature models can then be created by extending the abstract clafers `FeatureModel` and `Feature` as shown in Listing 1.2 (the symbol : indicates inheritance; ? indicates optionality). In Clafer, we use indentation to nest clafers (i.e., establish containment) and to indicate dependency that the feature `expressUp` requires `express`.

Similarly, the remainder of the reference model can be encoded in Clafer using abstract clafers [3]. While this approach is valid for modeling E/E architectures, it is limited by its inability to guide users in applying these concepts correctly. For example, a plain Clafer alone cannot ensure that a *feature* can only be defined inside (i.e., nested under) a *feature model* or another *feature*, because it is specific to the reference model.

In addition to being correctly nested, reference model concepts must also be constrained properly. For example, Listing 1.3 shows the definition of the functional analysis architecture concepts in plain Clafer. It consists of *analysis function*, *functional device*, and *function connector*. The latter has two nested reference clafers (indicated by ->), which represent the connector's endpoints (lines 14–15). Moreover, each functional analysis component or connector can be deployed into the hardware architecture (lines 2 and 16, respectively). The concepts also include many constraints, such as, that analysis functions can only be deployed to smart device nodes or that function connectors should not be deployed to anything when their sender and receiver are deployed to the same device node (e.g., the same ECU).

Listing 1.3. Encoding of functional analysis architecture concepts in plain Clafer

```
1   abstract FunctionalAnalysisComponent
2     deployedTo -> DeviceNode
3     latency -> integer
4
5   abstract AnalysisFunction : FunctionalAnalysisComponent
6     [deployedTo.type in SmartDeviceNode]
7     baseLatency -> integer
8     [latency = baseLatency*deployedTo.speedFactor]
9
10  abstract FunctionalDevice : FunctionalAnalysisComponent
11    [deployedTo.type in (SmartDeviceNode, EEDeviceNode)]
12
13  abstract FunctionConnector
14    sender -> FunctionalAnalysisComponent
15    receiver -> FunctionalAnalysisComponent
16    deployedTo -> HardwareDataConnector ?
17      [parent in this.deployedFrom]
18    [(sender.deployedTo.dref,receiver.deployedTo.dref) in (deployedTo.endpoint.dref)]
19    [(sender.deployedTo.dref = receiver.deployedTo.dref) <=> no this.deployedTo]
20    latency -> integer
21    messageSize -> integer
22    [latency = (if deployedTo then messageSize*deployedTo.transferTimePerSize else 0)]
```

Listing 1.4. A valid and an invalid function connector model example

```
1   WinSwitch : FunctionalDevice
2   WinArbiter : AnalysisFunction
3     [latency = 10]
4   WinControl : AnalysisFunction
5
6   // valid connector
7   winReq : FunctionConnector
8     [sender = WinArbiter]
9     [receiver = WinControl]
10
11  // underconstrained (invalid) connector
12  localWinReq : FunctionConnector
```

Fig. 3. Instances generated from Listing 1.4

Violating these constraints (e.g., deploying a function to a power device) will prevent the instance generator from producing any instances; instead it will report the set of mutually contradicting constraints, which then require model debugging. Furthermore, even if no constraints are violated, the instance generator can still produce correct (i.e., satisfying all constraints) but invalid instances (i.e., not making sense in terms of the domain) because the model can be underconstrained. For example, if the reference clafers on lines 14 and 15 for a function connector are not constrained to point to valid targets, the instance generator will be free to choose any function as a target, which is likely to result in a nonsensical architecture. Listing 1.4 contains a concrete example showing a correct (with respect to the stated constraints) yet invalid Clafer declaration of `localWinReq` (the connector should only be allowed between the `WinSwitch` and `WinArbiter` functions) and Fig. 3 shows the resulting instances. This example is *invalid* since it did not reflect the domain adequately. However, `winReq` is an example of a correct and valid function connector since the sender and receiver are properly constrained.

ClaferMPS solution. In order to minimize the need for writing constraints manually, we have designed and implemented a DSL on top of Clafer (using MPS' support for language extension), which provides E/E architecture concepts as first-class concepts to cover most of the reference model rules. Figure 4 shows a snippet of a functional analysis architecture modeled with the DSL. To ensure that users nest the reference model elements correctly, we restrict the usage context of the reference model concepts. This means that the DSL's auto completion menu shows only those concepts that are valid in the current context (i.e., *analysis function* is only shown in the context of *functional analysis architecture*) which can be seen at location ② in Fig. 4. If the user copy/pastes an element into the wrong context, the error will be presented as shown in Fig. 4, ①.

Next, the DSL syntax was designed to include values for all required reference clafers (from the plain Clafer approach) for the different concepts. Using the earlier example of function connectors, the DSL ensures that the user does not forget to set the targets of the sender and receiver, which are mandatory in the syntax. Additionally, the type system of the DSL ensures that the types of the chosen targets are correct, otherwise an error is reported (Fig. 4, ③). Thus,

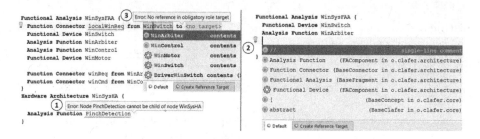

Fig. 4. ClaferMPS functional analysis example.

the DSL eliminates many common errors and minimizes the need for manually writing constraints and, consequently, model debugging.

Finally, the DSL supports semantic error detection. A simple example of a semantic rule can be formed from the constrains on lines 6 and 11 of Listing 1.3; it states that a device node of type *power* can't be given as a deployment target for an analysis function or functional device. Checking such rules informs users that there is a semantic error in the model (Fig. 6, ⑦).

5.2   Variability

In order to model more than one candidate architecture, the model must be augmented with variability. In plain Clafer, variability is expressed using multiplicities, group cardinalities, and reference clafers. For example, Listing 1.2 shows how variability can be expressed for the feature `express` by using a clafer multiplicity of 0..1 (denoted by ?). In ClaferMPS, we chose to model variability the same way as in plain Clafer, but using different keywords such as `optional` to help architects.

5.3   Quality Attributes

To evaluate quality of the candidate architectures, we need to annotate the different reference model components with *quality attributes*. These attributes can then differ among domains and even systems within a domain. For example, a power window system might not consider *security* as a quality, whereas a door locks system might.

In Clafer, quality attributes can be added to the reference model by nesting a clafer under the component type as shown on line 3 of Listing 1.3. Then, in the definitions of concrete components, the values can be defined using constraints as shown on line 3 of Listing 1.4. The challenge with this approach is that users have to directly modify the reference model and nest clafers appropriately without any guidance. Additionally, these modifications can lead to inconsistencies in the reference model over time or introduce subtle errors.

ClaferMPS solution. In ClaferMPS, users do not need to edit the reference model; instead, we provide a table shown in Fig. 5 whereby users define one or

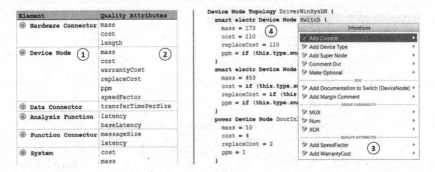

Fig. 5. User-defined quality attribute declarations for the architectural concepts (left). An intention menu for assigning values of quality attributes to model elements (right).

more *integer-valued* quality attributes ② for the chosen architectural concepts ①. Then, a user can immediately use the intention menu for a defined architectural concept (for example, the device node `Switch`) to add a value for that quality ③, ④. The intention menu is a contextual menu that allows users to perform various modifications of the model. Finally, quality attributes are properly inherited by subconcepts: the intention menu shows both concept-specific and inherited attributes.

Additionally, since the quality attributes are separate from the reference model, users can generate plain Clafer with or without the quality attributes. This allows the users to validate their architectural model (i.e., ensure that their model captures all possible candidates they intended to model) without taking the qualities into account. In plain Clafer, such a task requires manually commenting out the quality attributes in the reference model and all constraints which set their values. In Sect. 5.7, we describe how the generation process supports this functionality.

5.4   Extensibility

In plain Clafer, since the reference model is a set of abstract clafers included in the same file as the concrete system, users can perform arbitrary changes to the reference model and use all capabilities of the language in unrestricted ways. It is both an advantage for users who are Clafer experts as well as a disadvantage for non-expert users because they lack guidance and they can suffer from common errors.

ClaferMPS solution. As a result of building the Architecture DSL on top of the Clafer language in MPS, clafers and constraints can be mixed with the architectural elements. This is a common occurrence when a modeler wants to use Clafer's constraint language to write additional constraints that are not expressible using the Architecture DSL. For example, Fig. 6 shows a deployment specification of a functional architecture `WinSysFAA` to a hardware architecture

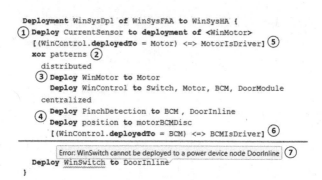

Fig. 6. Mixing clafers and constraints within a deployment (above the gray separator) and an example of semantic error for an invalid function deployment target (below the separator).

WinSysHA ①. The concepts `Deployment` and `Deploy` ① belong to the Architecture DSL; however, the element `patterns` ② is simply a clafer which, in this case, is used to group rules for the `distributed` ③ and `centralized` ④ deployment patterns. Also, the figure shows a few constraints which go beyond what is expressible using the `Deploy` concept: some of them must always hold because they are nested directly under deployment ⑤, some of them must only hold when an instance of the clafer `centralized` is present ⑥.

Additionally, ClaferMPS still provides guidance when adding Clafer to an architectural model through auto-completion and type checking.

The ability to mix clafers and constraints with DSL elements allows for lightweight extensibility of the reference model. In Fig. 6, the intention of the modeler is to specify a few alternative `DeploymentPattern`s, which is a concept currently not available in the reference model. Thanks to MPS, organizations can modularly extend the Architecture DSL by creating their own reference model which imports our reference model and adds new concepts, such as the `DeploymentPattern`. Next, they can create a new DSL which extends our Architecture DSL and adds the `DeploymentPattern` as a first-class concept together with an editor, typing, and other rules. The ability to mix clafers and constraints within the architectural models allows for working with the proposed extension before formally implementing it as a DSL in MPS.

5.5   Modularity

E/E architecture models can be quite large. Currently, Clafer does not have a module system and thus users have to define their model in a single, potentially large, text file. The model then becomes cumbersome to navigate, especially when modeling multiple subsystem architectures together.

ClaferMPS solution. ClaferMPS provides a simple module system that allows users to create *modules*, which export all contained definitions and which can import definitions from other modules. The modules are combined together during the generation process which we detail next in Sect. 5.7.

5.6   Presentation

The Clafer compiler can generate a static graphical representation of a model which shows the inheritance hierarchy and references as shown in Fig. 7. This graphical representation is complementary to the textual syntax which emphasizes clafer nesting; however, it is not suitable for visualizing architectures.

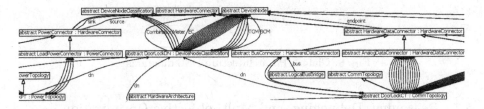

Fig. 7. Snippet of the graph for door locks generated by Clafer compiler

ClaferMPS Solution. In addition to textual syntax, the Architecture DSL provides a graphical representation of E/E architectures. This allows for architects to visualize the relationships and connections between different elements to ensure that their model matches what they intended. Figure 8 shows snippets of a few kinds of diagrams expressed with the graphical notations of the DSL; the diagrams are fully editable and, since they are projections of the same underlying model, they are always synchronized with the textual representation. Users can switch between textual and graphical projections and even view and edit both side-by-side.

The graphical editor is implemented using an MPS extension provided by the *mbeddr.platform*[2]. It does not only provide basic rendering functionality but also a set of helper tools such as automatic layout, alignment, and snapping, which reduce the effort for manually arranging the diagram elements. However, some manual layouting is still necessary.

In the Architecture DSL, diagrams focus on the structure and hide other information such as quality attributes or plain clafers. This allows users to view the model from a different perspective than offered by the textual representation. Additionally, thanks to support for modularity, users can see a graphical projection of their current module allowing them to work with a specific portion of the overall architecture.

---

[2] http://mbeddr.com/platform.html.

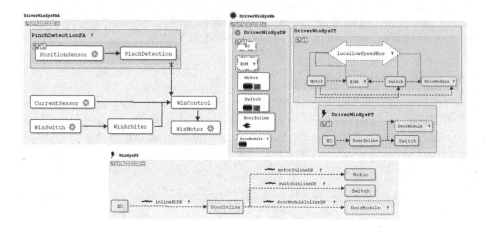

Fig. 8. ClaferMPS architecture DSL diagrams

5.7 Reasoning, Debugging, and Multi-objective Optimization

The typical workflow when modeling in plain Clafer is to write a small model fragment or temporarily comment out parts of a larger model irrelevant for the task at hand, execute the compiler to check whether the model is correct (syntax, name, type checking), execute the instance generator to validate the model (check that only valid instances are produced), and repeat. Murashkin described such micro-level and macro-level modeling patterns [5]. Next, users perform multi-objective optimization and impact and trade-off analyses [3,6].

Furthermore, the modelers often validate the model logic without the quality attributes, which requires commenting them out (cf. Sect. 5.3).

ClaferMPS Solution. The current reasoning, debugging, and multi-objective optimization tools require plain Clafer as input. Moreover, since Clafer tools do not have a module system, all imported modules, quality attributes, and the reference model must be combined into a single file.

Figure 9 shows how ClaferMPS generates plain Clafer. First, the Architecture DSL takes the predefined reference model without quality attributes expressed

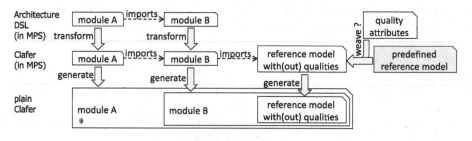

Fig. 9. Plain Clafer generation process

in Clafer in MPS (it contains Clafer code as shown in Listings 1.1 and 1.3, but written in MPS). If the user chooses to include quality attributes, ClaferMPS weaves them into the predefined reference model resulting in a reference model with quality attributes; otherwise, the predefined reference model is used directly. Next, the DSL transforms the modules expressed in the Architecture DSL into equivalent modules expressed in Clafer in MPS, while preserving the import structure. If the user has configured the DSL to exclude the quality attributes, ClaferMPS ignores all quality-related expressions during the transformation. Also, the resulting modules must now import the reference model. Finally, Clafer in MPS generates plain Clafer files for every module such that the resulting file contains all of its imported modules. For example, the generated plain Clafer for the module B contains the module's contents and the reference model with or without the quality attributes, whereas the plain Clafer for the module A has its contents as well as all contents of the module B.

This process allows the users to reason about, debug, and optimize each layer of the architecture separately with or without quality attributes. While the users still need to comment out unused parts of the reference model; their workload is greatly reduced.

6   Evaluation

The main goal of our work is make the modeling and reasoning power of Clafer accessible to practitioners. To evaluate and improve ClaferMPS, we performed the following exploratory case study. The objectives of the evaluation are to (O1) obtain feedback on usability of the DSL and tool support, (O2) demonstrate expressiveness of the DSL with respect to the case studies in the automotive body domain, and (O3) demonstrate support for modeling and analysis tasks, such as modular validation. First, we take two existing automotive system architectures, power window and door locks, which were previously modeled independently in plain Clafer by the second author [3].

The models for power window and door locks contain approximately 600 and 900 lines of Clafer and they encode 203,753,368 and 2,028 variants, respectively.

Next, we asked the second author (to whom we refer to as "the evaluator") to recreate both models in ClaferMPS and record his experience; the raw and detailed notes (40 pages) are available for the record [13]. The evaluator first modeled a single-door power window system, then he generalized it to a two-door system, and then he modeled the door-locks system. Finally, we discussed the notes with the evaluator, analyzed them, and extracted the main observations which we present here. The evaluator raised issues, reported bugs, made observations, and provided requirements. Some of the bugs and requirements were subsequently implemented in an iterative approach.

Case study completeness. Overall, the evaluator was able to completely model both case studies in ClaferMPS, generate equivalent but slightly different plain Clafer model when compared to the original model, and perform the same kinds of analyses using the Clafer toolchain as before [3,5].

Graphical projection. The evaluator frequently used the graphical projection to validate connections and he has actually discovered wrong connections once. In fact, the graph view was beneficial whenever references are used. Also, the graphical projection was useful for showing containment and ownership. However, the current graphical projection has a few shortcomings: the automatic layout sometimes requires manual rearrangement, and the evaluator could not view only a few selected elements because the projection always displays the entire module. The evaluator provided many observations about the advantages as well as suggestions for improving the graphical projection, including the ability to visualize a selected subset of elements.

In MPS, the evaluator divided the original single file plain Clafer models into many modules which was essential when working with such large models. Additionally, smaller modules make the graphical projection more useful and usable. The built-in "jump to definition" mechanism of MPS supports navigation across the modules.

Modeling, debugging, verification, and validation workflow. In ClaferMPS, the evaluator relied more on the Architecture DSL to create a more correct-by-construction model because the DSL enforces the proper structure and checks for typical errors during editing; this made the creation of the model faster in ClaferMPS. However, through the use of the Architecture DSL, the evaluator still created an invalid model, initially, by forgetting to assign some quality attributes and setting references to invalid targets. ClaferMPS helped with debugging, and finding such mistakes, because the evaluator no longer had to manually comment out fragments of a large model as ClaferMPS automatically generates code for every module and its imports, with or without the quality attributes. This allowed for testing each layer in isolation as well as testing the module logic while omitting quality attributes. In some situations, however, the evaluator still had to comment out the unused fragments of the reference model. For example, in order to test the functional architecture layer in isolation, the evaluator had to comment out the `deployedTo` reference, which induces a dependency on hardware architecture. As a result, we have implemented the separation of the deployment from the other layers and weaving of the deployment when needed during code generation; it has reduced the need for commenting out as above but can be improved further in the future to not require commenting out any portions of the model or reference model. Finally, the evaluator set up partial test modules which contain only a partial system and a subset of layers, which allowed testing the individual layers in isolation. These partial test modules allowed for testing and verifying logic associated with a specific layer of the system.

Autocomplete. The evaluator ranked autocomplete as the top feature of ClaferMPS because it prevents naming mistakes and helps in correctly selecting nested elements based on their type and the rules of the reference model. Although, autocomplete could also be provided for plain Clafer, it would not be able to interpret nesting constraints.

Inconsistencies between the reference model used in both case studies and reference model evolution. Chronologically, ClaferMPS was developed after the first version of the power window case study and the Architecture DSL was based on the reference model from that case study. The door locks case study was developed later and subsequently the power window case study was revised. In our evaluation, we observed that not only the reference models between the two case studies were slightly different but also the Architecture DSL was initially outdated. Eventually, we made all three reference models consistent.

This demonstrates the typical organizational problem which occurs when people apply a supposedly common reference model but are free to adjust it slightly in every project: the organization cannot easily enforce the consistent application of the reference model. By encoding the reference model in the DSL, providing limited extensibility, and enforcing domain-specific rules, the DSL ensures the consistent application of the reference model.

On the other hand, having a DSL creates the typical "schema migration" problem when a reference model evolves and the user models must be co-evolved consistently with the DSL. We observed this when we updated the DSL to be consistent with the reference model used in the power window case study. The architectural models became broken and the evaluator had to manually redo these broken parts. In practice, this problem is usually mitigated by versioning the reference model and providing migration scripts.

Required knowledge of Clafer. The evaluator stated that using the Architecture DSL requires basic understanding of object-orientation and navigation between objects by following the references. Building and using advanced models, such as the ones in our case studies, requires the ability to write propositional logic constraints and navigating among objects. Familiarity with constraint languages such as OCL, Alloy, or Clafer is very helpful to be able to create non-trivial architectural models. While a user could model an E/E architecture in ClaferMPS without a good understanding of Clafer, knowledge of Clafer is needed for debugging the models or creating ones with interesting variants.

6.1 Threats to Validity

A threat to the internal validity of our exploratory evaluation is that some of the development of ClaferMPS was performed in response to the evaluator's bug reports, issues, and requirements. This has not introduced any bias since the design of the DSL was originally based on the evaluator's case studies and the iterative process allowed completing the evaluation and ensuring that the DSL actually covers the entire scope of the case studies.

A threat to the external validity of our evaluation is that it was performed by a single person, who is an expert Clafer user, and therefore the observations cannot be generalized. It is possible that non-expert users of Clafer who are familiar with the reference model would not be capable of modeling the two case studies in the Architecture DSL. However, the evaluator was a novice user of MPS and his observations are likely to be valid for other users. In the future, we are planning to conduct a more extensive evaluation with many users with diverse backgrounds.

7 Related Work

Aleti et al. surveyed over 180 works concerning architecture optimization in the domains of information systems and embedded systems [14]. The surveyed methods, along with other related works [15–20], considered different design decisions or degrees of freedom (i.e., variability points) for hardware selection, deployment of software to hardware, task scheduling, redundancy allocation, communication topology design, hardware component placement, and wireharness sizing and routing. They also considered different design constraints such as memory capacity, functional dependencies, co-location restrictions, among many quality constraints such as mass, cost, and reliability. Lastly, these optimization works considered a number of different objectives such as performance, reliability, cost, mass, and energy consumption.

The majority of these works, however, only considered a handful of design decisions, constraints, and objectives where, in our work, we can consider a design decision for each reference model component. Additionally, in our MPS models, we were able to reason about mass, parts cost, warranty parts cost, and latency as in [3,5] since ClaferMPS is an extension of Clafer. In this work, we also consider decisions made about the features and their impact on the other layers of the system (functional and hardware) in E/E architectures which was first introduced by Murashkin [5].

Additionally, the works surveyed in [14] only consider the equivalent of the functional analysis architecture, device node classification, and the network buses in the communication topology. In other works that consider both the functional and hardware layers of the architecture as well as a graphical projection of the architecture, such as AF3 [21], OSATE [22], and PreeVision [23], they do not allow for expressing variability about almost any component in the model along with a supporting reasoner, as we do.

8 Conclusion

We presented the design and implementation of an Architecture DSL for modeling automotive E/E architectures. The goal of the DSL is to make the reasoning power of Clafer accessible to practitioners by guiding them in the correct application of the reference model, minimizing the need for writing constraints, and automatically generating plain Clafer files that can be used with the existing Clafer toolchain. This paper reports on the progress towards that goal.

This work opens up new possibilities in the design exploration of automotive architectures. As has been previously demonstrated in plain Clafer [3,5], architects can now include design decisions and alternatives about any element in their architectural model, automatically synthesize candidate architectures to see the impact of their decisions, enrich the model with quality attributes and multi-objectively optimize the model to find the set of Pareto-optimal candidates and explore the tradeoffs among them. This work is also applicable to modeling automotive product-line architectures and synthesizing concrete architectures for products.

In the future, we would like to address the remaining limitations and requirements uncovered by our evaluation, such as reference model slicing to eliminate the need for commenting out unused fragments of the reference model, separation of variability similar to the quality attributes and deployment, and integration of the instance generator and support for working with the candidate architectures to provide a smooth workflow within MPS. We would also like to perform experimental evaluation with external users to assess the practicality of the approach and the required expertise in Clafer.

References

1. Bąk, K., Diskin, Z., Antkiewicz, M., Czarnecki, K., Wąsowski, A.: Clafer: unifying class and feature modeling. Soft. Syst. Model. 1–35 (2014)
2. Voelter, M., Warmer, J., Kolb, B.: Projecting a modular future. IEEE Softw. **32**(5), 46–52 (2015)
3. Ross, J.: Case studies on E/E architectures for power window and central door locks systems, May 2016. http://gsd.uwaterloo.ca/node/667
4. EAST-ADL Association: EAST-ADL domain model specification, version V2.1.12. http://east-adl.info/Specification/V2.1.12/EAST-ADL-Specification_V2.1.12.pdf
5. Murashkin, A.: Automotive electronic/electric architecture modeling, design exploration and optimization using Clafer. Master's thesis, University of Waterloo (2014). https://uwspace.uwaterloo.ca/handle/10012/8780
6. Antkiewicz, M., Bąk, K., Murashkin, A., Olaechea, R., Liang, J., Czarnecki, K.: Clafer tools for product line engineering. In: SPLC (2013)
7. Murashkin, A., Antkiewicz, M., Rayside, D., Czarnecki, K.: Visualization and exploration of optimal variants in product line engineering. In: SPLC (2013)
8. Khalilov, E., Voelter, M., Antkiewicz, M.: ClaferMPS source code repository. https://github.com/gsdlab/claferMPS/. Accessed 2 May 2016
9. Fowler, M.: Language Workbenches: Killer-App for DSLs? ThoughtWorks (2005). http://www.martinfowler.com/articles/languageWorkbench.html
10. Voelter, M., Lisson, S.: Supporting diverse notations in MPS' projectional editor. In: GEMOC Workshop
11. Voelter, M.: Language and IDE modularization and composition with MPS. In: Lämmel, R., Saraiva, J., Visser, J. (eds.) GTTSE 2011. LNCS, vol. 7680, pp. 383–430. Springer, Heidelberg (2013). doi:10.1007/978-3-642-35992-7_11
12. Voelter, M., Ratiu, D., Kolb, B., Schaetz, B.: mbeddr: instantiating a language workbench in the embedded software domain. ASE **20**(3), 339–390 (2013)
13. Khalilov, E., Ross, J.: Supplemental material for the paper 'modeling and optimizing automotive electric/electronic (E/E) architectures: towards making Clafer accessible to practitioners', May 2016. http://gsd.uwaterloo.ca/node/668
14. Aleti, A., Buhnova, B., Grunske, L., Koziolek, A., Meedeniya, I.: Software architecture optimization methods: a systematic literature review. IEEE Trans. Softw. Eng. **39**(5), 658–683 (2013)

15. Voss, S., Eder, J., Schaetz, B. (eds.): Scheduling Synthesis for Multi-Period SW Components
16. Glaß, M., Lukasiewycz, M., Wanka, R., Haubelt, C., Teich, J.: Multi-objective routing and topology optimization in networked embedded systems. In: SAMOS, pp. 74–81 (2008)
17. Lin, C.W., Rao, L., Giusto, P., D'Ambrosio, J., Sangiovanni-Vincentelli, A.L.: Efficient wire routing and wire sizing for weight minimization of automotive systems. IEEE Trans. Comput. Aided Des. Integr. Circ. Syst. **34**(11), 1730–1741 (2015)
18. Biondi, A., Di Natale, M., Sun, Y.: Moving from single-core to multicore: initial findings on a fuel injection case study. Technical report, SAE Technical Paper (2016)
19. Hamann, A.: Iterative Design Space Exploration and Robustness Optimization for Embedded Systems. Cuvillier, Göttingen (2008)
20. Streichert, T., Glaß, M., Haubelt, C., Teich, J.: Design space exploration of reliable networked embedded systems. J. Syst. Archit. **53**, 751–763 (2007)
21. Aravantinos, V., Voss, S., Teufl, S., Hölzl, F., Schätz, B.: AutoFOCUS 3: tooling concepts for seamless, model-based development of embedded systems. In: ACES-MB 2015, p. 19 (2015)
22. Software Engineering Institute: OSATE, version 2. http://osate.github.io/
23. Schäuffele, J.: E/E architectural design and optimization using PREEvision. Technical report, SAE Technical Paper (2016)

Variability-Based Design of Services for Smart Transportation Systems

Maurice H. ter Beek[1], Alessandro Fantechi[1,2], Stefania Gnesi[1],
and Laura Semini[1,3(✉)]

[1] ISTI–CNR, Pisa, Italy
[2] University of Florence, Florence, Italy
[3] University of Pisa, Pisa, Italy
semini@di.unipi.it

Abstract. A smart transportation system can be seen as an aggregate of transportation opportunities and services, accompanied by advanced management services that make the access to the system easier for the user. In this paper, we exploit the product line paradigm to address the variability of an exemplary smart transportation system: a bike-sharing system. Improving the satisfaction of a user of a bike-sharing system includes providing information at runtime on the filling degree of the docking stations in the near future. To fulfill this expectation, a prediction service is needed to infer the probability that at a certain time of the day a user will return a bike to or take one from a station. In earlier studies, several possible advanced smart predictive services were identified. The choice of which services to offer to users by the managers of a bike-sharing system is influenced by minimizing the costs while maximizing customer satisfaction. To aid the managers, we modeled a family of smart bike-sharing services, after which an attributed feature model was used to augment the model with quantitative attributes related to cost and customer satisfaction, allowing for a multi-objective optimization by dedicated tools. We observe that the performance of the smart prediction services, and therefore of the related customer satisfaction, is highly dependent on the amount of collected historical data on which the predictive analysis is based. Therefore the result of the optimization also depends on this factor, which evolves over time.

1 Introduction

A smart transportation system can be considered as an aggregate of transportation opportunities and services, accompanied by advanced management services that make the access to the system easier to the final user. An example is a bike-sharing system. Bike-sharing systems are becoming more and more popular as a sustainable means of smart transportation in urban environments [19]. Ever more advanced services that aim to improve their usability are being developed and they moreover constitute a challenging case study with numerous interesting optimization problems [6,8–14,16,21]. Many cities are currently adopting fully automated public bike-sharing system as a green urban mode of transportation.

© Springer International Publishing AG 2016
T. Margaria and B. Steffen (Eds.): ISoLA 2016, Part II, LNCS 9953, pp. 465–481, 2016.
DOI: 10.1007/978-3-319-47169-3_38

The concept is simple: a user arrives at a docking station, takes a bike (using e.g. an RFID card), uses it for a while and eventually returns it to a station.

Improving the satisfaction of a user of a bike-sharing system includes informing her about the status of the stations at runtime. Most current systems provide information in terms of the number of bikes parked in each station, by means of services available via the Web. In case the arrival station is full or the departure station is empty, the user might be pleased to know it if there is any chance that this situation will change within a reasonable amount of time. To fulfill this expectation, a prediction service is needed to infer the probability that at a certain time of the day a user is going to return a bike to or to free a slot of a station. Different kinds of prediction services, with different cost and performance, can be envisaged for this purpose, using e.g. machine-learning techniques.

As part of a collaboration with the company that has installed a bike-sharing system in Pisa, two studies were conducted recently, with the aim of applying advanced design techniques to provide the users with a better service. In the first study [7], the product line paradigm was applied, at the level of systems engineering, in order to jointly address variability issues and quantitative analysis of the possible options that a generic bike-sharing system can exhibit. To this aim, first a reference feature model was defined and then feature attributes and global quantitative constraints were added, thus creating an attributed feature model suitable to conduct multi-objective optimization analyses. The focus was on the selection of physical components of the overall system, like the number and kind of stations. In the second study [3,4], a series of advanced predictive software services for the user of a bike-sharing system were envisaged, and partly implemented, using a machine-learning approach to analyze usage patterns and to learn computational models of such services from logs of actual system usage.

Here we aim to combine these efforts by proposing a product line framework defining a family of advanced prediction services. The services are evaluated with respect to their performance, expressed in terms of the accuracy of the prediction [3,4], on which customer satisfaction depends. The accuracy is the outcome of the use of several machine-learning techniques, based on the availability of data logs from system usage. The multi-objective analysis as applied in [7] is then used to assist the maintainers of the system in choosing the optimal configuration.

It turns out that the performance of the prediction services, and therefore of the related customer satisfaction, is highly dependent on the amount of collected historical data on which the predictive analysis is based. Therefore the result of the optimization also depends on this factor, which evolves over time. A typical scenario is the one of a newly installed bike-sharing system that initially has no historical data, and hence predictive services are inaccurate (and therefore have a low benefit/cost ratio) and only after years of usage the collected historical data can make a predictive service accurate enough to be safely provided to the user. The quantity of data needed may differ from service to service, though. Hence, the optimal configurations of the product line of services for bike-sharing systems evolves over time as well. The idea is to gradually introduce more advanced prediction services as over time more data on the system in operation becomes available. The availability of a set of tools to support this evaluation will aid the maintainers of the bike-sharing system in dynamically choosing the optimal configuration during its life cycle.

Based on concrete experiments with data concerning the bike-sharing system of Pisa (our 'testbed'), we show how preliminary results teach us that the relation between the size of available logged usage data and performance is not easy to capture with machine-learning techniques. Actually, it turned out that below a given threshold (a few months of usage) the prediction service is highly unreliable. We therefore tailored the analysis techniques applied in [7] to cope with this discrete relation between the size of available data and performance indicators. The described techniques are actually considered as an initial step in a research activity aimed at a full study of these kind of dependencies. Nevertheless, in our opinion, the resulting variability-based design process can be applied not only to bike-sharing systems of other cities, but in general to smart transportation systems which rely on the availability of advanced prediction services.

The paper is organized as follows. In Sect. 2, we introduce the bike-sharing system testbed. In Sect. 3, we discuss possible new smart prediction services that could be added to the bike-sharing system and we show how to estimate their performance based on machine-learning techniques. In Sect. 4, we address the quantitative analysis and optimization issues by adding quantitative attributes to features (e.g. performance in case of the prediction services) and show how to perform multi-objective quantitative analyses of the system. In Sects. 5 and 6, we discuss the results of our preliminary analyses and conclude the paper.

2   A Smart Transportation System

In this section, we briefly describe Pisa's bike-sharing system *CicloPi*. It will be the running example in this paper. *CicloPi* was introduced in town three years ago by PisaMo S.p.A., an in-house public mobility company of the Municipality of Pisa, with whom we started a fruitful collaboration. This bike-sharing system, which controls some 150 bikes and 15 stations, was supplied by Bicincittà S.r.l., together with a few basic services, described next. This is hence a relatively small bike-sharing system, which makes it an excellent testbed for our research.

Currently, *CicloPi* offers two basic services, one reserved to its administrators and one meant for its users. The first, which we call `Bikes Hired`, registers, for each hired bike, the user ID and the departure station and time of departure. It is needed to control whether all bikes are returned and it makes it possible to offer a billing service to the administrators (e.g. a fee applies for rides longer than 30 min). Up to now this service has collected way more than 300.000 entries of the following form: $\langle$ `ID`, $\underbrace{\texttt{station, slot, date\&time}}_{departure}, \underbrace{\texttt{station, slot, date\&time}}_{arrival} \rangle$

In [3,4], we exploited about 280.000 entries of this form, collected in two years, to design a number of predictive services, discussed in the next section.

The second basic service of *CicloPi* that is currently available is one that we call Stations Snapshot. It allows the user to perform a real-time check, for each docking station, of the availability of bikes at that station. Users can access this service using a Web browser to find the closest station with an available bike (or with a free slot, for returning a bike) before actually going there.

We note that the bike-sharing system administrators can also use this service, e.g. to plan redistributions. Redistribution of bikes (usually by trucks) is used to balance the number of bikes: bikes are taken from (nearly) saturated stations and parked in (nearly) empty stations. As such, the usual flow of bikes from one group of stations to another (e.g., from stations located in residential areas to those located in work areas in the morning and vice versa in the afternoon) can be balanced. However, to do this efficiently is a major issue for bike-sharing systems, but out of the scope of this paper (cf. [8,12,14]).

3   New Smart Prediction Services

To improve the satisfaction of users of a bike-sharing system, we propose several new smart services that provide information at runtime on the filling degree of the docking stations. In our testbed, customer satisfaction may be enhanced by offering hints on the status of the stations in the next few minutes. If the station of interest is currently empty, a user may be pleased to know that, with a high probability, one of the circulating bikes will be returned there soon. Likewise, for stations that are full it may be worthwhile to know the chances that someone will soon free a slot by renting a bike. However, vendors and installers of such bike-sharing systems would likely prefer to analyze and assess different solutions before actually putting them into operation in a specific setting.

To this aim, we propose to organize the new services as a family of services in an *attributed feature model* (i.e. a feature model enriched with attributes containing non-functional information on features). Feature models are a useful means to structure systems with variability. In our case study, the attributed feature model supports the stakeholders in understanding the system architecture and in deciding which product of a line to deploy, since we provide an estimate of the cost and customer satisfaction for each variant. We base the customer satisfaction attribute on a predictive performance measure, which is obtained by applying machine learning to analyze usage patterns and learn computational models of the respective features from logs of usage of the bike-sharing system.

Machine learning (ML) is concerned with computational models and methodologies to realize data-driven adaptive approaches to data analysis, pattern discovery and recognition, as well as to the predictive modeling of input-output data relationships. The term data-driven refers to the fact that ML approaches rely on (numerical) information encoded in the data [15]. In our case, ML methodologies allow us to learn the (unknown) relationship between the feature and its inputs by exploiting historical data representing examples of such input-output map. A trained model can then be used to provide predictions on future values of the feature in response to new input information, i.e. providing an implementation of the feature. The advantage of such an approach is twofold. On the one hand, such methodologies provide a powerful means to realize a wide choice of predictive features for which there exists meaningful historical data. On the other hand, trained ML models are provided with a measure of predictive performance that can be used as a metric to assess the customer satisfaction of the feature.

In [3,4], we put forward the idea of using ML methodologies to implement a preview service for a bike-sharing system. Here we combine this solution with the design capabilities offered by software product line engineering, exploiting the second characteristic of an ML approach, viz. the ability of trained ML models to return a performance measure.

3.1   A Feature Model of a Family of Services

Our starting point is the current set of basic services offered by *CicloPi*, viz. **Bikes Hired** and **Stations Snapshot** concerning the status of bikes and stations.

Subsequently, we add several further preview services, described next, which can be offered in the presence of a minimum of historical data.

The feature model of the resulting family of services is depicted in Fig. 1. The existing services that keep the status of the bike-sharing system updated are mandatory, while the new smart prediction services are optional.

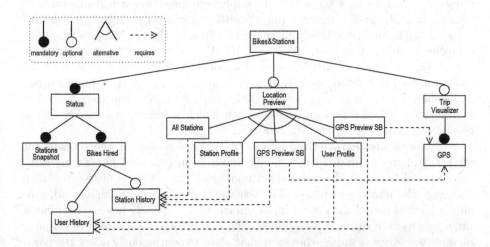

Fig. 1. Feature model for a product line of services of a bike-sharing system

The **Location Preview** service is concerned with the prediction of the destination of a circulating bike and is implemented using one of its sub-features, all of whose services are based on training ML models. They differ in the data they use and consequently in their performance, as we discuss in this section.

The services All Stations, Station Profile and User Profile use historical data, but they differ in the aggregation/disaggregation of data: the first being the simplest to implement and maintain but with the lowest predictive performance. They require one of the Station History and User History features of the basic Bikes Hired service, based on the type of profile.

The station-based and user-based services GPS Preview SB and GPS Preview UB, respectively, combine historical data with traces of the circulating bikes as communicated by GPS trackers, which is why they require GPS (trackers) next to the Station History and User History features of the basic Bikes Hired service, based on the type of profile. We will describe these services (sub-features of Location Preview) in Sect. 3.2, after an introduction to relevant ML techniques.

Trip Visualizer, finally, is a service that permits to track the circulating bikes, and to offer a trace visualization service to the user so that she can have the real-time position and direction of all bikes and figure out if one is approaching. Obviously, to implement this feature, each bike must have a GPS tracker.

GPS trackers are already in use in some bike-sharing systems, either as anti-theft or to eliminate docking stations: bikes are parked and locked anywhere, a user locates the closest one using the GPS and unlocks it with a code.

3.2   Machine Learning for Location Preview

ML is an active and wide research field comprising several paradigms, e.g. neural-inspired, probabilistic, kernel-based approaches, and addressing a variety of computational learning task types [15]. To implement the preview features we have focused in [3,4] on ML models and algorithms targeted at solving *supervised learning tasks*. Supervised learning refers to a specific class of ML problems that comprise learning of an (unknown) map $M : \mathcal{X} \to \mathcal{Y}$ between input information $x \in \mathcal{X}$ (e.g. a vector of attributes) and an output prediction $y \in \mathcal{Y}$. Such an unknown map is learned from couples $\{(x_1, y_1), \ldots, (x_N, y_N)\}$ of input-output data, referred to as *training examples*, following a numerical routine targeted at the optimization of a performance function which measures the quality of the predictions generated by the ML model.

ML models are characterized by two operational phases. In the *training* (or *learning*) phase, ground-truth teaching information (encoded in training samples) is used to adapt the parameters regulating the response of the model so that its performance is increased. The *testing* (or *prediction*) phase, instead, supplies a trained model with novel input information (typically unseen at training time) to generate runtime predictions. The two phases are not always disjoint: *incremental learning* approaches exist that allow to continuously adapt the parameters of a ML model, while this keeps providing its predictions in response to new input data. In general, the resulting quality of the ML model predictions is influenced, on the one hand, by the quality of the training data, which should represent a sufficient and significative sample of the relationship to be modeled, and, on the other hand, by the adequacy of the learning model for the specific learning task. In this sense, different tasks, associated with different features to be modeled, may require to use learning models with different capabilities.

The actual form of the performance measure depends on the nature of the learning task, but it typically evaluates the discrepancy between the output predicted and the actual output. Here, the most significative performance measure, which we will use in Sect. 4 to feed an attributed feature model of the feature model in Fig. 1, is an aggregated performance score (in %), called $F1$-score, calculated as follows: $F1 = \frac{2TP}{2TP+FP+FN}$, where TP, FP and FN are the number of true positive, false positive, and false negative classifications, respectively. Higher $F1$ values denote better classification performances. Other well-known performance measures are precision (the number of true positives per predicted positive) and recall (the number of true positives per real positive), of which $F1$ is the harmonic mean.

All services implicitly use the data offered by `Stations Snapshot` to combine data on actual occupancy with the prediction of the destination of circulating bikes, and have a prediction of the number of bikes that will be at a station.

ML for Location Preview: Static Data. As said before, `All Stations`, `Station Profile` and `User Profile` offer similar services. They all use data of a static type. This means that each training sample is a pair of identically and independently distributed vectors: departure and arrival data. Differences among the features depend on aggregation and/or abstraction of these data. To implement `All Stations` one learning model was built, and usage data was not partitioned into any subset, whereas to implement `Station Profile` usage data was split in order to build a different learning model for each station. In both cases the learning task abstracts from the user ID. On the contrary, `User Profile` analyzes the behaviour of single users, by building a learning model for each of them.[1]

Both `All Stations` and `Station Profile` require `Station History` to train the models (this feature maintains the history of all station-to-station movements with date and time) and the (mandatory) `Bikes Hired` feature in the prediction phase, to know the departure station of the circulating bikes.

`User Profile` uses the data maintained by `User History`, the history of all movements of each user, in the training phase, and uses `Bikes Hired` in the prediction phase, as above.

We trained and validated learning models for these services, using real-world usage data comprising more than 280.000 entries of the form discussed in Sect. 2.

The obtained results are reported and discussed in detail in [3, 4]. For the purposes of the present paper, the table on the right summarizes the obtained performance measures.

Service	$F1$-score
All Stations	18 %
Station Profile	34.9 %
User Profile	69 %

---

[1] To guarantee privacy protection, we only used anonymized data. In fact, the data from Bicincittà did not contain any information from which one could identify users.

ML for Location Preview: Sequential Data. The GPS Preview features (SB, station-based, and UB, user-based) can predict the same output as the other location features considered so far, using additional input data, that is GPS trajectories corresponding to journeys performed by users of the bike-sharing system. Trajectory data encodes a form of dynamical information of different nature with respect to the static vectorial data used in Sect. 3.2, requiring a radically different ML approach. A GPS trajectory is a form of sequential data, a type of structured information where the observation at a given point of the sequence is dependent on the context provided by the preceding or succeeding elements of the sequence. Such contextual information plays a role also in the learning task where, for instance, the decision on which will be the arrival station corresponding to a GPS trajectory cannot be taken based on the observation of a single element of the sequence, but should rather take into account the context provided by the full sequence or by at least a part of it.

We did not implement these features so far, due to the lack of data. Neither *CicloPi*, nor any of the bike-sharing systems provided by Bicincittà, have GPS trackers installed on the bikes. Recently, we contacted TMR S.r.l., which supplies the bike-sharing system of the municipality of Palermo. They did install GPS trackers on the bikes, to be used mainly as an anti-theft feature: bikes periodically communicate their position through a cellular network using the GPRS protocol. The service is brand new and they do not have a meaningful log of traces yet. As soon as this data will be available, we could decide to build learning models along the outline in [4]. We expect to obtain the scores given in the table below.

These values are based on discussions with domain experts, who foresee that the performance of the learning models will be improved by roughly 20 % with respect to the corresponding models built so far based on static data alone.

Service	F1-score
GPS Preview SB	41.88 %
GPS Preview UB	82.8 %

In the remainder of this section, we briefly describe how we would go about implementing the use of sequential data. A straightforward approach is to use models for static data feeding them with a fixed-size chunk of the input sequence. This window of observations can be slid across the full length of the sequence, providing a prediction for each sequence element that can take into consideration the surrounding elements up to the window length. The key issue of the approach is how to determine the correct size of the window for each learning problem. To address this issue, several learning models have been proposed that are capable of maintaining a memory of the history of the input signals and to use it to compute their predictions. We now describe one such model.

Recurrent Neural Networks (RNN) [17] were proposed specifically to deal with the dynamics of sequential information. They extend the original artificial neural networks paradigm with feedback connections that introduce a dynamic memory of the neuron activation which can be used to encode short to long term dependencies among the elements of the sequence, depending on the specific network architecture. In this context, the use of Reservoir Computing (RC) [18] gained increasing interest, due to its ability in conjugating computational efficiency with the RNN capability of dealing with learning in temporal sequence domains. The underlying idea of the RC approach is to use a layer of sparsely connected recurrent neuron whose connections are initialized and left untrained; adaptation of the neural weights is restricted to the layer of output neurons. This allows to considerably reduce the computational complexity of training, which is a key issue if performed at runtime. RC models appear well suited for the implementation of the Location Preview feature. In particular, they already showed considerable efficacy in closely related learning tasks, like the prediction of the destination room of trajectories of users walking in indoor environments [2].

4   A Family of Smart Services

In this paper, we set out to combine and extend the ideas of [3, 4, 7] by proposing a product line of a family of advanced prediction services. The services can be distinguished by the accuracy of the prediction obtained by using different ML techniques. To perform quantitative analyses, we add non-functional attributes and quantitative constraints over attributes to the feature model of our bike-sharing system (thus turning it into an attributed feature model).

4.1   Clafer and Multi-objective Optimization

Clafer is a general-purpose modeling language designed to represent domains, meta-models, components and variability models [5], including attributed feature models [1]. It can be used to model and optimize product lines [1, 20]. Clafer supports partial instances, i.e. a user can define a partial model with some undecided variability. The complete set of instances can be generated from the partial model. Alternatively, a user can define concrete instances with no variability.

A Clafer model is composed of definitions called *clafers*, which can represent either properties, types or references, depending on their nesting and syntactic modifiers. Here we use them to model features and from now on we speak of features rather than clafers. Constraints express dependencies among features or restrict allowed values. A feature can contain one or more sub-features and can include multiplicity, i.e. the number of times that the feature can be instantiated (not considered here). Optionality is denoted using a question mark. An optional feature may or may not be present in model instances.

Each feature can have one or more associated attributes and quality constraints can be specified either globally or in the context of a feature. Think, e.g., of associating a cost to each feature and a global constraint that only allows products (feature configurations) whose total costs remain within a predefined threshold value. This is an example of a single optimization objective, but usually there can be more than one attribute associated to a feature, leading to multiple optimization objectives. Imagine, e.g., that each feature also has a value for user satisfaction and while the objective might be to minimize the cost of a product it might at the same time be desirable to maximize user satisfaction.

The ClaferMoo extension of Clafer was specifically introduced to support attributed feature models and in particular the resulting complex multi-objective optimization goals [1,20]. A multi-objective optimization problem has a set of solutions, known as the Pareto front, representing trade-offs between two or more conflicting objectives. Intuitively, a Pareto-optimal solution is thus such that no objective can be improved without worsening another. A set of Pareto-optimal variants generated by ClaferMoo can be visualized (as a multi-dimensional space of optimal variants) and explored in the interactive tool ClaferMooVisualizer specifically designed to support product line scenarios [1,20].

4.2   Clafer Model of a Family of Services

We specified the attributed feature model of Fig. 1 in Clafer. Each feature of the bike-sharing system is defined as a clafer of the basic type `Feature` with three attributes of type integer: `csat` models the customer satisfaction, `cost` models the (estimated) additional cost in euros to implement the (prediction) service and `time` models the number of months of operation of the bike-sharing system that is needed before it can become operational.

For the new prediction services, customer satisfaction reflects their performance measure, expressed in terms of the accuracy of the prediction, i.e. the $F1$-score (cf. Sect. 3), since we believe this to constitute also a good indication for customer satisfaction. The more precise the prediction, the happier the user. For this reason, we simply take the $F1$-score values (in %) returned by the experiments as the integer value of the customer satisfaction of these services, and indeed we use the same 0–100 range to indicate the customer satisfaction for the other services, i.e. the mandatory ones and `Trip Visualizer`. The total customer satisfaction is then considered as the sum of the values of the features involved. The values for these other services were extracted from the results of an online poll concerning the features considered most useful for Pisa's planned (at the time) bike-sharing system [16,21] (these features include most of the services considered in this paper) and from discussions with PisaMo and Bicincittà.

The cost attribute has a component that was obtained from the ML experiments (described in detail in [3,4] and discussed in the previous section) and another component that was extracted from documents provided by Bicincittà and from documents concerning the cost of similar systems implemented in other Italian cities (and in one case from a private communication). The latter component concerns the additional cost required to implement the specific service.

The time attribute, finally, was derived from the ML experiments described in detail in [3,4] and discussed in the previous section.

The full Clafer model in Listing 1.1 contains a main abstract clafer `BikesAndStations`, composed of a set of features of type `Feature`.

Listing 1.1. Full Clafer Model of *CicloPi*

```
abstract Feature
  csat : integer
  cost : integer
  time : integer

abstract BikesAndStations
  Status
    StationsSnapshot
    BikesHired
      StationHistory : Feature ?
        [ csat = 68 ]
        [ cost = 500 ]
        [ time = 0 ]
      UserHistory : Feature ?
        [ csat = 79 ]
        [ cost = 500 ]
        [ time = 0 ]
  xor LocationPreview ?
    AllStations : Feature
      [ csat = 18 ]
      [ cost = 300 ]
      [ time = 24 ]
    StationProfile : Feature
      [ csat = 35 ]
      [ cost = 400 ]
      [ time = 24 ]
    UserProfile : Feature
      [ csat = 69 ]
      [ cost = 500 ]
      [ time = 24 ]
```

```
    GPSPreviewSB : Feature
      [ csat = 42 ]
      [ cost = 100 ]
      [ time = 12 ]
    GPSPreviewUB : Feature
      [ csat = 83 ]
      [ cost = 100 ]
      [ time = 12 ]
  TripVisualizer : Feature ?
    [ csat = 35]
    [ cost = 0 ]
    [ time = 0 ]
  GPS : Feature
    [ csat = 0 ]
    [ cost = 3000 ]
    [ time = 0 ]
  [ AllStations => StationHistory ]
  [ StationProfile => StationHistory ]
  [ UserProfile => UserHistory ]
  [ GPSPreviewSB => StationHistory ]
  [ GPSPreviewSB => GPS ]
  [ GPSPreviewUB => UserHistory ]
  [ GPSPreviewUB => GPS ]

  total_csat : integer = sum Feature.csat
  total_cost : integer = sum Feature.cost
  total_time : integer = sum Feature.time

Services : BikesAndStations

  << max Services.total_csat >>
  << min Services.total_cost >>
  << min Services.total_time >>
```

In Clafer, sub-features implicitly form an **and**-group, but they can also explicitly be declared as **or**-group or **xor**-group (i.e. modeling alternative features). For instance, `xor LocationPreview` means that any product must contain exactly one of the new smart prediction services. The additional (cross-tree) constraints are expressed as implications on the presence of features (keywords `=>` and `<=>`), e.g., `GPSPreviewSB => GPS` indicates that a product (i.e. a configuration) must require feature `GPS` whenever feature `GPSPreviewSB` is part of the product.

The clafers `total_csat`, `total_cost` and `total_time` do not represent features, but contain the total value of each attribute for a product instance (e.g. the total cost of the product is calculated as the sum of the cost of each of its features). When ClaferMooVisualizer instantiates all concrete products of a model, these clafers are used to compare product configurations and to place them on the Pareto front during the multi-objective optimization. To this aim, an additional part of any Clafer model contains the optimization goals. To actually optimize the model, Clafer needs a specific instance (`Services : BikesAndStations`) together with a set of goals, each of them enclosed in double brackets, e.g., `<<min Services.total_cost>>` represents the goal of minimizing the cost.

For our testbed, we are thus interested in maximizing the customer satisfaction while minimizing both the cost and the time required for the introduction of new prediction services (to become operational).

4.3   Quantitative Analysis with ClaferMoo

Now that we have an attributed feature model in Clafer, its associated tool ClaferMooVisualizer can help to understand the differences among variants, to establish their positioning with respect to various quality dimensions, to select the most desirable variants, possibly by resolving trade-offs, and, finally, to understand the impact that changes made during a product line's evolution have on a variant's quality dimensions. ClaferMooVisualizer is a Web-based tool that allows users to load a Clafer model and to visualize and compare instances of the model. It comes with the following four possible visualizations. *Bubble Front Graph* produces a bubble chart where each bubble represents an instance (also called variant). The graph supports up to four dimensions: the x- and y-axes, bubble color and bubble size. *Feature and Quality Matrix* lists all variants and their properties. *Variant Comparer* shows the commonalities and differences of two or more selected variants. In *Parallel Coordinates Chart*, each variant is represented by a line and each attribute is represented by a vertical axis. The point of intersection between a line and the axis corresponds to the value that the attribute holds for that variant. Especially the first two are very useful when one is interested in comparing a number of variants and we will illustrate their usage shortly. The third is particularly useful when one wants to understand better the subtle differences between a small number of variants, say up to three.

Evaluation of Adding Smart Prediction Services to CicloPi. The bubble chart resulting from a multi-objective optimization with ClaferMooVisualizer of the Clafer model presented in the previous section is shown in Fig. 2a.

The bubble chart is composed of 12 variants. Customer satisfaction is shown on the x-axis and cost on the y-axis, while the color of each bubble shows the time needed before the new smart prediction service of the respective variant can become operational (only assuming values 0, 12 or 24 in this case).

Next we inspected each of these variants by making use of the Feature and Quality Matrix reported in Fig. 3. As expected, the three variants that contain the smart Trip Visualizer service (4, 7 and 10) are far more expensive than the other ones, due to the need to equip all bikes with expensive GPS trackers. Variant 7, which also includes the GPS Preview UB service and both Station History and User History, is the variant with the highest customer satisfaction (265), which thus comes at a price. If the budget is limited, variant 12 might offer an excellent alternative with the User Profile prediction service, without having to give up on the either Station History or User History. It scores the second-best customer satisfaction at a reasonable cost, but the time needed to be fully operational is 24 months. This is unavoidable, though, for all new prediction services based on ML models that do not require GPS trackers.

Evaluation of Adding Smart Prediction Services Elsewhere. Now suppose we want to evaluate the installation of one of the smart prediction services in a city with a bike-sharing system that has been operating for over two years

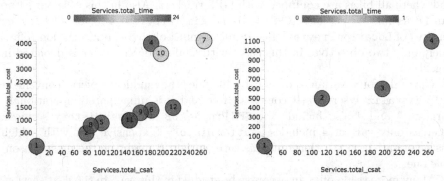

(a) 12 variants: bubbles 1, 2 and 4 are red (indicating `total_time`=0); bubbles 7 and 10 are yellow (`total_time` = 12); all further bubbles are green (`total_time`=24).

(b) 4 variants: four bubbles of the same color (red) indicating `total_time`=0.

Fig. 2. Bubble front graphs of the two evaluations of adding smart prediction services (Color figure online)

Model \ Variants	X 1	X 2	X 3	X 4	X 5	X 6	X 7	X 8	X 9	X 10	X 11	X 12
Services												
Status												
StationsSnapshot												
BikesHired												
StationHistory ?												
csat	-	-	68	68	68	68	68	68	68	-	-	68
cost	-	-	500	500	500	500	500	500	500	-	-	500
time	-	-	0	0	0	0	0	0	0	-	-	0
UserHistory ?												
csat	-	79	79	79	-	79	79	-	79	79	79	79
cost	-	500	500	500	-	500	500	-	500	500	500	500
time	-	0	0	0	-	0	0	-	0	0	0	0
LocationPreview ?												
AllStations ?												
csat	-	-	-	-	-	-	-	18	18	-	-	-
cost	-	-	-	-	-	-	-	300	300	-	-	-
time	-	-	-	-	-	-	-	24	24	-	-	-
StationProfile ?												
csat	-	-	-	-	35	35	-	-	-	-	-	-
cost	-	-	-	-	400	400	-	-	-	-	-	-
time	-	-	-	-	24	24	-	-	-	-	-	-
UserProfile ?												
csat	-	-	-	-	-	-	-	-	-	-	69	69
cost	-	-	-	-	-	-	-	-	-	-	500	500
time	-	-	-	-	-	-	-	-	-	-	24	24
GPSPreviewSB ?												
csat												
cost												
time												
GPSPreviewUB ?												
csat	-	-	-	-	-	-	83	-	-	83	-	-
cost	-	-	-	-	-	-	100	-	-	100	-	-
time	-	-	-	-	-	-	12	-	-	12	-	-
TripVisualizer ?												
GPS												
csat	-	-	-	0	-	-	0	-	-	0	-	-
cost	-	-	-	3000	-	-	3000	-	-	3000	-	-
time	-	-	-	0	-	-	0	-	-	0	-	-
csat	-	-	-	35	-	-	35	-	-	35	-	-
cost	-	-	-	0	-	-	0	-	-	0	-	-
time	-	-	-	0	-	-	0	-	-	0	-	-
total_csat	0	79	147	182	103	182	265	86	165	197	148	216
total_cost	0	500	1000	4000	900	1400	4100	800	1300	3600	1000	1500
total_time	0	0	0	0	24	24	12	24	24	12	24	24

Fig. 3. Feature and Quality Matrix of the 12 variants depicted in Fig. 2a

and where all bikes are equipped with GPS trackers. Also in this case our setup can be useful. We set cost(GPS) = 0 and time(Preview) = 0 for all Preview services of Location Preview. The result of multi-objective optimization (effectively only two objectives in this case) with ClaferMooVisualizer is depicted in Fig. 2b.

Now all four variants obviously include the suddenly very convenient Trip Visualizer service (it comes for free and it is immediately operational), variants 3 and 4 also include the GPS Preview UB and User History services, whereas only variant 4 includes Station History (expensive, yet with a high customer satisfaction). Hence in this case, variant 3 might be the most reasonable one.

Many more trade-offs can of course be studied in this way. In the next section, we discuss the implications of our experiments.

5   Lessons Learned and Discussion

The analysis with ClaferMooVisualizer shown in the previous section aims to provide a means to assist the management of a bike-sharing service. It offers support for the decisions as to which services are the most valuable ones to be suggested to and eventually implemented for clients, based on a trade-off between cost and customer satisfaction mainly. However, the conducted analysis shows how a third dimension was added, viz. the deployment time which influences the availability of logged data. This is a peculiar aspect of 'smart transportation' services, which need to anticipate to the user the actual availability of a transport service, in an as accurate as possible way, in order to be accepted by them as an important added value in terms of reliability of the whole service. Predictive services based on ML clearly show that the accuracy of their forecasts are heavily dependent on the significance and size of the training set. In the smart transportation domain, these two factors depend on the amount and quality of logged data, and on the implicit assumption that the average origin/destination demand of transportation services is quite stable in the long run.

The experiments with data concerning our testbed bike-sharing system show how the relation between the size of available logged usage data and performance is not easy to capture. In fact, it turned out that below a given threshold (a few months of service, and hence of accumulated data) the prediction service is highly unreliable. We therefore tailored the analysis techniques applied in [7] to cope with three discrete steps of observation length, viz. at time zero and after one or two years. We need more experiments to elaborate a more accurate definition of the dependance of the performance indicators on the size of available data. However, the preliminary results already provide support to decide whether and when to introduce an advanced smart transportation service (in the form of a predictive service for the users) in an already deployed bike-sharing system. In fact, we considered a family of services and we indicated tools to support such decisions, corresponding to selecting the most convenient services to be offered at a given deployment time. These decisions can be reconsidered by repeating the analysis once more usage data has been accumulated.

Notice that the appeal of ML-based solutions that only use historical data is outperformed as soon as a more advanced localization technology (GPS, in this case) is able to provide more accurate real-time data. The cost of such outperforming technology is a drawback that allows ML-based surrogates to still be a convenient solution; but if the cost of the technology is absorbed by other improvements (in our case, the desire to provide anti-theft capabilities), ML-based solutions that do not exploit the real-time trajectories loose their appeal. GPS-based solutions, moreover, can be applied sooner (i.e. with less data available). For instance, `Trip Visualizer` can be made available as soon as a new bike-sharing system is put in place. Solutions that apply ML techniques to analyse GPS trajectories can show a good performance also with a smaller dataset than those only using static data. Moreover, we have seen that the situation can be different for settings in which one of the (optional) features has already been foreseen (in which case it is as if it were a mandatory feature), drastically changing the outcome of the multi-objective optimization.

Note that once a more advanced predictive service should become available, then it could be included in the service family model as a new feature of the feature model, and associated with cost and customer satisfaction measures, possibly dependent on available logged usage data. Also note that training this new service might require more detailed data, not previously accommodated for, and which hence requires to start a new data logging period. Hence, the new service could be delivered to the users only when it is mature enough according to the time-dependent performance indicators. So this is actually an evolution of the product line, followed by the evolution of the decision support analysis.

6   Conclusions

The added value of *smart transportation systems* consists in offering the user a set of services that allow for a more comfortable usage of the provided transportation means, using the most advanced technologies available. A proper trade-off between the cost of offering such services and the related customer satisfaction has to be defined to obtain the most advantage from their introduction.

Organizing the possible services in a product line offers a means to support the determination of such a trade-off. This requires quantitative analysis of the involved parameters. We moreover extended to software services a previously defined process, which was originally employed to study—by means of a quantitative analysis and at the level of systems engineering—the possible options that a generic bike-sharing system can exhibit at the physical level.

Although the experiments presented in this paper are quite preliminary, and limited to a bike-sharing system, we believe that the envisaged variability-based decision support process and tools can be adopted not only in bike-sharing systems of other cities, but in general in a wide range of smart transportation systems which rely on the availability of advanced prediction services.

Acknowledgments. Research supported by EU project QUANTICOL, 600708. We are very grateful to Marco Bertini of PisaMo S.p.A. and Bicincittà S.r.l. for generously sharing with us information and actual usage logs of Pisa's bike-sharing system *CicloPi*. We thank Davide Bacciu and Antonio Carta for discussions and for having conducted the machine-learning experiments.

References

1. Antkiewicz, M., Bąk, K., Murashkin, K., Olaechea, R., Liang, J.H., Czarnecki, K.: Clafer tools for product line engineering. In: Kishi, T., Jarzabek, S., Gnesi, S. (eds.) SPLC, vol. 2, pp. 130–135. ACM (2013)
2. Bacciu, D., Barsocchi, P., Chessa, S., Gallicchio, C., Micheli, A.: An experimental characterization of reservoir computing in ambient assisted living applications. Neural Comput. Appl. **24**(6), 1451–1464 (2014)
3. Bacciu, D., Carta, A., Gnesi, S., Semini, L.: Using a machine learning approach in the design of smart transportation systems (2016, submitted)
4. Bacciu, D., Gnesi, S., Semini, L.: Using a machine learning approach to implement and evaluate product line features. In: ter Beek, M.H., Lluch-Lafuente, A. (eds.) WWV. EPTCS, vol. 188, pp. 75–83 (2015)
5. Bąk, K., Diskin, Z., Antkiewicz, M., Czarnecki, K., Wąsowski, A.: Clafer: unifying class and feature modeling. Softw. Syst. Model. **15**(3), 811–845 (2016)
6. ter Beek, M.H., Fantechi, A., Gnesi, S.: Challenges in modelling and analyzing quantitative aspects of bike-sharing systems. In: Margaria, T., Steffen, B. (eds.) ISoLA 2014, Part I. LNCS, vol. 8802, pp. 351–367. Springer, Heidelberg (2014)
7. ter Beek, M.H., Fantechi, A., Gnesi, S.: Applying the product lines paradigm to the quantitative analysis of collective adaptive systems. In: Schmidt, D.C. (ed.) SPLC, pp. 321–326. ACM (2015)
8. ter Beek, M.H., Gnesi, S., Latella, D., Massink, M.: Towards automatic decision support for bike-sharing system design. In: Bianculli, D., et al. (eds.) SEFM 2015 Workshops. LNCS, vol. 9509, pp. 266–280. Springer, Heidelberg (2015). doi:10.1007/978-3-662-49224-6_22
9. ter Beek, M.H., Legay, A., Lluch Lafuente, A., Vandin, A.: Quantitative analysis of probabilistic models of software product lines with statistical model checking. In: Atlee, J.M., Gnesi, S. (eds.) FMSPLE. EPTCS, vol. 182, pp. 56–70. EPTCS (2015)
10. ter Beek, M.H., Legay, A., Lluch Lafuente, A., Vandin, A.: Statistical model checking for product lines. In: Margaria, T., Steffen, B. (eds.) ISoLA. LNCS. Springer, Heidelberg (2016)
11. Ciancia, V., Latella, D., Massink, M., Pakauskas, R.: Exploring spatio-temporal properties of bike-sharing systems. In: SCOPES, pp. 74–79. IEEE (2015)
12. Fricker, C., Gast, N.: Incentives and redistribution in homogeneous bike-sharing systems with stations of finite capacity. EURO J. Transp. Logist. **5**, 261–291 (2016)
13. Froehlich, J., Neumann, J., Oliver, N.: Sensing and predicting the pulse of the city through shared bicycling. In: IJCAI, pp. 1420–1426 (2009)
14. Gast, N., Massonnet, G., Reijsbergen, D., Tribastone, M.: Probabilistic forecasts of bike-sharing systems for journey planning. In: CIKM, pp. 703–712. ACM (2015)
15. Getoor, L., Taskar, B. (eds.): Introduction to Statistical Relational Learning. The MIT Press, Cambridge (2007)

16. Gianfrotta, L., Topazzini, S., Pubblici, P.S.: Elaborazione di un Modello per lo Sviluppo di Nuovi Servizi e sua Applicazione al caso Bike Sharing di Pisa. Master's thesis, Università di Pisa (2013) (In Italian)
17. Kolen, J.F., Kremer, S.C. (eds.): A Field Guide to Dynamical Recurrent Networks. IEEE Press, New York (2001)
18. Lukoševičius, M., Jaeger, H.: Reservoir computing approaches to recurrent neural network training. Comput. Sci. Rev. **3**(3), 127–149 (2009)
19. Midgley, P.: Bicycle-Sharing schemes: enhancing sustainable mobility in Urban areas. Background Paper CSD19/2011/BP8, Commission on Sustainable Development, United Nations Department of Economic and Social Affairs, May 2011
20. Murashkin, A., Antkiewicz, M., Rayside, D., Czarnecki, K.: Visualization and exploration of optimal variants in product line engineering. In: Kishi, T., Jarzabek, S., Gnesi, S. (eds.) SPLC, pp. 111–115. ACM (2013)
21. Niccolai, C., Zanzi, E.: Progettare i servizi: Creazione di un modello di validità generale e applicazione al servizio di Bike Sharing a Pisa. Master's thesis, Università di Pisa (2013) (In Italian)

Comparing AWS Deployments Using Model-Based Predictions

Einar Broch Johnsen, Jia-Chun Lin$^{(\boxtimes)}$, and Ingrid Chieh Yu

Department of Informatics, University of Oslo, Oslo, Norway
{einarj,kellylin,ingridcy}@ifi.uio.no

Abstract. Cloud computing provides on-demand resource provisioning for scalable applications with a pay-as-you-go pricing model. However, the cost-efficient use of virtual resources requires the application to exploit the available resources efficiently. Will an application perform equally well on fewer or cheaper resources? Will the application successfully finish on these resources? We have previously proposed a model-centric approach, ABS-YARN, for prototyping deployment decisions to answer such questions during the design of an application. In this paper, we make model-centric predictions for applications on Amazon Web Services (AWS), which is a prominent platform for cloud deployment. To demonstrate how ABS-YARN can help users make deployment decisions with a high cost-performance ratio on AWS, we design several workload scenarios based on MapReduce benchmarks and execute these scenarios on ABS-YARN by considering different AWS resource purchasing options.

1 Introduction

Cloud computing is currently the main driver of an on-going change in how companies develop and exploit software by providing utility computing services [4]: IT resources and applications over the Internet are delivered on demand with a pay-as-you-go cost model. Cloud computing enables the infrastructure on which a software is deployed to be specialized to the needs of the software and even adapted at runtime by means of various adjustments of the configuration of the infrastructure. However, if the software does not adapt in an agile way to the changing deployment decisions (which are decisions of determining the capacity of computation resources, the scale of computation resources, or other parameters), we may experience a wasteful over-provisioning of resources or require substantial reengineering of the software, which might increase either the operational or the development costs of the software or both. Shifting deployment decisions from the deployment phase to the design phase of a software development process can significantly reduce such costs by performing model-based validation of the chosen decisions during the software design [10]. This shift

Supported by the EU projects H2020-644298 *HyVar: Scalable Hybrid Variability for Distributed Evolving Software Systems* (http://www.hyvar-project.eu).

T. Margaria and B. Steffen (Eds.): ISoLA 2016, Part II, LNCS 9953, pp. 482–496, 2016.
DOI: 10.1007/978-3-319-47169-3_39

requires that deployment decisions can be captured in formal models of the virtualized and distributed software and that these models enable us to assess the impact of different deployment decisions on the performance and operational cost of our software.

There are many providers of cloud computing technologies on the market today to offer a plethora of services in cloud ecosystems for both computing and data storage, e.g., virtual machine instances, containers, ready-made solutions for resource management and auto-scaling, service endpoints, as well as support for data storage, databases, and caching at many different costs. It is not easy to select a solution which best balances performance and incurred costs for a particular application. Even for very basic virtual machine instances, a company such as Amazon offers approximately 40 different so called instance types with different prices and resource specifications for on-demand virtual servers alone.

In this paper, we compare—at the modeling level—the effect of selecting different instance types for virtual servers from Amazon Web Services (AWS) in terms of performance and accumulated cost. Using a model-based approach, we design a set of workload scenarios consisting of a number of MapReduce benchmarks and consider different AWS instance type deployments to execute these scenarios so as to study the impacts of these deployments in terms of performance, cost, workload completion, etc.

The method used in this paper for model-based comparisons is based on the authors' previous work on ABS-YARN [15]. ABS-YARN is a highly configurable modeling framework for applications running on Apache YARN [21], a popular open-source distributed software framework for big data processing on cloud environments provided by vendors such as Amazon, HP, IBM, Microsoft, and Rackspace. ABS-YARN is defined in Real-Time ABS [5], a formal executable language for modeling deployed virtualized software by introducing a separation of concerns between the resource costs of the execution and the resource provisioning at (virtual) locations [14]. The focus of ABS-YARN is on obtaining results based on easy-to-use rapid prototyping, using the executable semantics of Real-Time ABS, defined in Maude [7], as a simulation tool for ABS-YARN. In previous work [15], we have shown through comprehensive experiments that ABS-YARN provides a satisfactory modeling accuracy as compared with a real YARN cluster. In this paper, we will base on the designed scenarios to demonstrate how users can utilize ABS-YARN to better understand the cost-performance trade-offs between different AWS resource purchasing options and make appropriate purchase decisions.

Paper overview. Section 2 discusses AWS, focusing on how to understand the specification of instance types for on-demand virtual servers. Section 3 describes YARN and ABS-YARN. Section 4 presents the modeling and comparison of different AWS instances in several scenarios. Section 5 discusses related work and Sect. 6 concludes the paper.

2   Amazon Web Services

Amazon Web Services (AWS) is the dominating player on today's market for cloud computing with an approximate 30 % market share for Q4, 2015 [6], especially for Infrastructure as a Service (IaaS). AWS offers an extensive ecosystem of services to help users to deploy, scale, and manage virtualized services on AWS infrastructure, including computing resources such as virtual servers, containers, load balancers, auto-scalers, etc. However, the pricing options in this ecosystem are complex: considering only the instance types of AWS itself (i.e., the different kinds of virtual machines), different types of instances may be acquired on demand, with no, partial, or all upfront payments with commitment for shorter or longer time periods, or at spot price[1].

As a customer of cloud computing services, it is important to understand the consequences that specific choices in this ecosystem may have for your software, both with respect to the *performance* of the software and to its incurred *operational costs*. In this paper, we focus on *on-demand* instance types, which do not require long-term commitments and therefore might be a good option for most customers who only run their applications sporadically.

Within this range of on-demand instance types, there are instance types which are suggested for general purpose applications as well as for compute-intensive and memory-optimized applications. Currently, there are around 40 different instance types available for on-demand instances. However, it is non-trivial to answer questions such as "what kind of instances should we choose for an application to achieve the best trade-off between performance and cost?".

Table 1. The specifications of five AWS instance types.

Instance type	vCPU	ECU	Memory (GB)	Price per hour
m4.large	2	6.5	8	$ 0.143
m4.xlarge	4	13.0	16	$ 0.285
m4.2xlarge	8	26.0	32	$ 0.57
m4.4xlarge	16	53.5	64	$ 1.14
m4.10xlarge	40	124.5	160	$ 2.85

Table 1 lists five on-demand instance types which all belong to AWS m4 category. M4 instances are the latest generation of general purpose instances, which provides a balance of compute, memory, and network resources, and it is a good choice for many applications [2]. Each row of Table 1 presents the specification of a particular instance type. We can see that each instance type roughly doubles the resources of the instance type on the previous row, but the instance type "m4.10xlarge" deviates slightly from this format. It is interesting to observe that deploying software on a utility computing model is different

---

[1] For details, see https://aws.amazon.com/ec2/pricing.

from how developers are used to think about CPU resources. Using the cloud, on-demand processing capacity is rented by the hour whereas, using a traditional provisioning model, a specific processor is bought with a long lifespan. AWS uses commodity hardware which is continually being replaced, so different hardware may be used to deliver the same virtual machine instances [1]: "Our goal is to provide a consistent amount of CPU capacity no matter what the actual underlying hardware." The actual processing capacity of an instance type is thus given in terms of *elastic compute units* (ECU) whereas the column vCPU suggests a traditional understanding in terms of hardware.

3 YARN and ABS-YARN

In this section, we will briefly introduce YARN ·and then describe how ABS-YARN models YARN.

YARN [21] (short for Yet Another Resource Negotiator) is an open-source software framework supported by Apache for distributed processing and storage of high data volumes. It inherits the advantages of its well-known predecessor Hadoop [3], including resource allocation, distributed data processing, fault tolerance, and data replication. YARN further improves Hadoop's limitations in terms of scalability, multi-tenancy support, cluster utilization, and reliability.

YARN supports the execution of different types of applications (or jobs), including MapReduce, graph, and streaming. Each job is divided into a set of smaller tasks which are executed in parallel on a cluster of machines. The key components of a YARN cluster are as follows:

- *ResourceManager* (RM): RM allocates resources to various competing jobs and applications in a cluster. The scheduling provided by RM is job level, rather than task level. Thus, RM does not monitor each task's progress or restart any failed task.
- *ApplicationMaster* (AM): An AM is an instance of a framework-specific library class for a particular job. It acts as the head of the job to manage the job's lifecycle, including requesting resources from RM, scheduling the execution of all tasks of the job, monitoring task execution, and re-executing failed tasks.
- *Slave nodes*: Each slave node provides both computation resources and storage to execute tasks and store data.
- *Containers*; Each container is a logical resource collection of a particular slave node (e.g., 1 CPU and 2 GB of RAM). Clients can specify the resource requirement of a container when they submit jobs to RM and run any kind of application on containers.

Given RM and a set of slave nodes, a YARN cluster provides both computation resources and storage capacity to execute applications and store data. Assume that RM only has one queue, the execution of a job on YARN is as follows:

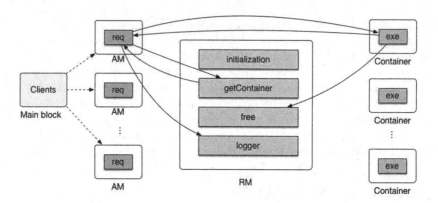

Fig. 1. The structure of the ABS-YARN framework.

1. Whenever RM receives a job request from a client, RM follows a FIFO scheduling policy to find a container from an available slave and initiate the AM of the job on the container.
2. Once the AM has been initiated, it starts requesting containers from RM based on the container resource requirements and the number of tasks of the job. Each task will be run on one container.
3. When RM receives a container request from the AM, it inserts the request into its queue and follows its job scheduling algorithm to allocate the desired container from an available slave node to the AM.
4. Upon receiving a container, the AM executes one task of the job on the container and monitors this task execution. If a task fails due to some errors such as an underlying container failure or slave node failure, the AM will re-request a container from RM to restart the task.
5. When all tasks of a job finish successfully, implying that the job is complete, the AM notifies the client about the completion.

ABS-YARN [15] is an executable model of YARN written in Real-Time ABS [5], which is a formal, executable, object-oriented language for modeling distributed systems by means of concurrent object groups [13]. Real-Time ABS uses *deployment components* to capture a location with a given resource specification in the deployment architecture, on which a number of concurrent objects can be deployed [14]. ABS-YARN follows the same execution flow as a YARN cluster.

Figure 1 shows the ABS-YARN architecture, which consists of interfaces AM, RM, and Container to model AM, RM, and containers, respectively. Interface RM has four methods. When a user starts ABS-YARN, method initialization initializes the entire cluster environment, including RM and slaves. Each slave has its own CPU, speed, and memory capacities. After the initialization, the cluster can start serving client requests. The method getContainer allows an AM to obtain containers with given resource requirements from RM. The method free is used to release container resources, and the method logger is used to record job execution statistics, including job ID and job execution time.

Currently, ABS-YARN focuses on the modeling of MapReduce jobs, which are the most common jobs in YARN. Each MapReduce job has two phases to process data: map phase and reduce phase. In the map phase, all map tasks are executed in parallel. When all the map tasks have completed, the reduce tasks are executed. The job is completed when all the map and reduce tasks have finished. Interface AM has only one method req, which is designed to request containers from RM and then ask the allocated containers to the execute the tasks of its job. For an AM, the total number of times that method req is called corresponds to the total number of the map tasks and reduce tasks of a job (e.g., if a job is divided into 10 map tasks and one reduce task, this method will be called 11 times). When all map tasks of the job have successfully completed, the AM proceeds with a container request to run the reduce task of the job. Only when all map and reduce tasks have completed successfully, the job is considered completed.

Interface Container has method exe to execute a task. The execution time of a task in a real YARN cluster might be influenced by many factors, e.g., the size of the processed data and the computational complexity of the task. To reduce the complexity of modeling the task execution time, ABS-YARN adopts the cost annotation functionality of Real-Time ABS to associate cost to the execution of a task. Hence, the task execution time will be the task cost divided by the CPU capacity of the container that executes the task.

ABS-YARN allows users to freely determine the scale and resource capacity of a YARN cluster by configuring the following parameters:

- the number of slave nodes in the cluster,
- the CPU capacity of each slave node, and
- the memory capacity of each slave node.

In addition, to support dynamic and realistic modeling of job execution, ABS-YARN also allows users to define the following parameters:

- Number of clients submitting jobs
- Number of jobs submitted by each client
- Number of map tasks and reduce tasks per job
- Cost annotation for each task
- CPU and memory requirements for each container
- Job inter-arrival pattern. Users can determine any kind of job inter-arrival distributions in ABS-YARN.

In the next section, we will apply ABS-YARN to study different instance types provided by AWS.

4   AWS Instances Study

As discussed in Sect. 2, AWS provides different kinds of instances to meet the resource requirements of different customers, including the on-demand instances, reserved instances, and spot instances. Here, we focus on comparing the on-demand instances which we believe are the best suited for sporadic YARN jobs because renting this type of instance does not need a long-term commitment. Different operating systems, such as Linux, Red Hat, and Windows, are also available for the on-demand instances. In this paper, we focus on Linux because this operating system is supported by YARN and commonly used by the software development community. We chose EU (Frankfurt) as the region of instance and consider five general-purpose instance types. Table 1 in Sect. 2 lists the corresponding specifications and prices.

Table 2. The average map-task execution time (AMT) and average reduce-task execution time (ART) of each benchmark job [15].

Benchmark	AMT (sec)	ART (sec)
WordCount	295.47	430.24
WordMean	139.98	201.11
WordSD	238.46	312.38
GrepSort	37.38	62.06
GrepSearch	173.92	205.94

To compare the five chosen AWS instance types, we create realistic workloads using the following MapReduce benchmark jobs as in [15]: WordCount, WordMean, WordSD, GrepSort, and GrepSearch. Each benchmark job processes 1 GB of enwiki data [8] with 128 MB block size (which is the default block size of YARN [16]). Therefore, each job has 8 (=1 GB/128 MB) map tasks and one reduce task, implying that 9 containers are required to execute each job. Based on the average task execution time of each benchmark job shown in Table 2, we configure the ABS-YARN framework with the corresponding task cost annotation for each benchmark job (following [15]). We use 350 s as a threshold to classify the five benchmark jobs based on their execution time as below:

- Type 1: The summation of the AMT and ART of a job is larger than or equal to the threshold.
- Type 2: Otherwise.

Hence, the WordCount, WordSD, and GrepSearch jobs are classified as type 1 (i.e., long jobs), whereas the WordMean and GrepSort jobs are classified as type 2 (i.e., short jobs). Based on this information, we create two scenarios to compare the five AWS instance types. In the first scenario, we create a non-urgent workload to compare the five instance types. The goal is to see which instance type provides the best cost-efficiency. In the second scenario, we create three workloads in which each task of a job has a time limit to obtain its required container. The purpose is to further study if employing a different number of instances affects workload completion rate under the given time limit or not.

Table 3. The specification of the five clusters tested in Scenario 1. Note that the # of vCores and memory are calculated based on Table 1.

Cluster	Instance type	# of instances	# of vCores	Memory (GB)
1	m4.large	80	160	640
2	m4.xlarge	40	160	640
3	m4.2xlarge	20	160	640
4	m4.4xlarge	10	160	640
5	m4.10xlarge	4	160	640

4.1 Scenario 1: Non-urgent Workload

In Scenario 1, the non-urgent workload consists of 100 MapReduce jobs without any time limit to get containers. As a consequence, each task of the jobs in this workload will eventually be executed on a container allocated by RM, implying that the workload completion rate will be 100 %. In the workload, half of the jobs are of Type 1 and the other half of the jobs are of Type 2. All the jobs are submitted by a user at the same time, i.e., these jobs have zero inter-arrival time. The purpose is to understand the cost efficiencies of different instance types when all jobs compete for containers simultaneously.

To compare the five instance types in a fair way, we use ABS-YARN to establish five clusters (see Table 3) with the same resource capacity, i.e., 160 vCPUs and 640 GB of memory, and then execute the workload.

The total workload execution time and the total instance cost spent by the five clusters to execute the non-urgent workload are shown in Fig. 2(a) and (b), respectively. It is clear that all the clusters have very close workload execution time and total instance costs. Therefore, as shown in Fig. 3, they have similar cost-efficiencies. The results confirm that the five instance types have no difference in terms of workload execution performance when the total instance cost is identical. However, when other issues such as management efforts or reliability are further considered, choosing different instance types might result in different

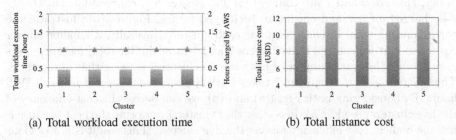

(a) Total workload execution time   (b) Total instance cost

Fig. 2. The total workload execution time and instance costs of clusters 1 to 5. Note that in (a) the first y axis is for the bar plot, whereas the second y axis is for the line plot.

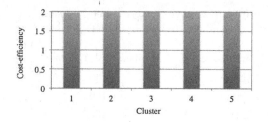

Fig. 3. The cost-efficiencies of clusters 1 to 5.

Table 4. The details of clusters 6 to 10.

Cluster	# of m4.large instances	# of vCores	Memory (GB)
6	80	160	640
7	40	80	320
8	20	40	160
9	10	20	80
10	5	10	40

effects. However, this depends on users' preferences, and it is outside of the scope of this paper.

We can see from Fig. 2(a) that each cluster only spent about 0.44 h to finish the entire workload, but all of them are charged by AWS for an entire hour (see the line plot in Fig. 2(a)). Based on these results, our next question is whether users can find a suitable number of instances to achieve a better cost-efficiency. To answer this, we conduct additional simulations to see how different numbers of the same instance type affect the cost-efficiency. We chose the m4.large instance type as an example and use ABS-YARN to establish another five clusters (see Table 4) and execute the same non-urgent workload.

Figure 4(a) shows that when a cluster employs fewer instances of the same type (implying that total number of available containers is smaller), the time to finish the entire workload increases. Based on the AWS hour-based charge policy, clusters 6 and 7 are charged for 1 h, cluster 8 is charged for 2 h, cluster 9 is charged for 3 h, and cluster 10 is charged for 5 h. Figure 4(b) illustrates the corresponding total instance cost for each cluster. Naturally, a smaller cluster costs less, but we can see that clusters 7 and 8 have similar total instance costs even though the total number of instances in cluster 7 is twice that of cluster 8. The key reason is that cluster 7 takes 1 AWS hour, but cluster 8 takes 2 AWS hours. By considering both Fig. 4(a) and (b), we can derive the cost-efficiency of the five clusters (see Fig. 5). It is clear that cluster 7 performs the best because it has the highest cost-efficiency among the five clusters. This result is not obvious by just looking at the specifications of AWS instances.

Based on all above simulations, we observe the following phenomenon: First, choosing different AWS m4 instance types makes no difference in terms of performance when the total instance cost is identical. Second, for a particular AWS instance type, employing different numbers of the instance leads to different cost efficiencies.

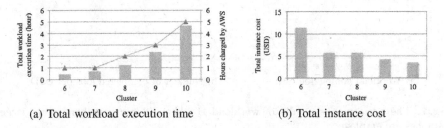

(a) Total workload execution time   (b) Total instance cost

Fig. 4. The total workload execution time and instance costs of clusters 6 to 10. Note that in (a) the first y axis is for the bar plot, whereas the second y axis is for the line plot.

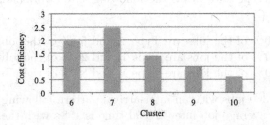

Fig. 5. The cost-efficiencies of clusters 6 to 10.

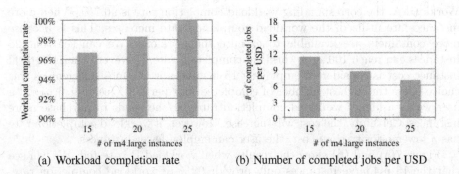

(a) Workload completion rate   (b) Number of completed jobs per USD

Fig. 6. The performance results of workload A when different numbers of m4.large instances are employed.

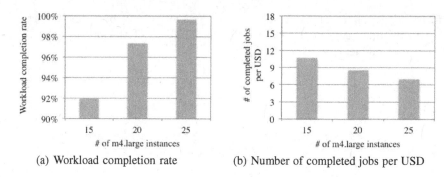

(a) Workload completion rate   (b) Number of completed jobs per USD

Fig. 7. The performance results of workload B when different numbers of m4.large instances are employed.

4.2   Scenario 2: Workload with a Time Limit

Recall that the goal of the second scenario is to investigate if different numbers of instances affect workload completion rate. In this scenario, we continue with the m4.large instance type and create the following three workloads with different job compositions:

– Workload A: 50 % of the jobs are Type 1, and 50 % of the jobs are Type 2.
– Workload B: 80 % of the jobs are Type 1, and 20 % of the jobs are Type 2.
– Workload C: 20 % of the jobs are Type 1, and 80 % of the jobs are Type 2.

All of them have 300 jobs with an inter-arrival pattern following an exponential distribution. The average job inter-arrival time is 158 s with the standard deviation of 153 s [15]. In addition, the three workloads have the same time limit for each task to get a container. In this experiment, we assume that the time limit is 2 min, i.e., each task of a job in the three workloads will be considered as failed if it cannot obtain its desired container within 2 min.

Figure 6(a) shows that when 15 m4.large instances are employed to execute Workload A, the corresponding workload completion rate is 96.7 %. When more instances are utilized, the workload completion rate increases. This is because more containers are available to execute the workload. We can see that 25 instances can reach 100 % of workload completion rate. However, when the total instance cost is considered, employing 15 instances is the most efficient as this choice offers the highest number of completed jobs per USD (see Fig. 6(b)). If a user wants a higher workload completion rate, he/she needs to purchase more instances. Certainly, the cost will increase. However, if workload completion rate has a lower priority than cost, the user can employ fewer instances.

Figure 7(a) and (b) show the results when workload B is tested. We can see that the 15 m4.large instances only provide 92 % of workload completion rate, and the 25 m4.large instances can no longer complete the entire workload B. The main reason is that workload B has more long jobs than workload A, implying that more containers for workload B are occupied for a longer period than those

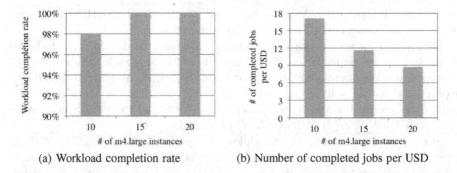

(a) Workload completion rate   (b) Number of completed jobs per USD

Fig. 8. The performance results of workload C when different numbers of m4.large instances are employed.

for workload A. Nevertheless, using 15 m4.large instances still perform the best in terms of the number of completed jobs per USD among the three options. Figure 8(a) and (b) show the results when workload C is tested. Different from workloads A and B, the completion rate of workload C is higher on the same number of instances. This is because workload C has more short jobs than the other two. Based on the simulation results of Scenario 2, it is clear that when a workload has different job compositions, employing the same number of AWS instances does not guarantee the same workload completion rate.

Note that our experiments are based on model-based simulations. Hence, the results (e.g., number of completed jobs per USD and workload completion rate) may differ from the actual price and completion. Although there exists some performance deviation [15], with ABS-YARN users can still easily compare different instance deployments and predict the corresponding consequences at the design phase of their applications.

5   Related Work

Many researchers have conducted performance studies by running their scientific applications in cloud environments. For examples, Hazelhurst [11] evaluated the performance of a bioinformatics application and Ramakrishnan et al. [19] studied the performances of e-Science applications in cloud computing. Several works have been introduced to study Amazon Elastic Compute Cloud (Amazon EC2). Napper et al. [17] analyzed the performance of the Linpack benchmarks on different EC2 instance types. Osterman et al. [18] conducted a variety of micro-benchmarks on Amazon EC2.

Garfinkel [9] presented a comprehensive introduction of Amazon's EC2, Simple Storage Service (S3), and Simple Queue Service (SQS) in their securities, privacy controls, legal issues, API limitations, and pricing models. Furthermore, a series of experiments are also provided to study the performances of EC2, S3, and SQS, including average daily throughput, average daily transaction, bandwidth speed, and availability. Jackson et al. [12] performed a comprehensive evaluation for comparing Amazon EC2 and two conventional HPC platforms (Franklin and Lawrencium) by using real application workloads.

Different from all previous work, the comparison of deployment decisions conducted in this paper is based on a model-centric approach to determine an appropriate deployment configuration at the design time. We compared different deployment decisions by using ABS-YARN [15]. In addition, our comparison focused on several instance types provided by AWS and their tradeoffs, rather than comparing different cloud or HPC platforms.

Stantchev [20] presents a methodology for performance evaluation of cloud computing configurations. The methodology consists of five steps: identify benchmark, identify configuration, run tests, analyze, and recommend. The author conducted a real experiment evaluation by deploying several configurations of a web service benchmark in Amazon EC2, and focused on analyzing the results of two nonfunctional properties: transactions rate and response time. Although this methodology can help users to compare different deployment decisions, the users have to conduct such comparisons in real cloud environments. In other words, the cost to purchase resource instances cannot be reduced.

6   Conclusions

In this paper, we have introduced different instance purchasing options provided by AWS, and also studied different AWS deployments using ABS-YARN. We considered two workload scenarios. In the first scenario, we created a non-urgent workload consisting of 100 MapReduce jobs with the same submission time. The goal was to investigate which AWS instance provides the best cost-efficiency. In the second scenario, we designed additional workloads to further study whether employing different numbers of instances affects workload completion rate.

The results demonstrated that AWS provides a fair instance pricing, i.e., the instance cost doubles when the performance of an instance doubles. Hence, from a performance perspective, choosing a better or worse instance makes no difference when the total instance cost is fixed. However, this may not be the case when other issues such as management efforts, reliability, and data locality are further considered. Furthermore, purchasing different numbers of a particular instance type may lead to different workload execution time and instance costs. Our results in the second scenario also showed that purchasing different numbers of the same AWS instances significantly affected workload completion rate, especially when workloads consist of different compositions of long jobs and short jobs.

In general, if users want to achieve a high cost-efficiency and a high workload completion rate, they need to conduct multiple tuning and comparisons between different instance options. With ABS-YARN, they can easily evaluate and compare different deployment decisions with less cost and effort.

References

1. Amazon EC2 FAQs. Q: What is an "EC2 compute unit" and why did you introduce it? https://aws.amazon.com/ec2/faqs/#hardware-information. Accessed 27 April 2016
2. Amazon EC2 Instance Types. https://aws.amazon.com/ec2/instance-types/?nc1=h_ls
3. Apache Hadoop. http://hadoop.apache.org/
4. Armbrust, M., Fox, A., Griffith, R., Joseph, A.D., Katz, R., Konwinski, A., Lee, G., Patterson, D., Rabkin, A., Stoica, I., Zaharia, M.: A view of cloud computing. Commun. ACM **53**(4), 50–58 (2010)
5. Bjørk, J., de Boer, F.S., Johnsen, E.B., Schlatte, R., Tapia Tarifa, S.L.: User-defined schedulers for real-time concurrent objects. Innovations Syst. Softw. Eng. **9**(1), 29–43 (2013)
6. Bort, J.: Amazon still dominates the \$16 billion cloud market. UK Business Insider, February 2015. http://uk.businessinsider.com/synergy-research-amazon-dominates-16-billion-cloud-market-2015-2
7. Clavel, M., Durán, F., Eker, S., Lincoln, P., Martí-Oliet, N., Meseguer, J., Talcott, C.L.: All About Maude - A High-Performance Logical Framework: How to Specify, Program and Verify Systems in Rewriting Logic. LNCS, vol. 4350. Springer, Heidelberg (2007)
8. enwiki. http://dumps.wikimedia.org/enwiki/
9. Garfinkel, S.L.: An evaluation of Amazon's grid computing services: EC2, S3, and SQS. Technical report TR-08-07, Center for Research on Computation and Society School for Engineering and Applied sciences, Harvard University, August 2007. https://dash.harvard.edu/handle/1/24829568
10. Hähnle, R., Johnsen, E.B.: Designing resource-aware cloud applications. IEEE Comput. **48**(6), 72–75 (2015)
11. Hazelhurst, S.: Scientific computing using virtual high-performance computing: a case study using the Amazon elastic computing cloud. In: Proceedings of the 2008 Annual Research Conference of the South African Institute of Computer Scientists and Information Technologists on IT research in Developing Countries: Riding the Wave of Technology, SAICSIT 2008, pp. 94–103. ACM (2008)
12. Jackson, K.R., Ramakrishnan, L., Muriki, K., Canon, S., Cholia, S., Shalf, J., Wasserman, H.J., Wright, N.J.: Performance analysis of high performance computing applications on the amazon web services cloud. In: 2nd IEEE International Conference on Cloud Computing Technology and Science, CloudCom 2010, pp. 159–168. IEEE (2010)
13. Johnsen, E.B., Hähnle, R., Schäfer, J., Schlatte, R., Steffen, M.: ABS: a core language for abstract behavioral specification. In: Aichernig, B.K., de Boer, F.S., Bonsangue, M.M. (eds.) FMCO 2010. LNCS, vol. 6957, pp. 142–164. Springer, Heidelberg (2011)
14. Johnsen, E.B., Schlatte, R., Tapia Tarifa, S.L.: Integrating deployment architectures and resource consumption in timed object-oriented models. J. Logical Algebraic Methods Programm. **84**(1), 67–91 (2015)
15. Lin, J.-C., Yu, I.C., Johnsen, E.B., Lee, M.-C.: ABS-YARN: a formal framework for modeling hadoop YARN clusters. In: Stevens, P., et al. (eds.) FASE 2016. LNCS, vol. 9633, pp. 49–65. Springer, Heidelberg (2016). doi:10.1007/978-3-662-49665-7_4
16. Murthy, A., Vavilapalli, V., Eadline, D., Niemiec, J., Markham, J.: Apache Hadoop YARN: Moving Beyond MapReduce and Batch Processing with Apache Hadoop 2. Addison-Wesley Professional, Reading (2014)

17. Napper, J., Bientinesi, P.: Can cloud computing reach the top 500? In: Proceedings of the Combined Workshops on UnConventional High Performance Computing Workshop Plus Memory Access Workshop, UCHPC-MAW 2009, pp. 17–20. ACM (2009)
18. Ostermann, S., Iosup, A., Yigitbasi, N., Prodan, R., Fahringer, T., Epema, D.: An early performance analysis of cloud computing services for scientific computing. Technical report PDS-2008-006, Delft University of Technology, December 2008. http://www.ds.ewi.tudelft.nl/reports/2008/PDS-2008-006.pdf
19. Ramakrishnan, L., Jackson, K.R., Canon, S., Cholia, S., Shalf, J.: Defining future platform requirements for e-science clouds. In: Proceedings of the 1st ACM Symposium on Cloud Computing, SoCC 2010, pp. 101–106. ACM (2010)
20. Stantchev, V.: Performance evaluation of cloud computing offerings. In: 2009 Third International Conference on Advanced Engineering Computing and Applications in Sciences, ADVCOMP 2009, pp. 187–192. IEEE (2009)
21. Vavilapalli, V.K., Murthy, A.C., Douglas, C., Agarwal, S., Konar, M., Evans, R., Graves, T., Lowe, J., Shah, H., Seth, S., Saha, B., Curino, C., O'Malley, O., Radia, S., Reed, B., Baldeschwieler, E.: Apache hadoop YARN: yet another resource negotiator. In: Lohman, G.M. (ed.) ACM Symposium on Cloud Computing (SOCC 2013), pp. 5:1–5:16 (2013)

A Toolchain for Delta-Oriented Modeling of Software Product Lines

Cristina Chesta[1], Ferruccio Damiani[2], Liudmila Dobriakova[1],
Marco Guernieri[1], Simone Martini[3], Michael Nieke[4(✉)], Vítor Rodrigues[2],
and Sven Schuster[4]

[1] Santer Reply S.p.A., Turin, Italy
[2] Universitá degli Studi di Torino, Turin, Italy
[3] Magneti Marelli S.p.A., Turin, Italy
[4] Technische Universität Braunschweig, Braunschweig, Germany
m.nieke@tu-braunschweig.de

Abstract. Software is increasingly individualized to the needs of customers and may have to be adapted to changing contexts and environments after deployment. Therefore, individualized software adaptations may have to be performed. As a large number of variants for affected systems and domains may exist, the creation and deployment of the individualized software should be performed automatically based on the software's configuration and context. In this paper, we present a toolchain to develop and deploy individualized software adaptations based on Software Product Line (SPL) engineering. In particular, we contribute a description and technical realization of a toolchain ranging from variability modeling over variability realization to variant derivation for the automated deployment of individualized software adaptations. To capture the variability within realization artifacts, we employ delta modeling, a transformational SPL implementation approach. As we aim to fulfill requirements of industrial practice, we employ model-driven engineering using statecharts as realization artifacts. Particular statechart variants are further processed by generating C/C++ code, linking to external code artifacts, compiling and deploying to the target device. To allow for flexible and parallel execution the toolchain is provided within a cloud environment. This way, required variants can automatically be created and deployed to target devices. We show the feasibility of our toolchain by developing the industry-related case of emergency response systems.

Keywords: Software Product Lines · Delta modeling · Model-driven engineering · Statecharts

1 Introduction

Software is increasingly individualized and adapted to the needs of specific customers. Moreover, after development and deployment, it may often have to be

---

The authors of this paper are listed in alphabetical order.

T. Margaria and B. Steffen (Eds.): ISoLA 2016, Part II, LNCS 9953, pp. 497–511, 2016.
DOI: 10.1007/978-3-319-47169-3_40

adapted to changing needs and environments. To this end, the software may be replaced by a different variant of the software having different functionality. As also these software adaptations may be individualized depending on the software's configuration and the host device's environment (e.g., sensor data), such software is often developed as a *Software Product Line (SPL)* capturing its commonalities and variabilities across different variants [15,18]. Moreover, such software variants often run distributed on remote devices in heterogeneous environments, e.g., on a car's *Electronic Control Unit (ECU)*. To allow for individualized adaptations of these distributed variants based on the software's configuration and the device's environment, an individual reconfiguration and deployment is required. Furthermore, a development environment is necessary to describe the particular domain variability as well as to develop variability-aware realization artifacts.

In this paper, we present an integrated toolchain for the development of SPLs as well as the automated derivation and deployment of their respective software variants. We employ *Feature Models (FMs)* [10] to capture the commonalities and variabilities of the different variants. Furthermore, we employ *delta modeling* [17], a transformational variability realization mechanism, to express variability within realization artifacts. As statecharts are common industrial practice to model the behavior of a system, we follow a model-driven engineering process employing statecharts as realization artifacts to integrate the toolchain in existing industrial processes. To deploy the variants, we generate C code from the variant statecharts and link this code, e.g., to device-specific code artifacts. As also these external code artifacts may be customizable, we combine the coarse-grained delta-oriented variability on statecharts with fine-grained preprocessor-based variability within the code artifacts. Finally, we deploy the generated, linked and compiled variant to the respective target device.

The variant derivation for a software adaptation is triggered based on the deployed variant's configuration and the device's environment (e.g., changing context information such as GPS coordinates) [12,13]. Therefore, environmental information has to be received from the target device and a flexible and scalable infrastructure must be available to perform multiple parallel reconfiguration processes for a potentially immense number of variants. To this end, the variant derivation, code generation, linking and compilation are performed in a cloud environment.

In particular, we make the following contributions:

- We present a toolchain for modeling an SPL using statecharts and C code as realization artifacts. We provide automatic variant derivation of a statechart variant as well as C code generation, linking to external code artifacts, compilation and automatic deployment of the variant to a target device.
- We employ a combination of two different variability mechanisms: delta-oriented modeling for coarse-grained variability on the level of statecharts, as well as preprocessors for fine-grained variability on the code level.
- To employ delta modeling, a language to express transformations must exist, which is specific to the respective target language. To this end, we present a

delta language for statecharts and a delta language for adding external code artifacts to the variant, which we call metadata.

The paper is structured as follows. Section 2 describes relevant foundations that are used throughout the toolchain. Section 3 elaborates on the running example used throughout the paper. Section 4 introduces the general workflow and the components of our toolchain. Section 5 describes how to specify an SPL using the tool suite *DeltaEcore* and our provided extensions to it. Section 6 describes the process of variant generation, code generation, linking, compilation and deployment of a particular variant. Section 7 contrasts our work to related work. Finally, Sect. 8 gives a conclusion and and an outlook on future work.

2   Background

In this section, we present technology and concepts of the toolchain. In particular, we present the technologies to realize variability on metamodels, to create models defining variants, to compile and link source code created from our models to existing source code.

2.1   Model-Driven Software Development with the Eclipse Modeling Framework (EMF)

In Model-Driven Software Development, models represent an abstraction of the reality [7]. A metamodel is an abstraction of models and specifies types of models. The Object Management Group (OMG) specified a standard for metamodels, i.e., a meta-metamodel, in the Meta-Object Facility (MOF)[1] and also a reduced Essential MOF (EMOF) standard. With the EMF, it is possible to specify ECORE metamodels, which are mostly based on the EMOF standard. ECORE models are specified by classes, attributes for the classes and references between them. EMF also provides a code generator, which generates Java code for metamodels defined in ECORE.

2.2   Yakindu Statecharts

As the explicit goal of our toolchain is to integrate into common industrial practice, we mainly use statecharts as realization artifacts which specify the behavior of software products. As a representative for tool support, we use the open source YAKINDU statechart tools[2]. YAKINDU statecharts are defined as an ECORE metamodel. With YAKINDU, it is possible to define statecharts with states and transitions between these states. Moreover, it is possible to define so-called *specifications* for the statechart. These specifications can consist of variables which are accessible from transactions or states. To this end, YAKINDU defines several primitive and platform independent types. Moreover, it is possible

---

[1] http://www.omg.org/mof.

[2] https://www.itemis.com/en/yakindu/statechart-tools.

to specify interfaces and external *operations*. Each operation has a signature and can also be used in transactions or states. YAKINDU provides a graphical editor to ease the creation of statecharts in a visual representation similar to UML state diagrams[3].

To generate an executable application out of a YAKINDU statechart, there are three different code generators for the C/C++/Java programming languages. As input, the code generators take a fully specified statechart and produce the source code for traversing the different states and transactions in the respective target language. Moreover, the generators create definitions for the variables, interfaces and external operations specified in the *specification* of a statechart in the respective programming language. Additionally, YAKINDU supports the specification of customized code generators that are able to generate source code for arbitrary languages.

2.3 Autotools

AUTOTOOLS, also known as The GNU Build System[4], is a set of tools designed to allow source code compilation for different Unix-based environments. Compilation of C/C++ source code can be very different from one Unix-based system to another, among others, because system headers and library functions can change decisively. To this end, AUTOTOOLS automatically generate *Makefiles* for certain platforms and environments. As input, AUTOTOOLS receive user-specified high-level configuration and makefiles, as Fig. 1 illustrates. In the *Makefile.am*, the user writes an abstracted makefile in a high-level specification, which is then translated to a template, the *Makefile.in*, for a concrete makefile. Users write a meta script, which abstracts over different execution environments for the script, which is called *configure.ac*. From this meta script, a portable concrete *configure* script is created, which is used to generate a concrete *makefile* out of the *Makefile.in*.

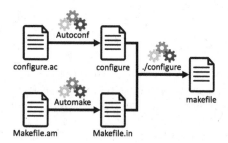

Fig. 1. Workflow to generate a makefile

---

[3] http://www.omg.org/spec/UML.

[4] https://www.gnu.org/software/software.en.html.

2.4 Software Product Lines

Software Product Lines (SPLs) are a methodology for large-scale reuse for families of closely related software systems in terms of variabilities and commonalities [15]. Conceptually, in the *problem space*, the variabilities and commonalities of an SPL are captured in a variability model, .e.g., a Feature Model (FM) [9]. Variability models define all possible configurations of an SPL. FMs consist of multiple features representing functionality of the SPL, independent of the implementation. Features are structured hierarchically and can be *optional* or *mandatory*. Moreover, features can be grouped into *alternative* or *or* groups. In *alternative* groups, exactly one feature has to be selected, whereas in *or* groups, at least one feature has to be selected. Moreover, cross-tree constraints (CTC) in terms of propositional formulas can be used to define dependencies between features independent of their hierarchical structures. Figure 2 illustrates an example of a visual representation of an FM.

The features in the *problem space* represent conceptual functionality, the realization artifacts, e.g., code or documentation, reside in the *solution space*. The realization artifacts are the artifacts, which are suitable for reuse in the SPL. The *configuration knowledge* defines the relations between the problem and the solution space, i.e., Boolean formulas defining under which feature selection certain realization artifacts are selected. Individual systems created from a configuration of an SPL are called variants or products.

Different variability realization mechanisms exist to describe variability in the realization artifacts [18]. In compositional approaches, e.g., Feature-Oriented Programming (FOP), new functionality, representing the selected features, is added to a base implementation [5,16]. In FOP, feature modules are specified, which define the new functionality and target for composition. In annotative approaches, for instance pre-processor directives (#ifdefs) in C [8], the variable code is annotated and removed if not needed. In transformational approaches, for instance delta modeling [6], a certain base artifact is transformed by means of adding, removing or modifying functionality. Delta languages define domain-specific delta operations, specifying add, remove and modify operations. In delta modeling, delta modules are specified, which contain a set of delta operation calls to realize the changes associated with certain combinations of features.

During the variant derivation, variability is resolved for a specific configuration, i.e., feature selection. For #ifdefs, a pre-processor removes the code whose annotations are not satisfied by the feature selection. In FOP and delta modeling, the feature and delta modules are selected and applied to the base code based on the feature selection using the configuration knowledge.

2.5 Delta Modeling with DeltaEcore

DELTAECORE is a tool suite, which supports developers in defining delta languages for their ECORE[5] metamodels [20]. Moreover, delta modules defined using

---

[5] https://eclipse.org/modeling/emf/.

the created language can be applied to a base variant. The different delta modules and the base variant represent the solution space of an SPL.

When creating a language for an ECORE metamodel, DELTAECORE provides a set of pre-defined delta operations based on the structure of the metamodel. Standard operations in a delta language of DELTAECORE can access arbitrary elements of a model of the respective metamodel and, additionally, can have Java primitives, String types and model elements as attributes. In addition, *custom operations* can be created by defining a signature of complex operations with user defined semantics. DELTAECORE then generates stubs for these operations which merely have to be implemented by the developer. Finally, if a delta language is completely specified, a text editor is generated, in which it is possible to define delta modules, potentially consisting of multiple *delta blocks*. Each delta block specifies a base variant which is transformed by delta operations called in this block. Note that it is possible to define delta blocks in different delta languages in one delta module to realize logically cohesive changes to realization artifacts of different languages.

To be able to support the whole workflow of an SPL, DELTAECORE also supports the definition of FMs, covering the problem space of an SPL. Moreover, it is also possible to define a mapping between the FM and available delta modules, covering the configuration knowledge. When delta modules, an FM and a mapping are defined, it is possible to define configurations, consisting of selected features. Using such a configuration, DELTAECORE provides the possibility to generate variants by applying delta modules if their respective expression in the mapping is satisfied.

3   Running Example – Emergency Response Systems

In this section, we present the running example used throughout the paper, which is based on a real scenario of the automotive domain: emergency response systems for cars. An emergency response system aims to automatically dial emergency numbers in the event of a serious road accident and to wirelessly send impact sensor information and location coordinates to local emergency agencies. Different programs exist such as the eCall/E112 program of the European Union as well as the Russian ERA GLONASS system.

As different requirements for different countries exist, software for the emergency response system must behave differently depending on the current location of the car. For example, the eCall/E112 program uses the Global Positioning System (GPS) for location information, whereas the Russian ERA GLONASS system employs the Russian Global Navigation Satellite System (GLONASS). Hence, depending on the current location of the vehicle, the system needs to be reconfigured to use a different satellite navigation system.

The feature model of the emergency response system for the particular use case of supporting both the (European) "eCall" and the "EraGlonass" features is presented in Fig. 2. Depending on which system is used, a different satellite system (i.e., "GPS" or "GLONASS") and a different language ("Russian" or

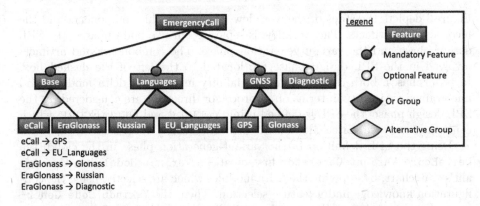

Fig. 2. Feature model and constraints for the emergency response system

"EU_Languages") is used. Moreover, the feature "ERA_GLONASS" requires the "Diagnostic" feature to be selected, whereas it is optional for the case of "eCall".

To implement emergency response systems in vehicles, an Electronic Control Unit (ECU) must be deployed inside, which can connect to cellular communication networks and integrates a localization module. The Autonomous Telematics Box (ATB2)[6] is such an ECU. It integrates a telephone modules for connection to cellular communication networks and a multi-constellation satellite localization module (e.g., GPS and GLONASS). The ATB2 is particularly suitable in the eCall/E112 use case because it supports remote updates of the running firmware.

4   Overall Concept and Architecture

In this section, we introduce the general workflow and the components of our toolchain.

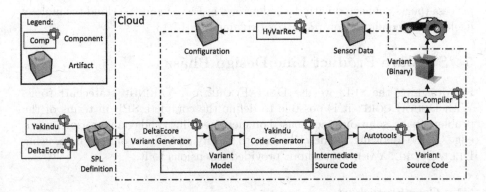

Fig. 3. Components of the Toolchain

---

[6] Magneti Marelli http://www.magnetimarelli.com.

Figure 3 depicts the steps of the workflow, the responsible components and the incorporated artifacts. The workflow is separated in two main phases: the SPL design phase and the variant-generation phase. The components and artifacts involved in the SPL design phase are located to the left of the dashed box. In both phases, both coarse-grained variability in terms of delta modules and fine-grained variability in terms of preprocessor directives are considered. In the SPL design phase, the SPL is defined using YAKINDU and DELTAECORE, which consists of the core statechart and the delta modules.

Using the SPL definition in the variant-generation phase in the cloud, the `DeltaEcore Variant Generator` first creates a `Variant Model`, i.e., the variant's statechart, by applying the delta modules which are selected using the configuration knowledge and a feature selection. Then, the `Yakindu Code Generator` creates code out of the statechart. Additionally, the `DeltaEcore Variant Generator` generates build automation files. To this end, it defines suitable metadata, which specify which features are selected, which external code artifacts should be linked and the name of the variant. The statechart's code together with the build automation files result in the `Intermediate Source Code`. AUTO-TOOLS link existing source code artifacts with the statechart's code and create a concrete makefile which is contained in the `Variant Source Code`. The existing source code artifacts may be annotated with pre-processor directives, whose values may be filled by `Autotools`. The `Cross-Compiler` compiles the source code using the provided makefile. The binary code is then deployed to the end device.

On the end device, the new binary is installed. Subsequently, it collects sensor data and sends it to the cloud. The sensor data is processed by HYVARREC which, if necessary, computes a new configuration and then starts a new loop of the variant-generation phase.

Our architecture is strongly component based. Distributed to the cloud, it achieves very flexible scaling. For instance, if the `Yakindu code generator` is very slow, multiple instances of it could be created in the cloud. In this paper, we explain the complete toolchain except for the deployment, the reconfiguration process (parts connected with dashed arrows in Fig. 3) and the cloud technology itself. The reconfiguration process is explained in [12,13].

5   Software Product Line Design Phase

For designing the SPL, we use DELTAECORE and YAKINDU statechart tools. With DELTAECORE, it is possible to define the complete SPL in terms of the problem space, solution space (based on metamodeling) and configuration knowledge. In the following, we describe how to specify an SPL for our use case, using DELTAECORE, YAKINDU and our provided extensions to it.

5.1   Core Statechart

As DELTAECORE is relying on delta modeling, which is a transformational approach, we need to specify a core statechart that can serve as source for

```
//...
deltaOperations:
    modifyOperation modifySpecificationOfStatechart(String value,
    Statechart [specification] element);
    customOperation addState(State state, Region region);
    customOperation removeState(State state);
    customOperation modifyNameOfState(State state, String newName);
//...
```

Fig. 4. Excerpt of delta dialect for Yakindu statecharts

transformation. In our toolchain, we specify the core statechart by using the standard YAKINDU statechart editor. This allows us to use the complete functionality provided by YAKINDU and does not break the workflow with statecharts that system engineers are used to. This core statechart is then modified by delta modules to create variants.

5.2 Managing Variability

In the problem space, we use FMs which are implemented in DELTAECORE. DELTAECORE provides an editor, which allows us to define FMs. Figure 2 depicts an FM representing the problem space of our running example.

In the solution space, DELTAECORE relies on delta modeling for metamodels. To be able to transform these models, it is necessary to define a delta language for each metamodel, which consists of a common base delta language and a metamodel-specific delta dialect. In our case, we need to define two delta dialects. One for the statecharts and one for the metadata. Figure 4 shows an excerpt of the delta dialect for the YAKINDU statecharts. With this dialect, it is possible to modify an existing statechart, e.g., by adding, removing or modifying states and transitions. Moreover, it is possible to modify the specification of the statechart via the delta operation modifySpecificationOfStatechart(...). In the specification of a statechart, it is possible to define variables, events, operations and interfaces. This is very important as these operations can be used to call existing external code artifacts. This will be explained later in more detail.

```
deltaOperations:
  customOperation preMetadata();
  customOperation addSourceFile(String filename);
  customOperation addFeature(String feature);
  customOperation setVariantName(String variant, String version);
  customOperation postMetadata();
```

Fig. 5. Delta dialect for metadata

The second dialect is defined to create metadata, which can be seen in Fig. 5. As the metadata is not available as ECORE metamodel, we only use the delta dialect to trigger operations provided for the metadata libraries. To this end, we introduced the operations preMetadata() and postMetadata(), which initialize and write out the metadata, respectively. The delta operation addSourceFile(...) defines external code artifacts which should be integrated by AUTOTOOLS and which should be linked to operations of the statechart. With the delta operation addFeature(...), the values for annotative variability in the external code artifacts is set. Finally, the setVariantName(...) delta operation is used to provide information on how to pack the final binary of a variant.

With these two dialects, it is possible to define delta modules consisting of a set of delta operations. Figure 6 depicts an excerpt of delta module of our running example. Among others, this delta module adds a state which is responsible for adding diagnostic information of the feature "Diagnostic" of Fig. 2. In each delta module, a core model can be specified with the keyword modifies, which should be modified by the delta module. Additionally, it is possible to define whether a delta module is dependent on another delta module via the keyword requires. As Fig. 6 shows, in one delta module, multiple delta dialects can be used. In our case, this is sensible, as we define operations in the statechart's specification which need to be linked to existing code artifacts. Thus, it is necessary to specify the respective code artifact to be integrated. However, in each delta module, it is possible to reference existing elements of the modified model. For example, the addState(...) operation adds the newly created state to an existing region of the statechart. In particular, the state initAdditionalDataState is added to the region identified by <eCall.main region.init_ecallmessage.InitEcallMessage>. Additionally, a new transition is added from an existing state to the new state. For the metadata, a source file, i.e., the encode_optionaldata.c, is marked for integration. Moreover, it is specified that the feature Diagnostic has been selected and the variant's name is russia_comb in version 1.0.

```
delta "Russia_Comb"
        dialect <http://www.yakindu.org/sct/sgraph/2.0.0>
    modifies <../core/eCall.sct>
{   //...
State initAdditionalDataState = new State(name: "init_additionaldata");
addState(initAdditionalDataState,
<eCall.main region.init_ecallmessage.InitEcallMessage>);
addTransition(<eCall.main region.init_ecallmessage.InitEcallMessage.init_ecallmessage>,
<eCall.main region.init_ecallmessage.InitEcallMessage.init_additionaldata>,"always");
    //...
}
dialect <http://eu/hyvar/metadata>
{
preMetadata();
addSourceFile("encode_optionaldata.c");
//...
addFeature("Diagnostic");
//...
setVariantName("russia_comb", "1.0");
postMetadata();
}
```

Fig. 6. Excerpt of a delta module of the running example

```
EraGlonass && Russian && Diagnostic :
<deltas/Russia comb.decore>
```

Fig. 7. Exemplary mapping of features to a delta module

In the problem space, we defined the features of our product line. In the solution space, we defined delta modules, which specify how a given statechart is modified and which existing code artifacts should be integrated. It is further necessary to link the problem and the solution space. This is done by the configuration knowledge, consisting of mappings between features and delta modules. Figure 7 depicts part of the configuration knowledge for our running example. First, an application condition needs to be specified. This is a Boolean expression on features, defining in which feature selection this mapping should be executed. In the example, the application condition is EraGlonass && Russian && Diagnostic, saying that the following deltas should only be applied if the features "EraGlonass", "Russian" and "Diagnostic" of our running example are selected together. The second part is a list of delta modules that should be applied if the application condition is true. In our example, this is only one delta module, i.e., the Russia_comb.decore.

6   Variant-Generation Phase

The second phase of the workflow consists of the variant generation. The variant generation is triggered by receiving a new configuration. For our running example, this could be a configuration consisting of the features "EmergencyCall", "Base", "Languages", "GNSS", "EraGlonass", "Russian" and "Diagnostic". After having the SPL defined, the component DeltaEcore Variant Generation uses the SPL artifacts and selects the delta module according to the feature selection in the configuration and the mapping in the configuration knowledge. Assuming the above mentioned configuration and the mapping of Fig. 7, this would be the delta module Russia_comb.decore. Then, the delta modules are applied to the core statechart. According to the delta module Russia_comb.decore depicted by Fig. 6, a new state for collecting the diagnostic information and an external operation call would be added. Moreover, new source files are specified in the metadata. As a result, this component produces the variant model (i.e., the variant's statechart) and the build automation files. In our case, the build automation files consist of an .am file and an .ac file, which are both used as input for Autotools. Assuming the application of the Russia_comb.decore delta module, the build automation files contain references to the newly added source files.

In the next step, the Yakindu Code Generator receives the variant's statechart as input and generates code out of it. In our case, this is currently C code but it is also possible to generate C++ or Java code. However, this code includes interfaces/header files, which represent the operations of the statechart (see Sect. 5.2). These interfaces/header files do not yet have an implementation but will be linked in a following phase.

Figure 8 illustrates the general workflow of the `Autotools` component. As input, the `Autotools` component receives the build automation files (i.e., the `Makefile.am` and the `configure.ac`), the source code repository, in which existing code artifacts are stored and the generated code from the variant's statechart. It processes these artifacts in three phases: In the first phase, it collects the existing code artifacts from a repository, which were specified in the metadata (see Sect. 5.2). In the second phase, the generated interfaces/header files of the `Yakindu Code Generator` are linked to the concrete implementations of the existing code artifacts. In the third phase, a makefile is created as Fig. 1 illustrates. The `Autotools` component's output is the variant's source code, i.e., the generated source code and the linked existing code artifacts as well as the makefile.

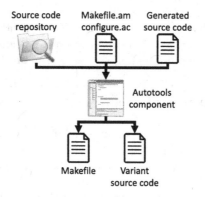

Fig. 8. Overview on the workflow of the `Autotools` component

The `Cross-Compiler` component receives the variant's source code as well as the makefile and compiles the code for a certain target platform. In our case, the target platform is the Autonomous Telematics Box (ATB2) which is based on an ARM platform. As a result, we receive a binary, which is deployed to the end device. In our case, the binary code is packed to a firmware image for the ATB2 and then deployed. For brevity, we do not explain the process of deployment in this paper. After having a new firmware installed, the end device continuously collects sensor data and sends it to our cloud infrastructure. The component `HyVarRec` receives the data as input and, if necessary, computes a new configuration. This new configuration triggers a new cycle of the variant generation phase. However, a description of how `HyVarRec` works can be found in [12, 13].

7 Related Work

A prominent framework for research on Feature-Oriented Software Development is FEATUREIDE [21], which is based on the ECLIPSE platform[7]. FEATUREIDE provides comprehensive tools for variability modeling with feature models as well as the ability to include different variability realization mechanisms. However, FEATUREIDE focuses on the development of SPLs, their analysis, configuration and finally, the variant derivation for different variability realization mechanisms. In contrast, we present an integrated toolchain for the development and deployment of software variants for distributed host devices.

DELTAECORE [20] is a tool suite for delta modeling on languages based on EMF ECORE metamodels. Using DELTAECORE, it is possible to semi-automatically create a delta languages for a particular EMF-based target language consisting of delta operations specific to that target language. Moreover, DELTAECORE provides comprehensive tools for variability modeling and configuration as well as variant derivation using the custom delta languages. In this work, we employ DELTAECORE for the development of SPLs and the variant derivation. However, using our toolchain, we further process the model variant by producing an executable variant and deploying it to the target device (cf. Sect. 4).

DELTAJAVA [11,17] is a custom-tailored delta language for the JAVA programming language. Thus, DELTAJAVA provides delta operations to transform legacy JAVA software to another variant of that software. However, DELTA-JAVA is tailored to JAVA, whereas our target language is C/C++. To this end, FEATUREC++ [3], employing FOP as the variability realization mechanism for SPLs based on C/C++, would be more suitable. However, delta modeling allows for more flexibility and improves expressiveness over FOP as elements may be removed. Other implementation approaches to SPLs include FEATURE-HOUSE [2], a language-independent composition tool that requires a general structure model of the base language called Feature Structure Tree (FST), as well as AHEAD [4], an algebraic foundation for module composition, which is implemented for JAVA.

PURE:VARIANTS[8] is a tool suite that uses family models as 150 % models of supported realization artifacts. Configuring these family models, a variant can be generated. BigLever's[9] GEARS PRODUCT LINE ENGINEERING TOOL AND LIFECYCLE FRAMEWORK[TM] is an SPL development tool suite based on feature models and an annotative variability realization mechanism. However, neither PURE:VARIANTS nor GEARS PRODUCT LINE ENGINEERING TOOL AND LIFECYCLE FRAMEWORK[TM] support delta modeling as a variability realization mechanism. Moreover, PURE:VARIANTS does not support C/C++ as the target language.

CLAFER TOOLS [1] is an integrated set of tools based on CLAFER, a language for structural modeling of SPLs. Using CLAFER TOOLS, variability modeling,

---

[7] http://www.eclipse.org.
[8] https://www.pure-systems.com.
[9] http://www.biglever.com.

configuration, and variant derivation of structural models (e.g., class diagrams) can be performed. However, CLAFER TOOLS does not support behavioral modeling of systems, such as statecharts. Therefore, generating executable variants is not possible using CLAFER TOOLS, which is essential to our work.

8 Conclusion and Future Work

In this paper, we presented an integrated toolchain for the development and deployment of increasingly individualized software that is adapted to changing contexts. To this end, we employed SPL engineering in a model-driven context where realization artifacts are modeled as YAKINDU statecharts and variability is realized using delta modeling with DELTAECORE. After variant derivation, the model variant is further processed to derive executable C/C++ code, including metadata consisting of build automation files. To allow a flexible and parallel reconfiguration, the variant derivation, linking and compilation processes are performed in a cloud infrastructure. Using the industry-related case of emergency response systems, we showed the feasibility of our toolchain for developing the SPL and deriving and deploying specific variants to target devices.

In the future, we plan to extend the application of the toolchain to a different and more challenging scenario where the generation of Java code is required. Moreover, we plan to support evolution of features (i.e., feature versions) [19] and evolution of the feature model [14] within the toolchain. This way, we would enable distributing different (e.g., older) versions of particular (parts of) variants.

Acknowledgments. This work was partially supported by the European Commission within the project HyVar (grant agreement H2020-644298), by ICT COST Action IC1402 ARVI (www.cost-arvi.eu), by the DFG (German Research Foundation) under grant SCHA1635/2-2, and by the Ateneo/CSP D16D15000360005 project RunVar. We thank Christoph Seidl from Technische Universität Braunschweig for sharing with us his useful comments and knowledge on DELTAECORE in particular and also the helpful comments of the anonymous reviewers.

References

1. Antkiewicz, M., Bąk, K., Murashkin, A., Olaechea, R., Liang, J., Czarnecki, K.: Clafer tools for product line engineering. In: Software Product Line Conference, Tokyo, Japan (2013). Accepted for publication
2. Apel, S., Kästner, C., Lengauer, C.: FeatureHouse: language-independent, automated software composition. In: Proceedings of the 31st International Conference on Software Engineering, ICSE 2009, pp. 221–231. IEEE Computer Society, Washington, DC (2009)
3. Apel, S., Leich, T., Rosenmüller, M., Saake, G.: FeatureC++: on the symbiosis of feature-oriented and aspect-oriented programming. In: Glück, R., Lowry, M. (eds.) GPCE 2005. LNCS, vol. 3676, pp. 125–140. Springer, Heidelberg (2005). doi:10.1007/11561347_10
4. Batory, D., Sarvela, J.N., Rauschmayer, A.: Scaling step-wise refinement. In: Proceedings of ICSE, pp. 187–197. IEEE (2003)

5. Batory, D., Sarvela, J.N., Rauschmayer, A.: Scaling step-wise refinement. IEEE Trans. Softw. Eng. **30**, 355–371 (2004)
6. Clarke, D., Helvensteijn, M., Schaefer, I.: Abstract delta modeling. ACM SIGPLAN Not. **46**(2), 13 (2011)
7. Greenfield, J., Short, K.: Software factories: assembling applications with patterns, models, frameworks and tools. In: Companion of the 18th Annual ACM SIGPLAN Conference on Object-Oriented Programming, Systems, Languages, and Applications, OOPSLA 2003, pp. 16–27. ACM, New York (2003)
8. ISO/IEC 9899:1990 - Programming Languages–C. Standard, International Organization for Standardization (1999)
9. Kang, K.C., Cohen, S.G., Hess, J.A., Novak, W.E., Peterson, A.S.: Feature-Oriented Domain Analysis (FODA) Feasibility Study. Technical report, Carnegie Mellon Software Engineering Institute (1990)
10. Kang, K.C., Kim, S., Lee, J., Kim, K., Shin, E., Huh, M.: Form: A feature-oriented reuse method with domain-specific reference architectures. Ann. Softw. Eng. **5**(1), 143–168 (1998)
11. Koscielny, J., Holthusen, S., Schaefer, I., Schulze, S., Bettini, L., Damiani, F.: Deltaj 1.5: delta-oriented programming for java 1.5. In: Proceedings of PPPJ, pp. 63–74. ACM (2014)
12. Mauro, J., Nieke, M., Seidl, C., Yu, I.C.: Context aware reconfiguration in software product lines. In: Proceedings of the Tenth International Workshop on Variability Modelling of Software-Intensive Systems, VaMoS 2016 (2016)
13. Nieke, M., Mauro, J., Seidl, C., Yu, I.C.: User profiles for context-aware reconfiguration in software product lines. In: Margaria, T., Steffen, B. (eds.) ISoLA 2016, Part II. LNCS, vol. 9953, pp. 563–578. Springer, Cham (2016)
14. Nieke, M., Seidl, C., Schuster, S.: Guaranteeing configuration validity in evolving software product lines. In: Proceedings of the Tenth International Workshop on Variability Modelling of Software-intensive Systems, VaMoS 2016, pp. 73–80. ACM, New York (2016)
15. Pohl, K., Böckle, G., van der Linden, F.: Software Product Line Engineering-Foundations, Principles, and Techniques. Springer, Heidelberg (2005)
16. Prehofer, C.: Feature-oriented programming: a fresh look at objects. In: Akşit, M., Matsuoka, S. (eds.) ECOOP 1997. LNCS, vol. 1241, pp. 419–443. Springer, Heidelberg (1997). doi:10.1007/BFb0053389
17. Schaefer, I., Bettini, L., Bono, V., Damiani, F., Tanzarella, N.: Delta-oriented programming of software product lines. In: Bosch, J., Lee, J. (eds.) SPLC 2010. LNCS, vol. 6287, pp. 77–91. Springer, Heidelberg (2010). doi:10.1007/978-3-642-15579-6_6
18. Schaefer, I., Rabiser, R., Clarke, D., Bettini, L., Benavides, D., Botterweck, G., Pathak, A., Trujillo, S., Villela, K.: Software diversity: state of the art and perspectives. Int. J. Softw. Tools Technol. Transf. **14**(5), 477–495 (2012)
19. Seidl, C., Schaefer, I., Aßmann, U.: Capturing variability in space, time with hyper feature models. In: Collet, P., Wasowski, A., Weyer, T. (eds.) The Eighth International Workshop on Variability Modelling of oftware-intensive Systems, VaMoS 2014, Sophia Antipolis, France, 22–24 January 2014, pp. 6:1–6:8. ACM (2014)
20. Seidl, C., Schaefer, I., Aßmann, U.: Deltaecore - A model-based delta language generation framework. In: Modellierung, Wien, Österreich, 19–21 März, pp. 81–96 (2014)
21. Thüm, T., Kästner, C., Benduhn, F., Meinicke, J., Saake, G., Leich, T.: Featureide: an extensible framework for feature-oriented software development. Sci. Comput. Program. **79**, 70–85 (2014)

A Technology-Neutral Role-Based Collaboration Model for Software Ecosystems

Ştefan Stănciulescu[1(✉)], Daniela Rabiser[2], and Christoph Seidl[3]

[1] IT University of Copenhagen, Copenhagen, Denmark
scas@itu.dk
[2] CD Lab MEVSS, Johannes Kepler University Linz, Linz, Austria
daniela.rabiser@jku.at
[3] Technische Universität Braunschweig, Braunschweig, Germany
c.seidl@tu-braunschweig.de

Abstract. In large-scale software ecosystems, many developers contribute extensions to a common software platform. Due to the independent development efforts and the lack of a central steering mechanism, similar functionality may be developed multiple times by different developers. We tackle this problem by contributing a role-based collaboration model for software ecosystems to make such implicit similarities explicit and to raise awareness among developers during their ongoing efforts. We extract this model based on realization artifacts in a specific programming language located in a particular source code repository and present it in a technology-neutral way. We capture five essential collaborations as independent role models that may be composed to present developer collaborations of a software ecosystem in their entirety, which fosters overview of the software ecosystem, analyses of duplicated development efforts and information of ongoing development efforts. Finally, using the collaborations defined in the formalism we model real artifacts from Marlin, a firmware for 3D printers, and we show that for the selected scenarios, the five collaborations were sufficient to raise awareness and make implicit information explicit.

Keywords: Software ecosystem · Collaboration · Role modeling · Marlin

1 Introduction

The software product line methodology allows to manage similar software systems by developing the core assets that are common to all systems and developing variant assets that are product specific [7]. Software ecosystems [5] (SECOs) provide a common platform to develop a family of closely related software systems having distinct characteristics. SECOs address development contexts which typically involve multiple organizations and product lines. However, both methodologies try to maximize reuse of software, reducing efforts in development as well as during maintenance of the products. With the advent of Github[1], projects

---

[1] http://www.github.com.

© Springer International Publishing AG 2016
T. Margaria and B. Steffen (Eds.): ISoLA 2016, Part II, LNCS 9953, pp. 512–530, 2016.
DOI: 10.1007/978-3-319-47169-3_41

share a common repository where changes can be pushed to from private repositories. This development process follows a similar path to the one of software ecosystems, where vendors contribute and maintain the platform without having a centralized mechanism.

Motivation: Products are frequently developed using a clone-and-own reuse approach by adapting existing solutions to create new customer-specific products. However, deviations from the reusable platform code (e.g., customer-specific features) remain largely undocumented. Empirical studies present this as an emerging challenge [11,12,21,22,33]. A lightweight solution for improving knowledge is to enhance awareness between developers. Lettner[2] et al. [23], propose the feature feed approach, which supports making specific implementations visible to interested users within the SECO via notifications.

Problem: Finding existing features or similar ones in the ecosystem is hard even for the community members. This is consistent with an observation of Berger et al. [4] that an excessive use of clone-and-own variants in industrial projects leads to loss of overview of the available functionality. Decentralization of information also leads to a loss of overview [12]. For example, in an open source 3D printer firmware project, 14 % of pull requests were rejected because of concurrent development [33].

Contribution: The main contribution of this paper is a formalism based on role models to describe collaborations of contributors and artifacts in an ecosystem, with the main purpose of providing an overview of the ecosystem in terms of relations between users, repositories and features. For example, one developer that develops a similar feature to already existing one in another repository could be informed of the already existing code, and a link that describes the two features as being similar would be created. We describe the formalism and how it can be used to tackle existing challenges, i.e., raising developer awareness of concurrent feature development. Our long term goal is to build an automatic process of constructing collaboration models in a SECO. We use an exploratory case study to test and evaluate the feasibility and expressiveness of the formalism in the context of Marlin, a firmware for 3D printers developed and maintained as an open source project on Github.

The paper is structured as following: in Sect. 2 we introduce required background knowledge. In Sect. 3 we motivate this work using an example and extract requirements for the collaboration role model, and present the collaboration role model in Sect. 4. We present our evaluation on an exploratory case study in Sect. 5, related work in Sect. 6, and we conclude in Sect. 7.

2   Background

In this section, we introduce the basic notions of role models, features, and Github's forking mechanism.

---

[2] Daniela Rabiser's previous work was published under the name Daniela Lettner.

Role models. A role model describes a (possibly infinite) set of object collaborations using role types [27]. Its focus lies on representing a single purpose of an object collaboration. Each role type specifies the behavior of one particular object with respect to the model's purpose. Role types relate to each other via relationships such as association and aggregation. To describe a concrete instance of a collaboration, roles may be mapped to various elements, e.g., source code fragments, users or repositories, depending on the respective collaboration. Role models may be complemented with formal ontologies providing standard terminologies and rich semantics to facilitate knowledge sharing and reuse [18,34].

Features. Commonalities and variability of a product portfolio are often captured using the abstract concept of features [3]. A feature has been defined as distinguishable characteristic of a concept (e.g., system, component) that is relevant to some stakeholder of the concept [8]. In the context of SECOs, a feature denotes a unit of configurable functionality. Software artifacts that implement specific program functionalities, i.e., features, can be discovered using feature location techniques [28]. However, there is no optimal feature location technique and the notion of feature varies widely in practice [3].

Github forking. Github[3] is a social coding platform that allows collaborative development. Github offers the *forking* mechanism to create a copy of a repository, together with a traceability link between the copied repository, the fork, and the original project. On Github, users can create pull requests which resemble traditional change requests. A pull request consists of a description, possible comments from users, and a set of commits. A pull request can be created either in the same repository, e.g., to allow a team to discuss the change, or from a fork to the original project. Forking in this sense is also known as the *pull-based development model*. Most often, forks are used to develop and test changes in isolation, and then those changes are integrated into the original repository using pull requests.

3   Challenges Arising in Software Ecosystems

The pull-based software development was investigated on its usage in practice by Gousios et al. [16], who found that around 14 % of the repositories in GitHub used the pull request mechanism (data until 2013). The most common reasons for rejecting a pull request are concurrent modifications, the way a project handles distributed development (e.g., newer pull requests are chosen over older pull requests addressing the same problem), or changes not matching a project's road map. Duc et al. [12] also confirmed in an industrial setting that there is a loss of overview of which elements exist and who is working on which element, when clone-and-own is used as a reuse mechanism between teams. Berger et al. [4] found in their empirical investigation on industrial systems that too much cloning of variants obscures what functionality is available. The same issues were also observed by Stănciulescu et al. [33] in an open source project that has been

---

[3] https://github.com.

heavily forked on GitHub. The authors identified that many pull requests were closed because of double development, overlapping or already existing code. This leads to time and effort wasted. Moreover, one of the maintainers explained that they are unaware of which elements exist in the SECO (e.g., forks, bug-fixes, improvements).

3.1 Motivating Example

Marlin[4] is a 3D printer firmware that is being developed as open source since 2011. Marlin has been forked by more than 2900 people on Github, with many of them contributing new features and testing the firmware. Due to the sheer amount of forks, it is difficult to get and maintain an accurate overview of what exists in the firmware's ecosystem, what features are being developed and what collaborations exist.

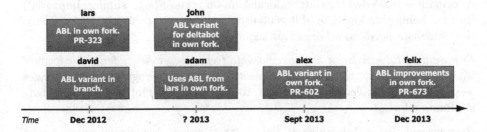

Fig. 1. Timeline showing the evolution of the ABL feature.

We use the feature *Auto Bed Leveling (ABL)* from Marlin to illustrate the challenges developers are faced with when they try to get an accurate overview of what exists related to a specific feature. The ABL feature is for computing bed tilt compensation for better results printing on a non-level bed. We extracted the example feature from Marlin's history. Figure 1 shows the evolution of the ABL feature. Initially, it was developed experimentally in a fork by user *lars*[5] without being integrated in the main repository. From pull request PR-323[6], we can see that there was another version being developed by user *david* (one of the repository maintainers and developer of Marlin at that time) but not made public. Yet another form of this feature existed in another fork of Marlin that was a variant to support a different type of printers developed by user *john*. In September 2013, the ABL feature was ported and integrated into Marlin from the initial fork by user *alex* who had commit access to Marlin. It is unclear if there existed other variants of this feature at that time. Somewhere in between, user *adam* has integrated the ABL feature from *lars'* fork. Following the integration

---

[4] http://github.com/MarlinFirmware/.

[5] We anonymized the names of the Github users to respect their privacy.

[6] https://github.com/MarlinFirmware/Marlin/pull/323.

of ABL in September 2013, other users (e.g., user *felix*) started contributing with improvements and bug fixes of the ABL feature in their own fork. These users created pull requests (PR-673) to integrate their changes back into Marlin.

Even when having access to this data offhand, it is difficult to understand the evolution of the ABL feature and to reveal what existed at different points in time. Furthermore, since information related to the ABL feature is spread across multiple repositories, it is hard to get an accurate overview. Moreover, the notion of a feature is not explicit in many cases but has to be made explicit from code annotations or developer documentation. When considering other SECOs, the problems in analyzing data are even amplified by different realization technologies, such as programming languages (e.g., Java, C++, Python) or repositories (e.g., Git, Mercurial, SVN, CVS).

3.2 Derived Requirements

A formalism is needed that lifts information on related (e.g., similar, improved) features being developed by different users in diverse repositories. Specifically, the formalism needs to address four requirements:

Requirement R1 – Analyze and present data technology-independent. The formalism needs to be agnostic of specific repository types and programming languages used. The main challenge is to be able to deal with different technologies using minimum effort.

Requirement R2 – Lift implicit knowledge. Implicit knowledge needs to be revealed and made explicit using repository analysis techniques. Furthermore, introducing a dedicated feature concept seems promising to link artifacts (e.g., source code, configuration options, documentation, tests) spread across repositories realizing a particular feature. Additionally, developers being responsible for specific feature implementations would be able to document their expert knowledge and, thus, make it available for other developers planning to reuse a feature or contributing to a feature.

Requirement R3 – Improve developer awareness. Developers should be aware of relevant features developed in other repositories of the SECO. The decision on whether a feature is relevant or not may be based on clone detection techniques or recommendation mechanisms and the features a developer has worked on or is currently working on.

Requirement R4 – Support modularization of strongly related elements. The formalism needs to support multiple levels of abstraction to facilitate zooming in to a specific feature, user or repository [26]. Such compartmentalization of strongly related entities (i.e., adhering to divide-and-conquer strategies and breaking down large-scale SECOs into smaller parts) further supports developers in understanding and reasoning about specific parts of a SECO. On the other hand, composing smaller parts into large ones could be effective in cases where an overview has to be included.

4   Collaboration Role Modeling

The main contribution of this paper is a *SECO collaboration role model* describing the relationships between repositories, users and features. Role modeling is not the same as programming language, even though concepts of relations, types and instances exist in role modeling as well. Role models are technology-neutral and can be used to guide collaboration between developers and to monitor communications. Collaboration models not just lift explicit information, they also provide insights into implicit communication edges. Role modeling focuses mostly on collaborations and is more fine-grained than class modeling. Furthermore, roles can be attributed to artifacts other than source code, such as repositories or users.

We use the collaboration role model as a way of understanding what entities and what kinds of collaborations between entities exist in a SECO. The mentioned entities—repositories, users and features—can be represented differently in concrete implementations (e.g., repositories: SVN, Git, CVS, Perforce, TeamServer; users: different account management systems; features: implicit or explicit, different realizations techniques such as annotations or feature-oriented programming). The collaboration role model is technology-neutral in the sense that it captures the relations and discards any information regarding the technologies used.

We present five distinct collaborations, each containing relevant roles and their relations for a specific concern of the SECO. These collaborations can be classified as either presenting inherent knowledge available implicitly in the repositories and making it explicit, such as the collaborations *development and usage* and *storage* do, or providing added information, such as, *subscription* and *recommendation* do. The collaboration *origin* provides both inherent (e.g., integrated feature) and added information (e.g., similar feature). In the following, we first describe each of the individual collaborations along with the concerns they address before elaborating on how to compose them to form a comprehensive SECO model.

4.1   Development and Usage Collaboration

The role model depicted in Fig. 2 defines roles related to feature development and feature usage. A user may either develop or implement a feature or re-use an existing feature implementation in her own context. Features are typically related to a dedicated feature location, e.g., a development branch in the repository. This role is needed to be able to create links between users and features. Knowing who uses the feature provides the basis for informing appropriate users of important fixes. Moreover, developers working on a feature can find other developers that have worked on the feature, or on similar features, and establish collaborations with them. It makes implicit information explicit, e.g., it introduces an explicit feature concept even if the underlying technology captures features only implicitly using different technologies (e.g., C preprocessor directives).

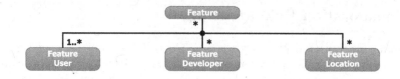

Fig. 2. Development and usage collaboration

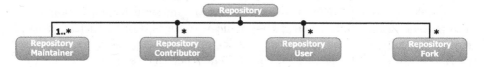

Fig. 3. Storage collaboration

4.2 Storage Collaboration

Repositories are one of the most important elements in a SECO. They store all artifacts related to a concrete project. A repository is managed by at least one maintainer. Furthermore, contributors or users work with a repository, as depicted in Fig. 3. A maintainer is a user who is responsible for managing issues, incoming changes and other artifacts of the repository. The maintainer is allowed to accept and merge changes from external collaborators to the repository. A repository user benefits from a repository without contributing or having any maintenance tasks. A repository fork indicates that one repository is a clone of an existing repository. This collaboration model offers coarse grained information about the users of the repository and is particularly useful to document the origin of per forked repository.

4.3 Origin Collaboration

The role model depicted in Fig. 4 shows the relations between several features that exist in the ecosystem. For example, a newly developed feature can be similar to another feature that already exists. This can be represented by using the relation between an original feature (the older one), and a similar feature (the newer one). This information could be (semi-)automatically extracted by a clone detection system [29] using the SECO and repository information. Furthermore, a feature may be enhanced by additional functionality to consider it as an improved feature of the original feature. Finally, an integrated feature represents a feature that is integrated in the main repository of the SECO.

4.4 Subscription Collaboration

In addition to the roles depicted in Fig. 2, we define a subscription collaboration in Fig. 5 which follows the publish-subscribe pattern [13]. A user can subscribe to a dedicated artifact. Based on a subscription, notifications are pushed to the

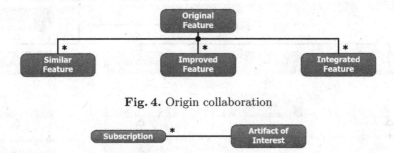

Fig. 4. Origin collaboration

Fig. 5. Subscription collaboration

subscribers. Such artifacts of interest can be of different granularity, from entire repositories (coarse) over features to lines of code in a file (fine-grained). This is similar to what exists currently in social coding platforms (e.g., Github or Bitbucket), but it is less restrictive allowing different levels of granularity. The role is designed specifically towards increasing developer awareness by using a notification system.

4.5 Recommendation Collaboration

As in the case of the subscription collaboration, the main purpose of the recommendation collaboration depicted in Fig. 6 is to enhance visibility of existing features in the ecosystem, and provide useful recommendations of existing features. Feature recommendations could be automatically provided using a recommender system based on a database of preferences for items by users. For instance, a new user would be matched against the database to discover neighbors, which are other users who have historically had similar interests. Items that the neighbors like would then be recommended to the new user [30].

4.6 Collaboration Role Relations

The five collaborations provide a unified way to represent individual concerns of a SECO relevant to determine the relation of features, users and repositories. However, the collaborations are not completely isolated from one another. In fact, part of our notation connects selected roles of different collaborations implicitly. We define concrete *collaboration role relations* to specify how specific roles of individual or different collaborations are related to one another as depicted in Fig. 7. These relations further ensure flexibility regarding adding new

Fig. 6. Recommendation collaboration

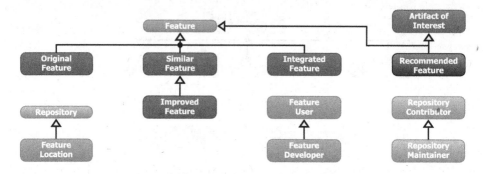

Fig. 7. Collaboration role relations connecting roles of individual collaborations

collaboration types. For instance, if the model needs to be extended regarding the relation of product variants and features, one would integrate a parent-child relation into Fig. 7 indicating that a feature is the child of one or more product variant(s).

In many cases, the fact that an element plays one role automatically entails that it plays a certain other role as well. We describe this using the *role implication* (arrow with hollow arrow tip) as relation between roles of potentially different collaborations. The role implication denotes that, whenever an element plays the role of the premise, it implicitly also plays the implied role in the conclusion. For example, the roles *original feature, similar feature, improved feature* and *integrated feature* from the *origin* collaboration all implicitly play the role *feature* from the *development and usage* collaboration. Furthermore, the enhancements in the role *improved feature* over those of the role *original feature* entail that each element playing the role *improved feature* also plays the role *similar feature*. Likewise, the role *recommended feature* from the *recommendation* collaboration entails the role *feature* and the role *artifact of interest* from the *subscription* collaboration. Furthermore, the *feature location* from the *development and usage* collaboration entails a *repository* role from the *storage* collaboration being mapped to the same element. Finally, being a *feature developer* also means being a *feature user* as well as being a *repository maintainer* means being a *repository contributor*.

The visual representations depicted in Figs. 8, 9 and 10 make the implied roles explicit for easier legibility but it would also be possible to determine the implied rules via a reasoning mechanism instead.

4.7   Instantiating Collaborations and Composing a SECO Model

To apply our notation to a concrete SECO, the collaborations are applied by mapping the individual roles to concrete elements to signal that element plays that role. This forms a comprehensive SECO model, which can be used for analyses, due to two reasons:

First, roles of different collaborations may be mapped to the same element to signal that one individual acts in multiple roles at once. For example, in Fig. 8, the roles *feature* and *original feature* are both mapped to the *AutoBedLeveling* functionality to signal both roles of the functionality. In consequence, it is possible to determine that user *lars* was the developer of the original feature for auto bed leveling by navigating from *feature developer* to *feature* and then *original feature*.

Second, the described collaboration role relations specify how relevant roles of individual or different collaborations are related to one another to allow navigation accross collaboration boundaries. For example, in Fig. 8, the fact that *lars/Marlin* plays the role *feature location* of the *development and usage collaboration* automatically entails that it also plays the role *repository* of the *storage* collaboration. Furthermore, the fact that user *lars* plays the role *feature developer* automatically entails that he plays the role *feature user* as well. This allows navigation of the SECO model even if part of this information are only available implicitly.

It is worth noting that, in the mapping process, each collaboration may be applied multiple times with a different context, e.g., the *storage* collaboration could be instantiated multiple times if one person contributes to or maintains multiple different repositories. Hence, our notation of five individual collaborations and the collaboration role relations of Fig. 7 permits the creation of comprehensive SECO models.

5   Exploratory Case Study

We illustrate the introduced SECO collaboration role model in the context of our case study subject system Marlin [33]. Marlin exhibits the main challenges we want to address and we have access to a database containing commits, issues, pull requests and other meta-data[7]. Our research objective aims at studying the expressiveness and feasibility of the SECO collaboration role model. Specifically, we investigate two research questions:

- *RQ1: Is the expressiveness of the SECO collaboration role model sufficient to address the discussed challenges arising in software ecosystem environments?*
- *RQ2: Is the SECO collaboration role model useful for revealing redundant development efforts?*

We investigate three selected scenarios and discuss them in terms of the requirements derived in Sect. 3. Two of the three investigated scenarios deal with redundant development of features. We present how the introduced SECO collaboration role model can be used to inform developers about double developments and further recommend potentially interesting artifacts.

---

[7] http://bitbucket.org/modelsteam/2015-marlin.

5.1   Data Collection Methods and Sources

Our main data source, a database containing information about repositories, users, forks, commits, pull requests, issues and other meta-data, has been created in earlier work [33]. Specifically, closed pull requests have been analyzed and the information regarding the reasons of closing them has also been stored in the database. As Marlin is a 3D printing firmware, the scenarios we inspect revolve around the functionality of 3D printers. In particular, we inspect three scenarios as part of the exploratory case study:

1. *AUTO_BED_LEVELING (ABL)*: Shows the evolution through different forks of a feature that computes a bed tilt compensation.
2. *FAN_CONTROL*: Shows the development of similar features in different forks using different ways to regulate ventilation.
3. *SWITCH*: Shows the development of similar features in different forks using the switching of an operation model of a hardware device.

We used information available in the database to conduct a pre-analysis to select the three scenarios. The analysis used keywords of known features, that the first author was aware of, due to previous experience with Marlin. For each of the selected scenarios, we further queryied the database to better understand the details of that scenario, and manually analyzed the results.

We then performed the following five steps to create the SECO role collaboration model per selected scenario.

S1. Inspect pull requests closed due to double development that are related to the scenario at hand
S2. Select interesting contributions (i.e., successfully merged pull request, pull request not merged due to double development)
S3. Break down contributions in terms of collaboration roles described in Sect. 4
S4. Instantiate the *development and usage, storage* and *origin* collaborations to represent inherent knowledge of the SECO
S5. Instantiate the *subscription* and *recommendation* collaborations to represent additional information of the SECO

5.2   Results

We instantiated the role-based collaboration model for each of the three inspected scenarios: *ABL* in Fig. 8, *FAN_CONTROL* in Fig. 9, and *SWITCH* in Fig. 10. Each diagram comprises information on (i) the feature under investigation (left side of the diagrams); (ii) the users[8] involved in the scenario (see diagram centers); (iii) the relations between repositories and users (see right side of the diagrams). For instance, in Fig. 8, the feature *ABL* was developed by the user *lars*, as indicated by the relation between the roles *original feature* and

---

[8] We anonymized the names of the Github users to respect their privacy.

feature developer. The developer *lars* is both a maintainer and a contributor to the *lars/Marlin* repository.

There are two features with the same name. However, the one in the bottom left is an improved feature of the original feature developed in *lars/Marlin* fork. Furthermore, we can see that this improved feature was integrated in the *erik/Marlin* repository by user *alex*, who thus becomes a repository contributor to the *erik/Marlin* repository.

Both Figs. 9 and 10 show the development of similar features. The fan control collaboration depicted in Fig. 9 covers two related features which have been implemented by different developers in different forks. The feature *FAN_CONTROL* by *david* supports reducing the controller fan speed which can reduce unwanted airflow and noise. However, the described functionality is also supported by *robbie*'s feature *EXTRUDER_FAN_CONTROL*. This was discovered while discussing *davids*'s pull request with the repository maintainer of *erik/Marlin*. As *robbie*'s feature *EXTRUDER_FAN_CONTROL* provides more advanced fan control based on extruder hot-end temperatures, the developers decided to merge *robbie*'s feature to the main repository *erik/Marlin* and close *david*'s pull request.

Figure 10 shows the duplication of the feature *M42* which has been developed by the user *erik* in his fork. The developer *anthony* submitted his new feature *M250* as a pull request. At a later time, the user realized that it was already implemented as *M42*. As the two features are almost identical, *anthony* is made a subscriber to the *M42* feature. Hence, the feature *M42* is recommended to *anthony* even though he was aware that it already existed.

The three scenarios show how the collaboration models use technology-dependent information and present it in a technology-neutral way. Implicit information that exists usually in the repository's issue tracker (if one exists) or developer's memory (e.g., if a feature was integrated) is made explicit by showing relations between features, repositories and users. This improves greatly the overview of existing features and their relation to raise developer awareness.

With respect to RQ1, in this scenario the five collaboration role concepts are sufficient to describe the relations between users, features and repositories in a SECO. The formalism is technology independent as required by R1, transforms relevant implicit information in explicit information (R2) such as who is contributing to an artifact and where does that artifact reside, and increases the awareness of developers using the subscription and recommendation collaboration roles as needed by R3. We hypothesize that in other similar scenarios, the collaboration role model would be sufficient, but further studies need to be conducted to understand if the model is general enough.

Regarding RQ2, using the formalism, we can create models that offer a simple view of artifacts and their relations in the SECO, thus increasing awareness of current developments and limiting concurrent development of features or even of existing ones. Querying the database is more difficult than using the diagrams to inform a user of existing features. One reason is that a user would need to perform several queries to retrieve the same information that is presented in the

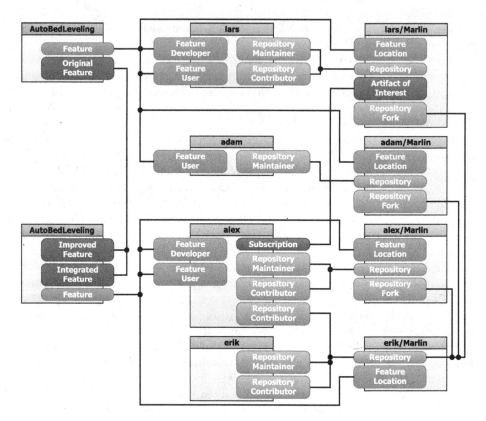

Fig. 8. Instance of the collaboration model for the *AUTO_BED_LEVELING* (*ABL*) scenario

diagram and to filter the queries. For example, querying for the string 'FAN' results in 194 commits that contain that string in the commit message. In such cases, a trivial task becomes harder to complete. Our formalism allows a more swift usage of the available information, decreasing the burden on developers.

5.3   Discussion

The main difficulty we encountered was to process a large quantity of data to retrieve only parts that we are interested in. The database used in this exploratory case study has a lot of information but it becomes less appealing to use when simple information needs to be retrieved. However, in the case of complex information–which code from what pull request of specific user was integrated in which repository–the database is extremely useful due to its querying capacities. Hence, in the future, our approach might be extended by a similar querying mechanism to limit the amount of information to a specific inquiry.

Regardless of the technology used, to create collaboration models in a SECO we need to mine and use available information from bug trackers, issue systems,

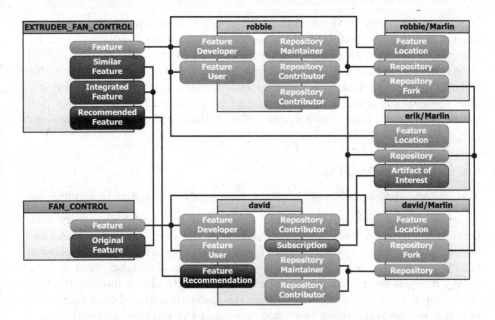

Fig. 9. Instance of the collaboration model for the *FAN_CONTROL* scenario.

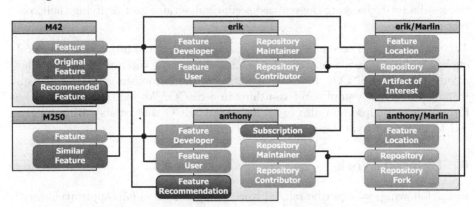

Fig. 10. Instance of the collaboration model for the *SWITCH* scenario

version control systems and other meta-data. Collecting such information can be automated to a high degree, for example by using GHTorrent [15], that facilitates querying a MySQL database containing Github meta-data about repositories, users, commits, pull requests, issues and others. The difficulty lies in transforming the data into the collaboration format model, though some parts can be automated, e.g., extracting users, repositories, contributors. Creating roles, discovering features, similar features and integrated features is more laborious and difficult, and requires less trivial computations.

Compositionality as demanded in R4 is principally supported by our formalism through the possibility to map collaborations multiple times (e.g., for different features) with some roles being mapped to the same element, which allows describing complex structures from basic constituents. Furthermore, the collaboration role relations connect cohesive collaborations. However, we still have to devise dedicated tool support, e.g., to semantically zoom in on a particular feature and only show relevant collaborations in order to make the sheer size of the collaboration model manageable.

5.4 Threats to Validity

As with any empirical evaluation, there are a number of threats to validity:

Internal Validity. For our evaluation, we considered only one repository with detailed information from an existing database. However, our method and formalism can be used for other types of repositories (Mercurial, CVS etc.), hosted on different hosting services (Bitbucket, Github, Sourceforge etc.) as it is technology independent. To ensure correctness of our method and models, the first two authors each executed several scenarios independently of each other and recorded all the steps taken. We then compared the recorded steps, discussed them and agreed on steps S1-S5 presented in Sect. 5.1. Finally, we cross-validated the results by exchanging the realized scenario diagrams and verifying their correctness.

External Validity. There is a threat in concluding that the formalism is general enough to be applied to any SECO. While we have not run an extensive evaluation using other SECOs, from our experience, the formalism is general enough to model different complex relationships in a SECO. We plan on applying the formalism to Eclipse and also in an industrial SECO that exists within KEBA AG to verify our hypothesis.

6 Related Work

In the following, we describe related work grouped by its main application area.

Software Ecosystems (SECOs). Existing approaches supporting SECO modeling [6,31], do not specifically focus on distributing knowledge about collaborations of contributors and artifacts (e.g., a new feature developed by a specific contributor). For instance, although software supply networks (SSNs) [6] provide a business and management view, they can hardly cover technical development aspects of SECOs. In contrast, the TECMO meta-model [31] provides a technical viewpoint on a SECO and models the variability of a SECO and its evolution in terms of products. However, this rather coarse-grained and product-focused view may not sufficiently support developers in revealing duplicate development of features.

Developer Collaboration Networks. Joblin et al. [19] present an automated approach to capture a view on developer coordination. Their fine-grained approach is based on commit information and source-code structure, mined from version-control systems. Their main goal is to identify developer communities. Another study by Panichella et al. [25] investigates how collaboration links vary and complement each other when they are identified through analyzing data from different kinds of communication channels (i.e., mailing lists, issue trackers, and chat logs) and how revealed collaboration links overlap with relations mined from code changes. Begel et al. [2] conducted a survey on inter-team coordination and found that it is most challenging to find and keep track of activities among the engineers. We provide a formalism that could be used by future research to describe collaborations between developers in SECOs.

Forked Code Bases. An exploratory study by Gousios et al. [16] investigates pull-based software development practices. Specifically, reasons for not merging pull requests are inspected. Results show that 29 % of unmerged pull requests are closed because the pull request is no longer relevant, or the feature is currently being implemented in another branch, a new pull request solves the problem better, or the pull request duplicates already available functionality. Another study by Gousios et al. [17] specifically examines managing and integrating contributions in a pull-based development environment. Pull requests are often rejected due to code quality, but also because newer pull requests already solved the same issue. Duc et al. [12] conducted semi-structured interviews to understand multi-platform development practices. The results show that diverged code bases lead to redundant development effort and to a lack of knowledge of the whole system.

Role-based Feature Management. Muthig and Schroeter [24] present a feature management framework including a software product line information model. The proposed information model comprises a role model which is used to formally model individuals and their access on system resources and operations. The collaboration role model presented in this paper is not concerned with access control or permissions. We focus on describing relationships between features, developers and repositories.

Awareness. Researchers have recognized awareness as an essential aspect of successful collaborative software development. Awareness has been defined as *an understanding of the activities of others providing a context for your own activity* [10]. It has also been stressed that building mental models of others' activities is important for software engineering tasks [9]. A recent study indicates that code reviews can provide additional benefits such as knowledge transfer or increased team awareness [1]. Most of the related work on awareness support for software development has focused on collaborative coding rather than requirements management, project management or design [32]. However, there are attempts focusing on higher levels of abstraction. An example is IBM's Jazz software development environment, which aggregates data to improve awareness of higher-level as well as low-level aspects [14]. Kintab et al. present a framework for recommending experts to developers needing help with a specific code fragment or system component [20]. A ranked list of potential helpers is created based on code similarities and social relationships. In comparison, our work tries to lay the fundamental concepts that allow to use frameworks as this one for a specific goal.

7   Conclusion and Outlook

In this paper, we have introduced a formalism based on role modeling that describes collaborations between contributors and artifacts in a software ecosystem. The formalism is designed to tackle several challenges that currently exist in software ecosystems, such as generating a better overview of the software ecosystem, and transforming implicit knowledge into explicit knowledge to aid developers during the development phase of features. We have conducted an exploratory case study on the Marlin open source software ecosystem and selected three scenarios to apply our formalism. For the inspected scenarios, the five collaborations defined in the formalism were sufficient to model real artifacts, transform implicit knowledge into explicit knowledge, and improve awareness of existing artifacts.

This work is a step forward in understanding how to use existing data to improve the knowledge of developers in the SECO. We plan on applying the formalism to other open source and industrial projects to gain further experience and inspect any shortcomings. Furthermore, we would like to address requirement R4 in more detail and provide dedicated tool support for semantic zoom on selected elements and their collaborations. Finally, it would also be interesting to explore how to incorporate changes to the SECO appearing as part of software evolution into our modeling notation.

Acknowledgments. This work was partially supported by the Christian Doppler Forschungsgesellschaft, Austria and KEBA AG, Austria. Further, this work was partially supported by the DFG (German Research Foundation) under grant SCHA1635/2-2 and by the European Commission within the project HyVar (grant agreement H2020-644298).

References

1. Bacchelli, A., Bird, C.: Expectations, outcomes, and challenges of modern code review. In: Proceedings of ICSE 2013 (2013)
2. Begel, A., Khoo, Y.P., Zimmermann, T.: Codebook: discovering and exploiting relationships in software repositories. In: Proceedings of ICSE 2010 (2010)
3. Berger, T., Lettner, D., Rubin, J., Grünbacher, P., Silva, A., Becker, M., Chechik, M., Czarnecki, K.: What is a feature?: a qualitative study of features in industrial software product lines. In: Proceedings of SPLC 2015 (2015)
4. Berger, T., Nair, D., Rublack, R., Atlee, J.M., Czarnecki, K., Wąsowski, A.: Three cases of feature-based variability modeling in industry. In: Dingel, J., Schulte, W., Ramos, I., Abrahão, S., Insfran, E. (eds.) MODELS 2014. LNCS, vol. 8767, pp. 302–319. Springer, Heidelberg (2014)
5. Bosch, J.: From software product lines to software ecosystems. In: Proceedings of SPLC 2009 (2009)

6. Boucharas, V., Jansen, S., Brinkkemper, S.: Formalizing software ecosystem modeling. In: Proceedings of 1st International Workshop on Open Component Ecosystems (2009)
7. Clements, P., Northrop, L.: Software Product Lines: Practices and Patterns. SEI Series in Software Engineering. Addison-Wesley, Boston (2001)
8. Czarnecki, K., Eisenecker, U.W.: Generative Programming: Methods, Tools, and Applications. Addison-Wesley, Boston (2000)
9. Dabbish, L., Stuart, C., Tsay, J., Herbsleb, J.: Social coding in github: transparency and collaboration in an open software repository. In: Proceedings of CSCW 2012 (2012)
10. Dourish, P., Bellotti, V.: Awareness and coordination in shared workspaces. In: Proceedings of CSCW 1992 (1992)
11. Dubinsky, Y., Rubin, J., Berger, T., Duszynski, S., Becker, M., Czarnecki, K.: An exploratory study of cloning in industrial software product lines. In: Proceedings of CSMR 2013 (2013)
12. Duc, A.N., Mockus, A., Hackbarth, R., Palframan, J.: Forking, coordination in multi-platform development: a case study. In: Proceedings of ESEM 2014 (2014)
13. Eugster, P.T., Felber, P.A., Guerraoui, R., Kermarrec, A.-M.: The many faces of publish/subscribe. ACM Comput. Surv. 35(2), 114–131 (2003)
14. Frost, R.: Jazz and the eclipse way of collaboration. IEEE Softw. 24(6), 114–117 (2007)
15. Gousios, G.: The ghtorrent dataset and tool suite. In: Proceedings of the 10th Working Conference on Mining Software Repositories, MSR 2013, pp. 233–236. IEEE Press, Piscataway (2013)
16. Gousios, G., Pinzger, M., van Deursen, A.: An exploratory study of the pull-based software development model. In: Proceedings of ICSE 2014 (2014)
17. Gousios, G., Zaidman, A., Storey, M.-A., van Deursen, A.: Work practices, challenges in pull-based development: the integrator's perspective. In: Proceedings of ICSE 2015 (2015)
18. Gruber, T.R.: Toward principles for the design of ontologies used for knowledge sharing. Int. J. Hum.-Comput. Stud. 43(5–6), 907–928 (1995)
19. Joblin, M., Mauerer, W., Apel, S., Siegmund, J., Riehle, D.: From developer networks to verified communities: a fine-grained approach. In: Proceedings of ICSE 2015 (2015)
20. Kintab, G.A., Roy, C.K., McCalla, G.I.: Recommending software experts using code similarity and social heuristics. In: Proceedings of CASCON 2014 (2014)
21. Lettner, D., Angerer, F., Grünbacher, P., Prähofer, H.: Software Evolution in an industrial automation ecosystem: an exploratory study. In: Proceedings of SEAA 2014 (2014)
22. Lettner, D., Angerer, F., Prähofer, H., Grünbacher, P.: A case study on software ecosystem characteristics in industrial automation software. In: Proceedings of ICSSP 2014 (2014)
23. Lettner, D., Grünbacher, P.: Using feature feeds to improve developer awareness in software ecosystem evolution. In: Proceedings of VaMoS 2015 (2015)
24. Muthig, D., Schroeter, J.: A framework for role-based feature management in software product line organizations. In: Proceedings of SPLC 2013 (2013)
25. Panichella, S., Bavota, G., Di Penta, M., Canfora, G., Antoniol, G.: How developers' collaborations identified from different sources tell us about code changes. In: Proceedings of ICSME 2014 (2014)
26. Reiser, M.-O., Weber, M.: Multi-level feature trees. Requirem. Eng. 12(2), 57–75 (2007)

27. Riehle, D., Gross, T.R.: Role model based framework design and integration. In: Proceedings of OOPSLA 1998 (1998)
28. Rubin, J., Chechik, M.: A survey of feature location techniques. In: Domain Engineering, Product Lines, Languages, and Conceptual Models, pp. 29–58 (2013)
29. Sajnani, H., Saini, V., Svajlenko, J., Roy, C.K., Lopes, C.V.: Sourcerercc: Scaling code clone detection to big code. CoRR, abs/1512.06448 (2015)
30. Sarwar, B., Karypis, G., Konstan, J., Riedl, J.: Item-based collaborative filtering recommendation algorithms. In: Proceedings of the 10th International Conference on World Wide Web, WWW 2001, pp. 285–295. ACM, New York (2001)
31. Seidl, C., Aßmann, U.: Towards modeling and analyzing variability in evolving software ecosystems. In: VaMoS (2013)
32. Sengupta, B., Chandra, S., Sinha, V.: A research agenda for distributed software development. In: Proceedings of ICSE 2006 (2006)
33. Stănciulescu, S., Schulze, S., Wąsowski, A.: Forked and integrated variants in an open-source firmware project. In: Proceedings of ICSME 2015 (2015)
34. Studer, R., Benjamins, V.R., Fensel, D.: Knowledge engineering: principles and methods. Data Knowl. Eng. 25(1–2), 161–197 (1998)

Adaptable Runtime Monitoring
for the Java Virtual Machine

Andrea Rosà[✉], Yudi Zheng, Haiyang Sun, Omar Javed, and Walter Binder

Faculty of Informatics, Università della Svizzera italiana (USI), Lugano, Switzerland
{andrea.rosa,yudi.zheng,haiyang.sun,omar.javed,walter.binder}@usi.ch

Abstract. Nowadays, many programming language implementations and programming frameworks target the Java Virtual Machine (JVM). Examples include the Java and Scala compilers, Oracle's Truffle framework and the interpreters built on top of it for a variety of dynamic programming languages, as well as big-data frameworks such as Apache Spark, Apache Flink, and Apache Storm. Unfortunately, the JVM provides only limited support for runtime monitoring. The JVM Tool Interface (JVMTI) offers only a very low-level programming model, often introduces high overhead, and does not guarantee proper isolation of the monitoring logic from the observed program. Aspect-Oriented Programming (AOP), in particular AspectJ, is often used to implement runtime monitoring tools. While offering a convenient programming model, the use of such technologies acerbates performance- and isolation-related problems. In this paper, we advocate the use of our dynamic program analysis framework DiSL for runtime monitoring on the JVM. DiSL reconciles an AOP-based programming model, full coverage of all executed bytecodes, optimizations of the monitoring logic, and support for isolation of the monitoring logic. Moreover, DiSL also offers an API to deploy, adapt, and remove monitoring logic at runtime, and it provides seamless support for monitoring also applications running on Android devices.

Keywords: Runtime monitoring · Runtime adaptation · Bytecode optimization · Bytecode instrumentation · Partial evaluation · Java Virtual Machine

1 Introduction

Nowadays, the Java platform is becoming adopted by an increasing number of programming languages and frameworks. Apart from Java, a growing set of programming languages (such as Scala[1], Groovy[2], and Clojure[3]) targets the Java Virtual Machine (JVM), while frameworks such as Oracle's Truffle [1,2] focus on the development of high-performance language runtimes based on the Java

---

[1] http://www.scala-lang.org.
[2] http://www.groovy-lang.org.
[3] https://clojure.org.

© Springer International Publishing AG 2016
T. Margaria and B. Steffen (Eds.): ISoLA 2016, Part II, LNCS 9953, pp. 531–546, 2016.
DOI: 10.1007/978-3-319-47169-3_42

compiler. Moreover, the JVM has recently become a popular target for big-data frameworks, including Apache Spark [3], Apache Flink[4], and Apache Storm[5].

While the JVM is becoming increasingly adopted for many purposes, it provides only limited support for runtime monitoring, a fundamental technique in software development and analysis. Runtime monitoring plays an important role in all stages of software development, from initial software debugging and testing to system deploying and maintenance. Indeed, there is large body of monitoring tools supporting several software engineering tasks, such as profiling, debugging, testing, software optimization, program comprehension, and reverse engineering.

Ideally, monitoring tools for the JVM should guarantee complete and correct coverage of all bytecodes executed by the target application (including the core class library), low monitoring overhead, and isolation of the monitoring logic from the observed program. Unfortunately, existing solutions for runtime monitoring present severe limitations. On the one hand, the Java platform offers the JVM Tool Interface (JVMTI)[6], an Application Programming Interface (API) that enables the development of tools for monitoring the execution of Java applications and inspect JVM internal state. In particular, JVMTI enables bytecode manipulation via external tools which can be used to collect specific metrics and track desired events. However, such API is considered to be rather low-level, often introduces high overhead, and does not guarantee proper isolation of the monitoring logic from the observed program. Moreover, JVMTI is often not available in Java-like platforms for embedded systems such as the Dalvik Virtual Machine (DVM) on Android devices, preventing the reuse of JVMTI-based runtime monitoring tools on embedded applications.

On the other hand, a popular choice in implementing runtime monitoring tools is to use Aspect-Oriented Programming (AOP)[7] languages such as AspectJ [4]. While offering a convenient programming model, AspectJ provides a limited set of join points to be instrumented and reduced code coverage. In particular, join points that are important for runtime monitoring (e.g., the execution of bytecodes or basic blocks) are missing, access to reflective dynamic join point information is expensive, and mixing low-level bytecode instrumentation with high-level AOP code is not supported. As a result, the category of events that can be monitored with AspectJ is rather limited. Tools relying on AspectJ (such as JavaMOP [5]) incur large runtime overhead when monitoring multiple properties simultaneously, and lack isolation of the monitoring logic from the observed program.

In this paper, we advocate the use of our dynamic program analysis framework DiSL for runtime monitoring on the JVM. DiSL [6] is an AOP-based framework that reconciles a convenient model offered by join points, pointcuts

---

[4] https://flink.apache.org.

[5] https://storm.apache.org.

[6] https://docs.oracle.com/javase/8/docs/technotes/guides/jvmti/.

[7] In AOP languages, *join points* represent specific points in the execution of a program, *pointcuts* denote a set of join points of interest, while an *advice* refers to code to be executed whenever a join point of interest is reached.

and advice. The DiSL weaver guarantees complete bytecode coverage to ensure that analysis results represent overall program execution. Moreover, DiSL integrates a partial evaluator to optimize woven advices, reducing analysis overhead via adaptive runtime instrumentation, and supports a deployment setting to enforce isolation by executing analysis code in a separate address space. DiSL support is not limited to the standard JVM and is extended to applications running on the DVM on the Android operating system, enabling runtime monitoring on an increasing number of mobile devices. This invited paper is based on the work presented in [6–8].

The rest of the paper is organized as follows. Section 2 presents an overview of the DiSL architecture and key characteristics. Section 3 describes DiSL's mechanism to dynamically adapt monitoring logic. Section 4 introduces a partial evaluator embedded in DiSL, while we outline DiSL's support for Android in Sect. 5. We present evaluation results on DiSL in Sect. 6. Finally, we discuss related work in Sect. 7, and give our concluding remarks in Sect. 8.

2   DiSL Overview

Below we give an overview of basic language constructs supported by DiSL. We refer the reader to our comprehensive description of the DiSL language [6] for further information.

Join point model. DiSL has an *open join point model* in which any region of bytecodes can be used as a join point. Pointcuts are expressed with *markers* that select bytecode regions. DiSL provides an extensible library of such markers including ones for selecting whole method bodies, basic blocks, single bytecodes, and exception handlers. DiSL relies on *guards* to further restrict the join points selected by a marker. Guards are predicate methods free of side-effects that are executed at weave-time which have access to static context information.

Advice. Advice in DiSL are expressed in the form of code *snippets*. Snippets serve as code templates to be inserted at certain join points indicated by their annotations. These snippets are instantiated by the weaver using contextual information. In contrast to mainstream AOP languages such as AspectJ, DiSL does not support around advice (synthetic local variables [6] mitigate this limitation).

Context information. Snippets and guards have access to complete context information in the form of method arguments. We classify the context information into two categories: static context information (that is, static reflective join point information, limited to constants: primitive values, strings, or class literals) and dynamic context information (including local variables and the operand stack). DiSL provides an extensible library of both context information.

When a snippet is selected to be woven at a join point, it is first instantiated with respect to the context of the join point. The DiSL weaver first replaces invocations of static context methods with the corresponding constants. That is, static context method invocations in the snippet are pseudo-method calls that are substituted with concrete constants. Dynamic context method invocations in the snippet are also pseudo-method calls that are replaced with bytecode sequences to access local variables respectively to copy operands from the stack.

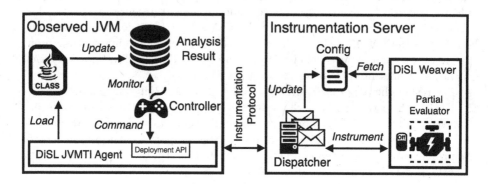

Fig. 1. DiSL architecture.

The overall architecture of DiSL is shown in Fig. 1. We base the architecture around two processes, since instrumentation occurs in a separate process from the observed program. The separation of the instrumentation from the instrumented classes reduces interferences and perturbations in the observed JVM, and hence enables the instrumentation and observation of the Java class library. All classes (including those from the Java class library) being loaded are intercepted by the DiSL JVMTI agent and forwarded to the instrumentation server, which employs the DiSL weaver equipped with a pluggable partial evaluator. The instrumented classes are then returned to the observed JVM for resuming the class loading. The user-defined controller module in the observed JVM is responsible for monitoring the analysis result and adapting the instrumentation. At runtime, the controller instructs DiSL via the deployment API to change the scope of the instrumentation and trigger retransformation of existing classes.

DiSL also supports a dedicated deployment setting to enforce isolation between analysis code and application code [9]. In this setting, analysis code is executed in a separate address space. Avoiding sharing state between analysis and the observed program greatly reduces perturbation and avoids known classes of bugs inherent to not-isolated approaches [10].

3   Runtime Adaptation of Monitoring Logic

Besides ordinary deployment, DiSL also includes a mechanism for dynamic undeployment and redeployment of instrumentation [7]. In certain scenarios, dynamic analysis applying runtime adaptation gains performance speedup without sacrificing accuracy or completeness.

We assume that such analysis employs instrumentation to update the analysis state. This analysis state can be structured as a table, or mapping from keys to values. The keys in the table typically represent some programmer-recognizable program elements of interest to the analysis (e.g., statements, basic blocks, methods, program paths, etc.), whereas the values in the table associated with the keys represent the data being collected (e.g., execution count, execution time, etc.). For example, a method-based profiler can be considered as maintaining a table of per-method counts or accumulated time values which are continually updated during execution. In this view, each value in the table is now a *state variable* with a defined state machine. For example, our method profiler has one state variable for each distinct method executed, and each variable's state machine is that of a counter, that is, the ascending chain of natural numbers starting from zero. Similarly, a simple coverage tool might define one state variable per basic block executed so far, and its state machine would be a "ratcheted boolean": it starts at false, may progress to true, and once true remains in that state.

Suppose that an instrumentation site J exists to update a state variable v. If J can no longer advance the state machine of v into a different state, the instrumentation site J can be removed. For example, once a basic block has been covered, its boolean state variable can never change to a different state, so the instrumentation covering the basic block can be removed. In practice, we often need to consider *sets* of state variables $v \in V$ affected by a given instrumentation site J (e.g., whenever state variables are *per-object*, such as lock sets in a data race detector, since a given instrumentation site can affect many objects).

3.1 Running Example

Having introduced our approach in general terms, we now step through a specific example based on *Stationary Field Analysis* (SFA). Stationary fields represent a generalization of final fields [11] found, e.g., in the Java language. However, unlike final fields, stationary fields can be initialized by multiple writes spanning multiple methods, as long as all the writes to the field happen before all the reads. Knowing what fields are stationary simplifies reasoning about object aliases and opens up opportunities for aggressive compiler optimizations.

SFA associates a per-class and per-instance state variable with every instance field of every class loaded during execution. Each variable represents the state of a simple state machine (see Fig. 2), which tracks the per-class and per-instance status of each field during execution. Once any of the per-instance state variables

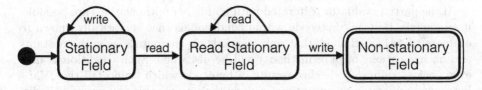

Fig. 2. State machine tracking an observed field's stationarity.

determines a field to be non-stationary, the per-class status of the field, which is the one we are interested in, cannot change for the rest of the execution.

A notable SFA implementation is the rprof tool developed by Nelson et al. [12]. The tool intercepts field accesses to identify fields that can be considered final or stationary, that is, fields that are modified once before the constructor method returns and fields that are not modified after they have been read, respectively. The original rprof makes use of a map/reduce framework to speed up the analysis and to avoid out-of-memory situations when performed on real-world programs. We have reimplemented the rprof tool using our framework. Instead of using map/reduce to mitigate performance problems, we use a simple in-process analysis and rely on adaptive instrumentation to mitigate the overhead.

Our implementation of SFA can be therefore factored into two parts: a straightforward implementation of SFA using DiSL, and additional logic to control the adaptation of instrumentation over the course of the analysis.

The control logic in this example is straightforward: once a field is determined to be non-stationary, we can notify the controller to remove all instrumentation intercepting accesses to that field. In the case of instrumentation on hot paths, this will significantly reduce the overhead being imposed on the observed program.

We expect the performance of our system to be much better than a comparable implementation without adaptive instrumentation, since we can gradually eliminate large amounts of instrumentation as the status of more and more fields becomes known. Reduced instrumentation also improves opportunities for dynamic compiler optimizations (reducing method sizes, thus enabling method inlining), further improving performance. To experimentally validate these claims, we examine the performance of our system quantitatively in Sect. 6.1.

4   Bytecode Optimization by Partial Evaluation

The DiSL weaver is equipped with an on-the-fly partial evaluator [8]. If enabled, the partial evaluator performs code optimizations during the process of snippet instantiation. As discussed in Sect. 2, the DiSL weaver instantiates snippets by replacing invocations of static context methods with bytecodes that load the corresponding constants. The partial evaluator can perform any computation in snippets that depends only on constants and does not produce any side effects at weave-time, thus avoiding repetitive runtime computations.

If the partial evaluator is iterated until no further optimizations are possible, it guarantees that any bytecode within conditionals that is statically known to evaluate to **false** (that is, that only depends on computations with constants and on invocations of pure methods) will be discarded. Such conditionals may even enclose snippet code that results in bytecode which would fail the JVM's bytecode verification when instantiated; as the unreachable snippet code is discarded, this otherwise unverifiable bytecode can neither cause a weave-time error nor a verification error when the instrumented class is linked.

The partial evaluation is divided into three major steps: (1) constant propagation, (2) conditional reduction, and (3) pattern-based code simplification.

Constant propagation. The constant interpreter performs constant propagation on the input snippet. It symbolically executes the bytecodes in the control-flow graph by transforming an input frame (which represents the local variables and the operand stack) into an output frame according to the bytecodes' semantics. For each bytecode, the partial evaluator stores a frame containing the constant status of each local variable and stack operand before executing it. If a bytecode is reachable through multiple execution paths, the partial evaluator merges the input frames. This operation will replace a constant with a dedicated value indicating that the local variable respectively stack operand is not constant or not the same constant for all merged input frames.

Besides symbolically executing bytecodes, our partial evaluator also executes pure methods at weave-time, thus enabling constant propagation across pure method calls. To this end, the DiSL programmer must annotate such methods with @Pure and ensure that the annotated methods indeed have no side effects and that their output does not change for subsequent invocations with the same arguments. Moreover, the methods have to be static with parameters of primitive (resp. wrapper) types or strings. Out-of-the-box, our partial evaluator also supports the removal of calls to pure methods in the Java class library.

Conditional reduction. After constant propagation, some branch instructions can be resolved to either if(true) or if(false). The partial evaluator discards the branch that is not taken and replaces the branch bytecode with a number of pop bytecodes corresponding to the number of operands that would be consumed by the branch bytecode. This code transformation ensures that the snippet code remains valid. After all branch bytecodes have been processed, the inaccessible basic blocks are removed from the control-flow graph.

Pattern-based code simplification. After each iteration, the partial evaluator eliminates superfluous code matching one of several different patterns, such as jumping to the next instruction. Another code pattern is the sequence of pop bytecodes introduced by conditional reduction. For each pop bytecode, the partial evaluator finds out the source bytecodes that push the operand. If all those bytecodes are free of side effects, the partial evaluator removes both the pop bytecode and its source bytecodes; for each bytecode thus removed, the partial evaluator inserts pop bytecodes corresponding to the number of stack operands that would be consumed by the removed source bytecode.

4.1   Running Example

To illustrate how the partial evaluation simplifies the programming of efficient dynamic analysis tools, we compare real-world dynamic analyses using (1) plain DiSL without partial evaluation, and (2) DiSL with partial evaluation enabled.

Figure 3a shows a profiler that traces each executed basic block of code, identified by an unique string comprising the fully qualified method name (package,

```
public class ExecutionTraceProfiler {
  @Before(marker = BasicBlockMarker.class, order = 1, guard = ClassInitGuard.class)
  static void onClassInit(MethodStaticContext msc) {
    ... /* profile class initialization */
  }

  @Before(marker = BasicBlockMarker.class, order = 0)
  static void onBB(CustomBasicBlockStaticContext cbbsc) {
    String bbID = cbbsc.thisBBID();
    ... /* profile basic block entry */
  }
}

public class CustomBasicBlockStaticContext extends BasicBlockStaticContext {
  public String thisBBID() {
    String methodFullName = staticContextData.getClassNode().name
      + "." + staticContextData.getMethodNode().name;
    return methodFullName + ":" + String.valueOf(getBBindex());
  }
}

public class ClassInitGuard {
  @GuardMethod
  static boolean evalGuard(BasicBlockStaticContext bbsc, MethodStaticContext msc) {
    return (bbsc.getBBindex() == 0) && msc.thisMethodName().equals("<clinit>");
  }
}
```

(a)

```
public class ExecutionTraceProfiler {
  @Before(marker = BasicBlockMarker.class)
  static void onBB(BasicBlockStaticContext bbsc, MethodStaticContext msc) {
    if (bbsc.getBBindex() == 0 && msc.thisMethodName().equals("<clinit>")) {
      ... /* profile class initialization */
    }
    String bbID = msc.thisMethodFullName() + ":" + String.valueOf(bbsc.getBBindex());
    ... /* profile basic block entry */
  }
}
```

(b)

Fig. 3. (a) Execution trace profiler using a custom static context class and a guard. (b) Execution trace profiler relying on partial evaluation. Code snippets in this figure are taken from [8].

class, method, signature) and a basic block ID (an integer value that is unique within the scope of a method body). In addition, the execution of the first basic block in each class initializer (method <clinit> at the bytecode level) is specially tracked by the profiler. The DiSL code in Fig. 3(a) is complicated; it comprises two snippets and requires both a custom static context and a guard. The static context ensures that the special basic block identifiers are built at weave-time, while the guard identifies the first basic block of class initializers. The snippet order guarantees that the special profiling of the first basic block in a static initializer happens before the normal basic block profiling.

Figure 3(b) shows a naïve single-snippet implementation with a conditional; the basic block ID is built within the snippet code. While this implementation is sound, it incurs excessive runtime overhead, since the conditional is evaluated and the identifier is built at runtime for each woven join point, i.e., for each basic block in the observed program. However, with partial evaluation, the woven bytecode for both versions of the profiler will be the same, as the conditional depends on static information only and the string operations are pure. Hence, DiSL evaluates these parts of the snippet code at weave-time. We will compare weave-time and runtime performance of both versions of the profiler in Sect. 6.2.

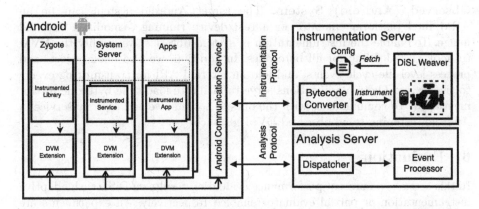

Fig. 4. Architecture of the dynamic program analysis framework on Android. Note that Zygote is the parent process of all applications in Android, responsible for preloading and sharing all necessary system libraries.

5   Android Support

Beyond the support for instrumentation on the JVM, DiSL can also be used to support development of on-the-fly dynamic program analysis tools for the DVM employed in Android. In such a scenario, the analysis runs outside the observed system in a separate analysis process, on a separate machine. This architecture enables flexible analyses over the same instrumentation, makes it possible to run analysis in parallel with the application, and separates the analysis from the observed program. As a result, it enforces strong isolation, cutting down the analysis' memory and performance impact upon the observed program [9].

We have developed a full-coverage dynamic program analysis framework for Android using DiSL. Below, we outline the three main components of the framework, while we refer the reader to [13] for more details and our evaluation results. Figure 4 summarizes the architecture of our framework.

Instrumentation Server. The instrumentation server receives Dalvik byte-code from Android, transforms it to Java bytecode with a bytecode converter, instruments it using the DiSL weaver, and converts the result again to Dalvik bytecode before sending it back. The framework solves the difficulty in instrumenting not only the application code but also system libraries and dynamically loaded code. Additionally, for library code, which is shared among processes, the user can specify in advance names of Android processes in which the instrumentation will be active.

Analysis Server. The analysis server receives analysis data emitted from the instrumented application as well as internal events from the DVM via a dispatcher. A separate event processor allows to analyze multiple processes observable as distinct contexts.

Observed (Android) System. The target Android system can be an ARM/Intel platform emulator or a real device running a modified Android image. To enable the instrumentation of system libraries, we modify the DVM to hook class loading for all bytecodes. In addition, we also hook object- and process-level life-cycle events, and add an internal API for transmitting events to the server. These modifications serve to facilitate load-time bytecode instrumentation. To communicate with the outside servers, we add a proxy service in Android, listening to all observed DVM instances.

6 Evaluation

In this section, we present performance evaluation results on DiSL with adaptive instrumentation or partial evaluator enabled respectively. All experiments are conducted on selected benchmarks from the DaCapo 9.12 suite[8] on a 64-bit multicore platform[9].

6.1 Performance Impact of Adaptive Instrumentation

In Sect. 3.1, we described SFA as a running example of the adaptive instrumentation. To assess the influence of adaptive instrumentation on SFA, we evaluate

---

[8] http://www.dacapobench.org/. We excluded tomcat, tradebeans, and tradesoap benchmarks due to well known issues (see http://sf.net/p/dacapobench/bugs/70/ and http://sf.net/p/dacapobench/bugs/68/).

[9] Dell PowerEdge M620, 1 NUMA node with 64 GB of RAM, Intel Xeon E5-2680 CPU 2.7 GHz with 8 cores, CPU frequency scaling and Turbo Mode disabled, Oracle JDK 1.6.0 b43 Hotspot Server VM (64-bit) running on Ubuntu Linux Server 64-bit version 12.04.2 64-bit with kernel 3.5.0-25-generic.

two variants of our DiSL-based reimplementation of rprof [12]. One is designed to mimic the original rprof tool (referred to as *Fixed SFA*) and only uses fixed instrumentation. We use this variant as the baseline. The other uses adaptive instrumentation (referred to as *Adaptive SFA*) with a controller thread that periodically (that is, every 100 milliseconds) triggers removal of instrumentation for fields that are known to be non-stationary. Like the original rprof tool, our DiSL-based SFA implementations report the stationary status of each field accessed during program execution. With respect to performance, we generally expect *Adaptive SFA* to perform better than *Fixed SFA*. The adaptive variant of the analysis incurs additional overhead due to class retransformation, which will temporarily undo optimizations performed not only on the retransformed classes, but also on methods in other classes containing, e.g., inlined code from the methods in the retransformed classes. However, in the long run, the adaptive analysis should incur lower overhead.

To evaluate the performance of both analysis variants, we execute them on the benchmarks from the DaCapo suite, and calculate their overhead compared to uninstrumented execution of the benchmarks. Since a developer would typically run such tool on her code once, our evaluation targets startup performance. Thus, we collect data from a single iteration of each benchmark.

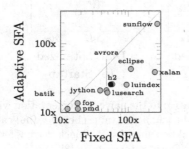

Fig. 5. Overhead factors for *Fixed SFA* and *Adaptive SFA*. The gray marks refer to the individual benchmarks; the black mark refers to the geometric mean of all speedup factors.

The results of the performance evaluation are summarized in Fig. 5. The diagonal line indicates data points for which the performance of *Fixed SFA* and *Adaptive SFA* is the same. As expected, the results for *Adaptive SFA* show a significant speedup compared to *Fixed SFA*: we observe the highest speedup of a factor of 6.36 with xalan, average speedup of a factor of 2.54 (calculated from total execution time), and the smallest speedup of a factor of 1.12 with batik. For the three longest-running benchmarks (eclipse, h2, and avrora, accounting for approx. 72 % of the total execution time of the whole uninstrumented benchmark suite), the speedup factor is over 2. This is consistent with our expectation that the adaptive instrumentation will have the biggest impact on long-running analyses. Based on the measurements, we conclude that adaptive instrumentation significantly improves SFA performance.

6.2   Performance Impact of Partial Evaluation

To assess the impact of partial evaluation on weave-time performance and the impact of code quality on runtime performance, we evaluate three versions of the execution trace profiler presented in Sect. 4.1: (1) the naïve implementation shown in Fig. 3(b) (*without PE*), which serves as a baseline for the comparison; (2) the manually optimized implementation shown in Fig. 3(a) (*without PE*), henceforth called *DiSL optimized*; and (3) the naïve implementation of Fig. 3(b) (*with PE*), called *DiSL PE*. Moreover, we consider three performance metrics: (a) the weave-time, that is, the time to weave all classes loaded during a single benchmark iteration; (b) the startup time, that is, the process time from creation to the termination of the first benchmark iteration; and (c) the steady-state execution time, that is, the median of the execution times of 15 benchmark iterations within the same JVM process.

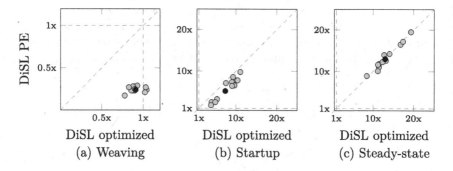

Fig. 6. Speedup factors relative to the naïve implementation without partial evaluation for the considered DaCapo benchmarks (values below 1x indicate slowdowns). The gray marks refer to the individual benchmarks; the black mark refers to the geometric mean of all speedup factors. This figure is taken from [8].

For each metric, Fig. 6 illustrates the speedup of *DiSL optimized* and *DiSL PE* relative to the baseline. The diagonal line indicates data points for which the performance of *DiSL optimized* and *DiSL PE* is the same. Regarding weave-time, (see Fig. 6(a)), the baseline is generally faster than both the *DiSL optimized* and *DiSL PE* versions. The reason is that, for the baseline, the partial evaluator is deactivated and there is no guard to be evaluated at weave-time. However, in a few benchmarks, *DiSL optimized* outperforms the baseline because the reduced complexity of the inlined snippet code outweighs the cost of guard evaluation. On average, *DiSL optimized* is only 10 % slower than the baseline, while the use of the partial evaluator increases weave-time by a factor of 4.2. This result clearly shows the drawback of partial evaluation: a considerable increase in weave-time.

Regarding startup performance, (see Fig. 6(b)), *DiSL optimized* outperforms the baseline by a factor of 7.4, and *DiSL PE* outperforms the baseline by a factor of 5.18. Interestingly, a single benchmark iteration (which includes weave-time) is sufficient to achieve a significant speedup by partial evaluation. The manually tuned version is faster still, as it does not significantly increase weave-time.

Regarding steady-state performance, (see Fig. 6(c)), *DiSL optimized* and *DiSL PE* reach the same high speedup of about 13x. This result highlights the strengths of our partial evaluator; high steady-state performance is achieved without having to write complicated, manually tuned code. The fact that *DiSL PE* significantly outperforms the baseline clearly shows that the just-in-time compiler of the JVM is not able to perform the same kind of optimizations as our partial evaluator.

7   Related Work

AspectJ [4] is a language often used for the kind of bytecode instrumentation tasks DiSL is designed for. The standard AspectJ compiler (ajc) already performs partial evaluation of the aspects' pointcuts, which are akin to DiSL's markers, scopes, and guards. It does not, however, partially evaluate the aspects' advice, which are akin to DiSL's snippets. Moreover, in the domain of runtime monitoring, there are many existing tools which use AspectJ to instrument systems for generating events. However, the use of AspectJ imposes several serious limitations, such as a join-point model which is not suitable for many types of analyses, reduced code coverage, lack of support for analyzing Android applications, as well as high instrumentation overheads.

Masuhara et al. describe AOP in terms of a semantics-based compilation model [14]. This model follows an interpretative approach to compilation, based on partially evaluating the AOP interpreter itself (written in Scheme) to remove unnecessary pointcut tests. In contrast to DiSL, advice code is not partially evaluated, but rather the partial evaluator verifies whether the advice should be inserted in the compiled code or not.

There is a number of frameworks for runtime monitoring, among which Java-MOP [5] is a full-fledged framework which enables parametric properties and supports multiple logical formalisms to express properties. JavaMOP incorporates knowledge of specific properties and uses static analysis to avoid creating or retaining unnecessary monitors [15,16]. Differing from JavaMOP, DiSL does not focus on checking runtime properties. Meanwhile, the optimizations in Java-MOP focus on creating fewer monitors or removing useless ones via garbage collection. DiSL is based on hotswapping techniques, thus it can also support optimizations by lazily creating monitors, that is, monitors can be created on-demand and enabled at runtime. It is also worth noting that our framework is more flexible than AspectJ, which JavaMOP relies on, in terms of choosing locations for program instrumentation. By replacing the AspectJ backend of JavaMOP with DiSL, the benefits of monitor optimization provided by Java-MOP and those of adaptive optimizations of the monitoring logic provided by DiSL could be combined. This work is among our ongoing investigations.

Partial evaluation (also called program specialization) enables aggressive inter-procedural constant propagation, constant folding, and control-flow simplifications [17]. An online partial evaluator makes decisions about what to specialize during the specialization process, while an offline partial evaluator makes all the decisions before specialization. Hybrid Partial Evaluation (HPE) [18] combines both approaches by letting the programmer guide the specialization process through annotations, e.g., to indicate which objects are to be instantiated at compile time. This is similar to DiSL's annotations used to guide the partial evaluation, without which not all optimization decisions can be made in an offline-fashion. Thus, DiSL can be considered to follow a hybrid approach, too.

Some approaches to partial evaluation are based on translating the source program into another programming language that provides more powerful specialization mechanisms. For example, Albert et al. use partial evaluation to automatically generate specialized programs by transforming Java bytecode into Prolog to apply powerful constraint logic programming [19]. The Prolog code is then interpreted by the CiaoPP abstract interpreter [20]. While this approach allows for powerful interpretative partial evaluation, it only handles a subset of Java that lacks exception handling, multi-threading, and reflection. In contrast, DiSL's partial evaluator is less powerful, but does not have such limitations.

Finally, existing dynamic analysis frameworks for Android are implemented with various techniques at different levels of the Android platform, ranging from the application level (Java) [21], through native library level [22], operating system level [23], to emulator level [24]. However, most of the work on dynamic analysis targets only a specific topic, that is, Android security, and has limitations towards developing custom dynamic program analysis tools.

8   Conclusions and Future Works

In this paper, we have shown how our dynamic program analysis framework DiSL can be efficiently used for runtime monitoring on the JVM and the DVM, thanks to full bytecode coverage, support for optimization and isolation of the monitoring logic, as well as runtime adaptation of instrumentation to gain performance speedup.

As future work, we plan to complement and improve DiSL along several directions. We intend to conduct further evaluations in the context of runtime monitoring tools. Moreover, given the large body of runtime monitoring tools based on AspectJ, porting existing tools to DiSL via an AspectJ-to-DiSL translator can overcome severe AspectJ limitations for several monitoring tools. This solution would not be applicable to all applications (for example, those making use of around advice that may skip or replicate the execution of intercepted join points are not suitable). Furthermore, use of inter-type declaration, in which an aspect can declare a new type such as class, interface or even another aspect is not currently supported by DiSL.

Finally, a further direction is to extend DiSL to support runtime monitoring and verification of systems that make use of dynamic code evolution. One approach is to leverage the existing DiSL infrastructure for the monitoring logic and for dynamic evolution of the observed program. In this context, dynamic code evolution may require additional runtime verification to ensure that the program behaves correctly during the transitional phase between two code versions. Another approach is to improve DiSL adaptation infrastructure by building it on top of a JVM that offers dedicated support for dynamic code evolution [25], such that the monitoring code could be changed even for methods active on the stack of some threads. This approach would raise concerns about the consistency of the monitoring information, that is, self-verifying monitoring logic might be needed.

DiSL is available open-source at http://disl.ow2.org.

Acknowledgments. This work has been supported by Oracle (ERO project 1332), by the Swiss National Science Foundation (project 200021_141002), and by the European Commission (contract ACP2-GA-2013-605442).

References

1. Würthinger, T., Wöß, A., Stadler, L., Duboscq, G., Simon, D., Wimmer, C.: Self-optimizing AST interpreters. ACM SIGPLAN Not. 2012 **48**, 73–82 (2012)
2. Duboscq, G., Würthinger, T., Stadler, L., Wimmer, C., Simon, D., Mössenböck, H.: An intermediate representation for speculative optimizations in a dynamic compiler. In: VMIL, pp. 1–10 (2013)
3. Zaharia, M., Chowdhury, M., Das, T., Dave, A., Ma, J., McCauley, M., Franklin, M.J., Shenker, S., Stoica, I.: Resilient distributed datasets: a fault-tolerant abstraction for in-memory cluster computing. In: NSDI, pp. 2:1–2:15 (2012)
4. Kiczales, G., Hilsdale, E., Hugunin, J., Kersten, M., Palm, J., Griswold, W.G.: An overview of AspectJ. In: Knudsen, J.L. (ed.) ECOOP 2001. LNCS, vol. 2072, pp. 327–354. Springer, Heidelberg (2001). doi:10.1007/3-540-45337-7_18
5. Jin, D., Meredith, P.O., Lee, C., Roşu, G.: JavaMOP: efficient parametric runtime monitoring framework. In: ICSE, pp. 1427–1430 (2012)
6. Marek, L., Villazón, A., Zheng, Y., Ansaloni, D., Binder, W., Qi, Z.: DiSL: a domain-specific language for bytecode instrumentation. In: AOSD, pp. 239–250 (2012)
7. Zheng, Y., Bulej, L., Zhang, C., Kell, S., Ansaloni, D., Binder, W.: Dynamic optimization of bytecode instrumentation. In: VMIL, pp. 21–30 (2013)
8. Zheng, Y., Ansaloni, D., Marek, L., Sewe, A., Binder, W., Villazón, A., Tuma, P., Qi, Z., Mezini, M.: Turbo DiSL: partial evaluation for high-level bytecode instrumentation. In: Furia, C.A., Nanz, S. (eds.) TOOLS 2012. LNCS, vol. 7304, pp. 353–368. Springer, Heidelberg (2012). doi:10.1007/978-3-642-30561-0_24
9. Marek, L., Kell, S., Zheng, Y., Bulej, L., Binder, W., Tůma, P., Ansaloni, D., Sarimbekov, A., Sewe, A.: ShadowVM: robust and comprehensive dynamic program analysis for the Java platform. In: GPCE, pp. 105–114 (2013)
10. Kell, S., Ansaloni, D., Binder, W., Marek, L.: The JVM is not observable enough (and what to do about it). In: VMIL, pp. 33–38 (2012)
11. Unkel, C., Lam, M.S.: Automatic inference of stationary fields: a generalization of Java's final fields. In: POPL, pp. 183–195 (2008)
12. Nelson, S., Pearce, D.J., Noble, J.: Profiling object initialization for Java. In: RV, pp. 292–307 (2012)

13. Sun, H., Zheng, Y., Bulej, L., Villazón, A., Qi, Z., Tůma, P., Binder, W.: A programming model and framework for comprehensive dynamic analysis on Android. In: MODULARITY, pp. 133–145 (2015)
14. Masuhara, H., Kiczales, G., Dutchyn, C.: A compilation and optimization model for aspect-oriented programs. In: Hedin, G. (ed.) CC 2003. LNCS, vol. 2622, pp. 46–60. Springer, Heidelberg (2003). doi:10.1007/3-540-36579-6_4
15. Chen, F., Meredith, P.O., Jin, D., Rosu, G.: Efficient formalism-independent monitoring of parametric properties. In: ASE, pp. 383–394 (2009)
16. Jin, D., Meredith, P.O., Griffith, D., Rosu, G.: Garbage collection for monitoring parametric properties. In: PLDI, pp. 415–424 (2011)
17. Jones, N.D., Gomard, C.K., Sestoft, P.: Partial Evaluation and Automatic Program Generation. Prentice Hall, Englewood Cliffs (1993)
18. Shali, A., Cook, W.R.: Hybrid partial evaluation. In: OOPSLA, pp. 375–390 (2011)
19. Albert, E., Gómez-Zamalloa, M., Hubert, L., Puebla, G.: Verification of Java bytecode using analysis and transformation of logic programs. In: Hanus, M. (ed.) PADL 2007. LNCS, vol. 4354, pp. 124–139. Springer, Heidelberg (2006). doi:10. 1007/978-3-540-69611-7_8
20. Hermenegildo, M.V., Puebla, G., Bueno, F., López-García, P.: Integrated program debugging, verification, and optimization using abstract interpretation (and the Ciao system preprocessor). Sci. Comput. Program. 58, 115–140 (2005)
21. Hao, H., Singh, V., Du, W.: On the effectiveness of API-level access control using bytecode rewriting in Android. In: CCS, pp. 25–36 (2013)
22. Hornyack, P., Han, S., Jung, J., Schechter, S., Wetherall, D.: These aren't the droids you're looking for: retrofitting Android to protect data from imperious applications. In: CCS, pp. 639–652 (2011)
23. Dietz, M., Shekhar, S., Pisetsky, Y., Shu, A., Wallach, D.S.: Quire: Lightweight provenance for smart phone operating systems. In: USENIX Security, pp. 23:1–23:16 (2011)
24. Yan, L.K., Yin, H.: DroidScope: seamlessly reconstructing the OS and Dalvik semantic views for dynamic Android malware analysis. In: USENIX Security, pp. 29:1–29:16 (2012)
25. Würthinger, T., Ansaloni, D., Binder, W., Wimmer, C., Mössenböck, H.: Safe and atomic run-time code evolution for Java and its application to dynamic AOP. In: OOPSLA, pp. 825–844 (2011)

Identifying Variability in Object-Oriented Code Using Model-Based Code Mining

David Wille[1]([⊠]), Michael Tiede[1], Sandro Schulze[2], Christoph Seidl[1], and Ina Schaefer[1]

[1] TU Braunschweig, Braunschweig, Germany
{d.wille,m.tiede,c.seidl,i.schaefer}@tu-brauschweig.de
[2] TU Hamburg-Harburg, Hamburg, Germany
sandro.schulze@tuhh.de

Abstract. A large set of object-oriented programming (OOP) languages exists to realize software for different purposes. Companies often create variants of their existing software by copying and modifying them to changed requirements. While these so-called clone-and-own approaches allow to save money in short-term, they expose the company to severe risks regarding long-term evolution and product quality. The main reason is the high manual maintenance effort which is needed due to the unknown relations between variants. In this paper, we introduce a model-based approach to identify variability information for OOP code, allowing companies to better understand and manage variability between their variants. This information allows to improve maintenance of the variants and to transition from single variant development to more elaborate reuse strategies such as software product lines. We demonstrate the applicability of our approach by means of a case study analyzing variants generated from an existing software product line and comparing our findings to the managed reuse strategy.

1 Introduction

Object-oriented programming (OOP) languages are widely used to develop software for different applications. Depending on the systems' requirements, different languages provide a suitable degree of abstraction from the underlying hardware. For instance, C++ allows development of software with real-time requirements (e.g., in embedded systems), while PYTHON or JAVA are often used to develop software for desktop applications (e.g., administration tools).

Software companies often are specialized in developing solutions for a certain domain (e.g., logistics software) and their applications have a common functionality. However, customers often have differing requirements and, thus, *variants* of the software need to be developed. For instance, a certain functionality is required by a customer for a company-specific process (e.g., the way stock

This work was partially supported by the DFG (German Research Foundation) under grant SCHA1635/2-2 and by the European Commission within the project HyVar (grant agreement H2020-644298).).

© Springer International Publishing AG 2016
T. Margaria and B. Steffen (Eds.): ISoLA 2016, Part II, LNCS 9953, pp. 547–562, 2016.
DOI: 10.1007/978-3-319-47169-3_43

data is stored). Thus, copying existing variants and modifying them to changed requirements is common practice to reuse functionality and reduce the development time for variants. This so-called *clone-and-own* practice allows companies to save money during the creation of a *software family* consisting of related variants with slight differences. However, companies rarely document the relations of created variants and existing errors are propagated between variants. As a consequence, identifying and fixing errors becomes a time-consuming and costly task because corresponding parts have to be identified by manually comparing the variants. Thus, the practice of clone-and-own is considered harmful to the long-term development process [5,7,12].

One solution to overcome clone-and-own related problems is introducing managed reuse of functionality to the created family of product variants instead of maintaining independent variants in isolation. Reverse engineering *variability information* (i.e., common and varying parts) from the related product variants allows developers to identify relations between them and use these insights during maintenance. For instance, changes can be propagated more easily between the variants and managed reuse of existing functionality is possible. Thus, the software quality improves and shorter development times for new products are possible [13]. In previous work, we successfully demonstrated *family mining*, a variability mining technique for block-based modeling languages [18,19].

In this paper, we introduce a model-based *code mining* framework, which allows to identify the variability between related variants realized in source code of OOP languages. The framework uses a language-independent meta-model as a data structure and executes all comparisons between the analyzed artifacts on this basis. In particular, we make the following contributions:

- We present a language-independent meta-model for OOP languages.
- We introduce a model-based code mining framework allowing to identify the variability between OOP code variants.
- We demonstrate the applicability of our approach by means of a case study.

This paper is structured as follows: Sect. 2 gives an overview of OOP languages, model-based software development, and family mining. Section 3 describes our model-based code mining approach and the language-independent meta-model for OOP languages. Section 4 provides a case study to show applicability of model-based code mining for OOP code. Section 5 discusses related work and Sect. 6 concludes with an outlook to future work.

2   Background

In this section, we give an overview of OOP languages (cf. Sect. 2.1), model-based development (cf. Sect. 2.2), and variability mining (cf. Sect. 2.3).

2.1   Object-Oriented Programming Languages

OOP languages are widely used in different domains to develop software systems for various application scenarios. For this reason, a large number of OOP languages exists to realize information structures supporting different requirements (e.g., developing desktop and server software).

In Listings 1.1 to 1.4, we show code examples for PYTHON, JAVA, and C++. All three languages provide similar concepts but use different names for some of them. They consist of *classifiers* (also referred to as *classes*), which are part of a *namespace* to organize and encapsulate them. Classes define the structure for objects containing *variables* to store values with different *types* (e.g., integers or characters) and *methods* to execute operations on them. Each example shows a `Rectangle` class storing two integers a and b to calculate the rectangle's area using the method `calculateArea()`. Methods have a *signature*, which is defined by their *visibility modifier* (e.g., `public` or `private`), *return type* (i.e., the type of the method's result), method name, and *parameters*. Visibility modifiers are used to control the accessibility of variables and methods inside of classes (i.e., whether other classes can access them). Parameters pass information to *constructors* (i.e., the method initializing objects during object creation) or methods to further process them. Although the basic structure of most OOP languages is very similar, certain differences exist. For example, C++ classes are normally defined in *header* files (cf., Listing 1.3), while their concrete implementation is defined in a separate implementation file (cf. Listing 1.4). Another example is PYTHON as it does not provide explicit visibility modifiers (i.e., all class variables and methods are accessible by other classes).

```
1   class Rectangle:
2     def __init__(self, a, b):
3       self.a = a
4       self.b = b
5
6     def calculateArea(self):
7       return self.a * self.b
```

Listing 1.1. PYTHON class

```
1   public class Rectangle {
2     private int a, b;
3
4     public Rectangle(int a, int b) {
5       this.a = a;
6       this.b = b;
7     }
8
9     public int calculateArea() {
10      return a * b;
11    }
12  }
```

Listing 1.2. JAVA class

```
1   #ifndef RECTANGLE_H
2   #define RECTANGLE_H
3   class Rectangle {
4     private:
5       int a, b;
6     public:
7       Rectangle(int a, int b);
8       int calculateArea();
9   };
10  #endif /* RECTANGLE_H */
```

Listing 1.3. C++ header

```
1   #include "Rectangle.h"
2
3   Rectangle::Rectangle(int a, int b) {
4     this->a = a;
5     this->b = b;
6   }
7
8   int Rectangle::calculateArea() {
9     return a * b;
10  }
```

Listing 1.4. C++ class

2.2 Model-Based Software Development

Model-based software development uses *meta-models* to define the language elements that can be used for a specific language. *Models* as concrete instances of meta-models allow to store data with regard to the provided language elements. With a suitable parser, source code can be perceived as a model conforming with a specific meta-model. The *concrete syntax* of a language is defined by a *grammar* and allows parser technology to create such a model representation from source code by transforming it to an instance of the meta-model. Developers use the concrete syntax (e.g., the textual syntax of JAVA source code) provided by many languages to implement their software (i.e., models). Meta-models are also referred to as a language's *abstract syntax* because they define how model instances have to be realized in order to conform with the language.

2.3 Family Mining

Companies often develop software for a specific domain (e.g., the logistics domain) with a large number of customers. These customers mostly use the same functionality but often have requirements to support certain company-specific tasks (e.g., a tax calculation module for a specific country). As a result, software companies need to develop *variants* of their products. A common strategy to create new variants is cloning-and-owning, which allows to reuse existing functionality, but also introduces risks to the development process (e.g., duplicate bug fixing of errors that were propagated between variants) [5].

A possible solution is to introduce managed reuse of existing functionality to the product family. Software product lines (SPLs) provide a suitable reuse mechanism as they manage all implementation artifacts (e.g., source code) for multiple variants in a single location. *Features* represent configuration options for such SPLs [13] and allow to configure and generate variants from the product family. In previous work, we successfully introduced *family mining*, a variability mining technique, to reverse engineer the *variability information* (i.e., common and varying parts) for block-based languages by using a metric-based compare algorithm [18,19]. After identifying relations between the compared variants, we merge all analyzed variants in a *150 % model* annotating all implementation artifacts with their variability. This information allows to analyze relations between variants and, thus, to improve the maintenance (e.g., by applying changes to all variants more easily). Furthermore, the variability information allows to gradually introduce SPL reuse strategies by mapping artifacts to features [1]. In this paper, we introduce family mining for source code of OOP languages.

3 Model-Based Code Mining Framework

In this section, we introduce our model-based code mining framework allowing to identify variability information for related OOP code variants. In Fig. 1, we show the corresponding workflow. Our framework expects source code in a supported OOP language (i.e., currently JAVA and C++), which is transferred to

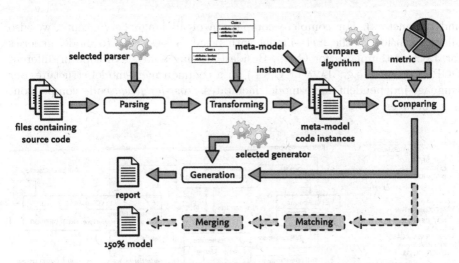

Fig. 1. Workflow for the model-based code mining framework.

an instance of our meta-model (cf. Sect. 3.1). For our comparisons, we utilize a metric (cf. Sect. 3.2) to calculate the similarity of compared elements. The identified variability can be exported in form of a summarizing report or a 150 % model storing all implementation artifacts from the analyzed variants together with their annotated variability.

The first step during variability analysis is to parse the selected OOP code variants using a corresponding parser and to transfer the resulting information to an instance of our meta-model (cf. Sect. 3.3). Afterwards, we utilize the defined metric to compare the models of the different variants (cf. Sect. 3.4). The identified variability information can be exported as a summarizing report (cf. Sect. 3.5). In addition, we discuss the creation of an annotated 150 % model but leave a concrete concept and its realization for future work (cf. Sect. 3.6).

3.1 Language-Independent Meta-Model

Using a model representation to identify variability between related code variants allows to abstract from the language-specific textual syntax of the analyzed programming language. This is possible because of the underlying abstract syntax of all programming languages captured in the meta-model. In theory, it would be possible to reuse an existing meta-model (e.g., used to define the language's abstract syntax) or to build one meta-model per analyzed language. However, as a result, our compare algorithms would have to be implemented for each individual meta-model. Instead, we created a language-independent meta-model to have a common data-structure for OOP languages and, thus, can use the same implementation of our algorithms for a large set of these languages (e.g., JAVA or C++). Such a generic meta-model is possible due to the common language elements of all OOP languages (e.g., classes, methods, and parameters). For complete comparison of all language concepts, we also allow extension of the meta-model with nested types, e.g., to model generics for JAVA or templates for C++. Besides allowing analysis of code in different OOP languages (e.g., JAVA or C++) on a common meta-model structure, our language-independent meta-model facilitates *cross-language* code comparisons (e.g., between JAVA and C++).

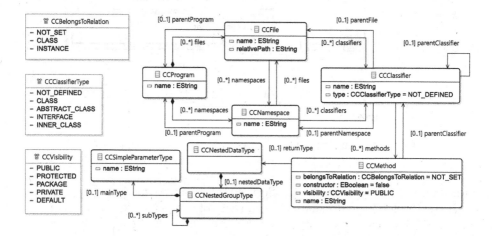

Fig. 2. Excerpt from the language-independent meta-model.

In Fig. 2, we show an excerpt from our language-independent meta-model. As we can see, *programs* contain a set of *files* and *namespaces*. Files are contained in a namespace and contain *classifiers* with different types (e.g., abstract classes or interfaces). Classifiers can contain further classifiers (i.e., inner classes) and define a set of methods. Methods can be declared as constructors and have a name, visibility, and *belongs-to-relation*. This relation allows to distinguish between *class methods* (also called *static methods*) and *instance methods*. These methods have a return type, which is represented as a nested data structure allowing to model more complex nested types for different languages. This nested type is used for all data types in the meta-model (e.g., method parameters).

3.2   Metric Definition

Using the specified meta-model, we define a metric for the comparison of code elements from OOP programs. This metric allows to assign different importance to the properties of compared elements and, thus, to influence their impact on the elements' similarity. The overall sum of all weights for an element (e.g., methods or fields) is normalized to be in the interval [0..1] to make calculated similarity values comparable. In Table 1, we present the properties considered during the comparison of methods and fields together with the corresponding weights, which have empirically proven to be sensible values and have been used for our

case study (cf. Sect. 4). During the comparison of methods, we assign the highest
weight to their names because developers select these names for specific reasons
and, thus, these properties are an important indicator for similarity. We are
not just interested in equality but also in cases, which are related variants with
reduced similarity (i.e., we allow minor deviations in the names). The return
type highly influences the behavior of corresponding methods as it determines
the expected result. However, multiple methods can exist with the same return
type and, thus, we assign a lower weight to them. During the comparison of
method parameters, we assign a lower weight to their types than to corresponding names. Here, multiple methods with the same parameter types might exist
and only their names make the parameters distinguishable. Finally, the modifiers of methods are weighted with the lowest value as they have relatively little
impact on the similarity. The weight for modifiers is subdivided into four weights
for the corresponding visibility, constant (i.e., the method cannot change class
fields), static (i.e., the method can be invoked without creating a class object),
and abstract modifiers (i.e., the method has to be overridden by a concrete implementation). In addition to the methods' signatures, we also consider their body
during comparison. For the overall similarity of two methods, we empirically
identified that weighting the signature similarity with 0.6 and the body similarity with 0.4 allows to calculate sensible results. During comparison of fields,
we consider names, data types and modifiers. Here, we assigned a low weight to
the modifiers as they only slightly influence the behavior of fields. The weight
for field modifiers is subdivided into weights for the visibility, constant (i.e., the
field cannot be changed), and belongs-to-relation modifiers.

Table 1. Metric used for the variability mining of OOP code

Method weights		Field weights	
Property	*Weight*	*Property*	*Weight*
Overall Modifier	0.05	Name	0.4
o *Visibility*	*0.25*	Data Type	0.4
o *Constant*	*0.25*	Overall Modifier	0.2
o *Static*	*0.25*	o *Visibility*	*0.33*
o *Abstract*	*0.25*	o *Constant*	*0.33*
Return Type	0.2	o *Belongs-to-Relation*	*0.33*
Name	0.45		
Parameter Names	0.2		
Parameter Types	0.1		

For configuring the overall mining process and particularly the metric, we
allow developers to define configuration values to specify programs that should
be compared, to select the used compare algorithms, and to configure the metric's
weights. Here, we allow to define relations and corresponding similarity weights

for similar types, which are not 100 % equal but still can be regarded as similar types (e.g., lists and arrays). This way, we allow adaptability and custom-tailored code mining when applying our algorithms to programs with different settings.

3.3 Parsing and Transforming Source Code Files

The first step is to parse the source code files that should be analyzed using a suitable parser. Our current implementation supports the import of JAVA and C++ source code. For JAVA source code we use the JAVA MODEL PARSER AND PRINTER (JAMOPP)[1], which parses provided JAVA code to the JAMOPP meta-model. The resulting meta-model instances are transformed to our language-independent meta-model in order to make the parsed information available for our variability mining algorithms or analysis by users. Our framework allows users to implement and select further parsers to parse and analyze files from other languages. For instance, we used the SCRML[2] parser to parse C++ code. The resulting SRCML XML output of the parsed code is transformed to an instance of our language-independent meta-model and afterwards can be used as input for our code mining algorithms.

3.4 Comparing the Source Code Variants

After parsing the source code variants and storing the parsed information in an instance of our language-independent meta-model, we now compare them using our algorithms. Besides utilizing our existing metric and compare algorithm, our framework allows users to realize their own custom-tailored algorithms implementing own metrics. We execute a pairwise comparison for the selected program variants. Our algorithm uses the first program as a basis and compares all other programs with this variant. For all comparisons between two programs, we currently use an $n{:}m$ algorithm. For instance, when comparing the fields of two classes Class1 and Class2, we compare all combinations of the fields.

First, we compare the file names and namespaces of the classes contained in the analyzed programs to identify whether they are contained in the same package and have the same name. Each comparison between two elements is stored in the overall *result model* together with the corresponding similarity value, which is calculated according to the weights from the selected metric. The *result model* allows us, e.g., to analyze and further process the identified relations after the comparisons. Next, we compare the classes contained in the files of analyzed programs. We start class comparisons by comparing their names and the contained fields. Next, we compare the methods' signatures and bodies. Currently, we compare the method bodies by regarding each line of the body as a single string. By comparing these strings, we identify the number of coinciding lines and can calculate the bodies' overall similarity.

---

[1] http://www.jamopp.org/.
[2] http://www.srcml.org/.

For the comparison of names, we calculate the strings' similarity by identifying their edit distance using the *Levenshtein algorithm* [9]. For methods, we split the name into groups starting with upper case characters (camel case notation) and identify the number of equal groups. As OOP languages use differing naming conventions, we allow configuring the used string compare algorithms.

Currently, we regard all elements with a similarity greater or equal to 85 % as *mandatory* (i.e., they are regarded as identical). All elements with a similarity below 60 % are regarded as *non-related* making each individual *optional* for the software family as they are not similar enough. Elements with a similarity between the mandatory threshold and the optional threshold (i.e., $\geq 60\,\% \wedge <85\,\%$) are regarded as *alternative*, because they still have a high degree of similarity but differ in minor parts (e.g., a method variant has an additional parameter).

3.5 Generating a Report About the Variability Information

After comparing the selected source code variants, we can export the resulting information. Currently, we provide the possibility to store the identified variability in a JSON format or in form of an HTML report. Both formats contain all executed comparisons and, thus, do not contain distinct matchings between elements (i.e., *1:1* relations). The JSON format allows users to further process and analyze the information with other programs. The HTML report is realized with technologies for dynamic websites, allowing users to interactively analyze the information (i.e., the employed metric and the results) and to make annotations. Most importantly, the report allows users to remove relations between elements, which enables them to narrow down the possible relations until distinct *1:1* relations are identified. In Fig. 3, we present an excerpt from a report generated during our case study (cf. Sect. 4). Here, two variants of the method addEntityType__wrappee__Fly with differing bodies were compared.

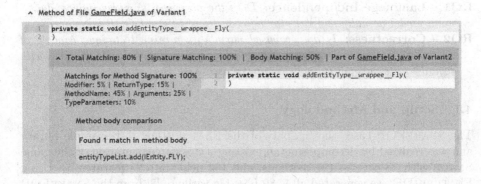

Fig. 3. Excerpt from an example report output.

3.6   Creating 150% Model Using the Variability Information

In addition to the report generation, we present another export possibility. Using the identified relations, it is possible to create an SPL in the form of a 150% model containing all implementation artifacts from the compared variants annotated with explicit variability information and their containing variants. We realized such a solution in previous work for family mining of block-based languages [18,19], thus, it seems sensible for code as well. However, as we currently did not realize this option, we marked the corresponding path in Fig. 1 with dashed arrows and plan to realize the 150% model generation in future work. To merge the variability information into a 150% model, we first need to identify distinct matches between the different elements from the compared source codes. Thus, we need to transform the $n{:}m$ comparison results into $1{:}1$ relations, allowing to identify unique variability between the corresponding elements. The resulting list of distinct matches can be used to merge a 150% model by adding all compared elements to a single file and annotating their variability (i.e., whether they are part of all variants or only contained in particular variants). In previous work, for block-based models [18,19], we already implemented semi-automatic algorithms for distinctively matching model elements, which can easily be adapted for our use case. These algorithms identify all comparisons containing a certain element and select the comparison with the highest similarity. After merging the variability information, the resulting 150% model can be used to analyze the variability of a software family and to generate all contained variants.

4   Case Study

We applied the presented variability mining technique in a case study to source code variants generated from an SPL case study. During this case study, we evaluated the following research questions to analyze the approach's feasibility.

RQ1 – Language Independence: *Does the proposed language-independent meta-model actually support storing code from different OOP languages?*

RQ2 – Correctness: *Is the proposed variability mining technique capable of correctly identifying variability information between related code variants with regard to the variability modeled in the used SPL case study?*

4.1   Setup and Methodology

The SNAKEFOP case study is part of the FEATUREIDE [17] example library and was realized by decomposing an existing JAVA implementation of the game SNAKE with 28 classes, 197 methods, and 133 fields into 21 features [8]. Using FEATUREIDE, we generated all 5580 possible variants [8] from the SNAKEFOP implementation. Although the SNAKEFOP case study was not realized using clone-and-own techniques, it allows to evaluate whether our code variability mining approach is able to identify variability between variants correctly by

Table 2. Details of the selected variants for the case study.

Size	Avg. LOC	Avg. Comparisons	Avg. Features	Avg. Runtime
SMALL	2037.3	33189.8	8.7	25457,0 ms
MEDIUM	2124.3	48150.0	13.6	30301,2 ms
LARGE	2274.0	54744.0	16.5	45278,1 ms

providing a ground truth. For our evaluation, we selected 30 variants subdivided into three subsets each containing 10 variants. We selected the variants by sorting them into three categories (SMALL, MEDIUM, and LARGE) according to their average number of *lines of code (LOC)*. In Table 2, we show the three categories together with information about the average LOC per variant, the average number of executed comparisons, the average number of selected features, and the average runtime of the comparisons. All comparisons were executed by a single developer using HTML report generation and the metric weights from Table 1 in Sect. 3.2 on a laptop with a 2.7 GHz Intel i7 processor and 12 GB RAM. For each category, the first variant was compared with all remaining variants (i.e., in total 27 comparisons were executed) and each comparison between two variants was executed 10 times to reduce the influence of inaccurate runtime measuring.

In addition, to demonstrate the language-independence of our meta-model, we used a set of C++ examples with a variety of language features (i.e., classes, methods, and fields). Executing a preliminary evaluation, we used these examples to analyze whether we can transform them to our meta-model and execute our variability analysis on the resulting meta-model instances.

4.2   Results and Discussion

Next, we report our results and discuss them to answer our research questions.

RQ1 – Language Independence: During the preliminary analysis of the meta-model's language independence, we successfully transformed the used JAVA variants and the C++ examples to our meta-model. Using the discussed compare algorithms, we were able to generate sensible results conforming with expectations of two consulted developers with experience in SPL design. Although, we only analyzed the meta-model's capabilities with two languages, we are confident that the meta-model is capable of storing code for different OOP languages because of their common structure.

RQ2 – Correctness: After executing the comparisons for the selected categories, we manually compared the identified possible relations from the generated HTML reports with the ground truth (i.e., the SNAKEFOP SPL). During this analysis, we found that our algorithms were able to identify all variability relations correctly, which can be accounted for by the used *n:m* algorithms as they generate each possible combination. However, we used the dynamic functionality of the HTML reports to manually reduce the relations to distinct combinations (i.e., each element from one variant is matched to exactly one element from the other variant) and assessed the corresponding similarity values. After consulting two developers with experience in SPL design, we identified that about 70 % of the values were reasonable. Here, we identified that the calculated field similarities were sensible and only the similarity for methods did not always meet the expectations. While, we classified about 90 % of the method signature similarities as sensible, only 50 % of the method body similarities met the expectations. Main reasons were methods of different size where the statements from the smaller method were all contained in the larger method but the overall similarity was calculated in accordance to the larger method.

4.3   Threats to Validity

During the case study, a single developer manually evaluated the results of our algorithms and compared them to the ground truth (i.e., the variability information from the SNAKEFOP SPL). The intuition of other researchers or developers might differ. However, the evaluating developer consulted two developers with experience in SPL design during the classification of the results and, thus, we are confident that the results are close to the expectations by other developers. In addition, our approach uses metrics as heuristic weights to calculate the similarity of compared elements. These metrics are highly dependent on human intuition and the created results might not always conform with expectations of other developers. However, we already gained experience in identifying variability during our research on block-based languages [18–20] and, thus, we argue that the employed metrics create results close to the domain experts' intuition.

Our case study is limited to a single scenario from an SPL with JAVA as OOP language and a preliminary analysis for C++ code. Thus, we cannot generalize the applicability of our algorithms to all OOP languages. However, we are confident that our ideas are transferable to further languages as the JAVA case study and the analysis of C++ code variants showed promising results. In addition, we realized our algorithms by iteratively adding functionality to support comparison of different OOP language features. Only afterwards, we executed comparisons using the selected variants. Thus, we did not overfit our implementation for the used case study and are confident that the algorithms are capable of handling other code. Furthermore, due to the extensible design of our framework and the common elements of all OOP languages considered during the design of our meta-model, we are confident that our algorithms are able to handle further OOP languages (e.g., PYTHON).

5   Related Work

Several techniques have been proposed that aim at revealing the similarity of source code. We contrast this work to our technique proposed in this paper.

Clone Detection: Clone detection is a prominent technique that has been proposed to detect similarities in source code within or between software systems [14]. As such, it is paramount to cope with implementations that result from clone-and-own. While many techniques exist that mainly differ in the underlying program representation (e.g., text-based, token-based, or tree-based), all of them focus on detecting similarities between code fragments. For example, *Hemel et al.* analyze the result of clone detection to perform a large-scale variability analysis with the goal to detect non-propagated patches across LINUX distributions [4]. In contrast to our work, these techniques only focus on cloned parts (except for defining different clone types) and, most notably, do not consider variability semantics, such as relations between similar code fragments.

Code Merging: Using identified variability information, approaches exist to merge software variants in different contexts. *Yoshimura et al.* merge several individual systems in a software family by using a clone classification and analysis approach [21]. However, since their focus is on migration, they do not define variation points (e.g., optional or alternative parts) but only assess the technical opportunities of merging parts of the analyzed systems. *Rubin et al.* propose an advanced algorithm with n-way comparison, which tackles the combinatorial explosion when comparing multiple software systems [16]. However, we provide variability information that could be used for merging in a migration process, while Rubin et al. only focus on merging, thus, omitting variability information.

Reverse Engineering: In addition to the mentioned approaches, there exists work to explicitly reverse engineer variability information. *Klatt et al.* use program dependency graphs (PDGs) and difference analysis to recover variability information between variants of features [6]. Their approach aims at reducing the manual effort of merging these features and focuses on corresponding differences in the code. In contrast, we focus on identifying variability between entire variants. While their approach exploits a language-dependent PDG, we use a flexible meta-model allowing to analyze different languages. *Martinez et al.* propose a generic framework that aims at identifying variability across multiple artifacts (e.g., models, code, and documentation) [11]. To this end, they provide a generic feature-oriented process, where features are explicitly identified, analyzed, and located. Based on this information, a concept for migration to an SPL is proposed. In contrast, we solely focus on source code and do not use feature information while still revealing variability across variants. Moreover, we do not strictly couple our approach with SPL migration (although it could be used in such a process) but also support other use cases such as change propagation. *Linsbauer et al.* provide an approach for extracting variation points between variants and the corresponding feature-to-code mapping [10]. While they also work on implementation artifacts, they require upfront knowledge about features implemented in each variant. In contrast, we do not include feature information and just relate code elements to each other by means of variability relations. *Duszynski et al.* transform variants to a more abstract representation of the system and identify commonalities of variants by building unions of occurrence matrices [2]. While their approach is limited to comparisons of these matrices, we also exploit more syntactical information of the underlying languages. Similar to Duszynski et al., we are able to apply our approach to different languages because our meta-model abstracts from too specific language elements. However, our approach provides a more detailed summary of the results on statement level, complemented by an overall assessment of similarity on block level (e.g. for methods).

Rubin et al. propose a framework for refactoring products into a more feature-centric SPL engineering process [15]. Similar to us, their approach encompasses dedicated phases for comparing and matching. However, it is only applicable to UML and EMF models and mainly focuses on formalizing the merge operator. In contrast, we focus on explicating variability between variants for maintenance activities. *Frenzel et al.* propose an approach to compare product variants on the architectural level [3]. Compared to our approach, their work differs in the considered artifacts (architectural models instead of source code), the general technique (clone detection instead of similarity analysis with variability semantics), and the objective (migration instead of maintenance).

6   Conclusion and Future Work

In this paper, we introduced a model-based variability mining technique for OOP programming languages. Our approach parses a set of source code variants to a language-independent meta-model and executes comparisons between the variants based on this representation. Currently, we realized an $n{:}m$ algorithm to identify the corresponding variability and to generate summarizing reports.

In future work, we plan to optimize our algorithm by automatically exploring the parsed models and ruling out improbable relations to reduce the overall number of comparisons. Furthermore, we plan to adapt algorithms from previous work [18,19] to identify distinct matches from the comparisons and merge all implementation artifacts into a 150 % model together with their annotated variability information. Using the resulting 150 % models, we plan to realize seamless transition from clone-and-own based variant creation to software product lines, for example, by generating annotated code (e.g., using C preprocessors) and corresponding feature mappings. Furthermore, we plan to improve the similarity calculation for method bodies by analyzing them on a more fine grained level.

References

1. Antkiewicz, M., Ji, W., Berger, T., Czarnecki, K., Schmorleiz, T., Lammel, R., Stănciulescu, S., Wąsowski, A., Schaefer, I.: Flexible product line engineering with a virtual platform. In: Proceedings of the International Conference on Software Engineering (ICSE), ICSE 2014, pp. 532–535. ACM (2014)
2. Duszynski, S., Knodel, J., Becker, M.: Analyzing the source code of multiple software variants for reuse potential. In: Proceedings of the Working Conference on Reverse Engineering (WCRE), WCRE 2011. IEEE, pp. 303–307 (2011)
3. Frenzel, P., Koschke, R., Breu, A.P.J., Angstmann, K.: Method for consolidating software variants into product lines. Softw. Qual. J. **17**(4), 331–366 (2009)
4. Hemel, A., Koschke, R.: Reverse engineering variability in source code using clone detection: a case study for linux variants of consumer electronic devices. In: Proceedings of the Working Conference on Reverse Engineering (WCRE), WCRE 2012, pp. 357–366. IEEE (2012)

5. Kapser, C., Godfrey, M.W.: "Cloning Considered Harmful" considered harmful. In: Proceedings of the Working Conference on Reverse Engineering (WCRE), WCRE 2006, pp. 19–28. IEEE (2006)
6. Klatt, B., Krogmann, K., Seidl, C.: Program dependency analysis for consolidating customized product copies. In: Proceedings of the International Conference on Software Maintenance and Evolution (ICSME), ICSME 2014, pp. 496–500. IEEE (2014)
7. Koschke, R.: Survey of research on software clones. In: Duplication, Redundancy, and Similarity in Software. Dagstuhl Seminar Proceedings 06301. Internationales Begegnungs- und Forschungszentrum fur Informatik (IBFI), Schloss Dagstuhl, Germany, Dagstuhl, Germany (2007)
8. Krieter, S., Schroter, R., Fenske, W., Saake, G.: Use-case-specific source- code documentation for feature-oriented programming. In: Proceedings of the International Workshop on Variability Modeling in Software-intensive Systems (VaMoS), VaMoS 2015, pp. 27:27–27:34. ACM (2015)
9. Levenshtein, V.I.: Binary codes capable of correcting deletions, insertions, reversals. Soviet Phys. Doklady **10**(8) (1966)
10. Linsbauer, L., Lopez-Herrejon, R.E., Egyed, A.: Variability extraction, modeling for product variants. Softw. Syst. Model., 1–21 (2016)
11. Martinez, J., Ziadi, T., Bissyande, T.F., Klein, J., Le Traon, Y.: Bottomup adoption of software product lines: a generic and extensible approach. In: Proceedings of the International Software Product Line Conference (SPLC), SPLC 2015, pp. 101–110. ACM (2015)
12. Monden, A., Nakae, D., Kamiya, T., Sato, S., Matsumoto, K.: Software quality analysis by code clones in industrial legacy software. In: Proceedings of the International Symposium on Software Metrics (METRICS), METRICS 2002, pp. 87–94. IEEE (2002)
13. Pohl, K., Bockle, G., van der Linden, F.J.: Software Product Line Engineering: Foundations, Principles and Techniques. Springer, Heidelberg (2005)
14. Roy, C.K., Cordy, J.R., Koschke, R.: Comparison and evaluation of code clone detection techniques and tools: a qualitative approach. Sci. Comput. Program. **74**(7), 470–495 (2009)
15. Rubin, J., Chechik, M.: Combining related products into product lines. In: Lara, J., Zisman, A. (eds.) FASE 2012. LNCS, vol. 7212, pp. 285–300. Springer, Heidelberg (2012). doi:10.1007/978-3-642-28872-2_20
16. Rubin, J., Chechik, M.: N-way model merging. In: Proceedings of the European Software Engineering Conference/Foundations of Software Engineering (ESEC/FSE), ESEC/FSE 2013, pp. 301–311. ACM (2013)
17. Thum, T., Kastner, C., Benduhn, F., Meinicke, J., Saake, G., Leich, T.: FeatureIDE: an extensible framework for feature-oriented software development. Sci. Comput. Program. **79**, 70–85 (2014)
18. Wille, D.: Managing lots of models: the FaMine approach. In: Proceedings of the International Symposium on Foundations of Software Engineering (FSE), FSE 2014, pp. 817–819. ACM (2014)
19. Wille, D., Schulze, S., Seidl, C., Schaefer, I.: Custom-tailored variability mining for block-based languages. In: Proceedings of the International Conference on Software Analysis, Evolution, and Reengineering (SANER), SANER 2016. IEEE (2016)
20. Wille, D., Holthusen, S., Schulze, S., Schaefer, I.: Interface variability in family model mining. In: Proceedings of the International Workshop on Model-Driven Approaches in Software Product Line Engineering (MAPLE), SPLC 2013, pp. 44–51. ACM (2013)

21. Yoshimura, K., Ganesan, D., Muthig, D.: Assessing merge potential of existing engine control systems into a product line. In: Proceedings of the International Workshop on Software Engineering for Automotive Systems (SEAS), SEAS 2006, pp. 61–67. ACM (2006)

User Profiles for Context-Aware Reconfiguration in Software Product Lines

Michael Nieke[1]([✉]), Jacopo Mauro[2], Christoph Seidl[1], and Ingrid Chieh Yu[2]

[1] Technische Universität Braunschweig, Braunschweig, Germany
{m.nieke,c.seidl}@tu-braunschweig.de
[2] University of Oslo, Oslo, Norway
{jacopom,ingridcy}@ifi.uio.no

Abstract. Software Product Lines (SPLs) are a mechanism to capture families of closely related software systems by modeling commonalities and variability. Although user customization has a growing importance in software systems and is a vital sales argument, SPLs currently only allow user customization at deploy-time. In this paper, we extend the notion of context-aware SPLs by means of user profiles, containing a linearly ordered set of preferences. Preferences have priorities, meaning that a low priority preference can be neglected in favor of a higher prioritized one. We present a reconfiguration engine checking the validity of the current configuration and, if necessary, reconfiguring the SPL while trying to fulfill the preferences of the active user profile. Thus, users can be assured about the reconfiguration engine providing the most suitable configuration for them. Moreover, we demonstrate the feasibility of our approach using a case study based on existing car customizability.

Keywords: Dynamic Software Product Line · User profiles · Preferences · Reconfiguration · Context-awareness

1 Introduction

SPLs are a technique to capture families of closely related software systems and to allow large-scale reuse [21]. In a *variability model*, the conceptual commonalities and variabilities of software systems are captured, thus defining the set of all possible configurations. Feature Models (FMs) represent the commonalities and variabilities in terms of a hierarchical structure of features. Features can be enriched by feature attributes, extending the variability of a feature by additional variables. A *configuration* is a set of selected features and values for attributes.

User customization already is of big importance in several domains, e.g., in the automotive domain, you can configure your car based on your own preferences. Multiple drivers of a car may have different preferences regarding how the car is configured and which features are most desirable under certain contexts. For instance, the Volkswagen AG presented a prototypical car at the Consumer Electronic Show (CES) 2015 which supports several user customizations

© Springer International Publishing AG 2016
T. Margaria and B. Steffen (Eds.): ISoLA 2016, Part II, LNCS 9953, pp. 563–578, 2016.
DOI: 10.1007/978-3-319-47169-3_44

at runtime, such as the change of the engine profile, allowing a more powerful or power-saving engine performance [6,25]. Moreover, nowadays, most devices have to interact and adapt based on their environment. Consequently, the context of a device needs to be considered in the configuration process of an SPL. Additionally the desire of users to customize a product may arise at runtime under certain contexts. For instance, drivers may want to activate a line assistance systems only when they are driving on a highway. For practical purposes, it may be important also to minimize the number of changes that are required to be performed, thus generating configurations that should be similar to the initial one as much as possible.

In standard SPL development, users can customize the product only when ordering a product or at runtime using settings in the software. The first case lacks the possibility to customize the user's end device after ordering it, while the second case always requires user interaction.

In [15], we already consider and propose an integrated approach to model the influence of contextual information on SPLs. To this end, we use a model-based representation of contextual information and represent the influence of the context on particular features. Based on this representation, we developed HyVarRec, a context-aware reconfiguration engine which incorporates the FM, the influence of contextual information on features and the current context to reconfigure the product accordingly. This approach, however, lacks the possibility to take the user preferences into account and, similar to other context-aware approaches, it does not distinguish between required adaptation due to context information and desired customization wishes of users.

In this paper, to overcome these limitations, we integrate customization wishes of users into SPLs. To this end, we introduce a notion of *user profiles* containing sets of prioritized *preferences* reflecting the wishes of users. However, in contrast to constraints, it is not mandatory to satisfy preferences as they only need to be satisfied if it is possible. As a main contribution, we extended our approach [15] to take user profiles into consideration, thus, creating a reconfiguration engine that incorporates contextual information, user profiles and the current context at once. To prove the feasibility of our approach, we extend HyVarRec and we apply it to reconfigure and maximize the preferences of some users and minimize the changes to be performed within scenarios inspired by an existing Volkswagen AG SPL for cars.

In Sect. 2, we present background on the concepts our methodology is founded on. In Sect. 3, we introduce a running example based on a real car SPLs and the CES example of Volkswagen as well as exemplary contextual information and user preferences. In Sect. 4, we explain how SPLs can be enriched by user profiles and preferences. In Sect. 5, we present the extension of HyVarRec to cope with user preferences. In Sect. 6, we show the feasibility of our methodology by applying HyVarRec to several scenarios. In Sect. 7, we discuss related work. In Sect. 8, we close with a conclusion and an outlook to future work.

2   Background

Feature Models (FMs) are a hierarchical representation of the variability of an SPL. FMs consist of features representing configurable functionality of a system [12]. Each feature can have several child features and an FM has exactly one root feature. As an example, Fig. 1 depicts an instance of a FM. In this case, the root feature is `Car` while `Engine Profile` and `Gear Shift` are two of its children. Features can be *mandatory* or *optional* and can be organized in *alternative* or *or* groups. In alternative groups, exactly one feature has to be selected, whereas in or groups, at least one feature has to be selected. For instance, in Fig. 1, the feature `Lane Assist` is optional and the feature `Engine Profile` is mandatory and has its children organized as alternative group. Feature attributes are typed variables associated with a feature which are used to express more fine-grained variability [2]. It is possible to specify a domain for each attribute to limit its value range. For example, in Fig. 1, the feature `Cruise Control` owns an attribute `maxSpeed` of type `int` that has a domain of $[0, 300]$.

Features are realized by other artifacts (e.g., code or documentation) that may evolve and exist in different *versions*. To keep track of the evolution of features, it is necessary to explicitly capture these feature versions: old versions of a feature may indeed be preferred over the newer versions, e.g., to preserve the compatibility to other systems. Moreover, feature versions may have dependencies among each other. Following [27], we use Hyper Feature Models (HFMs) to represent the different versions and new restrictions for them. HFMs define a first-class concept for *feature versions* to represent different revisions of the artifacts associated with a feature (e.g., source code). For example, in Fig. 1, the feature `Lane Assist` has two different versions: a first one denoted as `1.0` and its following version denoted as `2.0`.

In FMs, cross-tree constraints (CTCs) are used to specify additional dependencies between features which are not specified via the hierarchical structure of the FM. CTCs can be defined as Boolean formulas on features and expressions on feature attributes. Additionally, CTCs can be used to restrict the version range of a feature by having a version-aware constraint language [27]. A *configuration* of an FM is a set of selected features, feature versions and values for the relevant feature attributes. A configuration is *valid* if it conforms with the hierarchy of the FM and the CTCs.

In [15], we presented an extension to FMs to capture contextual information allowing to model the dependencies of the selected features or attributes with respect to some external parameters and environmental situations. Contextual information is captured with identifier-value pairs where a context is associated with a value. For instance, in Fig. 1, the context capturing the air pollution is represented by an identifier `Pollution` that can take a value in the domain $[0, 100]$. This context is used to force the selection of a more conservative driving setting when the pollution increases over certain thresholds. This is done by enforcing Validity Formulas (VFs), i.e., propositional formulas associated with a feature that can relate features and attributes with context values. For instance, in Fig. 1, the feature `Progressive` has associated the VF `Pollution ¡ 50` that forces the feature to be selectable only if the value of the `Pollution` is below 50.

As a configuration of an SPL may be invalidated due to changed values for contextual information and the violation of VFs, the product needs to be reconfigured. In [15], we proposed a first version of a reconfiguration engine that was able to verify if a configuration was valid when given a certain context. In case of invalidity, the reconfiguration engine returned a new valid configuration that was most similar to the original one.

3   Running Example

In this section, we introduce a SPL based on a CES car prototype of Volkswagen that we use to show the feasibility of our approach. The running example is taken from our case study.

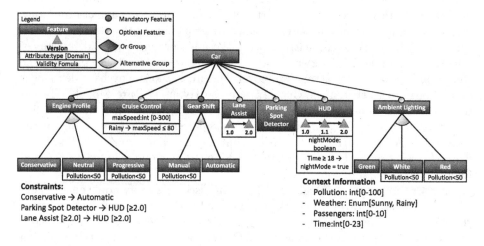

Fig. 1. Hyper feature model and context model for a car SPL.

Figure 1 shows the HFM of our running example. To customize the driving experience itself, it is possible to select different `Engine Profiles` and `Gear Shift` mechanisms as it is already state of the art in current cars. Thus, to drive sporty, it is possible to select a `Progressive Engine Profile` and a `Manual Gear Shift`, whereas a more comfortable driving experience can be achieved by selecting the `Conservative Engine Profile` and an `Automatic Gear Shift`. For drivers who do not want to drive very sporty, but sometimes accelerate to pass other cars, the `Neutral Engine Profile` is a suitable configuration option.

To provide even more comfort, several configurable driver assistance systems are modeled, which are already common in modern cars. For instance, the `Cruise Control` automatically accelerates to a given speed but always keeps a safe distance to cars in front of the own car. However, as some drivers never want to drive faster than a certain speed, the `Cruise Control` may be customized by defining a maximum speed using the attribute `maxSpeed`, e.g., to conform with the maximum speed permitted by law. As assistance systems are evolving and use new techniques, we model different versions of the `Lane Assist` and the `HUD` which is a heads up display providing additional information to the driver. The `HUD` in versions `1.0` and `1.1` is projecting information alongside the central field of view of the driver such as the current speed limit. To provide even more information and to reduce distraction of the driver, the `HUD` starting with version `2.0` is extended by augmented reality functionality and is able to show information on the windshield which is projected as overlay on the real world. For instance, a navigation system may show an arrow indicating a turn directly on the road at the position of the turn in the real world. Version `2.0` of the `Lane Assist` is using the augmented reality feature of the `HUD 2.0` to indicate the line which was exceeded by the driver. Other features are the `Parking Spot Detector`, which facilitates the parking of the car by indicating free parking spots, and the `Ambient Lighting` of the car, which can be configured to the users' tastes with colors `Green` (useful to influence a more calm and power saving mood), `White` (standard mood) and `Red` (powerful mood).

To allow a more convenient way to configure the car, we introduce the following *partial pre-configurations*:

$$
\begin{array}{ll}
\textit{Sport} & : \texttt{Progressive, Manual, Red} \\
\textit{Comfort} & : \texttt{Neutral, Automatic, White} \\
\textit{Eco} & : \texttt{Conservative, Automatic, Green}
\end{array}
$$

Each of these partial pre-configurations represents a certain type of driver: the sporty, the comfortable, and the eco-minded.

3.1 Contextual Information

The environment may have influence on the software system of the car. For instance, as a result of a changed GPS position of a car, the maximum allowed speed of the `Cruise Control` may be changed to conform to local jurisdiction of a country. To capture the impact of the environment on the software system of the car, we provide the following four types of contextual information.

- `Pollution` captures the amount of contaminants in the air
- `Weather` captures the current weather condition
- `Passengers` captures the number of passengers currently in the car
- `Time` captures the current hour of a day

The values of this context are collected by the car itself (i.e., `Passengers`, `Time`) or by external services (i.e., `Pollution`, `Weather`).

As air pollution is a severe problem in bigger cities, local authorities enforce the usage of the *Eco* partial pre-configuration for each car to keep the air pollution as low as possible. This is captured by making the features contradicting the *Eco* partial pre-configuration only selectable if the `Pollution` is less than 50.

To reduce the frequency of car accidents, local authorities limit the maximum allowed speed depending on the current weather. This is captured by limiting the attribute maxSpeed to be less than or equal to 80 km/h if the Weather is Rainy.

The last context dependent constraint regulates the use of the nightMode of the HUD. The night mode of electronic devices is a common feature activated to not distract users with the brightness of a display during night. Displays are dimmed and the colors are turned to darker ones. As the nightMode is an additional configuration explicitly for the HUD it is modeled as an attribute. Furthermore, this allows us to keep the HUD customizable, as the nightMode could be enabled following the drivers desires. As a safety restriction, a VF is used to enforce the activation of the nightMode after 18:00 (6 pm).

3.2   User Preferences

Multiple drivers may want to have different configurations of a car under certain contexts. In this paper, to mimic the preferences of two different drivers, we created two profiles: the *sporty driver* and the *safety-minded* driver.

The *sporty driver* (see Listing 1.1) has a passion for speed and wants to drive very sporty when driving alone. However, when he is accompanied, his highest priority becomes the comfort of the passenger. As he is not familiar with Manual Gear Shift, he still prefers the Automatic feature. He uses his portable media player in combination with the HUD. However, since his media player is very old and not compatible with the latest version of the HUD, he prefers the older version of the Heads Up Display. As the *sporty driver* often passes other cards when driving fast, he does not like to use the Lane Assist as it vibrates when crossing lanes. However, when driving with Cruise Control, he loses joy in passing other drivers and, as a result, he wants the support of the Lane Assist in this case.

The *safety-minded driver* (see Listing 1.2) is concerned about ecological and safety features. She wants to have all possible assistance systems in the newest version to receive as much support as possible for the driving process, such as the Parking Spot Detector or Cruise Control. Additionally, as her eyesight has worsened in the last few years, she prefers to enable the nightMode of the HUD already after 16:00 (4 pm).

4   Modeling Software Product Lines with User Preferences

In this section, we present the two major extensions for the meta model of context-aware SPLs presented in [15]: versions and user profiles.

Modeling Versions

To be able to constrain and target specific versions of the feature, we extend the propositional language to take into account as possible atom a single version of a feature. We use a dedicated construct to restrict the version selection for a feature. Each feature reference can have such a restriction for its versions. In particular, there are two different types of version restrictions: range restrictions (e.g., $[1.0 - 2.1]$) and relative restrictions (e.g., $[\geq 2.0]$ or $[1.1]$ specifying an exact version number). Thus, the expression language maintains the same expressive power of [15] being able to use the standard Boolean operators and arithmetic operators for the VFs and CTCs.

Modeling User Profiles

To allow more fine-grained user customization at runtime, we introduce *user profiles* which represent the desires of users. In particular, this means the desire to select or deselect features under certain circumstances. *User profiles* consist of a set of preferences which are linearly ordered according to their importance and priority. Preferences are "weak" or "soft" constraints in the sense that they only have to be satisfied if no other constraint or more important preference contradicts them [26]. Therefore, while CTCs and VFs can potentially forbid the possibility of having admissible valid configuration, this is not possible for preferences.

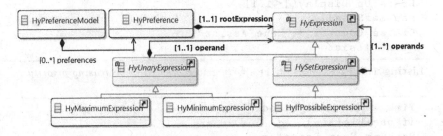

Fig. 2. Preference meta model (excerpt of meta model).

Similarly to VFs, we represent preferences as propositional formulas having as atoms features, versions, attributes, contexts and literal values. The excerpt of the meta model used to formalize the preference is presented in Fig. 2. However, in comparison to VFs, preferences may require a more expressive power. In particular, we consider the wish of users to select as many features as possible from a set of features. As our former expression language does not support expressions to support operations on a set of operands, we extend our expression language with the `HySetExpression`.

A user profile is represented as a `HyPreferenceModel`. Each `HyPreference-Model` consists of a list of `HyPreferences`. The order of the preferences in the list represents their priority, higher importance first. Moreover, each preference is described by a propositional formula, modeled with a `HyExpression`. To allow for giving a preference on a group of features, we introduce as syntactic sugar the `HyIfPossibleExpression` type, which is a subtype of the `HySetExpression`. Intuitively, this expression is used to state the preference that as many of its operands as possible should be satisfied. For instance, an expression such as `ifPossible({Progressive, Manual})` tries to select both `Progressive` and

`Manual` if possible, just one of the two if one of them can not be selected or none if both can not be selected. Only one `HyIfPossibleExpression` expression can be used per preference. Moreover, based on the common preferences usually stated, we also restrict the use of `HyIfPossibleExpression` to the root of an expression or as a right-hand side of a non nested implication.

Finally, as additional construct to require the preference to maximize or minimize the value of an attribute, we define the `HyMaxmimumExpression` and `HyMinimumExpression`, which may be used to state that a given attribute should be set to its maximum or minimum possible value, respectively.

As an example, the preferences of the *sporty driver* and the *safety-minded driver* presented in Sect. 3 can be formalize as presented in Listings 1.1 and 1.2, respectively.

```
1    Passengers ≥ 2 → ifPossible(Comfort)
2    Passengers ≥ 2 → Cruise Control
3    Automatic
4    ifPossible(Sport)
5    Heads Up Display [≤1.1]
6    max(maxSpeed)
7    Cruise Control → Lane Assist
8    ¬Lane Assist
```

Listing 1.1. Preferences of the *sporty driver* ordered in decreasing priority.

```
1    Time ≥ 16 → nightMode = true
2    ifPossible(Eco)
3    Parking Spot Detector
4    Heads Up Display [≥2.0]
5    Cruise Control
6    Lane Assist [≥2.0]
7    Lane Assist
```

Listing 1.2. Preferences of the *safety-minded driver* ordered in decreasing priority.

Note that, as the *sporty driver* does not want to have the `Lane Assist` assistance system, his profile contains the ¬`Lane Assist` preference. However, as he wants to select the `Lane Assist` when using `Cruise Control`, the preference `Cruise Control → Lane Assist` has higher priority than the other preference. As far as the *safety-minded driver* is concerned, we would like to remark that since she wants to have a `Lane Assist` activated, but preferably in version `2.0`, we have to model this in two different preferences requiring the activation of the version `2.0` with a higher priority.

5   Reconfiguration Engine

In this section, we describe the contextual reconfiguration tool `HyVarRec` and explain how the problem of reconfiguration in the presence of preferences is

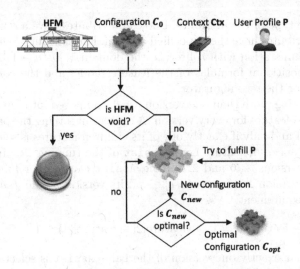

Fig. 3. Work-flow of the contextual reconfigurator.

modeled as a multi-objective optimization problem. We first describe the general execution flow of HyVarRec before entering more into the details of the encoding of the constraints and how the FM entities are translated into an optimization problem.

HyVarRec requires different sources of input, as depicted in Fig. 3: the HFM, the current configuration C_0 of the remote device, the current values of the contextual information Ctx, and the user profile P. The primary function of the contextual reconfigurator is to provide valid configurations C_{new} for the context Ctx that maximize the preferences of user profile P. In case of two configurations of equal quality regarding the maximization of the user preferences, the one that minimizes the difference between the initial configuration C_0 is provided. This means that HyVarRec first tries to minimize the number of feature removals needed to transform C_0 into C_{new} and, later, to maximize the number of attributes which values could be kept the same. Finally, HyVarRec outputs the configuration C_{opt}, which is the optimal configuration in the given context, satisfying as many preferences of P as possible.

The reconfiguration engine relies on Constraint Programming (CP). A Constraint Problem consists of a set of variables, each of which is associated with a finite domain of values that it can assume and a set of constraints defining all the admissible assignments of values to variables [13]. In particular, HyVarRec tries to solve a Constraint Optimization Problem (COP), a constraint problem where constraints are used to narrow the space of admissible solutions and the goal is to not just find any solution but a solution that minimizes (or maximizes) a specific objective function.

In accordance with the methodology presented in [2], we transform the "standard" feature model part of an HFM into propositional formulas on features. Then, we translate each feature and feature attribute to an integer variable. Whereas features have the domain of $[0, 1]$, for feature attributes, the domain depends on the type of the attribute. Boolean attributes have a domain of $[0, 1]$ and integer attributes have their specified domain. For attributes which can have values of an enumeration with n literals, the domain is $[0, (n-1)]$. These variables, the propositional formulas of the feature model and the constraints are used as input for the reconfigurator.

Features having more than one version are decomposed into a parent feature having one child feature for every version. A constraint forcing the parent feature to be selected if and only if exactly one of its children features is selected is then added. For instance, for feature `Lane Assist` of the running example in Fig. 1, there are two versions: `1.0` and `2.0`. `Lane Assist` can be therefore encoded in $feature[1]$, its version `1.0` in $feature[2]$ and its version `2.0` in $feature[3]$ with the following requirement.

$$\text{feature}[1] = 1 \leftrightarrow (\text{feature}[2] + \text{feature}[3]) = 1$$

This ensures that exactly one version of the `Lane Assist` is selected if the feature itself is selected. Moreover, if any version is selected, the feature itself has to be selected, as well. Hence, the remaining constraints of the HFM can still use `Lane Assist`. Version-aware constraints can encompass multiple versions defined by the expressions introduced in Sect. 4. Considering the following constraint: $e \rightarrow LaneAssist[\geq 1.0]$ encompasses the versions `1.0` and `2.0`. To determine all involved versions, we use the successor/predecessor relation following the approach introduced in [27]. Afterwards, we translate such an expression to the sum of all encompassed versions.

The expressions of the constraints are translated to their respective textual representation. For instance, a `HyAdditionExpression` with operands *op1* and *op2* is translated to: *op1* + *op2*. Also the preferences of the user profiles are encoded as expressions over a set of numerical variables. The only element which can not be translated trivially is the `ifPossible` expression. As we mentioned in Sect. 4, we can use the `isPossible` expression in two situations: as root of an expression or as right-hand side of a non-nested implication. In the first case, we translate it as the sum of its operands, as the optimizer tries to maximize the value of all operands in the sum. For instance, we translate the expression `ifPossible({A,B,C})`, with feature `A` translated to $feature[1]$, `B` to $feature[2]$ and `C` to $feature[3]$, to:

$$(\text{feature}[1] = 1) + (\text{feature}[2] = 1) + (\text{feature}[3] = 1)$$

In the second case, we translate the implication to a sum of implications of the single operands of the `ifPossible` expression. For instance, we translate the expression $e \rightarrow ifPossible(\{A, B\})$, with feature `A` translated to $feature[1]$, `B` to $feature[2]$ to:

$$(e_t \rightarrow feature[1] = 1) + (e_t \rightarrow feature[2] = 1)$$

where e_t is the translation of the `ifPossible`-free expression. In this way the semantics of the `ifPossible` is preserved and the maximal amount of the `ifPossible` features is selected when the left-hand side of the implication is true. Note that `HyVarRec`automatically transforms Boolean expression into integers, thus, allowing the user to write arithmetic expression over Boolean terms that are treated as 1 if true, 0 otherwise.

To potentially allow `HyVarRec` to support different FM modeling engines, we require the FM with its entities and constraints to be given as a list of propositional constraints as described before. In contrast, the preferences are given as arithmetic expressions or preferences to maximize or minimize a given attribute. The EBNF grammar defining the propositional constraint and the preferences is formally defined in https://github.com/HyVar/hyvar-rec/blob/master/SpecificationGrammar/SpecificationGrammar.g4 following the ANTLR conventions.[1]

`HyVarRec` is an anytime solver: it first determines a valid configuration, if one exists, and then proceeds in finding those that satisfy more preferences or are more similar to the initial configuration. The optimization proceeds in phases: when a valid configuration is found, additional constraints are imposed to search only valid configurations that satisfy additional user preferences. The process terminates when no other valid configuration can be found, meaning that the last determined configuration is the one maximizing the preferences and similarities with the initial configuration. In this way, `HyVarRec` allows users to interrupt the computation as soon as a good-enough configuration was found even though it might not be the best possible configuration. This may be extremely useful when handling large and complex SPLs and there are strong limitations on the computation and time resources to get a valid configuration as with Dynamic Software Product Lines (DSPLs).

`HyVarRec` relies on *MiniSearch* [24] to conduct the search and on *MiniZinc* [18] for the definition of the constraints. `HyVarRec` uses the Gecode constraint solver [10], the default solver adopted by MiniSearch because it implements natively the incremental API needed by MiniSearch to post additional constraint without restarting the solving process from scratch. However, other MiniZinc solvers that do not support the recently defined MiniZinc incremental API could still be used at the price of restarting their engine during the optimization process. Hence, the majority of the other state of the art solvers (e.g., the Java-based Choco [22], the SAT based MiniSatid [16]) can be integrated in `HyVarRec` by relying directly on the MiniSearch capabilities.

The output of `HyVarRec` is a sequence a JSON objects each of which represents a configuration satisfying more preferences or more similar to the initial one. When the entire search space is explored and the optimal configuration is found, we translate the respective configuration to an output format and notify the user that this is the optimal configuration. The schema of the JSON output format of `HyVarRec` is formalized in https://github.com/HyVar/hyvar-rec/blob/master/spec/hyvar_output_schema.json.

The main difference of `HyVarRec` w.r.t. its previous version is the introduction of the language to express the preferences. This has an impact also on the

---

[1] ANTLR (ANother Tool for Language Recognition) - http://www.antlr.org/.

formalization of the COP problem due to the fact that the metrics to optimize are established by the preferences. Moreover, to ease it use by external tools, HyVarRec now requires a unique JSON object that unifies all the input entities in a unique representation.

HyVarRec is written in python, open source, and freely available from https://github.com/HyVar/hyvar-rec.

6   Case Study

In this section we show the feasibility of our approach by applying HyVarRec on the car SPL detailed in Sect. 3.

Imagine that the *sporty driver* leaves home in the morning driving alone. In the residential areas, the measurement of the Pollution level is below 50. Due to his preferences, the car is running on Automatic Gear Shift and Progressive Engine Profile. The Ambient Lighting is selected and configured to Red and he is using the HUD in version 1.1 to connect his media player. As he is not using the Cruise Control, the Lane Assist is disabled.

On the way, he picks up a friend, which causes the *Comfort* partial pre-configuration to be prioritized over *Sport* as he is no longer alone in the car. Consequently, the car configuration is changed to Neutral Engine Profile and White Ambient Lighting. The Automatic Gear Shift is kept but the Cruise Control gets activated. However, the Weather is Sunny with low traffic on the highway. Therefore, the maxSpeed of the Cruise Control allows him to speed up to the maximum speed of 300 km/h. As the Cruise Control was activated, the Lane Assist is enabled too, but uses version 1.0 as the HUD is activated in version 1.1.

The car enters the city and the Pollution increases to 75. This contextual change enforces the car to reconfigure to the *Eco* partial pre-configuration. Therefore, the car now runs on Conservative engine mode with Green Ambient Lighting. As he prefers an older version of the HUD, the Parking Spot Detector is not enabled when he arrives at his destination.

Assume that the time is now 15:00 (3 pm) and the friend, who is the safety-minded driver, is driving the car home. As she prefers the *Eco* partial pre-configuration, the car remains in Conservative engine mode with Green Ambient Lighting and Automatic Gear Shift. Additionally, the HUD is updated to the newest version and, based on her preferences, the Parking Spot Detector is enabled with augmented reality support of the HUD. For a convenient ride, the Cruise Control is enabled, as well as the newest version of the Lane Assist.

During the ride back, the time passes 16:00 (4 pm) and it starts to rain. These two contextual changes cause the car to reconfigure. The maximum speed of Cruise Control is reconfigured to 80 km/h. Moreover, her preference causes the nightMode of the HUD to be switched on. The rain causes the Pollution level to drop to below 50, which would potentially enable a new reconfiguration of the car, but as she prefers the Eco profile, the selected sub-features of Engine Profile, Gear Shift, and Ambient Lightning remain unchanged.

Using our implementation, we were able to model all necessary features, constraints, contextual information, validity formulas, and preferences contained in the case study. Furthermore, we were able to provide the modeled case study as input for `HyVarRec`, generating the first initial configuration by hand and simulate the effects of the context changes. The resulting configurations match the scenario we described in this section, thus showing the suitability of our methodology to provide optimal configurations with respect to the user preferences.

`HyVarRec` has recently been adopted as the reconfiguration engine in an integrated toolchain to develop, deploy and reconfigure SPLs in an industrial setting [4].

7 Related Work

Preferences are a widely studied topic in the field of social sciences and artificial intelligence. Preferences are often assumed to be given by users. However, there are approaches where preferences are derived by inpsecting the history or use of an application or software. For instance, in [30], preferences are learned by analyzing the history of the different users, creating a profile of preferences for every user. Similarly, in [1], user preferences for web search engine optimization are learned from user behavior. In particular, preferences are widely investigated in the domain of product recommendation systems, e.g., in [29], which deals with preferences for music recommendation systems. While these approaches are extremely interesting and may prove useful for our future work, in this work, we assume that users elicit their preferences explicit.

Preferences are also well studied in a qualitative or quantitative way in the field of decision theory [8] and in Constraint Programming [26]. Preferences are often incorporated in COPs [3,7] and are also denoted as soft constraints [26]. `HyVarRec` is built on top of these approaches and it exploits all the experience accumulated in the Constraint Programming community to speed up the search of the configuration maximizing user preferences.

In the domain of SPLs, multiple work has been done on modeling contextual information to be used in software systems. Several authors introduce an additional feature model which consists of the contextual information modeled as features [9,11,28]. The relation of context and features is modeled as CTCs between the original feature model and the context feature model. However, the expressiveness of feature models is relatively coarse grained. Thus, for contexts which may have a big value domain, e.g., the `Pollution` or the `Time` contexts of our running example, features are not suitable to model each of these values. Additionally, for the sake of separation of concerns, a different and suitable notation for contextual information seems sensible instead of using feature models for it. To the best of our knowledge, none of these methodologies consider the reconfiguration of the SPL based on user preferences.

Other related works are [5,14], which propose approaches for reconfiguration similar to ours encompassing contextual information in the feature model. However, differently from us, for the reconfiguration, they explicitly model *triggers* which are fired based on values of the contextual information and have composition rules which model how the SPL has to be reconfigured. Additionally, they do not consider user preferences. The afore mentioned approaches model the influence of context on the feature selection directly, i.e., prescribing the selection of a feature in a certain context. In our approach, we model in which contexts a certain feature is selectable, allowing a better integration with user preferences.

In [20] a concept for DSPLs encompassing contextual information and user preferences is introduced. A *Decision Maker* decides if and how the DSPL has to be reconfigured. However, no notion of user preferences or contextual information is given, thus making unclear how to model and incorporated preferences with the DSPL. Moreover, there are no details on how the *Decision Maker* processes these information.

Some approaches like [17,19] assign values or costs to features that allows during the (re-)configuration to optimize certain properties (e.g., costs and productivity) to create a best configuration considering a multi-dimensional optimization problem. However, to simulate user preferences, these approaches require each user to specify values and cost for each feature which is not suitable for large models. Moreover, optimizing certain properties severely differentiates from trying to fulfill an ordered set of preferences.

8   Conclusion

In this paper, we introduced an approach to allow users to influence the reconfiguration of a context-aware SPL based on their preferences. To this end, we extended our preliminary work [15] to propose a formalism that can capture, in a concise way, not only contextual information but also user preferences as weak or soft constraints [26]. Conceptually, user preferences differ from (hard) constraints in the sense that they specify desired features of users and are not mandatory to be satisfied. Therefore, users can customize their SPL based on their desires and, additionally, can make them dependent on the current context. The preferences are summarized in *user profiles* as a linearly ordered set, ordered by priority.

Furthermore, we extended the context-aware reconfiguration engine HyVarRec to be able to consider user profiles. The new version of HyVarRec tries to maximize the number of satisfied preferences contained in the current profile while generating a valid configuration. We showed the feasibility of our methodology by modeling a realistic SPL of a customizable car, encompassing contextual information. We modeled two different user profiles and defined a scenario in which the car is influenced by contextual changes. We simulated the scenario by utilizing HyVarRec with the respective input. HyVarRec successfully created new valid configurations and maximized the given user profiles.

For future work, we are interested in extending our concepts by means of capturing evolution of the Feature Model (FM) and the user profiles and to address some limitations of the current model. For instance, we would like to allow the possibility to use context to force directly the selection of a particular feature. Additionally, we are interested in creating user profiles by learning from user behavior or understanding their polices [23] and how they can be enforced. Finally, we are interested in evaluating our approach using the toolchain presented in [4], analyzing the scalability of our approach considering varying and larger FMs.

Acknowledgments. This work was partially supported by the DFG (German Research Foundation) under grant SCHA1635/2-2 and by the European Commission within the project HyVar (grant agreement H2020-644298).

References

1. Agichtein, E., Brill, E., Dumais, S., Ragno, R.: Learning user interaction models for predicting web search result preferences. In: Proceedings of the 29th Annual International ACM SIGIR Conference on Research and Development in Information Retrieval, SIGIR 2006. ACM, New York (2006)
2. Benavides, D., Trinidad, P., Ruiz-Cortés, A.: Automated reasoning on feature models. In: Pastor, O., Falcão e Cunha, J. (eds.) CAiSE 2005. LNCS, vol. 3520, pp. 491–503. Springer, Heidelberg (2005). doi:10.1007/11431855_34
3. Boutilier, C., Brafman, R.I., Domshlak, C., Hoos, H.H., Poole, D.: Preference-based constrained optimization with CP-nets. Comput. Intell. **20**, 137–157 (2004)
4. Chesta, C., et al.: A toolchain for delta-oriented modeling of software product lines. In: Margaria, T., Steffen, B. (eds.) ISoLA 2016. LNCS, vol. 9953, pp. 497–511. Springer, Cham (2016)
5. da Silva Costa, P.A., Marinho, F.G., de Castro Andrade, R.M., Oliveira, T.: Fixture - A tool for automatic inconsistencies detection in context-aware SPL. In: ICEIS (2015)
6. Darryll Harrison, W.G.: CES 2016: Volkswagen brings gesture control to mass production with the E-Golf Touch (2016). http://media.vw.com/release/1123/
7. Domshlak, C., Rossi, F., Venable, K.B., Walsh, T.: Reasoning about soft constraints, conditional preferences: complexity results and approximation techniques. arXiv (2009)
8. Doyle, J., Thomason, R.H.: Background to qualitative decision theory. AI Mag. **20**(2), 55–68 (1999)
9. Fernandes, P., Werner, C., Murta, L.: Feature modeling for context-aware software product lines. In: Seke (2008)
10. GECODE (2015). http://www.gecode.org/
11. Hartmann, H., Trew, T.: Using feature diagrams with context variability to model multiple product lines for software supply chains. In: SPLC IEEE Computer Society (2008)
12. Kang, K.: Analysis, Feature-oriented Domain (FODA): Feasibility Study; Technical report CMU/SEI-90-TR-21 - ESD-90-TR-222. Software Engineering Inst., Carnegie Mellon Univ. (1990)
13. Mackworth, A.K.: Consistency in networks of relations. Artif. Intell. **8**(1), 99–118 (1977)
14. Marinho, F.G., Andrade, R.M.C., Werner, C.: A verification mechanism of feature models for mobile and context-aware software product lines. In: Software Components, Architectures and Reuse (SBCARS) (2011)

15. Mauro, J., Nieke, M., Seidl, C., Yu, I.C.: Context aware reconfiguration in software product lines. In: Proceedings of the Tenth International Workshop on Variability Modelling of Software-Intensive Systems - VaMoS 2016 (2016)

16. Minisatid. https://github.com/broesdecat/Minisatid

17. Murashkin, A., Antkiewicz, M., Rayside, D., Czarnecki, K.: Visualization and exploration of optimal variants in product line engineering. In: Proceedings of the 17th International Software Product Line Conference, SPLC 2013. ACM, New York (2013)

18. Nethercote, N., Stuckey, P.J., Becket, R., Brand, S., Duck, G.J., Tack, G.: MiniZinc: towards a standard CP modelling language. In: Bessière, C. (ed.) CP 2007. LNCS, vol. 4741, pp. 529–543. Springer, Heidelberg (2007). doi:10.1007/978-3-540-74970-7_38

19. Ochoa, L., González-Rojas, O., Thüm, T.: Using decision rules for solving conflicts in extended feature models. In: Proceedings of the ACM SIGPLAN International Conference on Software Language Engineering, SLE. ACM, New York (2015)

20. Parra, C., Blanc, X., Duchien, L.: Context awareness for dynamic service-oriented product lines. In: Proceedings of the 13th International Software Product Line Conference, SPLC 2009. Carnegie Mellon University, Pittsburgh (2009)

21. Pohl, K., Böckle, G., van der Linden, F.J.: Software Product Line Engineering: Foundations: Principles and Techniques. Springer, New York (2005)

22. Prud'homme, C., Fages, J.-G., Lorca, X.: Choco3 Documentation. TASC, INRIA Rennes, LINA CNRS UMR 6241, COSLING S.A.S. (2014)

23. Reiff-Marganiec, S.: A structured approach to VO reconfigurations through policies. In: Proceedings Third Workshop on Formal Aspects of Virtual Organisations. EPTCS, FAVO 2011, Sao Paolo, Brazil, 18 October 2011, vol. 83, pp. 22–31 (2011)

24. Rendl, A., Guns, T., Stuckey, P.J., Tack, G.: MiniSearch: a solver-independent meta-search language for MiniZinc. In: Pesant, G. (ed.) CP 2015. LNCS, vol. 9255, pp. 376–392. Springer, Heidelberg (2015). doi:10.1007/978-3-319-23219-5_27

25. Robarts, S.: Volkswagen's Golf R touch concept shows off the car cockpit of the future (2015). http://www.gizmag.com/volkswagen-golf-r-touch/35472/

26. Rossi, F., van Beek, P., Walsh, T. (eds.) Handbook of Constraint Programming. Elsevier (2006)

27. Seidl, C., Schaefer, I., Aßmann, U.: Capturing variability in space and time with hyper feature models. In: Proceedings of the Eighth International Workshop on Variability Modelling of Software-Intensive Systems - VaMoS 2014 (2014)

28. Ubayashi, N., Nakajima, S.: Context-aware feature-oriented modeling with an aspect extension of VDM. In: Proceedings of the ACM Symposium on Applied Computing, SAC 2007. ACM, New York (2007)

29. Yoshii, K., Goto, M., Komatani, K., Ogata, T., Okuno, H.G.: Hybrid collaborative and content-based music recommendation using probabilistic model with latent user preferences. In: ISMIR, vol. 6 (2006)

30. Young, S., Hong, J.-H., Kim, T.-S.: A formal model for user preference. In: Proceedings of IEEE International Conference on Data Mining (2002)

Refactoring Delta-Oriented Product Lines to Enforce Guidelines for Efficient Type-Checking

Ferruccio Damiani and Michael Lienhardt[✉]

University of Torino, Turin, Italy
{ferruccio.damiani,michael.lienhardt}@unito.it

Abstract. A Software Product Line (SPL) is a family of similar programs generated from a common code base. Delta-Oriented Programming (DOP) is a flexible and modular approach to construct SPLs. Ensuring type safety in an SPL (i.e., ensuring that all its programs are well-typed) is a computationally expensive task. Recently, five guidelines to address the complexity of type checking delta-oriented SPLs have been proposed. This paper presents algorithms to refactor delta-oriented SPLs in order to follow the five guidelines. Complexity and correctness of the refactoring algorithms are stated.

1 Introduction

A *Software Product Line* (SPL) is a family of similar programs, called *variants*, with well documented variabilities [4]. *Delta-Oriented Programming* (DOP) [3, 14] is a flexible and modular transformational approach to implement SPLs. A DOP product line comprises a *Feature Model* (FM), a *Configuration Knowledge* (CK), and an *Artifact Base* (AB). The FM provides an abstract description of variants in terms of *features* (each representing an abstract description of functionality): each variant is described by a set of features, called a *product*. The AB provides the (language dependent) code artifacts used to build the variants, namely: a (possibly empty) base program from which variants are obtained by applying program transformations, described by *delta modules* which can add, remove or modify code. The CK provides a mapping from products to variants by describing the connection between the code artifacts in the AB and the features in the FM: it associates to each delta module an *activation condition* over the features and specifies an *application ordering* between delta modules. In DOP, variants are generated by selecting a valid set of features from the FM, which activates the corresponding delta modules that are then applied in order to the base program. Delta modules are constructed from *delta operations* that can

---

The authors of this paper are listed in alphabetical order. This work has been partially supported by project HyVar (www.hyvar-project.eu), which has received funding from the European Union's Horizon 2020 research and innovation programme under grant agreement No. 644298; by ICT COST Action IC1402 ARVI (www.cost-arvi.eu); and by Ateneo/CSP D16D15000360005 project RunVar.

© Springer International Publishing AG 2016
T. Margaria and B. Steffen (Eds.): ISoLA 2016, Part II, LNCS 9953, pp. 579–596, 2016.
DOI: 10.1007/978-3-319-47169-3_45

add, modify and *remove* content to and from the base program (e.g., for Java programs, a delta module can add, remove or modify classes interfaces, fields and methods). As pointed out in [15], such flexibility allows DOP to support *proactive* (i.e., planning all products in advance), *reactive* (i.e., developing an initial SPL comprising a limited set of products and evolving it as soon as new products are needed or new requirements arise), and *extractive* (i.e., gradually transforming a set of existing programs into an SPL) SPL development [11].

Different type checking approaches for DOP have been studied [3,5,7] and some of them have been implemented for the ABS modeling language [1,10]. Recently [5], five programming guidelines that makes type checking more efficient have been proposed. Some of these guidelines are quite straightforward to follow, like the absence of useless operation (Sect. 4), others include subtleties and transforming an existing SPL into one that follows such guidelines can be quite challenging. This paper recalls the five guidelines and introduces for each of them an algorithm to refactor any delta-oriented SPL into an equivalent one that follows the given guideline. We illustrate these algorithms on a simple running example and discuss the complexity and correctness of the refactoring algorithms.

Section 2 introduces the example that will be used throughout the paper and recalls the IMPERATIVE FEATHERWEIGHT DELTA JAVA (IFΔJ) core calculus for delta-oriented SPLs of Java programs. Section 3 introduces some auxiliary notations. Sections 4, 5, 6, 7 and 8 present the five guidelines and their refactoring algorithms, respectively. Section 9 briefly discusses related work. Section 10 concludes the paper.

2   The Imperative Featherweight Delta Java Calculus

In this section, we introduce the structure of an IFΔJ SPL, the running example of this paper and briefly recall the IFΔJ [3] core calculus. In IFΔJ there is no concrete syntax for the feature model and the configuration knowledge of an SPL L. We instead use the following notations: $L.\texttt{features}$ is the set of features; $L.\texttt{products}$ specifies the products (i.e., a subset of the power set $2^{L.\texttt{features}}$); $L.\alpha$ maps each delta module name d to its activation condition; and $L.\texttt{order}$ (or $<_L$, for short) is the application ordering between the delta modules. Both the set of valid products and the activation condition of the delta modules are expressed as propositional logic formulas Φ where propositional variables are feature φ. A formula Φ represents the set of products $\{\overline{\varphi} \mid \overline{\varphi} \text{ validates } \Phi\}$ (see [2] for a discussion on other possible representations) and is described with the following syntax:

$$\Phi ::= \mathbf{true} \mid \varphi \mid \Phi \Rightarrow \Phi \mid \neg\Phi \mid \Phi \wedge \Phi \mid \Phi \vee \Phi.$$

As usual, we say that a propositional formula Φ is *valid* if it is true for all values of its propositional variables. To avoid over-specification, the order $<_L$ can be partial. We assume *unambiguity* of the product line, i.e., for each product, any total ordering of the activated delta modules that respects $<_L$ generates the same variant (see [3,12] for a discussion on effective means to ensure unambiguity).

$$EPL.\texttt{features} \;=\; \{\text{fLit, fAdd, fToInt, fToString, fEval1, fEval2}\}$$
$$EPL.\texttt{products} \;=\; \text{fLit} \wedge \text{fToInt} \wedge (\text{fEval1} \Rightarrow \text{fToString}) \wedge (\text{fEval1} \vee \text{fEval2}) \wedge \neg(\text{fEval1} \wedge \text{fEval2})$$

$$EPL.\texttt{order} \;=\; \{\text{dAdd}\} <_L \{\text{d\_notTostr, dAdd\_notTostr}\} <_L \{\text{dRMEval1}\} <_L \{\text{dEval2}\}$$
$$EPL.\alpha \;=\; \text{dAdd} \mapsto \text{fAdd},$$
$$\text{d\_notTostr} \mapsto (\neg\text{fToString}), \quad \text{dAdd\_notTostr} \mapsto (\text{fAdd} \wedge \neg\text{fToString}),$$
$$\text{dRMEval1} \mapsto \neg\text{fEval1}, \quad \text{dEval2} \mapsto \text{fEval2}$$

```
// Base program
class Exp extends Object { // To be used only as a type (i.e., not to be instantiated)
  Int toInt() { return new Int(); }
  String toString() { return ""; }
  Lit eval() { return (new Lit()).setLit(this.toInt()); }
}
class Lit extends Exp {
  Int val;
  Lit setLit(Int x) { this.val=x; return this; }
  Int toInt() { return this.val; }
  String toString() { return this.val.toString(); }
}
class Test extends Object {
  String test(Exp x) { return x.eval().toString(); }
}
// Delta Modules
delta dAdd {
  adds class Add extends Exp {
    Exp a;    Exp b;
    Int toInt() { return this.a.toInt().add(this.b.toInt()); }
    String toString() { return this.a.toString() + "+" + this.b.toString(); }
  }
}
delta d_notTostr {
  modifies class Exp { removes toString; }
  modifies class Lit { removes toString; }
}
delta dAdd_notTostr {  modifies class Add { removes toString; }  }
delta dRMEval1 {  modifies class Exp { removes eval }  }
delta dEval2 {  modifies class Exp { adds Int eval() {return this.toInt();} }  }
```

Fig. 1. Expression Product Line: FM (top), CK (middle), AB (bottom)

The running example of this paper is derived from the *Expression Product Line* (EPL) benchmark [13] (see also [3]) which encodes the following grammar for expressions over integers:

Exp ::= Lit | Add   Lit ::= <non−negative−integers>   Add ::= Exp "+" Exp

The EPL has 6 products, described by two feature sets: one concerned with data—fLit, fAdd—and one concerned with operations —fToInt, fToString, fEval1, fEval2. Features fLit and fToInt are mandatory, while the other features are optional with the two following constraints: exactly one between fEval1 and fEval2 must be selected; and fEval1 requires fToString. Each variant of the EPL contains a class Exp that represents an expression equipped with a subset of the following operations: toInt returns the value of the expression as an integer (an object of class Int); toString returns the expression as a String; and eval returns in some variants the value of the expression as a Lit (the subclass of Exp representing literals), and in the other variants the value of the expression as an Int. The definition of the EPL example is given in Fig. 1. The partial order

$$
\begin{array}{llr}
P & ::= \overline{CD} & \text{Program} \\
CD & ::= \textbf{class C extends C} \, \{ \, \overline{AD} \, \} & \text{Class} \\
AD & ::= FD \mid MD & \text{Attribute (Field or Method)} \\
FD & ::= \text{C f} & \text{Field} \\
MD & ::= \text{C m}(\overline{\text{C x}}) \, \{\textbf{return } e; \} & \text{Method} \\
e & ::= \text{x} \mid e.\text{f} \mid e.\text{m}(\overline{e}) \mid \textbf{new } \text{C}() \mid (\text{C})e \mid e.\text{f} = e \mid \textbf{null} & \text{Expression}
\end{array}
$$

$$
\begin{array}{llr}
L & ::= FM \quad CK \quad AB & \text{Product Line} \\
AB & ::= P \quad \overline{\Delta} & \text{Artifact Base} \\
\Delta & ::= \textbf{delta d} \, \{ \, \overline{CO} \, \} & \text{Delta Module} \\
CO & ::= \textbf{adds } CD \mid \textbf{removes C} \mid \textbf{modifies C [extends C$'$]} \, \{ \, \overline{AO} \, \} & \text{Class Operation} \\
AO & ::= \textbf{adds } AD \mid \textbf{removes a} \mid \textbf{modifies } MD & \text{Attribute Operation}
\end{array}
$$

Fig. 2. Syntax of IFJ (top) and of IFΔJ (bottom)

L.order is expressed as a total order on a partition of the set of delta modules. To make the example more readable, in the artifact base we use the JAVA syntax for operations on strings and sequential composition —encoding in IFΔJ syntax is straightforward (see [3] for examples). Note that, in the method Test.test (in the base program), the expression x.eval() has type Lit if feature fEval1 is selected (for this reason feature fEval1 requires feature fToString) and type Int otherwise.

In the following, we first introduce the IMPERATIVE FEATHERWEIGHT JAVA (IFJ) calculus, which is an imperative version of FEATHERWEIGHT JAVA [9], and then we introduce the constructs for variability on top of it. The abstract syntax of IFJ is presented in Fig. 2(top). Following [9], we use the overline notation for (possibly empty) sequences of elements: for instance $\overline{e}$ stands for a sequence of expressions. Variables x include the special variable this (implicitly bound in any method declaration MD), which may not be used as the name of a method's formal parameter. A program P is a sequence of class declarations $\overline{CD}$. A class declaration **class C extends** C$'$ $\{ \, \overline{AD} \, \}$ comprises the name C of the class, the name C$'$ of the superclass (which must always be specified, even if it is the built-in class Object), and a list of field and method declarations $\overline{AD}$. All fields and methods are public, there is no field shadowing, there is no method overloading, and each class is assumed to have an implicit constructor that initializes all fields to **null**. The subtyping relation $<:$ on classes, which is the reflexive and transitive closure of the immediate subclass relation (given by the **extends** clauses in class declarations), is assumed to be acyclic. Type system, operational semantics, and type soundness for IFJ are given in [3].

The abstract syntax of the IMPERATIVE FEATHERWEIGHT DELTA JAVA (IFΔJ) language is given in Fig. 2(bottom). An IFΔJ program L comprises: a feature model FM, a configuration knowledge CK, and an artifact base AB. Recall that we do not consider a concrete syntax for FM and CK and use the notations L.features, L.products, $L.\alpha$, and L.order ($<_L$ for short) introduced above. The artifact base comprises a possibly empty or incomplete IFJ program P, and a set of delta modules $\overline{\Delta}$.

A delta module declaration Δ comprises the name d of the delta module and class operations $\overline{CO}$ representing the transformations performed when the delta module is applied to an IFJ program. A class operation can add, remove, or modify a class. A class can be modified by (possibly) changing its super class and performing attribute operations $\overline{AO}$ on its body. An *attribute name* a is either a field name f or a method name m. An attribute operation can add or remove fields and methods, and modify the implementation of a method by replacing its body. The new body may call the special method `original`, which is implicitly bound to the previous implementation of the method and may not be used as the name of a method. The operational semantics of IFΔJ variant generation is given in [3].

Definition 1 (Getter on *FM* and *CK*). *Let Φ be extended to include module names* d *as propositional variables. The formula* $L.\text{FMandCK} \triangleq L.\text{products} \land \bigwedge_d (d \Leftrightarrow L.\alpha(d))$ *specifies the products and binds each variable* d *to the activation condition of module* d *(i.e., it specifies which modules are activated for each product).*[1]

3 Auxiliary Notations

In this section we introduce some auxiliary notations that will be used in the definition of our different refactoring algorithms. The following notation unifies delta operations on classes and on attributes in a single model, in order to uniformly manage these two kinds of operations in our refactoring algorithms.

Notation 1. *A reference, written ρ, is either a class name* C *or a qualified attribute name* C.a. *We abstract a delta module by a set of* Abstract Delta Operations *(ADO) which are triplets* (**dok**, ρ, D) *where: i)* **dok** *is a delta operation keyword* (**adds, removes** *or* **modifies**), *ii)* ρ *is the reference on which* **dok** *is applied, and iii)* D *is the data associated with this operations. The data corresponding to adding an element (a class or an attribute) is the element itself; the data corresponding to removing an element is empty; and the data corresponding to modifying a class (resp. a method) is the new* **extends** *statement (resp. the new version of the method). Given an ADO* o, *we denote its operator as* o.**dok**, *its reference as* o.ρ, *and its data as* o.D.

This notation is illustrated by the following examples. In particular, the first example shows that a **modifies** operation on a class C that contains only **adds** operations on attributes is represented by the set of ADOs containing only the **adds** operations: the **modifies** C operation is only a syntactic construction to introduce these **adds** operations and is not included in our representation.

Example 1. The delta module dEval2 in Fig. 1 that modifies classes Exp by adding a method eval to it, is modeled with one ADO:

---

[1] The last occurrence of d in $L.\text{FMandCK}$ is not used as a variable: it is used as argument of the map $L.\alpha$ to obtain the activation condition of module d.

(**adds**, Exp.eval, Lit eval() {**return** this.toInt();})

The following notation introduces the *Family Class Signature Table* (FCST) that is used to retrieve important type information from an SPL L.

Notation 2. *An* Attribute Type T *is either a field type* C *or a method type* $(\overline{C}) \to C'$*. Given the data of an attribute* D*, we write* type(D) *the type of this data (e.g.,* type(C m(C' x)) *is* $(C') \to C$*). Given an attribute reference* ρ = C.a*,* $L.\text{FCST}[\rho]$ *returns the mapping* $[T_i, \Phi_i]_{i \in I}$ *stating which are the possible types* T_i *of* C.a *in* L*, with* Φ_i *being the condition for that attribute to have that type. We write* dom($L.$FCST) *the set of references* ρ *such that* $L.\text{FCST}(\rho) \neq \emptyset$*. Given two class names* C_1 *and* C_2*,* $L.\text{FCST}(C_1 <: C_2)$ *returns the condition* Φ *for which* C_2 *is the super class of* C_1 *in* L*. Finally,* $L.\text{FCST}(\rho)$ *is defined similarly to* $L.\text{FCST}[\rho]$*, except that it follows the inheritance relation (e.g., if* C.a $\in$ dom($L.$FCST) *and* $L.\text{FCST}(C' <: C) \neq$ **false***, we have* C'.a $\in$ dom($L.$FCST))*,*

Finally, our last notation is used to iterate over the delta modules of an SPL.

Notation 3. *The set of delta module names declared in* L *is denoted as* dm(L) *and we write* $L.$d *the delta module named* d *in* L*. When* L *is clear from the context, we write* before(d) *the set of delta module names that are before* d *for* $L.$order*.*

4   G1: Absence of Useless Operations

A simple way to make typing SPL more efficient is to avoid cluttering it with code that will never be included into the SPL's variants. We call *useless operation* a delta operation that introduces some code or subtyping relation that will never be present in a variant, and avoiding such operation has two benefits: first, it makes typing quicker because part of the typing process is not lost on checking useless declarations; and second, it makes typing complete as all discovered typing errors correspond to an error in one of the SPL's variants. The guideline and the definition of the enforced property are presented as follows:

G1. Ensure that the product line does not contain useless operations.

Definition 2 (Useless operation and module). *The declaration, addition or modification of an element* ρ *in a module* d *is* useless *iff there exists a set of delta modules* $\{d_i \mid 1 \leq i \leq n\}$ *that are applied after* d *and that either remove or replace (i.e., modifies it without calling* original*)* ρ *such that* $(L.\text{FMandCK} \wedge d) \Rightarrow \bigvee_{1 \leq i \leq n} d_i$ *is valid. A module* d *is* useless *iff* $L.\text{products} \Rightarrow \neg L.\alpha(d)$ *is valid.*

The avoidance and removal of useless operations is a classic concept in software product lines, and some refactoring algorithms and code smells have already been defined to address this problem. In particular, [16] proposes a large set of code smells and refactoring algorithms for delta-oriented programming, which includes the smells *Dead Delta Action*, *Dead Delta Module*, and *Empty Delta Module* with corresponding refactoring algorithms. Applying these code smells to identify which operations and delta modules can safely be removed, and the corresponding refactoring algorithms to actually remove them would enforce G1 in any delta-oriented SPL.

5   G2: Type Uniformity

One of the causes of the complexity of type checking a delta-oriented SPL is the fact that two different modules may declare the same attribute with two different types. For instance, our EPL example contains two variations of the method eval: one that returns an Int and one that returns a Lit. Hence, for the type system to be complete, it needs to check the method Test.test twice, once for each possible type of the eval method. In general, the fact that a unique attribute can have several types may cause a method to be type-checked an exponential number of times.

Type uniformity is the property that all attributes declared in the SPL only have one type. Type checking is thus simpler (a method must be type-checked only once), and also using and extending such SPL is simpler.

The guideline and the definition of the enforced property are presented as follows:

G2. Ensure that the product line is type-uniform.

Definition 3 (Type-uniformity). *A product line L is* type-uniform *iff for all* C.a $\in$ dom(L.FCST), *the set L.FCST(C.a) is a singleton.*

Figure 3 presents the refactorG2 refactoring algorithm that transforms any IFΔJ SPL to enforce G2. It uses an auxiliary algorithm refactorG2Data, presented in Fig. 4. The algorithm takes in input the SPL L to refactor and a *renaming function* σ. This function σ is injective, takes in input an attribute with its type and returns a new attribute name.

The algorithm is constructed with a loop iterating over all the delta operations in the SPL that renaming all encountered attributes. We distinguish two kind of operations: **removes** that does not associate data nor a type to the attribute it removes; while **adds** and **modifies** do associate data and a type to the manipulated attribute. The **removes** operation is handled in lines 4–17. An interesting property of the **removes** operation is that it can be applied on an attribute, whatever its type is. Consider for instance adding the operation (**removes**, Exp.eval, $\emptyset$) to the EPL example: such operation can be applied to both variations of the eval method. Therefore, if the first and second variations of eval were respectively renamed eval1 and eval2, the remove operation must be duplicated so to still capture the two variations of the eval method. This duplication is handled as follows: line 5 identifies all the possible types of the attribute and either there is just one type, in which case no duplication is required and the renaming is directly applied to the attribute (line 7); or there are several types,

```
1    RefactorG2(L, σ) =
2      for d ∈ dm(L) do
3        for o ∈ L.d do
4          if (o.dok = removes) and (∃C, a, o.ρ = C.a) then  // 1. the removes case
5            {Tᵢ ↦ Φᵢ}₁≤ᵢ≤ₙ ←L.FCST[o.ρ]
6            if n = 1 then
7              o.ρ ←C.σ(T₁, a) // in place renaming
8            else
9              L.d ←L.d \ o // extract the operation from the module: we duplicate it
10             for i ∈ [1..n] do
11               L ←L + d' fresh with {
12                 L(d') ←{ (o.dok, C.σ(Tᵢ, a), ∅) }
13                 L.α(d') ←L.α(d) ∧ Φᵢ
14                 L.order(d') ←L.order(d)
15               }
16             done
17           fi
18         else if ∃C, a, o.ρ = C.a then  // 2. the adds and modifies case
19           o.ρ ←C.σ(type(o.D), a)
20           (Dᵢ, Φᵢ)₁≤ᵢ≤ₙ ← refactorG2Data(L, σ, o.D)
21           if n = 1 then
22             o.D ←D₁ // in place renaming
23           else
24             L.d ←L.d \ o // extract the operation from the module: we duplicate it
25             for i ∈ [1..n] do
26               L ←L + d' fresh with {
27                 L(d') ←{ (o.dok, o.ρ, Dᵢ) }
28                 L.α(d') ←L.α(d) ∧ Φᵢ
29                 L.order(d') ←Lorder(d)
30               }
31             done
32           fi
33         fi
34       done
35     done;
```

Fig. 3. The type uniformity refactoring algorithm

in which case the operation is extracted from its module (line 9), and duplicated in a fresh delta module, one new operation for each type of the attribute (the **for** loop in lines 10–16). When duplicating, the orders of the new delta modules are the same as before but the activation conditions are restricted to be active only for the considered variation of the attribute (line 13). The **adds** and **modifies** operations are handled in lines 18–32. Here, the type of the attribute is given in the data o.D so that renaming the attribute can be done directly (line 19). However, if the attribute is a method, its data (i.e., its body) can contain field accesses and method calls that must be renamed as well. Moreover, as the types of these field accesses and method calls are not given, we need to consider all the possible types of these attributes (similarly to the **removes** case), and duplication may occur. The renaming and duplication of data is done in the auxiliary algorithm refactorG2Data presented in Fig. 4 and follows the same principle as the duplication done in the **removes** case. This refactorG2Data algorithm takes in input the SPL L (to have access to its type information L.FCST), the renaming function σ and the data to be renamed and duplicated. It returns a set of renamed data D_i, together with the condition Φ_i in which this data is valid

E:Var
$$\frac{\Gamma(x) = C}{\Gamma, \sigma \vdash x : [(x, C) \mapsto \textbf{true}]}$$

E:Null
$$L, \Gamma, \sigma \vdash \textbf{null} : [(\textbf{null}, \bot) \mapsto \textbf{true}]$$

E:Access
$$\frac{L, \Gamma, \sigma \vdash e : [(e_i, T_i) \mapsto \Phi_i]_{i \in I} \quad I' = \{i \mid i \in I \wedge T_i.\textbf{f} \in dom(L.\text{FCST})\} \quad \forall i \in I', L.\text{FCST}(T_i.\textbf{f}) = [C_j \mapsto \Phi_j]_{j \in J_i}}{L, \Gamma, \sigma \vdash e.\textbf{f} : [(e_i.\sigma(T_j, \textbf{f}), T_j) \mapsto \Phi_i \wedge \Phi_j]_{i \in I', j \in J_i}}$$

E:Call
$$\frac{\begin{array}{c} L, \Gamma, \sigma \vdash e : [(e_i, T_i) \mapsto \Phi_i]_{i \in I} \\ L, \Gamma, \sigma \vdash e_k : [(e_l, T_l) \mapsto \Phi_l]_{l \in L_k} \quad I' = \{i \mid i \in I \wedge T_i.\textbf{m} \in dom(L.\text{FCST})\} \\ \forall i \in I', L.\text{FCST}(T_i.\textbf{m}) = [((C_{1,j}, \dots C_{m_j,j}) \to C_j) \mapsto \Phi_j]_{j \in J_i} \quad J_i' = \{j \mid j \in J_i \wedge m_j = n\} \end{array}}{L, \Gamma, \sigma \vdash e.\textbf{m}(e_1, \dots, e_n) : \left[\begin{array}{c} (e_i.\sigma((C_{1,j}, \dots C_{m_j,j}) \to C_j, \textbf{m})(e_{l_1}, \dots, e_{l_n}), C_j) \\ \mapsto \Phi_i \wedge (\bigwedge_{1 \le k \le n} \Phi_{l_k}) \wedge \Phi_j \end{array} \right]_{i \in I, j \in J_i', l_k \in L_k}}$$

E:New
$$L, \Gamma, \sigma \vdash \textbf{new } C() : [(\textbf{new } C(), C) \mapsto \textbf{true}]$$

E:Cast
$$\frac{L, \Gamma, \sigma \vdash e : [(e_i, T_i) \mapsto \Phi_i]_{i \in I}}{L, \Gamma, \sigma \vdash (C)e : [((C)e_i, C) \mapsto \Phi_i]_{i \in I}}$$

E:Assign
$$\frac{L, \Gamma, \sigma \vdash e.\textbf{f} : [(e_i, C_i) \mapsto \Phi_i]_{i \in I} \quad L, \Gamma, \sigma \vdash e' : [(e_j, T_j) \mapsto \Phi_j]_{j \in J}}{L, \Gamma, \sigma \vdash e.\textbf{f} = e' : [(e_i = e_j, C_i) \mapsto \Phi_i \wedge \Phi_j]_{i \in I, j \in J}}$$

R:Field
$$\text{refactorG2Data}(L, \sigma, C) = [C \mapsto \textbf{true}]$$

R:Method
$$\frac{L, \overline{x : C}, \sigma \vdash e : [(e_i, T_i) \mapsto \Phi_i]_{i \in I}}{\text{refactorG2Data}(L, \sigma, (\overline{\{C\ x\}}) \to C' \ \{ \ \textbf{return } e; \ \}) = [(\overline{\{C\ x\}}) \to C' \ \{ \ \textbf{return } e_i; \ \} \mapsto \Phi_i]_{i \in I}}$$

Fig. 4. Renaming and duplicating method bodies

(similarly to the **removes** case, where the renaming $\sigma(T_i, \textbf{a})$ was valid only when Φ_i was true). The computation of the duplicated data is done in line 20, and is handled as before: either there is just one data, in which case no duplication is required and the renaming is applied in place (line 22); or there are several data, in which case the operation is extracted from its module (line 24), and duplicated in a fresh delta module, one new operation for each data (the **for** loop in lines 25–31). When duplicating, the orders of the new delta modules are the same as before but the activation conditions are restricted to be active only for the considered variation of the data (line 28).

Application to the EPL example. As we previously discussed, our EPL example is not type uniform: the method Exp.eval may return an Int or a Lit. Applying our refactoring algorithm on this example, with the first (resp. second) variation of eval renamed in eval1 (resp. eval2) has two effects on the EPL. First it simply changes the name of eval in the base program and in the delta modules dRMEval1 and dEval2 (line 19 of our algorithm). Second, because Exp.eval has two types, the duplication of the method Test.test raises two data, and so that method is extracted from its class and duplicated in two new delta modules, one where eval1 is called while the second calls eval2. The following excerpt shows the modification done by our refactoring algorithm to the EPL example:

```
// Base program
class Exp extends Object { // To be used only as a type (i.e., not to be instantiated)
    ...
    Lit eval1() { return (new Lit()).setLit(this.toInt()); }
}
    ...
class Test extends Object { }

    ...
// Delta Modules
    ...
delta dRMEval1 {   modifies class Exp { removes eval1 } }
delta dEval2 {   modifies class Exp { adds Int eval2() {return this.toInt();} } }
delta dTestEval1 {   modifies class Test { adds String test(Exp x) { return x.eval1().toString(); } } }
delta dTestEval2 {   modifies class Test { adds String test(Exp x) { return x.eval2().toString(); } } }
```

Properties. Correctness and complexity of the refactoring algorithm are stated as follows.

- **Correctness of refactorG2.** Given a software product line L and an injective renaming function σ, for all product p of L such that the variant P of p can be generated, p is also a product of $\mathsf{RefactorG2}(L, \sigma)$, its variant P' can also be generated and we have that $P' = \sigma(P)$.
- **Complexity of refactorG2.** The refactoring algorithm $\mathsf{RefactorG2}$ is exponential in time and space.

6   G3: Acyclic Inheritance

The acyclicity of the inheritance graph is an important property that must be enforced in most object-oriented programming languages such as Java. In general, checking this property is exponential in time (as it must be enforced for every variant of the SPL). However, this complexity can be reduced to linear if the global inheritance graph defined by the different **extends** statements present in the SPL is itself acyclic. Indeed, the inheritance graph of every variant is included into this global one so that the acyclicity of the global one implies the acyclicity of the inheritance graph of all the variants. It is thus natural to propose the following guideline:

G3. Ensure that the product line's inheritance graph is acyclic.

Definition 4. *Given a product line L, we write $\mathsf{C}_0 <: \mathsf{C}_1 <: \ldots <: \mathsf{C}_n \in L.\mathsf{FCST}$ iff for all $0 \le i < n$, we have $L.\mathsf{FCST}(\mathsf{C}_i <: \mathsf{C}_{i+1}) \ne$ **false**. We say that the inheritance graph of a product line L is acyclic if there exists no sequence of classes $(\mathsf{C}_i)_{1 \le i \le n}$ such that $\mathsf{C}_0 <: \ldots <: \mathsf{C}_n <: \mathsf{C}_0 \in L.\mathsf{FCST}$ holds.*

To illustrate how our refactoring algorithm resolves inheritance loops, let us consider the example in Fig. 5 which represents an inheritance loop between the classes C_i with $0 \le i \le 4$. Here, we suppose that the variants of the SPL are well-typed so that every variant includes just a part of this loop: in particular, the class C_0 has a maximal ancestor, C_3 in our example, meaning that there exists no variant in which C_4 is an ancestor of C_0. Therefore, it is correct to split

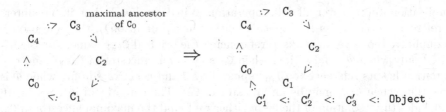

Fig. 5. Example of inheritance loop resolution

```
1   refactorG3(L) =                              18   refactorG3Dup(L, C, C′, Φ) =
2     for C₀ <: ... <: Cₙ <: C₀ ∈ L.FCST do     19     for d ∈ dm(L) do
3       Φ ← L.FCST(C₀ <: C₁)                     20       for o ∈ L.d do
4       i ← 0                                     21         if (o.ρ = C or C ∈ o.D)
5       C ← C₀                                    22            and (⊨ L.products ∧ L.α(d) ∧ Φ) then
6       while(⊨ L.products ∧ Φ) and (i < n) do   23            L.d ← L.d \ o
7         C ← fresh                               24            L ← L + d₁ fresh with {
8         refactorG3Dup(L, Cᵢ₊₁, C, Φ)
9         i ← i + 1;                              25               L(d₁) ← { (o.dok, C′, o.D[ᶜ′/c]) ) }
10        Φ ← Φ ∧ L.FCST(Cᵢ <: Cᵢ₊₁)             26               L.α(d₁) ← L.α(d) ∧ Φ
11      done                                      27               L.order(d₁) ← Lorder(d)
12      if i < n then                             28            } +d₂ fresh with {
13        L.FCST(C <: Object) ← L.FCST(C)         29               L(d₂) ← { (o.dok, C, o.D) }
14      else                                      30               L.α(d₂) ← L.α(d) ∧ ¬Φ
15        error                                   31               L.order(d₂) ← Lorder(d)
16      fi                                        32            }
17    done;                                       33         fi
                                                  34       done
                                                  35     done;
```

Fig. 6. The acyclic inheritance refactoring algorithm

(or duplicate) the classes C_1, C_2 and C_3 in two: one copy that can be ancestors of C_0 and that do not extend C_4, and one copy that inherit from C_0. The result of this duplication on our example is shown on the right side of Fig. 5.

Figure 6 presents our refactoring algorithm called refactorG3 that transforms any IFΔJ SPL into an equivalent that follows G3. Our algorithm takes in argument the SPL L to refactor, and iterates over all the inheritance loops to resolve them. The core of the algorithm is the **while** loop in lines 6–11 that iterates from the class C_0 and duplicates all its ancestors until finding the maximal ancestor of C_0. Our algorithm uses several variables. i is the index of the last class we considered in our algorithm; it is initialized to 0 (we start from the class C_0) and incremented at each iteration of the while loop. Φ has two purposes but is principally the constraint that we use to find the maximal ancestor: it accumulates the activation condition of all the $C_j <: C_{j+1}$ statements, thus stating at each iteration of the **while** loop which products have the $C_0 <: \ldots <: C_i$ inheritance relation. Hence, when the formula $L.\text{products} \wedge \Phi$ has a solution (written $\models L.\text{products} \wedge \Phi$ in line 6), a variant with such inheritance relation exists, and the first time that formula does not have any solution, C_i is the maximal ancestor of C_0. Finally, C is the name of the last duplicated class: it is initialized to C_0, and at each iteration of the **while** loop, it is set to a fresh name, i.e., the name of the replica of the class C_{i+1}. The duplication of the class C_{i+1} is done in the auxiliary function refactorG3Dup, presented in the right part of Fig. 6. The duplication iterates over all delta operations o in L, and each time it encounters a reference to the class to duplicate (either in $o.\rho$ or in $o.D$), the operation o is duplicated: one variation keep referencing the original C_{i+1} name, but is activated only when Φ is false (i.e., when C_0 may be an ancestor of C_{i+1}), and one variation has its reference to C_{i+1} replaced by C and is activated only when Φ is true (i.e., when C_{i+1} may be an ancestor of C_0). The conditional in lines 12–16 concludes the resolution of the loop: either we found the maximal ancestor of C_0, in which case we set its super class to Object (in line 13), or there is no maximal ancestor, in which case there exists a product that contains the full loop: hence, L is ill-typed and our algorithm returns an error (in line 15).

Properties. Correctness and complexity of the refactoring algorithm are stated as follows.

- **Correctness of refactorG3.** Given a software product line L such that non of its variant contains an inheritance loop, for all product p of L such that the variant P of p can be generated, p is also a product of RefactorG3(L, σ), its variant P' can also be generated and we have that P' is identical to P, up to class renaming (due to the fresh class name creation in line 7).
- **Complexity of refactorG3.** The refactoring algorithm RefactorG3 is exponential in time and space.

7   G4: Non Overlapping Modules

Due to the possibly exponential duplication of code it introduces, refactoring an SPL into a type-uniform equivalent may not be advisable in some cases. The following guideline aims at helping the understanding of an SPL implementation by decoupling the sources of non type-uniformity.

G4. Ensure that, for all distinct modules d_1 and d_2, if the set comprising d_1 and d_2 is not type-uniform then their activation conditions are mutually exclusive.

Figure 7 presents our refactoring algorithm called refactorG4 that transforms any IFΔJ SPL into an equivalent that follows G4. This algorithm is based on the fact that G4 is a direct consequence of L not containing any remove operation on an element ρ being followed by an opposite **adds** operation. Therefore, our algorithm iterates over all the delta operations in the input SPL L and looks for an **adds** operation that follows a **removes** operation. The iteration is done in *descending order*: we use the operator $\downarrow_L$ that orders its input set following the opposite order of $<_L$. When a **adds** and an opposite and preceding **removes** operations are found (in lines 10–11), the algorithm calls the function refactorG4Ext which updates the activation condition of the **removes** operation and then calls the function refactorG4Upd which updates the activation condition of the **adds** and **modifies** operations that could occur before.

```
 1   refactorG4(L) =
 2     for d ∈↓_L(dm(L)) do
 3       for o ∈ L.d do
 4         if o.dok = adds then
 5           Φ ←¬L.α(d)
 6           for d' ∈↓_L(before(d)) do
 7             for o' ∈ L.d' do
 8               if (o'.dok = removes)
 9                  and (o'.ρ = o.ρ) then
10                 L ←refactorG4Ext(L, d', o', Φ)
11                 L ←refactorG4Upd(L, d', o'.ρ, Φ)
12               fi
13             done
14           done
15         fi
16       done
17     done;
```

```
18   refactorG4Ext(L, d, o, Φ) =
19   .  L.d ←L.d \ o
20      L ←L + d' fresh with {
21        L(d') ←{ o }
22        L.α(d') ←L.α(d) ∧ Φ
23        L.order(d') ←L.order(d)
24      }
25      return L;
26
27   refactorG4Upd(L, d, ρ, Φ) =
28      for d' ∈↓_L(before(d)) do
29        for o ∈ L.d' do
30          if o.ρ = ρ then
31            if o.dok = removes then
32              return L
33            else
34              L ←refactorG4Ext(L, d', o, Φ)
35            fi
36          fi
37        done
38      done
39      return L;
```

Fig. 7. Changing the activation condition of operations to achieve G4

Application to the EPL example. Our EPL example does not follow the G4 guideline: the **true** activation condition of the base program (which introduces the first variation of the **eval** method) has a non-empty intersection with the delta module **dEval2**. Applying our refactoring algorithm on this example has two effects on the EPL. First, the activation condition of **dRMEval1** is changed to ¬fEval1 ∧ ¬fEval2 due to the call to refactorG4Ext in line 10. Note that, following Definition 2, this delta module is now *useless* as it can never be activated anymore. Second, the method **Exp.eval** is extracted from the base program and put in a fresh delta module with ¬fEval2 as activation condition due to the call to refactorG4Upd in line 11.

Properties. Correctness and complexity of the refactoring algorithm are stated as follows.

- **Correctness of refactorG4.** Given a software product line L, the two following statements are equivalent:
  (i) p is a product of L and P is its corresponding variant
  (ii) p is a product of refactorG4(L) and P is its corresponding variant
- **Complexity of refactorG4.** The refactoring algorithm RefactorG4 is quadratic in time and space.

8   G5: Uniform Partitioning

We introduce our final guideline with the following consideration: implementing or modifying a product line involves editions of the feature model, the configuration knowledge and the artifact base that may affect only a subset of the

```
1   partitionG5(L) =
2     S_m ←∅
3     for (T, D) ∈ im(L.dFCST) do
4       if #D > 1 then
5         S_m ←S_m ∪ {D}
6       fi
7     done
8     res ←∅
9     for p ∈ L.products do
10      D ←∅
11      for d ∈ ⋃_{D'∈S_m} D' do
12        if p ⊨ L.α(d) then
13          D ←D ∪ {d}
14        fi
15      done
16      placed ←false
17      for (P, D') ∈ res do
18        if ∀D'' ∈ S_m, D ∩ D' ∩ D'' = ∅ then
19          placed ←true;
20          P ←P ∪ {p}
21          D' ←D' ∪ D
22          break;
23        fi
24      done
25      if ¬placed then
26        res ←res ∪ {({p}, D)}
27      fi
28    done
29    return res;
```

Fig. 8. Type-Uniform partitioning of products

products. For example, adding, removing or modifying a delta module d and its activation condition will affect only the products that activate d. Therefore, only the projection of the product line on the affected products needs to be re-analyzed. If such a projection is type-uniform, then a more efficient type-checking technique can be used (see [5] for more details). The following guideline naturally arises.

G5. (i) Ensure that the set of products is partitioned in such a way that: each part S is type-uniform (i.e., the projection of the SPL on S is type uniform), and the union of any two distinct parts is not type-uniform.
(ii) If the number of parts of such a partition is "too big", then merge some of them to obtain a "small enough" partition where only one part is not type-uniform.

Figure 8 presents our algorithm to compute a partition following the guideline G5.i, named partitionG5. To simplify the description of our algorithm, we will say in the rest of the section that two modules are in conflict iff they add the same attribute with two different types. The algorithm takes in input an SPL following G4 (so two conflicting delta modules cannot be activated by the same product) and is structured in two parts. First (in lines 2–7), we compute the sets of conflicting delta modules S_m by using an annex getter on L, L.dFCST. L.dFCST is an extention of L.FCST which maps every qualified attribute C.a declared in the SPL to a set of pairs (T, D) where T is a possible type of the attribute, and D is the set of delta modules that add the attribute C.a with the type T. The second part (in lines 8–28) compute the actual partition **res** tagged with annex information used during the computation: basically, **res** is a set of pairs (P, D) where P is the set of products in the partition, and D is the set of modules conflicting with other modules used by the products in P. The computation of **res** is done by iterating over all the products p of the SPL (written $p \in L$.products in line 9). First (in lines 10–15), the algorithm computes the set D of possibly conflicting modules activated by p (we write $p \models \Phi$ when p validates the formula Φ). Then (in lines 16–24), we try to add p in existing partitions (P, D') by iterating over them and checking if a module in D is in conflict with a module in D'. If all existing partitions are in conflict with p, we add to **res** a new partition containing only p (in lines 25–27).

Additionally, we propose in Fig. 9 an algorithm that performs an incremental type-check. As mentioned in the beginning of this section, it is common that well-typed software product lines are modified, and to ensure the well-typedness of the result, it is necessary to only verify a small part of the SPL. The algorithm in Fig. 9, named typeG5, takes in input the originally well typed SPL L, the set of the added modules' names D, and the set of deleted modules U (modified modules are considered removed and added). The principle of this algorithm is to extract from L a much smaller SPL L' that contains all the necessary data to ensure that the well-typedness of P' is equivalent to the well-typedness of L. The construction of L' is done in three steps. First (in line 2), the auxiliary function typeG5Init creates L' with the same feature model as L, and all the modules in D. Moreover, it computes the set of elements E that are used or manipulated (i.e., added, removed or modified) by the modules in D: all delta operations manipulating these elements must be added to L' to type-check correctly the modules in D. To do so, it uses the function els that extracts the set of used or manipulated names from a delta operation o. Finally, it also computes the elements E' that were manipulated by the deleted modules in U: all delta operations manipulating or using these elements must be added to L' as they may not be well-typed anymore. The addition in L' of the delta operations manipulating or using the elements in E' is done in lines 3–14 by iterating over all the delta modules in L (except those in D that are already included in L'). In addition, this part of the algorithm extends E with the dependencies of the added delta operations: like before, all delta operations manipulating these elements must be added to L' to correctly type-check the added operations. The auxiliary function typeG5AddManip efficiently integrates E into L': as stated, this function adds to L' all the delta operations that manipulate the elements in E but also replaces all the method bodies with "**return null**": that way, there is no need to also add the dependencies of these operations in L'. Finally, we can type-check L' in line 16 to see if L is well-typed. Note that this algorithm does not require for the input SPL to follow the G4 guideline.

Application to the EPL example. As mentioned in Sect. 2, the EPL example has 6 products. Moreover, if we consider the variation of this example that follows G4 (discussed in Sect. 7), there are two conflicting modules: dEval2 and the one created by the refactorG4 algorithm. Therefore, the partition computed by our algorithm, which is unique in this case, has two elements P_1 and P_2 constructed as follows:

$$P_1 \triangleq \left\{ \begin{array}{l} \{fLit, fToInt, fEval1, fToString\} \\ \{fLit, fToInt, fEval1, fToString, fAdd\} \end{array} \right\} \quad P_2 \triangleq \left\{ \begin{array}{l} \{fLit, fToInt, fEval2\} \\ \{fLit, fToInt, fEval2, fToString\} \\ \{fLit, fToInt, fEval2, fAdd\} \\ \{fLit, fToInt, fEval2, fToString, fAdd\} \end{array} \right\}$$

```
1    typeG5(L, D, U) =                          30   typeG5AddManip(L, E, L') =
2      (L', E, E') ←typeG5Init(L, D, U)          31     for d ∈ dm(L) do
3      for d ∈ dm(L) \ D do                      32       for o ∈ L.d do
4        for o ∈ L.d do                          33         if o.ρ ∈ E then
5          if els(o) ∩ E' ≠ ∅ then               34           L' ←L' + d' fresh with {
6            E ←E ∪ els(o)                        35             L'(d') ←{ (o.dok, o.ρ, typeG5Simple(o.D)) }
7            L' ←L' + d' fresh with {             36             L'.α(d') ←L.α(d)
8              L'(d') ←{ o }                      37             L'.order(d') ←Lorder(d)
9              L'.α(d') ←L.α(d)                   38           }
10             L'.order(d') ←Lorder(d)           39         fi
11           }                                   40       done
12         fi                                    41     done
13       done                                    42     return L';
14     done                                      43
15     L' ←typeG5AddManip(L, E, L')              44   typeG5Simple(D) =
16     type_check(L');                           45   if D = (⟨c x⟩) → C' { return e; } then
17                                               46     return D[^null/e]
18   typeG5Init(L, D, U) =                       47   else if D = class C extends C' { ... } then
19     L' ←L.products                            48     return D[^null/e]
20     E ←∅                                      49   else
21     for d ∈ D do                              50     return D
22       L' ←L' ∪ L.d                            51   fi;
23       E ←E ∪ {els(o) | o ∈ L.d}
24     done
25     E' ←∅
26     for Δ ∈ U do
27       E' ←E' ∪ {o.ρ | o ∈ Δ}
28     done
29     return (L', E, E');
```

Fig. 9. Efficient typing of modified delta modules

To illustrate our typeG5 algorithm, let consider that a programmer modifies the EPL example by removing the dRMEval1 module (thus causing an error in the generation of all the variant with the feature fEval2 activated). Our algorithm, with the typeG5Init function, first initializes L' to contain only the feature model of the EPL example, E is empty and $E' = \{\text{Exp.eval}\}$. The second part of the algorithm adds to L' the method Exp.eval declared in the base program of EPL and the delta module dEval2. As the method Exp.eval depends on the class Lit and the methods Lit.setLit and Exp.toInt, these elements are added to L' by the function typeG5AddManip. The resulting SPL L' has the following form:

```
// Base program
class Exp extends Object { // To be used only as a type (i.e., not to be instantiated)
  Int toInt() { return new Int(); }
  Lit eval() { return (new Lit()).setLit(this.toInt()); }
}
class Lit extends Exp {
  Lit setLit(Int x) { return null; }
}
delta dEval2 {  modifies class Exp { adds Int eval() {return this.toInt();} }  }
```

Finally, our algorithm tries to type-check L' and fails as dEval2 redefines Exp.eval on top of its original definition in the base program: the typing error in the modified EPL is thus correctly detected by simply looking at the smaller SPL L'.

Properties. The properties of the two algorithms are stated as follows.

- **Correctness of partitionG5.** Given a software product line L and $\{(P_i, D_i) \mid i \in I\} = \mathsf{partitionG5}(L)$, the partition of products $\{P_i \mid i \in I\}$ follows G5.i.
- **Complexity of partitionG5.** The algorithm partitionG5 is exponential in time and space.
- **Correctness and Completeness of typeG5.** Given a well-typed software product line L and another product line L', a set of delta module names D and a set of delta modules U such that L' is the result of removing the delta modules U from L, and adding to it the delta modules in D. Then, the two following properties are equivalent:
  - L' is well-typed
  - $\mathsf{typeG5}(L', D, U)$ is well-typed
- **Complexity of typeG5.** The algorithm partitionG5 is linear in time and space.

9   Related Work

To the best of our knowledge, refactoring in the context of DOP has been studied only in [6,8,16]. We refer to [16] for the related work in the FOP or annotative approaches.

In [16], a catalogue of refactoring and code smells is presented, and most of them focus on changing one delta module, one feature at a time. In particular, the code smells and corresponding refactoring algorithms *Dead Delta Action*, *Dead Delta Module*, and *Empty Delta Module* presented in this paper can be combined to achieve the guideline G1, as described in Sect. 4. In [8], similar refactoring primitives are considered, for delta-oriented programming over components.

In [6] we have presented two refactoring algorithms that, like the algorithm presented in this paper, change the full structure of a given SPL to enforce some property. The properties considered in [6] are *increasing-* and *decreasing-monotonicity*, which focus on which delta operations are used in the SPL. The main intended use of these fully automated algorithms is to transform an SPL into an auxiliary variation more suited for static analysis, such as type checking. In fact, these algorithms might introduce major changes to the structure of an SPL leading to a result that might confuse the developers.

10   Conclusion and Future Work

In this paper, we presented refactoring algorithms for delta-oriented SPL s to enforce the guidelines introduced in [5] and have stated their main properties.

In future work, we would like to prove the properties that we have stated, to implement the algorithms, and to develop case studies to evaluate them. Moreover, these algorithms can be straightforwardly adapted in two ways that could be useful in practice. First, they can be made user-driven, so a programmer could use them to change his working copy of the SPL. Second, they can be transformed into simple analysis tools which could identify where some properties (such as uniformity or inheritance acyclicity) are invalidated in an SPL.

References

1. https://github.com/abstools/abstools/tree/master/frontend/src/abs/frontend/delta
2. Batory, D.: Feature models, grammars, and propositional formulas. In: Obbink, H., Pohl, K. (eds.) SPLC 2005. LNCS, vol. 3714, pp. 7–20. Springer, Heidelberg (2005). doi:10.1007/11554844_3
3. Bettini, L., Damiani, F., Schaefer, I.: Compositional type checking of delta-oriented software product lines. Acta Inf. **50**(2), 77–122 (2013). doi:10.1007/s00236-012-0173-z
4. Clements, P., Northrop, L., Lines, S.P.: Practices and Patterns. Addison Wesley, Boston (2001)
5. Damiani, F., Lienhardt, M.: On type checking delta-oriented product lines. In: Ábrahám, E., Huisman, M. (eds.) IFM 2016. LNCS, vol. 9681, pp. 47–62. Springer, Heidelberg (2016). doi:10.1007/978-3-319-33693-0_4
6. Damiani, F., Lienhardt, M.: Refactoring delta-oriented product lines to achieve monotonicity. In: Proceedings of FMSPLE, volume abs/1604.00346 of CoRR (2016). doi:10.4204/EPTCS.206.2
7. Damiani, F., Schaefer, I.: Family-based analysis of type safety for delta-oriented software product lines. In: Margaria, T., Steffen, B. (eds.) ISoLA 2012. LNCS, vol. 7609, pp. 193–207. Springer, Heidelberg (2012). doi:10.1007/978-3-642-34026-0_15
8. Haber, A., Rendel, H., Rumpe, B., Schaefer, I.: Evolving delta-oriented software product line architectures. CoRR, abs/1409.2311 (2014). doi:10.1007/978-3-642-34059-8_10
9. Igarashi, A., Pierce, B., Wadler, P.: Featherweight Java: a minimal core calculus for Java and GJ. ACM TOPLAS **23**(3), 396–450 (2001). doi:10.1145/503502.503505
10. Johnsen, E.B., Hähnle, R., Schäfer, J., Schlatte, R., Steffen, M.: ABS: a core language for abstract behavioral specification. In: Aichernig, B.K., Boer, F.S., Bonsangue, M.M. (eds.) FMCO 2010. LNCS, vol. 6957, pp. 142–164. Springer, Heidelberg (2011). doi:10.1007/978-3-642-25271-6_8
11. Krueger, C.: Eliminating the adoption barrier. IEEE Softw. **19**(4), 29–31 (2002). doi:10.1109/MS.2002.1020284
12. Lienhardt, M., Clarke, D.: Conflict detection in delta-oriented programming. In: Margaria, T., Steffen, B. (eds.) ISoLA 2012. LNCS, vol. 7609, pp. 178–192. Springer, Heidelberg (2012). doi:10.1007/978-3-642-34026-0_14
13. Lopez-Herrejon, R.E., Batory, D., Cook, W.: Evaluating support for features in advanced modularization technologies. In: Black, A.P. (ed.) ECOOP 2005. LNCS, vol. 3586, pp. 169–194. Springer, Heidelberg (2005). doi:10.1007/11531142_8
14. Schaefer, I., Bettini, L., Bono, V., Damiani, F., Tanzarella, N.: Delta-oriented programming of software product lines. In: Bosch, J., Lee, J. (eds.) SPLC 2010. LNCS, vol. 6287, pp. 77–91. Springer, Heidelberg (2010). doi:10.1007/978-3-642-15579-6_6
15. Schaefer, I., Damiani, F.: Pure delta-oriented programming. In: Proceedings of FOSD 2010. ACM (2010). doi:10.1145/1868688.1868696
16. Schulze, S., Richers, O., Schaefer, I.: Refactoring delta-oriented software product lines. In: Proceedings of the 12th Annual International Conference on Aspect-Oriented Software Development, AOSD 2013, pp. 73–84. ACM, New York (2013). doi:10.1145/2451436.2451446

Detecting and Understanding Software Doping

Detecting and Understanding Software Doping — Track Introduction

Christel Baier[1] and Holger Hermanns[2]

[1] Faculty of Computer Science, Technische Universität Dresden,
Dresden, Germany
[2] Saarland University — Computer Science, Saarland Informatics Campus,
Saarbrücken, Germany

It is by now understood that embedded software might provide features and function-alities that are not in the interest of the device's user or even of an entire society. The diesel car emissions scandal serves as a promiment current example. Such "software doping" is deeply intertwined with market strategies of embedded device manufacturers and comes with a strong trend towards proprietary problem solutions. Embedded software doping is what enables inkjet printers to reject third-party cartridges, and it enables cars to secretly pollute our environment. In general terms, embedded software doping locks the users out of the products they own. Efforts to counteract this trend by empirical evaluation and thus comparison for singular points (e.g. NOx emission tests under lab conditions) are clearly insufficient.

The ISOLA 2016 track "Detecting and Understanding Software Doping" discusses the research challenges for reasoning about doping-free programs and systems. First of all, there is agreement that richer models are needed to characterize the intended behaviour of an embedded device. These models must enable us to tell apart the required and the disallowed behaviour of a device over a broad range of operational conditions, not under lab conditions. They must represent quantifiable behaviour, so as to support reasoning about exhaust emissions, power consumption, temperature, and so on.

In order to detect and understand software doping in all its facets, these behaviour models need to be equipped with novel and thorough verification and analyis tech-niques in order to get provable assurance of device's functionality, if possible at design time. This goes far beyond lab testing, and bridges to strong approaches to model-based analysis. In order to arrive there, we need to bring together researchers working on interface technology, on quantitative models, on algorithmic verification, and other related fields. This track adresses this challenge. Four submitted papers have been selected for inclusion in the proceedings.

The paper *Facets of Software Doping* by Barthe, D'Argenio, Finkbeiner and Hermanns [1] develops and dicusses a sequence of characterizations of software doping and of dope-free programs, illustrated by real life cases and blueprint-style examples.

The paper *Software that meets its Intent* by Huisman et al. [4] describes research perspectives for developing software with formally specified intents and corresponding techniques for their analysis based on verification, testing and monitoring.

The paper *Compliance, Functional Safety & Fault Detection by Formal Methods* by Fetzer, Weidenbach and Wischnewski [3] proposes an auditor-based approach to ensuring formal safety, compliance and fault detection at run time.

Finally, ethical aspects of software doping are dicussed in the paper *What the Hack is wrong with Software Doping?* by Baum [2]. The contribution illustrates the views and justifiable interests of different stakeholders such as the owner and the manufacturer of the software in question and thereby identifies moral aspects of software doping.

These contributions alltogether shed light on the software doping phenomenon from four very different angles.

References

1. Barthe, G., D'Argenio, P.R., Finkbeiner, B., Hermanns, H.: Facets of software doping. In: T. Margaria and B. Steffen (Eds.) ISoLA 2016, Part II, LNCS 9953, pp. 601–608. Springer, Switzerland (2016)
2. Baum, K.: What the hack is wrong with software doping? In: Margaria, T., Steffen, B. (eds.) ISoLA 2016, Part II, LNCS 9953, pp. 633–648. Springer, Switzerland (2016)
3. Fetzer, C., Weidenbach,C., Wischnewski, P.: Compliance, functional safety and fault detection by formal methods. In: Margaria, T., Steffen, B. (eds.) ISoLA 2016, Part II, LNCS 9953, pp. 626–632. Springer, Switzerland (2016)
4. Huisman, M., Bos, H., Brinkkemper, S., van Deursen, A., Groote, J.F., Lago P., van de Pol, J., Visser, E.: Software that meets its Intent. In: Margaria, T., Steffen, B. (eds.) ISoLA 2016, Part II, LNCS 9953, pp. 609–625. Springer, Switzerland (2016)

Facets of Software Doping

Gilles Barthe[1], Pedro R. D'Argenio[2(✉)], Bernd Finkbeiner[3],
and Holger Hermanns[3]

[1] IMDEA Software, Madrid, Spain
[2] FaMAF, Universidad Nacional de Córdoba – CONICET, Córdoba, Argentina
dargenio@famaf.unc.edu.ar
[3] Saarland University – Computer Science, Saarland Informatics Campus,
Saarbrücken, Germany

Abstract. This paper provides an informal discussion of the formal aspects of software doping.

1 Introduction

Software is the great innovation enabler of our times. Software runs on hardware. Usually, software is licensed to the hardware owner, instead of being owned by her. And while the owner is in full physical control of the hardware, she usually has neither physical nor logical control over the software. That software however does not always exploit the offered functionality of the hardware in the best interest of the owner. Instead it may be tweaked in various manners, driven by interests different from those of the owner or of society. This situation may be aggravated if the software is not running on local hardware but remotely (e.g. in the cloud) since the software user has now little or no control of its execution.

There is a manifold of facets to this phenomenon, summarised as software doping. It becomes more widespread as software is embedded in ever more devices of daily use. Yet, we are not aware of any systematic investigation or formalisation from the software engineering perspective.

This paper reviews known real cases of software doping, and provides a conceptual account of characteristic behaviour that distinguishes doped from clean software.

2 Software Doping in the Wild

The simplest and likely most common example of software doping is that of ink printers [4] refusing to work when supplied with a toner or ink cartridge of a third party manufacturer [8], albeit being technically compatible. More subtle

This work is partly supported by the ERC Grants 683300 (OSARES) and 695614 (POWVER), by the Sino-German CDZ project 1023 (CAP), by ANPCyT PICT-2012-1823, by SeCyT-UNC 05/BP12 and 05/B497, and by the Madrid Region project S2013/ICE-2731 N-GREENS Software-CM.

T. Margaria and B. Steffen (Eds.): ISoLA 2016, Part II, LNCS 9953, pp. 601–608, 2016.
DOI: 10.1007/978-3-319-47169-3_46

variations of this kind of doping just issue a warning message about the risk of using a "foreign" cartridge [11]. In the same vein, it is known that printers emit "low toner" warnings [12] earlier than needed, so as to drive or force the customer into replacing cartridges prematurely. Similarly, cases are known where laptops refuse to charge [3] the battery if connected to a third-party charger.

Characteristic for these examples is that the functionality in question is in the interest of the device manufacturer, but against the customer interest. However, there are also variations of software doping that can be considered to be in the interest of the customer, but not in the interest of society: In the automotive sector, "chip-tuning" [19] is a remarkable variation of the software doping phenomenon, where the owner initiates a reprogramming of some of the vehicle's electronic control units (ECU) so as to change the vehicle characteristics with respect to power, emissions, or fuel consumption. By its nature, chip-tuning appears to be in the owner's interest, but it may well be against the interest of society, for instance if legally-defined and thus built-in speed limitations are overridden. Examples include scooters [9] and electric bikes [2,10].

Some cases of software doping are clearly neither in the interest of the customer, nor in the interest of society. This includes as prominent examples the exhaust emission scandal of Volkswagen [20] (and other manufacturers). Here, the exhaust software was manufactured in such a way that it heavily polluted the environment, unless the software detected the car to be fixed on the particular test setup used to determine the NOx footprint data officially published.

The same sort of behaviour has been reported in the context of smart phone designs [7], where software was tailored to perform better when detecting it was running a certain benchmark, and otherwise running in lower clock speed. Another smart phone case, disabling the phone [5] via a software update after "non-authorized" repair, has later been undone [1]. Often, software doping is a part of a lock-in strategy: The customer gets *locked-in* on the manufacturer or unit-supplier for products, maintenance and services [13].

3   Characterising Software Doping

It is difficult to come up with a crisp characterisation of what constitutes software doping. Nevertheless we consider it a worthwhile undertaking to explore this issue, with the intention to eventually enable a formal characterisation of software doping. That characterisation can be the nucleus for formulating and enforcing rigid requirements on embedded software driven by public interest, so as to effectively ban software doping. In order to sharpen our intuition, we offer the following initial characterisation attempt.

A software system is doped if the manufacturer has included a hidden   (1) functionality in such a way that the resulting behaviour intentionally favors a designated party, against the interest of society or of the software licensee.

So, a doped software induces behaviour that can not be justified by the interest of the licensee or of society, but instead serves another usually hidden interest. It thereby favors a certain brand, vendor, manufacturer, or other market participant. This happens intentionally, and not by accident.

However, the question whether a certain behaviour is intentional or not is very difficult to decide. To illustrate this, we recall that the above mentioned iPhone-6 case, where "non-authorized" repair rendered the phone unusable [5] after an iOS update, seemed to be intentional when it surfaced, but was actually tracked down to a software glitch of the update and fixed later. Notably, if the iOS designers would have had the particular intention to mistreat licensees who went elsewhere for repair, the same behaviour could well have qualified as software doping in the above sense (1).

As a result, we will look at software doping according to the above characterisation, but without any attempt to take into account considerations of intentionality.

In the sequel, we shall investigate this phenomenon by synthetic examples, that however are directly inspired by the real cases of software doping reviewed above.

3.1 Doping by Discrimination

Think of a program as a function that accepts some initial parameters and, given (partial) inputs, it produces (partial) outputs. As an example, (an abstraction of) the embedded software in a printer is given in Fig. 1. The program PRINTER has the parameter *cartridge_info* (which is not yet used within the function), two input variables (*document* and *paper_available?*) and two output variables (*alert_signal* and *page_out*).

A printer manufacturer may manipulate this program in order to favor its own cartridge brand. An obvious way is displayed in Fig. 2: This is a sort of discrimination based on parameter values. Therefore, a first formal approach to characterising a program as *clean* (or *doping-free*) is that it should behave in a similar way for all parameter values, where by

```
procedure PRINTER(cartridge_info)
    READ(document)
    while PAGESTOPRINT(document) > 0 do
        READ(paper_available?)
        if ¬paper_available? then
            TURNON(alert_signal)
            WAITUNTIL(paper_available?)
            TURNOFF(alert_signal)
        end if
        PRINTNEXTPAGE(page_out, document)
    end while
end procedure
```

Fig. 1. A simple printer.

```
procedure PRINTER(cartridge_info)
    if BRAND(cartridge_info) = my-brand then
        (··· same code as Fig. 1 ···)
    else
        TURNON(alert_signal)
    end if
end procedure
```

Fig. 2. A doped printer.

similar behaviour we mean that the visible output should be the same for any given input in two different instances of the same (parameterized) program. Obviously, "all parameter values" refers to all values within a given domain. In the case of the printer, we expect that it works with any *compatible* cartridge. Such compatibility domain defines a first scope within which a software is evaluated to be clean or doped. So, we could say the following.

A program is *clean* (or *doping-free*) if for every standard parameter it (2) exhibits the same visible outputs when supplied with the same inputs.

Under this view, the program of Fig. 2 is indeed doped. Also, note that this characterisation entails the existence of a contract which defines the set of standard parameters.

3.2   Doping vs. Extended Functionality

We could imagine, nonetheless, that the printer manufacturer may like to provide extra functionalities for its own product which is outside of the standard for compatibility. For instance (and for the sake of this discussion) suppose the printer manufacturer develops a new file format that is more efficient at the time of printing, but this requires some new technology on the cartridge. The manufacturer still wants to provide the usual functionality for standard file formats that works with standard compatible cartridges and comes up with the program of Fig. 3. Notice that this program does not conform to the specification of a clean program given by (2) since it behaves differently when a document of the new (non-standard) type is given. This is clearly not in the spirit of the program in Fig. 3 which is actually conforming to the standard specification. Thus, we relax the previous characterisation and only require that two instances of the program behave similarly if the provided inputs adhere to some expected standard. Therefore we propose the following weaker notion of clean program:

A program is *clean* if for every standard parameter it exhibits the same (3) visible outputs when supplied with any possible input complying with a given standard.

```
procedure PRINTER(cartridge_info)
    READ(document)
    if ¬NEWTYPE(document) ∨ SUPPORTSNEWTYPE(cartridge_info) then
        (··· proceed to print as in Fig. 1 ···)
    else
        TURNON(alert_signal)
    end if
end procedure
```

Fig. 3. A clean printer.

This characterisation is based on a comparison of the behaviour of two instances of a program, each of them responding to different parameter values. A second, different characterisation may instead require to compare a reference specification capturing the essence of clean behaviour against any possible instance of the program. The first approach seems more general than the second one in the sense that the specification could be considered as one of the possible instances of the (parameterized) program. However, the second characterisation is still reasonable and it could turn to be equivalent to (3) under mild conditions (namely, under behavioural equivalence.)

3.3 Doping by Switching

Let us draw the reader's attention to a different facet of software doping. We consider the ECU of a diesel vehicle, in particular its exhaust emission control module. For diesel engines, the controller injects a certain amount of a specific fluid (an aqueous urea solution) into the exhaust pipeline in order to lower NOx emissions.

```
procedure EMISSIONCONTROL()
    READ(throttle)
    def_dose = SCRMODEL(throttle)
end procedure
```

Fig. 4. A simple emission control.

We simplify this control problem to a minimal toy example. In Fig. 4 we display a function that reads the *throttle* position and calculates which is the dose of diesel exhaust fluid (DEF) that should be injected to reduce the NOx emission (this is stored in *def_dose*). Variable *throttle* is an input variable while, though *def_dose* is an output variable, it is not the actual visible output. The actual visible output is the NOx emission measured at the end of the exhaust system. Therefore, the behaviour of this system needs to be analyzed through testing. In this setting, we may only consider the standard input behaviour as the one defined in the laboratory emission tests.

The Volkswagen emission scandal arose precisely because their software was instrumented so that it works as expected *only if* operating in or very close to the lab testing conditions [6]. For our simplified example, this behaviour is exemplified by the algorithm of Fig. 5. Of course, the real case was less

```
procedure EMISSIONCONTROL()
    READ(throttle)
    if throttle ∈ throttle TestValues then
        def_dose = SCRMODEL(throttle)
    else
        def_dose = ALTERNATESCRMODEL(throttle)
    end if
end procedure
```

Fig. 5. A doped emission control.

simplistic. Notably, a software like this one still meets the characterization of *clean* given in (3). However, it is intentionally programmed to defy the regulations when being unobserved and hence it falls directly within our intuition of what a doped software is (see (1)).

The spirit of the emission tests is to verify that the amount of NOx in the car exhaust gas does not exceed a given threshold *in general*. Thus, one would expect that if the input values of the EMISSIONCONTROL function deviates within "reasonable distance" from the *standard* input values provided during the lab emission test, the amount of NOx found in the exhaust gas is still within the regulated threshold, or at least it does not exceed it more than a "reasonable amount". Similar rationale could be applied for regulation of other systems such as speed limit controllers in scooters and electric bikes. Therefore, we propose this alternative characterisation:

> A program is *clean* if for every standard parameter, whenever it is sup- (4) plied with any input (being it complying to the standard or not) that deviates within "reasonable distance" from a given standard input, it exhibits a visible output which does not deviate beyond a "reasonable distance" from the specified output corresponding to such standard input.

The "reasonable distances" are values that should be provided (together with the notion of distance) and are part of the contract that ensures that the software is clean. Also, the limitation to this "reasonable distance" has to do with the fact that, beyond it, particular requirements (e.g. safety) may arise. For instance, a smart battery may decide to stop accepting charge if the current emitted by a standardized but foreign charger is higher than "reasonable", but it may still proceed in case it is instead dealing with a charger of the same brand for which it may know that it can resort to a customized protocol allowing ultra-fast charging in a safe manner.

These 'reasonable distances' need to come with application-specific metrics on possible input and output values. Since these metrics are often related to real physical quantities, the metric spaces might be continuous. They might also be discrete, or superpositions of both.

Characterisation (4) This situation arises in cases like the exhaust emission system and almost any embedded system: input and output values will be as precise as sensors and actuators allow. In this case, the "reasonable distance" is going to be defined according to the precision of these devices.

4   Concluding Remarks

This paper has reviewed facets of software doping. Starting off from real examples a first intuitive characterisation of software doping was derived. We then discussed a sequence of – still informal — definitions of absence of software doping.

We are currently working on the formalisation of these definitions. We expect that many definitions will fall in the general class of hyperproperties [15]— informally, hyperproperties are sets of sets of program executions and capture behaviours of multiple runs of a program—which encompasses continuity [14] and non-interference [16,18]. These formal characterisations are expected to help to understand better the requirements on embedded software imposed by public interest, hence providing a framework to specify contracts or regulations pertaining to such technology, and to rigorously discriminate between doping and reasonably acceptable deviations from the normal behaviour. They will also help clarify the specificities of software doping with respect to malware, software sabotage, and substitution attacks that have been studied in the context of security [17]. Furthermore, rigorous definitions will provide the necessary foundations for developing analysis methods (verification or testing) against doping.

References

1. Apple apologizes and updates iOS to restore iPhones disabled by error 53. https://techcrunch.com/2016/02/18/apple-apologizes-and-updates-ios-to-restore-iphones-disabled-by-error-53/. Accessed 07 July 2016
2. BionX tuning. http://www.ebiketuning.com/comparison/bionx-tuning.html. Accessed 07 July 2016
3. Dell laptops reject third-party batteries and AC adapters/chargers. Hardware vendor lock-in? https://nctritech.wordpress.com/2010/01/26/dell-laptops-reject-third-party-batteries-and-ac-adapterschargers-hardware-vendor-lock-in/. Accessed 07 July 2016
4. Epson firmware update = no to compatibles. http://www.wasteink.co.uk/epson-firmware-update-compatible-problem/. Accessed 07 July 2016
5. 'Error 53' fury mounts as Apple software update threatens to kill your iPhone 6. https://www.theguardian.com/money/2016/feb/05/error-53-apple-iphone-software-update-handset-worthless-third-party-repair. Accessed 07 July 2016
6. The exhaust emissions scandal ("Dieselgate"). https://events.ccc.de/congress/2015/Fahrplan/events/7331.html. Accessed 07 July 2016
7. Galaxy S4 on steroids: Samsung caught doping in benchmarks. http://forums.appleinsider.com/discussion/158782/galaxy-s-4-on-steroids-samsung-caught-doping-in-benchmarks. Accessed 07 July 2016
8. Has a printer update rendered your cartridges redundant? https://conversation.which.co.uk/technology/printer-software-update-third-party-printer-ink/. Accessed 07 July 2016
9. How it works: The basics of ECU tuning. https://rideapart.com/articles/hows-work-ecu-tuning. Accessed 07 July 2016
10. How to get access to your bionx console code menu (codelist included). http://electricbikereview.com/community/threads/how-to-get-access-to-your-bionx-console-code-menu-codelist-included.519/. Accessed 07 July 2016
11. The secret printer companies are keeping from you. http://uk.pcmag.com/printers/60628/opinion/the-secret-printer-companies-are-keeping-from-you. Accessed 07 July 2016
12. Take that, stupid printer! http://www.slate.com/articles/technology/technology/2008/08/take_that_stupid_printer.html. Accessed 07 July 2016
13. Arthur, W.B.: Competing technologies, increasing returns, and lock-in by historical events. Econ. J. **99**(394), 116–131 (1989). http://www.jstor.org/stable/2234208
14. Chaudhuri, S., Gulwani, S., Lublinerman, R.: Continuity analysis of programs. In: Hermenegildo, M.V., Palsberg, J. (eds.) Proceedings of the 37th ACM SIGPLAN-SIGACT Symposium on Principles of Programming Languages, POPL 2010, pp. 57–70 (2010)
15. Clarkson, M.R., Schneider, F.B.: Hyperproperties. In: Proceedings of CSF 2008. pp. 51–65 (2008)

16. Goguen, J.A., Meseguer, J.: Security policies and security models. In: 1982 IEEE Symposium on Security and Privacy, Oakland, CA, USA, 26–28 April 1982, pp. 11–20. IEEE Computer Society (1982). http://dx.doi.org/10.1109/SP.1982.10014

17. Schneier, B., Fredrikson, M., Kohno, T., Ristenpart, T.: Surreptitiously weakening cryptographic systems. Cryptology ePrint Archive, Report 2015/097 (2015). http://eprint.iacr.org/2015/097

18. Volpano, D.M., Irvine, C.E., Smith, G.: A sound type system for secure flow analysis. J. Comput. Secur. 4(2/3), 167–188 (1996). http://dx.doi.org/10.3233/JCS-1996-42-304

19. Wikipedia: Chip tuning –Wikipedia, the free encyclopedia (2016). https://en.wikipedia.org/wiki/Chip_tuning. Accessed 07 July 2016

20. Wikipedia: Volkswagen emissions scandal – Wikipedia, the free encyclopedia (2016). https://en.wikipedia.org/wiki/Volkswagen_emissions_scandal. Accessed 07 July 2016

Software that Meets Its Intent

Marieke Huisman[1]([✉]), Herbert Bos[2], Sjaak Brinkkemper[3], Arie van Deursen[4],
Jan Friso Groote[5], Patricia Lago[2], Jaco van de Pol[1], and Eelco Visser[4]

[1] University of Twente, Enschede, The Netherlands
M.Huisman@utwente.nl
[2] Vrije Universiteit Amsterdam, Amsterdam, The Netherlands
[3] Utrecht University, Utrecht, The Netherlands
[4] Delft University of Technology, Delft, The Netherlands
[5] Eindhoven University of Technology, Eindhoven, The Netherlands

Abstract. Software is widely used, and society increasingly depends on its reliability. However, software has become so complex and it evolves so quickly that we fail to keep it under control. Therefore, we propose *intents*: fundamental laws that capture a software systems' intended behavior (resilient, secure, safe, sustainable, etc.). The realization of this idea requires novel theories, algorithms, tools, and techniques to discover, express, verify, and evolve software intents. Thus, future software systems will be able to verify themselves that they meet their intents. Moreover, they will be able to respond to deviations from intents through self-correction. In this article we propose a research agenda, outlining which novel theories, algorithms and tools are required.

1 Introduction

Problem. Software is everywhere: the estimated number of connected devices today ranges in the tens of billions and will be up in the hundreds of billions very soon. While society increasingly depends on its reliability and trustworthiness, the inconvenient truth is that software is very fragile. Software is so complicated that we have no clear idea of what a program may or may not do. And when something is working, we are afraid to touch it. For instance, many critical infrastructures do not update their software for fear of breaking things, even in the case of crucial security updates. As it stands we lack real control over software in virtually all areas. Both criminals and intelligence services employ this to hack into our computers. This is today. Tomorrow will be worse.

Solution. In 1942, the science fiction writer Isaac Asimov formulated a number of laws for robots. For instance, no matter how complex they became, they should never injure a human being, or through inaction, allow a human being to come to harm. In other words, the laws should govern the robot's behavior, independent of its normal functionality or complexity.

Today, some 75 years later, we take up this idea and apply it to software: by defining simple laws or *"intents"* for software, we want to govern a program's

T. Margaria and B. Steffen (Eds.): ISoLA 2016, Part II, LNCS 9953, pp. 609–625, 2016.
DOI: 10.1007/978-3-319-47169-3_47

behavior, independent of the implementation of its functionality: it should not crash, it should resist attacks, it should adhere to its functional specification. It should revert buggy updates, it should keep sensitive data private, etc.

Moreover, the intents should be met under any condition – even if the software evolves, or the environment changes. Where needed, the software should correct itself automatically to fulfil the intents. And whenever the intents change, the software has to adjust itself. In case conflicting intents for software are discovered, ethical considerations should be made to resolve the conflict.

This requires a research agenda, to investigate methods for discovering the dynamic intents of living software, techniques to specify and verify intents, and new mechanisms to make software self-correcting, *i.e.*, to make it adapt itself to deviations from the current intents. This requires the concerted efforts from a broad range of software technologies, combining formal analysis, experimental software laboratory research, and empirical research on deployed software. Developing and evaluating the methods also requires intimate collaboration with a number of embedded software application domains, like health care, robotics, automotive, and science experiments.

Software is becoming so versatile, all-embracing and intelligent that it is inconceivable that we can control all detailed aspects of its behavior. But by using intents we can guarantee that software adheres always to its essential purpose, avoids unnecessary harm, and operates within the boundaries of the law. With the same aim as Asimov's robot laws, intents guarantee that software can be used safely and reliably.

2   The Software Reliability Challenge

Software runs the world. Software plays an integral role in our daily lives. There is an 'app' for everything, from the energy grid that powers our infrastructure to the social media that mediate our social interactions. It is hard to recall what life was before all that software, and it is even harder to imagine what we would do without. Society would grind to a halt if the software running it would break down. This dependence on software *will keep growing* in the years to come. Gartner Inc. estimates that the number of connected devices today ranges in the tens of billions and that this will grow to hundreds of billions very soon [42].

The enormous growth in software [87] has led to many advances. Office software and information systems have revolutionized information processing in all sectors, from finance to retail to government. Software is now a crucial and often complex component in many *embedded systems* such as medical surgery robots; control systems for aviation, traffic, and nuclear equipment; and robot companions for elderly people. Software is also having a transforming impact on *science*: scientific experiments are often replaced by much faster, cheaper and safer software simulations, and scientific discoveries often result from automated analysis of large amounts of measurement data.

These successes stem from the fact that *computers outperform humans* in many tasks: computers are faster and more reliable; they can perform many tasks simultaneously, and can process astounding quantities of data. Already, there are many cases where software 'knows' more about the tasks at hand than the humans involved, and this development has only just started.

However, the tremendous growth of software also has a downside. All software systems contain errors that cause them to behave in unintended ways [41,62]. Studies show that even tested and deployed software has on average between 1 and 16 errors per 1000 lines of code [70,71]. As a consequence, dormant software faults persist even in mature code bases [20]. With code bases that often exceed a million lines of code, modern software systems easily contain thousands of bugs, many of which may bring down the entire system, or worse, produce wrong results that go undetected. Most software errors are introduced by developers accidentally violating the (informal) expectations on a system. However, errors may also be introduced consciously to actively fool the users [88], which makes error detection even more challenging. Almost daily, we are exposed to news reports on the consequences of failures and other malbehavior of software.

Thus, even though many people think they can depend on the *reliability* of software, the truth is that is just an idealized dream. Software has become *too complex*, and it *evolves* so quickly, that we are not really in control. Using artificial intelligence and autonomous learning techniques, software can adapt itself to its environment to outwit people, operating in a better way than any human could ever have programmed. This makes it scientifically very challenging to predict all possible emergent behaviors of a large, complex, and evolving software system, and thus to ensure that it is and will remain free of flaws, or to guarantee that it will always avoid foul play in obtaining its objectives.

Meanwhile, engineers keep developing new systems, for which new software has to be developed, while the software of old systems grows due to maintenance and adding new features. The resulting complexity is abused by various parties, such as criminals and intelligence services, actively searching for flaws in software systems in order to exploit them for their own advantage. There are even cases where software developers designed "features" in order to mislead customers and users, e.g. to circumvent environmental emission restrictions in cars. As a result, as a society we cannot guarantee the security and integrity of data, ultimately threatening the identity of our citizens. Moreover, as devices become increasingly *connected* and exchange information, the privacy of their users is at stake.

The root cause of this software reliability crisis is that the policies that software systems implement are buried in low-level code, which makes it hard to establish what exactly those policies are, whether they are implemented correctly, and whether these are indeed the policies that we intended. This problem is exacerbated by the rapidly increasing complexity of software systems. This would be akin to a society consisting of individuals that operate by doing as they please, driven by their own particular desires.

By contrast, modern society operates by *rule of law*, imposing constraints on the behavior of its citizens and institutions. While a modern society is a highly complex system with millions of entities interacting in many ways, rule of law keeps this system in check by imposing clear and objective criteria for judging the legality of the behavior of all these entities. To ensure that we can keep depending on software and to prevent it from running wild, software should be governed by rule of law, just like our society!

3   Software Intents

Software laws, which we will call *software intents*, explicitly describe the essential limits on and expectations on the *behavior* of a software system. Software intents often cover functional requirements, but they should also cover non-functional requirements (e.g., intended performance, response time), and security properties (e.g., resilience against attackers). A crucial property of software intents is that they describe high-level requirements that reflect the goals of a software system, not (just) the low-level effects of a particular realization of those goals on a particular computing substrate.

Common examples of software intents are: Software should not crash; When software crashes nevertheless, it should do so gracefully; Software should not cause any harm to its users, or to any other human being; Software should be resistant to attacks; Software should satisfy its specifications; and: Software should not violate the privacy of its users. For a telling example, consider the recent case of the Japanese satellite Hitomi, which tumbled out of control five weeks after launch, because of a software error [94]: in an attempt to stop itself from spinning, the control system fired a thruster jet in the wrong direction, causing an acceleration, instead of a slow down. An implicit intent for a satellite is that it should stay in its orbit. By making this intent explicit, and providing support to ensure that this intent is fulfilled at all times, the error could have been detected and corrected.

Software intents serve multiple purposes. First, each software system should explicitly *declare* its intents, which serves as a promise and explanation what it intends to do. Second, intents should be usable to *verify* that a software system is indeed realizing its intended behavior (and no others). Finally, intents should facilitate the *evolution* of software systems, by ensuring that software maintenance is intent preserving. Technically, *intents* can be viewed as a form of redundancy, which will allow to increase software reliability fundamentally, *i.e.*, reduce the chance of software errors to less than 10^{-10}.

Therefore, we propose a novel research agenda, revolving around the *paradigm of software intents*. This agenda should address at least the following areas:

- *Expression of Intent:* How to discover and define software intents?
- *Verification of Intent:* How to ensure that software systems *always* behave as intended?
- *Evolution of Intent:* How to ensure that software systems keep behaving as intended, also in the future?

While continuous change, reliability and trustworthiness regard any type of software system, they are especially critical in embedded software where intents derived from safety, ethics and performance concerns play an essential role. Therefore, this research agenda can only be effective in close collaboration with a selected number of embedded software application domains. Clear candidate domains are robotics, in industry, autonomous automotive, or home care situations, other health care applications, and science experiments in physics and biology. Here, reliability, safety, ethics, and performance play a prominent role.

3.1   Expression of Intent

The first challenge is *how to discover the implicit intents* of software systems. Generally, people have all kinds of expectations on software, but are incapable of making that precise. What are the fundamental properties that should continue to hold throughout the lifetime of a software system, no matter how it evolves? And how can we be sure that all relevant intents have been formulated? Intents might be specified upfront, but another interesting challenge is to discover intents for existing (legacy or open source) systems by observing their use, or mining user or developer data like logs, chats, code repositories, bug trackers, test suites, etc.

A particular interesting question is whether different intents can be *combined* or when intents are *conflicting*. In case of conflicting intents, we need to understand how to resolve these conflicts, which quickly becomes an *ethical question*, as it requires prioritizing one intent over the other. For example, in principle all user data should remain private, but if the user is a suspected terrorist, the privacy restriction might be released in favor of the society's security.

The next challenge is *how to express software intents*. There can be many sources of intents: they can be linguistic expressions of intent by human developers or users; they can be legal restrictions, imposed by laws on safety, privacy and security; or formal specifications, models, test cases etc. Thus, intents may be formal, but they do not have to be. How should suitable *languages of intent*, covering different classes of intents, be defined? For example, as a language of intent for a specific application domain, or as a language of intent for a particular class of properties? Rather than requiring a single language, we stress the usability and understandability of the languages, so that when an intent is expressed, all stakeholders have a common understanding of how the software should behave. Thus, these languages of intent will provide a common framework for all developers and users of software to express what they believe to be the intended program's behavior. Moreover, the advantage of having a well-defined language is that its underlying *semantics of intents* can be defined precisely and formally. This makes it possible to demonstrate that intents are compatible, and ultimately that software satisfies its intent.

3.2   Verification of Intent

There are many different ways to verify intents on software. This can be done at *design time* using logic-based techniques, which can provide high-correctness guarantees. It is possible to do this by testing applications in a *software laboratory* setting before deployment. But it can also be done after deployment, by *monitoring applications* in real-life situations in the specific environment in which the software is run.

Design-time verification (or static verification), is done on the basis of models of the program code or on the code itself. Instead of executing the program, it analyses all the possible program executions (for example, by exploring the complete state space of a program, or by representing program executions at a suitably abstract level in a symbolic way). Over the last decade, significant progress has been made to apply design-time verification to large-scale examples [27,53,69]. However design-time verification still requires a significant amount of user intervention. For design-time verification of intent-based software, the major research challenges that need to be addressed are:

1. to *fully automate* this process by automatically generating all the information that is necessary to capture all possible program behaviors in a suitable way;
2. to investigate how design-time verification can be *generalized* to other classes of intents than traditional functional specifications; and
3. to apply design-time verification when one only has control over parts of the software system only.

Testing, or run-time verification, considers concrete program executions, and verifies in a software laboratory whether software does not violate the intended behavior of the program. Because of the lab situation, one has full control over the program, and can rerun it, applying smart (or dangerous) test cases. The main challenges are:

1. to guide the testing process to test cases that might lead to discovering potential intent violations, or can support certifying their absence;
2. while at the same time optimizing the time and effort put in the testing process, possibly taking into account a suitable risk assessment.

Finally, **monitoring** is needed to verify that the software fulfils its intent even after software deployment. Verification and testing typically assume a particular environment in which the software is run, but after deployment the environment might change in unforeseen ways. Monitoring provides a first step, when a violation of intent is detected or predicted, to adapt the behavior of the system, or if necessary to completely interrupt it before any real harm can be done. The major challenges are to understand how the monitoring can be done effectively for all classes of intents:

1. without significant *overhead on the performance* of the software; and
2. in the presence of *great uncertainty* due to the dynamic environment in which the software is running.

3.3   Evolution of Intent

A fact of life (which makes it interesting) is that both the intents that software should satisfy as well as the environment in which it must run are continuously changing. If the environment changes, the software should live up to its intents, and if needed, adjust itself automatically. In case the intent itself changes, for example because of a change in user requirements, or a new law imposing new rules that the software must satisfy, the software has to be adjusted to live up to its intents. In traditional software engineering, the software has to be re-engineered. Because of the enormous size of software this is a costly, error prone and time consuming affair. Avoiding this requires novel techniques such that the software can correct itself autonomously, and then provide guarantees that it behaves according to its (new) intent again. Exciting new research shows that it is possible to achieve this on small programs, with search-based techniques, [58,73]. However, turning this into a scalable technique will require a major effort.

The first challenge is to investigate how software can *establish* itself that it is still fulfilling its intents, especially when there are changes in the environment. The software *should take responsibility for its own intent*. The next challenge is to understand the different techniques for *efficient correction* of the software in case the intents are violated. Due to the size and complexity of software, repairing software at one place can have an unwanted and unexpected impact on other parts of its behavior. Efficient methods are required, to show that local software reparations do not adversely affect the rest of the code. The challenge is to show that the intent is fulfilled again without a complete re-verification. Finally, the last major challenge is to understand if and how these correction techniques can be applied autonomously, i.e., to make the software *self-correcting*. For this, techniques are required that select the appropriate corrections for the diagnosed source of the problem automatically, and then apply these corrections.

Just as modern spellcheckers effectively apply auto-correction to natural language texts by pattern recognition, in our vision future software systems should

1. *detect software patterns* that violate their own intents; and.
2. *identify and apply correction patterns automatically* to make software respect its intents again.

4   Current State-of-the-Art

The quest for reliable software is not new, but started right after the conception of programmable machines. In this section, we provide a broad overview of the current state of the art on the topics covered by the proposed research agenda.

4.1   Expression of Intent

Requirements engineering is traditionally used to understand and model the software's intended behavior. Requirements engineering typically focuses on identifying, modeling and analyzing the goals of the stakeholders [89]. Usually, every stakeholder has a different perspective on what the software should do [37,78]. These *viewpoints* can be independent or partially overlapping. Various proposals exist to resolve the inconsistencies between viewpoints [5,36]. A common approach is to prioritize the requirements.

A systematic approach to incorporate ethical and legal questions into requirement prioritization is still largely missing. From a legal perspective, the formulation of norms and regulations on software is slowly gaining traction, especially in the field of security and privacy [15,54]. Recently, [24] formalized intents about a wide range of security requirements. Lago et al. started a library of intents in the domain of cloud-based software [61,76]. Despite their long history, the adoption of goal modelling techniques is still low. Software requirements are often written in natural language [90], so they cannot be linked directly to the other activities of software development.

At the other side of the spectrum, we have formal languages. For instance, modal logics specify external system behaviour [8,48]. They operate on idealized system models rather than on actual code. For program verification, several program annotation languages have been introduced [51,59]. These approaches are precise, but limited in expressivity. They are based on formal semantics, detailing the intended behavior of substantial parts of widely used programming languages, like C [34,60] and sequential and concurrent Java [6,52]. Other formal specification notations, like B and VDM, operate at the system level [3,38].

Formal notations are precise and often very expressive, but hard to use, even by insiders. Domain-specific languages (DSLs) [40,86] provide a good middle ground between informal natural language and low-level formal logics. DSLs provide domain-specific notation, analysis, verification, and optimization. A key complication is the cost of their implementation and maintenance, as studied by Van Deursen et al. [84]. This can be alleviated by the development of programming environments for the domain-specific programming languages [35,39]. A limitation of the current generation of language workbenches is the lack of support for guaranteeing the safety and reliability of languages, which is crucial for the software intent paradigm. This requires integrating verification of language properties in language workbenches [68].

4.2 Verification of Intent

In industry, testing is currently the prevalent way to discover faults, and to assess the quality of software. It became the most expensive part of system development, calling for test automation to reduce the costs. However, testing is poorly understood: while testing does reveal many software faults, it is currently unknown how much testing is sufficient to gain some justified level of confidence. Also, testing is often focused at small components (unit testing) while the actual challenges arise at system integration. An advanced test automation technique for control-intensive software is model-based testing [82]. This provides a sound and complete theory for deriving, executing, and evaluating test cases from a model of a system. However, systematic research on computing the next best optimal test case is still missing. For data generation, search-based testing has been investigated [79], which uses meta-heuristic search for steering random test suites towards optimizing a test fitness function. For both technologies, there is a gap between the intents of the system and the used test models.

Another challenge is to establish the likelihood that software satisfies its intent after testing, or to generate optimal test cases that lower that likelihood. This challenge is tough. An overview of the field is presented in [96], providing nice and intricate theoretical testing models. Aligning these models with practical observation is a big challenge. Viewing testing as a learning activity is promising, but not yet widespread. It is most prominent in the field of *exploratory testing* [50,93]. Our notion of intent could be used to record the knowledge obtained by exploratory testing. An algorithmic interpretation is provided by automaton learning [19,30,63,64], which has been used complementary to testing [1].

Automated verification of software at design-time raises confidence in program correctness. Its two fundamental pillars are modularity and automated reasoning. *Modularity* forms the cornerstone to scale up verification technology to full systems. It is rooted in proper abstractions of program behavior. In his seminal work, Robin Milner [66] introduced bisimulation as the appropriate equivalence notion. This allowed to reason about the abstract behavior of a program in its wider context. Hoare logic [51] provides modularity at the level of program code. Pre- and post-conditions abstract away from the implementation of software functions. Other parts of the program need to deal with their specification only.

Automated reasoning has been revolutionized by SAT solving. Although SAT solving is NP-hard, a series of breakthroughs [17,25,33,49,80] led to algorithms that allowed to solve instances of propositional formulas of tremendous size. Many problems have been translated into SAT solving. An early example is the verification of PLC programs by Groote [47] that guard the safety of railway yards, bridges and sluices. More recently, SAT solvers were extended with mathematical theories, leading to SMT solvers (satisfiability modulo theories), like Z3 and Mathsat [21,29], reasoning about data types automatically.

The three main branches in automated program verification are: (1) *Interactive proof checkers*. The Dutch mathematician De Bruijn observed in 1967 that proof checking could be mechanized. He built Automath [26], the first program to check mathematical proofs. Modern proof checkers, like Coq [11], follow the same principle. The user constructs a proof interactively, which is checked by an independent procedure, to eliminate all reasonable doubt on the validity of a theorem. This approach is versatile, but not feasible for non-trivial software, since a correctness proof is extremely detailed.

(2) *Model checkers* [8], invented by the Turing Award winners Clarke, Emerson and Sifakis, operate fully automatically in principle. They take a (model of a) program and a specification, and check the property by brute force computation. One of the most expressive model checkers is the mCRL2 toolset [48]. Tremendous progress was made by automated abstraction techniques [14,22], the use of BDD and SAT-solving technology [12], and the use of high-performance graph algorithms for model checking, e.g. [55]. Model checkers operate on finite systems of limited size only; checking realistic software with datatypes and concurrency remains a challenge.

(3) *Automated program verifiers*, like OpenJML and KeY [4,23] strike a balance between expressivity and automation. They directly operate on software programs, generating a sufficient set of verification conditions, which are automatically discharged by SMT solvers. Non-trivial programs can be handled, which is demonstrated by revealing an error in the popular TIMsort routine in the Java library with KeY [27]. Extending Hoare Logic [51] by Separation Logic [32] allowed handle concurrency and data structures of modern software. This led to tools that can reason about parallel Java programs, like the VerCors tool [13]. Still, program verifiers can only be used by verification experts, since they require manual annotations of pre- and post-conditions, as well as auxiliary properties like invariants and thread permissions. This doesn't scale beyond medium size programs.

Monitoring deployed software is common to all programming languages and even computer hardware. An example is checking memory accesses, to prevent violation of the intent that programs should access only their own memory. This can be supported by hardware, guaranteed by the Operating System, and is built-in in many modern programming languages (like Java and C#).

In the security context, the versatility and unpredictability of attacks on software make it hard to verify against *a priori* defined intent. Besides monitoring violation of well-defined security intents, software is often monitored globally and any unusual activity (such as extreme network activity) is reported for further investigation. Whenever a security breach is detected, this is generally transformed into an explicit intent that can be checked. Advanced security monitoring techniques are pioneered by Bos et al [81,83]. Likewise, Lago's team has pioneered monitoring of sustainability intents [57,75,77].

In the run-time verification community, attention has shifted to the dynamic verification of behavioural properties on programs [10,31]. These techniques are often limited to safety properties, which guarantee absence of malbehavior. Like user-inserted asserts, all these forms of monitoring typically lead to a stop-the-world whenever some intent violation is detected.

4.3   Evolution of Intent

Programming by contract [65] emerged as a systematic approach. When the software intent or the environment change, it can be checked whether the environment still offers sufficient functionality, such that the software can still guarantee its renewed contract. To establish that the software itself ends up undamaged in core memory, traditional methods are self-tests, checksums and oblivious hashing. These can be circumvented, so security researchers introduced tamper-proof software, which relies on encryption [7,95].

To localize faults, spectrum-based fault diagnosis attributes observed failures to the responsible software components [2,74]. A different perspective is origin tracking [85], where the contribution of a certain source element to some external effect is carefully traced. A promising new localisation approach is proof carrying code [9,67]. Here, the program correctness proof is encoded within the software.

If the intent changes, proof reconstruction might point to the relevant parts of the proof and program that must be changed.

There are a number of fields where returning to a safe situation has been investigated in depth. Examples are file storage [91], database transactions [56] and networking [18]. Generally, such techniques rely on external operators to restart systems and bring them back in a working state. A whole research line on software engineering considers self-* systems (e.g. self-adaptation, self-management, self-healing, self-configuration). Here a system must preserve its operation at run-time even in the presence of changes in environment, resources, security breaches, faults [28]. Solutions come from various areas, like software architecture, fault-tolerance, and bio-inspired computing [16,72,92]. These techniques typically protect against environment uncertainty.

If the software contains errors, or when the intents themselve change, software must be updated. There are several techniques to update software while it is running (hot swappable). Reliable dynamic updates and error recovery are studied in [44,45]. There is little systematic research into the question how software can handle its own mishap completely autonomously. Only very recently, some indications that self-correcting code might work were published [43,58,73]. The question is whether these observations carry over to software on a larger scale. In particular, it will be challenging to compute the best update on the software that removes the problem.

The fundamental challenge in self-correcting code lies in guaranteeing that code adapts itself in such a way that it will continue to behave in the right way, even if the intent has not been formulated explicitly and completely. In the past, various forms of self-adaptation of software have been used, generally with an adverse effect. An excellent example is the programming language COMAL [46], which would correct simple programming errors by itself. Superficial typos were sometimes transformed in deep, hard to spot programming errors, undoing the beneficiary effect of type checking.

5   Perspectives

We conclude by summarizing our perspective on achieving software that meets its intents. In particular, we identify technical challenges that will need further research in the next decade.

First, intents must be discovered and expressed. The goal is that all stakeholders can express, understand, and prioritize their expectations on software. Domain specific languages should bridge the enormous gap between human intent and low-level machine readable code.

Second, intents must be verifiable, both statically during design (verification), dynamically in a laboratory setting (testing), and on deployed code (monitoring). The big challenge is to make an automation leap: human effort to annotate or instrument programs, construct proofs, derive test cases, or operate verification tools should be avoided. Technically, this requires an advance of annotation and invariant generation. At the same time, verification should bridge the gap between detailed code and its high-level, emerging properties.

Finally, software should correct itself when it contains errors, when its environment changes, or when the intents of people or organizations evolve. Current runtime adaption and software update technology should be complemented by an auto-correction facility for code. Building in explicit and executable notions of intent make it possible in principle that software adapts itself to its intent.

These technical developments require the coordinated effort of researchers in theoretical computer science, programming languages, and empirical software engineering. When successful, they could form the basis for intents as software laws that can be verified and guaranteed. Only automatically self-correcting software will enable us to regain grip on the complex, evolving software systems that run our society. Ultimately, this development allows that software providers can be held accountable for their product.

References

1. Aarts, F., Kuppens, H., Tretmans, J., Vaandrager, F.W., Verwer, S.: Improving active Mealy machine learning for protocol conformance testing. Mach. Learn. **96**(1–2), 189–224 (2014)
2. Abreu, R., Zoeteweij, P., Van Gemund, A.J.C.: A new Bayesian approach to multiple intermittent fault diagnosis. In: International Joint Conference on Artificial Intelligence, IJCAI 2009, pp. 653–658 (2009)
3. Abrial, J.: Modeling in Event-B - System and Software Engineering. Cambridge University Press, Cambridge (2010)
4. Ahrendt, W., Beckert, B., Hähnle, R., Rümmer, P., Schmitt, P.H.: Verifying object-oriented programs with KeY: a tutorial. In: de Boer, F.S., Bonsangue, M.M., Graf, S., de Roever, W.-P. (eds.) FMCO 2006. LNCS, vol. 4709, pp. 70–101. Springer, Heidelberg (2007)
5. Ali, R., Dalpiaz, F., Giorgini, P.: Reasoning with contextual requirements: detecting inconsistency and conflicts. Inf. Softw. Technol. **55**(1), 35–57 (2013)
6. Amighi, A., Haack, C., Huisman, M., Hurlin, C.: Permission-based separation logic for multithreaded Java programs. Logical Methods Comput. Sci. 11(1:2), 1–66 (2015) paper 2
7. Andriesse, D., Bos, H., Slowinska, A.: Parallax: implicit code integrity verification using return-oriented programming. In: IEEE/IFIP IC on Dependable Systems and Networks, DSN 2015, pp. 125–135. IEEE Computer Society (2015)
8. Baier, C., Katoen, J.-P.: Principles of Model Checking. The MIT Press, Cambridge (2008)
9. Barthe, G., Grégoire, B., Kunz, C., Rezk, T.: Certificate translation for optimizing compilers. ACM Trans. Program. Lang. Syst. **31**(5), 18 (2009)
10. Bauer, A., Leucker, M., Schallhart, C.: Runtime verification for LTL and TLTL. ACM Trans. Softw. Eng. Methodol. **20**(4), 14 (2011)
11. Bertot, Y., Castéran, P.: Interactive Theorem Proving and Program Development - Coq'Art: The Calculus of Inductive Constructions. Texts in Theoretical Computer Science. An EATCS Series. Springer, Heidelberg (2004)
12. Biere, A., Cimatti, A., Clarke, E.M., Strichman, O., Zhu, Y.: Bounded model checking. Adv. Comput. **58**, 117–148 (2003)
13. Blom, S., Huisman, M.: The VerCors tool for verification of concurrent programs. In: Jones, C., Pihlajasaari, P., Sun, J. (eds.) FM 2014. LNCS, vol. 8442, pp. 127–131. Springer, Heidelberg (2014)

14. Bradley, A.R.: IC3 and beyond: incremental, inductive verification. In: Madhusudan, P., Seshia, S.A. (eds.) CAV 2012. LNCS, vol. 7358, p. 4. Springer, Heidelberg (2012)

15. Breaux, T.D., Vail, M.W., Antón, A.I.: Towards regulatory compliance: extracting rights and obligations to align requirements with regulations. In: IEEE International Requirements Engineering Conference, pp. 46–55 (2006)

16. Brun, Y., Di Marzo Serugendo, G., Gacek, C., Giese, H., Kienle, H., Litoiu, M., Müller, H., Pezzè, M., Shaw, M.: Engineering self-adaptive systems through feedback loops. In: Cheng, B.H.C., Lemos, R., Giese, H., Inverardi, P., Magee, J. (eds.) Software Engineering for Self-Adaptive Systems. LNCS, vol. 5525, pp. 48–70. Springer, Heidelberg (2009). doi:10.1007/978-3-642-02161-9_3

17. Bryant, R.E.: Symbolic manipulation of Boolean functions using a graphical representation. In: Ofek, H., O'Neill, L.A. (eds.) 22nd ACM/IEEE Conference on Design Automation, (DAC 1985), pp. 688–694. ACM (1985)

18. Cachin, C., Guerraoui, R., Rodrigues, L.E.T.: Introduction to Reliable and Secure Distributed Programming, 2nd edn. Springer, Heidelberg (2011)

19. Cassel, S., Howar, F., Jonsson, B., Steffen, B.: Active learning for extended finite state machines. Formal Aspects Comput. 28(2), 233–263 (2016)

20. Chen, T.-H., Nagappan, M., Shihab, E., Hassan, A.E.: An empirical study of dormant bugs. In: 11th Working Conference on Mining Software Repositories, MSR 2014, pp. 82–91. ACM (2014)

21. Cimatti, A., Griggio, A., Schaafsma, B.J., Sebastiani, R.: The MathSAT5 SMT solver. In: Piterman, N., Smolka, S.A. (eds.) TACAS 2013 (ETAPS 2013). LNCS, vol. 7795, pp. 93–107. Springer, Heidelberg (2013)

22. Clarke, E.M., Gupta, A., Strichman, O.: SAT-based counterexample-guided abstraction refinement. IEEE Trans. CAD Integr. Circ. Syst. 23(7), 1113–1123 (2004)

23. Cok, D.R.: OpenJML: software verification for Java 7 using JML, OpenJDK, and Eclipse. In: Dubois, C., Giannakopoulou, D., Méry, D. (eds.) 1st Workshop on Formal Integrated Development Environment, (F-IDE 2014). EPTCS, vol. 149, pp. 79–92 (2014)

24. Dalpiaz, F., Paja, E., Giorgini, P.: Security Requirements Engineering: Designing Secure Socio-Technical Systems, 1st edn. MIT Press, Cambridge (2016)

25. Davis, M., Logemann, G., Loveland, D.W.: A machine program for theorem-proving. Commun. ACM 5(7), 394–397 (1962)

26. de Bruijn, N.: A survey of the project AUTOMATH. In: To H.B. Curry: Essays in Combinatory Logic, Lambda Calculus and Formalism, pp. 579–606. Academic Press (1980)

27. de Gouw, S., Rot, J., de Boer, F.S., Bubel, R., Hähnle, R.: OpenJDK's Java.utils.Collection.sort() is broken: the good, the bad and the worst case. In: Kroening, D., Păsăreanu, C.S. (eds.) CAV 2015. LNCS, vol. 9206, pp. 273–289. Springer, Heidelberg (2015)

28. de Lemos, R., et al.: Software engineering processes for self-adaptive systems. In: Lemos, R., Giese, H., Müller, H.A., Shaw, M. (eds.) Software Engineering for Self-Adaptive Systems II. LNCS, vol. 7475, pp. 51–75. Springer, Heidelberg (2013). doi:10.1007/978-3-642-35813-5_3

29. de Moura, L., Bjørner, N.S.: Z3: an efficient SMT solver. In: Ramakrishnan, C.R., Rehof, J. (eds.) TACAS 2008. LNCS, vol. 4963, pp. 337–340. Springer, Heidelberg (2008)

30. van Deursen, A.: Testing web applications with state objects. Commun. ACM 58(8), 36–43 (2015)

31. Diekert, V., Leucker, M.: Topology, monitorable properties and runtime verification. Theor. Comput. Sci. **537**, 29–41 (2014)
32. Distefano, D., O'Hearn, P.W., Yang, H.: A local shape analysis based on separation logic. In: Hermanns, H., Palsberg, J. (eds.) TACAS 2006. LNCS, vol. 3920, pp. 287–302. Springer, Heidelberg (2006)
33. Eén, N., Sörensson, N.: An extensible SAT-solver. In: Giunchiglia, E., Tacchella, A. (eds.) SAT 2003. LNCS, vol. 2919, pp. 502–518. Springer, Heidelberg (2004)
34. Ellison, C., Rosu, G.: An executable formal semantics of C with applications. In: 39th ACM SIGPLAN-SIGACT Symposium on Principles of Programming Languages (POPL 2012), pp. 533–544. ACM (2012)
35. Erdweg, S., et al.: Evaluating and comparing language workbenches: existing results and benchmarks for the future. Comput. Lang. Syst. Struct. **44**, 24–47 (2015)
36. Finkelstein, A., Gabbay, D., Hunter, A., Kramer, J., Nuseibeh, B.: Inconsistency handling in multiperspective specifications. IEEE TSE **20**(8), 569–578 (1994)
37. Finkelstein, A., Kramer, J., Nuseibeh, B., Finkelstein, L., Goedicke, M.: Viewpoints: a framework for integrating multiple perspectives in system development. Int. J. Softw. Eng. Knowl. Eng. **2**(1), 31–57 (1992)
38. Fitzgerald, J., Larsen, P.G.: Modelling Systems: Practical Tools and Techniques for Software Development, 2nd edn. Cambridge University Press, Cambridge (2009)
39. Fowler, M.: Language workbenches: The killer-app. for domain specific languages? (2005). http://www.martinfowler.com/articles/languageWorkbench.html
40. Fowler, M.: Domain-Specific Languages. Addison Wesley, Boston (2010)
41. Ganapathi, A., Patterson, D.A.: Crash data collection: a windows case study. In: DSN, pp. 280–285. IEEE Computer Society (2005)
42. Gartner Inc. Smart cities will include 10 billion things by 2020 (2015). https://www.gartner.com/doc/3004417/smart-cities-include-billion
43. Ghardallou, W., Diallo, N., Mili, A.: Program derivation by correctness enhancements. In: Refinement (2015)
44. Giuffrida, C., Cavallaro, L., Tanenbaum, A.S.: Practical automated vulnerability monitoring using program state invariants. In: DSN, October 2013
45. Giuffrida, C., Iorgulescu, C., Kuijsten, A., Tanenbaum, A.S.: Back to the future: fault-tolerant live update with time-traveling state transfer. In: LISA, October 2013
46. Gratte, I.: Starting with COMAL. Prentice-Hall, Englewood Cliffs (1985)
47. Groote, J., Koorn, J., van Vlijmen, S.: The safety guaranteeing system at station Hoorn-Kersenboogerd (extended abstract). In: 10th Annual Conference on Computer Assurance (COMPASS 1995), pp. 57–68 (1995)
48. Groote, J., Mousavi, M.: Modeling and Analysis of Communicating Systems. The MIT Press, Cambridge (2014)
49. Groote, J.F., Warners, J.P.: The propositional formula checker HeerHugo. J. Autom. Reasoning **24**(1/2), 101–125 (2000)
50. Hendrickson, E.: Explore It!: Reduce Risk and Increase Confidence with Exploratory Testing. The Pragmatic Bookshelf, Raleigh (2013)
51. Hoare, C.: An axiomatic basis for computer programming. Commun. ACM **12**(10), 576–580 (1969)
52. Huisman, M.: Reasoning about Java Programs in Higher Order Logic with PVS and Isabelle. Ph.D. thesis, University of Nijmegen (2001)
53. Hwong, Y., Keiren, J., Kusters, V., Leemans, S., Willemse, T.: Formalising and analysing the control software of the compact muon solenoid experiment at the large hadron collider. Sci. Comput. Program. **78**, 2435–2452 (2013)

54. Ingolfo, S., Siena, A., Mylopoulos, J.: Establishing regulatory compliance for software requirements. In: Jeusfeld, M., Delcambre, L., Ling, T.-W. (eds.) ER 2011. LNCS, vol. 6998, pp. 47–61. Springer, Heidelberg (2011). doi:10.1007/978-3-642-24606-7_5

55. Kant, G., Laarman, A., Meijer, J., van de Pol, J., Blom, S., van Dijk, T.: LTSmin: high-performance language-independent model checking. In: Baier, C., Tinelli, C. (eds.) TACAS 2015. LNCS, vol. 9035, pp. 692–707. Springer, Heidelberg (2015)

56. Kemme, B., Jiménez, R., Patiño-Martinínez, M.: Database Replication. Synthesis Lectures on Data Management. Morgan & Claypool Publishers, San Rafael (2010)

57. Lago, P., Koçak, S.A., Crnkovic, I., Penzenstadler, B.: Framing sustainability as a property of software quality. Commun. ACM **58**(10), 70–78 (2015)

58. Le Goues, C., Nguyen, T., Forrest, S., Weimer, W.: GenProg: a generic method for automatic software repair. IEEE Trans. Softw. Eng. **38**(1), 54–72 (2012)

59. Leavens, G., Poll, E., Clifton, C., Cheon, Y., Ruby, C., Cok, D.R., Müller, P., Kiniry, J., Chalin, P.: JML Reference Manual, Dept. of Computer Science, Iowa State University, February 2007. http://www.jmlspecs.org

60. Leroy, X.: Formal verification of a realistic compiler. Commun. ACM **52**, 107–115 (2009)

61. Lewis, G.A., Lago, P., Avgeriou, P.: A decision model for cyber-foraging systems. In: Proceedings of the 13th Working IEEE/IFIP Conference on Software Architecture (WICSA 2016), pp. 51–60. IEEE (2016)

62. Matias, R., Prince, M., Borges, L., Sousa, C., Henrique, L.: An empirical exploratory study on operating system reliability. In: 29th Annual ACM Symposium on Applied Computing, SAC 2014, pp. 1523–1528. ACM (2014)

63. Mesbah, A., van Deursen, A., Lenselink, S.: Crawling Ajax-based web applications through dynamic analysis of user interface state changes. ACM Trans. Web **6**(1), 3 (2012)

64. Mesbah, A., van Deursen, A., Roest, D.: Invariant-based automated testing of modern web applications. IEEE Trans. Softw. Eng. **38**(1), 35–53 (2012)

65. Meyer, B.: Touch of Class: Learning to Program Well with Objects and Contracts. Springer, Heidelberg (2009)

66. Milner, R.: Calculus of Communicating Systems. Lectures in Computer Science, vol. 92. Springer, Heidelberg (1980)

67. Necula, G.C.: Proof-carrying code. In: Principles of Programming Languages (1997)

68. Neron, P., Tolmach, A., Visser, E., Wachsmuth, G.: A theory of name resolution. In: Vitek, J. (ed.) ESOP 2015. LNCS, vol. 9032, pp. 205–231. Springer, Heidelberg (2015)

69. Osaiweran, A., Schuts, M., Hooman, J., Groote, J., van Rijnsoever, B.: Evaluating the effect a lightweight formal technique in industry. Int. J. Softw. Tools Technol. Transf. **18**, 93–108 (2016)

70. Ostrand, T.J., Weyuker, E.J.: The distribution of faults in a large industrial software system. In: 2002 ACM SIGSOFT International Symposium on Software Testing and Analysis, ISSTA 2002, pp. 55–64. ACM (2002)

71. Ostrand, T.J., Weyuker, E.J., Bell, R.M.: Where the bugs are. In: 2004 ACM SIGSOFT International Symposium on Software Testing and Analysis, ISSTA 2004, pp. 86–96. ACM (2004)

72. Patikirikorala, T., Colman, A., Han, J., Wang, L.: A systematic survey on the design of self-adaptive software systems using control engineering approaches. In: Proceedings of the 7th International Symposium on Software Engineering for Adaptive and Self-Managing Systems, pp. 33–42. IEEE Press (2012)

73. Pei, Y., Furia, C.A., Nordio, M., Wei, Y., Meyer, B., Zeller, A.: Automated fixing of programs with contracts. IEEE Trans. Softw. Eng. **40**(5), 427–449 (2014)

74. Perez, A., Abreu, R., van Deursen, A.: A unifying metric for test adequacy and diagnosability. In: Automated Software Engineering (2016, Submitted)

75. Procaccianti, G., Fernández, H., Lago, P.: Empirical evaluation of two best practices for energy-efficient software development. J. Syst. Softw. **117**, 185–198 (2016)

76. Procaccianti, G., Lago, P., Lewis, G.A.: A catalogue of green architectural tactics for the cloud. In: Maintenance and Evolution of Service-Oriented and Cloud-Based Systems (MESOCA 2014), pp. 29–36. IEEE (2014)

77. Procaccianti, G., Lago, P., Vetro, A., Fernández, D.M., Wieringa, R.: The green lab: experimentation in software energy efficiency. In: Proceedings of the 37th International Conference on Software Engineering-Volume 2 (2015)

78. Rozanski, N., Woods, E.: Software Systems Architecture: Working with Stakeholders using Viewpoints and Perspectives. Addison-Wesley, Boston (2012)

79. Salvesen, K., Galeotti, J.P., Gross, F., Fraser, G., Zeller, A.: Using dynamic symbolic execution to generate inputs in search-based GUI testing. In: Gay, G., Antoniol, G. (eds.) 8th IEEE/ACM International Workshop on Search-Based Software Testing, SBST 2015, pp. 32–35. IEEE (2015)

80. Sheeran, M., Stålmarck, G.: A tutorial on Stålmarck's proof procedure for propositional logic. Formal Methods Syst. Des. **16**(1), 23–58 (2000)

81. Slowinska, A., Stancescu, T., Bos, H.: Body armor for binaries: preventing buffer overflows without recompilation. In: Proceedings of USENIX Annual Technical Conference, Boston, MA, June 2012

82. Tretmans, J.: Model based testing with labelled transition systems. In: Hierons, R.M., Bowen, J.P., Harman, M. (eds.) FORTEST. LNCS, vol. 4949, pp. 1–38. Springer, Heidelberg (2008)

83. van der Veen, V., Goktas, E., Contag, M., Pawlowski, A., Chen, X., Rawat, S., Bos, H., Holz, T., Athanasopoulos, E., Giuffrida, C.: A tough call: mitigating advanced code-reuse attacks at the binary level. In: Proceedings of the 37th IEEE Symposium on Security and Privacy (Oakland), San Jose, CA, USA, IEEE, May 2016

84. van Deursen, A., Klint, P.: Little languages: little maintenance? J. Softw. Maintenance **10**(2), 75–92 (1998)

85. van Deursen, A., Klint, P., Tip, F.: Origin tracking. J. Symbolic Comput. **15**(5/6), 523–545 (1993)

86. van Deursen, A., Klint, P., Visser, J.: Domain-specific languages: an annotated bibliography. SIGPLAN Not. **35**(6), 26–36 (2000)

87. van Genuchten, M., Hatton, L.: Metrics with impact. IEEE Softw. **30**, 99–101 (2013)

88. van Genuchten, M., Hatton, L.: When software crosses a line. IEEE Softw. **33**, 29–31 (2016)

89. van Lamsweerde, A.: Requirements engineering in the year 00: a research perspective. In: Proceedings of the IEEE International Symposium on Requirements Engineering, pp. 5–19 (2000)

90. van Lamsweerde, A.: Requirements Engineering: From System Goals to UML Models to Software Specifications. Wiley, Hoboken (2009)

91. von Hagen, W., Filesystems, U.: UNIX Filesystems: Evolution, Design, and Implementation. SAMS, Indianapolis (2002)

92. Weyns, D., Iftikhar, M.U., de la Iglesia, D.G., Ahmad, T.: A survey of formal methods in self-adaptive systems. In: Proceedings of the IC on Computer Science and Software Engineering, pp. 67–79. ACM (2012)

93. Whittaker, J.A.: Exploratory Software Testing: Tips, Tricks, Tours, and Techniques to Guide Test Design. Addison-Wesley, Boston (2009)
94. Witze, A.: Software error doomed Japanese Hitomi spacecraft. Nature **533**, 18–19 (2016)
95. Wurster, G., van Oorschot, P.C., Somayaji, A.: A generic attack on checksumming-based software tamper resistance. In: 2005 IEEE Symposium on Security and Privacy (S&P 2005), pp. 127–138. IEEE Computer Society (2005)
96. Yamada, S.: Software Reliability Modeling. Springer, Heidelberg (2014)

Compliance, Functional Safety and Fault Detection by Formal Methods

Christof Fetzer[1]([⊠]), Christoph Weidenbach[2], and Patrick Wischnewski[3]

[1] Technical University Dresden, Dresden, Germany
christof.fetzer@tu-dresden.de
[2] Max Planck Institute for Informatics, Saarbrücken, Germany
weidenbach@mpi-inf.mpg.de
[3] Logic4Business GmbH, Saarbrücken, Germany
patrick.wischnewski@logic4business.com

Abstract. With the increasing complexity of today's cars functional safety and compliance guarantees are more and more difficult to obtain. During the life time of a vehicle the detection of malfunctioning non-mechanical components requires meanwhile more attention than the maintenance of its mechanical counterparts. A full fledged formal verification of the overall car is not realistic and even hard to obtain for single non-trivial components such as assistant systems. Furthermore, it does not support fault detection at run time. We suggest an approach towards formal safety, compliance and fault detection at run time via an auditor. The auditor is automatically fed out of the engineering and production process by a suitable abstract specification and respective model of the car and can detect then detect violations and faulty components.

1 Introduction

The big advantage of cars as a system compared to software is robustness. A single spark ignition failure during an engine run is hardly ever recognized by the driver nor does it significantly influence the behavior of an engine. In contrast to the robustness of an engine, a single faulty line of code in a big piece of software typically causes undesired behavior of the overall system. On the other hand and in contrast to software, all parts of a car can unexpectedly break at life time. Therefore, instead of a rigid formal verification of a car, the robustness offers another possibility: the verification of the car's behavior with respect to an abstract specification and model at run time. The approach is not unrealistic. Car manufactures are typically able to predict the behavior of their cars with respect to such an abstract model on the basis of a few hundred specification parameters. For example, acceleration from 0 to 100 can be predicted up to an accuracy of at least 5 % already at the design time of a new car. Similarly, emission values of fuel consumption can be predicted as well.

This motivates our approach to guarantee functional safety, compliance and fault detection. An auditor is added to the car. It reads the run time parameters while driving, knows the abstract model and specification of the specific

© Springer International Publishing AG 2016
T. Margaria and B. Steffen (Eds.): ISoLA 2016, Part II, LNCS 9953, pp. 626–632, 2016.
DOI: 10.1007/978-3-319-47169-3_48

car, and may obtain further information, e.g., GPS information, by communicating to the outside world. The auditor compares the run time parameters with the abstract model. In case of a violation beyond the accuracy of the abstract model, it can act accordingly. Online monitoring has been already investigated previously, for example, in the context of a gear box [5]. Also, some auditing functionality is today already build into modern cars, e.g., for engine safety, our approach is generic in the sense that it can be applied to functional safety, compliance and fault detection, in general. Furthermore, because it is built on top of a formal model through engineering and manufacturing, it can even consider parameters at the level of a specific car. Any property that can be supported by a sufficiently accurate abstract model can be subject to the auditor. Furthermore, while the currently deployed auditors are hand-coded, we indicate that our auditor approach can be actually automatically generated out of an engineering and manufacturing process supported by an overall formal model. Because it is automatically generated, it can even be more accurate and potentially cheaper than today's approaches. For example, it might be able to distinguish hardware from software failures at run time [4] and may consider car specific properties such as electricity consumption.

The paper is now organized as follows: Sect. 2 explains how the formal abstract model and needed input parameters can be obtained out of an engineering and manufacturing process supported by formal methods. In Sect. 3, we explain our auditor approach, where a generic auditor is fed by the parameters and models from Sect. 2. The paper concludes with a discussion of the obtained results and its potential impact in practice.

2   Development

All car manufacturers already have a logical description of the cars they can build, they can produce, and they want to sell. This description is typically based on the parts of the car, including software at the same level as the mechanical parts, and also contains key specification properties. From the engineering process abstract models representing specific aspects of the overall car are available as well. For our approach, we accumulate all this information into one formal model.

We propose a rigid development, manufacturing and sales process that is build on top of a formal, consistent overall formal model representing all eventual products. Aftersales can make use of this model at a car specific level. The model is based on the *parts* of a car. Attached to parts are *attributes*. *Rules* in form of formulas of an appropriate logic state how the different parts can be combined to *components*, and eventually to *products*, i.e., cars. Furthermore, *constraints* on attributes, assigned to components and products further enable the fulfillment of properties beyond the bill of material.

For example, a *component* may be a particular engine, that contains as its *parts* a specific block, cylinder head etc. It carries as its *attributes* the overall volume and number of cylinders. Together with further parts, including a particular engine software, transmission, etc., the engine becomes an application for

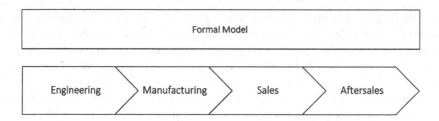

Fig. 1. Formal model representing all product variants over the product-life-cycle

a particular car. Its emission values are measured in the respective test-stand cycle and become *attributes* of the application and eventually parameters of the final abstract model (Fig. 1) .

Typical constraints with respect to engineering, manufacturing and legal requirements could be:

- the size of the gasoline tank of the car stays in a sound relation to its fuel consumption and desired reachability,
- the engine software properly matches the number of cylinders of the engine and considers the attached turbo charger, and
- the fuel consumption, and hence respective emission values, is limited at particular state of the engine, determined, e.g., by its current load,

respectively. If all this information is in fact the basis for the overall building process of the car, the parameters of the auditor for a particular car variant can be automatically set during manufacturing.

A formal model representing all product variants with its attributes comes with the big advantage that formal verification becomes available early in the process and can be used in order to prove that all specified rules are fulfilled. Consequently, the proof serves as a certificate for the correctness of the formal model in terms of safety, manufacturing and compliance requirements and the parameters for the auditor are automatically extracted from the certificate. With these parameters, the auditor observes and, hence, ensures that the correctness of the formal model is properly implemented and kept during life time in the real car. Consequently, the correctness of the overall system (car) is ensured over the complete life-cycle.

Furthermore, building, maintaining and automatically deriving properties of such an overall model of all car variants and its attributes provides the opportunity to perform optimizations on the formal model with respect to a wide range of parameters. This is not completely beyond scope of today's performance of automated reasoning tools. In [6], it is shown that the emission class of a car can be automatically obtained out of a model of the above form. For example, the weight of the car, one input parameter of the emission class formula, is accurately computed in this abstract model out of weight of the different parts of the car. It is even shown that optimization problems, e.g., answering questions of the form "what is the cheapest car with emission class x that contains the components $y, z, \ldots$" can be solved by appropriate usage of automated reasoning technology.

Although a rigid management of the product built process is a well known topic in the engineering and manufacturing science [3], an approach based on an overall formal model has not yet been developed. There is work on certain aspects of a formal model build on top of bill of material for the product [7] but it does not consider complex constraints and attributes as suggested here. These are needed to eventually and automatically provide an abstract model and specification to an auditor. A first step into this direction is described in [6].

3 Auditor

The objective of the online auditor is to monitor at runtime if all requirements (e.g., clean air regulations) are satisfied. To be able to do so, the car and in particular, its components like the engine controller, have to provide the auditor with all information that are needed to perform this real-time compliance check (see Fig. 2). The auditor has a formal model of the car together with its specific parameters that permits it to perform this compliance check, e.g., to ensure that emissions regulations and safety regulations are satisfied. This formal model is a result of configuration information generated in the development process (see Sect. 2).

The idea is that the auditor computes the compliance information and reports not only to the OEM but also during the next motor vehicle inspection if there were any violations. This report is certified to show that this report was generated by a valid auditor. An inspection station is permitted to download and analyze this report, in particular also for the detection and repair of faulty components.

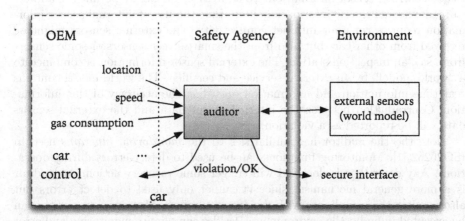

Fig. 2. The online auditor runs inside the car. The car provides the auditor with real-time information that permit it to check if requirements are satisfied. The auditor has access to external sensor data to crosscheck and to extend the real-time information

Note that the auditing of the emission data could in principle be performed outside of the car. For example, a car could upload all necessary information in real-time to some cloud service. This might, however, expose privacy relevant data to the cloud and might, moreover, require constant Internet connectivity. Similarly, if we would store all sensor data, one could process the data, say, at an inspection station. However, this would imply that all data must be stored for long durations (> 2years) - which would be too much data to store.

An online auditor does not need to store massive amounts of data nor does it need to send data across the Internet. It has to store only minimal amount of data: any violation of regulations is stored persistently until the next motor vehicle inspection. The auditor could even be configured to report violations immediately, e.g., to ensure that safety violations are immediately addressable. The auditor will not reveal any private data during normal operations. The auditor is the result of a formal car model, therefore, it can even be verified whether private data of the driver or intellectual property of the OEM is leaked to the outside. However, if a violation of some regulations has occurred, this information needs to be verifiable: the location of this violation might need to be reported as well as all sensor data relevant for proving that a violation has happened.

If a violation can be shown based on the information provided by the car, the auditor needs to show that the sensor data was indeed been provided by the car. Hence, we require that the car certifies all sensor data and the auditor only accepts certified sensor data. In this way, the auditor could formally prove to an external auditor, that a violation has happened. This proof could also be used to provide evidence to car manufacturers to fix the detected issues.

If a car would consistently lie to the auditor, the auditor might never detect a violation since a good liar will, of course, appear to satisfy all requirements. Since the auditor does not have any sensor itself, it cannot use its own sensing to detect wrong sensor information. To address this issue, we permit the auditor to read external sensor information. Note that the use of external sensor information requires constant Internet connectivity. The external sensors might be received from other cars but also from the smart street sensors or some sensors from, say, an inspection station. The external sensor information is combined to a "world model" by an external service and certified. The world model contains real/time information and information regarding the accuracy of this information. Contradiction between the internal sensor data and the external sensors data will be reported as a violation.

Note the the auditor has similarities to the *monitoring functions* used in ISO26262 [1]. Monitoring functions can be used to detect errors during operations. Any error that is detected will trigger some recovery action. An auditor is a more general mechanism since it cannot only used to detect errors but also monitor the compliance with various regulations. Moreover, an auditor can be executed in an hostile environment. Besides compliance monitoring and error detection, auditors could also be used to support the *field monitoring process* [2]. Field monitoring is used to collect data about any potential safety violation during operations. This cannot only be used to detect issues in safety critical software but also to support *proven in use arguments*.

4   Conclusions

Technical systems are highly complex and the verification that they are functionally safe and in compliance with all applicable regulations is very difficult to ensure using design time verification. In addition, design time verification does not support run time fault detection. Our proposal is to perform a continuous verification of the compliance of a technical system with its specification at run time. This should ensure a level playing field for all manufacturers - independent of their interpretation of legal regulations. Our approach balances regulatory compliance, protection of intellectual property by the manufacturer and the privacy of the users. It requires a formal-methods supported development process by using artifact created during the development with the auditor-based compliance checking. The auditor protects the IP of the manufacturer by processing in real-time all data and only keep data in case a violation of regulation was detected. Moreover, the auditor protects the privacy of the car user. Only in case of a violation, anonymized data may be forwarded.

We can think of a wide range of potential instances of the auditor. It may be an external component that is only attached to the car by a regulation authority to check compliance. It may be an external component used by the garage for fault cause detection. It may be a permanent part of the car and generalize the mechanisms already in place today.

References

1. ISO/DIS 26262–1 - Road vehicles Functional safety Part 1 Glossary, July 2009
2. ISO/DIS 26262–7 - Road vehicles Functional safety Part 7 Production and operation (2009)
3. ElMaraghy, H., Schuh, G., ElMaraghy, W., Piller, F., Schönsleben, P., Tseng, M., Bernard, A.: Product variety management. CIRP Ann. Manuf. Technol. **62**(2), 629–652 (2013)
4. Ghadhab, M., Kuntz, M., Kuvaiskii, D., Fetzer, C.: A controller safety concept based on software-implemented fault tolerance for fail-operational automotive applications. In: Artho, C. (ed.) FTSCS 2015. CCIS, vol. 596, pp. 189–205. Springer, Heidelberg (2016). doi:10.1007/978-3-319-29510-7_11
5. Heffernan, D., Macnamee, C., Fogarty, P.: Runtime verification monitoring for automotive embedded systems using the ISO 26262 functional safety standard as a guide for the definition of the monitored properties. IET Softw. **8**(5), 193–203 (2014)
6. Junk, C., Rößger, R., Rock, G., Theis, K., Weidenbach, C., Wischnewski, P.: Model-based variant management with v. control. In: Curran, R., Wognum, N., Borsato, M., Stjepandic, J., Verhagen, W.J. C. (eds.) Transdisciplinary Lifecycle Analysis of Systems - Proceedings of the 22nd ISPE Inc., International Conference on Concurrent Engineering, Delft, The Netherlands, July 20–23, 2015, vol. 2 of Advances in Transdisciplinary Engineering, pp. 194–203. IOS Press (2015)

7. Mendonça, M., Wasowski, A., Czarnecki, K.: SAT-based analysis of feature models is easy. In: Muthig, D., McGregor, J.D. (eds.) Software Product Lines, 13th International Conference, SPLC 2009, San Francisco, California, USA, August 24–28, 2009, Proceedings, vol. 446 of ACM International Conference Proceeding Series, pp. 231–240. ACM (2009)

What the Hack Is Wrong with Software Doping?

Kevin Baum[✉]

Saarland University, Saarbrücken, Germany
k.baum@uni-saarland.de

Abstract. Today we often deal with hybrid products, i.e. physical devices containing embedded software. Sometimes, e.g., in the VW emission scandal, such hybrid systems aims rather at the fulfillment of interests of the manufacturers than at those of the customers. This often happens hidden from and unbeknown to the owners or users of these devices and especially unbeknown to supervisory authorities. While examples of such *software doping* can be easily found, the phenomenon itself isn't well understood yet. Not only do we lack a proper definition of the term "software doping", it is also the moral status of software doping that seems vague and unclear. In this paper, I try, in the tradition of computer ethics, to first understand what software doping is and then to examine its moral status. I argue that software doping is at least pro tanto morally wrong. I locate problematic features of software doping that are in conflict with moral rights that come with device ownership. Furthermore, I argue for the stronger claim that, in general, software doping also is morally wrong all things considered – at least from the point of view of some normative theories. Explicitly, the VW emission scandal is adduced as a significant specimen of software doping that unquestionably is morally wrong all things considered. Finally, I conclude that we ought to develop software doping detection if only for moral reasons and point towards the implications my work might have for the development of future software doping detection methods.

1 Introduction

How many computers do you own? Many people cannot answer this question correctly these days – because we are typically not aware of the fact that we deal more and more often with mixtures of physical devices and software. Those *hybrid* products are, strictly speaking, computers – or, at least, contain one or more of them. Such hybrid devices come in many shapes and sizes, ranging from obvious examples like printers and smartphones to cars and toys. Hybrid devices raise a number of important legal as well as philosophical questions.

For instance, recently the case of the VW emission scandal hit the news: The German car manufacturer used an embedded software for detecting emission

K. Baum want to thank Holger Hermanns, Stephan Schweitzer, Stephan Padel, Deborah Hirth, and David McCann for their helpful comments on the ideas presented here.

T. Margaria and B. Steffen (Eds.): ISoLA 2016, Part II, LNCS 9953, pp. 633–647, 2016.
DOI: 10.1007/978-3-319-47169-3_49

testing and tweaking the engine's behavior to fit the legal emission requirements. We can learn a lesson from this case: Not every software embedded in a
device is essential to the purpose and proper functionality of it. Rather, it may
modify the device in ways that solely aim at the fulfillment of the manufacturers interests, and – by doing so – ignore the interests of the users and owners.
Typically, such software works in the background, hidden from and unbeknown
to the users and owners of the devices; it is often even clandestinely added
to deceive supervisory authorities. This so-called *software doping* allows VW
to pass nitrogen oxide emission tests by cheating, manufacturers of printers to
reject third-party cartridges, and point-and-shoot camera manufacturers to hide
a bunch of features from their users in cheaper models, making them available
only in more expensive models. Examples of software doping can be easily found,
it seems. However, the phenomenon itself isn't well understood yet. Although
the term "software doping" is made-up and rather a technical term, it has yet
to be properly defined. While we have an intuitive grasp, conceptual work is
pending. But even putting these conceptual worries aside, questions concerning
the moral status of the practice of software doping are in need of answers.

This paper aims at taking a step towards solving both of these issues, putting
to use methods of moral philosophy, especially from the fields of normative and
computer ethics. First, I suggest a definition of "software doping" in terms of
input-output modification of devices aiming at the benefits of the manufacturers
at costs of certain owner interests in Sect. 2. Then, in Sect. 3, I first argue that
software doping is necessarily, by definition, pro tanto wrong, followed by the
stronger claim that, in general, software doping also morally impermissible in an
overall sense – at least from the point of view of some normative theories. This
will be made clear by exploiting the VW emission scandal as a vivid example.
Finally, I will distill some lessons to learn from the result and sum up my findings
in Sect. 4.

2   What Is Software Doping?

Analytic philosophy is often concerned with providing conceptual clarity – not
as a task for its own sake, but because it is taken to be a necessary precondition
for achieving deeper knowledge about our understanding of the world. Some
observations turn out to be fundamental for such philosophical endeavors: Terms
and concepts are often understood and used without us being able to clearly
define them. Sometimes, we can even *apply* conditions of correct and incorrect
usage of terms *without being able to spell out* those conditions immediately – we
may be able to correctly say that in a certain context the use of some word is
clearly incorrect without being able to say why this is so and how we know.

Note, that this is not a grammatical point. Rather, it is the idea that an
intuitive understanding of a term is enough to correctly apply the term without
being able to formulate some criterion: We can apply every-day terms like "love"
or technical terms like "internet" correctly/adequately (and also can identify
incorrect/inadequate usage) without being able to spell out proper definitions of

the terms or explicit rules of correct usage.[1] However, in order to find answers to deep questions regarding the nature of certain concepts (denoted by some terms), we need at least something like characterization, operationalizations, or even better real definition of the corresponding terms: We need to do *conceptual work*. This methodology can be applied to all kinds of terms, even to artificial and technical terms like "software doping". This results in a better understanding of the related concepts.

While conceptual work is central to analytic philosophy in general, it is also perfectly in line with what James Moor identified as the classical nature of computer ethics in his very influential paper "What is Computer Ethics?":

> A typical problem in computer ethics arises because there is a policy vacuum about how computer technology should be used. [...] A difficulty is that along with a policy vacuum there is often a conceptual vacuum. Although a problem in computer ethics may seem clear initially, a little reflection reveals a conceptual muddle. What is needed in such cases is an analysis that provides a coherent conceptual framework within which to formulate a policy for action.[2]

Accordingly, this section deals with conceptual work, striving to identify and overcome a conceptual muddle. I try to explicate different aspects from the intuitive notion of software doping and then test these particular aspects against some example cases in order to sharpen our intuitive notion and to arrive at a full-blown and – most importantly – useful concept.

2.1 Defining "Software Doping"

Every conceptual work needs a starting point. Fortunately, the track organizers offer a useful characterization of "software doping" in intuitive terms: "Embedded software might provide features and functionalities that are not in the interest of the device's user or even of an entire society." And then:

> Embedded software doping is what enables inkjet printers to reject third-party cartridges, and it enables cars to secretly pollute our environment. In general terms, embedded software doping locks the users out of the products they own.

The term's meaning seems clear on an intuitive level, but the provided definition seems extensionally inadequate. Besides, these passages don't seem to tell the full story: for instance, providing features that are not in the interests of the device's

---

[1] Especially, such capabilities are not sufficient for philosophical work concerned with more theory-laden (philosophical) terms. For instance, while many of us use the terms "responsibility" or "knowledge" frequently and without any further thoughts about correctness conditions or definitions, a lot of philosophical work is concerned with how these terms can be defined or at least characterized properly.

[2] [8], p. 266.

users is neither equivalent nor obviously or immediately linked to being locked out of a product one owns. So the questions remains what software doping is exactly.

We can start answering the question by having a look at term's origins: The term "doping" is obviously borrowed from the field of sports. This already suggests two features: First of all, the device's 'behavior' is modified in some sense – and in the case of *software* doping this is achieved by the use of software (we are not concerned with doped software). Secondly, this is done intentionally with the aim to secure an (unfair and improper) advantage for the manufacturer. Accordingly, it is typically done secretly. To stretch the analogy to its limits, think of the manufacturers as the countries, trainers or teams of doped athletes and of the owners and users as fans. Now, let us take a look at the different aspects, I have extracted so far and clarify why and whether they are necessary for adequate definition of software doping.

A Device's Behavior. Taking a black-box perspective on the device allows us to shift the focus on the 'behavior' of a device is and enables us to express the influences of software doping: it may modify the inputs accepted by the device (as in the printer example) or the outputs that are generated, given specific inputs and a context (as in the VW emission case).

Intentionality and Aiming at Advantages. It is central for the concept of software doping that manufacturers add the software intentionally and with the aim to take (unfair) advantage of it, as an example makes clear: Recently, a U.S. federal magistrate judge ordered Apple to backdoor the iPhone that was used by one of the perpetrators of the San Bernardino shootings in December 2015.[3] The legal case was closed after the FBI was able to access data without the help of Apple. Now, assume – contrary to the current facts – that all manufacturers of smart phones are enforced by law to implement backdoors into every smart phone. These cases don't seem to be software doping in the relevant sense. Therefore, an appropriate account of software doping should consider the intention of the manufacturers in order to exclude such cases.

Secretly? Furthermore, it has to be stressed that according to the above characterization software doping isn't *necessarily* done in secret. Typically, it is – especially when it is done illegally. But the case of the voluntary self-restraint of most German car companies to a top speed of about 155 mph isn't something unknown to the public. Nevertheless, it seems to be at least a borderline case of software doping[4], since it was originally done in the interest of the manufacturer: First and foremost because they assumed future problems with safe tires for higher speeds, but second to forestall possible interventions by legislature (in fact, the self-restraint is crumbling the last years).

Against the Owner's Interests. This is, however, still not the full story. Imagine that a manufacturer adds a feature to its devices with the sole

---

[3] See the original order on documentcloud, [10], the statement of Apple, [4], and the statement of the Electronic Frontier Foundation, [9].

[4] Only if it is done by using software, which is not the case in general, but is becoming more common.

intention to benefit from it relative to competing companies. This doesn't
mean that the feature is not as well in the interest of the users or owners of the devices, even if this wasn't originally thought of. For example, in
the early ages of digital media, companies could have decided to completely
ignore Digital Rights Management *just because* it was complicated to implement. This clearly would have been in the interest of many if not all owners
of such devices. Thus, one should add that software doping modifies the
affected device's functionality against the legitimate and justified interests of
the owners – something I will explain in detail in a second.

All in all, this leads to the following definition:

Definition 1. *Embedding software[5] S in a device D is software doping if and
only if S was put there intentionally and modifies the device's behavior (the
inputs accepted or the outputs generated by D) in a way that isn't in line with
the justified interests of the owner/user, but instead serves the interests of the
manufacturer.*

However, whether this definition is satisfactory highly depends on how "justified
interests" is spelled out in detail – the endeavor of the next section.

2.2   Owner's Justified Interests

What distinguishes justified interests of owners from interests of owners that a
manufacturer is permitted to ignore or dismiss isn't a trivial question. In the
following, I first give a negative answer, i.e., what kind of interests are paradig-
matic cases of unjustified interests. Then, in a second step, I provide a positive
answer to the question by introducing a kind of interest that clearly qualifies as
justified.

Types of interest that are not justified interests of owners are easy to identify. Although one might be inclined to believe that every interest regarding the
use of one's property is justified, this turns out to be an overstatement. Some
interests of owners may well be neglected by embedded software without intuitively rendering these cases instances of software doping – even if it is done
intentionally by the manufacturers and in their own interests:

Interests in Unrealistic Purposes. Assume you buy some product that you
would like to use for a specific purpose, but that purpose is beyond the scope
of what the device could do. If you have an interest in using it for such
a purpose, then these interests are unjustified, because you don't have any
entitlement to expect the unrealistic.

For example, think of a customer who wants to turn the volume up on his
amplifier, but the software blocks at a certain level – a level, though, that

---

[5] My use of the term "software" here should apply also to components and/or sub-
routines of whole programs. Programs that might well be necessary for the hybrid
device's overall functionality.

corresponds to what the hardware can maximally achieve (and this is not due to some suboptimal wiring or so). Since the interest simply cannot be fulfilled, it is thus unjustified.

Interests against Essential Functionality. Assume you buy a product and it does what it is supposed to do. However, there is a piece of software that somehow conflicts with your interests in a deep sense – i.e. you don't just dislike a contingent feature like some color or sound choice, but something that is essential to its functionality. Without the software, a basic feature of the device wouldn't work anymore, but you nevertheless want it that way. As long as you were free to buy the product and you knew (or to be more precise: an *idealized* version of a consumer in the same circumstances easily could have known[6]) what you bought, this is not a justified interest.

Take as an example a new navigation device: After using it for the first time, you notice that you hate the fact that a computer is giving you directions. You don't just dislike the implemented voices, but the very idea of being guided by a computer.

Interests in Illegal Purposes. Assume you buy a product that in principle could be used for illegal ends, but you are prevented from using it for that purpose by embedded software and this limitation is even enforced by (morally acceptable[7]) laws. If you have interests in using it for this illegal purpose, then these interests are illegitimate and thus count as unjustified. Assume you want to play a pirated copy of a movie on your standard player device, but your player doesn't accept the copied Blu-ray disc due to missing DRM information. This might not count as a clear case of a justified interest of the owner. If we further assume that the manufacturer of the player was under a legal obligation to implement that DRM checking routine, it seems to be clearly no case of a justified interest.

This list may well be not exhaustive. Nevertheless, the idea behind what is *not meant* by "justified interests" should be clear now.

However, at least one positive example is needed to clarify what *is meant* by "justified interests of owners". Looking at examples of unjustified interests, we can summarize that by talking about justified interests of owners in their property we mean interests in using property in ways at least compatible with the originally intended way. Nevertheless, there might well be justified interests that go further, beyond the originally intended use and proper functionalities of the devices owned. To that end, I derive only a sufficient condition from this first aspect here. For this, I first need to try to make sense of the idea of the proper functionality of devices in terms of a black-box view on them.

---

[6] For instance, the consumer's lack of intellectual capacities should not suffice to render the interests justified.

[7] To be precise, this qualification is needed: If the laws are highly morally inadequate, my interests in using my device against the law may well be legitimate. However, to make things easier, for the rest of the paper, I make the pragmatic assumption that the laws relevant in cases of software doping of interest are morally acceptable in the relevant sense.

Definition 2. *Let D be a device. D's proper functionality can be expressed by·
a set of input types* $\tau_{\mathcal{I}_D}$*, a set of outputs* $\mathcal{O}_D$*, and a function* $f_D : \mathcal{I}_D \times \mathcal{C} \rightarrow \mathcal{O}_D$
where $\mathcal{I}_D$ *is the set of possible inputs of the types in* $\tau_{\mathcal{I}_D}$ *and* $\mathcal{C}$ *stands for the
set of contexts for the use of D.*[8] *It must hold that, in the process of acquisition,
these three components were knowable in a transparent way to the future owner
or at least they were reasonable to assume for her.*

Here we may assume something to be *knowable in a transparent way* if it is
advertised in that way, it was told by the authorized salesman to be that way, or it
is part of all the principally openly accessible information (handbooks, necessary
features to be compliant with the law, et cetera). Similarly, we may understand
something to be *reasonable to assume*, if there is something, I obviously can do
with the product, or there is a standard or default that normally is in place for
that type of product – like, e.g., laws. In the case of the VW emission scandal, it
was a necessary feature of the diesel cars sold to be in compliance with the laws
to respect certain emission thresholds. Thus, consumers justifiably assumed that
the cars they bought emit no more than the allowed amount of NO_x. Regarding
the input side, note that constraints may be in place by default, determining
admissible types in $\tau_{\mathcal{I}_D}$ – mostly, they are legal issues. E.g., it is reasonable to
assume that if my car drives on some specific *type* of gas, the *brand* won't be
a distinctive feature: you can buy gas of a certain type at a filling station of
your free choice. So it is – or ought to be – the case with ink: if my printer can
achieve the same quality in print with ink having certain chemical and physical
properties, delivered in specific cartridges of a fitting shape, then, again, the
brand should not matter.

Definition 2 allows us to arrive at a clearer view on justified interests:

Condition 1. *An owner has* justified interests *regarding her property D, if her
interests are compatible with the proper functionality of D, i.e., it is possible that
those interests are fulfilled while the proper functionality is in place.*

Note that none of the unjustified interests from the last subsection fulfill this
sufficient condition: In the mentioned examples it cannot be the case that the
sketched interests are fulfilled in light of what is being transparently knowable or
reasonable to assume by the owners about the $\tau_{\mathcal{I}_D}$, $\mathcal{O}_D$, and f_D as components of
the proper functionality of the products in question. Hence, the interests in those
examples are not compatible with the proper functionalities of the products.

Condition 1 may seem unspectacular in the sense that it only allows for a
very limited number of kinds of interests or a pretty 'boring' sort. But on the
contrary, it also allows for more special sorts of interests. For instance, take the
following kind of interests:

Interests in Originally Unintended Purposes. Assume you buy some product, which, in principle, could be used for an originally unintended purpose.

---

[8] This is, admittedly, a very simplistic model. But, I am confident it suffices to make
clear the general idea while being easily adoptable to more sophisticated models.

If you have interests in using your property for such unintended purposes, but you are prevented from that by some embedded software, then your interests should not necessarily count as unjustified – by definition –, because your interests still may be in line with the proper functionality of the device. To see this, forget for a moment about hybrid devices and think instead of 'good old' property. For instance, there is a whole community that is concerned with so-called "life hacks", i.e., the creative usage of things in an originally unintended way in order to make life easier or to come up with more efficient solutions to everyday problems. Indeed, nobody would declare your use of some binder clips as, say, cable holders as an expression of an unjustified interest in using them. This use also would be perfectly in line with their proper functionality: After all, they are sold as something you can use to clip something to something else. Even if the original intention of the manufacturer or seller may have been that you clip a bunch of papers together, this just means that they didn't had all plausible 'inputs' in mind originally. However, remember that the frustration of such (justified) interests does not suffice to render the candidate case an instance of software doping since for this it must additionally hold that these interests are frustrated to serve the interests of the manufacturer instead.[9]

Now that we have a useful and intelligible characterization at hand, we are able to analyze the moral status of software doping.

3   The Wrongness of Software Doping

So far we thinned out the conceptual fog around the concept of software doping by giving a sufficient condition for software doping. This enables us to analyze the moral properties of the concept. In a first step, I explain what is pro tanto morally wrong with software doping.[10] Then, I work out the role of normative background assumptions when it comes to the question whether, as default, software doping should be considered morally wrong all things considered. Finally, I argue for such default view motivated by the VW emission scandal.

---

[9] Nevertheless, there might be something morally wrong with the frustration of the owner's justified interests in such cases. This even might be the case for very similar reasons, I invoke in a moment to show the wrongness of software doping.

[10] The terms "pro tanto" and "all things considered" are common technical terms in analytic philosophy. For instance, there is a difference between *pro tanto wrongness/rightness* and *all things considered wrongness/rightness* or *overall wrongness/rightness*. Or so it is often assumed in ethics, at least by many mainstream views. A pro tanto wrongful action may well be the right thing to do all things considered. For example, think of harming someone (a pro tanto wrong thing to do) in order to prevent a lot of much more intense harm to many others. Or think of lying to someone (pro tanto the wrong thing to do) in order to save another's live. In both cases people have strong intuitions that a pro tanto morally wrong thing is the overall right thing to do.

3.1   Why Software Doping Is Pro Tanto Wrong

With ownership comes property. According to modern theories of property, ownership and property come with – or even define or constitute – certain rights.[11] The two least controversial rights, which are also assumed to be most fundamental, are the *right to exclude* and the *right to use*. The first allows an owner to exclude someone from their property and its usage, while the latter allows the owner to use their property appropriately. One may be inclined to think that one could choose to do with one's property whatever one wants to. But this is, in general, an overstatement. For example, we are typically not allowed to use our property in ways that interferes with fundamental rights of others.

The central problem with hybrid devices is often lurking around ownership rights and it is not always clear how to analyze and solve the conflicts resulting from the tension of those rights and the role embedded software plays. For example, while you in fact buy and, thus, own the hardware part of your hybrid devices, you typically neither buy nor own their software components: You rather license them in terms of some license agreement – even though many don't realize that fact. The distinction between owning and having licensed something is not a purely semantic issue. The rights (legally, but also morally speaking) that come with ownership are typically much richer and more far-reaching than the rights which are granted by license agreements. You are under a restriction imposed by a license agreement – those pages you never read when downloading, buying or installing some software. For instance, you are often prohibited to resell software you bought, because you never really *bought* the software but only a permission to install and use it.[12] But since you are typically allowed to sell what you own, the questions arises: Are you allowed to sell your hybrid devices? You own them, thus you have permission to sell them. But the software within is only licensed by you and the agreement may well be such that you have not the permission to sell the software. But whenever you sell such a device, you factually sell the embedded software as well. So, do you have the permission to sell your property or do you not have that permission? If you don't have this permission, this goes far beyond the limitations we already experience in the field of software reselling: E.g., imagine, you are no longer allowed to sell your car, because nowadays cars do contain many embedded systems, including embedded software. There is an ongoing discussion how to handle cases like this given the laws applicable. But also it is discussed in more general and philosophical terms how reasonable laws *ought* to handle such cases to be in accordance with natural, moral rights – rights often assumed to be more fundamental.[13]

While this is not the conflict-afflicted feature of those hardware-software hybrid entities this paper is concerned with, it points to the fact that there is

---

[11] The idea is at least as old as the foundation of modern law, e.g., it can be traced back to [2]. It can be found more informatively stated in modern terms in the very influential [7]. For a detailed discussion and summary of those two rights see [5].

[12] See [11].

[13] For a broad overview of different aspects see the Owner's Rights Initiative, an organization that fights for adequate rights: http://www.ownersrightsinitiative.org/.

a pending conflict that can emerge from rights connected to ownership and the role software plays in hybrid devices. In the case of software doping, I argue, this is the case, too.

Even if owners are not allowed to choose to do with their property whatever they desire to do, at least in typical cases there is an owner's right to use her property in *some* way. If in a case where the owner of some property is allowed to use her property in a certain way, someone or something hinders the owner to exercise her right, then this violates her right and, hence, is at least pro tanto morally wrong. I argue that software doping does exactly that: It hinders owners from exercising their rights to use and is, therefore, pro tanto morally wrong.[14] The argument has two steps.

First, notice that if an owner wants to use one of her devices D in a way compatible with D's proper functionality, then this doesn't interfere with rights at least equally as fundamental as the rights of others – at least not in general: If the proper functionality of some devices of a certain type were in general violating fundamental rights of others, this output, by definition of proper functionality, was reasonably to assume or be expectable in a transparent way. This, however, would make it extremely implausible for devices of this type to be allowed by any acceptable legal system, because an essential feature of such morally acceptable legal systems is that it prevents any systematic violation of fundamental rights of persons. Since, I assume such legal systems to be in place in the relevant cases, I am therefore allowed to conclude that, in general, it holds that if an owner wants to use some freely available device D in a way compatible with D's proper functionality, then this doesn't interfere with rights at least as fundamental as their rights of others. This observation is compatible with the existence of cases where one can use D in a way compatible with its proper functionality that nevertheless conflicts with such rights of others, but then – for the above given reasons – this is in exceptional circumstances. For example, you can drive your car on a proper street, but crash into a group of children passing the road. Then you used the car in its proper way, but under special and inauspicious circumstances.

Secondly, realize that by its very definition, software doping modifies someone's device's behavior intentionally in a way that isn't in line with the owner's interests for serving the interests of the manufacturer instead. Therefore, whenever there is software doping, it by definition hinders the owner from exercising the owner's right just established. By neglecting the justified interests of owners, software doping violates rights of owners. Hence, software doping is necessarily (by definition) pro tanto morally wrong.

---

[14] In terms of standard normative ethical theories, what is wrong is typically an action or a type of action. I therefore use "software doping" as an ellipsis for the act of implementing software doping. However, there is an influential idea in computer ethics (the so-called *embedded value approach*) that holds that computer systems and software are not morally neutral. For a deeper discussion of that topic see [3].

3.2 The All Things Considered Wrongness of Software Doping Relative to Normative Theories

Let us accept the conclusion of the last section, that is, accept that software doping is pro tanto morally wrong. But is it reasonable to hold the stronger claim that software doping is generally wrong all things considered? This depends, as I explain, on two aspects: the normative background assumptions and (possibly empirical) facts about cases of software doping. While the latter is a rather complicated issue not easy to generalize and at least in some cases subject of empirical science and not of philosophical investigation, the next subsection nevertheless hints at a certain direction motivated by a recent example, the VW emission scandal. This subsection, however, sheds light on the role of the mentioned normative background assumptions.

In normative ethics we find at least three families of theories: *Consequentialist* theories evaluate the normative status (being demanded, permitted, or forbidden) respectively the moral status (being morally right or morally wrong) solely on the qualities of the (actual or reasonably expectable) outcomes of available options, e.g. actions; *Deontologist* theories judge actions based on their compliance with certain rules. Typically duties, obligations, and rights play central roles in those theories. Finally, there are so called *virtue ethics*, which rather accent the role of the agent's character than the properties of her actions. All three families are 'densely populated' by a variety of theories, all basically claiming to be the correct theory of the morally right and wrong, the permitted, the forbidden, and the demanded.

Since it isn't even clear what kind of agent we are confronted with in the case of software doping, I focus on consequentialist and deontologist theories.[15] They are the most frequently held, anyway.

The idea of pro tanto wrongness in contrast to all-things-considered wrongness is compatible with and commonly accepted by all three families of normative ethical theories.[16] Also the connection between ownership and certain rights can be agreed upon by all three theories, albeit for very different reasons. A consequentialist, e.g., may accept such bundles of rights coming with ownership for pragmatic reasons and judge the violation of such rights as morally bad. It becomes clear that everything I showed to this point is, loosely speaking, independent from the choice of any kind of ethical theory.

---

[15] Is it the manufacturer, a single software engineer, a group of engineers, or the managers of the company? It is even more hazy whether these agents, whoever they might be, can be addressees of virtues.

[16] Immanuel Kant seems to be a special case: According to his specific deontological ethical theory around the categorical imperative, acting such that you don't meet one of your duties means you have acted wrongly, period. Therefore, even if you lie to the end of saving someone's life, you are acting wrongly by doing so, since according to Kant you are under a moral duty to speak the truth. However, it turns out that nowadays even Kantians, i.e., philosophers that agree with Kants thoughts, don't subscribe to the original – radical and rigorous – view anymore.

That being said, the theories don't always agree in their moral evaluations. They especially disagree when it comes to questions of all things considered wrongness: It can be the case that, while theories of different families of normative ethical theories agree in the pro tanto wrongness of some act, they disagree whether the act is morally wrong all things considered. E.g., if we can save two innocent persons from a painful death by killing a third one – someone that otherwise would have remained unaffected from our decision – this is indisputably pro tanto wrong according to most if not all plausible normative ethical theories: After all, we would kill an innocent person. However, according to many consequentialist theories such an act would be nevertheless overall morally right (if there are no better alternatives, of course), because the outcome of two innocent persons being alive and unharmed is better than the alternative outcome where only the third remains so. According to most deontologist theories, however, it would be wrong to kill one, even in order to save two, period.

Hence, the question we are concerned with comes down to the following: Can we reasonably assume in general that (i) other duties, obligations or rights are in place that 'overwrite' the pro tanto wrongness of software doping or that (ii) there are other good outcomes to be expected in such cases that 'outweigh' this pro tanto wrongness? Whether (i) or (ii) is pertinent depends on the choice of deontologist or consequentialist normative ethical theories respectively as background assumption.

3.3 A Clear Example of Wrongful Software Doping: The VW Emission Manipulation

Recently, VW was caught using a software version of a *defeat device*. A defeat device is defined as "an auxiliary emission control device [...] that reduces the effectiveness of emission controls under conditions that the locomotive may reasonably be expected to encounter during normal operation and use."[17] The software is able to detect laboratory emission testing and to adapt the engine such that the classical empirical evaluation for singular points under laboratory conditions become insufficient. The software was intentionally programmed for this purpose and used in Turbocharged Direct Injection (TDI) diesel engines during model years 2009 through 2015, affecting about half a million cars in the US and about eleven millions worldwide. It thereby constitutes a clear example of software doping, because, e.g., it serves the interests of the manufacturers – as long as not detected –, since it means a competitive advantage for them, and frustrates the interests of the users/owners, namely not being lied about the features of their car.

Most fundamentally, the NO_x outputs were adapted to meet US standards during regulatory testing, while in real-world driving emitting up to 40 times more NO_x. As a recent study, [1], suggests, approximately 59 estimated premature deaths have been caused by the excess pollution produced between 2008 and

---

[17] According to Code of Federal Regulations Title 40 - Protection of Environment by the Environmental Protection Agency: https://www.gpo.gov/fdsys/pkg/CFR-2015-title40-vol33/xml/CFR-2015-title40-vol33-sec1033-115.xml.

2015 by vehicles equipped with the defeat device – in the U.S. alone. Current investigations of the German Federal Motor Transport Authority (Kraftfahrt-Bundesamt, or KBA) may reveal further irregularities and similar cases of software doping involving Mercedes, BMW, Renault, and others.[18]

Maybe in the VW case, software doping was at least a rational choice, since it allowed the company to sell more cars. But even that may be disputed for good reasons.[19]

Since software doping in many cases aims at circumventing regulations and laws and because normally, acceptable regulation and laws aim at the public good, one can hold for good reasons that cases of software doping normally (under normal circumstances) don't aim at the public good. Obviously, in general, manufacturers have reasons to do what is *not* in the interest of the society: often their interests are contrary or even contradictory to the public interest. Software doping, thus, often causes harm additionally to the rights violation it necessarily causes. It need not be as harmful as the VW emissions, which in fact killed people, but it will often cause more harm than benefits compared to alternative options. Therefore, in consequentialist terms, we can easily and plausibly prima facie[20] ascribe all-things-considered wrongness to software doping in general.

From a deontologic point of view we must look out for duties of VW that may speak in favor of deception. True, VW was under a duty of success towards its shareholders. True, the company was under a duty of assuring its 'survival' towards its employees. And perhaps the only way to act according to these duties was applying the defeating device software into their diesel engines. But by no plausible view can those duties justify the eleven million times committed right violations of owners and even less they can justify their moral misconduct towards the rights of those seriously harmed or even of those killed by the illegal emissions.

Therefore, we can be sure that all cases of software doping are morally wrong even all things considered in light of deontologic views. And even from a consequentialist point of view we can hold such a default view on software doping for good reasons. Still, such theories may allow more space for exceptions.

---

[18] The data is not yet published, but first media reports suggest so, see http://www. spiegel.de/auto/aktuell/kba-misst-auch-bei-anderen-autoherstellern-erhoehte-abga-swerte-a-1062251.html.

[19] Either the responsible managers at VW thought they wouldn't get caught or they were only interested in short term benefits. Because it was obviously not in their interest to pay a billion dollar penalty – not to mention the awful stock market effects – and loose reputation in magnitudes hard to express in monetary value. But maybe they thought that, even if they were caught, that wouldn't be that bad – for what reasons ever –, or that all possible bad effects might be weighed out by the expectable (competitive) advantages.

[20] This evaluation can only be prima facie since there may well be exceptional cases, where (expectable) positive outcomes weigh out the general badness of a specific instance of software doping.

4   Conclusion

I developed a proposal of a definition of "software doping", then analyzed the moral features of the concept. I noted that software doping is necessarily pro tanto morally wrong because, by definition, it is in conflict with certain rights of owners. This leaves room for the possibility that it might nevertheless be morally right all things considered under specific circumstances, relative to some normative ethical theory as background assumption, first and foremost consequentialist theories. I argued, based on the example of the VW emission scandal, that it is reasonable to assume that such circumstances are not in place in general. It is thus also reasonable to think of software doping as something morally wrong as a default.

From this conclusion it follows that for moral reasons alone we ought to overcome software doping and thus ought to develop promising methods that allow to detect software doping, since this seems to be the most promising way to fight software doping from a pragmatic point of view. If the proposed definition is appropriate in its central aspects, such a development of software doping detection methods must proceed in two steps. First, one needs an explicit specification of a device's proper functionality to gain transparency. This comprises the final hybrid device, but surely also all smaller hybrid components with behavior dependent from embedded software. For this, models of the expected input-output-behavior of devices must be introduced. Second, one needs methods that allow for testing actual device's behavior against such specifications. This must be done on a much broader basis than under laboratory conditions, because more or less all realistic circumstances must be considered. In a nutshell: transparency must be achieved with regard to the de facto influences embedded software has on the behavior of modern hybrid devices.

References

1. Barrett, S.R.H., et al.: Impact of the Volkswagen emissions control defeat device on US public health. Environ. Res. Lett. **10**, 114005 (2005)
2. Blackstone, W.: Commentaries on the Laws of England. Clarendon Press, Oxford (1776)
3. Brey, P.: Values in technology and disclosive computer ethics. In: Floridi, L. (ed.) The Cambridge Handbook of Information and Computer Ethics, pp. 41–58. Cambridge University Press, Cambridge (2010)
4. Cook, T.: A message to our customers. www.apple.com/customer-letter/. Accessed Mar 2016
5. Douglas, S., McFarlane, B.: Defining property rights. In: Penner, J., Smith, H.E. (eds.) Philosophical Foundations of Property Law, pp. 219–243. Oxford University Press, New York (2013)
6. Grenoble, R.: Political protest or just blowing smoke? anti-environmentalists are now rolling coal'. Huffington Post. www.huffingtonpost.com/2014/07/06/rolling-coal-photos-video_n_5561477.html. Accessed Apr 2016
7. Honoré, A.M.: Ownership. In: Guest, A.G. (ed.) Oxford Essays in Jurisprudence, pp. 107–147. Oxford University Press, New York (1961)

8. Moor, J.H.: What is computer ethics? Metaphilosophy **16**(4), 266–275 (1985)
9. Opsahl, K.: EFF to support apple in encryption battle. Electronic Frontier Foundation. www.eff.org/de/deeplinks/2016/02/eff-support-apple-encryption-battle. Accessed Mar 2016
10. Pym, S., (U.S. Magistrate Judge): Order compelling Apple, Inc. To Assist Agents in Search. www.documentcloud.org/documents/2714001-SB-Shooter-Order-Compelling-Apple-Asst-iPhone.html. Accessed Mar 2016
11. von Lohmann, F.: You bought it, you own it: vernor v. autodesk. Electronic Frontier Foundation. www.eff.org/deeplinks/2010/02/you-bought-software-you-own-it-vernor-v-autodesk. Accessed Mar 2016

Learning Systems: Machine-Learning in Software Products and Learning-Based Analysis of Software Systems

Learning Systems: Machine-Learning in Software Products and Learning-Based Analysis of Software Systems

Special Track at ISoLA 2016

Falk Howar[1]([⊠]), Karl Meinke[2], and Andreas Rausch[1]

[1] Clausthal University of Technology, Clausthal-Zellerfeld, Germany
falk.howar@tu-clausthal.de
[2] KTH Royal Institute of Technology, Stockholm, Sweden

We are entering the age of learning systems! On the one hand, we are surrounded by devices that learn from our behavior [3]: household appliances, smart phones, wearables, cars, etc.—the most recent prominent example being Tesla Motor's autopilot that learns from human drivers. On the other hand, man-made systems are becoming ever more complex, requiring us to learn the behavior of these systems: Learning-based testing [8,13,17], e.g., has been proposed as a method for testing the behavior of systems systematically without models and at a high level of abstraction. Promising results have been obtained here using active automata learning technology in verification [6,16] and testing [1,8]. At the same time, active automata learning has been extended to support the inference of program structures [5,10] (it was first introduced for regular languages).

Advances in both areas raise the same questions cornering properties of inferred models: *How accurate are the descriptions that can be obtained of some behavior?* and: *How can we reason about and assure the safety of such systems?* This track aims at bringing together practitioners and researchers to explore the practical impact and challenges associated with using learning-based products as well as learning-based approaches in the analysis and verification of software. The track continues a series of special tracks focused on the application of automata learning techniques in testing and verification at ISoLA conferences [7,15] and [9]. This year's special track has three contributions and two tutorials.

The first contribution *"ALEX: Mixed-Mode Learning of Web Applications at Ease"* by Alexander Bainczyk, Malte Isberner, Tiziana Margaria, Johannes Neubauer, Alexander Schieweck, and Bernhard Steffen [2] (in this volume) presents ALEX, a Browser-based tool that enables non-programmers to fully automatically infer models of other Web applications via active automata learning. These models can be used for documentation, testing, and verification of such applications. ALEX guides a user in setting up dedicated learning scenarios, and invites her to experiment with the available options in order to infer models at adequate levels of abstraction. Characteristic for ALEX is its support for mixed-mode learning: Rest and Web services can be executed simultaneously in one learning experiment, which is ideal when trying to compare back-end and front-end functionality of a Web application. The authors present results from

T. Margaria and B. Steffen (Eds.): ISoLA 2016, Part II, LNCS 9953, pp. 651–654, 2016.
DOI: 10.1007/978-3-319-47169-3_50

an evaluation of ALEX in a comparative study with 140 undergraduate students. The contribution documents recent advances in the usability of learning-based analysis tools.

The second contribution *"Assuring the Safety of Advanced Driver Assistance Systems through a Combination of Simulation and Runtime Monitoring"* by Malte Mauritz, Falk Howar and Andreas Rausch [12] (in this volume) addresses one of the open challenges in the domain of autonomous driving: the lack of established and cost-efficient approaches for assuring the safety of advanced driver assistance systems. The authors present a method for ensuring that an advanced driver assistance system satisfies its safety requirements at runtime and operates within safe limits that were tested in simulations. This can be the basis for reducing the cost of quality assurance by transferring a significant part of the testing effort from road tests to (system-level) simulations. The approach utilizes runtime monitors that are generated from safety requirements and trained (i.e., learned) using simulated test cases. The contribution shows that relevant driving scenarios can be learned from data recorded in road tests. It presents an interesting usecase for data analysis and learning in the realm of safety assurance.

The third contribution *"Enhancement of an adaptive HEV operating strategy using machine learning algorithms"* by Mark Schudeleit, Meng Zhang, Xiaofei Qi, Ferit Küçükay, and Andreas Rausch [18] (in this volume) presents two approaches for reducing CO_2 emissions of a hybrid electric vehicle. The first approach is an adaptive heuristic operating strategy. It classifies current driving style and driving environment into predefined categories and chooses a corresponding strategy for switching between combustion and electric engine. The second approach optimizes this adaptive operating strategy for individual drivers using multigene symbolic regression and supervised machine learning. This contribution demonstrates the potential positive impact of learning products that can be trained to work optimally with their respective user.

The first tutorial *"Learning-based Testing of Procedural and Reactive Systems"* will be given by Karl Meinke from KTH Royal Institute of Technology in Sweden. Learning-based testing (LBT) is an emerging paradigm for black-box requirements testing that is based on combining machine learning with model checking [8,13,17]. The basic idea is to incrementally reverse engineer an abstract model of a system under test (SUT) by using machine learning techniques applied to black-box test cases and their results. Test verdict generation (pass/fail/warning) is fully automatic, based on a simple equality test. So a high degree of test automation is achieved. In practice many thousands of test cases per hour can be executed, with greater effectiveness than random testing. LBT is a general paradigm that can be applied to any class of software systems for which there exist efficient machine learning and model checking algorithms. We can illustrate this generality with research on testing: (1) imperative "C"-style programs against Hoare style pre- and postconditions, (2) reactive systems, based on automata learning algorithms and temporal logic model checkers, and (3) hybrid automata, based on combining methods from (1) and (2). The tutorial will address practical aspects of the methodology using the tool LBTest [14].

The second tutorial *"Active Automata Learning with LearnLib"* will be given by Falk Howar from Clausthal University of Technology in Germany. The tutorial will provide an introduction to active learning of Mealy machines, an automata model particularly suited for modeling the behavior of realistic reactive systems. Active learning is characterized by its alternation of an exploration phase and a testing phase. During exploration phases, so-called membership queries are used to construct hypothesis models of a system under learning. In testing phases, so-called equivalence queries are used to compare respective hypothesis models to the actual system. These two phases are iterated until a valid model of the target system is produced. The tutorial will demonstrate this simple algorithmic pattern using LearnLib [11] and its extension to register automata [4]. It will also address the underlying correctness argument, its limitations, and, in particular, methods to overcome apparent hurdles for practical application. This comprises ways to address real world applications, as well as the treatment of infinite data domains by abstraction refinement.

References

1. Aarts, F., Kuppens, H., Tretmans, G.J., Vaandrager, F.W., Verwer, S.: Learning and testing the bounded retransmission protocol. In: Heinz, J., de la Higuera, C., Oates, T. (eds.) Proceedings of 11th International Conference on Grammatical Inference (ICGI 2012), 5–8 September 2012. JMLR Workshop and Conference Proceedings, vol. 21. pp. 4–18. University of Maryland, College Park (2012)
2. Bainczyk, A., Isberner, M., Margaria, T., Neubauer, J., Schieweck, A., Steffen, B.: ALEX: mixed-mode learning of web applications at ease. In: ISoLA 2016 (2016)
3. Bosch, J., Olsson, H.H.: Data-driven continuous evolution of smart systems. In: Proceedings of the 11th International Symposium on Software Engineering for Adaptive and Self-Managing Systems, SEAMS 2016, pp. 28–34. ACM, New York (2016)
4. Cassel, S., Howar, F., Jonsson, B.: RALib: a LearnLib extension for inferring EFSMs. In: DIFTS 2015 at FMCAD 2015 (2015) (published online)
5. Cassel, S., Howar, F., Jonsson, B., Steffen, B.: Learning extended finite state machines. In: Giannakopoulou, D., Salaün, G. (eds.) SEFM 2014. LNCS, vol. 8702, pp. 250–264. Springer, Heidelberg (2014). doi:10.1007/978-3-319-10431-7_18
6. Cobleigh, J.M., Giannakopoulou, D., Păsăreanu, C.S.: Learning assumptions for compositional verification. In: Garavel, H., Hatcliff, J. (eds.) TACAS 2003. LNCS, vol. 2619, pp. 331–346. Springer, Heidelberg (2003). doi:10.1007/3-540-36577-X_24
7. Giannakopoulou, D., Păsăreanu, C.S.: Learning techniques for software verification and validation – special track at ISoLA 2010. In: Margaria, T., Steffen, B. (eds.) ISoLA 2010, Part I. LNCS, vol. 6415, pp. 640–642. Springer, Heidelberg (2010). doi:10.1007/978-3-642-16558-0_51
8. Hagerer, A., Hungar, H.: Model generation by moderated regular extrapolation. In: Kutsche, R.-D., Weber, H. (eds.) FASE 2002. LNCS, vol. 2306, pp. 80–95. Springer, Heidelberg (2002). doi:10.1007/3-540-45923-5_6
9. Howar, F., Steffen, B.: Learning models for verification and testing — special track at ISoLA 2014 Track Introduction. In: Margaria, T., Steffen, B. (eds.) ISoLA 2014, Part I. LNCS, vol. 8802, pp. 199–201. Springer, Heidelberg (2014). doi:10.1007/978-3-662-45234-9_14

10. Isberner, M., Howar, F., Steffen, B.: Learning register automata: from languages to program structures. Mach. Learn. **96**(1–2), 65–98 (2014)
11. Isberner, M., Howar, F., Steffen, B.: The open-source LearnLib. In: Kroening, D., Păsăreanu, C.S. (eds.) CAV 2015. LNCS, vol. 9206, pp. 487–495. Springer, Heidelberg (2015). doi:10.1007/978-3-319-21690-4_32
12. Mauritz, M., Howar, F., Rausch, A.: Assuring the safety of advanced driver assistance systems through a combination of simulation and runtime monitoring. In: ISoLA 2016 (2016)
13. Meinke, K., Sindhu, M.A.: Incremental learning-based testing for reactive systems. In: Gogolla, M., Wolff, B. (eds.) TAP 2011. LNCS, vol. 6706, pp. 134–151. Springer, Heidelberg (2011). doi:10.1007/978-3-642-21768-5_11
14. Meinke, K., Sindhu, M.A.: Lbtest: a learning-based testing tool for reactive systems. In: Sixth IEEE International Conference on Software Testing, Verification and Validation, ICST 2013, Luxembourg, Luxembourg, 18–22 March 2013, pp. 447–454 (2013)
15. Pasareanu, C.S., Bobaru, M.: Learning techniques for software verification and validation. In: Margaria, T., Steffen, B. (eds.) ISoLA 2012, Part I. LNCS, vol. 7609, pp. 505–507. Springer, Heidelberg (2012). doi:10.1007/978-3-642-34026-0_37
16. Peled, D., Vardi, M.Y., Yannakakis, M.: Black box checking. J. Automata Lang. Comb. **7**(2), 225–246 (2002)
17. Raffelt, H., Merten, M., Steffen, B., Margaria, T.: Dynamic testing via automata learning. Int. J. Softw. Tools Technol. Transfer **11**(4), 307–324 (2009)
18. Schudeleit, M., Zhang, M., Qi, X., Küçükay, F., Rausch, A.: Enhancement of an adaptive hev operating strategy using machine learning algorithms. In: ISoLA 2016 (2016)

ALEX: Mixed-Mode Learning of Web Applications at Ease

Alexander Bainczyk[1]($\boxtimes$), Alexander Schieweck[1]($\boxtimes$), Malte Isberner[1]($\boxtimes$),
Tiziana Margaria[2]($\boxtimes$), Johannes Neubauer[1]($\boxtimes$), and Bernhard Steffen[1]($\boxtimes$)

[1] Chair for Programming Systems, TU Dortmund University, Dortmund, Germany
{alexander.bainczyk,alexander.schieweck,malte.isberner}@tu-dortmund.de,
{johannes.neubauer,steffen}@cs.tu-dortmund.de
[2] The Irish Software Research Center, University of Limerick/Lero,
Limerick, Ireland
tiziana.margaria@lero.ie

Abstract. In this paper, we present ALEX, a web application that enables non-programmers to fully automatically infer models of web applications via active automata learning. It guides the user in setting up dedicated learning scenarios, and invites her to experiment with the available options in order to infer models at adequate levels of abstraction. In the course of this process, characteristics that go beyond a mere "site map" can be revealed, such as *hidden states* that are often either specifically designed or indicate errors in the application logic. Characteristic for ALEX is its support for mixed-mode learning: REST and web services can be executed simultaneously in one learning experiment, which is ideal when trying to compare back-end and front-end functionality of a web application. ALEX has been evaluated in a comparative study with 140 undergraduate students, which impressively highlighted its potential to make formal methods like active automata learning more accessible to a non-expert crowd.

Keywords: Active automata learning · Mixed-mode learning · Specification mining · Web services · Web applications

1 Introduction

With the surge of the cloud, an increasingly large share of communication, knowledge sharing, remote management of people and tools, and enterprise applications are designed, upgraded, or retrofitted as web applications. In the first two cases, these applications should work "as before"; if they are newly designed, they should behave "just right". Unfortunately, especially with the industrial adoption of agile and lean software development, the practice of comprehensive specification writing is in a decline, leaving it to the code itself to constitute the only reliable documentation of what the system does. The frequency of updates increases as well, driven by market demands as well as by the increasing adoption of a *DevOps* approach, where rapid and incremental development is coupled to

T. Margaria and B. Steffen (Eds.): ISoLA 2016, Part II, LNCS 9953, pp. 655–671, 2016.
DOI: 10.1007/978-3-319-47169-3_51

frequent and often targeted releases. Daily releases going live seamlessly, without the users noticing, are not uncommon.

Accountability on the other hand gains importance: data leaks, security and privacy breaches, as well as a lack of compliance with norms and regulations increasingly often lead to litigations or at least bad press, causing economic and reputation damage that are difficult to make up for. In this landscape, how can a company gain confidence that the web applications which drive their daily business work correctly, without exception? These demands resemble closely the profile of high assurance software. However, there are no models, often the code is not available, and even if it is, it is commonly a collection of scripts, programs, and services, written in a large variety of (often dynamically typed) languages, and relying on functionalities provided by the hosting platform.

Specification mining from observations has proven itself as a viable way to overcome the.dynamic and heterogeneous nature of this world. Using testing as a primary interrogation tool, it is possible to extract information from running web applications, and to mould this information into *behavioral* models, often as some variant of automata or Petri Nets. Passive learning, based on non-interfering observation of the behavior, can however lead to very partial results: what is not used cannot be observed, and thus will not become part of the model.

Active automata learning [6,31] on the contrary interrogates the system in a systematic fashion, thus promising a way out of this dilemma. By executing carefully constructed test cases on an actual system, a model reflecting the *actual* runtime behavior is constructed.

Applying the technique in practice comes with a number of challenges: how can one discover and distinguish behaviors that arise only after a complex sequence of actions? Without code or other auxiliary information (e.g., by application-specific fine tuning [18,31]), the correct identification of internal states is a major challenge.

Another central obstacle for fully automated model construction techniques to become reality is the definition of an adequate *learning alphabet* along with a corresponding *test driver* interfacing with the *System Under learning* (SUL). In fact, using a state-of-the-art active automata learning framework such as *Learn-Lib* [21], a user still needs to define the semantics of the learning alphabet by writing (Java) code. This setup, which requires significant technical knowledge, is shown in Fig. 1 (a). As a consequence, these tools are unsuitable for parties

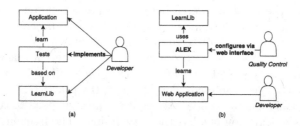

Fig. 1. Usage of existing approaches in comparison. (a) Manual approach with the LearnLib (b) ALEX

with limited programming expertise, such as the quality control department in a company.

As a consequence, there is a strong demand of tools that apply formal techniques such as automata learning without requiring their users to have a technical background. While there exist some software packages that offer an intuitive graphical user interface (e.g., *LearnLib Studio* [23], which offers a process-oriented approach to active automata learning), the need for writing code to communicate with an SUL is never fully eliminated. Furthermore, these approaches add an additional intermediate step between the development of an application and the process of using automata learning to test it, which costs time and may impact the release cycle of a software.

In this paper, we present ALEX[1], an extension of the open source LearnLib that enables non-programmers to fully automatically infer models of web applications via active automata learning [6,31], as shown in Fig. 1 (b). Being a web application itself, ALEX allows users to setup learning scenarios in a guided fashion. As will be illustrated in the paper, this concerns

- the definition and realization of the learning alphabet, i.e. the abstract model entities that reflect the web application's actions. Using the *HTML Element Picker* (Fig. 5) the user only has to select corresponding alternatives from a list of entries that have been extracted from the HTML code, and, if necessary, to provide a few exemplary input data like credentials.
- the concrete learning process. Users can conveniently select from a number of alternative algorithms, equivalence oracles, visualization features, resetting options, and interaction modalities.

Where the definition of the learning alphabet is a convenient way to tailor the learning process to cover specific aspects, like learning the registration modalities (Fig. 2), or focusing on the application behavior after successful registration, the specification of the learning process allows users to determine the precise intended model structure, the depth of search, and the modalities of interaction during the learning process: users may, e.g., challenge unintuitive execution paths of the model by posing them as a potential counter example. This either validates that these paths are indeed a valid run of the application, or it results in a refined model where a path is no longer possible.

Thus, by combining the automata-learning based approach with HTML-code-based setup support and the option to easily interact with the learning process just by clicking on the current hypothesis model, opens model learning, also called specification mining, from running web applications to a public without programming expertise. Moreover, being based on active automata learning, ALEX is able to deal with *hidden states*, i.e., states that cannot be distinguished on the basis of the HTML-code, because they are characterized by the runtime history. This is illustrated in Fig. 2 which shows the authentication protocol of the todo application. Even though this whole protocol is based on a single web page, the five state model obtained using ALEX clearly reveals that three

---

[1] http://learnlib.github.io/alex/.

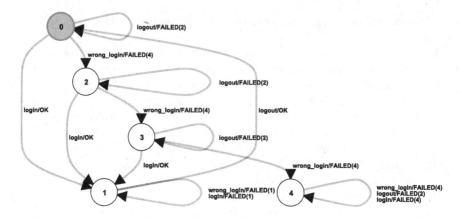

Fig. 2. Authentication protocol of our example Todo-App

successive erroneous authentication attempts lead to complete blocking of the account.

Characteristic for ALEX is its support for mixed-mode learning: REST and web services can be executed simultaneously in one learning experiment, which does not only allow to conveniently compare back-end and front-end functionality of a web application, but is also a means for optimization: the faster back-end learning can be used for establishing a model which can be used for checking the front-end functionality (cf. Table 1).

In the following, we will focus on the usability aspect of ALEX. The study with 140 student of our *Web Technologies II* lecture clearly revealed that ALEX impressively lowers the entry hurdle. The percentage of adequate corresponding solutions as part of the accompanying practical project increased from 5 % to 70 %.

After sketching active automata learning in Sect. 2, we will present ALEX in Sect. 3, and illustrate its usage and impact on a case study in Sect. 4. Subsequently, Sect. 5 discusses related work before we conclude with Sect. 6.

2   Active Automata Learning

Active automata learning, originally developed by Dana Angluin [6], is a technique to generate behavioral models (often in the form of finite-state machines) of black-box systems through testing. More concretely, a *learner* interacts with a *system under learning (SUL)* by posing two kinds of so-called *queries*: *membership queries (MQs)* correspond to feeding a number of inputs to the system (i.e., executing a test case), and observing the output in response to these inputs. *Equivalence queries (EQs)*, on the other hand, correspond to the question of whether a given *hypothesis*, i.e., a finite-state machine that reflects the learner's conjectured explanation of the observed behavior, correctly and completely models the system's behavior. In the negative case, a *counterexample* is provided to the learner, i.e., a test case that shows a discrepancy between the actual system's behavior and the behavior predicted by the hypothesis.

The names of these concepts originate from the theoretical setting that the problem was originally formulated in. In fact, the technique only became of practical relevance nearly 15 years after it was originally presented. This development was triggered by the seminal works of Peled *et al.* [26] and Steffen *et al.* [17,19], who independently recognized active automata learning as a means of extending the range of formal techniques such as model checking [15] or model-based testing [11] to systems that lack a formal description.

Since then, much effort has been spent on bridging the gap between the theoretical assumptions underlying active automata learning on one hand, and the constraints when dealing with realistic systems on the other hand. New learning algorithms for automaton models better suited for realistic systems have been presented [20,25], and tools and frameworks such as *LearnLib* [21] and *Tomte* [1,3] have been developed. As a result, automata learning has been successfully applied for a wide variety of systems, such as the biometric passport [5], bank cards [2], botnets [12], telephony and communication protocols [4,9].

While the mentioned tools provide a rich infrastructure along with a large array of learning algorithms, they still leave the user with considerable challenges, most of which can only be solved in application-specific ways. Some of the most common of these challenges include (cf. [31] for a more complete overview):

- Defining a *learning alphabet:* a learning alphabet is the set of basic operations (*symbols*) that a learner can make use of to assemble membership queries. These can, for example, include method invocations, RPC calls, or combinations thereof. Closely related to the specification of a learning alphabet is the definition of a so-called *mapper* [22], which takes care of handling dynamic data dependencies, as introduced by, e.g., session tokens.
- Specifying a *reset* mechanism: active automata learning relies on the assumption that membership queries are independent of each other. That is, after each query, the system has to be *reset* to its initial state. As this is often infeasible, workarounds such as creating a fresh session or registering a fresh user account are employed. It is common to treat the reset as a specially designated symbol in the learning alphabet.
- Realizing *equivalence queries:* while membership queries correspond to executing test cases on a system, realistic systems typically do not offer a functionality corresponding to equivalence queries. In fact, the absence of a precise behavioral specification is often the prime motivation for applying automata learning in the first place. Equivalence queries are therefore typically approximated through membership queries, using methods from conformance testing [10,14] or random testing.

In the next section, we will show how our tool ALEX supports the user in overcoming these challenges by focusing on a specific, yet widely relevant class of systems, namely web application and services.

3 ALEX

Current solutions for learning applications require users to acquire knowledge in handling the presented tools, the ability to write code in some programming language and a certain setup time for creating input symbols. This leads to the idea of a further abstraction and simplification of certain tasks. In this work, we focus on learning specific kinds of systems which are:

Web application: A deterministic system that runs on a server and can be accessed by clients over the HTTP protocol, e.g. with the help of a web browser. In this model, clients send requests that are always answered by the server, e.g. with an HTML file that can be rendered in the web browser.

Web service: Since the term "web service" can be interpreted in different ways, in this paper we understand it as an HTTP-based interface of a web application which one can communicate with via HTTP requests in order to work with its resources.

Automata Learning EXperience (ALEX) is a mobile friendly, multi-user web application that simplifies the process of testing web applications and RESTful styled web services to the point that users do not need to have programming knowledge nor any insights of an applications inner structure at all. It uses the functionalities of the LearnLib which are made available via a RESTful API. With this tool, we simplify the common steps it takes to learn an application via an easy to use, graphical interface. This includes

- the construction of a learning alphabet through direct interaction with the target SUL,
- the configuration of a learn process,
- the ability to search and verify counterexamples manually and automatically,
- the visualization of generated models and
- the generation of statistics of learn processes.

In Fig. 3 a part of the front-end of ALEX is shown. The sidebar on the left holds the navigation points to the items in the list above. In the following sections of this work a more detailed view on each item is given.

The tool is publicly available under the *Apache 2* license and can be downloaded from our GitHub repository[2].

3.1 Alphabet Modeling

Modeling the learning input alphabet is central to the learning process setup. A learning input alphabet is the list of symbols representing the different real functionalities of an application, like a *login* and *logout* operators for an authentication system. Previous approaches required testers to have knowledge in Java, to become familiar with the theory of active automata learning, the LearnLib and to work with further third party technologies just to get started.

---

[2] https://github.com/LearnLib/alex.

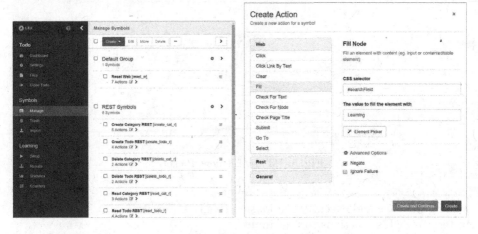

Fig. 3. Management of symbols

Fig. 4. Graphical editor to create and edit actions

Imagine a realistic enterprise application offering hundreds of features: the code needed to model their behavior properly would (a) require a lot of time of an experienced Java developer and (b) need to be modified or rewritten when the application changes. ALEX makes the creation of symbols less complicated and more user friendly by offering an easy to use web interface to model symbols. This may not result in the same flexibility as the manual approach offers, but it helps to get started quickly and enables a far larger and less skilled target user group to use this technology.

Symbols consist of a sequence of actions, i.e. atomic components that represent real individual interactions with web applications and web services. In order to create an action, the editor as shown in Fig. 4 is given. It allows a user to choose from a set of actions and parameterize it as he needs. Each action is then mapped to a corresponding piece of Java code that takes the arguments from the form and executes it on an SUL.

This list of actions is ordered and executed sequentially by the learner as soon as the symbol is called. Each action represents an executable call to an SUL. In the following, we present three different categories of actions.

Web Actions. Actions of this category simulate real user interactions on the graphical user interface of a web application. The functions of these actions lean on the ones given by Selenium[3], a framework used for automating user interactions in real browsers, which makes it useful for testing web applications via their front-end. Actions include, among other things, clicking on elements, filling out and submitting web forms and searching for strings or regular expression. Selenium offers so called web drivers for various web browsers and methods for

---

[3] http://www.seleniumhq.org/.

Fig. 5. HTML Element Picker

loading websites and executing actions on them. ALEX uses it on its server side
to test an SUL's reactions to user input.

A common problem when creating symbols with Selenium is the need to
know about the websites front-end code, and especially to be confident with web
technologies such as HTML and CSS. The *HTML Element Picker*, as depicted
in Fig. 5, is introduced in order to not require any programming knowledge anymore. It provides an easy way to extract the unique CSS selector of an element on
a website. Concretely, the website to be learned is loaded within the application,
enabling the interaction with its elements. Selected elements are highlighted with
a thick red border and their selector is displayed in the bar on the top. Selectors
serve as arguments for Selenium-based symbols in order to learn a web application via interactions with its front-end interface. For example in order to click
on an element, Selenium executes a click on its unique selector.

REST Actions. The second group holds actions used for the interaction with
RESTful APIs. An API and a client communicate by sending HTTP requests
and receiving HTTP responses. The idea is thus to create actions that can send
parameterized HTTP requests to a URI and analyze HTTP responses. Contrary
to web actions, which function independently from each other, REST symbols
should always start with a request, followed by actions to analyze the response.
To send HTTP requests to an SUL, one action allows to create a request with
a method in {GET,POST,PUT,DELETE}, a URI, and a content body that is
send with it.

General Actions. General actions have no specific logical connection with web
or with REST, but define methods that can be used in both contexts or allow
interaction between those groups. In some use cases symbols have to share some
kind of state or information, because their behavior can depend on previous
executed symbols. We realized this with two concepts:

   Variables: Variables contain string values and are persisted for a single membership query. With additional actions to extract and save strings from dif-

ferent sources and actions to manipulate them, they are useful to share, e.g., identifiers of objects.

Counters: Counters are defined as integer values and are persisted over multiple learn processes as long as the user does not delete them explicitly. This property comes in handy when the reset of an application is modeled by creating a new instance of a work object, like a new user. This allows the tester to not have to manually reset the application after each process.

Variables and counters are used to embed dynamic values in string arguments for actions, using the notation {{$VARIABLE_NAME}} for variables and {{#COUNTER_NAME}} for counters.

After the task was successfully created, the first response of the server contains a JSON object with the new task ID. This ID is required if we want to refer to this task in successive symbols or actions, so the ID is stored in a variable called *task_id*. Then the task can be deleted by sending an HTTP DELETE request to the URL, which has to contain the ID of the tasks to delete. To achieve this we tell ALEX to call "/rest/task{{$task_id}}" and the task ID will be inserted before sending the request.

3.2   Learn Process Configuration

To configure the learn processes, in contrast to previous approaches that used a programmatic or a process-oriented approach, ALEX uses a form-based solution optimized for usability without loss of flexibility where users configure the learning process (Fig. 6).

Users compose the learning alphabet by selecting a set of previously created symbols from a list. Since the logic to reset an application is also implemented in the behavior of a symbol it has to be explicitly specified which symbol should be used for the reset during the configuration. Optionally, the configuration can be refined in two ways: by choosing one of four supported learning algorithms

Fig. 6. Configuration of a learn process

(L*, Discrimination Tree, DHC and the TTT), and by choosing from a set of equivalence oracles (*Complete*, *Random Word* and *Sample*).

ALEX generates the learn process related statistics and the generation and visualization of hypotheses is automatic, without the user to model this explicitly. Concerning the statistics, it saves in the database the number of conducted membership queries, equivalence queries, symbol calls as well as the duration of the process, so that they are available for later examination.

The advantage of this approach, in contrast to the manual implementation, is that the learning alphabet can be easily adjusted for every test run. This enables users to learn an application iteratively, feature per feature, or learn it as a whole, without having to write a single line of code. It is not necessary any longer to read and understand the documentation of the various tools one had to use otherwise, thus reducing the effort and the time of testing an application.

Furthermore, since all statistics and learn results are persisted in a database, it is possible to compare them later with newer test results.

3.3 Testing Counterexamples

Once the learner has generated a hypothesis, ALEX displays its automaton. Counterexamples can be searched and specified manually in order to refine the learned model of an application in the next iteration. In ALEX, this is designed as an interactive and explorative process and executed directly on the displayed automaton.

As described in Fig. 7, counterexamples are words. In a first step, they are generated by clicking on the labels of the model that show the input symbol. In a next step, ALEX tests automatically whether the selected sequence actually is a counterexample. An integrated mechanism prevents passing wrong counterexamples that would otherwise cause the learner to break or never stop learning. Before refining the model, the assumed counterexample is posed to the SUL

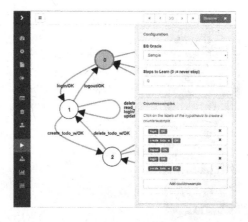

Fig. 7. Manually testing counterexamples on the hypothesis

first. If the output of the SUL differs from the given word, the counterexample is verified and can be used for the refinement process.

3.4   Learn Result Analysis

ALEX simplifies the analysis of the results of learned processes as well. This includes the generation of statistics from the characteristics of used learn algorithms in combination with differently parameterized equivalence oracles. Charts of the statistics can be generated and downloaded for an arbitrary number of results.

Furthermore, observing learned models and visually comparing them next to each other makes it easier to spot differences in multiple versions and allows the continuous documentation of the software evolution.

4   Evaluation

ALEX was already used in the Summer term 2015 by students of the "Web Technologies 2" course at our university. Comparing retrospectively with the same course in 2014, we had a test group size of approximately 140 students. Overall the use of ALEX lead to a drastic increase from 5 % to 70 % of the percentage of adequate corresponding solutions as part of the accompanying practical project.

In this paper, we present one examplary application to further evaluate the practical applicability of ALEX. Moreover we also learned Wordpress[4] as a real-life application. The setup can be found on our project homepage because it is too complex to be discussed in this paper. This example demonstrates the capabilities of our tool by learning the REST interface of Wordpress, an open source, PHP based content management system (CMS) for creating web applications. It is widely used as a content publishing platform and features an editorial system where users of different roles can, among other things, manage the publication process of articles and handle user generated comments related to an article. With the demonstration, we want to show how ALEX can be used to learn multi-user enabled applications via their REST APIs and see how different algorithms perform in this task. The result with a hypothesis with 31 states can also be seen online.

4.1   Use Case: ToDo

ToDo is a sample application for managing tasks that was developed as an exercise of the "Web Technologies 2" course in Summer 2014. It has a graphical front-end and supports the manipulation of its business objects via an integrated web service. This makes it an ideal example to showcase the features of ALEX.

---

[4] https://wordpress.org.

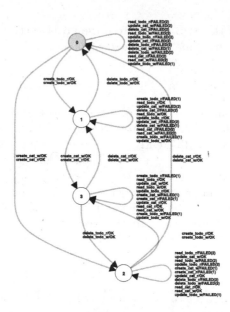

Fig. 8. Hypothesis ToDo Web and REST, generated in ALEX. The initial state is marked in green

To set up this application, a set of 16 symbols is modeled in a relatively short period of time using ALEX. The first half handles CRUD[5] operations on task objects and categories via the web interface, the second half executes the equivalent functionality via ToDo's API. There is an additional symbol to reset the application.

The learned ToDo model displayed in Fig. 8 shows that it is possible to concurrently learn the web and REST functionality of an application. There, symbols with the suffix _r execute the REST API and those with _w have been executed via a browser. ALEX's mixed-mode learning makes it easy to identify possible deviations, that would result in more states in the one or the other interface.

Results. The results from Table 1 have been generated using a virtual machine running Debian 8 "Jessie" with 4 GB of memory on a computer that runs Ubuntu 12.04 with 16 GB memory and an Intel Core i5-2500 with 4×3.3 GHz. For each test run, the *random word* equivalence oracle has been used with the same configuration. These results can be replicated by downloading the virtual box image and running these tests.

It is interesting to see that, depending on the chosen algorithm, running both symbol types together - which doubles the amount of input symbols - must not necessarily have a huge impact on the learn process execution time. Indeed, where the L^*, the Discrimination Tree and the DHC algorithm took about double

---

[5] Create, Read, Update, Delete.

Table 1. Impact of algorithm on various configurations on ToDo, generated with ALEX

Type	Alg.	$|\Sigma|$	#MQs	#EQs	#Calls	Time (ms)
Web	L^*	8	316	1	948	725959
REST	L^*	8	316	1	948	275960
Both	L^*	16	1124	1	3324	1560534
Web	DHC	8	248	1	884	630034
REST	DHC	8	248	1	884	234851
Both	DHC	16	1060	1	3192	1537986
Web	DT	8	90	2	390	181522
REST	DT	8	90	2	322	51232
Both	DT	16	154	2	914	411443
Web	TTT	8	141	3	466	266206
REST	TTT	8	129	2	416	88144
Both	TTT	16	306	4	930	286987

the time it took to learn only one type of symbols, the TTT algorithm takes advantage of the use of REST Symbols.

As expected, the execution of REST symbols is faster than their web counterparts in all cases. This is because in most cases, a REST action only needs to make a few HTTP requests in order to do the same as an equivalent web symbol, which has the overhead of using a (headless) web browser to load and navigate through several sites.

This speed improvement can be explained by the mix of REST and web symbols. Because REST symbols do not require to simulate the user interaction through a browser they are inherently faster than web symbols. So if membership queries contain more REST than web symbols the overall performance increases.

Finally, in order to take full advantage of this observation and speed up the learning process, one has to research more into this topic. One possibility is, if there is given an equivalent set of REST symbols, that these are used exclusively for the approximation of equivalence queries, which is, in praxis, a performance costly process, if done only with a browser.

Testing the Login Process. In the test setup above we assumed that the user was already logged in and only focused on the tasks and categories. Now we want to focus on the aspect of the login procedure itself, which is important, too.

Besides that only valid pairs of emails and passwords should identify an user and grant him access, the ToDo-App has one additionally security constraint: After the third invalid login the account should be blocked. This means that no login will be possible any more and the administrator of the system has to unblock the user.

To test this behavior the working *Login* and *Logout* symbols from the previous section are used together with a new *Invalid Login* action. The model in Fig. 2 shows the result. It is easy to see that the mechanism works as intended and after the third invalid login a blocking state (node 4) is reached.

5   Related Work

That web applications are particularly attractive targets of automata learning technology or more generally of process mining was first illustrated in [28] by automatically inferring a (partial) model of the bugtracking system Mantis. Despite using the LearnLib [27] this was still a quite programming intensive task. It required to establish the required test harness for automatic test execution and the realization of a corresponding so-called learning alphabet, essentially the abstract, application specific language to interact with the web application. Whereas in this approach the availability of the HTML code was only used for the construction of the learning alphabet, other approaches to web application mining are directly based on this code [8,29,30] and are therefore more syntax-driven. They follow the offered links in order to establish the site map structure and identify states by a notion of similarity of the pages' HTML code. Similar approaches have been presented for Android applications [13] and Windows applications [7]. These identify states based on the visible GUI elements (buttons, input boxes etc.) on the screen. Thus conceptually these approaches work in a dual fashion on the states visited during the testing-based exploration: Whereas automata learning is based on distinguishing states on the basis of the Nerode theorem [24] (state splitting), the other approaches identify states on the basis of code similarity (state fusion). This also explains their quite different application profile. Page code-based approaches are highly efficient, but fail to detect *hidden states*, i.e. state difference that are not apparent on the pages' HTML code [16]. In contrast, automata learning-based approaches, in their pure version, inherit the weaknesses (incompleteness) of the so-called equivalence query (essentially an oracle to provide counter examples typically realized via randomized search or conformance testing), but it allow to detect hidden states as e.g. illustrated in Fig. 2. Moreover, ALEX is unique in supporting mixed mode learning, e.g., learning the front-end and back-end behavior of a web application simultaneously in one model. This does not only support easy comparison, but is also a means for optimization: the faster back-end learning can be used for establishing a model which can be used for checking the front-end functionality (Table 1).

ALEX can be regarded as an extension of the open source LearnLib [21], which allows one to detect hidden states as e.g. illustrated in Fig. 2, that makes explicit use of the available HTML code.

6   Conclusion

We have presented ALEX, a web application that enables non-programmers to fully automatically infer models of web applications via active automata learning.

Its simplicity-oriented design guides the user to setup her dedicated learning scenarios, and to play at ease with the available options in order to infer models at adequate levels of abstraction. This may reveal characteristics beyond mere site maps like, e.g., hidden states that often need special attention. We have also seen that ALEX's ability of mixed-mode learning allows an easy comparison of front-end and back-end functionality of a web application, while it, at the same time supports optimization. ALEX has been evaluated in a comparative study with 140 students which revealed an impressive lowering of the entry hurdle.

Capturing the essential features of real world applications requires a continuous effort. Currently, we are working on the authentication in RESTful environments of users via protocols such as OAuth or OAuth2 or systems that use third party providers, and on support for reading and interacting with hyperlinks in emails, enabling to capture registration processes or applications that require its users to validate their account via email.

References

1. Aarts, F., Tomte: bridging the gap between active learning and real-world systems. Ph.D. thesis, Radboud University Nijmegen (2014)
2. Aarts, F., de Ruiter, J., Poll, E.: Formal models of bank cards for free. In: 2013 IEEE Sixth International Conference on Software Testing, Verification and Validation Workshops (ICSTW), pp. 461–468, March 2013
3. Aarts, F., Heidarian, F., Kuppens, H., Olsen, P., Vaandrager, F.: Automata learning through counterexample guided abstraction refinement. In: Giannakopoulou, D., Méry, D. (eds.) FM 2012. LNCS, vol. 7436, pp. 10–27. Springer, Heidelberg (2012). doi:10.1007/978-3-642-32759-9_4
4. Aarts, F., Jonsson, B., Uijen, J.: Generating models of infinite-state communication protocols using regular inference with abstraction. In: Petrenko, A., Simão, A., Maldonado, J.C. (eds.) ICTSS 2010. LNCS, vol. 6435, pp. 188–204. Springer, Heidelberg (2010). doi:10.1007/978-3-642-16573-3_14
5. Aarts, F., Schmaltz, J., Vaandrager, F.: Inference and abstraction of the biometric passport. In: Margaria, T., Steffen, B. (eds.) ISoLA 2010, Part I. LNCS, vol. 6415, pp. 673–686. Springer, Heidelberg (2010). doi:10.1007/978-3-642-16558-0_54
6. Angluin, D.: Learning regular sets from queries and counterexamples. Inf. Comput. **75**(2), 87–106 (1987)
7. Arlt, S., Ermis, E., Feo-Arenis, S., Podelski, A.: Verification of GUI applications: a black-box approach. In: Margaria, T., Steffen, B. (eds.) ISoLA 2014, Part I. LNCS, vol. 8802, pp. 236–252. Springer, Heidelberg (2014). doi:10.1007/978-3-662-45234-9_17
8. Bertolino, A., Inverardi, P., Pelliccione, P., Tivoli, M.: Automatic synthesis of behavior protocols for composable web-services. In: Proceedings of the the 7th Joint Meeting of the European Software Engineering Conference and the ACM SIGSOFT Symposium on the Foundations of Software Engineering, ESEC, FSE 2009, pp. 141–150. ACM, New York (2009)
9. Bohlin, T., Jonsson, B.: Regular inference for communication protocol entities. Technical report, Department of Information Technology, Uppsala University, Schweden (2009)

10. Brinksma, E.: Formal methods for conformance testing: theory can be practical. In: Halbwachs, N., Peled, D. (eds.) CAV 1999. LNCS, vol. 1633, pp. 44–46. Springer, Heidelberg (1999). doi:10.1007/3-540-48683-6_6

11. Broy, M., Jonsson, B., Katoen, J.-P., Leucker, M., Pretschner, A.: Part I. testing of finite state machines. In: Broy, M., Jonsson, B., Katoen, J.-P., Leucker, M., Pretschner, A. (eds.) Model-Based Testing of Reactive Systems. LNCS, vol. 3472, pp. 1–3. Springer, Heidelberg (2005). doi:10.1007/11498490_1

12. Cho, C.Y., Babić, D., Shin, R., Song, D.: Inference and analysis of formalmodels of botnet command and control protocols. In: Proceedings of the 2010 ACM Conference on Computer and Communications Security, CCS 2010, Chicago, Illinois, USA, pp. 426–440. ACM (2010)

13. Choi, W., Necula, G., Sen, K.: Guided GUI testing of android apps with minimal restart and approximate learning. In: Proceedings of the 2013 ACM SIGPLAN International Conference on Object Oriented Programming Systems Languages and Applications, OOPSLA 2013, pp. 623–640. ACM, New York (2013)

14. Chow, T.S.: Testing software design modeled by finite-state machines. IEEE Trans. Softw. Eng. 4(3), 178–187 (1978)

15. Clarke, E.M., Grumberg, O., Peled, D.A.: Model Checking. The MIT Press, Cambridge (1999)

16. Dallmeier, V., Burger, M., Orth, T., Zeller, A.: WebMate: generating test cases for web 2.0. In: Winkler, D., Biffl, S., Bergsmann, J. (eds.) SWQD 2013. LNBIP, vol. 133, pp. 55–69. Springer, Heidelberg (2013). doi:10.1007/978-3-642-35702-2_5

17. Hagerer, A., Hungar, H.: Model generation by moderated regular extrapolation. In: Kutsche, R.-D., Weber, H. (eds.) FASE 2002. LNCS, vol. 2306, p. 80. Springer, Heidelberg (2002). doi:10.1007/3-540-45923-5_6

18. Howar, F., Isberner, M., Steffen, B.: Tutorial: automata learning in practice. In: Margaria, T., Steffen, B. (eds.) ISoLA 2014, Part I. LNCS, vol. 8802, pp. 499–513. Springer, Heidelberg (2014). doi:10.1007/978-3-662-45234-9_34

19. Hungar, H., Steffen, B.: Behavior-based model construction. Int. J. Softw. Tools Technol. Transf. 6(1), 4–14 (2004)

20. Isberner, M., Howar, F., Steffen, B.: Learning register automata: from languages to program structures. Mach. Learn. 96(1), 65–98 (2014). doi:10.1007/s10994-013-5419-7

21. Isberner, M., Howar, F., Steffen, B.: The Open-source LearnLib: a framework for active automata learning. In: CAV 2015 (2015, accepted)

22. Jonsson, B.: Formal methods for eternal networked software systems. In: 11th International School on Formal Methods for the Design of Computer, Communication and Software Systems, SFM 2011, Bertinoro, Italy, 13–18 June 2011, pp. 327–349 (2011). Advanced lectures

23. Merten, M., Steffen, B., Howar, F., Margaria, T.: Next generation LearnLib. In: Abdulla, P.A., Leino, K.R.M. (eds.) TACAS 2011. LNCS, vol. 6605, pp. 220–223. Springer, Heidelberg (2011). doi:10.1007/978-3-642-19835-9_18

24. Nerode, A.: Linear automaton transformations. Proc. Am. Math. Soc. 9(4), 541–544 (1958)

25. Niese, O.: An integrated approach to testing complex systems. Ph.D. thesis, University of Dortmund, Germany (2003)

26. Peled, D., Vardi, M.Y., Yannakakis, M.: Black box checking. In: Wu, J., Chanson, S.T., Gao, Q. (eds.) Proceedings of FORTE 1999, pp. 225–240. Kluwer Academic (1999)

27. Raffelt, H., Steffen, B.: LearnLib: a library for automata learning and experimentation. In: Baresi, L., Heckel, R. (eds.) FASE 2006. LNCS, vol. 3922, pp. 377–380. Springer, Heidelberg (2006). doi:10.1007/11693017_28

28. Raffelt, H., Steffen, B., Margaria, T.: Dynamic testing via automata learning. In: Yorav, K. (ed.) HVC 2007. LNCS, vol. 4899, pp. 136–152. Springer, Heidelberg (2008). doi:10.1007/978-3-540-77966-7_13

29. Schur, M., Roth, A., Zeller, A.: Mining behavior models from enterprise web applications. In: Proceedings of the 2013 9th Joint Meeting on Foundations of Software Engineering, pp. 422–432. ACM (2013)

30. Schur, M., Roth, A., Zeller, A.: Mining workflow models from web applications. IEEE Trans. Softw. Eng. 41(12), 1184–1201 (2015)

31. Steffen, B., Howar, F., Merten, M.: Introduction to active automata learning from a practical perspective. In: Bernardo, M., Issarny, V. (eds.) SFM 2011. LNCS, vol. 6659, pp. 256–296. Springer, Heidelberg (2011). doi:10.1007/978-3-642-21455-4_8

Assuring the Safety of Advanced Driver Assistance Systems Through a Combination of Simulation and Runtime Monitoring

Malte Mauritz[✉], Falk Howar, and Andreas Rausch

Institute for Applied Software Systems Engineering (IPSSE),
Clausthal University of Technology, Clausthal, Germany
{malte.mauritz,falk.howar,andreas.rausch}@tu-clausthal.de

Abstract. Autonomous vehicles will share the road with human drivers within the next couple of years. One of the big open challenges is the lack of established and cost-efficient approaches for assuring the safety of Advanced Driver Assistance Systems and autonomous driving. Product liability regulations impose high standards on manufacturers regarding the safe operation of such systems. Today's conventional engineering methods are not adequate for providing such guarantees in a cost-efficient way. One strategy for reducing the cost of quality assurance is transferring a significant part of the testing effort from road tests to (system-level) simulations. It is not clear, however, how results obtained from simulations transfer to the road. In this paper, we present a method for ensuring that an Advanced Driver Assistance System satisfies its safety requirements at runtime and operates within safe limits that were tested in simulations. Our approach utilizes runtime monitors that are generated from safety requirements and trained using simulated test cases. We evaluate our approach using an industrial prototype of a lane change assistant and data recorded in road tests on German highways.

Keywords: Advanced driver assistance systems · Lane change assistant · Simulation-based testing · Runtime verification

1 Introduction

The automotive industry is heading towards autonomous vehicles that are expected to share the road with human drivers within the next couple of years (cf. [16]). Today, Adaptive Cruise Control (ACC) systems already take over longitudinal control and parking assistants take over lateral control in cars. With the release of its autopilot in 2015, Tesla Motors has rolled out a system that controls lateral and longitudinal movement of its cars autonomously on highways. All major car manufacturers, and even companies like Google, are working on sophisticated Advanced Driver Assistance Systems (ADAS) [23].

One of the big open challenges is the current lack of established and cost-efficient approaches for assuring the safety of such driving assistants [25]. Regulatory authorities require such systems to meet highest standards for ensuring

© Springer International Publishing AG 2016
T. Margaria and B. Steffen (Eds.): ISoLA 2016, Part II, LNCS 9953, pp. 672–687, 2016.
DOI: 10.1007/978-3-319-47169-3_52

road safety. The product and producer liability (e.g., in Germany: ProdHaftG §1, BGB §823 I, BGB §433) oblige manufacturers to ensure that ADAS safely operate in their highly dynamic environments and to eliminate harm for drivers, vehicles, and any persons or objects in their environments.

Today's conventional engineering methods are not adequate for providing such guarantees in a cost-efficient way: Common vehicle field tests are too expensive; they require too many miles to be driven in order to demonstrate that a system is sufficiently safe (cf. [25]). One strategy for reducing the cost of quality assurance is transferring a significant part of the testing effort from road tests to (system-level) simulations. Two challenges have to be addressed in order to use results obtained in simulations for assuring the safety of ADAS on the road (cf. [2]); First, it has to be ensured that the behavior of the tested system is comparable on the road and in simulations. Second, it has to be ensured that simulations cover relevant and realistic driving situations.

In this paper, we report the results of a research project that conducted initial research on novel approaches for combining simulations and road tests for ensuring the safety of ADAS. We have developed a framework for combining a pair of runtime monitors that record relevant driving situations and ensure that an ADAS operates within specified and tested limits. In system-level simulations, one monitor checks functional correctness, the other one observes and learns new driving situations. Together, these two monitors allow to test and verify the behavior of an ADAS. During road tests or operation the ADAS can then be monitored in order to identify unsafe or untested operation conditions and behavior. These conditions and behavior can then be transferred back to the simulation. We evaluate our method using an industrial prototype of a lane change assistant (LCA), and data recorded in road tests on national highways in Germany.

One of the main technical challenges of this approach is that the monitors have to abstract from concrete tested driving scenarios in order for our approach to become effective—otherwise testing will never cover a significant fraction of relevant driving situations. On the other hand, an abstraction cannot be too coarse. Otherwise unsafe concrete driving situations might be identified as tested. We show how we derived such an abstraction from safety requirements.

We have presented the research project in which we have developed our approach in [14] and reported preliminary findings from a small case study that we implemented in Java in a workshop paper [13]. In this paper, we present the complete approach and report on the results of an evaluation with the LCA.

Outline. The remainder of this paper is organized as follows. In Sect. 2, we describe the basic concepts and architecture of our runtime monitoring solution. Section 3 describes the abstraction of traffic situations used in our case study-a lane change assistant (LCA). In Sect. 4, we present results from the evaluation of our approach. We conclude and discuss future work in Sect. 6.

2   Core Concept and Architecture

In this section, we present our approach for transferring results obtained from simulations to the road. We ensure that the ADAS behaves consistently in both worlds, and that realistic driving conditions are simulated, by utilizing a set of runtime monitors.

Advanced Driver Assistance Systems. Modern ADAS consist of many components and often multiple assistants have to be coordinated. We group those components following the Input-Process-Output (IPO) pattern, where the environment is perceived by the vehicle's sensors and then preprocessed for a consistent view of the vehicle's environment (Input). Based on this internal view of the environmental situation the main function of the ADAS computes the necessary actions (Process). Finally, the computed actions are post-processed, coordinated, and transformed into commands for actuators, e.g., the braking system or the engine (Output).

Our work addresses the safety of the main function (IPO-Part: Process) of an ADAS by combining the runtime monitoring in simulations and at operation. Safety assurance for sensors, sensor fusion, and for actuators are complex challenges in their own domain. Please note that in this work we do not address the on-line selection and execution of appropriate counter measures but only evaluate if it is safe to operate the ADAS in the current situation.

We use a lane change assistant (LCA) as running example and as a basis for our evaluation (cf. Sect. 3). A LCA is an automated driving function that controls a vehicle on highways and performs lane changes autonomously. The main function of the LCA receives *traffic situations* as input, i.e., a map, containing roads with lanes, and objects with positions and velocities in the vehicles vicinity. Based on this map, the function computes a *target point*, i.e., a geo-spatial point that should be incorporated in the future trajectory of the controlled vehicle (the so-called *ego vehicle*).

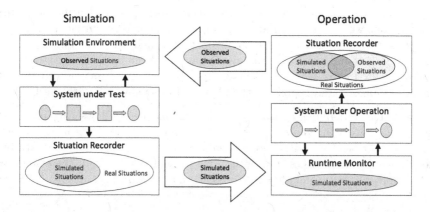

Fig. 1. Bridging the gap between simulation and road tests by (a) training driving situations in simulations, and (b) monitoring and recording driving situations on the road.

Relating Simulation and Road Tests. One of the challenges when verifying the correctness and safety of ADAS arises from the complex environments these systems operate in: Field tests will never cover the uncountable number of situations an ADAS may encounter on the road. In order for simulations to become efficient substitutes for field tests, simulations have to model realistic traffic situations. Our approach for transferring information between simulations and road tests is sketched in Fig. 1: Initially, a set of test cases is executed in a system-level simulation (left half of the Fig. 1). In these simulations, sequences of traffic situations are recorded and the behavior of the ADAS is verified using test oracles generated from safety requirements. The simulated and verified traffic situations are recorded in a database. This database is used by a runtime monitor to check if an observed situation has been tested. During operation (cf. right side of the Fig. 1), we check the ADAS with this monitor[1]. New situations encountered during operation are used to enhance the set of test cases (derived from sequences of traffic situations) for the ADAS in further simulations.

In order for the approach to be efficient, it is essential to abstract from concrete traffic situations. Figure 2 details this: A concrete traffic situation $c \in C$ consist of a set of objects with attributes from infinite domains, e.g., precise geo-spatial positions and velocities. It is thus impossible to simulate and record all real concrete situations. We introduce *abstract traffic situations* that abstract the position and other properties of a concrete object, to, e.g., *behind the ego vehicle on the lane to the left*. An abstract traffic situation $a \in A$ is a set of objects with predicates as indicated in the upper left of the figure. Due to the limited range of a cars sensors, we can assume that the number of objects in concrete and abstract traffic situations is finite.

Table 1. Combination of two monitors checking if traffic situations are deemed safe during operation, i.e., if encountered situations have been tested and if the ADAS behaves correctly.

Tested	Correct	Safe
Yes	Yes	Yes
Yes	No	No
No	Yes	No
No	No	No

When abstracting concrete traffic situations to abstract ones, it is important that the abstraction $A_I : C \mapsto A$ is not too coarse. Otherwise one abstract traffic situation could correspond to safe and unsafe concrete traffic situations. We ensure this as follows. We derive the predicates for our abstraction (e.g., *behind the ego vehicle*) from the safety-critical requirements of the system (for details cf. Sect. 3). This allows us to generate monitors for the functional requirements at the level of abstract traffic situations. These monitors serve two purposes. First, they are used as test oracles in simulations. Secondly, the monitors are used during road tests or operation to monitor if the abstraction is fine enough: We test the behavior of the ADAS for one concrete instance of an abstract (i.e., specified) situation in a simulation. The ADAS is supposed to behave identically (at the abstract level) for all other concrete instances of the same abstract situation. The monitors check this during operation (as shown in Table 1).

---

[1] The development environment in our industrial case study allows running identical components in simulations and on the real road.

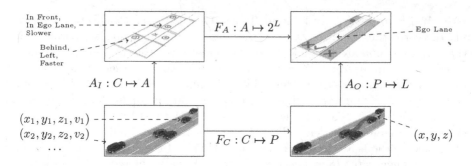

Fig. 2. A pair of abstractions A_I and A_O and an abstract function F_A are derived from safety requirements and enable the monitoring of abstract driving situations. (Color figure online)

Monitoring Architecture. The architecture of our runtime monitoring consists of two layers as shown in Fig. 3. The lower layer is the ADAS itself. We depict the ADAS following the Input-Process-Output (IPO) pattern. The upper layer depicts our runtime monitoring addressing the monitoring of the correctness of the system's behavior and of tested environmental situations. The architecture has two important features: First, monitoring components simply use the existing interfaces between components of the ADAS. Monitoring can easily be added to existing functions without compromising other assurance efforts. Second, identical components are used for simulation and operation. The only difference is the initialization of the abstract situation database.

The main function F_C of the ADAS takes concrete traffic situations from C as input and computes target points $p \in P$. The correctness of the main function of the ADAS is monitored by the *abstract function* F_A at the level of abstract traffic situations. The abstract function $F_A : A \mapsto 2^L$ computes a set of actions (in our concrete example: lane change operations) that the ADAS may perform in the current situation. The set of actions is used by the *conformance monitor* for the evaluation of the concrete action taken by the ADAS. The concrete action of the ADAS is abstracted to the level of the abstract function by function $A_O : P \mapsto L$. For a lane change, e.g., the concrete target point is abstracted to a target lane. The conformance monitor evaluates if the abstracted action of the ADAS is in the set of safe actions processed by the abstract function, i.e., if $A_O(F_C(x)) \in F_A(A_I(x))$ for $x \in C$ (cf. also Fig. 2).

A second set of components monitors the encountered environmental situations. The *situation monitor* (upper left of Fig. 3) records encountered abstract traffic situations. For each encountered situation, the situation monitor evaluates at runtime if the encountered abstract traffic situation has been tested in simulations. We use a canonical representation of abstract traffic situations and identify situations that are equivalent up to names of objects as equal. We refer to these canonic abstract situations as *unique* situations.

Combining the verdicts of monitoring of the conformance of the ADAS and familiarity of environmental situations, we can deduce a verdict about the safety of the ADAS. In case an observed situation has not yet been tested in simulations

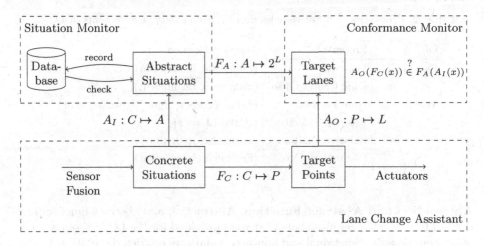

Fig. 3. Runtime monitoring architecture.

or if the ADAS does violate its requirements, operation of the ADAS is not safe, as detailed in Table 1.

3 Case Study: The Lane Change Assistant

In this section we describe how we have implemented the approach discussed in the previous section for testing the prototype of an industrial lane change assistant (LCA). We start by presenting a brief overview of how the lane change assistant operates on concrete traffic situations. We then describe how the *abstraction* (A_I, A_O) was derived from a set of functional safety requirements and how monitors for these requirements constitute the *abstract function* F_A used for monitoring the LCA.

LCA and Abstract Domain. As sketched in Fig. 2, the LCA operates on *concrete traffic situations*. A concrete traffic situation is a geo-spatial map of the ego vehicle's surroundings, containing information produced by environment recognition (i.e., sensing and sensor fusion) about driving lanes and other vehicles and objects. Two concrete traffic situations may differ only in the distance of one surrounding vehicle (and by as little as a couple of inches). The LCA (F_C) computes a *concrete target point* (marked in orange in the lower right corner of Fig. 2). This target point is an actual point in space that is processed together with target points of other assistants (e.g., an Advanced Cruise Control) into the final future trajectory of the ego vehicle.

As described in the previous section, abstraction A_I maps concrete traffic situations to *abstract traffic situations*. The abstraction A_O maps concrete target points to *target lanes*. The abstract function F_A computes the set of *target lanes* allowed for the lane change assistant in the current abstract situation. The LCA operates in safe limits as long as the abstracted concrete target point is in the set of allowed target lanes.

Table 2. Properties of other vehicles derived from safety requirements of LCA.

Object	Property	Abstract Domain
Ego Vehicle	Velocity	{Sufficient; Insufficient}
	Lane Center Offset	{Sufficient; Insufficient}
Vehicle	Lane Position	{Left_Neighbor; Ego; Right_Neighbor}
	Relative Velocity	{Higher; Lower}
	Relative Position	{Front; Next; Behind}
	Distance to Ego	{Sufficient; Insufficient}

Abstraction and Abstract Function. Abstraction and abstract function are derived from a set of requirements that were provided for the LCA: From a total of 58 requirements (functional and non-functional), we restricted our attention to the 17 safety-relevant requirements restricting the performance of lane changes based on position and behavior of objects in the vicinity of the ego vehicle. These 17 requirements were decomposed and formalized into abstraction and abstract function.

We used a pattern based analysis to derive formal predicates and formulas from requirements based on their structure (following the ideas of [10]). We exemplify the steps and result of the analysis the specific requirement;

> "The system shall be able to handle fast objects approaching the ego vehicle from behind with at least 10 m/s relative velocity".

In a first step, we discussed the requirements with the developers of the LCA and replaced imprecise language in requirements by more precise expressions. In this case we specified "to handle" to mean "not to perform a lane change" since it is deemed unsafe to perform a lane change into a lane if a vehicle on this lane approaches the ego vehicle from behind with a higher relative velocity.

In a second step, we reformulated requirements in a conditional structure consisting of an activity and a condition under which the activity is prohibited, resulting in properties like

> "No lane change to right lane if vehicle on right lane behind ego vehicle with more than 10 m/s relative velocity".

Abstraction. We derive the abstraction from the conditional parts of the requirements. We are interested in relations between objects. In our example relations are: *(vehicle) behind the ego vehicle*, and *(vehicle's) relative velocity is more than* 10 m/s, and *vehicle on right lane*. In each relation there is one subject (the vehicle in this case). We derive properties of subjects and abstract domains for those properties from the relations: This, e.g., yields *relative position* as a property of other vehicles and *behind* as one of its abstract values. Table 2 shows the properties and corresponding abstract values for the ego vehicle and other vehicles.

Overall, we defined 14 properties for ego vehicle, other vehicles, lanes, the general environment, and the human driver from the 17 analyzed safety requirements. A concrete traffic situation is abstracted by keeping all objects (lanes, vehicles, etc.) and by computing the abstract values of their properties.

Abstract Function. The conditional parts of the 17 safety requirements can be implemented as checks on ego vehicle, lanes, other vehicles, and their properties in abstract traffic situations. The abstract function evaluates these checks for each road lane and surrounding object. For each unsatisfied check, the corresponding lane is excluded from the set of valid target lanes. As result remains the set of lanes the vehicle may safely change to.

For this work, we analyzed requirements that are formulated in natural language and manually implemented abstractions and abstract function. We envision that this process can be automated by using formal specification languages (e.g., Alloy [9] or Z [21]).

From Simulations to the Road and Back. The ultimate goal of this work is to bridge the gap between simulations and road tests as is shown in Fig. 1.

Simulation to Road. In our case study with the LCA, we used the described abstractions and abstract function to record abstract traffic situations during simulations. The simulation was driven by manually designed test scenarios. These scenarios were designed to test the conformance of the LCA to its specification. We then used the database of recorded unique abstract traffic situations as a basis for the situation monitor (cf. Fig. 3) when evaluating the LCA in road tests.

Road to Simulation. We extracted abstract situations from data recorded during road tests and used these situations as a basis for defining new test cases that were then replayed in simulations. Please note, that this is not trivial: The simulator computes concrete vehicle trajectories. These have to be generated from abstract traffic situations, which only contain relational information (e.g., behind, slower, left, etc.). For this work, we manually designed test cases that simulate a sequence of abstract traffic situations. This was sufficient for an initial evaluation of the loop between simulation and road tests.

In a next step we plan to generate models from the recorded sequences of abstract traffic situations and use these models as a basis for generating realistic

Table 3. Coverage of traffic situations after training the situation monitor.

Experiment	Duration [Min:Sec]	Situations [#]		Tested [%]		Not tested [%]	
		Sum	Unique	Correct	Incorr	Correct	Incorr.
Simulated (1)	10:38	17,879	518	16.74	0.0	82.63	0.63
Simulated (2)	10:37	18,419	567	14.92	0.0	85.07	0.01
Road (3-lane, A2)	5:53	7,078	1,078	0.68	0.0	96.62	2.70
Road (2-lane, A39)	6:34	7,885	974	1.57	0.0	96.45	1.98

traffic situations in simulations. We plan to use automata learning algorithms (e.g. [12]) for generating probabilistic abstract models.

4   Evaluation

We have evaluated our approach on a prototype of a LCA that is being developed as part of an industrial highway autopilot. Our partner's development[2]- and simulation[3]- environment allows running the same LCA components in simulations and on the road. Since our monitors only listen to situations and target points on existing interfaces, it possible to use recorded data in our evaluation.

We use two sets of data as a basis for our evaluation.

Simulated. Data recorded while the LCA operates in randomly generated traffic on two tracks in the simulation environment.

Road. Data recorded in two road tests with the LCA on German highways A2 and A39; A2 is a three lane highway, A39 is a two lane highway.

Using the simulation environment, we can replay these recordings with our monitoring components in the loop. During replay, the situation monitor operates in *checking mode* in which observed abstract traffic situations are compared to situations in the database (as detailed in Sect. 2). The database is initialized with data recorded while simulating the LCA in 23 manually developed test cases. These test cases were designed by project partners to test the conformance of the LCA to its specification.

We use our monitoring components to compute some statistics over the abstract traffic situations on the individual recordings (e.g., frequencies and distribution).

We evaluate the following three conjectures.

H1. *The abstraction generated from the functional requirements is not too coarse.* We evaluate this hypothesis by analyzing abstract traffic situations that are classified as incorrect when replaying the *Simulated* and *Road* data sets.

H2. *Randomly simulated and manually tested traffic situations are not realistic in the simulation environment that is used for validating the LCA.* We evaluate this hypothesis by comparing frequencies and distribution of abstract traffic situations in the *Simulated* and *Road* data sets.

H3. *It is possible to achieve satisfiable coverage of situations when training monitors with realistic traffic.* We evaluate this hypothesis by initializing the situation monitor using increasing sets of realistic test cases and then replaying the *Road (A2)* data set while analyzing the performance of the situation monitor.

---

[2] ADTF - http://www.elektrobit.com/products/eb-assist/adtf/.
[3] Virtual Test Drive (VTD) - http://www.vires.com/products.html.

H1: Coarse Abstraction. Table 3 reports duration, numbers of total and unique abstract traffic situations, and coverage results for the *Simulated* and *Road* (A2 and A39) data set. In the *Simulated* data set, approximately 18,000 situations are observed. The number of unique abstract traffic situations is between 500 and 600 for both experiments. The percentage of safe (i.e., tested and correct) abstract traffic situations ranges from 14.92 % to 16.74 %. The vast majority of abstract situations (82.63 % and 85.07 %) is untested while the LCA conforms to its safety-critical requirements. Only 0 % to 0.63 % of abstract traffic situations were untested while the LCA violates its safety-critical requirements.

For the *Road* data set, the recordings each contain data for about six minutes. The more complex abstract traffic situations recorded by the situation monitor lead to an absolute increase in the number of unique abstract traffic situations (in comparison to the *Simulated* data set) to around 1,000. The percentage of tested abstract traffic situations drops to around 1 % for these experiments. Around 96 % of all observed abstract traffic situations are untested while the LCA performs within the limits of the functional requirements. The fraction of situations in which the LCA violates the functional requirements in untested abstract traffic situations increases to 1.98 % and 2.70 %.

We did not encounter any tested abstract traffic situations in which the LCA does not conform to its safety-critical requirements. This indicates that the used abstraction is adequate. We have manually analyzed the untested situations in which the LCA apparently does not conform to the specification. We did not find any indication of the abstraction being too coarse for these cases but rather discovered that the implementation on the LCA actually violates the functional requirements by performing a lane change to the right onto a lane with a slower vehicle ahead of the ego vehicle.

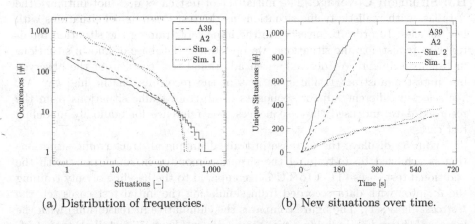

(a) Distribution of frequencies.   (b) New situations over time.

Fig. 4. Unique abstract traffic situations and distribution of frequencies and discovery of new situations over time. (a) Distribution of frequencies. (b) New situations over time.

H2: Realistic Traffic. As an indicator for the complexity of traffic we analyze the rate at which new unique abstract traffic situations are discovered over time as well as the total of unique abstract traffic situations in one experiment.

Figure 4a shows the number of occurrences for each unique abstract traffic situation. Both axes are scaled logarithmically. The *Simulated* series exhibit a similar distribution. The number of occurrences is distributed exponentially: there are many abstract traffic situations with few occurrences and only few abstract traffic situations with many occurrences. For the *Road* data set, the exponential distribution of occurring situations is more pronounced than for *Simulated* data set. This indicates that the exponential distribution becomes less expressed for longer experiments when a representative sample of situations is observed.

Figure 4b shows how the number of observed unique abstract traffic situations evolves over time in the experiments. The rates are significantly lower in the *Simulated* data set than the rates for the *Road* data set. On the two lane highway (A39) new situations occur at a slightly lower rate than on the three lane highway (A2). This indicates that the traffic generated by the simulation environment is less complex than real traffic on German highways and hence not realistic enough for testing the LCA in simulations sufficiently. Though we were not able to observe this in our experiments due to their limited duration, we expect that in longer data sets the increase in new situations to tail off at some point.

Additionally, the data presented in Table 3 suggests that test cases derived from the system's requirements are simpler than real traffic (and rightfully so: those tests are minimal scenarios for testing certain behavior of the LCA). Trained with these tests, the situation monitor classifies as little as $0,69\%$ (resp. 1.57%) of abstract traffic situations from the *Road* data set as tested.

H3: Situation Coverage. The initial set of test cases does not initialize the database with realistic traffic situations as the test cases model situations with few vehicles. In order to investigate the impact of training the situation monitor with realistic traffic situations, we update the database of known situations in this experiment. We derived seven additional test cases from the observed but untested abstract traffic situations of the recording on the highway A2. We selected different adjoint sequences of abstract traffic situations from the recorded data and used these sequences as a reference for manually modeling test cases.

Figure 5a displays the increase in trained unique abstract traffic situations that is achieved by re-training the situation monitor in simulations with the additional test cases (TC 1 to TC 7)—compared to the baseline of only training the monitor with data recorded from simulating the initial test cases (cf. the *test case* data set). The figure compares the cumulative increase (line) with the increase achieved by individual test cases (circles). From 77 tested abstract traffic situations for the initial set of test cases, the seven test cases increased the total number of trained unique abstract traffic situations to 369. The encountered situations in independent simulations of each test case correlate with the

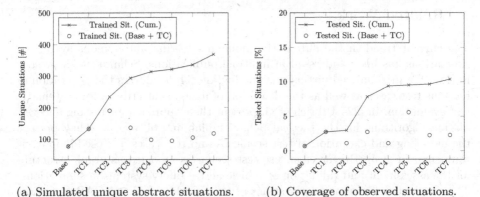

(a) Simulated unique abstract situations.   (b) Coverage of observed situations.

Fig. 5. Coverage after training monitors with additional test cases generated from observed situations. (a) Simulated unique abstract situations. (b) Coverage of observed situations.

increase of the set of trained unique abstract traffic situations of all test cases accumulated.

The graph in Fig. 5b shows the changes in the percentage of tested abstract traffic situations for the re-monitoring of the recording on the highway A2 with the trained abstract traffic situations of the additional test cases. The graph compares cumulative percentage (line) with the changes achieved by individual test cases (circles). The cumulated set of 369 trained abstract traffic situations increases the accumulated percentage of tested abstract traffic situations for the recording on the highway A2 from originally 0.67 % to 10.37 % (cf. Fig. 5b).

In comparison to the results for trained abstract traffic situations of the test cases (cf. Fig. 5a), the recorded abstract traffic situations of each test case do not directly correspond to the percentage of tested abstract traffic situations at the operation of the LCA. As for the test case TC 2, the accumulated percentage of tested abstract traffic situations does not directly correspond to its large number of trained abstract traffic situations.

Discussion. Our evaluation shows promising results: We were able to find evidence for the effectiveness of the proposed approach. The experiments show that test cases derived from real traffic situations enable a more efficient and realistic simulation of traffic situations. The results also show that state-of-the-art simulation (at least in this particular case) does not generate operation conditions that resemble conditions on the road closely enough.

Finally, our experiments indicate that abstracting concrete traffic situations to the level of the considered requirements is a valid idea. Engineers tend to reason about systems' behavior on an abstract level similar to the level of the requirements. This idea is even more valid in the context of safety-critical functions, where every line of code can be traced to a functional requirement.

5   Related Work

The current trend in the automotive domain - testing autonomous system in simulations has been addressed in multiple publications. Schuldt et al. present in [18,19] a modularized virtual test tooling kit. They address the generation of relevant test cases as well as the definition of assessment criteria for systematic test evaluation. In [22], Ulbrich et al. present their approach for testing and validating algorithms for the tactical behavior planning of a LCA. They present the modeling and execution of test scenarios and test cases in closed-loop environments. In [3,5], Berger et al. use test scenarios modeled as graph structure for the assessment and validation of vehicle active safety systems in simulations. The graph structures model variations of US NCAP and EuroNCAP scenarios. In [4], the authors enhance the evaluation of the test results by introducing tolerance ranges. Olivares et al. use in [17] a stochastic approach for the construction of test scenarios with respect to relevant parameter combinations, which might have been omitted by manually defined sets of scenarios. Zofka et al. employ in [26] parameterizable simulation models to define relevant test scenarios. None of the approaches considers real road traffic as input for the generation of test cases. Without consideration of real traffic, it is unlikely that an ADAS is tested in realistic situations.

For the validation of ADAS, several authors have proposed approaches combining field tests with simulations. In [6], Bock describes the use of augmented reality to inject virtual obstacles into the view of human drivers. In [20], Sefati et al. describe the integration of scientific objects into the object recognition of the ADAS for testing purposes. Both approaches are only used in field tests and do no benefit from the performance and reproducibility of simulations.

Other authors use data from field tests as input for simulations and testing. Lages et al. describe in [11] the semi-automatic generation of test scenarios for Software-in-the-Loop tests from recorded real world drivings. Bach et al. describe in [1] the problem of inadequate domains of the recorded test data for usage in virtual verification. They transform the test data into coherent stimuli for the system under test (SUT) by identifying dependencies between the input data streams of the SUT. Wachenfeld et al. present in [24] a runtime validation method called Virtual Assessment of Automation in Field Operation (VAAFO). VAAFO accesses automation's safety and identifies relevant test cases for closed-loop simulations by simulating the ADAS and its world alongside the human driver in the vehicle at operation.

None of these approaches generate data for new test cases at the abstract level of a specification. Neither does any approach transfer results of the simulation back to the road. Our approach introduces a comprehensive methodology to iteratively improve the safety of ADAS by using results from the road in the simulation and also results from simulations on the road.

6   Conclusion and Future Work

We have presented a method for ensuring that an advanced driver assistance system satisfies its safety requirements at runtime and operates within safe limits that were tested in simulations. Our main technical contribution is a conceptual framework for establishing a relation between simulations and road tests using a set of monitoring components for computing, checking, and learning relevant abstract traffic situations. We have evaluated our approach using an industrial prototype of a LCA and data recorded in road tests on German highways. We were able to identify relevant traffic situations in road tests, train monitors with abstract traffic situations in simulations, and then use those monitors to check tested and correct behavior of the ADAS.

There are many open questions for future research: One obvious question is how monitors perform aboard an actual vehicle under real-time conditions. A second direction of research would be extending our monitoring framework to stateful and time-dependent behavior, e.g., to cover maneuvers that require different phases. We plan to investigate how automata learning (e.g. [12,15]) can be used for producing stateful models of traffic situations. These stateful models can then become the basis for generating realistic traffic in simulations. Then, for our evaluation, abstraction and abstract function were implemented manually based on the derived properties and abstract values. We imagine that abstraction and abstract function could be generated from requirements in future applications in an automated fashion when using a formal specification language (e.g., Alloy [9] or Z [21]). In this work we did not address the refinement of a chosen abstraction that may become necessary. We plan to investigate if counterexample-guided abstraction refinement (CEGAR) can be applied in our setting [7]. Some automata learning algorithms already incorporate abstraction refinement [8]. Using such an algorithm would allow us to integrate model generation and abstraction refinement.

Finally, the ultimate goal is the integration of safety monitors into the planning of autonomous behavior of higher-level functions.

References

1. Bach, J., Bauer, K.-L., Holzpfel, M., Hillenbrand, M., Sax, E.: Control based driving assistant functions test using recorded in field data. In: Proc. 7. Tagung Fahrerassistenzsysteme (2015)
2. Berger, C.: From autonomous vehicles to safer cars: selected challenges for the software engineering. In: Ortmeier, F., Daniel, P. (eds.) SAFECOMP Workshops 2012. LNCS, vol. 7613, pp. 180–189. Springer, Heidelberg (2012)
3. Berger, C., Block, D., Heeren, S., Hons, C., Kuhnel, S., Leschke, A., Plotnikov, D., Rumpe, B. Simulations on consumer tests: a systematic evaluation approach in an industrial case study. In: ITSC 2014 (2014)
4. Berger, C., Block, D., Heeren, S., Hons, C., Kühnel, S., Leschke, A., Plotnikov, D., Rumpe, B.: Simulations on consumer tests: systematic evaluation of tolerance ranges by model-based generation of simulation scenarios. In: Proceedings of the Fahrerassistenzsysteme und Integrierte Sicherheit (2014)

5. Berger, C., Block, D., Heeren, S., Hons, C., Kuhnel, S., Leschke, A., Plotnikov, D., Rumpe, B.: Simulations on consumer tests: a systematic evaluation approach in an industrial case study. IEEE Intell. Transp. Syst. Mag. **7**(4), 24–36 (2015)

6. Bock, T.: Bewertung von Fahrerassistenzsystemen mittels der vehicle in the loop-simulation. In: Winner, H., Hakuli, S., Wolf, G. (eds.) Handbuch Fahrerassistenzsysteme. Vieweg+Teubner Verlag, Wiesbaden (2012)

7. Clarke, E., Grumberg, O., Jha, S., Lu, Y., Veith, H.: Counterexample-guided abstraction refinement for symbolic model checking. J. ACM (JACM) **50**(5), 752–794 (2003)

8. Howar, F., Steffen, B., Merten, M.: Automata learning with automated alphabet abstraction refinement. In: Jhala, R., Schmidt, D. (eds.) VMCAI 2011. LNCS, vol. 6538, pp. 263–277. Springer, Heidelberg (2011)

9. Jackson, D., Abstractions, S.: Logic, Language, and Analysis. The MIT Press, Cambridge (2006)

10. Kane, A.: Runtime monitoring for safety-critical embedded systems. Ph.D. thesis, Carnegie Mellon University (2015)

11. Lages, U., Spencer, M., Katz, R.: Automatic scenario generation based on laser-scanner reference data and advanced offline processing. In: 2013 IEEE Intelligent Vehicles Symposium Workshops (IV Workshops) (2013)

12. Mao, H., Chen, Y., Jaeger, M., Nielsen, T.D., Larsen, K.G., Nielsen, B.: Learning probabilistic automata for model checking. In: 2011 Eighth International Conference on Quantitative Evaluation of Systems (QEST), pp. 111–120. IEEE (2011)

13. Mauritz, M., Howar, F., Rausch, A.: From simulation to operation: using design time artifacts to ensure the safety of advanced driving assistance systems at runtime. In: International Workshop on Modelling in Automotive Software Engineering (2015)

14. Mauritz, M. Rausch, A., Schaefer, I.: Dependable ADAS by combining design time testing and runtime monitoring. In: 10th International Symposium on Formal Methods, FORMS/FORMAT 2014, pp. 28–37 (2014)

15. Merten, M., Steffen, B., Howar, F., Margaria, T.: Next generation LearnLib. In: Abdulla, P.A., Leino, K.R.M. (eds.) TACAS 2011. LNCS, vol. 6605, pp. 220–223. Springer, Heidelberg (2011)

16. Okuda, R., Kajiwara, Y., Terashima, K.: A survey of technical trend of ADAS and autonomous driving. In: Proceedings of Technical Program - 2014 International Symposium on VLSI Technology, Systems and Application, VLSI-TSA 2014 (2014)

17. Olivares, S.P., Rebernik, N., Eichberger, A., Stadlober, E.: Virtual stochastic testing of advanced driver assistance systems. In: Schulze, T., Müller, B., Meyer, G. (eds.) Advanced Microsystems for Automotive Applications 2015. Springer, Cham (2016)

18. Schuldt, F., Lichte, B., Maurer, M., Scholz, S.: Systematische Auswertung von Testfällen für Fahrfunktionen im modularen virtuellen Testbaukasten. In: 9. Workshop Fahrerassistenzsysteme (2014)

19. Schuldt, F., Saust, F., Lichte, B., Maurer, M.: Effiziente systematische Testgenerierung für Fahrerassistenzsysteme in virtuellen Umgebungen. In: Automatisierungssysteme, Assistenzsysteme und eingebettete Systeme für Transportmittel, AAET 2013 (2013)

20. Sefati, M., Stoff, A., Winner, H.: Testing method for autonomous safety functions based on combined steering/braking maneuvers for collision avoidance and mitigation. In: 6. Tagung Fahrerassistenz (2013)

21. Spivey, J.M., Abrial, J.: The Z Notation. Prentice Hall, Hemel Hempstead (1992)

22. Ulbrich, S., Schuldt, F., Homeier, K., Steinhoff, M., Menzel, T., Krause, J., Maurer, M.: Testing and validating tactical lane change behavior planning for automated driving. In: Horn, M., Watzenig, D. (eds.) Automated Driving - Safer and More Efficient Future Driving. Springer, Cham (2016)
23. Verband der Automobilindustrie e.V.: Automation: From Driver Assistance Systems to Automated Driving. VDA Magazine - Automation (2015)
24. Wachenfeld, W., Winner, H.: Virtual assessment of automation in field operation a new runtime validation method. In: 10. Workshop Fahrerassistenzsysteme (2015)
25. Winner, H.: ADAS, Quo Vadis? In: Winner, H., Hakuli, S., Lotz, F., Singer, C. (eds.) Handbook of Driver Assistance Systems: Basic Information, Components and Systems for Active Safety and Comfort. Springer, Cham (2014)
26. Zofka, M.R., Kuhnt, F., Kohlhaas, R., Rist, C., Schamm, T., Zllner, J.M.: Data-driven simulation and parametrization of traffic scenarios for the development of advanced driver assistance systems. In: 18th International Conference on Information Fusion (2015)

Enhancement of an Adaptive HEV Operating Strategy Using Machine Learning Algorithms

Mark Schudeleit[1(✉)], Meng Zhang[2], Xiaofei Qi[1], Ferit Küçükay[1], and Andreas Rausch[2]

[1] Institute of Automotive Engineering, Technische Universität Braunschweig, Braunschweig, Germany
{m.schudeleit,x.qi,f.kuecuekay}@tu-braunschweig.de
[2] Institute of Informatics, Technische Universität Clausthal, Clausthal, Germany
{meng.zhang,andreas.rausch}@tu-clausthal.de

Abstract. For vehicle manufacturers as well as for many drivers saving fuel has been a popular issue. In order to maximize the potential of the consumption-savings, optimization of operating strategy of vehicles, particularly of HEV (HEV: hybrid electric vehicle.), becomes an increasingly important task.

To enhance the current rule-based operating strategy of HEV, an adaptive heuristic operating strategy has been developed, which identifies driving patterns and chooses the best parameter set for the control strategy from a database. However, this strategy does not fit to the driving behavior of individual drivers.

Therefore, a further knowledge-based approach that independently optimizes the operating strategy has been developed using of multigene symbolic regression by utilizing supervised machine learning.

The investigation showed that a knowledge-based approach is able to save about 18.3 % CO_2 and fuel compared to a basic heuristic strategy.

1 Introduction

As a result of the limitation of fossil energy resources and negative influences of the growing transport sector on the environment due to pollutants, regulations have been adopted in order to decrease emissions. An example is the 95 g/km CO_2 limitation for OEM fleet emissions [1]. Nevertheless, the fuel consumption of a conventional vehicle, which directly correlates with the CO_2 emissions, can already be reduced significantly by enhancing it to a HEV. This is done by adding an electric motor and a battery to the conventional drivetrain consisting of an ICE[1] and a transmission. In situations where the ICE efficiency is poor, i.e. while driving in the city at low power, the vehicle can be driven electrically and emission free. Thus, the design of the operating strategy, which decides on the use of the two power sources, is key to drive optimally with regard to efficiency.

There has been research conducted on commonly used heuristic operating strategies. They control the ICE and EM based on fixed rules. Their behavior is transparent to drivers and the code is easily applicable on vehicles control devices. In [2, 3] the

---

[1] ICE: internal combustion engine.

T. Margaria and B. Steffen (Eds.): ISoLA 2016, Part II, LNCS 9953, pp. 688–702, 2016.
DOI: 10.1007/978-3-319-47169-3_53

basic heuristic operating strategy of this paper has been identified by optimization. It minimize CO_2 and pollutant emissions. [4] proposes a robust operating strategy with has a stable behavior in cycles as well as in real driving, which leads to overall improvements of about 3 %. [5, 6] integrate the thermal management of the vehicle in operating strategy focusing on different warm-up strategies. The authors came to the conclusion that heating up the engine in early phases reduces overall emissions due to improved engine efficiency. After all, rule-based operating strategies are usually solely optimized on legislated driving cycles and therefore, cannot exploit the full fuel saving potential applied to other driving scenarios occurring in real driving.

A conventional solution to overcome this weakness is to provide drivers different possibilities of driving modes. For example, the approach of Porsche Innodrive expands the ACC[2] functionality by deriving a speed band from a static map. Based on this speed band and algorithms of dynamic programming, a predictive operating strategy is developed. In this case the driver's individual intention has not been considered, but dictated by choosing one of the modes: comfort, efficiency or dynamic [7].

Another solution is based on adaptive approaches. To take the real world operation of vehicles into account, an adaptive heuristic approach using physical modeling has been developed in our work. This approach enhances the basic operating strategy by respectively classifying different driving styles and driving environments into three predefined categories. Based on the classification, the adaptive approach adopts different suitable operating strategies for different driving scenarios. To determine these operating strategies, the approach needs to build the physical models of the driving styles and the driving environments. However, the modeling is complex and not entirely precise. For example, the mood of the driver, which is impossible accurately to model, might also influence the driving style.

Performance limits already forces manufacturers today to strongly simplify the physical models implemented on the ECUs. Against this weakness, knowledge-based approaches based on machine learning algorithms offer significant advantages. These approaches use vehicle data and information about the vehicle's direct environment, which are collected through the pre-existing vehicle sensors and additional surrounding sensors like radar, infrared and camera systems [8]. Considering the past experience with the driver, individual vehicle and specific environment, the approaches can optimize the operating strategy of the vehicle by themselves.

Many vehicle manufacturers and research institutes are currently focusing on the predictive operating strategy of vehicles. One example of such approaches is the Audi PEA[3] [9]. This approach uses high-resolution map material and topographical data to provide anticipatory advice that helps the driver adopt an economical driving style. Therefore, considerable data about the following route needs to be processed to construct physical models. It requires a higher computing performance. In this case, continually increasing complexity of physical models will reach limits due to the ECU[4] performance.

---

[2] ACC: adaptive cruise control.

[3] PEA: predictive efficiency assistant.

[4] ECU: engine control unit.

To overcome the weaknesses of the latter adaptive heuristic approach, a knowledge-based approach as a further enhancement has been developed. According to the adaptive approach, the driving environments are classified into three categories by using statistic method. For each class of the driving environment, the knowledge-based approach attempts to optimize the current configuration of the operating strategy for individual vehicle as well as its driver.

This paper consists of 6 sections. Section 1 introduces the motivation as well as the structure of this paper. In Sect. 2, a simulation model of a full-HEV is introduced. This model is used to evaluate the adaptive heuristic as well as the knowledge-based approach. An approach for determining adaptive heuristic operating strategy of HEV according to different categories of driving styles as well as driving environments, is illustrated in Sect. 3. Subsequently, the knowledge-based approach, which further improves the operating strategy of the adaptive heuristic approach, is introduced in Sect. 4. Section 5 deals with the evaluation of the knowledge-based approach. A summary of the entire paper is included in the last section.

2 Preliminaries

2.1 Vehicle Topology

Object of this paper is a full hybrid electric sedan-sized vehicle. The modeled HEV[5] (see Fig. 1) has in addition to the conventional ICE[6] and a DCT[7] an additional shaft between ICE[8] and gearbox which is separated by two clutches, clutch 0 and clutch 1. The electric motor[9] is located on this shaft.

2.2 Basic Heuristic Operating Strategy

The basic operating strategy of the HEV is displayed in Fig. 2. It chooses the current operating mode according to the SOC[10] of the battery and the driving power P. Available hybrid operating modes are recuperation, pure electric drive (only EM), pure ICE drive (only ICE) and LPS[11]. The parameter $P_{ICE,lim}$ controls the maximum power of electric driving and transitions between pure electric driving and LPS. With $SOC_{ICE,lim}$ and $SOC_{EM,lim}$ the operating modes are chosen depending on the state of charge of the battery. Transition areas with a hysteresis are implemented to avoid

---

[5] full-HEV: hybrid electric vehicle with an electric motoric power to vehicle mass ratio of more than 20 kW/t.

[6] Internal combustion engine.

[7] DCT: double clutch transmission.

[8] ICE: internal combustion engine.

[9] EM: electric motor.

[10] SOC: state of charge; current state of energy saved in a battery in percent.

[11] LPS: load point shift; the necessary propulsion power is distributed to the combustion engine and the electric motor. Therefore the operating point of the combustion engine is shifted (usually to points of higher efficiency) compared to the operation without the electric motor.

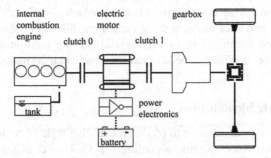

Fig. 1. HEV topology [10].

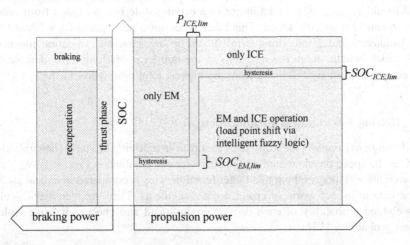

Fig. 2. SOC-power based operating strategy of a parallel HEV with intelligent fuzzy control in the operating mode "load point shift" (LPS) (not shown in this figure) [10].

alternating between two operating modes. The operating strategy parameters are constant. In the LPS an intelligent fuzzy logic controller controls the torque distribution between ICE and EM through numerous rules to shift the operating point of the ICE to its optimum efficiency as well as enabling SOC-leveling.

3 Adaptive Heuristic Operating Strategy

Using heuristic operating strategies with fixed parameter sets has advantages. The strategies are always plausible in the eyes of the customer as they always work as expected. Furthermore, these strategies can be implemented easily on the control devices. It also provides good robustness and is widely adopted in HEVs. Nevertheless, it offers neither predictions nor adaptions on the current driving situation. As the parameter sets are optimized on legislated driving cycles, it is not parameterized optimally for real driving, which then leads to higher emissions. An approach is therefore suggested to use the driving style and driving environment identifier, which uses current vehicle data (v, a) in order to classify into three different drivers and three different driving environments in real-time. For each combination of drivers and driving environments, an optimal parameter set can be identified to be selected for a particular scenario.

3.1 Driving Style Identification

The DSI[12] was developed in order to predict the driving style of customer in a car and to adopt driver assistance systems accordingly [11]. Hence, it can also be used to supply parameters for an adaption of the operating strategy of a HEV to the driving behavior.

Input signals are the speed v and the acceleration while accelerating a_{accel} as well as while breaking a_{break}. The probabilities of a driving style is determined from acceleration signals at a specific speed. This takes place for a retrospect of 1 s (short-term), 30 s (midterm) and 2 min (long-term). In the *priorization* an evaluation function is used, which benefits more recent results in the mid-term and long-term identification. The current driving style follows from the highest total probability [12].

3.2 Driving Environment Identification

The driving environment identifier uses past data in a driving scenario (here: 60 s) and analyses the speed profile regarding the characteristic parameters v_{max}, v_{min}, v_{mean}, and v_{std}, weights and merges them to a target function. This is compared to a database with offline data from real world of customer measurements. Then the identifier calculates the weighted probability of each driving environment and chooses the one with the highest probability [13].

3.3 Results

In order to test the potential of the alternative operating strategy the emissions have been determined by tracing speed profiles of legislated driving cycles and some from different customer measurements by the modeled vehicle. The results are shown in Fig. 3.

It can be seen that the emissions of CO_2 are reduced by using the adaptive operating strategy in contrast to the basic one. In NEDC[13], WLTP[14] and FTP-75[15], CO_2 emissions have been reduced by up to 10 percent. Using customer driving cycles the CO_2

---

[12] DSI: driving style identification.

[13] NEDC: New European Driving Cycle. Up to 2020 the emission and fuel economy test cycle in Europe.

[14] WLTP: Worldwide Harmonized Light-Duty Vehicles Test Procedures define a global harmonized standard for determining the levels of pollutants and CO2.

[15] FTP-75: Federal Test Procedure. A driving cycle defined by the US Environmental Protection Agency.

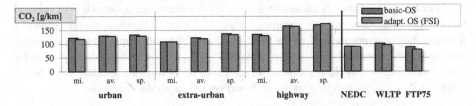

Fig. 3. CO_2 emissions of basic and adaptive strategy [14]

reduction potential highly depends on the driving style as well as on the driving environment. Whereas the adaptive operating strategy has benefits especially in urban driving scenarios, while driving on a highway it only reduces emissions for drivers with a mild or average driving style. Overall, the adaptive operating strategy shows improvement in customer driving scenarios without deteriorating emissions in legislated driving cycles. However, in real world, both, the speed profile and the driving style of individual customers are unknown and will differ, which leaves reduction potential unexploited. To tackle this the driving behavior must be assessed and the database must be enlarged continuously.

4 Self-learning Operating Strategy Based on Machine Learning

As a further enhancement of the adaptive operating strategy of HEV, a knowledge-based approach has been developed. This section deals with the motivation as well as the concept of this approach. With the help of a machine learning algorithm, the knowledge-based approach attempts to optimize the configuration of the adaptive operating strategy of HEV.

4.1 Motivation

The adaptive heuristic operating strategy shows improvements particulary in real driving by adapting to the driver. However, this is only an approximated method, which classifies all driving styles into several predefined categories such as sporty, average and mild.

In the operating strategy of the adaptive heuristic approach, a parameter $P_{ICE,Lim}$ decides when the vehicle drives in pure electric mode or hybrid mode. As introduced in Sect. 2, an individual value of this parameter is determined for each class of driving styles as well as driving environments. Since driver's are classified into three styles: sporty, average and mild (see Sect. 3.2), the adaptive approach only offers restricted variants of operating strategies, which are possibly not optimal for an individual driver. On the other hand, a long-term aging effect of machines in the vehicle, which also indirectly affects the driving style of the driver, is impossible to be considered by using static physical modeling as it is done in the adaptive approach.

In order to overcome these weaknesses, a knowledge-based approach is developed to optimize the value of the parameter $P_{ICE,lim}$ for an individual driver. Figure 4 indicates the structure as well as the process flow of the entire approach. A modeling module is used to model the function between $P_{ICE,lim}$ and the vehicle consumption by using multigene symbolic regression. In addition, an optimizing module attempts to optimize $P_{ICE,lim}$ by changing its value based on the modeled function.

4.2   Concept

As illustrated in the adaptive heuristic approach, the driving styles and the driving environments are respectively classified into three categories. Each combination of classes of driving styles and driving environments represents an individual scenario. For each scenario, an initial value of the parameter $P_{ICE,Lim}$ is determined as the operating strategy according to the adaptive heuristic approach. The developed knowledge-based approach focuses on further optimizing the value of this parameter.

Initially based on the operating strategy in the adaptive approach, the value of the parameter $P_{ICE,lim}$ and all data about the driving profile as well as vehicle consumption profile are collected while driving. According to the adaptive operating strategy, the collected driving profile is classified into different driving environments such as urban, extra-urban and highway. For each environment an individual average driving profile of the driver is generated after each trip based on the driving profiles from the last as well as from the former trips. All driving and consumption profiles of the vehicle (as input) and the current value of $P_{ICE,lim}$ (as output) are used as training data for a machine learning algorithm in the modeling module. This algorithm works on multigene symbolic regression (by using supervised learning) to model a function between the parameter $P_{ICE,lim}$ and the vehicle consumption based on the generated average driving profile. In our work, an open-source toolbox GPTIPS[16], which allows developers to set an individual configuration, is utilized to implement the MGSR-algorithm[17]. Based on genetic programming and symbolic regression, the MGSR algorithm builds 250 functions for each generation by combining predefined basic mathematical functions such as "sin", "cos" and "exp". 30 % of the models with the least errors in comparison with the original in- and output data, are selected and inherited to the next iteration step. By selecting and inheriting the functions over generations, the algorithm optimizes the modeled function by itself and finally, selects the best one. Commonly, the functions in the first generation are randomly generated. Since they might also influence the final modeling quality, the algorithm performs four individual runs[18] that are merged at the end of the entire modeling process. Each run terminates after a predefined time period of 60 s.

Once the MGSR-algorithm has completed to approximate the function of the vehicle consumption profile and the parameter $P_{ICE,lim}$, in each driving environment,

---

[16] GPTIPS is a open-source symbolic data mining platform and interactive modelling environment for MATLAB [15].

[17] MGSR: multigene symbolic regression [15].

[18] Each run means that the algorithm begins to model the functions again from the first generation.

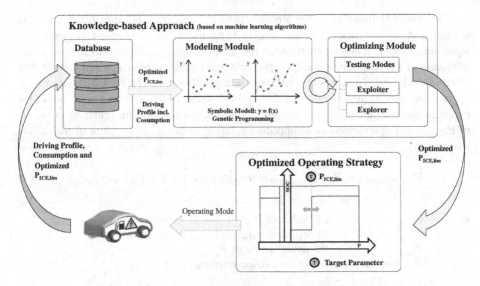

Fig. 4. Overview of concept of the knowledge-based approach

the optimizing module attempts to find the best value of $P_{ICE,lim}$ through evaluating the vehicle consumption with the help of the average driving profile. The module has two modes in total: explorer and exploiter, which are randomly activated according to a predefined probability distribution.

A classic mathematical problem by optimizing parameter is how to find the global minima and avoid the local minima. Figure 5 illustrates an example of this problem based on our application. Imagine that the algorithm has already changed the value of $P_{ICE,lim}$ for several times, minimum and maximum values ($P_{minKnown}$ and $P_{maxKnown}$) build a known range of values. In this case, the algorithm will always find the optimum as the local consumption minimum once the searching range of the values is not extended. This would not lead to the desired global minimum, so the explorer-mode is designed to eliminate this problem by randomly extend the actual range of values of $P_{ICE,lim}$.

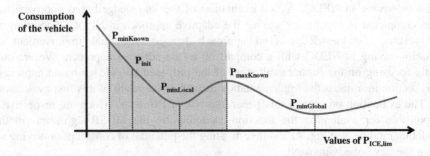

Fig. 5. Schematic diagram of vehicle consumption by different values of $P_{ICE,Lim}$

The modeled function in the algorithm could sometimes be unrealistic, once the training data is insufficient, which usually happens in the early phase by using the algorithm. Once the algorithm changes the value of $P_{ICE,lim}$ directly to an unrealistic minimum of the function, it could be possible that the algorithm cannot find any better value in the future. To avoid this problem, the algorithm only updates the value of $P_{ICE,lim}$ step by step in the direction of the optimal value in the known range, while the exploiter-mode is activated. In the current algorithm, a function for updating the value of $P_{ICE,min}$ is implemented as a simplified solution to avoid the problem of unrealistic minimum:

$$P_{ICE,min\_next} = P_{ICE,min\_current} + \alpha \cdot \left(P_{ICE,min\_known} - P_{ICE,min\_current}\right) \qquad (1)$$

with P_{ICE,min_next}:   the value of $P_{ICE,lim}$ for next attempt
P_{ICE,min_known}:   the optimal value of $P_{ICE,lim}$ in the known range
$P_{ICE,min\_current}$:   the actual value of $P_{ICE,lim}$
α: discount factor to avoid unrealistic minima (< 1)

In a further development, different mathematical functions for updating the value of $P_{ICE,min}$ will be tested in the algorithm to guarantee a more stable optimization effect.

4.3 Summary

This section deals with the concept of a knowledge-based approach to optimize the operating strategy of a HEV, which further enhances the adaptive heuristic approach (see Sect. 3). With the help of this knowledge-based approach, the value of a parameter $P_{ICE,lim}$ in the operating strategy is continually optimized for an individual driver and his vehicle in different driving environments. In the next section, the entire approach is evaluated with several different tests. A potential of consumption-saving of the approach is determined as the final result of this paper.

5 Evaluation

As shown in Fig. 3 the adaptive approach offers insignificant potential of emission-saving in NEDC. A first evaluation of the knowledge-based approach has been completed to benchmark against the adaptive approach in NEDC. According to our results, the knowledge-based approach has a substantial improvement of emission-saving in NEDC with a comparison to the adaptive approach. We are currently focusing on the further evaluation of the proposed knowledge-based approach. This section introduces the implementation as well as the result of this first evaluation.

The evaluation process in this paper consists of two tests, which are respectively responsible for evaluating the function modeling by the MGSR-algorithm (in the modeling module, see Fig. 4) and investigating the potential of consumption-saving by using the developed approach.

The first test focuses on validation of the algorithm based on multigene symbolic regression. As introduced in the section on preliminaries, a simulation model of a full HEV is developed in our work. For a HEV, the vehicle consumption consists of two parts: the consumption of the ICE and the consumption of the EM. Our first step to validate the algorithm is aimed to investigate the influence of the parameter $P_{ICE,lim}$ on the total consumption of the vehicle by testing the simulation model in the NEDC. Based on the vehicle model, a simulation with input as different values of $P_{ICE,lim}$[19] is performed. The outputs of this simulation are the consumption of ICE and SOC-difference, which is seen as the consumption of EM.

Figure 6 illustrates the relation between the parameter $P_{ICE,lim}$ and the ICE and EM consumptions. It is clear that the consumption of the ICE is affected by $P_{ICE,lim}$ and the difference of SOC for a certain driving cycle. By fixing the value of $P_{ICE,lim}$, we can note that ICE consumption is antiproportional to the difference of SOC, which is equivalent to the consumption of the EM. The points in the figure represent the real simulated data. After training with these data points, the MGSR algorithm models a plane function of the ICE consumption of the vehicle using $P_{ICE,lim}$ and the SOC-difference (used to describe the EM consumption) before and after driving:

$$\text{ICE consumption} = f\left(P_{ICE,lim}, \text{SOC-difference}\right) \tag{2}$$

It is worth emphasizing that this plane function is only a mathematical model, which means that the value range of the model is restricted because of boundary conditions in reality such as the current SOC of the battery and the realistic range of performance of the machines in the vehicle.

After the simulation, an error analysis has been performed to validate the MGSR-algorithm. As introduced before, the algorithm executes four individual runs to model the target function. For each run, a total of the 250 best models is inherited in the algorithm. These models from the 4 runs are merged together at the end of modeling phase. That means, after the entire test, a total of 1000 mathematical models are inherited as the final result. Each model contains a summarized mathematical function, which could be also described as a curve (2d) or a spline (3d). Thus, the modeling quality can be evaluated based on a criteria related to the squared correlation coefficient (R^2), which describes the similarity between the summarized curve/spline and the vectors of original data points. Figure 7 shows the square of the correlation coefficient (y-axis) and generation indexes (x-axis) of these 1000 models. In the figure, the triangles represent best models in each generation. The best model in the entire test is represented by the squares.

In this paper, 70 % (training set) of all simulated data are used for training the model while the rest 30 % (test set) are used for validating the algorithm. In the validation phase, the original input data (SOC-difference and $P_{ICE,lim}$) are used as inputs for the modeled function. The corresponding outputs (ICE consumption) can be calculated with the help of the function and be seen as prediction results. Based on the deviations between the prediction results (as the dashed line in Fig. 8) and the original

---

[19] In this test, the value of $P_{ICE,lim}$ varies between 4 and 15 kW.

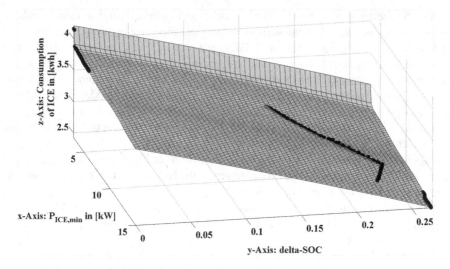

Fig. 6. ICE and SOC consumption of the vehicle

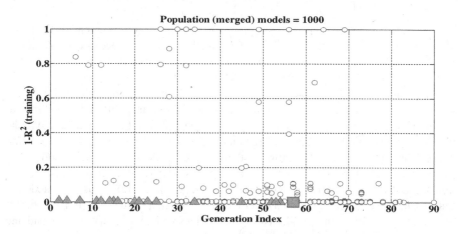

Fig. 7. Population models of MGSR algorithm

output data (as target data, the solid line in Fig. 8), RMS-errors as well as the square of
the correlation coefficient (R^2) are calculated and illustrated in Fig. 8. Since the errors
are low ($R^2 > 0.99$[20]), it is clear that the algorithm has shown a significant good ability
to model the target function.

After validating the MGSR-algorithm, the next step during evaluation focuses on
determining the potential of consumption-saving by using the developed knowledge-

---

[20] R^2 of 1.0 relates to a 10 % match of predicted result and the original output data.

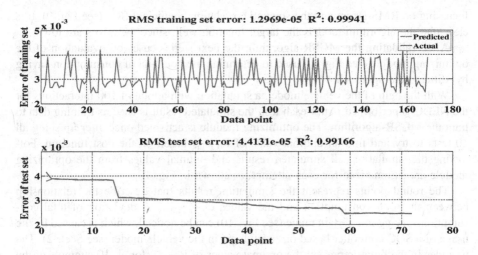

Fig. 8. RMS errors and Square of the correlation coefficient of training set and test set

based approach. Since the total consumption consists of the ICE consumption and the EM consumption, it is necessary to define a cost function.

In the first step of this study, the cost function is defined as follows:

$$\text{Total Consumption} = \text{Consumption of ICE}_{\text{Tank}} + \text{Consumption of EM}_{\text{Tank}} \qquad (3)$$

where the consumptions of both motors are converted to equivalent consumptions on tank level in the vehicle. In this step, the MGSR-algorithm is used to model a function between $P_{\text{ICE,lim}}$ and the total consumption. It is necessary to verify, whether the algorithm can model the target funciton. After the learning process, similar to the last test for validating the MGSR-algorithm, an error analysis has been performed,

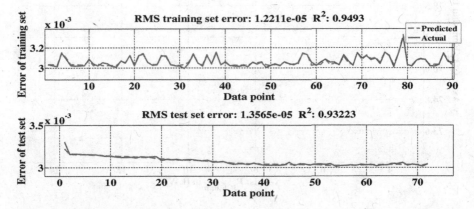

Fig. 9. RMS error and the squared correlation coefficient of training and test set for 10 optimizing processes

focussing on RMS-errors and the squared correlation coefficient (R^2) (see Fig. 9). It is clear that the algorithm models the target function well, since the errors are low.

After validating the MGSR-algorithm, the next step focuses on evaluation of the optimizing module (see Fig. 4), used to determine the potential of consumption-saving by utilizing the approach.

With the help of the vehicle model, a simulation with a total of 100 interactions for the NEDC is performed. After each test, the simulated result is used as training data to train the MGSR-algorithm. The optimizing module is activated once after finishing all 10 tests to try and find an optimal value of $P_{ICE,lim}$ based on the cost funciton. Following the simulation, all simulated results and optimal values from the optimizing module are summarized for each attempt, as shown in Fig. 10.

The round points represent the simulation results that describe the relationship between the total consumption and the values of $P_{ICE,lim}$. A deviation of total consumption varying in a certain range (see Fig. 10) can be noticed, which is caused by the usage of a SOC controller based on fuzzy logic in the vehicle model (see Sect. 2). The triangles in the figure represent the optimal values of $P_{ICE,lim}$ for all 10 attempts of the optimizing module. The found optimal values might be not realistic for the first couple of optimization processes (see the triangle on the bottom right in Fig. 10), which is a disadvantage of the learning approach, since insufficient data are used to train the algorithm. This causes an error risk. To work against this problem, the function for updating the value of $P_{ICE,min}$ (see Sect. 4.2) needs to be further investigated. However, the learning approach shows a significant potential for the long term. Once the training data are sufficient, the algorithm models a smooth function and ignores the small

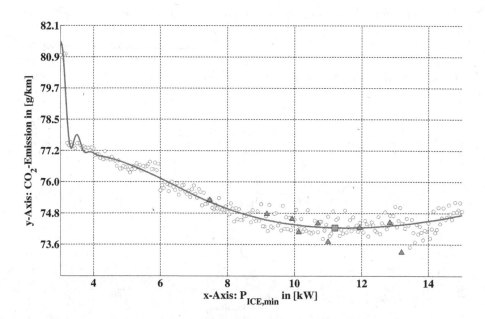

Fig. 10. Modeled function after 100 learning processes

deviations of the training data, which might be caused by external disruptions such as sensor errors (see Fig. 10).

According to the results in Fig. 3 CO_2 emissions generally decreased in real driving using the adaptive instead of the basic operating strategy. However, the improvements in the NEDC (from 90.6622 g/km to 90.0293 g/km) of about 0.7 % are slight. Based on the modeled function in Fig. 10, it is possible to find the minimum of total consumption with a value of about 74.0431 g/km, meaning that in the NEDC the knowledge-based approach offers a CO_2 emission saving potential about 18.3 % in comparison to the basic operating strategy.

It is worth emphasizing that the EM consumption is considered in our evaluation of the knowledge-based approach. Therefore, SOC leveling (initial SOC is equal to the final SOC) must not be achieved in simulation, whereas the evaluation result of the adaptive approach, represented in Fig. 3 did this. That means, the effective potential by using the knowledge-based approach might be smaller. Furthermore, it must be proofen that the SOC leveling can be achieved as the vehicle with the knowledge-based operating strategy would drive primarily electrical due to the increase of $P_{ICE,lim}$. In further evaluation, this point will be particularly investigated.

6   Conclusion and Outlook

The study introduced a learning operating strategy for hybrid electric vehicles using supervised learning algorithms, developed to achieve emission reduction in real driving by learning patterns of occurring driving scenarios.

Coming from a rule-based operating strategy with fixed thresholds for engine power and SOC level controlling the ICE and EM power distribution, optimizations have been carried out regarding multiple emissions in NEDC. Afterwards the basic operating strategy has been enhanced by implementing a classifying identification of the driving conditions (driving style and driving environment), and creation of an operating strategy database, which leads to improvements.

In order to accurately adapt the operating strategy to a certain driver without classification and the driving environment a knowledge-based approach was developed to enhance the heuristic one. With this the value of the parameter $P_{ICE,lim}$, which switches between pure electric and hybrid mode, is optimized using a machine learning algorithm based on multigene symbolic regression also taking a possible SOC-difference into account.

To proof the concept the algorithm is tested in the legislated driving cycle NEDC. It is possible to extend it by other cycles as well as real driving profiles of customers likewise. Over 170 data points were tested in the NEDC. The algorithm created about 1000 models and selected the one fitting best regarding RMS and square of the correlation coefficient. The results show that the CO_2-emission in the NEDC could be reduced from 90.6622 g/km (basic operating strategy) to 74.0431 g/km. It means that the potential of CO_2 emission savings using the developed learning algorithm is up to 18.3 %.

Based on the proofen concept, further enhancements towards a neural operating strategy can take place by automation of the learning process and testing the algorithm for different real driving profiles as well as for fleet-based energy management optimization of HEV.

References

1. Barsali, S., et al.: A control strategy to minimize fuel consumption of series hybrid electric vehicles. IEEE Trans. Energy Convers. **19**, 187–195 (2004)
2. Schudeleit, M., Küçükay, F.: Effects of customer use on emissions for optimised operation HEV. In: Proceedings of the 5th IET Hybrid and Electric Vehicles Conference (HEVC 2014) (2014). 978-1-84919-911-7
3. Schudeleit, M., Eghtessad, M., Küçükay, F.: Simulative determination of CO_2 and pollutant emissions of a HEV with multicriteria-optimised operation strategy in customer use. In: Energy Efficient Vehicles 2014: Visions, Trends and Solutions for Energy Efficient Vehicle Systems, Dresden (2014)
4. Schudeleit, M., Küçükay, F.: Control strategy for a parallel hybrid drive. MTZ Worldwide **76**, 48–53 (2015). Springer Verlag
5. Mustafa, R., Schulze, M., Eilts, P., Küçükay, F.: Intelligent Energy Management Strategy for a Parallel Hybrid Electric Vehicle for Different Driving Conditions, SAE Technical Paper, 2014-01-1909 (2014)
6. Mustafa, R.: Intelligent Energy Management for a Parallel Hybrid Electric Vehicle in Customer Use. Shaker Verlag, Aachen (2015)
7. Roth, M., et al.: Porsche InnoDrive – An Innovative Approach for the Future of Driving, 20. Aachen Colloquium Fahrzeug- und Motorentechnik, Aachen, Germany (2011)
8. Mauk, T.: Learning, reliability-oriented prediction of energetic relevant measures in vehicles [Selbstlernende, zuverlässigkeitorientierte Prädiktion energetisch relevanter Größen im Kraftfahrzeug]. University Stuttgart, Stuttgart, Germany (2011)
9. Audi: Predictive efficiency assistant, Audi 2015 Annual Report, p. 155 (2015)
10. Schudeleit, M., Küçükay, F.: Emission-robust operation of diesel HEV considering transient emissions. Int. J. Automot. Technol. **17**(3), 523–533 (2016)
11. Pion, O.: Determination of the driver performance to adapt driving assistance systems [Bestimmung des Fahrerleistungsvermögens zur Adaption von Fahrerassistenzsystemen]. Shaker Verlag, Aachen (2015)
12. Qi, X.: Development of a cycle-independent control strategy with driving situation dependent adaption, Technische Universität Braunschweig (2015)
13. Sternberg, M.: Development and online integration of a street classifier [Entwicklung und Online-Integration eines Straßenklassenschätzers], Technische Universität Braunschweig (2015)
14. Schudeleit, M.: Development of an adaptive learning operating strategy, company conference of the Institute of Automotive Engineering, Technische Universität Braunschweig (2015)
15. Searson, D.P., et al.: GPTIPS: an open source genetic programming toolbox for multigene symbolic regression. In: Proceedings of the International MultiConference of Engineers and Computer Scientists, IMECS 2010, vol. I, Hong Kong (2010)

Testing the Internet of Things

Testing the Internet of Things

Michael Felderer[1] and Ina Schieferdecker[2]

[1] University of Innsbruck, Innsbruck, Austria
`michael.felderer@uibk.ac.at`
[2] Fraunhofer Institute FOKUS & TU Berlin, Berlin, Germany
`ina.schieferdecker@fokus.fraunhofer.de`

Internet of Things (IoT) is achieving wide application and playing a more and more significant role in todays smart world. It is designed to make objects sensed and controlled remotely across network infrastructure, building integration of the physical world into information networks. The IoT connects every device with the internet for switching information and co-working with other devices. It extends and expands the communication between human and human, human and machine, or machine and machine, where a machine can be any physical entity [1]. In Gartner's 2015 Hype Cycle for Emerging Technologies [2] — which illustrates how a technology stacks up against others in terms of maturity — the Internet of Things (IoT) is presented at the peak of the curve with high expectations as the new digital business paradigm that will offer fundamentally new ways for service- and value creation and extends previous approaches to manage eternal networked systems [3].

The different application domains and scenarios of the IoT are enormous and will impact all areas of our daily lives [4]. Typical application scenarios are the transportation and logistics domain (i.e. intelligent decisions on routing of products), healthcare domain (i.e. personalize patient care) and smart cities, homes and factories (i.e. energy savings and property protection, Industry 4.0) [5–7]. Gartner estimates there will be 50 billion connected devices by 2020 [8]. Such massive-scale interconnections are built on multiple levels of technology support, from physical devices, to communications, to data, and to applications, which are heterogeneous by nature but are glued dynamically with various middlewares. To link and share everything as promoted by IoT, the scale and complexity of the system have been greatly increased.

Consequently, quality assurance of the IoT system faces new risks and threatens that are hardly addressed by conventional approaches. Furthermore, with the emergence of the IoT and its characteristics, the environment for software engineers radically changes related to development and delivery of high quality and error-free IoT software applications. Hence, software quality assurance and software testing activities must meet these new requirements and be adapted to be compliant with the new and rapidly changing environment caused by the IoT. Marwah and Sirshar [1] even claim that software quality assurance in the IoT can be seen as a new era in research.

Due to the architecture, IoT systems are constructed in a rather different way from traditional software systems. A common IoT system would be built on the foundation of collaboration among various components at various levels and involve components from hardware elements to top-level programs. Test and validation ensuring correct functionality, workflow control, resilience to attacks, data authentication, and client privacy for such a complex system requires great efforts and novel approaches. Test perspectives vary as different levels and qualities are concerned in IoT. For instance, at device-level, connectivity, energy and network transport between devices are main issues threatening to correctness and performance of IoT systems. The cloud-level involves most test perspectives including functionality, performance and security. At the mobile-level testing is more focused on mobile application correctness over any network in the whole lifecycle scenarios. Finally, end-to-end testing takes all previous levels into consideration to validate the whole systems. Due to the complexity, the importance of data and the need for testing of several level (including the device, cloud and mobile level), especially model-based testing [9, 10] and risk-based testing [11, 12] approaches are well-suited to support quality assurance of IoT applications.

This special track on Testing the Internet of Things serves as a platform for researchers and practitioners to present approaches, results, experiences and advances on all level of IoT testing, i.e., device, cloud, mobile and end-to-end testing level. The objective of the Testing the Internet of Things track was to establish a fruitful and meaningful dialog among systems practitioners and with systems engineering researchers in embedded systems, cyber-physical systems, and the Internet of Things on the challenges, obstacles, results (both good and bad), and lessons learned associated with the massive deployment of Internet of Things solutions in various safety- and security-critical environments.

In the special track two papers, one by Foidl and Felderer [13] and another one by Ahmad et al. [14] are presented.

Foidl and Felderer [13] present data science challenges to improve quality assurance of IoT applications. Due to the massive amount of data generated in workflows of IoT applications, data science plays a key role in their quality assurance. Therefore, the authors present respective data science challenges to improve quality assurance of Internet of Things applications. Based on an informal literature review, they outline quality assurance requirements evolving with the IoT grouped into six categories (Environment, User, Compliance/Service Level Agreement, Organizational, Security and Data Management) and present data science challenges to improve the quality assurance of Internet of Things applications in four categories (Defect prevention, Defect analysis, User incorporation and Organizational) derived from the six quality assurance requirement categories.

Ahmad et al. [14] present Model-Based Testing As A Service (MBTAAS) for testing data and IoT platforms. To manage things heterogeneity and data streams over large scale and secured deployments, IoT and data platforms are becoming a central part of the IoT. MBTAAS responds to the fast growing demand to systematically test such IoT and data platforms. For this purpose, MBTAAS combines model-based testing techniques and service-oriented solutions. Besides the approach itself, the authors also present experiments with MBTAAS on FIWARE, one of the EU most emerging IoT enabled platforms.

References

1. Marwah, Q.M., Sirshar, M.: Software quality assurance in internet of things. Int. J. Comput. Appl. **109**(9), 16–24 (2015)
2. Gartner: Gartner's 2015 hype cycle for emerging technologies identifies the computing innovations that organizations should monitor. Technical report, Gartner (2015)
3. Issarny, V., Steffen, B., Jonsson, B., Blair, G.S., Grace, P., Kwiatkowska, M.Z., Calinescu, R., Inverardi, P., Tivoli, M., Bertolino, A., Sabetta, A.: CONNECT challenges: towards emergent connectors for eternal networked systems. In: 14th IEEE International Conference on Engineering of Complex Computer Systems, ICECCS 2009, Potsdam, Germany, 2–4 June 2009, pp. 154–161 (2009)
4. Santucci, G., L.S.: Internet of things in 2020 - a roadmap for the future. Technical report (2011)
5. Vermesan, O., Friess, P.: Internet of Things-from Research and Innovation to Market Deployment. River Publishers Aalborg (2014)
6. Lee, I., Lee, K.: The internet of things (iot): Applications, investments, and challenges for enterprises. Bus. Horiz. **58**(4), 431–440 (2015)
7. Foidl, H., Felderer, M.: Research challenges of industry 4.0 for quality management. In: Felderer, M., Piazolo, F., Ortner, W., Brehm, L., Hof, H. (eds.) Innovations in Enterprise Information Systems Management and Engineering, vol. 245, pp. 121–137. Springer, Switzerland (2016)
8. Evans, D.: The internet of things - how the next evolution of the internet is changing everything. Technical report, Cisco Internet Business Solutions Group (IBSG) (2011)
9. Schieferdecker, I.: Model-based testing. IEEE Softw. **29**(1), 14 (2012)
10. Felderer, M., Zech, P., Breu, R., Büchler, M., Pretschner, A.: Model-based security testing: a taxonomy and systematic classification. Softw. Test. Verification Reliab. **26**(2), 119–148 (2016)
11. Felderer, M., Schieferdecker, I.: A taxonomy of risk-based testing. Int. J. Softw. Tools Technol. Transf. **16**(5), 559–568 (2014)
12. Felderer, M., Wendland, M.F., Schieferdecker, I.: Risk-based testing. In: Margaria, T., Steffen, B. (eds.) ISoLA 2014, Part II, LNCS 8803, pp. 274–276. Springer, Switzerland (2014)
13. Foidl, H., Felderer, M.: Data science challenges to improve quality assurance of internet of things applications. In: Margaria, T., Steffen, B. (eds.) ISoLA 2016, Part II, LNCS 9953, pp. 707–727. Springer, Switzerland (2016)
14. Ahmad, A., Bouquet, F., Le Gall, F., Legeard, B., Fourneret, E.: Model-based testing as a service for data fiware generic enablers. In: Margaria, T., Steffen, B. (eds.) ISoLA 2016, Part II, LNCS 9953. Springer, Switzerland (2016)

Data Science Challenges to Improve Quality Assurance of Internet of Things Applications

Harald Foidl and Michael Felderer[(✉)]

Institute for Computer Science, University of Innsbruck, Innsbruck, Austria
{harald.foidl,michael.felderer}@uibk.ac.at

Abstract. With the increasing importance and complexity of Internet of Things (IoT) applications, also the development of adequate quality assurance techniques becomes essential. Due to the massive amount of data generated in workflows of IoT applications, data science plays a key role in their quality assurance. In this paper, we present respective data science challenges to improve quality assurance of Internet of Things applications. Based on an informal literature review, we first outline quality assurance requirements evolving with the IoT grouped into six categories (Environment, User, Compliance/Service Level Agreement, Organizational, Security and Data Management). Finally, we present data science challenges to improve the quality assurance of Internet of Things applications sub-divided into four categories (Defect prevention, Defect analysis, User incorporation and Organizational) derived from the six quality assurance requirement categories.

Keywords: Software quality assurance · Software testing · Internet of Things · Data science · Process mining · Software quality engineering

1 Introduction

As the third phase of the Internet revolution, the Internet of Things (IoT) has attracted a lot of attention from practitioners, researchers and industries from all over the world [1, 2]. Compared to its predecessors, the World Wide Web (1990's) and the mobile Internet (the 2000's), the IoT aims to connect and link *all physical entities and objects of the real world* with the Internet and with each other [1, 3]. Thus, information and communication systems will be invisibly embedded in our environment and enable connectivity for anything and anyone at anytime and anyplace with anything and anyone [1]. This opens tremendous opportunities for a variety of new and innovative applications [4] that promise a significant improvement of our everyday lives [5] (e.g. smart homes where smart fridges monitor the expiration date of food and reorder consumed food completely autonomous online). Beside the huge number of opportunities which are coming along with the IoT, the emergence of the IoT also unveils several challenges in data privacy, safety and security [3]. In addition, the IoT requires the handling of a huge number of heterogeneous devices from simple sensors and RFID tags to intelligent cars and fridges. This in turn leads to the challenge to deal with the *growing complexity caused by the IoT*. Therefore, developers of the IoT have to deal

T. Margaria and B. Steffen (Eds.): ISoLA 2016, Part II, LNCS 9953, pp. 707–726, 2016.
DOI: 10.1007/978-3-319-47169-3_54

with a massive amount of data and a great number of different devices which cannot be envisioned by them [6].

This resulting new and challenging environment consequently increases the requirements to develop and deliver high quality and error-free IoT software applications. With the emergence of the IoT, especially the amount of available data literally explodes and accumulates at an unpredictable speed bringing humanity finally in the big data era [7–9]. This poses new challenges to software quality assurance and requires radically new quality assurance methods and techniques. Hence, typical software quality assurance processes, which can be seen as "a set of activities and tasks that enable software suppliers to produce, collect, and validate evidence [...] that the software product conforms to its established requirements" [10], must be adapted to address these new requirements. Marwah et al. [3] even claim that *software quality assurance in the IoT* can be seen as a *new era of research.*

However, researchers and practitioners realized that analyzing and exploiting data and information provides a great opportunity to gain several significant benefits in different application scenarios [7]. Therefore, *data science* is currently gaining a lot of attraction and becoming an important topic of investigation [8, 11]. Provost and Fawcett [12] describe data science at a high level as "a set of fundamental principles that support and guide the principled extraction of information and knowledge from data". The application of data science principles in the field of software engineering already emerged as a successful research direction with a lot of contributions (i.e. mining software repositories, mining software engineering data, software analytics) [13–15]. Bird et al. [16] even state that there is currently an unsustainable "bubble" in data science for software engineering.

Nevertheless, with the advent of the IoT and the associated tremendous increase of available data there arises the promising opportunity to apply data science techniques for assuring the challenging quality requirements of IoT applications. Hence, this paper first presents *software quality assurance requirements of the IoT* based on an informal literature review. Afterwards, *challenges of data science relating to improve quality assurance of IoT applications* are illustrated.

The remainder of this paper is structured as follows. Section 2 briefly introduces the IoT and its main characteristics. Afterwards, Sect. 3 presents basic background information on data science. Section 4 then presents the upcoming requirements of IoT compared to traditional software regarding software quality assurance. Based on these requirements, Sect. 5 outlines challenges and opportunities how data science can be applied in quality assurance of the IoT. Finally, Sect. 6 concludes the paper and suggests possible future work in this area.

2   Internet of Things

As a promising area of future technology [2] the IoT is defined by various researchers and practitioners in different ways depending on the perspective taken [17]. Semantically, the term "Internet of Things" describes a world-wide network of seamlessly integrated and uniquely addressable objects and devices interacting via standard communication protocols [1, 4, 17]. Such "smart" objects and devices will communicate and interact completely wireless by using emerging technologies like real-time localization or near-field communication and in synergy within a network of various different sensors and actuators [17].

The different application domains and scenarios of the IoT are large and therefore also the expected increase in the quality of our lives [17]. Typical application scenarios are the transportation and logistics domain (i.e. intelligent decisions on routing of products), healthcare domain (i.e. personalize patient care) and smart cities, homes and factories (e.g. energy savings and property protection, Industry 4.0) [2, 4, 18]. These are by far not all the possible application domains, but they clearly demonstrate the three categories where IoT can be applied: *Monitoring and control, big data and business analytics* and *information sharing and collaboration* [2].

Monitoring and control IoT applications allow the user to constantly track the performance or condition of devices, equipment or other things which generate data and are connected to the IoT network (e.g. tracking temperature and humidity of transported goods, tracking body temperature, heart beat rate, blood pressure). Therefore, decisions can be taken based on real time data and future outcomes can be predicted or areas of potential improvement can be identified (i.e. predictive maintenance). By using business analytics someone is able to discover and resolve critical business issues based on real time data generated by different embedded sensors and actuators of IoT machines and devices (e.g. changes in market conditions or customer behavior). Through information sharing and collaboration between all participants of the IoT (things as well as people), information delay can be avoided and situational awareness can be significantly enhanced (e.g. increasing customer engagement, increasing productivity in plants) [2, 4, 17–20].

To implement and deploy the concept of the IoT there are several technologies used [2, 18]. The most essential and widely used are *radio-frequency identification* (RFID), *wireless sensor networks* (WSN), *middleware, cloud computing* and *IoT applications* [2]. As the IoT is currently in its infancy, there is a lack of common underlying software to *build IoT applications* and developers must build coherent IoT applications out of several unrelated software modules. Therefore, a big challenge for developers of IoT applications is to combine the numerous different user- and industry-specific IoT applications in order to build stable systems ensuring robust and reliable interactions and communication. [2, 21].

To put it simply, the IoT is characterized by the facts that anything can communicate and interact with anything and anything is uniquely identified [22]. In more detail, Miorandi et al. [22], Zhang et al. [23] and Liu and Zhou [24] describe the main characteristics and features of the IoT as: *Devices heterogeneity, Scalability and Real-time, Localization and tracking capabilities, Self-organization capabilities, Semantic interoperability and data management, Embedded security and privacy-preserving mechanisms, Reliability and Energy-optimized solutions.*

3   Data Science

This section aims to give a brief overview about data science. First, Subsect. 3.1 introduces the emerging field of data science. Subsection 3.2 then illustrates related work of the application of data science techniques on software engineering data.

3.1   Background

Driven by the large amount of abundantly available data, van der Aalst [25] states that we currently see the birth of a new discipline called "*data science*". Although the term "data science" was already first used by Peter Naur in 1966 [26] as a suitable replacement for the term "computer science", its common usage in academic and research began not before the 1990's [8, 27]. In accordance with the emerging of data science in research, several journals dealing with scientifically data and its application were founded (e.g. Data Science Journal [28], Journal of Data Science [29]).

Although several research contributions dealt with the content, scope and topics of data science [8, 12, 30–32], a common definition of it is still missing or varies between researchers [8]. Waller and Fawcett [33] define data science as "the application of quantitative and qualitative methods to solve relevant problems and predict outcomes". A more detailed definition was stated by Smith [27] who defines data science as "the study of the capture of data, their analysis, metadata, fast retrieval, archiving, exchange, mining to find unexpected knowledge and data relationships, visualization in two and three dimensions including movement, and management". In this paper we want to use the in our opinion most intuitive definition given by Provost and Fawcett [12] who describe data science at a high level as "a set of fundamental principles that support and guide the principled extraction of information and knowledge from data".

However, data science is multidisciplinary and draws from many fields of study [12, 34]. Van der Aalst [34] depicts data science as a broad discipline which combines different sub-disciplines as Fig. 1 illustrates.

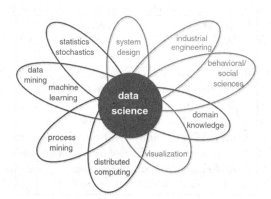

Fig. 1. Data science [34]

It is important to realize that data science is more than analytics, statistics and mining data. Beside knowledge about methods to visualize, analyze and interpret data, data scientists should also have practical knowledge about information technology and programming to realize solutions. Further, data science is a discipline where intuition, common sense and creativity are needed. In addition, it is an essential capability of every data scientist to view business problems from a data perspective. Therefore, successful data scientists must have beside excellent analytical skills also deep domain knowledge, knowledge about business models and the ability to communicate their message [12, 33, 34]. Basically, the application domains of data science are manifold (e.g. marketing, finance, manufacturing) [12]. In the course of this paper we will focus on data science and its application on software engineering.

The next subsection describes some related work about the application of data science in the field of software engineering.

3.2 Data Science in Software Engineering

In order to make daily decisions, software engineers and managers typically have to answer several questions (i.e. which parts of a software system to change and test? when to release a new feature and who uses this feature?) [15]. As different types and volume of software engineering data had grown with an vast rate over the past few years, manual investigation and browsing through these data becomes impossible [35]. Therefore, practitioners and researchers need automated tools and methods to analyze this huge amount of data in order to get valuable information out of it [16, 35]. As a result, the application of data science methods to software projects became a normal course in research [16, 36]. How valuable and important the application of data science on software engineering for software practitioners is, show two surveys of Begel and Zimmermann [37]. They presented a catalog of 145 questions grouped into 12 categories that software engineers would like to ask data scientists about software projects, processes and practices.

Hence, mining software engineering data (e.g. execution traces, bug databases, mailing lists, code bases, historical code changes) emerged as a successful research direction over time by providing valuable information about the status, progress and evolution of a software project [14]. Various published papers and many studies underpinned the successful application of data science and mining techniques in software engineering (e.g. Mockus et al. [38], Zimmermann et al. [39], Cheatham [40], Gorla et al. [41], or Chaturvedi et al. [42]).

Concluding, the usage of data science techniques in the area of software engineering already resulted in a variety of successful applications and promises a great potential by the steadily increasing amount of data generated in software development processes.

4 Software Quality Assurance Requirements of the IoT

Today, software applications and systems govern and permeate nearly all aspects of our daily life [43]. Resulting from this great dependence of today's society on software, there is a strong demand for software products representing the highest quality [44]. Therefore, assuring the quality of software products is an essential part of current software development practices.

In general, quality assurance is "a planned and systematic pattern of all actions necessary to provide adequate confidence that an item or product conforms to established technical requirements" [45]. Hence, "quality assurance includes all techniques we use to build products in a way to increase our confidence as well as techniques to analyze products" [46]. As an essential quality assurance technique for modern software-intensive systems, software testing aims to improve the quality of software products by finding and correcting defects. Therefore, we treat software testing in the following as an essential main part of software quality assurance. Thus, we especially focus on software testing in the remainder of this paper as an essential quality assurance technique.

With the emergence of the IoT and its characteristics, the environment for developers and software engineers radically changes related to develop and deliver high quality and error-free IoT software applications. Hence, software quality assurance and software testing activities must meet these new requirements and must be adapted to be compliant with the new and rapidly changing environment caused by the IoT. As already stated, Marwah et al. [3] even claim that software quality assurance in the IoT can be seen as a new era of research.

This section outlines the requirements which are evolving with the IoT related to software quality assurance and software testing activities. Therefore, the *main differences* to traditional software quality assurance and testing are described. The presented requirements are based on an informal literature review considering grey as well as academic literature [47]. *Google* as web search engine and renowned databases as *jstor, Ebsco, emeraldinsight, Elsevier ScienceDirect* and *AISEL* (only abstract and title were browsed to limited number of hits) were used for reviewing the literature. Following keywords were used: "testing" "internet of things", "quality assurance". The word order of the keywords was changed (i.e. "internet of things" "testing") and slightly modified (i.e. "assuring quality" "IoT") in order to increase the number of hits.

Since the IoT is still in its infancy, not much academic literature on quality assurance and testing the IoT was available. Hence, we focused on grey literature including whitepaper, articles, presentations, blog entries and websites. We grouped the identified requirements based on the identified literature into six categories, namely *Environment (E), User (U), Compliance/Service Level Agreements (C/SLA), Organizational (O), Security (S)* and *Data Management (DM)* requirements. Whereas the most requirement categories are self-explanatory, we briefly want to describe the Environment and Organizational requirement categories. The Environment category describes the surrounding field in which IoT devices must operate. All managerial and organizational activities (e.g. planning, communication, social interaction, monitoring, controlling, or project management) of the software development life cycle are summarized under the requirement category Organizational.

Table 1 shows the result of the literature review and the assigned requirement categories. We assigned the requirements categories to a contribution if the contribution at least mentioned or dealt with requirements within the defined category.

Environment. With the emergence of the IoT, the environment in which quality assurance and testing activities are executed radically changes. As classical software quality assurance and testing activities are typically applied in defined environments (e.g. personal computer with a defined operating system and a network connection), testing and assuring the quality of IoT applications and solutions demands a shift to a *complex dynamic environment* with millions of sensors, actuators and different types of devices in conjunction with intelligent software engines. Due to this great number of different devices and components in the IoT, many of them will not be available when IoT applications are developed and tested.

In order to develop IoT applications, developers must understand and know the *architecture of used third party hardware and devices*.

Often, vendors of used third party *subcomponents restrict the access* to their components and devices which increases the effort of development and further also quality assurance activities. Therefore, an authentic replication of such a dynamic and fully connected environment (e.g. smart cars, smart cities) is sheer impossible and *classical integration testing is not feasible* anymore. In addition to this, IoT devices must operate correctly and reliable under *different physical conditions* as extreme heat, cold, rain, snow or humidity which are also costly and complex to simulate.

Quality assurance and testing of IoT applications and solutions requires testing the ability of devices to support the required functionality among other external devices and implementations. IoT devices must be able to deal with *different messaging protocols, operating systems, software versions, types of networks* and *communication channels*. Due to the fact that IoT devices are movable, they *move in and out of different networks*. This requires testing the functionality in different networks including all possible circumstances (e.g. bandwidth, dropped connections, lost packets). IoT applications must ensure that data is stored in case of a dropped connection or loss of power. The energy consumption of some IoT devices can be critical (for instance, for wearable devices). Therefore, quality assurance activities must also consider testing *different power modes* to ensure the device also works properly in each power mode. Further, many smart devices in the IoT have integrated self-healing abilities which recover the device's state in case of failures. The purposely creation of such failures in order to evaluate the *devices ability to recover* itself properly is an upcoming challenge in testing and assuring quality of smart IoT devices.

Due to IoT devices typically interact with clouds and mobile apps, quality assurance and testing IoT applications does not mean focusing only on the devices itself. Cloud services must be able to deal with increasing user demand (e.g. on Christmas, typically many new devices will go online) and user requests (e.g. on New Year's Eve, typically many people interact with their devices in order to send new year celebrations). Therefore, *scalability* and *reliability testing* of services which are used by IoT applications and offered by cloud computing is essential.

Table 1. Literature review

Whitepapers				
Title	Company/Institution	Author	Year	Category
The Internet of Things: QA Unleashed [48]	Cognizant	Muthiah Subbiah, Venkatasubramanian Ramakrishnan	2015	**E, U, C/SLA, O, S**
Testing for Internet of Things (IOT) [49]	TechArcis Solutions	n/a	n/a	**E, U, S, DM**
Testing the Internet of Things [50]	Polarion Software	n/a	2015	**E, S**
The Importance of Quality Assurance Testing for the Internet of Things [51]	Ayla Networks	n/a	2016	**E, U, C/SLA, S**
Keeping up with the Internet of Things (IoT): 10 Hints on Testing and Optimizing a Connected World [52]	Testbirds	n/a	n/a	**E, U, S**
Internet of Everything – Test Strategy [53]	Gerrard Consulting	Gerrard Paul	2015	**E, U, DM**
Presentations				
Title	Event	Author	Year	Category
How to test the Internet of Things [54]	German Testing Night Munich	Böger, Henning	2013	**E, U**
Testing the Internet of Things [55]	Presentation TMF	n/a	n/a	**E, U, S**
Articles				
Title	Journal	Author	Year	Category
Testing the Internet of Things [56]	Printed Circuit Design and Fab	Lau Mark	2014	**E**
Websites/Blogs				
Title	Website/Blog	Author	Year	Category
Functional Testing for IoT [57]	DevOps	Riley Chris	2015	**E, C/SLA, O, S**
How do we test the Internet of Things? [58]	LeanTesting	Hill Simon	2015	**E, U, S**
Performance Testing 101: How to Approach the Internet of Things [59]	Neotys	Rexed Henrik	2015	**E, U, C/SLA**
How To Cut Verification Costs For IoT [60]	Semiconductor Engineering	Bailey Brian	2014	**E**
Testing the Internet of Things [61]	SmartBear	Rohrman Justin	2015	**E, U, S**
Testing the Internet of Things? It's time to plan your test strategy [62]	IoT-Now	Lanka Venkata Ramana	2015	**E, C/SLA, S, DM**
Security Testing the Internet of Things IoT [63]	Beyond Security	n/a	n/a	**E, S**
The Function of Quality Assurance (QA) with the Internet of Things [64]	CenturyLink Cloud	Townsend Jonathan	2016	**E, U, C/SLA, S**
The testing challenges ahead for the Internet of Things [65]	embedded	Hammerschmidt Christoph	2014	**E**
Testing Strategy for the IoT [66]	LogiGear	Hagar Jon	2014	**E, O, S**
Internet-of-Things [67]	TestPlant	n/a	2016	**E, U**
Academic Literature				
Title	Journal	Author	Year	Category
Software Quality Assurance in Internet of Things [3]	Int. Journal of Computer Applications	Marwah, Mateen Qudsia, Sirshar Mehreen	2015	**E, S**

As a lot of IoT applications operate and deliver data in real time, quality assurance and testing activities should also incorporate *evaluating the real time behavior* of IoT applications. In general, testing real time ability is challenging because of the *variety of possible real time use case scenarios* and the complexity which emergences in combination with the applications intelligence. The real time replication, simulation and mimic of data generated by real world business processes is difficult (e.g. for stock exchange business processes). Further, testing and validating all analytical real time rules of a business process (e.g. which drug dose related to health parameters) can result in a massive effort due to the *huge amount of different application scenarios of IoT applications*. Nevertheless, testing real time ability is challenging but important for IoT applications. Therefore, *logging* to get time-stamped events is a very important prerequisite to evaluate and assess the real time ability of IoT devices.

With the deployment of IoT devices, the feature to update and upgrade device software and firmware over the network (over-the-air) [68] will become common. Therefore, *over-the-air testing* will be needed in order to ensure that this feature works properly. Automatic regression testing routines can ensure that each device works correctly after each upgrade. In case of failures, *remotely initiated downgrading* to earlier versions must be possible and *remote debugging procedures* should be considered in the architecture of IoT applications.

User. As already stated, classical integration testing is not feasible anymore in the new emerging IoT environment. IoT devices can communicate and interact with various other devices such that a lot of bugs and failures will only emerge when the IoT device *is used in the real world*. Therefore, quality assurance and testing of IoT applications must *incorporate user behavior and experience*. Testers and quality assurance personal should *mimic user behavior* and test "as a user" to identify and correct as many failures as possible before the product is released. Based on the *huge amount of different application scenarios* of IoT products, testing and quality assurance activities should focus on evaluating functions and features that are *important for the user*.

Nevertheless, user behavior strongly varies between different concurrent users and IoT applications offer many possible ways to use it that sufficient quality assurance and testing is not feasible without incorporating users. Therefore, quality assurance and testing of IoT applications and devices should consist of *field testing* executed by different user groups. Hence, data of how the users use the product can be *collected and tracked* in order to use it for assuring quality and testing. The *user experience* must be considered in order to guarantee a high quality and error free product as well as to satisfy user requirements.

Along with the integration of the user in the quality assurance and testing procedure, new demand for *remote and immediate user support* arises. Failures of IoT devices must be immediately notified and *remote debugging* and *error correction methods* must be available. Otherwise, user satisfaction will dramatically decrease.

Organizational. Assuring the quality of IoT deployments incorporates devices, network infrastructure and cloud services which will require *different teams or persons testing different parts* of the IoT deployment. The *coordination* of all involved people, exchanging information and data, is a new challenge which must be considered in the quality assurance of the IoT. Moreover, testing IoT devices and applications includes a lot of different components of different vendors. In case of failures or questions about unexpected behavior of these components, fast and efficient *communication with third party vendors* is essential to meet the strict quality assurance time plan.

Compliance/Service Level Agreements. IoT solutions can be used at different *geographic locations in different countries*. Therefore, large scale releases of IoT devices and solutions *must meet the governmental standards and regulations* related to each country. Assuring that the IoT deployment is compliant to these standards and regulations is an important activity in the quality assurance of the IoT.

In addition, vendors of third party components that are integrated in IoT solutions typically validate parameters of their components (e.g. performance) in defined environments. Assuring that these parameters are also met in *new environments and in conjunction with other subcomponents* of IoT devices must be done while testing the IoT application. This is essential because IoT devices must be *compliant to service level agreements* in order to meet user requirements.

Moreover, a failure in one component of an IoT deployment can cause a *ripple effect* that leads to a wrong behavior of another IoT device which results in an undesired outcome. In such a case it must be *clearly defined who is responsible* for the consequences.

Security. Through the distributed nature of IoT devices communicating and interacting in a worldwide network several security issues arise. Quality assurance activities must ensure that *sufficient authentication methods* are integrated in every IoT device. The transmitted data must be properly *protected* and data storage in web clouds must fulfill *stringent requirements*. Different *data privacy regulations*, depending on the business sector in which the IoT applications are used, must be considered and evaluated while testing IoT applications. Moreover, a lot of devices will be upgraded with internet and network connections to enter the demanding IoT market. Therefore, the *used hardware of these devices is rather old* and can bear various vulnerabilities for hackers as soon as being connected to the Internet. Resulting, quality assurance activities must consider already existing hardware and software which were not designed for being connected to the world wide web.

Data Management. With the advent of the IoT the amount of data generated and transmitted will explode. IoT devices will create tons of varying data in differing formats and quality. Resulting, quality assurance activities must deal with a *diversity of data sources* creating *several different data types incorporating complex data structures in real time*. The management of these data will play a key role in order to ensure feasible and efficient quality assurance of IoT applications (e.g. regarding the usage of recorded data from different types of devices and environments for validating IoT applications).

Summarizing, the advent of the IoT causes several new requirements for the domain of software quality assurance and software testing. In order to meet these new requirements, quality assurance and testing activities must be adapted accordingly. The next section presents data science challenges in order to address these new emerging requirements.

5   Data Science Challenges

In this section we present challenges, opportunities and application scenarios of data science related to software quality assurance and software testing activities of the IoT. As stated in Sect. 3, the field of data science is very broad including many different sub-disciplines. Each of these disciplines is in itself very comprehensive, incorporating dozens of algorithms, methods and techniques. Moreover, a lot of algorithms and methods are used interchangeably in several disciplines [69, 70]. In order to avoid confusion and ambiguity, the challenges, opportunities and application scenarios presented in this section focus especially on the sub-disciplines data mining, process mining, statistics, machine learning and visualization.

Concretely, we aim to motivate the application and usage of algorithms and techniques (e.g. *classification, characterization, association* and *clustering* algorithms) as well as methods (e.g. *predictive modeling, findings patterns* and *relations*) of these disciplines to support the quality assurance of IoT solutions and deployments. As the IoT will generate a massive amount of data, we see promising potential for innovative applications.

Following, we present data science challenges grouped into four categories (*Defect prevention, Defect analysis, User incorporation* and *Organizational*) for which we see promising opportunities to apply data science techniques and methods in order to improve quality assurance for IoT applications. These four categories are derived from the six requirement categories of the previous section as shown in Fig. 2 by the dashed framed rectangles. Due to the large amount of data which becomes available with the emergence of the IoT the quality assurance requirement category Data Management influences all four data science challenge categories. The IoT with its huge amount of generated and available data is illustrated as an ellipsis in Fig. 2. The six software quality assurance requirements of the IoT are illustrated by rounded rectangles. Further, the field of data science with its methods, techniques and algorithms is outlined by the rectangle with the two cut corners. The four remaining rectangles with the cut corners represent the four categories which contain the data science challenges. Moreover, the double arrows outline on the one hand the derivation of the four data science challenge categories from the six software quality assurance requirements and on the other hand which data science challenges can support which quality assurance requirements of IoT solutions and deployments.

The challenges, opportunities and application scenarios of each of the four categories presented in the following subsection are, as not otherwise stated, inspired by the work of Kim et al. [36], Menzies and Zimmermann [35] as well as Buse and Zimmerman [71]. Further, we underpin the mentioned challenges with related work and example applications presented in published academic contributions. In order to avoid misunderstandings, we use the term defect in the following according to Wagner [46] as a superset of faults and failures.

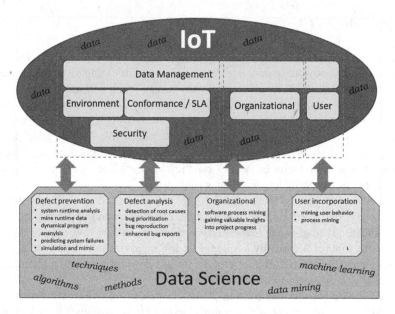

Fig. 2. Derived Data Science challenges

5.1 Defect Prevention

Preventing IoT applications and solutions from defects is an important and essential quality assurance task. Defect prevention aims to identify defects and unexpected behavior of the software as early as possible and to ensure that these defects and anomalies do not occur again. Applied at each stage of development, it can reduce overheads, costs, resources and the time needed for building IoT applications with a minimum of defects. [72, 73] Following, we present some data science opportunities to improve the defect prevention of IoT applications and solutions.

One example to prevent IoT applications and solutions from defects is to exactly monitor their behavior. By applying data science techniques to *monitor applications* and to *mine runtime data*, valuable information can be gained. For example, Han et al. [74] proposed an approach that mines call stack traces to effectively discover performance bugs. Further, Jiang et al. [75] presented an approach that automatically analyzes execution logs of a load test and flags possible performance problems. Hindle et al. [76] investigated how software changes are impacting the software power consumption by mining software repositories. Moreover, Rubin et al. [77] suggest the usage of process mining techniques to *application monitoring*, *predicting system failures* and *discovering architectural anti-patterns*. As one sub-discipline of data science [34], *process mining* is typically applied to extract knowledge from event logs of information systems in order to discover, monitor and improve real processes [78, 79]. Hence, process mining "connects process models and data analytics" [25]. According to van der Aalst [78], there are already a lot of mature process mining techniques available which can be directly used in everyday practice.

Another application scenario of data science techniques for preventing defects is the *injection of telemetry* to *detect anomalies*. Also the *dynamical program analysis* can be enhanced by applying methods from data science. Shershakov and Rubin [80] presented several examples how process mining techniques can be successfully applied for *system runtime analysis*. Moreover, determining *defect predictors* is a promising way to apply data science techniques (i.e. data miners [81]) for preventing IoT applications from defects. For example, Ostrand et al. [82] developed a negative binomial regression model to predict the numbers of faults for a large inventory system by using information from previous releases.

Using simulation for testing software products is not new [83]. With the large amount of available data in the IoT, the application of data science techniques provides promising opportunities to *simulate and mimic* the complex and distributed IoT environment. This becomes rather important due to the variety and the sheer number of IoT devices. Mimic sensor data, middleware functionality and communication is an essential task of future quality assurance of the IoT and demands strong support of data science techniques.

5.2   Defect Analysis

Analyzing defects is a very useful and vital task to assure and continuously improve the quality of IoT applications and solutions [73, 84]. Basically, defect analysis seeks to identify possible causes of defects in order to eliminate them [73]. However, the analysis of defects is according to Kumaresh and Baskaran [73] limited and restricted by human investigation capabilities. Hence, data science provides promising potential for improvement.

Data science techniques can be used to *detect root causes* of defects. Hence, the exact localization of faults in the code can be determined. For example, Wong and Qi [85] successfully applied a machine learning model (back-propagation neural network) to exactly localize program faults in software programs. Also Kannadhasan and Maheswari [86] successfully applied a machine learning algorithm to classify fault and non-fault statements in object oriented applications. Further, efficient *bug prioritization* and *bug reproduction* can be realized by applying data science methods. In addition, the application of data science techniques generates *richer information about defects* and enables the generation of *more detailed bug reports*. Also the dependencies of different software modules, components as well as third party software can be illustrated in an effective way by applying data science techniques.

5.3   User Incorporation

Academia and practice already recognized that a strong user involvement in software development is very important to meet user requirements and expectations. Hence, the ISO/IEC 25010:2011 [87] defines beside the software product quality model which describes a software product's quality also the quality-in-use model which represents the perspective of a user interacting with the software product [46]. As outlined in the previous section, functional testing is no longer feasible in the IoT area. Hence, a strong user involvement and incorporation is essential in assuring quality of the IoT.

Users who test IoT applications generate a lot of data which can be used to extract valuable information about different attributes (e.g. performance or user habits). For example, Cao et al. [88] proposed an approach that *mines behavior patterns* of mobile users by analyzing context logs. Moreover, Rubin et al. [79] presented how *process mining techniques* can be used to analyze and predict user behavior as well as to discover usability anti-patterns [77]. A quite different, but also promising approach was presented by Gruska et al. [89]. They mined more than 6,000 open source Linux projects in order to extract rules which reflect normal interface usage. By using these usage rules they were able to *efficiently determine anomalies* (i.e. code smells, defects) in new software projects.

Applying data science techniques on user data of IoT applications promise great potential to increase user satisfaction. Moreover, it is an effective mean to address the new requirements evolving with the IoT where a classical integration testing approach is no longer feasible and testers should "test as a user" in order to better understand the final customers.

5.4   Organizational

As stated earlier, we use the term "organizational" in this paper to summarize all managerial and organizational activities (e.g. planning, communication, social interaction, monitoring, controlling, or project management) of the software development life cycle. Mining and analyzing software development processes can provide significant and valuable insights into how organizations execute software projects [90]. Rubin et al. [77] even mention *software process mining* as a new area which opens numerous challenges and research directions.

One interesting approach how data science techniques can be applied was proposed by Bacchelli et al. [91]. They presented an approach which exploits valuable information (i.e. design choices) embedded in emails related to software development. Additional work on this was done by Bird et al. [92] who mined the email social network on an open source software project. This is very valuable in order to *understand and uncover misunderstandings* related to user requirements between software engineers and therefore to improve the quality of the developed application. Moreover, the variety and amount of different devices and components used while developing IoT solutions offers great opportunities to *measure and monitor the progress* of a software project on the basis of each involved software engineer. This could be further used to exactly determine which engineers are the most suitable choice for specific development projects that demand special technical skills. According to Begel and Zimmermann [37] software engineers are very interested in comparing each other as well as assessing their individual performance.

The emergence of the IoT causes organizations to tailor their software quality assurance processes in order to meet the new evolving requirements. Applying data science techniques promises great potential to enhance the organizational perspective of software development related to quality assurance of the IoT.

6   Conclusion and Future Work

With the advent of the IoT the amount of available data literally explodes and accumulates at an unpredictable speed [7]. This poses promising opportunities to apply data science techniques for assuring the challenging quality requirements of IoT applications. Although the application of data science algorithms and techniques in the field of software testing is not new [93, 94] we expect sustainable improvement in this area caused by the large amount of data becoming available with the IoT.

One of the main challenges will be to deal with the huge amount of data which becomes available with the emergence of the IoT. Applying the right techniques, algorithms and methods on this data to extract valuable knowledge and using this gained knowledge in proper application scenarios will be a further big upcoming challenge which opens promising new research directions. This is also in line with Zimmermann and Menzies [35] who state that "this is an exciting time for those of us involved in data science and software analytics".

In this paper, we presented data science challenges to improve the quality assurance of IoT applications. Therefore, we first described the main characteristics of the IoT. Afterwards, we provided a brief introduction of data science and its application in the software engineering domain. Based on an informal literature review, we further outlined requirements grouped into six categories (*Environment, User, Compliance/Service Level Agreements, Organizational, Security* and *Data Management*) which are evolving with the emergence of the IoT related to software quality assurance. Finally, we presented data science challenges related to quality assurance of the IoT sub-divided into four categories derived from the six quality assurance requirements categories. Namely, we see promising potential of data science applications in the following four categories: *Defect prevention, Defect analysis, User incorporation* and *Organizational.*

The outlined challenges in this paper constitute the motivation of the following future work. First, existing algorithms and methods of data science and its sub-disciplines must be investigated in order to determine their meaningful application addressing the stated challenges. After selecting possible algorithms and methods, concerns must be made about their specific application. Secondly, their application must be roughly evaluated and their successful usage must be documented. Currently, implementing IoT solutions lack on the availability of generic methodologies, tool support and automation. Therefore, also the quality assurance of such solutions is done without structure and tool support. Hence, methodologies, frameworks and tool support should be developed incorporating the selected and evaluated algorithms and methods. This would contribute to improving the quality assurance of IoT deployments. Further possible future work comprises the development and evaluation of new algorithms and methods as well as their innovative application to address the stated challenges.

References

1. Santucci, G.: The Internet of Things: between the revolution of the internet and the metamorphosis of objects. In: Sundmaeker, H., Guillemin, P., Friess, P., Woelfflé, S. (eds.) Vision and Challenges for Realising the Internet of Things, pp. 11–24. CERP-IoT – Cluster of European Research Projects on the Internet of Things, Luxembourg (2010)
2. Lee, I., Lee, K.: The Internet of Things (IoT): applications, investments, and challenges for enterprises. Bus. Horiz. **58**, 431–440 (2015)
3. Marwah, Q.M., Sirshar, M.: Software quality assurance in Internet of Things. Int. J. Comput. Appl. **109**, 16–24 (2015)
4. Gubbi, J., Buyya, R., Marusic, S., Palaniswami, M.: Internet of Things (IoT): a vision, architectural elements, and future directions. Future Gener. Comput. Syst. **29**, 1645–1660 (2013)
5. Xia, F., Yang, L.T., Wang, L., Vinel, A.: Internet of Things. Int. J. Commun Syst **25**, 1101–1102 (2012)
6. Prasad, N.R., Eisenhauer, M., Ahlsén, M., Badii, A., Brinkmann, A., Hansen, K.M., Rosengren, P.: Open source middleware for networked embedded systems towards future Internet of Things. In: Sundmaeker, H., Guillemin, P., Friess, P., Woelfflé, S. (eds.) Vision and Challenges for Realising the Internet of Things, pp. 153–163. CERP-IoT – Cluster of European Research Projects on the Internet of Things, Luxembourg (2010)
7. Cai, L., Zhu, Y.: The challenges of data quality and data quality assessment in the Big Data Era. Data Sci. J. **14**, 1–10 (2015)
8. Zhu, Y., Xiong, Y.: Towards data science. Data Sci. J. **14**, 1–7 (2015)
9. Katal, A., Wazid, M., Goudar, R.H.: Big Data: issues, challenges, tools and good practices. In: Sixth International Conference on Contemporary Computing (IC3 2013), pp. 404–409. IEEE (2013)
10. IEEE: IEEE Standard for Software Quality Assurance Processes, vol. 730™-2014 (Revision of IEEE Std. 730-2002). IEEE Computer Society, New York (2014)
11. May, T.: The New Know: Innovation Powered by Analytics. Wiley, New Jersey (2009)
12. Provost, F., Fawcett, T.: Data science and its relationship to Big Data and data-driven decision making. Big Data **1**, 51–59 (2013)
13. Taylor, Q., Giraud-Carrier, C.: Applications of data mining in software engineering. Int. J. Data Anal. Tech. Strat. **2**, 243–257 (2010)
14. Xie, T., Pei, J., Hassan, A.E.: Mining software engineering data. In: 29th International Conference on Software Engineering (ICSE 2007 Companion), pp. 172–173. IEEE, Minneapolis (2007)
15. Hassan, A.E., Xie, T.: Software intelligence: the future of mining software engineering data. In: Proceedings of the FSE/SDP Workshop on Future of Software Engineering Research, pp. 161–165. ACM, Santa Fe (2010)
16. Bird, C., Menzies, T., Zimmermann, T.: The Art and Science of Analyzing Software Data. Morgan Kaufmann, Waltham (2015)
17. Santucci, G., Lange, S.: Internet of Things in 2020 - a roadmap for the future. INFSO D.4 Networked Enterprise & RFID INFSO G.2 Micro & Nanosystems (2008)
18. Agrawal, S., Vieira, D.: A survey on Internet of Things. Abakós **1**, 78–95 (2013)
19. Atzori, L., Iera, A., Morabito, G.: The Internet of Things: a survey. Comput. Netw. **54**, 2787–2805 (2010)

20. Foidl, H., Felderer, M.: Research challenges of industry 4.0 for quality management. In: Felderer, M., Piazolo, F., Ortner, W., Brehm, L., Hof, H.-J. (eds.) ERP Future 2015 - Research. LNBIP, vol. 245, pp. 121–137. Springer, Heidelberg (2016). doi:10.1007/978-3-319-32799-0_10

21. Vermesan, O., Harrison, M., Vogt, H., Kalaboukas, K., Tomasella, M., Wouters, K., Gusmeroli, S., Haller, S.: Strategic research agenda. In: Sundmaeker, H., Guillemin, P., Friess, P., Woelfflé, S. (eds.) Vision and Challenges for Realising the Internet of Things, pp. 39–82. CERP-IoT – Cluster of European Research Projects on the Internet of Things, Luxembourg (2010)

22. Miorandi, D., Sicari, S., De Pellegrini, F., Chlamtac, I.: Internet of Things: vision, applications and research challenges. Ad Hoc Netw. **10**, 1497–1516 (2012)

23. Zhang, D., Yang, L.T., Huang, H.: Searching in Internet of Things: vision and challenges. In: Ninth IEEE International Symposium on Parallel and Distributed Processing with Applications (ISPA 2011), pp. 201–206. IEEE (2011)

24. Liu, Y., Zhou, G.: Key technologies and applications of Internet of Things. In: Fifth International Conference on Intelligent Computation Technology and Automation (ICICTA 2012), pp. 197–200. IEEE, Zhangjiajie (2012)

25. van der Aalst, W.M.P.: Extracting event data from databases to unleash process mining. In: Vom Brocke, J., Schmiedel, T. (eds.) BPM - Driving Innovation in a Digital World. Management for Professionals, pp. 105–128. Springer, Switzerland (2015)

26. Naur, P.: The Science of datalogy. Commun. ACM **9**, 485 (1966)

27. Smith, J.F.: Data Science as an academic discipline. Data Sci. J. **5**, 163–164 (2006)

28. Data Science Journal. http://datascience.codata.org/

29. Journal of Data Science. http://www.jds-online.com/about

30. Hayashi, E.C.: What is data science? Fundamental concepts and a heuristic example. In: Hayashi, C., et al. (eds.) Data Science, Classification, and Related Methods. Studies in Classification, Data Analysis, and Knowledge Organization, pp. 40–51. Springer, Japan (1996)

31. Liu, L., Zhang, H., Li, J., Wang, R., Yu, L., Yu, J., Li, P.: Building a community of data scientists: an explorative analysis. Data Sci. J. **8**, 201–208 (2009)

32. Dhar, V.: Data science and prediction (2012)

33. Waller, M.A., Fawcett, S.E.: Data science, predictive analytics, and big data: a revolution that will transform supply chain design and management. J. Bus. Logistics **34**, 77–84 (2013)

34. van der Aalst, W.M.P.: Data scientist: the engineer of the future. In: Mertins, K., Bénaben, F., Poler, R., Bourrières, J.-P. (eds.) Enterprise Interoperability VI - Interoperability for Agility, Resilience and Plasticity of Collaborations. Proceedings of the I-ESA Conferences, vol. 7, pp. 13–26. Springer, Switzerland (2014)

35. Menzies, T., Zimmermann, T.: Software analytics: so what? IEEE Softw. **30**, 31–37 (2013)

36. Kim, M., Zimmermann, T., DeLine, R., Begel, A.: The emerging role of data scientists on software development teams - Technical report. MSR-TR-2015-30. Microsoft Research (2015)

37. Begel, A., Zimmermann, T.: Analyze this! 145 questions for data scientists in software engineering. In: Proceedings of the 36th International Conference on Software Engineering (ICSE 2014), pp. 12–23. ACM (2014)

38. Mockus, A., Weiss, D.M., Zhang, P.: Understanding and predicting effort in software projects. In: Proceedings of the 25th International Conference on Software Engineering (ICSE 2003), pp. 274–284. IEEE Computer Society (2003)

39. Zimmermann, T., Weißgerber, P., Diehl, S., Zeller, A.: Mining version histories to guide software changes. In: Proceedings of the 26th International Conference on Software Engineering (ICSE 2004), pp. 563–572. IEEE (2004)

40. Cheatham, T.J.: Software testing: a machine learning experiment. In: 23rd Annual Conference on Computer Science (CSC 1995), pp. 135–141. ACM (1995)

41. Gorla, A., Tavecchia, I., Gross, F., Zeller, A.: Checking app behavior against app descriptions. In: 36th International Conference on Software Engineering (ICSE 2014), pp. 1025–1035. ACM (2014)

42. Chaturvedi, K.K., Singh, V.B., Singh, P.: Tools in mining software repositories. In: 13th International Conference on Computational Science and Its Applications (ICCSA 2013), pp. 89–98. IEEE (2013)

43. Fuggetta, A., Di Nitto, E.: Software process. In: Proceedings of the Future of Software Engineering, FOSE 2014, pp. 1–12. ACM (2014)

44. Trendowicz, A., Kopczynska, S.: Adapting multi-criteria decision analysis for assessing the quality of software products. Current approaches and future perspectives. In: Hurson, A., Memon, A. (eds.) Advances in Computers, vol. 93, pp. 153–226. Academic Press, Waltham (2014)

45. ISO/IEC/IEEE: ISO/IEC/IEEE 24765:2010 - Systems and software engineering — Vocabulary. ISO (2010)

46. Wagner, S.: Software Product Quality Control. Springer, Heidelberg (2013)

47. Garousi, V., Felderer, M., Mäntylä, M.V.: The need for multivocal literature reviews in software engineering: complementing systematic literature reviews with grey literature. In: 20th International Conference on Evaluation and Assessment in Software Engineering (EASE 2016). ACM, Limerick (2016)

48. Cognizant. http://www.cognizant.com/InsightsWhitepapers/the-internet-of-things-qa-unleashed-codex1233.pdf

49. TechArcis Solutions. http://techarcis.com/whitepaper/testing-for-internet-of-things/

50. Polarion Software. https://www.polarion.com/resources/download/testing-the-internet-of-things?utm_campaign=Blog-2016-Embedded-Q1&utm_medium=Blog&utm_source=Blog

51. Ayla Networks. http://theinternetofthings.report/Resources/Whitepapers/7f4b81fe-25c3-4fa1-a1fb-a12fa6d42f44_Ayla_Whitepaper_Art-of-IoT-QA.pdf

52. Testbirds. https://www.testbirds.com/fileadmin/Whitepaper-Studies/Whitepaper-Internet-of-Things-EN.pdf

53. Gerrard Consulting. http://gerrardconsulting.com/sites/default/files/IoETestStrategy.pdf

54. Henning, B.: http://de.slideshare.net/HenningBoeger/german-testing-nightiothenningboeger20130228enexport

55. Test and Verification Solutions. http://www.testandverification.com/wp-content/uploads/Testing%20the%20Internet%20of%20Things.pdf

56. Lau, M.: Testing the Internet of Things. Printed Circuit Design and Fab, 43, April 2014

57. DevOps. http://devops.com/2015/02/24/functional-testing-iot/

58. LeanTesting. https://leantesting.com/resources/how-do-we-test-the-internet-of-things/

59. Neotys. http://www.neotys.com/blog/performance-testing-101-how-to-approach-the-internet-of-things/

60. Semiconductor Engineering. http://semiengineering.com/how-to-cut-verification-costs-for-iot/

61. SmartBear. http://blog.smartbear.com/user-experience/testing-the-internet-of-things/

62. IoT-Now. http://www.iot-now.com/2015/05/25/33241-testing-the-internet-of-things-its-time-to-plan-your-test-strategy/

63. Beyond Security. http://www.beyondsecurity.com/security_testing_iot_internet_of_things.html

64. CenturyLink Cloud. https://www.ctl.io/blog/post/qa-with-the-iot/
65. Embedded. http://www.embedded.com/electronics-news/4437315/The-testing-challenges-ahead-for-the-Internet-of-things
66. LogiGear. http://www.logigear.com/magazine/issue/past-articles/testing-strategy-for-the-iot/
67. TestPlant. http://www.testplant.com/explore/testing-use-cases/testing-the-internet-of-things-set-top-boxes/
68. Nilsson, D.K., Larson, U.E.: Secure firmware updates over the air in intelligent vehicles. In: ICC Workshops - 2008 IEEE International Conference on Communications Workshops, pp. 380–384. IEEE (2008)
69. Zumel, N., Mount, J.: Practical Data Science with R. Manning Publications, New York (2014)
70. Schutt, R., O'Neil, C.: Doing Data Science. O'Reilly, Sebastopol (2014)
71. Buse, R.P.L., Zimmermann, T.: Information needs for software development analytics. In: Proceedings of the 34th International Conference on Software Engineering (ICSE 2012), pp. 987–996. IEEE (2012)
72. Suma, V., Nair Gopalakrishnan, T.R.: Effective defect prevention approach in software process for achieving better quality levels. Proc. World Acad. Sci. Eng. Technol. **42**, 258–262 (2008)
73. Kumaresh, S., Baskaran, R.: Defect analysis and prevention for software process quality improvement. Int. J. Comput. Appl. **8**, 42–47 (2010)
74. Han, S., Dang, Y., Ge, S., Zhang, D., Xie, T.: Performance debugging in the large via mining millions of stack traces. In: Proceedings of the 34th International Conference on Software Engineering (ICSE 2012), pp. 145–155. IEEE (2012)
75. Jiang, Z.M., Hassan, A.E., Hamann, G., Flora, P.: Automated performance analysis of load tests. In: International Conference on Software Maintenance (ICSM 2009), pp. 125–134. IEEE (2009)
76. Hindle, A.: Green mining: a methodology of relating software change to power consumption. In: 9th IEEE Working Conference on Mining Software Repositories (MSR), pp. 78–87. IEEE (2012)
77. Rubin, V., Lomazova, I., van der Aalst, W.M.P.: Agile development with software process mining. In: Proceedings of the 2014 International Conference on Software and System Process (ICSSP 2014), pp. 70–74. ACM (2014)
78. van der Aalst, W.M.P.: Process Mining – Discovery, Conformance and Enhancement of Business Processes. Springer, Heidelberg (2011)
79. Rubin, V.A., Mitsyuk, A.A., Lomazova, I.A., van der Aalst, W.M.P.: Process mining can be applied to software too! In: Proceedings of the 8th ACM/IEEE International Symposium on Empirical Software Engineering and Measurement (ESEM 2014). ACM, Torino (2014)
80. Shershakov, S.A., Rubin, V.A.: System runs analysis with process mining. Model. Anal. Inf. Syst. **22**, 813–833 (2015)
81. Menzies, T., Greenwald, J., Frank, A.: Data mining static code attributes to learn defect predictors. IEEE Trans. Softw. Eng. **32**, 2–13 (2007)
82. Ostrand, T.J., Weyuker, E.J., Bell, R.M.: Where the bugs are. In: International Symposium on Software Testing and Analysis (ISSTA 2004), pp. 86–96. ACM (2004)
83. Lazic, L., Velasevic, D.: Applying simulation and design of experiments to the embedded software testing process. Softw. Test. Verification Reliab. **14**, 257–282 (2004)
84. Wagner, S.: Defect classification and defect types revisited. In: International Symposium on Software Testing and Analysis (ISSTA 2008) – Workshop on Defects in Large Software Systems (DEFECTS 2008), pp. 39–40. ACM (2008)
85. Wong, E.W., Qi, Y.: BP neural network-based effective fault localization. Int. J. Softw. Eng. Knowl. Eng. **19**, 573–597 (2009)

86. Kannadhasan, N., Maheswari, U.B.: Machine learning based methodology for testing object oriented applications. J. Eng. Appl. Sci. **10**, 7400–7405 (2015)

87. ISO/IEC: ISO/IEC 25010:2011 - Systems and software engineering – Systems and software Quality Requirements and Evaluation (SQuaRE) – System and software quality models. ISO/IEC (2011)

88. Cao, H., Bao, T., Yang, Q., Chen, E., Tian, J.: An effective approach for mining mobile user habits. In: 19th ACM International Conference on Information and Knowledge Management (CIKM 2010), pp. 1677–1680. ACM (2010)

89. Gruska, N., Wasylkowski, A., Zeller, A.: Learning from 6,000 projects: lightweight cross-project anomaly detection. In: Proceedings of the 19th International Symposium on Software Testing and Analysis (ISSTA 2010), pp. 119–130. ACM (2010)

90. Santos, R.M.S., Oliveira, T.C., Brito e Abreu, F.: Mining software development process variations. In: 30th Annual ACM Symposium on Applied Computing (SAC 2015), pp. 1657–1660. ACM (2015)

91. Bacchelli, A., Dal Sasso, T., D'Ambros, M., Lanza, M.: Content classification of development emails. In: 34th International Conference on Software Engineering (ICSE 2012), pp. 375–385. IEEE (2012)

92. Bird, C., Gourley, A., Devanbu, P., Gertz, M., Swaminathan, A.: Mining email social networks. In: International Workshop on Mining Software Repositories (MSR 2006), pp. 137–143. ACM (2006)

93. Noorian, M., Bagheri, E., Du, W.: Machine learning-based software testing: towards a classification framework. In: 23rd International Conference on Software Engineering & Knowledge Engineering (SEKE 2011), pp. 225–229 (2011)

94. Lenz, A.R., Pozo, A., Vergilio, S.R.: Linking software testing results with a machine learning approach. Eng. Appl. Artif. Intell. **26**, 1631–1640 (2013)

Model-Based Testing as a Service
for IoT Platforms

Abbas Ahmad[1,2(✉)], Fabrice Bouquet[2], Elizabeta Fourneret[3], Franck Le Gall[1],
and Bruno Legeard[2,3]

[1] Easy Global Market, Sophia-Antipolis, France
[2] Université de Franche-Comté - Femto-ST, Besançon, France
[3] Smartesting Solutions and Services, Besançon, France
abbas.ahmad@eglobalmark.com

Abstract. *The Internet of Things* (IoT) has increased its footprint
becoming globally a 'must have' for today's most innovative companies.
Applications extend to multitude of domains, such as smart cities, healthcare, logistics, manufacturing, etc. Gartner Group estimates an increase
up to 21 billion connected things by 2020. To manage 'things' heterogeneity and data streams over large scale and secured deployments, IoT and
data platforms are becoming a central part of the IoT. To respond to this
fast growing demand we see more and more platforms being developed,
requiring systematic testing. Combining Model-Based Testing (MBT)
technique and a service-oriented solution, we present *Model-Based Testing As A Service* (MBTAAS) for testing data and IoT platforms. In this
paper, we present a first step towards MBTAAS for data and IoT Platforms, with experimentation on FIWARE, one of the EU most emerging
IoT enabled platforms.

Keywords: Model Based Testing · Testing As A Service · Internet of
Things · Standard compliance

1 Introduction

Internet of Things (IoT) applications can be found in almost all domains, with
use cases spanning across areas such as healthcare, smart homes/buildings/
cities, energy, agriculture, transportation, etc. **FIWARE** [4] is an emerging
IoT platform, funded by the European Union (EU), which is pushing for an
ecosystem providing APIs and open-source implementations for lightweight and
simple means to gather, publish, query and subscribe context-based, real-time
"things" heterogeneous information. This independent community includes 60
cities across Europe in the Open and Agile Smart Cities alliance, which adopted
FIWARE standardised APIs to avoid vendor lock-in of proprietary solutions.

FIWARE provides an enhanced Open Stack-based cloud environment including a rich set of open standard APIs that make it easier to connect to the heterogeneous IoTs, process and analyse Big Data and real-time media or incorporate

© Springer International Publishing AG 2016
T. Margaria and B. Steffen (Eds.): ISoLA 2016, Part II, LNCS 9953, pp. 727–742, 2016.
DOI: 10.1007/978-3-319-47169-3_55

advanced features for user's interaction. These platforms, strongly dependent on the cloud, need to be properly tested to cover all necessary points to achieve success in their adoption. Scalability, security, performance, conformance, interoperability are the main points that must be ensured, for instance through white, gray or blackbox testing [13]. Moreover, as IoT is an emerging technology retooling and changes are frequent, requiring reducing the cost of testing by rethink the way of testing. In this context, Model-Based Testing (MBT) offers tool and language independence thus aiming to lower the testing effort of IoT [3].

In this paper, we focus on Model-Based Testing in terms of conformity and interoperability. We demonstrate through the FIWARE [4] case study that for these purposes, MBT as a Service is a suitable and scalable approach for testing IoT Platforms. We introduce the basic concepts of MBT and how it applies for the testing of IoT systems as a Service. Indeed, most recent IoT platforms are using standardized protocols to communicate (MQTT, CoAP, HTTP). This makes MBT testing deployment very suited by enabling design of a generic model, based on these standards and producing test cases that can be used over multiple applications.

FIWARE has defined its own standard starting from the Open Mobile Alliance Next Generation Services Interface (NGSI) standard [2] in order to make the development of future internet applications easier and interoperable. This standard is used as part of general-purpose platform functions available through APIs, each being implemented on the platform, noted as GEi (Generic Enabler Implementation). We used our MBT solution to increase confidence in the development of the FIWARE platform applications. We show through our experiment on the FIWARE Orion Context Broker [4] how it indeed helps developers to create high quality applications.

The paper is organised as follows. Section 2 poses the challenges of testing IoT platforms and the context of our approach, MBT and FIWARE. Section 3 defines our approach for MBT as a Service for IoT platforms testing. Section 4 summarizes the results and lessons learnt on the case study. We discuss related works in Sect. 5. Finally we conclude and provide a roadmap for future works in Sect. 6.

2   Challenges and Context of Testing IoT Platforms Through FIWARE

We identify the challenges and define the context for our approach based on the analysis of the FIWARE IoT Platform, which is a perfect representative for this domain due to its presence in the European market. We further applied MBT to FIWARE, which was already an ongoing project. We illustrate the MBT approach and the test generation later in Sects. 2.2 and 2.3.

2.1   The FIWARE IoT Platform

The **FIWARE** [4] cloud and software platform is the perfect catalyst for an open ecosystem of entrepreneurs aiming at developing state-of-the-art data-driven applications. This ecosystem is formed by application developers, technology and infrastructure providers and entities that aim to leverage the impact of developing new applications based on the produced data. Building applications based on FIWARE is intended to be quick and easy thanks to the use of pre-fabricated components in its cloud, sharing their own data as well as accessing "open" data. However, the challenge remains to build developers' trust and confidence into this FIWARE underlying platform. This is achieved by setting up quality assurance (QA) processes relying on effective testing of the platform. This raises questions such as balancing of test coverage with time and cost. However, several questions arise when testing IoT platforms with respect to the specificities of the communication protocols, devices and the heterogeneity of the data.

Connecting "things" as devices, requires to overcome a set of problems arising in the different layers of the communication model. Using devices' produced data or responding to device's requests requires interacting with an heterogeneous and distributed environment of devices running **several protocols** (such as HTTP, MQTT, COAP), through multiple wireless technologies.

Devices have a lot of particularities so it is not feasible to provide a testing solution where one size fits all. Devices are resource constrained and cannot use full standard protocol stacks: they cannot transmit information too frequently due to battery drainage, they are not always reachable due to wireless connection based on low duty-cycles, their communication protocols are IoT specific and lack integrated approach [3] and use **different data encoding languages**, which makes global deployment hardly existing.

Developers face complex scenarios where **merging the information** is a real challenge. For this reason, an IoT platform must enable intermediation and data gathering functions to deal with devices variety and it must be configurable and adaptable to market needs.

Figure 1 exposes the FIWARE architecture that deals with all these specific elements, which remain a challenge when testing them in a real situation. More specifically, the figure illustrates a connector (IoT Agent) solving the issues of

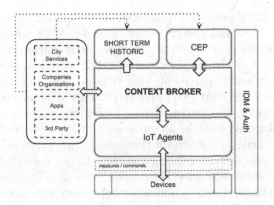

Fig. 1. FIWARE IoT platform architecture

heterogeneous environments where devices with different protocols are translated into to a common data format: NGSI. While several enablers are improving the capacities of the platform to manage stored information (security tools, advanced data store models, historical retrieval of information, linkage to third party applications...), a core component known as Orion Context Broker allows to gather and manage context information between data producers and data consumers at large scale. This context broker is at the centre of the exposed MBT based evaluation.

2.2 Introducing MBT in FIWARE

FIWARE was an ongoing project facing testing problems when we introduced MBT to its community. The introduction required to adapt the existing FIWARE testing process. In Fig. 2, we illustrate this introduction through the FIWARE use-case: `Orion Context Broker`. The focus is to bring examples over the method `registerContext`. This method enables the registration of a new "thing" in the Context broker implementation.

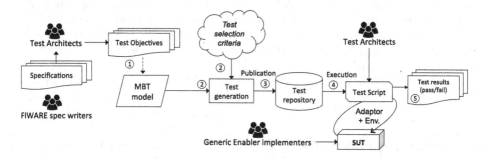

Fig. 2. FIWARE MBT process

Classicaly an MBT process [17] includes activities such as test planning and controls, test analysis and design (which includes MBT modelling, choosing suitable test selection criteria), test generation, test implementation and execution [11]. Figure 2 illustrates the classical MBT process applied to FIWARE. The test analyst takes requirements and defines tests objectives as input to model the System Under Test (SUT) (step ①). This MBT model contains static and dynamic views of the system. Hence, to benefit as much as possible from the MBT technology, we consider an automated process, where the test model is sent as an input to the test generator that automatically produces abstract test cases and a coverage matrix, relating the tests to the covered model elements or according to another test selection criteria (step ②). These tests are further exported, automatically (step ③), in a test repository to which test scripts can be associated. The automated test scripts in combination with an adaptation layer link each step from the abstract test to a concrete command of the SUT and automate the test execution (step ④). In addition, after the test execution, tests results and metrics are collected (step ⑤) and feedback is sent to the user.

From one MBT model different test selection criteria exist to drive the test generation approach [17]. In Fig. 2 we illustrate the general FIWARE MBT process that is based on different test selection criteria, depending on the tool being used.

In our approach for compliance testing we used the Smartesting CertifyIt tool [12], as it has already shown its benefits in compliance testing [7]. The CertifyIt tool uses coverage-based test selection criteria (see Sect. 2.3) and it considers, among others, UML class and object diagrams to develop MBT models. Each type has a separate role in the test generation process. The class diagram describes the system's structure, namely the set of classes that represents the static view of the system: (*i*) Its entities, with their attributes, (*ii*) Operations that model the API of the SUT, (*iii*) Observations (usually denoted as *check* operations) that serve as oracles, for instance an observation returns the current state of the user's connection on a web site.

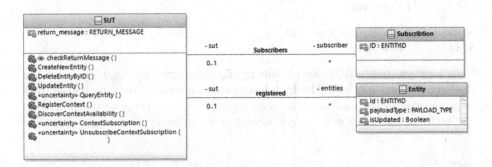

Fig. 3. MBT Orion Context Broker UML model - static view (class diagram)

The MBT model given in Fig. 3 shows the architecture of the SUT - the Orion Context Broker. The classes have attributes and functions. For instance in the *SUT* class we model respectively **return_message**, the SUT response to the sent messages and the function **RegisterContext**, that registers the entities (for instance a sensor).

Next, from the previous class diagram we instantiate an object diagram (Fig. 4). This data view provides the initial state of the system and also the objects that will be used for test generation as input data for the operation parameters.

The dynamic view of the system or its behaviours are described by Object Constraint Language (OCL) constraints written as pre/postcondition in operations in a class (Fig. 5). The test generation engine sees these behaviour objects as test targets. The operations can have several behaviours, identified by the presence of the conditional operator if-then-else. The precondition is the union of the operation's precondition and the conditions of a path that is necessary

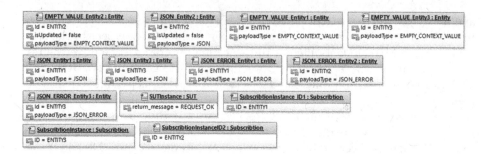

Fig. 4. MBT Orion Context Broker UML model - input data (object diagram)

to traverse for reaching the behaviour's postcondition. The postcondition corresponds to the behaviour described by the action in the `then` or `else` clause of the conditional operator. Finally, each behaviour is identified by a set of tags, which refers to a requirement covered by the behaviour. For each requirement, two types of tags exist:

- `@REQ` - a high-level requirement
- `@AIM` - its refinement

Both tags are followed by an identifier. Figure 5 shows the OCL code for the Register Context method. The high level requirement is to test the registration of an entity. Its refinement is the case where an error in the destination URL can be found, an error in the payload sent or its success.

```
RegisterContext

1 let entity : Entity = Entity.allInstances()->any(
2 e : Entity | e.sut.oclIsUndefined() and e.payloadType = IN_PAYLOAD_TYPE and e.Id = IN_ENTITYID) in
3 ---@REQ:RegisterContext
4 if(IN_URL = URL::INVALIDURL)
5 then ---@AIM:UrlError
6     self.return_message = RETURN_MESSAGE::URL_ERROR
7 else if(IN_PAYLOAD_TYPE = PAYLOAD_TYPE::JSON_ERROR)
8     then ---@AIM:JSONPayloadError
9         self.return_message = RETURN_MESSAGE::BAD_REQUEST
10    else if(IN_PAYLOAD_TYPE = PAYLOAD_TYPE::JSON)
11        then ---@AIM:JSONPayloadSuccess
12            self.entities->includes(entity) and
13            self.return_message = RETURN_MESSAGE::REQUEST_OK
14 endif endif endif and
15 result = self.return_message
16 and checkReturnMessage()
```

Fig. 5. Orion Context Broker "Register Context" method OCL - dynamic view

Deducing the test oracle from our model is a major advantage of the used tool (Smartesting CertifyIt). A specific type of operations, called observations are used to assign the test verdict. The tester with these special operations can define the system parts or variables to observe, for instance a function `checkReturnMessage()`. Thus, based on these observations, the test oracle is automatically generated for each test step, based on the `return_message` variable expected and actual (from the execution) result.

2.3   Test Generation with CertifyIt

The CertifyIt tool uses the object diagram and the OCL constraints to extract automatically a set of test targets. The test targets are used to drive the test generation process. As discussed previously each test has a set of tags associated for which it will ensure the coverage.

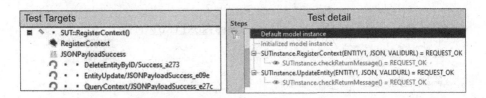

Fig. 6. `Register Context` test case

Figure 6 illustrates a test target associated to the success behaviour depicted in Fig. 5 and its corresponding test in the CertifyIt tool. The tool lists all generated tests clustered per covered requirement. We can visualize the test case and for each step a test oracle is generated. As discussed, the tester with the observation manually defines the system point to observe when calling any function. As we can see on Fig. 6, `checkReturnMessage()` observes the return code of each Orion Context Broker function with respect to the activated requirement. One test covers one or more test targets. Moreover, the tool's engine generates fewer tests then test targets, because it uses the *light merge* of tests method, which considers that one test is covering one or more test objectives (all test objectives that have been triggered by the test steps) [8]. The *light merge* of tests means that the generator will not produce separate tests for the previously reached test targets but will consider the test targets as covered by a specific test. The generated tests are exported as an XML file gathering the description of each test suite with its test cases containing parametrized abstract test steps. Generated tests are abstract and to execute them on the system an adaptation layer is required, as classically done in MBT.

3   MBTAAS for IoT Platforms Testing

IoT platforms offer services to applications users. The question of conformance testing and validation of IoT platforms can be tackled with the same *"as a service"* approach. This section presents the general architecture of our **Model Based Testing As a Service** (MBTAAS). We then present in more details, how each service works individually in order to publish, execute and present the tests/results.

3.1   Architecture

An overview of the general architecture can be found in Fig. 7. In this figure we find the four main steps of the MBT approach (MBT modeling, test generation, test implementation and execution) presented in Sect. 2.2.

However, to the difference of a classical MBT process, MBTAAS implements several webservices, which communicate with each other in order to realise testing steps. A webservice, uses web technology such as HTTP, for machine-to-machine communication, more specifically for transferring machine readable file formats such as XML[1] and JSON[2].

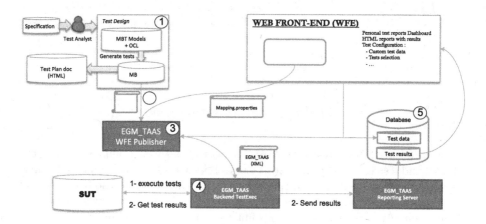

Fig. 7. MBTAAS architecture

In addition to the classical MBT process, the central piece of the architecture is the database service ⑤ that is used by all the other services. We will see its involvement as we describe each service individually. Nevertheless, the database service can be separated from all the other services, it can be running in the cloud where it is accessible. The database stores important information such as test data (input data for test execution) and test results. The entry point of the system is the web-front end service (customization service). This service takes a user input to customize a testing session and it communicates it to a Publication service ③. The purpose of the publisher service is to gather the MBT results file and user custom data in order to produce a customized test description file (EGM_TAAS file). This file is then sent to an Execution service ④ which takes in charge the execution of the customized tests. It stimulates the SUT with input data in order to get response as SUT output data. The execution service then finally builds a result response and sends it to a last service, the Reporting service. The reporting service is configured to feed the database

---

[1] https://www.w3.org/XML/.
[2] http://www.json.org.

service with the test results. These test results are used by the web-front end service in order to submit them to the end-user. This testing architecture is taken to a modular level in order to respond to the heterogeneity of an IoT platform. In the following sections, a detailed description of each services is provided.

3.2 Customization Service

In order to provide a user friendly testing as a service environment, we created a graphical web-front end service to configure and launch test campaigns[3]. The customization service is a web site where identified users have a private dashboard. The service offers a pre-configured test environment. The user input can be reduced to the minimum, that is: `defining a SUT endpoint` (URL). User specific test customization offers a wide range of adjustments to the test campaign. The web-service enables:

- **Test Selection:** from the proposed test cases, a user can choose to execute only a part of them.
- **Test Data:** pre-configured data are used for the tests. The user is able to add his own specific test data to the database and choose it for a test. It is a test per test configurable feature.
- **Reporting:** by default the reporting service will store the result report in the web-front end service database (more details on this in Sect. 3.5). The default behaviour can be changed to fit the user needs for example, having the results in an other database, tool, etc.

After completion of the test configuration and having the launch tests button pressed, a configuration file is constructed. The configuration file can be seen in Fig. 8: *Configuration File excerpt*, defines a set of {key = value}. This file is constructed with default values that can be overloaded with user defined values.

```
14  ***********************************************************************************
15  ****************      REQUIRED PARAMETERS  ****************************************
16  ***********************************************************************************
17
18  #NAME OF THE OWNER OF THE REPORT
19  OWNER=EGM_TE_XML_PUBLISHER
20  #REPORT LOCATION AFTER TESTS (FOR EGM_TAAS_BACKEND)
21  REPORT_LOCATION=http://193.48.247.210:8081/report
22  #HOW TO REPORT (FOR EGM_TAAS_BACKEND)
23  REPORT_TYPE=POST_URL
24  #URL OF SUT TO TEST WITH THE PORT (FULL PATH)
25  ENDPOINT_URL=http://193.48.247.246:1026
26  #URL of EGM_TAAS backend that will execute the tests
27  EGM_TAAS_BACKEND = localhost:8080/executeTests
28  #Name of the Model file to be Used by EGM_TAAS_BACKEND
29  EGM_TAAS_MODEL = OrionCB_GE.xml
30  #Where to Output the results in the EGM_TAAS_BACKEND
31  EGM_TAAS_OUTPUT = tmp
```

Fig. 8. Configuration File excerpt

---

[3] http://193.48.247.210/egm_taas/users/login (for reviewing purpose login:isola, password:isola).

The configuration file is one of three components that the publisher service needs to generate the test campaign. The next section describes the publication process in more details.

3.3   Publication Service

The publisher service, as it name states, publishes the abstract tests generated from the model into concrete test description file. It requires three different inputs (Fig. 7 step ②) for completion of its task: the model, the configuration file and test data. The model provides test suites containing abstract tests. The concretization of abstract tests is made with the help of the database and configuration file. For example, the abstract value ENDPOINT_URL taken from the model, is collected from the configuration file and PAYLOAD_TYPE (Fig. 5) parameter is gathered from the database service ⑤.

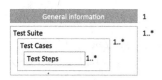

Fig. 9. Published file parts

The concrete test description file is for our use case, an XML file that instantiates the abstract tests. The test description file has two main parts, general informations and at least one test suite (Fig. 9). A test suite is composed by one or more test cases and a test case itself is composed of one or more test steps. This hierarchy respects the IEEE 829-2008, Standard for Software and System Test Documentation.

The general information part of the file is useful to execute the tests (Sect. 3.4) and report the results. Here are some of the most important parameters that can be found in that part:

- **owner:** used for traceability purposes. It allows to know who is the detainer of the test in order to present it in his personal cloud dashboard.
- **sut_endpoint:** the hostname/ip address of the System Under Test. This address should be reachable from the execution service point of view.
- **location:** the hostname/ip address of the reporting service (Sect. 3.5).

The test suites contain all useful test information. In our case, for FIWARE, the applications are HTTP-based RESTful applications. The mandatory informations required to succeed a RESTful query are: the URL (SUT endpoint) and the HTTP method (GET, POST, PUT, DELETE). The Test suite and test cases purpose is the ordering and naming of the test but the test information and test data are stored in the test steps. Each test step have its own configuration. Once the file published, it is sent to the execution service in order to execute the tests.

3.4   Execution Service

The execution service is the functional core of the MBTAAS architecture. The execution service will run the test and collect results depending on the configuration of the received test description file. FIWARE RESTful interface tests are executed with the REST execution module. Each test is run against the SUT and a result report (Listing 1.1) is constructed on test step completion. The result report contains information on date-time of execution, time spent executing the step and some other test specific values. The "endpoint" represent the URL value and validity of where the step should be run. An invalid endpoint would allow to skip the type check on the endpoint value and thus allowing to gather an execution error. The response of each step is validated within the "assertion_list" tags (test oracle). It validates each assertion depending on the assertion type and values with the response received.

Listing 1.1 – Test step result report

```
<teststep name="UpdateEntity1">                        <key>code</key>
    <executionResults>                                 <value>404</value>
        <timestamp>{TIMESTAMP}</timestamp>             <result>false</result>
        <executionTimeMs>22</executionTimeMs>      </assertion>
    </executionResults>                            </assertion_list>
    <endpoint>                                     <result>false</result>
        <value>{IP}:{PORT}/upContext</value>       <response>{
        <isinvalid>false</isinvalid>                   "errorCode" : {
    </endpoint>                                            "code" : "400",
    <method>POST</method>                                  "reasonPhrase" : "Bad Request",
    <headers>{HEADERS}</headers>                           "details" : "JSON Parse Error"
    <payload>{PAYLOAD}</payload>                       }
    <assertion_list>                               }
        <assertion>                                </response>
            <type>JSON</type>                  </teststep>
```

Figure 10 shows an excerpt of the execution service log. In order to execute one test step, the endpoint (URL) must be validated. Then a REST request is created and executed. A response is expected for the assertions to be evaluated. At the end, an overall test result is computed. The overall assertion evaluation algorithm is as simple as: "All test assertions have to be true", that implies if one assertion is false, the step is marked as failed.

```
[egm.modelTools.HttpRequestExecuter] Validating url : http://          :1026/v1/updateContext
[egm.modelTools.HttpRequestExecuter] URL is VALID
[egm.modelTools.HttpRequestExecuter] Starting Jetty HTTP Client
[egm.modelTools.HttpRequestExecuter] Jetty HTTP Client Started with Success
[egm.modelTools.HttpRequestExecuter] Creating request : URL = http://          :1026/v1/updateContext, HTTPMETHOD = POST
[egm.modelTools.HttpRequestExecuter] Request created
[egm.modelTools.HttpRequestExecuter] Request status code: 200
[egm.modelTools.HttpRequestExecuter] Response content: {
    "errorCode" : {
        "code" : "400",
        "reasonPhrase" : "Bad Request",
        "details" : "JSON Parse Error"
    }
}
[egm.modelTools.HttpRequestExecuter] Stopping Jetty HTTP Client
[egm.modelTools.HttpRequestExecuter] Jetty HTTP Client Stopped
[egm.modelTools.HttpRequestExecuter]

[egm.model.Assertion] Asserting...expression to be assert: is key "code" contains value: "404"
[egm.modelTools.TestStepResponseParser] is JSON data key "code" contains value: "404"
[egm.modelTools.TestStepResponseParser] no value of : "404" has been found for id: "errorCode"
[egm.modelTools.TestStepResponseParser] no value of : "404" has been found for id: "code"
[egm.model.TestStep] Execution Result of step UpdateEntity148 : false
```

Fig. 10. Execution snapshot

Once the execution service has finished all test steps, their results are gathered within one file, we call this file **Test Results**, and it is sent to the reporting service.

3.5 Reporting service

After executing the test, a file containing the test description alongside their results are sent to and received by the reporting service. The reporting service configuration is made in the web front-end service. The configuration is passed with the test configuration file where the publisher service re-transcribes that information to the file sent to the execution service. The execution service then includes the reporting configuration in the report file where it is used in the reporting service once it receives it. By default the reporting service will save the results in the database service ⑤ . For our use case, the database is implemented as a MySQL database. This database is afterwards used by the web front-end service to present the test results to the user.

4   Evaluation

We present results on requirements coverage, test execution and time spent to apply the approach in order to show the cost-benefits of MBTAAS.

4.1 Results

We have created two test suites for the Orion Context Broker. One test suite for automated test generation (to cover compliance requirements) and an other test suite with user defined scenarios to use the tester's experience (to cover specific functional requirements (as also available with CertifyIt [8]). For our FIWARE scope 22 requirements were manually extracted from the FIWARE standard, traced into the MBT model using the tagging feature with REQ/AIM. This automatically produced a coverage matrix between the generated test cases and the requirements, which in our case is 100 % (for more details consider the following report [1]. To further evaluate our approach we gathered information on the test case generation (number of generated tests) and test execution time. We compare these results with respect to a manual approach, a tester crafting the test cases to cover the same test objectives.

In total, the two CertifyIt test suites contain together 31 test cases and 172 test steps. The execution time including the response evaluation is accomplished in less than six seconds (5438 ms). Compared to a manual test step execution, where the execution and the evaluation can take up to approximatively 1 min by test step in the best conditions (all testing environment pre-set up) we have a 1720 times improvement in time consumption. The test execution resulted in 165 successful test steps (25 tests) and 7 failed test steps (6 tests). Failed tests are due to a gap between specification and implementation. The model showed that some test result were noted as "success" in specification and does not state a clear result which we could match with actual implementation results. Applying our MBT approach on an enablement API made possible to clearly identify the benefits of applying a service oriented MBT approach in terms of APIs interoperability verification thus ensuring the respect of the specifications.

In terms of project planning, it took us 26 person/hours to create the MBT model. More specifically, it took 10 person/hours to model the static view of the system (the class diagram) suitable for testing and 16 person/hours to model the dynamic view of the system (to write the OCL). These metrics abstract away the domain knowledge on FIWARE standards and the FIWARE NGSI specification itself. If the MBT approach is integrated within the project, the testing teams have already this knowledge. This is linked to the developers/testers experience and we consider the process of getting additional knowledge of the platform as negligible. The MBT part of our approach is transparent for the community, thus the community will simply submit their application for FIWARE compliance testing and use the MBT output artefacts i.e. the test cases produced by our MBT approach. Additionally, time spent on building the service approach is also given. And it is important to notice that the services are modular. They are only developed once for RESTFul application and each new model comes as input to the MBTAAS system already in place. In case of an other IoT platform protocol, lets take MQTT (http://mqtt.org/) for example, adjustments to the services is required. The web front-end service should include the possiblity to choose the new type of platform and a new execution module needs to be developped and integrated in the execution service. The same modifications are needed in the reporting service if we want to propose for example to export the results to a mongo-DB (https://www.mongodb.org/) database rather than MySQL.

4.2   Discussion

We are confident in our work and results following that the paper user case "Orion Context Broker" testing is a continuation of a preceding proof of concept on FIWARE enablers testing. The last use case was on the *Espr4FastData* enabler: a complex event processing tool [5]. We demonstrated that a classical MBT approach is suited to test an IoT platform thus encouraging us move forward and bring the service layer to our proof of concept.

One major advantage we saw in applying the MBT approach on FIWARE is that the test repository remains stable, while the project requirements and specification may evolve within the time. MBT is a suitable approach for emerging technologies and especially on IoT platforms where the maturity level is still increasing while technology development is still on going. Being able to generate tests automatically and in a systematic way, as we did, makes possible to constitute a test suite covering the defined test objectives. The MBT further allows generating reports to justify the test objective coverage, which can be easily used for auditing for instance. These couple of examples show the usefulness of an automated and systematic use of an MBT approach on applications that should comply to specific standards. Combined with a user friendly and ease of access through service oriented solution, first experiments with MBTAAS show that it is a promising powerful tool.

5   Related Works

In this section, we review work related to our proposed approach in the areas
of model-based testing (MBT) related to Internet of things (IoT) systems, more
specifically mobile and cloud testing, and Model-Based Testing as a service.
Model-based testing has been extensively studied in the literature [16,17]. However, the majority of existing approaches in connexion to the IoT domain are
mostly designed for mobile application. For instance, authors in [6] design a GUI
(Graphical User Interface) ripping approach based on state machine models for
testing Android applications. Other work concentrates on vulnerability testing
of mobile application based on models, for instance authors in [15] propose an
MBT approach to generate automatically test cases using vulnerability patterns,
that target specifically the Android instant Messaging mechanism.

In addition, recent survey by Incki et al. [10] reports on the work done on
testing in the cloud, including mobile, cloud applications and infrastructures,
testing the migration of applications in the cloud. They realized a categorization
of the literature on cloud testing based on several elements among which: test
level and type, as well as contribution in terms of test execution, generation and
testing framework. They underlined that testing as a service for the interoperability for cloud infrastructures today remains still a challenge. Authors in [9]
propose a model-based testing approach based on graph modeling for system
and functional testing in cloud computing. Hence, contrary to these approaches
that refer to testing approaches of the different layers of the cloud: Software as a
service, Platform as a service and Infrastructure as a service, our approach proposes Model-Based Testing as a service for compliance testing of IoT systems,
were the cloud is one element of it.

Testing service can be provided to cloud consumers as well as cloud providers
generally called Testing as a Service (TaaS) [14]. Previous work on testing as a
service, to the best of our knowledge, specifically relates to web services and cloud
computing. Zech et al. in [18] propose a model-based approach using risk analysis
to generate test cases to ensure the security of a Cloud computing environment
when outsourcing IT langscapes. More recently Zech et al. [19] proposed a model-
based approach to evaluate the security of the cloud environment by means
of negative testing based on the Telling Test Stories Framework. Model-Based
Testing provides the benefit of being implementation independent. In this paper,
we propose MBT as service to the Internet of Things, making thus the test cases
available for any platform implementation of the specification. Contrary to the
existing works, our approach proposes an abstraction on model construction, it is
configuration over development. Our model-based test generation does not take
into account risk analysis elements neither security requirements, which can be
one possible extension of this module of our Model-Based Testing as a Service
approach.

6   Conclusion and future works

This paper presented a successful application of an MBT approach with a service oriented solution. We believe that this approach can be generally applied on a wide range of specifications defining APIs for FIWARE. Within the FIWARE context, the created MBT model, NGSI compliant, can be reused for testing any range of enablers respecting that specification. New developments focus on the test configuration layer which is made in the front-end service, in order to make the tests compatible with the System Under Test. The modularity, will be explored to be used in *integration testing* between IoT platform applications (Fig. ,1). Furthermore, one of our concerns was to provide the IoT platform tests to the community in the easiest way possible, including the possibility to choose the version of standard compliance only by model selection. This is done with the service oriented approach, providing to all involved stakeholders (not only testers) the capacity to test their generic enabler installation remotely from an online webpage in a Plug and Test approach. IoT platforms can be used by third party entities (data consumers/providers) that connect to the platform to verify their compliance to the platform's standard. The next step of the research work is to explore to what extent the models of an IoT platform can be used to test those third party applications in order to validate their behaviour on the platform.

Acknowledgments. This research was supported by the projectS FP7 FI-CORE & H2020 ARMOUR.

References

1. FIWARE test repository and requirements matrix. http://fiware.eglobalmark. com/html/. Accessed 29 Apr 2016
2. Open Mobile Alliance. http://technical.openmobilealliance.org/Technical/ technical-information/release-program/current-releases/ngsi-v1-0. Accessed 18 Apr 2016
3. Reinhart Richter, Xcerra Corporation: Does the Internet of Things force us to rethink our test strategies? http://xcerra.com/ep_doestheinternetofthingsforce ustorethinkourteststrategies-vision
4. The FIWARE Project. https://www.fiware.org/2015/03/27/build-your-own-iot-platform-with-fiware-enablers/. Accessed 8 Apr 2016
5. Ahmad, A.: Iot interoperability model-based testing, a fiware case study: poster at UCAAT. ETSI, Sophia-Antipolis, France (2015)
6. Amalfitano, D., Fasolino, A.R., Tramontana, P., De Carmine, S., Memon, A.M.: Using GUI ripping for automated testing of android applications. In: 27th IEEE/ACM ICSE, ASE 2012, NY, USA, pp. 258–261. ACM, New York (2012). http://doi.acm.org/10.1145/2351676.2351717
7. Bernabeu, G., Jaffuel, E., Legeard, B., Peureux, F.: MBT for global platform compliance testing: experience report and lessons learned. In: 25th IEEE ISSRE Workshops, Naples, Italy, pp. 66–70 (2014)

8. Botella, J., Bouquet, F., Capuron, J., Lebeau, F., Legeard, B., Schadle, F.: Model-based testing of cryptographic components - lessons learned from experience. In: 6th IEEE ICST, Luxembourg, pp. 192–201 (2013)

9. Chan, W.K., Mei, L., Zhang, Z.: Modeling and testing of cloud applications. In: Services Computing Conference, APSCC 2009, IEEE Asia-Pacific, pp. 111–118, December 2009

10. Incki, K., Ari, I., Sozer, H.: A survey of software testing in the cloud. In: 6th IEEE International Conference, SERE-C, pp. 18–23, June 2012

11. Kramer, A., Legeard, B.: Model-Based Testing Essentials - Guide to the ISTQB Certified Model-Based Tester: Foundation Level. Wiley, Hoboken (2016)

12. Legeard, B., Bouzy, A.: Smartesting CertifyIt - model-based testing for enterprise IT. In: ICST 2013, 6th IEEE International Conference on Software Testing, Verification and Validation, Testing Tool Track, pp. 192–201. IEEE, Luxembourg (2013)

13. Nebut, C., Traon, Y.L., Jezequel, J.M.: System testing of product lines: from requirements to test cases. In: Käköla, T., Duenas, J.C. (eds.) Software Product Lines, pp. 447–478. Springer, Heidelberg (2006). http://dx.doi.org/10.1007/978-3-540-33253-4_12

14. Riungu, L.M., Taipale, O., Smolander, K.: Research issues for software testing in the cloud. In: 2nd IEEE International Conference CloudCom, pp. 557–564, November 2010

15. Salva, S., Zafimiharisoa, S.R.: Data vulnerability detection by security testing for android applications. In: Information Security for South Africa, pp. 1–8. IEEE (2013)

16. Utting, M., Legeard, B., Bouquet, F., Fourneret, E., Peureux, F., Vernotte, A.: Chapter 2 - Recent advances in model-based testing. Adv. Comput. **101**, 53–120 (2016). http://dx.doi.org/10.1016/bs.adcom.2015.11.004

17. Utting, M., Pretschner, A., Legeard, B.: A taxonomy of model-based testing approaches. STVR **22**(5), 297–312 (2012). http://dx.doi.org/10.1002/stvr.456

18. Zech, P., Felderer, M., Breu, R.: Towards a model based security testing approach of cloud computing environments. In: 6th International Conference SERE-C, pp. 47–56 (2012)

19. Zech, P., Kalb, P., Felderer, M., Breu, R.: Chapter 40 - Threatening the cloud: securing services and data by continuous, model-driven negative security testing. Transportation Systems and Engineering: Concepts, Methodologies, Tools, and Applications, vol. 3, pp. 789–814 (2015)

Doctoral Symposium

ISoLA Doctoral Symposium

Anna-Lena Lamprecht

Lero - The Irish Software Research Centre, University of Limerick,
Limerick, Ireland
anna-lena.lamprecht@lero.ie

In 2014 for the first time, ISoLA hosted a Doctoral Symposium as a scientific and networking event specifically targeted at young academics, complementing the different thematically focused research tracks of the main symposium. Master and PhD students were invited to participate and to present their research ideas and projects, to discuss them with the scientific community, and to establish collaborations in their field of research. It was very well received, with 15 young researchers participating and several seniors attending the sessions, and featured high-quality works on a wide range of topics.

ISoLA 2016 will again comprise a Doctoral Symposium. It will be held as combination of poster sessions and short presentations. Posters will be on display all along the ISoLA symposium, and the coffee breaks will offer plenty of time for elaborate discussions of the posters. Additionally there will be Doctoral Symposium sessions in the conference program, where all participants get the opportunity to give a brief presentation of their work.

To participate in the Doctoral Symposium, candidates have to submit a research abstract of up to four pages that has be structured and formatted according to a specific template. The template defines five sections, and for each section includes a list of hints and questions that provide guidance on what to address in the respective sections:

1. **Problem and Research Question**
   Which problem do you address with your research? Why is this important? What is the central research question and what do you want to find out? What knowledge do you expect to gain?
2. **Related Work**
   What are the three most important works of other groups to which your research is related? How did these works influence you? What do you do better than existing works?
3. **Methods**
   How do you conduct your research? Which methods do you use? How do you verify or evaluate your results?
4. **Preliminary Results**
   Describe your preliminary results. Why should we trust these results? How did you check them?
5. **Next Steps**
   What are the next steps in your work? What is missing before your work can become a dissertation?

It can be quite a challenge to cover all these points on just four pages, but enforcing this structure helps the young researchers to reflect very concretely and precisely on the status of their own thesis work. This can be a stark contrast to other research papers they have written, which are often a result of joint work with more senior members of the research groups and thus are embedded in a broader thematic range. Focussing on their own contributions in their respective research context for the Doctoral Symposium contributions supports them to clarify the profile and "story" for their dissertation project, but also provides other researchers with a better basis to give adequate and purposeful feedback.

Submissions to the Doctoral Symposium will be accepted until shortly before the conference, and the participants will be invited to submit a full-length article on their work to a post-conference proceedings volume, which allows them to incorporate the feedback received during the symposium. In addition there was the possibility of including selected early submissions in the main conference proceedings (this volume), and it was decided to include Kahina Hacid's research abstract on "Handling domain knowledge in formal design models: An ontology based approach" [1]. The author has succeeded particularly well in describing her research work along the lines of the template, and thus her abstract can serve as a concrete example and provide orientation for other young researchers who would like to reflect on their work in this way - be it for the upcoming Doctoral Symposium or in any other context.

We are looking forward to meeting all participants of the Doctoral Symposium in October, to another series of interesting posters and presentations, and to lively discussions about the various research topics.

Reference

1. Hacid, K.: Handling domain knowledge in formal design models: an ontology based approach. In: Margaria, T., Steffen, B. (eds.) ISoLA 2016, Part II, LNCS 9953, pp. 747–751. Springer, Switzerland (2016)

Handling Domain Knowledge in Formal Design Models: An Ontology Based Approach

Kahina Hacid[✉]

Université de Toulouse, INPT, IRIT, Institut de Recherche
en Informatique de Toulouse, Toulouse, France
kahina.hacid@enseeiht.fr

1 Problem and Research Question

During the development of complex systems, several models corresponding to different analyses are built. These analyses refer to different engineering domains. In general, the knowledge carried out by an engineering domain is not explicitly taken into account during system development process. The system development process leads to the production of several heterogeneous models corresponding to different views or analyses of the same system. In this context, the most important heterogeneity factor, in addition to the one due to the use of different modelling languages, is related to information, knowledge and assumptions of the domain (the environment and context where designed systems evolve). In general, this knowledge is not explicitly formalised and therefore not used in the models associated to the design of these systems. One of the reasons is the absence, in the modelling languages, of resources to model such domain knowledge. As a consequence, very few domain knowledge information is handled by the designed models. The developer handles this information by himself in the development process. Indeed, although systems are developed in accordance with development standards and good practices, a large part of the knowledge required for the interpretation and validation of these models of systems remains implicit. This situation may lead to inconsistent model verification and/or validation and models may loose some of their properties if the information related to their domain, context and environment are integrated to the models.

Our research question results from the above observations. The objective of our thesis research work is to propose a sound and operationalised approach to enrich and strengthen formal design models with domain knowledge modelled as formal ontologies. Decomposing this overall research objective, we formulate three research goals that we address during our thesis work.

1. Provide a formal framework supporting the explicit modelling of domain knowledge.
2. Establish an explicit link or reference between domain knowledge models and the design models.
3. Express and verify, on the enriched design models, the properties entailed by the domain knowledge reference.

© Springer International Publishing AG 2016
T. Margaria and B. Steffen (Eds.): ISoLA 2016, Part II, LNCS 9953, pp. 747–751, 2016.
DOI: 10.1007/978-3-319-47169-3_54

2 Related Work

Semantic enrichment of models has drawn the attention of several research communities. Annotation is promoted as the main mechanism to link design models and domain knowledge models. Different methods and techniques emerged with the aim to enrich the semantics of models using annotation mechanisms. Below, we recall the three main categories of approaches for semantic annotation. More details can be found in [1,2].

First, in [3,4], the authors use ontologies for raw data annotation in an informal context. Web pages and documents are annotated with semantic information formalized within linguistic ontologies. Once annotations achieved, formal reasoning can be performed.

In the second category of approaches, ontologies are used for the semantic enrichment of models in a semi-formal context. [5] propose a fully automated technique for integrating heterogeneous data sources called "ontology-based database". This approach assumes the existence of a shared ontology and guarantees the autonomy of each source by extending the shared ontology to define its local ontology. In [6–10] annotations are made in an interoperable context in order to improve common understanding and re-usability of the models and thus enabling unambiguous exchange of models. In [11], a reasoning phase is performed based on the output of the annotation phase. The reasoning rules produce inferred results : (1) Suggestion of semantic annotation, (2) Detection of inconsistencies between semantic annotations and (3) Conflict identification between annotated objects. These approaches addressing interoperability issues focused on improving the common understanding of models. They do not deal with the formal correctness of models with respect to domain properties and constraints.

The third category of approaches address the semantic enrichment of design models related to an application domain using formal annotations. Some approaches use annotations with expressions that make explicit references to ontologies. Indeed, in [12–14], the authors argue that many problems in the development of correct systems could be better addressed through the separation of concerns. [12,13] advocate the re-definition of design models correctness as a ternary relation linking the requirements, the system and the application domains. Domain concepts are then explicitly modelled as first-class objects. Furthermore, they propose the formalisation of ontologies by Event-B contexts. The formalised information can then be integrated incrementally and directly in the behavioural requirements using refinements. In [14] a DSL abstract syntax and references to domain ontologies are axiomatised into logic theories. These two models are related using a third logical theory. The authors use Alloy [15] to check the consistency of the unified theory.

Positioning of our approach. Compared to our thesis research work, the approaches cited above use, through annotations, domain information and knowledge directly (i.e. as built-in concepts) in the design model. Our approach improves these approaches. It advocates to first separate the ontology and the design model and second to make the annotation explicit using an annotation model. In this way, models are separated from the domain model and thus ontologies and models can evolve separately and asynchronously.

3   Methods

Our research method is inspired by practice. We have observed that several models implicitly include domain knowledge without making reference to or sharing descriptive models, leading to heterogeneous models. The integration of such models becomes difficult to achieve. The modularity decomposition principle has been followed. We have described domain knowledge as modules that are referenced by design models. Our approach is based on the exploitation of domain ontologies. We consider that on the one hand, ontologies are good candidates for describing and making explicit a domain knowledge [16], and on the other hand, annotation of model resources by references to ontologies makes it possible to handle domain knowledge in design models. More precisely, in order to reach our objectives, we propose the stepwise methodology detailed below [1].

Step 1. Domain Knowledge Formalization. Domain information (concepts, properties, constraints) of the studied domain are represented and formalised within a knowledge model, carried out by domain ontologies. The ontology referencing mechanism (URI) is the ground model for the annotation process. An ontology modelling language can be used to describe this model. The choice of this modelling language depends on the kind of reasoning to be performed.

Step 2. Specific Domain Knowledge. Specific design models to enrich are defined at this step. They correspond to a given specification and are formalised within a specific modelling language supporting different analyses.

Step 3. Annotation Model. The relationships between design model entities and the corresponding knowledge concepts are identified. They are made explicit and formalised within an annotation model. Relationships are themselves described with a modelling language. As discussed in [17], three different kinds of relationships can be set up.

Step 4. Properties Expression and Verification. The annotated model is analysed to determine whether the constraints associated to the knowledge domain, carried out by the annotations, can or cannot be expressed in the new enriched design model.

At the end of this process, a new design model enriched with new information of the domain knowledge is obtained. Verification and validation of this model are required to check if the domain knowledge properties, resulting from the annotation still hold, and if the new ones can be expressed.

4   Preliminary Results

The proposed approach has been exploited to strengthen static design models. It has been deployed for two design model development approaches: a model driven engineering (MDE) approach [17] and a correct by construction formal modelling one based on refinement and proof using the Event-B method [1].

An ontology meta-model as well as a formal ontology language with axioms and theorems have been defined. We have used the Eclipse modelling framework to support the MDE based approach and the Rodin platform for the formal approach. In both cases, the approach proved powerful enough to enrich design models with knowledge domain properties. Note that, in case of proof based formal developments, ontologies are strengthened with proved theorems that are directly deduced from axioms. This deduction mechanism is not available in the case of the MDE based approach. Indeed, in this case, theorems can only be expressed as constraints in the constraints description language.

5   Next Steps

Several aspects of our work can be improved. First, the semantic enrichment of dynamic design models, describing complex information systems, with domain knowledge needs to be addressed. An extension of the developed ontology language is then required to be able to describe dynamic entities (e.g. services). Then, the ontology validation issue needs to be addressed, as well as the reasoning mechanisms offered by ontological reasoners (e.g. racer [18], etc.). The case of semantic mismatch, where ontologies and design models are not described in the same modelling language, needs to be addressed. Semantic alignment shall be studied. Finally, we are interested in describing an ontological language in an upper level using event-B theories.

References

1. Hacid, K., Aït Ameur, Y.: Strengthening MDE and formal design models by references to domain ontologies, a model annotation based approach. In: ISOLA (2016, to appear)
2. Hacid, K.: Explicit definition of prperties by model annotation. Technical report, Institut de Recherche en Informatique de Toulouse, Toulouse university (2014)
3. Cunningham, H., Maynard, D., Bontcheva, K.: Text Processing with Gate. Gateway Press, Murphys (2011)
4. Handschuh, S., Volz, R., Staab, S.: Annotation for the deep web. IS (2003)
5. Bellatreche, L., Pierra, G., Xuan, D.N., Hondjack, D., Ameur, Y.A.: An a priori approach for automatic integration of heterogeneous and autonomous databases. In: Galindo, F., Takizawa, M., Traunmüller, R. (eds.) DEXA 2004. LNCS, vol. 3180, pp. 475–485. Springer, Heidelberg (2004). doi:10.1007/978-3-540-30075-5_46
6. Boudjlida, N., Panetto, H.: Annotation of enterprise models for interoperability purposes. In: Advanced Information Systems for Enterprises (2008)
7. Wang, Y., Li, H.: Adding semantic annotation to UML class diagram. In: Computer Application and System Modeling (ICCASM) (2010)
8. Lin, Y., Strasunskas, D.: Ontology-based semantic annotation of process templates for reuse. In: CAiSE (2005)

9. Lin, Y., Strasunskas, D., Hakkarainen, S.E., Krogstie, J., Solvberg, A.: Semantic annotation framework to manage semantic heterogeneity of process models. In: Martinez, F.H., Pohl, K. (eds.) CAiSE 2006. LNCS, vol. 4001, pp. 433–446. Springer, Heidelberg (2006). doi:10.1007/11767138_29

10. Zouggar, N., Vallespir, B., Chen, D.: Semantic enrichment of enterprise models by ontologies-based semantic annotations. In: EDOC. IEEE (2008)

11. Liao, Y., Lezoche, M., Panetto, H., Boudjlida, N., Loures, E.R.: Formal semantic annotations for models interoperability in a PLM environment (2014)

12. Ait-Ameur, Y., Gibson, J.P., Méry, D.: On implicit and explicit semantics: integration issues in proof-based development of systems. In: Margaria, T., Steffen, B. (eds.) ISoLA 2014, Part II. LNCS, vol. 8803, pp. 604–618. Springer, Heidelberg (2014). doi:10.1007/978-3-662-45231-8_50

13. Méry, D., Sawant, R., Tarasyuk, A.: Integrating domain-based features into eventb: a nose gear velocity case study. In: Bellatreche, L., Manolopoulos, Y., Zielinski, B., Liu, R. (eds.) MEDI 2015. LNCS, vol. 9344, pp. 89–102. Springer, Heidelberg (2015). doi:10.1007/978-3-319-23781-7_8

14. de Carvalho, V.A., Almeida, J.P.A., Guizzardi, G.: Using reference domain ontologies to define the real-world semantics of domain-specific languages. In: Jarke, M., Mylopoulos, J., Quix, C., Rolland, C., Manolopoulos, Y., Mouratidis, H., Horkoff, J. (eds.) CAiSE 2014. LNCS, vol. 8484, pp. 488–502. Springer, Heidelberg (2014). doi:10.1007/978-3-319-07881-6_33

15. Jackson, D.: Software Abstractions - Logic, Language, and Analysis (2006)

16. Aït Ameur, Y., Méry, D.: Making explicit domain knowledge in formal system development. Sci. Comput. Program (2015, to appear)

17. Hacid, K., Ait-Ameur, Y.: Annotation of engineering models by references to domain ontologies. In: Bellatreche, L., Pastor, Ó., Almendros Jiménez, J.M., Aït-Ameur, Y. (eds.) MEDI 2016. LNCS, vol. 9893, pp. 234–244. Springer, Heidelberg (2016). doi:10.1007/978-3-319-45547-1_19

18. RACER Ontology Reasoner. https://www.w3.org/2001/sw/wiki/RacerPro

Industrial Track

A Retrospective of the Past Four Years with Industry 4.0

Axel Hessenkämper

Hottinger Baldwin Messtechnik GmbH, Darmstadt, Germany

Since the "Umsetzungsempfehlung für das Zukunftsprojekt Industrie 4.0" [1] was published in 2012, industries and enterprises are trying to define and implement their Industry 4.0 and digitalization strategy. The past four years are embossed by papers, conferences, speeches, tracks and all kinds of information. But what is Industry 4.0 and what does that mean for businesses of tomorrow?

After having read thousands of lines of text, tried to interpret charts and sheets, and been creative to understand the meaning of doodle designs of new processes and procedures, there is no proper and general defined guideline to implement Industry 4.0. Enterprises and mid to large sized companies are left alone. Every Enterprise has to define and find its own way towards Industry 4.0 and make the step from linear product development towards exponential business. Even major enterprises struggle and might disappear in the future like those famous examples of Nokia and Motorola. An important question each enterprise has to answer is whether they want to make that shift internally or whether they get the support from external partners to boost their business. Many businesses chose for the latter. To prepare themselves, enterprises started to spend the previously used budget for R&D topics on consultants and expert opinions to become "digitalized". But is it actually successful? Which *REAL INNO-VATION* was launched by this strategy employed by enterprises with a long history and a common way of thinking and working? When looking at the results of the past four years it becomes clear that *REAL INNOVATIONS* will not evolve just by reading those articles, being consulted by experts or maybe buying a Think Tank with Software Experts. Especially, the de-location of the R&D budget to other areas is questionable if the introduction of innovations to the market are the ultimate goal.

There are two major success factors for successfully becoming innovative. First, the mindset change, which has to start at the top-management level! Especially, boundaries and hierarchical structures need to be broken down and adapted to allow for creativity and changes. Second, the management has to trust its first movers that the proposed innovation could lead to a success and needs to be willing to support changes triggered by the enterprise's first movers e.g. by spending money into the required infrastructure, people with the right expertise and time. Additionally, time is a crucial factor to give the innovator-team a chance to set things up. Success factors like "fail often, but early", "be agile" etc. may have the same weighting like the two success factors mentioned above, but they are used so often in the context of Industry 4.0 that they fulfil the role of *Buzzwords* reducing their importance to the reader. The early history teaches us that a lot of money is spent and a lot is said but the real change is missing! Who will make the race towards Industry 4.0 and the digitalization? How will companies with long mechanical background look like in 5–10 years from now?

Barbara Steffen, Steve Boßelmann and Axel Hessenkämper [2] will present how enterprises with a high value of single unit solutions can handle their complexity with higher efficiency in the future.

The Model-Based One Thing Approach is in an early stage of development, but coming up with a running prototype and first presentable results. Here, the entire development and customization of a customer order for process machines and plants will be handled out of one source without information leaking. Nils Wortmann, Malte Michel and Stefan Naujokat [3] will present the results and first results of the actual status from the proof-of-concept.

The automotive industry, too, is currently racing towards Industry 4.0 and digitalization: Car manufacturers explore new business models (e.g., on-demand delivery of driving assistants) and investigate ways to leverage the data that can be produced by huge fleets of vehicles on the road. In the automotive world, these two trends are complemented by a third one. Not only production and business are becoming smart and digital, the products themselves are as well: Autonomous vehicles that are expected to share the road with human drivers within the next couple of years [4], which is expected to lead to a major shift towards mobility as a service. Prof. Andreas Rausch, chairman of the board of the Institute for Applied Software Systems Engineering (Clausthal University of Technology) and board member of the Automotive Research Centre Niedersachsen, will share his perspective on these trends with a particular emphasis on the technical challenges of assuring the safety of advanced driver assistance systems.

References

1. Kagermann, W.H.: Umsetzungsempfehlung für das Zukunftsprojekt Industrie 4.0. Büro der Forschungsunion im Stifterverband für die Deutsche Wissenschaft e.V., Berlin (2012)
2. Steffen, B., Boßelmann, S., Hessenkämper, A.: Effective and Efficient Customization through Lean Trans-Departmental Configuration. ISoLA 2016
3. Wortmann, N., Michel, M., Naujokat, S.: A Fully Model-Based Approach to Software Development for Industrial Centrifuges. ISoLA 2016
4. Okuda, R., Kajiwara, Y., Terashima, K.: A survey of technical trend of ADAS and autonomous driving. In: Proceedings of Technical Program - 2014 International Symposium on VLSI Technology, Systems and Application. VLSI-TSA 2014 (2014)

Effective and Efficient Customization Through Lean Trans-Departmental Configuration

Barbara Steffen[1,2]([✉]), Steve Boßelmann[3], and Axel Hessenkämper[4]

[1] University of Twente, Enschede, Netherlands
barbarasteffen@gmx.net
[2] GEA Westfalia Separator Group GmbH, Oelde, Germany
[3] Chair of Programming Systems, TU Dortmund, Dortmund, Germany
steve.bosselmann@cs.tu-dortmund.de
[4] Hottinger Baldwin Messtechnik GmbH, Darmstadt, Germany
axel.hessenkaemper@gmx.de

Abstract. Today's organizations tend to offer customized products and services to satisfy challenging customer needs. In this context, product customization spans product variant configuration as well as actual custom engineering. Particularly custom engineering induces various obstacles that organizations must overcome in order to effectively and efficiently realize inter-departmental communication and smooth internal order processing. Both are mandatory to achieve customer satisfaction and outcompete competitors. These obstacles span topics in the fields of recommendation-driven and knowledge-centered customization, knowledge engineering and maintenance, organizational learning, as well as intra-departmental process alignment. Based on first-hand insights and expert interviews, we identify the main business requirements when faced with process innovations and technological challenges in this context and discuss shortcomings of available approaches in common practice. We also report preliminary results that include the conceptual design of a knowledge-centric configuration framework designed to overcome the obstacles raised.

Keywords: Knowledge-driven product configuration · Organization-wide knowledge sharing · Inter-& Intra-departmental process alignment · Technological gatekeeper · Process innovation implementation

1 Introduction

Global manufacturing enterprises supplying customized solutions on the Business-to-Business market have to steadily improve and adapt to survive in the continuously changing competitive environment that asks for global availability and technical support 24/7. Understanding the customer, offering the best product and service solution timely and with the highest quality are only the top drivers to succeed. In Business-to-Business markets, the organizations are in direct competition with each other to get customer orders. Their goal is to convince the customer of the own organization's superiority in fulfilling their needs, which is often translated into offering the best suiting customization solution. Customer needs comprise the perfect technical performance of the product, at a fair price and a short delivery time while ensuring

© Springer International Publishing AG 2016
T. Margaria and B. Steffen (Eds.): ISoLA 2016, Part II, LNCS 9953, pp. 757–773, 2016.
DOI: 10.1007/978-3-319-47169-3_57

supplier's reliability and trustworthiness. Depending on the customers' wishes, the actual customer and supplier dependency, transaction, relationship and end-product can differ a lot. Backhaus and Voeth differentiate between the *product, project, system* and *integration* business models, describing the dependencies and relationship required for each of them to be successful [1]. Firstly, the *product* can be sold as (standard) product, meaning that neither the customer nor the supplier are dependent on each other, with no need for a relationship if the customer chooses a standard product. Secondly, the *product* can result from a project, calling for a relationship at least until the project is completed. In the project business, the supplier is dependent on the customer as he can choose between different suppliers' offers and determine which supplier receives the order based on the customer's wishes. Thirdly, in the *system* business, the customer is dependent on the supplier due to the buy-in effect that leads to a long-term relationship. This means that the initial transaction entails follow-up purchases that can only be delivered by the same supplier. An example for this type is SAP's business model. This dependency enables the supplier to exploit his position with respect to the customer. Lastly, *integration* leads to a situation where customer and supplier are mutually dependent and therefore build a tight and long-term relationship. Here, the customer is the only one demanding and the supplier the only one offering a specific product. There would not be a business transaction without these two parties interested in it.

If an organization wants to offer the full customization spectrum, it has to cover several of these business models simultaneously. This is a huge challenge due to the fact that these business models require different handling and management, asking for high flexibility in the internal processes. However, manufacturing enterprises are not prepared to satisfy this demand of flexibility efficiently and effectively.

To address this issue, we previously introduced the Global Communication Infrastructure (GCI) [2], a very ambitious conceptual approach that aims at efficiently aligning organization-wide knowledge management with the production processes. While the considerations presented in this article augment the GCI concept, they represent only a first step of its realization and focus on organizations operating in the Business-to-Business market.

In the following, in Sect. 2 we present the state-of-the-art by means of today's common practice of knowledge management in organizations, then we describe the actual research approach in Sect. 3, and list preliminary results in Sect. 4. Finally, Sect. 5 provides notes on related work followed by a conclusion with future perspectives.

2   State of the Art and Problem Definition

The four kinds of business models introduced above differ especially in the handling of the **first process phase**, from customer request to the offer composition: based on it, the customer chooses which supplier will get the order. This initial process phase is therefore particularly important, as it lays the foundation for the product specification, the relationship between the supplier and customer, the perception of the supplier's image, and it leads to a potential competitive advantage. Additionally, it is crucial to fulfil or outperform the contract, also generating positive references that may lead to potential new orders in the future.

To make that possible, a lot has to change. Nowadays most globally operating manufacturing enterprises lack a departmental-wide let alone organization-wide single knowledge source. Currently, employees have no other chance than to maintain their expert knowledge in their heads, saving it as (printed or electronic) documents on their desktops or exploiting the advantage of working with simple configurators, which can depict the simplest product configurations the organization offers.

The major issues to be addressed in this context are:

1. Narrowness and rigidity of the available 'State of the Art' systems,
2. A landscape of isolated tools inside the global enterprises,
3. Inflexible ERP-Solutions,
4. Missing integration and process support,
5. Not implementable requirements from the users to follow the process.

The need for internal process improvement and enterprise-wide knowledge transfer is well known to everybody, starting from the Executive Boards, via the CIOs, to every single (process-) contributor, as there are no adequate 'State of the Art' off-the-shelf solutions available today. Thus, enterprises are typically trying to use their own processes and solutions, using their decades-old filled and installed ERP systems and databases to handle knowledge, processes, and know-how. This individual approach requires enormous customization efforts and costs, and transforms the originally standardized ERP systems successively into a costly individual solution, even though they originally were not designed for this new purpose: The ERP system(s)' restricted structure hampers the smooth implementation of solutions that fit the organization's (daily) needs. Even minor changes require the help of external specialized consultants, who are uniquely able to implement the new requirement into the ERP system. This state of affairs is very costly, takes a long time, and exacerbates the lock-in situation and causes even higher future costs.

As a result, simple to use and often spreadsheet based tools are created to collect and process local knowledge, mostly stored on local servers with local access-rights. To overcome this locality, some enterprises install intranet solutions with global access rights for all the relevant parties within the organization. This leads to redundancy and inconsistency of the data, which are still incomplete and need to be manually enriched case by case. In particular, there is currently no systematic way to aggregate knowledge or to structurally and consistently enrich the knowledge with new concepts as they may arise during the manufacturing process. Thus only few of the process participants' needs are satisfied: information and knowledge are still spread all over the enterprise and there is still no alignment of offers, discussions, and negotiations within the enterprise. As a consequence, the interdisciplinary communication, in particular between (regional-) sales, development and engineering, is still too error prone.

However, to enable the internal processes to meet the needs of the Business-to-Business markets, they have to be adapted to fulfil the requirements of all four business models in a standardized manner, ensuring that this process step clearly defines the offer's scope, becomes cheaper and faster while offering a higher quality. Therefore, best-in-class processes and an interdisciplinary alignment are mandatory to supply all internal departments with the needed information, and to run the order with full customer satisfaction. Especially, the (regional) sales department has to be provided with the best possible information from development, construction, production, internal sales and various other departments. Thus, processes providing all these information and data 24/7 without any delay have to be installed to provide 'just in time' offers with a maximum of liability and reliability.

Concluding, it can be said that the main problem of most organizations is that they fail to accomplish a continuous, streamlined and directed information exchange, which is required for the efficient division of labor needed to successfully specialize and coordinate the internal processes between an organization's different departments. Based on the conducted interviews it appears that the reason why organizations nowadays often fail, is that they are confronted with the power of the *not-knowing barrier* leading to an internal coordination problem and the *not-wanting barrier* representing the motivation problem [3]. Correspondingly, this paper addresses this complex problem from a technical perspective as well as from a business perspective, each tackling the barriers independently.

This paper's technical approach focuses on overcoming the coordination problem by proposing an internal process innovation through a Holistic in-the-Loop Configurator (HiLC) aligning the different departments, offering smoothly working cooperation and functioning as technological gatekeeper, while the business approach focuses on tackling the motivation problem with change and innovation management practices. The business perspective faces especially in large manufacturing firms (which typically follow a mechanistic organization structure) a powerful and widespread resistance to process innovations, as it is particularly invasive and complex and affects the organization's culture and way of working. Moreover, it is typically complicated to communicate their need as they only indirectly translate into a tangible advantage. On the contrary, affected stakeholders often fear disadvantages, like endangered jobs through rationalization [4, 5], which makes it difficult to obtain the required support, openness and willingness to change. This has to be overcome by applying approaches to individual change that address these fears and explain the advantages.

In three interview rounds with 6, 7, and 5 interviewees respectively at different project stages, the newest ideas and prototypes were demonstrated and feedback was gathered. On this basis we identified and refined several consequences resulting from the above mentioned main problem. These must be overcome by technical support via means of the HiLC and business approaches regarding change management and form internal processes satisfying the requirements of customization offerings:

1. *Misalignment:* There is little inter- and intradepartmental coordination resulting in faulty budget and timespan planning.
2. *Non-conformity:* Previously developed (project) solutions are overlooked.
3. *Staff education:* New employees need long training to become fit for service.
4. *Lost knowledge:* On-site work remains undocumented and/or information is distributed over various types of files or sources.
5. *No detailed process overview:* In theory the processes are clear, however in practice it is difficult to determine who is responsible for what and when.
6. *No clearly defined scope of supply:* The contracts are too vague, leaving too much space for customers to renegotiate or to claim changes after delivery.

7. **Dependency on experts:** Expert knowledge is only saved in the experts' heads, making the firm and products' quality dependent on them and this bottleneck.
8. **No integrated feedback loop:** Customers' feedback is not linked to the development of new products.
9. **No overview of actual machine performance:** Lab data might not correspond to actual machine performance. However, it would be beneficial for guarantees and delivery promises to analyze the actual machine performance.
10. **Process innovation resistance:** Process innovations are not regarded necessary.
11. **Resistance to change:** Organizations are resistant to intrusive changes of their processes, as they impact their culture, require a lot of time and effort, and rarely promise direct benefits.

Research Question. Based on the identified main problem and its consequences the following research question was developed aiming at overcoming the problem.

How to develop and implement flexible, effective and efficient internal processes supporting manufacturing enterprises in offering customization?

This breaks down into a technical and a business part:

– What are the technical requirements to improve and support the internal processes?
– How to prepare the organization for the internal process innovation and change?

We will answer it from the technological perspective and business perspective, which are individually discussed in their dedicated sub-sections throughout all chapters.

3 Research Approach

The research is based on interviews with practitioners and experts from the applied research fields, to identify the theoretical and practical requirements along our research project and to ensure that it fulfils and prepares for those requirements. We first conducted an industry analysis with interviewees from different industries, revealing which industries struggle the most. Here, the interviewees held different positions in several globally operating enterprises. This diversity was important to collect sufficient and extensive information about the real problems of the target group. To identify the major problems, the interviewees were asked about their internal handling processes, the occurring challenges, the internal support system, the project team composition, the time-frame of projects, the extent of enterprise-wide exchange of experiences made and knowledge gained, and where they see the major errors and points of improvement in the process. Based on the analysis of the interviewees' answers we identified the "first mover" on which we focused then the further research and progress. Currently, the research is focused on a small cross-functional team composed of supporters of the first-mover, who actually pushes the project's progress forward and aims at fast results. The applied research approach is a combination of Maurya's running lean approach [6], focusing on close contact for validating the progress with the actual target group, and Hevner's three-cycle-view of the design science research cycle, consisting of the relevance, design and rigor cycle [7]. Throughout the relevance cycle, the environment was observed to identify problems and opportunities which could be translated into requirements to be handled in the design cycle. The arising solutions were then grounded in accordance to state of the art research in the rigor cycle, to ensure that they fit the experience, expertise and scientific theories and methods of up-to-date research. The quality and fit of the developed solution were then evaluated and validated through field testing when reconnecting the design and relevance cycle.

Throughout our research project the goal is to stay in close contact with the target group of experts in order to validate the problem hypotheses, envisioned solution, and future project steps and plans. The research just finished the fourth sweep of the design research cycle, as the project benefits from early feedback ensuring that the project's progress is actually still in line with the first mover's needs. This approach was able to ensure that the project's scope and the faced problems could be refined and possible solution aspects could be validated. The interviewees are convinced that the proposed process changes actually could overcome many problems and prevent their occurrence, and have the potential to standardize the handling even of customized and engineering products. Therefore, they are looking forward to a first prototype demonstrating the actual benefits of the envisioned solution.

3.1 Technical Approach

As argued in [2], there is no (such) tool that realizes organization-wide knowledge management in an out-of-the-box fashion. Even worse, there is no such thing as a best practice approach regarding how to accomplish this goal by integrating a decent set of software solutions. Knowledge management in general and organizational learning in particular are rather young research fields, only receiving increased attention for the last decade. When it comes to knowledge-centric product configuration, the first attempts of transferring academic results to business practice have been formulated just recently [8].

In order to tackle the issues raised in the course of problem definition, a consistent knowledge-driven software solution is conceptualized. It is constructed around a product configurator that is embedded in a process-driven environment with continuous interlinking of knowledge-centric data and activities to push process performance and improve inter-departmental communication. However, setting up the rules and logic behind a configurator as well as defining interactions and processes often requires specialized programming knowledge, but certainly significant investments of money and time in development. In particular, this means huge investment upfront due to the difficult and tedious task of knowledge acquisition, i.e. the transfer of expert knowledge to a structured knowledge base. In order to reduce costs and effort, we continuously strive for simple and efficient solutions wherever applicable.

Product Configuration Framework. In practice, the general understanding and use of product configurators differs depending on its actual area of application. In the Business-to-Consumer market they are commonly used as software tools that typically are integrated into web shops and online order systems. As an example, car configurators can be found on the website of nearly every car manufacturer today. These configurators are consumer-oriented and represent an essential building block in the order processing chain to effectively realize so-called mass customization. That means the customer, the purchaser, configures a product according to its needs. However, this term is slightly misleading in this context, as in this setting customers can choose from pre-defined options to configure variants that nonetheless result in a standardized or at least expected product. On the contrary, customization in the scope of this project triggers an individual or small-scale production process to produce a unique product or small batches, respectively. This also holds true for the Business-to-Business market, where product configurators are commonly used by sales staff to configure machines, control cabinets or components of consumer products to customer needs. In this context as well, custom engineering triggers adapted order processing routines.

The requirement for enabling this kind of customization directly influences the development of a solution that covers both the configuration of standard product variants as well as the support for out-of-standard customization requests. However, this means leaving trodden paths by means of commercial ERP-centric product configurators that only cover the standard case, i.e. well-defined product variants. This does not mean to replace existing ERP systems, but rather to integrate its data management capabilities into the envisioned solution that adds the required functionality. In fact, the integration of tailored engineering aspects introduces new requirements regarding the inter-departmental communication as well as additional needs for knowledge access, coordination processes and business unit alignment. This touches various topics of software engineering and bringing them together to come up with an integrated solution is one of the main challenges. Throughout the project, we proceed to identify particular use cases in this context, sketch potential realizations and appropriate workflows in order to conceptualize a suitable solution. We apply continuous validation to the concept by means of presenting it to the expert contacts and evaluating the feedback. Lessons learned will have immediate impact on the further development.

Technological Requirements. The technical solution needs to fulfil the requirements of the process contributors in terms of the following three criteria to be successfully implemented and adopted:

1. *usability,* to have an easy interface and a high and fast learning curve,
2. *ease in adaptability to changing processes,* to be agile in a fast changing global enterprise environment and
3. *accessibility,* to be able to use the technical solution everywhere at every time.

Next to the process contributor requirements, the IT departments have to put effort into supporting the solution of the new product. Here, installation routines, user-access and product care are only some tasks they have to execute. First, the IT departments have to ensure the interface to the existing ERP system. All relevant data from different departments are already stored and used. To overcome the ERP system as the main data storage of the enterprise is not the purpose of this technical solution, while this will use the data. Second, the technical solution has to be executable on the corporate hardware and operating systems. Especially, changes to the operating system and the IT landscape could be hard to convince the IT departments.

3.2 Business Approach

As defined by Davenport, *"process innovation combines the adoption of a process view of the business with the application of innovation to key processes. What is new and distinctive about this combination is its enormous potential for helping any organization achieve major reductions in process cost or time, or major improvements in quality, flexibility, service levels, or other business objectives"* [9]. However, this only goes hand in hand with adapting the way of working, which faces strong resistance. This resistance can be partly reduced to the learning dip concept stating that whenever one has to do things differently than one is used to, one's performance reduces drastically, as one first has to adapt and relearn how to excel at the new task [10]. This costs time and effort and requires motivation explaining why people try to resist change whenever they can and therefore often act as inhibitors of innovations asking for adaption. Accordingly, when aiming at introducing and implementing process innovations it is important to identify the possible negative reactions, arguments and strategies of the inhibitors so that the roles and tasks of the power, process, expert and relationship promoters as well as of the process innovation's supporters can be defined to prepare everyone involved upfront for the upcoming barriers.

In addition to this direct confrontation of inhibitors and promoters it is important to have pro- and re-active approaches of change management in place. Armstrong defined *change management* as "the process of achieving the smooth implementation of change by planning and introducing it systematically, taking into account the likelihood of being resisted" [11]. For such an invasive process innovation as aimed at here, to be successfully implemented it is crucial to understand and analyze the organization's culture and willingness to change, to identify the affected stakeholders and address them in accordance to their needs. Only this way it is possible to align them in compliance to the organization's overall strategy for change, without overruling their identity. This requires to empathise with the stakeholders, see the big picture, address it by thinking out of the box and be patient as the process' uprising hurdles slow down the progress and to eventually address the given situation with the support of innovation and change management approaches.

The radical process innovation acts as need recognition for change triggering the *change process* [12]. The change processes' goal is to reach a state at which the organization actually desires to change. To make that possible it is important to decide upon whom to involve in the project to pursue and support it further. This is actually a crucial decision the process and power promoter have to take, as if this envisioned change reaches the attention of a power inhibitor too early, the project may not get a chance to prove its superiority over the status quo. In the next step it is important to critically review the present state and to define the preferred future state by articulating a guiding vision. After the vision is set, the change plan and the supportive interventions need to be developed accordingly. At this stage *Lewin's Three-Step Model* can be adapted which is defined as "unfreezing the status quo, movement to a desired end state, and refreezing the new change to make it permanent" [13]. The movement is enabled by either increasing the power of the driving forces, decreasing the restraining forces' power or both. This can be done by e.g. reducing the learning dips impact through suited incentives, feedback, skills development and trainings etc. on the individual level. The change plan guides the actual implementation of the change. For changes as radical as the one considered here it is preferable to handle it as an emergent change meaning that the desired end-state adapts dependent on the changes' and plans' progresses. When the change is successfully implemented, it is of major importance to ensure its sustainability in order to prevent that employees fall back into old habits. This step can be supported by guiding feedback and incentives. Throughout the whole organizational change process special attention must be paid on managing people.

4   Preliminary Results

Based on the received feedback testing and validating the project's intermediate results along the way this chapter provides an overview of the preliminary results from the technical and business perspective.

4.1   Technical Perspective

In the course of developing a product configuration framework, we have conceptualized a solution that covers both the standard case (i.e. the configuration of multi-variant products) and the out-of-standard case in terms of product customization involving engineering activities. The framework is meant to be integrated into the general GCI concept. It comprises the essential aspects discussed in the following sections.

Component Catalogue. A very basic requirement for enabling the configuration of products is a catalogue of components that might potentially be used as building blocks. Each component holds a description and is configurable by means of a set of component-specific attributes. But instead of providing a flat collection, these components need to be coherently structured according to an appropriate classification. This enables both reasoning about the type of a component as well as searching the catalogue for specific components in a structured manner. Obviously, the task of identifying, for example, all engines in a catalogue of machine components is simple if respective items are classified as such.

While the component classification induces an almost intuitive hierarchical arrangement, i.e. a taxonomy, the component attributes hold detailed information about each component. And when it comes to searching they enable the application of filters based on attribute values. This allows for listing all components that, for example, are made of stainless steel or marked as heat resistant. Additionally, filters might be combined to create more complex queries like listing all components that are made of stainless steel *and* marked as heat resistant. However, this requires the attributes to not being component-specific but rather type-specific. Hence we explicitly consider this for the proposed structure of the component database.

The described approach based on product classification and attribute-based filtering is commonly used, e.g. in sophisticated online shops. We propose it as a crucial feature for the product configurator that enables an intuitive and efficient interface in the first place. Additionally, it is a mandatory prerequisite for the definition of type-based composition rules and combination constraints we discuss in a subsequent section.

Definition of the Product Structure. To configure a product, its structure needs to be well defined, i.e. the amount and arrangement as well as required characteristics of components from which a specific product may actually be composed of. In this context, a component may represent a module that itself may consist of multiple components, hence inducing a hierarchical perspective to be considered as functionality for the development of a structuring tool.

In order to support structure design in an understandable and convenient way, we emphasize the need for an intuitive solution as the main users in this context are engineers that typically lack programming knowledge. Though they need to convey structural descriptions in a sound and consistent manner, they should not be urged to first learn complex specification languages. Hence we propose a modelling approach based on a graphical representation of the product and its configuration points. We created a prototype to demonstrate the feasibility of this graphical approach. This prototype is an enhancement of the early prototype we have been creating in the course of the development of the GCI vision. Users can create shapes that represent place-holders for actual components. Hence, they need to be linked to suitable types of components that later on can be used to replace these placeholders in the actual product configuration step. But apart from the component's type, there is need for more sophisticated ways of defining restrictions regarding suitable components and dependencies between them. To achieve this, rules and constraints are required.

Composition Rules and Combination Constraints. The configuration logic comprises the Do's and Don'ts in the context of composing a product from a set of components. This logic is typically specified as a set of complex rules that comprise various constraints and dependencies. However, setting up the rules and logic behind a configurator often requires specialized programming knowledge and the coping of propositional logic. On the other hand, the experts that provide the respective knowledge are foremost engineers that often lack these skills. But bringing programmers and engineers together to create the desired solution introduces a semantic gap and significant delay to the design process.

In order to overcome these drawbacks, or at least to reduce the hurdle, we aim at providing the experts with intuitive tools that allow them to specify rules and constraints themselves even without sophisticated skills in programming or formal logics. Some of the rules are already embedded in the definition of the product structure based on component types and hence covered by the model-driven approach just mentioned. But more complex constraints might depend on the presence or absence of specific components as well as on specific component attributes. However, we propose to enrich the graphical model that holds the information about the product structure to additionally hold information about interdependencies and conflicts between components. These may be designed as directed edges that represent the respective relation. We have found that this approach has the potential to cover the most recurring constraints in the context of product configuration. And though it might be necessary to fall back to writing formulas or programming in order to cover the complex cases, an intuitive solution for the majority of cases has the potential to significantly speed up the task of defining a product's structure.

Domain-Specific Views. So far, the discussion focused on the role of the engineer in the product structuring process. However, the main users of the product configurator are salesmen that configure products according to customer needs. But customers and salesmen are specifically interested in product features and performance, but not so much in technical details of components. Hence we propose to provide each user group with appropriate views according to the respective expertise and competencies. In particular, the default entry point should be a feature-centric view for the sales staff while engineers are expected to prefer a rather technical view. However, while the respective information from another view should be hidden in the first place, it must be accessible on demand, for example to enable salesmen to answer detailed questions of customers.

In order to enable these domain-specific views, product features need to be defined and put in relation to the product's components and their characteristics. This is important because product features are not component-specific, but are related to partial configurations, i.e. specific combinations of components with appropriate characteristics. As an example, the throughput of a liquid processing machine does not solely depend on the size of its outlet, but also on the size of installed pipes and the power of its engine. A realization of this concept can build on the product structure and enable the specification of partial configurations to be linked to respective feature descriptions.

Again, in order to provide an intuitive solution to non-programmers, we propose a model-driven approach based on the graphical representation of the product structure that has been introduced in the preceding sections. Figure 1 shows the graphical approach by means of screenshots from the prototype that has been created.

Configuration Recommendation via Profile Matching. A strong focus in the conceptualization regarding a product configuration framework lies on the integration of a recommender system to support the finding of a specific product variant that best fits feature requirements, which might be incomplete or defined in a vague manner. In particular, in the context of identifying suitable product configurations we propose the configurator to support user-centric prioritization of features. This would allow salesmen to specify whether requirements to the product are mandatory or rather nice-to-have. An integrated recommendation system evaluates and interprets the request and as a result

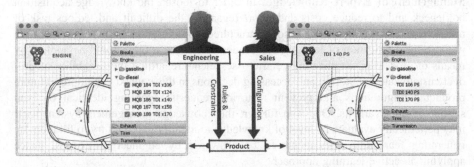

Fig. 1. Product structure definition and product configuration

provides a list of feasible products. The latter may comprise both, standard product variants as well as potential customizations.

The main objective of this approach is to provide the user with a list of suitable alternatives to choose from what he or she considers best-fitting. To further support this decision making, the list of alternatives should be sortable according to relevant criteria, including aspects like the product's price, availability or production time as well as expected profit margin.

Any recommended configuration needs to be consistent with the product-specific rules and constraints regarding the combination of components and the configurator needs to assure this via internal validation. However, in order to provide extended support for the product-finding process we propose the recommendation system to include customized product variants that are induced by the evaluation of rules and constraints, but not necessarily known solutions in terms of having been built before. As this type of recommendations may as well cover unrealizable variants, i.e. configurations that have not yet been excluded by means of respective rules and constraints, it is mandatory to mark them as such and handle them differently throughout the product configuration task.

Feasibility Assessment based on inter-departmental Communication. If any of the uncertain product variants just introduced are of interest for the sales rep, he or she might trigger a feasibility assessment workflow involving engineering experts in order to clarify whether the solution can be build or not. If triggered, the configuration framework translates the feature-centric view regarding the proposed configuration into a component-centric view with technical details to be presented to an engineer. Based on expertise, he or she decides on the feasibility. The answer should be structured and comprise the decision, possible restrictions and supplementary requirements. If not feasible, the engineer should be able to justify the decision (e.g. by naming incompatible components) and it should be supported to propose alternatives that are feasible and fulfil the requested features, if existent. The alternative-finding task again should be supported by a recommendation system that according to composition rules and constraints induces possible configurations that might fit the requirements.

We propose that this inter-departmental communication should explicitly be supported by the product configuration framework in order to avoid media gaps and to enable subsequent processing and storing of the actual assessment.

Management of Expert Knowledge. In order to loosen the knowledge acquisition bottleneck and to reduce costs and effort regarding the difficult and tedious task of transferring expert knowledge into a structured configuration knowledge base, we propose the application of learning techniques. Passive learning should be applied by means of processing engineering-centric assessments regarding the feasibility of product customizations. Storing and accessing decisions in this context can improve future product configurations and prevent recurring requests regarding identical or even similar product variants. One step further, the knowledge management system itself may periodically evaluate its level of knowledge to identify gaps and try to fill them by generating feasibility assessments to be answered by engineering experts, hence applying an active learning approach.

Table 1. Possible inhibitors' arguments and promoters' reactions

Inhibitors' Arguments	Promoters' Reactions	Change Management Approach
Fear of uncertainty	The process promotor must outline the path of change to inform the employees about what they have to expect and integrate them.	The uncertainty's impact must be reduced by defining the change's goal and process clearly. It increases the likelihood of achieving change and decreases employees' internal chaos.
Not-wanting barrier	The power promoter can use his force to overcome this barrier and sanction inhibitors if necessary.	Incentives/ Rewards/ Motivators Sanctions/ Punishments Reducing the learning dip's impact
Not-knowing barrier	The expert promoter's task is to explain the innovation and its goal, and to convince the inhibitors with technical arguments.	Skill development Training Information meetings: explaining the change process and effects on employees
Technological arguments: Mistrust in feasibility & functional capabilities Does not fit the organization's culture → it is better to wait	The proof-of-concept supported by the affected departments will demonstrate how the project will be approached. Organizational change must be aligned with the process changes and the HiLC's implementation.	Motivate employees to change their perspectives by explaining the purpose of the change, the benefits and herewith win their trust. State the need and urgency for the organization to change in order to stay competitive.
Economic arguments: Employees are satisfied with the current state Already used tools become obsolete Change costs too much money, time, and effort	Current processes are not compatible with the customization market. HiLC is more enhanced than the other tools and applicable to all industry sectors and products. In the long-run HiLC will lead to major time and cost reductions and will improve time and quality to market.	Create dissatisfaction with the state of the art to enable required change. To change the status quo a clear end must be marked, rendering tools and routines obsolete and enabling the movement to the desired state. Explain how the change investments will pay off in the future and lead to performance and quality improvement.
Existential fear: Fear of becoming dispensable	The innovation's goal is to support the internal processes, align the departments, prevent errors, and achieve a fully utilized production chain instead of staff reduction.	It is important to make the vision of the desired state clear: increase the organization's competitiveness, leading to more orders, which requires all employees and internal resources available.

This continuous maintenance and extension of the configuration knowledge is consistent with the continuous improvement cycle formulated in the general concept of the GCI.

4.2 Business Perspective

Based on the conducted interviews, we created the overview of possibly arising barriers and arguments of the inhibitors detailed in Table 1. Each of the inhibitors' argument was opposed by possible reactions of the promoters, which are based on several change management techniques. When enabling change, especially in cases of radical change due to process innovations, it is crucial to reduce the uncertainty accompanying it by defining a goal and constantly updating and involving the employees in the process [9].

The employees need reassurance and confirmation demonstrating that they are an important part of the change, and that the change actually offers benefits for them and that it is not just forced onto them. To motivate the employees to embrace change, incentive and sanction schemes are useful to regulate the driving and restraining forces of change, steering the movement from the status quo to the desired state of the art.

5   Related Work

In business practice, the utilization of product configurators is steadily increasing. Research in this context spans knowledge-based configuration methods, the acquisition and representation of knowledge as well as the transfer of academic results to practice.

Knowledge-driven Configuration. Configuration tools enable the aggregation of a specific product by combining predefined components, thereby respecting well-defined constraints and rules that represent relations and dependencies between them. A constraint solver processes this knowledge, solves the dependencies and that way it ensures that the configured variant is consistent with the structural requirements, concretely by solving a Constraint Satisfaction Problem [14]. The improvement of knowledge engineering processes has been researched since the late 1970s. Early research developed model-based knowledge representations that enable the separation of domain knowledge and problem-solving algorithms. Component-oriented configuration models have been developed and integrated into commercial configuration tools, as most configuration domains in business practice are component-oriented [15]. Additionally, graphical knowledge representations that are more compact have been developed [16], as well as intelligent diagnosis methods that support the maintenance of configuration knowledge [17]. The application of recommendation technologies [18] to support domain experts and engineers in creating configuration knowledge is a recent research approach [19]. It tackles the major challenge to overcome the difficult and tedious transfer of expert knowledge into a knowledge base, which is known as the knowledge acquisition bottleneck [20].

Product Configurators. The problem-solving methodology that underlies product configurators has been researched since the development of expert systems in the late

1970s. A prominent example of an early product configurator is the R1/XCON [21] that enabled the configuration of computers and enhanced the order process by preventing infeasible configurations. In today's Business-to-Consumer market, product configurators typically are integrated into web shops and online order systems. The customer itself configures a product according to its needs. The benefits and challenges for organizations have recently been discussed [22] and a comprehensive survey on the state of the art has been published [23].

Product customization in the context of this article triggers an individual or small-scale production process to produce a unique product or small batches, respectively. This aspect of customization is not covered by commercial product configurators.

In the Business-to-Business market product configurators enable salesmen to offer customer-specific products and that way improve order specification and project planning by means of generating bills of materials and routing. Most of the product configurators in this context are integrated into ERP systems that manage product components in a bill of material. As an example, SAP manages a maximum bill of material as well as maximum routing [24]. Based on specified relationship knowledge, the system chooses the components and the operations that are required for a specific product variant, respectively. Other examples of ERP-centered solutions are BAAN [25], ORACLE [26], proALPHA [27] and unipps [28].

Knowledge Management. In practice, business content and organizational knowledge are typically stored in a variety of ways, often dispersed over a heterogeneous system landscape, and most of a company's intellectual capital is under-used or even lost [2]. There exist content management systems (CMS) like Livelink [29], Microsoft Share-Point [30] and ShareNet [31], but none meets and exploits the needs of global enterprises as they do not offer the possibility to globally and systematically share and search the organization's internal information and knowledge enabling employees to find the information they are looking for on time.

6 Conclusion and Next Steps

Last year the GCI was presented in the doctorial symposium session of the International Conference on Software Business (ICSOB 2015). Based on the received feedback at the conference and from industry representatives throughout the subsequent year, it became evident that the proposed approach is very ambitious. Hence, the project proceeds stepwise, by focusing on individual aspects of organization-wide knowledge management. In this article, we have presented a first step focusing on organizations operating in the Business-to-Business market, and discussed how they would benefit from the HiLC supporting the process. We conceptualized an early prototype to be validated by domain experts and promoters that have the role and responsibility to stay alert and foresee possibly upcoming barriers of the inhibitors. Being prepared and fast are the major criteria for successful change management as it limits the inhibitors' potential for intervention. We argued that it is crucial to make the employees part of the change to reduce their perceived uncertainty.

In the next step, we plan to extend the prototype based on the results and feedback received through the technical and business approach at the first mover consisting of a small cross-departmental group of supporters pushing the project forwards. Further development comprises a model-driven constraint editor, a recommendation system and the realization of process-driven inter-departmental consultation. The goal is to create an integrated proof of concept. We plan to apply it to a limited but meaningful product field, which allows to demonstrate its benefits more clearly and to be validated by domain experts and promoters.

Simultaneously, the supportive base of the project will be expanded and prepared for the actual confrontation with the inhibitors for the point in time when the project becomes official. Here, it is important to actually analyze the organization's culture more in depth to apply the rather broad recommendations addressed in chapter three to the specific situation in this particular organization. The employees and their reasons for resisting the change must be understood to prepare detailed change plans and approaches suiting the given situation.

Acknowledgement. We are very grateful to the interviewees, and, in particular, to Moritz Kröplin who provided us with practical insights and helped organizing the interviews.

References

1. Backhaus, K., Voeth, M.: Industriegütermarketing. Grundlagen des Business-to Business Marketings. 10. Auflage. Vahlen, München (2014)
2. Hessenkämper A., Steffen B., Boßelmann S.: Global communication infrastructure: towards standardization of customized projects via profile matching. Post-proceedings of the 6th International Symposium on Leveraging Applications of Formal Methods (ISoLA 2014) (2014)
3. Hauschildt, J., Salomo, S.: Innovationsmanagement, 5th edn. Vahlen, München (2011)
4. Rechberg, I., Syed, J.: Ethical issues in knowledge management: conflict of knowledge ownership. J. Knowl. Manag. **17**(6), 828–847 (2013)
5. Riege, A.: Three-dozen knowledge-sharing barriers managers must consider. J. Knowl. Manag. **9**(3), 18–35 (2005)
6. Maurya, A.: Running Lean Iterate from Plan A to a Plan That Works, 2nd edn. O'Reilly, Sebastopol (2012)
7. Hevner, A.: A three cycle view of design science research. Scand. J. Inf. Syst. **19**, 87–92 (2007)
8. Felfernig, A., Hotz, L., Bagley, C., Tiihonen, J.: Knowledge-Based Configuration: From Research to Business Cases, 1st edn. Morgan Kaufmann Publishers Inc., San Francisco (2014)
9. Davenport, T.H.: Process Innovation Reengineering Work through Information Technology. Harvard Business School Press, Boston (1993)
10. Cameron, E., Green, M.: Making Sense of Change Management, 4th edn. Kogan Page, London (2015)
11. Armstrong, M.: A Handbook of Human Resource Management Practice, 11th edn., p. 424. Kogan Page (2009)

12. Hayes, J., Hyde, P.: Managing the Merger, a Change Management Simulation. Organisation Learning Tools, Novi (1998)
13. Robins, S., Judge, T.: Essentials of Organizational Behavior, 12th edn. Pearson, Boston (2012)
14. Apt, K.: Principles of Constraint Programming. Cambridge University Press, New York (2003)
15. Mittal, S., Frayman, F.: Towards a generic model of configuration tasks. In: 11th International Joint Conference on Artificial Intelligence (IJCAI 1989), vol. 2, Detroit, Michigan, pp. 1395–1401 (1989)
16. Stumptner, M., Friedrich, G., Haselböck, A.: Generative constraint-based configuration of large technical systems. In: Artificial Intelligence for Engineering Design, Analysis and Manufacturing, vol. 12(4), pp. 307–320. Cambridge University Press, New York (1998)
17. Felfernig, A., Friedrich, G., Schubert, M., Mandl, M., Mairitsch, M. Teppan, E.: Plausible repairs for inconsistent requirements. In: 21st International Joint Conference on Artificial Intelligence (IJCAI 2009), Pasadena, CA, pp. 791–796 (2009)
18. Jannach, D., Zanker, M., Felfernig, A., Friedrich, G.: Recommender Systems. Cambridge University Press, New York (2010)
19. Felfernig, A., Reiterer, S., Stettinger, M., Reinfrank, F., Jeran, M., Ninaus, G.: Recommender systems for configuration knowledge engineering. In: Workshop on Configuration, Vienna, Austria, pp. 51–54 (2013)
20. Hoekstra, R.: The knowledge reengineering bottleneck. Semant. Web 1(1–2), 111–115 (2010)
21. McDermott, J.: R1: A rule-based configurer of computer systems. Artif. Intell. 19, 39–88 (1982)
22. Heiskala, M., Tiihonen, J., Paloheimo, K.S., Soininen, T.: Mass Customization with Configurable Products and Configurators: A Review of Benefits and Challenges. Mass Customization Information Systems in Business, pp. 1–32. Idea Group Publishing, London (2007)
23. Zhang, L.: Product configuration: a review of the state of the art and future research. Int. J. Prod. Res. 52(21), 6381–6398 (2014)
24. Haag, A.: Sales configuration in business processes. IEEE Intell. Syst. 13(4), 78–85 (1998)
25. Yu, B., Skovgaard, H.: A configuration tool to increase product competitiveness. IEEE Intell. Syst. 13(4), 34–41 (1998)
26. ORACLE. http://www.oracle.com. Accessed 08 August 2016
27. proALPHA. http://www.proalpha.com. Accessed 08 August 2016
28. unipps. http://www.comtri.de/it-dienstleistungen/erp-system-unipps.html. Accessed 08 August 2016
29. Livelink. http://www.opentext.com/what-we-do/products/opentext-product-offerings-catalog/rebranded-products/livelink-is-now-part-of-the-opentext-ecm-suite. Accessed 08 August 2016
30. SharePoint. https://products.office.com/en-us/sharepoint/sharepoint-2013-overview-collaboration-software-features. Accessed 08 August 2016
31. ShareNet. http://www.share-netinternational.org/. Accessed 08 August 2016

A Fully Model-Based Approach to Software Development for Industrial Centrifuges

Nils Wortmann[1], Malte Michel[2], and Stefan Naujokat[3(✉)]

[1] Software Design, GEA Group AG, Oelde, Germany
nils.wortmann@gea.com
[2] TU Dortmund University, Dortmund, Germany
malte.michel@tu-dortmund.de
[3] Chair for Programming Systems, TU Dortmund University, Dortmund, Germany
stefan.naujokat@tu-dortmund.de

Abstract. We present a model-based approach to software development for industrial process automation, overall aiming at decreased development efforts, increased quality, and reduced time to market. Key to this approach is the high-level specification of all required aspects using dedicated domain-specific modeling languages. This abstraction provides both a standardized framework supporting the communication between experts on industrial processes and PLC software developers, as well as the reduction of implementation overhead through full code generation. As a proof of concept, processes for industrial centrifuges are considered. We present the standardized models and tools used to fully generate code for Beckhoff Twin CAT 3. The presented work is the result of a cooperation project at TU Dortmund with the GEA Group AG involving 12 students.

Keywords: Industrial automation · Model-based development · Domain-specific languages · Full code generation

1 Introduction

In the fast growing technological environment of industrial automation, a product's time to market has become more and more important to its success. The development of the corresponding software often has significant influence on this time to market, as experts from multiple disciplines – such as mechanical engineering, electrical engineering, process chemistry, PLC programming, etc. – have to tightly cooperate, but usually lack a clear channel of communication; especially one that successfully bridges the gaps between these disciplines.

One promising way to approach this communication and cooperation issue is the standardization of the development process, and in particular software design, by establishing standardized models that abstract from technical details. However, to prevent developers from occasionally "bending" these standards to their individual needs, a highly specialized tool is required that guides and constrains them according to the developed standards. Such a tool establishes "Archimedean Points" [11], i.e. unchangeable aspects of the domain it specializes to.

© Springer International Publishing AG 2016
T. Margaria and B. Steffen (Eds.): ISoLA 2016, Part II, LNCS 9953, pp. 774–783, 2016.
DOI: 10.1007/978-3-319-47169-3_58

With models powerful enough to describe a product as a whole – so they can be automatically generated to complete running code – this tool-supported standardization will significantly decrease the products' time to market. This idea closely follows the *One-Thing Approach* (OTA) [5] where interconnected models of different types form one consistent and comprehensive specification for the addressed domain.

This paper presents a proof of concept for such a model-based generative approach in a specific domain of the automation industry, in particular considering production processes involving industrial centrifuges. An intial prototype of a corresponding tool was created, which is named IPSUM: **I**ndustrial **P**rocess **S**oftware **U**tilizing **M**odelization. It was developed with CINCO [9], a generative meta-level specification framework that facilitates the fast development of OTA tools, providing early prototypes that gradually evolve into sophisticated solutions.

In the following, Sect. 2 gives a short introduction on common problems of the traditional development workflow for process automation software. Section 3 then discusses how these problems can be approached with standardized models and their full generation to executable code. Afterwards, Sect. 4 provides a detailed introduction to the model types available in IPSUM, followed by a brief presentation of the code generation concepts in Sect. 5. The paper concludes with a summary and directions to future work in Sect. 6.

2 Current Industrial Workflow

The machine and plant engineering industry has to solve complex processes in many different areas for which they need highly qualified process technicians. This becomes even more difficult if a company provides machines that are not only used in single processes, but in many different areas and many different ways. If this is the case, it is very important that a process technician develops a solution in cooperation with the customer. After this, the process technician usually designs a *Piping and Instrumentation Diagram* (P&ID), a common diagram used in the process industry to show the piping and the material flow between the components [1,6]. Also, a flow graph diagram is often used to illustrate the solution of that specific process. One major problem at this point is, that the process technicians' designs might not be within their own company's norms or standards, which are more often than not only implicitly 'defined' by the combined knowledge of experts from different fields. In particular, there is no tool to specifically guide and constrain the process technician.

This problem carries on to the next step of the development. Usually, a process technician has to pass the diagrams to a programmer to implement the specifications on a *Programmable Logic Controller* (PLC) or *Industrial PC* (IPC). As the programmer may receive such diagrams from different process technicians with different design rules, this usually results in a large communication overhead between the process technician and the programmer, which considerably slows down the development.

This is the reason why actual standards and norms for these type of diagrams are of huge interest for companies suffering from these problems. Thus, the machine and plant engineering industry tries to optimize the workflow by creating standards for all involved steps, beginning with the customer conversation and going all the way down to the implementation. However, the approach we present even goes further: It does not only standardize the workflow and the involved models, but also completely removes the necessity of an implementation phase by introducing model to model transformations and code generators for the full automatic generation of all required code.

3   IPSUM Workflow

The design of the *IPSUM workflow* is based on the analysis of the *industrial workflow* discussed in the previous section. It primarily aims at reducing implementation overhead. Thus, the first goal of this optimization is that no task should be done twice, i.e. as much information as possible should be carried over from one tasks to the other, so that changes in every part of the development process are automatically propagated to all other parts. This does not only result in a reduction of work, but also ensures the consistency of the whole design. Closely related to the traditional workflow, the design process starts with the customer conversation the P&ID design will be based on. This P&ID already provides a lot of information for other phases of the workflow (cf. Sect. 4.2). This is illustrated in Fig. 1 by the two edges labeled *a*, representing model to model transformations to create initial versions of the hardware diagram (cf. Sect. 4.3) and the HMI diagram (cf. Sect. 4.4). After this, only those elements not already defined by the P&ID have to be added to those diagrams.

All information needed for the logical diagrams (cf. Sect. 4.5) is now available. The tool provides a dedicated view for the process technician to access this information (Fig. 1, edges *b* and *c*). On this foundation the process technician can model the process within defined constraints, ensuring the aspired standardization. At this point the designer models on two different abstraction layers, each represented with a dedicated diagram type: the State Machine Diagram and the Flow Graph Diagram.

Usually, the models are created according to the described workflow. However, all diagrams contribute to a huge entwined model where every change in a diagram is automatically adapted to the other diagrams to keep them consistent and meaningful. This makes sure that the developer can always return to previous design steps and adjust them, without invalidating the parts of the design process that are built upon those steps, resulting in an overall much more agile development process.

The last step of our workflow is the code generation. At this point all information needed for the process solution is specified with the models, and an executable project can be generated without any additional work. In the current proof of concept, three different components are created for a full Beckhoff Twin-CAT 3 [2] Project (cf. Sect. 5). After this step, a fully model-driven deployment is available.

4   IPSUM Model Types

In order to describe the industrial process with IPSUM, the process technician is provided with a number of different diagrams, representing a model. Each of these diagrams holds specific information about the process and its components, that is needed to create executable code for a wide range of target systems. As shown in Fig. 1, these diagrams are dependent on each other.

One of the main goals of this standardized collection of diagrams is to describe everything needed for the industrial process independent from the target system the process will later be executed on. Thus, the user is not only able to describe the process without deep knowledge about programming, but can also distribute it to different types of systems without any difference in the models he uses and creates. This is our approach to the standardization discussed in Sect. 3. The target platform that was used for testing is the Beckhoff Embedded PC, executing a Beckhoff TwinCAT 3 project, that can be fully generated through our toolset.

4.1   Overview Diagram

The core of the IPSUM diagrams is the Overview Diagram. It contains all the other diagrams describing the process and is not only used as a fast access and as an overview for the user, but also shows specific dependencies between them, as shown in Fig. 1.

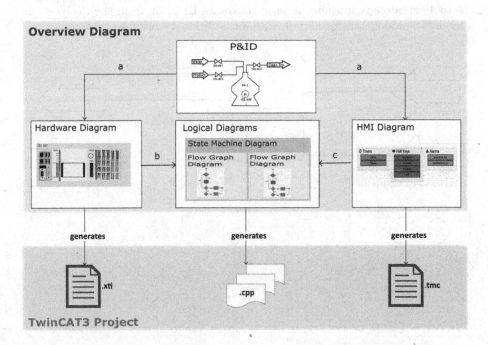

Fig. 1. Relationships and dependencies between all models from IPSUM

More specifically, it contains the Piping and Instrumentation Diagram specifying the phsyical layout of the process, the Hardware Diagram describing the hardware that the software will be generated for, the Human Machine Interface Diagram holding timers, alarms and other variables, and the Logical Diagrams representing the procedure in detail. In summary, the overview diagram shows how these diagrams are used as a huge entwined model as described in Sect. 3.

If the process is controlled by multiple systems, these can be specified as different modules in the Overview Diagram. Each of these modules can then include their own Hardware Diagram, HMI Diagram and Flow Graph Diagram, thus representing its own computational unit.

4.2   Piping and Instrumentation Diagram

The development of an industrial process usually starts with the P&ID, as introduced in Sect. 2. This already standardized diagram type describes the layout of the machine, depicting its different functional units like centrifuges, pumps, valves, etc., and how they are connected to each other (cf. Fig. 2). It also contains abstract information about the control systems, showing details on monitoring and control.

In the *IPSUM workflow* the information this diagram holds is also used to support the preparation of other diagrams. As the P&ID holds valuable information about measuring and control points, this can be used to automatically determine the minimum number of inputs and outputs the hardware needs, so the tool can already initialize a basic Hardware Diagram from the P&ID using a model to model transformation, without additional work for the user.

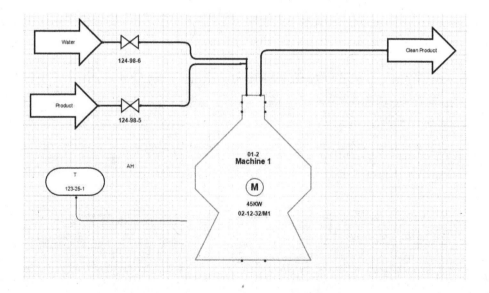

Fig. 2. Piping and Instrumentation Diagram

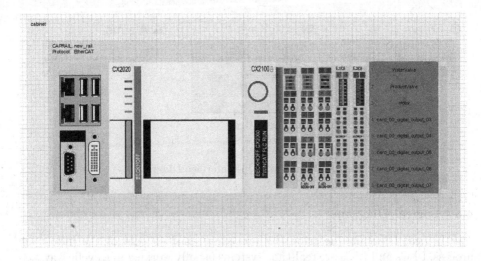

Fig. 3. Hardware Diagram

4.3   Hardware Diagram

The Hardware Diagram (cf. Fig. 3) specifies the arrangement of the hardware the generated software will later be executed on. It includes not only the IPC (in our case study a Beckhoff Embedded PC), but also the input and output components that link the software to the real-world control elements of the system.

This diagram is meant to be a direct representation of its real-world counterpart. The user can specify names for the different input and output ports, which are then used directly in the Logical Diagrams to read from or write to the according ports. Thus, this diagram defines the input and output variables for the Logical Diagrams.

As described in Sect. 3, one primary goal of our solution is the standardization. Since different target hardware from different manufacturers is of course not standardized, this Hardware Diagram will look different for different target platforms. However, the concept of the hardware diagram is still applicable, as the kind of information a (manufacturer-specific) variant holds can very well be standardized.

4.4   Human Machine Interface Diagram

In addition to the input and output variables of an industrial process, which are specified in the Hardware Diagram, a usual process also contains other variables. This includes timers, counters, alarms and HMI keys (user input variables). Later on, those variables will also be used to display the current situation of the system on the so-called Human Machine Interface (HMI), that is also providing the user with a way to interact with the machine. All those variables are managed in the Human Machine Interface Diagram (cf. Fig. 4). Like input and output variables, they can be read and modified (used) within the Logical Diagrams.

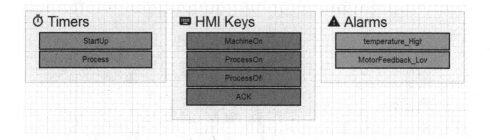

Fig. 4. Human Machine Interface Diagram

4.5   Logical Diagrams

The Logical Diagrams describe the procedure used to control the industrial process. PLCs and IPCs are real-time systems usually working in a cyclic way, i.e. a control cycle of fixed duration (usually a few milliseconds) consists of reading inputs, followed by calculating and setting outputs. Thus, in our diagrams the logical procedure is also modeled in a "per cycle" manner, stating the procedure that is happening in a single control cycle of the system.

To provide a more comprehensible representation of the process, the *IPSUM workflow* divides this logic into two layers. One layer represents *what* is happening using a state machine, the other defines *how* exactly it is happening using a flow chart.

State Machine Diagram. The upper layer of the Logical Diagrams is the State Machine Diagram. Most industrial processes include different stages of operation. In the case of our focus on industrial centrifuges these stages could, for example, be "filling the centrifuge", "processing the product", and "emptying the centrifuge". Each of these stages follows a different procedure and acts on different variables. Since most processes are much more complex, the State Machine Diagram gives the user the opportunity to sketch out the basic procedure. Similar to statecharts [3] and MathWorks Stateflow [7] the transitions between the stages are controlled through guard conditions, i.e. logical expressions over the variables of the system, which are evaluated on each control cycle. Each state contains its own Flow Graph Diagram, representing the control cycle for that state. In each cycle of the system, the current state's Flow Graph is executed, and afterwards the state for the upcoming cycle is determined.

Flow Graph Diagram. The Flow Graph models the logical procedure of a single process stage as introduced in Sect. 4.5. This diagram is loosely based on other sequential programming languages like Siemens' SIMATIC S7-GRAPH [10]. At the beginning of a cycle the Flow Graph Diagram of the currently active state from the State Machine Diagram is entered through a dedicated *start node*, and from there on the diagram is executed along its edges, controlled through boolean

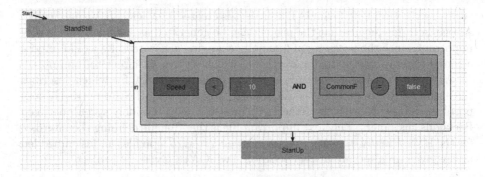

Fig. 5. State Machine Diagram

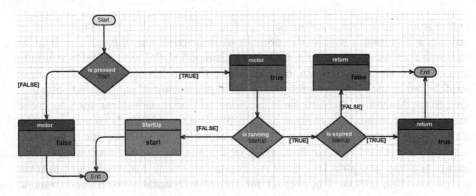

Fig. 6. Flow Graph Diagram

decisions, as well as *operations* performed on all types of variables provided by the Hardware Diagram (cf. Sect. 4.3) and the HMI Diagram (cf. Sect. 4.4). One cycle is finished as soon as the *end node* is reached.

Similar to classic flowcharts, the Flow Graph Diagram is basically providing the user with a type of "graphical programming language", which is easy to use, but powerful enough to fully generate code from.

5   Code Generation

After the creation of the different model types, code for the deployment on PLC or IPC is needed. The general idea of the code generation is to use the abstract specification provided by the models and translate it into executable code. At this point it doesn't matter which system is used for deployment. In our case study we used a Beckhoff IPC (as mentioned in Sect. 4), because their TwinCAT3 application allows an easy access for machine control programming. C++ is used as programming language and the files for the hardware and the HMI interface are written in XAML [8]. Moreover, the structure of the project folder is easy to verify, as the Beckhoff TwinCAT 3 project is created in Microsoft Visual Studio. Altogether, this means that the project can be generated as a whole. This is very important, since the necessity of manually changing generated files would impose a round-trip problem inducing overhead, which we overall intent to minimize.

As depicted in Fig. 1, the code generator generates an .xti file which describes the entire hardware and thus is the interface to I/O ports. IPSUM currently supports the hardware with the EtherCAT protocol, as it is widely spread between Beckhoffs customers. The next important file is the .tmc file defining the interface for the HMI. Finally, the program logic is generated to .cpp files and is embedded in the given architecture of the Beckhoff TwinCAT3 Cycle IO project.

6   Conclusion

Our project provided a proof of concept for model-driven development of automation software within the domain of industrial centrifuges. The IPSUM tool was successfully tested on a Beckhoff Embedded PC with simulated inputs and outputs, showing that standardization of the workflow and formalization of models can actually achieve fully automatic generation of the needed software. Our State Machine Diagram even provides an abstraction layer for the cyclic programming common in control systems like PLC and IPC. Currently, only the Flow Graph Diagram directly exposes this cyclic execution semantics, and their use can be reduced to a minimium by expressing all state-related information within a State Machine Diagram. As gaining feedback and realizing improvements based on it is very important for ensuring acceptance with practitioners, we are currently conducting user tests with process technicians to evaluate the usability of the IPSUM tool with our target group.

A crucial idea behind IPSUM is to provide an abstract level of modeling for industrial process automation that supports deployment on various kinds of different PLC or IPC systems (cf. Fig. 7). Ideally, a single tool can provide a fast solution for many different systems a customer may ask for. Thus, to validate our model abstraction, we plan to develop further code generators targeting different platforms, without needing to change the model structures. Furthermore, we will extend the scope of the project to also include the complete generation of

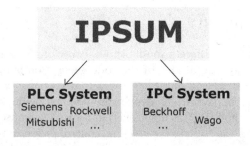

Fig. 7. IPSUM provides a model-based abstraction from PLC and IPC technologies

an HMI view using Beckhoff's ADS protocol in combination with our already existing HMI Diagram. With the upcoming "Industry 4.0" in mind and the development of standardized machine to machine communication [4], support for these protocols can even further expand the target market.

Acknowledgements. We thank the GEA Group AG for their constant support and for providing us with the necessary hardware. Also, a big thanks to the other members of the project team: Alexander Hornung, Fabian König, Clemens Classen, Johannes Lohmann, Johannes P. Neumann, Kristof Wilke, Laurette M. T. Mefowe, Niklas Ueter, Phillip A. Goldap and Viktor Noniev.

References

1. ISO 10628–1: 2015. International Organization for Standardization, 1st edn. Geneva, Switzerland, September 2014
2. Beckhoff: TwinCAT 3. http://www.beckhoff.de/twincat3, August 2016
3. Harel, D.: Statecharts: a visual formalism for complex systems. Sci. Comput. Program. **8**(3), 231–274 (1987)
4. Jeschke, S.: Standardization in the Era of 4.0. Presentation DKE-Conference 2016, May 2016
5. Margaria, T., Steffen, B.: Business process modelling in the jABC: the one-thing-approach. In: Cardoso, J., van der Aalst, W. (eds.) Handbook of Research on Business Process Modeling. IGI Global, Hershey (2009)
6. Marrano, S.J.: Process and Instrumentation Diagram Development in Water and Waste Water Treatment Plants
7. MathWorks: MathWorks.   http://www.mathworks.com/products/stateflow/, August 2016
8. Microsoft   Corporation: XAML.   https://msdn.microsoft.com/en-us/library/cc189054, August 2016
9. Naujokat, S., Lybecait, M., Kopetzki, D., Steffen, B.: CINCO: a simplicity-driven approach to full generation of domain-specific graphical modeling tools (2016, to appear)
10. Siemens: S7 Graph V5.1 for S7–300/400 Programming Sequential Control Systems, 5th edn. Siemens (2001)
11. Steffen, B., Naujokat, S.: Archimedean points: the essence for mastering change. In: LNCS Transactions on Foundations for Mastering Change (FoMaC), vol. 1(1) (2016)

RERS Challenge

RERS 2016: Parallel and Sequential Benchmarks with Focus on LTL Verification

Maren Geske[1]([✉]), Marc Jasper[1,2], Bernhard Steffen[1], Falk Howar[3],
Markus Schordan[2], and Jaco van de Pol[4]

[1] TU Dortmund University, Programming Systems, 44227 Dortmund, Germany
{maren.geske,marc.jasper,steffen}@cs.tu-dortmund.de
[2] Lawrence Livermore National Laboratory, Livermore, CA 94551, USA
{jasper3,schordan1}@llnl.gov
[3] Clausthal University of Technology, Clausthal-Zellerfeld, Germany
falk.howar@tu-clausthal.de
[4] University of Twente, Formal Methods and Tools, Enschede, The Netherlands
J.C.vandePol@utwente.nl

Abstract. The 5th challenge of Rigorous Examination of Reactive
Systems (RERS 2016) once again provided generated and tailored benchmarks suited for comparing the effectiveness of automatic software
verifiers. RERS is the only software verification challenge that features
problems with linear temporal logic (LTL) properties in larger sizes that
are available in different programming languages. This paper describes
the revised rules and the refined profile of the challenge, which lowers
the entry hurdle for new participants. The challenge format with its
three tracks, their benchmarks, and the related LTL and reachability
properties are explained. Special emphasis is put on changes that were
implemented in RERS — compared to former RERS challenges. The
competition comprised 18 sequential and 20 parallel benchmarks. The
20 benchmarks from the new parallel track feature LTL properties and a
compact representation as labeled transition systems and Promela code.

1 Introduction

The RERS challenge is an annual verification challenge that focuses on LTL
and reachability properties of reactive systems. The benchmarks are generated
automatically from automata which allows to generate new problems each year
that are previously unknown to the participants. The challenge was designed to
explore, evaluate and compare the capabilities of state-of-the-art software verification tools and techniques. Areas of interest include but are not limited to static
analysis [14], model checking [2,5,7], symbolic execution [11], and testing [4].

The focus of RERS is on principal capabilities and limitations of tools and
approaches. The RERS challenge is therefore "free-style", i.e., without time and
resource limitations and encouraging the combination of methods and tools.
Strict time or resource limitations in combination with previously known solutions encourage tools to be tweaked for certain training sets, which could give a

© Springer International Publishing AG 2016
T. Margaria and B. Steffen (Eds.): ISoLA 2016, Part II, LNCS 9953, pp. 787–803, 2016.
DOI: 10.1007/978-3-319-47169-3_59

false impression of their capabilities. It also leads to abandoning time consuming problems in the interest of time. The main goals of RERS[1] are:

1. encouraging the combination of methods from different (and usually disconnected) research fields for better software verification results,
2. providing a framework for an automated comparison based on differently tailored benchmarks that reveal the strengths and weaknesses of specific approaches,
3. initiating a discussion about better benchmark generation, reaching out across the usual community barriers to provide benchmarks useful for testing and comparing a wide variety of tools, and
4. collecting (additional) interesting syntactical features that should be supported by benchmark generators.

To the best of our knowledge there is no other software verification challenge with a profile that is similar to that of RERS. The SV-COMP[2] [3] challenge is also concerned with reachability properties and features a few benchmarks concerning termination and memory safety. In direct comparison, SV-COMP does not allow the combination of tools and directly addresses tool developers. It has time and resource limitations, does not feature achievements, but has developed a detailed ranking system for the comparison of tools and tries to prevent guessing by imposing high penalties on mistakes. An important difference to SV-COMP is that RERS features benchmarks that are generated automatically for each challenge iteration, ensuring that all results to the verification tasks are unknown to participants.

Another challenge concerned with the verification of parallel benchmarks in combination with LTL properties is the Model Checking Contest [12] (MCC). The participants have to analyze Petri nets as abstract models and check LTL and CTL formulas, the size of the state space, reachability, and various upper bounds. The benchmark set consists of a large set of known models and a small set of unknown models that were collected among the participants. Participants submit tools, rather than problem answers. Tools that participate in MCC have to adhere to resource restrictions, which is not the case when participating in RERS. MCC uses randomly generated LTL formulas, but uses no mechanism to generate models that match them. In direct comparison to RERS, MCC features hand-written or industrial problems instead of automatically generated benchmarks.

Finally, VerifyThis [10] features program verification challenges. Participants get a fixed amount of time to work on a number of challenges, to prove the functional correctness of a number of non-trivial algorithms. That competition focuses on the use of (semi-)interactive tools, and submissions are judged by a jury. In direct comparison, RERS participants submit results that can be checked and ranked automatically; only the "best approach award" involves a jury judgment.

---

[1] As stated online at http://www.rers-challenge.org/.

[2] https://sv-comp.sosy-lab.org/.

This paper describes the challenge procedure of RERS 2016 and presents the three different tracks: Sequential LTL, Sequential Reachability, and Parallel LTL. Parallel benchmarks are a new addition to the RERS challenge. Their structure and the format of the Parallel LTL track are introduced within the following sections. Simplifications for the sequential benchmarks that were made to lower the entry hurdle for new participants are explained and a new solution verification tool for training problems is introduced. Throughout this paper, special focus is set on the changes compared to former RERS challenges.

Section 2 describes the overall layout and timeline of the RERS challenge 2016. The three tracks and their benchmarks are explained in Sect. 3. Section 4 presents the structure of individual benchmark programs, whereas Sect. 5 showcases examples of the provided properties that participants have to analyze. The scoring scheme and the submission format are defined in Sect. 6. Section 7 briefly discusses the benchmark generation process before Sect. 8 presents a conclusion and an outlook to future developments.

2   Challenge Procedure

The RERS challenge 2016 features sequential and parallel benchmarks. The sequential problems are divided into two tracks according to their verification tasks, LTL properties and reachability of errors. The parallel track only focuses on LTL properties. All challenge tasks are newly generated for each competition so they are unknown to the participants prior to the competition. No training of verifiers on the benchmarks is possible as the solutions are only released after the challenge is completed. Instead, sets of training problems help participants to test their tools before submitting actual results.

2.1   Sequential Benchmarks

In every year RERS provides a couple of training problems that are available with solutions. These problems allow contestants to get a feeling for the sequential programs, the related verification tasks, and the syntactical features that are newly introduced in a particular year. In order to ease the initial adaptation effort for participants, a tool is provided that takes a training solution file and a proposed solution of the participant and calculates the correct and wrong answers and total points scored for the problem[3].

The challenge procedure starts off with the release of the training problems and their solutions. This is consistent with all former editions of the challenge [6, 9]. For this year's challenge, 8 training problems are provided for both sequential tracks, 16 problems in total with 100 properties each. A detailed description of the problem format can be found in Sect. 3. The training problems are small in size, but have the same complexity and syntax as the challenge problems for each category (i.e., plain, arithmetic, and data structures).

---

[3] www.rers-challenge.org/2016/index.php?page=trainingphase.

The challenge phase starts with the release of the actual benchmarks. The time between the release of the problems and the submission deadline was set to four and half months. There are 18 benchmarks, 9 for each of the two tracks, LTL and Reachability verification. Each benchmark comes with 100 properties of the track category that need to be verified or falsified. The verifiers do not have to be submitted. Only the given answers are evaluated for the final ranking and achievements. In addition, an award for the best approach is given out by the competition committee based on submitted descriptions.

2.2 Parallel Benchmarks

The parallel benchmarks of RERS are a new addition in 2016 and were released a few months later than the sequential problems. These 20 different problems from the parallel category feature from 1 to 20 parallel automata. They each come with 20 LTL properties that participants can analyze.

Participants had about four weeks for analyzing the parallel benchmarks. Because of this shorter time frame, separate training problems were omitted in favor of a structured sequence of problems with an increasing number of parallel automata. The first 5 problems can be analyzed completely by existing tools such as SPIN [8]. Their results can be used as a reference by participants which lowers the hurdle to enter the challenge.

3   Challenge Format and Categories

This section describes the verification tasks of the individual benchmarks and the different categories that the RERS 2016 challenge consists of.

3.1 Verification Tasks

Each sequential or parallel problem comes with 100 or 20 properties respectively. The participants have to check whether or not the individual properties are satisfied. The possible answers are defined as follows:

True. The property is satisfied, there exists no path that violates the property.
False. The property is violated, there exists at least one path that violates the property.
No answer given. The participant was not able to find an answer to this question.

The submission of counterexample traces for violated properties is not a requirement. Only the answers described above are used for the ranking and achievement evaluation (see Sect. 6).

3.2   Sequential Benchmarks

The sequential benchmarks are grouped into two tracks, i.e., LTL and Reachability, that correspond to the property type that has to be analyzed (see Sect. 5). The LTL properties are specified in additional files and distributed with the benchmark programs. Figure 1 gives an overview of the generated benchmarks and their respective category and track (dashed lines for Reachability, solid lines for LTL) and the achievements that can be gained (see Sect. 6 for details and thresholds). For each track there are three categories that represent the syntactical features included in the benchmarks belonging to the respective category.

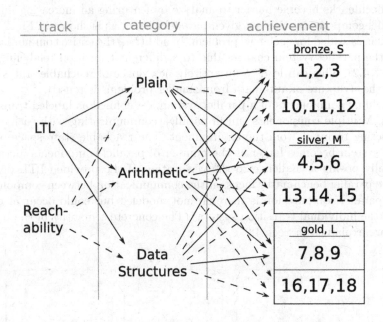

Fig. 1. Sequential benchmarks for RERS 2016

Plain. The program only contains assignments, with the exception of some scattered summation, subtraction, and remainder operations in the reachability problems.

Arithmetic. The programs frequently contain summation, subtraction, multiplication, division, and remainder operations.

Data structures. Arrays and operations on arrays are added. Other data structures are planned for the future.

Some of this year's problems from the plain category in the Reachability track also contain a few arithmetic operations. The LTL track is not affected. The reason for the existence of these operations is an improved method of inserting (un-)reachable errors into the program. Arithmetic operations in the plain category are planned to be removed for next year's challenge.

In the rightmost column of Fig. 1, the problem numbers are grouped according to the type of achievement that can be gained. The achievement levels also correspond to the size of the benchmarks: bronze are small, silver are medium-sized, and gold are large programs. In each line the first problem is of the *Plain* category, the middle of the *Arithmetic* and the last of the *Data Structures* category.

3.3   Parallel Benchmarks

The benchmarks in the parallel track of RERS 2016 form a sequence of problems with increasing difficulty. Instead of scaling complexity through code obfuscation, these benchmarks become harder to analyze by featuring an increasing number of parallel components within a given parallel system as is shown in Fig. 2. One component is added for each new problem. In addition, the entire communication within the parallel system changes due to a different transition relabeling (see also Sect. 4.2). This can lead to an entirely new space of reachable states even though the structure of automata from smaller problems is reused.

Individual components of a parallel system are defined as labeled transition systems. Multiple components run in parallel, communicating with each other, and reacting to input from the environment. The reachable state space of the parallel system becomes larger as the number of parallel components increases, potentially posing a challenge to the verification of the provided LTL properties. The parallel benchmarks focus on the communication between components. Actual parallel computation is therefore not modeled but could occur at every state of the individual transition systems. The concrete semantics of the benchmarks are explained in Sect. 4.2.

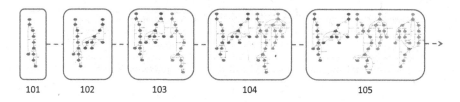

101   102   103   104   105

Fig. 2. Sequence of parallel benchmarks

4   Program Structure and Available Formats

The different types of programs that are part of the RERS 2016 benchmarks are explained in the following paragraphs, along with their structural properties and changes compared to previous challenge iterations.

4.1   Sequential Benchmarks

The sequential programs are available as C and Java code. The overall structure of the source code is the same for all of these benchmarks. They represent

```
int x1 = 1;                    int main() {
int x2 = 2;                      while (1) { // main i/o-loop
 ...                               int input;
void calc_output(int);           scanf("%d", &input);
                                 if((input != 2) && (input != 5)
int calc_output(int in) {        && (input != 1) &&
  if(in == 3 && x7 != 0) {       (input != 3) && (input != 4))
   x9 = 4;                            return -2;
   return 24;                     calc_output(input);
 }                             }
 ...                         }
}
```

(a) Variables and Control Logic   (b) Main Function with Infinite Loop

Fig. 3. Example of a sequential benchmark program in C

instances of event-condition-action systems that are used for example in logic controllers [1] and database management systems [13]. An illustrating code snippet is depicted in Fig. 3. Each program consists of a main function with an infinite while-loop that reads an input and passes it to the calc_output-function[4] that contains the program logic and computes an output. The logic is organized in nested if-else-blocks and contains syntactical operations according to the benchmark's category. Compilation instructions are provided on the website[5].

Improved Benchmark Code. In contrast to former challenges, all inputs that are not eligible are rejected before the internal logic is evaluated. This way the problems are now self-contained and it is not necessary anymore to pass the input alphabet to the verifier. Moreover, this change makes the main function equal to the versions of RERS 2012 benchmarks that are used in SV-COMP [3], allowing all participants to use their tools without modifications on the new benchmarks for 2016. In order to assure that the code is valid C++ code, all functions are previously defined.

Predefined Functions. In order to ease the entry level for new participants, the former "error syntax" (i.e., an assertion with the error number) has been removed from the benchmarks. It was replaced by an external function for C99 and C++ programs, e.g., _VERIFIER_error(5) for the error number 5, and by a static function of a fictional Errors class in Java, e.g., Errors._VERIFIER_error(5) for the error number 5. An implementation that simulates the semantics

---

[4] The name was shortened for space reasons, in the challenge the function is named calculate_output.
[5] Java version: http://rers-challenge.org/2016/index.php?page=java-code
C version: http://rers-challenge.org/2016/index.php?page=c-code.

```
void __VERIFIER_error(int);

void __VERIFIER_error(int i) {
  fprintf(stderr,"error_%d_",i);
  assert(0);
}
```

```
public class Errors {
  public static void
    __VERIFIER_error(int i) {
      throw new
      IllegalStateException(
        "error_" + i );
  }
}
```

(a) Reference Implementation in C99/C++

(b) Reference Implementation in Java

Fig. 4. Reference implementations for simulating pre-2016 error behavior

used in RERS prior to 2016 can be viewed in Fig. 4. The reference implementation can be replaced by a suitable implementation for the verifier or can just be interpreted semantically.

4.2   Parallel Benchmarks

The new parallel programs are available in two different formats. First, the benchmarks are represented as a cluster of labeled transition systems. Second, a Promela [8] version is provided that implements the transition systems as parallel processes.

Cluster of Labeled Transition Systems. Each benchmark is available as a DOT[6] graph (.dot file) containing the components of the parallel systems as clusters in a directed graph (Fig. 5). These clusters are understood as nondeterministic labeled transition systems. A run of such a transition system starts at the single state without incoming transitions. There are three types of labels within the transition systems:

Environment Input. Labels that only occur in a single transition system can be triggered independently, when they are enabled (e.g. "c1_t0" in Fig. 5b).
Empty Label. Similarly, transitions without a label are understood as internal transitions that can be triggered at any time. For RERS 2016, these only exist as initial transitions because they do not add to the communication with other components or the environment. As initial transitions however, empty labels help to ensure that both the DOT graph and the Promela code feature the same semantics regarding LTL properties.
Communication. Non-empty labels that occur in multiple transition systems are synchronized (rendezvous communication). They only exist in pairs and can only be triggered simultaneously, when they are both enabled (e.g., "c0_t0_c1_t2" in Fig. 5b).

---

[6] http://www.graphviz.org/content/dot-language.

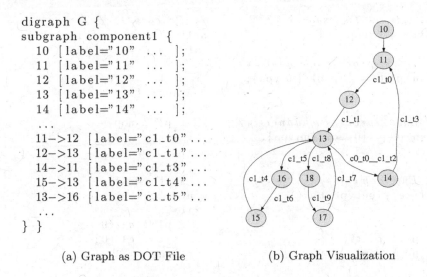

```
digraph G {
subgraph component1 {
   10 [label="10" ... ];
   11 [label="11" ... ];
   12 [label="12" ... ];
   13 [label="13" ... ];
   14 [label="14" ... ];
   ...
   11->12 [label="c1_t0" ...
   12->13 [label="c1_t1" ...
   14->11 [label="c1_t3" ...
   15->13 [label="c1_t4" ...
   13->16 [label="c1_t5" ...
   ...
} }
```

(a) Graph as DOT File   (b) Graph Visualization

Fig. 5. Component of a parallel system as DOT graph

A transition is enabled if and only if the corresponding components are currently in the states preceding that transition. The only known fact about the environment is that it does not introduce new deadlocks: One of the enabled transitions (if any) will eventually be triggered.

Promela Code. Each parallel benchmark is available as Promela code. An example is shown in Fig. 6: Within this version, every component of the parallel system is implemented as a parallel process (proctype). The environment is represented by an additional parallel process and sends random messages to the parallel components which triggers their transitions. All message channels are unbuffered to realize rendezvous communication. For simplicity, transition-system-internal empty labels in the graph representation are also triggered by the environment process in the Promela version (nop message). The rendezvous communication between different parallel components is also realized via message passing.

The Promela program contains a single global variable lastAction and an additional parallel process Listener. This listener gets notified about every message that is sent in between the parallel components or between the parallel system and the environment. The listener always stores the most recent message in lastAction. The sequence of values stored in variable lastAction describes an abstract trace of the Promela program that matches the trace of transitions in the respective cluster of labeled transition systems. The LTL properties are therefore defined based on the content of variable lastAction (see also Sect. 5.1). Note that the addition of this variable increases the state space, which would be unnecessary for solutions that are based on action-based properties.

```
/* Actions (messages) */
mtype = { nop, c1_t7, ...
```

```
/* Inter-process channels */
chan p1_0 = [0] of {mtype};
...
```

```
/* Env<->process channels */
chan p0 = [0] of {mtype};
...
```

```
/* Environment */
active proctype Env()
{
do
:: p1 ! c1_t7
:: p0 ! nop
...
od
}
```

```
/* Action channel */
chan act = [0] of {mtype};
```

```
/* Most recent message */
mtype lastAction = nop;
```

```
/* Action listener */
active proctype Listener() {
atomic {
do
:: act ? lastAction ->
step: skip
od
} }
```

```
/* Process 1 */
active proctype Proc1() {
int state = 10;
do
:: state == 10 ->
atomic {
if
:: p1 ? nop ->
state = 11;
fi
}
:: state == 11 ->
atomic {
if
:: p1 ? c1_t0 ->
act ! c1_t0;
state = 12;
fi
}
...
:: state == 13 ->
atomic {
if
:: p1 ? c1_t5 ->
act ! c1_t5;
state = 16;
:: p1 ? c1_t8 ->
act ! c1_t8;
state = 18;
:: p1_0 ! c0_t0__c1_t2 ->
state = 14;
fi
}
...
}
```

(a) channels, environment, and listener　　　(b) parallel component from Figure 5

Fig. 6. Promela code example

5　Properties and Their Representation

The sequential benchmarks contain the two tracks: LTL and Reachability. The new parallel problems only provide LTL properties. As mentioned in Sect. 4, the sequential benchmarks are now designed to only contain properties of their respective track type instead of both (which was the case in former challenges). The separation of properties leads to a more understandable semantics of the LTL properties: In past challenges, a definition of "error-free behavior" was required to specify on which execution paths the LTL properties needed to be checked.

5.1 LTL Properties

This section explains the structure of the LTL properties provided as part of the RERS challenge benchmarks.

Sequential Benchmarks. For each sequential problem in the LTL track there are 100 LTL formulas that have to be checked. The properties are provided in a property file (extension .txt) and contain the input and output symbols that are used within these formulas. Figure 7 shows an exemplary property file for a sequential benchmark. Each formula has an identifying number marked by # and ranging from 0 to 99. This identifier is followed by a textual description of the property. The following line contains the actual LTL property formulated in the syntax and semantics already explained in [16].

```
#inputs  [[A, B, C, D, E]]
#outputs  [[X, Y, Z, U, V, W, S, T]]
#0: output W, output V responds to input C after output U
( false R (! oU | ( false R (! iC | (oW & X ( true U oV ))))))

#1: input B precedes output Y before output X
(! ( true U oX) | (! oY U (iB | oX)))
```

Fig. 7. Extract from an LTL property file (sequential benchmark)

Parallel Benchmarks. The parallel benchmarks include property files similar to the sequential ones described above. Instead of specifying input-output behavior, they contain LTL formulas over transition labels in the respective parallel automata. For the LTL verification, a trace of a parallel benchmark is always understood as its sequence of transition labels. The declaration of specific alphabets is therefore omitted. To simplify the representation, these LTL formulas contain some additional operators such as => for the regular implication[7]. Currently, no textual description of the LTL properties is provided for parallel benchmarks.

In addition to being included in the property files (.txt), the LTL properties are directly part of the Promela code (.pml). Within the Promela file, the formulas are represented in an equivalent SPIN syntax. Figure 8 shows an example of one LTL property in both RERS and SPIN representations (see Footnote 7) (W and V meaning "weak until" and "release", respectively). The #define statements are taken from the Promela code and ensure that only those messages received by the listener count as transitions for the LTL properties (see Sect. 4.2).

---

[7] For detailed definitions, please refer to https://spot.lrde.epita.fr/trans.html.

#4:
(G(c2_t9 => (! c2_t6 W c4_t3)))

(a) RERS Property File

```
#define  p_c2_t9  (lastAction == c2_t9)
#define  p_c4_t3  (lastAction == c4_t3)
#define  p_c2_t6  (lastAction == c2_t6)

ltl  p4 { [](! p_c2_t9 || (p_c4_t3 V (! p_c2_t6 || p_c4_t3))) }
```

(b) Promela Version

Fig. 8. An LTL property from a parallel benchmark

5.2   Reachability Properties

Each sequential Reachability problem comes with 100 properties that have to be analyzed. Other than the LTL properties, the Reachability properties are implicitly provided in the program's source code in form of error function calls that are described in Sect. 4.1. The number that is passed to the predefined function call corresponds to the error number and falls in the range of 0 and 99. A property to be verified or falsified is that the error function _VERIFIER_error(x) is never executed for some particular x in the range of 0 to 99.

6   Scoring Scheme

RERS has a 3-dimensional reward structure that consists of a competition-based ranking on the total number of points, achievements for solving benchmarks, and an evaluation-based award for the most original idea or a good combination of methods. Apart from the evaluation-based ranking, both the achievements and the competition rules have been changed for this year's competition to make the challenge more appealing to participants.

The new parallel benchmarks only feature a ranking based on the achieved score, achievements in this track are left for future iterations of RERS. As participating with someone else's tool is possible in all tracks, each tool used by the participant is listed with his or her submission. This ensures that no tool can be discredited by improper usage.

6.1   Achievements

To honor the accomplishments of verification tools and methods without the pressure of losing in a competition despite good results, RERS introduced achievements for different nuances of difficulty. For every sequential category there are 3 achievements: bronze, silver and gold. Achievements are awarded for reaching a threshold of points that is equal to the number of counterexamples that can be witnessed for the corresponding group of benchmarks, as long as no wrong answer is given. Counterexamples are paths reaching an error function for the Reachability track and paths violating LTL properties for the LTL track. Only the highest achievement for every category is awarded and the thresholds for every category are calculated as follows:

- $bronze$ = #falsifiable properties of small problem
- $silver$ = $bronze$ + #falsifiable properties of medium problem
- $gold$ = $silver$ + #falsifiable properties of large problem

The participant's achievement score within a category is computed from all submitted results (verified or falsified):

$$
\text{achievement\_score}(category) = \begin{cases} (\#\text{submitted}(category, small) & \text{if } 100\,\% \\ + \#\text{submitted}(category, medium) & \text{correct} \\ + \#\text{submitted}(category, large)) & \text{results} \\ 0 & \text{otherwise} \end{cases}
$$

For example let achievement_score($plain$) $>=$ $bronze(plain)$ and achievement_score($plain$) $<$ $silver(plain)$, then the participant is awarded the Bronze Achievement in the plain category. In total it is possible to gain 6 achievements, 3 for each sequential track, matching the number of different categories within a track.

6.2 Competition-Based Ranking

The most significant change compared to previous iterations is that RERS 2016 has no overall ranking for the whole challenge anymore, but separate rankings for each track. This will highlight specialized tools that are excellent in a single track, but do not contribute to other tracks. Moreover, only one submission is allowed for both the achievements and the ranking for sequential problems. Reducing the submission to a single set of answers should prevent guessing of unknown properties. Previous RERS issues allowed a restricted form of guessing by having a mild penalty for wrong answers. The motivation was to differentiate incomplete approaches that cover large parts of the state space from approaches that only covered a small part. The current issue discourages guessing, since we want to focus on solutions for complete verification or falsification. Therefore, we considerably raised the penalty for wrong solutions. Participants can opt out of the ranking and will thus only appear on the website if they successfully gained an achievement. The scoring scheme for the competition ranking works as follows.

Correct answer. The participant receives 1 point.

No answer. The score remains unchanged if no answer was submitted.

Incorrect answer. The penalty is calculated over all mistakes in a track and corresponds to an exponential penalty for all mistakes of 2 to the power of n, where n is the number of mistakes made.

The revised penalty for mistakes hardly punishes unexpected mistakes, which can always happen by programming mistakes for example. However, the penalty for systematic guessing, which usually produces several mistakes, is severe.

6.3   Solution Format

The solution format is straightforward and has to be submitted in comma-separated value (CSV) format. An example can be seen in Fig. 9 where

- **no** is the problem number (unique for the challenge)
- **spec** is the property specification number (error code or number of the LTL property in the LTL property file)
- **answer** expresses whether or not the property is satisfied, i.e., the LTL formula is satisfied or the error function call is unreachable. It can be specified as true/false, yes/no or 1/0.

$$<\text{no}1>,<\text{spec}1>,<\text{answer}1>$$
$$<\text{no}2>,<\text{spec}2>,<\text{answer}2>$$
$$\dots$$

Fig. 9. Format for submitted solutions

7   Generation Process

This section explains how the sequential benchmark generation in 2016 differs when compared to previous iterations of the RERS challenge and briefly sketches the generation of the parallel benchmarks. An overview of the abstract generation process and all generated files is included in Fig. 10.

The parallel benchmark generation uses a new concept and has been implemented in the tool CodeThorn that is based on the ROSE compiler infrastructure [15]. As a first step, the set of parallel automata is generated and a graphical DOT representation is exported to give an overview of the system. LTL formulas are then automatically generated, tested, and 20 difficult properties are selected. Afterwards, a Promela version of the parallel system is generated that includes the LTL formulas. These properties are also exported as separate solution and property files. Details of the generation process will be explained in an upcoming paper.

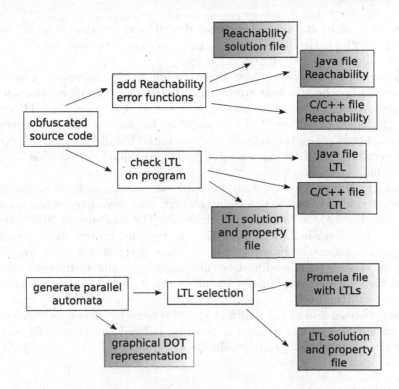

Fig. 10. Benchmark generation for RERS 2016

The process to generate the sequential benchmarks remained the same as in [16]. Figure 10 shows how it diverges after the basic skeleton of the obfuscated source code has been created. In former challenges all properties were used for all types of benchmarks. In comparison, RERS 2016 separated LTL and Reachability properties to make the challenge more transparent. The only change to the generator when compared to former challenges is that instead of inserting error function into all problems, they are only added to the Reachability benchmarks for which no property file is exported. Only for the LTL benchmarks the LTL properties are checked and exported as a solution and property file. The language export of the sequential benchmarks is not specific to the benchmark track or category and generates a Java and C99 version for each benchmark.

8   Conclusion and Perspectives

The RERS challenge 2016 was the fifth iteration of the challenge and was used to establish a clearer profile and strengthen the position as an LTL challenge. The reachability properties were separated from LTL properties to ease the entry hurdle and to remove misunderstandings concerning the semantic of an "error-free" behavior from former challenges. The rules were slightly adapted to further discourage guessing of results. This paper describes all changes compared to the challenge of 2015 in detail and gives a clear overview of the structure and rules that are valid for the 2016 RERS challenge.

Furthermore, we added a new aspect to automatic benchmark generation with parallel benchmarks that are provided both as a graph representation and as Promela code. Parallel benchmarks are used to strengthen the LTL aspect of the challenge, by adding 20 LTL properties for each of the 20 problems in the parallel track. We plan to build on these initial parallel benchmarks during future iterations of RERS, for example by adding additional versions in other programming languages.

Looking back at the evolution of RERS, the challenge in 2012 contained only simple programs from the plain category that were later enhanced with arithmetic calculations for the online challenge. The challenge in 2013 featured white-box and black-box problems with more complex control structures. 2014 added data structures to the set of available syntactical features and extended the variety of available small modifications like larger input alphabets. The challenge in 2015 finally added benchmarks for monitoring as it was co-located with the conference on Runtime Verification[8].

The long-term goal of the RERS challenge is to establish open source benchmark generators that can be used to generate tailored benchmarks for an easy comparison of different tools and techniques.

References

1. Almeida, E.E., Luntz, J.E., Tilbury, D.M.: Event-condition-action systems for reconfigurable logic control. IEEE Trans. Autom. Sci. Eng. **4**(2), 167–181 (2007)
2. Beyer, D.: Status report on software verification. In: Ábrahám, E., Havelund, K. (eds.) TACAS 2014. LNCS, vol. 8413, pp. 373–388. Springer, Heidelberg (2014). doi:10.1007/978-3-642-54862-8_25
3. Beyer, D.: Reliable and reproducible competition results with benchexec and witnesses (report on SV-COMP 2016). In: Chechik, M., Raskin, J.-F. (eds.) TACAS 2016. LNCS, vol. 9636, pp. 887–904. Springer, Heidelberg (2016). doi:10.1007/978-3-662-49674-9_55
4. Broy, M., Jonsson, B., Katoen, J.-P., Leucker, M., Pretschner, A. (eds.): Model-Based Testing of Reactive Systems. LNCS, vol. 3472. Springer, Heidelberg (2005)
5. Clarke, E.M., Grumberg, O., Peled, D.: Model Checking. MIT Press, Cambridge (2001)
6. Geske, M., Isberner, M., Steffen, B.: Rigorous examination of reactive systems: the RERS challenge 2015. In: Bartocci, E., Majumdar, R. (eds.) RV 2015. LNCS, vol. 9333, pp. 423–429. Springer, Heidelberg (2015). doi:10.1007/978-3-319-23820-3_28
7. Holzmann, G.J., Smith, M.H.: Software model checking: extracting verification models from source code. Softw. Test. Verification Reliab. **11**(2), 65–79 (2001)
8. Holzmann, G.: The SPIN Model Checker: Primer and Reference Manual, 1st edn. Addison-Wesley Professional (2011)

---

[8] http://rv2015.conf.tuwien.ac.at/.

9. Howar, F., Isberner, M., Merten, M., Steffen, B., Beyer, D., Păsăreanu, C.: Rigorous examination of reactive systems. The RERS challenges 2012 and 2013. Softw. Tools Technol. Transfer **16**(5), 457–464 (2014)

10. Huisman, M., Klebanov, V., Monahan, R.: VerifyThis 2012 - a program verification competition. STTT **17**(6), 647–657 (2015)

11. King, J.C.: Symbolic execution and program testing. Commun. ACM **19**(7), 385–394 (1976)

12. Kordon, F., Garavel, H., Hillah, L.M., Hulin-Hubard, F., Chiardo, G., Hamez, A., Jezequel, L., Miner, A., Meijer, J., Paviot-Adet, E., Racordon, D., Rodriguez, C., Rohr, C., Srba, J., Thierry-Mieg, Y., Trinh, G., Wolf, K.: Complete Results for the 2016 Edition of the Model Checking Contest, June 2016. http://mcc.lip6.fr/2016/results.php

13. McCarthy, D., Dayal, U.: The architecture of an active database management system. ACM Sigmod Rec. **18**(2), 215–224 (1989). ACM

14. Nielson, F., Nielson, H.R., Hankin, C.: Principles of Program Analysis. Springer, Heidelberg (1999)

15. Schordan, M., Quinlan, D.: A source-to-source architecture for user-defined optimizations. In: Böszörményi, L., Schojer, P. (eds.) JMLC 2003. LNCS, vol. 2789, pp. 214–223. Springer, Heidelberg (2003). doi:10.1007/978-3-540-45213-3_27

16. Steffen, B., Isberner, M., Naujokat, S., Margaria, T., Geske, M.: Property-driven benchmark generation: synthesizing programs of realistic structure. Softw. Tools Technol. Transfer **16**(5), 465–479 (2014)

STRESS

Introduction

Welcome to STRESS 2016, the *4th International School on Tool-based Rigorous Engineering of Software Systems* held in Imperial, Corfu (Greece) on October 2016, 5–9th in association with ISoLA 2016.

Following the tradition of its predecessors held 2006 in Dortmund, 2012 in Crete, and 2014 in Corfu, this year's School followed aims to provide top-quality lectures and innovative pedagogical material that provide young researchers with instruction in existing and emerging formal methods and software engineering techniques that are tool-supported and process-oriented, providing insights into how software is developed in the real world. This includes domains such as safety/mission-critical software and embedded systems where the development effort associated with tool-based formal methods promises greatest returns. It also presents case studies and example domains where formal methods have been successfully translated into actual development, along with insights in how to bridge the gap between research tools and actual development processes.

The School program includes four units of core STRESS instruction

- **Simplicity-Driven Development of Domain-Tailored Modeling Environments**, by Stefan Naujokat, Johannes Neubauer, and Bernhard Steffen (TU Dortmund, Germany), described in detail [1].
- **Towards a Holistic Security Concept**, by Tiziana Margaria and Anna-Lena Lamprecht (University of Limerick and Lero – The Irish Software Research Centre, Ireland) and Antonio Varriale (Blu5 Labs, Malta).
- **Verification Techniques for Hybrid Systems**, by Pavithra Prabhakar (Kansas State University, USA), described in detail in [2].
- **On the Power of Statistical Model Checking**, by Axel Legay (INRIA, Rennes, France) and Kim G. Larsen (Aalborg University, Denmark), described in detail in [3].

This year it also incorporates a fifth element

- **Soft Skills: Getting to Yes**, by Barry D. Floyd (California Polytechnic University), Tiziana Margaria (University of Limerick and Lero – The Irish Software Research Centre, Ireland), and Barbara Steffen (Erasmus University Rotterdam, The Netherlands) that delivers additional pedagogical resources and personal interactive experiences in the area of "graduate attributes", for the purpose of increasing the communication and negotiation skills of the participants.

In **Towards a Holistic Security Concept**, the presenters build on the ongoing work in a joint project between Lero and Blu5 Labs that tackles the model driven design and enforcement of holistic security, from the chip to the application layer. One of the limiting factors to achieve integrated security is the lack of coordination between the different layers of security that individually cover the layers of the IT stack. Today, hardware, operating system, middleware, virtualization layer, and the many layers and components that constitute a user-facing application - including data and persistency, and the communication over networks - are still developed and protected largely independently, with little inherent integration. Data at rest, data in motion, communication access and governance, as well as system evolution (e.g., through updates) are managed individually, too often under the responsibility of different actors, different technologies, different products and vendors. In this context, concerns of holistic security are growing, and call for a better integration and communication across the different layers.

This contribution, based on the work presented at the Special Track "End-to-end security and Cybersecurity: from the Hardware to application" held at SAM 2016 this July [4], illustrates how a partnership of different actors (SME vendors in security, leading edge research institutions, customers/users) gathers to create an open source platform based on the technologies presented during the previous day that integrates all these layers.

We thank the ISoLA organizers, the local Organization Chair, Petros Stratis, and the EasyConferences team for their continuous precious support during the week. Special thanks are due to our home institutions for their endorsement.

October 2016

Kerkyra, Corfu
John Hatcliff
Tiziana Margaria
Robby
Bernhard Steffen

References

1. Boßelmann, S., et al.: DIME: a programming-less modeling environment for web applications. In: Margaria, T., Steffen, B. (eds.) ISoLA 2016, Part II, LNCS 9953, pp. 809–832. Springer, Switzerland (2016)
2. Prabhakar, P., Soto, M.G., Lal, R.: Verification techniques for hybrid Systems. In: Margaria, T., Steffen, B. (eds.) ISoLA 2016, Part II, LNCS 9953, pp. 833–842. Springer, Switzerland (2016)
3. Legay, A., Larsen, K.G.: On the power of statistical model checking. In: Margaria, T., Steffen, B. (eds.) ISoLA 2016, Part II, LNCS 9953, pp. 843–862. Springer, Switzerland (2016)
4. Margaria, T., Varriale, A.: Special track on end-to-end security and cybersecurity: from the hardware to application (6 papers). In: Proceedings of SAM 2016, International Conference on Security and Management, pp. 131–173 (2016)

DIME: A Programming-Less Modeling Environment for Web Applications

Steve Boßelmann, Markus Frohme, Dawid Kopetzki, Michael Lybecait,
Stefan Naujokat, Johannes Neubauer[(✉)], Dominic Wirkner,
Philip Zweihoff, and Bernhard Steffen

Chair for Programming Systems, TU Dortmund, Dortmund, Germany
{steve.bosselmann,markus.frohme,dawid.kopetzki,michael.lybecait,
stefan.naujokat,johannes.neubauer,dominic.wirkner,philip.zweihoff,
bernhard.steffen}@tu-dortmund.de

Abstract. We present DIME, an integrated solution for the rigorous
model-driven development of sophisticated web applications based on
the Dynamic Web Application (DyWA) framework, that is designed to
accelerate the realization of requirements in agile development environments. DIME provides a family of Graphical Domain-Specific Languages
(GDSLs), each of which is tailored towards a specific aspect of typical
web applications, including persistent entities (i.e., a data model), business logic in form of various types of process models, the structure of
the user interface, and access control. They are modeled on a high level
of abstraction in a simplicity-driven fashion that focuses on describing
what application is sought, instead of *how* the application is realized. The
choice of platform, programming language, and frameworks is moved to
the corresponding (full) code generator.

1 Introduction

The *DIME* (DyWA Integrated Modeling Environment) approach [3] is a consequent refinement of the realization of *jABC4* [14] for process modeling
and *DyWA* [13] (Dynamic Web Application) for data modeling, empowering
prototype-driven application development. In the spirit of its predecessors, DIME
follows *OTA* (One Thing Approach) [4] and *XMDD* (eXtreme Model-Driven
Design) [7] and puts the application expert (a potential non-programmer) in the
center of the development process. Hence, the different aspects of an application are described with the most adequate form of model, respectively. All these
models are interdependently connected, shaping the "one thing" in a very formal
yet easy to understand and to use manner to the extend that it can be one-click-generated to a running application. DIME can be used to realize a wide range
of web applications. We are just starting to explore its potential. Central design
goals on this journey are simplicity [11], agility [6], and quality assurance [19].

An application modeler specifies various graphical models of dedicated
Graphical Domain-Specific Languages (GDSLs) in DIME that cover different
aspects of the target application, raising development tasks to the user level.

© Springer International Publishing AG 2016
T. Margaria and B. Steffen (Eds.): ISoLA 2016, Part II, LNCS 9953, pp. 809–832, 2016.
DOI: 10.1007/978-3-319-47169-3_60

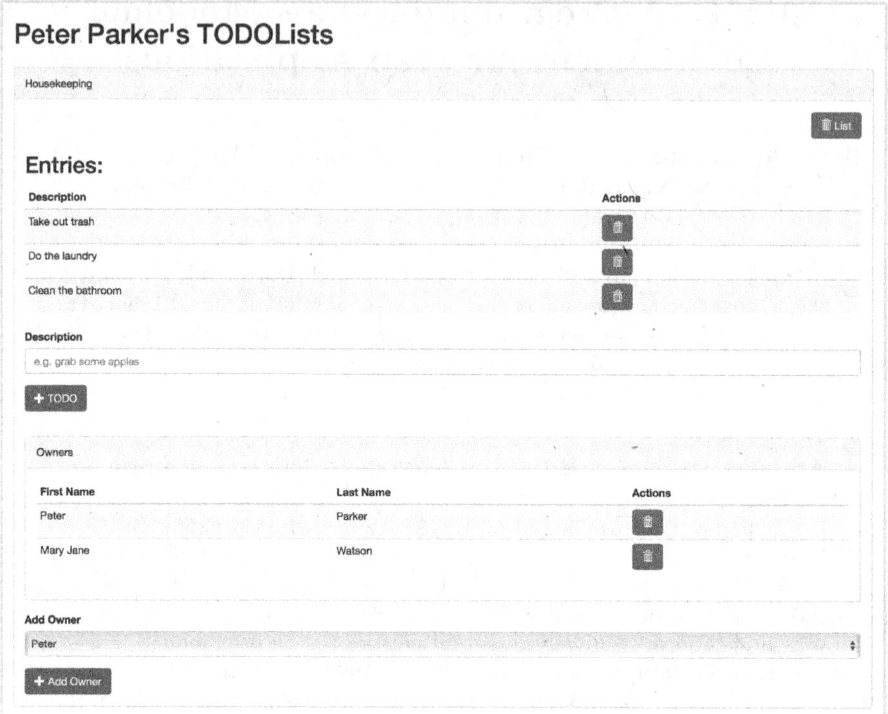

Fig. 1. Screenshot of the TODO-app

Each model is validated at design time to guide the correct syntactical and semantical use of components, ensuring the intended behavior. These models form the input for a subsequent product generation step by means of model to code transformation. The target application is assembled from a variety of generated files that contain the respective source code. The runtime environment for this product generation is the DyWA framework that fosters prototype-driven development of web applications throughout the whole application life-cycle in a service-oriented manner [9]. In short, modeling and code generation is done in DIME whereas DyWA supports the product deployment phase, constitutes the actual runtime environment, and manages data persistence. Furthermore, DyWA explicitly enables and supports continuous evolution in the sense of continuous model-driven engineering [5] in a rigorous manner, which supports iterations through the product re-design, re-generation and re-deployment cycle.

The DIME approach provides the user with both an early prototype of an up-and-running web application from the very beginning of the development process as well as explicit support for product evolution due to the agile nature of version management regarding data handling and persistence by the DyWA framework. Altogether, the approach has the potential to tremendously shorten development cycles in an agile but consistent manner.

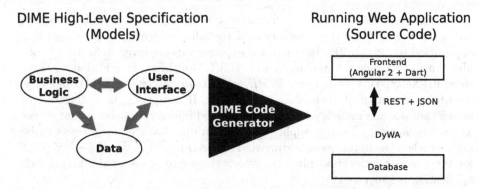

DIME High-Level Specification (Models)

Running Web Application (Source Code)

Fig. 2. The DIME concept: full generation of web applications from abstract model specifications

In the course of this tutorial paper the presented modeling concepts are illustrated by means of a simple example application called *TODO-app*. Basically this application allows (logged-in) users to manage *lists of todos*, i.e. tasks that need to be done. Every user can create multiple todo lists as well as multiple *todo entries* per list. In addition to this, todo lists may be shared with other users allowing them to also add or delete entries. Figure 1 gives an impression of the finished web application generated with DIME. The TODO-app presented in this paper is a simplified variant (for presentation purposes) of the one shipped with the example projects of DIME, which are accessible via the "New DIME Example App" action in DIME's project explorer.

For an easy distinction between concepts and tutorial-like descriptions, the latter are presented in grey boxes. The autumn school STRESS[1] comprises a corresponding step-by-step tutorial introduction.

The rest of the paper is organized as follows: While Sect. 2 briefly introduces the high-level modeling concepts realized with DIME, its user interface is described in Sect. 3. The GDSLs for data, processes, and presentation are explained in Sects. 4, 5, and 6, respectively. Section 7 summarizes and provides an outlook to future development.

2 High-Level Modeling Concept

Each model type in DIME is a graphical modeling language specialized to certain aspects of the target web application. They all comprise (different types of) *nodes* and *edges* as the basic components of graph models as well as *containers*, which are special nodes that can contain other nodes. Graphical modeling is primarily done by means of drag and drop of components in interaction with the *canvas* of the *diagram editor*.

---

[1] http://santos.cs.ksu.edu/STRESS/2016/index.html.

Available model types are briefly introduced in the following subsections to give an overview of how they together form the full specification of the target web application (cf. Figure 2). More detailed explanations are given in Sects. 4 (Data Modeling), 5 (Process Modeling) and 6 (GUI Modeling). In addition to these three model types, a designated *DIME application descriptor* (DAD) model is used to specify artifacts belonging to a project. It comprises the declaration of all relevant domain models as well as a dedicated interaction process that serves as the landing page for the application and an optional startup process to be invoked when the application is started. The DAD model is also the entry point for the product generation phase in which the source code of the target web application is generated.

2.1   Data

Data models form the basic domain model for any DIME application. The model structure is based on common data modeling concepts in terms of (concrete and abstract) types with inheritance, attributes, and relations (i.e. unidirectional and bidirectional associations) between them. Visually, they resemble *UML class diagrams* [16] as they are widespread and usually quite well understood.

Web applications usually rely on a database for persisting information. Applications generated with DIME do so as well, but only behind the scenes. Its programming-free data modeling on the user level provides an abstraction layer. The actual database access is done by the DyWA framework. The generated code just calls the API of the DyWA framework, so that the modeler does not need to handle technical details like table designs, file I/O, or transactions.

2.2   Business Logic

Process models define the *business logic* in DIME. They are conceptually based on jABC4 [8,15,18], a framework for graphically modeling an application's business logic with so-called *service logic graphs* (SLGs). Most important for jABC's SLGs (and thus also for DIME process models) is the notion of *service independent building blocks* (SIBs), which are executable and reusable modeling components the process models are composed of. A SIB can directly represent an implementation (called *native SIB* in DIME) or another process (called *process SIB* in DIME), with the latter enabling to model hierarchical service structures [17]. SIBs are integrated by dragging from a list of available SIBs and dropping on the modeling canvas. This triggers the creation of a node representing the respective SIB.

In DIME, business logic is defined with different process model types, each of them tailored towards specific aspects of a web application's behavior: short-running data processing, long-running workflows, structures for the frontend resembling a sitemap and access control decisions based on the logged-in user as well as his relation to entities in the system. Each of those process types follows certain rules regarding which kind of SIBs may be integrated. However,

to provide a consistent usability experience for the modeler, the general handling
.and graphical syntax is basically the same for all types of SIBs and processes.

Data-flow is also explicitly modeled within process models. SIBs have input
and output ports that can be either connected directly with each other or used
to read and write from/to variables placed in a dedicated container representing
the *data context*. This is a consequent evolution of the jABC principles: jABC
already had a data context for over a decade, but access to it was implicit, i.e. hidden within the SIBs' implementations. Then, jABC4[2] introduced typed, explicit
data-flow declarations (with inputs and outputs on SIBs) including parametric
polymorphism, but they were not directly visible in the model. DIME's process
models now show the data-flow information within the graphical representation
of the models in a dedicated view.

Native SIBs are defined with an additional model type, which is currently
the only textual modeling language of DIME. Models of this type form *native
SIB libraries* that essentially declare SIBs with their branches (cf. Sect. 5.1)
as well as input/output types and assign Java methods that contain the SIBs'
implementations. Additionally, special *native types*, which map to an arbitrary
Java type, can be declared and used in variables and native SIBs. However, in
contrast to the types defined in DIME's data model, the native types' inner
structure is not visible on the modeling level so that their instances are just
annotated with a type and can be passed through processes and native SIBs.
This is an important design-decision: similar to native SIBs, which facilitate
service orientation on a behavioral level, native types enable interoperability on
a structural level.

2.3   User Interface

For the definition of the target web application's user interfaces DIME supports
dedicated *GUI models* which reflect the structure of the individual web pages.
They can be included as *GUI SIBs* within the *sitemap processes* and are also
reusable within other GUI models to build hierarchical structures and prevent
redundancy in modeling.

While GUI models do not express control-flow, they have a data-binding
mechanism very similar to the data-flow modeling in DIME's process models,
i.e. a container representing the data context. Various types of edges for data-
binding exist to connect those variables with data-sensitive GUI components.
This way, both data visualization as well as write operations can be modeled.

3   Modeling Environment

DIME has been specifically tailored towards simplification of recurrent modeling
steps, i.e. to provide guidance for the user by means of quick access to available
model entities and relevant properties. This section provides a short overview of
the DIME user interface as well as more details on the structural properties of
the various models and on features supporting the developer during modeling.

---

[2] http://hope.scce.info.

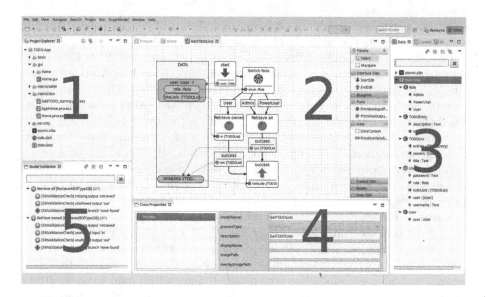

Fig. 3. User interface of DIME with exemplary arrangement of views: (1) *project explorer*. (2) *diagram editor* with *built-in component palette*. (3) *model component views*. (4) *properties view*. (5) *model validation view*

DIME is based on the *Eclipse Rich Client Platform* (RCP) [10] and developed with the Cinco *SCCE Meta Tooling Suite* [12]. As an RCP application, DIME consists of a set of plug-ins for the Eclipse framework that provide support for effective model editing and specific *views*[3] on models in the current workspace. DIME's view components provide dense overviews as well as quick access to the models, their components, and to detailed model information. Figure 3 exemplarily depicts an arrangement of these views constituting the user interface of DIME. They follow simple and standard principles of user interface design. The shown information is structured in tree-based views. Moreover, the model component views as well as the model validation view share the same arrangement of user interface components (see Fig. 4): a button to refresh the view and buttons to fully expand or collapse the tree. Additionally, there is a full-text search underneath the toolbar to filter subtrees based on the displayed tree node labels, and from the context menu opened with a right-click on a model or data type the respective model is opened with the corresponding node (if applicable) being highlighted.

3.1 Project Explorer

The *project explorer* is a standard user interface component of Eclipse and lists all projects contained in the *workspace* selected on launch. It mostly serves the purpose to navigate through folders for opening models and other files.

---

[3] In the context of Eclipse views denote the 'subwindows' usually arranged around the main editor.

3.2 Diagram Editor

The *diagram editor* is situated in the middle of the DIME interface and provides the canvas to create graphical models. A *built-in component palette* on the right of the canvas contains the basic modeling components for the respective model type.

A new node is created via drag and drop of an entry in the palette to the canvas. Hovering with the mouse over a node overlays a menu with actions like "delete node" and "create edge". Two nodes can be connected via an edge by drag and drop of the corresponding action onto the target node. A fixed set of rules defines whether an edge may connect a node to another. If multiple edge types are allowed, a context menu for selection appears after the aforementioned drag and drop. The route of an edge can be modified via *bending points*.

It is possible to have multiple models opened at the same time. They are arranged in tabs, but only one model can be active at a time and is shown in the canvas.

3.3 Model Component Views

The *data component view* (Fig. 4a) lists all data models and native types in the current project. They can be dragged and dropped on the canvas in order to model data exchange or data manipulation in various contexts. An icon indicates the type of an element. To simplify handling of multiple and very large data models, the user can switch between two *display modes*: *hierarchical* and *flat*. They can be selected in the menu next to the *tool bar* and are described in the following.

While the top levels of both display modes are models, they differ on how data types and attributes are arranged beneath them. The tree of the hierarchical mode reflects the modeled type hierarchy. On the level of a specific type all attributes defined by this type as well as existing subtypes are shown. This

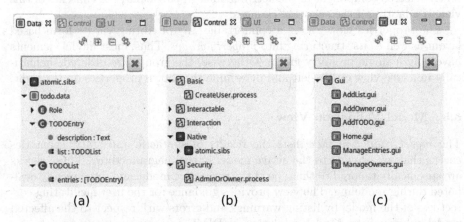

(a)   (b)   (c)

Fig. 4. Model Component Views: (a) *Data* (b) *Control* (c) *UI*

pattern then repeats for subtypes. The flat mode flattens the type hierarchy and therefore has only three levels of depth: data models, types and attributes. In contrast to the hierarchical mode, all inherited attributes are listed alphabetically under a specific data type. Figure 4(a) shows the view in hierarchical mode.

The *control component view* provides the user with components that represent services implementing business logic, like process models and native SIBs. From this view, a model can be dragged to the canvas in the diagram editor, whenever the currently edited model supports the inclusion of models of that respective type. Like the data component view, tree nodes are marked with an icon to help quickly identifying the model type and different display modes are provided to support more flexibility when modeling.

While the *flat mode* sorts available models according to their types into different categories(cf. Figure 4(b)), the *hierachical mode* at first sight seems very similar to the Eclipse project explorer, as it reflects the folder structure of the underlying file system. However, in both display modes additional useful features tailored to the environment of DIME are offered. For instance, an option to hide models whose type cannot be included in the active model removes unnecessary elements for the user to choose from. Additionally, cross-reference information for each model can be displayed. This means another level is added below each model in the view that indicates in which other models the specific one is used.

The *UI component view* is quite similar to the control component view, but provides access to available user interface models instead of control-flow elements. It also offers the same context-sensitive component filter, display modes, search filter and cross-reference information.

3.4   Properties View

The *properties view* shows attributes as well as their actual values for the currently selected component in the active model. In particular, the contents of this view is adapting if the selection changes.

The properties view allows a comfortable way of editing via its form-based layout as well as its structuring into *property groups*. Thus, most model elements have only a single property group. Otherwise, the groups are ordered thematically in a tree view on the left and determine the shown properties on the right.

3.5   Model Validation View

The *model validation view* lists the results of syntactic and static semantics checks that are applied to the active model in the diagram editor. These checks are specifically tailored to the type of the respective model and dynamically evaluated during modeling. The view provides guidance for the user facilitating correctness of the model by listing warnings and errors with respect to the affected model substructure. Model validation in DIME comprises various aspects, for instance, the enforcement of unique names, type correctness of data-flow, identification of missing edges, etc.

The model validation view provides two display modes that differ in how the check results are listed: by check or by the affected model component. In both modes an icon next to a check or model component indicates whether it contains errors or just warnings. Thus, the user can quickly identify important messages to refine the model. Also, to provide information about validation results of the whole project, the view can be configured to globally check all available models.

4   Data Modeling

In DIME the application domain is defined via data models. We differentiate between different kinds of data types: While *primitive types* are built-in concepts forming the foundation of the data model, *complex types* are defined by the user and aggregate both *primitive attributes* and *associations* to other complex types. *Enum types* are used to define a complex type with a fixed set of (named) instances. A *User type* defines the type that holds user credentials (i.e. username and password) and can be used to log into the system.

4.1   Primitive Types

Data models provide six primitive types that can be used for attributes in complex types and directly for variables in process models and GUI models:

Text a sequence of characters
Integer an integer number
Real a real number
Boolean a logical value, namely `true` or `false`
Timestamp a point in time.
File a file on disk. Instances of this type consist of some meta-information:

    – content type (e.g. pdf)
    – the name of the file
    – a reference to its actual content.

All of this information is gathered automatically whenever a file variable is set in the course of *data binding*. As an example, GUI models provide special components to manage file upload and download that take care of providing this information.

When defining an attribute or variable, the user can decide whether it should hold a single value or a list of values of the primitive type.

Furthermore, following the philosophy of simplicity, the primitive types are interpreted semantically rather than technically. This in particular means that, unlike in many programming languages, no differentiation between sizes and precision is made on the modeling level.

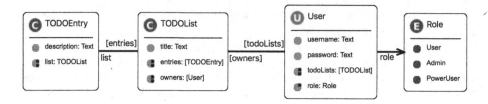

Fig. 5. Data model of the TODO-app

4.2   Complex Types

Complex types can hold multiple attributes and associations to other types. The latter are displayed both as (complex) attributes in the type and as association edges to the target types. Bidirectional associations are also supported, resulting in two cohesive complex attributes in the respective types and an bidirectional (undirected) edge between them.

A double-click on a node representing a complex type adds a primitive attribute. Initially, its type is Text. This can be changed to one of the six primitive types via a dropdown list in the properties view. The TODO-app – serving as running example in this paper – defines three complex and one enum type. The entire data model for the TODO-app is shown in Fig. 5.

The type TODOList is created via drag and drop to store the information about a *todo list* (cf. Fig. 5). To create an attribute the type is double-clicked and the added primitive attribute is renamed to title. Furthermore, a second type to describe *todo entries* is created and renamed to TODOEntry. To store information about the task described by such a todo list entry, the primitive textual attribute description is added. To manage users in the TODO-app, a *user type* is created, named User, and extended with an attribute role, which associates a single value of the type Role.

An association is created by drawing an edge between two complex types. To determine whether an unidirectional or bidirectional association is desired, the user is provided with a selection dialog listing the respective options. While a bidirectional association is depicted as a simple line, an unidirectional association is depicted as directed edge with an arrow head pointing towards the target type. The definition of bidirectional associations triggers the creation of attributes in both types. We will refer to them as *bidirectional attributes*.

For the TODO-app a bidirectional association between the types TODOList and TODOEntry is created. The left of Fig. 5 shows the edge representing this association as well as the respective attributes that are named accordingly. To express that a todo list can manage multiple entries, the bidirectional attribute `entries` of the type `TODOList` is set to be a list via the according property in the properties view.

In the process and GUI models, this association offers the possibility to access `TODOEntry` objects from a `TODOList` object and vice versa. As mentioned in the application description, a todo list should belong to a list of users, who are allowed to modify it by adding and deleting entries.

In Fig. 5 the corresponding bidirectional association is called `owners` on the `TODOList` side and `todoLists` on the opposite side. After using the properties view to set both attributes to be lists, it expresses that a user owns multiple todo lists while a todo list has multiple owners, resulting in a many-to-many relation.

5   Process Modeling

Process models in DIME comprise both, a control-flow aspect as well as a data-flow aspect. We provide five different process types, which each cover different aspects of the business logic. Since DIME applications are realized with a multi-layer architecture and even more importantly in the spirit of *separation of concerns* the different process types are organized in layers, too. In the following we illustrate the main design concepts as well as the impact of the layered architecture on which model types can reference which other model types.

5.1   Control-Flow

Process models contain a single start node and may have multiple end nodes. In between, the control-flow is modeled by means of connecting multiple SIBs via directed control-flow edges. In this context, SIBs can not only represent other process models (i.e., process SIBs) but also GUI models (i.e., GUI SIBs). Whereas integrating process SIBs fosters model reuse by means of sub-processes, integrating GUI SIBs introduces an interaction with the user. The subsequent control-flow depends on the actual outcome of the executed sub-process or the user's input, respectively. We reflect the distinction of outcomes with *branches*. SIBs as components of process models consist of a node, representing the "activity", and multiple branches to model a decision between a fixed set of outcomes. In modern programming languages branches can be emulated with special enumeration types[4]. The control-flow follows only one branch of a SIB at a time.

---

[4] For example, these are called *sealed classes* in Kotlin, *case classes* in Scala, and *enumerations with associated values* in Swift.

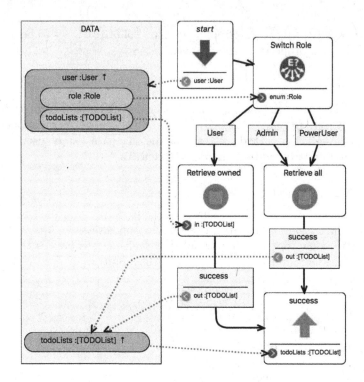

Fig. 6. Process model GetTODOLists

As an example, Fig. 6 shows a process model that contains a SIB labeled Switch Role with three branches represented by outgoing edges labeled User, Admin and PowerUser. In this example, the SIB represents an activity that identifies the actual role of the currently logged-in user. Its branches cover all possible cases (cf. Fig. 5). It is also apparent from Fig. 6 that the subsequent control-flow depends on the actual branch taken at runtime.

For GUI models, each user interaction with the respective web page, like clicking a submit button in a form or following a hyperlink to another page, is represented by a branch.

As an example, the GUI model Home (cf. also Fig. 8 in Sect. 6) is integrated into the process model AppHome in Fig. 7 by means of a GUI SIB labeled Home. Consequently, the buttons in this GUI model as well as those in any of the hierarchically integrated GUI sub-models are mapped to branches of the GUI SIB in the process model.

The branch Add List corresponds to the button in the GUI model AddList (cf. Fig. 10) that is integrated in GUI model Home. As different outcomes of a SIB might convey different data output, each branch may

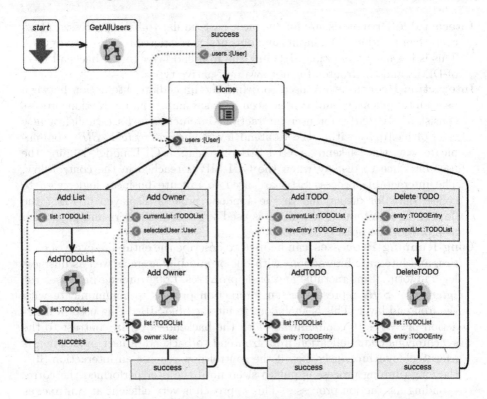

Fig. 7. Process model `AppHome`

have multiple output ports. For instance, in Fig. 7 the GUI SIB `Home` has a branch `Add List` with one output `list` returning the list to add, whereas branch `Add Owner` provides two outputs: `currentList` and `selectedUser`.

5.2 Process Types

DIME offers five process types. The type of SIBs that can be integrated into each of them depends on the application layer (see Fig. 2) the process type corresponds to:

Basic Processes characterize the smallest parts of the application's business logic. They consist of native SIBs and *built-in SIBs* from the palette as well as other embedded basic processes to hide complexity and enable reuse. Basic processes are usually used to model so-called *CRUD*[5] and data processing operations on entities.

---

[5] i.e., create, read, update, and delete.

Interactable Processes are for the most part similar to basic processes. However, their interface (i.e., inputs and outputs) is restricted to non-native types. This is because interaction SIBs link the frontend layer to the backend layer of DIME and the frontend is not aware of native types.

Interaction Processes are used to define the immediate interaction between user and application and can be seen as a sitemap. The interaction process consist of GUI SIBs for user interaction, *interaction SIBs* establish a new level of hierarchy within the frontend layer, and *interactable SIBs* communicate with the backend. A GUI SIB represents a GUI model defining the user interface to display when the GUI SIB is reached in the control-flow. The interactable process SIBs are used to execute business logic, e.g., to collect data for displaying. In the `AppHome` process displayed in Fig. 7 the `GetAllUsers` interactable process is used to retrieve all users and pass them as input for the `Home` GUI SIB.

Long-Running Processes can be used to describe the entire life-cycle of entities, and integrate interactions with one or multiple users as well as business logic in form of interactable and basic processes. Long-running processes use *interaction SIBs* representing an interaction process to communicate with the frontend layer. This is analogous to interactable SIBs being used in interaction processes to communicate with the backend layer. In contrast to the synchronous communication from frontend to backend, a user interaction is executed asynchronously. I.e., if the control-flow reaches an interaction SIB, the long-running process is put to sleep until the user performed the corresponding interaction processes. This approach is very efficient at runtime, as processes are not 'busy waiting' for user interactions.

Security Processes are used to realize access control. They are mostly similar to interactable processes, but with a predefined interface: the start node must include the currently signed-in user as an input and end nodes are restricted to be labelled with `granted`, `denied` and `permanently denied`, where permanently denied nodes cancel the entire underlying long-running process.

5.3   Data-Flow

Data-flow in processes is modeled in a graphical manner, too. For this purpose, the concepts of *input ports* and *output ports* as well as the *data context* are introduced.

For modeling data communication process models provide a specific container that holds nodes representing a *variable* of primitive, native, or complex types. In the following, this container is referred to as the data context. While SIBs can have input ports, branches in turn can have output ports.

For example, in Fig. 6, each of the `success`-branches of the retrieval activities `Retrieve owned` and `Retrieve all` have one output port representing the retrieved todo lists. The connection of these ports with the variable `todoLists` in the data context via a *data-flow edge* expresses that at runtime the data object is provided by the output port of the respective branch. As both the data output of the branches as well as the data object in the data context are typed as [TODOList] (i.e. a list of TODOList instances) the data-flow edge is type safe. In turn, data-flow edges violating type constraints are recognized via model validation. Additionally, Fig. 6 shows how the data object represented by the todoLists variable is provided as data for the input port todoLists of the end node success. Altogether, the process depicted in Fig. 6 describes that at runtime either the todo lists owned by the current application user or all todo lists are retrieved from the database, depending on the role of the user.

The variables present in the data context can be connected to input ports by *read edges* and to output ports by *update edges*. When the control-flow reaches a SIB the read operation on the connected variable is executed. Analogously, the update operation is performed, when a branch is reached. As a shortcut, process models offer *direct data-flow* for the connection of an output port to an input port without the need to put a variable in between. In Fig. 7, only this type of data-flow is used.

Complex variables offer their attributes as embedded nodes of the variable (cf. variable user in Fig. 6). The modeler can toggle between *folding* and *unfolding* the attributes of a variable's type. A small icon on the right of the node with an arrow pointing up or downwards shows the current state of folding.

A complex attribute which associates another complex type can be *expanded* by dragging the corresponding embedded node out of the variable to the data context. An edge with a filled circle from parent variable to expanded attribute symbolizes the association. *Expanded attributes* again offer their attributes as embedded nodes allowing for chaining (cf. variable currentUser → lists → owners in Fig. 8).

Furthermore, list variables of both primitive and complex types can be unfolded. Instead of offering the attributes of the corresponding type they provide *list attributes* for accessing the size of the list as well as the first, last and current element. The current element can be accessed, if the list is used in an iteration.

If a process model is integrated into another model by means of a process SIB, each of its end nodes is mapped to a separate branch of this process SIB. Furthermore, the branches of the process SIB contain an output port for each input port of the corresponding end node. Analogously, the output ports of a process' start node are mapped to input ports of corresponding process SIBs. These are referred to as *model parameters*. The mapping between a process SIB and the referenced subprocess relates to the concept of formal and actual parameters of functions in programming languages.

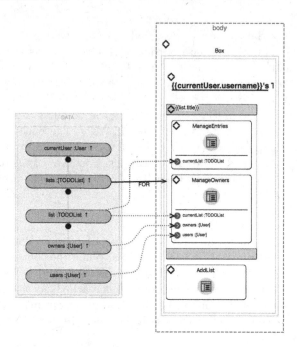

Fig. 8. GUI model Home

6   GUI Modeling

GUI models are declarative structures representing a user interface, enriched with basic state control via concepts like *control edges* and *data bindings*. One of the main design goals is supporting reuse for rapid prototyping and agile development. In the following the data-driven and event-driven concepts regarding the core *GUI components* and control edges are described alongside our example TODO-app. The GUI models provide a rich set of basic components for accepting user input and displaying data, and advanced components for structuring pages. In addition, every component is highly customizable to personalize the look and feel of a page.

6.1   Data-Flow

The GUI model is data-driven, i.e., data changes result in a modification of the viewable page. The life-cycle of a GUI model starts with rendering, including the injection of initially specified data. Similar to process models, GUI models provide a data context. However, in contrast to processes the model parameters of a GUI model are not defined in a start node. Instead, the initially needed data is specified by marking a variable as *input variable*. These inputs are mapped to input ports of the corresponding GUI SIB.

In the context of the TODO-app example, the Home GUI model in Fig. 8 requires one input variable users to receive a list of users from the calling interaction process. After the rendering is finished, data binding triggers a re-rendering of the affected components for every change to the available data. For example, when one of the user's lists changes[6], the components ManageEntries and ManageOwners shown in Fig. 8 are refreshed.

Further on, there is some information that can be provided by the environment. For example, the currently authenticated user will be available in the *injected variable* currentUser without the need to be explicitely modeled. If the user is not authenticated the system will automatically redirect to a login page.

Variables can be read in multiple ways. Besides using data-flow edges to connect variables with GUI components, every GUI component which displays static, continuous text can be extended with *template expressions*. All variables in the scope of the current GUI model can be accessed in an expression. Reminiscent of expressions in Angular [2] and the template language mustache [1] we use *double curly braces* to start an expression in static text and *dot-notation* to navigate through the associations of a value. Each time an expression has been adapted, the model validation parses it and validates, whether all variables and associations used are available in the data context and the data model, respectively.

As an example, in Fig. 8 the expression {{currentUser.username}} displays the username text attribute of the currentUser variable in a headline component. The dot-operator can be chained to step through the associations and attributes of the variable's type.

Additionally, certain GUI model components facilitate bi-directional data binding, i.e., the GUI component is live-updated when the value changes and the value is updated as soon as the GUI component is changed without reloading the page (e.g., text fields and text areas).

The life-cycle of a GUI model ends, when a button (or hyperlink) is clicked, since every button of a GUI model results in a branch of the corresponding GUI SIB. The calling interaction process redirects to the successor GUI SIB or process SIB via the corresponding branch. In most cases, it is necessary to retrieve data from a GUI model when it is terminated, like a selected entry of a combo box. Therefore, the GUI model provides the *submit edge*, which can be drawn between any variable and a button component. The connected variable will be propagated to the branch present in the calling interaction process as an output port.

The data binding between the variables in the data context and the components ensures that every part of the page is always up-to-date without any additional effort. A modeler can focus on describing the data dependencies and the structure of the GUI, instead of juggling with technical details.

6.2 Components

A GUI model is used to describe the structure of the rendered page declaratively. This user interface structure is called *template*. The template can be built up using different components which represent common parts of a user interface like tables, forms with input fields and parts to render content. The different components can be nested to customize the page and create a unique styling. The available components in the GUI models are divided into multiple groups, according to different requirements of a user interface. The most important ones for the TODO-app, namely tables and forms, are described in more detail in the following paragraphs.

Tables can be used to display interrelated information (i.e. entries of lists) in multiple columns. To bind a list variable to the table, a *table load* edge is provided. Besides the basic presentation of data, the table component offers features to sort and filter the displayed rows. To take advantage of these features, columns have to be specified for the table. The corresponding built-in component, which is available in the palette of the GUI model, is the *table entry* component. Multiple properties can be set on a table entry, like the label and a sorting and filter option. If the options are enabled, the source variable for the column has to be specified by a *table column load* edge. This edge should be connected to a

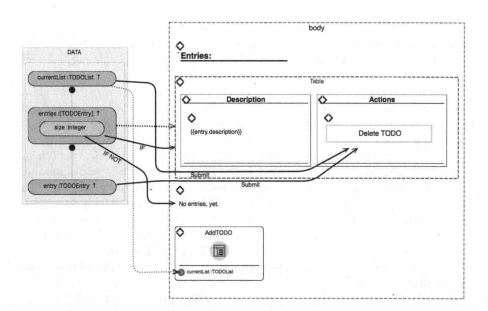

Fig. 9. GUI model `ManageEntries`

member of the expanded *current* list attribute of the source list. The expansion of attributes in GUI models is similar to the process data handling described in Sect. 5.3. The actually displayed content of a table column, represented by a table entry, can show the value of the bound variable and it can be highly customized by nesting GUI components.

In the TODO-app, a table component is required to list the single todo entries of a todo list (cf. Figure 9). As a result of this, the table load edge connects the list variable `entries` of the `TODOEntry` complex type with the table component, to assign the source. We decided that every todo entry should be represented by its variable `description`. A new table entry component is dragged to the table and its label is set to `Description` as shown in Fig. 9. To actually display the value of the `TODOEntry`'s description, a text component is inserted in the table entry. The content property of the text component is filled with the expression `{{entry.description}}`, which accesses the attribute `description` of the table's iteration variable. A second table entry is present in Fig. 9, which is labeled `Actions`. This column is used to offer the possibility to remove a todo entry, when it is finished. The included button component `Delete TODO` results in an according branch of the corresponding GUI SIB in the calling interaction process. To trace the selected `TODOEntry` to be removed from the list `currentList`, both are bound to the button component using *submit edges*. The resulting branch for the `Delete TODO` button contains two corresponding output ports (cf. Fig. 7).

Forms. Encapsulate components which enable the user to modify values of variables. In the GUI model only two different types of modifications are distinguished: *Field components* for editing primitive variables, and *selection components* (like *radio button*, *combo box*, and *check box*) for choosing from a list of options. A target variable has to be specified which is modified when the user triggers a change. The connection between a form component and the target variable can either be done by a *form submit* edge for uni-directional editing and *form load submit* edge for bi-directional editing.

Primitive data types like `text`, `real`, `timestamp` (e.g. date picker), and `file` (e.g. file upload) are supported by field components. In addition, more concrete kinds can be selected in the properties view. This enables additional semantics, since the expected input can be defined as e.g. a color, a phone number or a URL. The generated input field will validate and parse the inserted values and offers advanced editing assistance to the user at runtime, without any additional effort for the GUI modeler.

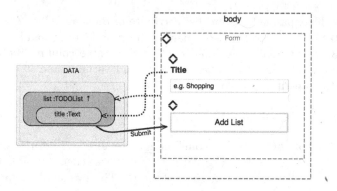

Fig. 10. GUI model `AddList`

In the TODO-app example, multiple form components are required. A form component is present in the `AddList` GUI model in Fig. 10, which is used in the `Home` GUI model of Fig. 8. The `AddList` button enables the user of the application to create a new `TODOList`. To create a new `TODOList`, an appropriate variable is placed in the data context. The user should define a title for the new `TODOList`, which requires a form field component, to edit the primitive attribute `title` of the `TODOList`. A form component is placed in the template and extended with a form field and a button to trigger the creation. The form field is connected to the attribute using a form submit edge, which will write the inserted text of the form field to the attribute. Since the newly created `TODOList` has to be propagated to the calling interaction process for further processing, the variable is connected to the button by a submit edge.

Additional groups of built-in components are provided for GUI models. The *navigation* components enable a modeler to realize a sophisticated layout, which keeps track of and highlights the last selected navigation menu entry. In combination with a strict decoupling of layout and content, consequent reuse of recurrent GUI components is supported. Furthermore, we provide components to display images, progress bars and alerts to support the users in their creativity. GUI models can be used hierarchically to the extend of being *second-order* where a GUI model is used as a parameter to another GUI model.

6.3 Control Edges

Besides the different components placed in the template to display and modify the values of variables in the data context, dedicated *control edges* can be used to dynamically adapt GUI components to the value of variables: *if edges* provide conditional control and *for edges* to repeat components.

The *if edge* can be used to display or hide a component and all of their inner components at runtime. To define a conditional indication, the if edge can be dragged from a variable to an arbitrary component. An inverted condition can be created by setting the **negate** property of an if edge. Based on a boolean evaluation[7] of the variable, the connected component is either shown or hidden. Similar to the data binding with edges or expressions, the condition of the if edge is re-evaluated automatically, iff the corresponding variable is modified.

The use of the if edge is demonstrated in Fig. 9. The table component should not be displayed if the list variable **entries** is empty. Instead, the text component with the content "no entries, yet." has to be displayed. To realize these conditions, two **if** edges are drawn between the **entries** variable's size and the table and the text components. The second edge to the text component is negated to enable the switching behavior. As a result, the text will be displayed, if the size of the list is lower than one, otherwise the table is shown.

Dynamic data structures like lists cannot be displayed statically with a fixed set of components. To access every item of a list variable the *for edge* is provided. The connection of a list variable to a component in the template using a *for edge* results at runtime in the repetition of the target component for each element in the list. The iteration variable, which can be expanded from the list variable, is available in the scope of the target and all inner components.

In the TODO-app, a for edge is used in the **Home** GUI model of Fig. 8 displaying all todo lists of the **currentUser**. The edge connects the panel component in the template (which surrounds the GUI SIBs for handling one todo list) and the list variable **lists** in the data context of the model. This results in the iterative rendering of the panel and its inner components (i.e. **ManageEntries** and **ManageOwners**) for every todo list. Furthermore, the iterator variable **list** is expanded from the **lists** variable to be used in the inner components.

---

[7] Apart from the obvious semantics of boolean, an integer or real variable is considered **true** if it is not 0, whereas a text or a list (of any tpye) must be neither **null** nor empty. All other types (including the primitive types timestamp and file) must not be **null**.

7   Conclusion and Perspectives

In this paper we have presented DIME, an integrated solution for model-driven development of sophisticated web applications. Following the paradigms OTA (One Thing Approach) and XMDD (Extreme Model-Driven Design), DIME enables agile user-level software development and rapid prototyping of applications. To achieve this a whole family of gaphical domain-specific languages was introduced, each of which covers in a declarative way a specific aspect of a modern web application. The data model is reminiscent to UML class diagrams and represents the application's domain model that is used to generate the persistence layer. Business logic as well as access control rules are defined in five interdependent variants of process models in the spirit of separation of concerns. Additionally, the user interface is designed in GUI models. With model validation we guide the modeler, facilitating high quality products. DIME is in particular suited for agile and evolutionary development life-cycles due to its prototype-driven technical foundation, the DyWA (Dynamic Web Applications) framework.

This paper gives first insights to DIME and its model types. A more complete presentation would go beyond the scope of this tutorial. Please refer to the official DIME website[8] for more information and news.

DIME itself is in a very early stage of development. We still have to explore its full impact and potential to improve it further. A brief outlook is given in the following. The presentation and editing of GUI models is subject to improvement in terms of becoming more WYSIWYG-like and to introduce a fast preview. Another opportunity lies in refining how search queries are modeled. Currently, as seen in Fig. 6, filtering of data sets is done imperatively in process models. This mingles the concerns of data retrieval and processing, leading to both bigger and less comprehensive process models as well as less information for optimizations (e.g. executing as much as possible directly with database queries). This issue will be addressed with a new model type, in which data queries can be modeled. As we do not want to simply model SQL statements, an appropriate abstraction for model components needs to be found.

A present-day, real-world web application is not isolated, it needs to interact via various communication channels with other services and no matter how many features are integrated into DIME, there will always be requirements that are not covered. Therefore, the concept of service-orientation, which is already very mature in the backend via native SIBs, has to be extended to native interaction SIBs for frontend models allowing for integration of third-party (web) services and libraries as well as native GUI components in order to display arbitrary visual components.

We are confident that the rigorous modeling approach of DIME is a game-changing technology with a great future. We plan to go open source with DIME soon, and are very excited how others will adopt this new and promising way of software development.

---

[8] http://dime.scce.info.

References

1. {{mustache}} Logic-less templates. https://mustache.github.io/. Accessed 05 Aug 2016
2. One framework - Angular 2. https://angular.io/. Accessed 05 Aug 2016
3. Boßelmann, S., Neubauer, J., Naujokat, S., Steffen, B.: Model-driven design of secure high assurance systems: an introduction to the open platform from the user perspective. In: Margaria, T., Solo, M.G.A. (eds.) The 2016 International Conference on Security and Management (SAM 2016). Special Track "End-to-end Security and Cybersecurity: from the Hardware to Application", pp. 145–151. CREA Press (2016)
4. Margaria, T., Steffen, B.: Business process modelling in the jABC: the one-thing-approach. In: Cardoso, J., van der Aalst, W. (eds.) Handbook of Research on Business Process Modeling. IGI Global (2009)
5. Margaria, T., Steffen, B.: Continuous model-driven engineering. IEEE Comput. **42**(10), 106–109 (2009)
6. Margaria, T., Steffen, B.: Simplicity as a driver for agile innovation. Computer **43**(6), 90–92 (2010)
7. Margaria, T., Steffen, B.: Service-orientation: conquering complexity with XMDD. In: Hinchey, M., Coyle, L. (eds.) Conquering Complex., pp. 217–236. Springer, London (2012)
8. Margaria, T., Steffen, B., Reitenspieß, M.:Service-oriented design: the jABC approach. In: Cubera, F., Krämer, B.J., Papazoglou, M.P. (eds.) Service Oriented Computing (SOC). No. 05462 in Dagstuhl Seminar Proceedings, Internationales Begegnungs- und Forschungszentrum für Informatik(IBFI), Schloss Dagstuhl,Germany, Dagstuhl, Germany (2006)
9. Margaria, T., Steffen, B., Reitenspieß, M.: Service-oriented design: the roots. In: Benatallah, B., Casati, F., Traverso, P. (eds.) ICSOC 2005. LNCS, vol. 3826, pp. 450–464. Springer, Heidelberg (2005)
10. McAffer, J., Lemieux, J.M., Aniszczyk, C.: Eclipse Rich Client Platform, 2nd edn. Addison-Wesley Professional (2010)
11. Merten, M., Steffen, B.: Simplicity driven application development. J. Integr. Des. Process Sci. (SDPS) **16**, 9–23 (2013)
12. Naujokat, S., Lybecait, M., Kopetzki, D., Steffen, B.: CINCO: A Simplicity-Driven Approach to Full Generation of Domain-Specific Graphical Modeling Tools (2016, to appear)
13. Neubauer, J., Frohme, M., Steffen, B., Margaria, T.: Prototype-driven development of web applications with DyWA. In: Margaria, T., Steffen, B. (eds.) ISoLA 2014, Part I. LNCS, vol. 8802, pp. 56–72. Springer, Heidelberg (2014)
14. Neubauer, J., Steffen, B.: Plug-and-play higher-order process integration. IEEE Comput. **46**(11), 56–62 (2013)
15. Neubauer, J., Steffen, B., Margaria, T.: Higher-order process modeling: product-lining, variability modeling and beyond. Electron. Proc. Theor. Comput. Sci. **129**, 259–283 (2013)
16. Rumbaugh, J., Jacobsen, I., Booch, G.: The Unified Modeling Language Reference Manual. The Addison-Wesley Object Technology Series, 2 edn. Addison-Wesley Professional (2004)
17. Steffen, B., Margaria, T., Braun, V., Kalt, N.: Hierarchical service definition. Ann. Rev. Commun. ACM **51**, 847–856 (1997)

18. Steffen, B., Margaria, T., Nagel, R., Jörges, S., Kubczak, C.: Model-driven development with the jABC. In: Bin, E., Ziv, A., Ur, S. (eds.) HVC 2006. LNCS, vol. 4383, pp. 92–108. Springer, Heidelberg (2007)
19. Windmüller, S., Neubauer, J., Steffen, B., Howar, F., Bauer, O.: Active continuous quality control. In: 16th International ACM SIGSOFT Symposium on Component-Based Software Engineering, CBSE 2013, pp. 111–120. ACM SIGSOFT, New York (2013)

Verification Techniques for Hybrid Systems

Pavithra Prabhakar[1]([✉]), Miriam Garcia Soto[2], and Ratan Lal[1]

[1] Department of Computer Science, Kansas State University, Manhattan, KS, USA
{pprabhakar,ratan}@ksu.edu
[2] IMDEA Software Institute, Madrid, Spain
miriam.garcia@imdea.org
http://people.cs.ksu.edu/~pprabhakar/

Abstract. A brief introduction to the state-of-the-art techniques in verification of hybrid systems is presented. In particular, the hybrid automaton model is introduced, important correctness properties are discussed and a brief overview of the analysis techniques and tools is presented.

1 Introduction

Software that interacts with physical components is an integral part of modern systems. These include autonomous road vehicles, smart buildings, smart grids, process control systems, autopilots in aircraft and medical monitoring and control devices. An integral feature of these systems is the mixed discrete-continuous behaviors that arise as a result of the interaction of (discrete) software with a (continuous) physical system. Since, these systems manifest so frequently and are safety critical, it is important to understand how their behaviors can be formally modeled and analysed. These STRESS 2016 lectures will provide a brief introduction to state of the art techniques in modeling and analysis of hybrid systems, and will include the following content:

- formal definition of hybrid systems,
- use of several state-of-the-art tools for modeling, simulation, and verification of hybrid systems,
- a detailed overview of automated techniques used in hybrid system analysis for two important classes of correctness specifications: reachability (e.g., establishing that a hybrid system does not enter an undesired state) and stability (e.g., small perturbations in the initial state or input to the system lead to only small deviations in the system behaviors; they capture notions of robustness of system behaviors),
- presentation of the above using three different example systems: a simple dimmable light switch (used to illustrate basic system timing aspects), a automobile dynamics model (used to illustrate discrete logic that controls the trajectory evolution, e.g., in wheeled robots, airplanes and underwater vehicles), and a automobile cruise control model (used to illustrate the interaction between

---

The original version of this chapter was revised: Two author names with affiliation were added. The Erratum to this chapter is available at 10.1007/978-3-319-47169-3_63

© Springer International Publishing AG 2016
T. Margaria and B. Steffen (Eds.): ISoLA 2016, Part II, LNCS 9953, pp. 833–842, 2016.
DOI: 10.1007/978-3-319-47169-3_61

discrete and continuous dynamics, namely, velocity evolution and gear changes that influence each other),

- a discussion of challenging open research questions in hybrid systems.

In the rest of the paper, we provide a bird's eye view of the contents to be covered in the tutorial.

2   Hybrid System Examples

We discuss a few examples of hybrid systems with increasing complexity. As a simple example, let us consider a model for a light that is controlled using a button [1]. Pressing the button once will switch the light on in a dim state. On the other hand, to switch the light on in the bright state, the button needs to be pressed twice within an interval of 10 s. Figure 1 shows a timed (hybrid) automaton model of the light switch. A clock is used to enforce the time constraints, the clock evolves according to the following differential equation:

$$\dot{x} = 1$$

Here, x is a clock variable whose value depends on time t, $\dot{x}$ refers to the derivative of the variable x with respect to time t. Since the value of x increases at rate 1, $x(t)$, the value of x at time t, is given by, $x(t) = x_0 + t$, where x_0 is the initial value of the clock, that is, $x(0) = x_0$. In the off state, if the button is pressed, then the automaton/light switches to the dim state. During the switch, the clock x is reset to $0, x := 0$. Hence, the clock x measure the time that has passed since the last press of the button. If the button is pressed again within 10, seconds then the light switches to the bright state, where as if the button is pressed much later, then the light switches off. This example illustrates the role of continuous dynamics to capture timing constraints.

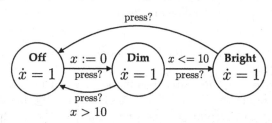

Fig. 1. Timed automaton for a light switch

Next, let us consider the Dubin's car dynamics, used to model the trajectories of wheeled robots, airplanes and underwater vehicles [9]. The trajectories are controller by applying appropriate angular velocities at different times. Let $\omega(t)$ be the angular velocity at time t. Let us explore how this effects the position and velocities of the vehicle. Let $x(t), y(t)$ represent the position of the vehicle in some two dimensional coordinate system. Note that $(\dot{x}(t), \dot{y}(t))$ represent the rate of change of position, namely, velocity $(v_x(t), v_y(t))$. Here v_x represents the horizontal velocity and v_y the vertical velocity. Hence,

$$\dot{x} = v_x, \dot{y} = v_y$$

The angular velocity ω is the rate of change of the heading angle θ of the vehicle. Hence, $\omega = \dot{\theta}$. Let $v = \sqrt{v_x^2 + v_y^2}$ and $\theta = \tan^{-1}(v_y/v_x)$. Then $v_x = v\cos(\theta)$ and $v_y = v\sin(\theta)$. Note that $\dot{v}_x = -v\sin(\theta)\dot{\theta} = v_y\omega$ and $\dot{v}_y = v\cos(\theta)\dot{\theta} = v_x\omega$. Therefore,

$$\dot{v}_x = -\omega v_y, \dot{v}_y = \omega v_x$$

Since, the derivatives of the variables depend linearly on the variable, the above dynamics can be represented using a matrix as:

$$\begin{bmatrix} \dot{x} \\ \dot{y} \\ \dot{v}_x \\ \dot{v}_y \end{bmatrix} = \begin{bmatrix} 0 & 0 & 1 & 0 \\ 0 & 0 & 0 & 1 \\ 0 & 0 & 0 & -\omega \\ 0 & 0 & \omega & 0 \end{bmatrix} \begin{bmatrix} x \\ y \\ v_x \\ v_y \end{bmatrix}$$

An automaton representing a navigation algorithm may provide the time or state at which the angular velocity needs to be changed as well as the new angular velocity. This example illustrates the modeling of physical entities such as distance and velocity. A supervisory control that measures the state of the system and decides the angular velocity shows how the discrete logic can influence the continuous evolution of the system.

As a last example, consider a cruise control that interacts with the gear box to set the velocity of vehicle to the desired/set velocity [20]. Let $v(t)$ be the velocity of the vehicle at a given time t and M its mass. The net force on the vehicle $M\dot{v}$ is obtained by adding all the forces acting on the vehicle.

$$M\dot{v} = p_q\frac{T}{r} - g\sin(\alpha)$$

Here, α is the gradient of the road. The first term represents the positive force on the vehicle due to torque T generated by the engine. In particular, engine torque T translates into a corresponding torque p_qT on the wheels, where p_q is the transmission ratio that is unique to the current gear q, and r is the radius of the wheels. The second term corresponds to the resistance on the road (friction) to the motion of the vehicle. Here, we ignore other resistances such as that due to air.

The cruise control measures the velocity v of the vehicle, and uses the deviation of the current velocity v from the desired velocity v_d to apply a corrective action by setting the appropriate engine torque. This is captured using the following PI controller (proportional integral controller), where the engine torque T is a sum of a proportional term and an intergral term with respect to the error $v_d - v$. Hence,

$$T = T_P + T_I, T_P = K_q(v_d - v), T_I = \frac{K_q}{\tau}\int (v_d - v)dv$$

where K_q is a gain constant associated with each gear position q and τ is the integration time constant. Considering T_I and $E = (v_d - v)$ as variables of the state-space representation, we obtain:

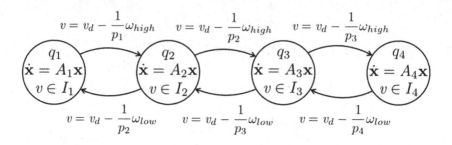

Fig. 2. Hybrid automaton of the automatic gearbox

$$\dot{E} = -\frac{p_q}{Mr}K_q E - \frac{p_q}{Mr}T_I + \frac{g}{M}\sin(\alpha)$$
$$\dot{T}_I = \frac{K_q}{\tau}E$$

Note that if the slope of the road $\alpha = 0$, then the above system of differential equations is again a linear dynamical system that can be expressed using a matrix. Let A_1, A_2, A_3 and A_4 denote the matrices corresponding to the dynamics of the cruise control/gear box when in gears $1, 2, 3$ and 4, respectively. Figure 2 shows a hybrid automaton modeling the cruise control interacting with the gear box. Note that the gear change is enabled when the vehicle velocity satisfies certain constraints (annotating the corresponding edges). In turn, the evolution of the velocity is dictated by the current gear.

3   Hybrid System Syntax and Semantics

In this section, we provide a formal definition of a hybrid system using a combination of differential equations and finite state automata.

Definition. A *hybrid system* $\mathbb{H}$ is a tuple $(\mathbb{Q}, \mathbb{A}, \mathbb{E}, \mathbb{X}, \mathbb{F}, \mathbb{I}, \mathbb{J})$, where:

- $\mathbb{Q}$ is a finite set of locations or discrete states;
- $\mathbb{A}$ is a finite set of actions;
- $\mathbb{E} \subseteq \mathbb{Q} \times \mathbb{A} \times \mathbb{Q}$ is a finite set of edges;
- $\mathbb{X} = \mathbb{R}^n$ is a set of continuous states;
- $\mathbb{F} : \mathbb{Q} \times \mathbb{X} \to \mathbb{X}$ is the vector field function;
- $\mathbb{I} : \mathbb{Q} \to 2^{\mathbb{X}}$ is the invariant function; and
- $\mathbb{J} : \mathbb{E} \to 2^{\mathbb{X} \times \mathbb{X}}$ is the jump function.

Here, $\mathbb{Q}, \mathbb{A}, \mathbb{E}$ represent a finite state automaton; $\mathbb{X}$ captures the continuous variables, $\mathbb{F}$ captures the differential equation, $\mathbb{I}$ specifies certain constraints on the statespace within which the solution should evolve in a location, and $\mathbb{J}$ captures the set of continuous state changes allowed when an edge is taken.

The semantics of the hybrid system is defined as a set of executions that consist of continuous trajectories that correspond to the system evolution in a particular location and discrete transitions that correspond to instantaneous changes during a mode switch. Given a hybrid system $\mathbb{H} = (\mathbb{Q}, \mathbb{A}, \mathbb{E}, \mathbb{X}, \mathbb{F}, \mathbb{I}, \mathbb{J})$:

- A *trajectory* is a pair $\eta = (q, \tau)$, where $q \in \mathbb{Q}$ and $\tau : [0, T] \to \mathbb{X}$ satisfies

$$\frac{d}{dt}\tau(t) = \mathbb{F}(q, \tau(t)), \tau(t) \in \mathbb{I}, \forall t \in [0, T]$$

The first and last states of η, denoted $first(\eta)$ and $last(\eta)$, are the states $(q, \tau(0))$ and $(q, \tau(T))$, respectively; the states of η, denoted $states(\eta)$, is $\{(q, \eta(t)) \mid t \in [0, T]\}$. We define $\eta_{\downarrow t}$ to be the trajectory η starting at time t, that is, $\eta_{\downarrow t}$ is the trajectory with domain $[0, T - t]$ such that $\eta_{\downarrow t}(t_1) = \eta(t + t_1)$ for all $t_1 \in [0, T - t]$. We let $size(\eta)$ to be T.

- A *transition* is a pair of states $\eta = ((q_1, x_1), (q_2, x_2))$ such that $(q_1, q_2) \in \mathbb{E}, (x_1, x_2) \in \mathbb{J}(e)$. Again, we define $first(\eta) = (q_1, x), last(\eta) = (q_2, x)$ and $states(\eta) = \{(q_1, x), (q_2, x)\}$. We let $size(\eta)$ to be 0.

An *execution* is a (finite or infinite) sequence $\sigma = \eta_1 \eta_2 \cdots$ where η_i is either a trajectory or a transition, and $first(\eta_i) = last(\eta_{i+1})$ for all i. $first(\sigma) = first(\eta_1)$ and if σ is a finite sequence, then $last(\sigma) = last(\eta_n)$, where η_n is the last element of σ. Also, $states(\sigma) = \cup_i states(\eta_i)$. Finally, we define $\sigma_{\downarrow t}$ to be the execution σ starting at time t, that is, $\sigma_{\downarrow 0} = \sigma$, and for $t > 0, \sigma_{\downarrow t} = \eta_{i \downarrow t_i} \eta_{i+1} \cdots$, where i is the first index in σ corresponding to a trajectory such that $\sum_{j=1}^{i} size(\eta_i) \geq t$ and $t_i = \sum_{j=1}^{i} size(\eta_i) - t$.

4   Correctness Specifications

We discuss here two important classes of correctness specifications, namely, safety and stability. Safety property states that the system remains in a safe state along any execution of the system. For instance, in a robot navigation protocol, the robot is expected to avoid collision with certain obstacles or other navigating robots.

Definition. A hybrid system $\mathbb{H}$ starting from a state in I is said to be *safe* with respect to a set of unsafe states U, if for every finite execution σ of $\mathbb{H}$ with $first(\sigma) \in I, last(\sigma) \notin U$.

In a robot navigation protocol, the unsafe states correspond to the states in which the robot occupies the same space as an obstacle or another navigating robot. Violating a safety property could be disastrous, for instance, lead to an accident.

Stability is another fundamental property that is expected out of hybrid control system designs. It stipulates that small perturbations in the initial state or input lead to small deviations in the system behavior. For instance, we not only expect the cruise control to drive the system to the desired velocity, but also expect it to maintain the vehicle at the desired velocity even in the presence of perturbations that arise due to the vehicle moving uphill or downhill. There are two classical notions of stability, namely, Lyapunov and asymptotic stability, that are defined with respect to an equilibrium point, which is a state in which the system can remain in the absence of perturbations. We will assume the origin $\bar{0}$ is the equilibrium point. Below, we use $B_r(x)$ to denote an r-open ball around x in the Euclidean space.

Definition. A hybrid system $\mathbb{H}$ is said to be *Lyapunov stable*, if for every $\epsilon > 0$, there exists a $\delta > 0$ such that for every execution σ of $\mathbb{H}$ with $x \in B_\delta(\bar{0})$, where $first(\sigma) = (q, x)$, we have $x' \in B_\epsilon(\bar{0})$ for all $(q', x') \in states(\sigma)$.

Lyapunov stability captures a graceful degradation property that stipulates that small perturbations in the initial state of the system lead to small deviations in the corresponding executions. Asymptotic stability requires, in addition to Lyapunov stability, convergence of the executions to the equilibrium state.

Definition. An execution $\sigma \in Exec(\mathbb{H})$ is said to be *convergent* to $\bar{0}$ if for every $\epsilon > 0$, there exists a time $T \geq 0$ such that $x \in B_\epsilon(\bar{0})$ for all $(q, x) \in states(\sigma_{\downarrow T})$.

Definition. A hybrid system $\mathbb{H}$ is said to be *asymptotically stable* if it is Lyapunov stable and there exists a value $\gamma > 0$ such that every execution σ of $\mathbb{H}$ with $x \in B_\gamma(\bar{0})$, where $first(\sigma) = (q, x)$, is convergent to $\bar{0}$.

While Lyapunov stability ensures that the system behavior does not change drastically, asymptotic stability ensures that the system will in fact move towards the desired state.

Next, we present a brief overview of the verification techniques for safety and stability analysis.

5   Safety Verification

Safety verification typically consists of computing the reachable states of the system and checking that they are disjoint from the unsafe states. Reach set is computed by an iterative application of continuous and discrete post computation operators starting from the set of initial states until a fix point is reached, that is, no further states can be added; the continuous post computation operator computes the set of states reached by using one trajectory and the discrete post computation operator computes the set of states reached by using one transition. There are broadly two difficulties with the computation of the reachable states:

- Computing the exact continuous post set, the states reached by an application of a continuous post operator, is infeasible, in general;
- The iterative procedure does not terminate, in general.

Safety verification is undecidable for a relatively simple class of hybrid systems [13]. Hence, abstraction/approximation methods have been developed to overcome the computational challenges. One class of techniques consist of computing an over-approximation of the continuous post set using a sampling based method, called the flowpipe computation. Flowpipe construction algorithms have been applied for computing over approximation of the reachable set of linear [24], uncertain linear [2,12], affine [11], and non-linear dynamical systems [6]. Flowpipe construction for a dynamical system in an interval $[0, T]$ is illustrated in Fig. 3. First, the solution of the dynamical system is sampled at uniform time intervals, that is, $s_0, \cdots, s_6$ are the values of the solution at times

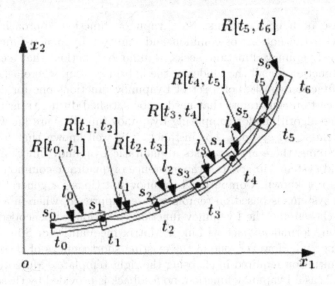

Fig. 3. Flow pipe construction for a single initial point

$0 = t_0 < t_1 < \cdots < t_6 = T$, respectively, where the times are uniformly sampled. The convex hull, $CH(s_i, s_{i+1})$ is computed, resulting in a straight line. The over-approximate reach set in the interval $[t_i, t_{i+1}]$ is computed by bloating the set $CH(s_i, s_{i+1})$ by an upper bound on the error between the actual reach set in interval $[t_i, t_{i+1}]$ and $CH(s_i, s_{i+1})$. Several methods for approximating the error have been proposed; extensions to non-uniform sampling have been investigated. In addition, algorithms extend these ideas to a set of initial states as opposed to a single initial state.

To address the termination problem, finite/infinite state abstractions have been proposed that compute a simplified system on which the reachable set computation is guaranteed to terminate and which provides an over approximation of the actual set. These include predicate abstraction [4], hybridization [8] and counter-example guided abstraction refinement [3,7].

6   Stability Analysis

Stability is a well-studied problem in the realm of control theory. The extensively used methods for stability verification rely on exhibiting a function called Lyapunov function, that provides a certificate of stability [15]. For a dynamical system $\dot{x} = f(x)$, where f is a function from $\mathbb{R}^n$ to $\mathbb{R}^n$, a Lyapunov function is a function $V : \mathbb{R}^n \to \mathbb{R}$ satisfying:

- $V(\bar{0}) = 0$,
- $V(x) > 0$ for every $x \neq 0$, and
- $\dfrac{dV(x)}{dx} f(x) < 0$ for every $x \in \mathbb{R}^n \backslash \bar{0}$.

For the case of hybrid systems, the Lyapunov function approach has been extended with the notions of common and multiple Lyapunov functions [17]. A common Lyapunov function seeks a unique function that serves as a Lyapunov function for all the modes of the hybrid system, where as, a multiple Lyapunov function consists of a set of Lyapunov functions one for each mode, along with certain constraints that need to be satisfied during transitions.

Decidable algorithms for computing Lyapunov functions are known only for certain subclasses of systems. For instance, it is well known that for the case of linear systems, there always exists a quadratic Lyapunov function. Even for linear hybrid systems, in general, the existence of quadratic common Lyapunov functions is not known. Computing Lyapunov functions for general non-linear and hybrid systems is based on template based approach, wherein a candidate function is chosen and the Lyapunov function conditions are encoded in a constraint solving formalism such as Linear Matrix Inequalities or Sum-of-Squares programming [19]. However, one of the existing shortcomings of these methods is the user intuition required in choosing the right templates. Moreover, when a template fails as a Lyapunov function, no feedback is provided by these methods regarding the reason for instability or the choice of the new template. To overcome some of these shortcomings, a new abstraction/refinement based methodology for stability analysis has been proposed that uses counter-examples in the abstractions that fail to prove stability to guide the choice of useful abstractions [21,23].

7   Verification Tools

The hybrid system research has resulted in the development of several verification tools. Reachability analysis tools include UPPAAL [5] for timed automata, HyTech [14] for polyhedral hybrid automata, SpaceEx [10] for linear hybrid systems, BEAVER [16] for parameterized linear hybrid systems, Flow* for non-linear hybrid systems [6]. Stability verification tools include Stabhyli [18] and AVERIST [22]. In this tutorial, we will introduce SpaceEx and BEAVER to illustrate safety verification of (parameterized) linear hybrid systems, and AVERIST to illustrate stability verification. The students will learn how to use these verification tools, how to model hybrid systems in the tools, how to use the tool for verification include how to set different parameters, and what they mean.

8   Conclusion

In this paper, we presented a brief overview of the models, properties and methods that will be discussed during the lectures. In addition, tools implementing these methods will be used to provide hands on experience in using hybrid system verification tools.

Acknowledgments. The author would like to thank Miriam García Soto and Ratan Lal for discussions and inputs towards writing this draft.

References

1. Aceto, L., Ingólfsdóttir, A., Guldstrand Larsen, K., Srba, J.: Reactive Systems: Modelling, Specification and Verification. Cambridge University Press, New York (2007)
2. Althoff, M., Le Guernic, C., Krogh, B.H.: Reachable set computation for uncertain time-varying linear systems. In: Proceedings of the International Conference on Hybrid Systems: Computation and Control, pp. 93–102 (2011)
3. Alur, R., Dang, T., Ivanꞷić, F.: Counter-example guided predicate abstraction of hybrid systems. In: Garavel, H., Hatcliff, J. (eds.) TACAS 2003. LNCS, vol. 2619, pp. 208–223. Springer, Heidelberg (2003). doi:10.1007/3-540-36577-X_15
4. Alur, R., Dang, T., Ivancic, F.: Predicate abstraction for reachability analysis of hybrid systems. ACM Trans. Embed. Comput. Syst. **5**(1), 152–199 (2006)
5. Bengtsson, J., Larsen, K.G., Larsson, F., Pettersson, P., Yi, W.: UPPAAL - a tool suite for automatic verification of real-time systems. In: Hybrid Systems, pp. 232–243 (1995)
6. Chen, X., Ábrahám, E., Sankaranarayanan, S.: Flow*: an analyzer for non-linear hybrid systems. In: Sharygina, N., Veith, H. (eds.) CAV 2013. LNCS, vol. 8044, pp. 258–263. Springer, Heidelberg (2013). doi:10.1007/978-3-642-39799-8_18
7. Clarke, E.M., Fehnker, A., Han, Z., Krogh, B., Ouaknine, J., Stursberg, O., Theobald, M.: Abstraction and counterexample-guided refinement in model checking of hybrid systems. Int. J. Found. Comput. Sci. **14**(4), 583–604 (2003)
8. Dang, T., Testylier, R.: Hybridization domain construction using curvature estimation. In: HSCC, pp. 123–132 (2011)
9. Dubins, L.E.: On curves of minimal length with a constraint on average curvature, and with prescribed initial and terminal positions and tangents. Am. J. Math. **79**(3), 497–516 (1957)
10. Frehse, G., Le Guernic, C., Donzé, A., Cotton, S., Ray, R., Lebeltel, O., Ripado, R., Girard, A., Dang, T., Maler, O.: SpaceEx: scalable verification of hybrid systems. In: Gopalakrishnan, G., Qadeer, S. (eds.) CAV 2011. LNCS, vol. 6806, pp. 379–395. Springer, Heidelberg (2011). doi:10.1007/978-3-642-22110-1_30
11. Frehse, G., Kateja, R., Le Guernic, C.: Flowpipe approximation, clustering in space-time. In: Proceedings of the International Conference on Hybrid Systems: Computation and Control, pp. 203–212 (2013)
12. Girard, A.: Reachability of uncertain linear systems using zonotopes. In: Proceedings of the International Conference on Hybrid Systems: Computation and Control, pp. 291–305 (2005)
13. Henzinger, T.A., Kopke, P.W., Puri, A., Varaiya, P.: What's decidable about hybrid automata? In: Proceedings of the ACM Symposium on Theory of Computation, pp. 373–382 (1995)
14. Henzinger, T.A., Ho, P.-H., Wong-Toi, H.: HYTECH: a model checker for hybrid systems. In: Grumberg, O. (ed.) CAV 1997. LNCS, vol. 1254, pp. 460–463. Springer, Heidelberg (1997). doi:10.1007/3-540-63166-6_48
15. Khalil, H.K.: Nonlinear Systems. Prentice-Hall, Upper Saddle River (1996)
16. Lal, R., Prabhakar, P.: BEAVER: bounded error approximate verification (2015)
17. Liberzon, D.: Switching in Systems and Control. Birkhuser, Boston (2003)
18. Möhlmann, E., Theel, O.E.: Stabhyli: a tool for automatic stability verification of non-linear hybrid systems. In: Proceedings of the 16th International Conference on Hybrid Systems: Computation and Control, HSCC, Philadelphia, PA, USA, 8–11 April 2013, pp. 107–112 (2013)

19. Parrilo, P.A.: Structure semidefinite programs and semialgebraic geometry methods in robustness and optimization. Ph.D. thesis, California Institute of Technology, Pasadena, CA, May 2000

20. Pettersson, S., Lennartson, B.: Stability of hybrid systems using LMIs - a gear-box application. In: Lynch, N.A., Krogh, B.H. (eds.) HSCC 2000. LNCS, vol. 1790, pp. 381–395. Springer, Heidelberg (2000). doi:10.1007/3-540-46430-1_32

21. Prabhakar, P., Garcia Soto, M.: Abstraction based model-checking of stability of hybrid systems. In: Sharygina, N., Veith, H. (eds.) CAV 2013. LNCS, vol. 8044, pp. 280–295. Springer, Heidelberg (2013). doi:10.1007/978-3-642-39799-8_20

22. Prabhakar, P., Soto, M.G.: AVERIST: algorithmic verifier for stability. In: International Workshop on Numerical Software Verification (2015)

23. Prabhakar, P., Soto, M.G.: Counterexample guided abstraction refinement for stability analysis. In: Chaudhuri, S., Farzan, A. (eds.) CAV 2016. LNCS, vol. 9779, pp. 495–512. Springer, Heidelberg (2016). doi:10.1007/978-3-319-41528-4_27

24. Prabhakar, P., Viswanathan, M.: A dynamic algorithm for approximate flow computations. In: Proceedings of the International Conference on Hybrid Systems: Computation and Control, pp. 133–142 (2011)

On the Power of Statistical Model Checking

Kim G. Larsen[1,2] and Axel Legay[1,2(✉)]

[1] Aalborg University, Aalborg, Denmark
[2] Inria, Rennes, France
axel.legay@inria.fr

Abstract. This paper contains material for our tutorial presented at STRESS 2016. This includes an introduction to Statistical Model Checking algorithms and their rare event extensions, as well as an introduction to two well-known SMC tools: PLASMA and UPPAAL.

1 Context

This paper summarizes the content of our STRESS tutorial on Statistical Model Checking (SMC). More details about can be found in the papers presented in the SMC session at ISOLA 2016 (part of the same volume).

In short, in order to solve the model checking problem for probabilistic systems, the SMC approach *simulates* the system for finitely many runs, and use *hypothesis testing* or estimators to infer whether the samples provide *statistical* evidence for the satisfaction or violation of the specification [34,43].

SMC is thus based on the notion that since sample runs of a stochastic system are drawn according to the distribution defined by the system, they can be used to obtain estimates of the probability measure on executions. Starting from time-bounded Probabilistic Bounded Temporal Logic properties (PCTL) [43], the technique has been extended to handle properties with unbounded until operators [38], as well as to black-box systems [37,43]. Tools, based on this idea have been built [27,39,43], and have been used to analyse many systems that are intractable numerical approaches.

In this tutorial, we first introduce two SMC algorithms that work with a finite set of observations. The first one, which is based on hypothesis testing, can be used to check whether the probability to satisfy the property exceed some fixed valued. The second algorithm, which is based on Monte Carlo, can be used to estimate this probability. For the estimation case, it is well-known that Monte Carlo based approaches have trouble to estimate very low probabilities. To overcome this difficulty, we introduce two major extensions of Monte Carlo

The research has received funding from the European FET projects SENSATION (http://www.sensation-project.eu/), Grant Agreement № 2888917 (DALI (http://www.ict-dali.eu/dali/)), and CASSTING (http://www.cassting-project.eu/), the Sino-Danish Basic Research Center IDEA4CPS (www.idea4cps), the Danish Innovation Center DiCyPS (www.dicyps.dk), as well as the ERC Advanced Grant LASSO and a CREATIVE Grant from the Brittany region.

© Springer International Publishing AG 2016
T. Margaria and B. Steffen (Eds.): ISoLA 2016, Part II, LNCS 9953, pp. 843–862, 2016.
DOI: 10.1007/978-3-319-47169-3_62

that are importance splitting and sampling. Those can be used to estimate very low probability either by modifying the probability mass of the system, or by guiding the executions with respect to the property to be verified.

In the second part of the tutorial, we will introduce tools and SMC applications. The first tool that will be introduced is PLASMA. This tool is an efficient self-contained SMC tool and software library [12] written in Java. We will illustrate the portability of the tool with two applications coming from the assisted living and energy-centric worlds, respectively. Then, we will turn our focus to those systems whose behavior also depends on real-time information. We will introduce a SMC extension for the well-known tool UPPAAL. We will also show how the tool can be extended to synthesize good strategies for those systems whose behavior depends on both timed and stochastic informations. The rest of this paper gives some pointers to the content of the tutorial.

2   Statistical Model Checking: Algorithms

2.1   Qualitative and Quantitative Original SMC Algorithms

Consider a stochastic system $\mathcal{S}$ and a logical property φ that can be checked on finite executions of the system. Statistical Model Checking (SMC) refers to a series of simulation-based techniques that can be used to answer two questions: (1) *Qualitative*: Is the probability for $\mathcal{S}$ to satisfy φ greater or equal to a certain threshold? and (2) *Quantitative*: What is the probability for $\mathcal{S}$ to satisfy φ? In contrast to numerical approaches, the answer is given up to some correctness precision.

As we said above, SMC first consists in monitoring φ on a finite set of executions of the system. Then, an algorithm from the statistics is used to answer either the qualitative or the quantitative question. As we shall see in the rest of the section, the algorithm that is applied clearly depends on the question one wants to solve. It is important to notice that any SMC algorithm must terminates after producing a finite amount of executions, each of them being of finite length. As a consequence the answer of any SMC algorithm is correct up to some confidence.

In the sequel, we use B_i as a Bernouili variable associated with the *ith* simulation of the system. The outcome for B_i, denoted b_i, is 1 if the simulation satisfies φ and 0 otherwise. We also use $p = Pr(\varphi)$ as the true probability for the system to satisfy φ.

Qualitative Answer. The main approaches [37,43] proposed to answer the qualitative question are based on *sequential hypothesis testing* [40]. The idea is to reduce the qualitative question to the one of a test between two hypothesis. Concretely, to determine whether $p \geq \theta$, the algorithm will test the hypothesis $H : p \geq \theta$ against $K : p < \theta$.

As we shall see, the principle of any sequential hypothesis testing will be to simulate System $\mathcal{S}$ execution by execution. After each new execution, a check will be performed to decide between the two hypothesis. The algorithm will have to continue until a decision is taken (hence the term "sequential").

Of course, this decision must be taken after a finite number of executions have been monitored. Consequently, the algorithm may take the wrong decision. One thus has to elaborate on the quality of the answer that is provided. In hypothesis testing, this is called the *strength* of the test. It is determined by two parameters, α and β, such that the probability of accepting K (respectively, H) when H (respectively, K) holds, called a Type-I error (respectively, a Type-II error) is less or equal to α (respectively, β). A test has *ideal performance* if the probability of the Type-I error (respectively, Type-II error) is exactly α (respectively, β).

Another difficulty with sequential testing algorithm if p is really close to θ, then it will take a lot of simulation to decide between the two hypothesis. In fact, one can even show that if the two quantities are infinitely close, then one cannot converge in finite amount of time. A solution to this problem is to use an *indifference region* $[p_1, p_0]$ (given some δ, $p_1 = \theta - \delta$ and $p_0 = \theta + \delta$) and to test $H_0 : p \geq p_0$ against $H_1 : p \leq p_1$. Intuitively, this means that if the two quantities are infinitely close, then it does not matter to select one or the other hypothesis.

We now sketch the Sequential Probability Ratio Test (SPRT) that is the most well-known hypothesis testing algorithm. In this algorithm, one fixes two values A and B. Let m be the number of observations that have been made so far. The test is based on the following quotient:

$$\frac{p_{1m}}{p_{0m}} = \prod_{i=1}^{m} \frac{Pr(B_i = b_i \mid p = p_1)}{Pr(B_i = b_i \mid p = p_0)} = \frac{p_1^{d_m}(1 - p_1)^{m - d_m}}{p_0^{d_m}(1 - p_0)^{m - d_m}},$$

where $d_m = \sum_{i=1}^{m} b_i$.

The idea is to accept H_0 if $\frac{p_{1m}}{p_{0m}} \geq A$, and H_1 if $\frac{p_{1m}}{p_{0m}} \leq B$. The algorithm computes $\frac{p_{1m}}{p_{0m}}$ for successive values of m until either H_0 or H_1 is satisfied. In the work of Wald, it is showed how to select A and B such that the strength of the test (see type-error above) is respected. In practice as A and B are correlated to α and β, the number of simulations to terminates highly depends on α and β. The smaller those two values are and the more simulations one will need to terminate.

Quantitative Answer. The objective of a quantitative answer is to estimate the probability p to satisfy the property. As we will only have a finite number of executions to monitor, the best one can obtain is an estimate $\hat{p}$ that is at some distance δ from the true probability. Of course, there is always the possibility that the algorithm does not respect this distance. One thus seek for a confidence α on our estimator[1].

To obtain such an estimator $\hat{p}$, we will use a so-called Monte Carlo estimator approach. The idea is quite simple. Let m be a pre-computed number of executions on which the property is to be monitored. We set $\hat{p}$ to be the number of

---

[1] Please note that δ and α do not have the same meaning as for the qualitative question.

executions that does satisfy the property divided by m. The challenge is now to select an m such that δ and α are guaranteed.

Given a *precision* δ, the *Chernoff bound* of [36] is used to compute a value for $\hat{p}$ such that $|\hat{p} - p| \leq \delta$ with *confidence* $1 - \alpha$. Let $\hat{p} = \sum_{i=1}^{m} b_i/m$, then the Chernoff bound [36] gives $Pr(|\hat{p} - p| \geq \delta) \leq 2e^{-2m\delta^2}$. As a consequence, if we take $m = \lceil \ln(2/\alpha)/(2\delta^2) \rceil$, then $Pr(|\hat{p} - p| \leq \delta) \geq 1 - \alpha$.

Observe that there is a major difference between the qualitative and quantitative algorithm, that is the quantitative algorithm pre compute the number of executions it needs to terminate. There are however, sequential versions of the quantitative algorithms. Their study goes beyond this paper.

2.2   Towards Rare Events: On Extending SMC Algorithms

Statistical model checking avoids the exponential growth of states associated with probabilistic model checking by estimating probabilities from multiple executions of a system and by giving results within confidence bounds. Rare properties are often important but pose a particular challenge for simulation-based approaches, hence a key objective for SMC is to reduce the number and length of simulations necessary to produce a result with a given level of confidence. In the literature, one finds two techniques to cope with rare events: *importance sampling* and *importance splitting*.

In order to minimize the number of simulations, importance sampling works by estimating a probability using weighted simulations that favour the rare property, then compensating for the weights. For importance sampling to be efficient, it is thus crucial to find good importance sampling distributions without considering the entire state space. In [28], we presented a simple algorithm that uses the notion of cross-entropy minimisation to find an optimal importance sampling distribution. In contrast to previous work, our algorithm uses a naturally defined low dimensional vector of parameters to specify this distribution and thus avoids the intractable explicit representation of a transition matrix. We show that our parametrisation leads to a unique optimum and can produce many orders of magnitude improvement in simulation efficiency.

One of the open challenges with importance sampling is that the variance of the estimator cannot be usefully bounded with only the knowledge gained from simulation. Importance *splitting* achieves this objective by estimating a sequence of conditional probabilities, whose product is the required result. In [29] we motivated the use of importance splitting for statistical model checking and were the first to link this standard variance reduction technique [31] with temporal logical. In particular, we showed how to create *score functions* based on logical properties, and thus define a set of *levels* that delimit the conditional probabilities. In [29] we also described the necessary and desirable properties of score functions and levels, and gave two importance splitting algorithms: one that uses fixed levels and one that discovers optimal levels adaptively.

One interesting aspect of rare events is that the performances of algorithms for single core often degenerate when moving to distributed architectures. Details on this study can be found in [30].

3 Plasma: A Modular Toolset for Statistical Model Checking

PLASMA is a compact, efficient and flexible platform for statistical model checking of stochastic models. The tool offers a series of SMC algorithms which includes classical SMC algorithms and rare events ones presented above. The main difference between PLASMA and other SMC tools is that PLASMA proposes an API abstraction of the concepts of stochastic model simulator, property checker (monitoring) and SMC algorithm. In other words, the tool has been designed to be capable of using external simulators, input languages, or SMC algorithms. This not only reduces the effort of integrating new algorithms, but also allows us to create direct plug-in interfaces with industry used specification tools. The latter being done without using extra compilers. PLASMA is the focus of ongoing collaborations with companies Dassault, Thales, IBM, and EADS. PLASMA is also used by several European projects.

Figure 1 presents PLASMA architecture. More specifically, the relations between model simulators, property checkers, and SMC algorithms components. The simulators features include starting a new trace and simulating a model step by step. The checkers decide a property on a trace by accessing to state values. They also control the simulations, with a *state on demand* approach that generates new states only if more states are needed to decide the property. A SMC algorithm component, such as the Monte Carlo algorithm, is a runnable object. It collect samples obtained from a checker component. Depending on the property language, their checker either returns Boolean or numerical values. The algorithm then notifies progress and sends its results through the Controller API.

Usage. The GUI provides an integrated development environment (IDE) to facilitate the use of PLASMA as a standalone statistical model checker with multiple 'drop-in' modelling languages. PLASMA is usually invoked via its GUI. It may also be invoked from the command line or embedded in other software as a

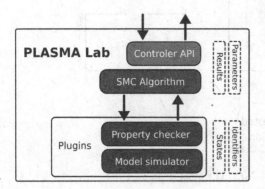

Fig. 1. PLASMA architecture

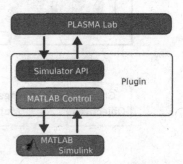

Fig. 2. Interface between PLASMA and Simulink

library. In addition to the GUI, PLASMA provides an SMC engine in the form of a pre-compiled jar file. A source template is also provided to create custom simulator classes. The minimum requirement to create a custom simulator is to implement methods that (*i*) initiate a new simulation and (*ii*) advance the simulation by one step. Dedicated language parsers are typically invoked in the constructor of the custom simulator class. In coordination with this architecture, we use a plugin system to load models and properties components. It is then possible to support new model or property languages. Adding a simulator, a checker or an algorithm component is pretty straigthforward as we will see with simulink below. One of the goal of PLASMA is also to benefit from a massive distribution of the simulations, which is one of the advantage of the SMC approach. Therefore PLASMA API provides generic methods to define distributed algorithms. We have used these functionalities to distribute large number of simulations over a computer grid[2].

3.1   Application to Motion Planning

PLASMA is used by the DALi project in a novel motion planning application of SMC. DALi aims to develop an autonomous device to help those with impaired ability to negotiate complex crowded environments (e.g. shopping malls). High level constraints and the objectives of the user are expressed in temporal logic, while low level behaviour is predicted by the 'social force model' [23]. The planner

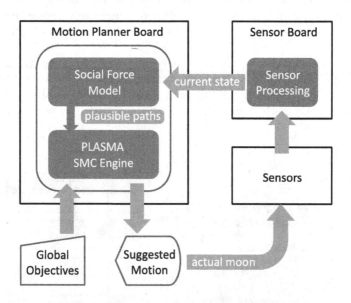

Fig. 3. Control loop of DALi motion planner.

---

2 https://project.inria.fr/plasma-lab/documentation/tutorial/
igrida-experimentation/.

first hypothesises many plausible futures for a range of possible user actions, then chooses the action which maximises the probability of success (Fig. 3).

PLASMA was integrated with MATLAB to develop the prototype algorithm. The final version is implemented directly in C on embedded hardware and finds the optimum trajectory in a fraction of a second [15]. PLASMA improves the social force model's ability to avoid collisions by a factor of five [15]. Using behavioural templates [14], the predictive power of our SMC-based motion planner can be even greater.

3.2 Integration Plasma with Simulink

We now show how to integrate PLASMA within Simulink, hence lifting the power of our simulation approaches directly within the tool. We will focus on those Simulink models with stochastic information, as presented in [44]. But our approach is more flexible because the user will directly use PLASMA within the Simulink interface, without third party.

Simulink is a block diagram environment for multi-domain simulation and Model-Based Design approach. It supports the design and simulation at the system level, automatic code generation, and the testing and verification of embedded systems. Simulink provides a graphical editor, a customizable set of block libraries and solvers for modeling and simulation of dynamic systems. It is integrated within MATLAB. The Simulink models we considered have special extensions to randomly behave like failures. By default the Simulink library provides some random generators that are not compatible with statistical model checking: they always generate the same random sequence of values at each execution. To overcome this limitation we use some C-function block calls that generate independent sequences of random draws.

Our objective was to integrate PLASMA as a new Simulink library. For doing so, we developed a new simulator plugin whose architecture is showed in Fig. 2. One of the key points of our integration has been to exploit MATLAB Control[3], a library that allows to interact with MATLAB from Java. This library uses a proxy object connected to a MATLAB session. MATLAB invokes, *e.g.* functions `eval`, `feval` ... as well as variables access, that are transmitted and executed on the MATLAB session through the proxy. This allowed us to implement the features of a model component, controlling a Simulink simulation, in MATLAB language. Calls to this implementation are then done in Java from the PLASMA plugin.

Regarding the monitoring of properties, we exploit the simulation output of Simulink. More precisely, BLTL properties are checked over the executions of a SDES, *i.e.*, sequences of states and time stamps based on the set of state variables SV. This set must be defined by declaring in Simulink signals as log output. During the simulation these signals are logged in a data structure containing time stamps and are then retrieved as states in PLASMA. One important point is that Simulink discretizes the signals trace, its sample frequency being parameterized

---

[3] https://code.google.com/p/matlabcontrol/.

by each block. In terms of monitoring this means that the sample frequency must be configured to observe any relevant change in the model. In practice, the frequency can be set as a constant value, or, if the model mixes both continuous data flow and state flow, the frequency can be aligned on the transitions, *i.e.*, when a state is newly visited.

Illustration of the integration. Let us now illustrate the approach with a concrete example (see also https://project.inria.fr/plasma-lab/). This model is taken from the Simulink/Stateflow examples library. It describes the fuel control system of a gasoline engine. The system is made robust by detecting failures in sensors and dynamically re-configuring its behavior to maintain a continuous operation. This is a typical example of hybrid system. It is modelled in Simulink by using Sateflow diagrams to to handle the discrete changes of the control system, and linear differential equations to model the continuous behaviors.

The system contains four separate sensors: a throttle sensor, a speed sensor, an oxygen sensor, and a pressure sensor. Each of these sensors is represented by a parallel state in Stateflow, that is say finite state machines concurrently active. In total the entire logic of the systems is implemented by six parallel states. Each parallel state of a sensor contains two sub-states, a normal state and a fail state (the exception being the oxygen sensor, which also contains a warm-up state). If any of the sensor readings is outside an acceptable range, then a fault is registered, and the state of the sensor transitions to the failed sub-state. If the sensor recovers, it can transition back to the normal state.

In the original model, sensors faults are decided by the user using manual switch block for each sensor. The interest of the SMC approach comes from the possibility to observe a large set of execution traces produced by a probabilistic procedure. Therefor we replaced the Speed, EGO and MAP manual switches by custom probabilistic switches. These switches use a Poisson distribution and are parameterized by a rate to decide when a fault happen. A sensor will repair itself after a duration of 1 s. This modified model is similar to the one use in [44].

The Poisson distribution block that we use draws a random time T in seconds, that is the time before the next fault happens, and we use a Stateflow diagram as a timer. The signal from the Poisson block is then used by the sensor's switch. A Stateflow repair timer is used to maintain the fault signal for a duration of 1 s.

The system uses its sensors to maintain the air-fuel ratio at a constant value. When one sensor fails, a higher ratio is targeted to allow a smoother running. If another sensors fails the engine is shutdown for safety reasons, which is detected by a zero fuel rate.

We estimate the probability of a long engine shutdown. We use the following BLTL property to monitors executions over a period of 100 t.u., and to check if the fuel remains at zero for 1 t.u.:

$$\Phi = \neg F_{\leq 100}(G_{\leq 0.999}\mathsf{Fuel} = 0)$$

We try to reproduce with this property the results of [44]. In this paper they use a Bayesian SMC technique to estimate the probability of this property with the bound 1 for G operator. We can almost reproduce their results using the Monte Carlo algorithm on our own implementation of the Simulink model with stochastic distributions, but only if we use the approximated bound 0.999. Indeed the property is false, mainly when the three sensors are faulty at the same time. In that case the second sensor to fail remains in fault condition for exactly one second, with at least one other sensor. When this second sensor is repaired, there remains only one faulty sensor and the engine is restarted. Whether the Fuel variable in the sample after exactly one second is monitored at 0 or 1 by the SMC checker, changes the evaluation of the property. By using the value 0.999 we avoid these approximation issues. Table 1 recaps our results and the one of [44] for different values of the sensors fault rates (expressed in seconds). Our results are obtained with PLASMA Monte Carlo (MC) algorithm after 1000 simulations. It takes approximately 2500 s to complete on a 2.7 GHz Intel Core i7 with 8 GB RAM and running MATLAB R2014b on Linux.

Table 1. Probability estimation of Φ with PLASMA and the results from [44]. The fault rates in seconds correspond to the Speed, EGO and MAP sensors, respectively.

Fault rates	PLASMA MC	Bayesian SMC [44]
(3 7 8)	0.396	0.356
(10 8 9)	0.748	0.853
(20 10 20)	0.93	0.984
(30 30 30)	0.985	0.996

4 UPPAAL: Statistical Model Checking and Beyond

In the following we give an overview of the classical UPPAAL toolbox (supporting model checking of timed automata base models), and the two recent branches UPPAAL SMC and UPPAAL STRATEGO, which supports statistical model checking of stochastic hybrid automata and synthesis learning for stochastic hybrid games, respectively.

4.1 UPPAAL

UPPAAL is a toolbox for verification of real-time systems represented by (a network of) timed automata extended with integer variables, structured data types, and channel synchronization. The tool is jointly developed by Uppsala University and Aalborg University. It has been applied successfully in case studies ranging from communication protocols to multimedia applications (see [5] and [6] for concrete examples). The first version of UPPAAL was released in 1995 [33]. In the same spirit as any other professional model checker such as SPIN, UPPAAL proposes efficient data structures [35], a distributed version of UPPAAL [3,10],

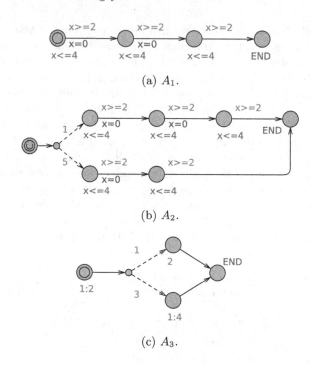

(a) A_1.

(b) A_2.

(c) A_3.

Fig. 4. Three stochastic timed automata.

guided and minimal cost reachability [8,9,32], work on UML Statecharts [22], acceleration techniques [24], and new data structures and memory reductions [7,11].

Example. Consider the three TAs A_1, A_2 and A_3 from Fig. 4 each using a single clock x. Ignoring (initially) the weight annotations on locations and edges, the END-locations in the three automata are easily seen to be reachable within the time-intervals $[6, 12]$, $[4, 12]$ and $[0, +\infty)$.

Example. To illustrate the extended input language of UPPAAL, we consider in Fig. 5 the Train Gate example adapted from [42]. The example model is distributed together with UPPAAL tool. A number of trains are approaching a bridge on which there is only one track. To avoid collisions, a controller stops the trains. It restarts them when possible to make sure that trains will eventually cross the bridge. There are timing constraints for stopping the trains modeling the fact that it is not possible to stop trains instantly. Each train has a designated clock x to constrain the timing between the different phases, e.g. the combination of the invariant in the location Cross and the guard its ouToing edge models that once the passing of the crossing takes between 3 and 5 time units. Figure 5b shows the gate controller that keeps track of the trains with an internal queue data-structure (not shown here). It uses functions to queue trains (when a train

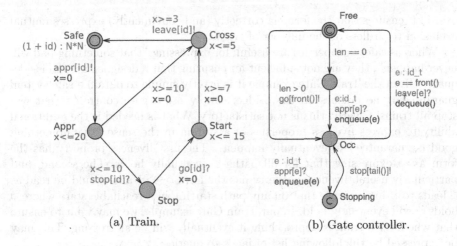

(a) Train.   (b) Gate controller.

Fig. 5. Templates for the train-gate example.

approaches and the bridge is occupied in Occ) or dequeue them (when some train leaves and the bridge is free).

Queries. The query language of UPPAAL consists of a subset of TCTL [1] allowing for reachability, safety and (time-bounded) liveness properties to be expressed.

Reachability properties are of the form E<>ϕ and means that there exists some path on which ϕ holds at some state. Reachability properties are useful for checking that models proposed at early design stages possess expected basic behaviours and to ask for diagnostic traces to confirm and study this more closely. For the Train Gate example such sanity properties could be:

```
E<> Gate.Occ
E<> Train(0).Cross
E<> Train(1).Cross
E<> Train(0).Cross and Train(1).Stop
E<> Train(0).Cross and (forall(i:id_t) i!=0 imply Train(i).Stop)
```

Safety properties are of the form A[]ϕ and mean that for all paths and for all states on those paths the property ϕ For the Train Gate example expected safety properties are:

```
A[] forall (i:id_t) forall (j:id_t) \
    Train(i).Cross && Train(j).Cross imply i==j
A[] not deadlock
```

Here the first safety property expresses that the gate controller correctly implements mutual exclusion of the bridge, in that no two different trains can be in the crossing simultaneously. The nested usage of the forall construct ranging over id t, ensures that the formula correctly (and conviniently) expresses mutual exclusion regardless of the number of trains.

Whereas safety properties are usefull for expressing "that something bad will never happen", they are not sufficient for ensuring that a designed system is adequate. Given the Train Gate example it is utterly simple to obtain a safe system guaranteeing no crashes on the bridge: simply use a gate controller that will stop all trains! Clearly, this is not satisfactory. What is needed is the additional ability to express liveness properties of a system in the sense "that something good is guaranteed to eventually happen". The first liveness property has the form A<>ϕ expressing that for all paths ϕ eventually holds. The second, and particularly useful, liveness property has the form ϕ-->ψ and should be read as ϕ leads to ψ in the sense that on any path starting in a reachable state where ϕ holds ψ will eventually hold. In our Train Gate example, we may want to ensure that whenever a train is approaching it eventually will be at crossing. This may be expressed by the following list of laads-to queries:

```
Train(0).Appr --> Train(0).Cross
Train(1).Appr --> Train(1).Cross
Train(2).Appr --> Train(2).Cross
...
```

4.2 UPPAAL SMC

Unfortunately, timed automata is not a panacea. In fact, albeit powerful, the model is not expressive enough to capture behaviors of complex cyber-physical systems. Indeed, the continuous time behaviors of those systems often rely on rich and complex dynamics as well as on stochastic behaviors. The model checking problem for such (stochastic hybrid) systems is in general undecidable, and approximating those behaviors with timed automata [25] was originally the best one could originally do in UPPAAL.

With UPPAAL SMC [21] we proposed an alternative to the above-mentioned problem. This new branch of UPPAAL proposes to represent systems via networks of automata whose behaviors may depend on both stochastic and non-linear dynamical features. Concretely, in UPPAAL SMC, each component of the system is described with an automaton whose clocks can evolve with various rates. Such rates can be specified with, e.g., ordinary differential equations. Moreover, each component chooses independently the point in time when it want to do its next discrete action, leading to a resulting *fully stochastic* combined system, with repeated time-races between the components.

To allow for the efficient analysis of probabilistic performance properties, UPPAAL SMC proposes to work with Statistical Model Checking (SMC) [37,43], an approach that has been proposed as an alternative to avoid an exhaustive exploration of the state-space of the model. The core idea of SMC is to monitor random simulations of the system (obtained from its stochastic semantics), and then use classical the statistical methods (e.g. sequential hypothesis testing or Monte Carlo simulation) to decide whether the system satisfies the property with some desired degree of confidence.

Modeling. The modeling formalism of UPPAAL SMC is based on a stochastic interpretation and extension of the timed automata (TA) formalism [2] used in the classical model checking version of UPPAAL [5]. For *individual TA components* the stochastic interpretation replaces the non-deterministic choices between multiple enabled transitions by probabilistic choices (that may or may not be user-defined). Similarly, the non-deterministic choices of time-delays are refined by probability distributions, which at the component level are given either uniform distributions in cases with time-bounded delays or exponential distributions (with user-defined rates) in cases of unbounded delays.

Example. Reconsider the three TAs A_1, A_2 and A_3 from Fig. 4. The stochastic interpretation of the three TAs provides probability distributions over the reachability time. For A_1, the delay of the three transitions will all be (automatically) resolved by independent, uniform distributions over $[2, 4]$. Thus the overall reachability time is given as the sum of three uniform distributions as illustrated in Fig. 6a. For A_2, the delay distributions determined by the upper and lower path to the END-location are similarly given by sums of uniform distributions. Subsequently, the combination ($\frac{1}{6}$ to $\frac{5}{6}$) of these as illustrated in distribution of the overall delay is obtained by a weighted Fig. 6b. Finally, in A_3 – in the absence of invariants – delays are chosen according to exponential distributions with user-supplied rates (here $\frac{1}{2}$, 2 and $\frac{1}{4}$). In addition, after the initial delay a discrete probabilistic choice ($\frac{1}{4}$ versus $\frac{3}{4}$) is made. The resulting distribution of the overall reachability time is given in Fig. 6c.

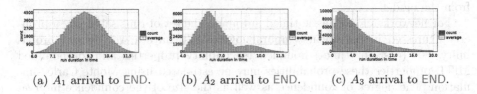

(a) A_1 arrival to END.	(b) A_2 arrival to END.	(c) A_3 arrival to END.

Fig. 6. Distributions of reachability time

Importantly, the distributions provided by the stochastic semantics are in agreement with the delay intervals determined by the standard semantics of the underlying timed automata. Thus, the distributions for A_1 and A_2 have finite support by the intervals $[6, 12]$ and $[4, 12]$, respectively. Moreover, as indicated by A_3, the notion of stochastic timed automata encompasses both discrete and continuous time Markov chains. In particular, the class of distributions over reachability-time from the stochastic timed automata (STA) of UPPAAL SMC includes that of phase-type distributions.

Example. Now reconsider the Train Gate example from Fig. 5 the interesting point w.r.t. SMC is the stochastic distribution of delays of the various trains in a given location. Figure 5 a shows the template for a train. The location Safe has no invariant and defines the rate of the exponential distribution for delays. Trains delay according to this distribution and then approach by synchronizing on appr[i] with the gate controller. Here we define the rational $\frac{1+id}{N^2}$ where id is the identifier of the train and N is the number of trains. Rates are given by expressions that can depend on the current states. Trains with higher id arrive faster. Taking transitions from locations with invariants is given by a uniform distribution over the time interval defined by the invariant. This happens in locations Appr, Cross, and Start, e.g., it takes some time picked uniformly between 3 and 5 time units to cross the bridge.

Queries. In addition to the standard model checking queries UPPAAL SMC provides a number of new queries related to the stochastic interpretation of timed automata. In particular UPPAAL SMC allows the user to visualize the values of expressions (evaluating to integers or clocks) along simulated runs, providinginsight to the user on the behavior of the system so that more interesting properties can be asked to the model-checker. On the Train Gate example we may monitor when Train(0) and Train(5) are crossing as well as the length of the queue. The query is

```
simulate 1 [<=300]
  { Train(0).Cross, Train(5).Cross, Gate.len }
```

This gives us the plot of Fig. 7a. Interestingly Train(5) crosses more often (since it has a higher arrival rate). Secondly, it seems unlikely that the gate length drops below 3 after some time (say 20), which is not an obvious property from the model.

For networks of stochastic timed automata the set of runs satisfying a property expressed in the linear-temporal logic MITL have a well-defined probability. For (cost- or time-) bounded reachability properties and for bounded MITL properties these probabilities may be estimated using Monte Carlo simulation. The degree of confidence as well as the size of the confidence interval may be user-specified. Also, exploiting sequential testing methods, such unknown

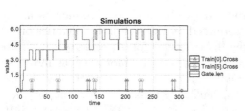

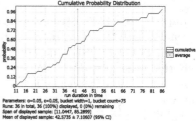

(a) Visualizing the gate length and when Train(0) and Train(5) cross on one random run.

(b) The cumulative probability distribution of Pr[<=T](<> Train(5).Cross).

Fig. 7. Simulation and distribution

property-probabilities may be tested against each other or against a given threshold. For the Train Gate example the following queries estimates that the Train(0) and Train(5) will be in the crossing before 100 time-units:

```
Pr[<=100](<> Train(0).Cross)
Pr[<=100](<> Train(5).Cross)
```

In fact with only 383 respectively 36 runs UPPAAL SMC returns the two 95 % confidence intervals [0.502421, 0.602316] and [0.902606, 1]. In addition more detailed information in terms of (cumulative, confidence interval, frequency histogram) probability distribution of the time-bounded reachability property, e.g. Fig. 7b.

UPPAAL SMC has been applied to a wide range of case studies, going from systems biology [19,20] to nash equilibrium analysis [13] or energy-centric systems [18,41].

4.3   UPPAAL Stratego

UPPAAL STRATEGO [16,17] is a novel branch which facilitates generation, optimization, comparison as well as consequence and performance exploration of strategies for stochastic (priced) timed games in a user-friendly manner. In particular, UPPAAL STRATEGO (statistical model checking), UPPAAL-TIGA [4] (synthesis for timed games) and the method proposed in [16] (synthesis of near optimal schedulers) have been integrated into one tool suite. UPPAAL STRATEGO comes with an extended query language where strategies are first class objects that may be constructed, compared, optimized and used when performing (statistical) model checking of a game under the constraints of a given synthesized strategy. Thus, the tool allows for efficient and flexible "strategy-space" exploration before adaptation in a final implementation by maintaining strategies as first class objects in the model-checking query language.

Example. Now consider a *game* version of the Train Gate example given in Fig. 8a, between an environment consisting of the various trains – with uncontrollable behaviour in terms of when to approach, and choice of time for crossing indicated by dashed transitions – and the control options for the gate – with controllability of stopping and restarting of trains indicated by full transitions. The aim is to synthesize a control strategy for the gate given a specified objective.

Assuming that the trains (i.e. the environment) chooses their delays according to the specified distributions (uniform or exponential) the game is really a $\frac{1}{2}$-player game (i.e. and infinite-state MDP), where the objective of the controller would be to optimize some cost-function. However, as illustrated in Fig. 9 we can abstract the $\frac{1}{2}$-player game into a 2-player timed game simply by ignoring the stochasticity and the (possible) price-decoration. In particular, given a safety (including time-bound reachability) objective ϕ, we may use the branch UPPAAL TIGA to synthesize a most permissive, non-deterministic and memoryless strategy σ which ensure that the objective ϕ is met. Constraining the game

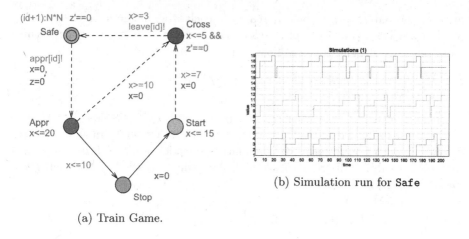

(b) Simulation run for Safe

(a) Train Game.

Fig. 8. Train game

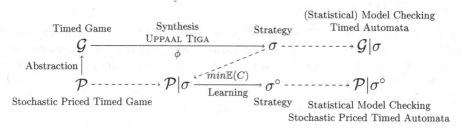

Fig. 9. Overview of models and their relations. The lines show different actions. The dashed lines show that we use the object.

$\mathcal{G}$ with respect to σ it is possible to perform additional (statistical) model checking of under the strategy using UPPAAL and UPPAAL SMC. For the Train Game example an obvious safety strategy is that no two different trains should ever be in the crossing at the same time. The following UPPAAL STRATEGO query asks for a strategy ensuring this objective to be synthesized:

```
strategy Safe =
    control: A[] forall (i : id_t) forall (j : id_t)
                Train(i).Cross && Train(j).Cross imply i == j
```

UPPAAL STRATEGO answers affirmative to this query and returns a nondeterministic strategy (named Safe) that ensures the objective. Now given a synthesized strategy (essential) all UPPAAL and UPPAAL SMC queries may be performed on the game restricted with the strategy. In particular – having added a local clock z – we may estimate the expected time from any particular train enters location Appr until it reaches Cross. The query:

```
E[<=200 ; 100] (max: Train(0).z) under Safe
```

estimates this expected time for Train(0) to 40.7866 ± 2.58574, and the following query:

```
simulate 1 [<=200]
   { Train(0).Safe + 2*Train(0).Appr + 3*Train(0).Stop
                   + 4*Train(0).Start + 5*Train(0).Cross,
     7+Train(1).Safe + 2*Train(1).Appr + 3*Train(1).Stop
                   + 4*Train(1).Start + 5*Train(1).Cross,
     14+Train(2).Safe + 2*Train(2).Appr + 3*Train(2).Stop
                   + 4*Train(2).Start + 5*Train(2).Cross
   } under Safe
```

generates a random run of duration 200 tracing three expressions that each indicate numerically the state of a one of three trains as illustrated in the plot of Fig. 8b. As can be seen (noticing that for each train the max value indicates that the particular train is in the crossing) – and as expected given the objective – there are never two different trains in the crossing at the same time. One objection to this strategy is that the expected time for Train(0) to enter the crossing is to high. To remedy this on may apply reinforcement learning as implemented in UPPAAL STRATEGO for the stochastic priced timed game to obtain a strategy which minimizes this expectation. The following query:

```
strategy GoFast =
        minE (Train(0).z) [<=100] : <> Train(0).Cross
```

leads in a total of 88 iterations to a strategy GoFast for which the expected time is only 15.6394 ± 0.411427 (thus a substantial improvement). However as can be seen from the plot the this strategy – though near-ideal in performance – is in no way safe, as there are several instances of this single random run where two different trains are simultaneously in the crossing.

Fortunately reinforcement learning strategies may also be subject to the restriction of already generated safety strategies. Thus the query:

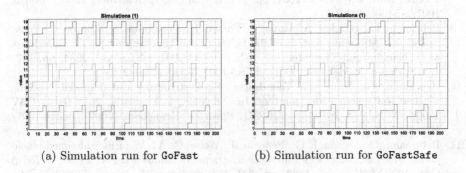

(a) Simulation run for GoFast   (b) Simulation run for GoFastSafe

Fig. 10. Simulation runs

```
strategy GoFastSafe =
       minE (Train(0).z) [<=100] : <> Train(0).Cross
            under Safe
```

uses reinforcement learning with a total of 42 iterations to generate the sub-strategy GoFastSafe. Here the expected time for Train(0) to reach the crossing is again attempted minimized, but now within the boundary of what are permitted by the safety strategy Safe. Now the expected time is 22.1332 ± 0.494325, which is still a lot better than the Safe strategy, but with the guarantee that safety is met in contrast to the GoFast strategy. The plot in Fig. 10b witnesses this. As can be seen from this plot, the optimization for Train(0) is on the expense of the performance for the other trains.

References

1. Alur, R., Courcoubetis, C., Dill, D.L.: Model-checking in dense real-time. Inf. Comput. **104**(1), 2–34 (1993)
2. Alur, R., Dill, D.L.: A theory of timed automata. Theor. Comput. Sci. **126**(2), 183–235 (1994)
3. Behrmann, G.: Distributed reachability analysis in timed automata. Int. J. Softw. Tools Technol. Transfer **7**(1), 19–30 (2005)
4. Behrmann, G., Cougnard, A., David, A., Fleury, E., Larsen, K.G., Lime, D.: UPPAAL-Tiga: time for playing games!. In: Damm, W., Hermanns, H. (eds.) CAV 2007. LNCS, vol. 4590, pp. 121–125. Springer, Heidelberg (2007)
5. Behrmann, G., David, A., Larsen, K.G., Håkansson, J., Pettersson, P., Yi, W., Hendriks, M.: Uppaal 4.0. In: QEST. IEEE Computer Society (2006)
6. Behrmann, G., David, A., Larsen, K.G., Pettersson, P., Yi, W.: Developing uppaal over 15 years. Softw. Pract. Exper. **41**(2), 133–142 (2011)
7. Behrmann, G., David, A., Larsen, K.G., Yi, W.: Unification & sharing in timed automata verification. In: Ball, T., Rajamani, S.K. (eds.) SPIN 2003. LNCS, vol. 2648, pp. 225–229. Springer, Heidelberg (2003). doi:10.1007/3-540-44829-2_15
8. Behrmann, G., Fehnker, A., Hune, T., Larsen, K., Pettersson, P., Romijn, J.: Efficient guiding towards cost-optimality in UPPAAL. In: Margaria, T., Yi, W. (eds.) TACAS 2001. LNCS, vol. 2031, pp. 174–188. Springer, Heidelberg (2001). doi:10.1007/3-540-45319-9_13
9. Behrmann, G., Fehnker, A., Hune, T., Larsen, K., Pettersson, P., Romijn, J., Vaandrager, F.: Minimum-cost reachability for priced time automata. In: Benedetto, M.D., Sangiovanni-Vincentelli, A. (eds.) HSCC 2001. LNCS, vol. 2034, pp. 147–161. Springer, Heidelberg (2001). doi:10.1007/3-540-45351-2_15
10. Behrmann, G., Hune, T., Vaandrager, F.: Distributing timed model checking — how the search order matters. In: Emerson, E.A., Sistla, A.P. (eds.) CAV 2000. LNCS, vol. 1855, pp. 216–231. Springer, Heidelberg (2000). doi:10.1007/10722167_19
11. Behrmann, G., Larsen, K.G., Pearson, J., Weise, C., Yi, W.: Efficient timed reachability analysis using clock difference diagrams. In: Halbwachs, N., Peled, D. (eds.) CAV 1999. LNCS, vol. 1633, pp. 341–353. Springer, Heidelberg (1999). doi:10.1007/3-540-48683-6_30

12. Boyer, B., Corre, K., Legay, A., Sedwards, S.: PLASMA-lab: A Flexible, Distributable Statistical Model Checking Library. In: Joshi, K., Siegle, M., Stoelinga, M., D'Argenio, P.R. (eds.) QEST 2013. LNCS, vol. 8054, pp. 160–164. Springer, Heidelberg (2013). doi:10.1007/978-3-642-40196-1_12

13. Bulychev, P.E., David, A., Larsen, K.G., Legay, A., Mikucionis, M.: Computing nash equilibrium in wireless ad hoc networks: a simulation-based approach. In: IWIGP. EPTCS, vol. 78 (2012)

14. Colombo, A., Fontanelli, D., Gandhi, D., De Angeli, A., Palopoli, L., Sedwards, S., Legay, A.: Behavioural templates improve robot motion planning with social force model in human environments. In: EFTA. IEEE (2013)

15. Colombo, A., Fontanelli, D., Legay, A., Palopoli, L., Sedwards, S.: Motion planning in crowds using statistical model checking to enhance the social force model. In: CDC. IEEE (2013)

16. David, A., Jensen, P.G., Larsen, K.G., Legay, A., Lime, D., Sørensen, M.G., Taankvist, J.H.: On time with minimal expected cost!. In: Cassez, F., Raskin, J.-F. (eds.) ATVA 2014. LNCS, vol. 8837, pp. 129–145. Springer, Heidelberg (2014). doi:10.1007/978-3-319-11936-6_10

17. David, A., Jensen, P.G., Larsen, K.G., Mikučionis, M., Taankvist, J.H.: UPPAAL STRATEGO. In: Baier, C., Tinelli, C. (eds.) TACAS 2015. LNCS, vol. 9035, pp. 206–211. Springer, Heidelberg (2015). doi:10.1007/978-3-662-46681-0_16

18. David, A., Larsen, K.G., Legay, A., Mikucionis, M.: Schedulability of herschel revisited using statistical model checking. Int. J. Softw. Tools Technol. Transfer 17(2), 187–199 (2015)

19. David, A., Larsen, K.G., Legay, A., Mikucionis, M., Poulsen, D.B., Sedwards, S.: Runtime verification of biological systems. In: Margaria, T., Steffen, B. (eds.) ISoLA 2012, Part I. LNCS, vol. 7609, pp. 388–404. Springer, Heidelberg (2012). doi:10.1007/978-3-642-34026-0_29

20. David, A., Larsen, K.G., Legay, A., Mikucionis, M., Poulsen, D.B., Sedwards, S.: Statistical model checking for biological systems. Int. J. Softw. Tools Technol. Transfer 17(3), 351–367 (2015)

21. David, A., Larsen, K.G., Legay, A., Mikučionis, M., Wang, Z.: Time for statistical model checking of real-time systems. In: Gopalakrishnan, G., Qadeer, S. (eds.) CAV 2011. LNCS, vol. 6806, pp. 349–355. Springer, Heidelberg (2011). doi:10.1007/978-3-642-22110-1_27

22. David, A., Möller, M.O., Yi, W.: Formal verification of UML statecharts with real-time extensions. In: Kutsche, R.-D., Weber, H. (eds.) FASE 2002. LNCS, vol. 2306, pp. 218–232. Springer, Heidelberg (2002). doi:10.1007/3-540-45923-5_15

23. Helbing, D., Molnár, P.: Social force model for pedestrian dynamics. Phys. Rev. E 51(5), 4282–4286 (1995)

24. Hendriks, M., Larsen, K.G.: Exact acceleration of real-time model checking. In: Electronic Notes in Theoretical Computer Science, vol. 65. Elsevier Science Publishers, April 2002

25. Henzinger, T.A., Ho, P.: Algorithmic analysis of nonlinear hybrid systems. In: CAV

26. Hérault, T., Lassaigne, R., Magniette, F., Peyronnet, S.: Approximate probabilistic model checking. In: Steffen, B., Levi, G. (eds.) VMCAI 2004. LNCS, vol. 2937, pp. 73–84. Springer, Heidelberg (2004). doi:10.1007/978-3-540-24622-0_8

27. Jegourel, C., Legay, A., Sedwards, S.: A platform for high performance statistical model checking – PLASMA. In: Flanagan, C., König, B. (eds.) TACAS 2012. LNCS, vol. 7214, pp. 498–503. Springer, Heidelberg (2012). doi:10.1007/978-3-642-28756-5_37

28. Jegourel, C., Legay, A., Sedwards, S.: Cross-entropy optimisation of importance sampling parameters for statistical model checking. In: Madhusudan, P., Seshia, S.A. (eds.) CAV 2012. LNCS, vol. 7358, pp. 327–342. Springer, Heidelberg (2012). doi:10.1007/978-3-642-31424-7_26

29. Jegourel, C., Legay, A., Sedwards, S.: Importance splitting for statistical model checking rare properties. In: Sharygina, N., Veith, H. (eds.) CAV 2013. LNCS, vol. 8044, pp. 576–591. Springer, Heidelberg (2013). doi:10.1007/978-3-642-39799-8_38

30. Jégourel, C., Legay, A., Sedwards, S., Traonouez, L.: Distributed verification of rare properties using importance splitting observers. ECEASST (2015)

31. Kahn, H., Marshall, A.W.: Methods of reducing sample size in Monte Carlo computations. Oper. Res. **1**(5), 263–278 (1953)

32. Larsen, K., Behrmann, G., Brinksma, E., Fehnker, A., Hune, T., Pettersson, P., Romijn, J.: As cheap as possible: effcient cost-optimal reachability for priced timed automata. In: Berry, G., Comon, H., Finkel, A. (eds.) CAV 2001. LNCS, vol. 2102, pp. 493–505. Springer, Heidelberg (2001). doi:10.1007/3-540-44585-4_47

33. Larsen, K.G., Pettersson, P., Yi, W.: Uppaal in a nutshell. Int. J. Softw. Tools Technol. Transfer **1**(1), 134–152 (1997)

34. Larsen, K.G., Skou, A.: Bisimulation through probabilistic testing. Inf. Comput. **94**(1), 1–28 (1991)

35. Larsson, F., Larsen, K.G., Pettersson, P., Yi, W.: Efficient verification of real-time systems: compact data structures and state-space reduction. In: Proceedings of the 18th IEEE Real-Time Systems Symposium. IEEE Computer Society Press, December 1997

36. Okamoto, M.: Some inequalities relating to the partial sum of binomial probabilities. Ann. Inst. Stat. Math. **10**(1), 29–35 (1959)

37. Sen, K., Viswanathan, M., Agha, G.: Statistical model checking of black-box probabilistic systems. In: Alur, R., Peled, D.A. (eds.) CAV 2004. LNCS, vol. 3114, pp. 202–215. Springer, Heidelberg (2004). doi:10.1007/978-3-540-27813-9_16

38. Sen, K., Viswanathan, M., Agha, G.: On statistical model checking of stochastic systems. In: Etessami, K., Rajamani, S.K. (eds.) CAV 2005. LNCS, vol. 3576, pp. 266–280. Springer, Heidelberg (2005). doi:10.1007/11513988_26

39. Sen, K., Viswanathan, M., Agha, G.A.: VESTA: a statistical model-checker and analyzer for probabilistic systems. In: QEST. IEEE Computer Society (2005)

40. Wald, A.: Sequential tests of statistical hypotheses. Ann. Math. Stat. **16**(2), 117–186 (1945)

41. Wognsen, E.R., Haverkort, B.R., Jongerden, M., Hansen, R.R., Larsen, K.G.: A score function for optimizing the cycle-life of battery-powered embedded systems. In: Sankaranarayanan, S., Vicario, E. (eds.) FORMATS 2015. LNCS, vol. 9268, pp. 305–320. Springer, Heidelberg (2015). doi:10.1007/978-3-319-22975-1_20

42. Yi, W., Pettersson, P., Daniels, M.: Automatic verification of real-time communicating systems by constraint-solving. In: Proceedings of the 7th IFIP WG6.1 International Conference on Formal Description Techniques VII. Chapman & Hall Ltd., London (1995)

43. Younes, H.L.S.: Verification and Planning for Stochastic Processes with Asynchronous Events. Ph.D. thesis, Carnegie Mellon (2005)

44. Zuliani, P., Platzer, A., Clarke, E.M.: Bayesian statistical model checking with application to Stateflow/Simulink verification. Formal Methods Syst. Des. **43**(2), 191–232 (2013)

Erratum to: Verification Techniques for Hybrid Systems

Pavithra Prabhakar[1]([⊠]), Miriam Garcia Soto[2], and Ratan Lal[1]

[1] Department of Computer Science, Kansas State University,
Manhattan, KS, USA
{pprabhakar, ratan}@ksu.edu
[2] IMDEA Software Institute, Madrid, Spain
miriam.garcia@imdea.org
http://people.cs.ksu.edu/~pprabhakar/

Erratum to:
Chapter 61 in: T. Margaria and B. Steffen (Eds.)
Leveraging Applications of Formal Methods, Verification
and Validation (Part II)
DOI: 10.1007/978-3-319-47169-3_61

In the original version of this paper, the names of two of the authors were erroneously omitted. This has been updated. The correct author list is as follows:

Pavithra Prabhakar[1], Miriam Garcia Soto[2], and Ratan Lal[1]

[1] Department of Computer Science, Kansas State University, Manhattan, KS, USA, pprabhakar@ksu.edu, ratan@ksu.edu, http://people.cs.ksu.edu/~pprabhakar/
[2] IMDEA Software Institute, Madrid, Spain, miriam.garcia@imdea.org

---

The updated original online version for this chapter can be found at 10.1007/978-3-319-47169-3_61

© Springer International Publishing AG 2016
T. Margaria and B. Steffen (Eds.): ISoLA 2016, Part II, LNCS 9953, p. E1, 2016.
DOI: 10.1007/978-3-319-47169-3_63

Author Index